BUSINESS LAW

UCC COMPREHENSIVE VOLUME

REVISED EDITION

TEXTBOOK SERIES

RONALD A. ANDERSON
Professor of Law and Government, Drexel University
Member of the Pennsylvania and Philadelphia Bars

IVAN FOX
Professor of Law and Chairman,
Business Law Department, Pace University
Member of the New York Bar

DAVID P. TWOMEY
Professor of Law, School of Management, Boston College
Member of the Massachusetts and Florida Bars

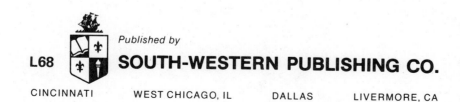

L68

Published by

SOUTH-WESTERN PUBLISHING CO.

CINCINNATI   WEST CHICAGO, IL   DALLAS   LIVERMORE, CA

ISBN: 0-538-12680-9

Library of Congress Catalog Card Number: 86-63843

3 4 5 6 7 8 D 5 4 3 2 1 0 9

Printed in the United States of America

COVER PHOTO: Courtesy of the Phillips Collection, Washington

PREFACE

Much has been written over the years about what ought to be taught in an introductory business law course and about how it ought to be taught. Some have advocated an environmental approach, some a traditional approach, and a growing number something in between. Our focus in preparing this revised edition of BUSINESS LAW: UCC COMPREHENSIVE VOLUME has been to create a flexible teaching tool with universally desirable qualities that can be adapted to each instructor's personal teaching philosophy. We have sought, in presenting a broad range of materials, to make this book (1) accurate, (2) understandable, (3) balanced, (4) life-oriented, and (5) thought-provoking.

By *accurate*, we mean that we have done everything possible to ensure that the content of the book is as up-to-date as modern publishing technology will permit. Accurate also means that new doctrines and minority trends should be identified. Accordingly, we have endeavored to make this book anticipatory as well as retrospective. In the process of so doing, we hope to emphasize the dynamic character of the law.

Understandable means that legalistic jargon and words of art must be translated into ordinary English. We have replaced linguistic provincialisms and obscure words with ordinary simple language that can be understood by the modern student.

Balanced means that from the myriad discrete legal topics that might have some significance for undergraduate students of business law, those with the greatest relevance have been selected. If all the volumes of professional treatises relating to business were added together, the number would exceed 1000. The beginning law student is given one book. Obviously, careful choice is necessary to bring the great mass of the law down into a one-volume book for beginners. In addition, great care must be exercised to treat all portions of the student's book with the appropriate degree of intensity.

Life-oriented requires the book to be devoted to those areas that the undergraduate student of today will most likely meet in future years. Conversely, it means avoiding the unusual, the bizarre, the headline cases which have no real value for the business person. Above all, life-oriented brings out the interrelationship between the law and life: the law is shaped by the "environment" and the law gives direction to the "environment." For the purpose of curriculum compartmentalization, "law" is a separate subject but as far as life is concerned it is an inseparable part of life. The more the student can appreciate this interrelationship, the better will be the student's understanding both of law and of life.

Thought-provoking means there are end-of-the-chapter materials that call for the student's developing skill in the analysis of data to identify basic questions, to apply existing principles to the solution of such basic questions, and to make intelligent decisions when there are no preexisting principles to govern the exact basic questions that are involved. This not only brings the student back to the orientation of law to life but also assures the teaching of law a permanent place in the pattern of higher education.

The objectives above set forth have guided the writing of this book for more than a third of a century. Though our focus on these objectives has never wavered, the specific content of the book has evolved to keep pace with changing times. The early 1960s witnessed the integration of the Uniform Commercial Code in the Seventh Edition as a result of the growth in the number of states adopting the UCC. In subsequent years that coverage has been continually updated to keep pace with amendments to the Code and other uniform and model acts. Most recently, current curriculum trends have us placing increasing emphasis on environmental and regulatory topics in this Revised Edition.

THE LEGAL AND SOCIAL ENVIRONMENT OF BUSINESS.

This is the title of an expanded Part I of the book. It brings together in one part various chapters relating to societal or "public law" that form the general background for individual business transactions. To borrow terms familiar to the economist, Part I deals with macro law while much of the balance of the book relates to micro law. It is important that the student see the background of macro law. It is also important the student recognize that the "legal environment of business" is the sum total of the macro and micro areas.

More specifically, the new Part I deals with the regulatory environment in which business operates. The social forces behind the creation and evolution of the specific principles and substantive rules that govern disputes and transactions between individuals are explored. A comprehensive discussion of the federal and state court structure and the procedures involved in a lawsuit from commencement to execution of the judgment is included. The Constitution, as the foundation of the legal environment of business, is presented. The increasing role played by the administrative agencies in the government regulation of business is fully discussed.

This allocation of the indicated material to Part I is in harmony with the increased concern for an environmental approach to the teaching of business law. At the same time, this focusing on societal or "public law" is not made at the expense of the treatment of the areas of "private law." There has been no lessening of attention to accuracy of the content, clarity of expression, and thoroughness of subject matter coverage.

In addition to the topics discussed in Part I, other chapters throughout the book are appropriate for a course which focuses on public law. While every chapter in the text possesses the raw potential for an environmental approach, some chapters lend themselves to this mode of teaching more readily than others. An outline of chapters emphasizing public law follows:

SUGGESTED LEGAL ENVIRONMENT OUTLINES

Chapters:

1. Law and Enforcement Agencies
2. Law as an Expression of Social Forces
3. The Constitution as the Foundation of the Legal Environment
4. Government Regulation of Business
44. Employment (Government Regulation of Employment)
49. Corporate Stock and Shareholders (Securities Regulation)
21. Personal Property (Protection of Trademarks, Copyrights, Patents, Computer Software and Chips)
5. International Legal Environment
6. Administrative Agencies
7. Environmental Law and Community Planning
8. Consumer Protection
9. Crimes
10. Torts
38. Bankruptcy

(or)

Chapters:

1. Law and Enforcement Agencies
2. Law as an Expression of Social Forces
3. The Constitution as the Foundation of the Legal Environment
4. Government Regulation of Business
5. International Legal Environment
6. Administrative Agencies
7. Environmental Law and Community Planning
8. Consumer Protection
9. Crimes
10. Torts
21. Personal Property (Protection of Trademarks, Copyrights, Patents, Computer Software and Chips)
38. Bankruptcy
44. Employment
49. Corporate Stock and Shareholders (Securities Regulation)

An introductory course which emphasizes societal or public law may include the chapters contained in either of the above outlines and other appropriate chapters selected for the course. An introductory course emphasizing private law may cover selected chapters from Part I, The Legal and Social Environment of Business, and chapters on Contracts, Personal Property, or Agency. The instructor may choose to cover additional topics in this introductory course, depending on the ability level of the students and time allotted to the course at the institution. The remainder of the book may be covered in advanced courses.

PREPARATION FOR CPA EXAM

As was true in previous editions, this Revised Edition includes material on topics essential to preparation for the business law section of the CPA exam. Topics generally tested on this exam (along with relative weight expressed as a percent) are:

The CPA and the Law (10%)
Business Organizations (20%)
Contracts (15%)
Debtor-Creditor Relationships (10%)
Government Regulation of Business (10%)
Uniform Commercial Code (25%)
Property (10%)

As this list suggests, the breadth and depth of CPA testing in the business law section necessitate inclusion of a great deal of material in any text purporting to prepare students for the exam. Adequate coverage of all these topics requires at least six semester hours. Consequently, this text is designed to accommodate a two-semester program in business law.

NEW TOPICS

New in this Revised Edition are chapters on Constitutional Law and International Law designed to satisfy AACSB curriculum requirements. Also new is the expanded coverage of white collar crimes and white collar torts in two separate chapters. Other chapters contain substantial updating, reflecting the Revised Model Business Corporations Act, new amendments to the Bankruptcy Act, and electronic funds transfer, among others.

CASE SUMMARIES

As in previous editions, this Revised Edition contains ample case summaries integrated with the text of each chapter. Popular summaries from previous editions have been retained while at the same time adding many new summaries (over 100 of which have been handed down since 1980).

NEW FEATURES

New to this edition are end-of-chapter summaries designed to assist students in assimilating the material presented in each chapter. Students will find the summaries helpful in highlighting important chapter concepts.

Also new is the addition of the text of the Constitution of the United States, excerpts from the ABA Revised Model Business Corporations Act, the

Uniform Limited Partnership Act, and a brief guide to legal research to the Appendix. Both instructor and student should find this expanded Appendix a convenient reference source.

STUDENT STUDY GUIDE

Accompanying this Revised Edition is a new student study guide authored by E. Clayton Hipp of Clemson University. This new, 100% larger study guide contains highlights of each chapter in the text, a new mix of questions and problems, and special exercises designed to demonstrate real-life application of legal rules and principles.

INSTRUCTOR'S MATERIALS

A completely revised and repackaged instructor's manual prepared by Kim Tyler of Shasta College and the authors contains a complete set of instructional transparencies, chapter outlines, lecture notes and teaching suggestions, and answers to end-of-chapter questions and case questions all packaged in a three-ring binder for ease of use. A set of 23 pre-printed achievement tests is separately available. The examination package is also available in an easy-to-use software package.

ABOUT THE AUTHORS

Ronald A. Anderson, Professor of Law and Government at Drexel University for nearly 40 years, is the internationally renowned author of the definitive, 10-volume treatise on the Uniform Commercial Code and other well-respected professional and educational works.

Professor Anderson graduated from the University of Pennsylvania in 1933 and earned his *Juris Doctor* degree from that school in 1936. He is a member of the American, Pennsylvania, and Philadelphia Bar Associations, and an active member of the legal community.

Ivan Fox, with Pace University since 1958, and currently Professor of Law and Chairman of the Business Law Department, is widely known for his work with the Fox-Kirschbaum-Lambers CPA Review Course, and has lectured extensively to professional and banking groups on various business law topics.

Professor Fox graduated from Pace University in 1954, earned his *Juris Doctor* from New York Law School in 1957 and received his LL.M. from New York University in 1963. He is a member of the New York Bar and the New York State Bar Association.

David P. Twomey is Professor of Law at Boston College and a nationally known labor arbitrator, having served as arbitrator in numerous disputes throughout the country in the private and public sectors. He has written a great number of books and articles on labor law and business law topics, and was elected to membership in the National Academy of Arbitrators in 1979.

Professor Twomey graduated from Boston College in 1962 and earned his MBA at the University of Massachusetts at Amherst in 1963. After two years of business experience, he entered Boston College Law School and earned his *Juris Doctor* in 1968. He is a member of the Massachusetts, Florida, and Federal Bars. Professor Twomey joined the faculty of the Boston College School of Management in 1968 and was promoted to professor in 1978. His special interest in curriculum development is demonstrated by his three-year chairmanship of his school's Educational Policy Committee.

CONTENTS

Preface   iii
About the Authors   viii

PART 1
THE LEGAL AND SOCIAL
ENVIRONMENT OF BUSINESS

1   Law and Enforcement Agencies   3
2   Law as an Expression of Social Forces   22
3   The Constitution as the Foundation of the Legal Environment   37
4   Government Regulation of Business   55
5   The International Legal Environment   71
6   Administrative Agencies   90
7   Environmental Law and Community Planning   109
8   Consumer Protection   121
9   Crimes   139
10 Torts   161

PART 2
CONTRACTS

11 Nature and Classes of Contracts   185
12 The Agreement   201
13 Contractual Capacity   221
14 Genuineness of Assent   234
15 Consideration   251
16 Legality and Public Policy   266
17 Form of Contract   284
18 Interpretation of Contracts   302
19 Third Persons and Contracts   319
20 Discharge of Contracts   334
21 Breach of Contract and Remedies   356

PART 3
PERSONAL PROPERTY AND BAILMENTS

22 Personal Property   381
23 Bailments   403
24 Special Bailments and Documents of Title   419

PART 4
SALES

25 Nature and Form of Sales   441
26 Risk and Property Rights   457
27 Obligations and Performance   472
28 Warranties and Other Product Liabilities   483
29 Remedies for Breach of Sales Contracts   502

PART 5
COMMERCIAL PAPER

30 Kinds of Paper, Parties, and Negotiability   521
31 Transfer of Commercial Paper   536
32 Rights of Holders and Defenses   550
33 Presentment of Paper for Payment and Acceptance   565
34 Discharge of Commercial Paper   580
35 Checks and Customer-Bank Relationship   590

PART 6
SECURED TRANSACTIONS,
CREDITORS' RIGHTS, AND INSURANCE

36 Secured Transactions Under Article 9   609
37 Other Security Devices   624
38 Bankruptcy   634
39 Insurance   647
40 Kinds of Insurance   661

PART 7
AGENCY AND EMPLOYMENT

41 Agency — Creation and Termination   683
42 Principal and Agent   702
43 Third Persons in Agency   718
44 Employment   739

PART 8
BUSINESS ORGANIZATIONS

45 Forms of Business Organizations   759
46 Creation and Termination of Partnerships   774
47 Powers and Duties of Partners   793
48 Nature, Creation, and Termination of Corporations   809
49 Corporate Powers   828

50   Corporate Stock and Shareholders   839
51   Management of Corporations   864

        PART 9
        REAL PROPERTY

52   Nature and Ownership of Real Property   881
53   Leases   904

        PART 10
        ESTATES

54   Decedents' Estates   927
55   Trusts   946
Appendices
How to Find the Law   957
U.S. Constitution   960
Uniform Commercial Code   969
Uniform Partnership Act   1072
Uniform Limited Partnership Act   1081
Revised ABA Model Business Corporation Act   1086
Glossary   1102
Subject Index   1123

PART 1

THE LEGAL AND SOCIAL

ENVIRONMENT OF BUSINESS

Chapter 1 Law and Enforcement Agencies
Chapter 2 Law as an Expression of Social Forces
Chapter 3 The Constitution as the Foundation of the Legal Environment
Chapter 4 Government Regulation of Business
Chapter 5 The International Legal Environment
Chapter 6 Administrative Agencies
Chapter 7 Environmental Law and Community Planning
Chapter 8 Consumer Protection
Chapter 9 Crimes
Chapter 10 Torts

CHAPTER 1

LAW AND ENFORCEMENT

AGENCIES

CHAPTER OBJECTIVES

After studying this chapter you will be able to:
1. Give two examples of the evolutionary character of legal rights.
2. List the agencies or bodies that interpret and apply law.
3. Describe the basic structure of federal and state court systems.
4. Name the officers of a court.
5. List the steps that may be involved in a lawsuit.

Why have law?

If you have ever been stuck in a traffic jam on a turnpike or crowded in a mob leaving a stadium, then you have been in a position to observe the need for order to keep things running smoothly and efficiently. What is true on a small scale for traffic jams and crowds is true on a large scale for society in general. The order, or pattern of rules, which society establishes to govern the conduct of individuals and the relationships among them we call law. Law is society's way of keeping things running smoothly and efficiently.

Stated another way, law is merely management at the societal level. You personally have objectives and make decisions to manage your life. Business people have objectives and make decisions to manage their businesses. Likewise, when society governs itself it determines its objectives and makes management decisions, albeit through a much more complex process. That which we call law is merely a particular aspect of the broad problem of management: the management of society.

In this text we will look generally at the process of managing society through the system of laws and enforcement agencies, and we will examine specifically those aspects of the system that deal with business. Perhaps the best place to start our study is with an explanation of the nature of law and legal rights.

A. NATURE OF LAW AND LEGAL RIGHTS

Law consists of the body of principles that govern conduct and that can be enforced in courts or by administrative agencies. Much of the difficulty in seeking to understand the law is the result of regarding it as an absolute and exact science. The ideal of a definite body of law is not only attractive to the student but is dear to the heart of everyone. Long-revered is the maxim that "in the known certainty of the law lies the safety of all." The purpose of establishing our Constitution was to the end that we may have a government of laws and not of people.

The truth of the matter is that the certainty, the precision, and the logic of the law are very relative matters. In truth the law is an arbitrary set of rules that we have agreed upon to govern ourselves. And our reason for so doing is the quest for justice and the advancement of the various social objectives that we hold dear.

§ 1:1.   Legal Rights.

What are legal rights? And who has them? In answering these questions, we tend to make the mistake of thinking of the present as being characteristic of what was and what will be. But consider the evolution of the concept of the "rights of the human being" and the right of privacy.

(a) **The "Rights of the Human Being" Concept.** Our belief in the American way of life and in the concepts on which our society or government is based should not obscure the fact that at one time there was no American way of life. While many religious leaders, philosophers, and poets spoke of the rights and dignity of people, rulers laughed at such pretensions and held people tightly in a society based on status. A noble had the rights of a noble. A warrior had the rights of a warrior. A slave had very few rights at all. In each case, the law saw only status; rights attached not to the human being but to the status.

In the course of time, serfdom displaced slavery in much of the Western world. Eventually feudalism disappeared and, with the end of the Thirty Years War, the modern nation-state began to emerge. Surely one might say that in such a "new order," a human being had legal rights. The person had rights, but not as a human being—only as a subject. Even when the English colonists settled in America, they brought with them not the rights of human beings but the rights of British subjects. Even when the colonies were within one year of war, the Second Continental Congress presented to King George III the Olive Branch Petition which beseeched the king to recognize the colonists' rights as English subjects. For almost a year the destiny of the colonies hung in the balance with the colonists unable to decide between remaining loyal to the Crown, seeking to obtain recognition of their rights as English subjects (a "status" recognition), or doing something else.

Finally, the ill-advised policies of George III and the eloquence of Thomas Paine's Common Sense tipped the scales and the colonies spoke on

July 4, 1776, not in terms of the rights of English subjects but in terms of the rights of people existing independently of any government. Had the American Revolution been lost, the Declaration of Independence would have gone rattling down the corridors of time with many other failures. But the American Revolution was won, and the new government that was established was based upon "human beings" as the building blocks rather than upon "subjects." Rights of human beings replaced the concept of rights of subjects. With this transition, the obligations of a monarch to faithful subjects were replaced by the rights of human beings existing without regard to will or authority of any kind. Since then, America has been going through additional stages of determining what is embraced by the concept of "rights of human beings."

(b) **The Right of Privacy.** Today everyone recognizes that there is a right of privacy. Before 1890, however, this right did not exist in American law. Certainly those who wrote the Declaration of Independence and the Bill of Rights were conscious of rights. How can we explain that the law did not recognize a right of privacy until a full century later?

The answer is that at a particular time people worry about the problems which face them. Note the extent of the fears and concern of the framers of the Bill of Rights. The Fourth Amendment states, "The right of the people to be secure in their persons, houses, papers, and effects, against unreasonable searches and seizures, shall not be violated, and no Warrants shall issue, but upon probable cause, supported by Oath or affirmation, and particularly describing the place to be searched and the persons or things to be seized." The people of 1790 were afraid of a recurrence of the days of George III.

The framers of the Fourth Amendment declared what we today would regard as a segment of privacy — protection from police invasion of privacy. The people of 1790 just were not concerned with invasion of privacy by a private person. While a snooping person could be prosecuted to some extent under a Peeping Tom statute, this was a criminal liability. The victim could not sue for damages for the invasion of privacy.

If we are honest with history, all that we can say is that modern people think highly of privacy and want it to be protected. And, knowing that the law is responsive to the wishes of society, we can also say that the right is protected by government. But note that we should go no further than to say that it is a right which society wishes to protect at the present time. If circumstances arise in our national life of such a nature that the general welfare is opposed to the right of privacy we can expect that the "right" of privacy will be limited or modified. For example, although the right of privacy prevents a bank from giving out information about a customer's bank account, the federal government, acting under a 1969 statute, can require such information to see if income taxes are due or if money has been paid or received in criminal transactions.[1]

§ 1:2.   What Is the Law?

The expression, "a law," is ordinarily used in connection with a statute enacted by a state legislature or the Congress of the United States,

[1]United States v Bisceglia, 420 US 141 (1975). But see § 35:4(a) of this book.

such as an act of the federal Congress to provide old-age benefits. However, the statutes enacted by legislative bodies are not the only source of law.

Constitutional law includes the constitutions in force in the particular area or territory. In each state, two constitutions are in force, the state constitution and the national constitution.

Statutory law includes statutes adopted by the lawmakers. Each state has its own legislature and the United States has the Congress, both of which enact laws. In addition, every city, county, or other subdivision has some power to adopt ordinances which, within their sphere of operation, have the same binding effect as legislative acts.

Of great importance are the **administrative regulations,** such as rules of the Securities and Exchange Commission and the National Labor Relations Board. The regulations promulgated by national and state administrative agencies generally have the force of statute and are therefore part of "the law."

Law also includes principles that are expressed for the first time in court decisions. This is **case law.** For example, when a court decides a new question or problem, its decision becomes a **precedent** and stands as the law for that particular problem in the future. This rule that a court decision becomes a precedent to be followed in similar cases is the doctrine of **stare decisis.**

Law also includes treaties made by the United States, and proclamations and orders of the President of the United States or of other public officials.

§ 1:3.   Uniform State Laws.

To secure uniformity as far as possible, the National Conference of Commissioners on Uniform State Laws, composed of representatives from all the states, has drafted statutes on various subjects for adoption by the states. The best example of such laws is the Uniform Commercial Code (UCC).[2] The Code regulates the fields of sales of goods; commercial paper, such as checks; secured transactions in personal property; bulk transfers; and particular aspects of banking, letters of credit, warehouse receipts, bills of lading, and investment securities.

National uniformity has also been brought about in some areas of consumer protection by the adoption of the federal Consumer Credit Protection Act (CCPA), Title I of which is popularly known as the Truth in Lending

---

[2]The Code has been adopted in every state except Louisiana. It has also been adopted for Guam, the Virgin Islands, and the District of Columbia. Louisiana has adopted Articles 1, 3, 4, 5, 7, and 8 of the Code. In 1972, a group of Amendments to the Code was recommended. These have been adopted in Alabama, Alaska, Arizona, Arkansas, California, Colorado, Connecticut, Delaware, Florida, Georgia, Hawaii, Idaho, Illinois, Indiana, Iowa, Kansas, Kentucky, Maine, Maryland, Massachusetts, Michigan, Minnesota, Mississippi, Montana, Nebraska, Nevada, New Hampshire, New Jersey, New Mexico, New York, North Carolina, North Dakota, Ohio, Oklahoma, Oregon, Pennsylvania, South Dakota, Tennessee, Texas, Utah, Virginia, Washington, West Virginia, Wisconsin, and Wyoming. The 1972 amendments have also been adopted for Guam and the District of Columbia. The changes made by the 1972 Amendment to the UCC are confined mainly to Article 9 on secured transactions. In 1977, Article 8 of the Code, relating to investment securities, was amended. This amended version has been adopted in Arkansas, California, Colorado, Connecticut, Delaware, Idaho, Massachusetts, Minnesota, Montana, Nevada, New York, North Dakota, Ohio, Oklahoma, Oregon, Texas, Virginia, West Virginia, and Wyoming.

Act.[3] A Uniform Consumer Credit Code (UCCC) has been proposed and is now before the states for adoption. To the extent that it is adopted, it will complement the Uniform Commercial Code.[4]

§ 1:4.   Classifications of Law.

Law is classified in many ways. For example, **substantive law,** which creates, defines, and regulates rights and liabilities, is contrasted with **procedural law,** which specifies the steps that must be followed in enforcing those rights and liabilities. Law may also be classified in terms of its origin, as coming from the Roman (or civil) law, the common law of England, or the law merchant. It may be classified as to subject matter, such as the law of contracts, the law of real estate, and the law of wills.

B. AGENCIES FOR ENFORCEMENT OF LEGAL RIGHTS

Legal rights are meaningless unless they can be enforced. Government, therefore, provides a system by which the rights of the parties under the law can be determined and enforced. Generally the instrumentality of government by which this is accomplished is a court; the process involved is an action or a lawsuit. Administrative agencies have also been created to enforce law and to determine rights within certain areas. At the same time private agencies have developed as an out-of-court method of dispute determination.

§ 1:5.   Courts.

A **court** is a tribunal established by government to hear and decide matters properly brought before it, to give redress to the injured or enforce punishment against wrongdoers, and to prevent wrongs. A **court of record** is one in which the proceedings are preserved in an official record. In a **court not of record** the proceedings are not officially recorded.

Each court is empowered to decide certain types or classes of cases. This power is called **jurisdiction.** A court may have original or appellate jurisdiction, or both. A court with **original jurisdiction** has the authority to hear a controversy when it is first brought into court. A court having **appellate jurisdiction,** on the other hand, has authority to review the judgment of an inferior court.

The jurisdiction of a court may be general as distinguished from limited or special. A court having **general jurisdiction** has power to hear and decide all controversies involving legal rights and duties. A court of **limited** or **special jurisdiction** has authority to hear and decide only those cases that fall within a particular class, such as cases in which the amounts are below a specified sum.

---

[3]15 United States Code § 1601 et seq., and 18 USC § 891 et seq.

[4]As of January, 1986, the 1968 version of the Uniform Consumer Credit Code has been adopted in Colorado, Indiana, Oklahoma, South Carolina, Utah, Wisconsin, and Wyoming. It has also been adopted for the Island of Guam. The 1968 version of the UCCC has been replaced by a 1974 version which has been adopted in Idaho, Iowa, Kansas, and Maine. In 1983, Idaho replaced the UCCC with the Idaho Credit Code.

Courts are frequently classified in terms of the nature of their jurisdiction. A **criminal court** is one that is established for the trial of crimes, which are regarded as offenses against the public. A **civil court,** on the other hand, is authorized to hear and decide issues involving private rights and duties and also noncriminal public matters. In like manner, courts are classified as equity courts, juvenile courts, probate courts, and courts of domestic relations, upon the basis of their limited jurisdiction.

Each court has inherent power to establish rules necessary to preserve order in the court or to transact the business of the court. An infraction of these rules or the disobedience to any other lawful order, as well as a willful act contrary to the dignity of the court or tending to pervert or obstruct justice, may be punished as **contempt of court.**

§ 1:6.   Administrative Agencies.

The difficulties of courts' administering laws regulating business, labor, agriculture, public utilities, and other phases of the economy led Congress and the state legislatures to establish commissions or agencies of experts to make the rules and to pass upon violations of the rules. Thus we find the Interstate Commerce Commission regulating interstate commerce and passing upon whether conduct of a carrier is a violation of its regulations. The Commission is thus a lawmaker, an executive that enforces the law, and a court which interprets and applies the law. This is also true of the Federal Trade Commission, the Securities and Exchange Commission, the National Labor Relations Board, and many other federal and state administrative agencies.

§ 1:7.   Private Agencies.

Because of the rising costs, delays, and complexities of litigation, business people often seek to resolve disputes out of court.

(a) **Arbitration.** By the use of **arbitration** a dispute is brought before one or more arbitrators (disinterested persons selected by the parties to the dispute) who make a decision which the parties have agreed to accept as final. This procedure first reached an extensive use in the field of commercial contracts. Parties to a contract which is to be in effect for some time may specify in the contract that any dispute shall be submitted to arbitrators to be selected by the parties. Arbitration today is encouraged as a means of avoiding expensive litigation and easing the workload of courts. Arbitration enables the parties to present the facts before the arbitrators who are trained experts and are familiar with the practices that form the background of the dispute.

A Uniform Arbitration Act has been adopted in a number of states.[5] Under this Act and similar statutes, the parties to a contract may agree in advance that all disputes arising thereunder will be submitted to arbitration.

---

[5]The 1955 version of the Uniform Arbitration Act has been adopted in Alaska, Arizona, Arkansas, Colorado, Delaware, Idaho, Illinois, Indiana, Iowa, Kansas, Maine, Maryland, Massachusetts, Michigan, Minnesota, Missouri, Montana, Nevada, New Mexico, North Carolina, Oklahoma, Pennsylvania, South Carolina, South Dakota, Tennessee, Texas, Utah, Vermont, and Wyoming; and the District of Columbia. The earlier 1925 version of the Act is in force in Wisconsin.

In some instances the contract will name the arbitrators for the duration of the contract.

In some states, by rule or statute, the arbitration of small claims is required. The losing party, however, may appeal from such compulsory arbitration to a court and the appeal will proceed just as though there never had been any prior arbitration. This is called an **appeal** *de novo* and is required to preserve the constitutional right to a jury trial. As a practical matter, however, relatively few appeals are taken from the arbitration decision.

(b) **Reference to Third Person.** An out-of-court determination of disputes under construction contracts is often made under a term of the contract that any dispute shall be referred to the architect in charge of the construction and that the architect's decision shall be final.

Increasingly, other types of transactions provide for a third person or a committee to decide rights of persons. Thus, employees and an employer may have agreed as a term of the employment contract that claims of employees under retirement and pension plans shall be decided by a designated board or committee. The seller and buyer may have selected a third person to determine the price to be paid for goods. Ordinarily the parties agree that the decision of such a third person or board shall be final and that no appeal or review may be had in any court. In most cases, the referral situation involves the determination of a particular fact in contrast to arbitration which seeks to end a dispute.

(c) **Association Tribunals.** Many disputes never reach the law courts because both parties to the dispute belong to a group or association and the tribunal created by the group or association disposes of the matter. Thus, a dispute between members of a labor union, a stockbrokers' exchange, or a church, may be heard by some board or committee within the association or group. Courts will review the action of such tribunals to determine that a fair and proper procedure was followed but generally the courts will not go any further and will not examine the facts of the case to see if the association tribunal reached the same conclusion that the court would have reached.

C. COURT ORGANIZATION

Courts in the United States are organized in two distinct systems: the federal courts and the state courts. Although created under separate governments, the methods of operation and organization of these two systems are similar.

§ 1:8.   Personnel of Courts.

Both the federal and state court systems require the assistance of many people. These include not only those in the direct employ of the court, but also those described as officers of the court and in many cases a jury as well.

(a) **Officers of the Court.** The **judge** is the primary officer of the court. A judge is either elected or appointed. **Attorneys** or counselors at law are also officers of the court. They are usually selected by the parties to the controversy — but in some cases by the judge — to present the issue of a case to the court.

The **clerk** of the court is appointed in some of the higher courts but is usually elected to office in the lower courts. The principal duties of the clerks are to enter cases upon the court calendar, to keep an accurate record of the proceedings, to attest the same, and, in some instances, to approve bail bonds and to compute the amount of costs involved.

The **sheriff** is the chief executive of a county. In addition to the duty of maintaining peace and order within the territorial limits of a county, the sheriff has many other duties in connection with the administration of justice in county courts of record: summoning witnesses, taking charge of the jury, preserving order in court, serving writs, carrying out judicial sales, and executing judgments. The **marshals** of the United States perform these duties in the federal courts. In county courts not of record, such as the courts of justices of the peace, these duties, when appropriate, are performed by a **constable.** Some of the duties of the sheriff are now performed by persons known as **court criers;** or by deputy sheriffs, known as **bailiffs.**

(b) The Jury. The **jury** is a body of citizens sworn by a court to try to determine by verdict the issues of fact submitted to them. A trial jury consists of not more than twelve persons. The first step in forming a jury is to make a **jury list.** This involves the preparation by the proper officers or board of a list of qualified persons from which a jury may be drawn.

A certain number of persons drawn from the jury list constitute the **jury panel.** A trial jury is selected from members of the panel.

§ 1:9. Federal Courts.

The Supreme Court of the United States is the highest court in the federal system. The courts of appeals are intermediate courts. The district courts and special courts are the lower courts.

(a) **Supreme Court of the United States.** The Supreme Court is the only court expressly established by the Constitution. Congress is authorized by the Constitution to create other federal courts.

The Supreme Court has original jurisdiction in all cases affecting ambassadors, other public ministers, and consuls, and in those cases in which a state is a party. Except as regulated by Congress, it has appellate jurisdiction in all cases that may be brought into the federal courts in accordance with the terms of the Constitution. The Supreme Court also has appellate jurisdiction of certain cases that have been decided by the supreme courts of the states. Thousands of cases are filed with this court each year.

(b) **Courts of Appeals.** The United States, including the District of Columbia, is divided into 12 judicial circuits. Each of the circuits has a court of appeals. These courts are courts of record.

A court of appeals has appellate jurisdiction only and is empowered to review the final decisions of the district courts, except in cases that may be taken directly to the Supreme Court. The decisions of the courts of appeals are final in most cases. An appeal may be taken as a matter of right on certain constitutional questions. Otherwise, review depends on the discretion of the Supreme Court and, in some cases, of the court of appeals.

(c) **District Courts.** The United States, including the District of Columbia, is further divided into a number of judicial districts. Some states form a single district, whereas others are divided into two or more districts. District courts are also located in the territories.

The district courts have original jurisdiction in practically all cases that may be maintained in the federal courts. They are the trial courts for civil and criminal cases.

Civil cases that may be brought in these district courts are (a) civil suits brought by the United States; (b) actions brought by citizens of the same state claiming land under grants by different states; (c) proceedings under the bankruptcy, internal revenue, postal, copyright, and patent laws; (d) civil cases of admiralty and maritime jurisdiction; (e) actions against national banking associations; (f) cases between citizens of different states or between citizens of one state and a foreign state involving $10,000 or more; and (g) cases that arise under the federal Constitution, or laws and treaties made thereunder.

(d) **Other Federal Courts.** In addition to the Supreme Court, the courts of appeals, and the district courts, the following tribunals have been created by Congress to determine other matters as indicated by their titles: Court of International Trade, Claims Court, Tax Court, Court of Military Appeals, and the territorial courts.

§ 1:10.   State Courts.

The system of courts in the various states is organized along lines similar to the federal court system, although differing in details, such as the number of courts, their names, and jurisdiction.

(a) **State Supreme Court.** The highest court in most states is known as the Supreme Court. In a few states it may have a different name, such as "Court of Appeals" in New York. The jurisdiction of a supreme court is ordinarily appellate, although in a few instances it is original. In some states the supreme court is required to render an opinion on certain questions that may be referred to it by the legislature or by the chief executive of the state. The decision of a state supreme court is final in all cases not involving the federal Constitution, laws, and treaties.

(b) **Intermediate Courts.** In some states, intermediate courts have original jurisdiction in a few cases but, in the main, they have appellate jurisdiction of cases removed for review from the county or district courts. They are known as superior, circuit, or district appellate courts. As a general rule, their decisions may be reviewed by the highest state court.

(c) **County and District Courts.** These courts of record have appellate jurisdiction of cases tried in the justice of the peace and police courts, as well as general original jurisdiction of criminal and civil cases. They also have jurisdiction of wills and guardianship matters, except when, as in some states, the jurisdiction of such cases has been given to special orphans', surrogate, or probate courts.

(d) **Other State Courts.** In addition to the foregoing, the following, which are ordinarily not courts of record, have jurisdiction as indicated by their titles: city or municipal courts, police courts, traffic courts, small claims courts, and justice of the peace courts.

D. COURT PROCEDURE

Detailed laws specify how, when, and where a legal dispute can be brought to court. These rules of procedure are necessary in order to achieve an orderly, fair determination of litigation and in order to obtain, as far as humanly possible, the same decisions on the same facts. It is important to remember, however, that there is no uniform judicial procedure. While there are definite similarities, the law of each state may differ from that of the others. For the most part the uniform laws that have been adopted do not regulate matters of procedure.

§ 1:11.   Steps in a Lawsuit.

The following are the steps in a lawsuit. Not every step is taken in every suit. The facts of a case may be such that the case ends before every possible step is taken. The parties may not want to fight it out to the very end or to raise every possible point.

(a) **Commencement of Action.** An action is begun by filing a complaint with the clerk of the appropriate court. The complaint generally consists of a description of the acts complained of by the plaintiff and a request for some sort of reparation or relief.

(b) **Service of Process.** The defendant must be served with **process** (a writ, notice, or summons; or the complaint itself) to give notice that the action is pending and to subject the defendant to the power of the court.

(c) **Pleadings.** After process has been served on the defendant and the plaintiff has filed a complaint, the defendant must make some reply after receiving the complaint, generally within 15 or 20 days. If the defendant fails to do so, the plaintiff ordinarily wins the case by default.

Before answering the plaintiff's complaint, the defendant may make certain preliminary objections, such as that the action was brought in the wrong court or that service was not properly made. If the objection is sustained, the case may be ended, depending upon the nature of the objection, or the plaintiff may be allowed to correct the mistake if that is possible. The defendant may also raise the objection, sometimes called a **motion to dismiss** or **demurrer**, that even if the plaintiff's complaint is accepted as true, the plaintiff is still not entitled to any relief.

If the defendant makes an objection but the objection is overruled or dismissed, the defendant must file an **answer**, which either admits or denies some or all of the facts asserted by the plaintiff. For example, if the plaintiff declared that the defendant made a contract on a certain date, the defendant may either admit making the contract or deny having done so. An admission of having made the contract does not end the case, for the defendant may then be able to plead defenses, for example, that at a later date the plaintiff and defendant had agreed to set the contract aside.

Without regard to whether the defendant pleads such new matter, the defendant may generally assert a **counterclaim** or **cross complaint** against the plaintiff. Thus, the defendant may contend the plaintiff owes money or is liable for damages and that this liability should be offset against any claim which the plaintiff may have.

After the defendant files an answer, the plaintiff may generally file preliminary objections to the answer. Just as the defendant could raise objections, the plaintiff may, in certain instances, argue that a counterclaim raised by the defendant could not be asserted in that action, that the answer is fatally defective in form, or that it is not legally sufficient. Again the court must pass upon the preliminary objections. When these are disposed of, the pleading stage is ordinarily over.

Generally, all of the pleadings in an action may raise only a few or perhaps one question of law, or a question of fact, or both. Thus, the whole case may depend on whether a letter admittedly written by the defendant amounted to an acceptance of the plaintiff's offer, thereby constituting a contract. If this question of law is answered in favor of the plaintiff, a judgment will be entered for the plaintiff; otherwise, for the defendant. By way of contrast, it may be that a certain letter would be an acceptance if it had been written by the defendant; but the defendant may deny having written it. Here the question is one of fact, and the judgment is entered for the plaintiff if it is determined that the facts happened as claimed by the plaintiff. Otherwise the judgment is entered for the defendant.

If the only questions involved are questions of law, the court will decide the case on the pleadings alone since there is no need for a trial to determine the facts. If questions of fact are involved, then there must be a trial to determine what the facts really were.

(d) Pretrial Procedure. Many states and the federal courts have adopted other procedural steps that may be employed before the trial, with the purpose of eliminating the need for a trial, simplifying the issues to be tried, or giving the parties information needed for preparation for trial.

(1) Motion for Judgment on the Pleadings. After the pleadings are closed, many courts permit either party to move for a **judgment on the pleadings.** When such a motion is made, the court examines the record and may then enter a judgment according to the merits of the case as shown by the record.

(2) Motion for Summary Judgment. In most courts a party may shorten a lawsuit by bringing into court sworn statements and affidavits which show that a claim or defense of the adverse party is false or a sham. This procedure cannot be used when there is substantial dispute of fact concerning the matters to be proved by the use of the affidavits.

(3) Pretrial Conference. In many courts either party may request the court to call a **pretrial conference,** or the court may take the initiative in doing so. This conference is in substance a round table discussion by a judge of the court and the attorneys in the case. The object of the conference is to eliminate matters that are not in dispute and to determine what issues remain for litigation. Some cases are settled at this stage.

(4) Discovery. The Federal Rules of Civil Procedure and similar rules in a large number of states now permit one party to inquire of the adverse party and of all witnesses about anything relating to the action. This includes asking the adverse party the names of witnesses; asking the adverse party and the witnesses what they know about the case; examining, inspecting, and photographing books, records, buildings, and machines; and making an examination of the physical or mental condition of a party when it has a bearing on the action. These procedures are classed as **discovery**.

(5) Depositions. Ordinarily a witness testifies in court at the time of the trial. In some instances it may be necessary or desirable to take such testimony out of court before the time of the trial. It may be that the witness is aged or infirm or is about to leave the state or country and will not be present when the trial of the action is held. In such case the interested party is permitted to have the testimony, called a **deposition**, of the witness taken outside of the court.

(e) **Determination of Facts.** A legal system must provide for someone to determine the facts of a case when the parties do not agree on the facts.

(1) The Trier of Facts. If the legal controversy is one which under the common law would have been tried by a jury, either party to the action has the constitutional right today to demand that the action be tried before a jury. If all parties agree, however, the case may be tried by the court or judge alone without a jury, and in some instances may be referred to a master or a referee appointed by the court to hear the matter.

In equity there is no constitutional right to a jury trial but a chancellor or equity judge may submit questions to a jury. There is the basic difference that in such cases the verdict or decision of the jury is only advisory to the chancellor; that is, the chancellor is not bound by the verdict. In contrast, the verdict of a jury in an action at law is binding on the court unless a basic error is present.

When new causes of action are created by statute, such as the right of an employee to obtain workers' compensation for an injury arising in the course of employment without regard to whether the employer was negligent, there is no constitutional right to a trial by jury. The trier of facts may accordingly be a judge without a jury, or a special administrative board or agency, such as a Workers' Compensation Board.

(2) Basis for Decision. The trier of fact, whether a jury, a judge, a referee, or a board, can only decide questions of fact on the basis of evidence presented before it. Each party offers evidence. The evidence usually consists of the answers of persons to questions in court. Their answers are called **testimony**. The evidence may also include **real evidence**, that is, tangible things, such as papers, books, and records. It is immaterial whether the records are kept in ordinary ledger books or stored on computer tapes because a computer printout of data made for trial is admissible as evidence of the information contained in the computer.[6] In some cases, such as a damage action for improper construction of a building, the trier of fact may be taken to view the building so that a better understanding can be obtained.

[6]Washington v Ben-neth, 34 Wash App 600, 663 P2d 156 (1983).

The witness who testifies in court is usually a person who had some direct contact with the facts in the case, such as a person who saw the events occur or who heard one of the parties say something. In some instances, it is also proper to offer the testimony of persons who have no connection with the case when they have expert knowledge and their opinions as experts are desired.

A witness who refuses to appear in court may be ordered to do so by a **subpoena**, and may also be compelled to bring relevant papers to the court by a **subpoena duces tecum.** If the witness does not obey the subpoena, the witness may be arrested for contempt of court. In some states the names of the order upon the witness and the procedure for contempt have been changed, but the substance remains the same.

(f) **Conduct of the Trial.** The conduct of a trial will be discussed in terms of a jury trial. Generally a case is one of several assigned for trial on a certain day or during a certain trial period. When the turn of the case is called, the opposing counsel seat themselves at tables in front of the judge and the jury is selected. After the jury is sworn, the attorneys usually make **opening addresses** to the jury. Details vary in different jurisdictions, but the general pattern is that each attorney tells the jury what will be proven. When this step has been completed, the presentation of the evidence by both sides begins.

The attorney for the plaintiff starts with the first witness and asks all the questions desired that are proper. This is called the **direct examination** of the witness since it is made by the attorney calling the witness. After the direct examination has been finished, the opposing counsel asks the same witness other questions in an effort to disprove the prior answers. This is called **cross-examination.**

After the cross-examination has been completed, the attorney for the plaintiff may ask the same witness other questions to overcome the effect of the cross-examination. This is called **redirect examination.** This step in turn may be followed by further examination by the defendant's attorney, called **recross-examination.**

After the examination of the plaintiff's witness has been concluded, the plaintiff's second witness takes the witness stand and is subjected to an examination in the same way as the first. This continues until all of the plaintiff's witnesses have been called. Then the plaintiff "rests," and the defendant calls the first defense witness. The pattern of examination of witnesses is repeated except that now the defendant is calling the witnesses, and the defendant's attorney conducts the direct and redirect examination while the questioning by the plaintiff's attorney is cross- or recross-examination.

After the witnesses of both parties have been examined and all the evidence has been presented, each attorney makes another address, a **summation,** to the jury which sums up the case and suggests that a particular verdict be returned by the jury.

(g) **Charge to the Jury and Verdict.** The summation by the attorneys is followed by a **charge** of the judge to the jury. This charge is a résumé of what has happened at the trial and an explanation of the law applicable. At its conclusion, the judge instructs the jury to retire and study the case in the light of the charge and then return a **verdict**. By such instructions, the judge leaves to the jury the problem of determining the facts but states the law that they must apply to such facts as they may find. The jury then retires to secret deliberation in the jury room.

(h) **Taking the Case from the Jury and Attacking the Verdict.** At several points during the trial, or immediately after it, a party may take a step to end the case or to set aside the verdict which the jury has returned.

(1) Voluntary Nonsuit. A plaintiff who is dissatisfied with the progress of the trial, may wish to stop the trial and begin again at a later date. In most jurisdictions this can be done by taking a **voluntary nonsuit.**

(2) Compulsory Nonsuit. After the plaintiff has presented the testimony of all witnesses, the defendant may request the court to enter a nonsuit on the ground that the case presented by the plaintiff does not entitle the plaintiff to recover. This is called a **compulsory nonsuit.**

(3) Mistrial. When necessary to avoid great injustice, the trial court may declare that there has been a **mistrial** and thereby terminate the trial and postpone it to a later date. While either party may move the court to enter a mistrial, it is discretionary with the court whether it does so. A mistrial is commonly entered when the evidence has been of a highly prejudicial character and the trial judge does not believe that the jury can ignore it even when instructed to do so, or when a juror has been guilty of misconduct.

(4) Directed Verdict. After the presentation of all the evidence at the trial, either party may request the court to direct the jury to return a verdict in favor of the requesting party. When the plaintiff would not be entitled to recover even if all the testimony in the plaintiff's favor were believed, the defendant is entitled to have the court direct the jury to return a verdict for the defendant. The plaintiff is entitled to a directed verdict when, even if all the evidence on behalf of the defendant were believed, the jury would still be required to find for the plaintiff. In some states, the defendant may make a motion for a directed verdict at the close of the plaintiff's proof.

(5) New Trial. After the verdict has been returned by the jury, a party may move for a new trial if not satisfied with the verdict or with the amount of damages that has been awarded. If it is clear that the jury made a mistake or if material evidence that could not have been discovered before the trial becomes available later, the court will award a new trial and the case will be tried again before another jury.

(6) Judgment N.O.V. If the verdict returned by the jury is clearly wrong as a matter of law, the court may set aside the verdict and enter a judgment contrary to the verdict. This in some states is called a **judgment** *non obstante veredicto* (notwithstanding the verdict), or as it is abbreviated, a judgment n.o.v.

(i) **Judgment and Costs.** The court enters a judgment conforming to the verdict unless a new trial has been granted, a mistrial declared after the return of the verdict, or a judgment n.o.v. entered. Generally whoever is the winning party will also be awarded costs in the action. In equity actions or those that had their origin in equity, and in certain statutory proceedings, the court has discretion to award costs to the winner or to divide them between the parties.

Costs ordinarily include the costs of filing papers with the court, the cost of having the sheriff or other officers of the court take official action, the statutory fees paid to the witnesses, the cost of a jury fee, if any, and the cost of printing the record when this is required on appeal. They do not include compensation for the time spent by the party in preparing the case or in being present at the trial, the time lost from work because of the case, or the fee paid to an attorney. Sometimes when a special statutory action is brought, the statute authorizes recovery of a small attorney's fee. Thus, a mechanics' lien statute may authorize the recovery of an attorney's fee of 10 percent of the amount recovered, or a "reasonable attorney's fee." As a general rule, the costs that a party recovers represent only a small part of the total expenses actually sustained in the litigation.

(l) **Appeal.** After a judgment has been entered, the party who is aggrieved thereby may appeal. This means that a party who wins the judgment but is not awarded as much as had been hoped, as well as a party who loses the case, may take an appeal.

The appellate court does not hear witnesses. It examines the record of the proceedings before the lower court, that is, the file of the case containing all the pleadings, the testimony of witnesses, and the judge's charge, to see if there was an error of law. To assist the court, the attorneys for the parties file arguments or briefs and generally make arguments orally before the court.

If the appellate court does not agree with the application of the law made by the lower court, it generally sets aside or modifies the action of the lower court and enters such judgment as it concludes the lower court should have entered. It may set aside the action of the lower court and send the case back to the lower court with directions to hold a new trial or with directions to enter a new judgment in accordance with the opinion that is filed by the appellate court.

(k) **Execution.** After a judgment has been entered or after an appeal has been decided, the losing party generally will comply with the judgment of the court. If not, the winning party may then take steps to execute or carry out the judgment.

If the judgment is for the payment of a sum of money, the plaintiff may direct the sheriff or other judicial officer to sell as much of the property of the defendant as is necessary to pay the plaintiff's judgment and the costs of the proceedings and of the execution. Acting under this authorization, the sheriff may make a public sale of the defendant's property and apply the proceeds to the payment of the plaintiff's judgment. In most states the defendant is allowed a limited monetary exemption and an exemption for certain articles, such as personal clothing and tools of trade.

If the judgment is for the recovery of specific property, the judgment will direct the sheriff to deliver the property to the plaintiff.

If the judgment directs the defendant to do or to refrain from doing an act, it is commonly provided that failure to obey the order is a contempt of court punishable by fine or imprisonment.

§ 1:12. Declaratory Judgment.

In this century, a new court procedure for settling disputes, authorized by statute, has made its appearance. This is the **declaratory judgment** procedure. Under it a person, when confronted with the early prospect of an actual controversy, may petition the court to decide the question before loss is actually sustained. A copy of the petition is served on all parties. They may file answers. After all the pleadings have been filed, the court then decides the questions involved just as though a lawsuit had been brought.

E. STREAMLINING JUDICIAL PROCEDURE

The judicial procedure described in this chapter can sometimes be long and costly. To some extent this can be corrected both within and outside of the existing formal legal system.

§ 1:13. Streamlining within the Legal System.

A judge can at many points of the lawsuit act in a proper way that will reduce the time and expense of the lawsuit. One of the greatest time-cost factors in modern litigation is the wide discovery that has been typical since the adoption of the Federal Rules of Civil Procedure in 1938. Such rules and similar state rules all contain a provision authorizing the court to limit discovery. Many judges do not attempt to exercise any control over the extent and scope of discovery with the result that the entire case is tried twice, once in the discovery proceeding phase and a second time in court. In addition, the discovery phase may go to great lengths on what has been nicknamed a "fishing expedition."

In the course of a pretrial conference, a judge can indicate the merit or lack of merit of a particular position of a litigant. Without in any way forcing a settlement on the parties, this insight into the mind of the judge will often persuade the attorneys to compromise the action. At the trial itself, the judge has the duty to admit proper evidence and to exclude improper and cumulative evidence. A strong judge will keep close reins on the evidence at the trial. Other judges will let the trial ramble on while time goes by and costs increase.

§ 1:14. Streamlining Outside of the Legal System.

Litigants may avoid the cost and delay of litigation by having their disputes settled by the private agencies of arbitration, reference to a third person, or in some cases, reference to an association tribunal.[7] In addition to these, various experiments have been made to provide a substitute method of dispute determination or a method of encouraging negotiation.

(a) **Summary Jury Trial.** This is in effect a dry run or mock trial in which the lawyers present their claims before a jury of six persons. The object is to get the reaction of a sample jury. No evidence is presented before this jury and it bases its opinion solely on what the lawyers state at this trial. The

[7] See § 1:7

determination of the jury has no binding effect but it has value in that it gives the lawyers some idea of what a jury might think if there would be an actual trial. This has special value when the heart of a case is whether something is reasonable under all the circumstances. When the lawyers see how the sample jury reacts, the lawyers may moderate their positions and reach a settlement.

(b) **Rent-a-Judge.** Under this plan, the parties hire a judge to hear the case. In many states this is done by the parties' voluntarily choosing the judge as a "referee," with the judge acting under a statute authorizing the appointment of referees.[8] Under such a statute, the referee hears all the evidence just as though there were a regular trial and the judge's determination is binding on the parties unless reversed on appeal. In some jurisdictions, special provision is made for the parties to agree that the decision of the judge selected as referee shall be final.

(c) **Mini-Trial.** When only part of a case is really disputed, the parties may stay within the framework of the legal lawsuit but agree that only the disputed issues be submitted to a jury. For example, when there is no real dispute over the liability of the defendant but the parties disagree as to the damages, the issue of damages alone may be submitted to the jury.

In some states, instead of submitting the matter to a regular jury, a mini-trial will be held with the agreement of the attorneys. Under this system, the parties agree that a particular person, frequently a retired judge, should listen to the evidence on the disputed issues and decide the case. The agreement of the parties for the mini-trial may specify whether this decision is binding on the parties. As a practical matter, the evaluation of the case by a neutral will often bring the opposing parties together to reach a settlement.

(d) **Contract Provisions.** The parties' contract may pave the way for the settlement of future disputes by containing clauses requiring the parties to submit disputes to arbitration or to make use of one of the extralegal procedures above described. In addition, contracts may provide that no action may be taken until after the expiration of a specified cooling off period, or that the parties shall continue in the performance of their contract even though there is a dispute between them.

Trade associations will commonly require their members to employ out-of-court methods of dispute settlement. Thus the National Association of Home Builders requires its member builders to employ arbitration. The National Automobile Dealers Association provides for panels to determine warranty claims of customers. The decision of such panels is final as to the dealer but the consumer is allowed to bring a regular lawsuit if he or she loses before the panel.

SUMMARY

Law consists of the pattern of rules established by society to govern conduct and relationships. These rules can be expressed as constitutional provisions, statutes, case decisions, and administrative regulations. Law can

[8]See § 1:7(b)

be further classified as substantive or procedural, and it can be described in terms of its historical origins or by the subject to which it relates.

Courts have been created to hear and resolve legal disputes. A specific court's power is defined by its jurisdiction, which may be original or appellate, general or special, and criminal or civil. The judge is the primary officer of a court. A jury may serve to determine issues of fact.

Courts in the United States are organized in two distinct systems, federal and state. The Supreme Court of the United States is the highest federal court. The United States Courts of Appeals are the intermediate appellate courts and the United States District Courts are the trial level courts. Most state court systems are similarly organized.

A lawsuit is begun by filing a complaint. The defendant named in the complaint must be served with process, that is, the defendant must be notified that an action has been commenced. The issues to be tried are developed through pleadings and pretrial procedures. Testimony and real evidence are presented at trial, where attorneys for the parties introduce evidence and examine the witnesses.

Because a formal trial can be time consuming and costly, the parties sometimes agree to an alternative method of resolving the dispute. Among common alternatives are the summary jury trial, the private judge/referee, the mini-trial, and contract arbitration.

QUESTIONS AND CASE PROBLEMS

1. Jones tells you that he has a business dispute with his partner Smith. He does not want to sue Smith. Is there any way in which the dispute can be settled without going to court?
2. How can parties to a dispute avoid the expense of litigation?
3. What is the difference between original and appellate jurisdiction of a court?
4. What is the most significant uniform law?
5. On learning of the many steps of a lawsuit, Elaine exclaimed that all lawsuits must take a very long time. Is she correct?
6. Tenton owed Orlando $1,000. Orlando has a friend, Helen, who is a judge in the Court of International Trade. Orlando wants to sue Tenton in that court. May he do so?
7. Carolyn, Elwood, and Isabella are involved in a real estate development. The development is a failure and Carolyn, Elwood, and Isabella want to have their rights determined. They could bring a lawsuit but they are afraid that the case is so complicated that a judge and jury not familiar with the problems of real estate development would not reach a proper result. What can they do?
8. Attorneys are and, at the same time, are not officers of the court. Explain this contradictory statement.
9. Ames brought an action against Jarvis Co. to recover damages resulting from a breach of contract. No process was served on the defendants, but Ames published notice of the action in the newspaper. Ames secured a judgment against the defendants. Later it was contended that the judgment was not valid. Do you agree? Why?

10. How does each of the following pretrial procedures contribute to the determination of legal disputes?
    (a) Motion for judgment on the pleadings
    (b) Motion for summary judgment
    (c) Pretrial conference
    (d) Discovery
11. A witness who is willing to testify concerning certain facts in a case lives in another state. How can the testimony be secured for use as evidence in the trial?
12. Outline briefly the steps in a trial beginning with the opening statements by the attorneys.
13. The right of privacy is a fundamental right which has always been recognized by American law. Appraise this statement.
14. The right to trial by jury is a fundamental procedure which must always be used whenever any issue of fact is to be determined. Appraise this statement.

CHAPTER 2

LAW AS AN EXPRESSION OF

SOCIAL FORCES

CHAPTER OBJECTIVES

After studying this chapter you will be able to:
1. Describe how social objectives make the law.
2. List the most common social objectives that make the law.
3. Explain the way in which the social objectives may sometimes conflict.
4. Show how a rule of law may be a synthesis of conflicting objectives.
5. Describe how law is an evolutionary process.

In Chapter 1, we defined "law" as a body of *enforceable* principles of conduct. In a democratic society, these principles of conduct are determined by the people — they represent an expression of the collective desires of the people to encourage conduct that is right, and good, and just, and to discourage conduct that is wrong, or evil, or unjust. In this regard, the law has its underpinnings in ethics, and the ethics of a society constitute a force that helps to mold that society's law.

But a society's law is an imperfect image of its ethics. The added element of enforceability, the notion that the society's resources will be brought to bear against an individual to either require or prohibit certain conduct, makes the translation from ethics to law a conservative one. In practice then, the law is not only reflective of a society's ethics but is also reflective of other social forces.

§ 2:1.   Ethics and the Law.

Ethics concern basic notions of what actions are right or wrong, good or evil. These notions vary from person to person, from society to society, and from time to time. The concepts are molded of human experience,

22

slowly and gradually taking form as tacit assumptions, oral or written traditions, expressions of public conscience, and eventually as working codes.

Today many companies have established codes of ethics as guides for their employees, requiring that company business be conducted not only in compliance with the law, but also in accordance with the highest standards of business integrity and honest dealings.

The law, as opposed to broad ethical standards, must be more definite and stable in order to be capable of consistent enforcement. Notwithstanding this distinction between law and ethics, it is clear that there is a strong relation between them. Laws are made and remade as notions of justice change. A society's sense of justice is in turn influenced by its laws. The interactions are unquestionably complex, but a few observations can nonetheless be made.

(a) **Law as the Crystallization of Ethics.** While all ethical values are not capable of expression as laws, certainly the more elemental ethical principles find their way into a society's legal framework. An ethical regard for the value of human life is crystallized as criminal codes detailing precisely defined degrees of offense — murder, manslaughter, negligent homicide. Similarly, an ethical obligation to look after the well-being of others takes the form of the parents' legally enforceable duty to care for their children. In these areas the law approaches the attainment of ethical values of society and locks the ethical concepts into binding rules of conduct.

But the law cannot equal the reach of ethical values, at least partly because some things are better left to individual choice and initiative. Criminal penalties for behavior that actively or negligently endangers human life stop short of imposing a general duty to intervene to save a life already in danger. And legal obligations to further the well-being of others are not extended to members of society generally, but only to those with a dependent relationship. In fact, it might be said that if a society's ethical codes constitute its concept of ideal behavior, then that society's law is its minimum standard of conduct.

(b) **Societal Ethics as the Blueprint for Future Law.** As we noted earlier, a society's ethical values change over time. The law similarly evolves to keep pace with changing technologies and values, though at a much more deliberate pace. Because of the close relation between law and ethics, the ethical values of today's society can be regarded as a blueprint for the law of tomorrow.

(c) **Particular Applications.** As you study this business law text, or any law text, you will find many instances of established legal principles that became inadequate to serve society's changing notions of what was right or just. You will see that, as public sentiment against a particular law or legal principle grew, a legal system that was otherwise resistant to change found various ways to relieve the pressure. The change sometimes took the form of a judicial decision that found a new exception to an established rule or simply overturned an earlier decision. Or the change may have been manifested as a new statute or a constitutional amendment. Here are a few illustrations.

As we have already discussed in Chapter 1, there was not always a legally recognized right of privacy. The very rapid dissemination of information to great numbers of people made possible by the development of the modern newspaper, and much later radio and television, created a need for enforceable protection against unwarranted intrusion upon private lives. This right was first cited as a basis for recovery in the lower courts of New York.[1] It has since been elevated to a constitutionally protected right.[2]

Another example of changes in societal ethics resulting in changes in the law involves consumerism. As of 1776, the concept of what was "right" in the marketplace meant that everyone was equal. That was the year in which the Declaration of Independence proclaimed the political equality of everyone and Adam Smith in his *The Wealth of Nations* declared that every person was the economic equal of every other person and should be allowed to move about in the marketplace freely and without restraint. But all this was before the rise of mass production, modern distribution, and giant sellers. Beginning in the middle of this century, society began to feel that it was just not "right" to treat the consumer as the equal of the giant seller. The result, consumer protection laws, gave the consumer special protection because of such inequality. Conversely, the Uniform Commercial Code places special duty on merchants. Our American ideal of equality has been modified in recognition of the fact that equality does not exist in the marketplace.

(d) **Implications for Business.** As the size, resources, and business patterns of society change, what seems right today may seem wrong in the future. While society's changing notions of what is right and just do not create binding obligations on businesses and business people, they do constitute a force that will help to mold future law. Businesses that act irresponsibly and with disregard for society's view of what is right will speed the transition from ethical concept to enforceable law. Business can only avoid society's tendency toward more stringent regulation and over "legalization" by acting responsibly and in harmony with societal ethics. In the remainder of this chapter, we will examine some of the basic principles that this society regards as important in making its ethical decisions and its laws.

§ 2:2.　Objectives of the Law.

Every rule has an objective, and it is helpful in understanding law to know the objectives of the law.

The more common objectives of the law are discussed against the background of the general objective of creating and providing order, stability, and justice.

(a) **Protection of the State.** A number of laws are designed to protect the existing governments, both state and national. Laws condemning treason, sedition, and subversive practices are examples of society taking measures to preserve governmental systems. Less dramatic are the laws that impose taxes to provide for the support of those governments.

(b) **Personal Protection.** At an early date, laws developed to protect the individual from being injured or killed. The field of criminal law is

---

[1]Manola v. Stevens, N.Y. Sup. Ct. 1890, in N. Y. Times, June 15, 18, 21, 1980 (unreported).

[2]Griswold v. Connecticut, 381 U.S. 479 (1965).

devoted to a large extent to the protection of the person. In addition, under civil law a suit can be brought to recover damages for the harm done by criminal acts. For example, a person who steals an automobile is subject to a penalty imposed by the state in the form of imprisonment or a fine, or both. In addition, the thief is liable to the owner for the money value of the automobile. Over the course of time, the protection of personal rights has broadened to include the protection of reputation, and privacy, and to protect contracts and business relations from malicious interference by outsiders.

FACTS:

The state of Arizona gave government employees the option to select one of several plans under which they would take only part of their regular pay and allow the remaining part to be held in a fund with payments being made to the employees on retirement. The amounts paid on retirement would be controlled by the use of standard actuarial tables showing the expectable life of people. These tables showed that women lived longer than men, from which it was concluded that the payment from the fund had to continue over a longer period for a woman than for a man. In order to make the money last, each plan offered provided that a woman should receive a smaller amount per month than a man although each of them had postponed the same amount of salary. Nathalie Norris claimed that this violated the federal Civil Rights Act which prohibits discrimination on the basis of sex.

DECISION:

Arizona violated the rights of women under the federal Civil Rights Act. Under that Act, a woman postponing part of her salary until retirement was entitled to receive the same monthly retirement payment as a man who had postponed the same number of dollars as the woman. The woman could not be deprived of this equality of treatment because actuarial tables showed that she had a longer life expectancy. [Arizona Governing Committee v Norris, 463 US 1073 (1983)]

It is a federal offense to knowingly injure, intimidate, or interfere with anyone exercising a basic civil right (such as voting), taking part in any federal government program, or receiving federal assistance. Interference with attendance in a public school or college, with participation in any state or local governmental program, with service as a juror in a state court, or with the use of any public facility (common carrier, hotel, or restaurant) is prohibited when based on race, color, religion, or national origin discrimination.[3]

Protection of the person is expanding to protect economic interests. Laws prohibiting discrimination in employment, in furnishing hotel accommodations and transportation, and in commercial transactions in the sale of property are an extension of the concept of protecting the person. Because membership in a professional association, a labor union, or a trade or busi-

---

[3]Civil Obedience Act of 1968, PL 90–284, 18 United States Code § 245.

ness group has economic importance to its members, an applicant can no longer be arbitrarily excluded from the membership, nor may a member be expelled without notice of the charges made and an opportunity to be heard.[4]

(c) **Protection of Public Health, Safety, and Morals.** The law seeks to protect the public health, safety, and morals in many ways. Laws relating to quarantine, food inspection, and compulsory vaccination protect the public health. Laws regulating highway speeds and laws requiring fire escapes or guard devices around moving parts of factory machinery are for the safety of the public. Laws prohibiting the sale of liquor to minors and those prohibiting obscenity protect the morals of the public.

FACTS:

A police broadcast stated that a named motel had been robbed by two men using a sawed-off shotgun. The men were reported fleeing in an automobile traveling northwestwardly. Police officers hearing this report assumed that the robbers were seeking to escape to Chicago and went to the nearest intersection of the road leading to that city. They saw a car which they thought might contain the suspects. They trailed the car to another intersection where the better lighting gave a better view of the driver. The police then stopped the car. After it was stopped, the police saw a shotgun in the back of the car and a man attempting to hide on the back seat. The men in the car were arrested and prosecuted for robbery of the motel. They claimed that the evidence of what was learned when their car was stopped could not be admitted at the trial because they had been stopped without a search warrant.

DECISION:

The evidence was admissible because the warrantless search was proper under the circumstances. While the Fourth Amendment to the federal Constitution prohibits unreasonable searches and seizures without a warrant, it is necessary in applying this prohibition to balance the rights of the public and the rights of the accused. Under the circumstances it was reasonable for the police officers to stop the automobile although they did not have a warrant, and what they saw after the automobile was stopped was admissible in evidence. [Williams v Indiana, 261 Ind 547, 307 NE2d 457 (1974)]

(d) **Property Protection.** Just as laws have developed to protect the individual's physical well-being, laws have developed to protect one's property from damage, destruction, and other harmful acts. As already noted, a thief who steals an automobile is civilly liable to the owner of the automobile for its value and is criminally responsible to the state.

(e) **Title Protection.** Because of the importance of ownership of property, one of the objectives of the law has been to protect the title of the owner of property. Thus, if property is stolen, the true owner may recover it from the thief, and even from a person who purchased it in good faith from the thief.

[4]Silver v New York Stock Exchange, 373 US 341 (1963); Cunningham v Burbank Board of Realtors, 262 Cal App 2d 211, 68 Cal Rptr 653 (1968).

(f) **Freedom of Personal Action.** In the Anglo-American stream of history, the desire for freedom from political domination gave rise to the American Revolution, and the desire for freedom from economic domination gave rise to the free enterprise philosophy. Today we find freedom as the dominant element in the constitutional provisions for the protection of freedom of religion, press, and speech,[5] and also in such laws as those against trusts or business combinations in restraint of trade by others.

This right of freedom of personal action, however, cannot be exercised by one person in such a way that it interferes to an unreasonable extent with the rights of others. Freedom of speech, for example, does not mean freedom to speak or write a malicious, false statement about another person's character or reputation. In effect, this means that one person's freedom of speech must be balanced with another person's right to be free from defamation of character or reputation.

(g) **Freedom of Use of Property.** Freedom of action is often stated in terms of freedom of use of property. For example, the owner of an automobile is free to drive the car or not, to say who shall ride in it, to sell or give it away, and so on.

It must be remembered, however, that there are often restrictions on the use of property, such as speed laws governing the automobile, zoning laws regulating buildings, and antipollution laws restricting factories.

FACTS:

The Great Atlantic & Pacific Tea Co. owned a building several hundred feet away from one of the boundaries of the grounds for the New York World's Fair of 1964. On the top of the building, approximately 110 feet above the ground, was a red neon A & P sign approximately 250 feet long with letters 10 feet high. The World's Fair placed artificial trees and shrubbery along the boundary line to hide the electric sign, which the Fair claimed was generally unesthetic and interfered with a fountain and electric light display of the Fair. A & P sued to enjoin the Fair from hiding its sign in this manner.

DECISION:

Injunction refused. The fact that an occupier's use of land causes harm to the owner of neighboring land is not controlling. Here the use by the Fair of its land was a reasonable use to protect its exhibits from outside interference. The fact that it was advantageous to A & P that the Fair make no use of its land did not justify the conclusion that the use which the Fair made was unreasonable and subject to injunction as a nuisance. [Great A & P Tea Co. v New York World's Fair, 42 Misc 2d 855, 240 NYS2d 256 (1964)]

(h) **Enforcement of Intent.** When persons voluntarily enter into a transaction, the law usually seeks to enforce their intent. This objective is closely related to the concept that the law seeks to protect the individual's freedom of action. For example, if a person provides by will for the distribution of property upon death, the law will generally allow the property to pass

[5]McLellan v Mississippi State Bar Ass'n (Miss) 413 So2d 705 (1982).

to the persons intended by the deceased owner. The law will likewise seek to carry out the intention of the parties to a business transaction.

The extent to which the intent of one person or of several persons will be carried out has certain limitations. Sometimes the intent is not effective unless it is manifested by a particular written formality. For example, a deceased person may have intended to leave property to a friend, but in most states that intent must be shown by a written will signed by the deceased owner. Likewise, in some cases the intent of the parties may not be carried out because the law regards the intent as illegal.

(i) **Protection from Exploitation, Fraud, and Oppression.** Many rules of law have developed in the courts and many statutes have been enacted to protect certain groups or individuals from exploitation or oppression by others.

FACTS:

Dr. Falcone was a licensed and qualified physician and surgeon, holding degrees from a Philadelphia school and from the College of Medicine of the University of Milan, who practiced surgery and obstetrics. He met all the requirements of the bylaws of the Middlesex County Medical Society. The Society, however, refused him membership on the ground that it had an unwritten rule requiring that every applicant have four years of study in a medical school recognized by the American Medical Association. Dr. Falcone did not meet this requirement since the Philadelphia school was not AMA-approved and, although the University of Milan was so approved, the course was not four years. The local hospitals refused to allow him to practice surgery because he was not a member of the County Medical Society. Dr. Falcone brought suit against the Society for refusing to admit him to membership. The Society defended on the ground that it was a private organization and could determine its own membership rules.

DECISION:

Judgment for Falcone. With the close relationship between the local hospitals and the County Medical Society, exclusion from the Society was in effect a revocation of Dr. Falcone's license to practice surgery. Membership in the Society therefore ceased to be a private social matter and became an economic necessity for the individual doctor and a matter of great concern to the public health and welfare. Consequently public policy prohibited any association from adopting a membership standard which imposed unreasonably higher requirements than were imposed by the state in licensing doctors. The Society regulation was arbitrary and unreasonable. It was therefore invalid and could not be enforced. [Falcone v Middlesex County Medical Society, 34 NJ 582, 170 A2d 791 (1961)]

Thus, the law developed that a minor (a person under legal age) could set aside contracts, subject to certain exceptions, in order to protect the minor.

Persons who buy food that is packed in tin cans are given certain rights against the seller and the manufacturer. Since they cannot see the contents, buyers of such products need special protection from unscrupulous canners. The consumer is also protected by laws against adulteration and poisons in food, drugs, and household products. Laws prohibiting unfair competition and discrimination, both economic and social, are also designed to protect from oppression.

(j) **Furtherance of Trade.** Society seeks to further trade in a variety of ways, as by establishing a currency as a medium of payment; by recognizing and giving legal effect to installment sales; by adopting special rules for checks, notes, and similar instruments so that they can be widely used as credit devices and substitutes for money; and by enacting laws to mitigate the harmful effects of alternating periods of depression and inflation.

Laws that have been considered in connection with other objectives may also serve to further trade. For example, laws protecting against unfair competition have the objective of furthering trade, as well as the objective of protecting certain classes from oppression by others.

(k) **Creditor Protection.** Society seeks to protect the rights of creditors and to protect them from dishonest or fraudulent acts of debtors. Initially, creditors are protected by the law that makes contracts binding and that provides machinery for the enforcement of contracts, and by the provision of the federal Constitution that prohibits states from impairing the obligation of contracts. Further, creditors may compel a debtor to come into bankruptcy. If the debtor has concealed property or transfers it to a friend in order to hide it from creditors, the law permits the creditors to claim the property for the payment of the debts due them.

(l) **Debtor Rehabilitation.** Society has come to regard it as unsound that debtors should be ruined forever by the burden of their debts. Imprisonment for debt has been abolished. Bankruptcy laws have been adopted to provide the debtor with a means of starting a new economic life. In times of widespread depression, the same objective has been served by special laws prohibiting the foreclosure of mortgages.

(m) **Stability.** Stability is particularly important in all business transactions. When you buy a house for example, you not only want to know the exact meaning of the transaction under today's law but you also want the transaction to have the same meaning in the future.

Because of the desire for stability, courts will ordinarily follow former decisions unless there is a strong reason to depart from them. Likewise, when no former case directly bears on the point involved, the court will reach a decision that is a logical extension of some former decision or which follows a former decision by analogy, rather than to strike off on a fresh path to reach a decision unrelated to the past.

(n) **Flexibility.** If stability were always required, the cause of justice would often be defeated. The reason that originally gave rise to a rule of law may have ceased to exist.[6] Also a rule may later appear unjust because it reflects a concept of justice that is outmoded or obsolete. For example, capital punishment which one age believed just, has been seriously questioned by

---

[6] "It is revolting to have no better reason for a rule of law than that it was laid down in the time of Henry IV. It is still more revolting if the grounds upon which it was laid down have vanished long since, and the rule simply persists from blind imitation of the past." Holmes, Collected Papers 187 (1920).

"The law must be stable, but it must not stand still." Roscoe Pound, *Introduction to the Philosophy of Law* (Connecticut: Yale University Press, 1922).

another age. We must not lose sight of the fact that the rule of law under question was created to further the sense of social justice existing at that time; and that our concepts of justice change.

Changes by legislative action are relatively easy to make. Furthermore, some statutes recognize the impossibility of laying down in advance a hard and fast rule that will do justice in all cases. The typical modern statute, particularly in the field of regulation of business will often contain an "escape clause" by which a person can escape from the operation of the statute under certain circumstances. Thus, a rent control law may impose a rent ceiling—that is, a maximum above which landlords cannot charge; but it may also authorize a greater charge when special circumstances make it just to allow such exception, as when the landlord has made expensive repairs to the property or when taxes have increased materially.

The rule of law may be stated in terms of what a reasonable or prudent person would do. Thus, whether you are negligent in driving your automobile is determined in court by whether you exercised the degree of care that a prudent person would have exercised in the same situation. This is a vague and variable standard as to how you must drive your car, but it is the only standard that is practical. The alternative would be a detailed motor code specifying how you should drive your car under every situation that might arise, a code that obviously could not foresee every possibility and which certainly would be too long for any driver to remember.

Even constitutions are flexible to the extent that they can be changed by amendment or judicial construction. Constitutions state the procedures for their amendment. Making changes in constitutions is purposely made difficult to serve the objective of stability, but change can be made when the need for change is generally recognized by the people of the state or nation.

(o) **Practical Expediency.** Frequently the law is influenced by what is practical or expedient in the situation. Often the law will strive to make its rules fit the business practices of society. For example, a signature is frequently regarded by the law as including a stamping, printing, or typewriting of a name, in recognition of the business practice of "signing" letters and other instruments by mechanical means. A requirement of a handwritten signature would impose a burden on business that would not be practically expedient.

With the advent of the computer, the law of evidence has changed to allow a computer printout to be admitted in evidence as against the old law that records could not be produced in court unless the person who prepared them was present as a witness.[7]

FACTS:

Williams was arrested for the murder of a small girl. The police promised his attorney that Williams would not be questioned in the absence of his attorney. Meanwhile two hundred volunteers were searching the area where the child's body might be. Contrary to the promise to the attorney, the police, in the absence of the attorney, asked Williams some questions, including the location of the body.

[7]Capital Marine Supply, Inc. v M/V Roland Thomas (CA5 La) 719 F2d 104 (1983).

Williams told the police where the body was. The search for the body was called off and the body was found where Williams had stated. At his trial, evidence was admitted of the location and condition of the body. Williams was convicted. He appealed on the ground that the evidence as to the location and condition of the body could not be admitted against him because it had been obtained by improperly asking questions in violation of his constitutional rights.

DECISION:

The evidence was admissible. Although the use of evidence illegally obtained is a violation of the constitutional rights of the accused, the searching party in the Williams' case would inevitably have located the body and therefore no harm was done to Williams because, by virtue of his answers, the body had been found sooner. [Nix v Williams, 467 US 431 (1984)]

---

§ 2:3. Conflicting Objectives.

The specific objectives of the law sometimes conflict with each other. When this is true, the problem is one of social policy, which in turn means a weighing of social, economic, and moral forces to determine which objective should be furthered. Thus, we find a conflict at times between the objective of the state seeking protection from the conduct of individuals or groups and the objective of freedom of action by those individuals and groups.

For example, while protection of the freedom of the individual urges the utmost freedom of religious belief, society will impose limitations on religious freedom where it believes such freedom will cause harm to the public welfare. Hence, state laws requiring vaccination against smallpox were enforced as against the contention that this violated religious principles. Similarly, parents failing to provide medical care for a sick child will be held guilty of manslaughter if the child dies, even though the parents sincerely believed as a matter of religious principle that medical care was improper. In contrast, when the harm contemplated is not direct or acute, religious freedom will prevail, so that a compulsory child education law will not be enforced against Amish parents who as a matter of religion are opposed to state education.[8]

As another example, the objective of protecting title may conflict with the objective of furthering trade. Consider again the example of the stolen property that was sold by the thief to one who purchased it for value and in good faith, without reason to know that the goods had been stolen. If we are to further the objective of protecting the title to the property, we will conclude that the owner can recover the property from the innocent purchaser. This rule, however, will discourage trade, for people will be less willing to buy goods if they run the risk that the goods were stolen and may have to be surrendered. If we instead think only of taking steps to encourage buying and selling, we will hold that the buyer takes a good title because the buyer acted in good faith and paid value. If we do this, we then destroy the title of the original owner and obviously abandon our objective of protecting title to property. As a general rule, American society has followed the objective of protecting title. In some instances, however, the objective of furthering trade is adopted by statute and the buyer is given good title, as in certain

[8]Wisconsin v Yoder, 406 US 205 (1972) (high school student).

cases of commercial paper (notes, drafts, and checks) or of the purchaser from a regular dealer in other people's goods.

FACTS:

Edwin Lee as an employer paid Social Security taxes. He paid under protest, claiming that the Social Security system was unconstitutional as to him and to his employees because they all belonged to a religious sect that believed that members of the sect have a duty to assist each other and that it was improper to accept benefits from the federal Social Security system. Lee sued the United States to get back the taxes that he had paid.

DECISION:

Judgment against Lee. The Social Security tax and system were constitutional and therefore the taxes were properly collected. It would not be practical to administer the Social Security system if any employer could avoid making the required tax payment on the ground of religious belief. The general welfare of those who would be benefited by the system thus comes into conflict with the religious beliefs of the individual employer. The interest of advancing the general welfare must be given priority over the protection of the religious freedom of the employer. The tax was therefore constitutional and payment of the tax was required without regard to the employer's religious beliefs. [United States v Lee, 455 US 252 (1982)]

---

§ 2:4. Law as an Evolutionary Process.

Law changes as society changes. Let us consider an example of this type of change. When the economy was patterned on a local community unit in which everyone knew each other and each other's product, the concept of "let the buyer beware" expressed a proper basis on which to conduct business. Much of the early law of the sale of goods was based on this view. In today's economy, however, with its interstate, national, and even international character, the buyer has little or no direct contact with the manufacturer or seller, and the packaging of articles makes their presale examination impossible. Under these circumstances, the consumer must rely on the integrity of others. Gradually practices that were tolerated and even approved in an earlier era have been condemned and the law has changed to protect the buyer.

Moreover, new principles of law are being developed to meet the new situations that arise. Every new invention and every new business practice introduces a number of situations for which there may be no existing rule of law. For example, how could there have been a law governing the liability of a food canner to the consumer before canning was invented? How could there have been a law relating to stocks and bonds before those instruments came into existence? How could there have been a law with respect to the liability of radio and television broadcasters before such methods of communication were developed?

New inventions and new techniques for investigation have changed or produced new rules of law because it has become possible to prove facts that could not have been proven before. Thus, fingerprint identification, ballistics, and advanced chemical analysis techniques have made identification a certainty. The use of radar to determine speed is now commonplace. Within the last decade the development of the human leukocyte antigen test has made it possible to determine parentage with over 90% accuracy.[9]

§ 2:5. Law as a Synthesis.

Many rules of law do not further one objective alone. Some rules are a combination of two or more objectives with each objective working toward the same result. In other instances, the objectives oppose each other and the rule of law that emerges is a combination or synthesis of the different objectives.

Law as a synthesis may be illustrated by the law as it relates to contracts for the sale of a house. Originally such a contract could be oral; that is, merely spoken words with nothing in writing to prove that there was such a contract. Of course, there was the practical question of proof — that is, whether the jury would believe that there was such a contract — but no rule of law said that the contract had to be evidenced by a writing. This situation made it possible for a witness in court to swear falsely that Jones had agreed to sell Jones' house for a specified sum. Even though Jones had not made such an agreement, the jury might believe the false witness and Jones would be required to give up the house on terms to which Jones had never agreed. To prevent such a miscarriage of justice, a statute was passed in England in 1677 declaring that contracts for the sale of houses had to be evidenced by a writing.

This law ended the evil of persons lying that there was an oral agreement for the sale of a house, but was justice finally achieved? Not always, for cases arose in which Jones did in fact make an oral agreement to sell land to Smith. Smith would take possession of the land and would make valuable improvements at great expense and effort, and then Jones would have Smith thrown off the land. Smith would defend on the ground that Jones had orally agreed to sell the land. Jones would then say, "Where is the writing that the statute requires?" To this, Smith could only reply there was no writing. No writing meant no binding legal agreement; and therefore Smith lost the land, leaving Jones with the land and all the improvements that Smith had made. That certainly was not just.

Gradually the courts developed the rule that even though the statute required a writing, the courts would enforce an oral contract for the sale of land when the buyer had gone into possession and made valuable improvements of such a nature that it would be difficult to determine what amount of money would be required to make up the loss to the buyer if the buyer were to be put off the land.

Thus, the law passed through three stages: (a) the original concept that all land contracts could be oral and did not require any written evidence.

[9]Callison v Callison, 687 P2d 106 (Okla, 1984).

Because the perjury evil arose under that rule, the law swung to (b) the opposite rule that no such contract could be oral without any written evidence. This rule gave rise to the hardship case of the honest buyer under an oral contract who made extensive improvements. The law then swung back, not to the original rule, but to (c) a middle position, combining both (a) and (b), that is, combining the element of a writing requirement as to the ordinary transaction, but allowing oral contracts in special cases to prevent hardship.

This example is also interesting because it shows the way in which the courts "amend" the law by decision. The flat requirement of the statute was "eroded" by decisions and by an exception created by the courts in the interest of furthering justice.

SUMMARY

A society's ethical code constitutes the foundation on which its laws are built. In contrast to ethics, however, the law must be more definite and stable in order to be enforceable. Nevertheless, a society's evolving ethical code can serve as a blueprint for the future form its laws will assume.

Some of the underlying principles that society regards as important in making its ethical decisions and formulating its laws include: protection of the state; protection of the person; protection of public health, safety, and morals; property protection; title protection; freedom of personal action; freedom of use of property; enforcement of intent; protection from exploitation, fraud, and oppression; furtherance of trade; creditor protection; debtor rehabilitation; stability; flexibility; and practical expediency. These individual concerns sometimes conflict with one another and so as laws are created and evolve society is continually seeking a proper balance or synthesis of its ultimate objectives.

Questions and Case Problems

1. What is the general purpose of the law?
2. What social force is involved in the rule that a professional association cannot arbitrarily exclude a person from membership?
3. Give an illustration of the social force of protection of title.
4. The social force in favor of freedom of personal action permits you to say anything you wish. Appraise the statement.
5. Does the law remain constant?
6. Of the specific objectives of the law, which do you consider to be the most important? Why?
7. (a) How can law be dynamic if stability is one of its specific objectives? (b) How do some statutes provide for "built-in" flexibility?
8. Sometimes the development of the law seems to follow a zigzag course. What is the explanation?
9. McCarthy owned a motor scooter. He obtained an insurance policy from the Foundation Reserve Insurance Company. This policy covered medical expenses when the insured was "struck by automobile." McCarthy rode his scooter into an automobile. The insurance company refused to pay his medical expenses on the ground that he had struck the automobile and

had not been struck by an automobile. What social forces are involved in deciding the case?

10. The Reader's Digest Association published an article on truck hijacking. In the article it stated that John Doe, giving his actual name, had taken part in a truck hijacking eleven years before and had thereafter reformed. John Doe sued the Reader's Digest for damages. It raised the defense that it was not liable because the information was true. What was the theory on which John Doe sued? What social forces are involved? Is John's claim valid?

11. Husband and wife filed a joint income tax return. The wife's mother-in-law signed the wife's name to the joint return filed by the husband. She did this without the consent or authorization of the wife. The wife sued the mother-in-law. Is the mother-in-law liable? [Schlessman v Schlessman, 50 Ohio App 2d 226, 361 NE2d 1347]

12. When O'Brien was prosecuted for burning his draft card, he raised the defense that the right of free speech gave him the privilege to express his disapproval of the draft and of the war in this manner. Was he correct? [United States v O'Brien, 391 US 367]

13. The City of Columbia, South Carolina, provided for the fluoridation of the city water supply. Hall claimed that this deprived him of his constitutional right to drink unfluoridated water since there was no other water supply, and further attacked the validity of the plan on the ground that dental cavities are not contagious and therefore a public health problem did not exist. Was he correct? [Hall v Bates, Mayor of Columbia, 247 SC 511, 148 SE2d 345]

14. The New York Social Services Law authorized the Social Services officials to replace necessary furniture and clothing of welfare recipients who lost such items by fire, flood, or other like catastrophe. Howard was on state welfare. Her clothing was stolen from her apartment by a burglar. She claimed that this was a "catastrophe" and that the Social Service official was required to replace the stolen clothing. Was she correct? [In re Howard, 28 NY2d 434, 271 NE2d 528]

15. Davidson was arrested for loitering. This was her first arrest. The Police Department made the standard police record, taking her photograph and fingerprints. She was acquitted and then brought suit against Dill, the chief of police, to remove her case from the police records or to give her the papers. Dill claimed that she was not entitled to any relief. Was he correct? [Davidson v Dill, 180 Colo 123, 503 P2d 157]

16. The United States Congress has passed several laws aimed at preventing the sale of narcotics and harmful drugs. One of these laws makes it illegal for an unauthorized person to sell or supply marihuana or LSD. Judith Kuch was prosecuted for violating this Act. She admitted that she had transferred the substances covered by the Act and that she did not have a license as required by the Act. She claimed, however, that she was protected by religious freedom. She was, in fact, an ordained minister of the Neo-American Church and the substances were only used by her as part of the religious services in her church. Decide. [United States v Kuch, (DC Dist Col) 288 FSupp 439]

17. Hodgeson was prosecuted for manslaughter. The district attorney wanted to show that a phone call had been made from a certain telephone. In order to do this, the records of the telephone company were offered in evidence. The records consisted of a computer printout. Hodgeson objected to admitting this printout in evidence without producing in court the persons who had supplied the information that was stored in the computer. Should the printout be admitted? [Louisiana v Hodgeson, (La) 305 So2d 421]

CHAPTER 3

THE CONSTITUTION AS

THE FOUNDATION OF THE

LEGAL ENVIRONMENT

CHAPTER OBJECTIVES

After studying this chapter you will be able to:
1. Describe the governmental system created by the U.S. Constitution.
2. List the branches and levels of government and describe their relationship to each other.
3. Explain how the U.S. Constitution adapts to change.
4. List and describe three significant federal powers.
5. List and describe two significant constitutional limitations on governmental power.

A basic principle of the American Revolution was that there should be limits to governmental power. The Americans saw the need for a central government, but did not want that government to have unlimited power. Consequently, the document creating that central government, the Constitution of the United States, contains not only the structure and powers of government but also the limitations on those powers. This constitution together with the constitutions of each of the states form the foundation of our legal environment.

A. THE FEDERAL SYSTEM

By creating a strong central government, which was to coexist with the governments of the individual states, the U.S. Constitution created a federal system. In a **federal system,** a central government is given power to administer to national concerns while the individual states retain the power to administer to local concerns.

§ 3:1.   What the Constitution Is.

The constitution of a state or a nation when spelled with a small letter "c" refers to the structure of the government and its relation to the people within its sphere or area of power. When the word is spelled with a capitalized "C," the word refers to the written document that specifies the structure and powers of the United States national government and its relation to the people within the territory of the United States.

In speaking of the Constitution it is often necessary to distinguish between the written Constitution and the living Constitution. This is required because the Constitution has grown and changed as described in § 3:6.[1]

§ 3:2.   The Branches of Government.

The written Constitution establishes a **tripartite** (3-part) division of government. That is, there is a **legislative branch** (Congress) that makes the laws, an **executive branch** (the President) to execute the laws, and a **judicial branch** (courts) to interpret the laws. The national legislature or Congress is a **bicameral** (two-house) body consisting of a Senate and a House of Representatives. Members of the Senate are popularly elected for a term of 6 years. Members of the House of Representatives, often called "Congressmen," are popularly elected for a term of 2 years. The President is elected by an Electoral College whose membership is popularly elected. The President serves for a term of 4 years and is eligible for re-election for a second term. Judges of the United States are appointed by the President with the approval of the Senate and serve for life, subject to removal only by impeachment because of misconduct.

§ 3:3.   The States and the Constitution.

The effect of the adoption of the Constitution was to take certain powers away from the states and to give them to the national government. Thus the power to wage war was exclusively given to the national government. Other powers given to the national government may be exercised concurrently by the states. For example, the power to tax granted to the federal government did not destroy the state power to tax, even though both governments were to tax the same subject or base. In contrast, some powers may be exercised by the state only as long as they are not exercised by the national government. Thus state safety appliance laws may apply until a federal law on the subject is adopted.

The Constitution prohibits states from doing certain acts, even though the federal government is also similarly prohibited. Thus neither states nor the national government may adopt *ex post facto* laws making criminal an act already committed that was not criminal when committed or increasing the penalty for an act already committed above the penalty in force at the time when it was committed.

(a) **Federal Supremacy.** When Congress has passed a law on a certain subject, that law overrides or displaces any state law that is in conflict.

---

[1]See generally, Anderson, Government and Business (4th ed) (South-Western Publishing Co., Cincinnati, Ohio, 1981).

This **federal supremacy** of the federal statute is expressly declared by the Constitution.[2] When there is a direct conflict between the federal and the state statutes, the decision is thus easy to make as to which prevails.

FACTS:

Southland Corporation sold franchises to run 7-Eleven stores. The franchise contracts required the parties to arbitrate any dispute. The Federal Arbitration Act makes arbitration agreements binding in contracts affecting commerce. Suit was brought by several holders of franchises claiming violation of the state franchisee protection statute. Southland claimed that the dispute should be submitted to arbitration. The court refused to require arbitration on the theory that the state statute required a trial of the issues.

DECISION:

The decision of the state court was overruled by the Supreme Court. The Federal Arbitration Act made the agreement to arbitrate binding and the supremacy clause of the Constitution made the federal statute the supreme law of the land. Any state law or state decision to the contrary could not be enforced. The controversy therefore had to be submitted to arbitration. [Southland Corp. v Keating, 465 US 1 (1984)]

If there is no obvious conflict because the federal statute covers only part of the subject matter, the question arises whether a state law can regulate the areas not regulated by Congress or whether the partial regulation made by Congress **preempts** the field so as to prohibit state legislation.

(b) **The Silence of Congress.** In some situations, the silence of Congress in failing to cover a particular phase of the subject, or in failing to have any law on the subject at all, is held to indicate that Congress does not want any law on the matter and that therefore no state law will be allowed to regulate the matter. When national uniformity is essential, it is generally held that the silence of Congress means that the subject has been preempted by Congress and that no state law on the subject may be adopted.[3]

§ 3:4.   Interpreting and Amending the Constitution.

Within a very few years after the Constitution was adopted, conflict arose as to whether the Constitution was to be interpreted strictly so as to give the federal government the least power possible, or broadly, so as to give the federal government the greatest power that the words would permit. These two views may be given the names of (a) the bedrock view and (b) the living document view.

By the bedrock view, the purpose of a constitution is to state certain fundamental principles for all time.[4] By the living document view, a constitution is merely a statement of goals and objectives, and is intended to grow and change with the time.

[2]US Const, Art VI, Cl. 2.
[3]Burbank v Lockheed Air Terminal, Inc. 411 US 624 (1972).
[4]Marbury v Madison, 1 (US) Cranch 137 (1803).

Whether the Constitution is to be liberally interpreted, under the living document view, or narrowly interpreted under the bedrock view has a direct affect upon the Constitution. For the last century, the Court has followed the living document view, which has resulted in strengthening the power of the federal government, permitting the rise of administrative agencies, and expanding the protection of human rights. If the Constitution had been strictly interpreted according to the bedrock theory, the central or federal government would have relatively little power today, administrative agencies would not be allowed, and many human rights would not be protected from governmental invasion. The living document view has given us the living constitution described in § 3:6. The living document view was first stated by the United States Supreme Court in the *McCulloch* case.

FACTS:

The first bank of the United States was chartered for 20 years in 1791 and again in 1816. Hostile state legislation attempted to drive the bank out of existence. In a lawsuit by the state of Maryland against McCulloch, the cashier of the bank, it was claimed that the federal government could not create a national bank because the Constitution did not authorize it to do so.

DECISION:

The federal government has the power to create a bank. The Constitution does not expressly give this power. However, the Constitution is to be interpreted to grow to meet the needs of government. The creation of a national bank was a reasonable way of carrying out the express powers of government, such as the handling of government funds, the payment of expenses, and other matters that were expressly authorized. This liberal interpretation of the Constitution would be adopted because it could not be foreseen what situations would arise and the liberal interpretation would enable the Constitution to grow to meet future situations that could arise. [McCulloch v Maryland, 4 Wheat 316 (1819)]

Can we decide that we should adopt the bedrock view or the living document view? We cannot select one view to the exclusion of the other for the simple reason that we want both. Contradictory as this sounds, it is obvious that we want our Constitution to be durable. We do not want a set of New Year's Resolutions that will be forgotten shortly. At the same time, we know that the world changes and therefore we do not want a constitution that will hold us tied in a straightjacket of the past.

In terms of social forces that make the law, we are torn between our desire for stability and our desire for flexibility. We want a constitution which is stable. At the same time, we want one which is flexible. There is probably no one living today who believes that the Constitution should be 100 percent stable nor, on the other hand, who believes that it should be 100 percent flexible. Everyone wants both qualities and the problem is how to reach a compromise. This is where the conflict arises: where do we draw the line between the extremes of never changing and of always changing? Some people will favor more change than others. That is why we have conflict.

It is essential that we recognize that our Constitution is in a sense torn between the conflicting desires of change and no change. To look only at the Constitution as it was written in 1789 and to ignore the stresses and strains of the "change/no change" conflict is misleading. If we do not see the conflict, we do not see the Constitution as it really is today. Even more important, we lack the understanding needed to meet the problems of tomorrow.

§ 3:5.   Amending the Constitution.

The United States Constitution has been amended in three ways: (a) expressly, (b) by interpretation, and (c) by practice.

(a) **Constitutional Method of Amending.**   Article V of the Constitution sets forth the procedure to be followed for making amendments to the Constitution. Relatively few changes have been made to the Constitution by this formal amending process although thousands of proposals for that purpose have been made.

(b) **Amendment by Judicial Interpretation.**   The greatest change to the written Constitution has been made by the Supreme Court in "interpreting" the Constitution. Generally this is done to apply the Constitution to a new fact situation that could not have been foreseen when the written Constitution was adopted.

(c) **Amendment by Practice.**   In actual practice, the letter of the Constitution is not always followed. This departing from the written Constitution began as early as 1793 when Washington refused to make treaties, as required by the Constitution, "by and with the consent of the Senate," and began the practice that has been followed since that time of the President's negotiating the treaty with the foreign country and then submitting it to the Senate for approval. Similarly, the Electoral College that was intended to exercise independent judgment in selecting the President, now automatically elects the official candidate of the party that elected them to the Electoral College.

Other aspects of practice have added to the Constitution things that are not there. As written, the Constitution contemplates that Congress will originate and adopt laws. With the rise of the party system, that was not anticipated by the framers of the Constitution, the President has become the leader of the legislative program. This position of leadership has been strengthened greatly by the modern media of communication, beginning with Roosevelt's radio "fireside chats" of the thirties and broadening out into television in later years.

§ 3:6.   The Living Constitution.

The constitution that has developed in the manner described in the preceding section is radically different from that which was written on paper. The living Constitution has the following characteristics:

(a) **Strong Government.** The characteristic of the new Constitution is strong government. The concept of Adam Smith of *laissez faire,* of a "hands off" policy of government, has been largely forgotten. While freedom of the individual as a human being has expanded, business enterprises can be regulated and the economy controlled.

(b) **Strong President.** Instead of being merely an officer who carries out the laws, the President has become the political leader of his party. As such he exerts a strong influence on the lawmaking process. If the President's political party is in control of both Houses of the Congress, the President is also the leader of the lawmaking process.

(c) **Eclipse of the States.** Under the new Constitution, all governments have powers which they never possessed before, but the center of gravity of power has shifted from the states to the nation. When the Constitution was adopted in 1789, the federal government was to have only the very limited powers specified in Article I, Sec. 8, of the Constitution. What regulation of business was permissible was to be imposed by the states. Today, the great bulk of the regulation of business is adopted by the federal government through the Congress or its administrative agencies. As the American economy moved from the local community stage to the nationwide stage, the individual states were obviously unable to regulate, so that it was inevitable that regulation would be drawn to the central government. Consequently, when we speak of government regulation of business, we ordinarily mean the national government, not the state or local governments.

(d) **Administrative Agencies.** These were virtually unheard of in 1789 and no mention is made of them in the Constitution of 1789. The vast powers of the new Constitution are exercised to a very large degree by administrative agencies. They are in effect a fourth branch of the government not provided for in the written Constitution. More importantly, for the vast majority of people it is the administrative agencies which come in contact with the business person and the citizen. The agencies are the "government" for most people.

In other words, the vast power of government to regulate business is not exercised directly by the branches of government that are most familiar to us; namely, the legislatures, the courts, and the executive officers. But rather, this power is exercised by persons or agencies known as administrators. They are not elected by the voters and their decisions are to a large degree not subject to effective review or reversal by the courts.

(e) **Human Rights.** The scope of human rights protected from governments has dramatically broadened. These rights are protected not merely from invasion by the federal government, but by any government. Most significant of all, "unwritten" rights are protected although not guaranteed by any express constitutional provision.

The study of the past evolution of the Constitution will serve us as a guide to understand the present and to foresee, even if dimly, the future, and to appreciate the problems that are involved. As people working in a business world, it is essential that we have this understanding. As citizens living and voting in an organized democratic society, it is our duty to ourselves and our nation to understand these problems so that we can take an intelligent part in their solution.

B. FEDERAL POWERS

The federal government possesses powers necessary to administer to matters of national concern. Some of those powers are of particular interest to businesses.

§ 3:7. Power to Regulate Commerce.

The desire to protect commerce from restrictions and barriers set up by the individual states was a prime factor leading to the adoption of the Constitution of 1789. To protect commerce, Congress was given, by Article I, § 8, Clause 3, the power "to regulate Commerce with foreign Nations, and among the several States, and with the Indian Tribes."

Down to 1937, the Supreme Court held that this provision only gave Congress the power to control or regulate that which crossed a state line, such as an interstate railway train or an interstate telegraph message.

(a) The Commerce Power Becomes a General Welfare Power.

Beginning in 1937, the Supreme Court began expanding the concept of interstate commerce so that by 1946 the power to regulate interstate commerce had become very broad. By that year, the power had expanded to the point that it gave authority to Congress to adopt regulatory laws that were "as broad as the economic needs of the nation."[5] By virtue of this broad interpretation, Congress can regulate manufacturing, agriculture, mining, stock exchanges, insurance, loan sharking,[6] monopolies, and conspiracies in restraint of trade. If desired, Congress can set standards, quotas, and priorities, for industries.

The case that was the starting point in this transition of the commerce clause was the *Jones & Laughlin Steel Corporation* case.

FACTS:

By the National Labor Relations Act, Congress prohibited unfair labor practices in industries affecting interstate commerce. A National Labor Relations Board (NLRB) was created to enforce the Act. A complaint was made that the Jones & Laughlin Steel Corporation was committing unfair labor practices. It defended on the ground that Congress had no power to impose the regulations that it had violated.

DECISION:

The Constitution does not give Congress the power to regulate labor or production but it does give it the power to regulate interstate commerce. The power to regulate includes the power to protect. Strikes and labor disputes in major industries slow down or stop the interstate flow of goods. This is a harm to interstate commerce and therefore Congress can adopt a law to prevent such a harm. This it had done by the Natonal Labor Relations Act and that Act was therefore constitutional. [NLRB v Jones & Laughlin Steel Corp. 301 US 1 (1937)]

---

[5]American Power & Light Co. v Securities and Exchange Commission, 329 US 90 (1946).

[6]Perez v United States, 402 US 146 (1971).

(b) **The Commerce Power as a Limitation on States.** The federal power to regulate commerce not only gives Congress the power to act but also prevents states from regulating commerce in any way that interferes with federal regulation or burdens interstate commerce. For example, if the federal government establishes safety device regulations for interstate carriers, a state cannot require different devices.

FACTS:

Iowa adopted a statute prohibiting the use of 65-foot double-trailer trucks. The use of such trucks was permitted in other western and midwestern states. A motor carrier using the prohibited size trucks would be forced to drive around Iowa or convert to the use of smaller trucks. Consolidated Freightways brought a suit claiming that either alternative placed such a burden on interstate commerce that the law was unconstitutional.

DECISION:

The cost of going around Iowa or of using smaller trucks imposed a substantial economic burden on interstate commerce by burdening those engaged in such commerce. No justification for this burden was established as by proving that the prohibition was justified in the interest of safety or in order to protect the highways. As there was a substantial burden but no justification for imposing such burden, the state law was unconstitutional as an unreasonable burden on interstate commerce. [Kassel v Consolidated Freightways Corp. 450 US 662 (1981)]

Because modern commerce is typically interstate in character, the silence of Congress, that is, the fact that Congress does not impose any regulation, is generally interpreted as excluding state action with respect to interstate commerce.

§ 3:8.   **The Financial Powers.**

The financial powers of the federal government include the powers to tax, borrow, spend, and coin money.

(a) **The Taxing Power.** The Federal Constitution provides that "Congress shall have Power To lay and collect Taxes, Duties, Imposts and Excises, to pay the Debts and provide for the common Defense and general Welfare of the United States:"[7] Subject to the express and implied limitations arising from the Constitution, the states may impose such taxes as they desire and as their own individual constitutions permit. The extent to which political subdivisions may tax is determined by the constitution and the statutes of each state, subject to the limitations arising from the federal Constitution. In addition to express constitutional limitations, both national and local taxes are subject to the unwritten limitation that they be imposed for a public purpose.

The federal government is subject to certain limitations on the form of the taxes imposed by it. Capitation or poll taxes and all direct taxes must

---

[7]US Const, Art 1, § 8, Cl 1.

be apportioned among the states according to the census-determined population.[8] Today, direct taxes include taxes on real estate or personal property and taxes imposed on persons because of their ownership of property. Income taxes, to the extent that they tax the income from property, are direct, although by virtue of the Sixteenth Amendment their apportionment is no longer required.

All other taxes imposed by the federal government are regarded as indirect taxes. These include customs duties, taxes on consumption (such as gasoline and cigarette taxes), taxes on the exercise of a privilege (such as an amusement tax), taxes on the transmission of property upon death (such as estate or inheritance taxes), taxes upon the privilege of making a gift (such as gift taxes), or taxes upon the privilege of employing workers (such as the federal employer's social security tax). In the case of a federal tax upon the exercise of a privilege, it is immaterial whether the privilege arises by virtue of a state or a federal law.

The only restriction upon the form of indirect federal taxes is that they be uniform throughout the continental United States and the incorporated territories. This requirement of uniformity does not prohibit a progressively graduated tax, by which the greater the monetary value of the tax base, the greater the rate of tax. The requirement of uniformity also is not violated by a provision allowing credits against the federal tax for taxes paid to a state, even though the amount of the federal tax paid will vary from state to state, depending upon the existence of a state tax for which credit is allowable.

(b) **The Borrowing Power.** Congress is authorized "to borrow Money on the credit of the United States."[9] No limitation is prescribed as to the purposes for which the United States can borrow.

Obligations of the United States issued to those lending money to the United States are binding, and the Congress cannot attempt to repudiate them or to make them repayable in a less valuable currency than called for by the obligations without violating the legal rights of the holders.

The states have an inherent power to borrow money. State constitutions and statutes may impose a limit on the amount that can be borrowed. Frequently, these limitations are evaded by the creation of independent authorities or districts which borrow money by issuing bonds. The bonded indebtedness of such independent authorities and districts is not regarded as a debt of the state and therefore is not subject to the limitations applicable to state borrowing.

(c) **The Spending Power.** The federal government may use tax money and borrowed money "to pay the debts and provide for the common defense and general welfare of the United States."[10] From the earliest days of the Constitution there was disagreement over whether there was any limitation on the power of the United States to spend the money which it raised by taxation or borrowing. Madison claimed that the money of the United States could only be spent on a subject which could be directly regulated or legis-

---

[8]US Const, Art 1, § 9, Cl 4.
[9]US Const, Art 1, § 8, Cl 2.
[10]US Const, Art 1, § 8, Cl 1.

lated upon by Congress. Hamilton claimed that as long as the money was spent for a public purpose rather than a private purpose, it was immaterial whether the Congress could legislate directly upon the object for which the money was spent.

This matter has become academic with the present interpretation of the commerce power as permitting federal regulation of anything. The situation can no longer arise in which Congress would be spending money for something that it could not regulate if it so chose.

(d) **The Currency Power.** The Constitution authorizes Congress "to coin money, regulate the value thereof" and "provide for the punishment of counterfeitting and securities and . . . coins of the United States."[11] This federal power is made exclusive by prohibiting the states from coining money, emitting bills of credit, or making anything but gold and silver coins legal tender in payment of debts.[12]

The national government can determine what shall be legal tender and is not restricted to the use of metallic money but may issue paper money.[13] Congress can establish such base as it desires for paper currency and may change the base of existing currency.

§ 3:9.   The Power to Own Businesses.

In a sense, government ownership of what would ordinarily be deemed private business represents the ultimate in the regulation of private business.

(a) **The Background of Government Ownership.** Government ownership may affect private business in one of three different ways. The operation of business by the government may remove a potential customer from other private enterprises. For example, the United States government maintains its own printing office, which deprives private printing houses of a very large customer. Government ownership may go a step further and sell goods or services to the public in competition with private enterprises that furnish the same goods or services to the public. This can be illustrated by the Tennessee Valley Authority (TVA), through which the United States government sells electrical power to public and private consumers in competition with private electrical power plants. The final stage of government ownership exists when the government maintains a monopoly of a particular type of enterprise, so that the private enterpriser cannot enter that field even if the enterpriser is willing to face the competition of the government-operated business. This total absorption by the government of a field of enterprise is more characteristic of nationalization or socialization programs than it has been of government ownership of business in the United States to date.

(b) **Reasons for Government Ownership.** It is significant to note that in the instances in which the federal government has embarked upon government ownership the move has rarely been influenced by a doctrine of state socialism. Three other factors have been more important in bringing the federal government into the operation of business.

[11]US Const, Art 1, § 8, Cls 5, 6.
[12]US Const, Art 1, §10.
[13]Julliard v Greenman, 110 US 421 (1884).

The first factor which has always been significant is that government is able to operate a business which private industry could not operate at a profit. This does not mean that governmental operation is more efficient than private enterprise, but only that private enterprise, in the last analysis, cannot exist unless it makes a profit, whereas government activity does not have to meet this standard. If the people of the nation or a state wish their government to offer a particular service, that service can be rendered at a loss and the deficit can be made up from public funds. The United States Postal System illustrates this situation, for the mail traffic in certain areas is so small that a private enterprise would not wish to furnish service to those areas.

The second significant factor in government ownership is that reform movements, convinced rightly or wrongly that certain evils in private management cannot be eliminated, have taken the business away from private hands and placed it under the government. This has been typical of many of the state moves to acquire and run industry.

The third factor in government operation of business has been the inability of government to transfer to private ownership enterprises entered into during times of war or emergency. This is true of the TVA, which began in 1917 as a plant for the generation of electricity. The electricity was to be used to make nitrates for explosives, for use in World War I. The actual working facilities were not completed until 1926. Partly because there was no feasible way of disposing of this large investment, the federal government began active development and operation of the TVA as a hydroelectric plant. In this connection it should be noted, however, that the advent of the New Deal was responsible to a large degree for expanding the TVA as a desirable asset, rather than regarding it as a liability to be scrapped as soon as possible.

(c) **Constitutionality of Government Ownership.** Speaking generally, there is no constitutional barrier against state or federal government ownership and operation of businesses. While it had formerly been assumed that there were certain purposes that were not public or for the general welfare which were clearly distinguished from those that were public or for the general welfare, it would seem that it is impossible today to draw such a line between public and private and to prohibit a government from entering into any particular business on the ground that to do so is not in furtherance of a public purpose or does not advance the general welfare.

(d) **Creation of New Business.** The statement that the United States may constitutionally engage in business leads to the conclusion that it may constitutionally spend its money in order to create a new business or build new plants. There is no requirement that limits the national government to acquiring existing businesses and plants.

(e) **Acquisition of Existing Businesses and Plants.** The power to engage in and own businesses embraces the right to acquire existing businesses and plants by purchase or gift. The national government may also acquire the property by eminent domain if the owner will not voluntarily sell to the government at a price that is satisfactory to the government.

In the case of the United States, it is to be noted that the United States as a sovereign state may acquire land or any other property by any means. It may do so by war, purchase, or treaty.

(f) **Sale and Distribution of Government Production.** A government may sell or otherwise dispose of the products which the government-owned business manufactured. Congress is authorized to "dispose of and make all needful rules and regulations respecting the territory or other property belonging to the United States."[14] The power of a government to dispose of its property permits the government to compete with a private enterprise and to dispose of its products at any price it chooses without regard to whether the price is below cost or not. No constitutional privilege of the private business is violated by being underpriced by the national, a state, or local government.[15]

C. CONSTITUTIONAL LIMITATIONS ON GOVERNMENT

The most significant limitations in the Constitution are found in the first ten amendments adopted in 1791 and in the post-Civil War amendments. Most state constitutions contain limitations similar to those of the national Constitution. The limitations discussed in the next three sections are the limitations that are most important to the person and to business.

§ 3:10. Due Process.

The most important limitation on the power of government is that found in the Fifth and Fourteenth amendments to the Constitution. Those amendments prohibit the national government and the state governments, respectively, from depriving any person of life, liberty, or property, without due process of law. By virtue of liberal interpretation of the Constitution, the **due process clause** is now held to be a guarantee of protection from unreasonable procedures[16] and unreasonable laws, and a guarantee of equal protection of the law and a guarantee of protection of significant interests.

(a) **Expansion of Due Process.** The Supreme Court extended the due process clause to protect the record or standing of a student.

FACTS:
Lopez and other public high school students were suspended for misconduct for periods up to ten days. A state statute authorized the principal of a public school to suspend a student for periods up to ten days without a hearing. A suit was brought by Lopez and others claiming that the statute was unconstitutional because it deprived them of due process by not giving them notice and a hearing to determine whether a suspension was justified.

DECISION:
The statute was unconstitutional. The education of a student is so important to future life that any action that interrupts that education or gives the student a bad record can not be taken without some type of hearing that will bring out both sides of the question. A suspension for ten days can not be regarded as so trivial that the requirement of a hearing can be ignored. The statute authorizing suspensions up to ten days without a hearing was therefore unconstitutional as a denial of due process. [Goss v Lopez, 419 US 565 (1975)]

---

[14]US Const, Art 4, § 3(2).
[15]Puget Sound Power & Light Co. v Seattle, 291 US 619 (1934).
[16]Mennonite Board of Missions v Adams, 462 US 792 (1983).

Through judicial construction, due process of law affords the individual a wide protection. The guarantee, however, affords no protection when the matter is reasonably debatable. In view of this conclusion, due process of law does not bar the regulation of business, for any regulation that would have sufficient support to pass a legislature or the Congress would have at least sufficient claim to validity as to be debatable. The fact that many persons would deem the law unsound, unwise, hazardous, or un-American does not in itself make the law invalid under the due process clause.

As the due process concept is a limitation upon governmental action, it does not apply to transactions between private persons, to private employment or other nonpublic situations. In some cases, however, statutes, such as the federal Civil Rights Act and consumer protection laws, apply due process concepts to private transactions.

§ 3:11. Equal Protection of the Law.

The Constitution prohibits both the state and national governments from denying any person the equal protection of the laws.[17] This guarantee prohibits a government from treating one person differently than another when there is no reasonable ground for classifying them differently.

(a) **Reasonable Classification.** The equal protection clause does not require that all persons be protected or treated equally, and a law is valid even though it does not apply to everyone or everything. Whether a classification is reasonable depends on whether the nature of the classification made bears a reasonable relation to the evil to be remedied or to the object to be attained by the law. In determining this, the courts have been guided generally by considerations of historical treatment in the past and by the logic of the situation. The trend is to permit the classification to stand unless it is clear that the lawmaking body has been arbitrary or capricious.

(b) **Improper Classification.** Laws that make distinctions in the regulation of business, the right to work, and the right to use or enjoy property in terms of race, alienage, or religion; or that impose restrictions on some but not all persons without any justification for the distinction[18] are invalid. A law prohibiting the ownership of land by aliens has been traditionally regarded as an exception to this rule, as the danger of large alien holdings of land is considered such a social evil as to justify legislation directly prohibiting such holding, although it appears that in course of time this discrimination may be declared invalid.[19]

The lawmaker may not discriminate on the basis of moral standards and culture patterns. People cannot be deprived of the same treatment given to other persons because they do not have the same moral standards or cul-

---

[17] US Const, Fourteenth amendment as to the states; modern interpretation of due process clause of Fifth amendment as to national government. Congress has adopted the Civil Rights Act to implement the concept of equal protection. Newport News Shipbuilding and Dry Dock Co. v EEOC, 462 US 669 (1983).

[18] Carey v Brown, 447 US 445 (1980).

[19] The alien land laws have been declared unconstitutional by the supreme courts of California, Montana, and Oregon, as being in violation of the Fourteenth amendment of the United States Constitution.

ture pattern as the lawmaker. Lawmakers cannot penalize people because they do not live, think, and dress the same as the lawmakers.

Can Congress refuse benefits to people that it does not like when it provides those benefits to others?

FACTS:

The Federal Food Stamp Act provided for the distribution of food stamps to needy "households." In 1971, [sec] 3(e) of the statute was amended to define "households" as limited to groups whose members were all related to each other. This was done because of Congressional dislike for the lifestyles of unrelated "hippies" who were living together in "hippie communes." Moreno and others applied for food stamps but were refused them because the "relationship" requirement was not satisfied. An action was brought to have the "relationship" requirement declared unconstitutional.

DECISION:

The "relationship" requirement did not bear any reasonable relationship to the object of the statute. The statute was designed to assist those in need. Persons without food were in need without regard to their relationship to other persons. The "relationship" requirement was therefore unconstitutional as a denial of equal protection. [United States Department of Agriculture v Moreno, 413 US 528 (1973)]

---

§ 3:12. Protection of the Person.

The Constitution does not contain any express provision protecting "persons" from governmental action. Persons are expressly protected by the Constitution with respect to particular matters, such as freedom of speech, ownership of property, right to a jury trial, and so on. There is, however, no general provision declaring that the government shall not impair "rights of persons." There is not a word in the Constitution as to the inalienable rights that were so important on July 4, 1776.[20]

(a) Rise of Constitutional Protection of the Person. During the last four decades, the Supreme Court has been finding constitutional protection for a wide array of rights of the person that are not expressly protected by the Constitution, such as the right of privacy, the right to marry the person one chooses, protection from unreasonable zoning, protection of parental control, protection from durational residency requirements,[21] protection from discrimination against poverty, and protection from sex discrimination.[22]

---

[20]The term "inalienable right" is employed in preference to "natural right," "fundamental right," or "basic right." Apart from the question of scope or coverage, the adjective "inalienable" emphasizes the fact that the right is still possessed by the people, as opposed to the contention that people have surrendered or subordinated such rights to the will of society. The word "alien" is the term of the old common law for transferring title or ownership. Today we would say transfer and, instead of saying inalienable rights, would say nontransferable rights. Inalienable rights of the people were therefore those which not only were possessed by the people, but which they could not give up, even if they wanted to. Therefore they are still owned by everyone.

[21]Zobel v Williams, 457 US 55 (1982); Scott v Gunter, (Fla App) 447 So 2d 272 (1983).

[22]In the earlier cases, the courts have given the due process and equal protection clauses a "liberal" interpretation in order to find a protection of the person, thereby making up for the fact that there is no express constitutional guarantee of protection of the person. Davis v Passman, 442 US 228 (1979) (due process); Orr v Orr 440 US 268 (1979) (equal protection).

(b) **Democracy and the Protection of the Person.** As the goal of a democracy is to promote the well-being and development of each individual, the concept of protecting a person and the goal of democracy would appear to be moving toward the same objective. This is ordinarily true but there may be a conflict between the democratic system of government and the protection of the person. We think of a democratic society as one in which the majority of the people govern. But is being governed by the majority sufficient for those who cherish the American ideal?

If we look closely at our individual and national desires, we see that the American way of life is not a society run by the will of the majority. Instead we find that the American way divides life into two zones. In one zone, the democratic concept is that the majority rules. In the other zone, that of the "person," not even the majority can interfere. To illustrate, the majority can declare by statute that before you marry you must have a health certificate. This is perfectly reasonable for the protection of the general health and welfare. But no one, not the majority, nor even the unanimous action of everyone in the United States, can command you to marry or not marry or choose your mate for you.

Most amazing is the fact that a relatively short time ago the second zone was unheard of and everything was thought to be in the zone which was controlled by the majority unless there was an express prohibition of such action by the Constitution. Even more startling, the emergence of the second zone has taken place for the most part within your lifetime. The expansion of the second zone will have a profound effect on the rest of your life.

SUMMARY

The U.S. Constitution created the structure of our national government and gave it certain powers. It also placed limitations on those powers. It created a federal system, with a tripartite division of government, and a bicameral national legislature.

Some governmental powers are possessed exclusively by the national government, while other powers are shared by both the states and the federal government. In areas of conflict, federal law is supreme.

The U.S. Constitution is not a detailed document. It takes much of its meaning from the way in which it is interpreted. In recent years, liberal interpretation has expanded the powers of the federal government.

Among the powers of the federal government that directly affect business are the power to regulate commerce; the power to tax, borrow, spend, and coin money; and the power to own and operate businesses. Among the limitations on government that are of interest to business are the requirement of due process and the requirement of equal protection of the law.

The due process requirement stipulates that no person shall be deprived of life, liberty, or property without due process of law. The due process requirement applies to both the state and federal governments, but does not apply to private transactions.

The equal protection clause of the U.S. Constitution prohibits both the state and federal governments from treating one person different from another unless there is a legitimate reason for doing so and unless the basis of classification is reasonable.

QUESTIONS AND CASE PROBLEMS

1. What are the characteristics of the Constitution as it is today?
2. Would an amendment to the United States Constitution be valid that deleted the present Article V and in its place provided that an amendment could be adopted by a majority of those voting at a Presidential election?
3. What decision would have been made in the *Goss* case if the Court applied the test that due process only guarantees historical procedure whenever life, liberty, or property is involved?
4. (a) Does equal protection prevent classification? (b) If not, when is classification proper?
5. A federal law is adopted providing that no one may operate a television station without a federal license. Is that statute constitutional?
6. Does the due process clause protect a business from being destroyed by taxation?
7. Perez was sued for damages arising from an automobile collision. A judgment was entered against Perez. He then filed a petition in bankruptcy. In due course, he was given a discharge in bankruptcy which discharged him from all debts, including the judgment. The state of Arizona then suspended Perez's automobile registration and operator's license pursuant to a state statute providing for such suspension whenever a judgment remained unpaid for 60 days, even though the judgment had been discharged in bankruptcy. Perez claimed that the state statute was unconstitutional and that the suspension of his licenses was therefore improper. Was he correct? [*Perez v Campbell,* 402 US 637]
8. The home of the Crafts was supplied with gas by the city gas company. Because of some misunderstanding, the gas company believed that the Crafts were delinquent in paying their gas bill. The gas company had an informal complaint procedure for discussing such matters, but the Crafts had never been informed that such procedure was available. The gas company notified the Crafts that they were delinquent and that the company was shutting off the gas. The Crafts brought an action to enjoin the gas company from so doing on the theory that a termination without any hearing was a denial of due process. The lower courts held that the interest of the Crafts in receiving gas was not a property interest protected by the due process clause and that the procedures which the gas company followed satisfied the requirements of due process. The Crafts appealed. Were they correct in contending that they had been denied due process of law? [*Memphis Light, Gas and Water Division v Craft,* 436 US 1]
9. An Oregon statute provides that a defendant may be convicted of a noncapital offense by a verdict of 10 out of 12 jurors. Apodaca was convicted of assault with a deadly weapon, a noncapital offense, on a verdict of 11 to 1 in favor of guilt. He appealed from the conviction on the ground that the due process clause required that the verdict of a jury be unanimous. Was he correct? [*Apodaca v Oregon,* 406 US 404]
10. Gladys Boddie lived on welfare in Connecticut. She wanted to obtain a divorce but she did not have the $60 required to commence a divorce action. She claimed that the state requirement of the prepayment of such

fees deprived her of her constitutional rights and that the statute was therefore invalid. Was she correct? [*Boddie v Connecticut*, 401 US 371]

11. The New York Civil Service law provided that only United States citizens could hold permanent civil service positions. Dougall was an alien who had lawfully entered and was lawfully residing in the United States. He held a job with the City of New York but was fired because of the state statute. He claimed that the statute was unconstitutional. Was he correct? [*Sugarman v Dougall*, 413 US 634]

12. For a person to register to vote in a state election, a Tennessee statute required that the person be a resident of the state for one year and of the county for three months. Blumstein moved into the state. He could not satisfy the residency requirements and therefore could not register to vote. He claimed that this deprived him of his constitutional right to vote and that therefore the residency requirements were invalid. The state claimed that the residency requirements were designed to insure that voters would be familiar with the issues involved in the elections and to give the voting officials time in which to verify any disputed claim to having a local residence. Were the residency requirements constitutional? [*Dunn v Blumstein*, 405 US 330]

13. A federal law prohibits interstate commerce in intoxicating liquor. A person buys a bottle of intoxicating liquor in Kentucky, puts it in his pocket, and then gets in a trolley car to ride from Kentucky to West Virginia. He is indicted for violating the federal statute prohibiting interstate commerce in intoxicating liquor. Is he guilty? [*United States v Simpson*, 252 US 465]

14. The city of Philadelphia, Pennsylvania, made a contract with owners of land in New Jersey under which the city could dump solid waste on the land of the New Jersey owners. New Jersey adopted a statute prohibiting the depositing in New Jersey of solid waste originating in other states. There was no prohibition against depositing New Jersey solid wastes in New Jersey. Philadelphia and the owners of the New Jersey land claimed that the New Jersey statute was unconstitutional. Was the law unconstitutional? [*Philadelphia v New Jersey*, 437 US 617]

15. The Jones Company made clothing from cloth that it purchased within the state and then resold within the state to distributors. It had no association or business transactions with anyone outside of the state. A complaint was filed before the National Labor Relations Board claiming that the Jones Company violated a national act. The company defended on the ground that it was not engaged in or producing for interstate commerce. If this defense was true, the Board did not have jurisdiction. Did the Board have jurisdiction over the complaint? [*NLRB v Fainblatt*, 306 US 601]

16. Heald was the executor of a deceased person who had lived in Washington, D.C. Heald refused to pay federal tax owed by the estate on the ground that the tax had been imposed by an act of Congress, but that, since residents of the District of Columbia had no vote in Congress, the tax law was necessarily adopted without their representation. In addition to having no voice in the adoption of the tax laws, the proceeds from taxes collected in the District were paid into the general treasury of the

United States and were not maintained as a separate District of Columbia fund. Heald objected that the tax law was void as contrary to the Constitution because it amounted to taxation without representation. Decide. [*Heald v District of Columbia*, 259 US 114]

17. California owns the Belt Railroad that serves San Francisco Harbor and, through connections with other lines, handles interstate traffic. It is a common carrier and files tariffs with the Interstate Commerce Commission. A collective bargaining agreement was entered into between the state and the employees of the Belt Railroad. A number of employees later presented claims arising under the agreement to the National Railroad Adjustment Board. The board refused to exercise jurisdiction over the matter, on the theory that the Railway Labor Act did not apply to a state-owned railroad. The employees then brought an action against the board to compel it to exercise jurisdiction. Decide. [*California v Taylor*, 353 US 553]

CHAPTER 4

GOVERNMENT

REGULATION

CHAPTER OBJECTIVES

After studying this chapter you will be able to:

1. State the extent to which government can regulate business.
2. State what Congress has done to protect free enterprise from unfair competition and from unfair restraints.
3. State when price discrimination is prohibited and when it is allowed.
4. List statutory and judicial exceptions to the Sherman Antitrust Act.
5. Describe the governmental regulation of employment.
6. Describe the statutory regulation of collective bargaining.
7. Describe the constitutional limitations on state regulation of business.
8. Solve problems involving government regulation of business.

In Chapter 3, you saw that government can regulate business and much of our lives. Whether government should exercise this power comes down to a question of policy whether we the people want government to do so. This in turn involves questions of economics, political science, the humanities, and related subjects. If society decides that there should be regulation by government, then questions arise as to what should be regulated and how. These questions involve important decisions for the welfare of society, because in every decision some social interest loses and some interest gains. Society must make the difficult management decision of how it should manage itself. For the last century, the American people have called upon government to regulate more and more of their way of life. While there is some movement towards deregulation, the overwhelming pattern continues to be regulation of business by government.

§ 4:1.   Power to Regulate.

The states, by virtue of their police power, may regulate business in all of its aspects so long as they do not impose an unreasonable burden on interstate commerce or any activity of the federal government. Local governments may also exercise this power to the extent each state permits. The federal government may impose any regulation upon any phase of business that is required by "the economic needs of the nation."[1]

§ 4:2.   Regulation of
Production, Distribution, and Financing.

In order to protect the public from harm, government may prohibit false advertising and labeling, and may establish health and purity standards for cosmetics, foods, and drugs. Without regard to the nature of the product, government may regulate business with respect to what materials may be used, the quantity of a product that may be produced or grown, and the price at which the finished product may be sold. Government may also engage in competition with private enterprises or own and operate an industry.

Regulation of production may take the form of providing encouragement or assistance for enterprises that would not prove attractive to private investors.[2]

Under its commerce power the federal government may regulate all methods of interstate transportation and communication, and a like power is exercised by each state over its intrastate traffic. The financing of business is directly affected by the national government in creating a national currency and in maintaining a federal reserve bank system. State and other national laws may also affect financing by regulating the contracts and documents used in financing, such as bills of lading and commercial paper.

The federal government may also establish standards for weights and measures. The Metric Conversion Act of 1975 declares that it is the policy of the United States to convert to the metric system. Various agencies have adopted regulations to carry out this policy.

§ 4:3.   Regulation of Competition.

The federal government, and the states in varying degrees, prohibit unfair methods of competition. Frequently, a commission is established to determine whether a given practice comes within the general class of unfair methods of competition. In other instances, the statutes specifically define the practices condemned.

The Congress has declared "unlawful" all "unfair methods of competition" and has created a Federal Trade Commission to administer the law. The FTC has condemned harassing tactics, coercing by refusing to sell, boycotting, discriminating, disparaging of a competitor's products, enforcing payment wrongfully, cutting off or restricting the market, securing and using confidential information, spying on competitors, and inducing breach of

---

[1]American Power & Light Co. v SEC, 329 US 90 (1946).
[2]Orphan Drug Act of January 4, 1983, PL 97–44, 96 Stat 2049, 21 USC §§ 301, 306 (encouraging development of drugs to fight diseases that are so rare that there is no commercial interest in doing so).

customer contracts. The law also prohibits misrepresentation by appropriating business or corporate names, simulating trade or corporate names, appropriating trademarks, simulating the appearance of a competitor's goods, simulating a competitor's advertising, using deceptive brands or labels, and using false and misleading advertising.

In the current decade, a shift of emphasis is taking place in appraising methods of doing business. Instead of harm to competitors being the sole consideration, the effect upon the consumer is being given increasing recognition. Many practices that were condemned earlier only because they would harm a competitor by diverting customers are now condemned because such practices prevent the customer from getting full value for the money spent.

§ 4:4. Regulation of Prices.

Governments, both national and state, may regulate prices. This may be done directly by the lawmaker, that is, the Congress or the state legislature, or the power to do so may be delegated to an administrative officer or agency. This power extends to "prices" in any form. It includes not only what a buyer pays for goods purchased from a store, but also what a borrower pays as interest on a loan and what a tenant pays for rent.

(a) **Price Discrimination Prohibited.** The Clayton Act of 1914, applicable to interstate and foreign commerce, prohibits price discrimination between different buyers of commodities "where the effect of such discrimination may be substantially to lessen competition or tend to create a monopoly in any line of commerce."

The federal law prohibits the furnishing of advertising or other services that, when rendered to one purchaser but not another, will have the effect of granting the former a price discrimination or lower rate. It is made illegal for a seller to accept any fee or commission in connection with a sale except for services actually rendered and unless the services are equally available to all on the same terms. The Act makes both the giving and the receiving of any illegal price discrimination a crime.

(b) **Permitted Price Discrimination.** Price discrimination is expressly permitted when it can be justified on the basis of: (1) difference in grade, quality, or quantity involved; (2) the cost of the transportation involved in performing the contract; (3) when the sale is made at the lower price in good faith in order to meet competition; (4) differences in methods or quantities; (5) deterioration of goods; or (6) when the seller in good faith is making a close-out sale of a particular line of goods. The Robinson-Patman Act of 1936 reaffirms the right of a seller to select customers and to refuse to deal with anyone as long as the refusal is in good faith and not for the purpose of restraining trade.

The meeting competition defense is available where the seller lowers the price for a general competitive area, as distinguished from doing so on an individual customer basis.[3]

---

[3]Falls City Industries, Inc. v Vanco Beverages, Inc. 460 US 428 (1983).

§ 4:5. Prevention of Monopolies and Combinations.

To protect competitors and the public from monopolies and combinations in restraint of trade, the federal government and almost all of the states have enacted antitrust statutes.

(a) **The Federal Antitrust Act.** The federal antitrust act, known as the Sherman Antitrust Act, is applicable to both sellers and buyers.[4] It provides that "[§ 1] Every contract, combination in the form of trust or otherwise, or conspiracy, in restraint of trade or commerce among the several states, or with foreign nations, is declared to be illegal. [§ 2] Every person who shall monopolize or attempt to monopolize, or combine or conspire with any other person or persons to monopolize any part of the trade or commerce among the several states, or with foreign nations, shall be deemed guilty of a misdemeanor."[5]

(b) **Conduct Prohibited.** Section 1 of the Sherman Act applies only when two or more persons agree or conspire to restrain trade. Under Section 2, one person or corporation may violate the law by monopolizing or attempting to monopolize interstate commerce. The Sherman Act applies not only to buying and selling activities generally associated with trade and commerce, but also to manufacturing and production activities without regard to whether consumers, brokers, or manufacturers are involved.

FACTS:

Three California sugar refiners agreed among themselves to pay California sugar beet farmers a uniform price for their crops. The refined sugar would be sold by the refiners in interstate markets. Mandeville Island Farms, a sugar beet farmer, sued American Crystal Sugar Co., one of the refiners, for treble damages under the Sherman Act. The defendant claimed that the Act was not applicable because the conduct of the refiners had not taken place in interstate commerce.

DECISION:

The combination of refiners was a conspiracy in interstate commerce. While their acts were committed locally, the consequences of those acts would be seen in the prices charged in distant markets in other states. This made their acts "in interstate commerce." [Mandeville Island Farms v American Crystal Sugar Co. 334 US 219 (1948)]

(c) **Bigness.** The Sherman Antitrust Act does not prohibit bigness. However, section 7 of the Clayton Act, as amended in 1950, provides that "no corporation... shall acquire the whole or any part of the assets of another corporation..., where in any line of commerce in any section of the country, the effect of such acquisition may be substantially to lessen competition, or to tend to create a monopoly." Does this statute prevent a manufacturer

---

[4]This Act has been amended by the Clayton Act, the Federal Trade Commission Act, the Shipping Act, and other legislation.

[5]15 United States Code, Ch. 1, §§ 1, 2.

from buying out a plant that makes a part that is used in the manufacturer's product?

FACTS:

From 1917 to 1919, Du Pont acquired a 23 percent stock interest in General Motors. During the following years General Motors bought substantial quantities of automotive finishes and fabrics from Du Pont. In 1949, the United States claimed the effect of the stock acquisition had been to lessen competition in interstate commerce on the theory that the sales to General Motors had not been the result of successful competition but were the result of the stock ownership, and therefore such stock ownership violated the Clayton Act. The United States brought an action against Du Pont, General Motors, and others.

DECISION:

The ownership of the General Motors stock by the Du Pont company was a violation of the Clayton Act since such stock ownership tended to lessen competition by making it less likely that General Motors would purchase its supplies from an outside supplier. It was immaterial that no unfair advantage had been taken of this power by supplying inferior products. [United States v E. I. du Pont de Nemours & Company, 353 US 586 (1957)]

---

(1) *Mergers.* The Clayton Act now declares that a merger of corporations doing interstate business is illegal when the effect of the acquisition by one corporation of all or any part of the assets of the other "may be substantially to lessen competition, or to tend to create a monopoly."[6]

(2) *Premerger Notification.* When large-size enterprises plan to merge, they must give written notice to the Federal Trade Commission and to the attorney in charge of the Antitrust Division of the Department of Justice and then wait a specified time to see if there is any objection to the proposed merger.[7]

(d) **Price Fixing.** Agreements fixing prices, whether horizontally or vertically, violate the federal antitrust law. Thus manufacturers cannot agree between themselves as to the price at which they will sell (horizontal price fixing); likewise a wholesaler cannot require a dealer to agree not to resell below a stated price (vertical price fixing).[8]

(e) **Exceptions to the Antitrust Law.** By statute or decision, associations of exporters, marine insurance associations, farmers' cooperatives, and

---

[6]15 USC § 18.

[7]Antitrust Improvement Act of 1976, PL 94–435, 90 Stat 1383, § 201, 15 USC §§ 1311 et seq.

[8]Vertical price-maintenance agreements were authorized by statutes in varying degrees from 1931 to 1975 but the Consumer Goods Pricing Act of 1975, PL 94–145, 89 Stat 801, abolished the immunity from the federal antitrust law which had been given to such agreements. Although the states may permit such agreements as long as interstate commerce is not involved, the area of intrastate commerce is so slight that for all practical purposes such agreements are now illegal.

labor unions are exempt from the Sherman Antitrust Act with respect to agreements between their members. Certain pooling and revenue dividing agreements between the carriers are exempt from the antitrust law when approved by the appropriate federal agency. The Newspaper Preservation Act of 1970 grants an antitrust exemption to operating agreements entered into by newspapers to prevent financial collapse. The Soft Drink Interbrand Competition Act[9] grants the soft drink industry a limited exemption when it is shown that in fact there is substantial competition in spite of the agreements.

(1) *The Rule of Reason.* The general approach of the Supreme Court of the United States to the trust problem has been that an agreement is not automatically or per se to be condemned as a restraint of interstate commerce merely because it creates a power or a potential to monopolize interstate commerce. It is only when the restraint imposed is unreasonable that the practice is unlawful.

(f) Punishment and Civil Remedy. A violation of either of the Sherman Act provisions stated above is punishable by fine or imprisonment or both in the discretion of the court. The maximum fine for a corporation is $1,000,000. A natural person can be fined a maximum of $100,000 or imprisoned for a maximum term of three years or both. In addition to this criminal penalty, the law provides for an injunction to stop the unlawful practices and permits suing the wrongdoers for damages.

(1) *Individual Damage Suit.* Any person or enterprise harmed may bring a separate action for treble damages (three times the damages actually sustained).

(2) *Class Action Damage Suit by State Attorney General.* When the effect of an antitrust violation is to raise prices, the attorney general of a state may bring a class action to recover damages on behalf of those who have paid the higher prices.[10] This action is called a *parens patriae* action, on the theory that the state is suing as the "parent" of its people.

§ 4:6.   Regulation of Employment.

Basically the parties are free to make an employment contract on any terms they wish. By statute, certain limitations are imposed on this freedom of contract. Thus, persons under a certain age cannot be employed at certain kinds of labor. Statutes commonly specify minimum wages and maximum hours which the employer must observe. A state may also require employers to pay employees' wages for the time that they are away from work for the purpose of voting.

(a) Fair Labor Standards Act. By this statute, which is popularly known as the Wage and Hour Act, Congress provides that, subject to certain exceptions, persons working in interstate commerce or in an industry producing goods for interstate commerce cannot be paid less than a specified minimum wage; and they cannot be employed for more than 40 hours a week unless they are paid time and a half for overtime.[11] The Act prohibits the em-

---

[9]Act of July 9, 1980, PL 96–308, 94 Stat 939, 15 USC §§ 3501 et seq.

[10]Antitrust Improvement Act of 1976, PL 94–435, 90 Stat 1383, Title III, 15 USC §§ 1311 et seq.

[11]Fair Labor Standards Amendment of 1977, PL 95–151, 91 Stat 1245, 29 USC §§ 201 et seq.

ployment of children under the age of 14 years. It permits the employment of children between the ages of 14 and 16 years in all industries, except mining and manufacturing, under certain prescribed conditions. This Act has been copied by a number of states in regulating those phases of industry not covered by the federal statute.

(b) **Fair Employment Practices Acts.** With some exceptions, employers of 15 or more persons are forbidden to discriminate as to compensation and other privileges, and conditions of employment against any person because of race, religious creed, color, sex, or national origin, or because of age.[12] Special protection for migrant farm workers is provided by the Federal Migrant and Seasonal Agricultural Work Protection Act.[13]

FACTS:

Griggs and other black workers were employed in the labor department of Duke Power Co. They sought promotion to higher paying departments of their employer but could not obtain promotion because the employer had established promotion standards of (1) high school education, and (2) satisfactory scores on two professionally prepared aptitude tests. The tests were not designed to measure ability to perform the work in the particular department to which they sought promotion. Griggs and other black employees brought a class action under Title VII of the federal Civil Rights Act of 1964, claiming the promotion criteria discriminated against them because of race. The Court of Appeals held that there was no prohibited discrimination even though white workers apparently obtained better scores in the tests because of having obtained a better public school education. Griggs appealed to the Supreme Court.

DECISION:

The tests were in violation of the federal law because they did not test for a skill or ability related to the desired work and had the effect of freezing the black worker in the labor department. [Griggs v Duke Power Co. 401 US 424 (1971)]

---

(1) *Sex Discrimination.* An employer cannot discriminate on the basis of sex.[14] An employer may not hire on the basis of a stereotype pattern of what is woman's work and what is man's work. Women, therefore, cannot be excluded from working as bartenders and men cannot be excluded from working as airline flight attendants. Indirect sex discrimination is also pro-

[12]Federal Civil Rights Act of 1964, Title VII, as amended by the Equal Employment Opportunities Act of 1972 and 1986. TWA v Thurston, 469 US ____, 83 L Ed 523 (1985). With minor exceptions, the federal law prohibits age discrimination. In some states and cities, state statutes and local ordinances also prohibit age discrimination.

[13]Act of January 14, 1983, PL 97–470, 96 Stat 2583, 29 USC § 1801.

[14]Washington County v Gunther, 452 US 161 (1981).

hibited, as when the employer establishes height and weight specifications for job applicants but such requirements have no bearing on the performance of the work and their effect is to exclude women from the job.

The equality of the sexes is literally applied so that a law is unconstitutional when it gives to women a protection or an advantage which it does not give to men performing the same work. Likewise, it is a discriminatory labor practice to allow women seniority rights which are not available to men on the same terms, or to prohibit women from working at jobs which involve the lifting of heavy weights. A standardized "compulsory pregnancy leave" regulation for public school teachers is unconstitutional because no consideration is given the fitness of the individual teacher to continue teaching and there is no proof that pregnant teachers as a class are necessarily and universally unfit to teach.[15] The protection against sex discrimination is not limited to situations that are customarily regarded as "employment." Thus it is held that a law partnership violates the Act if it refuses to invite an associate to become a partner because the associate is a woman.[16]

(2) *Allowable Distinctions.* The federal law does not require that every employee be treated the same as every other. It does not prohibit the testing or screening of applicants or employees for the purpose of determining whether a person is qualified to be hired, or promoted, or given a wage increase, or given special training. The Civil Rights Act has no effect upon the employer's right to establish compensation scales, to provide bonus pay and incentive pay, or to pay different rates in different geographic areas. The employer may also recognize seniority status, voluntarily or as a result of collective bargaining.

§ 4:7.   Labor Representation.

Statutes generally declare the right of employees to form a union and require the employer to deal with the union as the bargaining representative of the employees. An employer cannot refuse in advance to bargain with the proper representative of the employees on the ground that the employer is afraid that improper demands will be made by the representative.[17]

(a) **Machinery to Enforce Collective Bargaining.** To protect the rights of workers to unionize and bargain collectively, the federal government created the National Labor Relations Board (NLRB). The NLRB determines the proper collective bargaining unit and eliminates unfair practices by which the employer and the union might interfere with employees' rights.

Federal law preempts the area of labor relations so as to bar a supervisory employee from bringing a common-law tort action against the union for interfering with the supervisor's contractual relationship with the employer.[18]

(b) **Selection of Bargaining Representative.** Generally there is an election by secret ballot to select the bargaining representative of the employees within a particular collective bargaining unit.

(c) **Exclusive and Equal Representation of All Employees.** Any union selected by the majority of the workers within the unit is the exclusive representative of all the employees in the unit for the purpose of bargaining

[15]Cleveland Board of Education v La Fleur, 414 US 632 (1974).
[16]Hishon v King & Spalding, 467 US 69 (1984).
[17]Skyline Corp. v NLRB (CA5 NLRB) 613 F2d 1328 (1980).
[18]International Union of Operating Engineers v Jones, 460 US 669 (1983).

with respect to wages, hours of employment, or other conditions of employment. Whether or not all the workers are members of the representative union is immaterial for, in any case, this union is the exclusive representative of every employee. It is unlawful for any employee, whether a member or nonmember of the union, to attempt to make a contract directly with the employer. Except as to grievances, every worker must act through the representative union with respect to the contract of employment. At the same time, the union is required to represent all workers fairly, nonmembers as well as members. It is unlawful for the union, in bargaining with the employer, to discriminate in any way against any employee. It makes no difference whether a particular worker is a member of the representative union. The union cannot use its position as representative of all workers to further its interest as a union.

The fact that the representative of the bargaining unit must represent all employees fairly does not bar it from exercising independent judgment and from failing to prosecute the grievance of an employee the union honestly believes has no merit.[19]

§ 4:8.   Unfair Labor Practices.

The National Labor Relations Act prohibits certain practices as unfair and authorizes the NLRB to conduct proceedings to stop such practices.

(a) Unfair Employer Practices. The federal law declares that it is an unfair labor practice for an employer to interfere with unionization, to discriminate against any employee because of union activities, or to refuse to bargain collectively as to wages, hours, and other terms and conditions of employment.

FACTS:

James Brown was employed by City Disposal Systems as a truck driver. The collective bargaining agreement between the union to which he belonged and City Disposal specified that the employer would not require any employee to drive a truck that was not in safe operating condition. Brown was assigned a truck with bad brakes. He refused to drive it. Because of this he was fired. He then claimed that this was a violation of the National Labor Relations Act because it interfered with rights of employees guaranteed by the Act "to bargain collectively... and to engage in other concerted activities for the purpose of collective bargaining or other mutual aid or protection." The employer denied this because there was only one employee who was involved and therefore there was not any concerted action.

DECISION:

The discharge of Brown came under the protection of the federal statute. Although he was only one employee and there was no concerted action as to the discharge, he was claiming the benefit of a provision of the collective bargaining agreement. He was thereby protecting every employee in the enjoyment of the rights that were given them by the contract, which contract had been obtained through collective bargaining. Concerted action and collective bargaining were therefore involved although the specific practice of which complaint was made was the firing of only one employee. [NLRB v City Disposal Systems, Inc. 465 US 822 (1984)]

---

[19]Sanders v Youthcraft Coats and Suits, Inc. (CA8 Mo) 700 F2d 1226 (1983).

(b) **Unfair Union Practices.** The federal law declares it to be an unfair labor practice for a union to interfere with employees in forming a union or in refraining from joining a union; to cause an employer to discriminate against an employee for belonging to another union or no union; to refuse to bargain collectively; and under certain circumstances to stop work or refuse to work on materials or to persuade others to stop work.

(c) **Procedure for Enforcement.** Under the National Labor Relations Act, the NLRB issues a complaint whenever it appears that an unfair labor practice has been committed. The complaint informs the respondent of the charges made and gives notice to appear at a hearing before an administrative law judge (ALJ). The ALJ conducts a hearing and files a report to the parties and the five member Board in Washington, D.C. *recommending* either an order to "cease and desist" from an unfair labor practice or dismissal of the complaint. Unless either party files timely exceptions to the judge's findings, the judge's recommended order becomes an order of the Board. Where exceptions are filed the five member Board reviews the case and either finds the respondent guilty or not guilty. When the respondent is found guilty, the Board issues a cease and desist order, which can be enforced by the U.S. Court of Appeals.

(d) **Constitutional Protection.** Any employment practice that violates a constitutional right of a worker can be stopped by court action if not within the control of an administrative agency.

FACTS:

Finkel and Tabakman had county jobs as assistants to the public defender. There was a political change in the county elections and Branti, the new public defender for the county, fired Finkel and Tabakman because they belonged to the losing political party. They sued Branti to save their jobs. The lower court found that they were doing their work properly and that their work had nothing to do with making policies nor possessing confidential information.

DECISION:

They could keep their jobs. It was unconstitutional to deprive them of their jobs solely because of their political beliefs. This violated their constitutional rights as it is unconstitutional by virtue of the First and Fourteenth Amendment to deprive a government employee of employment merely because of political beliefs unless it is shown that the proper performance of the work was harmed by the political beliefs. As the plaintiffs had nothing to do with making official policies and did not handle confidential information of the government it was not essential to the proper performance of the duties of the office of the public defender that all employees therein have the same political views. There was therefore no basis for an exception to the protection given them by the Constitution and they could keep their jobs. [Branti v Finkel and Tabakman, 445 US 507 (1980)]

§ 4:9.   Union Organization and Management.

In order to insure the honest and democratic administration of unions, Congress adopted the Labor-Management Reporting and Disclosure Act of 1959 to regulate unions operating in or affecting interstate commerce. The Act protects the rights of union members within their unions by guaranteeing equality, the right to vote on specified matters, and the right to information on union matters and contracts. It also protects members from interference with the enjoyment of these rights.

FACTS:

A rule of the steelworkers' union provided that a union member was not eligible to hold office in a local union unless the member had attended at least one half of the regular meetings of the union in the preceding three years. The application of this rule to Local 3489 made 96.5% of the union members ineligible to hold office. This left only 23 members eligible. Nine of these were already officers of the local union. An election was held in the union. The Secretary of Labor of the United States then brought an action to invalidate the election on the ground that it was illegal because it had been conducted subject to the meeting-attendance rule and that such rule was invalid because it was not a "reasonable qualification" and therefore violated the Labor-Management Reporting and Disclosure Act, [sec] 401(e), 29 USC [sec] 481(e), which declared that "every member in good standing shall be eligible to be a candidate and hold office...subject to...reasonable qualifications uniformly imposed."

DECISION:

The meeting-attendance rule was invalid. It could not be justified as a rule designed to secure better attendance at union meetings because in fact it did not have that effect. Likewise it could not be justified as a regulation intended to secure union leadership which, through attendance at the meetings, was familiar with the problems of the union. The actual effect of the regulation outweighed all theoretical arguments: the rule placed control of the union in the hands of 3.5% of the membership. Accordingly the rule failed to obtain and in fact prevented the holding of "free and democratic" union elections and was therefore invalid under the Labor-Management Reporting and Disclosure Act. [United Steelworkers of America v Usery, 429 US 305 (1977)]

---

§ 4:10.   Social Security.

The federal Social Security Act establishes a single federal program of aid for the needy aged, the blind, and the disabled. This is called the Supplemental Security Income Program (SSI). Payments are administered directly by the Department of Health and Human Services.

The states also have plans of assistance for the unemployed, aged, and disabled. The federal law encourages the making of payments under state programs in addition to those received under the federal program. Such additional programs are called State Supplemental Payments (SSP). State plans typically establish an administrative board or agency with which claims for assistance are filed by persons coming within the category to be benefited by the statute. If the board approves a claim, assistance is given to the applicant in the amount specified by the statute for the number of weeks or other period of time designated by the statute.

Federal law allows a state which elects to supplement the SSI payments with an SSP program to choose whether it will retain control over the administration of such supplements or will delegate that responsibility to HHS.

Unemployment compensation laws generally deny the payment of benefits when the employee was discharged for good cause, or abandoned work without cause, failed or refused to seek or accept an offer of suitable employment, or when the unemployment was the result of a labor dispute.

§ 4:11.   Limitations on State Regulation of Business.

The states possess a general power to adopt laws to protect the general welfare, health, safety, and morals. This is called the **police power.** By virtue of this power, the states may regulate business to prevent the sale of harmful products, to protect from fraud, and so on. The power of the states is subject to two important limitations.

(a) **Constitutional Limitations.** A state law, although made under the police power, cannot (1) impose an unreasonable burden on or discriminate against interstate commerce, nor (2) invade a right which is protected by the federal Constitution.

FACTS:

Approximately 95% of all prescriptions filled by druggists require only the dispensing of pills, capsules, or liquid already prepared or packaged by the drug manufacturer. Virginia prohibited druggists from advertising the prices of their prescription drugs. A Virginia resident who was required to take prescription drugs daily and two consumer groups claimed that the anti-advertising law was unconstitutional as it prevented the consumer from learning where the drugs could be purchased at the lowest price. The Virginia Consumer Council claimed that the statute was void as a violation of the free speech guarantee of the First Amendment of the federal Constitution.

DECISION:

Judgment for Consumer Council. The freedom of speech guaranteed by the federal Constitution protects commerical speech as well as speech advancing political or social ideas. A real need for public knowledge of comparative prices of drugs existed because of the wide range of prices. This knowledge was essential to persons of limited income who, without such knowledge, could not make the most effective expenditure of their resources. The anti-advertising statute was unconstitutional. [Virginia State Board of Pharmacy v Virginia Citizens Consumer Council, Inc. 425 US 748 (1976)]

(b) **Federal Supremacy.** A state law cannot conflict with a federal law or regulation on the same subject matter. Moreover, when the federal government regulates a particular activity, state regulation is generally excluded even as to matters not covered by the federal regulation. That is, the federal government occupies or preempts the entire field even though every detail is not regulated.[20]

SUMMARY

Regulation by government has been made primarily to protect one group from the improper conduct of another group. Down until the middle third of this century, regulation of business was primarily directed at protecting competitors from misconduct of other competitors. Beginning with the middle third of this century, regulation has expanded in the interest of protecting consumers.

In the last one hundred years, the federal government has regulated advertising and food, drugs, and cosmetics. This protects the consuming public from false claims and from untested and possibly unsafe drugs. Unfair methods of competition are prohibited. Prices have been regulated both by the setting of the exact price or a maximum price and by prohibiting discrimination as to prices. Price discrimination as between buyers is prohibited when the effect of such discrimination could tend to create a monopoly or lessen competition. Certain exceptions are made where the circumstances are such that the price discrimination does not have the purpose or result of harming someone else. The Federal Antitrust or Sherman Act prohibits conspiracies in restraint of trade and the monopolization of trade. A partial attempt to solve the problem of bigness is made by the Clayton Act in prohibiting mergers or the acquisition of the assets of another corporation when such conduct would tend to lessen competition or give rise to a monopoly. Violation of these statutes subjects the wrongdoer to criminal prosecution and suit by persons harmed, for three times the damages caused them (treble damages). The application of these laws is modified to some extent by express exceptions and by the application of the rule of reason. Employment has been regulated in a variety of ways. The Federal Fair Labor Standards Act, also known as the Wage and Hour Act, requires that employees be paid not less than a specified minimum wage. Fair employment practice acts prohibit discrimination in employment because of race, religion, color, sex, or national origin. Discrimination because of age is partially prohibited. Special protection is afforded by statute to migrant farm workers. The right of employees to bargain collectively with their employer and the right to choose their representative for such purpose is guaranteed by the National Labor Relations Act. The representative selected by the employees to bargain on their behalf is required to represent all employees fairly and equally without regard to whether particular employees are members of the representative union. The National Labor Relations Act prohibits both employers and unions from committing specified acts that would violate the rights of employees. The enforcement of the National Labor Relations Act is entrusted to a General Counsel and the National Labor Relations Board (NLRB). In order to protect union members from misconduct within their own unions,

[20]Alessi v Raybestos-Manhattan, Inc. 451 US 504 (1981).

the Federal Labor-Management Reporting and Disclosure Act imposes certain limitations on unions to insure that they are run in an honest and democratic manner. As an aspect of regulating the rewards of labor, the Social Security system under the federal law provides for payment to workers retired because of age or disability. The federal Social Security payment (SSI) will in some cases be added to or supplemented by payments made under state programs (SSP).

Many of the regulations imposed by the federal government are paralleled or copied by state laws making a similar regulation as to local matters. The action of the states is limited by the limitations arising from the Constitution and by the doctrine of the supremacy of federal law.

QUESTIONS AND CASE PROBLEMS

1. What is the objective of each of the following rules of law?
   (a) Horizontal price-fixing is illegal under the federal law without regard to whether the price fixed is fair and reasonable.
   (b) Farmers' and dairy farmers' cooperatives are exempt by statute from the operation of the Sherman Antitrust Act.
2. What government can regulate business?
3. The Cotton Brand Oil Company and the Northwest Livestock Corporation made an agreement to market their products through a common agent who would set the prices for all products. They were prosecuted for violating the Sherman Antitrust Act. Could they prove that their agreement did not impose an unreasonable restriction on trade?
4. The Danabo Corporation paid the workers in its Pennsylvania factory $.50 an hour more than workers doing the same work in its Mississippi factory. Was the Danabo Corporation guilty of unfair employment practices?
5. Hart is employed by the Bulldog Concrete Forms Company. Her employer refused to promote her because she belonged to a labor union. She claimed that the employer violated a fair employment practices act. Was she correct?
6. Cressler owns a factory. She refuses to obey the state safety laws on the ground that there is no constitutional provision which grants the state the power to make such laws. Does this justify Cressler's refusing to obey the state law?
7. Compare the power to regulate competition and the power to regulate prices.
8. What limitations are imposed upon the purchasing of the assets of an existing enterprise?
9. Jim Mandell applied to the Conestago Airlines for a job as an airflight attendant. His application was rejected on the ground that the airline was only employing female stewardesses because the passengers preferred stewardesses. Jim claimed that the airline was guilty of an unlawful discrimination in its employment practices. Was he correct?
10. The Hines Cosmetic Company sold beauty preparations nationally to beauty shops at a standard or fixed price schedule. Some of the shops were also supplied with a free demonstrator and with free advertising

materials. The shops that were not so supplied with a free demonstrator and free materials claimed that the giving of the free services and materials was an unlawful price discrimination. Hines replied that there was no price discrimination because it charged everyone the same and what it was giving free was merely a promotional campaign and was not intended to discriminate against those who were not given anything free. Was Hines guilty of unlawful price discrimination?

11. A New Jersey statute provides that no rebates, allowances, concessions, or benefits shall be given, directly or indirectly, so as to permit any person to obtain motor fuel from a retail dealer below the posted price or at a net price lower than the posted price applicable at the time of the sale. An action was brought by Fried, a retail gasoline dealer, to prevent the enforcement of the statute. He claimed that it was invalid because it was discriminatory in that it related only to the sale of gasoline and that it denied due process by regulating the price. Was the law constitutional? [Fried v Kervick, 34 NJ 68, 167 A2d 380]

12. Moore ran a bakery in Santa Rosa, New Mexico. His business was wholly intrastate. Mead's Fine Bread Company, his competitor, engaged in an interstate business. Mead cut the price of bread in half in Santa Rosa but made no price cut in any other place in New Mexico or in any other state. As a result of this price cutting, Moore was driven out of business. Moore then sued Mead for damages for violation of the Clayton and Robinson-Patman Acts. Mead claimed that the price cutting was purely intrastate and therefore did not constitute a violation of federal statutes. Was Mead correct? [Moore v Mead's Fine Bread Co. 348 US 115]

13. The El Paso Natural Gas Company acquired the stock and assets of the Pacific Northwest Pipe Line Company. El Paso, although not a California enterprise, supplied over half of the natural gas used in California; all the other natural gas was supplied by California sources. No gas was sold in California by Pacific Northwest, although it was a strong, experienced company within the Northwest area and had attempted several times to enter the California market. United States claimed that the acquisition of Pacific by El Paso constituted a violation of § 7 of the Clayton Act, as amended, because the effect would be to remove competition between the two companies within California. The defense was raised that (a) California was not a "section" of the country within the Clayton Act, (b) the sale of natural gas was not a line of commerce, and (c) the acquisition did not lessen competition when there had not been any prior sales by Pacific within the area. Decide. [United States v El Paso Natural Gas Co. 376 US 651]

14. Sun Oil sells gasoline retail in its own gas stations, as well as selling gas to independently-owned gas stations. In selling to one independent, it gave that independent a price cut to enable it to meet the competition of other independent gas stations. The Federal Trade Commission claimed this was an unlawful price discrimination. Sun Oil defended on the ground that the price cut was made as authorized by the statute "in good faith to meet an equally low price of a competitor." Was this defense valid? [Federal Trade Commission v Sun Oil Co. 371 US 505]

15. The First National Maintenance Corporation supplies maintenance and cleaning services to commercial customers. It supplied the services for the Greenpark Care Center. Greenpark claimed that the work of the employees of First National was not satisfactory and that First National was charging too much for their services. First National did not believe that it was charging enough and finally decided that the best thing to do was to terminate the contract with Greenpark and to fire the employees who had been assigned to do the work for Greenpark. When the union that represented those employees learned of the above plan to terminate, it claimed that the decision to terminate a contract with a customer of the employer was subject to collective bargaining. Was it correct? [First National Maintenance Corp. v NLRB, 452 US 666]

16. Copperweld Corp. purchased Regal Tube Co. Some time later the Independence Tube Corp. sued Copperweld and Regal for damages for conspiring in violation of the Sherman Antitrust Act. They denied liability for "conspiring" because Regal was the wholly owned subsidiary of Copperweld. Were they liable? [Copperweld Corp. v Independence Tube Corp. 467 US 752

C H A P T E R   5

THE INTERNATIONAL

LEGAL ENVIRONMENT

CHAPTER OBJECTIVES

After studying this chapter you will be able to:

1. Identify seven major international organizations, conferences, and treaties.
2. Describe the forms of business organizations that exist for doing business abroad.
3. Identify extraterritorial conduct to which the U. S. antitrust laws will apply.
4. Differentiate between secrecy laws and blocking laws in regards to SEC enforcement of U.S. securities laws.
5. List and explain the laws which provide protection against unfair competition from foreign goods.
6. List and explain the laws that provide economic relief for those adversely affected by import competition.
7. List and explain the laws enacted to bolster the export performance of U.S. firms.

American business firms have become increasingly international in their orientation and operations in recent years as they seek to expand their participation in global markets. They must compete in world trade with the business firms of other nations, including host-country firms; and the success or failure of the firms may well depend on accurate information on the laws and customs of the host countries. In their domestic operations, American business firms compete against imports from the nations of the world, such as Japanese automobiles, German steel, French wine, Taiwan textiles, and Chilean copper. American business firms should be well aware of the business practices of foreign business firms in order to compete effectively, and also to ascertain if foreign firms are using unfair methods of competition in violation of American antitrust laws, anti-dumping laws, or international trade agreements. Individuals from all over the world participate in the U.S. securities markets, and special problems exist in the regulation and enforcement of American securities laws involving financial institutions of countries with secrecy laws.

§ 5:1.   International Trade Organizations, Conferences, and Treaties.

A large number of organizations exist which affect the multinational markets for goods, services, and investments. A broad world view of multinational trade consists of the "industrialized world" which generally favors free trade; the "centrally planned world" with its trade often focusing on providing for unplanned shortages or disposing of unplanned surpluses; and the developing countries of the world, sometimes called the **"third world"** who are not in favor of free trade and seek to use trade to structurally improve their own economies. A survey of major international organizations, conferences, and treaties follows.

(a) **GATT.** The **General Agreement on Tariffs and Trade (GATT)** is a multilateral treaty, subscribed to by 88 governments, including the United States, which together account for more than four-fifths of world trade. Its basic aim is to liberalize world trade, and place it on a secure basis, thereby contributing to economic growth and development of the world's peoples. The GATT is the only multilateral instrument that lays down agreed rules for international trade. Negotiations are conducted in rounds, like the Tokyo Round which started in 1973 and concluded in 1979. Although the GATT is a long and complicated document, it is based on the fundamental principles of trade without discrimination and protection through tariffs. The principle of trade without discrimination is embodied in its **most-favored nation** clause, and states that trade must be conducted on the basis of non-discrimination. All contracting parties are bound to grant, to each other, treatment as favorable as they give to any country in the application and administration of import and export duties and charges. Thus no country is to give special trading advantages to another: all are to be on an equal basis and share the benefits of any moves toward lower trade barriers. Exceptions to this basic rule are allowed in certain special circumstances involving regional trading arrangements, like the European Economic Community (the Common Market) and special preferences granted developing countries. The second basic principle is that where protection is given for domestic industry, it should be extended essentially through the customs tariff, and not through other commercial measures. The aim of this rule is to make the extent of protection clear, and to make competition possible.

(b) **UNCTAD.** The **United Nations Conference on Trade and Development (UNCTAD)** represents the interests of the less developed countries of the world. Its prime objective is the achieving of an international redistribution of income through trade. Through UNCTAD pressure, the developed countries of the world agreed to a system of preferences, with quota limits, for manufactured imports from the developing countries.

(c) **EEC.** The **European Economic Community** (**EEC**) was established in 1958 to remove trade and economic barriers between member countries and to unify their economic policies. The EEC's Treaty of Rome contains the governing principles of this regional trading group. This treaty was signed by the original six nations of Belgium, France, West Germany, Italy, Luxembourg, and the Netherlands. Membership in the EEC has expanded by the entry of Denmark, Ireland, Great Britain, Greece, Spain, and Portugal. It also has free trade agreements with other Western European countries such that Western Europe has become an industrial free trade area.

(d) **COMECON.** The **Council of Mutual Economic Cooperation** (**COMECON**) was formed in 1949 to coordinate trade and other forms of economic relations among the centrally planned economies of Eastern Europe. The council includes the countries of Bulgaria, Czechoslovakia, East Germany, Hungary, Poland, Romania, and the USSR.

(e) **Regional Trading Groups of Developing Countries.** In recent years numerous trading arrangements between groups of developing countries have developed.

(f) **IMF-World Bank.** The **International Monetary Fund** was created after World War II by a group of nations meeting in Bretton Woods, New Hampshire. The Articles of Agreement of the Fund state that the purpose is to "facilitate the expansion and balanced growth of international trade" and to "shorten the duration and lessen the disequilibrium in the international balance of payments of members." The Fund helps to achieve such purposes by administering a complex lending system through which a country can borrow money from other Fund members or from the Fund by means of **Special Drawing Rights** (**SDR**) sufficient to permit that country to maintain the stability of its currency's relationship to other world currencies. The Bretton Woods conference after World War II also set up the International Bank for Reconstruction and Development (World Bank) to facilitate the lending of money by capital surplus countries—such as the United States—to countries needing economic help and wanting foreign investments after the War.

(g) **OPEC.** The **Organization of Petroleum Exporting Countries** (**OPEC**) is a producer cartel whose two main goals have been to raise the taxes and royalties earned from crude oil production and to assume control from the major oil companies over production and exploration. Its early success in attaining these goals has led other nations who export raw materials to form similar cartels, such as copper and bauxite producing nations. More recently, an oversupply of oil combined with decreased demand have reduced the effectiveness of OPEC price structures.

§ 5:2.   Forms of Business Organizations.

The decision to participate in international business transactions, and the extent of that participation, depend on the financial position of the individual firm, production and marketing factors, and tax and legal considerations. A number of forms of business organization exist for doing business abroad.

(a) **Export Sales.** A direct sale to customers abroad by an American firm, with terms of payment commonly based on an irrevocable letter of credit is an **export sale.** No foreign presence exists for the American firm in such an arrangement. The export is subject to a tariff, but the firm is not subject to local taxation.

(b) **Agency Arrangements.** A United States manufacturer may decide to make a limited entry into international business by appointing an agent to represent it in a foreign market, who will receive commission income for sales made on behalf of the United States principal. The appointment of a foreign agent, with authority to make contracts for a United States firm, commonly constitutes "doing business" in that country, and subjects the U.S. firm to local taxation.

(c) **Foreign Distributorships.** A distributor takes title to goods and bears the financial and commercial risks for the subsequent sale of the goods. The decision to appoint a foreign distributor is often made to avoid a major financial investment by a United States firm or to avoid management of a foreign operation with its complicated local business, legal, and labor conditions. As will be seen in the *Grundig* decision, care is required in designing an exclusive distributorship for a European Economic Community (EEC) country, lest it be in violation of EEC antitrust laws.

(d) **Licensing.** American firms may select licensing as a means to do business in other countries. Licensing involves the transfer of technology rights in a product so that it may be produced by a different business organization in a foreign country in exchange for royalties and other payments as agreed to under the licensing contract. Patents, trademarks, and "knowhow" (trade secrets and unpatented manufacturing processes outside the public domain) are the internationally recognized categories of legally enforceable intellectual property rights that define the parameters of the technology being licensed. They may be licensed separately or incorporated into a single comprehensive licensing contract. Franchising, which involves granting permission to use a trademark, trade name, or copyright under specified conditions, is a form of licensing which is now very common in international business.

(e) **Wholly Owned Subsidiaries.** A firm seeking to maintain control and authority over its own operations, including the protection of its own technological expertise, may choose to do business abroad through a wholly owned subsidiary. In Europe the most common choice of foreign business organization similar to the United States corporate form of business organization is called the **société anonyme (S.A.),** while in German-speaking countries this form is called **Aktiengesellschaft (A.G.).**

Corporations doing business in more than one country pose many problems for the taxing governments in which the firm does business. The United States has established tax treaties with many countries, which treaties grant relief to corporations from double taxation. Credit is normally given to United States corporations for taxes paid to foreign governments.

A potential for tax evasion by U.S. corporations exists by their selling goods to overseas subsidiaries which they control at less than the fair market value of the goods to avoid a U.S. tax on the full profit for such sales, allowing the foreign subsidiaries located in countries with lower tax rates to make higher profits, and the company as a whole to minimize its taxes. Section 482 of the Internal Revenue Code allows the IRS to reallocate the income between the parent and the foreign subsidiary corporation it controls. The parent corporation is insulated from such a reallocation if it can show, based on independent transactions with unrelated parties, its charges were at arm's length.[1]

FACTS:

Dupont de Nemours (taxpayer) created a wholly-owned Swiss marketing and sales subsidiary: Du Pont International S.A. (DISA). Most of the Du Pont chemical products marketed abroad were first sold by the taxpayer to DISA, which then arranged for resale to the ultimate consumer through independent distributors. Du Pont's tax strategy was to sell the goods to DISA at prices below fair market value so that the greater part of the total profit would be realized by DISA upon resale. DISA's profits would be taxed at a much lower level by Switzerland than Du Pont would be taxed in the USA. The IRS, under section 482 of the Code, reallocated a substantial part of DISA's income to Du Pont, increasing Du Pont's taxes by considerable sums. Du Pont contends that the prices it charged DISA were valid under the "resale price method" of the Tax Code.

DECISION:

Judgment for the IRS. The reallocation of DISA's income to Du Pont was proper. Du Pont's prices to DISA were set wholly without regard to the factors which normally enter the setting of intercorporate prices on an arms' length basis, such as the economic correlation of prices to costs. Du Pont set prices for the two years in question based solely on estimates of the greatest amount of profits that could be shifted without causing IRS intervention. [E.I. Du Pont De Nemours & Company v United States, (U.S. Ct of Cl) 608 F2d 445 (1979)]

(f) **Joint Ventures.** A United States manufacturer and a foreign entity may form a joint venture whereby the two firms agree to perform different functions for a common result. The responsibilities and liabilities of such operations are governed by contract. For example, Hughes Aircraft Co. formed a joint venture with two Japanese firms, C. Itoh & Co. and Mitsui, and successfully bid on a telecommunications space satellite system for the Japanese government.

§ 5:3.   Antitrust.

As developed in Chapter 4, antitrust laws exist in the United States to protect the American consumer by assuring the benefits of competitive products from foreign competitors as well as domestic competitors. Private

---

[1]United States Steel Corp. v Commissioner, 617 F2d 942 (CA 2 NY 1980).

agreements between competitors designed to raise the price of imports or to exclude imports from our domestic markets in exchange for not competing in other countries are restraints of trade in violation of our antitrust laws. The antitrust laws also exist to protect American export and investment opportunities against privately imposed restrictions, whereby a group of competitors seek to exclude another competitor from a particular foreign market. Antitrust laws also exist in other countries where American firms compete. These laws are usually not directed at breaking up cartels, but rather at regulating them in the national interest.

(a) **Jurisdiction.** In United States courts the United States antitrust laws have a broad extraterritorial reach and must be reconciled with the rights of other interested countries as embodied in international law concepts such as sovereign immunity and comity.

(1) The Effects Doctrine. Judge Learned Hand's decision in *United States v Alcoa*[2] established the **effects doctrine** whereby United States courts will assume jurisdiction and apply the antitrust laws to conduct outside of the United States, where the activity of the business firms outside the United States have a direct and substantial effect on U.S. commerce. This basic rule has been modified to require that the effect on U.S. commerce also be foreseeable.

(2) The "Jurisdictional Rule of Reason." The "jurisdictional rule of reason" addresses the problems arising when conduct taking place outside of the United States has the requisite "effect" on United States commerce, but a foreign state also has a significant interest in regulating the conduct in question. The jurisdictional rule of reason balances the vital interests of the United States including its laws and policies with the vital interests of the foreign country involved and its laws and policies, and is based on the principle of comity. **Comity** is a principle of international law which contemplates that the laws of all nations deserve the respect legitimately demanded by equal participants in international affairs.

(b) **Defenses.** Three defenses are commonly raised to the extraterritorial application of the United States antitrust laws. These defenses are also commonly raised to attack jurisdiction in other legal actions involving international law.

(1) Act of State Doctrine. The classic enunciation of the **act of state doctrine** is that:

> Every sovereign state is bound to respect the independence of every other sovereign state, and the courts of one country will not sit in judgment of the acts of the government of another done within its own territory.[3]

The act of state doctrine is based on the judiciary's concern over its possible interference with the conduct of foreign relations, considering such matters "political," not judicial questions.[4]

[2]148 F2d 416 (CA2 NY 1945).
[3]Underhill v Hernandez, 108 US 250, 252 (1897).
[4]First City Bank v Banco National de Cuba, 406 US 759 (1972).

FACTS:

The Timberlane Lumber Company, an Oregon partnership, brought an antitrust suit alleging violations of sections 1 and 2 of the Sherman Act against the Bank of America, and others, alleging that the defendants conspired to prevent Timberlane, through Honduran subsidiaries, from milling lumber in Honduras and exporting it to the United States, thus maintaining control of the Honduran lumber business in the hands of individuals financed and controlled by the Bank. The defendants contend that the action must be dismissed because of the "act of state doctrine" since a Honduran court approved certain of the challenged activities.

DECISION:

Judgment for Timberlane. The "act of state doctrine" did not require dismissal of this action where the allegedly "sovereign" acts of Honduras consisted of judicial proceedings which were initiated by a private party rather than by the Honduran government itself. Timberlane's action under the Sherman Act did not seek to name Honduras or any Honduran officer as defendant nor to challenge Honduran policy or sovereignty or hold any threat to relations between Honduras and the United States. [Timberlane Lumber Co. v Bank of America, (CA 9 Cal) 549 F2d 597 (1976)]

(2) The Sovereign Compliance Doctrine. This doctrine allows a defendant to raise as an affirmative defense to an antitrust action the fact that the defendant's actions were compelled by a foreign state.[5] In order to establish this defense, compulsion by the government is required. The Japanese Government uses informal and formal contacts within an industry to establish a consensus on a desired course of action. Such governmental action is not a defense for a U.S. firm, however, because the activity in question is not compulsory.

(3) The Sovereign Immunity Doctrine. This doctrine states that a foreign sovereign generally cannot be sued unless an exception to the Foreign Sovereign Immunities Act of 1976 applies.[6] The most important exception covers the commercial conduct of a foreign state.

(c) Legislation. In response to business uncertainty as to the applicability of the antitrust laws to international transactions, Congress passed the Foreign Trade Antitrust Improvements Act of 1982, which in essence codified the "effects" doctrine, by requiring a direct, substantial, and reasonably foreseeable effect on United States domestic commerce or exports by U.S. residents before business conduct abroad may come within the purview of the United States antitrust laws.[7]

(d) Foreign Antitrust Laws. Because of the different attitudes of countries towards cartels and business combinations, antitrust laws vary among the countries of the world in content and application. Japan, for example, has stressed consumer protection against such practices as price fixing

[5]Mannington Mills, Inc. v Congoleum Corp., (CA 3 PA) 595 F2d 1287 (1979).
[6]*See* Verlinden B.V. v Central Bank of Nigeria, 461 US 574 (1983).
[7]Public Law 97–290, 96 Stat. 1233, 15 USC 6(a).

and false advertising. However with regards to mergers, corporate interlocking directorates, stock ownership, and agreements among companies to control production, Japanese law is much less restrictive than American law.

Europe is a major market for American products, services, and investments. American firms doing business in Europe are subject to the "competition" laws of the EEC. The Treaty of Rome uses the term "competition" rather than "antitrust." Articles 85 and 86 of the Treaty of Rome set forth the basic regulation on business behavior in the EEC.

Article 85 expressly prohibits agreements and concerted practices which:

1. even indirectly fix prices of purchases or sales, or fix any other trading conditions;
2. limit or control production, markets, technical development, or investment;
3. share markets or sources of supply;
4. apply unequal terms to parties furnishing equivalent considerations, thereby placing them at a competitive disadvantage; or
5. make a contract's formation turn upon acceptance of certain additional obligations which according to commercial usage, have no connection with the subject of such contracts.

FACTS:

Under an agreement made between Grundig, a German manufacturer of radios and televisions, and Consten a distributor, Consten was appointed exclusive distributor in France of Grundig products. Consten agreed not to deliver any Grundig products directly or indirectly outside France. Grundig undertook not to deliver to anyone in France except Consten and, in addition, imposed restrictions upon its distributors in each of the Member States not to export to France. After a ruling by the Commission that the distributorship agreement violated Article 85 paragraph 1 of the Treaty of Rome, Consten and Grundig appealed the matter to the EEC Court of Justice, contending that they were not competitors and that the relationship did not impair trade.

DECISION:

Judgment for the Commission. Since the contract between Grundig and Consten on the one hand prevented enterprises other than Consten from importing Grundig products into France and on the other hand prohibited Consten from re-exporting such products to other countries of the Common Market, it unquestionably impaired trade between Member States. An agreement between producer and distributor that is designed to restore the national barriers in trade between Member States conflicts with the basic objectives of the Community and is in violation of Article 85. [Grundig v EEC 1966 ECR 229]

Article 86 provides that it is unlawful for one or more enterprises, having a dominant market position within at least a substantial part of the Common Market, to take improper advantage of such a position if trade between the member states may be affected thereby.

§ 5:4.   Securities Regulation in an International Environment.

Illegal conduct in the United States security markets, which are the broadest, most active markets in the world, whether initiated in the United States or abroad, threatens the vital economic interests of the United States. Investigation and litigation concerning possible violations of the United States securities laws often have extraterritorial effects and may conflict with the laws of foreign countries.

(a) **Jurisdiction.** United States district courts have jurisdiction over violations of the anti-fraud provisions of the Securities Exchange Act where losses occur from sales to Americans living in the United States, whether or not the actions occurred in this country, and where losses occur to Americans living abroad, if the acts occurred in the United States. The anti-fraud provisions do not apply however to losses from sales of securities to foreigners outside the United States unless acts within the United States caused the losses.[8]

(b) **Impact of Foreign Secrecy Laws on SEC Enforcement. Secrecy laws** are confidentiality laws applied to home-country banks, which prohibit the disclosure of business records or the identity of bank customers. **Blocking laws** prohibit the disclosure, copying, inspection, or removal of documents, located in the territory of the enacting country, in compliance with orders from foreign authorities. These laws impede, and indeed sometimes foreclose, the SEC's ability to properly police its securities markets.

FACTS:

Banca Della Suizzerra Italiana (BSI), a Swiss bank with an office in the United States, purchased certain call options and common stock of St. Joe Minerals Corporation (St. Joe), a New York corporation, immediately prior to the announcement on March 11, 1981 of a cash tender offer by Joseph Seagram & Sons Inc. for all St. Joe common stock at $45 per share. On March 10, 1981, the stock traded at approximately $30 per share. On March 11, 1981, when BSI acted, the stock moved sharply higher in price and BSI instructed its broker to close out the purchases of the options and sell most of the shares of stock, resulting in an overnight profit of two million dollars. The SEC noticed the undue activity in the options market and initiated suit against BSI. The SEC, through the Departments of State and Justice and the Swiss government, sought without success to learn the identity of BSI's customers involved in the transactions, believing that the customers had used inside information in violation of the Securities Exchange Act of 1934. The SEC brought a motion to compel disclosure. BSI, a Swiss bank, objected on the ground that it might be subject to criminal liability under Swiss penal and banking laws if it disclosed the requested information.

DECISION:

Judgment for the SEC. BSI made deliberate use of Swiss nondisclosure law to evade the strictures of American securities law against insider trading. Whether acting solely as an agent or also as a principal (something which can only be clarified through disclosure of the requested information), BSI voluntarily engaged in transactions in American securities markets and profited in some measure thereby. It cannot rely on Swiss nondisclosure law to shield this activity. [SEC v Banca Della Suizzera, 92 FRD 111 (DC NY 1981)]

---

[8]Fidenas v Honeywell Bull, S.A., 606 F2d 5 (CA 2 NY 1979).

The SEC is not limited to litigation when a securities law enforcement investigation runs into secrecy or blocking laws. For example, the SEC may rely on the 1977 Treaty of Mutual Assistance in Criminal Matters between the United States and Switzerland.[9] While this treaty has served to deter the use of Swiss secrecy laws to conceal fraud in the U.S., its benefits for securities enforcement have been limited, because it applies only where there is a dual criminality, i.e., the conduct involved constitutes a criminal offense under the laws of both the U.S. and Switzerland.

§ 5:5.   Barriers to Trade.

The most common barrier to the free movement of goods across borders is the tariff barrier. A wide range of non-tariff barriers also restrict the free movement of goods, services, and investments. Governmental export controls used as elements of foreign policy have proven to be a major barrier to trade with certain countries.

(a) **Tariff Barriers.** A **tariff** is an import or export duty or tax placed on goods as they move into or out of a country. It is probably the most common method used by the countries of the world to restrict foreign imports, for the tariff raises the total cost and thus the price of the imported product in the domestic market, making the price of the domestically produced product, not subject to the tariff, more advantageous. The General Agreement on Tariff and Trade (GATT) has pursued seven rounds of negotiations since 1948 seeking, in part, the reduction of tariffs by its member nations through negotiations.

(b) **Non-tariff Barriers.** Non-tariff barriers consist of a wide range of restrictions, which inhibit the free movement of goods between countries. An import quota, such as the unilateral or bilateral limitation of the number of automobiles that can be imported from one country to another, is such a barrier. More subtle non-tariff barriers exist in all countries. For example, Japan's complex customs procedures resulted in the restriction of the sale of U.S. made aluminum baseball bats in Japan by requiring the individual uncrating and "destruction testing" of bats at the ports of entry. Government subsidies are also non-tariff barriers to trade. A major objective of the Tokyo Round of the GATT was to produce agreements on limiting the use of non-tariff measures.

(c) **Export Controls as Instruments of Foreign Policy.** U.S. export controls have been used as instruments of foreign policy in recent years. For example, the United States has sought to deny goods and technology of strategic or military importance to unfriendly nations and to deny goods such as grain, technology, or machine parts to the Soviet Union in protest or to punish activities it considered violative or human rights or world peace.

The Export Administration Act of 1979[10] is the principal statute imposing export controls on goods and technical data; and it empowers the President and the Department of Commerce to implement its directives.

---

[9]27 UST 2021.
[10]PL 96–72, 93 Stat 503, 50 USC § § 2401–20.

The system of export controls is implemented through a complicated licensing procedure designed to ensure that U.S. origin goods do not go to unauthorized locations.

The extra-territorial effects of embargoes under the Export Administration Act may be in conflict with international law.

FACTS:

Sensor, a Netherlands business organization, wholly owned by Geosource, Inc. of Houston, Texas, made a contract with C.E.P. to deliver 2,400 strings of geophones to Rotterdam by September 20, 1982, with the ultimate destination identified as U.S.S.R. Thereafter, in June of 1982, the President of the United States with a foreign policy objective of retaliating for the imposition of martial law in Poland and acting under regulations issued under the Export Administration Act of 1979, prohibited the shipment of equipment manufactured in foreign countries under license from U.S. firms. Sensor in July and August of 1982 notified C.E.P. that as a subsidiary of an American corporation it had to respect the President's embargo. C.E.P. filed suit in district court of the Netherlands asking that Sensor be ordered to deliver the geophones.

DECISION:

Judgment for CEP. Sensor's reliance on the American embargo as a defense for not fulfilling its contract is not compatible with international law. While it is the universally accepted rule of international law that in general it is not permissible for a state to exercise jurisdiction over acts performed outside its borders, an exception exists under the so-called "nationality principle." However, the nationality of a business entity is determined primarily by the place of the incorporation, as well as by other links to a particular jurisdiction, including the location of the registered office, accounts and share register, the place where its board meetings are held, and its listings in the tax records of a jurisdiction. It is not determined by who owns or controls the entity. Since Sensor, though owned by a U.S. corporation, was a Netherlands business corporation, it did not have to respect the American embargo. [Compagnie Europeenne Des Petroles v Sensor Nederland, 22 ILM 66 (1983)]

---

§ 5:6.   Relief Mechanisms for
Economic Injury Caused by Foreign Trade.

In the dynamic and profitable markets that the United States provides for foreign produced goods, certain U.S. industries may suffer severe economic injury as a result of foreign competition. American law provides protection against unfair competition from foreigners' goods and provides certain economic relief for U.S. industries, communities, firms, and workers adversely affected by import competition.

(a) **Antidumping Laws and Export Subsidies.** Selling foreign goods in the United States at less than their fair value is called **dumping** and is prohibited under the Trade Agreement Act of 1979[11]. Proceedings in anti-dumping cases are conducted by two federal agencies, which separately examine two distinct components. The International Trade Administration of the Department of Commerce (ITA) investigates the matter of whether specified foreign goods are being sold in the U.S. at less than fair value (LTFV). The International Trade Commission (ITC) conducts proceedings to determine if there is an injury to a domestic industry as a result of such sales. A finding of both LTFV sales and injury must be present before remedial action, including additional duties to reflect the difference between the fair value of the goods and the price being charged in the U.S., is taken.

FACTS:

In 1971, to protect the U.S. television industry from injury by sales of television receivers from Japan at less than fair value (LTFV), an antidumping duty order was issued by the International Trade Commission (ITC). In 1981, Matsushita Electric Ltd. (Panasonic) and other Japanese television receiver manufacturers petitioned the ITC to review the antidumping duty order, contending that the revocation of the order would not be injurious to the U.S. industry. American manufacturers opposed the petition. The ITC sent out questionnaires to domestic producers, importers, and purchasers and held two days of hearings. It determined that LTFV sales would resume or continue upon revocation of the antidumping order. Its decision not to revoke the order was reversed by the International Court of Trade. The matter was appealed to the U.S. Court of Appeals.

DECISION:

Judgment for the American manufacturers. The ITC used an appropriate standard for conducting a review investigation and its determination is supported by substantial evidence. While contrary evidence existed, the evidence relied on by the ITC indicated that excess tube production capacity in Japan and lower U.S. duty rates on complete sets would lead to increased exports from Japan to the attractive U.S. market. [Matsushita Electric Ltd v U.S., (CA Fed) 750 F2d 927 (1984)]

A settlement of the matter may be reached through a "suspension agreement," whereby prices are revised to completely eliminate any LTFV sales, and other corrective measures taken.

The 1979 Act also applies to subsidy practices by foreign countries selling subsidized goods in the United States at less than their fair value. Basically, countervailing duties are imposed when (1) the ITA determines that a subsidy from any source is being provided to a class of merchandise imported to the United States, and (2) the ITC determines that a domestic industry is materially injured, threatened with material injury, or that the establishment of an industry is materially injured, threatened with material injury, or that

[11]PL 96–39, § 106, 93 Stat 193.

the establishment of an industry in the U.S. is materially retarded by reason of the subsidized importation. Judicial review of both ITA and ITC decisions are before the Court of International Trade.

(b) **Relief from Import Injuries.** Title II of the Trade Act of 1974[12] provides relief for United States industries, communities, firms, and workers when any one or more of them are substantially adversely affected by import competition. The Department of Commerce, the Secretary of Labor, and the President have roles in determining eligibility. The relief provided may be import relief, such as the imposition of a duty or quota on the foreign goods, and, for workers found to be eligible, they may seek assistance in the form of readjustment allowances, job training, job search allowances, as well as certain unemployment compensation eligibility.

§ 5:7. Expropriation.

A major concern of United States businesses which do business abroad is the risk of expropriation of financial assets by a host government. Firms involved in the extraction of natural resources, banking, communications, or defense related industries are particularly susceptible to nationalization. Multinational corporations commonly have a staff of full-time political scientists and former Foreign Service officers studying the countries relevant to their operations to monitor and calculate risks of expropriation. Takeovers of American owned businesses by foreign countries may be motivated by a short-term domestic political advantage, or to demonstrate political clout in world politics. Takeovers may also be motivated by longer-term considerations associated with planned development of the country's economy.

Treaty commitments, or provisions in other international agreements between the U.S. and the host country, may serve to narrow expropriation uncertainties. Treaties commonly contain provisions whereby property will not be expropriated except for public benefit and with the prompt payment of just compensation.

One practical way to investigate the risk of traumatic investment loss due to foreign expropriation of a firm's property is to purchase insurance through private companies such a Lloyd's of London. Commercial insurance is also available against such risks as host governments' arbitrary recall of letters of credit and commercial losses due to embargoes.

The Overseas Private Investment Corporation (OPIC) is an agency of the United States under the policy control of the Secretary of State which supports private investments in less developed friendly countries. OPIC offers asset protection insurance against risk of loss to plant and equipment as well as losses of deposits in ovseas   bank accounts to companies who qualify on the basis of a "substantial U.S. interest" being involved.

§ 5:8.   Government-assisted Export Programs.

Massive U.S. trade deficits and the recognition that U.S. exporters encounter strong competition from foreign government-assisted enterprises which are aggressively structured to promote the export trade of the foreign

---

[12]PL 93–618, 88 Stat 1978, 19 USC § 2251–2298.

country have led the United States government to take legislative action to bolster the export performance of United States firms.

(a) **Export Trading Company Act.** The **Export Trading Company Act of 1982 (ETCA)**[13] is designed to stimulate and promote additional U.S. exports by promoting the formation of U.S.-based export trading companies and by allowing banks to invest in these export trading companies. The Act also clarified applicable antitrust restrictions and provided a limited exception from antitrust liability through a certificate of review process.

Trading companies exist in many European and East Asian countries, and are primary competitors of U.S. exporters. Japan's export trading companies, or **sogo shosha,** provide comprehensive export services, and may serve as models for U.S. trading companies created under the 1982 Act. For example a *sogo shosha* may participate in the purchase transaction of goods for export; it may then handle the paperwork and documents related to the export transaction. It may obtain insurance coverage and provide warehousing and transportation services. Through access to or ownership of banks, the *sogo shosha* may extend credit or make loans or loan guarantees to buyers, sellers, and suppliers. It has expertise in marketing research relative to target export markets, and expertise in foreign exchange and tariff requirements. By encouraging exporters to form trading companies with banking institutions (banks have been prohibited by law from engaging in "commercial" as opposed to "banking" activities), and specifically allowing and encouraging the bank-related firms to perform comprehensive export services, Congress believes that increased export activity will be generated.

(b) **Foreign Sales Corporations.** The **Foreign Sales Corporation** created by the Foreign Sales Corporation Act of 1984[14] replaces the Domestic International Sales Corporation (DISC) created by the Revenue Act of 1971, in response to complaints from several of the United States major trading partners who viewed certain DISC indefinite tax deferment rules as creating an illegal export subsidy in violation of the GATT.

The 1984 Act provides export incentives for U.S. firms that form Foreign Sales Corporations (FSC), so as to continue export incentives to United States firms, without violating GATT. In order to qualify for the tax incentives provided under the 1984 Act an FSC subsidiary of an American firm must be organized under the laws of a U.S. possession (such as the Virgin Islands, Guam, but not Puerto Rico), or under the laws of an acceptable foreign country, that is, a country with an income tax treaty with the United States containing an exchange-of-information program. The FSC must satisfy certain other organizational requirements in order to be eligible for the tax incentives provided by the law.

(c) **United States Export-Import Bank (Eximbank).** **Eximbank** is wholly owned by the United States Government. Its primary purpose is to facilitate U.S. exports by making direct loans in the form of dollar credits to foreign importers for the purchase of U.S. goods and services with payments

---

[13]PL 97–290, 96 Stat 1233 (1982).
[14]Title VIII of the Tax Reform Act of 1984, PL 98–369, 98 Stat 678. See IRC § § 921 through 927.

being made directly to the U.S. exporter of goods and services. Such loans are made where private financial sources are unwilling to assume the political and economic risks existing in the country in question. Loans are also made by Eximbank to enable U.S. suppliers of goods and services to compete for major foreign contracts on a competitive basis with the terms offered by competing foreign firms with government-subsidized export financing.

(d) **Other Programs.** As stated in the prior section, the Overseas Private Investment Corporation (OPIC) provides expropriation insurance for U.S. private investments in "friendly" less developed countries. The Commodity Credit Corporation (CCC) provides financing for agricultural exports. And, the Small Business Administration has an export loan program.

§ 5:9.   The Foreign Corrupt Practices Act.

Legal restrictions exist applicable to United States firms doing business abroad in connection with payments made to foreign government officials in the procurement of business from foreign governments. Passage of the Foreign Corrupt Practices Act of 1977[15] resulted from the bribery scandals connected to the Lockheed Aircraft Company's procurement of foreign government contracts. The Act requires strict accounting standards and internal control procedures to prevent the hiding of improper payments to foreign officials. The Act prohibits the offer, payment, or gift to foreign officials, or third parties who might have influence with foreign officials, to influence a decision on behalf of the firm making the payment. It provides for sanctions against the company of up to $1 million, and for fines and imprisonment for the employees involved. The Act does not apply however to payments to low level officials to expedite performance of routine government services.

SUMMARY

In order to understand the international legal environment in which American firms do business, information on certain international trade treaties and organizations is necessary. The General Agreement on Tariffs and Trade is a multilateral treaty which is subscribed to by the United States and most of the industrialized countries of the world, which is based on the principle of trade without discrimination. The European Economic Community is a regional trading group which includes most of Western Europe, making the area an industrial free trade zone for its member countries and certain other developing countries. COMECON is a regional trading group of Eastern European countries and Russia.

American firms may choose to do business abroad by making export sales or contracting with a foreign distributor to take title to their goods and sell them abroad. Such methods generally do not result in foreign presence by the United States firms. American firms may also license their technology or trademarks for foreign use. An agency arrangement, or the organization of a foreign subsidiary, may be required to effectively participate in foreign

[15]PL 95–213, 94 Stat 1494.

markets. This results in foreign presence for the U.S. firm, subjecting the firm to taxation in the host country. However, tax treaties commonly resolve the matter of double taxation.

In choosing the form for doing business abroad, U.S. firms must be careful not to violate the antitrust laws of host countries. For example, EEC "competition" rules prohibit the use of distributorships which set up exclusive territories or set prices. Anticompetitive foreign transactions may have an adverse impact on competition in U.S. domestic markets. U.S. antitrust laws have a broad extraterritorial reach, and the U.S. courts apply a jurisdictional rule of reason weighing the interests of the United States with the interests of the foreign country involved in making a decision on whether or not to hear the case. Illegal conduct may occur in the United States securities markets, which are used by citizens of most nations of the world; and it is in no nation's interest to interfere with enforcement efforts to preserve the integrity of these markets. However, U.S. enforcement efforts run into secrecy and blocking laws of foreign countries which hinder effective enforcement.

Tariff and non-tariff barriers exist to free trade. Additionally, the United States has used export controls as an instrument of foreign policy.

Relief exists for domestic firms threatened by unfair foreign competition through antidumping laws. Also, economic programs exist to assist industries, communities, and workers injured by import competition. Programs also exist to bolster the export performance of U.S. firms.

QUESTIONS AND CASE PROBLEMS

1. What social forces are affected by the extraterritorial application of United States antitrust laws?
2. What is "pipeline diplomacy?" Assess its effectiveness from both a political point of view and an economic point of view.
3. How does the "most favored nation" clause of the GATT work to foster the principle of trade without discrimination?
4. How does the selling of subsidized foreign goods in the United States adversely affect free trade?
5. Fabric House, Inc. (F-H), an American manufacturer of highly successful designer clothing in great demand in Europe, made individual distributorship agreements with British, French, Italian, and German firms to sell its products exclusively in the home country of each of these respective firms. Each firm signed an agreement with F-H that it would limit its activities to its own country and would follow the "suggested retail price" schedules accompanying each shipment of goods. The Commission of the EEC charges that F-H is in violation of Article 85 of the Treaty of Rome. F-H defends that it is good business to be represented in a host country by nationals of that country since they speak the language and understand the customs and tastes of the people. It points out as well that its price schedule is clearly labeled "suggested retail price." It denies that it is in violation of Article 85. Decide.
6. Mirage Investments Corporation (MIC) planned a tender offer for the shares of Gulf States International Corp. (GSIC). Archer, an officer of MIC, placed purchase orders for GSIC stock through the New York of-

fice of the Bahamian Bank (BB) prior to the announcement of the tender offer, making a $300,000 profit when the tender offer was made public. The Bahamas is a secrecy jurisdiction; and the bank informs the SEC that under its law it cannot disclose the name of the person for whom it purchased the stock. What, if anything, may the SEC do to discover whether or not the federal securities laws have been violated?

7. National Dynamics Corp. (ND), a large defense contractor, has been selected by the oil rich African nation of Nirombia to build and deliver 20 ND-21 jet fighter planes at an average price of $16,000,000 per plane. N.D.'s back orders are small, and it needs the contract to avoid layoffs of many hundreds of workers. At a meeting held in Nirombia to finalize the contract, the Prime Minister made it very clear to ND's senior representative that a .025% of the contract price "finder's fee" would be required to be deposited in his brother-in-law's account in Switzerland in order to finalize the contract. He pointed out that the contract was being made in Nirombia where American law did not apply. He stated that such a payment was an ordinary business custom in his country and on the African continent; and said such payment was offered by ND's European competitor if the contract were awarded to it. The Prime Minister laughed, saying "the percentage is so small you can consider it an entertainment expense if you want to." Advise National Dynamics.

8. Six major oil companies, four based in the United States and two in Western Europe, operate oil concessions in an African country. Five of these producers, concerned about the stability of their operations in this African country and seeking leverage in their dealings with that country, form a joint venture called Petro Supply Corp., incorporated in the Bahamas. The purpose of the joint venture is to arrange back-up commitments from other sources in Africa of scarce low-sulphur oil, required by environmental standards in the U.S. and Europe. They agreed to pool such oil on a pro-rata basis among the participants. The three American firms (A, B, and C) and the two European firms (D, in which the British Government owns 50 percent of the stock, and E, in which the French Government owns 50 percent of the stock) agree that the fourth American firm, Mesquite Petroleum of San Angelo, Texas, not be included in the joint venture, because of its cutthroat pricing tactics in both the United States and Europe, and the reckless takeover ventures of the corporate chairman. The U.S. Justice Department contends in a court action that the joint venture is a violation of the Sherman Act. The joint venture contends that the U.S. court has no jurisdiction over a Bahamian corporation seeking oil supplies outside of the United States; it contends that the ownership by the British and French governments entitles the venture to sovereign immunity and it contends that a joint venture to share the large and unusual risks involved in producing low-sulphur oil in the African nation is a justifiable business reason for the joint venture. Decide.

9. Assume that prior to the formation of the European Economic Community the lowest cost source of supply for a certain product consumed in France was the United States. Explain the basis by which, after the EEC was formed, higher cost producers in Germany could have assumed the position formerly held by the United States sources of supply.

10. Brannan filed suit in a Texas state court alleging that he was the owner of two ranches in Mexico which had been expropriated by the Mexican government without payment to him. Mexico contended that Brannan's petition was barred by the doctrine of sovereign immunity, Brannan disagreed. Decide. [United Mexican States v Ashley (Tex) 556 SW2d 784]

11. Timken Roller Bearing Co. of Ohio (American Timken) owns 30 percent of the outstanding shares of British Timken, a foreign competitor. In 1928 American Timken and British Timken organized French Timken, and since that date together own all the stock of the French Company. Beginning in that year and continuing in the years thereafter American Timken, British Timken, and French Timken have continuously kept operative "business agreements" regulating the manufacture and sale of antifriction bearings by the three companies and providing for the use by the British and French corporations of the trademark "Timken." Under these agreements the contracting parties have (1) allocated trade territories among themselves; (2) fixed prices on products of one of the parties sold in the territory of the others; and (3) cooperated to protect each other's markets and to eliminate outside competition. The United States Department of Justice contends that American Timken has violated Sections 1 and 3 of the Sherman Act. American Timken contends that its actions were legal, since it was entitled to enter a joint venture with British Timken to form French Timken, and was legally entitled to license the trademark "Timken" to the British and French companies. Decide. [Timken Roller Bearing Co. v United States, 341 US 593]

12. Roland Staemphfli was employed as the chief financial officer of Honeywell Bull S.A. (HB) a Swiss computer company operating exclusively in Switzerland. Staemphfli purportedly arranged financing for HB in Switzerland through the issuance of promisory notes for DM 7,500,000 with the assistance of Fidenas, a Bahamian company dealing in commercial paper. Unknown to Fidenas the HB notes were fraudulent, having been prepared and forged by Staemphfli, who lost all of the proceeds in a speculative investment. Staemphfli was convicted of criminal fraud. HB denied responsibility for the fraudulently issued notes when they came due. Fidenas' business deteriorated because of its involvement with the HB notes. It sued HB and others in the United States for violations of the United States securities laws. HB defended that the U.S. court did not have jurisdiction over the transactions in question. Decide. [Fidenas v Honeywell Bull, S.A., 606 F2d 5 [CA 2 NY)]

13. Marc Rich & Co., A.G., a Swiss commodities trading corporation, refused to comply with a grand jury subpoena requesting certain business records maintained in Switzerland relating to crude oil transactions and possible violations of United States income tax laws. Marc Rich contends that a U.S. court has no authority to require a foreign corporation to deliver to a U.S. court documents located abroad. The court disagreed and imposed fines, froze assets, and threatened to close a Marc Rich wholly-owned subsidiary which does business in the State of New York. The fines amounted to $50,000 for each day the company failed to comply

with the court's order. Marc Rich appeals the judge's decision. Decide. [Marc Rich v US, 707 F2d 633 (CA 2 NY)]

14. The United States Steel Corporation formed Orinoco Mining Company, a wholly owned corporation, to mine large deposits of iron ore that U.S. Steel had discovered in Venezuela. Orinoco, which was incorporated in Delaware, was subject to Venezuela's maximum tax of fifty percent on net income. Orinoco was also subject to United States income tax, but the United States foreign tax credit offset this amount. U.S. Steel Corp. purchased the ore from Orinoco in Venezuela. U.S. Steel formed Navios, Inc., a wholly owned subsidiary, to transport the ore for it. Navios, a Liberian corporation, was subject to a 2.5 percent Venezuelan excise tax and was exempt from United States income taxes. Although U.S. Steel was Navios's primary customer, it charged other customers the same price it charged U.S. Steel. U.S. Steel's investment in Navios was $50,000. In seven years Navios accumulated nearly $80 million in cash, but had not paid any dividends to U.S. Steel. The IRS used Internal Revenue Code section 482 to allocate $52 million of Navios's income to U.S. Steel and U.S. Steel challenged this action, contending its charges to U.S. Steel were at arm's length and the same it charged other customers. Decide. [United States Steel Corp. v Commissioner 617 F2d 942 (CA 2 NY)]

15. Toshiba of Japan accounts for 85% of all U.S. imports of electric motors between 5 horsepower and 150 horsepower. American producers of electric motors suspect Toshiba is selling certain of these motors at less than their fair value in U.S. markets and that the sale of these imported motors is causing a material injury to the small electric motor industry of the United States. Is Toshiba, having overcome the barrier of thousands of miles of ocean, and having paid a moderate import duty on its motors, free to sell these motors in the United States at any price it deems appropriate even if the prices are less than the fair value of the motors? What action, if any, may U.S. motor manufacturers take on the above facts? [45 Fed Reg. 73723, Nov. 6, 1980]

C H A P T E R   6

ADMINISTRATIVE

AGENCIES

CHAPTER OBJECTIVES

After studying this chapter you will be able to:

1. List and illustrate the functions that may be exercised by an administrator.
2. State the constitutional limitations on the power of an administrator to require the production of papers.
3. Describe the typical pattern of administrative procedure.
4. State the extent to which an administrator's decision may be reviewed and reversed by a court.
5. Define and state the purpose of the Federal Register.
6. Solve problems involving administrators.

In Chapter 4, we discussed the ability of governments—federal, state, and local—to regulate many aspects of business. Early in this country's history all of this regulation was accomplished through direct application of the powers of the legislative, executive, and judicial branches of government. As the pace of advancing technology outstripped this cumbersome tripartite government's ability to keep up with it, a new form of governmental specialist began to emerge—the administrative agency.

A. NATURE OF THE ADMINISTRATIVE AGENCY

§ 6:1. The Importance of the Administrative Agency.

In this new age of complex regulation, most people and businesses do not come into direct contact with the constitutional branches of government. Typically they deal with an administrative agency. To them, the agency is the "government."

Large areas of the American economy are governed by federal administrative agencies created to carry out the general policies specified by Congress. A contract must be in harmony with the law declared by Congress and the courts and also with the regulations and decisions of the appropriate administrative agency. For example, a contract to market particular goods might not be prohibited by any statute or court decision but it may still be condemned by the Federal Trade Commission as an unfair method of competition. When the proper commission has made its determination, a contract not in harmony therewith, such as a contract of a carrier charging a higher or a lower rate than that approved by the Interstate Commerce Commission, is illegal. Other federal administrative agencies include the Federal Communications Commission, the Federal Maritime Commission, the Federal Power Commission, the National Labor Relations Board, and the Securities and Exchange Commission. The law governing these agencies is known as administrative law.

State administrative agencies may also affect business and the citizen, because state agencies may have jurisdiction over fair employment practices, workers' compensation claims, and the renting of homes and apartments.

§ 6:2.   Uniqueness of Administrative Agencies.

The structure of government common in the states and the national government is a division into three branches — executive, legislative, and judicial — with the lawmaker selected by popular vote and with the judicial branch acting as the superguardian to prevent either the executive or the legislative branch from exceeding the proper spheres of their respective powers. In contrast, members of administrative agencies are ordinarily appointed (in the case of federal agencies, by the President of the United States with the consent of the Senate); and the major agencies combine legislative, executive, and judicial powers in that they may make the rules, police the community to see that the rules are obeyed, and sit in judgment to determine whether there have been violations of their rules.

FACTS:

Larkin was a doctor licensed under the laws of Wisconsin. The state medical licensing board conducted an investigaton after which it concluded that a hearing should be held by it to determine whether Larkin's license to practice should be suspended. Larkin claimed that his constitutional rights were violated if the same body which had investigated the case against him would also act as judge to determine whether his license should be suspended. He brought a lawsuit against Withrow and the other members of the licensing board to enjoin them from holding the hearing.

DECISION:

Injunction refused. There was no evidence that the board was prejudiced against Larkin as the result of its investigation nor any evidence that the board members would not judge the case fairly. The fact that the investigation and trial would not be conducted by separate bodies was therefore not unreasonable. There is no requirement in the Constitution that administrative powers be separated. [Withrow v Larkin, 421 US 35 (1975)]

§ 6:3. The Administrator's Powers.

The administrator may be an agency or commission of a few or many persons or the head of an executive department of the United States government. The name or size is not important. It is the function of "administering" which is here considered; and for the sake of brevity, the term **administrator** will be used to refer to all these administrators as a general class without indicating the number of persons or the structure of the agency involved.

The modern administrator typically possesses legislative, executive, and judicial powers. In order to meet the objection that the exercise of executive, legislative, and judicial powers by the same administrator is a potential threat to impartiality, some steps have been taken toward decentralizing the administrative functions. Thus the prosecutorial power of the National Labor Relations Board was severed from the Board and entrusted to an independent General Counsel by the Labor-Management Relations Act of 1947. In a number of agencies, such as the Federal Trade Commission, the judicial function is assigned to special members of the Commission, called Administrative Law Judges.

§ 6:4. Right to Know.

In order to avoid the evils of secret government, provision is made for public knowledge of the activity of administrators. This is done through (a) open records; (b) open meetings; and (c) public announcement of agency guidelines. The more recently adopted statutes creating new administrators will typically contain provisions regulating these matters. For most federal agencies not otherwise regulated, these matters are controlled by the Administrative Procedure Act (APA). A number of states have adopted statutes that copy the provisions of the APA.

(a) **Open records.** The Freedom of Information Act[1] provides that information contained in records of federal administrative agencies shall be made available on proper request. Numerous exceptions are made to this right in order to prevent persons from obtaining information that is not necessary to the protection of their legitimate interests. The state statutes creating a right to know typically exempt information the disclosure of which would constitute an invasion of the privacy of others.[2]

FACTS:

Robert Olson was the administrator of the county hospital of Itasca County. The County Board of Commissioners held an open meeting to evaluate Olson's work. Such an open meeting was required by the Minnesota Open Meeting Law. In the meeting, Olson's personnel record was talked about. He objected to this on the ground that the Minnesota Data Practices Act declared that personnel records were private matters and could not be made public.

[1]Added to the APA by Act of December 31, 1974, PL 93-579, 88 Stat 1897, as amended, 5 USC §§ 552 et seq.

[2]Kestenbaum v Michigan State University, 414 Mich 510, 327 NW2d 783 (1982).

DECISION:

Judgment against Olson. The general language of the Data Practices Act could not override the specific provison for open meetings. Thus the personnel record which ordinarily would be a private matter by virtue of the one statute became a public matter when it came within the scope of an open meeting held under the other statute. Consequently, when the personnel data had to be discussed at the meeting it could be discussed even though the meeting was an open meeting. Although there was a conflict between the two statutes, the open meeting statute should prevail and a court should not create exceptions that were not expressly made by the legislature. [Itasca County Board of Commissioners v Olson (Minn App) 372 NW2d 804 (1985)]

(b) **Open Meetings.** The Government in the Sunshine Act of 1976 requires most of the meetings of the major administrative agencies to be open to the public.[3] The object of this statute is to enable the public to know what is being done and to prevent administrative misconduct by making the administrator aware that the public is watching.

(c) **Public Announcement of Agency Guidelines.** In order to inform the public of the way in which administrative agencies operate, the APA, with certain exceptions, requires that each federal agency publish in the Federal Register a statement of the rules, principles, and procedures followed by the agency.[4]

B. LEGISLATIVE POWER OF THE ADMINISTRATOR

The modern administrator has power to make laws that regulate a particular segment of life or industry.[5]

§ 6:5.   The Administrator's Regulation as Law.

There once was a great reluctance to accept the fact that the administrator made law because of our constitutional doctrine that only the lawmaker, namely, the Congress or the state legislature, can make laws. It therefore seemed an improper transfer or delegation of power for the lawmaker to set up a separate body or agency and give to it the power to make the laws.

The same forces that led society initially to create the administrator caused society to clothe the administrator with the power to make the laws. Practical expediency gradually prevailed in favor of the conclusion that if we want the administrator to do a job, we must grant the administrator sufficient power to do it.

In the early days of administrative regulation, the legislative character of the administrative rules was not clearly perceived, largely because the administrator's sphere of power was so narrow that the administrator was, in

[3]PL 94-409, 90 Stat 1241, 5 USC § 552.
[4]APA codified to 5 USC § 552, Act of September 13, 1976, PL 94-409, 90 Stat 1247. See § 6:7 for a description of the Federal Register.
[5]Doe v Syracuse School District (DC NY) 508 F Supp 333 (1981).

effect, merely a thermostat. That is, the lawmaker told the administrator when to do what, and all that the administrator did was to act in the manner specified by such program. For example, the cattle inspector was told to take certain steps when it was determined that cattle had hoof-and-mouth disease. Here it was clear that the lawmaker had set the standard, and the administrator merely "swung into action" when the specified fact situation existed.

The next step in the growth of the administrative power was to authorize the cattle inspector to act upon finding that cattle had a contagious disease, leaving it to the inspector to formulate a rule or guide as to what diseases were contagious. Here again, the discretionary and the legislative aspects of the administrator's conduct were obscured by the belief that the field of science would define "contagious," leaving no area of discretionary decision to the administrator.

Today's health commission, an administrator, is authorized to make such rules and regulations for the protection or improvement of the common health as it deems desirable. Its rules thus make the "health law." In regulating various economic aspects of national life, the administrator is truly the lawmaker.

Gradually, the courts have come to recognize, or at least to tolerate, the entrusting of a job to an agency although the lawmaker did nothing more than state the goal or objective to be attained by the agency.

FACTS:

The practice developed for owners of trucks who drove their loaded trucks from one point to another to hire themselves and their trucks out to a common carrier so that the return trip would not be made with empty trucks. The Interstate Commerce Commission concluded that these one-trip rentals made it possible for the carriers to operate in part without satisfying the requirements otherwise applicable to them. In order to stop this, the commission adopted a set of rules which provided that trucks could not be rented by a carrier for less than 30 days. A number of suits were brought to prevent the enforcement of these rules on the ground that they were not authorized by the Interstate Commerce Act and their enforcement would cause financial loss and hardship.

DECISION:

The one-trip rental regulations were authorized. The fact that Congress had not authorized the Commission to adopt such regulations did not mean that the Commission did not have the power to do so. The Commission had the responsibility of making regulations to promote the transportation system of the country, and, if it deemed that the one-trip rental regulation was desirable to achieve this goal, the Commission could impose such regulation. As the Commission had the power to act, it was immaterial what the economic consequences would be. These would not be considered by the court as the court did not have the responsibility or power to consider the economic wisdom or effect of administrative regulations. [American Trucking Associations v United States, 344 US 298 (1953)]

Thus, it has been sufficient for a legislature to authorize an administrator to grant licenses "as public interest, convenience, or necessity requires;"

"to prohibit unfair methods of competition;" to regulate prices so that they "in [the administrator's] judgment will be generally fair and equitable;" to prevent "profiteering;" "to prevent the existence of intercorporate holdings, which unduly or unnecessarily complicate the structure [or] unfairly or inequitably distribute voting power among security holders;" and to renegotiate government contracts to prevent "excessive profits."

The authority of an administrator is not limited to the technology existing when the administrator was created. To the contrary, the sphere in which the administrator may act expands with new scientific developments. So it has been held that although community cable television (CATV) was developed after the Federal Communication Commission was created by the Federal Communications Act of 1934, the Commission can regulate CATV. This power to regulate includes both the mechanical aspects of broadcasting and reception and also the content of the broadcast. Thus the Commission may require such systems to originate local programs (cablecasting) in order to serve the local communities, in addition to their activity of transmitting programs from a distance.[6]

When the matter is a question of policy as to how to deal with an issue not specifically addressed by statute, the agency given the discretion to administer the statute may establish policies covering such issues without regard to whether the lawmaker had intentionally left such matters to the discretion of the administrator or had merely never foreseen the problem. In either case, the matter is one to be determined within the discretion of the administrator and a court will not review a decision as to policy that has been made by the administrator.[7]

§ 6:6.   Public Participation in Adoption of Regulation.

In some instances, nongovernmental bodies or persons play a part in furnishing information or opinions that may ultimately affect the adoption or nature of the rule adopted by the administrator. This pattern of cooperation with the administrator may be illustrated by the Federal Trade Commission practice begun in 1919, of calling together members of each significant industry so that the members can discuss which practices are fair trade practices and which are not. The conclusions of these conferences are not automatically binding on the Federal Trade Commission, but they serve as a valuable means of bringing to the Commission detailed information respecting the conduct of the particular industry or business in question. Under the Federal Trade Commission practice, the rules of fair practice agreed to at a trade conference may be approved or disapproved by the Commission. When the rules are approved, a further distinction is made between those rules that are "affirmatively approved" by the Commission and those that are merely "accepted as expressions of the trade." In the case of the former, the Com-

---

[6]United States v Midwest Video Corp. 406 US 649 (1972) (sustaining a Commission regulation which provided that "no CATV system having 3,500 or more subscribers shall carry the signal of any television broadcast station unless the system also operates to a significant extent as a local outlet by cablecasting and has available facilities for local production and presentation of programs other than automated services.")

[7]Chevron, U.S.A., Inc. v National Resources Defense Council, Inc. 467 US 837 (1984).

mission will enforce compliance by the members of the industry. In the case of the latter, the Commission will accept the practices as fair trade practices but will not enforce compliance by persons not willing to comply. This technique of industry participation has recently been followed by several other major federal administrative agencies. In addition, the APA, with certain exceptions requires that a Federal agency planning to adopt a new regulation must give public notice of such intent and then hold a hearing at which members of the public may be present to express their views and make suggestions.[8]

§ 6:7.   Public Knowledge of Regulation.

When the administrator adopts a regulation, a practical problem arises as to how to inform the public of its existence. Some regulations will have already attracted such public attention that the news media will give the desired publicity. The great mass of regulations, however, do not attract this attention. In order to provide publicity for all regulations, the Federal Register Act provides that an administrative regulation is not binding until it is printed in the Federal Register. This is a government publication, published five days a week, in which are printed all administrative regulations and all presidential proclamations and executive orders and such other documents and classes of documents as the President or Congress may from time to time direct.

The Federal Register Act provides that the printing of an administrative regulation in the Federal Register is sufficient to give notice of the contents of the regulation to any person subject thereto or affected thereby. This means that no one can claim ignorance of the published regulation as an excuse. This is so, even though the person in fact did not know that the regulation had been published in the Register.

C. EXECUTIVE POWER OF THE ADMINISTRATOR

The modern administrator has the power to execute the law and to bring proceedings against violators.

§ 6:8.   Execution of the Law.

The power of an administrator to execute the law is of course confined to matters within the administrator's jurisdiction. Within that sphere, the administrator typically has the power to investigate, to require persons to appear as witnesses and to produce relevant papers and records, and to bring proceedings against violators of the law. In this connection, the phrase "the law" embraces regulations adopted by the administrator as well as statutes and court decisions. Increasingly, administrators are required to file opinions, reports, or give an explanation for their actions.

---

[8]APA codified to 5 USC §§ 553, 556, by Act of September 6, 1966 PL 89-554, 80 Stat 383, as amended.

FACTS:

The Reserve Mining Company obtained a permit from the Minnesota Pollution Control Agency to dump waste water into a nearby river. The permit specified a maximum standard for the amount of pollutants allowed in the waste water. The agency did not make or file any explanation as to how or why that maximum was selected. Reserve Mining appealed from the maximum limitation.

DECISION:

The agency had acted arbitrarily and capriciously in setting the maximum without any explanation or justification as to how or why it selected that particular specified maximum. Because of the importance of waste pollution control to a tri-state area, reasonable action by an agency required it to explain and justify its action. Only in this way would the parties and an appellate court have the advantage of the expertise of the agency. Without such explanation, no one could know why the limitation was imposed or whether in fact it was a good limitation. Because the action of the agency had been arbitrary and capricious, the matter was sent back to the agency to do its job properly. [Reserve Mining Co. v Minnesota Pollution Control Agency (Minn App) 364 NW 2d 411 (1985)]

The administrator may investigate in order to see if there is any violation of the law or of its rules generally, to determine whether there is need for the adoption of additional rules, to ascertain the facts with respect to a particular suspected or alleged violation, and to determine whether its decisions are being obeyed.[9]

The federal Antitrust Civil Process Act is an example of the extent to which administrative investigation is authorized. The Act authorizes the Attorney General or the Assistant Attorney General in charge of the Antitrust Division of the Department of Justice to make a civil investigative demand (CID) upon any person believed to have knowledge relevant to any civil antitrust investigation, such as an investigation before bringing a suit to enjoin a monopolistic practice or an investigation made upon receiving a premerger notification. The person so notified can be compelled to produce relevant documents, furnish written answers to written questions, or appear in person and give oral testimony.[10] Similar power to require the production of papers is possessed by the Federal Trade Commission, the Federal Maritime Commission, the National Science Foundation, the Treasury Department, the Department of Agriculture, the Department of the Army, the Department of Labor, and the Veterans Administration.

[9]Polaris International Metals Corp. v Arizona Corporation Commission, 133 Ariz 500, 652 P2d 1023 (1982).
[10]Antitrust Civil Process Act of 1962, as amended by the Antitrust Improvement Act of 1976, §§ 101, 102, PL 94-435, 90 Stat 1383, 15 USC § 1311 et seq.

§ 6:9. Constitutional
Limitations on Administrative Investigation.

The Constitution does not impose any significant limitation on the power of an administrator to conduct an investigation.

(a) **Inspection of Premises.** In general, a person has the same protection against unreasonable search and seizure by an administrative officer as that person has against unreasonable search and seizure by a police officer.

In contrast, when the danger of concealment is great, a warrantless search is validly made of the premises of a business which is highly regulated, as that of selling liquor or firearms.[11] Likewise, when violation of the law is dangerous to health and safety, the law may authorize inspection of the workplace without giving advance notice or obtaining a search warrant when such a requirement could defeat the purpose of the inspection.

FACTS:

The Federal Mine Safety and Health Act of 1977 requires government inspectors to inspect mines and quarries a specified number of times each year to see if the safety laws are being observed. The statute also authorizes inspectors to make a warrantless inspection to see if prior violations have been corrected. An inspector may make such a checkup search without first giving notice or obtaining a search warrant. The federal inspector made an inspection of the quarry of the Waukesha Lime and Stone Company. The inspector reported twenty-five violations. Several months later he returned to re-inspect the quarry to see if the violations had been corrected. The president of the company refused to allow the inspector to make such inspection without first obtaining a search warrant to do so. The inspector stated that the federal statute authorized a warrantless search. The president claimed that this provision of the statute was unconstitutional and that a search warrant was necessary.

DECISION:

The statute was constitutional and the search could be made without first giving notice or obtaining a search warrant. The federal statute does not prohibit all searches of property but only "unreasonable" searches. In the case of business property, greater freedom to search may be allowed than in the case of a private home. The statute requirement of periodic inspections gave adequate notice to the owners of a mine or quarry that there would be such safety compliance inspections. To require that advance notice of a particular inspection be given and that a warrant be obtained could defeat the purpose of the inspection. No real purpose would be advanced by requiring the obtaining of a search warrant other than that of blocking or making inspection more difficult. The purpose of the inspection was closely related to national health and safety. The warrantless search of the business property that was subject anyway to periodic inspection was therefore proper for the purpose of determining whether prior violations had been corrected [Donovan v Dewey, 452 US 594 (1981)]

(b) **Production of Papers.** For the most part, the constitutional guarantee against unreasonable search and seizure does not afford much

[11]United States v Biswell, 406 US 311 (1972).

protection for papers and records against investigation by an administrator, since that guarantee does not apply in absence of an actual seizure. That is, a subpoena to testify or to produce records cannot be opposed on the ground that it is a search and seizure, as the constitutional protection is limited to cases of actual search and seizure rather than the obtaining of information by compulsion.

The protection afforded by the guarantee against self-incrimination is likewise narrow. It cannot be invoked (1) when the person compelled to present self-incriminating evidence is given immunity from future prosecution; nor can it be claimed as to (2) corporate records, even though the officer or employee of the corporation who produces them would be incriminated thereby; nor for (3) records which by law must be kept by the person subject to the administrative investigation.

FACTS:

A federal statute authorizes the Secretary of the Treasury to examine any books and papers "relevant or material" to an inquiry as to the amount of taxes owed to the United States. Arthur Young & Co., a firm of certified public accountants, had made an independent audit of Amerada Hess in order to comply with the requirements of the Securities and Exchange Commission. The IRS was making a routine audit or examination of the tax returns of Amerada Hess and, on detecting a questionable item, requested Arthur Young to give the IRS copies of Young's tax accrual workpapers that had been prepared by Young in connection with its independent audit. Young refused to produce the papers. The IRS, acting under 26 USC [sec] 7602, filed a petition in the District Court to compel Young to produce the papers.

DECISION:

The court could compel the production of the papers. The papers involved matter that was relevant to the question of tax liability. The production of the papers could therefore be required unless there was some exception providing otherwise. The statute did not make any exception. No work product exception would be implied because there is no confidential relationship between an independent auditor and the person whose records are examined. The case is not the same as that of an accountant and the client of that accountant. The independent auditor is a stranger to whom nothing is told in confidence. There is accordingly no reason to create by decision an exception for the workpapers of the independent auditor. [United States v Arthur Young & Co. 465 US 805 (1984)]

D. JUDICIAL POWER OF ADMINISTRATOR

The modern administrator possesses judicial powers.

§ 6:10.   The Administrator as a Specialized Court.

The modern administrator may be given power to sit as a court and to determine whether there have been any violations of the law or of its regulations. Thus, the National Labor Relations Board determines whether there has been a prohibited unfair labor practice, the Federal Trade Commission will act as a court to determine whether there is unfair competition, and so on.

At first glance, this is contrary to American tradition. For example, when an administrative agency sits as a judge as to the violation of a regulation that it has made, there is the element that the "judge" is not impartial because it is trying the accused for violating "its" law rather than "the" law. There is also the objection that the administrator is determining important rights but does so without a jury, which seems inconsistent with the long-established emphasis of our history upon the sanctity of trial by jury. In spite of these objections to the administrator's exercise of judicial power, such exercise is now firmly established.

§ 6:11.   Pattern of Administrative Procedure.

At the beginning of the era of modern regulation of business, the administrator was, to a large extent, a minor executive or police officer charged with the responsibility of enforcing laws applicable to limited fact situations. The health officer empowered to condemn and destroy diseased cattle was typical. In view of the need for prompt action and because of the relative simplicity of the fact determination to be made, it was customary for such administrator to exercise summary powers; that is, upon finding cattle believed to be diseased, the animals would be killed immediately without delaying to find their true owner and without holding a formal hearing to determine whether they were in fact diseased.

Today, the exercise of summary powers is the exceptional case. Concepts of due process generally require that some notice be given those who will be adversely affected and that some form of hearing be held at which they may present their case.

(a) **Preliminary Steps.** It is commonly provided that either a private individual aggrieved by the conduct of another, or the administrator, may file a written complaint. This complaint is then served on the alleged wrongdoer, who is given opportunity to file an answer. There may be other phases of pleading between the parties and the administrator, but eventually the matter comes before the administrator to be heard. After a hearing, the administrator makes a decision and enters an order either dismissing the complaint or directing the adverse party to do or not to do certain acts.

The complaint filing and prehearing stage of the procedure may be more detailed. In many of the modern administrative statutes, provision is made for an examination of the informal complaint by some branch of the administrator to determine whether the case comes within the scope of the administrator's authority. It is also commonly provided that an investigation be made by the administrator to determine whether the facts are such as to warrant a hearing of the complaint. If it is decided that the complaint is within the jurisdiction of the administrator and that the facts appear to justify it, a formal complaint is issued and served on the adverse party, and an answer is then filed as above stated.

With the rising complexity of the subjects regulated by administrative agencies, the trend is increasingly in the direction of greater preliminary examination upon the basis of an informal complaint.

(b) **The Administrative Hearing.** In order to satisfy the requirements of due process, it is generally necessary for the administrator to give notice and to hold a hearing at which all persons affected may be present. A significant difference between the administrator's hearing and a court hearing is that there is no right of trial by jury before an administrator. For example, a workers' compensation board may decide a claim without any jury. The absence of a jury does not constitute a denial of due process.

FACTS:

Under the Occupational Safety and Health Act of 1970 (OSHA), an employer may be ordered to eliminate or abate an unsafe working condition. On failing to do so, a civil penalty may be assessed against the employer. Atlas Roofing was ordered to abate a specified working condition and a penalty was assessed against it for failing to do so. It claimed that the procedure which had been followed violated the right to a jury trial declared by the 7th Amendment of the Federal Constitution: "In suits at common law, where the value in controversy shall exceed twenty dollars, the right of trial by jury shall be preserved, and no fact tried by a jury shall be otherwise re-examined in any court of the United States, than according to the rules of the common law."

DECISION:

Judgment against Atlas Roofing. The constitutional provision means only that where a jury was required at common law it must now be provided. The constitutional provision has no application to new duties and liabilities created by statute which were unknown to the common law. Such new duties and liabilities may therefore be determined without a jury. [Atlas Roofing Company, Inc. v Occupational Safety and Health Review Commission, 430 US 442 (1977)]

Another significant difference between an administrative hearing and a judicial determination is that the administrator may be authorized to make an initial determination without holding a hearing. If the administrator's conclusion is challenged, the administrator will then hold a hearing. A court, however, must have a trial before it makes a judgment. This has important practical consequences in that when a hearing is sought after the administrator has acted, the objecting party has the burden of proof and the cost of going forward. The result is that fewer persons go to the trouble of seeking such a hearing. This, in turn, reduces the amount of hearings and litigation in which the administrator becomes involved, with the resultant economy of money and personnel from the government's standpoint.

(c) **Streamlined Procedure.** Cutting across these procedures are the practical devices of informal settlement and consent decrees. In many instances, the alleged wrongdoer is willing to change upon being informally notified that a complaint has been made. It is therefore sound public relations, as well as expeditious handling of the matter, for the administrator to inform the alleged wrongdoer of the charge made prior to the filing of any formal complaint in order to encourage a voluntary settlement. A matter that has already gone into the formal hearing stage may also be terminated by agreement, and a stipulation or consent decree may be filed setting forth the terms of the agreement.

A further modification of this general pattern is made in the case of the Interstate Commerce Commission. Complaints received by the Commission are referred to the Bureau of Informal Cases, which endeavors to secure an amicable adjustment with the carrier. If this cannot be done, the complainant is notified that it will be necessary to file a formal complaint. At this stage of the proceedings, the parties can expedite the matter by agreeing that the case may be heard on the pleadings alone. In this event, the complainant files a pleading or memorandum to which the defendant files an answering memorandum, the plaintiff then filing a reply or rebuttal memorandum. If the parties do not agree to this procedure, a hearing is held after the pleadings have been filed.

§ 6:12.   Punishment and
Enforcement Powers of Administrators.

Originally administrators were powerless to impose any punishment or to enforce their decisions. If the person regulated did not voluntarily comply with the administrator's decision, the administrator could only petition a court to order that person to obey.

Within the last few decades, administrators have been increasingly given the power to impose a penalty and to issue orders which are binding on the regulated person unless an appeal is taken to a court and the administrative decision reversed. As an illustration of the first, the Occupational Safety and Health Act of 1970 provides for the assessment of civil penalties against employers failing to put an end to dangerous working conditions when ordered to do so by the administrative agency created by that statute. Likewise environmental protection statutes adopted by states commonly give the state agency the power to assess a penalty for a violation of the environmental protection regulations. As an illustration of the second type of administrative action, the Federal Trade Commission can issue a cease and desist order to stop a practice which it decides is improper. This order to stop is binding unless reversed on an appeal.

FACTS:
Moog Industries was ordered by the Federal Trade Commission to stop certain pricing practices. It raised the objection that its competitors were also guilty of the same practices and that Moog would be ruined if it were required to stop the practices without the FTC's requiring competitiors to stop such practices.

DECISION:
Judgment against Moog. The administrator has the discretion of determining where and how to begin solving a problem. The fact that the administrator does not act as to everyone at the same time does not constitute a defense to an enterprise which is subjected to an otherwise valid regulation. [Moog Industries v Federal Trade Commission, 355 US 411 (1958)]

(a) **Compliance Verification.** In order to assure itself that a particular person is obeying the law, including the agency's regulations and orders, an administrative agency may require proof of compliance. At times, the question of compliance may be directly determined by the administrator's making an investigation either of a building or plant or by examining witnesses and documents. An agency may require the regulated person or enterprise to file reports in the form specified by the administrator.[12] The administrator may also hold a hearing or audit on the question of compliance and may require the filing of a detailed statement or plan of operation showing that the regulated person or enterprise is acting properly.

§ 6:13.   Finality of Administrative Determination.

Basic to the Anglo-American legal theory is the belief that no one, not even a branch of the government, is above the law. Thus, the growth of powers of the administrative agency was frequently accepted or tolerated on the theory that if the administrative agency went too far the courts would review the administrative action. The typical modern statute provides that an appeal may be taken from the administrative action by any person in interest or by any person aggrieved. When the question which the administrator decides is a question of law, the court on appeal will reverse the administrator if the court disagrees with the decision. But if the controversy turns on a question of fact, a court will accept the conclusion of the administrator if it is supported by substantial evidence.[13] A court will not reverse an administrator's decision merely because the court would have made a different decision on the same facts. As most disputes before an administrator are based on questions of fact, the net result is that the decision of the administrator will, in most cases, be final.

The greatest limitation upon court review of the administrative action is the rule that a decision involving discretion will not be reversed in the absence of an error of law; or a clear abuse of, or the arbitrary or capricious exercise of, discretion.

The courts reason that since the administrator was appointed because of expert ability, it would be absurd for the court that is manifestly unqualified technically to make a decision in the matter to step in and determine whether the administrator made the proper choice. Courts will not do so unless the administrator has clearly acted wrongly, arbitrarily, or capriciously. As a practical matter, the action of the administrator is rarely found to be arbitrary or capricious. As long as the administrator has followed the proper procedure, the fact that the court disagrees with the conclusion reached by the administrator does not make that conclusion arbitrary or capricious. In areas in which economic or technical matters are involved, it is generally sufficient that the administrator had a reasonable basis for the decision made and a court will not attempt to second guess the administrator as to complex criteria with which an administrative agency is intimately familiar. The judi-

[12]United States v Morton Salt Co. 338 US 632 (1950).
[13]Inwood Laboratories, Inc. v Ives Laboratories, Inc. 456 US 844 (1982).

cial attitude is that for protection from laws and regulations which are un-wise, improvident, or out of harmony with a particular school of thought, the people must resort to the ballot box and not to the court.

§ 6:14.   Liability of Administrator.

The decision of the administrator may cause substantial loss to a business by increasing its operating costs or by making a decision that later is shown to be harmful to the economy. The administrator is not liable for such loss when the administrator had acted in good faith in the exercise of discretionary powers.[14]

SUMMARY

The administrative agency is unique because it combines the three functions that are kept separate under the traditional system: legislative, executive, and judicial. By virtue of legislative power, the administrator adopts regulations that have the force of law, although the administrator was not elected by those who are subject to the regulations. By virtue of the executive power, the administrator carries out and enforces the regulations, makes investigations, and requires the production of documents. By virtue of the judicial power, the administrator acts as a court to determine whether there has been a violation of any regulation. To some extent, the administrator is restricted by constitutional limitations in making inspection of premises and in requiring the production of papers. These limitations, however, have a very limited application in the case of administrators. The protection against unreasonable search and seizure and the protection against self-incrimination are so narrowed by judicial construction as to have little protective value. When the administrator acts as a judge, it is not required that there be a jury trial or that the ordinary courtroom procedures be followed. Typically the administrator will give notice to the person claimed to be acting improperly and a hearing will then be held before the administrator. When the administrator has determined that there has been a violation, the stopping of the violation may be ordered, and under some statutes, the administrator may go further and impose a penalty upon the violator.

An appeal may be taken from any decision of the administrator by a person harmed thereby. As a practical matter, this appeal will have little value. When the controversy turns on a determination of facts, a court will not reverse the decision of the administrator because it disagrees with the conclusion that the administrator drew from those facts. When the administrator is given discretion to act, a court will never reverse the administrator just because it disagrees with the choice that the administrator made. In contrast, if the administrator made a wrong decision as to a question of law, a court will reverse the administrator when the court disagrees with the administrator's decision. In the absence of an error of law, the administrator's decision will only be reversed if the court decides that the administrative action was arbitrary and capricious.

[14]Butz v Economou, 438 US 478 (1978). As to the liability of the administrator for traditional and constitutional torts, see § 10: 9(a) of this book.

Protection from secret government is provided by the right to know what is contained in most administrative agency records; the requirement that most agency meetings be open to the public; by inviting the public to take part in rule making; and by giving publicity, through publication in the Federal Register, to the guidelines followed by the administrator and to regulations that have been adopted.

QUESTIONS AND CASE PROBLEMS

1. What social forces are affected by the principle that the same administrator may conduct an investigation to determine if there is reason to believe that there has been a violation and then hold a hearing to determine whether in fact there was a violation?

2. Can an administrator make "laws"?

3. Caroline is a licensed physician. She is appointed State Health Administrator in 1984 under a statute adopted in 1960. The statute authorizes the Administrator to adopt regulations protecting from health hazards and disease. In 1985, certain candy manufacturers begin using a new artificial sweetener, Doucetran. Tests conducted by Caroline convince her that Doucetran may cause cancer. She adopts a regulation prohibiting the use of Doucetran. The candy manufacturers claim that she cannot do this on the theory that she could only regulate those health hazards which were known in 1960 when the legislature adopted the statute. Are they correct?

4. There is a department in the federal government called the Department of Housing and Urban Development. It decides to hold a conference of leading building contractors for the purpose of deciding patterns of urban development that should be encouraged by HUD. Jane Culpepper wants to attend the meeting. She is denied admission because she is neither a government official nor a building contractor. Is she entitled to attend the meeting?

5. Adams is appointed the state Price Control Administrator. By virtue of this position, he requires all sellers of goods and suppliers of services to keep records of the prices charged by them. He suspects that the Ace Overhead Garage Door Corporation is charging more than the prices permitted by law. To determine this, he notifies the company to produce the records which it was required to keep. It refuses to do so on the grounds that Adams does not have the authority to require the production of papers. Is this a valid defense?

6. Taggert, the state factory safety inspector, is authorized by statute to prohibit conditions which in his opinion tend to expose workers to unreasonable health hazards. He orders the Mancini Company to eliminate certain conditions in a factory on the ground that the conditions present an unreasonable fire hazard to the workers. Mancini appeals from the order and claims that the order is unreasonable and capricious and produces proof that many experts do not regard the prohibited conditions as unreasonably dangerous. Will the court reverse the order of Taggert?

7. Bella was employed by the Sinclair Radio Corporation. She was fired from her job and made a complaint to the National Labor Relations

Board that she was fired because she belonged to a union. The examiner
of the Board held a hearing at which Bella produced evidence of an anti-
union attitude of the employer. The employer produced evidence that
Bella was fired because she was chronically late, and did poor work. The
examiner and the Labor Relations Board concluded that Bella was
fired because of her union membership. Sinclair appealed. The court
reached the conclusion that had the court been the Board it would have
held that the discharge of Bella was justified because it would not have
believed the testimony of Bella's witnesses. Will the court reverse the decision of the National Labor Relations Board?

8. An agency created by an act of Congress
   (a) can only be given powers to carry out the terms of an act of Congress
   (b) can only be given executive power
   (c) can be given executive, legislative, and judicial powers
   Is any of these three alternatives correct? Explain.

9. Compare the procedure of a lawsuit with the procedure followed when
   an unfair labor practice complaint is made to the National Labor Relations Board.

10. Woodham held a license as insurance agent. He was notified to appear
    in person or by counsel at a hearing to be held by Williams, the State
    Insurance Commissioner, for the purpose of determining whether
    Williams should revoke Woodham's license because of improper prac-
    tices as agent. Woodham appeared at the hearing and testified in his own
    behalf. He did not make any objection that what he was asked would
    incriminate him. Williams revoked Woodham's license. Woodham ap-
    pealed and claimed, among other grounds, that the proceedings before
    Williams were invalid because Woodham had not been warned that what
    he would say could be used against him. Were the proceedings valid?
    [Woodham v Williams (Fla App) 207 So2d 320]

11. The New York City charter authorizes the New York City Board of
    Health to adopt a health code and declares that it "shall have the force
    and effect of law." The Board adopted a Code in 1964 that provided for
    the fluoridation of the public water supply. A suit was brought to enjoin
    the carrying out of this program on the ground that it was unconstitu-
    tional and that money could not be spent to carry out such a program in
    the absence of a statute authorizing such expenditure. It was also claimed
    that the fluoridation program was unconstitutional because there were
    other means of reducing tooth decay; fluoridation was discriminatory in
    that it benefited only children; it unlawfully imposed medication on the
    children without their consent; and fluoridation "is or may be" danger-
    ous to health. Was the Code provision valid? [Paduano v City of New
    York, 257 NYS2d 531]

12. The Federal Trade Commission directs the Essex Manufacturing Com-
    pany to install safety devices in its factory. Essex claimed that the Com-
    mission's order can be ignored because the members of the Commission
    were not elected by the voters and therefore the Commission cannot
    make an order that has the force of law. Is this defense valid?

13. The Congress of the United States adopted a law to provide insurance to
    protect the wheat farmers. The agency in charge of the program adopted

regulations to govern applications for this insurance. These regulations were published in the Federal Register. Merrill applied for insurance but his application did not comply with the regulations. He claimed that he was not bound by the regulations because he never knew they had been adopted. Is he bound by the regulations? [Federal Crop Insurance Corp. v Merrill, 332 US 380]

14. A commission of the City of Long Beach held a hearing to determine whether English was physically fit to perform the duties of his job with the city. English was present at this hearing. Thereafter, another hearing was held by the commission at which it considered additional evidence. English did not know that this second hearing was held and was not present at it. On the basis of the additional evidence presented at the second hearing, the commission decided that English was not physically fit to perform his duties as employee of the city. He appealed from this decision on the ground that the commission had acted improperly. Was he correct? [English v City of Long Beach, 35 Cal 2d 155, 217 P2d 22]

15. The Occupational Safety and Health Act of 1970 authorizes the Secretary of Labor to adopt job safety standards to protect workers from harmful substances. The Secretary is directed by the statute to adopt that standard "which most adequately assures, to the extent feasible, on the basis of the best available evidence" that no employee will suffer material impairment of health. Acting under this authorization, the Secretary adopted a Cotton Dust Standard to protect workers exposed to cotton dust. This dust causes serious lung disease which disables about one out of twelve cotton factory workers. The cotton industry attacked the validity of the Cotton Dust Standard on the ground that the Secretary in adopting the Standard had not considered the cost to the cotton industry of complying with the Standard, which cost would be $656.5 million. Was the Cotton Dust Standard valid? [American Textile Manufacturers Institute, Inc. v Donovan, 452 US 490]

16. In order to prevent inflation in World War II, Congress adopted the Emergency Price Control Act. This Act created the office of Price Administrator and authorized the Administrator to fix maximum prices above which goods could not be sold. In order to carry out the policies of the Act, the Price Administrator specified standard forms of records to be kept. William Shapiro was a wholesaler of fruit and produce. The Price Administrator believed that Shapiro was charging more than the ceiling prices allowed by the price regulation by requiring customers to purchase unwanted unregulated articles with the regulated articles they wanted. The Administrator requested Shapiro to produce his business records so that the Administrator could check on this. This procedure was authorized by the federal statute. At first, Shapiro refused to produce the records. Shapiro then produced the records but protested that his constitutional rights were violated because he was compelled to incriminate himself with his own business records. He was prosecuted for violating the price control regulation. The evidence on which the prosecution was based was obtained from the information found in the records that he had been required to produce before the administrator. Shapiro was convicted. Were the constitutional rights of Shapiro violated? [Shapiro v United States, 335 US 1]

17. The Fair Labor Standards Act of 1938 (FLSA) authorizes the Secretary of Labor to issue a subpoena directing an employer to produce papers relating to hours and wages of employees. Acting in the name of the Secretary of Labor, Donovan, an employee of the Department of Labor entered the lobby of Lone Steer Inc., a motel-restaurant, and served a subpoena on an employee of Lone Steer directing the production of papers relating to wages and hours of the employees. Lone Steer refused to comply with this subpoena, claimed that the administrative subpoena could not constitutionally be issued unless there first was a judicial subpoena issued by a court, and asserted that entering into the lobby to serve the administrative subpoena was an unreasonable search that violated the Fourth amendment of the Constitution. Was Lone Steer correct? [Donovan v Lone Steer, Inc. 464 US 408]

C H A P T E R 7

ENVIRONMENTAL LAW AND

COMMUNITY PLANNING

CHAPTER OBJECTIVES

After studying this chapter you will be able to:

1. List the significant statutes adopted to protect the environment.
2. List the methods for enforcing environmental protection controls.
3. Distinguish between private and public community planning.
4. Define and illustrate restrictive covenants as to real estate.
5. Compare zoning, eminent domain, and the law of nuisance with respect to interference with rights of owners of property.
6. Solve problems involving protection of environment and community planning.

For the first two centuries of national existence, Americans looked upon America as a country of unlimited resources. To them, there was no need to take care of, conserve, or protect. The answer to any shortage problem was always very easy, just move westward where there was more of everything. As long as the open west was there, there was no need to talk of protecting the environment. In 1912, the territories of New Mexico and Arizona became states and the United States was then 48 states reaching from the Atlantic to the Pacific. There was no open west any longer into which to go. Americans and American industry were thus locked into a land area that remained constant. While Hawaii and Alaska later became states, the problem for the continental United States remained unchanged. Increasing population and industrialization consumed national resources and created waste that threatened to destroy much of what was left. The result was that America had to begin to save what it had and to stop polluting the environment. Both the desire to protect people from the harmful effects of pollution and the desire to protect America from running out of resources merged and came to the surface in the last two decades as the movement for environmental protection at the governmental level. At the private level, added impetus was given to the concept of community planning.

Underlying these trends was the basic policy decision to restrict freedom of enterprise and the freedom of the use of property and of personal action in the interest of the general welfare.

A. PREVENTION OF POLLUTION

As America changed from rural and agricultural to urban and industrialized, new laws were needed to prevent the pollution of the environment.

§ 7:1.   Statutory Environmental Protection.

Beginning with the National Environmental Policy Act of 1969 (NEPA), Congress has adopted a series of laws designed to prevent the pollution of the air and water and to reduce noise.[1] Congress has adopted other statutes designed to reduce the problem of waste disposal by encouraging recycling or reuse of various products.[2]

State legislatures have also been active in this area, and many states have laws that are similar to the federal laws. A state law must not (a) conflict with a federal statute, nor (b) place an unreasonable burden on interstate commerce.

FACTS:

The City of Burbank, California, adopted an ordinance prohibiting the nighttime takeoffs of jet aircraft between 10 p.m. and 7 a.m. Lockheed Air Terminal owned and operated the Hollywood-Burbank Airport. It sued Burbank to prevent the enforcement of the ordinance.

DECISION:

Judgment for the airport. The federal government has adopted laws regulating aviation and noise (the federal Aviation Act of 1958 and the Noise Control Act of 1972) and such legislation preempted the field and excluded state action. Local regulations would place an unreasonable burden on interstate commerce because it would be very difficult to plan flight schedules if each airport had its own landing times. Moreover the bunching of flights to avoid local curfews would produce even greater noise and would increase the danger of collison by increasing traffic density. From the nature of the activity, a single, national control, excluding all local regulation was essential. Local state regulation was therefore prohibited. [Burbank v Lockheed Air Terminal, Inc. 411 US 624 (1973)]

---

[1]For example, see the Clean Air Act, 42 USC § 1857 et seq., the National Motor Vehicles Emissions Standards Act, 42 USC § 1857f-1 et seq., the Noise Control Acts of 1970 and 1972, 42 USC § 4901, the Water Pollution Control Act Amendments of 1972, 33 USC § 1251 et seq. The pollution of navigable waters had already been prohibited by the River and Harbor Appropriations Act of 1899.

[2]See for example, the Solid Waste Disposal Act, Act of October 20, 1965, 79 Stat 997, 42 USC §§ 3251 et seq., the Resource Recovery and Policy Act of 1970, Act of October 26, 1970, PL 91-512, 84 Stat 1227, 42 USC §§ 3251 et seq., the Resource Conservation and Recovery Act of 1976, Act of October 21, 1976, PL 94-580, 90 Stat 2795, 42 USC §§ 6901 et seq. These statutes have been amended many times.

§ 7:2.   Waste Control.

Modern industry and life styles produce a large quantity of waste materials. Some of the industrial waste can be used to make by-products. Some can be used again or recycled. Some wastes are biodegradable.

In contrast, some waste materials remain and some are dangerous to life, both human and animal, and to vegetation and water supplies. The state and federal governments have adopted programs for protecting the nation and the public from harmful wastes.[3]

(a) **Waste Site Cleanup.** The Comprehensive Environmental Response, Compensation and Liability Act of 1980 (CERCL)[4] provides for making a national inventory of inactive hazardous waste sites and the creation of a multi-million dollar Hazardous Waste Fund, commonly called "Superfund," to pay the cost of eliminating or containing the condemned waste sites.

§ 7:3.   Environmental Impact Statement.

Environmental protection legislation typically requires that any activity which might have a significant effect upon the environment be supported by an environmental impact statement (EIS). Whenever any bill is proposed in Congress and whenever any federal action significantly affecting the quality of the human environment is considered, a statement must be prepared as to the environmental impact of the action. A number of states impose the same requirement on government officials and some require an environmental impact statement for any large private building construction.

When the law requires that an environmental impact statement be filed before a particular construction or improvement can be made, a court will prohibit the making of the construction or improvement if no statement has been filed. It will also do so if a statement has been filed but is so deficient or poor that in effect it is no statement at all.

The duty of a federal agency does not end with its issuing an EIS. It has a continuing duty to gather relevant information, to evaluate such information, and to issue a revised or supplemental EIS if the new information indicates such course of action.[5]

§ 7:4.   Regulation by Administrative Agencies.

For the most part, the law against pollution is a matter of the adoption and enforcement of regulations by administrative agencies, such as the federal EPA (Environmental Protection Agency.) Administrative agency control is likely to increase in the future because of the technical nature of the problems involved, and because of the interrelationship of pollution problems and nonpollution problems.

§ 7:5.   Litigation.

A private person may bring a lawsuit to recover damages or obtain an injunction against a polluter if damages peculiar to such plaintiff can be

[3]See for example, the Nuclear Waste Policy Act of 1982, Act of January 7, 1983, PL 97–425, 42 USC §§ 10101-10226.
[4]Act of December 11, 1980, PL 96-510, 94 Stat 2767, 42 USC §§ 9601 et seq.
[5]Stop H-3 Ass'n v Dole (CA9 Hawaii) 740 F2d 1442 (1984).

shown. This requirement of harm to the plaintiff has to some extent been relaxed so that a person may sometimes sue without proving any harm different than that sustained by any other member of the general public. For example, federal statutes authorize a private suit by "any person" in a federal district court to stop a violation of the air, water, and noise pollution standards. Courts have been increasingly willing to recognize the right of organizations to sue on behalf of their members.

A private person does not always have the right to sue for violation of an environmental protection control.[6] In some instances the right to sue is restricted to a particular government agency. Likewise, an action brought for a violation of the Marine Protection, Research, and Sanctuaries Act of 1972 may only be brought by the Attorney General of the United States.[7]

It is reasonable to expect that courts will not take an active part in the solution of pollution problems. It is likely that on these technical problems they will defer to the decisions made or to be made by the appropriate administrative agency,[8] particularly when the matter before them is merely a small segment of the total pollution problem involved so that the exercise of jurisdiction by a court could hamper or disrupt the work of administrative agencies and study groups.[9]

§ 7:6.   Criminal Liability.

Knowingly doing an act prohibited by an evironmental protection statute is generally a crime. For example, the dumping of hazardous wastes without a federal permit is a crime.[10]

In a prosecution for such a crime, it is no defense that the defendant did not intend to violate the law or was not negligent. It is also no defense that the defendant operated a business in the customary way and did not produce a greater amount of pollution than other similar enterprises.

FACTS:

The Arizona Mines Supply Co. was prosecuted for violating the county air pollution regulations. It raised the defense that it did not intentionally violate the law and offered evidence that it had installed special equipment in order to meet the standards imposed by the law. The prosecution objected to the admission of this evidence on the ground that the absence of any intent to violate the law was not a defense and that accordingly evidence of an attempt to comply with the law was irrelevant.

DECISION:

The evidence could not be admitted on the question of guilt. If the air was polluted, the defendant was guilty even though it did not have any intent to pollute the air and even though it had sought to prevent it. This is so, because society makes the mere doing of the act

[6]Middlesex County Sewerage Authority v National Sea Clammers Ass'n, 453 US 1(1981).

[7]Act of October 21, 1972, PL 92-532, 86 Stat 1052, § 303(d), 16 USC § 1433(d).

[8]Boomer v Atlantic Cement Co. 26 NY2d 219, 309 NYS2d 312, 257 NE2d 870 (1970).

[9]Ohio v Wyandotte Chemicals Corp. 401 US 493 (1971) (Ohio sought to enjoin Canadian, Michigan, and Delaware corporations from dumping mercury into tributaries of Lake Erie, which allegedly polluted that lake which was used by parts of Ohio as a water supply. The Supreme Court refused to decide the case).

[10]United States v Johnson & Towers, Inc. (CA3 NH) 741 F2d 662 (1984).

a crime for the reason that society is harmed when the air is polluted regardless of why it was polluted. After the question of guilt was decided, the evidence could be considered, how-

ever, in determining what sentence to impose and whether to put the defendant on probation. [Arizona v Arizona Mines Supply Co. 107 Ariz 199, 484 P2d 619 (1971)]

B. COMMUNITY PLANNING

In order to provide for the orderly growth of communities, some planning and control is necessary. Community planning may be classified as private (restrictive covenants) and public (zoning).

§ 7:7.   Restrictive Covenants in Private Contracts.

In the case of private planning, a real estate developer will take an undeveloped tract or area of land, map out on paper an "ideal" community, and then construct the buildings shown on the plan. These are then sold to private purchasers. The deeds to the buyers will contain **restrictive covenants** that obligate the buyers to observe certain limitations in the use of their property, the nature of buildings that will be maintained or constructed on the land, and so on.

FACTS:
McCord owned two houses in a real estate development. His deed specified that the property "shall be used only as a residence property" and that "only a dwelling house, and for not more than two families, shall be built" on the land. Eight or more college students lived in McCord's houses. They were unrelated, and their homes were in different places. Pichel owned a neighboring house. He sued for an injunction to stop the occupancy by the students.

DECISION:
Judgment for Pichel. The restrictive covenant in McCord's deed limited the nature of the use of the land as well as the kind of buildings that could be erected on the land. The covenant therefore required use of the land by "families." As the unrelated students did not constitute a family, their occupancy was a breach of the restrictive covenant and would be stopped by injunction. [McCord v Pichel, 35 App Div 2d 879, 315 NYS2d 717 (1970)]

A restrictive covenant will be given its ordinary meaning but if there is any uncertainty the covenant will be construed strictly in favor of the free use of the land.[11]

§ 7:8.   Public Zoning.

By **zoning**, a governmental unit, such as a city, adopts an ordinance imposing restrictions upon the use of the land. The object of zoning is to insure an orderly physical development of the regulated area. In effect, zoning is the same as the restrictive covenants with the difference being the source of authority. In most cases, zoning is based upon an ordinance of a local po-

[11]Lake St. Louis Community Association v Leidy (Mo App) 672 SW2d 381 (1984).

litical subdivision, such as a municipality or a county. Restrictive covenants are created by agreement of the parties.

The zoning power permits any regulation that is conducive to advancing public health, welfare, and safety. The object of a particular zoning regulation may be to prevent high density of population.[12]

FACTS:

The zoning ordinance for the City of Cleburne, Texas, prohibited homes for the mentally retarded unless a special use permit was obtained from the city to run such home. The Cleburne Living Center applied for such a special use permit. The permit was denied. The Center then claimed that the requirement of a special use permit was unconstitutional.

DECISION:

The special use requirement was unconstitutional because it denied those who were mentally retarded the equal protection of the law that was guaranteed by the Constitution. There was no evidence that the living in one home of a number of retarded persons would in any way harm or threaten the legitimate interests of the city. Therefore there was no reason for requiring a special use permit and the requirement could not be justified on the ground that it was necessary in order to protect the city or the public. The zoning ordinance made the distinction between those who are retarded and those who are not. But as there was no sound reason for such classification, the classification was invalid as an unconstitutional denial of equal protection. [City of Cleburne v Cleburne Living Center, 87 L Ed 2d 313 (1985)]

(a) **Nonconforming Use.** When the use to which the land is already being put when the zoning ordinance goes into effect is in conflict with the zoning ordinance, such use is described as a **nonconforming use**. For example, when a zoning ordinance was adopted which required a setback of 25 feet from the boundary line, an already existing building that was only set back 10 feet was a nonconforming use.

A nonconforming use has a constitutionally protected right to continue. If the nonconforming use is discontinued, it cannot be resumed. The right to make a nonconforming use may thus be lost by abandonment; as when the owner of a garage stops using it for a garage and uses it for storing goods, a return to the use of the property as a garage will be barred by abandonment.

(b) **Variance.** The administrative agency charged with the enforcement of a zoning ordinance may generally grant a **variance**. This permits the owner of the land to use it in a specified manner inconsistent with the zoning ordinance.

[12]Charter Township v Dinolfo, 419 Mich 253, 351 N.W.2d 831 (1984).

The agency will ordinarily be reluctant to permit a variance when neighboring property owners object because, to the extent that variation is permitted, the basic plan of the zoning ordinance is defeated. Likewise, the allowance of an individual variation may result in such inequality as to be condemned by the courts as **spot zoning**. In addition, there is the consideration of practical expediency that if variances are readily granted, every property owner will request a variance and thus flood the agency with such requests. When the desired use of the land is in harmony with the general nature of the surrounding areas, it is probable that a zoning variance will be granted. A zoning variance will not be granted on the ground of hardship when the landowner created the hardship by purchasing a lot that was too small to satisfy the zoning requirements or by selling part of a larger tract until the remaining part was undersized.[13]

FACTS:

Stokes owned a house in the City of Jacksonville in a section which was zoned for one-family residences. He and other property owners wished to change the zoning to commercial. The city refused to rezone the area. When the property owners had purchased their homes, a two-lane highway ran through the area. This had been increased to six lanes and the increased noise and fumes made the area unfit for residential purposes. Gas stations were located on three of the four corners of the nearby intersection and the area contained a number of automobile dealers, a Super Burger restaurant, a fish market, and a cocktail lounge.

DECISION:

Rezoning ordered. The area was so definitely nonresidential that it was unreasonable to insist that it be used for residential purposes. To impose such a limitation on the landowner in effect took his property from him. [Stokes v Jacksonville (Fla App) 276 So2d 200 (1973)]

It is unlikely that a variance from the zoning standard will be granted when the only reason advanced for the variance is that it would enable the owner to make more money.

§ 7:9.   Eminent Domain.

Eminent domain is the power of government to take private property for a public purpose. The power of eminent domain plays an important role in community planning because it is the means by which the land required for housing, redevelopment, and other projects may be acquired. Eminent domain has not become important in the area of environmental protection, although it is always present as a possible alternative on the theory that a government owned plant would be more concerned with protection of the environment.

[13]Le Blanc v Barre City (Vt) 477 A2d 970 (1984).

When property is taken by government by eminent domain, it must be taken for a public purpose and the government must pay the owner the fair value of the property taken. The taking of property for a private purpose is void as a deprivation of property without due process of law.

The fact that a zoning restriction may have the effect of preventing the landowner from making the most profitable use of the land, and thereby lowers the value of the land, does not constitute an eminent domain taking of the land and does not entitle the landowner to compensation.[14]

§ 7:10.   Nuisances.

Conduct which unreasonably interferes with the enjoyment or use of land is a **nuisance**. This may be smoke from a chemical plant which damages the paint on neighboring houses. It may be noise, dirt, and vibration from the passing of heavy trucks. Some conduct is clearly so great an interference with others that it is easy to conclude that it constitutes a nuisance. Every interference is not a nuisance and it is frequently difficult to determine whether the interference is sufficiently great to be condemned as unreasonable and therefore as being a nuisance. The courts attempt to balance the social utility of the protection of a plaintiff, on the one hand, with the social utility of the activity of the defendant on the other.[15] Thus the mere fact that the plaintiff shows harm does not establish that the defendant's conduct is a nuisance, if the court believes that the conduct is socially desirable and therefore should be allowed to continue at the expense of the plaintiff's interest. For example, it has been held that smoke, fumes, and noise from public utilities and power plants were not nuisances although they harmed the complaining plaintiffs, the courts believing that the interests of the community in the activity of the defendants outweighed the interests of the plaintiffs affected. Similarly, the proper use of land does not constitute a nuisance as to a neighbor even though the neighbor does not like the use. For example, when trees and underbrush on the landowner's land serve as a screen to hide the neighbor's backyard from public view, the neighbor has no legal ground for objecting to the landowner's removing such trees and underbrush even though the neighbor has lost the "privacy" that such trees and underbrush had given.[16]

If conduct is held to constitute a nuisance, the persons affected may sue for money damages for the harm caused and may obtain an injunction or court order to stop the offending conduct.[17]

FACTS:

Judy Godwin began the construction of a home. About 6 months later Exxon Corporation constructed a separation plant 700 feet away. The plant was on a continuous round-the-clock operation. This caused intense vibration of the Godwin house and caused many cracks to appear. The vibration damaged the house to the extent that repairs would be useless. In addition, sulphur fumes from the plant, the release of steam, and the blowing of whistles were a constant source of annoyance and discomfort to persons in the Godwin home. Judy Godwin (now Dunn by marriage) and other persons living in the house sued Exxon for money damages to compensate for the harm caused by the plant activity.

[14]Scott v Sioux City (CA8 Iowa) 736 F2d 1207 (1984).
[15]Padilla v Lawrence (App) 101 NM 556, 685 P2d 964 (1984).
[16]Jones v Newton (Ala) 454 So 2d 1345 (1984).
[17]Meyer v 4-D Insulation Co., 60 Or App 70, 652 P2d 852 (1982).

DECISION:

The operation of the Exxon plant constituted a nuisance. As it was proven that the Godwin house was damaged beyond repair, it was properly concluded that the house was worthless and therefore Judy was entitled to damages equal to the full value of the house. Judy and the other persons who had lived in the house could also recover damages for their physical discomfort and annoyance, even though there was no evidence that anyone was hit by anything coming from the plant nor any evidence that anyone sustained a direct physical injury from the plant. [Exxon Corp. v Dunn (Fla App) 474 So 2d 1269 (1985)]

When a nuisance affects only one or a few persons, it is called a **private nuisance**. When it affects the community or public at large it is called a **public nuisance**. At this point, the law of nuisance is very close to environmental protection although there is a difference between the two as the new environmental protection law is more concerned with harm to the environment and is less concerned with the social utility of the defendant's conduct than is the law of nuisance.

The existence of a statutory environment protection procedure may bar or supersede the prior common law of nuisance.[18]

FACTS:

Prah brought an action to prevent the construction of his neighbor's house. Prah had been the first to build and had constructed a house heated by solar energy. Maretti later purchased the adjoining lot and proposed to build a house. Prah requested Maretti to change his building plans so that Maretti's house would be moved a few feet further away from the boundary line so that it would not interfere with the path of the sunlight to Prah's house. If Maretti built his house as originally planned, it would seriously interfere with the solar enery system of Prah's house. Maretti raised the defense that he could not be prevented from building as he desired because his building conformed to the restrictions in his deed and to the local zoning and building laws. Prah claimed that locating Maretti's house so as to interfere with the solar energy system of Prah's house was a nuisance even though the construciton of Maretti's house was by itself lawful. There was no evidence that the change in the building location desired by the plaintiff would have any effect upon the defendant or the use of the defendant's house.

DECISION:

Maretti could be prevented from locating his house where he originally desired because at that location it would constitute a private nuisance. A use of one's land so as to interfere with the lawful use of another's land constitutes a private nuisance. The fact that the defendant's proposed building was itself otherwise lawful, being in conformity with restrictions in the deed and with building and zoning laws, did not give the defendant the right to interfere unnecessarily with the solar energy system of the plaintiff. [Prah v Maretti, 108 Wis 2d 223, 321 NW2d 182 (1982)]

---

[18]Milwaukee v Illinois, 451 US 304 (1981).

SUMMARY

America has awakened to the fact that resources are not unlimited and that what is done to the resources and modern technology can be harmful to life. This realization has led to the adoption of numerous state and federal laws aimed at preventing the pollution of air, water, and the earth. With the advent of the nuclear age, the problem of disposing of wastes in such a way as to avoid environmental pollution has become increasingly acute. A person violating an environmental protection law is subject to administrative agency action, civil suit, and criminal prosecution.

Community planning has both governmental and private aspects. With respect to government, community planning ordinarily takes the form of a zoning statute or ordinance that regulates the kind of use to which land may be put. When a zoning ordinance is adopted, there may be some spots in the zoned area that are being used in a manner that violates the zoning plan. Such a nonconforming use can not be outlawed by the zoning ordinance. As the converse of allowing the nonconforming use to continue, the person wishing to use land in a way not permitted by the zoning ordinance may petition the zoning board or authority for a variance from the general zoning plan. Government may also take part in community planning by taking land by eminent domain for use for a public purpose.

At the private level, community planning is made by means of restrictive convenants in the deeds given by the planning owner of a large tract to the purchasers of individual lots of the tract. Traditional equity power authorizes enjoining (stopping) of nuisances. A public nuisance may also be stopped by direct government action.

QUESTIONS AND CASE PROBLEMS

1. "Smoke, fumes, and noise from public utilities and power plants are not to be condemned as nuisances merely because some harm is sustained from their activity by a particular plaintiff." Which of the objectives of the law listed in Chapter 2 are operative?
2. What is the purpose of an environmental impact statement?
3. The Federal Oil Company was loading a tanker with fuel oil. The loading hose snapped for some unknown reason and about one thousand gallons of oil poured into the ocean. The Federal Oil Company was prosecuted for water pollution. It raised the defense that it had exercised due care, was not at fault in any way, and had not intended to pollute the water. Is it guilty?
4. Annabel purchased a building in an area in the city which was zoned residential. She wanted to run a quick printing shop in the building. She was informed that she could not do so because of the zoning regulation. She replied that she could do so because the deed which transferred ownership of the property to her did not contain any restriction prohibiting such use. Was she correct?
5. Magnolia City wanted to build a thruway from one side of the city to the other in order to facilitate thru traffic. To acquire the land for such a highway, it purchased various parcels of land from private owners.

Thompson refused to sell his land. The city tendered to Thompson the fair value of his land and demanded that he surrender the land to the city. Thompson claimed that the city could not require him to sell the land. Was Thompson correct?

6. The Abington Corporation purchased a tract of vacant land. Thereafter, a zoning ordinance was adopted which required that a specified area of land be reserved for parking and air space. Abington claimed that this in effect prevented it from using 20% of the tract of land and that accordingly it should be compensated for the taking away of 20% of the value of the land. Was Abington correct?

7. Which two of the following three are most closely related?
   (a) Zoning
   (b) Restrictive covenants
   (c) Eminent domain

8. What remedies does a homeowner have when smoke from a nearby factory causes the paint on the home to peel?

9. Carlotta owns a grocery store. It is located in an area that is later zoned as exclusively residential. Can Carlotta continue to run the grocery store after the adoption of the zoning regulation?

10. Mark divides a large tract of land into small lots. He then sells the lots. In the deed to each buyer is a provision stating that the buyer will not build a house closer than six feet to any boundary line of the lot. Madeline buys one of these lots and begins to build two feet from the boundary line. Her neighbor, Jason, protests that Madeline cannot do this because of the six-foot restriction in her deed. Madeline replies that this restriction was made with Mark and that it has no effect between Jason and Madeline. Is Madeline correct?

11. SCA Services operated a dump or landfill for toxic chemical waste. The area of the landfill was approximately 130 acres, most of which was within the boundary limits of the Village of Wilsonville. SCA would haul the chemical waste from businesses producing such waste and would bury the waste in trenches in the landfill area. This area was over an old coal mine that had been shut down. Water passing through the chemical waste in the landfill would filter down through the mine area causing the land surrounding the landfill to subside. It was also probable that the waste would enter the streams that supplied water for the Village and would contaminate that water and could possibly contaminate the Mississippi River. The Village brought an action to enjoin the operation of the waste landfill and to order the removal of the waste that had already been deposited. Was the Village entitled to this relief? [Village of Wilsonville v SCA Services, Inc. 86 Ill 2d 1, 55 Ill Dec 499, 426 NE2d 824]

12. A zoning ordinance of the City of Dallas, Texas, prohibited the use of property in a residential district for gasoline filling stations. Lombardo brought an action against the City to test the validity of the ordinance. He contended that the ordinance violated the rights of the owners of property in such districts. Do you agree with this contention? [Lombardo v City of Dallas, 124 Tex 1, 73 SW2d 475]

13. Shearing was a homeowner in Rochester. The City burned trash on a nearby tract of land. Fires burned continuously on open ground, not in

an incinerator, at times within 800 yards of the plaintiff's house. The smoke and dirt from the fires settled on the house of the plaintiff and on those of other persons in the area. The plaintiff sued to stop the continuance of such burning and to recover damages for the harm done to his home. Decide. [Shearing v Rochester, 51 Misc 2d 436, 273 NYS2d 464]

14. The Belmar Drive-In Theatre Co. brought an ction against the Illinois State Toll Highway Commission because the bright lights of the toll road station interfered with the showing of motion pictures at the drive-in. Decide. [Belmar Drive-In Theatre Co. v Illinois State Toll Highway Commission, 34 Ill 2d 544, 216 NE2d 788]

15. The Stallcups lived in a rural section of the state. In front of their house ran a relatively unused unimproved public county road. Wales Trucking Co. transported concrete pipe from the plant where it was made to a lake where the pipe was used to construct a water line to bring water to a nearby city. In the course of four months Wales made 825 trips over the road carrying from 58,000 to 72,000 pounds of pipe per trip and making the same number of empty return trips. The heavy use of the road by Wales cut up the dirt and made it like ashes. The Stallcups sued Wales for damages caused by the deposit of dust on their house and for the physical annoyance and discomfort caused by the dust. Wales defended on the ground that it had not been negligent and that its use of the road was not unlawful. Decide. [Wales Trucking Co. v Stallcup (Tex Civ App) 465 SE2d 44]

16. Rogers Morton, the United States Secretary of the Interior, announced that the United States proposed to sell certain oil lands that were out in the ocean. Before this could be done, an environmental impact statement had to be filed by the Director of the Bureau of Land Management. He filed such a statement. The Natural Resources Defense Council claimed that the statement was not sufficient because it did not identify and consider the effects upon the environment of other alternatives to the proposed action. The Secretary replied that the alternatives had been omitted because he had no authority to put the alternatives into operation. Was this a valid excuse for omitting the alternatives? [Natural Resources Defense Council, Inc. v Morton (CA Dist Col) 458 F2d 827]

17. Gallagher owned a tract of land that was subject to the restriction that it be used "for residence only." He began to build a townhouse condominium on the land. The owners of the neighboring land, acting as the Don Cesar Property Owners Corporation, brought an action against Gallagher to prevent the construction of the condominium. Were they entitled to prevent the construction? [Don Cesar Property Owners Corp. v Gallagher (Fla App) 452 So 2d 1047]

CHAPTER 8

CONSUMER PROTECTION

CHAPTER OBJECTIVES

After studying this chapter you will be able to:

1. Describe the purpose of truth in advertising legislation.
2. Explain and apply the four installment rule.
3. Explain the effect of the Federal Warranty Disclosure Act of 1974.
4. State the extent to which the holder of a credit card is liable for purchases made by a person finding or stealing the card.
5. Explain the Federal Trade Commission regulation for the preservation of consumer defenses.
6. State what is provided for the protection of credit standing and reputation.
7. List the remedies available for a breach of a consumer protection law.
8. Solve problems involving consumer protection law.

In the world of today, the consumer does not stand on equal footing with the enterprise with which the consumer deals. When the consumer buys from the large store or business there is an economic inequality. When the consumer buys a modern product there is a wall of ignorance of technology that prevents the consumer from being able to determine the quality of the product by inspection. When the consumer buys a product in a cardboard package or a can, there is no way to know what there is inside without first opening the package or the can. Typically the consumer buys on credit and usually the credit terms will be the same wherever the consumer goes. In short the concept of equality is contradicted by the reality that the consumer is not an equal.

What should society do? Should it insist that no exceptions be made to the concept of equality or should it step in and regulate the marketplace for the purpose of protecting the consumer. In the last several decades, the social forces of protecting the person and preventing fraud, oppression, and hardship have convinced government to step in and adopt laws protecting consumers.[1]

§ 8:1.   Advertising.

Statutes commonly prohibit fraudulent advertising, but most advertising regulations are entrusted to an administrative agency, such as the Federal Trade Commission (FTC), which is authorized to issue orders to stop false, misleading advertising. Statutes prohibiting false advertising are liberally interpreted.

FACTS:

A Wisconsin statute prohibited sellers from making false and deceptive statements "to the public." Automatic Merchandisers advertised its products with truthful statements but when a salesperson would negotiate with individual customers, the salesperson would make false statements to that customer. An action was brought by the state of Wisconsin to enjoin the making of the false statements. Automatic defended on the ground that the false statements had not been made to the public but had been made to individual prospective customers.

DECISION:

Judgment for Wisconsin. The making of the false statements to the individual members of the public who were prospective customers was the making of "statements to the public" within the scope of the statute. [Wisconsin v Automatic Merchandisers of America, Inc. 64 Wis 2d 659, 221 NWd 683 (1974)]

(a) **Deception.** Under consumer protection statutes, deception, rather than fraud, is the significant element. This means that there is a breach of such statutes even though there is no proof that the wrongdoer intended to defraud or deceive anyone.[2]

This is a shift of social point of view. That is, instead of basing the law in terms of fault of the actor, the law is concerned with the problem of the buyer who is likely to be misled by statements made without regard to whether the defendant had any evil intent. The good faith of an advertiser or the absence of intent to deceive is immaterial, as the purpose of false advertising legislation is to protect the consumer rather than to punish the advertiser.

---

[1]Consumer protection is not limited to the protection of persons of limited education or economic means. See Weisz v Parke-Bernet Galleries, Inc. 67 Misc 2d 1077, 325 NYS2d 576 (1971); American Petrofina, Inc. v PPG Industries, Inc. (Tex App) 679 SW2d 740 (1984) (glass producer purchasing 3 million gallons of diesel oil fuel).
[2]Rollins, Inc. v Heller (Fla App) 454 So 2d 580 (1984).

The net effect of the truth in advertising legislation is that a seller must make an accurate and substantially complete description of the product and the terms on which it is sold and must do so in a way which the buyer can be expected to understand.

At common law, a seller was not liable when the product did not live up to the opinion expressed by the seller to the buyer. The theory of the common law was that the buyer should recognize that the statement was merely the opinion of the seller and that the buyer should not rely thereon. In the realities of the marketplace, buyers do rely on sellers' opinions and therefore the unfair trade practices laws condemn false opinions of sellers which mislead buyers.

The FTC requires that an advertiser maintain a file containing the data claimed to support an advertising statement as to safety, performance, efficacy, quality, or comparative price of an advertised product. The FTC can require the advertiser to produce this material. If it is in the interest of the consumer, the Commission can make this information public, except to the extent that it contains trade secrets or matter which is privileged.

FACTS:

The Colgate-Palmolive Co. ran a television commercial to show that its shaving cream "Rapid Shave" could soften even the toughness of sandpaper. The commercial showed what was described as the sandpaper test. Actually what was used was a sheet of plexiglas on which sand had been sprinkled. The FTC claimed that this was a deceptive practice. The advertiser contended that actual sandpaper would merely look like ordinary colored paper and that plexiglas had been used to give the viewer an accurate visual representation of the test. Could the FTC prohibit the use of this commercial?

DECISION:

Yes. The commercial made the television viewer believe that he was seeing with his own eyes an actual test, and this would tend to persuade him more than it would if he knew that he was seeing merely an imitation of a test. To that extent, the use of the mockup without disclosing its true character was deceptive, and it therefore could be prohibited by the FTC. [Federal Trade Commission v Colgate-Palmolive Co. 380 US 374 (1965)]

(b) Corrective Advertising. When an enterprise has made false and deceptive statements in advertising, the Federal Trade Commission may require that a new advertising be made in which the former statements are contradicted and the truth stated. This corrective advertising required by the Federal Trade Commission is also called **retractive advertising.**

§ 8:2. Seals of Approval.

Many commodities are sold or advertised with a sticker or tag stating that the article has been approved or is guaranteed by some association or organization. Ordinarily, when a product is thus sold, it will in fact have been approved by some testing laboratory and will probably have proven adequate to meet ordinary consumer needs. A seller who sells with a seal of approval of a third person makes, in effect, a guarantee that the product has been so approved, so that such a seller is liable, if the product was in fact not approved. In addition, the seller would ordinarily be liable for fraud if the statement is not true.

§ 8:3.   Labeling.

Closely related to the regulation of advertising is the regulation of labels and marking of products. Various federal statutes are designed to give the consumer accurate information about the product, while others require warnings as to dangers of use or misuse. Consumer protection regulations prohibit the use in the labeling or marking of products of such terms as "jumbo," "giant," "full," which tend to exaggerate and mislead.

§ 8:4.   Selling Methods.

Consumer protection statutes prohibit the use of improper and deceptive selling methods.[3] These statutes are liberally construed to protect consumers from improper practices.[4]

(a) **Disclosure of Transaction Terms.** The federal law requires the disclosure of all interest charges, points or fees for granting loans, and similar charges. These charges must be set forth as an annual percentage rate so that the consumer can see just how much the transaction costs a year.[5]

If sellers advertise that they will sell or lease on credit, they cannot state merely the monthly installments that will be due. They must give the consumer additional information: (1) the total cash price; (2) the amount of the down payment required; (3) the number, amounts, and due dates of payments; and (4) the annual percentage rate of the credit charges.[6]

In various ways, consumer protection statutes seek to protect the consumer from surprise or unbargained-for terms and from unwanted contracts.

(1) *Four Installment Rule.* Whenever a sale or contract provides for payment in more than four installments, it is subject to the Truth in Lending Act. This is so even though no service or financial charge is expressly added because of the installment pattern of paying.

When consumer credit is advertised as repayable in more than four installments and no financing charge is expressly imposed, the advertisement must "clearly and conspicuously" state that "the cost of credit is included in the price" quoted for the goods and services.

---

[3]As to states adopting the Uniform Consumer Credit Code (UCCC) see § 1:6. The Uniform Consumer Sales Practices Act has been adopted in Kansas, Ohio, and Utah; a Uniform Deceptive Trade Practices Act (1966 revision) has been adopted in Colorado, Georgia, Hawaii, Minnesota, Nebraska, New Mexico, Ohio, and Oregon: the 1964 version of the Uniform Deceptive Trade Practices Act was adopted in Delaware, Illinois, Maine, and Oklahoma; and a Model Land Sales Practice Act has been adopted in Alaska, Connecticut, Florida, Hawaii, Idaho, Kansas, Minnesota, Montana, South Carolina, and Utah.

[4]Haveriah v Memphis Aviation, Inc. _____ Tenn App _____, 674 SW2d 297 (1984).

[5]Consumer Credit Protection Act (CCPA), 15 USC §§ 1605, 1606, 1636; Regulation Z adopted by the Federal Reserve Board of Governors, § 226.5.

[6]Regulation Z, § 1210, Consumer Leasing Act of 1976, 15 USC § 1667.

FACTS:

Acting under the Truth in Lending Act, the Federal Reserve Board adopted a Regulation Z. Among other things, this Regulation declared that whenever a consumer paid the price for goods purchased on credit in more than four installments, the person dealing with him was subject to the Truth in Lending Act. The Family Publications Service sold a magazine to Leila Mourning but failed to disclose the information required by the Act although payment was to be made by her in 30 monthly installments. Family Publications claimed that the four month rule of Regulation Z was invalid and that the Federal Truth in Lending Act could not apply to it because it did not make any extra charge for the making of installment payments.

DECISION:

The Regulation applied to the sale and was valid in so doing. Such application of the Regulation was necessary to prevent evasion of the statute's disclosure provisions. If not so applied, a seller could conceal the items of which disclosure was required by increasing his price and then permitting the buyer to pay in installments on a price to which apparently no "charges" were added. [Mourning v Family Publication Service, Inc. 411 US 356 (1973)]

(2) Contract on Two Sides. In order to be sure that disclosures required by federal law are in fact seen by the consumer, special provision is made for the case when the terms of the transaction are printed on both the front and back of a sheet or contract. In such case, (1) both sides of the sheet must carry the warning: "NOTICE: see other side for important information," and (2) the page must be signed at the end of the second side. Conversely, the requirements of the federal law are not satisfied when there is no warning of "see other side" and the parties sign the contract on the face or the first side of the paper only.

(3) Particular Sales and Leases. The Motor Vehicle Information and Cost Savings Act requires the disclosure to the buyer of various elements in the cost of an automobile. The Act prohibits selling an automobile without informing the buyer that the odometer has been reset below the true mileage. A buyer who is caused actual loss by odometer fraud may recover from the seller 3 times the actual loss or $1500, whichever is greater.[7] There is a breach of the federal statute when the seller has knowledge that the odometer has turned itself at 100,000 miles but the seller then states that the mileage is 20,073 miles instead of 120,073.[8] The Consumer Leasing Act of 1976 requires that persons leasing automobiles and other durable goods to consumers make a full disclosure to the consumer of the details of the transaction. The Act also regulates advertising and seeks to protect lessees from loss if the property is resold by the lessor upon the expiration of the lease.

(b) Home Solicited Sales. A sale of goods or services for $25 or more made to a buyer at home may be set aside within 3 days. This right

[7]Act of October 20, 1972, §§ 403, 409, PL 92–513, 86 Stat 947, 15 USC §§ 1901 et seq., as amended.

[8]Suits v Little Motor Co. (CA5 Ga) 642 F2d 883 (1981).

may be exercised merely because the buyer does not want to go through with the contract. There is no requirement of proving any misconduct of the seller nor any defect in the goods or services.[9]

(c) **Referral Sales.** The technique of giving the buyer a price reduction for customers referred to the seller is theoretically lawful. In effect, it is merely paying the buyer a "commission" for the promotion of other sales. In actual practice, however, the referral sales technique is often accompanied by fraud or by exorbitant pricing, so that consumer protection laws variously condemn referral selling. As a result, the referral system of selling has been condemned as unconscionable under the UCC, and is expressly prohibited by UCCC.

§ 8:5.   Contract Terms.

Consumer protection legislation does not ordinarily affect the right of the parties to make a contract on such terms as they choose. It is customary, however, to prohibit the use of certain clauses which, it is believed, bear too harshly on the debtor or which have too great a potential for exploitive abuse by a creditor. For example, the UCCC prohibits provisions permitting a creditor to enter a judgment against a debtor without giving the debtor any chance to make a defense.[10]

The federal Warranty Disclosure Act of 1974 establishes disclosure standards for consumer goods warranties in order to make them understood by the consumer.[11]

The parties to a credit transaction may agree that payments should be made in installments but that if there is a default as to any installment, the creditor may declare the entire balance due at once. This cancels or destroys the schedule for payments by making the entire balance immediately due. Such *acceleration* of the debt can cause the debtor great hardship. Because of this, some statutes limit or prohibit the use of acceleration clauses.

(a) **Unconscionability.** To some extent, consumer protection has been provided under the UCC by those courts which hold that the "unconscionability" provision protects from "excessive" or "exorbitant" prices when goods are sold on credit.[12]

FACTS:

Romain sold "educational materials" on a house-to-house sales basis, catering to minority groups and persons of limited education and economic means. The materials were sold at a price approximately two and a half times the reasonable market value of the materials if they were fit for their intended purpose, but there was evidence that much of it was practically worthless. Kugler, the Attorney General, brought an action on behalf of all customers of Romain to declare their contracts invalid.

[9]Federal Trade Commission Regulation, 16 CFR § 429.1, Brown v Martinelli, 66 Ohio 2d 45, 419 NE2d 1081 (1981).
[10]UCCC §§ 2.415, 3.407.
[11]Act of January 4, 1975, PL 93–637, 88 Stat 2183, 15 USC § 2301.
[12]UCC § 2–302(1).

DECISION:

Judgment for Kugler. Under the circumstances, the price was unconscionable under UCC [sec] 2-302. Unconscionability is to be equated with fraud when there is an exploitation of persons of limited income and education by selling them goods of little or no value at high prices. [Kugler v Romain, 58 NJ 522, 279 A2d 640 (1971)]

(b) Form of Contract. Consumer protection laws commonly regulate the form of the contract, requiring that certain items be specifically listed, that payments under the contract be itemized, and indicate the allocation to principal, interest, insurance, and so on. Generally certain portions of the contract or all of the contract must be printed in type of a certain size and a copy must be furnished to the buyer. Such statutory requirements are more demanding than the statute of frauds section of the UCC. It is frequently provided that the copy furnished the consumer must be completely filled in. Back-page disclaimers are void if the front page of the contract does not call attention to the presence of such terms.

(c) Limitation of Credit. Various laws may limit the ability to borrow money or purchase on credit. In some states, it is prohibited to make "open end" mortgages by which the mortgage secures a specified debt and such additional loans as may thereafter be made. Consumer protection is also afforded in some states by placing a time limit on smaller loans.

§ 8:6.   Credit Cards.

Today's credit card may cover travel and entertainment; or a particular group of commodities, or it may be a general-purpose card, covering the purchase of any kind of goods and services.

(a) Unsolicited Credit Card. The unsolicited distribution of credit cards to persons who have not applied for them is prohibited.

(b) Surcharge prohibited. A seller cannot add any charge to the purchase price because the buyer uses a credit card instead of paying with cash or a check.[13]

(c) Unauthorized Use. A cardholder is not liable for more than $50 for the unauthorized use of a credit card. In order to impose liability up to that amount, the issuer must show that (1) the credit card was an accepted card,[14] (2) the issuer had given the holder adequate notice of possible liability in such case, (3) the issuer had furnished the holder with a self-addressed, prestamped notification form to be mailed by the holder in the event of the loss or theft of the credit card, (4) the issuer had provided a method by which

---

[13]Truth in Lending Act Amendment of 1976, 15 USC § 1666f. Ironically, the same section permits a merchant to offer a discount to cash paying customers and not customers using a credit card.

[14]A credit card is "accepted" when "the card holder has requested and received or has signed or has used, or authorized another to use [it], for the purpose of obtaining money, property, labor, or services on credit." CCPA § 103(1). Transamerica Ins. Co. v Standard Oil Co. (ND) 325 NW2d 210 (1982).

the user of the card could be identified as the person authorized to use it,[15] and (5) unauthorized use of the card had occurred or might occur as a result of loss, theft, or otherwise.

§ 8:7.   Payments.

Consumer legislation may provide that when a consumer makes a payment on an open charge account, the payment must be applied to pay the oldest items. The result is that, should there be a default at a later date, any right of repossession of the creditor is limited to the later unpaid items. This outlaws a contract provision by which, upon the default of the buyer, the seller could assert the right to repossess all purchases that had been made at any prior time. Such a provision is outlawed by the UCCC and is probably unconscionable under the UCC.

§ 8:8.   Preservation of Consumer Defense.

Consumer protection laws generally prohibit a consumer from waiving or giving up any defense provided by law.

FACTS:

Donnelly purchased a television set on credit from D.W.N. Advertising, Inc. He also contracted for service on the set. D.W.N. assigned the sales contract to the Fairfield Credit Corporation. D.W.N. went out of existence and the service contract was never performed. Fairfield sued Donnelly for the balance due on the purchase price. Donnelly raised the defense that the service contract had never been performed. Fairfield claimed that this defense could not be asserted against it because the sales contract contained a waiver of defenses.

DECISION:

The assignee was subject to the defenses which the obligor-consumer could have asserted against the assignor-seller. The waiver of defenses would not be given effect as it was contrary to public policy to permit an assignee to recover from a consumer when the assignor would not be able to do so. Donnelly therefore could assert his defenses against Fairfield Credit Corporation. [Fairfield Credit Corp. v Donnelly, 158 Conn 543, 264 A2d 547 (1969)]

In the ordinary contract situation, when goods or services purchased or leased by a consumer are not proper or are defective, the consumer is not required to pay the seller or lessor or is only required to pay a reduced amount. With the modern expansion of credit transactions, sellers and lessors have made use of several techniques for getting paid without regard to whether the consumer had any complaint against them.

To prevent this, the Federal Trade Commission has adopted a regulation which requires that in every sale or lease of goods or services to a con-

---

[15]Regulation Z of the Board of Governors of the Federal Reserve § 226.13(d), as amended, provides that the identification may be "signature, photograph, or fingerprint on the credit card or by electronic or mechanical confirmation."

sumer, the contract of the consumer contain a clause giving the consumer the right to assert defenses not only against the seller or lessor but also against a third person, such as a bank or finance company, to which the seller or lessor transfers the rights against the consumer. The Commission regulation requires that the following notice be included in boldface type at least ten point in size.

NOTICE

ANY HOLDER OF THIS CONSUMER CREDIT CONTRACT IS SUBJECT TO ALL CLAIMS AND DEFENSES WHICH THE DEBTOR COULD ASSERT AGAINST THE SELLER OF GOODS OR SERVICES OBTAINED PURSUANT HERETO OR WITH THE PROCEEDS HEREOF. RECOVERY HEREUNDER BY THE DEBTOR SHALL NOT EXCEED AMOUNTS PAID BY THE DEBTOR HEREUNDER.

§ 8:9.   Product Safety.

The health and well-being of consumers is protected by a variety of statutes and rules of law, some of which antedate the modern consumer protection era.

States typically have laws governing the manufacture of various products and establishing product safety standards. The federal Consumer Product Safety Act provides for research and the setting of uniform standards for products in order to reduce health hazards; establishes civil and criminal penalties for the distribution of unsafe products; recognizes the right of an aggrieved person to sue for money damages and to obtain an injunction against the distribution of unsafe products and creates a Consumer Product Safety Commission to administer the Act.[16]

A consumer, as well as various non-consumers, may hold a seller or manufacturer liable for *damages* when the product causes harm as discussed in Chapter 28 of this book.

The federal Anti-Tampering Act[17] makes it a federal crime to tamper with consumer products.

§ 8:10.   Credit, Collection, and Billing Methods.

Various provisions have been made to protect consumers from discriminatory and improper credit and collection practices.

(a) **Credit Discrimination.** It is unlawful to discriminate against an applicant for credit on the basis of race, color, religion, national origin, sex, marital status, or age; because all or part of the applicant's income is obtained from a public assistance program; or because the applicant has in good faith exercised any right under the Consumer Credit Protection Act. When a credit application is refused, the applicant must be furnished a written explanation why the application was rejected.

(b) **Correction of Errors.** When the consumer believes that an error has been made in billing by the issuer of a credit card, the consumer should

---

[16]Act of October 27, 1972, PL 92–573, 86 Stat 1207, 15 USC §§ 2051–2081.
[17]Act of October 13, 1983, PL 98–127, 97 Stat 831, 13 USC § 1365.

send the creditor a written statement and explanation of the error. The creditor or card issuer must investigate and make a prompt written reply to the consumer.[18]

(c) **Improper Collection Methods.** Unreasonable methods of debt collection are often expressly prohibited by statute or are held by courts to constitute an unreasonable invasion of privacy.[19] Statutes generally prohibit sending bills in such form that they give the impression that a lawsuit has been begun against the consumer and that the bill is legal process or a warrant issued by the court. The CCPA prohibits the use of extortionate methods of loan collection. A creditor may be prohibited from informing the employer of the debtor that the latter owes money.

When the seller made telephone calls to the buyer and the buyer's relatives and made obscene, threatening, and malicious statements which caused the buyer to become physically ill, the seller was liable for the tort of intentional mental disturbance. In order to give rise to such liability, the conduct must be more than mere insults, indignities, threats, and annoyances and must be so shocking and outrageous as to exceed all reasonable bounds of decency.

A creditor is liable for unreasonably attempting to collect a bill which in fact has been paid. This liability can arise under general principles of tort law as distinguished from special consumer protection legislation.

When a collection agency violates the Fair Debt Collection Practices Act, it is liable to the debtor for damages, and it is no defense that the debtor in fact owed the money that the agency was seeking to collect.[20]

§ 8:11.   **Protection of Credit Standing and Reputation.**

In many instances one party to a transaction wishes to know certain things about the other party. This situation arises when a person purchases on credit or applies for a loan, a job, or a policy of insurance. Between two and three thousand private credit bureaus gather such information on borrowers, buyers, and applicants and sell such information to interested persons.

The Fair Credit Reporting Act (FCRA) of 1970[21] seeks to protect from various abuses that may arise. FCRA applies only to consumer credit, which is defined as credit for "personal, family, and household" use, and does not apply to business or commercial transactions.

(a) **Privacy.** A report on a person based on personal investigation and interviews, called an **investigative consumer report,** may not be made without informing the person investigated of the right to discover the results of the investigation.[22] Bureaus are not permitted to disclose information to

---

[18]Fair Credit Billing Act, Act of October 18, 1974, PL 93–495, 15 USC § 1601.
[19]Fair Debt Collection Practices Act, Act of September 20, 1977, PL 95–109, 91 Stat 874, 15 USC §§ 1692 et seq.
[20]Baker v G. C. Services Corp. (CA9 Or) 677 F2d 775 (1982).
[21]Act of October 26, 1970, PL 91–508, 84 Stat 1128, 15 USC §§ 1681 seq.
[22]CCPA, § 606, 15 USC § 1681(d).

persons not having a legitimate use for it. It is a federal crime to obtain or to furnish a bureau report for an improper purpose.

On request, a bureau must tell a consumer the names and addresses of persons to whom it has made a credit report during the previous six months. It must also tell, when requested, which employers were given such a report during the previous two years.

A store may not publicly display a list of named customers from whom it will not accept checks, as such action is an invasion of the privacy of those persons.[23]

(b) **Protection from False Information.** Much of the information obtained by bureaus is based on statements made by persons, such as neighbors, when interviewed by the bureaus' investigator. Sometimes the statements are incorrect. Quite often they are hearsay evidence and would not be admissible in a legal proceeding. Nevertheless, they may go on the records of the bureau without further verification and will be furnished to a client of the bureau who will tend to regard them as accurate and true.

A person has a limited right to request an agency to disclose the nature and substance of the information possessed by the bureau. The right to know does not extend to medical information. It is not required that the bureau identify the persons giving information to its investigators. The bureau is not required to give the applicant a copy of, nor to permit the applicant to see, its file.

When a person claims that the information of the bureau is erroneous, the bureau must take steps within a reasonable time to determine the accuracy of the disputed item.

Adverse information obtained by investigation cannot be given to a client after 3 months unless verified to determine that it is still valid. Most legal proceedings cannot be reported by a bureau after 7 years. A bankruptcy proceeding cannot be reported after 14 years.

FACTS:

The San Antonio Retail Merchants Association (SARMA) was a credit reporting agency. It was asked by one of its members to furnish information on William Douglas Thompson, III. It supplied information from a file that contained data on William, III, and also on William Daniel Thompson, Jr. The agency had jumbled information related to William Jr., into the file relating to William, III; so that all information appeared to relate to William, III. This was a negligent mistake because each William had a different social security number and this should have raised a suspicion that there was a mistake. In addition, SARMA should have used a number of "checkpoints" to assure that incoming information would be put into the proper file. William, Jr., had a bad credit standing and because of its mistake, SARMA gave a bad report on William, III, who was denied credit by several enterprises. The federal Fair Credit Reporting Act makes a credit reporting agency liable to any consumer as to whom it furnishes a consumer report without following "reasonable procedures to assure maximum possible accuracy of information." William, III, sued SARMA for its negligence in confusing him with William, Jr.

[23]Mason v Williams Discount Center, Inc. (Mo App) 639 SW2d 836 (1982).

DECISION:

Judgment for William, III. The failure to search for an explanation of the two social security numbers and the failure to establish better filing procedures constituted negligence. This estabished that the agency had not fol- lowed reasonable procedures designed to insure accuracy of information and therefore it was liable under the federal statute for the damages sustained by William, III. [Thompson v San Antonio Retail Merchants Ass'n. (CA5 Tex) 682 F2d 509 (1982)]

---

§ 8:12.   Expansion of Consumer Protection.

Various state laws aimed at preventing fraudulent sales of corporate securities, commonly called blue sky laws, have been adopted. These statutes are discussed in Chapter 50 on corporate stock. Other statutes have been adopted to protect purchasers of real estate and buyers of services.

(a) **Real Estate Development Sales.** Anyone promoting the sale of a real estate development which is divided into fifty or more parcels of less than five acres each must file with the Secretary of Housing and Urban Development a **development statement** setting forth significant details of the development required by the federal Land Sales Act.[24]

Anyone buying or renting one of the parcels in the subdivision must be given a **property report.** This is a condensed version of the development statement filed with the Secretary of HUD. This report must be given to the prospective customer more than 48 hours before signing the contract to buy or lease.

If the development statement is not filed with the Secretary, the sale or renting of the real estate development may not be promoted through the channels of interstate commerce nor by the use of the mail.

If the property report is given to the prospective buyer or tenant less than 48 hours before signing a contract to buy or lease, or after it has been signed, the contract may be avoided within 48 hours. If the property report is never received, the contract may be avoided and there is no statutory limitation on the time in which to do so.

The federal statute prohibits the splitting of fees or the imposing or receiving of unauthorized payments in connection with a real estate settlement.

(b) **Service Contracts.** The UCCC treats a consumer service contract the same as a consumer sale of goods if payment is made in installments or a credit charge is made and the amount financed does not exceed $25,000. It defines "services" broadly as embracing work, specified privileges, and insurance provided by a noninsurer. The inclusion of "privileges" makes the UCCC apply to contracts calling for payment on the installment plan or including a financing charge for transportation, hotel and restaurant accom-

---

[24]Act of August 1, 1968, as amended, PL 90–448, 82 Stat 590, 15 USC §§ 1701–1720.

modations, education, entertainment, recreation, physical culture, hospital accommodations, funerals, and similar accommodations.

Some states have adopted statutes requiring that any present payments for future funeral services or goods must be deposited in a bank account or similar depository to be held for the benefit of the customer. A contract which does not provide for such deposit is void as being against public policy.

Consumer protection legislation commonly prohibits charging for services that in fact are not performed.

FACTS:

The Hotel Waldorf-Astoria in New York added a 2 percent charge to the bill of every guest. The charge was described as "sundries," but no further explanation or itemization was made. The hotel claimed that this charge was justified as covering messenger services, but only 77 percent of the guests used such service. The attorney general brought an action to enjoin the making of the charge for sundries and to refund the money which the guests had paid for such item.

DECISION:

Judgment against the hotel. The charge for unperformed and unexplained services was a fraud upon the guests and was therefore a violation of the consumer protection statute. [New York v Hotel Waldorf-Astoria, 323 NYS2d 917 (1971)]

---

§ 8:13. Consumer Remedies.

The theoretical right of the consumer to sue or to assert a defense is often of little practical value to the consumer because of the small size of the amount involved and the high cost of litigation. Consumer protection legislation provides special remedies.

(a) **Government Agency Action.** The UCCC provides for an administrator who will, in a sense, police business practices to insure conformity with the law. This is not regarded by some as an improvement and has been criticized because of the danger that the administrator may be creditor-oriented, and that the debtor might, as a consequence, be deprived of protection in many cases when it is a question of policy or discretion as to what action, if any, should be taken by the administrator.

(b) **Action by Attorney General.** A number of states provide that the state attorney general may bring an action on behalf of a particular group of consumers to obtain cancellation of their contracts and restitution of whatever they had paid.

FACTS:

Celebrezze, as Attorney General of Ohio, brought an action against Hughes Motors, claiming that Hughes had violated the federal and state consumer protection laws by setting back the odometers of used automobiles. The federal statute authorized the entry of a judgment for $1500 on proof of such tampering, even though there was no proof that actual harm had been sustained. Hughes defended on the ground that (1) the Attorney General could not sue without joining the consumers as co-plaintiffs, and (2) no judgment could be entered in favor of any consumer who did not sustain actual loss because of the tampering.

DECISION:

Judgment against Hughes on both points. The Attorney General was authorized by statute to sue without joining the consumers on whose behalf the suit was brought. The applicable statute allowed a minimum recovery of $1500 for every violation even though no specific loss was sustained by a consumer. [Celebrezze v Hughes, 18 Ohio 3d 71, 479 NE2d 886 (1985)]

Many states permit the attorney general to bring an action to enjoin violation of the consumer protection statute.

Consumer protection statutes commonly give the attorney general the authority to seek a voluntary stopping of improper practices before seeking to obtain an injunction from a court.

(c) **Action by Consumer.** Some consumer protection statutes provide that a consumer who is harmed by a violation of the statutes may sue the wrongdoing enterprise to recover a specified penalty or may bring an action on behalf of consumers as a class. Consumer protection statutes are often designed to rely on private litigation as an aid to enforcement of the statutory provisions. The Consumer Product Safety Act of 1972 authorizes "any interested person" to bring a civil action to enforce a consumer product safety rule and certain orders of the Consumer Product Safety Commission. But in some cases the individual consumer cannot bring any action, and enforcement of the law is entrusted exclusively to an administrative agency.

(d) **Scope of Relief.** The consumer protection statutes only provide relief as to conduct condemned by such statutes. They afford no protection to a consumer against a mere breach of contract.[25] Thus the fact that the seller never delivers the goods purchased by the buyer does not by itself constitute a violation of a consumer protection statute. However, there may be other circumstances which, when combined with the nondelivery of the goods, will show that the seller has violated a consumer protection statute.

§ 8:14.   Civil and Criminal Penalties.

The seller or lender engaging in improper consumer practices may be subject to civil penalties and criminal punishment. In some instances

[25]La Sara Grain Co. v First Nat. Bank (Tex) 673 SW2d 357 (1984).

the laws in question are the general laws applicable to improper conduct, while in other cases the laws are specifically aimed at the particular consumer practices.

Illustrative of the applicability of the general law, a contractor who falsely stated to a homeowner that certain repairs needed on the roof cost, with labor and materials, $650 when in fact they cost only $200, was guilty of the crime of obtaining money by false pretenses. Illustrative of specific consumer protection statutes, the Truth In Lending Act subjects the creditor to a separate claim for damages for each periodic statement which violates the disclosure requirements. Furthermore, consumer protection statutes of the disclosure type generally provide that the creditor can not enforce the obligation of the debtor if the required information is not set forth in the contract.

SUMMARY

With the modern era of consumer protection, society has accepted the premise that equality before the law, an essential part of the American way of life, is not appropriate to the marketplace where modern methods of marketing, packaging, and financing have reduced the ordinary consumer to a subordinate position. In order to protect the consumer from the hardship, fraud, and oppression that could result from being in such an inferior position, the law has at many points limited the freedom of action of the enterprise with which the consumer deals.

These consumer protection laws are directed at false and misleading advertising; misleading or false use of seals of approvals and labels; the methods of selling, as by requiring the disclosure of terms, permitting consumer cancellation of home-solicited sales, and, in some states, prohibiting referral sales; the contract made by the consumer, as by regulating its form, prohibiting unconscionable terms, and limiting the credit that can be extended to a consumer; credit cards, as by prohibiting the unauthorized distribution of such cards and limiting liability of the cardholder for the unauthorized use of a credit card; the application of payments; the preservation of consumer defenses as against a transferee of the consumer's contract; product safety; the protection of credit standing and reputation; and, to some extent, to real estate development sales and service contracts.

When a consumer protection statute is violated, an action may sometimes be brought by the consumer against the wrongdoer. More commonly, such action is brought by the administrative agency or by the attorney general of the state.

QUESTIONS AND CASE PROBLEMS

1. What is the object of each of the following rules of law:
   (a) Back-page disclaimers are void if the front page of the contract does not call attention to the presence of such terms.
   (b) A consumer's waiver of a statute designed for consumer protection is void, but the transaction otherwise binds the consumer.
2. Neil purchases a printing press from Guardian Press Company for $12,000, payment to be made in three installments of $4,000 each. Neil

later sued Guardian for failing to make the disclosures specified by the federal Truth In Lending Act. Was Guardian required to make disclosures under the Act?

3. Cora telephoned from her home to the Kimbell Music Supply Company and ordered an electric guitar. The employee of Kimbell answering the phone stated that Cora's order was accepted and the guitar would be sent to Cora within a few days. That night, Cora saw an ad in the newspaper for the same guitar for $100 less than the Kimbell price. Cora wrote and mailed a letter the next day to the Kimbell Company stating that she canceled her order. May Cora do so?

4. What is the purpose of corrective advertising?

5. The Madison Home Appliance Store charged its credit card customers a price slightly higher than the price charged customers paying cash. It did this to offset the discount which it was required to allow the companies issuing the credit cards used by the customers. May Madison charge this higher price to credit card purchasers?

6. The Merit Breakfast Food Company sold its breakfast cereal in ordinary sized packages. The packages, however, were labeled "jumbo" size. Merit was ordered to stop using this term by the Federal Trade Commission. Merit raised the defense that the term jumbo was not used with any intent to defraud and therefore its use was not improper. Is this a valid defense?

7. Compare the sale of a television by a dealer for $400 payable in (a) cash, (b) two installments, and (c) eight installments.

8. Thomas is sent a credit card through the mail by a company that had taken his name and address from the telephone book. Because he never requested the card, Thomas left the card lying on his desk. A thief stole the card and used it to purchase merchandise in several stores in the name of Thomas. The issuer of the credit card claims that Thomas is liable for the total amount of the purchases made by the thief. Thomas claims that he is not liable for any amount. The court decides that Thomas is liable for $50.00. Who is correct?

9. The state trade commission orders the Eagle Hotel to stop false advertising. The hotel does not admit or deny that its advertising is false but raises the defense that all the other hotels in the competitive area advertise in the same way and that it would be placed at a very serious disadvantage if it had to stop this kind of advertising while its competitors were allowed to continue to do so. The state commission ignores this defense. The Eagle Hotel appeals to the appropriate court. If it is true that the Eagle Hotel is the only one that has been ordered to stop, will the court overrule the order of the state trade commission?

10. A state statute prohibited false advertising. A bank advertised the "per annum" interest on its loans but did not state that the year to which it referred was a year of 360 days. An action was brought against the bank for false advertising. It raised the defense that in the banking industry it was customary to regard a year as consisting of 360 days and that in doing what all banks did it was clear that there was no intent to defraud anyone. Was this a valid defense? [Chern v Bank of America, 15 Cal 3d 866, 127 Cal Rptr 110, 544 P2d 1310]

11. A debtor borrowed money from a bank to construct a building. The promissory note signed by the debtor called for payments in installments and gave the bank the right to call the entire balance due if any installment were not paid. The debtor missed some payments on the note. The New England Mutual Life Insurance Company which then held the note brought an action for the entire balance of the note against the debtor, the Luxury Home Builders. The debtor raised the defense that it could not be held liable for the entire debt because the acceleration clause was contrary to public policy and that its failure to pay was excused because it did not make payment because of personal and business misfortune. Was Luxury Home liable? [New England Mut. Life Ins. Co. v Luxury Home Builders, Inc. (Fla App) 311 So2d 160]

12. A federal statute prohibits the interstate shipment of deceptively or fraudulently labeled goods. Acting under the authority of this statute, federal officers seized a shipment of 95 barrels that were labeled "apple cider vinegar." This vinegar had been made from dried apples that had been soaked in water. The government claimed that the label was false because "apple cider vinegar" meant to the average person that the vinegar had been made from fresh apples. The shipper claimed that as the barrels in fact contained vinegar that had been made from cider produced from apples, the labels were truthful in calling the contents by the name of "apple cider vinegar." Was the shipper correct? [United States v 95 Barrels of Alleged Apple Cider Vinegar, 265 US 438]

13. Wilke was contemplating retiring. In response to an advertisement, he purchased from Coinway 30 coin-operated testing machines. He purchased these because Coinway's representative stated that, by placing these machines at different public places, Wilke could obtain supplemental income. This statement was made by the representative although he had no experience as to the cost of servicing such machines or their income-producing potential. The operational costs of the machines by Wilke exceeded the income. Wilke sued Coinway to rescind the contract for fraud. Wilke defended on the ground that the statements made were merely matters of opinion and did not constitute fraud. Was Wilke entitled to rescission? [Wilke v Coinway, Inc. 257 Cal App 2d 126, 64 Cal Rptr 845]

14. Greif obtained credit cards from Socony Mobil Oil Co. for himself and his wife. The card specified, "This card is valid unless expired or revoked. Named holder's approval of all purchases is presumed unless written notice of loss or theft is received." Later Greif returned his card to the company, stating that he was canceling it, but that he could not return the card in his wife's possession because they had separated. Subsequently Socony sued Greif for purchases made by the wife on the credit card in her possession. He defended on the ground that he had canceled the credit card contract. Decide. [Socony Mobil Oil Co. v Greif, 10 App Div 2d 119, 197 NYS2d 522]

15. To what extent may the holder of a credit card be held liable for purchases made by the use of the card by a thief who has stolen the card?

16. A suit was brought against General Foods on the ground that it was violating the state law prohibiting false and deceptive advertising. It raised

the defense that the plaintiffs failed to show that the public had been deceived by the advertising, that the public in fact had not relied on the advertising, and that there was no proof that anyone had sustained any damage because of the advertising. Were these valid defenses? [Committee on Children's Television, Inc. v General Foods Corp. 35 Cal 3d 197, 197 Cal Rptr 783, 673 P2d 660]

17. Shelly Weisberg and his wife did business as a corporation with the name Shelly Weisberg Associates, Inc. The corporation acted as a sales representative for clothing manufacturers. In order to build a showroom for the clothing, Shelly borrowed $10,000 from the Puritan Finance Corporation. The loan was made to the corporation and was guaranteed by the Weisbergs. They made the required installment payments on the debt for two years and then stopped. When suit was brought against them, they claimed that the creditor was barred because the original loan transaction had not disclosed the matters required by the federal Truth In Lending Act. Was such breach of the federal statute a defense to the Weisbergs? [Northwest Federal Savings & Loan Ass'n v Weisberg, 97 Ill App 3d 470, 52 Ill Dec 92, 422 NE2d 1101]

CHAPTER 9

CRIMES

CHAPTER OBJECTIVES

After studying this chapter you will be able to:

1. Define crime.
2. Describe three ways of classifying crimes.
3. Identify persons who are not held responsible for criminal acts.
4. Define white collar crimes.
5. Distinguish one criminal offense from another on the basis of the elements of each offense.

Law sets the standards of conduct for all to follow. What happens when someone does not follow the law? There are two aspects to the problem. On the one hand, society wants to punish the wrongdoer and prevent others from repeating what was done. On the other hand, society, through the law, authorizes the victim to sue the wrongdoer for damages sustained by the victim. The first phase of punishment and prevention is governed by principles of criminal law, discussed in this chapter. The second phase is governed by the principles of tort law, discussed in the next chapter.

It is important to bear in mind that society has made a choice of having both criminal law and tort law, as contrasted with having only one and not the other; and, by having both, rejects any argument that it is unfair to punish a wrongdoer twice for the one wrong.

A. GENERAL PRINCIPLES

A **crime** is an offense against the sovereign, a breach of public duty. Most crimes have certain common characteristics. These are discussed in the following sections.

139

§ 9:1.   Classification of Crimes.

A crime may be classified according to the source of the criminal law, the seriousness of the offense, or its nature.

(a) **Source of Criminal Law.** Crimes are classified in terms of their origin, as common-law and statutory crimes. Some offenses that are defined by statute are merely declaratory of the common law. Each state has its own criminal law, although a common pattern among the states may be observed.

(b) **Seriousness of Offense.** Crimes are classified in terms of their seriousness; as treason, felonies, and misdemeanors. **Treason** is defined by the Constitution of the United States, which states that "Treason against the United States, shall consist only in levying war against them, or in adhering to their enemies, giving them aid and comfort.[1] " **Felonies** include the other more serious crimes, such as arson, murder, and robbery, which are punishable by confinement in prison or by death. Crimes not classified as treason nor felonies are **misdemeanors.** Reckless driving, weighing and measuring goods with scales and measuring devices that have not been inspected, and disturbing the peace by illegal picketing are generally classified as misdemeanors. An act may be a felony in one state and a misdemeanor in another.

(c) **Nature of Crimes.** Crimes are also classified in terms of the nature of the misconduct. **Crimes mala in se** are crimes that are inherently vicious or, in other words, that are naturally evil as measured by the standards of a civilized community. **Crimes mala prohibita** are acts that are only wrong because they are declared wrong by some statute.

§ 9:2.   Basis of Criminal Liability.

A crime generally consists of two elements (a) an act or omission, and (b) a mental state.

(a) **Mental State.** Mental state does not require an awareness or knowledge of guilt. In most crimes, it is sufficient that the defendant voluntarily did the act that is criminal, regardless of motive or intent.[2] In some instances, a particular mental state is required, such as the necessity that a homicide be with malice aforethought in order to constitute murder. In some cases, it is the existence of a specific intent that differentiates one crime from other offenses, as an assault with intent to kill is distinguished by that intent from an ordinary assault or from an assault with intent to rob.

(b) **Harm to Others.** Causing harm is typical of some crimes, such as murder or arson. Other crimes, however, are committed although no one is harmed. For example, a person may be guilty of the crime of speeding or reckless driving on the highway although no one is hurt. In such case, it is the social judgment that the act condemned as a crime has such a potential for harm to others that the act should be prohibited before it does cause harm to others.

---

[1]US Const, Art 3, § 3, Cl 1.
[2]California v Lynn, 159 Cal App 3d 715, 206 Cal Rptr 181 (1984).

§ 9:3.   Parties to a Crime.

Two or more parties may directly or indirectly commit or contribute to the commission of a crime. At common law, participants in the commission of a felony may be principals or accessories.

(a) **Principals.** Principals may be divided into two classes: (1) **principals in the first degree,** who actually engage in the perpetration of the crime, and (2) **principals in the second degree,** who are actually or constructively present and aid and abet in the commission of the criminal act. For example, a person is a principal in the second degree if that person assists by words of encouragement, stands by ready to assist or to give information, or keeps watch to prevent surprise or capture.

The distinction as to degree is frequently abolished by statute so that all persons participating in the felony are principals.

(b) **Accessories.** Accessories to a crime are divided into two classes: (1) accessories before the fact, and (2) accessories after the fact. An **accessory before the fact** differs from the principal in the second degree only by reason of absence from the scene of the crime. An **accessory after the fact** is a person who knowingly assists one who has committed a felony.[3] Thus, a person, who after the commission of the crime and with intent to assist the felon, gives warning to prevent arrest or shelters or aids in an escape from imprisonment is an accessory after the fact.

§ 9:4.   Responsibility for Criminal Acts.

In some cases, particular persons are not held responsible for their criminal acts. In other cases, persons are held criminally responsible for acts committed by others.

(a) **Employers.** An employer is liable for the crime committed by the employee when the employer directs or requires the commission of the crime. The fact that the employee is also guilty of a crime does not shield the employer and both the employer and the employee carrying out the wrongful plan are guilty of crimes. Thus, an employer is guilty of a crime when the employer gives the employee money to bribe a building inspector to overlook violations of the fire code. The employee is also guilty of the crime of bribery when the employee pays the money to the inspector.

When the employer has not directed the commission of the crime, the employer is not liable for the crime of the employee that is committed outside of the scope of the employment of the employee.

(b) **Corporations.** The modern tendency is to hold corporations criminally responsible for their acts. A corporation may also be held liable for crimes based upon the failure to act. Thus, a corporation may be held criminally responsible when an employee is killed because of the corporation's failure to install the safety devices required by law.

[3]Butler v United States (Dist Col App) 481 A2d 431 (1984).

In some instances, the crime may be defined by statute in such a way that it requires or is interpreted as requiring a living "person" to commit the crime, in which case a corporation can not be held criminally liable. Certain crimes, such as perjury, can not be committed by corporations.

It is also usually held that crimes punishable only by imprisonment or corporal punishment can not be committed by corporations. If the statute imposes a fine in addition to or in lieu of imprisonment or corporal punishment, a corporation may be convicted for the crime. Thus, a corporation may be fined for violating the federal antitrust law by conspiring to restrain interstate commerce.

(c) **Minors.** Some states have legislation fixing the age of criminal responsibility. At common law, a child under the age of seven was presumed incapable of committing a crime; after the age of 14, the child was presumed to have capacity as though an adult; and between the ages of 7 and 14, no presumption of law arose and it had to be shown that the minor had such capacity. The existence of capacity can not be presumed from the mere commission of the act.

(d) **Insane Persons.** An insane person is not criminally responsible. There is a confict of opinion over what constitutes such insanity as to excuse a person from criminal responsibility. All courts, however, agree that intellectual weakness alone is not insanity.

A test commonly applied is the **right and wrong test.** The responsibility of the defendant is determined in terms of the ability to understand the nature of the act committed and to distinguish right from wrong in relation to it.

Some courts also use the **irresistible impulse test,** the theory of which is that when the defendant acts under an uncontrollable impulse because of an unsound state of mind caused by disease of any nature, such act is not a voluntary act and the defendant is not criminally responsible. If the mental instability is not caused by disease, the irresistible impulse test is not applied.

Under the Model Penal Code of the American Law Institute, and under the law in many states and in the federal courts, the defense of insanity is not established by the mere inability to know right from wrong unless it is shown that there was a mental disease or defect that prevented the defendant from appreciating the wrongfulness of his or her conduct.[4]

(e) **Intoxicated Persons.** Involuntary intoxication relieves a person from criminal responsibility; voluntary intoxication generally does not.[5] An exception is made to this latter rule in the case of a crime requiring specific intent, when the accused was so intoxicated, whether voluntarily or not, as to be incapable of forming the required specific intent.

§ 9:5.   Attempts and Conspiracies.

Prior to the commission of an intended crime, there may be conduct that is itself a crime, such as an attempt or a conspiracy.

[4]Insanity Defense Reform Act of 1984, § 401, PL 98-473, 98 Stat 2057, 18 USC 402.
[5]Grayson v Oklahoma (Okla Crim) 687 P2d 747 (1984).

(a) **Attempts.** When the criminal fails to commit the crime intended it may be that what has been done constitutes an attempt. Attempts are punished as distinct crimes. It is, however, difficult to determine just what constitutes an attempt. Obviously, it is something less than committing the intended crime, but it must be more than merely preparing to commit that crime. Thus the purchasing of a gun with which to kill the victim is not regarded as an attempt but as mere preparation, and ordinarily is not itself a crime. However, when the cirminal points the gun at the door through which the victim is expected to leave the building, an attempt has been committed. The modern trend is to condemn as an attempt any conduct which has reached such a point that the potential for harm to others is unreasonably great. Thus a defendant firing a gun at the victim is guilty of an attempt even though the gun, unknown to the defendant, has a broken firing pin, so that it is impossible to shoot with the gun. Likewise a robber pointing a gun at the victim and demanding money is guilty of an attempt even though the robber changes his mind and does not take any money.

(b) **Conspiracies.** A conspiracy is an agreement between two or more persons to commit an unlawful act or to use unlawful means to achieve an otherwise lawful result. The crime is the agreement and it is immaterial that nothing is done to carry out the agreement. Some statutes, however, require that there be some act done to carry out the conspiracy before the crime is committed.[6]

(c) **Number of Offenses.** If the criminal actually commits the intended crime, there is no criminal attempt. There can only be an attempt when the intended crime is not committed.

In contrast with the concept of an attempt, a conspiracy is a separate crime. Consequently the fact that the intended crime is actually committed does not erase the conspiracy. Defendants may thus be prosecuted both for having conspired to commit the crime and for having committed the crime intended. They may be prosecuted for the conspiracy although the contemplated crime in fact is not committed.

§ 9:6.   Criminal Fines and Administrative Penalties Compared.

The differences between a money penalty imposed by an administrator and a fine imposed by a court are very slight and largely theoretical. In both the administrative proceeding and the criminal court prosecution, the money penalty represents dollars paid by the defending party to the government. Both the fine and the penalty are imposed because the defending party failed to follow a standard of conduct required by the government.

Minor points of difference are that in many jurisdictions the judges are elected so that the judge imposing the fine is directly responsible to the voters. In contrast, the administrator is typically appointed by someone who was elected by the voters, and thus the control of the voters over the administrator is "once removed."

---

[6]United States v Sarro (CA11 Fla) 742 F2d 1286 (1984).

Historically, courts and judges have for many centuries had the power to impose fines. The imposition of a money penalty by administrators is less than a half century old. Originally the administrators were not given any such power. Then administrators were given the power to impose a penalty, but the penalty could not be collected or enforced unless the administrator went to a court and obtained a court order directing the defending party to pay the penalty. The more recently created administrators have the power to make assessments for violation of the law and of their regulations, and these assessments are final and binding upon the defendant if no appeal is taken within a specified number of days. After the lapse of the specified time, the penalty can be collected as in the case of any other money judgment and the defendant can not attack the penalty on the ground that it was improperly entered or excessive.

There are certain practical differences between the administrator's money penalty and the court's fine. The administrative determination can be made without a jury. In contrast, most crimes that can be punished by the imposition of a substantial fine will be tried by a jury. Because a criminal conviction and fine is a stigma or blot on the reputation of the defendant, a jury is less likely to find a respectable business person guilty of a crime. Moreover, a judge does not like to treat the respected citizen as a criminal. Typically, these feelings are not shared by the administrator who will therefore be more likely to enforce the law and impose a substantial penalty in order to deter the defendant and others from violating the law.

In many instances, the administrative penalty will be significantly larger than fines imposed by a court. The reason is partly historical in that the statute defining a particular crime and specifying the maximum fine will ordinarily follow the statutory pattern of an earlier statute that may go back into the last century. What was then a large fine is today insignificant. Thus a fine maximum inherited from the past may specify that the fine that can be imposed for armed robbery may not exceed $1,000. In contrast, the administrator with power to impose a penalty is a creation of our time and therefore any penalties are stated in terms of the modern purchasing power of the dollar. Thus, it is not unusual to authorize an administrator to impose a penalty not to exceed $10,000. This difference in the penalty maximum may also be justified theoretically in terms of the fact that in the case of armed robbery there was but the one victim of the crime whereas in the case of the administrative agency situation the violator's act may, as in the case of the factory that pollutes the environment, affect many persons.

§ 9:7. Indemnification of Crime Victim.

Typically the victim of a crime does not benefit from the criminal prosecution and conviction of the wrongdoer. Any fine that is imposed upon the defendant is paid to the government and is not received in any way by the victim. Several states have adopted statutes to provide a limited degree of indemnification to victims of crime in order to compensate them for the harm or loss sustained.[7] The Victims of Crime Act of 1984 creates a federal Crime

---

[7]A Uniform Crime Victims Reparations Act has been adopted in Kansas, Louisana, Montana, North Dakota, Ohio, and Texas.

Victims Fund. This fund receives the fines paid into the federal courts and other moneys, from which grants are made to the states to assist them in financing programs to provide indemnity to and assistance for victims of crime.[8] The Victim and Witness Protection Act of 1982 authorizes the sentencing judge in a federal district court to order, in certain cases, that the defendant make restitution to the victim or pay the victim the amount of medical expenses or loss of income caused by the crime.[9] Mob violence statutes frequently impose liability for property damage upon the local government. The term "property" in such a statute generally applies to tangible property and does not authorize recovery for loss of profits or goodwill resulting from business interruption. The fact that the government was unable to prevent the harm or damage is not a defense to liability under such statutes.

Under some criminal victim indemnification statutes, dependents of a deceased victim are entitled to recover the amount of the support of which they were deprived by the victim's death.

(a) **Action for Damages.** While the criminal prosecution of a wrongdoer does not financially benefit the victim of the crime, the victim is typically entitled to bring a civil action for damages against the wrongdoer for the harm sustained. The modern pattern of statutes creating business crimes is to give the victim the right to sue for damages. Thus the wrongdoer violating the federal antitrust act or the Racketeer Influenced and Corrupt Organizations Act (RICO) is liable to the victim for three times the damages actually sustained. A number of states have adopted statutes following the pattern of RICO.

A damage suit may be brought under the federal Act without proof of a "racketeering injury" or the prior conviction of the defendant.[10]

§ 9:8. Sentencing.

The problem of sentencing the convicted criminal is one of the most difficult problems in the administration of justice. The difficulty lies in part in the fact that society is caught between conflicting social purposes. Uniformity and stability are desired. At the same time flexibility is desired in order to make the punishment fit both the crime and the criminal. For the earlier part of this century, the emphasis had been on flexibility in sentencing. This, however, has produced a very inconsistent pattern of sentencing, much of which can be explained in terms of the particular culture patterns in which the sentencing judge was trained. If that culture regards the particular crime as very serious, it is likely that the judge will impose a greater sentence than if the crime were not regarded as so serious. Variations in sentencing also arise from the fact that the offense in question may be a felony in one state while in another state it is merely a misdemeanor. Various reform movements are under way to secure more nearly uniform sentencing of criminals. The Sen-

---

[8]Act of October 12, 1984, PL 98-473, 98 Stat 2170, 18 USC § 1401 et seq.
[9]Act of October 12, 1982, PL 97-291, 96 Stat 1253, 18 USC § 3579.
[10]Sedima, S.P.R.L. v Imrex Co., Inc. _____ US _____, 87 L Ed2d 346 (1985).

tencing Reform Act of 1984 contains provisions designed to produce greater uniformity in sentencing.[11]

(a) **The Indigent Defendant.** When a court imposes sentence it can not impose an alternative (1) fine or (2) imprisonment if the defendant does not have the money with which to pay the fine. For example, it is unconstitutional to sentence a defendant to "$30 or 30 days."[12] This conclusion is reached on the ground that such a sentence in the alternative discriminates on the basis of poverty by making the poor person who can not pay the fine go to jail while the rich person pays the fine and walks out of the court.

(b) **White Collar Crimes.** There is much criticism about the sentencing of white collar criminals on the ground that the penalties are not sufficiently large to serve either the purpose of punishing the defendant or of deterring others from committing similar crimes. It can be recognized that there is a reluctance on the part of judges to send an otherwise respectable person to jail. But one of the fundamentals of our American system is equality before the law and therefore no exception should be made because the defendant had a good standing or a good education. In some instances, the lawmaker is at fault in failing to provide punishments that fit the crime.

(c) **Forfeiture of Crime-Related Property.** When a defendant is convicted of a crime, the court may also declare that the defendant's rights in any instrument of that crime is forfeited. When the forfeited property can only be used for a criminal purpose, as in the case of engraved plates used for making counterfeit paper money, there is no question of the right of the government to forfeit the property, even though this forfeiture in effect increases the penalty imposed on the defendant.

This right of forfeiture is not limited to property that can only be used for crime. Thus, an automobile that is used to carry illegal merchandise may itself be seized by the government, even though it is obvious that the automobile could also be put to a lawful use.

As we move into the area of the white collar crimes, this problem of defining crime-related property becomes increasingly difficult because the property involved is not by itself criminal or even potentially criminal in character. Legislation in this area has been directed at depriving the wrongdoer of the gains obtained by the crime or of taking away the power to benefit from the crime. Of the first class is the Sherman Antitrust Act under which a defendant guilty of unlawfully acquiring the stock of competing corporations may be ordered by the court to sell or otherwise dispose of such shares. This is called a divestiture order. Illustrative of both the first and the second class is the federal Racketeer Influenced and Corrupt Organizations Act (RICO) under which the court is required to enter an order against the defendant forfeiting any property acquired or used in exercising unlawful racketeering influence.

[11]Act of October 12, 1984, Chapter 227, PL 98-473, 98 Stat 1987, 18 USC § § 3551 et seq. The Commissioners on Uniform Laws have proposed a Model Sentencing and Corrections Act.

[12]Tate v Short, 401 US 395 (1971).

FACTS:

Joseph Russello was a member of an arson ring. He set fire to a building that he owned and then collected on the fire insurance policy covering the building. He was prosecuted and convicted for the crime of arson. The court ordered that he forfeit to the United States the insurance money that he had received.

DECISION:

The forfeiture was authorized by law. RICO provides for the forfeiture of "any interest" acquired by the criminal from his "racketeering" activity. The statute does not define what is meant by "an interest" but this would be liberally interpreted to cover any kind of ill-gotten gain. The history of RICO in Congress clearly shows the intent of Congress to strike at the economic roots of organized crime. The broad language of the statute would therefore not be limited and "any interest" would mean just that. Therefore "any interest" included insurance money obtained by defrauding the insurer by intentionally burning the insured property. [Russello v United States, 464 US 16 (1983)]

B. WHITE-COLLAR CRIMES

In common speech, those crimes that do not use or threaten to use force or violence or do not cause injury to persons or physical damage to property are called **white-collar crimes.** A particular defendant may be guilty of both a white-collar crime and a traditional crime described in part C of this chapter.

§ 9:9. **Crimes Related to Production, Competing, and Marketing.**

The person or enterprise in business may be guilty of the various crimes relating to labor and employment practices, conspiracies and combinations in restraint of trade, price discrimination, and environmental pollution discussed in Chapters 4 and 7.

(a) **Improper Use of Interstate Commerce.** The shipment of improper goods or the transmission of improper information in interstate commerce constitutes a crime under various federal statutes. Thus, it is a federal crime to send in interstate commerce a statement as part of a scheme to defraud; to send a blackmail or extortion threat; or to ship adulterated or misbranded foods, drugs, or cosmetics; or to ship into a state child-labor or convict-labor made goods or intoxicating liquor when the sale of such goods is prohibited by the destination state.

(b) **Securities Crimes.** In order to protect the investing public, both state and federal laws have regulated the issuance and public sale of stocks and bonds.[13] Between 1933 and 1940, seven such regulatory statutes were adopted by the Federal Congress. As a practical matter, these federal statutes have largely displaced state statutes by virtue of the principle of federal preemption. Violation of these statutes is typically made a crime.

§ 9:10. Computer Crimes.

Computer crimes may be divided into three classes in terms of seriousness.

(a) **Unauthorized Use of Computer.** The least serious is the unlawful use of the computer of somebody else. In most states the unlawful use of a computer is not a crime. Although the user is "stealing" the time of the computer, the wrongdoer is not regarded as committing the crime of larceny because the wrongdoer has no intent to deprive the owner permanently of the computer.

In most states the borrowing of another's automobile without the owner's permission is not a crime where there is no intention to deprive the owner permanently thereof. The same approach will undoubtedly be made in the case of the unauthorized use of a computer. In some states, the borrowing of an automobile for a joyride is made a separate crime. It can be anticipated that states will adopt laws making it a crime to use a computer without the consent of the owner.

FACTS:
Lund was a graduate student at a university. In working on his doctoral dissertation he made use of the university computer and was assisted by the personnel of the computer facility. The value of what he thus obtained was about $30,000. Lund had not been authorized to use the computer; he was prosecuted for grand larceny.

DECISION:
Lund was not guilty of larceny because larceny was limited to the unauthorized taking of "property" and does not include the unauthorized use of property or the services of others. [Lund v Virginia, 217 Va 688, 232 SE2d 745 (1977)]

(b) **Theft of Software.** When a thief takes software, either in the form of a program written on paper, or a program on a disc or tape, a situation arises that does not fit into the standard definitions of crimes. The thief commits larceny of the piece of paper or of the tape or disc, but the program is not something that can be stolen because it is not "property" within the traditional concept of what constitutes property for the purpose of crime.

The distinction between the program and the substance on which it is written or recorded is material. If the law ignores the program, the thief is guilty only of petty larceny in most states when he steals the piece of paper or the disc or tape carrying the program. This is so because the value of the

---

[13]See § 50:10 of this book

piece of paper or the disc or tape will be relatively small and thus bring the crime down to the category of petty larceny. In contrast, the program itself may have a value of thousands of dollars so that if the grade of larceny is determined by the value of the program, the thief is guilty of grand larceny, an offense which generally carries much more significant penalties and is typically a felony. In some states, the unauthorized taking of information may constitute a crime under a trade secrets protection statute. It can be expected that in the near future larceny statutes will be amended to make the theft of computer programs a distinct crime and classifying that crime as grand larceny and a felony.

(c) **Computer Raiding.** The most serious computer crime involves taking information from a computer without the consent of the owner of the information. Whether this is done by having the computer make a printout of stored information or by tapping into the data bank of the computer by some electronic means is not important. In many instances, the taking of information from the computer will constitute a crime of stealing trade secrets.

The Counterfeit Access Device and Computer Fraud and Abuse Act of 1984[14] makes it a federal crime to access a computer without authorization.

§ 9:11.   Electronic Fund Transfer Crimes.

The Electronic Fund Transfers Act (EFTA)[15] makes it a crime to use any counterfeit control device to obtain money or goods in excess of a specified amount through an electronic fund transfer system, to ship such devices or goods so obtained in interstate commerce, or to knowingly receive goods that have been obtained by means of the fraudulent use of the transfer system.

§ 9:12.   Bribery.

Bribery is the act of giving money, property, or any benefit to a particular person to influence that person's judgment in favor of the giver of the bribe. At common law, the crime was limited to doing such acts to influence a public official. In this century, the common-law concept has expanded to include commercial bribery. Thus, it is now a crime to pay a competitor's employee money in order to obtain secret information about the competitor.

The giving and the receiving of the bribe each constitutes a crime. In addition, the act of seeking to obtain a bribe is a crime of solicitation of bribery.

The crime of bribery is complete when the bribe has been paid or received. Whether the person paying the bribe obtains what was bargained for does not affect the guilt of either the giver or the receiver of the bribe.

§ 9:13.   Extortion and Blackmail.

Extortion and blackmail are crimes by which the wrongdoer seeks to force the victim to do some act, typically the payment of money, that the victim would not otherwise desire to do.

---

[14]Act of October 12, 1984, § 2102, PL 98-473, 98 Stat 2190, 18 USC § § 1030 et seq.
[15]Act of October 10, 1978, § 916(n), PL 90-321, PL 95-630, 92 Stat 3738, 15 USC § 1693n.

(a) **Extortion.** When a public officer acting under the apparent authority of the office makes an illegal demand, the officer has committed the crime of extortion. For example, if a health inspector threatens to close down a restaurant on a false charge of violation of the sanitation laws unless the restaurant pays the inspector a sum of money, the inspector has committed extortion. If the restaurant had voluntarily offered the inspector the money to prevent the restaurant's being shut down because of actual violations of the sanitation laws, the crime committed would have been bribery.

Modern statutes tend to ignore the "public officer" aspect of the common law and expand **extortion** to include any obtaining of something of value by threat, whether in connection with loan-sharking or labor racketeering. In a number of states, statutes extend the extortion concept to include the making of "terroristic threats."[16]

(b) **Blackmail.** In jurisdictions in which extortion is limited to conduct of public officials, a non-official person commits blackmail by making demands that would be extortion if made by public official. Ordinarily, the concept of blackmail is used in the context of a threat to give publicity to some matter that would damage the victim's personal or business reputation.

§ 9:14.   Corrupt Influence.

In harmony with changing concepts of right and wrong, society has increasingly outlawed practices on the ground that they exerted a corrupting influence on business transactions. To some extent this objective of the law was attained by applying the criminal law of extortion, blackmail, and bribery to the particular situations involved. In time, the definitions of these crimes were expanded to include practices similar to the old crimes but yet not within the technical definition of such crimes. Thus the crime of bribery was extended to include commercial bribery.

(a) **Improper Political Influence.** In order to protect from the improper influencing of political or governmental action, various new crimes have been created. Thus it is a crime for the holder of a government office to be financially interested in or receive money from an enterprise that is seeking to do business with the government, as such conflict of interests is likely to produce a result that is harmful to the public. Persons engaged in lobbying and foreign agents must register in Washington, D.C.,[17] and the giving and receiving of contributions for political campaigns is regulated in terms of amounts of contribution and disclosure of sources. Violation of these regulatory statutes is a crime.

(b) **Improper Commercial Influence.** The protection from improper influence is extended to the commercial world by statutes making it a crime to engage in commercial bribery, to engage in loan sharking, to use gangster methods to influence legitimate business, or to run a legitimate business for the purpose of laundering gangster money.

Under federal statutes, it is a crime to obtain a benefit by means of a threat of economic or physical loss or harm, to use racketeering methods or

---

[16]Pennsylvania v Bunting, 284 Pa Super 444, 426 A2d 130 (1981).
[17]Foreign Agents Registration Act, Act of June 8, 1938, 52 Stat 631, 22 USC §§ 611 et seq., as amended.

money obtained from racketeering to acquire an interest in a legitimate business, or to travel in interstate commerce for the purpose of engaging in racketeering activities. A person convicted of such crimes is subject to punishment by fine, imprisonment, and the forfeiture of money obtained by the criminal conduct. The convicted defendant is also subject to civil liability to the victims of the crime.[18]

§ 9:15.   Counterfeiting.

It is a federal crime to make, to possess with intent to pass, or to pass counterfeit coins, banknotes, or obligations or other securities of the United States. Legislation has also been adopted against the passing of counterfeit foreign securities or notes of foreign banks.

The various states also have statutes prohibiting the making and passing of counterfeit coins and banknotes. These statutes often provide, as does the federal statute, a punishment for the mutilation of banknotes or the lightening or mutilation of coins.

§ 9:16.   Forgery.

Forgery consists of the fraudulent making or material altering of an instrument, such as a check, which apparently creates or changes a legal liability of another person. The instrument must have some apparent legal efficacy in order to constitute forgery.

Ordinarily, forgery consists of signing another's name with intent to defraud. It may also consist of making an entire instrument or altering an existing one. It may result from signing a fictitious name or the offender's own name with the intent to defraud.

When the nonowner of a credit card signs the owner's name on a credit card invoice, such act is a forgery.

§ 9:17.   Perjury.

Perjury consists of knowingly giving false testimony in a judicial proceeding after having been sworn or having affirmed to tell the truth.[19] By statute, knowingly making false answers on any form filed with a government is typically made perjury or is subjected to the same punishment as perjury. In some jurisdictions, the out-of-court offense is called false swearing.

§ 9:18.   False Claims and Pretenses.

Many statutes declare it a crime to make false claims or to obtain goods by false pretenses.

(a) **False Claims.** A statute may expressly declare that the making of a false claim is a crime.

The federal False Statement statute makes it a crime to knowingly and willfully make a false material statement as to any matter within the

---

[18]Act of June 25, 1948, 62 Stat 793, 18 USC § 1951; Travel Act of September 13, 1961, PL 87-228, 75 Stat 498, 18 USC § 1952; Racketeer Influenced and Corrupt Organizations Act of October 15, 1970, PL 91-452, 84 Stat 941, 18 USC § § 1961 et seq.

[19]New York v Loizides, 479 NYS2d 663 (1984).

jurisdiction of any department or agency of the United States.[20] Thus, it is a crime for a contractor to make a false claim against the United States for payment for work that was never performed by the contractor. Other statutes indirectly regulate the matter by declaring that the signing of a false written claim constitutes perjury or is subject to the same punishment as perjury.

(b) **Obtaining Goods by False Pretenses.** In almost all of the states, statutes are directed against obtaining money or goods by means of false pretenses. These statutes vary in detail and scope. Sometimes the statutes are directed against a particular form of deception, such as the using of a bad check.

The Trademark Counterfeiting Act of 1984[21] makes it a federal crime to deal in goods and services under a counterfeit mark.

FACTS:
Randono and Dreyer were partners. They owned two bars and restaurants—Feliciano's and the Saddleback Inn. The Saddleback Inn was headed for bankruptcy. The partners decided to take advantage of this situation by ordering $20,000 worth of liquor on credit to be charged to the Saddleback Inn with the intent of immediately transferring the liquor to Feliciano's without paying for it. This was done and one of the partners was then prosecuted for obtaining property by false pretenses.

DECISION:
The partner was guilty. The false pretense consisted in ordering the merchandise from the sellers. This was a false pretense because an ordinary person would believe that payment would be made for the goods which were so ordered. As the partners had already formed the intent to avoid paying for the goods by going through bankruptcy, the act of ordering the goods constituted a misrepresentation of their intentions or a false pretense and each partner was guilty of obtaining property by false pretenses. [California v Randono, 32 Cal App3d 164, 108 Cal Rptr 326 (1973)]

False representations as to future profits or the identity of the defendant are common forms of false pretenses.

§ 9:19.   Cheats and Swindles.

Various statutes are designed to protect the public from being deceived.

(a) **False Weights, Measures, and Labels.** Cheating, defrauding, or misleading the public by use of false, improper, or inadequate weights, measures, and labels is a crime. Both the federal and state governments have adopted many statutes on this subject.

(b) **Swindles and Confidence Games.** The act of a person who, intending to cheat and defraud, obtains money or property by trick, decep-

---

[20]United States v Petullo (CA7 I11) 709 F2d 1178 (1983).
[21]Act of October 12, 1984, § 1502, PL 98–473, 98 Stat 2178, 18 USC § 113.

tion, fraud, or other device, is an act known as a swindle or confidence game. Bad stock and spurious works of art are frequently employed in swindling operations.

§ 9:20. Credit Card Crimes.

It is a crime to steal a credit card and, in some states, to possess the credit card of another person without the consent of that person. The use of a credit card without the permission of the rightful cardholder constitutes the crime of obtaining goods or services by false pretenses or with the intent to defraud. Likewise a person continuing to use a credit card with knowledge that it has been canceled is guilty of the crime of false pretenses.

When the wrongdoer signs the name of the rightful cardholder on the slip for the credit card transaction, the wrongdoer commits the crime of forgery. The district attorney has the discretion to choose the particular crime for which to bring a prosecution against the wrongdoer.

The Credit Card Fraud Act of 1984[22] makes it a federal crime to obtain anything of value in excess of $1,000 in a year by means of a counterfeit credit card, to make or traffic in such cards, or to possess more than 15 counterfeit cards at one time.

§ 9:21. Use of Mails to Defraud.

Congress has made it a crime to use the mails to further any scheme or artifice to defraud. To constitute this offense, there must be (a) a contemplated or organized scheme to defraud or to obtain money or property by false pretenses, and (b) the mailing or the causing of another to mail a letter, writing, or pamphlet for the purpose of executing or attempting to execute such scheme or artifice. Illustrations of schemes that come within the statute are false statements to secure credit, circulars announcing false cures, false statements to induce the sale of stock of a corporation, and false statements as to the origin of a fire and the value of destroyed goods for the purpose of securing indemnity from an insurance company. Federal law also makes it a crime to use a telegram or a telephone to defraud.

§ 9:22. Criminal Libel.

A person who falsely defames another without legal excuse or justification may be subject to criminal liability as well as civil liability. **Criminal libel** is made a crime because of its tendency to cause a breach of the peace. Under some statutes, however, the offense appears to be based upon the tendency to injure another.

No publication or communication to third persons is required in the case of criminal libel. The offense is committed when the defendant communicates the libel directly to the person libeled as well as when it is made known to third persons.

The truth of the statement is a defense in civil libel. In order to constitute a defense to criminal libel, the prevailing view requires that a proper motive on the part of the accused be shown as well as proof that the statement was true.

[22]Act of October 12, 1984, § 1029, PL 98-473, 98 Stat 2183, 18 USC § 1029.

In a number of states, slander or particular kinds of slander have also been made criminal offenses by statutes.

§ 9:23.   Lotteries and Gambling.

There are three elements to a lottery: (a) a payment of money or something of value for the opportunity to win (b) a prize (c) by lot or chance. If these elements are present it is immaterial that the transaction appears to be a legitimate form of business or advertising, or that the transaction is called by some name other than a lottery, such as a raffle. The sending of a chain letter through the mail is generally a federal offense both as a mail fraud and as an illegal lottery, when the letter solicits contributions or payments.

In many states, government lotteries are legal.

Gambling is a crime under modern statutes. It is similar to a lottery in that there are the three elements of payment, chance, and prize.[23] Equipment used in gambling is generally declared by law to be contraband and may be confiscated by the government. If the winner of an electronic video card game receives something of value as a prize, the game is an illegal gambling device.

§ 9:24.   Embezzlement.

Embezzlement is the fraudulent conversion of property or money owned by another by a person to whom it has been entrusted, as in the case of an employee receiving money for the employer. It is a statutory crime designed to cover the case of unlawful takings that were not larceny because the wrongdoer did not take the property from the possession of another, and which were not robbery because there was neither a taking nor the use of force or fear.

It is immaterial whether the defendant received the money or property from the victim or from a third person to deliver to the victim. Thus an agent commits embezzlement when the agent receives and keeps payments from third persons, which payments the agent should have remitted to the principal. Generally, the fact that the defendant intends to return the property or money embezzled, or does in fact do so, is no defense.

Today, every jurisdiction has not only a general embezzlement statute but also various statutes applicable to particular situations, such as embezzlement by trustees, employees, and government officials.

§ 9:25.   Receiving Stolen Goods.

The crime of **receiving stolen goods** is the receiving of goods which have been stolen with knowledge of that fact, and with the intent to deprive the owner of them. It is immaterial that the receiver does not know the identity of the owner or of the thief.

---

[23]Monte Carlo Parties, Ltd. v Webb, 253 Ga 508, 322 SE2d 246 (1984).

C. CRIMES OF FORCE AND CRIMES AGAINST PROPERTY

In contrast with the white-collar crimes are those that involve the use of force, threat of force, or that cause injury to persons or damage to property.

§ 9:26. Larceny.

Larceny is the wrongful or fraudulent taking and carrying away by any person of the personal property of another, with a fraudulent intent to deprive the owner of such property.[24] The place from which the property is taken is generally immaterial, although by statute the offense is sometimes subjected to a greater penalty when property is taken from a particular kind of building, such as a warehouse. Shoplifting is a common form of larceny. In many states, shoplifting is made a separate crime.

Although the term is broadly used in everyday speech, every unlawful taking is not a larceny. At common law, a defendant taking property of another with the intent to return it was not guilty of larceny. This has been changed in some states so that a person who "borrows" a car for a joyride is guilty of larceny, theft, or some other statutory offense.

Statutes in many states penalize as **larceny by trick** the use of any device or fraud by which the wrongdoer obtains the possession of, or title to, personal property from the true owner. In some states all forms of larceny and robbery are consolidated into a statutory crime of theft. At common law, there was no crime known as "theft."

§ 9:27. Robbery.

Robbery is the taking of personal property from the presence of the victim by use of force or fear.[25] In most states, there are aggravated forms of robbery, such as robbery with a deadly weapon. The crime of robbery may overlap with the crime of larceny. When the unlawful taking is not by force or fear, as when the victim does not know that the property is being taken, the offense is larceny but it can not be robbery. In contrast, when the property is taken from the victim by use of force or fear there is both robbery and larceny. In such case, the prosecuting attorney will determine for which crime the defendant is to be prosecuted.

§ 9:28. Burglary.

At common law, **burglary** was the breaking and entering in the night-time of the dwelling house of another, with the intent to commit a felony therein.[26] While one often thinks of burglary as stealing property, any felony would satisfy the definition. The offense was aimed primarily at protecting

---

[24]Meissner v Aetna Cas. & Surety Co. 195 NJ Super 462, 480 A2d 233 (1984).
[25]Harper v Texas (Tex App) 675 SW2d 534 (1984).
[26]Mason v Indiana, _____ Ind _____, 467 NE2d 737 (1984).

the habitation and thus illustrates the social objective of protection of the person, in this case, the persons living or dwelling in the building.

Modern statutes have eliminated many of the elements of the common-law definition so that under some statutes, it is immaterial when or whether there is an entry to commit a felony and the elements of breaking and entering are frequently omitted. Under some statutes, the offense is aggravated and the penalty is increased in terms of the place where the offense is committed, such as a bank building, freightcar, or warehouse. Related statutory offenses have been created, such as the crime of possessing burglar's tools.

§ 9:29. Arson.

At common law, **arson** was the willful and malicious burning of the dwelling house of another. As such, it was designed to protect human life, although the defendant was guilty if there was a burning of the building even though no one was actually hurt. In most states, arson is a felony so that if someone is killed in the resulting fire, the offense is murder by application of the felony-murder rule, under which a homicide, however unintended, occurring in the commission of a felony is automatically classified as murder.

In virtually every state, a special offense of **burning to defraud** an insurer has been created by statute. Such burning is not arson when the defendant burns the defendant's own house in order to collect the insurance money.

FACTS:
Chester James lived in a mobile home. He obtained fire insurance on the home. Some time later the home was intentionally set on fire by someone. At the time of the fire, James owed a substantial debt that was less than the amount of the insurance. A few minutes before the fire, James was seen removing clothing and exercise apparatus from the home. He was prosecuted and convicted for burning the home with intent to defraud the insurer.

DECISION:
Conviction affirmed. The circumstances were such that the jury properly deduced that the fire had been set by James and that he had done so with the intent to get the insurance money. He was therefore guilty of the crime of burning a dwelling place with the intent to defraud. [North Carolina v James, 77 NC App 219, 334 SE2d 452 (1985)]

---

§ 9:30. Riots and Civil Disorders.

Damage to property in the course of a riot or civil disorder is ordinarily a crime to the same extent as though only one wrongdoer were involved. That is, there is larceny or arson, and so on, depending on the nature of the circumstances, without regard to whether one person or many are involved. In addition, the act of assembling as a riotous mob and engaging in civil disorders is generally some form of crime in itself, without regard to the destruction or theft of property, whether under common-law concepts of disturbing the peace or under modern antiriot statutes.

A statute may make it a crime to riot or to incite to riot. However, a statute relating to inciting must be carefully drawn to avoid infringing constitutionally protected free speech.

SUMMARY

When a person does not live up to the standards set by the law, society may regard the conduct of the defendant as so dangerous to the government, or to people, or to property, that it will prosecute the defendant for such misconduct. This punishable conduct, called crime, may be common law or statutory in origin. In a few states, there are only statutory crimes. Crimes are classified as treason, felonies, and misdemeanors, with a felony being a crime that is punishable by imprisonment or death.

In terms of the parties taking part in a crime, there are principals in the first and second degree and accessories before and after the fact. The principals are the ones who do the actual wrong. Accessories provide assistance, comfort, or protection either in advance of the commission of the crime (before the fact) or after the crime has been committed (after the fact).

Employers and corporations may be criminally responsible for their acts and the acts of their employees. Minors, insane, and intoxicated persons are held criminally responsible to a limited extent. This means that in some cases they will not be held responsible for a crime when a normal, adult person would be held responsible.

Crimes are often classified in terms of whether force or violence is involved. The phrase of white collar crime is frequently used in reference to crimes that do not involve force or violence. Some white collar crimes are linked with modern technology. When modern technology is involved, the criminal law frequently lags behind the technology because it takes time for the lawmaker to become aware that the white collar criminal has found a new way to commit a crime. White collar crimes embrace the following: crimes relating to illegal methods of production, competing, and marketing, including the improper use of the means of interstate transportation and communication; crimes relating to securities, such as stocks and bonds; computer crimes, including the unauthorized use of a computer, the theft of computer software, and the raiding of a computer to obtain its information (The latter is now a federal crime. By federal statute, a group of crimes related to the electronic transfer of funds have been declared such as obtaining illegal access or use of the transfer system or using or transporting devices for gaining such access.); bribery, at common law consisting of the giving of some favor to a public official to obtain an advantage, now broadened to include the private person, such as the employees of a competitor (commercial bribery) and of athletes (extortion, as the counterpart of bribery, is the obtaining of an advantage from a public official by means of threats of harm; blackmail is the name given to extortion when the victim is not a public official.); crimes relating to the exercise of improper influence in politics and in business, as by outlawing the use of racketeering methods to influence or acquire a legitimate business (RICO); counterfeiting, forgery, perjury, the making of false claims against the government, and the obtaining of goods or money by false pretenses, the use of false weights, measures and labels, and swindles and confidence games; federal statutes make it a crime to deal in counterfeit credit cards and to possess more than 15 such cards at one time; it is a federal crime to use the mails to defraud; defamatory statements made about another may be so likely to cause retaliation of some sort that that defamation is condemned as criminal libel; lotteries and gambling, defined as the giving of consideration for a chance to win a prize, are illegal regardless of their name (In many states an exception is made to authorize public lotteries run by the government.); embezzlement is the keeping for oneself of money that was received as agent or as employee of another and that should have been remitted to that other person; receiving stolen goods consists of receiving goods that are in fact stolen with knowledge that they are.

In contrast with the foregoing crimes that are loosely called white-collar crimes, are the crimes of force and violence. Most common of these are: Larceny, the taking without permission of personal property from the possession of another with the intent to deprive that person permanently of the property (In some states, larceny has been expanded to include larceny by trick.); robbery, the taking without permission of personal property from the possession of another by means of force or fear (In some states all forms of larceny and robbery have been combined as a single crime of "theft."); burglary is the breaking and entering of the dwelling house of another in the nighttime for the purpose of committing a felony therein (Statutes have removed some of these restrictions as to time and place and have made felonious entry into certain places, such as a bank, an aggravated form of the crime.); arson is the burning of the dwelling house of another; burning to defraud an insurer is a statutory crime aimed at preventing a person from burning that person's own building in order to collect the insurance money on the building; taking part in a riot or civil disorder may be a crime in itself, in addition to the traditional forms of crime that may be committed in the course of the riot or disorder.

There is no uniform law of crimes. Each state and the federal government defines and punishes crimes as it chooses. While there is a tendency to follow a common pattern, there are many variations as to details between the law of different states and the federal law.

QUESTIONS AND CASE PROBLEMS

1. What is the objective of the rule of law that an irresistible impulse to commit a crime does not excuse criminal liability when the mental instability is not the result of disease?
2. What is a crime which is malum in se?
3. Hunter was employed by the Watson Corporation. He was killed at work by an explosion caused by the gross negligence of the corporation. The corporation was prosecuted for manslaughter. It raised the defense that only people could commit manslaughter and that therefore it was not guilty. Was this defense valid?

4. Johnny took a radio from the Englehart Music Store without the knowledge of any clerk that he was removing it. He was then prosecuted for larceny. He claimed that he could only be prosecuted for shoplifting because larceny was a serious felony and all that he had done was to take merchandise from a store. Was this defense valid?

5. Garrison purchased goods that she knew had been stolen. When the police traced some stolen articles and discovered Garrison's activities, Garrison was prosecuted for embezzlement. Was she guilty?

6. Compare larceny, robbery, and embezzlement.

7. Carlotta drove her automobile after having had dinner and several drinks. She fell asleep at the wheel and ran over and killed a pedestrian. She was prosecuted for manslaughter and raised the defense that she did not intend to hurt anyone and because of the drinks did not know what she was doing. Was this a valid defense?

8. Koonce entered a gas station after it was closed for the night. By means of force, he removed the cash box from a soft drink vending machine. He was prosecuted for burglarizing a "warehouse." Was he guilty? [Koonce v Kentucky (Ky) 452 SW2d 822; Shumate v Kentucky (Ky) 433 SW2d 340]

9. Buckley took a credit card from the coat of its owner with the intent to never return it. He then purchased some goods at a department store and paid for them by presenting the credit card to the sales clerk and then signing the credit card slip with the name of the owner of the credit card. How many crimes, if any, did Buckley commit? [Buckley v Indiana (IndApp) 322 NE2d 113]

10. Morse was convicted of forging the name "Hillyard Motors" as the drawer of a check. He appealed on the ground that signing such a name had no legal effect, and that therefore he was not guilty of forgery. Decide. [Washington v Morse, 38 Wash 2d 927, 234 P2d 478]

11. Wolfe gave some counterfeit money to Ballinger, telling her that the bills were counterfeit and that she should go "downtown" to pass them and that, being New Year's Eve, it was a good time to pass them. Ballinger thereafter spent two of the bills and attempted to destroy the balance. Wolfe was arrested and prosecuted for passing counterfeit obligations of the United States with intent to defraud. He raised the defense that he could not be guilty as Ballinger was told that the money was counterfeit. Decide. [United States v Wolfe (CA 7 Ill) 307 F2d 798 cert den 372 US 945]

12. Berman organized the Greatway Travel Ltd. Greatway sold travel consultant franchises and promised that the franchisees would receive various discounts and assistance. None of these promises were ever kept because Greatway lost all its money through mismanagement. Berman was prosecuted for obtaining money by false pretenses. Was he guilty? [Berman v Maryland (Md App) 370 A2d 580]

13. Lang and his wife lived in a trailer in a trailer park. Winhoven broke into the trailer in order to steal. He was prosecuted and convicted of breaking and entering "an occupied dwelling" with the intent to commit larceny. He raised the defense that he had not broken into an occupied dwelling

but into a trailer. Was he correct? [Michigan v Winhoven, 65 Mich App 522, 237 NW2d 540]

14. Socony Mobil Oil Co. ran a telephone bingo game series. The gasoline station dealers purchased the bingo cards from Socony and gave them free to anyone requesting them, whether a customer or not. It was not possible to play the game without a card. A cash prize was awarded the winner. The State of Texas brought an injunction action against Socony to stop this on the ground that it was a lottery. Socony raised the defense that since no value or consideration was given by the persons participating in the bingo games, it was not a lottery. Decide. [Texas v Socony Mobil Oil Co. (Tex Civ App) 386 SW2d 169]

15. Swanson wanted to procure a loan from the Lincoln Bank. He falsely represented to the bank that he owned 629 head of cattle when in fact he owned only 80. The bank made a loan to him of approximately $3,000 and credited his account with this amount. Before Swanson drew any money from the bank, the bank's agent learned of the falsity of Swanson's representation. Swanson thereafter drew out by check the amount of the loan. Swanson was then prosecuted by the state for obtaining property by false pretenses. He defended on the ground that he had not actually drawn any money from the bank until after the bank, through its agent, knew of the fraud and that since the bank took no steps to prevent the money from going out thereafter, it was in effect the bank's own negligence that made it sustain loss. Was this a valid defense? [Nebraska v Swanson, 179 Neb 693, 140 NW2d 618]

16. Bryant was indicted for having knowingly received stolen property. He raised the defense that the money that he had received had been embezzled by the person from whom he had received it and that it was therefore not "stolen" property. Was he correct? [New Mexico v Bryant, 99 NM App 149, 655 P2d 161]

17. Skelton attempted to rob a general store. He used a small wooden toy pistol. The attempt failed and he was arrested. He was prosecuted for attempted armed robbery. Was he guilty? [Illinois v Skelton, 83 Ill 2d 58, 46 Ill Dec 571, 414 NE2d 455]

18. In order to obtain uniformity in sentencing, Florida adopted a set of guidelines to be followed by judges. The guidelines allowed a judge to impose a greater sentence for "clear and convincing" reasons but prohibited increasing a punishment because of the social or economic status of the defendant. Karen Mischler was the bookkeeper of a small roofing contractor. She was convicted of embezzling between $14,000 and $19,000 of her employer's money. Both during her trial and after her conviction, Karen insisted that she was innocent. The judge imposed a harsher sentence than indicated by the guidelines because (1) he felt that white collar crimes should be punished more severely, (2) the defendant did not show remorse for her crime, (3) the amount embezzled was substantial when compared to the finances of the victim, and (4) she had violated a position of trust. She appealed from the sentencing on the ground that her sentence was excessive and unauthorized. Was she correct? [Mischler v Florida (Fla App) 458 So 2d 371]

CHAPTER 10

TORTS

CHAPTER OBJECTIVES

After studying this chapter you will be able to:
1. Define torts and distinguish them from contracts and from crimes.
2. Explain the basis of tort liability.
3. Define absolute liability and describe circumstances where the law imposes it.
4. Define negligence and explain its application.
5. Give examples of both negligent and intentional torts.

When a wrong has been done that has caused harm to someone, the law generally allows the injured person to recover money damages from the wrongdoer. When the wrong that has been done is the breaking of a contract, the right of the aggrieved person is governed by contract law. When there is no contract, the right of the aggrieved person is typically governed by tort law.

In this chapter you will see many points at which there is a gradual expansion of the law of torts, an expansion being made in response to what society thinks is right as it strives to promote the social forces described in Chapter 2.

§ 10:1. Tort and Crime Distinguished.

A crime is a wrong arising from a violation of a public duty, whereas a **tort** is a wrong arising from a violation of a private duty. More practically stated, a crime is a wrong of such a serious nature that the state steps in to take some action to punish the wrongdoer and to deter others from committing the same wrong. Whenever the act that is punished as a crime causes harm to an identifiable person, that person may sue the wrongdoer for money damages to compensate for the harm. As to the person harmed, the wrongful act is called a tort; as to the government the wrongful act is a crime. If, however, a crime does not hurt an identifiable person, it is not a tort. For example, bribing a public official is a crime but no individual person is harmed so that no tort is committed. Conversely, there may be a tort even though there is no crime. For example, if I walk away with your coat wrongly but honestly thinking that it is mine, I have committed the tort of conversion. That is, I have committed a wrongful act as to you. However, I have not committed any crime because I did not have the mental state necessary to constitute a crime such as larceny or theft.

§ 10:2.   Tort and Breach of Contract Distinguished.

The wrongs or injuries caused by a breach of contract arise from the violation of an obligation or duty created by the agreement of the parties. In contrast, a tort arises from the violation of an obligation or duty created by law. The same act may be both a breach of contract and a tort. For example, when an agent exchanges property instead of selling it as directed by the principal, the agent is liable for breach of contract and for the tort of conversion.

§ 10:3.   Basis of Tort Liability.

The mere fact that a person is hurt or harmed in some way does not mean that such person can sue and recover damages from the person causing the harm. There must exist a recognized basis for liability.

(a) **Voluntary Act.** The defendant must be guilty of a voluntary act or omission. Acts committed or omitted by one who is confronted with a sudden peril caused by another are considered involuntary acts.

(b) **Intent.** Whether intent to do an unlawful act or intent to cause harm is required as a basis for tort liability depends upon the nature of the tort involved. Liability is imposed for some torts even though the person committing the tort acted without any intent to do wrong. Thus a person going on neighboring land without consent of the landowner is liable for the tort of trespass even though such action was unintended and was caused by an honest mistake as to the location of the boundary line.

In other torts, the intent of the actor is an essential element. Thus in the case of slander and interference with contracts, it is necessary for the plaintiff to show that the defendant intended to cause harm or at least had the intent to do an act which a reasonable person would anticipate was likely to cause harm.

(c) **Motive.** As a general rule, motive is immaterial except as it may be evidence to show the existence of intent. In most instances, a legal right may be exercised even with bad motives, and an act that is unlawful is not made lawful by good motives.

(d) **Causal Relationship.** In order to put legal responsibility upon one as a wrongdoer, it is necessary to show that there was a relationship of cause and effect between the wrongful act and the harm sustained by the plaintiff. In some states, the wrongful act must have been the proximate (or immediate) cause of the plaintiff's harm. In many states, however, the requirement of a causal connection has been relaxed so that it is sufficient that the defendant's act or omission substantially contributes to the harm rather than being the sole and proximate cause.

FACTS:

George Nesselrode was a passenger in an airplane made by Beech Aircraft Corporation. A few minutes after taking off, the plane crashed and all occupants were killed. An action was brought by George's widow against Beechcraft on the theory that it was at fault because it did not take adequate precautions to prevent the improper installation of certain parts in its airplanes, in consequence of which the parts could be installed in reverse or backwards, and this improper installation had caused the fatal crash. Beechcraft claimed that it was the act of the persons making improper installation that had caused the harm and that it was that installation that was the proximate cause.

DECISION:

Judgment against Beech Aircraft Corp. Although no harm would have occurred if third persons had not made an improper installation, the fact remained that the prior failure of Beechcraft to give proper warning was a substantial factor in bringing about the harm. It therefore could not claim that the installation was an act that broke the causal chain. As a substantial contributing factor, the manufacturer was liable even though the wrong installation was the proximate cause and was the act of a third person. [Nesselrode v Executive Beechcraft, Inc. and Beech Aircraft Corp. (Mo) 707 SW2d 371 (1986)]

In many instances, the courts define causal relationship in terms of foreseeability. That is, if it was reasonably foreseeable that the conduct of the defendant could cause harm to the plaintiff there is a sufficient causal relationship between the defendant's conduct and the plaintiff's harm.[1]

(1) *Act of Third Person.* The fact that the wrongful act of a third person takes effect between the time that the defendant acted or failed to act and the time when the plaintiff is injured, does not establish that the causative chain between the defendant's conduct and the plaintiff's harm has been broken and the defendant therefore insulated from liability for the plaintiff's harm. If the conduct of the third person was foreseeable, it does not relieve the defendant from liability to the plaintiff.[2] To the contrary both the defendant and the third person are liable to the plaintiff and the question of division of liability discussed in § 10:7 of this book then arises.

[1]Bain v Gillispie, _____ Iowa App _____, 357 NW2d 47 (1984).
[2]Independent School District No. 14 v Ampro Corp. _____ Minn App _____, 361 NW2d 138 (1985).

(e) **Liability for Tort of Employee or Child.** A person may be innocent of wrong but yet be held liable for the tort committed by another person. As will be discussed later in the chapters on agency, the tort of an employee or agent may in some cases impose liability upon the employer or principal.

A parent is ordinarily not liable for the tort committed by a child. That is, the mere fact that the person sued is the parent of the child committing the wrong does not impose liability on the parent.

There are several instances, however, in which a parent will be held liable. If the parent knows that the child has a dangerous characteristic, such as a disposition to set houses on fire, and does not take reasonable steps to prevent this, the parent will be held liable for the harm caused by the child. If the child is a reckless driver and the parent allows the child to use the parent's car, the parent is liable on the theory that the parent was negligent in entrusting the car to the child. In about half of the states, a parent supplying a family car is liable for any harm negligently caused by any member of the family while driving the car. In some states, any person lending an automobile is liable for the harm caused by the negligence of the person borrowing or renting the car. In some states, statutes make a parent liable for willful or malicious property damage caused by minor children. Such statutes generally specify a maximum limitation on such liability.

§ 10:4.   Liability-Imposing Conduct.

Typically, American law imposes tort liability only when there is some fault on the part of the defendant. Thus it is required that the defendant either intended to cause the harm of the plaintiff or that the defendant was negligent. In a number of instances, the law of this century has made exceptions to the concept that liability can only be based on fault and has imposed liability solely because the plaintiff has been harmed by the act of the defendant.

§ 10:5.   Absolute Liability.

In some areas of the law, liability for harm is imposed without regard to whether there was any fault on the part of the defendant; that is, without regard to whether there was any negligence or intention to cause harm. For example, in most states when a contractor blasts with dynamite and debris is hurled onto the land of another, the landowner may recover damages from the contractor even though the contractor was not negligent and did not intentionally cause the harm.

By this concept of absolute liability, society is saying that the activity is so dangerous to the public that liability must be imposed even though no fault is present. Yet society will not go so far as to say that the activity is so dangerous that it must be outlawed. Instead, the compromise is made to allow the activity to continue but make the one who stands to benefit from the activity pay its injured victims regardless of the circumstances under which the injuries are inflicted.[3]

[3]Bunyak v Clyde J. Yancey and Sons Dairy, Inc. (Fla App) 438 So 2d 891 (1983).

(a) Industrial Activity. Generally there is absolute liability for harm growing out of the storage of inflammable gas and explosives in the middle of a populated city; crop dusting when the chemical used is dangerous to life and the dusting is likely to be spread by the wind; and for factories emitting dangerous fumes, smoke, and soot in populated areas.

FACTS:

Mallinckrodt produces nuclear and radioactive medical pharmaceuticals and supplies. An adjoining business owner, Maryland Heights Leasing, claimed that the low-level radiation emissions damaged its property and caused a loss of earnings. Maryland sued Mallinckrodt.

DECISION:

The defendant would be liable for damages caused by its ultrahazardous activity if it was shown that the harm could not be avoided and that the harm to the plaintiff significantly outweighted the value of the operation of the plant. [Maryland Heights Leasing, Inc. v Mallinckrodt, Inc. (Mo App) 706 SW2d 218 (1985)]

(b) Consumer Protection. Pure food statutes may impose absolute liability upon the seller of foods in favor of the ultimate consumer who is harmed by them. Decisions and statutes governing product liability impose liability although the defendant was not negligent and intended no harm.[4]

(c) Wild Animals. A person keeping a wild animal is absolutely liable for any harm caused by it. This liability is not affected by the fact that the animal was tamed and the owner had no reason to foresee that harm would occur.

(d) No-Fault Liability. No-fault liability is another name for absolute liability. However called, the defendant is liable for harm caused the plaintiff by virtue of the fact that such harm was caused the plaintiff. Liability is imposed without regard to the absence of any fault or intention to harm on the part of the defendant.

No-fault liability is based on statutes. Typically, recovery on no-fault liability is less than the liability that would exist if fault of the defendant could be established. Generally the plaintiff is allowed to prove such fault and recover a greater amount when serious injury or death has been caused.[5]

No-fault liability is today associated with automobiles. A half century before the no-fault concept was applied to automobile liability, it became the basis for workers' compensation. Under such statutes, the worker is compensated when the employment-related harm is sustained, without any question being raised as to the presence or absence of fault on the part of the employer. The amount recovered by a worker is smaller than could be recovered if a common-law action could by prosecuted and the worker would be successful therein. The injured worker who is covered by workers' compensa-

---

[4]See Chapter 28 of this book.
[5]Byer v Smith, 419 Mich 541, 357 NW2d 644 (1984).

tion is restricted to the recovery permitted by such law and does not have the choice of bringing a lawsuit to seek a larger recovery.

§ 10:6. Negligence.

The widest range of tort liability today arises in the field of **negligence,** which exists whenever the defendant has acted with less care than would be exercised by a reasonable person under the circumstances.[6] Such negligence must be causally related to the harm sustained by the plaintiff.

FACTS:

Metropolitan Gas Repair Service installed a new circulation pump in the heating system of Kulik's home. No safety inspection was made after the installation was completed. The safety release valve on the pump was plugged but this was not discovered because the safety inspection test was not made. When the heating system was put in operation, the pressure increased to the danger point, the safety release valve did not open because it was plugged, and there was an explosion that damaged Kulik's home. He sued Metropolitan for damages. It raised the defense that it had performed the contract by installing the pump.

DECISION:

Judgment for Kulik. The fact that Metropolitan had installed the pump as required by the contract did not mean that it had done everything that was required of it. The fact that Metropolitan had done the work called for by the contract did not excuse it for failing to exercise due care. If, as was the case, the release valve was plugged, and if a safety inspection was required to determine whether it was plugged, it was clear that a reasonable person would regard a safety inspection as necessary in the light of the circumstances. The failure to make such inspection was therefore negligent and Metropolitan was liable for the harm caused by its negligence. [Metropolitan Gas Repair Service, Inc. v Kulik _____ Colo _____, 621 P2d 313 (1980)]

(a) **The "Reasonable Person."** The reasonable person whose behavior is made the standard is an imaginary person. In a given case which is tried before a jury, the reasonable person is what appears to the composite or combined minds of the jurors to be a model person.

This reasonable person is not any one of the jurors nor an average of the jurors. The law is not concerned with what the jurors would do in a like situation, for it is possible that they may be more careful or less careful than the abstract reasonable person.

(b) **Variable Character of the Standard.** By definition, the standard is a variable standard for it does not tell you in advance what should be done. This is confusing to everyone, in the sense that you never know the exact answer in any borderline case until after the lawsuit is over. From the standpoint of society, however, this very flexibility is desirable because it is obviously impossible to foresee every possible variation in the facts that might

[6]McCaskill v Welch (La App) 463 So 2d 942 (1985).

arise and even more impossible to keep such a code of conduct up-to-date. Imagine how differently the reasonable person must act while driving today's automobile on today's superhighways than when driving a Model T on dirt roads three-quarters of a century ago.

(c) **Degree of Care.** The degree of care required of a person is that which an ordinarily prudent person would exercise under similar circumstances. It does not mean such a degree of care as would have prevented the harm from occurring, nor is it enough that it is just as much care as everyone else exercises. Nor is it sufficient that one has exercised the degree of care which is customary for persons in the same kind of work or business, or that one has employed the methods customarily used. If one is engaged in services requiring skill, the care, of course, must measure up to a higher standard. In any case, the degree of care exercised must be commensurate with the danger that would probably result if such care were lacking. In all cases, it is the diligence, care, and skill that can be reasonably expected under the circumstances. Whether one has exercised the degree of care that is required under the circumstances is a question that is determined by the jury.

(d) **Contributory Negligence.** At common law, a plaintiff could not recover for injuries caused by another's negligence if the plaintiff's own negligence had contributed to the injury. The plaintiff guilty of contributory negligence was denied recovery without regard to whether the defendant was more negligent. The common law did not recognize comparative degrees of negligence nor did it try to apportion the injury to the two parties in terms of the degree of their respective fault.

In order to avoid the harshness of the common-law rule as to contributory negligence, there developed a doctrine variously called the doctrine of last clear chance, the humanitarian doctrine, and the doctrine of discovered peril. Under this concept, although the plaintiff was negligent, the defendant was liable if the defendant had the last clear chance to avoid the injury. When the defendant had such opportunity but did not make use of it, the theory was that the plaintiff's negligence was not the cause of the harm sustained.

(e) **Comparative Negligence.** In most states, the common-law rule as to contributory negligence has been rejected because it is regarded as unjust that the plaintiff who has been contributorily negligent should forfeit all rights even when the plaintiff's negligence was slight in comparison to the defendant's negligence. These states provide that there should be a comparing of the negligence of the plaintiff and the defendant with the result that the negligence of the plaintiff does not bar recovery but only reduces the plaintiff's recovery to the extent that the harm was caused by the plaintiff's fault. For example, if the jury decides that the plaintiff had sustained damages of $100,000 but that the plaintiff's own negligence was one-fourth the cause of the damage, the plaintiff would be allowed to recover $75,000. At common law, the plaintiff in such case would have recovered nothing.

In some states the comparative negligence concept is modified by ignoring the negligence of the plaintiff if it is slight and the negligence of the defendant is great or gross. At the other extreme, some states refuse to allow the plaintiff to recover anything if the negligence of the plaintiff was more than 50% of the cause of the harm.

The trend of the law is to apply the concept of comparative fault to all actions even though the defendant's alleged liability is based on warranty, strict tort, or absolute liability.[7]

(f) Proof of Negligence. The plaintiff ordinarily has the burden of proving that the defendant did not exercise reasonable care. In some instances, however, it is sufficient for the plaintiff to prove that the injury was caused by something that was within the control of the defendant. If injury ordinarily results from a particular object only when there is negligence, the proof of the fact that injury resulted is held sufficient proof that the defendant was negligent. This is expressed by the maxim *res ipsa loquitur* (the occurrence or the thing speaks for itself).

This concept does not establish that the defendant was negligent but merely allows the jury to conclude or infer that the defendant was negligent. The defendant is not barred from proving lack of negligence or from explaining that the harm was caused by some act for which the defendant was not responsible; and the jury, if it believes the defendant's evidence, can refuse to infer negligence from the mere happening of the event and can conclude that the defendant was not negligent.

The burden of proving that the plaintiff was contributorily negligent is on the defendant both under common law and under the comparative negligence concept.

(g) Violation of Statute. By the general rule, if harm is sustained while the defendant is violating a statute, the defendant is deemed negligent and is liable for the harm. Many courts narrow this concept so that the defendant is liable only if the statute is intended to protect against the kind of harm which was sustained because of the violation of the statute and if the plaintiff was a member of the class that the statute was designed to protect.[8] For example, when the automobiles of the plaintiff and defendant are in a collision, the fact that the defendant was driving without proper tags in violation of an automobile registration law will be ignored as the purpose of that statute was not to describe negligent driving nor to protect other drivers from being negligently harmed.

§ 10:7. Division of Liability.

In some instances, when two or more defendants have caused harm to the plaintiff, it is difficult or impossible to determine what damage was done by each of such wrongdoers or tortfeasors. For example, suppose automobile #1 strikes automobile #2 which is then struck by automobile #3. Ordinarily, it is impossible to determine how much of the damage to automobile #2 was caused by each of the cars. Similarly, a tract of farmland down river may be harmed because two or more factories have dumped industrial wastes into the river. It is not possible to determine how much damage each of the factories has caused the farmland.

[7]Mills v Smith, 9 Kan App 2d 80, 673 P2d 117 (1983).
[8]Walker v Bignell, 100 Wis 2d 256, 301 NW2d 447 (1981).

By the older view, a plaintiff was denied the right to recover from any of the wrongdoers in these situations. The courts followed the theory that a plaintiff is not entitled to recover from a defendant unless the plaintiff can prove what harm was caused by that defendant. The modern trend of the cases is to hold all the defendants jointly and severally (collectively and individually) liable for the total harm sustained by the plaintiff.[9]

§ 10:8.   Who May Sue.

Ordinarily the person who brings suit for a tort is the person whose property has been damaged or who has sustained personal injury.

In some torts, not only the immediate victim has the right to sue but also persons standing in certain relationships to the victim. Thus, under certain circumstances, one spouse can sue for an injury to the other spouse or a parent can sue for an injury to the child. In a wrongful death action, members of the surviving group (typically the spouse, child, and parents of the person who has been killed) have a right to sue the wrongdoer for such death.

§ 10:9.   Immunity from Liability.

Basically, every person committing a tort is liable for damages for the harm caused thereby. However, certain persons and entities are not subject to tort liability. This is called **immunity from liability**.

(a) **Government.** Governments are generally immune from tort liability. This rule has been eroded by decision and in some instances by statutes, such as the Federal Tort Claims Act, which, subject to certain exceptions, permits the recovery of damages from the United States for property damage, personal injury, or death action claims arising from the negligent act or omission of any employee of the United States under such circumstances that the United States, "if a private person, would be liable to the claimant in accordance with the law of the place where the act or omission occurred." A fast-growing number of states have abolished governmental immunity although many still recognize it.[10]

(b) **Minors.** All persons are not equally liable for torts. A minor of tender years, generally under 7, can not be guilty of negligence or contributory negligence. Between the ages of 7 and 14, a minor is presumed to have capacity to commit a tort, although the contrary may be shown. Above 14 years, no distinction is made in terms of age. A minor who drives a motorcycle or automobile on a public highway must observe the same standard of care as an adult.[11]

(c) **Family Relationships.** At common law, no suit could be brought by a husband against his wife or vice versa. By statute, this immunity has been abolished as to torts involving property. The immunity continues in most states with respect to personal torts, whether intentional or negligent,

---

[9]Roberts v Rockwell International Corp. (Fla App) 462 So 2d 502 (1984).
[10]Mesina v Burden, 228 Va 301, 321 SE2d 657 (1984).
[11]Davis v Waterman (Miss) 420 So 2d 1063 (1982).

although a substantial number of states now allow personal tort actions between spouses. The trend of judicial decisions rejects the argument that the allowance of such suits would open the door to fraud and collusion between spouses when one of them is insured.

An immunity exists between parent and child in many states with respect to personal tort claims. This also is being gradually abolished.[12]

(d) **Charities.** Early in this century, charities were exempt from tort liability. For example, a hospital could not be held liable for negligent harm to a patient caused by its staff or employees. Within the last four decades this immunity has been rejected in nearly all of the states.

§ 10:10.   Causing of Mental Distress.

When the defendant commits an act which by itself is a tort, there is ordinarily recovery for the mental distress which is caused thereby. At common law there was no recovery for mental distress in the absence of a tortious act.

(a) **Intentionally Caused Mental Distress.** With the turn of this century, and particularly in the last four decades, recovery has been allowed in a number of cases in which no ordinary or traditional form of tort was committed and the common element in these cases was that the defendant had willfully subjected the plaintiff to unnecessary emotional disturbance. This result was reached when the common carrier or the hotel insulted a patron; an outrageous practical joke was played upon the plaintiff; the corpse of a close relative was concealed, mistreated, or interference was made with the burial; or statements were made to humiliate the plaintiff because of race, creed, or national origin.

The concept of liability for intentionally caused distress is applicable in a commercial setting, as when a collection agency uses harassing techniques to collect the debt owed by a consumer or when a manufacturer engages in a continuing campaign to intimidate a critic of the defendant's product, including illegal electronic eavesdropping. In either case, the tort may be called the tort of outrageous conduct, or the tort of outrage.[13] No distinction is made between causing mental distress or fear for the purpose of causing such distress or fear and the situation in which the wrongdoer seeks to thereby coerce the victim into acting or refraining from acting in a particular way.

When there is liability for intentionally caused distress, there is also liability for any physical harm that is caused by the distress.

(b) **Negligently Caused Mental Distress.** In many jurisdictions, the concept of liability for distress has been expanded to impose liability for negligently caused distress.

(c) **Bystander Recovery.** When a bystander is a spectator to the negligent conduct of the defendant and the witnessing of such conduct causes serious and reasonably foreseeable emotional distress, the bystander may re-

[12]Kirchner v Crystal, 15 Ohio 3d 326, 474 NE2d 275 (1984).
[13]Neufeldt v L. R. Foy Construction Co., Inc. 236 Kan 664, 693 P2d 1194 (1985).

cover damages for such harm from the wrongdoer.[14] Many courts limit this liability to spectators who are closely related to the person directly endangered by the defendant's conduct.

§ 10:11.   Invasion of Privacy.

As an aspect of protecting the person from unreasonable interference, the law has come to recognize a right of privacy. This right is most commonly invaded in one of the following ways: (a) invasion of physical privacy, as by planting a microphone in a person's home; (b) giving unnecessary publicity to personal matters of the plaintiff's life, such as financial status or past careers; (c) false public association of the plaintiff with some product or principle, such as indicating that the plaintiff endorses a product or is in favor of a particular law, when such is not the case; or (d) commercially exploiting the plaintiff's name or picture as in using them in advertising without permission.[15]

When a party has a legitimate business interest in making information known, such conduct is generally not regarded as an invasion of privacy and the conduct is protected by a privilege as long as good faith is exercised by the disclosing party.

FACTS:

The Medical Information Bureau (M.I.B.) was a nonprofit association formed by approximately seven hundred insurance companies. Whenever an application for insurance was made to any of these member companies, it would relay the medical information concerning the applicant to the M.I.B. Any other member could obtain this information from the data bank maintained by M.I.B. Senogles applied to the Security Benefit Life Insurance Company for a policy of health insurance. The medical information which he furnished the company was forwarded to the M.I.B. He sued Security for damages, claiming that his privacy had been invaded by the company's giving the information to M.I.B.

DECISION:

Judgment for Security. The circumstances showed that the communication was made for legitimate business reasons and therefore was conditionally privileged. The insurance companies had the interest of protecting themselves from writing policies for bad risks. This in turn benefitted the policy holders who would ultimately pay higher premiums if the companies insured bad risks. Because of these interests, Security was protected from liability by a conditional privilege which entitled it to make the communication in good faith. [Senogles v Security Benefit Life Insurance Co. 217 Kan 438, 536 P2d 1358 (1975)]

---

§ 10:12.   Malpractice.

Malpractice liability is a tort liability imposed for a poor or bad performance of a legal duty that results in harm. Usually, it will be a poor

---

[14]Paugh v Hanks, 6 Ohio 3d 72, 451 NE2d 759 (1983).
[15]Martin Luther King, Jr., Center v American Heritage Products, Inc. 250 Ga 135, 296 SE2d 697 (1982).

performance because of negligence, as distinguished from harm that is intentionally caused. Typically, the duty of performance will be a duty that arises from a contract and therefore the wrongdoer is guilty of both a breach of contract and a tort. Because of this interrelationship, the subject matter of malpractice will be considered in detail in Part Two relating to contracts, Chapter 21.

§ 10:13. Fraud.

A person is entitled to be protected from fraud and may recover damages for harm caused by fraud. This protects the plaintiff from false statements made with knowledge of their falsity or with reckless indifference as to whether they were true or not.[16]

In some instances, anti-fraud provisions have been adopted by consumer protection statutes. To illustrate, when the seller of a used car turns the odometer back with the intent to defraud, the seller is liable under the federal Motor Vehicle Information and Cost Savings Act to whoever purchases the automobile, without regard to whether the purchaser bought directly from that dealer or from an intermediate dealer.[17]

Fraud may be found in any commercial setting. Most commonly it is found when someone is trying to sell a house, goods, a business, or services. The *Midwest Supply* case involved the false advertising of services.

FACTS:
Midwest advertised that it possessed expertise in tax matters. Relying on such advertising, Waters had Midwest prepare his federal income tax return. Midwest assigned the preparation of the return to a new employee who was not qualified, and the tax return was defective. Waters was required to pay additional taxes and sued Midwest for damages. The jury returned a verdict in favor of Waters for extra damages of $100,000 to punish Midwest. Judgment was entered on this verdict and Midwest appealed.

DECISION:
Judgment affirmed. The defendant had misrepresented to the public that tax returns prepared by it were prepared by experts. The new employee preparing the Waters' returns was not qualified. He was a former construction worker and did not have any special training in tax return preparation. The claim of Midwest that expert service was provided its clients was fraudulent. The damages were therefore properly awarded. [Midwest Supply, Inc. v Waters, 89 Nev 210, 510 P2d 876 (1973)]

---

§ 10:14. Defamation by Slander.

A person is liable for defamation of another.

Reputation is injured by **defamation**, which is a publication tending to cause one to lose the esteem of the community. **Slander** is a form of

---

[16]State National Bank v Farah Manufacturing Co., Inc. (Tex App) 678 SW2d 661 (1984). The concept of fraud is more fully analyzed in § 14:5 of this book.
[17]Ryan v Edwards (CA4 Va) 592 F2d 756 (1979).

defamation consisting of the publication or communication to another of false, spoken words. Thus a false statement by the manager of a business that the plaintiff, who had formerly been manager, had been fired for stealing is slander.[18] The fact that language is offensive or derogatory does not in itself constitute slander.

(a) **Privilege.** Under certain circumstances, no liability arises when false statements are made even though they cause damage. This absolute privilege exists in the case of publication by a public officer when the publication is within the officer's line of duty. The rule is deemed necessary to encourage public officers in the performance of their public duties.

Other circumstances may afford a qualified or conditional privilege. A communication made in good faith, upon a subject in which the party communicating has an interest or right, is privileged if made to a person having corresponding interest or right. Thus, the owner of a watch may in good faith charge another person with the theft of the watch. A mercantile agency's credit report is conditionally privileged when made to an interested subscriber in good faith in the regular course of the agency's business. Also when a client tells an attorney that a customer of the client owes money, such statement does not impose liability for defamation even though it is wrong. The former employer of a job applicant has a qualified privilege to tell the prospective employer of the applicant why the former employer discharged the applicant.[19]

If a consumer makes false statements about a seller, such as that the consumer purchased a "lemon" from the automobile dealer, the consumer is liable for defamation.[20] The fact that a person is a consumer does not give rise to any privilege to make false statements.

§ 10:15.   Defamation by Libel.

The reputation of a person or a business may be defamed by written statements. This is known as **libel**. Although the defaming statement is described as a "writing" it may also be in print, picture, or in any other permanent, visual form. For example, to construct a gallows in front of another's residence is a libel. A written report falsely stating than an employee has falsified her time work records is libelous.[21]

§ 10:16.   Defamation by Computer.

A person's credit standing or reputation may be damaged because a computer contains erroneous information and the erroneous information is supplied to third persons. Will the data bank operator or service company be held liable to the person who is harmed? If the operator or the company had exercised reasonable care to prevent errors and to correct errors, it is

---

[18]Tandy Corp. v Bone, 283 Ark 399, 678 SW2d 312 (1984).
[19]Lewis v Equitable Life Assurance Society, _____ Minn App _____, 361 NW2d 875 (1985).
[20]Hajek v Bill Mowbray Motors, Inc. (Tex App) 645 SW2d 827 (1982), on appeal holding that such defamation could not be stopped by injunction. (Tex) 647 SW2d 253 (1983).
[21]Vinson v Linn-Mar Community School District, _____ Iowa _____, 360 NW2d 108 (1984).

probable that there will not be any liability on either the actual programmer-employee operating the equipment or the management providing the computer service. Conversely, if negligence or an intent to harm is shown, the wrongdoer could be held liable for what may be called defamation by computer. It is likely that liability could be avoided by supplying the person to whom the information relates with a copy of any printout of information which the data bank supplies the third person, as this would tend to show good faith and due care on the part of the management of the data bank operation and a reasonable effort to keep the information accurate.

Liability for defamation by computer may arise under the federal Fair Credit Reporting Act of 1970 when the person affected is a consumer. The federal Credit Card Act of 1970 further protects from defamation by computer. These acts, which are not limited to situations involving computers, are discussed in Chapter 8 on consumer protection.

§ 10:17. Disparagement of Goods and Slander of Title.

In the transaction of business, one is entitled to be free from interference by means of malicious, false statements made by others as to the title or the quality of goods sold by the business. Actual damage must be proved by the plaintiff to have resulted from the false communications by the defendant to a third person.[22] The plaintiff must show that in consequence thereof the third person had refrained from dealing with the plaintiff.

§ 10:18. Infringement of Trade and Service Marks.

A **trademark** or **servicemark** is a word, name, device, symbol, or any combination of these, used by a manufacturer or seller of goods or a provider of services to distinguish those goods and services from those of other persons. When the mark of a particular person is used or substantially copied by another, it is said that the mark is infringed. The owner of the mark may sue for damages and enjoin its wrongful use.[23]

§ 10:19. Infringement of Patents.

A grant of a patent entitles the patentee to prevent others for a period of 17 years from making, using, or selling a particular invention. Anyone so doing without the patentee's permission is guilty of a patent infringement. If the inventor does not have a patent or if the patent is invalid, anyone may copy the invention without liability.

An infringement occurs even though all parts or features of an invention are not copied, if there is a substantial identity of names, operations, and result between the original and the new device. In the case of a process, however, all successive steps or their equivalent must be copied. In the case of a combination of an ingredient, the use of the same ingredient with others constitutes an infringement, except when the result is a compound essentially different in nature.

---

[22]Advanced Training Systems, Inc. v Caswell Equipment Co. Inc. _____ Minn _____, 352 NW2d 1 (1984).
[23]§ 22:3 of this book.

§ 10:20.   Infringement of Copyrights.

A wrong similar to the infringement of a patent is the infringement of a copyright. A copyright is the right given by statute to prevent others for a limited time from printing, copying, or publishing a production resulting from intellectual labor. The right exists for the life of the author and for fifty years thereafter.[24]

Infringement of a copyright in general consists of copying the form of expression of ideas or conceptions. There is no copyright in the idea or conception itself, but only in the particular way in which it is expressed. In order to constitute an infringement, the production need not be reproduced entirely nor be exactly the same as the original. Reproduction of a substantial part of the original, although paraphrased or otherwise altered, constitutes an infringement; but appropriation of only a word or single line does not.

One guilty of infringement of copyright is liable to the owner for damages, which are to be determined by the court. The owner is also entitled to an injunction to restrain further infringement.

§ 10:21.   Unfair Competition.

Unfair competition is unlawful and the person injured thereby may sue for damages and an injunction to stop the practice, or may report the matter to the Federal Trade Commission or to an appropriate state agency.

It is unfair competition to imitate signs, storefronts, advertisements, and the packaging of goods of a competitor. Thus, when one adopts a box of distinctive size, shape, and color in which to market a product, and the package is imitated by a competitor, the latter is liable for unfair competition.

Every similarity to a competitor, however, is not necessarily unfair competition. For example, the term "downtown" is merely descriptive so that the Downtown Motel can not obtain an injunction against the use of the name Downtown Motor Inn, because a name that is merely descriptive can not be exclusively appropriated or adopted. As an exception, if the descriptive word has been used by a given business for such a long time as to be identified with the business in the public mind, a competitor can not use that name.

The goodwill that is related to a trade name is an important business asset; and there is a judicial trend in favor of protecting a trade name from a competitor's use of a similar name.

FACTS:

Anheuser-Busch holds a trademark registry for the names of Budweiser and Bud as applied to beer which it manufactured and sold under the slogan, "Where there's life...there's Bud." It spent millions of dollars advertising with this slogan. Chemical Corporation of America manufactured a combined floor wax and insecticide which it marketed under the slo-gan of "Where there's life...there's bugs." In addition, there was a similarity between the pattern, background, and stage settings of the television commercials employed by both companies. Anheuser-Busch sued for an injunction to prevent the use of such a slogan. The defendant objected on the ground that the parties were not in competing businesses.

[24]Copyright Act of 1976, Act of October 19, 1976, § 302, PL 94-553, 90 Stat 2541, 2572, 17 USC § 302.

DECISION:

It was improper practice for the defendant to imitate the advertising of another enterprise and thus get a "free ride" on the advertising image created by the other enterprise at great expense. It was immaterial that the other enterprise was not a direct competitor of the defendant. [Chemical Corp. v Anheuser-Busch (CA5 Fla) 306 F2d 433, cert den 372 US 965 (1962)]

Historically the law as to unfair competition was only concerned with protecting competitors from unfair competition by their rivals. Under consumer protection statutes, most states now give protection to the consumer who is harmed by unfair competitive practices.

§ 10:22.   Combinations to Divert Trade.

Business relations may be harmed by a combination to keep third persons from dealing with another who is the object of attack. Such a combination, resulting in injury, constitutes an actionable wrong known as conspiracy if the object is unlawful or if a lawful object is sought by unlawful means.

If the object of a combination is to further a lawful interest of the combination, no actionable wrong exists so long as lawful means are employed. For example, when employees are united in a strike they may peacefully persuade others to withhold their patronage from the employer. On the other hand, all combinations to drive or keep away customers or prospective employees by violence, force, threats, or intimidation are actionable wrongs.

Labor laws prohibit some combinations as unfair labor practices, while other combinations to divert trade are condemned as illegal trusts.

§ 10:23.   Interference with Contract.

The tort law relating to interference with contracts and other economic relationships has increased greatly in recent years as the result of the law's seeking to impose upon the marketplace higher ethical standards to prevent the oppression of victims of improper practices. In general terms, when the defendant interferes with and brings about the breach of the contract between a third person and the plaintiff, the circumstances may be such that the plaintiff has an action in tort against the defendant for interfering with contractual relations.

The mere fact that the defendant's voluntary conduct has the effect of interfering with the plaintiff's contract does not establish that the defendant is liable to the plaintiff. For example, when the defendant is acting for what the law regards as a legitimate economic end, a resulting breach of contract between a third person and the plaintiff does not impose liability on the defendant. However, the fact that the defendant is a competitor of the plaintiff does not constitute justification for the defendant's causing third persons to break their contracts with the plaintiff.[25]

[25]Memorial Gardens, Inc. v Olympian Sales & Management Consultants, Inc. _____ Colo _____, 690 P2d 207 (1984).

(a) **Contract Terminable at Will.** The fact that a contract is terminable at will does not deprive it of protection from interference. Likewise it is immaterial that the contract could be ignored because not evidenced by a writing that satisfies the statute of frauds,[26] the rationale of the law being that although the contract could not have been enforced in court, it was probable that the parties would have lived up to their contract had it not been for the interference of the defendant.

(b) **Prospective Contract.** In addition to protecting existing contracts from intentional interference, tort liability is imposed for acts intentionally committed to prevent the making of a contract.

To illustrate, an action may be brought for slander of title when the malicious false statements of the defendant as to the plaintiff's ownership of property scares a buyer away and prevents the plaintiff from making a sale.

§ 10:24.   Wrongful Interference with Business Relations.

One of the fundamental rights of an individual is to earn a living by working or by engaging in trade or business. A wrongful interference with this liberty is a tort.[27]

The right to conduct one's business is, nevertheless, subject to the rights of others. Hence, the injuries suffered by one in business through legitimate competition give no right to redress.

§ 10:25.   Trespass to the Person.

Trespass to the person consists of any contact with the victim's person for which consent was not given. It thus includes what is technically described as a **battery**. It also includes an **assault** in which the victim apprehends the commission of a battery but is in fact not touched, and includes false imprisonment.

In some instances, a person will have a right to use force which would otherwise constitute an unlawful battery.

§ 10:26.   False Imprisonment.

False imprisonment is the intentional, unprivileged detaining of a person without that person's consent.[28] It may take the extreme form of kidnapping. At the other extreme, a shopper who is detained in a store manager's office and questioned as to shoplifting is the victim of false imprisonment where there is no reasonable ground for believing that the shopper is a thief. False imprisonment also includes detention under an official arrest when there is no legal justification for the arrest.

(a) **Detention.** Any detention at any place by any means for any duration of time is sufficient. Stone walls are not required to make a false imprisonment. If a bank robber holds a bank teller at gun point for the pur-

[26]Consolidated Petroleum Industries, Inc v Jacobs (Tex App) 648 SW2d 363 (1983).
[27]Tamiami Trail Tours, Inc. v Cotton (Fla App) 463 So 2d 1126 (1985).
[28]Walker v Portland, 71 Or App 693, 693 P2d 1349 (1985).

pose of preventing the teller from attacking the other robbers or from escaping, there is a sufficient detention.

(b) Consent and Privilege. By definition, no false imprisonment occurs when the person detained consents thereto. For example, when a merchant without any justification detains a person on the suspicion of shoplifting, such detention is not a false imprisonment if the victim consents to it without any protest. If the merchant had reasonable ground for believing that the victim was guilty of shoplifting, the action of the merchant was not false imprisonment even though the victim was detained under protest and did not consent thereto. Statutes frequently give merchants a privilege to detain persons reasonably suspected of shoplifting.

§ 10:27.   Trespass to Land.

A **trespass to land** consists of any unpermitted entry below, on, across, or above land. This rule is modified to permit the proper flight of aircraft above the land so long as it does not interfere with a proper use of the land.

§ 10:28.   Trespass to Personal Property.

An illegal invasion of property rights with respect to property other than land constitutes a **trespass to personal property** whether done intentionally or negligently, as when one car hits another. When done in good faith and without negligence, there is no liability in contrast with the case of trespass to land where good faith and absence of negligence is not a defense.

Negligent damage to personal property imposes liability for harm done. Intentional damage to personal property will impose liability for the damage done and also may justify exemplary or punitive damages.

(a) Conversion. A **conversion** occurs when personal property is taken by the wrongdoer and kept from its true owner or prior possessor. For example, a bank clerk commits conversion by unlawfully taking money from the bank. Conversion is the civil side of the crimes relating to stealing. The good faith of the converter, however, is not a defense to civil liability.[29] Thus, an innocent buyer of stolen goods is liable for damages for converting them.

SUMMARY

Conduct that harms other people or their property is generally called a tort. The injured person may sue the wrongdoer to recover damages to compensate for the harm or loss caused. The conduct that is a tort may also be a crime and may sometimes be a breach of contract. Tort liability is generally imposed because of the fault of the wrongdoer and in some cases it is imposed without fault. In any case, the harm-causing conduct of the defendant must be voluntary and must have a causal relationship to the harm sustained. Motive is not required to constitute a tort. In some cases, intent is an essential element of the tort. In others, it is not. Liability is imposed without fault in connection with industrial activity, consumer protection, wild animals, and

[29]Trail Clinic v Bloch, 114 Mich App 700, 319 NW2d 638 (1982).

certain areas of liability to workers or to victims of automobile collisions. Negligence is the failure to follow the degree of care that would be followed by a reasonably prudent person in order to avoid foreseeable harm. If the negligence of the plaintiff contributes to the plaintiff's harm, the recovery obtained by the plaintiff may be reduced proportionately or barred depending upon the type of comparative negligence rule that is in force. In a minority of states, the common-law rule is still followed under which any negligence of the plaintiff bars all recovery. Negligence must be proven as a fact although the plaintiff may be aided by the doctrine of res ipsa loquitur which permits an inference of negligence of the defendant when things cause harm and, in the experience of society, harm would not result in the absence of negligence. In most states, the violation of a statute is proof that the defendant was negligent, provided the statute is designed to protect from the kind of harm that has been sustained and the plaintiff is a member of the class that the statute sought to protect. In general, any person aggrieved or harmed by a tort can sue the defendant. In some instances a relative of the injured person will have a right to sue the defendant because of the harm caused. When there are two or more persons causing harm in such a way that it is not possible to determine how much harm was caused by each person, all the persons causing the harm are jointly and severally liable to the plaintiff by the modern trend.

While ordinarily any wrongdoer may be sued, some wrongdoers have a limited immunity while others may be liable for the tortious acts of third persons. Governments may be immune from suit, to some extent minors, parents of the aggrieved person and the spouse of that person may be immune from suit. The trend of the law is to treat charities the same as other defendants and impose tort liability upon them.

Some specific torts include: the causing of mental distress of the victim or of a bystander, either intentionally or negligently; invasion of privacy; defamation by slander, libel, or computer; disparagement of goods and slander of title; infringement of trade and service marks, patents, and copyrights; unfair competition; combinations to divert trade; interference with contracts and with business relations; trespass to person; false imprisonment; trespass to land and to personal property; and conversion.

QUESTIONS AND CASE PROBLEMS

1. What is the objective of each of the following rules of law? (a) In some areas of law, liability for harm exists without regard to whether there was any negligence or intention to cause harm. (b) Geographical and descriptive names cannot ordinarily be adopted as trademarks.
2. Is proof of a bad motive essential to imposing tort liability?
3. The Coleman Construction Company was constructing a highway. It was necessary to blast rock with dynamite. The corporation's employees did this with the greatest of care. In spite of their precautions, some flying fragments of rock damaged a neighboring house. The owner of the house sued the corporation for the damages. The corporation raised the defense that the owner was suing for tort damages and that such damages could not be imposed because the corporation had been free from fault. Was this defense valid?

4. Burnstein drove a car on a country road at 35 miles an hour. The maximum speed limit was 45 miles an hour. He struck and killed a cow that was crossing the road. The owner of the cow sued Burnstein for the value of the cow. Burnstein raised the defense that as there was no driving above the speed limit there could be no liability for negligence. Was this defense valid?

5. The Brunswick Corporation manufactured and sold raincoats which it advertised to consumers as "waterproof" when in fact they were merely "water resistant." The Brunswick Corporation was sued for engaging in unfair competition. It raised the defense that it was not guilty because it was understood in the trade that "waterproof" meant only "water resistant" and therefore no unfair advantage was taken of any competitor. Was this defense valid?

6. Shortly before noon, Reech was jogging around the Broadmoor High School track. He tripped over a small dog owned by Bodin's son. Reech was severely injured when he fell. He sued Bodin on the theory that Bodin had been negligent in failing to restrain the dog. Bodin proved that Reech knew that the dog was on the track and had seen the dog some time prior to the moment when the dog ran between his legs and tripped him. Was Reech entitled to recover? [Reech v Bodin (La App) 286 So2d 477]

7. Jessica Sorensen was a minor. She was riding in an automobile driven by her father, Paul. The car collided with another car. Jessica was injured. She sued her father for her injuries. He raised the defense that a child could not sue its father for negligence. Was he correct? [Sorensen v Sorensen 369 Mass 350, 339 NE2d 907]

8. Henry Neiderman was walking with his small son. An automobile driven by Brodsky went out of control, ran up on the sidewalk, and struck a fire hydrant, a litter pole and basket, a newsstand, and Niederman's son. The car did not touch Niederman, but the shock and fright caused damage to his heart. He sued Brodsky for the harm that he sustained as the result of Brodsky's negligence. Brodsky defended on the ground that he was not liable because he had not touched Niederman. Was this a valid defense? [Niederman v Brodsky, 436 Pa 401, 261 A2d 84]

9. Catalano ran a gasoline service station which was licensed by the State of New York to conduct inspections of motor vehicles. Capital Cities Broadcasting Corporation prepared and televised a "news special" on the subject of the difficulty of obtaining an automobile inspection. It sent an on-the-spot interviewer and photographer to Catalano's station. Catalano, believing that the interviewer was a customer, told her that he could not inspect her automobile because the space in the station was filled with cars being repaired but that, as soon as one of the car stalls was empty, he would take the interviewer's car. This discussion was recorded by the interviewer by means of a concealed tape recorder; but before it was televised, it was edited by eliminating the explanation given by Catalano and thus merely broadcasted his flat refusal to inspect the car. Catalano claimed that this caused him a loss of business and sued Capital for damages. Was it liable? [Catalano v Capital Cities Broadcasting Corp. 313 NYS2d 52]

10. Carrigan, a district manager of Simples Time Recorder Company, was investigating complaints of mismanagement of the Jackson office of the company. He called at the home of Hooks, the secretary of that office. She expressed the opinion that part of the trouble was caused by stealing of parts and equipment by McCall, another employee. McCall was later discharged and sued Hooks for slander. Was she liable? [Hooks v McCall (Miss) 272 So2d 925]

11. Giles, a guest at a Pick Hotel, wanted to remove his brief case from the right-hand side of the front seat of his auto. To support himself while so doing, he placed his left hand on the center door pillar of the right-hand side of the car. The hotel bellboy closed the rear door of the car without noticing Giles' hand. One of Giles' fingers was smashed by the closing of the door and thereafter had to be amputated. Giles sued the Pick Hotels Corp. Was he entitled to recover? [Giles v Pick Hotels Corp. (CA6 Mich) 232 F2d 887]

12. Burdett repaired a neon sign on the restaurant of Cinquanta. They disagreed whether Cinquanta or his insurance company should pay for the work. Burdett and some friends went to the restaurant and ordered an expensive meal for which they refused to pay. A heated argument followed in which Burdett stated to Cinquanta, "I don't like doing business with crooks. You're a deadbeat. You've owed me $155 for three or four months. You're crooks." Cinquanta sued Burdett for slander but did not show in what way he had been damaged by these remarks. Burdett claimed that he was not liable for slander. Decide. [Cinquanta v Burdett, 154 Colo 37, 388 P2d 779]

13. A statute required that air vent shafts on hotel roofs have parapets at least 30 inches high. Edgar Hotel had parapets only 27 inches high. Nunneley was visiting a registered guest at the Edgar Hotel. She placed a mattress on top of a parapet. When she sat on the mattress, the parapet collapsed and she fell into the air shaft and was injured. She sued the hotel, claiming that its breach of the statute as to the height of the parapets constituted negligence. Decide. [Nunneley v Edgar Hotel, 36 Cal 2d 493, 225 P2d 497]

14. A, B, and C owned land. They did some construction work on their land which prevented the free flow of surface water and caused a flooding of land owned by D. D sued A for the damage caused his land by the flooding. A claimed that D could not hold him liable for any damage since D could not prove how much of the total damage had been caused by A, and how much by B and C, and that in any event, A could not be liable for more than 1/3 of the total damage sustained by D. Decide. [Thorson v Minot (ND) 153 NW2d 764]

15. Tom Lawrence took his automobile to Wayne Strand Pontiac-GMC, Inc., for repairs. Wayne left the car on its lot with the key in the ignition. Two weeks later Lawrence's car was stolen. Ronald Williamson was driving his car and came into the vicinity of the stolen car just as the thieves abandoned it and ran away on foot. In order to avoid hitting the thieves, Williamson swerved. In so doing, he struck the abandoned car and was injured. He then sued Wayne Strand for damages. Was Wayne liable for damages? [Williamson v Wayne Strand Pontiac-GMC, Inc. (Tex App) 658 SW2d 263]

16. Collete Bass worked in a building owned by Nooney Company. As part of her job she was going from one floor to another when the elevator stopped moving. She was alone in the elevator for about an hour before she was rescued. The emergency phone in the elevator was dead. She sued the Nooney Company for the mental distress to which she was subjected. The Nooney Company claimed that it was not liable because there was no proof that it had been negligent. Bass claimed Nooney had the burden of proving that it was not negligent. Was she correct? [Bass v Nooney Co. (Mo) 646 SW2d 765]

PART 2

CONTRACTS

Chapter 11 Nature and Classes of Contracts
Chapter 12 The Agreement
Chapter 13 Contractual Capacity
Chapter 14 Genuineness of Assent
Chapter 15 Consideration
Chapter 16 Legality and Public Policy
Chapter 17 Form of Contract
Chapter 18 Interpretation of Contracts
Chapter 19 Third Persons and Contracts
Chapter 20 Discharge of Contracts
Chapter 21 Breach of Contract and Remedies

CHAPTER 11

NATURE AND CLASSES OF

CONTRACTS

CHAPTER OBJECTIVES

After studying this chapter you will be able to:
1. List the essential elements of a contract.
2. Describe the way in which a contract arises.
3. State how contracts are classified.
4. Differentiate contracts from agreements that are not contracts.
5. Differentiate formal contracts from simple contracts.
6. Differentiate express contracts from implied contracts.
7. Differentiate contractual liability from quasi-contractual liability.
8. Solve problems involving the classification of contracts.

Practically every personal business activity involves a contract: an enrollment in college, the purchase of a color TV, the renting of an apartment. In each transaction relating to the acquisition of raw materials, their manufacture, and the distribution of the finished product by businesses, there are contracts that define the relationship and the rights and obligations of the parties. As pervasive as contracts are in our lives, the legal language of contracts is not very familiar to most of us. For that reason, this introductory chapter is devoted primarily to the terminology or vocabulary that is needed to work with contract law.

In addition, Chapter 11 deals with something called quasi contracts. These, as you might guess, are not true contracts. They lack some essential element that the law requires of a true contract. Nevertheless, society through its laws has created this special class of obligations that will be enforced in a limited way.

§ 11:1.   Definition of a Contract.

A **contract** is a binding agreement.[1] By one definition "a contract is a promise or a set of promises for the breach of which the law gives a remedy, or the performance of which the law in some way recognizes as a duty."[2] Contracts arise out of agreements; hence a contract may be defined as an agreement creating an obligation.

The substance of the definition of a contract is that by mutual agreement or assent the parties create enforceable duties or obligations that are legally binding. That is, each party is obligated to do or to refrain from doing certain acts.[3]

The substance of the definition of a contract is that by mutual agreement or assent the parties create enforceable duties or obligations that are legally binding.

§ 11:2.   Elements of a Contract.

The elements of a contract are: (1) an agreement, (2) between competent parties, (3) based upon the genuine assent of the parties, (4) supported by consideration, (5) made for a lawful objective, and (6) in the form required by law, if any. These elements will be considered in the chapters that follow.

§ 11:3.   Subject Matter of Contracts.

The subject matter of a contract may relate to the performance of personal services, such as contracts of employment to work on an assembly line in a factory, to work as a secretary in an office, to sing on television, or to build a house. The contract may provide for the transfer of ownership of property, such as a house (real property) or an automobile (personal property), from one person to another. A contract may also call for a combination of these things. For example, a builder may contract to supply materials and do the work involved in installing the materials, or a person may contract to build a house and then transfer the house and the land to the buyer.

§ 11:4.   Parties to a Contract.

A person who makes a promise is the **promisor,** and the person to whom the promise is made is called the **promisee.** If the promise is binding, it imposes upon the promisor a duty or obligation and the promisor may be called the **obligor.** The promisee who can claim the benefit of the obligation is also called the **obligee.** The parties to a contract are said to stand in privity with each other, and the relationship between them is termed **privity of contract.**

In written contracts, parties may be referred to by name. More often, however, they are given special names that serve better to identify each party.

---

[1]The Uniform Commercial Code defines "contract" to mean "the total legal obligation which results from the parties' agreement as affected by [the Code] and any other applicable rules of law," UCC § 1-201(11).

[2]Restatement, Contracts, 2d § 1.

[3]Matherly v Hanson, _____ Iowa _____, 359 NW2d 450 (1984).

For example, the parties to a contract by which one person agrees that another may occupy a house upon the payment of money are called landlord and tenant, or lessor and lessee, and the contract between them is known as a lease. Other parties have their distinctive names, such as vendor and vendee, for the parties to a sales contract; shipper and carrier, for the parties to a transportation contract; and insurer and insured, for the parties to an insurance policy.

A party to a contract may be an individual, a partnership, a corporation, or a government. A party to a contract may be an agent acting on behalf of another person. There may be one or more persons on each side of the contract. In some cases there are three-sided contracts, as in the case of a credit card transaction, which involves the company issuing the card, the holder of the card, and the business furnishing goods and services in reliance on the credit card.

In addition to the original parties to the contract, other persons may have rights or duties with respect to it. For example, one party may to some extent assign rights under the contract to a third person. Also, the contract may have been made for the benefit of a third person, as in a life insurance contract, in which case the third person (the beneficiary) is permitted to enforce the contract.

✗ (b) § 11:5.   How a Contract Arises.

A contract is based upon an agreement. An agreement arises when one person, the **offeror**, makes an offer and the person to whom the offer is made, the **offeree**, accepts.[4]

FACTS:

Kalalinick was injured by Knoll. The claim for the injuries was covered by insurance that Knoll carried with the Country Mutual Insurance Company. Country Mutual made an offer to Kalalinick to settle the claim. Kalalinick accepted the offer. Later Country Mutual refused to pay as required by the settlement agreement. Kalalinick sued Knoll and Country Mutual. Country Mutual claimed that the settlement agreement was not binding because Knoll had not acted in reliance on the agreement.

DECISION:

Judgment for Kalalinick. A bilateral contract was formed as soon as the insurer's offer was accepted by Kalalinick. There was no requirement that Kalalinick do any act in reliance on the agreement in order to make it a binding contract. [Kalalinick v Knoll, 97 Ill App 3d 660, 52 Ill Dec 802, 422 NE2d 1011 (1981)]

There must be both an offer and an acceptance. If either is lacking, there is no contract.

[4]Dura-wood Treating Company v Century Forest Industries, Inc. (CA5 Tex) 675 F2d 745 (1982).

An offeror may make an offer to a particular person or it may be made to the public at large. The latter case arises, for example, when a reward is offered to the public for the return of lost property.

It is frequently said that a meeting of minds is essential to an agreement or a contract. Modern courts do not stress the meeting of the minds, however, because in some situations the law finds an agreement even though the minds of the parties have not in fact met. The real test is not whether the minds of the parties met, but whether under the circumstances one party was reasonably entitled to believe that there was an offer and the other to believe that there was an acceptance.

§ 11:6. Intent to Make a Binding Agreement.

Because a contract is based on the consent of the parties and is a legally binding agreement, it follows that there must be an intent to enter into an agreement which is binding.

FACTS:

A movement was organized to build a Charles City College. Hauser and others signed pledges to contribute to the college. At the time of signing, Hauser inquired what would happen if he should die or be unable to pay. The representative of the college stated that the pledge would not then be binding and was merely a statement of intent. The college failed financially and Pappas was appointed receiver to collect and liquidate the assets of the college corporation. He sued Hauser for the amount due on his pledge. Hauser raised the defense that the pledge was not a binding contract.

DECISON:

Judgment for Hauser. From the statements of the representative of the college, it was clear that the pledge had not been intended by the parties as a binding agreement. It was therefore not a contract and could not be enforced against Hauser. [Pappas v Hauser, 293 Iowa 102, 197 NW2d 607 (1972)]

Sometimes the parties are in agreement but their agreement does not produce a contract. Sometimes there is merely a preliminary agreement but the parties never actually make a contract. It may be merely an agreement as to future plans or intentions without any contractual obligation to carry out those plans or intentions.

§ 11:7. Enclosed Printed Matter.

Frequently a contract is mailed or delivered by one party to the other in an envelope which contains additional printed matter. Similarly, when goods are purchased, the buyer often receives with the goods a manufacturer's manual and various pamphlets. What effect do all these papers have upon the contract?

CONTRACT

Parties	This contract is executed between the Lookout Alarm System, herein called "System," of 276 West Jackson Street, Phoenix, Arizona, and A.J. Armstrong herein called "Homeowner," of 737 Inwood Drive, Phoenix, Arizona.
Installation	System agrees to install a burglar alarm system at the above address of the Homeowner, in accordance with the specifications that are attached hereto.
Payment	Homeowner agrees to pay System for the above installation the sum of $3,863.00, $663.00 being paid upon execution of this contract and the balance of $3,200.00 being paid within 90 days following satisfactory completion of the work by System.

Lookout Alarm System

By _S.J. McRory_   _A. J. Armstrong_
S.J. McRory, President   A.J. Armstrong

July 1, 19--   _July 1, 19--_
Date   Date

CONTRACT. Note that this contract includes the important items of information: (1) the name and address of each party, (2) the promise or consideration of the seller, (3) the promise or consideration of the buyer, (4) the signatures of the two parties, (5) the date.

(a) **Incorporation of Other Statement.** The contract itself may furnish the answer. Sometimes the contract will expressly refer to and incorporate into the contract the terms of the other writing or printed statement. For example, a warehouse contract may expressly state that it covers the "goods" of the customer, but instead of listing the goods, the contract will continue by following the words "goods of the customer" with the words "as set forth in Schedule A which is delivered to the customer with this contract." Frequently such a schedule will be stapled or otherwise attached to the contract itself. Or the contract may say that the customer will be charged at the rates set forth in the approved tariff schedule posted on the premises of the warehouse, and may continue with the words, "a copy of which is attached hereto and made part of this contract."

(b) **Exclusion of Other Statement.** As the opposite of incorporation, the contract may declare that there is nothing outside of the contract. This means that either there never was anything else or that any prior agreement was merely a preliminary step which is finally canceled out or erased and the contract in its final form is stated in the writing. For example, the seller of goods may state in the contract that no statements as to the goods have been made to the buyer and that the written contract contains all of the terms of the sale.

(c) **Reduction of Contract Terms.** The effect of accompanying or subsequently delivered printed matter may be to reduce the terms of the written contract. That is, one party may have had a better bargain under the original contract. In this case the accompanying matter will generally be ignored if it is not shown that the party who would be harmed had agreed that it be part of the contract.

This is so because a contract once made cannot be changed by unilateral action; that is, by the action of one party or one side of the contract without the agreement of the other.

FACTS:

The School District mailed a teaching contract to Adamick. In the same envelope there was a copy of the school calendar. Adamick and other teachers later brought an action against the school to prevent it from holding classes on three dates specified in the calendar as holidays. The District defended on the ground that the calendar could be changed by the District.

DECISION:

The contract did not make any specific reference to the school calendar which had been mailed in the same envelope. The school calendar was therefore not part of the contract and there was no contract obligation on the school district to treat as holidays any days which were so specified in the calendar. [Adamick v Ferguson-Florissant School District (Mo App) 483 SW2d 629 (1972)]

---

 § 11:8.   Formal and Informal Contracts.

Contracts can be classified as formal or informal contracts.

(a) **Formal Contracts. Formal contracts** are enforced because the formality with which they are executed is considered sufficient to signify that the parties intend to be bound by their terms. Formal contracts include (1) contracts under seal, (2) contracts of record, and (3) negotiable instruments.

A **contract under seal** is executed by affixing a seal or making an impression upon the paper or upon some tenacious substance, such as wax, attached to the instrument. Although at common law an impression was necessary, the courts now treat various signs or marks to be the equivalent of a seal. Most states hold that there is a seal if a person's signature or a corporation's name is followed by a scroll or scrawl, the word "seal," or the letters "L.S." In some jurisdictions the body of the contract must recite that the parties are sealing the contract, in addition to their making a seal following their signatures.[5]

FACTS:

Square D Company made a contract with C.J. Kern Contractors, Inc. The corporate seal of Kern appeared on the contract. Was the contract a sealed contract?

DECISION:

The contract with Kern was not a sealed contract. The mere presence of the corporate seal on the paper did not by itself make it a sealed contract without some statement in the contract or other evidence that it was intended to be a sealed contract. [Square D Co. v C.J. Kern Contractors, Inc. 314 NC 423, 334 SE2d 63 (1985)]

A contract under seal was binding at common law solely because of its formality. In many states, this has been changed by statute. The Uniform Commercial Code abolishes the law of seals for the sale of goods. In some states the law of seals has been abolished generally without regard to the nature of the transaction involved.

A **contract of record** is an agreement or obligation that has been recorded by a court. One form of contract of record arises when one acknowledges before a proper court the obligation to pay a certain sum unless a specified condition is met. For example, a party who has been arrested may be released on a promise to appear in court and may agree to pay a certain sum on failing to do so. An obligation of this kind is known as a **recognizance.**

Similarly, an agreement made with an administrative agency is binding because it has been so made. For example, when a business agrees with the Federal Trade Commission that the enterprise will stop a particular practice which the Commission regards as unlawful, the business is bound by its agreement and cannot thereafter reject it.

Negotiable instruments are contracts governed by the law of commercial paper. These special purpose contracts must meet certain formal requirements in order to be enforceable.

[5]Lumbermen's Mutual Cas. Co. v Pattillo Constr. Co. 172 Ga App 452, 323 SE2d 649 (1984).

(b) **Informal Contracts.** All other contracts are called **informal,** or **simple, contracts** without regard to whether they are oral or written. These contracts are enforceable not because of the form of the transaction but because they represent the agreement of the parties.

§ 11:9.   Express and Implied Contracts.

Simple contracts may be classified in terms of the way in which they are created, as express contracts or implied contracts.

(a) **Express Contracts.** An **express contract** is one in which the agreement of the parties is manifested by their words, whether spoken or written.[6]

(b) **Implied Contracts.** An **implied contract** (or, as sometimes stated, a contract implied in fact) is one in which the agreement is not shown by words, written or spoken, but by the acts and conduct of the parties.[7] Such a contract arises, for example, when one person renders services under circumstances indicating that payment for them is expected, and the other person, knowing such circumstances, accepts the benefit of those services. Similarly, when an owner requested a professional roofer to make repairs to the roof of a building, an obligation arose to pay the reasonable value of such services although no agreement had been made as to compensation.

FACTS:

Anisgard was a tennis professional. He suggested to Bray and his partner a plan for constructing a tennis facility that would be managed by Anisgard. Anisgard gave Bray all the information that he had acquired as to the proper location of the facility, the feasibility study that he had obtained, the arrangements that he had made for the leasing of a building, and the identity of a bank willing to finance the operation. Bray used this information in constructing the tennis facility but never paid Anisgard anything for the information or the work involved in developing the information. Anisgard had expected to be paid for such information and there had been several discussions with Bray as to the amount to be paid. No agreement was ever reached by the parties. Anisgard sued Bray for compensation for the reasonable value of his services. Bray defended on the ground that there was no contract calling for such payment.

DECISION:

Judgment for Anisgard. Although no express contract had been made for compensation, that did not bar recovery. The services were rendered with the expectation of receiving compensation and the benefit of the services was accepted by Bray with knowledge that payment was expected. Accordingly there arose an implied contract to pay the reasonable value of those services. [Anisgard v Bray, 11 Mass App 726, 419 NE2d 315 (1981)]

---

[6]Gratkowski v United States, 6 Ct Cl 458 (1984).
[7]Gary-Wheaton Bank v Burt, 104 Ill App 3d 767, 60 Ill Dec 518, 433 NE2d 315 (1982).

In terms of effect, there is no difference between an implied contract and an express contract. The difference relates solely to the manner of proving the existence of the contract.

An implied contract cannot arise when there is an existing express contract on the same subject. Likewise, no contract is implied when the relationship of the parties is such that by a reasonable interpretation the performance of services or the supplying of goods was intended as a gift.[8]

§ 11:10.   Valid and Voidable Contracts and Void Agreements.

Contracts may be classified in terms of enforceability or validity.

(a) **Valid Contracts.** A **valid contract** is an agreement that is binding and enforceable.

(b) **Voidable Contracts.** A **voidable contract** is an agreement that is otherwise binding and enforceable but, because of the circumstances surrounding its execution or the lack of capacity of one of the parties, it may be rejected at the option of one of the parties. For example, a person who has been forced to sign an agreement which that person would not have voluntarily signed may in some instances avoid the contract.

(c) **Void Agreements.** A **void agreement** is without legal effect. An agreement that contemplates the performance of an act prohibited by law is usually incapable of enforcement; hence it is void. Likewise, it cannot be made binding by later approval or ratification.[9]

§ 11:11.   Executed and Executory Contracts.

Contracts may be classified, in terms of the extent to which they have been performed, as executed contracts and executory contracts.

(a) **Executed Contracts.** An **executed contract** is one that has been completely performed. In other words, an executed contract is one under which nothing remains to be done by either party.[10] A contract may be executed at once, as in the case of a cash sale; or it may be executed or performed in the future.

(b) **Executory Contracts.** In an **executory contract**, something remains to be done by one or both parties. For example, if a utility company agrees to furnish electricity to a customer for a specified period of time at a stipulated price, the contract is executory. If the entire price is paid in advance, the contract is still deemed executory; although, strictly speaking, it is executed on one side and executory on the other.

§ 11:12.   Bilateral and Unilateral Contracts.

In making an offer, the offeror is in effect extending a promise to do something, such as to pay a sum of money, if the offeree will do what the

---

[8]Beecham's Estate, _____ Minn App _____, 361 NW2d 86 (1985).

[9]See § 16:1. Although the distinction between a void agreement and a voidable contract is clear in theory, there is frequently confusion because some courts describe a given transaction as void while others regard it as merely voidable.

[10]Lockheed Missiles v Gilmore Industries, 135 Cal App 3d 556, 185 Cal Rptr 409 (1982).

offeror requests. If the offeror extends a promise and asks for a promise in return and if the offeree accepts the offer by making the promise, the contract is called a **bilateral contract** because one promise is given in exchange for another and each party is bound by the obligation. For example, when the house painter offers to paint the owner's house for $1,000 and the owner promises to pay $1,000 for the job, there is an exchange of promises and the agreement gives rise to a bilateral contract.

In contrast, the offeror may offer to do something only when something is done by the offeree. As only one party is obligated to perform after the contract has been made, this kind of contract is called a **unilateral contract**. This is illustrated by the case of the reward for the return of lost property because the offeror does not wish to have promises by members of the public that they will try to return the property. The offeror wants the property and promises to pay anyone who returns the property. The offer of a unilateral contract calls for an act and a promise to do the act does not give rise to a contract.[11]

FACTS:

Cook took employment with Heck's Inc. Some time thereafter she was fired. She brought suit against Hecks's for breach of contract. She claimed that the contract was to be found in the employer's manual that was given to her in which the employer stated the terms of employment and of employment security.

DECISION:

The employment provisions of the employer's manual constituted the offer of a unilateral contract because the employer was seeking the performing of work in return for the promises in the handbook. This offer was accepted by Cook's continuing to work at Heck's. Once accepted, the terms of the manual bound Heck's by a contract. [Cook v Heck's Inc. _____ WVa _____, 342 SE2d 453 (1986)]

---

§ 11:13.   Quasi Contracts.

In some cases, the courts will pretend that there is a contract when in fact there is no contract. Such a "make believe" contract is called a **quasi contract**.[12]

(a) **Prevention of unjust enrichment.** These quasi contracts are recognized in a limited number of situations in order to attain an equitable or just result. These instances may be classified in terms of situations in which there is no contract between the parties, those in which there was a contract between the parties but it has been avoided, and those in which there was an attempted contract but for some reason the agreement is held illegal and therefore void.

(1) No Contract. In some cases the hoped for contract is never formed. The parties expect there will be a contract but something happens

[11]Deer Creek, Inc. v Clarendon Hot Springs Ranch, Inc. 107 Idaho 286, 688 P2d 1191 (1984).

[12]Stanley Smith & Sons v Limestone College, 283 SC App 430, 322 SE2d 474 (1984).

that prevents their reaching a final agreement. Meanwhile, one or more of the parties may have jumped the gun and begun performing as though there were a contract. When it is finally clear that there is no contract, a party who had rendered some performance will seek to be paid for what was done. The claim will be made that if payment is not made the other party will be unjustly enriched.

The "no contract" case may arise in a situation where there is a mistake as to the subject matter of the contract. For example, a painter may begin painting the house of A because of a mistake as to the address of the building. A sees the work going on and realizes the painter is making a mistake. Nevertheless, A does not stop the painter. When the painter finishes the work and presents a bill for painting, A then refuses to pay because there never was a contract. This is true because A never expressly agreed for the painting. Likewise, the conduct of A never caused the painter as a reasonable person to believe that A was entering into a contract. The painter just assumed that everything was all right.

In such case, the law deems it inequitable that A should have remained silent and then reaped the benefits of the painter's mistake. A will therefore be required to pay the painter the reasonable value of the painting. This liability is described as quasi contractual.

(2) *The Avoided Contract.* In some situations, one party to the contract may be able to avoid it or set it aside. As will be seen in Chapter 13, the contract of a minor can be avoided. If the contract was for a necessary received by the minor, the minor must pay the reasonable value of what was received. The minor is not required to pay the contract price but only the reasonable value of the benefit received. As the liability enforced against the minor is not based on the contract, it is called quasi contractual.

(3) *The Void Agreement.* In some instances, the parties make a contract, one party receives the benefit of the contract, and then the benefited party seeks to avoid paying on the ground that the contract was void because of illegality. For example, governmental units, such as cities, must generally advertise for the lowest responsible bidder when a contract is to be made to obtain supplies or to construct buildings. In some instances, the city officials may improperly skip the advertising. This might be done either because of a corrupt purpose or because the officials honestly but wrongly believed that the particular contract came within an exception to the requirement of advertising. Whatever the reason, the city officials enter into a contract with a contractor without following the statutory procedures. The contractor fully performs the contract. When the contractor requests to be paid, the city officials refuse to live up to the contract on the ground that the contract violated the statutory requirements and therefore was illegal and therefore was void. In such cases, it will be held that although the contract is void, the city must still pay the reasonable value of what has been done. In this way, the contractor gets paid for what the contractor really did. The city is not required to pay for any more than it has actually received. The danger of the city's paying out inflated prices, which was the evil that the advertising statute sought to avoid, does not arise because the court does not require the city to pay the contract price but only the reasonable value of the benefit conferred upon the city.

(b) When Quasi-Contractual Liability Does Not Exist. While the objective of the quasi contract is to do justice, one must not jump to the conclusion that a quasi contract will arise every time there is an injustice. The mere fact that someone has benefited someone else and has not been paid will not necessarily give rise to a quasi contract. For example, no quasi-contractual obligation arises when the plaintiff merely confers upon the defendant a benefit to which the defendant was already entitled.

(1) Unexpected Cost. The fact that performance of a contract proves more difficult or more expensive than had been expected does not entitle a party to extra compensation when there was no misrepresentation as to the conditions that would be encountered or the events that would occur and particularly when the party complaining is experienced with the particular type of contract and the problems which are likely to be encountered. That is, the contractor is not entitled to quasi-contractual recovery for extra expense on the theory that the extra work had conferred a greater benefit than had been contemplated.

(2) Contract with Third Person. When a person has a binding contract with a third person, only that person is required to pay for the performance made under the contract. Even though performance did benefit the defendant, the person cannot sue the defendant for quasi contract when the third person fails to make payment under the contract. For example, a subcontractor doing work which benefits the homeowner can only sue the contractor on the contract between the subcontractor and the contractor. The subcontractor cannot sue the owner merely because the owner was benefited by the work done by the subcontractor.[13]

FACTS:

Lombard insured his car. When it was damaged, the insurer took the car to General Auto Service for repairs. The insurance company did not pay the repair bill. General Auto Service sued Lombard for the repair bill because he had benefited by the repair work.

DECISION:

Judgment for Lombard. General Auto Service had a contract with the insurance company. The fact that the insurance company did not pay in accordance with its contract did not give General the right to sue Lombard, even though he had benefited by the work done. General could only sue the insurance company on its contract and could not sue Lombard in quasi contract. [General Auto Service, Inc. v Lombard (La) 151 So2d 536 (1963)]

---

(3) No Unjust Enrichment. In order to recover in quasi contract the plaintiff must prove that the defendant was enriched, the extent or dollar value of such enrichment, and that such enrichment was unjust.[14] If the

[13]Note that state statutes generally give unpaid laborers and suppliers of material a mechanics' lien on the building they construct in order to overcome the inability to sue the owner. See § 44:5(b) in this book.

[14]Otworth v Southern Pacific Transportation Co. 166 Cal App 3d 452, 212 Cal Rptr 743 (1985)

plaintiff can not prove all these elements, there can be no recovery in quasi contract.

SUMMARY

A contract is an agreement of two or more parties that they intend to be binding (contractual intent). A contract arises when an offer is accepted with such intent. When more than one document is involved or more than one conversation is held, a question arises as to how much is to be regarded as part of the agreement of the parties. When a written contract is sent with additional printed matter, the question arises whether the additional matter is part of the contract or is excluded from the contract and whether it reduces or modifies the terms of the contract.

Contracts may be classified in a number of ways, as to parties, subject matter, form, manifestation, validity, and obligations. With respect to form, a contract may be formal, such as those under seal or those appearing on the records of courts or administrative agencies. The manifestation of the agreement distinguishes between agreements that are expressed by words, written or oral, and those that are expressed by or deduced from conduct. The question of validity requires distinguishing between contracts that are valid, those that are voidable, and those that are not contracts at all but merely void agreements. Contracts can be distinguished, on the basis of the obligations created, as executed contracts in which everything has been performed and executory contracts in which something remains to be done. The bilateral contract is formed by exchanging a promise for a promise and therefore each party has the obligation of thereafter rendering the promised performance. In the unilateral contract, which is the doing of an act in exchange for a promise, no performance is required of the offeree performing the act and the only obligation is that of the promisor. In certain situations, the law regards it as unjust that a person should receive a benefit and not pay for it. In such case, the law of quasi contracts allows the performing person to recover the reasonable value of the benefit conferred upon the benefited person, even though there is no contract of any kind between them requiring any payment. The unjust enrichment that the concept of quasi contract is designed to prevent sometimes arises when there never was any contract between the persons involved or when there was a contract but for some reason it was avoided or held that it was merely a void agreement. Quasi contractual recovery is not allowed merely because someone loses money. It is not allowed merely because the cost of performance under a contract rises above that contemplated; because a third person breaks a contract with the performing person to pay for services rendered under that contract; or because the performing party is unable to prove that there was any enrichment, the extent of such enrichment, or that any enrichment was unjust.

QUESTIONS AND CASE PROBLEMS

1. State the specific objective(s) of the law (from the list in Chapter 2, § 2:2) illustrated by the following quotation: "A person shall not be allowed to enrich himself unjustly at the expense of another."

Note: As you study the various rules of law in this chapter and the chapters that follow, consider each rule in relationship to its social, economic, and moral background. Try to determine the particular objective(s) of each important rule. To the extent that you are able to analyze law as the product of society striving for justice, you will have a greater insight into the law itself, the world in which you live, the field of business, and the human mind.

2. What is a contract?

3. Ackerman went to the phone book and sent letters to randomly selected names. The letter to each stated, "It is agreed that we will paint your house for a price based on the cost of our labor and paint plus an additional 10% for profit." He sent such a letter to Maria. Is there a contract between Ackerman and Maria?

4. Henry makes a written contract to paint Betty's house for $500. The reasonable value of such work is $1,000. Henry made the price low in the hope that Betty's neighbors would have him paint their houses. He painted Betty's house. He got no work from the neighbors. He then sent Betty a bill for $1,000 on the ground that an implied contract existed to pay him the reasonable value of his services. Was he entitled to recover $1,000?

5. Henry said to Hilda, "I want to buy your old automobile." She replied, "It's yours for $400.00." Henry replied, "I'll take it." Later Henry changed his mind and refused to take or pay for the car. When Hilda sued him for damages he raised the defense that he had never made a contract with her because they had never expressly stated, "We hereby make a contract for the sale of the automobile." Henry claimed that in the absence of such an express declaration showing that they intended to make a contract there could be no binding agreement to purchase the automobile. Was he correct?

6. The Acme Machinery Company installed a furnace in the home of Milton. Milton has not yet paid the balance due. Is the contract executed or executory?

7. Cynthia took a package of food from the shelf of the Royal Supermarket and paid for it at the cashier's counter. Cynthia later sued Royal because of a defect in the product. Royal raised the defense that it could not be sued because it had never made a contract with Cynthia for the sale of the product. Was Royal correct?

8. Compare an implied contract and a quasi contract.

9. A made a contract to construct a house for B. Subsequently, B sued A for breach of contract. A raised the defense that the contract was not binding because it was not sealed. Is this a valid defense? [Cooper v G. E. Construction Co. 116 Ga App 690, 158 SE2d 305]

10. Prior to the death of Emma Center, her nephew's wife, Clara Stewart, rendered various household services to Emma. All of the parties lived in the same house as a family group. During most of the time in question, Clara also had a full-time job. After Emma's death, Clara sued Emma's estate for the value of her household services. Was Clara entitled to recover? [Stewart v Brandenburg (Ky) 383 SW2d 1122]

11. Martha Parker reared Louis Twiford as a foster son from the time he was 6 or 7 years of age. He lived with her until he was 27 years of age when he married and moved into another house. During the next few years Martha was very ill, and Louis took care of her. She died, and Louis made a claim against Waterfield, her executor, for the reasonable value of the services he had rendered. Was he entitled to recover? [Twiford v Waterfield, 240 NC 582, 83 SE2d 548]

12. Dozier and his wife, daughter, and grandson lived in the house Dozier owned. At the request of the daughter and grandson, Paschall made some improvements to the house. Dozier did not authorize these, but he knew that the improvements were being made and did not object to them. Paschall sued Dozier for the reasonable value of the improvements. Dozier defended on the ground that he had not made any contract for such improvements. Was he obligated to pay for such improvements?

13. Harriet went away for the summer. In her absence, Landry, a house-painter, painted her house. Landry had a contract to paint a neighbor's house but painted Harriet's house by mistake. The painting of Harriet's house was worth $1,000.00. When she returned from her vacation, Landry billed her for $1,000.00. She refused to pay. He claimed that she had a quasi-contractual liability for that amount. Was he correct?

14. Bidwell took his auto to German Motors, Inc. for repairs. He specifically directed the mechanic to repair the engine. Instead of repairing the engine, the mechanic replaced it with a rebuilt engine. Bidwell did not know this until he was handed the bill for the work. The mechanic claimed that the replacement of the engine was the most economical thing to do. Was Bidwell liable for the cost of the new engine and the labor involved? [Bidwell v German Motors, Inc. 41 Colo App 284, 586 P2d 1003]

15. William was a certified public accountant. He did all the accounting work for his wife, Frances. William and Frances were divorced but remained friendly. William continued to perform the accounting services as before and also for North Star Motors, a business operated by the brother of Frances. When Frances sued William on a promissory note, he counterclaimed for compensation for his accounting services rendered to his ex-wife and her brother on the theory that an implied contract arose to pay him for such services. Was he entitled to recover on the counterclaim? [Ryan v Ryan (Del Super) 298 A2d 343]

16. Margrethe and Charles Pyeatte were married. They agreed that she would work so that he could go to law school and that when he finished law school she would go back to school for her Master's degree. After Charles was admitted to the Bar and before Margrethe went back to school, the two were divorced. She sued Charles for breaking their contract. The court held that there was no contract because the agreement between them was too vague to be enforced. Margrethe then claimed that she was entitled to quasi contractual recovery of the money that she had paid for Charles' support and law school tuition. He denied liability. Was she entitled to recover for the money she spent for Charles' maintenance and law school tuition? [Pyeatte v Pyeatte (App) 135 Ariz 346, 661 P2d 196]

17. Thomas M. Maddux and his wife Helen owned a tract of land. They gave Ralph Greene and Edward Lewis the option to purchase part of the land. The buyers agreed that at their expense they would have twelve irrigation wells drilled, seven on the part retained by the sellers and five on the land subject to the option. The agreement further provided that if the buyers exercised the option the purchase price would be reduced by the cost of the seven wells on the part retained by the sellers. The buyers made a contract with the Haggard Drilling Company to drill the wells. Lewis exercised the option to purchase the portion of the tract. Haggard was not paid and sued Greene, Lewis, and Maddux for breach of contract. Maddux raised the defense that he had not made any contract with Haggard. Haggard then claimed that Maddux was liable in quasi contract for the wells. Was Maddux liable? [Haggard Drilling, Inc. v Greene, 195 Neb 136, 236 NW2d 841]

CHAPTER 12

THE AGREEMENT

CHAPTER OBJECTIVES

After studying this chapter you will be able to:
1. Tell whether a statement is an offer.
2. Tell whether an agreement is too indefinite to be enforced.
3. Describe the exceptions that the law makes to the requirement of definiteness.
4. List the ways in which an offer is terminated.
5. Compare offers, firm offers, and option contracts.

As described in Chapter 11, a contract consists of enforceable obligations that have been voluntarily assumed. Thus, one of the essential elements of a contract is an agreement. The importance of requiring an agreement is that it shows that the parties have voluntarily surrendered a part of their freedom of action—they have bound themselves to act in the manner specified in the contract. Because freedom of action is so essential to the American way of life, society is very careful to be sure that there is a proper agreement whenever any part of that freedom is surrendered. Therefore, it is necessary to show that there was an offer and that while the offer was still existing it was accepted without any qualification. Only then can it be said that both parties have assented to the terms of the contract and only then is each party bound by the obligations stated in the contract.

A. REQUIREMENTS OF AN OFFER

An **offer** expresses the willingness of the offeror to enter into a contractual agreement regarding a particular subject. It is a promise which is conditional upon an act, a forbearance, or a return promise that is given in exchange for the promise or its performance.

§ 12:1.   Contractual Intention.

To constitute an offer, the offeror must intend to create a legal obligation or must appear to intend to do so.[1] It is not necessary, however, for the parties to expressly state that they are making a contract.

There is no contract when a social invitation is made or when an offer is made in jest or excitement because a reasonable person would not regard such an offer as indicating a willingness to enter into a binding agreement.

(a) **Invitation to Negotiate.** The first statement made by one of two persons is not necessarily an offer. In many instances there may be a preliminary discussion or an *invitation* by one party to the other to *negotiate* or to make an offer.

Ordinarily a seller sending out circulars or catalogs listing prices is not regarded as making an offer to sell at those prices, but as merely indicating a willingness to consider an offer made by a buyer on those terms. The reason for this rule is in part the practical consideration that since a seller does not have an unlimited supply of any commodity, the seller cannot possibly intend to make a contract with everyone who sees the circular. The same principle is applied to merchandise that is displayed with price tags in stores or store windows and to most advertisements. A "for sale" advertisement in a newspaper is merely an invitation to negotiate and is not an offer which can be accepted by a reader of the paper, even though the seller in fact has only one of the particular item advertised.[2]

The circumstances may be such, however, that even a newspaper advertisement constitutes an offer. Thus the seller may make an offer when the advertisement states that specific items will be sold at a clearance sale at the prices listed and adds the words "first come, first served."

Quotations of prices, even when sent on request, are likewise not offers in the absence of previous dealings between the parties or the existence of a trade custom which would give the recipient of the quotation reason to believe that an offer was being made. Whether a price quotation is to be treated as an offer or merely an invitation to negotiate is a question of the intent of the party making such quotations. Although sellers are not bound by quotations and price tags, they will as a matter of goodwill ordinarily make every effort to deliver the merchandise at those prices.[3]

In some instances, it is apparent that an invitation to negotiate and not an offer has been made. When construction work is done for the national government, for a state government, or for a political subdivision, statutes require that a printed statement of the work to be done be published and circulated. Contractors are invited to submit bids on the work, and the statute generally requires that the bid of the lowest responsible bidder be accepted.

---

[1]Lininger v Dine Out Corporation, 131 Ariz App 160, 639 P2d 350 (1981).
[2]Osage Homestead, Inc. v Sutphin (Mo App) 657 SW2d 346 (1983).
[3]Statutes prohibiting false or misleading advertising may also require adherence to advertised prices.

Such an invitation for bids is clearly an invitation to negotiate, both from its nature and from the fact that it does not specify the price to be paid for the work. The bid of each contractor is an offer, and there is no contract until the government accepts one of these bids. This procedure of advertising for bids is also commonly employed by private persons when a large construction project is involved.

FACTS:

The Board of Education decided to construct a building. The Board advertised for bids by contractors. Rofra, Inc. submitted a bid. Later the Board of Education entered into a contract with Harrison. Rofra sued the Board, claiming that the Board had broken its contract with Rofra.

DECISION:

Rofra did not have any contract with the Board of Education. The invitation to submit bids was merely an invitation to negotiate. It was not an offer and the making of the bid was not an acceptance. The making of a bid was merely an offer. As the Board never accepted the offer of Rofra, there was no contract between the Board and Rofra. [Rofra, Inc. v Board of Education, 28 Md App 538, 346 A2d 458 (1975)]

In some cases the fact that material terms are missing serves to indicate that the parties are merely negotiating and that an oral contract has not been made. When a letter or printed promotional matter of a party leaves many significant details to be worked out later, the letter or printed matter is merely an invitation to negotiate and is not an offer which may be accepted and a contract thereby formed.

(b) **Statement of Intention.** In some instances a person may make a statement of intention but not intend to be bound by a contract. For example, when a lease does not expressly allow the tenant to terminate the lease because of a job transfer, the landlord might state that should the tenant be required to leave for that reason, the landlord would try to find a new tenant to take over the lease. This declaration of intention does not give rise to a binding contract, and the landlord cannot be held liable for breach of contract should the landlord fail to obtain a new tenant or not even attempt to obtain a new tenant.

(c) **Agreement to Make a Contract at a Future Date.** No contract arises when the parties merely agree that at a future date they shall consider making a contract or shall make a contract on terms to be agreed upon at that time. In such a case, neither party is under any obligation until the future contract is made. Similarly there is no contract between the parties if essential terms are left open for future negotiation.[4] Thus, a promise to pay a bonus or compensation to be decided upon after three months of business operation is not binding.

---

[4]Casper v Harrison Hatchery, Inc. 172 Ga App 35, 321 SE2d 785 (1984).

FACTS:

A cable television company, T.V. Transmission, Inc., made a contract to use the utility poles of the Lincoln Electric System, a utility owned by the City of Lincoln. The contract was to expire on a specified date but could be extended on such terms as would be agreed to by the parties. A lawsuit was brought to determine the effect of the contract after the specified expiration date.

DECISION:

There was no contract after the expiration date. There was merely an agreement to agree, which by itself is not a contract. In the absence of the making of a new contract, the contract would expire on the specified date. [T.V. Transmission, Inc. v City of Lincoln, 220 Neb 887, 374 NW2d 49 (1985)]

§ 12:2.   Definiteness.

An offer, and the resulting contract, must be definite and certain.[5] If an offer is indefinite or vague or if an essential provision is lacking, no contract arises from an attempt to accept it. The reason is that the courts cannot tell what the parties are to do. Thus, an offer to conduct a business for such time as should be profitable is too vague to be a valid offer. The "acceptance" of such an offer does not result in a contract that can be enforced. Likewise, a promise to give an injured employee "suitable" employment that the employee was "able to do" is too vague to be a binding contract. Likewise a statement by a landlord to the tenant that "some day it [the rented land] will be your own" is too indefinite to be an offer and no contract for the sale of the land arises when the tenant agrees to the statement.[6]

FACTS:

Fearless Farris Wholesale, Inc. agreed to supply gas to Harvey who ran a service station. The agreement left the price open. It was agreed that if Farris did not give the lowest price, Harvey could buy where he could get the lowest price. Was there a contract?

DECISION:

No. There was no obligation on the part of the buyer to purchase from the seller if the buyer could get the gas from another source at a better price than that offered by the seller. The agreement in effect only required the buyer to purchase from the seller when it was to his advantage to do so. As there was no fixed or definite obligation on the buyer to purchase there was no contract. [Harvey v Fearless Farris Wholesale, Inc. (CA9 Idaho) 589 F2d 451 (1979)]

(a) **Definite by Incorporation.** An offer and the resulting contract which by themselves may appear "too indefinite" may be made definite by

[5]Gegg v Kiefer (Mo App) 655 SW2d 834 (1983).
[6]First National Bank v Minke, 99 Ill App 3d 10, 54 Ill Dec 999, 425 NE2d 11 (1981).

reference to another writing. For example, an agreement to lease property which was too vague by itself was made definite because the parties agreed that the lease should follow the standard form with which both were familiar. An agreement may also be made definite by reference to the prior dealings of the parties and to trade practices.

(b) **Implied Terms.** Although an offer must be definite and certain, not all of its terms need be expressed. Some of the omitted terms may be implied by law. For example, an offer "to pay $50 for a watch" does not state the terms of payment. A court, however, would not condemn this provision as too vague but would hold that it required that cash be paid and that the payment be made upon delivery of the watch. Likewise terms may be implied from conduct. As an illustration, where the borrowed money was given to the borrower by a check on which there was written the word "loan," the act of the borrower in indorsing the check constituted an agreement to repay the amount of the check.

(c) **Divisible Contracts.** When the agreement consists of two or more parts and calls for corresponding performances of each part by the parties, the agreement is a **divisible contract.** Thus, in a promise to buy several separate articles at different prices at the same time, the agreement may be regarded as separate or divisible promises for the articles. When a contract contains a number of provisions or performances to be rendered, the question arises whether the parties intended merely a group of separate, divisible contracts or whether it was to be a "package deal" so that complete performance by each party is essential.

FACTS:

Fincher was employed by Belk-Sawyer Co. as fashion coordinator for the latter's retail stores. The contract of employment also provided for additional services of Fincher to be thereafter agreed upon in connection with beauty consultation and shopping services to be established at the stores. After Fincher had been employed as fashion coordinator for several months, Belk-Sawyer Co. refused to be bound by the contract on the ground that it was indefinite.

DECISION:

Judgment for Fincher. The contract was sufficiently definite as to the present employment, and the intention of the parties to have a present contract on that subject was not to be defeated because they recognized that an additional agreement might be made by them as to other work. [Fincher v Belk-Sawyer Co. (Fla App) 127 So2d 130 (1961)]

(d) **Unimportant Vague Details Ignored.** If the term of an agreement which is too vague is not important, it may sometimes be ignored. If the balance of the agreement is definite, there can then be a binding contract. For example, where the parties agreed that one of them would manage a motel which was being constructed for the other and it was agreed that the contract would begin to run before the completion of the construction, the management contract did not fail because it did not specify any date on which it was to commence, as it was apparent that the exact date was not essential and could not be determined at the time when the contract was made.

(e) **Exceptions to Definiteness.** As exceptions to the requirement of definiteness, the law has come to recognize certain situations where the practical necessity of doing business makes it desirable to have a "contract," yet the situation is such that it is either impossible or undesirable to adopt definite terms in advance. In these cases, the indefinite term is often tied to the concept of good faith performance or to some independent factor that will be definitely ascertainable at some time in the future, for example, market price, cost to complete, or production requirements. Thus, the law recognizes binding contracts in the case of a contract to buy all requirements of the buyer from the seller and the contract of a producer to sell the entire production or output to a given buyer. These are binding contracts although they do not state the exact quantity of goods that are to be bought or sold. Contracts are also binding although they run for an indefinite period of time; or require a buyer to pay the "costs" plus a percentage of costs as profit; or require one person to supply professional services as needed.

FACTS:

Heat Incorporated made an agreement with Griswold, an accountant, by which it agreed to pay him $200 a month for rendering such accounting services "as he, in sole discretion, may render." Griswold had done the accounting work of the corporation for the preceding six years, and it was desired that he should continue to render the services as in the past. When the corporation refused to pay on the ground that the agreement was so indefinite that it was not binding, Griswold sued for damages.

DECISION:

Judgment for Griswold. The parties to the contract had had six years experience with the rendering of services by Griswold. It was their intention that such pattern of rendering service should continue in the future. Because of uncertainties of the future and possible changes in the law, it was obvious that the parties could not specify in precise detail the services which were to be rendered. The law should therefore allow them to make a vague contract if they so desire, and the duty to perform contracts in good faith would be a sufficient protection for the corporation. [Griswold v Heat Inc. 108 NH 119, 229 A2d 183 (1967)]

---

§ **12:3.   Communication of Offer to the Offeree.**

The offer must be communicated to the offeree. Otherwise the offeree cannot accept even though knowledge of the offer has been indirectly acquired. Internal management communications of an enterprise that are not intended for outsiders or employees do not constitute offers and can not be accepted by them.[7] Sometimes, particularly in the case of unilateral contracts,

---

[7]Tobias v Montgomery Ward and Company, Inc. _____ Minn App _____, 362 NW2d 380 (1985).

the offeree performs the act called for by the offeror without knowing of the offer's existence. Thus, without knowing that a reward is offered for the arrest of a particular criminal, a person may arrest the criminal. In most states, if that person learns thereafter that a reward has been offered for the arrest, the reward cannot be recovered.[8]

Not only must the offer be communicated, but it must be communicated by the offeror or at the offeror's direction.

B. TERMINATION OF OFFER

An offer gives the offeree power to bind the offeror by contract. This power does not last forever, and the law specifies that under certain circumstances the power ends or is terminated.

Once the offer is terminated, the offeree cannot revive it. If an attempt is made to accept the offer after it has been terminated, this attempt is meaningless, unless the original offeror is willing to regard the "late acceptance" as a new offer which the original offeror then accepts.

Offers may be terminated in any one of the following ways: (1) revocation of the offer by the offeror, (2) counteroffer by offeree, (3) rejection of offer by offeree, (4) lapse of time, (5) death or disability of either party, and (6) subsequent illegality.

§ 12:4.   Revocation of the Offer by the Offeror.

Ordinarily the offeror can revoke the offer before it is accepted.[9] If this is done, the offeree cannot create a contract by accepting the revoked offer. Thus, the bidder at an auction sale may withdraw (revoke) a bid (offer) before it is accepted. The auctioneer cannot thereafter accept that bid.

An ordinary offer may be revoked at any time before it is accepted, even though the offeror had expressly promised that the offer would be good for a stated period and that period had not yet expired, or even though the offeror had expressly promised to the offeree that the offer would not be revoked before a specified later date.

(a) **What Constitutes a Revocation.** No particular form of words is required to constitute a revocation. Any words indicating the offeror's termination of the offer is sufficient. A notice sent to the offeree that the property which is the subject of the offer has been sold to a third person is a revocation of the offer. An order for goods by a customer, which is an offer to purchase at certain prices, is revoked by a notice to the seller of the cancellation of the order, provided such notice is communicated before the order is accepted.

(b) **Communication of Revocation.** A revocation of an offer is ordinarily effective only when it is made known to the offeree. Until it is communicated to the offeree, directly or indirectly, the offeree has reason to believe that there is still an offer which may be accepted; and the offeree may rely on this belief.

[8]With respect to the offeror, it should not make any difference as a practical matter whether the services were rendered with or without knowledge of the existence of the offer. Only a small number of states have adopted this view, however.

[9]T.M. Cobb Co., Inc. v Superior Court, 36 Cal 3d 273, 204 Cal Rptr 143, 682 P2d 338 (1984).

Except in a few states, a letter or telegram revoking an offer made to a particular offeree is not effective until received by the offeree. It is not a revocation at the time it is written by the offeror nor even when it is mailed or dispatched. A written revocation is effective, however, when it is delivered to the offeree's agent, or to the offeree's residence or place of business under such circumstances that the offeree may be reasonably expected to be aware of its receipt.

It is ordinarily held that there is a sufficient "communication" of the revocation when the offeree learns indirectly of the offeror's revocation. This is particularly true in a land sale, when the seller-offeror, after making an offer to sell the land to the offeree, sells the land to a third person, and the offeree indirectly learns of such sale and necessarily realizes that the seller cannot perform the original offer and therefore must be deemed to have revoked it.

If the offeree accepts an offer before it is effectively revoked, a valid contract is created. Thus, there may be a contract when the offeree mails or telegraphs an acceptance without knowing that a letter of revocation has already been mailed.

When an offer is made to the public it may usually be revoked in the same manner in which it was made. For example, an offer of a reward that is made to the general public by an advertisement in a newspaper may be revoked in the same manner. A member of the public cannot recover the amount of the reward by thereafter performing the act for which the reward was originally offered. This exception is made to the rule requiring communication of revocation because it would be impossible for the offeror to communicate the fact that the offer was revoked to every member of the general public who knows of the offer. The public revocation of the public offer is effective even though it is not seen by the person attempting to accept the original offer.

(c) **Option Contracts.** An **option contract** is a binding promise to keep an offer open for a stated period of time or until a specified date. This requires that the promisor receive consideration, that is, something, such as a sum of money, as the price for the promise to keep the offer open. In other words, the option is a contract to refrain from revoking an offer.

(d) **Firm Offers.** As another exception to the rule that an offer can be revoked at any time before acceptance, statutes in some states provide that an offeror cannot revoke an offer prior to its expiration when the offeror makes a **firm offer**, that is, an offer which states that it is to be irrevocable, or irrevocable for a stated period of time. Under the Uniform Commercial Code, this doctrine of firm offers applies to a merchant's signed, written offer to buy or sell goods, but with a maximum of three months on its duration.[10]

FACTS:

Gordon, a contractor, requested bids on structural steel from various suppliers. Coronis submitted an offer by letter. He later withdrew the offer. Gordon sued Coronis for breach of contract on the ground that he could not revoke his offer.

[10]UCC § 2–205.

DECISION:

Judgment for Coronis. The mere making of an offer without an express declaration therein which "gives assurance that it will be held open" does not constitute a firm offer but is merely an ordinary offer which can be revoked at any time. [Coronis Associates v Gordon Construction Co. 90 NJ Super 69, 216 A2d 246 (1966)]

(e) Detrimental Reliance. There is growing authority that when the offeror foresees that the offeree will rely on the offer's remaining open, the offeror is obligated to keep the offer open for a reasonable time. Thus, it has been held that a subcontractor cannot revoke a bid made to the general contractor after the general contractor had used the subcontractor's bid in computing the general bid given to the owner and the contractor's general bid was then accepted by the owner.[11]

§ 12:5.   Counteroffer by Offeree.

Ordinarily if *A* makes an offer, such as to sell a used automobile to *B* for $1,000, and *B* in reply makes an offer to buy at $750, the original offer is terminated. *B* is in effect saying, "I refuse your original offer, but in its place I make a different offer." Such an offer by the offeree is known as a **counteroffer.**[12]

Counteroffers are not limited to offers that directly contradict the original offers. Any departure from, or addition to, the original offer is a counteroffer even though the original offer was silent as to the point added by the counteroffer.[9] For example, when the offeree stated that the offer was accepted and added that time was of the essence, the "acceptance" was a counteroffer because the original offer had been silent on that point.

§ 12:6.   Rejection of Offer by Offeree.

If the offeree rejects the offer and communicates this rejection to the offeror, the offer is terminated, even though the period for which the offeror agreed to keep the offer open has not yet expired. It may be that the offeror is willing to renew the offer; but unless this is done, there is no longer any offer for the offeree to accept.

§ 12:7.   Lapse of Time.

When the offer states that it is open until a particular date, the offer terminates on that date if it has not yet been accepted.[13] This is particularly so where the offeror declares that the offer shall be void after the expiration of the specified time. Such limitations are strictly construed. For example, it has been held that the buyer's attempt to exercise an option one day late had no effect.

If the offer does not specify a time, it will terminate after the lapse of a reasonable time. What constitutes a "reasonable" time depends upon the

---

[11]Powers Construction Co., Inc. v Salem Carpets, 283 SC App 302, 322 SE2d 30 (1984).

[12]Normille v Miller, 313 NC 98, 326 SE2d 11 (1985).

[13]Sullivan v Economic Research Properties (Fla App) 455 So 2d 630 (1984).

circumstances of each case; that is, upon the nature of the subject matter, the nature of the market in which it is sold, the time of the year, and other factors of supply and demand. If the commodity is perishable in nature or fluctuates greatly in value, the reasonable time will be much shorter than if the subject matter is a staple article. An offer to sell a harvested crop of tomatoes would expire within a very short time. When a seller purports to accept an offer after it has lapsed by the expiration of time, the seller's acceptance is merely a counteroffer and does not create a contract unless that offer is accepted by the buyer.

FACTS:

Morrison wished to purchase land owned by Rayen Investments. Morrison gave a real estate agent a writing stating the desire to purchase and specifying that Rayen must accept in fifteen days. On the sixteenth day, Rayen sent Morrison a telegram accepting Morrison's offer. Rayen later refused to go through with the transaction and Morrison brought suit for breach of contract.

DECISION:

Judgment for Rayen. There was no contract upon which suit could be brought. The offer of Morrison could only be accepted within fifteen days. It lapsed with the expiration of the fifteen days. The "acceptance" telegram on the sixteenth day therefore had no effect and there was no contract. [Morrison v Rayen Investments, Inc. 97 Nev. 58, 624 P2d 11 (1981)]

---

§ 12:8.   Death or Disability of Either Party.

If either the offeror or the offeree dies or becomes insane before the offer is accepted, it is automatically terminated.[14]

§ 12:9.   Subsequent Illegality.

If the performance of the contract becomes illegal after the offer is made, the offer is terminated. Thus, if an offer is made to sell alcoholic liquors but a law prohibiting such sales is enacted before the offer is accepted, the offer is terminated.

C. ACCEPTANCE OF OFFER

Once the offeror expresses or appears to express a willingness to enter into a contractual agreement with the offeree, the latter may accept the offer. An acceptance is the assent of the offeree to the terms of the offer. No particular form of words or mode of expression is required, but there must be a clear expression that the offeree agrees to be bound by the terms of the offer.

§ 12:10.   Privilege of Offeree.

Ordinarily the offeree may refuse to accept an offer. If there is no acceptance, by definition there is no contract.

[14]Watts v Dickerson, 162 Cal App 3d 1160, 208 Cal Rptr 846 (1984).

Certain partial exceptions exist to the privilege of the offeree to refuse to accept an offer.

(a) **Places of Public Accommodation and Public Utilities.** These are under a duty to serve any fit person. Consequently, when a fit person offers to register at a hotel, that is, offers to hire a room, the hotel has the obligation to accept the offer and to enter into a contract for the renting of the room. This is a partial exception to the general rule because there is no duty to accept on the part of the hotel unless the person is fit and the hotel has space available.

(b) **Antidiscrimination.** When offers are solicited from members of the general public, an offer may generally not be rejected because of the race, nationality, religion, or color of the offeror. If the solicitor of the offer is willing to enter into a contract to rent, sell, or employ, as the case may be, antidiscrimination laws compel the solicitor to accept an offer from any otherwise fit person.

(c) **Consumer Protection.** Statutes and regulations designed to protect consumers from false advertising may require a seller to accept an offer from a customer to purchase advertised goods and may impose a penalty for an unjustified refusal.

§ 12:11.   Nature of the Acceptance.

An **acceptance** is the offeree's manifestation of intent to enter into a binding agreement on the terms stated in the offer.[15] In the absence of a contrary requirement in the offer, an acceptance may be indicated by an informal "O.K.," by a mere affirmative nod of the head, or, in the case of an offer of a unilateral contract, by performing the act called for. However, while the acceptance of an offer may be shown by conduct, it must be very clear that the offeree intended to accept the offer.

The acceptance must be absolute and unconditional. It must accept just what is offered. If the offeree changes any terms of the offer or adds any new term, there is no acceptance because the offeree does not agree to what was offered.

Where the offeree does not accept the offer exactly as made, the addition of any qualification converts the "acceptance" into a counteroffer and no contract arises unless such counteroffer is accepted by the original offeror.

FACTS:

Wayne State University advertised for bids for the construction of a building. A bid was submitted by the Building Systems Housing Corporation. The University accepted the bid "subject to approval of federal agency and sale and delivery of financing bonds." Thereafter Building Systems withdrew its bid. The University sued for breach of contract.

[15]Prince Enterprises, Inc. v Griffith Oil Co. 8 Kan App 2d 664, 664 P2d 877 (1983).

DECISION:

Judgment for Building Systems. There was no contract. The bid was an offer. The "acceptance" by the University was conditional in that it added the two conditions of government approval and the sale of bonds. As this acceptance was not identical to the offer, it had the effect of rejecting the offer made by Building Systems. No contract arose because there was no acceptance of the offer. [Wayne State University v Building Systems Housing Corp. 62 Mich App 77, 233 NW2d 195 (1975)]

The addition of new terms in the acceptance, however, does not always mean that the attempted acceptance fails. The acceptance is still unqualified if the new terms are merely those that (1) would be implied by law as part of the offer; (2) constitute a mere request; or (3) relate to a mere clerical detail.

FACTS:

Alpha Venture/Vantage Properties rented property to Creative Carton Corporation. Thereafter Creative wanted to get out of the lease and made an offer to pay three months rent in return for being released. Alpha sent Creative a letter of acceptance and a form for termination of lease that was to be signed by Creative. The acceptance letter referred to the commission being charged by a real estate broker involved and stated that such commission "should be shared" between Alpha and Creative. Creative later claimed that the letter from Alpha was not an acceptance but was a counteroffer because of the provision as to the sharing of the broker's commission.

DECISION:

The acceptance letter was an acceptance. The provision as to broker's commissions was made as merely a suggestion and not as a condition to the acceptance. The intent to accept was made obvious by sending Creative a termination form for it to sign. Consequently, the acceptance letter accepted the offer and parties were then bound by the terms of the offer. [Alpha Venture/Vantage Properties v Creative Carton Corp. _____ Minn App _____ , 370 NW2d 649 (1985)]

---

§ 12:12.   Who May Accept.

An offer may be accepted only by the person to whom it is directed. If anyone else attempts to accept it, no agreement or contract with that person arises.

If the offer is directed not to a specified individual but to a particular class, it may be accepted by anyone within that class. If the offer is made to the public at large, it may be accepted by any member of the public at large who has knowledge of the existence of the offer.

When a person to whom an offer was not made attempts to accept it, the "acceptance" has the effect of an offer. If the original offeror is willing to accept this offer, a binding contract arises. If the offeror does not accept the new offer, there is no contract.

FACTS:

Shuford offered to sell a specified machine to the State Machinery Co. The Nutmeg State Machinery Corp. heard of the offer and notified Shuford that it accepted. When Shuford did not deliver the machine, the Nutmeg Corp. sued him for breach of contract. Could the Nutmeg Corp. recover?

DECISION:

No. Nutmeg did not have a contract with Shuford since Shuford had made the offer to State Machinery. Only the person to whom an offer is made can accept an offer. No contract arises when a third person accepts the offer. [Nutmeg State Machinery Corp. v Shuford, 129 Conn 659, 30 A2d 911 (1943)]

§ 12:13.   Manner of Acceptance.

The acceptance must conform to any conditions expressed in the offer concerning the manner of acceptance. When the offeror specifies that there must be a written acceptance, no contract arises when the offeree makes an oral acceptance. If the offeror calls for an acceptance by a specified date, a late acceptance has no effect. When an acceptance is required by return mail, it is usually held that the letter of acceptance must be mailed the same day that the offer was received by the offeree. If the offer specifies that the acceptance be made by the performance of an act by the offeree, the latter cannot accept by making a promise to do the act but must actually perform it.

When a person accepts services offered by another and it reasonably appears that compensation was expected, the acceptance of the services without any protest constitutes an acceptance of the offer and a contract exists for the payment for such services.

When the offeror has specified a particular manner of acceptance, the offeree cannot accept in any other way. However, acceptance in some other way is effective (1) if the manner of acceptance specified was merely a suggested alternative and was not clearly the exclusive method of acceptance, or (2) if the offeror has proceeded on the basis that there had been an effective acceptance.

FACTS:

Brown made an offer to purchase the house of Overman. Brown made the offer on a standard printed form. Underneath Brown's signature was the statement: "ACCEPTANCE ON REVERSE SIDE." Overman did not sign the offer on the back but sent Brown a letter accepting the offer. Later Brown refused to perform the contract. Overman sued him for breach of contract. Brown claimed that there was no contract because the offer had not been accepted in the manner specified by the offer.

DECISION:

Judgment for Overman. The printed form of offer did not make accepting the offer depend upon signing on the reverse side of the paper. Consequently a letter that would make a reasonable person believe that the offer had been accepted was effective as an acceptance. Overman's letter expressed that intent and therefore constituted an acceptance of Brown's offer, thereby giving rise to a contract, [Overman v Brown, 220 Neb 788, 372 NW2d 102 (1985)]

(a) **Silence as Acceptance.** In most cases, the offeree's silence and failure to act cannot be regarded as an acceptance. Ordinarily the offeror is not permitted to frame an offer in such a way as to make the silence and inaction of the offeree operate as an acceptance.[16]

FACTS:

Everlith obtained a one-year liability policy of insurance from the insurance company's agent, Phelan. Prior to the expiration of the year, Phelan sent Everlith a renewal policy covering the next year, together with a bill for the renewal premium. The bill stated that the policy should be returned promptly if the renewal was not desired. Everlith did not return the policy or take any other action relating to the insurance. Phelan sued for the renewal premium.

DECISION:

The silence of Everlith did not constitute an acceptance since there was not a sufficient prior course of conduct between the parties which would lead a reasonable person to believe that the silence indicated an acceptance. The single transaction that had occurred in the past did not establish a course of conduct. [Phelan v Everlith, 22 Conn Supp 377, 173 A2d 601 (1961)]

In the case of prior dealings between the parties, as in a record or book club, the offeree may have a duty to reject an offer expressly and the offeree's silence may be regarded as an acceptance.

(b) **Unordered Goods and Tickets.** When a seller writes to a person with whom the seller has not had any prior dealings that, unless notified to the contrary, specified merchandise will be sent to be paid for at stated prices, there is no acceptance if the recipient of the letter ignores the offer and does nothing. The silence of the person receiving the letter is not an acceptance, and the sender as a reasonable person should recognize that none was intended.

This rule applies to all kinds of goods, books, magazines, and tickets sent to a person through the mail when they have not been ordered. The fact that the items are not returned does not mean that they have been accepted; that is, the offeree is neither required to pay for nor return the goods or other items. If desired, the recipient of the unordered goods may write "Return to Sender" on the unopened package and put the package back into the mail without any additional postage. This is not required and the Postal Reorganization Act of 1970 provides that the person who receives unordered mailed merchandise from a commercial (noncharitable) sender has the right "to retain, use, discard, or dispose of it in any manner the recipient sees fit without any obligation whatsoever to the sender."[17] It provides further that any unordered merchandise that is mailed must have attached to it a

---

[16]Club Chain of Manhattan, Ltd. v Christopher & Seventh Gourmet, Ltd. 74 App Div 2d 277, 427 NYS2d 627 (1980).

[17]Federal Postal Reorganization Act § 3009.

clear and conspicuous statement of the recipient's rights to treat the goods in this manner.

§ 12:14.   Communication of Acceptance.

If the offeree accepts the offer, must the offeror be notified? The answer depends upon the nature of the offer.

If the offeror makes an offer of a unilateral contract, communication of acceptance is ordinarily not necessary. In such a case, the offeror calls for a completed or accomplished act. If that act is performed by the offeree with knowledge of the offer, the offer is accepted without any further action by way of notifying the offeror. As a practical matter, there will eventually be some notice to the offeror because the offeree who has performed the act will ask the offeror to pay for the performance which has been rendered.

If the offer pertains to a bilateral contract, an acceptance is not effective unless communicated.[18] The acceptance must be communicated directly to the offeror or the offeror's agent.

FACTS:

Mrs. Hodgkin told her daughter and son-in-law, Brackenbury, that if they would leave their home in Missouri and come to Maine to care for her, they could have the use of her house during her life and that she would will it to them. The daughter and son-in-law moved to Maine and began taking care of the mother. Family quarrels arose, and the mother ordered them out of the house. They brought an action to determine their rights. Mrs. Hodgkin defended on the ground that the plaintiffs had not notified her that they would accept her offer.

DECISION:

Judgment for daughter and son-in-law. The contract offered by the mother was a unilateral contract. She called for the moving to Maine of the plaintiffs and their taking care of her. This they did and, by so doing, they accepted the offer of the mother. The fact that they did not notify the mother of their acceptance of the offer or did not make a counter-promise to her was immaterial since neither is required in the case of a unilateral contract. [Brackenberry v Hodgkin, 116 Maine 399, 102 A 106 (1917)]

---

§ 12:15.   Acceptance by Mail or Telegraph.

When the offeree sends an acceptance by mail or telegraph, questions may arise as to the right to use such means of communication and as to the time when the acceptance is effective.

(a) **Right to Use Mail or Telegraph.** Express directions of the offeror, prior dealings between the parties, or custom of the trade may make it clear that only one method of acceptance is proper. For example, in negotiations with respect to property of rapidly fluctuating value, such as wheat or corporation stocks, an acceptance sent by mail may be too slow. When there is no

[18]Rosin v First Bank of Oak Park, 126 Ill App 3d 230, 81 Ill Dec 443, 466 NE2d 1245 (1984).

indication that mail or telegraph is not a proper method, an acceptance may be made by either of those instrumentalities without regard to the manner in which the offer was made. The trend of the modern decisions supports the following provision of the Uniform Commercial Code relating to sales of personal property: "Unless otherwise unambiguously indicated by the language or circumstances, an offer to make a sales contract shall be construed as inviting acceptance in any manner and by any medium reasonable in the circumstances."

(b) **When Acceptance by Mail or Telegraph Is Effective.** If the offeror specifies that an acceptance shall not be effective until received, the law will respect the offeror's wish. If there is no such provision and if acceptance by letter is proper, a mailed acceptance takes effect when the acceptance is properly mailed.

FACTS:

The Thoelkes owned land. The Morrisons mailed an offer to the Thoelkes to buy their land. The Thoelkes agreed to this offer and mailed back a contract signed by them. While this letter was in transit, the Thoelkes notified the Morrisons that their acceptance was revoked. Were the Thoelkes bound by a contract?

DECISION:

Yes. The acceptance was effective when mailed, and the subsequent revocation of the acceptance had no effect. [Morrison v Thoelke (Fla App) 155 So2d 889 (1963)]

The letter must be properly addressed to the offeror, and any other precaution that is ordinarily observed to insure safe transmission must be taken. If it is not mailed in this manner, the acceptance does not take effect when mailed, but only when received by the offeror.

The rule that a properly mailed acceptance takes effect at the time it is mailed is applied strictly. The rule applies even though the acceptance letter never reaches the offeror.

An acceptance sent by telegraph takes effect at the time that the message is handed to the clerk at the telegraph office, unless the offeror specifies otherwise or unless custom or prior dealings indicate that acceptance by telegraph is improper.

(c) **Proof of Acceptance by Mail or Telegraph.** How can the time of mailing be established, or even the fact of mailing in the case of a destroyed or lost letter? A similar problem arises in the case of a telegraphic acceptance. In either case, the problem is not one of law but one of fact: a question of proving the case to the jury. The offeror may testify in court that an acceptance was never received or that an acceptance was sent after the offer had been revoked. The offeree may then testify that the acceptance letter was mailed at a particular time and place. The offeree's case will be strengthened if postal receipts for the mailing and delivery of a letter sent to the offeror can be produced, although these of course do not establish the contents of the letter. Ultimately, the case goes to the jury, or to the judge, if a jury trial has been waived, to determine whether the acceptance was made at a certain time and place as claimed by the offeree.

§ 12:16.   Acceptance by Telephone.

Ordinarily acceptance of an offer may be made by telephone unless the circumstances are such that by the intent of the parties or the law of the state no acceptance can be made or contract arise in the absence of a writing.

A telephoned acceptance is effective when and where the acceptance is spoken into the phone.[19] Consequently, where an employee who lived in Kansas applied for a job to work in Missouri and the employer telephoned from Missouri to Kansas accepting the application, the employment contract was a Missouri contract because the acceptance by the employer was spoken into the phone in that state and therefore the Kansas Workers' Compensation statute did not apply when the employee was subsequently injured.

§ 12:17.   Auction Sales.

At an auction sale the statements made by the auctioneer to draw forth bids are merely invitations to negotiate. Each bid is an offer, which is not accepted until the auctioneer indicates that a particular offer or bid is accepted. Usually this is done by the fall of the auctioneer's hammer, indicating that the highest bid made has been accepted. As a bid is merely an offer, the bidder may withdraw the bid at any time before it is accepted by the auctioneer.

Ordinarily the auctioneer may withdraw any article or all of the property from the sale if not satisfied with the amounts of the bids that are being made. Once a bid is accepted, however, the auctioneer cannot cancel the sale. In addition, if it had been announced that the sale was to be made "without reserve," the goods must be sold to the person making the highest bid regardless of how low that may be.

SUMMARY

As a contract arises when an offer is accepted, it is necessary to find that there was an offer and that it was accepted. If either element is missing there is no contract.

An offer does not exist unless the offeror has contractual intent. This intent is lacking if the statement of the person is merely an invitation to negotiate, a statement of intention, or an agreement to agree at a later date. Newspaper ads, price quotations, and catalog prices are ordinarily merely invitations to negotiate and cannot be accepted. In addition to the contractual intent, an offer must be definite. If an offer is indefinite, its acceptance will not create a contract because it will be held that the resulting agreement is too vague to enforce. In some cases an offer that is by itself too indefinite is made definite because some writing or standard is incorporated by reference and made part

---

[19]O'Briant v Daniel Construction Co. 279 SC 254, 305 SE2d 241 (1983).

of the offer. In some cases, the offer is made definite by implying terms that were not stated. In other cases, the indefinite part of the offer is ignored when that part can be divided or separated from the balance of the offer. In other cases, the requirement of definiteness is ignored either because the matter that is not definite is unimportant or because there is an exception to the rule requiring definiteness. Assuming that there is in fact an offer that is made with contractual intent and that is sufficiently definite, it still does not have the legal effect of an offer unless it is communicated to the offeree by or at the direction of the offeror.

In some cases, no contract arises because there is no offer that satisfies the requirements just stated. In other cases, there was an offer but it was terminated before it was accepted. By definition, an attempted acceptance made after the offer has been terminated has no effect. The ordinary offer may be revoked at any time by the offeror. All that is required is the manifestation of intent to revoke and the communication of that intent to the offeree. The offeror's power to revoke is barred by the existence of an option contract under common law, a firm offer under the Uniform Commercial Code or local non-Code statute, and by the application of the doctrine of detrimental reliance by the offeree. An offer is also terminated when the offeree rejects the offer or makes a counteroffer, or by the lapse of the time stated in the offer or of a reasonable time when none is stated, by the death or disability of either party, and by a change of law that makes illegal a contract based on the particular offer.

When the offer is accepted, a contract arises. Only the offeree can accept an offer and the acceptance must be of the offer exactly as made without any qualification or change. Ordinarily the offeree may accept or reject as the offeree chooses. Limitations on this freedom of action have been imposed by antidiscrimination and consumer protection laws. The acceptance is any manifestation of intent to agree to the terms of the offer. Ordinarily silence or failure to act does not constitute acceptance and the recipient of unordered goods and tickets may make any disposition thereof without such action constituting an acceptance. An acceptance does not exist until the words or conduct manifesting assent to the offer are communicated to the offeror. Acceptance by mail or telegraph takes effect at the time and place when or where the letter is mailed or the telegram dispatched. A telephoned acceptance is effective when and where spoken into the phone.

In an auction sale, the auctioneer asking for bids makes an invitation to negotiate, a person making a bid is making an offer, and the acceptance of the highest bid by the auctioneer is an acceptance of that offer and gives rise to a contract. When the auction sale is without reserve the auctioneer must accept the highest bid. If not expressly made without reserve, the auctioneer may refuse to accept any of the bids.

QUESTIONS AND CASE PROBLEMS

1. What objective of the law (from the list in § 2:2) is illustrated by each of the following statements?
   (a) Economic life would be most uncertain if we did not have the assurance that contracts once made would be binding.

(b) An offer is terminated by the lapse of a reasonable time when no time has been stated.

2. The Hamilton store ran a newspaper ad stating that a certain television set was on sale for $400. Nora phoned the store that she wanted one of the sets. The store stated that it was sold out and could not fill her order. She sued Hamilton for breach of contract. Was it liable?

3. The Croft Cement Works agreed to supply Grover with as much cement as Grover would buy at a specified price per unit. Was this a requirements contract?

4. Katherine mailed Paul an offer which stated that it was good for ten days. Two days later she mailed Paul another letter stating that the original offer was revoked. That evening, Paul phoned Katherine that he accepted the offer. She said that he could not do so because she had mailed him a letter of revocation and that he would undoubtedly receive the letter of revocation in the next morning's mail. Was the offer revoked by Katherine?

5. When an offer is rejected by the offeree, can the offeree thereafter accept the offer if the offeror refuses to make a better offer?

6. Compare the communication of an offer, the communication of the revocation of an offer, and the communication of the acceptance of an offer.

7. The Lessack Auctioneers advertised an auction sale which was open to the public and was to be conducted with reserve. Gordon attended the auction and bid $100 for a work of art which was worth much more. No higher bid, however, was made but Lessack refused to sell the item for $100 and withdrew the item from the sale. Gordon claimed that as he was the highest bidder, Lessack was required to sell the item to him. Was he correct?

8. The Willis Music Co. advertised a television set at $22.50 in the Sunday newspaper. Ehrlich ordered a set, but the company refused to deliver it on the ground that the price in the newspaper ad was a mistake. Ehrlich sued the company. Was it liable? Reason? Ehrlich v Willis Music Co. 93 Ohio App 246, 113 NE2d 252]

9. A buyer sent an order to a seller for some goods. The seller never took any action with respect to the order and did not reply to the buyer's letter. The buyer later sued the seller for breach of contract. Was the seller liable?

10. Hall, the owner of a tract of land wanted to have an office building constructed on it. He advertised for bids for the construction of the building. Davis, a contractor, sent in a bid accompanied by a letter stating that he accepted Hall's offer and thanked him for the contract. Did Davis have a contract with Hall?

11. Thompson and Liquichimica of America discussed the sale of the latter's business to Thompson. After some discussion, a letter was written that stated in part "it is understood that all parties will exercise their best efforts to reach an agreement on or before May 15, 1979." Thompson claimed that this gave him a contract to purchase the business. Was he correct? Thompson v Liquichimica of America (SD NY) 481 F Supp 361]

12. A dealer received a purchase order from a customer. In order to fill the order for the customer, the dealer ordered from the factory the goods

called for by the buyer's purchase order. The buyer thereafter canceled the order. Could the buyer do so? Antonucci v Stevens Dodge, Inc. 73 Misc 2d 173, 340 NYS2d 979]

13. Hubbard owed the Hahnemann Medical College a bill for medical services. Hahnemann sued Hubbard. The plaintiff's attorney requested the defendant's attorney to extend the time for taking certain steps in the lawsuit. The defendant's attorney wrote a letter stating that an extension would be agreed to if certain conditions then stated in the letter were satisfied. The plaintiff's attorney never replied to this letter. Later in the lawsuit it was claimed that there was a contract to extend the time. Was this correct? [Hahnemann Medical College v Hubbard, 486 Pa Super 536, 406 A2d 1120]

14. A owned land. He signed a contract agreeing to sell the land but reserving the right to take the hay from the land until the following October. He gave the contract form to B, a broker. C, a prospective buyer, agreed to buy the land and signed the contract but crossed out the provision as to the hay crop. Was there a binding contract between A and C?

15. Soar was a professional football player in the National Football League. He claimed that a commissioner of the league had agreed that he would be included in the league's pension plan "if sufficient funds become available." Soar brought suit against the football league players' association to enforce this promise. Was he entitled to recover? [Soar v National Football League Players' Ass'n (Cal RI) 550 F2d 1287]

16. Benny Tenenbaum owned land. Al Weiner offered to purchase the land from him and gave him a deposit and a written offer that specified a time limit within which the offer had to be accepted. Tenenbaum signed the offer and gave it to his agent to deliver to Weiner. The time for acceptance expired while the paper was still held by Tenenbaum's agent. Weiner claimed that there was no contract and demanded the return of his deposit. Is he entitled to it? [Weiner v Tenenbaum (Fla App) 452 So 2d 986]

17. A. H. Zehmer discussed selling a farm to Lucy. After 40 minutes discussion of a first draft of a contract, Zehmer and his wife, Ida signed a second draft stating: "We hereby agree to sell to W. O. Lucy the Ferguson Farm complete for $50,000 title satisfactory to buyer." Lucy agreed to purchase the farm on these terms. Thereafter the Zehmers refused to transfer title to Lucy and claimed that they had made the contract for sale as a joke. Lucy brought an action to compel performance of the contract. The Zehmers claimed that there was no contract. Were they correct? [Lucy v Zehmer, 198 Va App 493, 84 SE2d 516]

CHAPTER 13

CONTRACTUAL CAPACITY

CHAPTER OBJECTIVES

After studying this chapter you will be able to:

1. Define contractual capacity.
2. State the extent and effect of avoidance of a contract by a minor.
3. Define the extent of a minor's liability for necessaries.
4. Compare the liability of third persons with respect to the contract of a minor.
5. List those classes of persons who lack contractual capacity.
6. Solve problems involving the question of contractual capacity.

If society desired to treat all persons as equal, everyone would be able to make a contract and, conversely, all persons would be fully bound by their contracts. Such a rule of law would lay a trap for minors, intoxicated persons, and incompetents, because they would enter into contracts and find themselves bound thereby, even though the contracts were foolish and unwise from the standpoint of their best interests. To prevent this, society departs from the concept of equality and declares that certain persons can not make contracts that will bind them. Thus minors, intoxicated persons, and insane persons may have the right to avoid their contracts. This is described technically as being that they lack contractual capacity.

Historically, married women and aliens were also considered to lack contractual capacity. It should be no surprise that society has moved away from this discriminatory incapacity, and today there are only slight traces of it remaining.

§ 13:1. Definition.

Contractual capacity is the ability to understand that a contract is being made and to understand its general nature. The fact that a person does not understand the full legal meaning of a contract does not mean that contractual capacity is lacking.

If any party to a contract does not have contractual capacity, the contract is either void or voidable.[1]

Some persons, such as minors, are deemed by the law to lack contractual capacity. Ordinarily, however, every party to a contract is presumed to have contractual capacity until the contrary is shown. When there is evidence that a party has some illness, the question often arises whether that illness or medication taken for it had impaired the contractual capacity of the party.

§ 13:2. Double Aspect of Capacity.

In order to give rise to a contract, all parties to the agreement must have contractual capacity. This has both a negative and a positive aspect.

As to the negative, if capacity is lacking, the contract is voidable and in some instances, is void. As this chapter will show, many concepts of incapacity have been abolished. This is understandable in terms of the growing importance and recognition of the social force of protecting the person. That is, a person is not to be denied the capacity to make a binding contract unless there is some actual physical or mental disability that the law should recognize in order to protect that person. Incapacity based on discrimination against sex, alienage, or as punishment for crime is disappearing from the law.

As to the positive aspect, contractual capacity is in most instances the equivalent of freedom of contract.[2] That is, persons with capacity to contract may make whatever contract they choose, and the law will not lightly nullify or reject their desires.

FACTS:

Sinclair Oil Corporation obtained a contract of insurance from the Columbia Casualty Company to protect it from liability to third persons. An accident occurred in the unloading of a tanker and Sinclair was sued by the injured person for both compensatory and punitive damages.* Columbia claimed that the provision of the policy obligating it to pay punitive damages was invalid.

DECISION:

The parties to the contract had contractual capacity. They therefore could make any contract that they chose unless there was some principle of law prohibiting the contract. Although there is a conflict of authority as to whether it is against public policy to provide insurance covering punitive damages, the sounder view is that it is not and therefore the parties could make such a contract as they chose and

[1]V. G. A. S. v S. I. S. (Del) 407 A2d 253 (1978).
[2]Fidelity & Deposit Co. v Sun Life Ins. Co. 174 Ga App 214, 329 SE2d 517 (1985).

could make the provision that they did as to punitive damages. [Sinclair Oil Corp. v Columbia Gas. Co (Wyo 682 P2d 975 (1984)] *Authors' Comment: Compensatory damages are those which are equal to the loss sustained by the plaintiff and thus compensate for that loss. Punitive damages consist of an additional amount imposed upon the defendant to punish the defendant for highly improper conduct.

§ 13:3.   Minors.

At common law any person, male or female, under twenty-one years of age was a **minor** (or an infant). At common law, minority ended the day before the 21st birthday. The "day before the birthday" rule is still followed, but the 21 years has been reduced to 18 years in most states and to 19 in a few.

§ 13:4.   Minor's Power to Avoid Contracts.

With exceptions that will be noted later, a contract made by a minor is voidable at the election of the minor. The minor may affirm or ratify the contract upon attaining majority by performing the contract or by an express statement of approval. After so doing, the contract can no longer be avoided.

(a) **Minor's Misrepresentation of Age.** Generally the fact that the minor has misrepresented age does not affect the minor's power to avoid the contract. A few states hold that such fraud of the minor prevents the minor from avoiding the contract. A few states permit the minor to avoid the contract in such case but require the minor to pay for any damage to the property received under the contract.

In any case, the other party to the contract may avoid it because of the minor's fraud.

(b) **Time for Avoidance.** The minor can avoid a contract only during minority and for a reasonable time after attaining majority. After the lapse of such reasonable time, the contract is deemed ratified and cannot be avoided by the minor. A few states permit the former minor to avoid a wholly executory contract thereafter in the absence of an express affirmance.

§ 13:5.   What Constitutes Avoidance.

Avoidance or disaffirmance of a contract by a minor may be accomplished by any expression of an intention to repudiate the contract. Any act inconsistent with the continuing validity of the contract is also a disaffirmance. Thus, when a minor sold property to A and later, on reaching majority, made a sale of the same property to B, the second sale was an avoidance of the first.

§ 13:6.   Restitution by Minor after Avoidance.

When a minor avoids a contract, the question arises as to what must be returned by the minor to the other contracting party.

(a) **Original Consideration Intact.** When a minor still has what was received from the other party, the minor, on avoiding the contract, must return it to the other party or offer to do so. That is, the minor must put things back to the original position, or as it is called, restore the **status quo ante.** If the minor who is able to return the consideration does not do so, the minor cannot avoid the contract. By virtue of this rule, when a contract is avoided, the minor must avoid all of it. Part of it cannot be kept.

(b) **Original Consideration Damaged or Destroyed.** What happens if the minor cannot return what has been received because it has been spent, used, damaged, or destroyed? The minor's right to avoid the contract is not affected thereby. The minor can still avoid the contract and is only required to return what remains. The fact that nothing remains or that what remains is damaged does not bar the right to avoid the contract. In those states which follow the common-law rule, the minor can thus refuse to pay for what has been received under the contract or can get back what had been paid or given, even though the minor does not have anything to return or returns any property in a damaged condition. There is, however, a trend which would limit this rule.

FACTS:

Kevin Green purchased an automobile from Star Chevrolet Company. He later notified Star that he was a minor and was avoiding the contract. Star refused to take back the car and to refund the purchase price. Kevin continued to use the car. He was involved in a collision. His insurance company paid his claim and he transferred the car to the company. The company later sold the car for salvage for $1500. Kevin sued Star for the price that he had paid for the car.

DECISION:

Kevin was entitled to the purchase price less $1500 representing the salvage value of the car. A minor may avoid a contract and recover whatever the minor has paid to the other party. If the minor still has what was received from the other party, the minor must return it in whatever condition it then is. Kevin should have returned the wrecked car to Star which then would have been able to make the salvage sale. This amount should therefore be deducted from the refund of the purchase price to which Kevin was entitled. [Star Chevrolet Co. v Green (Miss) 473 So 2d 157 (1985)]

---

§ 13:7.   Recovery of Property by Minor upon Avoidance.

When a minor avoids a contract, the other contracting party must return the money received from the minor. Any property received from the minor must also be returned. If the property has been sold to a third person who did not know of the minority of the original seller, the minor cannot get the property back, but in such cases the minor is entitled to recover the money value of the property or the money received by the other contracting party from the third person.

§ 13:8.   Contracts for Necessaries.

A minor can avoid a contract for necessaries but must pay the reasonable value for furnished necessaries. This duty of the minor is called a quasi-contractual liability.[3] It is a duty which the law imposes upon the minor rather than one created by contract.

Originally **necessaries** were limited to those things absolutely necessary for the sustenance and shelter of the minor. Thus limited, the term would extend only to the most simple foods, clothing, and lodging. In the course of time, the rule was relaxed to extend generally to things relating to the health, education, and comfort of the minor. Thus, the rental of a house used by a married minor is a necessary. And services reasonably necessary to obtaining employment by a minor have been held to be necessaries.

The rule has also been relaxed to hold that whether an item is a necessary in a particular case depends upon the financial and social status, or station in life, of the minor. The rule as such does not treat all minors equally. To illustrate, college education may be regarded as necessary for one minor but not for another, depending upon their respective stations in life.

Property other than food or clothing acquired by a minor is generally not regarded as a necessary. Although this rule is obviously sound in the case of jewelry and property used for pleasure, the same view is held even though the minor is self-supporting and uses the property in connection with work, as tools of trade, or an automobile used to go to and from work. The more recent decisions, however, hold that property used by a minor to earn a living is a necessary. Thus, it has been held that a tractor and farm equipment were necessaries for a married minor who supported a family by farming.

It is likely that necessaries will in time come to mean merely that which is important by contemporary standards.

These changes have come about because in this century minors have taken a greater part in the business and working world, in many cases leaving the parental home to lead independent lives as young adults.

FACTS:

Bobby Rogers, a minor, married, quit school, and looked for work. He agreed with the Gastonia Personnel Corporation, an employment agency, that if he obtained employment through it, he would pay a stated commission. Rogers obtained work through the agency but refused to pay the agreed commission of $295, for which he denied liability on the ground of minority.

DECISION:

Rogers must pay the reasonable value of the agency's services. The services of an employment agency should be deemed a "necessary" on the theory that they enable a minor "to earn the money required to pay [for] the necessities of life for himself and those who are legally dependent upon him." [Gastonia Personnel Corporation v Rogers, 276 NC 279, 172 SE2d 19 (1970)]

[3]See § 11:13 as to quasi-contractual liability generally.

§ 13:9. Minor's Ratification of Voidable Contract.

A minor can not avoid a contract after it has been ratified. The ratification can not be canceled or set aside.

(a) **What Constitutes Ratification. Ratification** consists of any words or conduct of the minor manifesting an intent to be bound by the terms of the contract.

FACTS:

While still a minor, Jones made a contract with Free Flight Sport Aviation which entitled Jones to use Free Flight's sky diving facilities. The contract contained a provision exempting Free Flight from liability for any harm or injury to Jones. Jones attained his majority in December 1973. In October 1974 he made use of the privileges provided by the contract but was injured because of the alleged negligence of the pilot of the plane furnished by Free Flight. He sued the owner and operator of the plane and Free Flight. Free Flight raised the defense that the contract shielded it from liability. Jones denied this on the ground that he was a minor when the contract was made and he avoided the contract.

DECISION:

Judgment for Free Flight. When Jones used the facilities in October 1974 he was an adult. His use of the facilities was a ratification of the contract that he had made when a minor. He therefore could not evade the clause of the contract limiting liability, by saying that he avoided the entire contract. [Jones v Dressel, ____ Colo ____, 623 P2d 370 (1981)]

The making of payments after attaining majority may constitute a ratification. Many courts, however, refuse to recognize payment as ratification in the absence of further evidence of an intent to ratify, an express statement of ratification, or an appreciation by the minor that such payment might constitute a ratification.

An acknowledgment by the minor that a contract had been made during minority, without an intent to be bound thereby, is not a ratification.

(b) **Form of Ratification.** Generally no special form is required for ratification of a minor's voidable contract, although in some states a written ratification or declaration of intention is required.

(c) **Time for Ratification.** A minor can avoid a contract any time during minority and for a reasonable time thereafter but, of necessity, can only ratify a contract after attaining majority. The minor must have attained majority or the "ratification" would itself be regarded as voidable.

§ 13:10.   Contracts That Minors Cannot Avoid.

Statutes in many states deprive a minor of the right to avoid an education loan,[4] a contract for medical care, a contract made while running a business, a contract approved by a court, a contract made in performance of a legal duty, or relating to bank accounts, insurance policies, or corporate stock. In most states, the contract of a veteran, although a minor, is binding, particularly one for the purchase of a home. In some states, by court decision, a minor who is nearly an adult or who appears to be an adult cannot avoid a contract, particularly when it is made in connection with a business or employment.

Some courts take an intermediate position with respect to employment contracts by allowing the minor to avoid the contract but prohibiting the use of any secret information obtained in the course of the employment or from competing with the former employer when the avoided contract contained a noncompetitive clause. It is also held that when a minor has settled a claim and received the amount specified in a release, the release is binding upon the minor and cannot be set aside when the minor attains majority.

As an exception to the right to disaffirm a contract during minority, a minor cannot fully avoid a conveyance for the transfer of land until majority is attained.

§ 13:11.   Liability of Third Person for Minor's Contract.

The question arises whether parents are bound by the contract of their minor child. The question also arises whether a person cosigning a minor's contract is bound after the contract is avoided.

(a) **Liability of Parent.** Ordinarily a parent is not liable on a contract made by a minor child. The parent may be liable, however, if the child is acting as the agent of the parent in making the contract. Also, the parent is liable to a seller of necessaries for the reasonable value of the necessaries supplied by the seller to the child if the parent had deserted the child.

(b) **Liability of Cosigner.** When the minor makes a contract, another person, such as a parent or a friend, may sign the contract along with the minor for the purpose of accommodating the minor by making the contract more attractive to the third person.

With respect to the other contracting party, the cosigner is bound independently of the minor. Consequently, when the minor avoids the contract the cosigner remains bound by the contract. If the debt to the creditor is actually paid, the obligation of the cosigner is discharged.

If the minor avoids a sales contract but does not return the goods, the cosigner remains liable for the purchase price.

---

[4]A Uniform Minor Student Capacity to Borrow Act makes educational loans binding on minors in Arizona, Mississippi, North Dakota, Oklahoma, and Washington. This uniform act was reclassified as a model act by the Commissioners on Uniform Laws, indicating that it was recognized that uniformity was not important and that the matter was primarily local in character.

§ 13:12. Incompetents.

A person who is mentally deranged is generally called an **incompetent** and lacks capacity to make a contract. The cause of the incapacity is immaterial. It may be the result of insanity, senile dementia, imbecility, the result of excessive use of drugs or alcohol, or it may be the result of a stroke.[5] If the person is so mentally deranged as to be unable to understand that a contract is being made or the general nature of the contract, the person lacks contractual capacity.

An incompetent may have lucid intervals. If a contract is made during such an interval and is not affected by any delusion the contract is valid and binding.

(a) **Effect of Incompetence.** An incompetent person may ordinarily avoid a contract in the same manner as a minor. Upon the removal of the disability, that is, upon becoming normal, the former incompetent person either can ratify or disaffirm the contract.

FACTS:

Chiara in Texas purchased furniture from Ellard. He sold some to a third person and moved the balance of it to New York. Chiara, who was of unsound mind, later brought an action to set aside the purchase from Ellard. The latter claimed that Chiara must first return all of the property.

DECISON:

Judgment for Chiara. As to the property resold by him, he was only required to return so much of the proceeds of the sale as he still held. As to the furniture that he still owned, he was required to account for it. This would not require the actual return of the property as it did not have any unique value and its return from New York would be expensive. It was sufficient that he pay the seller the value of the property that he had moved to New York as of the date of the sale. [Ellard v Chiara (Tex Civ App) 252 SW2d 991 (1952)]

As in the case of minors, the other party to the contract has no right to disaffirm the contract merely because the incompetent has the right to do so.

(b) **Appointment of Guardian.** If a proper court appoints a guardian for the incompetent person, a contract made before that appointment may be ratified or disaffirmed by the guardian. If the incompetent person makes a contract after a guardian has been appointed, the contract is void and not merely voidable.

§ 13:13. Intoxicated Persons.

The capacity of a party to contract and the validity of the contract are not affected by the party's being drunk at the time of making the contract as long as the party knew that a contract was being made. The fact that the contract was foolish and would not have been made if sober does not

[5]Gallagher v Central Indiana Bank, _____ Ind App _____, 448 NE2d 304 (1983).

make the contract voidable unless it can be shown that the other party purposely caused the person to become drunk in order to induce the making of the contract.

If the degree of intoxication is such that a person does not know that a contract is being made, the contract is voidable by that person. The situation is the same as though the person were so insane at the time as to not know what was being done. Upon becoming sober, the person may avoid or rescind the contract. An unreasonable delay in taking steps to set aside a known contract entered into while intoxicated, however, may bar the intoxicated person from asserting this right.

§ 13:14.   Aliens.

An **alien** is a national or subject of a foreign country. Originally aliens were subject to many disabilities. These have been removed in most instances by treaty between the United States and the foreign country, under which each nation agrees to give certain rights to the citizens of the other. Generally an alien's right to make a contract is recognized.[6]

If this country is at war with a nation of which an alien is a subject, the alien is called an *enemy alien* without regard to whether the alien is actually assisting that country in the prosecution of the war. An enemy alien is denied the right to make new contracts or to sue on existing ones, but if sued on an existing contract, may defend the action. A contract made by an enemy alien, even though made before the war began, will at least be suspended during the war. In some instances, if the contract calls for continuing services or performance, the war terminates the contract.

§ 13:15.   Married Women.

At common law a married woman could not make a binding contract. The common-law disability of a married woman has almost been abolished by statute in practically all the states.[7] There are still a few restrictions in some jurisdictions. It is probable that these will disappear in the near future.

FACTS:

An Alabama statute provided that a married woman could not sell her land without the consent of her husband. Montgomery made a contract to sell to Peddy land owned by her. Montgomery's husband did not consent thereto. Montgomery did not perform the contract and was sued by Peddy. The defense was raised that the contract was void and could not be enforced because of the statute. Peddy claimed that the statute was unconstitutional.

DECISION:

The statute was unconstitutional. Constitutions, both federal and state, guarantee all persons the equal protection of the law. Married women are denied this equal protection when they are treated differently than married men and unmarried females. The fact that such unequal treatment had once been regarded as proper does not justify its modern continuation. [Peddy v Montgomery (Ala) 345 So2d 631 (1977)]

---

[6]A state cannot restrict or prohibit the employment of aliens in private or public employment. Truax v Raich, 239 US 33 (1915); Purdy & Fitzpatrick v California, 79 Cal Rptr 77, 456 P2d 645 (1969).
[7]United States v Yazell, 382 US 341 (1966).

SUMMARY

An agreement that otherwise appears to be a contract may not be binding because a party thereto lacks contractual capacity. In such case, the contract is ordinarily voidable at the election of that party who lacks contractual capacity, and in some cases is void. Ordinarily contractual incapacity is the inability for mental or physical reasons to understand that a contract is being made and its general terms and nature. This is typically the case when it is claimed that incapacity exists because of insanity or intoxication. In other cases, the incapacity arises because society is discriminating either in favor of or against a particular group or class. The incapacity of minors is a discrimination in favor of that class designed to protect them from unwise contracts. The incapacity of aliens and married women illustrates discrimination against a particular class. The modern trend is to reduce or eliminate incapacity based on discrimination against a class.

Historically minors were persons under 21 years of age. In the large majority of states today the age has been reduced to 18 years. Typically a minor can avoid any contract. If the minor had received anything from the other party, the minor on avoiding the contract must return what had been received from the other party, if the minor still has it. If what was received has been destroyed, lost, or spent, the minor is not required to make any return or to pay damages for the value of what has not been returned. If what was received has been damaged, the minor must return such property but is not required to pay money for the damage sustained by the property. If the minor had originally transferred property to the other contracting party, as a minor buyer making a trade-in, the minor may recover such property on avoiding the contract. This right to recover property exists only as long as the minor's former property is owned by the other contracting party. If the other contracting party has resold the property to a third person buying in good faith and for value, the minor can not recover the property from such third person.

A minor can avoid all contracts which means that the minor can not be required to pay the purchase price or perform any obligation of such contracts. By statute and decision, however, exceptions have been made to this general rule and certain kinds of contracts may no longer be avoided by a minor, such as contracts of insurance, contracts to purchase stock, or contracts made by a minor running a business. A minor may avoid a contract regardless of the subject matter but when it relates to a necessary the minor must pay the reasonable value of any benefit received. At common law, a "necessary" was limited to the minimal needs of food, clothing, and shelter. The concept of a necessary has expanded so that it now embraces needs reasonably necessary for the minor's existence and employment, taking into consideration the social position and background of the minor. By this modern view, an automobile used in connection with the minor's work and the services of an employment agency are "necessaries."

Only a minor is liable for the minor's contract. Parents of the minor are not liable on the contracts of the minor merely because they are the parents. Frequently, an adult will enter into the contract as a co-party of the minor. Such an adult, whether a parent or a non-relative, is liable on the contract made by such person and the minor without regard to whether the minor has avoided the contract. However, the co-signer is released if every-thing in its original condition is returned by the minor to the other contract-ing party.

The contract of an insane person is voidable to much the same extent as the contract of a minor, with the important distinction that if a guardian has been appointed for the insane person, a contract made by that person is void and not merely voidable.

An intoxicated person lacks contractual capacity to make a contract if the intoxication is such that the person does not understand that a contract is being made. Modern law abandons the earlier distinction between volun-tary and involuntary intoxication.

Historically aliens were subject to a contractual incapacity but this has generally been removed by reciprocal treaties between nations. When nations that have entered into such a treaty are at war with each other, the subjects or nationals of each nation are generally denied the right to make or enforce contracts against the subjects or nationals of the other nation.

At common law, married women lacked contractual capacity but this has been generally abolished and today exists only in a small number of states and then only with respect to contracts by which a wife would promise to pay the husband's debt if it were not paid by the husband.

QUESTIONS AND CASE PROBLEMS

1. (a) What is the objective of the rule of law that a minor who avoids a contract usually cannot recover property if the other party has trans-ferred it to a third person who did not know of the minority and purchased the property for value?

   (b) How is the evolutionary nature of the law illustrated by the changes in the definition of a minor's necessaries?

2. What contracts of a minor can be avoided?

3. Michael was sixteen years old. He purchased a motorcycle to go on a summer camping trip. After having driven the motorcycle approximately 5,000 miles and after having wrecked and repaired it once, he brought it back to the dealer who sold him the motorcycle and demanded the return of the full purchase price. The dealer refused to take back the motorcycle or to return any part of the purchase price. Was the dealer required to take back the motorcycle and refund the purchase price?

4. Oscar Adams, aged 16, purchased a radio from Braverman Brothers. The radio was stolen from Oscar. He then avoided the contract with Braver-man. Braverman Brothers then demanded that Oscar's mother, Joyce, pay for the radio set. Was she liable?

5. Helen, age 17, wanted to buy a motorcycle. She did not have the money to pay cash but persuaded the dealer to sell a cycle to her on credit. He did so partly because she said that she was 22. Helen showed the dealer an identification card that falsely stated that her age was 22. Helen drove the motorcycle away. A few days later she damaged it and then returned it to the dealer and stated that she avoided the contract because she was a minor. The dealer said that she could not do so because (a) she had

misrepresented her age and (b) the motorcycle was damaged. Can she avoid the contract?

6. Joe Venuto left his home in Italy where he was born and came to the United States. He settled in North Dakota and obtained a job from the Fabricare Corporation. He was later fired on the ground that the contract of employment was void because he was an alien and therefore lacked capacity to make a contract. Was the contract of employment valid?

7. Compare ratification by a minor of a contract when (a) the minor ratifies the contract while still a minor, and (b) the minor ratifies the contract a day after becoming an adult.

8. Compare the avoidance of a minor's contract for (a) a luxury, and (b) a necessary.

9. Martinson executed a note payable to Matz. At the time Martinson was drunk. The next day he was told that he signed the note. Five years later, Martinson's wife told Matz's attorney that Martinson would not pay the note as he was drunk at the time he executed the note. Matz brought suit on the note two years after that. Could he recover? [Matz v Martinson, 127 Minn 262, 149 NW 370]

10. On February 28, 1958, Alice Sosik signed a note promising to make certain payments to Conlon. She later sued to have the note set aside on the ground that she lacked mental capacity. A letter from a physician was presented which stated that he had examined her on July 3, 1959, and that she "is suffering from a chronic mental illness and is totally incapable of managing her affairs." Did the letter provide sufficient proof to allow her to set the note aside? [Sosik v Conlon, 91 RI 439, 164 A2d 696]

11. Stuhl was 20 years of age. At that time, 21 years was the age of majority. He gave a check to Eastern Airlines to pay for a flight ticket. By the time his check was dishonored by the bank for insufficient funds, Stuhl had already flown on the flight. Eastern Airlines then sued him on the check. He filed an answer in the lawsuit in which he stated that he was a minor when he bought the flight ticket and that he now disaffirmed the contract with Eastern Airlines for the flight. Could he avoid the contract? [Eastern Airlines, Inc. v Stuhl, 65 Misc 2d 901, 318 NYS2d 996, aff'd 68 Misc 2d 269, 327 NYS2d 752]

12. A, who appeared to be over 21 years of age but made no statement regarding his age, purchased an automobile from B. He later informed B that he was a minor and avoided the contract. A gave as his explanation that there were certain defects in the car. B claimed that these defects were trivial. Assuming that the defects were trivial, could A avoid the contract?

13. Helen purchased a refrigerator for her new apartment. Because she was not employed, the store did not want to sell it to her on credit unless her father, who had a good job, would sign a promissory note for the amount of the purchase price. Both Helen and her father signed such a note. Six months later, the refrigerator was destroyed by a fire in the apartment house. Helen and her father refused to make any more

payments for the refrigerator. The store sued both of them for the balance of the purchase price. Were they liable?

14. Thomas Bell, a minor, went to work in the beauty parlor of Sam Pankas and agreed that when he left the employment, he would not work in or run a beauty parlor business within a ten-mile radius of downtown Pittsburgh, Pennsylvania, for a period of two years. Contrary to this provision, Bell and another employee of Pankas opened up a beauty shop three blocks from Pankas's shop and advertised themselves as former employees of Pankas. Pankas sued Bell to stop the breach of the non-competition or restrictive covenant. Bell claimed that he was not bound because he was a minor when he had agreed to the covenant. Was he bound by the convenant? [Pankas v Bell, 413 Pa 494, 198 A2d 312]

15. Hillhouse, while a minor, purchased an automobile from Haydon. After becoming of age, Hillhouse made ten additional monthly payments, was in three collisions with the automobile, and collected insurance for the damage, purchased a new top for the car from Haydon, and drove the car 35,000 miles. He then brought an action to rescind the contract on the ground that he was a minor when the contract was made. Can he rescind the contract? [Haydon v Hillhouse, 223 Ark 957, 270 SW2d 910]

16. Saccavino made a contract with Carl Gambardella, then 15 years of age, and Carl's parents, that he would train Carl to be a horse rider and that he would receive in return a share of Carl's earnings from exhibitions and racing. When Saccavino sued on the contract years later, Carl claimed that it was void. Was he correct? [Saccavino v Gambardella, 22 Conn Supp 168, 164 A2d 304]

17. Laura Jesset, who had been committed to a mental institution in 1940, was released by 1944 as "improved." In 1955, her husband died. She and her son made a contract for his funeral with Melbourne, the undertaker. Shortly thereafter, her son had Laura committed to a mental institution because of the effect of the shock of the husband's death. Melbourne sued the Jessets for the funeral bill. Laura claimed that she was not liable because she was incompetent. Decide. [Melbourne v Jesset, 110 Ohio App 502, 163 NE2d 773]

CHAPTER 14

GENUINENESS OF ASSENT

CHAPTER OBJECTIVES

After studying this chapter you will be able to:
1. List the reasons why an agreement is not binding because the assent thereto was in fact not genuine.
2. List the kinds of mistake that can be made and their effect upon contracts.
3. Compare the effect of an innocent false statement, a failure to volunteer information, and fraud.
4. Distinguish between undue influence, physical duress, and economic duress.
5. List the remedies available when the assent of a party to the agreement is not genuine.
6. Solve problems involving the question whether assent to an agreement was genuine.

In order to protect the voluntary character of contractual agreements, special rules had developed to meet the situation in which the apparent agreement does not reflect the true intentions of the parties whether because of mistake, a false statement, concealment, or pressure. This chapter considers the scope of these factors and the remedies that are available to the contracting party who is the victim of such practices.

§ 14:1. Unilateral Mistake.

A unilateral mistake as to a fact does not affect the contract. As exceptions to this statement, the agreement has no effect if it states that it shall be void if the fact is not as believed. The party making the mistake may also avoid the contract if the mistake is known or should be known or recognized by the other contracting party.

A unilateral mistake as to (a) expectations or (b) the law, does not have any effect upon the contract. Thus, the fact that a signer of a contract would not have signed if the signer had understood the legal effect of the contract is not a defense.

FACTS:

Sanif, Inc. made a contract with The Protection People by which the latter provided burglar alarm service for Sanif's place of business. The place of business was burglarized. Sanif sued Iannotti and other persons involved and The Protection People, suing the latter on the theory that there was negligent failure of the alarm system. The Protection People raised the defense that the contract expressly limited its liability in case of failure. The officer of the plaintiff claimed that this limitation was not binding because it had not been explained to him when the contract was signed.

DECISION:

The limitation was binding. The officer of the plaintiff had voluntarily signed the contract on behalf of the corporation. There was no evidence that the other contracting party had committed any fraud and therefore the failure to have explained the limitation clause to the other contracting party did not affect the validity of the limitation clause. [Sanif, Inc. v Iannotti, _____App Div 2d _____, 500 NYS2d 798 (1986)]

(a) **Mistake as to Nature of Paper.** When a party makes a negligent mistake as to the nature of a paper, the party is bound according to its terms. For example, when the printed form for applying for a loan to a corporation contained a guaranty by the president of the corporation of the corporate debt, the president signing the application without reading it was bound by this guaranty, even though the president did not know that it was in the application and the application was headed merely "application for credit."

(b) **Mistake as to Terms of Paper.** A person who has the ability and the opportunity to read a paper before signing is bound by its terms even though such person signed without reading. Such a signer can not avoid liability on the ground that there had not been any explanation given of the terms of the writing.[1]

A person unable to read or to understand the terms of a paper is bound by signing the paper without obtaining an explanation of it, unless the other contracting party knows or has reason to know of the signer's disability or educational limitation.

(c) **Mistakes as to Releases.** An insurance claimant is bound by the release given to the insurance company when there is a unilateral mistake

[1]Tank v Peterson, 219 Neb 438, 363 NW2d 530 (1985).

as to its meaning resulting from carelessness in reading the release. When a release is given and accepted in good faith, it is initially immaterial that the releasor or both of the parties were mistaken as to the seriousness or possible future consequences of a known injury or condition.[2] If the release covers all claims "known or unknown," the courts following the common-law view hold the releasor is bound even though there were other injuries of which the releasor was unaware because the effects of the unknown injuries had not yet appeared. Some courts depart from this and hold the release effective only with respect to the conditions or consequences that were known as of the time when the release was given.

§ 14:2. Mutual Mistake.

When both parties make the same mistake of fact, the agreement is void. Thus, the contract is void if both parties mistakenly believe that the contract can be performed, when in fact, it is impossible to perform it. Assume that A meets B downtown and makes a contract to sell to B an automobile, which both believe is in A's garage. Actually the automobile was destroyed by fire an hour before the agreement was made. Since this fact is unknown to both parties, there is a mutual mistake as to the possibility of performing the contract, and the agreement is void.

When a sale was made of a business and both the seller and buyer believed that it was operating at a profit, there was a mutual mistake of fact when the business was actually running at a loss, and the agreement was therefore not binding.[3]

(a) **Mistake as to Expectations.** A bilateral mistake with respect to expectations ordinarily has no effect on the contract unless the realization of those expectations is made an express condition of the contract. This means that the mistake has no effect unless the contract says that it shall be void if the matter is not as believed.

(b) **Mistake of Law.** When the mutual or bilateral mistake is one of law, the contract generally is binding. Thus, even if both parties to a lease mistakenly believe that the leased premises can be used for boarding animals because they are unaware of a zoning regulation that prohibits such a use of the property, the tenant does not have a right to rescind the lease for mutual mistake of law. In the eyes of the law the parties should have known what the zoning regulations allowed. A few courts have refused to follow this rule, and in several states statutes provide that a mutual mistake of law shall have the same effect as a mutual mistake of fact.

(c) **Collateral Matters.** When a mutual mistake occurs as to a collateral matter, it has no effect on the contract thereafter executed. For example, where the plaintiff asks the fire insurer to issue a policy and both the insured and the insurance company wrongly believed that there was no other policy, the policy which was then issued to the insured was not void because of the mutual mistake that there was no other policy. That mistake was as to a collateral matter.

[2]Indiana Bell Telephone Co., Inc. v Mygrant, _____ Ind _____, 471 NE2d 660 (1984).

[3]Simonson v Fendell, 101 Wash 2d 88, 675 P2d 1218 (1984).

FACTS:

Couri Pontiac made a contract with Interstate Industrial Uniform Rental, Inc. by which the latter agreed to supply Couri with clean uniforms for its personnel. At the time, Couri was already under a contract with Standard Uniform Rental, Inc. Both Couri and Interstate knew this but both believed that Couri could terminate the contract with Standard whenever it chose to do so. This was a mistake. The contract with Standard obligated Couri to take its service on a year to year basis, with the contract continuing to exist each year unless timely notice was given to terminate the agreement. Couri refused to go through with its contract with Interstate. Interstate sued Couri for breach of contract. Couri claimed that there was no contract because the parties had made a mutual mistake as to the existence of a binding contract with Standard.

DECISION:

Judgment for Interstate. No mistake had been made with respect to Interstate's contract with the customer. The mistake that was made was whether the customer had another contract with a third person. That mistake was not related to Interstate's contract with the customer but was outside or collateral to it. Therefore the fact that that mistake had been made did not alter the fact that Interstate and the customer had made an agreement, and that agreement was therefore binding. [Interstate Industrial Uniform Rental, Inc. v Couri Pontiac, Inc. (Me) 355 A2d 913 (1976)]

§ 14:3.   Innocent Misrepresentation.

Suppose that one party to a contract makes a statement of fact which is false but which is innocently made without intending to deceive the other party. Can the other party set aside the contract on the ground of being misled by the statement?

Equity will permit the rescission of the contract when the innocent misstatement of a material fact induces another to make the contract. If the deceived person is a defendant in an action at law, it is generally held that such innocent deception by the plaintiff cannot be asserted as a defense. There is a tendency, however, for the law courts to adopt the rule of equity. For example, it may be possible for an insurance company to avoid its policy because of an innocent misstatement of a material fact by the applicant. Contracts between persons standing in confidential relationships, such as guardian and ward, or parent and child, can be set aside for the same reason. Some courts go beyond this and permit the recovery of damages sustained because of the misrepresentation.

§ 14:4.   Nondisclosure.

In contrast to innocent misrepresentation, nondisclosure by one party to a contract generally will not make a contract voidable by the other party. Under certain circumstances, however, nondisclosure will serve to make a contract voidable, especially when the nondisclosure consists of active concealment.

(a) **General Rule of Non-liability.** Ordinarily there is no duty on a party to a contract to volunteer information to the other.[4] If *A* does not ask *B* any questions, *B* is not under any duty to make a full statement of material facts. Consequently, the nondisclosure of information which is not asked for does not impose fraud liability nor impair the validity of a contract.

(b) **Exceptions.** In some instances, the failure to disclose information which was not requested is regarded as fraudulent and the party to whom the information was not disclosed has the same remedies as though a known false statement were intentionally made.

(1) Unknown Defect or Condition. There is developing in the law a duty on a party who knows of a defect or condition to disclose that information to the other party where the defect or condition is obviously unknown to the other person and is of such a nature that it is unlikely that the other person would discover the truth or inquire about it.

FACTS:

The City of Salinas entered into a contract with Souza & McCue Construction Co. to construct a sewer. The city officials knew that unusual subsoil conditions, including extensive quicksands, existed, which would make performance of the contract unusually difficult; but it did not make that information known when it advertised for bids. The advertisement for bids directed bidders to "examine carefully the site of the work" and declared that the submission of a bid would constitute "evidence that the bidder has made such examination." Souza & McCue was awarded the contract, but because of the subsoil conditions it could not complete the contract on time and was sued by Salinas for breach of contract. Souza & McCue counterclaimed on the basis that the City had not revealed its information of the subsoil conditions and was liable for the loss caused thereby.

DECISION:

Judgment for contractor. An owner is liable for not informing the contractor of unusual difficulties known to the owner which the contractor will encounter in the performance of a contract. As the City knew that the contractor would base its bid on the incomplete information, the City had misled the contractor by such concealment and was liable to the contractor for the loss caused thereby. The provision as to the examination of "site of the work" did not alter this conclusion since there was nothing in that provision which would call to the contractor's attention the conditions that would be encountered nor which disclaimed liability for concealed subsoil conditions. [City of Salinas v Souza & McCue Construction Co. 66 Cal App 2d 217, 57 Cal Rptr 337, 424 P2d 921 (1967)]

(2) Confidential Relationship. If *A* and *C* stand in a confidential relationship, such as that of attorney and client, *A* has a duty to reveal anything that is material to *C's* interest when dealing with *C*, and *A's* silence has the same legal consequence as a knowingly made false statement that there was no material fact to be told to *C*.

The relationship between the buyer of a house and a financial institution lending the money to finance the purchase is not a confidential relationship and therefore the lender is not under any duty to disclose information posessed by it.[5]

[4]Osterberger v Hites Constr Co. (Mo App) 599 SW2d 221 (1980).
[5]Lee v United Federal Savings & Loan Ass'n (Ala) 466 So 2d 131 (1985).

(3) Fine Print. An intent to conceal may be present when a printed contract or document contains certain clauses in such fine print that it is reasonable to believe that the other contracting party will never take the time nor be able to read such provisions.

In some instances, legislatures have outlawed certain fine print contracts. Statutes commonly declare that insurance policies may not be printed in type of smaller size than designated by statute. Consumer protection statutes frequently require that particular clauses be set in large type. When a merchant selling goods under a written contract disclaims the obligation that goods be fit for their normal use, the Uniform Commercial Code requires the waiver to be set forth in "conspicuous" writing[6] which is defined as requiring "a term or clause... [to be] so written that a reasonable person against whom it is to operate ought to have noticed it. A printed heading in capitals...is conspicuous. Language in the body of a form is 'conspicuous' if it is in larger or other contrasting type or color...."[7]

There is a growing trend to treat a fine print clause as not binding upon the party who would be harmed thereby, without considering whether fraud was involved. A provision freeing the other contracting party from liability is not binding when it is printed in type that is so small that a person with normal vision would have difficulty in reading it.[8]

(4) Active Concealment. Nondisclosure may be more than the passive failure to volunteer information. It may consist of a positive act of hiding information from the other party by physical concealment, or it may consist of furnishing the wrong information. Such conduct is fraud.[9]

§ 14:5.   Fraud.

Fraud is (1) the making of a false statement of fact (2) with knowledge of its falsity or with reckless indifference as to its truth, (3) with the intent that the listener rely thereon and (4) the listener does so rely and (5) is harmed.[10]

The boundary line between fraud and nondisclosure may sometimes be very thin and frequently cases involve elements of both.

FACTS:

Karan purchased a used truck from a dealer, Bob Post, Inc. In selecting his purchase, he asked whether the odometer reading of 27,000 miles was correct. The salesman did not know whether it was or not but assured Karan that it was correct and also stated that certain parts of the truck were still covered by the manufacturer's 50,000 mile warranty. The actual mileage of the truck was over 48,000 miles and the truck was not eligible for any warranty protection. After taking possession of the truck, Karan discovered its poor condition and then learned that the statements of the salesman had been false. Karan sued the dealer for the fraud. The defense was made that the salesman had not known that his statements were false and did not have any reason to know that they were false and therefore he could not have been guilty of fraud.

[6]Uniform Commercial Code § 2-316(2).
[7]UCC § 1-201(10).
[8]Robinson v National Association for Stock Car Auto Racing, Inc. 158 Cal App 3d 138, 205 Cal Rptr 513 (1984).
[9]Mancini v Morrow, 321 Pa Super 184, 458 A2d 580 (1983).
[10]Martin v Brune (Mo App) 631 SW2d 77 (1982).

DECISION:

The salesman was guilty of fraud even though he did not actually know that his statements were false. He knew that he did not have definite knowledge that what he said was true, but he made his statements as being true. He therefore took the risk that they might be false and if they were false, his statements constituted fraud. [Karan v Bob Post, Inc. _____ Colo App _____ , 521 P2d 1276 (1974)]

(a) **Statement of Intention.** A statement of intention can constitute fraud when a promise is made by a person who does not intend to keep it.[11] To illustrate, a customer purchases goods from a merchant on credit and agrees to pay for them in 60 days. If the customer does not intend to pay for the goods and does not do so, the customer is guilty of fraud by misrepresenting intention.

(b) **Statement of Opinion or Value.** Ordinarily a misstatement of opinion or value is not regarded as fraudulent on the theory that the person hearing the statement recognizes or should recognize that it is merely the speaker's personal view and not a statement of fact.

If, however, the defendant, in making a statement as to the future, had knowledge not available to the plaintiff which showed that such expectations could not be realized, the statement as to the future expectations can be held fraudulent. Thus, a statement that a business would make a stated profit in the future is actionable when the speaker knew that on the basis of past events such prediction was false.

Likewise a statement of opinion may be fraud when the speaker knows of past or present facts that make the opinion false.[12]

(c) **Statement of Law.** A misstatement of law is treated in the same manner as a misstatement of opinion or value. Ordinarily, the listener is regarded as having an opportunity of knowing what the law is, an opportunity equal to that of the speaker, so that the listener is not entitled to rely on what the speaker says. When the speaker has expert knowledge of the law or claims to have such knowledge, however, the misstatement of law can be the basis for fraud liability.

(d) **Use of Assumed Name.** The use of an assumed name is not necessarily fraudulent or unlawful. It is only such when the user of the name uses the name of another person or makes up a name for the purpose of concealment to avoid arrest or to avoid creditors or to imitate a competitor and deceive customers.

FACTS:

Euge opened a checking account under the assumed name of Horn with the Manchester Bank. He drew a check for an amount greater than his account and was prosecuted for the crime of issuing a bogus check. The prosecution claimed that the check was drawn by a fictitious person on a fictitious account.

[11] Wagstaff v Protective Apparel Corp. (CA10 Okla) 760 F2d 1074 (1985).
[12] Trenholm v Ratcliff (Tex) 646 SW2d 927 (1983).

DECISION:

Euge was not guilty since there was an actual account although under the fictitious name he had assumed. The contract with the bank was lawful, and the bank would have been protected had it honored Euge's checks in the assumed name that he used. The account was an existing account under a fictitious name, but this did not constitute the crime charged. [State v Euge (Mo) 400 SW2d 119 (1966)]

In the absence of any intent to evade or deceive by the use of the assumed name, it is lawful for a person to go by any name, although other persons may refuse to enter into contracts unless the actual name is used. If a person makes a contract in an assumed or fictitious name or in a trade name, such person is bound by the contract because that name was in fact used to identify that person.

A married woman has the right to retain her maiden name. Moreover, a married woman who has taken her husband's name may return to her maiden name after they are divorced.[13]

§ 14:6.   Undue Influence.

An aged parent may entrust all business affairs to a trusted child; an invalid may rely on a nurse; a client may follow implicitly whatever an attorney recommends. The relationship may be such that for practical purposes the one person is helpless in the hands of the other. When such a confidential relationship exists, it is apparent that the parent, the invalid, or the client is not in fact exercising a free will in making a contract suggested by the child, nurse, or attorney, but is merely following the will of the other person. Because of the great possibility that the person dominating the other will take unfair advantage, the law presumes that the dominating person exerts **undue influence** upon the other person whenever the dominating person obtains any benefit from a contract made with the dominated person. The contract is then voidable and may be set aside by the dominated person unless the dominating person can prove that at the time the contract was made no unfair advantage had been taken.

The class of confidential relationships is not well-defined. It ordinarily includes the relationships of parent and child, guardian and ward, physician and patient, attorney and client, and any other relationship of trust and confidence in which one party exercises a control or influence over another.

FACTS:

Studley and Bentson made a contract by which the latter agreed to transfer to the former certain property in consideration of the promise of Studley to provide a home and take care of Bentson for life. The contract was prepared by a third person, and its effect was explained to Bentson by the president of the bank where he deposited his money. Bentson died, and the administratrix of his estate sued to set aside the contract, claiming undue influence.

[13]Thomas v Thomas, 100 Ill App 3d 1080, 56 Ill Dec 604, 427 NE2d 1009 (1981).

DECISION:

Judgment for Studley. The fact that Studley and Bentson had been friends and that the latter had confidence in the former did not make the relationship a confidential relationship so as to cast on Studley the burden of sustaining the validity of the contract. [Johnson v Studley, 80 Cal App 538, 252 P 638 (1926)]

Whether undue influence exists is a difficult question for the court (ordinarily the jury) to determine. The law does not regard every "influence" as undue. Thus, nagging may drive a person to make a contract, but that is not ordinarily regarded as undue influence. Persuasion and argument are not in themselves undue influence.

An essential element of undue influence is that the person making the contract does not exercise free will. In the absence of a recognized type of confidential relationship, such as that between parent and child, the courts are likely to take the attitude that the person who claims to have been dominated was merely persuaded and consequently there was no undue influence.

§ 14:7.   Duress.

A party may enter into a contract to avoid a threatened danger. The danger threatened may be a physical harm to person or property, called **physical duress;** or it may be a threat of financial loss, called **economic duress.**

(a) Physical Duress. A person makes a contract under **duress** when there is such violence or threat of violence that the person is deprived of free will and makes the contract to avoid harm. The threatened harm may be directed at a near relative of the contracting party as well as against a contracting party. If a contract is made under duress, the resulting agreement is voidable at the victim's election.

Agreements made to bring an end to mass disorders or violence are ordinarily not binding contracts because they were obtained by duress.

FACTS:

Rollins was a prisoner in a state prison. There was an uprising of the prisoners accompanied by violence and the holding of prison personnel as hostages. The director of the Department of Corrections promised Rollins and others immunity from prosecution if they would stop. They did so and were later indicted and prosecuted for the crimes committed in the course of the uprising. Rollins and the others raised the defense that a promise of immunity had been made to them. The prosecution claimed that the promise of immunity was not binding because it had been obtained by duress. The trial court refused to enforce the promise of immunity.

DECISION:

The promise of immunity was not binding because it had been obtained under duress. The threat of continuing the uprising and the danger to the hostages constituted duress which made the promise of immunity voidable by the promisor. [Rhode Island v Rollins, 116 RI 1528, 359 A2d 315 (1976)]

(b) **Economic Duress.** The economic pressure on a contracting party may be so great that it will be held to constitute duress. Economic duress occurs when the victim is threatened with irreparable loss for which adequate recovery could not be obtained by suing the wrongdoer.[14]

FACTS:

Loral was awarded a $6 million contract by the United States Navy for the production of radar sets. To perform this contract, Loral required 40 precision-gear component parts. Loral advertised for bids on these parts and let a subcontract to Austin to supply 23 gear parts. In the following year Loral was awarded a second Navy contract. Austin declared that it would not make further deliveries under its subcontract unless Loral agreed to a price increase, both as to parts already delivered and parts to be delivered and also unless Loral gave Austin a subcontract under the second Navy contract for all 40 component gear parts. Loral did not want to increase the prices under the original contract and wished to let subcontracts for parts under the second Navy contract on the basis of individual subcontracts for each part with the lowest bidder thereon. Loral communicated with 10 manufacturers of precision gears but could find none that could supply gears in time to perform its contract with the Navy. Loral then agreed to the price increase in connection with the first Navy contract and awarded Austin the subcontract for all 40 parts under the second Navy contract. After performance of the contracts was completed, Austin sued Loral for the balance due under the contracts. Loral sued Austin to recover the amount of the price increase on the theory that such increase had been agreed to under economic duress.

DECISION:

Judgment for Loral. The circumstances showed that Loral could not have obtained the goods from other sources and was therefore exposed to the peril of a costly default under the first contract unless Loral agreed to Austin's terms. Loral had communicated with the 10 manufacturers that it knew were competent to do the precision work required under the Navy contract. Loral was not required to take a chance with any unknown manufacturer. The contract modification which Austin obtained by its economic duress could be avoided by Loral and Loral could recover any money which it had lost as the result thereof. [Austin Instrument, Inc. v Loral Corp. 29 NY2d 124, 324 NYS2d 22, 272 NE2d 533 (1971)]

Generally, a threat of economic loss or pressure caused by economic conditions does not constitute duress which makes a contract voidable. The fact that the plaintiff drove a hard bargain does not give rise to the defense of economic duress. When money is in fact owed a creditor, a threat by the creditor to sue the debtor to collect the amount owed does not constitute

[14]Houston North Hospital Properties v Telco Leasing, Inc. (CA5 Tex) 680 F2d 19 (1982).

unlawful duress as it is merely a statement of what the law entitles the creditor to do.[15]

(c) **Adhesion contracts.** Pressure on a contracting party that is not as extreme as physical duress or economic duress may still be sufficient to justify the conclusion that there was no genuine assent freely given and that accordingly the basic element of a voluntary agreement was lacking and that what appears to be a contract is merely a voidable transaction. Such a situation is frequently described as involving a **contract of adhesion.** Such a contract is one that is offered by a dominant party to a party with inferior bargaining power on a "take-it-or-leave-it" basis and the weaker person can not go elsewhere to obtain the goods or services desired and therefore must deal on the terms dictated by the superior party or do without.

With the rise of the concept of unconscionability[16] and the adoption of consumer protection laws[17] the need to apply the adhesion contract concept has diminished greatly. In most cases it is held that the concept is not applicable either because there is not a gross inequality of bargaining power or because the goods or services could be obtained elsewhere.[18]

§ 14:8.   Remedies.

Mistake, fraud, undue influence, and duress may make the agreement voidable or, in some instances, void. The following remedies are then available.

(a) **Rescission.** If the contract is voidable, it can be rescinded or set aside by the party who has been injured or of whom advantage has been taken. If not avoided, however, the contract is valid and binding. In no case can the other party, the wrongdoer, set aside the contract. If the agreement is void, neither party can enforce it and no act of avoidance is required by either party to set the contract aside.

FACTS:

Thompson bought an automobile on credit from Central Motor Co. The contract required him to pay 35 monthly installments of $125 and a final installment of $5,265. The sales manager fradulently assured Thompson that when the last payment was due it could be refinanced by signing another note for that amount at 8 percent interest. Thompson agreed to make the purchase and signed the contract and a note in reliance on the assurance that he could refinance the final payment. Thereafter Central Motor refused to finance the final

payment unless Thompson promised to pay 12 percent interest. He refused to do so, and returned the car. Central sold the car and then sued Thompson for the balance remaining due.

DECISION:

Judgment for Thompson. The misrepresentation of the sales manager constituted fraud which permitted Thompson as the victim of the fraud to avoid the contract and the note. [Central Motor Co. v Thompson (Tex Civ App) 465 SW2d 405 (1971)]

---

[15]Fields v Thompson, 164 Ga App 331, 297 SE2d 100 (1982).
[16]See § 16:5 of this book.
[17]See Chapter 7 of this book.
[18]Muscat v Lawyers Title Ins. Corp. 135 Mich App 26, 351 NW2d 893 (1984).

(b) **Damages.** If the other party was guilty of a wrong, such as fraud, as distinguished from making an innocent mistake, the injured party may sue for damages caused by such a wrong. In the case of the sale of goods, the aggrieved party may both rescind and recover damages; but in other contracts, the victim must choose one of these two remedies.[19] Thus, a buyer rescinding a contract for the sale of a house because of fraud cannot also recover damages for the fraud.

(c) **Reformation of Contract by Court.** When a written contract does not correctly state the agreement already made by the parties, either party can have the court correct or reform the writing to state the agreement actually made. An action for reformation may be necessary because a change of circumstances or the occurrence of certain events may cause the other party to refuse to change the contract. For example, if A obtains a collision insurance policy on an automobile but through mistake the policy describes the wrong car, A can obtain a decree of court declaring that the policy covers the car that A and the insurance company intended to insure rather than the car wrongly identified in the policy. The insurance company would have gladly made the correction prior to any loss being sustained, but if the car A intended to insure had been damaged, court reformation would be necessary.

FACTS:

Kadish Pharmacy and other pharmacies made a contract with Blue Cross Blue Shield to provide prescription drugs to subscribers of Blue Cross Blue Shield, which in turn would reimburse the pharmacies. Kadish and the other pharmacies claimed that the contract with Blue Cross Blue Shield should have specified that the reimbursement to them would be at the customary rate charged by them. There was no proof that the parties had ever agreed to this as a term of their contract. Kadish sued to reform the contract.

DECISION:

Reformation will not be allowed to rewrite a contract to include a provision that one party subsequently realized should have been included. It is only allowed to correct the written contract to state what in fact had been agreed to by the parties. [Kadish Pharmacy, Inc. v Blue Cross Blue Shield, _____ App Div 2d _____, 494 NWS2d 354 (1985)]

SUMMARY

The assent of a party to an agreement is not genuine or voluntary in certain cases of mistake, misstatement, concealment, or pressure. When this is so, the agreement of the parties does not give rise to a contract and what appears to be a contract can be avoided by the victim of such circumstances or conduct.

As to mistake, it is necessary to distinguish between unilateral mistakes that are unknown to the other contracting party and those that are known. Mistakes that are unknown to the other party typically do not affect

[19]UCC § 2-721.

the binding character of the agreement while a unilateral mistake of which the other contracting party has knowledge or reason to know makes the contract avoidable by the victim of the mistake.

The misstatement situation may be one of innocent misrepresentation, nondisclosure, or fraud. The innocent misrepresentation generally has no effect on the binding quality of an agreement, although there is a trend to recognize it as a ground for avoiding the contract and a few courts allow the recovery of damages. When one party to the contract knows of a fact that has a bearing on the transaction, the failure to volunteer information as to that fact to the other contracting party is called nondisclosure. The law ordinarily does not attach any significance to nondisclosure, deeming that it is preferable that the party lacking the knowledge ask questions of the party with knowledge, rather than to impose a duty on the party with knowledge to volunteer information. Thus the agreement of the parties is not affected by the fact that one party did not disclose information to the other party. Contrary to this rule, there is a duty to volunteer information when a confidential relationship exists between the possessor of the knowledge and the other contracting party. A strong modern trend in the law imposes a duty to disclose or volunteer information relating to matters that are not likely to be inquired about by the other contracting party, such as a hidden defect or condition that a stranger is not likely to perceive and is not likely to inquire about.

When concealment goes beyond mere silence and consists of actively taking of steps to hide the truth, the conduct is classified as fraud rather than nondisclosure. There is a growing trend to hold fine print clauses not binding on the theory that they are designed to hide the truth from the other contracting party. Consumer protection statutes often outlaw fine print clauses by requiring particular contracts or particular clauses in contracts to be printed in type of a specified size. Fraud is the making of a false statement with knowledge of its falsity or reckless indifference as to its truth with the intent that the other person rely thereon and such person does rely on such false statement and sustains harm or loss. Ordinarily the false statement can not be a statement of intention or a promise although it is fraud when made with the present secret intention contrary to the stated one. Likewise a statement of opinion, value, or of the law can not ordinarily be the basis for fraud liability although it can when the maker of the false statement claims to be an expert as to the particular subject matter and is making the statement as an expert. The use of an assumed name is not fraudulent when not done for the purpose of deceiving.

The free will of a person, essential to the voluntary character of a contract, may be lacking because the agreement had been obtained by pressure. This may range from undue influence, which is something more than nagging or continuous hounding; through the array of threats of extreme economic loss, called economic duress; to the threat of physical force that would cause serious personal injury or damage to property, called physical duress. The mere fact that one party to the contract has great bargaining power and offers the other party a printed contract on a "take-it-or-leave-it" basis, that is an adhesion contract, does not prove that the agreement was not voluntary. However, some courts have held that in such cases the agreement is not voluntary if the weaker party can not obtain the desired goods or services elsewhere.

When the voluntary character of an agreement has been destroyed by mistake, misstatement, concealment, or by pressure, the victim may avoid or rescind the contract or may ratify the contract and obtain money damages from the wrongdoer sufficient to put the victim in the position that the victim would have held had there been a voluntary agreement. In cases of fraud, some jurisdictions depart from this rule and limit the plaintiff to recovering the out of pocket expenses. All these remedies may be lost by delay. Rescission is also lost if the aggrieved party is not able to put things back the way they were before the contract was made (restore the status quo ante). When the mistake consists of an error in putting an oral contract in writing, either party may ask the court to reform or correct the writing so that it states what the parties had actually agreed to.

QUESTIONS AND CASE PROBLEMS

1. What is the objective of each of the following rules of law?
   (a) One party generally cannot set aside a contract because the other party failed to volunteer information which the complaining party would desire to know.
   (b) In certain close relationships that are regarded as confidential, it is presumed that a contract which benefits the dominating person was obtained by undue influence, and the dominating person has the burden of proving the contrary.
2. How is a contract affected by a unilateral mistake?
3. Lester purchased a used automobile from MacKintosh Motors. He asked the seller if the car had ever been in a wreck. The MacKintosh salesperson had never seen the car before that morning and knew nothing of its prior history, but quickly answered Lester's question by stating: "No. It has never been in a wreck." In fact, the auto had been seriously damaged in a wreck and, although repaired, was worth much less than the value it would have had if there had not been any wreck. When Lester learned the truth, he sued MacKintosh Motors and the salesperson for damages for fraud. They raised the defense that the salesperson did not know that the statement was false and had not intended to deceive Lester. Did the conduct of the salesperson constitute fraud?
4. For convenience, Henry Hanschlagel wants to shorten and change his name. May he open a bank account using the name of "Henry Shaw" without his first obtaining a court order approving this change of name?
5. Helen and Richard make a contract for the sale of an automobile. They orally agree that the price Richard is to pay is $2,000 but when the written contract is typed, the amount is wrongly stated as $3,000 and this contract is signed before anyone notices the mistake. Helen then claims that the written contract is binding and that Richard is required to pay $3,000. He claims that he is only required to pay the originally agreed to amount of $2,000. Is he correct?
6. Compare (a) misrepresentation, (b) nondisclosure, and (c) fraud.

7. Mary purchased a home from the Mitchell Developers. She was told that the house was free from termites. Actually the house was infested with termites, and there was extensive termite damage in the house which was known to Mitchell and which Mitchell had intentionally concealed by paint and paper. When Mary learned of the actual termite condition, she sued Mitchell for damages for fraud and to set aside the contract. How will her claims be decided by the court?

8. If a buyer makes an arithmetic mistake in calculating the quantity of goods to purchase, what effect does such mistake have upon the contract to purchase the excessive amount?

9. Tucker purchased an automobile from Central Motors, relying on the representation that it was the latest model available. The sale was completed on February 9. On February 10, Tucker learned that the representation that the automobile was the latest model was false. He continued to drive the car; and after having driven it in excess of one thousand miles, he demanded on April 7 that the purchase be set aside for fraud. Decide. [Tucker v Central Motors, 220 La 510, 57 So2d 40]

10. The Browns were having a house built. The contractor purchased brick from the Georgia Carolina Brick and Tile Co. The contract required the brick company to supply the entire quantity ordered from the same "run" or manufacturer's lot of brick. Bricks from two different runs were sent. The color for the two was not exactly the same. The representative of the brick company falsely stated to the Browns that when the bricks dried out they would all be the same color. The representative knew that this was false. When the company was sued for fraud, it raised the defense that the statement of its representative was merely an opinion and therefore could not give rise to fraud liability. Was this defense valid? [Georgia-Carolina Brick & Tile Co. v Brown, 153 Ga App 747, 266 SE2d 531]

11. Hylton was arrested on the complaint of the Cox Construction Company. The admitted facts showed that there was no legal basis for the arrest. The deputy sheriffs of the county, Phillips and Bay, put Hylton in a jail cell and dressed him in prison clothing. They told him that he could get out if he signed a paper releasing them from any liability for false imprisonment. Hylton signed the paper. He was released. Hylton then sued Phillips and Bay. They defended by proving that Hylton had released them from liability. Hylton claimed the release was void. Was he correct? [Hylton v Phillips, 270 Or 766, 529 P2d 906]

12. A claimed that B owed him money. A was under the impression that B did not have much money. On the basis of this impression, A made a settlement agreement with B for a nominal amount. When A later learned that B was in fact reasonably wealthy, A sought to set the agreement aside. Was A entitled to do so?

13. An agent of Thor Food Service Corp. was seeking to sell Makofske a combination refrigerator-freezer and food purchase plan. Makofske was married and had three children. After being informed of the eating habits of Makofske and his family, the agent stated that the cost of the freezer and food would be about $95 to $100 a month. Makofske carefully

examined the agent's itemized estimate and made some changes to it. Makofske then signed the contract and purchased the refrigerator-freezer. The cost proved to be greater than the estimated $95 to $100 a month, and Makofske claimed that the contract had been obtained by fraud. Decide. [Thor Food Service Corp. v Makofske, 28 Misc 2d 872, 218 NYS2d 93]

14. A corporation was about to be sued by the First National Bank on a large loan that was overdue. Such a lawsuit would have caused the value of the stock of the corporation to drop on the stock exchange. A owned the majority of the shares of stock of the corporation. In order to protect the value of those shares, A promised the bank to pay the debt owed by the corporation if the bank would not sue the corporation. The bank agreed that it would not sue the corporation. However, the debt was not paid and the bank sued A. A claimed that the promise to pay the corporate debt was not binding because it had been obtained by economic duress. Is A correct?

15. On December 1, 1964, Neely, a senior in college, made a contract to play the following year for the Houston Oilers professional football team. It was agreed orally that the making of this contract would be kept secret so that Neely would appear to be eligible for a postseason college game. Neely then received a better offer from the Dallas Cowboys and after college went to play for them. Houston sought an injunction against Neely to prevent him from playing with the Dallas Cowboys. Neely claimed Houston could not enforce the contract because of its fraud in stating that the contract would be effective on January 2, 1965, and in filing the contract with the League Commissioner before that time in violation of the agreement to keep the execution of the contract secret so as to make him appear eligible for the postseason college football game. Was Neely's defense valid? [Houston Oilers, Inc. v Neely (CA10 Okla) 361 F2d 36]

16. Portland General Electric Company desired to have some construction work done. It advertised for bids. A bid from the Ace Electric Company was the lowest received but it was so low that Portland thought something must be wrong and that Ace must have overlooked the cost of certain reenforced ducts. Portland telephoned Ace and asked if Ace was satisfied with its bid but did not state that Portland thought that there was some mistake nor indicate what that mistake could be. Ace stated that it was satisfied with the bid. Portland accepted Ace's bid. Ace did not discover until after the contract was signed that it was obligated to perform the work on the reenforced ducts and that such work had not been considered in calculating its bid. Ace performed the work for the ducts and then sued Portland for additional compensation for this work. Was it entitled to recover? [Ace Electric Co. v Portland General Electric Co. 55 Or App 382, 637 P2d 1366]

17. In 1622, a fleet of Spanish treasure ships sank 40 nautical miles off the Florida coast. In 1971, Treasure Salvors, Inc. located one of the wrecked ships, the Atocha. Treasure Salvors and the Department of State of Florida believed that the wreck was located on the Florida coastal strip.

On this basis, the State of Florida and Treasure Salvors made successive annual contracts giving Treasure Salvors the right to search for sunken treasure of the wreck in return for its giving Florida 25% of everything that was found. In a subsequent lawsuit, it was determined that the wreck was not on Florida land. Treasure Salvors claimed that it was not bound by its contract with Florida. Was it correct? [Florida v Treasure Salvors, Inc. (CA5 Fla) 621 F2d 1340]

CHAPTER 15

CONSIDERATION

CHAPTER OBJECTIVES

After studying this chapter you will be able to:

1. Define what constitutes consideration.
2. State the effect of the absence of consideration.
3. Identify promises that can serve as consideration.
4. Distinguish between present consideration and past consideration.
5. State when forbearance can be consideration.
6. Recognize situations when adequacy of consideration has significance.
7. List the exceptions to the requirement of consideration.
8. Solve problems involving the existence of consideration.

kay

In Chapter 12, you saw that an agreement between the parties is one of the essential ingredients of a binding contract. The existence of an agreement ensures that the obligations created by the contract have been voluntarily assumed. But society will not muster its resources to enforce every promise. As a condition for enforceability, society requires that a promise be supported by a consideration, that is, the promise must have been obtained in return for something else. Does it matter what is offered in return? Historically, no. In the days of Adam Smith, the law left it to the contracting parties to determine what each party wanted as consideration. Whether that was too much or too little was no concern of the law. In the last few decades, this social desire for unrestricted bargaining freedom has lost much of its appeal when it is seen that those with inferior economic power or education can not take care of themselves. In order to prevent their exploitation, consumer protection statutes and the concept of unconscionability have made the law examine the sufficiency or adequacy of the consideration. Going

251

in the opposite direction, society has chosen to enforce certain promises when made in certain situations even though no consideration at all was present. Thus in some instances, no consideration is required to make a promise binding.

§ 15:1.   Definition.

Consideration is what a promisor demands and receives as the price for the promise.[1] Consideration is something to which the promisor is not otherwise entitled and which the promisor specifies as the price for the promise. It is not necessary that the promisor expressly use the word "consideration."

Since consideration is the price paid for the promise, it is unimportant who pays that price as long as it has been agreed that it should be paid in that way. For example, consideration may be the extending of credit to a third person, as extending credit to the corporation of which the promisor is a stockholder.

FACTS:

Joy Manufacturing Company sold goods to the Marrick Company on credit. Joy was not paid for the goods. In order to induce Joy to continue to sell on credit, an agreement was made by which Walter Kennedy, shareholder and vice-president of Marrick, promised that he would pay if the corporation did not. He later refused to live up to his promise on the theory that it was not supported by consideration and therefore was not binding.

DECISION:

The promise of Joy to continue to sell to the corporation on credit was consideration for the promise of Kennedy to pay if the corporation did not. [Kennedy v Joy Manufacturing Co. (Ky App) 707 SW2d 362 (1986)]

(a) **Nature of Contract.** In a unilateral contract, the consideration for the promise is the doing of the act called for. The doing of the act in such case is also the acceptance of the offer of the promisor.

FACTS:

Radio Station KSCS broadcast a popular music program. It announced that it would pay $25,000 to any listener who detected that it did not play three consecutive songs at a time. Steve Jennings listened and heard a program in which two songs were followed by a commercial. He claimed the $25,000. The station refused to pay on the ground that there was no consideration for its promise to pay that amount.

---

[1]Pink v Busch, 100 Nev 684, 691 P2d 456 (1984).

DECISION:

The obvious purpose of the offer of the radio station was to increase its listening audience. It purchased conduct, namely listening, by its promise. The conduct of the plaintiff in listening to the program was thus consideration for the promise of the station to pay the money if a listener satisfied the specified condition. The station was therefore bound by contract to pay the money to Jennings when he detected that there was not a three song sequence. [Jennings v Radio Station KSCS (Tex App) 708 SW2d 60 (1986)]

In a bilateral contract, which is an exchange of promises, each promise is the consideration for the other promise. When a lawsuit is brought for breaking a promise, it is the consideration for the promise on which suit is brought to which attention is directed.

(b) **Agreed exchange.** Consideration is what is agreed to in return for the promise of the defendant. In most cases, this will directly benefit the defendant, the promisor, and will be some burden or detriment to the plaintiff, the promisee. For example, an employer who promises to pay wages sustains detriment by promising to pay the wages in exchange for the benefit of receiving the employee's promise to work. The important thing, however, is that what is received is what was asked for as the price of the promise.

As long as someone gives what was asked for by the promisor, the promisor's obligation is supported by consideration even though the economic benefit of the promise is received by a third person. Thus when a third person comes to the financial aid of a debtor by making some promise to the creditor, there is consideration for the promise to the creditor if that promise is in exchange for some promise from the creditor, even though the creditor's promise benefits the debtor rather than the third person. A promise guaranteeing a loan to a corporation is binding although the money loaned was all received by the corporation and nothing was received by the promisor.[2]

FACTS:

Kemp leased a gas filling station from Baehr. Kemp, who was heavily indebted to the Penn-O-Tex Oil Corporation, transferred to it his right to receive payments on all claims. When Baehr complained that the rent was not paid, he was assured by the corporation that the rent would be paid to him. Baehr did not sue Kemp for the overdue rent but later sued the corporation. The defense was raised that there was no consideration for the promise of the corporation.

DECISION:

The promise of the corporation was not binding because there was no consideration for it. While the concept of consideration developed as the way of determining which agreements were serious and intended by the parties to be binding, the converse does not follow that every serious agreement is binding. It is necessary in every case to find that the promisor received the required price of his promise. Although Baehr's not suing Kemp could have been specified by the corporation as the price of its promise to pay Kemp's obligation, the corporation had not done so and hence there was no consideration. [Baehr v Penn-O-Tex Oil Corporation, 258 Minn 533, 104 NW2d 661 (1960)]

[2]Blalock v Central Bank of Georgia, 170 Ga App 87, 316 SE2d 474 (1984).

§ 15:2.   Effect of Absence of Consideration.

The absence of consideration makes a promise not binding. Thus, a person sued for breaking a promise will not be held liable when no consideration was received for the promise. For example, when the promise of an employee to refrain from competing with the employer is not supported by consideration, the promise is not binding and the employee may compete with the employer.[3] Likewise an offer that is to be held open for a specified number of days may be revoked at any time when no consideration is given for the promise to keep the offer open.

While the absence of consideration ordinarily prevents enforcing a promise, the absence of consideration has no greater effect. That is, the agreement is not illegal because there was no consideration. Consequently, when a person keeps the promise, the performance rendered cannot be thereafter revoked on the ground that there was no consideration. To illustrate, a promise to make a gift cannot be enforced because there is no consideration for the promise, but once the gift is made, the donor cannot take the gift back because there was no consideration.

§ 15:3.   A Promise as Consideration.

In a bilateral contract, each party makes a promise to the other. The promise which one party makes is consideration for the promise made by the other.

(a) **Binding Character of Promise.** To constitute consideration, a promise must be binding; that is, it must impose a liability or create a duty. An unenforceable promise cannot be consideration. Suppose that a coal company promises to sell to a factory at a specific price all the coal which it orders, and that the factory agrees to pay that price for any coal which it orders from the coal company. The promise of the factory is not consideration because it does not obligate the factory to buy any coal from the coal company. If, however, the factory promises to purchase all the coal it requires for a specific period and the coal dealer agrees to supply it at a specific price per ton, there is a valid contract.

(b) **Conditional Promise.** Can a conditional promise be consideration? Assume that an agreement states "buyer promises to buy provided buyer can obtain financing." Is such a promise consideration for the seller's promise to sell, or is the buyer's promise not consideration because it does not impose any obligation on the buyer at the time that the promise is made?

(c) **Cancellation Provision.** Although a promise must impose a binding obligation, it may authorize one or either party to terminate or cancel the agreement under certain circumstances or upon giving notice to the other party. The fact that the contract may be terminated in this manner does not make the contract any less binding prior to such termination.

§ 15:4.   Promise to Perform Existing Obligation.

Ordinarily a promise to do what one is already under a legal obligation to do is not consideration. Similarly, a promise to refrain from doing

[3]Insurance Agents, Inc. v Abel (Iowa App) 338 NW2d 531 (1983).

what one has no legal right to do is not consideration. This preexisting duty or legal obligation can be based upon statute, upon general principles of law, upon responsibilities of an office held by the promisor, or upon a preexisting contract.

FACTS:

Through a mistake, Midwest Recovery Bureau wrongfully took Cobb's truck. In so doing, the truck was damaged. Later Cobb gave Midwest a release by which he released Midwest from liability for wrongfully taking his truck. The release was given in consideration of the repairing and the returning of the truck. After the truck was repaired and returned, Cobb sued Midwest for damages. It raised the defense that Cobb had released it from liability.

DECISION:

Judgment for Cobb. The release was not binding because there was no consideration for it. As the truck had been wrongfully taken, Midwest was under the duty to return the truck and to return it in the same condition as when taken. Therefore Cobb was only obtaining that to which he was entitled when the truck was repaired and returned. Therefore the repairing and the returning of the truck was not consideration and the release was not binding. [Cobb v Midwest Recovery Bureau Co. _____ Minn _____, 295 NW2d 232 (1980)]

(a) **Completion of Contract.** When a contractor refuses to complete a building unless the owner promises a payment or bonus in addition to the sum specified in the original contract, and the owner promises to make that payment, the question arises whether the owner's promise is binding. Most courts hold that the second promise of the owner is without consideration.

If the promise of the contractor is to do something that is neither expressly nor impliedly a part of the first contract, then the promise of the other party is binding. For example, if a bonus of $1,000 is promised in return for the promise of a contractor to complete the building at a date earlier than that specified in the original agreement, the promise to pay the bonus is binding. Similarly, when a cement subcontractor is obligated by contract to pour cement for the construction of a building on five working days during working hours, and then promises to pour round-the-clock, seven days a week, the subcontractor is promising a performance that was not already required and therefore such promise constitutes consideration for the contractor's promise to make an additional payment to the subcontractor.[4]

(1) *Good Faith Adjustment.* There is a trend to enforce a second promise to pay a contractor a greater amount for the performance of the original contract when there are extraordinary circumstances caused by unforseeable difficulties and when the additional amount promised the contractor is reasonable under the circumstances.

When parties to a contract in a good faith effort to meet the business realities of a situation agree to a reduction of contract terms, there is some authority that the promise of the one party to accept the lesser performance

[4]Hobbs Construction & Development, Inc. v Colonial Concrete Co. (Fla App) 461 So 2d 255 (1984).

of the other is binding even though technically the promise to render the lesser performance is not consideration because the obligor was already obligated to render the greater performance. Thus, a landlord's promise to reduce the rent was binding when the tenant could not pay the original rent and the landlord preferred to have the building occupied even though receiving a smaller rental.

(2) Contract for Sale of Goods. When the contract is for the sale of goods, any modification made by the parties to the contract is binding without regard to the existence of consideration for the modification.

(b) Compromise and Release of Claims. The rule that doing or promising to do what one is bound to do is not consideration applies to a part payment made in satisfaction of an admitted debt. For example, if one person owes another $100, the promise of the latter to accept $50 in full payment is not binding and will not prevent the creditor from demanding the remainder later because the part payment made by the debtor was not consideration for the promise to release the balance of the claim.

If the debtor pays before the debt is due, there is, of course, consideration since on the day when the payment was made, the creditor was not entitled to demand any payment. Likewise if the creditor accepts some article, even of slight value, in addition to the part payment, the agreement is held to be binding.

If there is a bona fide dispute as to the amount owed or as to whether any amount is owed, a payment by the debtor of less than the amount claimed by the creditor is consideration for the latter's agreement to release or settle the claim. It is generally regarded as sufficient if the claimant believes in the merit of the claim. Conversely, if the claimant knows that the claim does not have any merit and is merely pressing it in order to force the other party to make some payment to buy peace from the annoyance of a lawsuit, the settlement agreement based on the part payment is not binding.

(c) Part Payment Checks. The acceptance and cashing of a check for part of a debt releases the entire debt when the check bears a notation that it is intended as final or full payment and the total amount due is disputed or unliquidated. It probably has this same effect even though the debt is not disputed or unliquidated.[5]

In some jurisdictions, this principle is applied without regard to the form of payment or whether the claim is disputed, it being required only that the part payment was in fact received and accepted as discharging the obligation. The California Civil Code § 1541, provides: "An obligation is extinguished by a release therefrom given to the debtor by the creditor upon a new consideration, or in writing, with or without new consideration."

(d) Composition of Creditors. In a **composition of creditors,** the various creditors of one debtor mutually agree to accept a fractional part of their claims in full satisfaction thereof. Such agreements are binding and are supported by consideration. When creditors agree to extend the due date of their debts, the promise of each creditor to forbear is likewise consideration for the promise of other creditors to forbear.

---

[5]Upper Avenue National Bank v First Arlington National Bank, 81 Ill App 3d 208, 36 Ill Dec 325, 400 NE2d 1105 (1980); Uniform Commercial Code § 3–408. Official Comment, point 2.

§ 15:5.   Present Consideration Versus Past Benefits.

Since consideration is what the promisor states must be received in return for the promise, the consideration must be given when or after the promisor states what is demanded. Past benefits already received by the promisor cannot be consideration for the later promise.[6]

FACTS:

Warner & Co. procured a purchaser for the property of Brua and submitted to Brua sales papers to be signed. The papers contained a promise to pay Warner & Co. commissions for finding a purchaser. Brua signed the paper but later refused to pay Warner & Co. Thereafter Warner & Co. brought a suit to recover the commissions from Brua, who contended that there was no consideration for his promise.

DECISION:

There was no consideration for the owner's promise to pay the broker since the broker's services which the owner promised to compensate had been performed and were therefore past consideration. A promise given because of past consideration is not binding. [Warner & Co. v Brua, 33 Ohio App 84, 168 NE 571 (1929)]

(a) **Complex Transactions.** In applying the rule that past benefits cannot be consideration, care must be taken to distinguish between the situation in which the "consideration" is in fact "past" and the situation in which the earlier consideration and the subsequent promises were all part of one complex transaction. In such cases, the earlier consideration is not regarded as "past" and supports the later promises.

§ 15:6.   Forbearance as Consideration.

In most cases, consideration consists of the performance of an act or the making of a promise to act. But consideration may also consist of forbearance, which is refraining from doing an act, or a promise of forbearance. In other words, the promisor may desire to buy the inaction of the other party or a promise not to act.

The waiving or giving up of any right can be consideration for the promise of another. Thus, the relinquishment of a right in property or of a right to sue for damages will support a promise given in return for it.

When the creditor agrees to extend the time for paying the debt in return for the debtor's promise of a higher return of interest, the agreement to extend is consideration for the promise to pay the higher rate of interest.

When a supplier has the right to terminate the contract with the dealer selling its products, the promise of the supplier to refrain from revoking the contract with the dealer is consideration for the dealer's agreement to reduce the commissions deducted on the resale of the supplier's product.

The right that is surrendered in return for a promise may be a right against a third person, as well as against the promisor.

As under the rule governing compromises, forbearance to assert a claim is consideration when the claim has been asserted in good faith, even

---

[6]Hayes v Plantations Steel Co. _____ RI _____, 438 A2d 1091 (1982).

though it is without merit.[7] In the absence of a good faith belief, forbearance with respect to a worthless claim is not consideration.

FACTS:

Dale Dyer was employed by National By-Products, Inc. He was seriously injured while at work because of a job-related accident. He agreed to give up his right to sue the employer for damages in consideration of the employer's giving him a lifetime job. The employer later claimed that this agreement was not binding because Dyer's promise to not sue could not be consideration for the promise to employ because in fact Dyer had no right to sue as his only remedy was to make a claim under workers' compensation.

DECISION:

It could not be determined without a trial whether the settlement agreement was binding. The fact that Dyer did not have any right to sue was not controlling. If the jury found that Dyer honestly believed that he could sue the employer, his surrender of that right constituted consideration for the promise of the employer, even though in fact Dyer did not have any legal right. [Dyer v National By-Products, Inc. (Iowa) 380 NW2d 732 (1986)]

---

§ 15:7.   Adequacy of Consideration.

Ordinarily courts do not consider the adequacy of the consideration given for a promise. The fact that the consideration supplied by one party is slight when compared with the burden undertaken by the other party is immaterial. It is a matter for the parties to decide when they make their contract whether each is getting a fair return. In the absence of fraud or other misconduct, the court usually will not interfere to make sure that each side is getting a fair return.[8]

FACTS:

Upon the death of their mother, the children of James Smith gave their interest in the mother's estate to their father in consideration of his payment of $1 to each and of his promise to leave them the property on his death. The father died without leaving them the property. The children sued their father's second wife to obtain the property in accordance with the agreement.

DECISION:

Judgment for children. The promises between the father and the children created a binding contract, as against the objection that the contract was not binding because the children got so little from the father, since all they received was the $1 and the chance that when the father died, there would be something in his estate which could be left to them. This argument was rejected because the law will not consider the adequacy of consideration when there is no element of fraud. [Smith v Smith, 340 Ill 34, 172 NE 32 (1930)]

---

[7]Todd v Berner, _____ Mont _____, 693 P2d 506 (1984).
[8]Okeson v Jack Dempsey Drywall, Inc. (Neb) 301 NW2d 356 (1981).

§ 15:8.   Exceptions to Adequacy of Consideration Rule.

The insufficiency or inadequacy of the consideration may lead a court to the conclusion that a contract is not binding because unconscionable or that fraud was practiced on the promisor.

The inadequacy of the consideration may be evidence of the exercise of undue influence or the taking advantage of the condition of the other contracting party. Several factors may combine to challenge the validity of the contract.

§ 15:9.   Exceptions to Requirement of Consideration.

By statute or decision, consideration is no longer required in a number of situations.

(a) **Charitable Subscriptions.** When charitable enterprises are financed by voluntary subscriptions of a number of persons, the promise of each is generally enforceable. For example, when a number of people make pledges or subscriptions for the construction of a church, for a charitable institution, or for a college, the subscriptions are binding.

The theories for sustaining such promises vary. Consideration is lacking according to the technical standards applied in ordinary contract cases. Nevertheless, the courts enforce such promises as a matter of public policy.

FACTS:

A college was planned. Salsbury obtained a pledge from the Northwestern Bell Telephone Company to contribute to the college. When the Company did not pay, Salsbury sued the Company. It raised the defense that there was no consideration for the Company's promise and that nothing had been done by the college in reliance on the promise.

DECISION:

Judgment for Salsbury. As a matter of public policy, a promise of a charitable contribution is binding even though there is no consideration for the promise and without regard for whether the charity had done any acts in reliance on the promise. The Company was therefore liable on its promise to contribute. [Salsbury v Northwestern Bell Telephone Co. ____Iowa ____, 221 NW2d 609 (1974)]

(b) **Uniform Commercial Code.** In a number of situations, the Uniform Commercial Code abolishes the requirement of consideration. For example, under the Code, consideration is not required for (1) a merchant's written firm offer as to goods, stated to be irrevocable; (2) a written discharge of a claim for an alleged breach of a commercial contract; or (3) an agreement to modify a contract for the sale of goods.[9]

(c) **Sealed and Written Instruments.** At common law, consideration was not necessary to support a promise under seal. In a state which gives the seal its original common-law effect, the gratuitous promise or a promise to make a gift is enforceable when it is set forth in a sealed instrument.

[9]UCC § 2–209(1).

In some states, a promise under seal must be supported by consideration, just as though it did not have a seal. Other states take a middle position and hold that the presence of a seal is prima facie proof that there is consideration to support the promise. This means that if nothing more than the existence of the sealed promise is shown, it is deemed supported by consideration. The party making the promise, however, may prove that there was no consideration. In that case, the promise is not binding.

In some states a presumption arises whenever a contract is in writing that the promises of the parties thereto are supported by consideration.[10]

§ 15:10.   Promissory Estoppel.

Most courts enforce promises that are not supported by consideration by applying the doctrine of **promissory estoppel**. By this doctrine, if a person makes a promise to another under such circumstances that the promisor should reasonably foresee that the promisee will be induced to rely thereon and that the promisee will then sustain substantial loss if the promise is not kept, the promise is binding even though there is no consideration for it. In applying the doctrine of promissory estoppel, courts are ignoring the requirement of consideration in order to attain a just result.

Promissory estoppel differs from consideration in that the reliance of the promisee is not the bargained-for price or response sought by the promisor. Under promissory estoppel, it is sufficient that the promisor foresees that there will be such reliance. The doctrine of promissory estoppel applies only when (1) the promisor has reason to foresee the detrimental reliance by the promisee, and (2) the promisee in fact would sustain a substantial loss because of such reliance if the promise is not performed. In the absence of detrimental reliance on the promise, the doctrine of promissory estoppel is not applicable. Thus a promise made to the debtor by the creditor that the creditor would collect only $20 a month on the debt of approximately $12,000 was not binding because there was no proof that the debtor relied in any manner upon such promise.[11]

FACTS:

Hoffman wanted to acquire a franchise as a Red Owl grocery store, Red Owl being a corporation that maintained a system of chain stores. The agent of Red Owl informed Hoffman and his wife that if they would sell their bakery in Wautoma, acquire a certain tract of land in Chilton, another city, and put up a specified amount of money, they would be given a franchise as desired. Hoffman sold his business, acquired the land in Chilton, but was never granted a franchise. He and his wife sued Red Owl, which raised the defense that there had only been an assurance that Hoffman would receive a franchise but no promise supported by consideration and therefore no binding contract to give him a franchise.

DECISION:

Judgment for the Hoffmans. Injustice would result under the circumstances of the case if the Hoffmans were not granted relief because of the failure of Red Owl to keep the promise made by its authorized agent. The plaintiffs had acted in reliance on such promise and would be harmed substantially if the promise were not held binding. [Hoffman v Red Owl Stores, Inc. 26 Wis 2d 683, 133 NW2d 267 (1967)]

---

[10]Pinney v Tarpley (Tenn App) 686 SW2d 574 (1985).
[11]Southeastern Equipment Co. v Mauss (Utah) 696 P2d 1187 (1985).

Legal difficulties often arise because parties take certain things for granted. Frequently they will be sure that they have agreed to everything and that they have a valid contract. Sometimes they do not and the courts are then faced with the problem of leaving them with their broken dreams or coming to their rescue.

§ 15:11.   Legality of Consideration.

The law will not permit persons to make contracts that violate the law. Accordingly, a promise to do something which the law prohibits or a promise to refrain from doing something which the law requires is not valid consideration and the contract is illegal.[12] This subject is further discussed in Chapter 16.

§ 15:12.   Failure of Consideration.

When a promise is given as consideration, the question arises as to whether the promisor will perform the promise. If the promise is not performed, the law describes the default as a "failure of consideration."[13]

The fact that performance of the contract by the other party does not have the result that one hoped for does not mean that there is a failure of consideration. For example, when one buys a store building in a real estate development, the buyer obviously does so in the expectation of obtaining a large volume of trade by virtue of the location. It may be that this will not occur because of the continuing of earlier shopping habits of the public. While the buyer of the store building is disappointed, there has not been any failure of consideration with respect to the contract for the purchase of the store from the owner.

FACTS:

The Aqua Drilling Company made a contract to drill a well for the Atlas Construction Company. It was expected that this would supply water for a home being constructed by Atlas. Aqua did not make any guarantee or warranty that water would be produced. Aqua drilled the well exactly as required by the contract but no water was produced. Atlas refused to pay and asserted that the contract was not binding on the theory that there had been a failure of consideration because the well did not produce water.

DECISION:

The contract was binding. Atlas obtained the exact performance required by the contract. While Atlas had expected that water would be obtained, Aqua did not make any guarantee or warranty that this would be so. Hence there was no failure of consideration. [Atlas Construction Co., Inc. v Aqua Drilling Co. ＿＿Wyo ＿＿, 559 P2d 39 (1977)]

---

[12]Lewkowicz v El Paso Apparel Corp. (Tex) 625 SW2d 301 (1982).
[13]Narus v Narus (Fla App) 382 So2d 144 (1980).

SUMMARY

A promise is not binding if there is no consideration for the promise. Consideration is the price required by the promisor as the price for the promise. That price may be the doing of an act or refraining from doing an act or merely a promise to do or to refrain. In a bilateral contract, it is necessary to find that the promise of each party is supported by consideration. If either promise is not so supported, it is not binding and the agreement of the parties is not a contract, with the consequence that the agreement can not be enforced. When a promise is the consideration it must be a binding promise. The binding character of a promise is not affected by the circumstance that there is a condition precedent to the performance promised. Likewise the binding character of the promise and of the contract is not affected by a provision in the contract for its cancellation by either one or both of the parties. A promise to do what one is already obligated to do is not consideration, although some exceptions are made when the rendering of a partial performance or a modified performance is accepted as a good faith adjustment to a changed situation, a compromise and release of claims, a part payment check, or a compromise of creditors. As consideration is the price that is given to obtain the promise, past benefits conferred upon the promisor can not be consideration, although in the case of a complex transaction, the past benefit and the subsequent transaction relating to the promise may in fact have been intended by the parties as one transaction. In such a case, the earlier benefit is not past consideration but is the consideration contemplated by the promisor as the price for the promise subsequently made.

A promise to refrain from doing an act can be consideration. A promise to refrain from suing or asserting a particular claim can be consideration. Generally the promise to forebear must be for a specified time, as distinguished from agreeing to forebear at will. When consideration is forebearance to assert a claim, it is immaterial whether the claim is valid as long as the claim has been asserted in good faith in the belief that it was valid.

When the promisor obtains the price specified for the promise, the law is not concerned with the value or adequacy of that price (the consideration), although exceptions are sometimes made in the case of fraud or unconscionability and under consumer protection statutes. There is a trend to abandon the requirement of consideration and exceptions are made in the case of charitable subscriptions, contracts governed by certain statutory provisions, such as a contract for the modification of a sale of goods under the Uniform Commercial Code. In some states, the common-law effect of the seal continues and makes a promise binding although there is no consideration to support it. The most extensive repudiation of the requirement of consideration is seen in the application of the doctrine of promissory estoppel. Under this doctrine, a promise is binding although not supported by consideration when the promisor should have realized that the promise would induce the promisee to rely thereon and the promisee relies on the promise to the extent that substantial loss would be sustained by the promisee if the promisor did not keep the promise.

In harmony with the basic principle that all transactions must be lawful, consideration for a promise must be legal. If it is not, there is no consideration and the promise is not binding.

When the promisor does not actually receive the price promised for the promise, it is said that there is a "failure of consideration." This is merely a default in performance and the binding character of the agreement is not affected by the subsequent failure to perform or "failure of consideration." Such failure merely constitutes a breach of the contract.

Although consideration is required to make a promise binding, the promise that is not supported by consideration is not unlawful or illegal. If the promisor voluntarily performs the promise, the promisor can not undo the performance and restore matters to their position prior to the making of the agreement. The parties are free to perform their agreement but the courts will not help either of them because there is no contract because consideration is lacking.

QUESTIONS AND CASE PROBLEMS

1. What is the objective of each of the following rules of law?
   (a) An executed gift or a performance that has been rendered without consideration cannot be rescinded for lack of consideration.
   (b) In the absence of fraud, the adequacy of consideration is usually immaterial.
2. What is consideration?
3. Marvin's house caught on fire. Through the prompt assistance of his neighbor, Odessa, the fire was quickly extinguished. In gratitude, Marvin promised to pay Odessa $1,000. Can Odessa enforce this promise if Marvin does not pay the money?
4. Clifton agreed to work for Acrylics Incorporated for $400 a month. Clifton later claimed that there was no contract because the consideration for the services to be rendered was inadequate. Is there a binding contract?
5. Frank promised to paint Cynthia's house. There was nothing given in return for the promise. Frank did not paint the house. Cynthia sued Frank for damages on the theory that the promise was binding because of promissory estoppel as she had waited for him to paint the house. Is Frank liable?
6. Compare (a) adequate consideration, (b) moral consideration, and (c) past consideration.
7. Galloway induced Marian to sell Marian's house to Galloway by false statements that a factory was going to be built on the vacant lot adjoining Marian's house. No factory was ever built and Marian then sued Galloway for damages for fraud. Marian offered to prove that Galloway had paid Marian only a fraction of the true value of Marian's house. Galloway claimed that this evidence as to value could not be admitted because it was immaterial whether the consideration paid Marian was adequate. Is Galloway correct?
8. What is the legal difference between an employer's promise to give an employee a bonus for an idea when the promise to pay the bonus is made (a) before or (b) after the employee discloses the idea to the employer?
9. Koedding hired the West Roofers to put a roof on his house. He later claimed that the roofing job was defective and threatened to sue West. Both parties discussed the matter in good faith and finally West guaran-

teed that the roof would be free from leaks for 20 years in return for which guarantee Koedding agreed not to sue West for damages. The roof leaked the next year. Koedding sued West on the guarantee. West claimed that the guarantee was not binding because there was no consideration for it because Koedding's promise not to sue West had no value because Koedding in fact did not have any valid claim against West and therefore was not entitled to sue West. Was this defense valid?

10. Gage borrowed money from Freeman and agreed to repay the amount borrowed with interest at the legal rate at the end of five years. As the due date approached, Freeman agreed to allow Gage to take such additional time as he needed provided Gage agreed that interest should be paid on the debt at the legal rate until the debt was paid. When the original due date arrived, Freeman demanded payment and refused to recognize the extension agreement. Was the extension agreement binding?

11. Fedun rented a building to Gomer who did business under the name of Mike's Cafe. Later, Gomer was about to sell out the business to Brown and requested Fedun to release him from his liability under the lease. Fedun agreed to do so. Brown sold out shortly thereafter. The balance of the rent due by Gomer under the original lease agreement was not paid, and Fedun sued Gomer on the rent claim. Could he collect after having released Gomer? [Fedun v Mike's Cafe, 204 Pa Super 356, 204 A2d 776]

12. Alexander Proudfoot Company was in the business of devising efficiency systems for industry. It told the Sanitary Linen Service Company that it could provide an improved system for Sanitary Linen that would save it money. It made a contract with Sanitary Linen to provide a money-saving system. The system was put into operation and Proudfoot was paid the amount due under the contract. The system failed to work and did not save money. Sanitary Linen sued to get the money back. Was it entitled to do so? [Sanitary Linen Service Co. v Alexander Proudfoot Co. (CA5 Fla) 435 F2d 292]

13. Before Youngman went to work for the Nevada Irrigation District, the superintendent promised him that he would receive a specified pay increase in April of each year. When he did not receive the increase he sued the District. He claimed that he had relied on the promise that he would receive such increase and that accordingly, the promise was binding. Was he correct? [Youngman v Nevada Irrigation District, 70 Cal 2d 235, 74 Cal Rptr 398, 449 P2d 462]

14. Allen owned land which was being developed. Her brother, Norburn, wrote to the vice-president of [Investment Properties of Asheville, Inc., stating that "this is to certify that I will stand personally liable" for the land preparation expenses. When Investment Properties sued him on this guaranty, he raised the defense that he did not receive any consideration for his promise and therefore it was not binding. Was this a valid defense? [Investment Properties of Asheville, Inc. v Norburn, 281 NC 300, 188 SE2d 342]

15. Sears, Roebuck & Co. promised to give Forrer "permanent employment." Forrer sold his farm at a loss in order to take the job. Shortly after commencing work, he was discharged by Sears which claimed that the contract could be terminated at will. Forrer claimed that promissory

estoppel prevented Sears from terminating the contract. Was he correct? [Forrer v Sears, Roebuck & Co., 36 Wis 2d 388, 153 NW2d 587]

17. Elena O'Brien was an interior decorator. The owner of two condominium buildings agreed to hire her to decorate the building interiors if she promised to split her commission with Victor Hovas, the son-in-law of the owner. She promised to do so and was given the job. Elena and Hovas then signed a separate contract in which she agreed to split the commission. Elena did not split the commission and Hovas sued her on their contract. She raised the defense that there was no consideration for her promise. Was she correct? [Hovas v O'Brien (Tex App) 654 SW2d 801]

18. Slattery was a licensed polygraph (lie detector) operator. He was a freelance operator. He administered lie detector tests at the request of certain state and county law-enforcement officers. He was paid by the hour and his contract required him to give the officials any information that was learned through the tests that might assist them in the performance of their duties.

A Wells Fargo armored car was robbed and an employee in the car was killed. Wells Fargo offered a reward of $25,000.00 for information leading to the arrest and conviction of the criminals. Slattery was examining a suspect on a matter that had nothing to do with the Wells Fargo case, but in the course of the examination obtained a statement from the person that he had committed the Wells Fargo crime. That person was subsequently tried and convicted for the Wells Fargo crime. Slattery then claimed the reward from Wells Fargo. It refused to pay. Slattery sued Wells Fargo. Was he entitled to recover the reward? [Slattery v Wells Fargo Armored Service Corp. (Fla App) 366 So 2d 157]

CHAPTER 16

LEGALITY AND PUBLIC

POLICY

CHAPTER OBJECTIVES

After studying this chapter you will be able to:

1. State the effect of illegality upon a contract.
2. Compare illegality and unconscionability.
3. Distinguish between illegality in performing a legal contract and the illegality of a contract.
4. Recognize when a contract is invalid because it obstructs legal processes.
5. State the elements of a lottery.
6. State the extent to which agreements not to compete are lawful.
7. Solve problems involving the question of the legality of a contract.

If society were totally committed to free enterprise and freedom of contract, anyone could make a contract on any subject. But as you might suspect, society does not wish to go that far. In Chapters 9 and 10 you saw that certain conduct is prohibited as crimes and torts. Logically it follows that society will not allow the making of a contract that calls for conduct that would be a crime or a tort.

In its most obvious form, the rule has developed that a contract calling for the commission of a crime is void. However, the criminal law generally lags behind the societal judgment of what is right and what is wrong. What happens when a court is faced with a contract that it believes is wrong but there is no statute making the transaction illegal? In such case, it will be declared that the contract is void as contrary to public policy. In recent years the judges have ventured even further in order to declare a contract or a contract provision invalid because unconscionable. All three limitations: (1) illegality, (2) contrary to public policy, and (3) unconscionability, represent society, speaking through the lawmaker or the judge for the purpose of striking a balance between freedom of contract and protection of the public.

A. GENERAL PRINCIPLES

An agreement is illegal when either its formation or performance is a crime or a tort, or is contrary to public policy. Ordinarily an illegal agreement is void.

§ 16:1.   Effect of Illegality.

When an agreement is illegal, the parties are usually not entitled to the aid of the courts. If the illegal agreement has not been performed, neither party can sue the other to obtain performance or damages. If the agreement has been performed, neither party can sue the other for damages or to set it aside.

FACTS:
Siddle purchased a quantity of fireworks from the Red Devil Fireworks Company. The sale was illegal because Siddle did not have a license to make the purchase. The seller knew this because it had been so informed by the Attorney General of the state. Siddle did not pay for the fireworks. Red Devil sued him. He defended on the ground that the contract could not be enforced because it was illegal.

DECISION:
Judgment for Siddle. The contract was illegal and the parties knew that it was illegal. Therefore public policy would not enforce the sales contract or compensate the seller for the reasonable value of the benefit received by the buyer. Although this meant that Siddle was getting something for nothing, it was more important to the public welfare to show that the courts would not assist parties to an illegal contract than it was to make Siddle pay for what he had received. [Red Devil Fireworks Co. v Siddle, 32 Wash App 521, 648 P2d 468 (1982)]

(a) **Exceptions.** The following are exceptions to the general rule that the court will not aid a party to an unlawful agreement:

(1) *Protection of One Party.* When the law which the agreement violates is intended for the protection of one of the parties, that party may seek relief. For example, when, in order to protect the public, the law forbids the issuance of securities or notes by certain classes of corporations, a person who has purchased them may recover the money paid.

(2) *Unequal Guilt.* When the parties are not equally guilty, or as it is said, are not *in pari delicto,* the one less guilty is granted relief when public interest is advanced by so doing. For example, when a statute is

adopted to protect one of the parties to a transaction, as a usury law adopted to protect borrowers, the person to be protected will not be deemed to be in pari delicto with the wrongdoer when entering into a transaction which is prohibited by the statute.

§ 16:2.   Partial Illegality.

An agreement may involve the performance of several promises, some of which are illegal and some legal. The legal parts of the agreement may be enforced, provided that they can be separated from the parts which are illegal.[1] The same rule applies when the consideration is illegal in part. The rule is not applied, however, to situations in which the illegal act or consideration is said to taint and strike down the entire agreement.

If a contract is susceptible of two interpretations, one legal and the other illegal, the court will assume that the legal meaning was intended unless the contrary is clearly indicated.[2]

§ 16:3.   Crimes and Civil Wrongs.

An agreement is illegal and therefore void when it calls for the commission of any act that constitutes a crime. To illustrate, one cannot enforce an agreement by which the other party is to commit an assault, to steal property, to burn a house, or to kill a person.

An agreement that calls for the commission of a civil wrong is also illegal and void. Examples are agreements to slander a third person; to defraud another; or to infringe another's patent, trademark, or copyright; or to fix prices.

§ 16:4.   Good Faith and Fairness.

The law is evolving toward requiring that contracts be fair and be made in good faith. The law is becoming increasingly concerned with whether A has utilized a superior bargaining power or superior knowledge to obtain better terms from B than A would otherwise have obtained.

In the case of goods, the seller must act in good faith, which is defined as to merchant sellers as "honesty in fact and the observance of reasonable commercial standards of fair dealing in the trade."[3]

§ 16:5.   Unconscionable and Oppressive Contracts.

Ordinarily a court will not consider whether a contract is fair or unfair, wise or foolish, or operates unequally between the parties. However, in a number of instances the law holds that contracts or contract clauses

---

[1]Fukuhara v Frank Huff Agency, Ltd (Hawaii) 607 P2d 1304 (1980).
[2]Haley v Pagan Lewis Motors, Inc. (Tex App) 647 SW2d 319 (1982).
[3]Uniform Commercial Code § 2–103(a)(b). Higher standards are also imposed on merchant sellers by other provisions of UCC. See § 2–314, as to warranties; § 2–603, as to duties with respect to rightfully rejected goods; and § 2–509(3), as to the transfer of risk of loss. While the provisions of the Code above noted do not apply to contracts generally, there is a growing trend of courts to extend Article 2 of the Code, which relates only to the sale of goods, to contract situations generally, on the theory that it represents the latest restatement of the law of contracts made by expert scholars and the legislators of the land.

will not be enforced because they are too harsh or oppressive to one of the two parties. This principle is most commonly applied to invalidate a clause providing for the payment by one party of a large penalty upon breaking the contract or a provision declaring that a party shall not be liable for the consequences of negligence. This principle is extended in connection with the sale of goods to provide that "if the court . . . finds the contract or any clause of the contract to have been unconscionable at the time it was made, the court may refuse to enforce the contract, or it may enforce the remainder of the contract without the unconscionable clause, or it may so limit the application of any unconscionable clause as to avoid any unconscionable result." [4]

A provision which gives what the court believes is too much of an advantage over a buyer is likely to be held void as **unconscionable**.

In order to bring the unconscionability provision into operation, it is not necessary to prove that fraud was practiced. When there is a grossly disproportionate bargaining power between the parties so that the weaker or inexperienced party "cannot afford to risk confrontation" with the stronger party but "just signs on the dotted line," courts will hold that "grossly unfair" terms obtained by the stronger party are void as contrary to public policy.

Under the UCCC a particular clause or an entire agreement relating to a consumer credit sale, a consumer lease, or a consumer loan is void when such provision or agreement is unconscionable. [5]

However, the fact that a contract is a bad bargain does not make it unconscionable. Moreover, unconscionability is to be determined in the light of the circumstances existing at the time when the contract was made. The fact that later events make the contract unwise or undesirable does not make the contract unconscionable. Hence the fact that there is a sharp rise in the market price of goods after the contract has been made does not make the contract unconscionable. The decision that a provision or a contract is unconscionable can only be made by a court after holding a hearing in order to determine the real effect of the contract when viewed in its commercial setting. In a particular state, the concept of unconscionability may be based on the Uniform Commercial Code, the Uniform Consumer Credit Code, local non-uniform code statutes, or general principles of equity absorbed by the common law. The concept of unconscionability is given the same interpretation by the courts regardless of the source of the concept. [6]

FACTS:

The Walker-Thomas Furniture Co. sold furniture on credit under contracts which contained a provision that a customer did not own the purchase as long as any balance on any purchase remained due. It sold goods to Williams. At the time when the balance of her account was $164, Walker-Thomas Furniture Co. sold her a $514 stereo set with knowledge that she was supporting herself and seven children on a government relief check of $218 a month. From 1957 to 1962 Williams had purchased $1,800 worth of goods and made payments of $1,400. When she stopped making payments in 1962,

[4]UCC § 2–302(1).
[5]Uniform Consumer Credit Code § 5.108.
[6]McMellon v Adkins, _____ WVa _____, 300 SE2d 116 (1983).

Walker-Thomas sought to take back everything she had purchased since 1957. Williams defended on the ground that the contract was unconscionable and could not be enforced. Walker-Thomas insisted that the contract could be enforced according to its terms.

DECISION:

Judgment against Walker-Thomas. A contract will not be enforced according to its terms if those terms are unconscionable. This means that because of the inferior bargaining power of one of the parties that party had no "meaningful choice" in agreeing to the contract terms and those terms unreasonably favored the other party. The terms of the contract with Walker-Thomas were very favorable to the seller and therefore it was necessary to hold a hearing to determine whether Williams in fact had made a meaningful choice and the terms of the contract would not be enforced unless the court found that she had made such a choice. [Williams v Walker-Thomas Furniture Co. (CA Dist Col) 350 F2d 445 (1965)]

---

§ 16:6.   Social Consequences of Contracts.

The social consequences of a contract are an important element today in determining its validity and the power of government to regulate it. The social consequences of a contract are related to the concept of unconscionability, although the latter concept would seem to be concerned with the effect of the contract as between the parties, whereas social consequences have a broader concern for the effect of the particular contract and other similar contracts upon society in general.

(a) **The Private Contract in Society.** The law of contracts, originally oriented to private relations between private individuals, is moving from the field of bilateral private law to multi-party societal considerations. The Supreme Court has held that private contracts lose their private and "do-not-touch" character when they become such a common part of our way of life that society deems it necessary to regulate them.

The significance of the socioeconomic setting of the contract is seen in the minimum wage law decisions. The Supreme Court at first held such laws unconstitutional as an improper interference with the rights of two adult contracting parties. Thereafter it changed its point of view to sustain such laws because of the consequences of substandard wages upon the welfare of the individual, society, and the nation.

This reevaluation of old standards is part of the general move to make modern law more "just."

(b) **The *n* Factor.** With the expansion of the concepts of "against public policy" and "unconscionability" on the one hand, and government regulation of business on the other, the importance of a given contract to society becomes increasingly significant in determining the validity of the contract as between the parties. Less and less are courts considering a contract as only a legal relationship between *A* and *B*. More and more, the modern court is influenced in its decision by the recognition of the fact that the contract before the court is not one in a million but is one of a million.

For example, *J* Company makes an insurance contract with *K* that is of the same nature as one that *J* makes with *M*. Also these contracts are the same as the one that Company *R* makes with *S*, and so on. A like similarity or industry-wide pattern is seen in the case of the bank loan made by bank *O* to borrower *P*, by bank *Q* to borrower *T*, and so on.

The appreciation that a particular contract is merely one of many has not only influenced the courts in the interpretation of such contracts but has also been held to justify regulation of the contract by government. The view has been adopted that "when a widely diffused public interest has become enmeshed in a network of multitudinous private arrangements, the authority of the state 'to safeguard the vital interests of its people' . . . is not to be gainsaid by abstracting one such agreement from its public context and treating it as though it were an isolated private contract constitutionally immune from impairment." [7]

B. AGREEMENTS AFFECTING PUBLIC WELFARE

Agreements that may harm the public welfare are condemned as contrary to public policy and are not binding.[8] Agreements that interfere with public service or the duties of public officials, obstruct legal process, or discriminate against members of minority groups are considered detrimental to public welfare, and as such are not enforceable.

§ 16:7.   Agreements Contrary to Public Policy.

A given agreement may not violate any statute but may still be so offensive to society that the courts feel that to enforce the contract would be contrary to public policy.

FACTS:
Lorraine Capazzoli was suing her husband for a divorce. Harry Holzwasser promised to support Lorraine and her children for the rest of her life if she would go through with the divorce, abandon her marriage, and keep Harry's name out of the divorce proceedings. Lorraine did all this and Harry supported her and her children for several years. He then stopped and she sued him for breach of contract.

DECISION:
Judgment for Harry. Protection of the marriage relationship is of great importance to society. A contract that encourages one spouse to divorce the other is contrary to public policy and will not be enforced by the courts. [Capazzoli v Holzwasser, 397 Mass 158, 490 NE2d 420 (1986)]

The concept of **"public policy"** can not be defined accurately, but is loosely described as "protecting from that which tends to be injurious to the public or contrary to the public good, or which violates any established interest of society." Courts are slow and cautious in invalidating a contract on the

---

[7]East New York Savings Bank v Hahn, 326 US 230, 232 (1945).
[8]Hazelwood v Mandrell Industries Co., Ltd. (Tex Civ App) 596 SW2d 204 (1980).

ground that it is contrary to public policy. This is so because the courts recognize that, on the one hand, they are applying a very vague standard, and, on the other hand, they are restricting the freedom of the contracting parties to contract freely as they choose.[9]

(a) **Agreements Evading Statutory Protection.** Statutes frequently confer benefits or provide protection. If an agreement is made that deprives a person of such a statutory benefit, it is generally held that the agreement is invalid because it is contrary to the public policy declared by the statute. For example, where a state law provided that automobile insurance policies should cover certain persons, a policy provision that excluded certain persons who would be covered by the statutory provision is not valid because it is contrary to the public policy declared in this statute.[10]

§ 16:8.   Agreements Injuring Public Service.

An agreement that tends to interfere with the proper performance of the duties of a public officer—whether legislative, administrative, or judicial—is contrary to public policy and void. Thus, an agreement to procure the award of a public contract by corrupt means is not enforceable. Other examples are agreements to sell public offices, to procure pardons by corrupt means, or to pay a public officer more or less than legal fees or salary.

One of the most common agreements within the class is the **illegal lobbying agreement.** This term is used to describe an agreement to use unlawful means to procure or prevent the adoption of legislation by a lawmaking body, such as Congress or a state legislature. Such agreements are clearly contrary to the public interest since they interfere with the workings of the democratic process. They are accordingly illegal and void.

Some courts hold illegal all agreements to influence legislation, regardless of the means contemplated or employed. Other courts adopt the rule that such agreements are valid in the absence of the use of improper influence or the contemplation of using such influence.

§ 16:9.   Agreements Involving Conflicts of Interests.

Various statutes prohibit government officials from being personally interested, directly or indirectly, in any transaction entered into by such officials on behalf of the government. When there is a prohibited conflict of interests, a contract is invalid without regard to whether its terms are fair or advantageous to the public.[11]

§ 16:10.   Agreements Obstructing Legal Processes.

Any agreement intended to obstruct or pervert legal processes is contrary to public interest and therefore void. Agreements that promise to pay money in return for the abandonment of the prosecution of a criminal case, for the suppression of evidence in any legal proceeding, for initiating litigation, or for the perpetration of any fraud upon the court are therefore void.

[9]Walker v American Family Mut. Ins. Co. (Iowa) 340 NW2d 599 (1983).
[10]Meyer v State Farm Mut. Automobile Ins. Co. ＿＿ Colo ＿＿, 689 P2d 585 (1984).
[11]Thomson v Call, 38 Cal 3d 633, 214 Cal Rptr 139, 699 P2d 316 (1985).

An agreement to pay an ordinary witness more than the regular witness fee allowed by law or a promise to pay a greater amount if the promisor wins the lawsuit is void. The danger here is that the witness will lie in order to help win the case.

(a) **Selection of the Court.** Contracts representing a substantial obligation will generally contain a provision for dispute settlement and tribunal selection. Sometimes it will be specified that any dispute shall be referred to arbitrators. In some instances it will be specified that any lawsuit must be brought in the courts of a particular state. Such provision will ordinarily be held valid as an aspect of the parties' freedom of contract to agree on such terms as they choose.

(b) **Unconscionability and Public Policy.** When the obvious purpose of the tribunal designation provision is to erect a hurdle against being sued, the provision will be held void when the parties are not in an equal bargaining position. Thus, it has been held that where the contract of the seller of prefabricated homes specified that any suit brought against the seller by a buyer must be brought in a third state which had no relationship to either the consumer buyer, the seller, or to the performance of the contract, the provision was void as unconscionable because it was clearly aimed at discouraging litigation by the consumer purchaser.

§ 16:11.   Illegal Discrimination Contracts.

A contract that a property owner will not sell to a member of a particular race cannot be enforced because it violates the Fourteenth Amendment of the federal Constitution.[12] Hotels and restaurants may not deal with their customers on terms that discriminate because of race, religion, color, or national origin.[13]

§ 16:12.   Wagers and Lotteries.

Largely as a result of the adoption of antigambling statutes, wagers or bets are generally illegal. Private lotteries involving the three elements of prize, chance, and consideration, or similar affairs of chance, also are generally held illegal, though in many states public lotteries (lotteries run by a state government) have been legalized by statute. Raffles are usually regarded as lotteries. Sales promotion schemes calling for the distribution of property according to chance among the purchasers of goods are held illegal as lotteries, without regard to whether the scheme is called a guessing contest, raffle, or gift.

Giveaway plans and games are lawful as long as it is not necessary to buy anything or to give anything of value in order to participate. If participation is "free," the element of consideration is lacking and there is no lottery.

An activity is not gambling when the result is solely a matter of skill. In contrast, it is gambling when the result is solely a matter of luck. Rarely is any activity one hundred percent skill or one hundred percent luck.

---

[12]Shelley v Kraemer, 334 US 1 (1948).
[13]Federal Civil Rights Act of 1964, 42 United States Code § 2000a et seq.

FACTS:

The Seattle Times ran a football forecasting contest called "Guest-Guesser." The Chief of Police claimed this was illegal as a lottery. The Times brought a declaratory judgment action to determine the legality of the contest.

DECISION:

The contest was a lottery because winning the prize was fundamentally a matter of chance. [Seattle Times Co. v Tielsch, 80 Wash App 2d 502, 495 P2d 1366 (1972)]

C. REGULATION OF BUSINESS

Local, state, and national laws regulate a wide variety of business activities and practices. A person violating such regulations may under some statutes be subject to a fine or criminal prosecution or under others to an order to cease and desist by an administrative agency or commission.

Whether an agreement made in connection with business conducted in violation of the law is binding or void depends upon how strongly opposed the public policy is to the prohibited act. Some courts take the view that the agreement is not void unless the statute expressly so specifies. In some instances, as in the case of the failure to register a fictitious name under which the business is done, the statute expressly preserves the validity of the contract by permitting the violator to sue on a contract made while illegally conducting business after the name is registered as required by the statute.

§ 16:13.   Statutory Regulation of Contracts.

In order to establish uniformity or to protect one of the parties to a contract, statutes frequently provide that contracts of a given class must follow a statutory model or must contain specified provisions. For example, statutes commonly specify that particular clauses must be included in insurance policies in order to protect the persons insured and their beneficiaries. Others require that contracts executed in connection with credit buying and loans contain particular provisions designed to protect the debtor.

Consumer protection legislation gives the consumer the right to rescind the contract in certain situations. Laws relating to truth in lending, installment sales, and home improvement contracts commonly require that an installment sale contract specify the cash price, the down payment, the trade-in value, if any, the cash balance, the insurance costs, the interest and finance charges.

When the statute imposes a fine or imprisonment for violation, the court should not hold that the contract is void since that would increase the penalty which the legislature had imposed. If a statute prohibits the making of certain kinds of contracts or imposes limitations on contracts that can be made, the attorney general or other government official may generally be able to obtain an **injunction** or court order to stop the parties from entering into a prohibited kind of contract.

§ 16:14.   Licensed Callings or Dealings.

Statutes frequently require that a person obtain a license, certificate, or diploma before practicing certain professions, such as law or medicine, or to carry on a particular business or trade, such as that of a real estate broker, peddler, stockbroker, hotelkeeper, or pawnbroker. If a license is required to protect the public from unqualified persons, a contract made by an unlicensed person is void.

Thus, an agreement with an unlicensed physician for services cannot be enforced by the physician. The patient of the unlicensed physician, however, may sue for damages if the contract is not properly performed.

The illegality of contracts often comes into the picture when parties seek to set up some arrangement to evade government regulations, prohibitions of the criminal law, or to avoid paying taxes.

FACTS:

Thiede was a licensed tavern owner. Schara wished to purchase the business but he did not have a license. To enable Schara to run the business under Thiede's license, the parties executed an agreement by which Schara was described as running the business as manager for Thiede for the balance of the period of Thiede's license, after which Thiede was to lease the business to Schara. Thiede refused to execute the lease and Schara brought an action against him for breach of his agreement to lease the business.

DECISION:

Judgment for Thiede. The contract could not be enforced because it was illegal. The contract was not in fact what it appeared to be: a contract to employ Schara as manager with a leasing of the business to Schara after one year. This was just a cover up to hide the fact that Schara who actually was operating the tavern as owner had no license to do so. A court will not enforce a contract which has such a criminal purpose. [Schara v Thiede, 58 Wis 489, 206 NW2d 129 (1973)]

In contrast with the protective license, a license may be required solely as a revenue measure by requiring the payment of a fee for the license. In that event, an agreement made in violation of the statute by one not licensed is generally held valid. The contract may also sometimes be held valid when it is shown that no harm has resulted from the failure to obtain a permit to do the work contemplated by the particular contract.

It is frequently held that the absence of a license cannot be raised as to transactions between persons who should all be licensed, such as dealers, when the purpose of the license requirement is not to protect such persons as against each other but to protect the public generally against such persons. Likewise, irregularities in licensing for construction work contracts will be overlooked when there has been substantial compliance with the requirements of the statute and the construction contract has been fully performed, and the other party would not be given any greater protection by insisting on complete compliance with the statute. For example, when a contractor obtained a license for his single proprietorship which did business under an assumed name, it was technically a violation of the licensing statute for the contractor to then make a contract in his own name rather than in the name of the licensed proprietorship. However, after the contractor had fully performed the contract with the owner, the latter could not avoid paying the contractor on the ground that the improvement had been made by an unlicensed contractor. While this was true, in that it was the proprietorship that was licensed, there was no way in which the owner would be benefited by insisting on a strict compliance with the licensing statute and, to the contrary, it would be most unjust to allow the owner to keep the benefit of the performance without paying for it. Accordingly, the licensing statute was to be deemed satisfied on the theory that there had been substantial compliance with its terms and the owner could not attack the validity of the contract because there had not been a literal compliance with the statute.[14]

§ 16:15.   Fraudulent Sales.

Statutes commonly regulate the sale of certain commodities. Scales and measures of grocers and other vendors must be checked periodically, and they must be approved and sealed by the proper official. Certain articles must be inspected before they are sold. Others must be labeled in a particular way to show their contents and to warn the public of the presence of any dangerous or poisonous substance. Since these laws are generally designed for the protection of the public, transactions in violation of such laws are void.

§ 16:16.   Administrative Agency Regulation.

Large areas of the American economy are governed by federal administrative agencies created to carry out the general policies specified by Congress. A contract must be in harmony with public policy not only as declared by Congress and the courts but also as applied by the appropriate administrative agency. For example, a particular contract to market goods might not be prohibited by any statute or court decision but may still be condemned by the Federal Trade Commission as an unfair method of competition. When the proper commission has made its determination, a contract not in harmony therewith, such as a contract of a railroad charging a higher or a lower rate than that approved by the Interstate Commerce Commission, is illegal.

§ 16:17.   Contracts in Restraint of Trade.

An agreement that unreasonably restrains trade is illegal and void on the ground that it is contrary to public policy. Such agreements take many forms, such as a combination to create a monopoly or to obtain a corner on the market, or an association of merchants to increase prices. In addition to the illegality of the agreement based on general principles of law, statutes frequently declare monopolies illegal and subject the parties to various civil and criminal penalties.[15]

§ 16:18.   Agreements Not to Compete.

When a going business is sold, it is commonly stated in the contract that the seller shall not go into the same or a similar business again within a

[14]Asdourian v Araj, 38 Cal 3d 276, 211 Cal Rptr 703, 696 P2d 95 (1985).
[15]Sherman Antitrust Act. 15 USC §§ 1–7; Clayton Act, 15 USC §§ 12–27; Federal Trade Commission Act, 15 USC §§ 41 to 58.

certain geographical area, or for a certain period of time, or both. In early times, such agreements were held void since they deprived the public of the service of the person who agreed not to compete, impaired the latter's means of earning a livelihood, reduced competition, and exposed the public to monopoly. To the modern courts, the question is whether under the circumstances the restriction imposed upon one party is reasonably necessary to protect the other party. If the restriction is reasonable, it is valid.

Restrictions to prevent competition by an employee are held valid when reasonable and necessary to protect the interest of the employer. For example, a provision that a doctor employed by a medical clinic would not practice medicine for one year within a 50-mile radius of the city in which the clinic was located is reasonable and will be enforced.

If there is no sale of a business or the making of an employment contract, an agreement not to compete is illegal as a restraint of trade and a violation of the antitrust law. The agreement is therefore void.

When a restriction of competition agreed to by the parties is invalid because its scope as to time or geographical area is too great, how does this affect the contract? Some courts trim the restrictive covenant down to a scope that the court deems reasonable and require the parties to abide by that revision.

FACTS:

Todd sold his business to Hodges. The contract stated that Todd would not compete with Hodges for five years. In violation of this restriction, Todd started a new business and competed with Hodges. Hodges sued to stop this competition. The lower court held that the restriction on competition was void because it was too broad as it did not place any geographic boundary on the zone of no competition. Hodges appealed.

DECISION:

While the restrictive covenant prohibiting competition was invalid because it was too broad, the court was not required to take an "all or nothing" approach and hold that there was no restriction whatever on competition. Instead, the court would add reasonable boundaries to the contract and enforce the covenant within that area. The court therefore sent the case back to the lower court to determine and set reasonable geographic boundaries for the no competition zone and to enjoin competition within that zone. [Hodges v Todd (Ky App) 698 SW2d 317 (1985)]

Other courts hold that this is rewriting the contract of the parties, which courts ordinarily cannot do, and refuse to revise the covenant. However, this does not invalidate the entire contract and the balance of the contract is enforced as though the contract had never contained the illegal restrictive covenant. Consequently, the buyer of a business can not avoid paying for the business on the ground that the contract of sale contained an invalid anti-competitive provision.[16]

[16]Mann v Cherry Bekaert and Holland (Ala) 414 So 2d 921 (1982).

§ 16:19.   Usurious Agreements.

Usury is committed when money is loaned at a greater rate of interest than is allowed by law. Most states prohibit by statute the taking of more than a stated amount of interest. These statutes provide a **maximum contract rate** of interest which is the highest annual rate that can be exacted or demanded under the law of a given state. This maximum is often stated as a flat percentage rate though there is a trend to tie the usury ceilings to current market rates. Intentionally charging greater interest on a loan than allowed by law constitutes usury. It is not necessary to prove that the defendant knew that there was a violation of the usury law.[17]

§ 16:20.   Credit Sale Contracts.

Sales of goods and services on credit are not technically within the scope of the usury laws as the seller does not make an express "loan" to the buyer. When the sale is made on credit, the price which the seller charges is ordinarily not controlled by the usury law.

(a) Credit Sale Price. A seller may charge one price for cash sales and a higher price for credit or installment sales. The difference between these two prices is called the **time price differential.** As the usury law is not applicable, the time price differential may be greater than the maximum amount of interest which could be charged on a loan equal to the cash price.

FACTS:
Grannas and his partner purchased heavy equipment from Aggregates Equipment on credit, agreeing to pay in 36 monthly installments including a "credit service charge" of $11,713.44. Aggregate assigned the contract and security agreement to a finance company, Equipment Finance, which later sued Grannas and his partner when they stopped paying the installments. Grannas and his partner raised the defense that the credit service charge was usurious because the cash price of the equipment was $65,075.28.

DECISION:
Judgment for finance company. The usury statute applied only to a loan. No loan is involved when the seller agrees to accept payment in installments. The fact that an assignment was made to a finance company did not alter the basic nature of the transaction nor require the court to conclude that the transaction was a sham transaction to disguise a loan. These principles were established before and had not been changed by the Uniform Commercial Code. In addition, both parties to the contract were businessmen who must be regarded as knowing what they were doing. The plaintiff was therefore entitled to enforce the contract. [Equipment Finance, Inc. v Grannas, 207 Pa Super 363, 218 A2d 81 (1966)]

---

[17]Western Auto Supply Co. v Vick, 303 NC 30, 277 SE2d 360 (1981).

A few states, however, hold that the time price differential is subject to the usury law or have amended their usury laws or have adopted statutes to regulate the differential between cash and time prices charged by the seller. Such statutes, however, are sometimes limited to sales by retailers to consumers or apply only to sales under a stated dollar maximum.

Many states have adopted retail and installment sale laws which apply whenever the sale price is to be paid in installments and the seller retains a security interest in the goods. These laws frequently fix a maximum for the time price differential thereby remedying the situation created by the fact that the price differential is not subject to the usury laws.

(b) **Revolving Charge Accounts.** When a merchant sells on credit and puts the bill on a charge account and then adds a charge to the unpaid balance due by the customer, most courts hold that the amount of such charge is not controlled by the usury law.

FACTS:

Sears, Roebuck and Co. issued credit cards by which the holder of a card could buy on credit and would be billed monthly for purchases. If payment of the balance shown on a monthly statement was made within thirty days, no service charge was added. This charge was 1.5 percent a month on the balance but no less than fifty cents. On an annual basis, this amounted to 18 percent. Overbeck made purchases on a Sears credit card and paid the monthly service charges. Thereafter he brought suit claiming that the 18 per cent rate was usurious as the maximum legal rate was 6 per cent and sought to recover the "excess" interest on behalf of himself and all other credit card holders.

DECISION:

Judgment for Sears. The credit card system did not make loans to the customers of Sears and therefore the usury law did not apply. The practical effect of the credit card charges was that a person buying on such credit cards paid a higher price than a person purchasing for cash. As a time price differential does not violate the usury law, a credit card charge which amounts to a time price differential likewise does not violate the usury law. [Overbeck v Sears, Roebuck and Co. 169 Ind App 501, 349 NE2d 286 (1976)]

SUMMARY

When an agreement is illegal, it is ordinarily void and no contract arises therefrom. Courts will not allow one party to an illegal agreement to bring suit against the other party. There are some exceptions to this, as when the parties are not equally guilty or when the law's purpose in making the agreement illegal is to protect the person who is bringing suit. When possible, an agreement will be interpreted as being lawful and even when a particular provision is held unlawful, the balance of the agreement will generally be saved, so that the net result is that there is a contract minus the clause that was held illegal.

The term illegality embraces an array encompassing situations in which a statute declares that certain conduct is unlawful or a crime, contracts requiring the commission of a tort, contracts that are contrary to public policy, contracts that are unconscionable, and to some extent to contracts that are oppressive, unfair, or made in bad faith. The question of the legality of an agreement is not considered in the abstract but the effect of the decision upon the rest of society is considered, for the reason that increasingly a given contract is not in a class by itself but is the same as thousands and even millions of other contracts just like it.

Whether a contract is contrary to public policy may be difficult to determine because public policy is not precisely defined. That which is harmful to the public welfare or general good is contrary to public policy. Contracts condemned as contrary to public policy include those designed to deprive the weaker party of a benefit that the lawmaker desired to provide; agreements injuring public service, such as an agreement to buy a government job for an applicant; agreements involving conflicts of interests, as when the purchasing officer of a government buys from a company that the officer privately owns; agreements obstructing legal process, such as an agreement with a witness to disappear; illegal discrimination contracts; and wagers and lotteries. Statutes commonly make the wager illegal as gambling. The lottery is any plan under which for a consideration a person has a chance to win a prize.

Illegality may consist of the violation of a statute or administrative regulation adopted to regulate business. Statutes may make it illegal to do business unless a particular form of contract is used or unless the moving party is licensed. The protection of buyers from fraud of sellers may make it unlawful to sell under certain circumstances or without making certain disclosures. Contracts in restraint of trade are generally illegal as violating federal or state antitrust laws. An agreement not to compete is illegal as a restraint of trade except when reasonable in its terms and when it is incidental to the sale of a business or to a contract of employment.

The charging by a lender of a higher rate of interest than allowed by law is usurious. Courts must examine transactions carefully to see if there is a usurious loan disguised as a legitimate transaction. When sellers of goods offer their buyers one price for a cash sale and another higher price for a credit sale, the higher price is lawful and is not usurious even though the difference between the cash price and the credit price is greater than the amount that could be charged as interest on a loan equal to the cash price. This concept is called the time price differential. A minority of states reject or abolish it or limit the increase of the credit price over the cash price to a specified percentage or to the maximum amount that could be charged on a loan equal to the cash price. Most states do not apply the usury law to a revolving charge account but a minority do so, with the result that the charges imposed on the account must not exceed the amount that could be charged as interest on a loan of the amount due in the account.

QUESTIONS AND CASE PROBLEMS

1. What social forces are affected by the rule that a credit sale price is not usurious although the difference between the credit price and the cash

price is greater than the interest which could be charged on a loan in the amount of the cash price?

2. When are the parties to an illegal agreement in pari delicto?

3. Isabel made a contract to purchase an automobile from Crockett Motors on credit. Isabel failed to make payments on time. When Crockett sued to enforce the contract, Isabel raised the defense that the price of the car had been increased because she was buying on credit and that this increase was unconscionable. Crockett proved that the automobile was exactly what it was represented to be and that no fraud had been committed in selling the car to Isabel. Does Crockett's evidence constitute a defense to Isabel's claim of unconscionability?

4. The Civic Association of Plaineville raffled off an automobile in order to raise funds to build a hospital. Laura won the automobile but the Association refused to deliver it to her. She sued the Association for the automobile. Can Laura enforce the contract?

5. Oakes made a contract with the Guarantee Insurance Co. to act as its agent. He should then have obtained a certificate from the State Board of Insurance showing his authority to act as agent for the company. A statute imposed a penalty on agents failing to obtain the required certificate. No penalty was imposed upon insurance companies employing agents who did not obtain the necessary certificate. Oakes did not obtain the certificate required by statute but just went ahead and acted as agent. He collected over six thousand dollars of premiums that he should have paid over to the Guarantee Insurance Co. He did not make such payment and Guarantee sued him. He raised the defense that Guarantee could not recover because the obligation to pay the premiums was based on the contract of agency with the company but that that contract was illegal because the certificate of authority had not been obtained. Was this a valid defense?

6. The Creswell Department Store sold for cash and for credit. A customer purchasing on credit paid in twelve monthly installments and paid a purchase price that was 20 percent higher than a person buying for cash. Rose purchased a refrigerator from Creswell on the credit plan. After paying for it in full, she sued Creswell for the penalties prescribed by the state usury law. She claimed that the price increase of 20 percent for the credit sale violated the state usury law which allowed a maximum of only 6 percent interest on loans. Was she entitled to recover the penalties?

7. Compare the legality of a prize drawing with winners selected by a random drawing from (a) names in the telephone book, (b) names of persons attending a television show, and (c) names of persons written on entry blanks obtained on purchasing goods from the sponsoring store.

8. Burgess, a salesman for Bowyer, failed to turn over to Bowyer an indefinite amount of money collected by him. In order to avoid a criminal prosecution of Burgess by Bowyer, Burgess and his brother-in-law entered into a contract with the employer by which they agreed to pay Bowyer $5,000 if full restitution was not made. No restitution was made, and Bowyer sued Burgess and his brother-in-law on the contract for $5,000. Was he entitled to recover?

9. Compare the legality of (a) a door prize given to the lucky customer of a supermarket on its opening day, and (b) a door prize given to the lucky person coming to the opening of the supermarket.

10. A person borrowed money and executed a promissory note for the loan. The note called for the payment of interest at a usurious rate. Under the local law this made the note void. The lender sued on the note. When the borrower raised the defense that the note was void because of usury, the creditor asserted that he was only claiming the amount of interest which could be lawfully claimed and that therefore the usury aspect was eliminated and he could recover on the note. Was he correct? [Yakutsk v Alfino, 43 App Div 2d 552, 349 NYS2d 718]

11. A entered a retirement home operated by B. The contract between A and B required A to make a specified monthly payment that could be increased by B as the cost of operations of the home increased. The contract and the payment plan were thoroughly explained to A. As the cost of operations rose, the monthly payments were continually raised by B. A objected to the increases on the ground that the increases were far more than had been anticipated and the contract was therefore unconscionable. Was his objection valid? [Onderdonk v Presbyterian Homes, 171 NJ Super 529, 410 A2d 252]

12. Smith was employed as a salesman for Borden, Inc., which sold food products in 63 counties in Arkansas, 2 counties in Missouri, 2 counties in Oklahoma, and 1 county in Texas. The contract with Smith prohibited him from competing with Borden after leaving its employ. Smith left Borden and went to work for a competitor, Lady Baltimore Foods. Working for this second employer, Smith sold in three counties of Arkansas. He had sold in two of these counties while he worked for Borden. Borden brought an injunction action against Smith and Lady Baltimore to enforce the anticompetitive covenant in Smith's former contract. Was Borden entitled to the injunction? [Borden, Inc. v Smith, 252 Ark 295, 478 SW2d 744]

13. Colonial Stores was looking for someone to build a store in the city and lease it to Colonial. McArver and Gerukos agreed between themselves that they would obtain options to buy some land for a store site and resell the options to a third person who would build a store and lease it to Colonial. All of this was successfully done, but Gerukos kept all of the profits from the transaction. When McArver sued him for his share of the profits, Gerukos raised the defense that McArver could not recover because a statute required that all real estate brokers and salesmen be licensed and McArver did not have such a real estate license. Was this defense valid? [McArver v Gerukos, 265 NC 413, 144 SE2d 277]

14. Connolly was a professional engineer but did not have a license in California. Carlotta was an architect licensed in California. She consulted Connolly in designing an apartment complex that was to be constructed in San Francisco. Carlotta did not pay Connolly for his services. Connolly sued Carlotta to recover for such services. She raised the defense that he could not sue for the services rendered by him because he did not have a license to render such services. Is this defense valid?

15. Doherty ran a lounge and bar known as the Orchid Room in California where betting is illegal. Bradley was a patron in the Orchid Room who

made bets with Doherty on the scores he could attain on the pinball machine. Bradley lost $70,000 on such bets. He later sued Doherty to recover the money. Doherty raised the defense that Bradley was in pari delicto and therefore could not recover. Bradley claimed that this defense did not apply because the pinball machines were fixed by electronic devices and also because he, Bradley, was a compulsive gambler. Was Bradley correct? [Bradley v Doherty, 30 Cal App 3d 991, 106 Cal Rptr 725]

16. Credit Alliance Corporation loaned money to Westland Machine Company, Inc. Both companies had business experience and the contract was signed on behalf of Westland by its president, who was also an attorney. He apparently did not read the contract and did not see that buried in standard clauses there was a provision waiving trial by jury. Credit Alliance later sued Westland on the debt. Westland demanded a jury trial and claimed that the waiver was invalid because unconscionable and contrary to public policy. Should a jury trial be granted? [Credit Alliance Corp. v Westland Machines Co. Inc. (Fla App) 439 So 2d 332]

CHAPTER 17

FORM OF CONTRACT

CHAPTER OBJECTIVES

After studying this chapter you will be able to:
1. State when a contract must be evidenced by a writing.
2. List the requirements of a writing that evidences a contract.
3. State the effects of the absence of a sufficient writing when a contract must be evidenced by a writing.
4. List the exceptions that have been made by the courts to the laws requiring written evidence of contracts.
5. Compare statute of frauds requirements with the parol evidence rule.
6. List exceptions to the parol evidence rule.
7. Solve problems involving the statute of frauds and the parol evidence rule.

There was a time, in the history of the common law, when there was no requirement that a promise be in writing in order to be enforceable—a promise was a promise irrespective of its form (oral or written). Experience proved that this degree of freedom created too great an opportunity for abuse and perjury became commonplace. In order to prevent this type of fraud, the law was changed to require that certain kinds of contracts be evidenced by a writing. In actual practice, this flat requirement was found also to open the door to fraud when in fact there was an oral contract but the existence of the contract was falsely denied. So the law shifted once again and now recognizes certain exceptions to the writing requirement. As an example, the requirement may be satisfied by a sufficient part performance. Some courts have gone further to ignore the writing requirement in certain cases of detrimental reliance upon an oral contract.

Assuming that a contract is evidenced by a writing, whether or not the writing was required by statute, society was next faced with the policy of what effect was to be given the writing. Specifically, was the writing the final word or could it be modified or contradicted by the testimony of witnesses? Society has made a compromise between two extremes, holding by what is called the parol evidence rule that ordinarily the writing is the final word but that in certain circumstances it is not.

A. STATUTE OF FRAUDS

In Chapter 11 it was stated that a contract is a binding agreement. Must the agreement be evidenced by a writing?

§ 17:1. Oral Contracts Valid.

Generally a contract is valid whether it is written or oral. By statute, however, some contracts must be evidenced by a writing. Such statutes are designed to prevent the use of the courts for the purpose of enforcing certain oral agreements or alleged oral agreements. The statutes do not apply when an oral agreement has been voluntarily performed by both parties.

The failure to sign and return a written contract does not establish that there is no contract as there may have been an earlier oral contract. If one of the parties, with the knowledge or approval of the other contracting party, undertakes performance of the contract before it is reduced to writing, it is generally held that the parties intended to be bound from the moment the oral contract was made.

Although ordinarily oral agreements are binding and are therefore contracts, an exception will arise when it is the intent of the parties that there is no binding agreement until a written contract is prepared and signed. In such case there is no contract until the written contract is executed.[1]

§ 17:2. Contracts That Must Be Evidenced by a Writing.

Ordinarily a contract, whether oral or not, is binding if the existence and terms of the contract can be established to the satisfaction of the trier of fact, ordinarily the jury. In some instances a statute, commonly called a **statute of frauds,**[2] requires that certain kinds of contracts be evidenced by a

---

[1]James Noel Flying Service, Inc. v Rockwell International Corp. (La App) 421 So 2d 979 (1982).

[2]The name is derived from the original English Statute of Frauds and Perjuries, which was adopted in 1677 and became the pattern for similar legislation in America. The seventeenth section of that statute governed the sale of goods, and its modern counterpart is § 2-201 of the Uniform Commercial Code, discussed in Chapter 25. The fourth section of the English statute provided the pattern for American legislation with respect to contracts other than for the sale of goods described in this section of the chapter. The English statute was repealed in 1954, except as to land sale and guaranty contracts. The American statutes remain in force, but the liberalization by Uniform Commercial Code § 2-201 of the pre-Code requirements with respect to contracts for the sale of goods may be regarded as a step in the direction of the abandonment of the statute of frauds concept.

When the English Statute of Frauds was adopted, the parties to a lawsuit were not permitted to testify on their own behalf, with the result that a litigant had difficulty in disproving perjured testimony of third persons offered as evidence on behalf of the adverse party. The Statute of Frauds was repealed in England partly because it was felt that it permitted the assertion of a "technical" defense as a means of avoiding just obligations and partly on the ground that with parties in interest now having the right to testify there is no longer the need for a writing to protect the parties from perjured testimony of third persons. Azevedo v Minister, 86 Nev 576, 471 P2d 661 (1970).

writing or they cannot be enforced. This means that either (a) the contract itself must be in writing and signed by both parties, or (b) there be a sufficient written memorandum of the oral contract signed by the person being sued for breach of contract.

(a) **Agreement That Cannot Be Performed Within One Year after the Contract Is Made.** A writing is required when the contract by its terms or subject matter cannot be performed within one year after the date of the agreement. Thus a joint venture agreement to construct a condominium complex was subject to the one-year provision of the statute of frauds where the contract could not reasonably have been performed within one year, as seen from the complex nature of the project and from the fact that the plans of the parties projected a development over the course of three years.[3] The year runs from the time of the making of the oral contract rather than from the date when performance is to begin. In computing the year, the day on which the contract was made is excluded. The year begins with the following day and ends at the close of the first anniversary of the day on which the agreement was made.

FACTS:

In February or March, Corning Glass Works orally agreed to retain Hanan as a management consultant from May 1 of that year to April 30 of the next year for a total fee of $25,000. Was this agreement binding?

DECISION:

No. Since it was not to be performed within one year from the making of the oral agreement, it was not enforceable because of the statute of frauds. [Hanan v Corning Glass Works, 63 Misc 2d 863, 314 NYS2d 804 (1970)]

The statute of frauds does not apply if it is possible under the terms of the agreement to perform the contract within one year. Thus, a writing is not required when no time for performance is specified and the performance will not necessarily take more than a year. In this case the statute is inapplicable without regard to the time when performance is actually begun or completed.

As a contract of indefinite duration is terminable by either party at will, the statute of frauds is not applicable since the contract may be terminated within a year.

(b) **Agreement to Sell or a Sale of Any Interest in Real Property.** All contracts to sell and sales of land, buildings or interests in land, such as mortgages which are treated as such an interest, must be evidenced by a writing.

The statute applies only to the agreement between the owner and purchaser, or between their agents. It does not apply to other or collateral agreements, such as those which the purchaser may make in order to raise the money to pay for the property or to agreements to pay for an examination or

---

[3]Dean v Myers (Ala) 466 So 2d 952 (1985).

search of the title of the property. Similarly, a partnership agreement to deal in real estate is generally not required for that reason to be in writing. The statute ordinarily does not apply to a contract between a real estate agent and one of the parties to the sales contract employing the agent.

(c) **Promise to Answer for the Debt or Default of Another.** When *A* promises *C* to pay *B*'s debt to *C* if *B* does not do so, *A* is promising to answer for the debt of another. Such a promise must usually be evidenced by a writing to be enforceable. Thus, the oral promise of the president of a corporation to pay the debts owed by the corporation to its creditors if they will not sue the corporation does not bind the president.

If the promise is made directly to the debtor that the promisor will pay the creditor of the debtor what is owed, the statute of frauds is not applicable. In contrast, if the promisor makes the promise to the creditor, it comes within the category of a promise made for the benefit of another and must therefore be evidenced by a writing which satisfies the statute of frauds.

(d) **Promise by the Executor or Administrator of a Decedent's Estate to Pay a Claim against the Estate from Personal Funds.** The personal representative (executor or administrator) has the duty of winding up the affairs of a deceased person, paying the debts from the proceeds of the estate and distributing any balance remaining. The executor or administrator is not personally liable for the claims against the estate of the decedent. If the personal representative promises to pay the decedent's debts with the representative's own money, the promise cannot be enforced unless it is evidenced by a writing that complies with the terms of the statute.

If the personal representative makes a contract on behalf of the estate in the course of administering the estate, a writing is not required since the representative is then contracting on behalf of the estate. Thus if the personal representative employs an attorney to settle the estate or makes a burial contract with an undertaker, no writing is required.

(e) **Promise Made in Consideration of Marriage.** If a person makes a promise to pay a sum of money or to give property to another in consideration of marriage or a promise to marry, the agreement must be evidenced by a writing. This provision of the statute of frauds is not applicable to ordinary mutual promises to marry, and it is not affected by the statutes in some states that prohibit the bringing of any action for breach of promise of marriage.

(f) **Sale of Goods.** When the contract price for goods is $500 or more, the contract must ordinarily be evidenced by a writing.[4]

(g) **Miscellaneous Statutes of Frauds.** In a number of states, special statutes require other agreements to be in writing or evidenced by a writing. Thus, a statute may provide that an agreement to name a person as beneficiary in an insurance policy must be evidenced by a writing.

The Uniform Commercial Code contains three statutes of frauds relating to sales of personal property: (1) goods, (2) securities, such as stocks and bonds; (3) personal property other than goods and securities.

[4]See Chapter 25 of this book.

In some states contracts with brokers relating to the sale of land are also subject to the statute of frauds.[5]

§ 17:3.   Note or Memorandum.

The statute of frauds requires a writing to evidence those contracts which come within its scope. This writing may be a note or memorandum, as distinguished from a contract. It may be in any form because its only purpose is to serve as evidence of the contract. The statutory requirement is, of course, satisfied if there is a complete written contract signed by both parties.

(a) **Signing.** The note or memorandum must be signed by the party sought to be charged or that person's agent. A letter from an employer setting forth the details of an oral contract of employment satisfies the statute of frauds in a suit brought by the employee against the employer, as the writing was signed by the party "sought to be charged." If the employer had sued the employee in such case, the employer's letter would not satisfy the statute of frauds as it would not be signed by the employee.

Some states require that the authorization of an agent to execute a contract coming within the statute of frauds must also be in writing.[6] In the case of an auction, it is the usual practice for the auctioneer to be the agent of both parties for the purpose of signing the memorandum.

FACTS:

Griffith purchased land at an auction sale. Following the sale, the seller and the auctioneer signed a written memorandum reciting the sale of the land to Griffith. He later refused to complete the transaction and claimed that he was not bound by any contract because he had not signed any writing to satisfy the statute of frauds.

DECISION:

Judgment against Griffith. He was correct that he had not signed any writing that satisfied the statute of frauds but he had purchased the land at an auction sale and the auctioneer had executed a memorandum of sale. For the purpose of the statute of frauds the auctioneer is to be deemed to have the agency power to act on behalf of the buyer with respect to signing a writing to satisfy that statute. Accordingly Griffith could not claim that the memorandum had not been properly signed so as to satisfy the statute of frauds. [Schwinn v Griffith, ——Minn ——, 303 NW2d 258 (1981)]

The signature may be made at any place on the writing, although in some states it is expressly required that the signature appear at the end of the writing. The signature may be an ordinary one or any symbol that is adopted by the party as a signature. It may consist of initials, figures, or a mark. When a signature consists of a mark made by a person who is illiterate

[5]United Listing Service v Shepherd, 96 Mich App 547, 293 NW2d 624 (1980).
[6]Cammorata v Woodruff (Ala) 445 So 2d 867 (1983).

or physically incapacitated, it is commonly required that the name of the person be placed upon the writing by someone else, who may be required to sign the instrument as a witness. A person signing a trade or assumed name is liable to the same extent as though the contract had been signed with the signer's name. In the absence of a local statute that provides otherwise, a signature may be made by pencil, pen, or by typewriter, by print, or by stamp.[7]

(b) **Content.** Except in the case of a sale of goods, the note or memorandum must contain all the material terms of the contract so that the court can determine just what was agreed. Thus, it is insufficient if the contract is partly oral and partly written. The subject matter must be identified either within the writing itself or in other writings to which it refers. A writing is not sufficient that does not identify the subject of the contract. A deposit check given by the buyer to the seller does not take the oral land sales contract out of the statute of frauds as the check does not set forth the terms of the sale.[8]

FACTS:

Howell and Inland Empire Paper Co. signed a paper by which they agreed to transfer to Howell "portions of tracts" 55 to 59 and 62 to 64 "to consist of approximately 55.5 acres." The company did not make the transfer and Howell brought suit against it.

DECISION:

Judgment for Inland Empire. A contract for the transfer of an interest in land must set forth all material terms. The exact land to be transferred is a material term. A description as "portions" totalling a specified number of acres did not identify which land was being sold. This identification could only be done by admitting parol evidence to show what portions of the tracts identified were being sold. This is prohibited by the statute of frauds which requires that the writing declare the entire contract. [Howell v Inland Empire Paper Co. 28 Wash App 494, 624 P2d 739 (1981)]

In some states a description of real estate by street number, city or county, and state, is not sufficient; the writing must show the lot and block numbers of the property as well as name the city or county and state. When the writing does not contain a description which satisfies the statute of frauds, the land may not be identified by the testimony of witnesses.

It is not necessary that the writing specifically state a term that would be implied, as that the price therein stated is to be paid in "cash." Some states make a further exception to the general rule and do not require that the writing set forth the consideration or terms of payment.

A writing claimed to satisfy the statute of frauds as to a contract which cannot be performed within one year must set forth all the material

[7]Department of Banking and Finance v Wilken, 217 Neb 796, 352 NW2d 145 (1984).
[8]Hemingway v Gruener, 106 Idaho 422, 679 P2d 1140 (1984).

terms of the contract. Consequently, a letter is not sufficient as a writing to evidence an oral contract of employment for more than one year when the letter does not state the salary.

The note or memorandum may consist of one writing or of separate papers, such as letters or telegrams, or of a combination of such papers.[9]

Separate writings cannot be considered together unless they are linked, either by express reference in each writing to the other or by the fact that each writing clearly deals with the same subject matter.

It is not necessary that the writing be addressed to the other contracting party or to any other person, nor is it necessary that the writing be made with the intent to create a writing to satisfy the statute of frauds. When a corporation made an oral contract of employment with an employee, the minutes of the corporation reciting the adoption of the resolution to employ the employee (which minutes were signed by the president of the corporation) together with the salary check paid the employee constituted a sufficient writing to satisfy the statute of frauds.

The memorandum may be made at the time of the original transaction or at a later date. It must, however, ordinarily exist at the time a court action is brought upon the agreement.

§ 17:4.   Effect of Noncompliance.

The majority of states hold that a contract which does not comply with the statute of frauds is voidable. A small minority of states hold that such an agreement is void. Under either view, if an action is brought to enforce the contract, the defendant can raise the objection that it is not evidenced by a writing. No one other than the defendant, however, can make the objection. Thus, an insurance company cannot refuse to pay on its policy on the theory that the insured did not have any insurable interest in the insured property because there was no writing relating to the property that satisfied the statute of frauds.

(a) **Recovery of Value Conferred.** In most instances, a person who is prevented from enforcing a contract because of the statute of frauds is nevertheless entitled to recover from the other party the value of any services or property furnished or money given under the oral contract. Recovery is not based upon the terms of the contract but upon the quasi-contractual obligation of the other party to restore to the plaintiff what was received in order to prevent unjust enrichment at the plaintiff's expense. For example, when an oral contract for services cannot be enforced because of the statute of frauds the person performing the work may recover the reasonable value of the services rendered.

FACTS:

Richard Golden orally agreed to sell his land to Earl Golden who paid a deposit of $3,000. The transaction was never completed and Earl sued for the return of his deposit.

Richard claimed that the statute of frauds prevented Earl from proving that there ever was an oral contract under which a deposit of money had been paid.

[9]McNabb v Norine, _____ Mont _____, 664 P2d 927 (1983).

DECISION:

Judgment for Earl. The statute of frauds bars enforcement of an oral contract for the sale of land. It does not prevent proof of the contract for the purpose of showing that the seller has received a benefit which would unjustly enrich him if retained by him. Earl could therefore prove the existence of the unperformed oral contract in order to show that Richard had received a deposit which should be returned. [Golden v Golden, 273 Or 506, 541 P2d 1397 (1975)]

(b) Proof of Fraud. The statute of frauds does not bar proof that the promisor had no intention to pay the debt of the third person but had made such promise fraudulently to induce the promisee to supply goods.[10]

§ 17:5. Judicial Relief from Statute of Frauds.

The requirements of the statute of frauds are easily met. Often, however, because people are in a hurry or do not know the law, transactions consist only of spoken words. No writing is made that satisfies the statute of frauds. If one of the parties double-crosses the others by claiming that the transaction is not binding because of the statute of frauds, a real injustice can be inflicted. To prevent this hardship, the courts have created certain exceptions to the statute of frauds.

(a) Part Performance of Land Contract. In spite of the statute of frauds, an oral contract for the sale of an interest in land will be enforced if the buyer has gone into possession of the land and has made substantial valuable improvements to the land, and the value of such improvements cannot be easily measured in dollars.

(b) Promisor Benefited by Promise to Pay Debt of Another. If a person orally promises a creditor to pay the debt owed to that creditor by a debtor, the promise is ordinarily not binding because of the statute of frauds. If the promise is not made by the promisor to help the debtor but is made primarily to benefit the promisor, the courts refuse to apply the statute of frauds. In such case, the promise to pay the debt of the third person is binding even though it is oral and benefits the debtor by discharging the debt that was due.[11]

For example, when a contractor promises to pay the debt owed by a subcontractor to the supplier of materials needed by the subcontractor for the construction work, it can be found that the primary purpose of the contractor's making such promise was to assure the uninterrupted work on the construction and thus protect the contractor from liability for delay that would result from an interruption. If so found, the contractor is liable on the promise although there is no writing as would be required by the statute of frauds for a promise to pay the debt of another.[12]

---

[10]Colonial Ford Truck Sales, Inc v Schneider, 228 Va 671, 325 SE2d 91 (1985).

[11]Morrison-Knudsen Co., Inc v Hite Crane & Rigging, Inc. 36 Wash App 860, 678 P2d 346 (1984).

[12]Barboza v Liberty Contractors Co., Inc. 18 Mass App 971, 469 NE 1303 (1984).

FACTS:

Boeing Airplane Co. contracted with Pittsburgh-Des Moines Steel Co. for the latter to construct a supersonic wind tunnel. R.H. Freitag Mfg. Co. sold material to York-Gillespie Co., which subcontracted to do part of the work. In order to persuade Freitag to keep supplying materials on credit, Boeing and the principal contractor both assured Freitag that he would be paid. When Freitag was not paid by the subcontractor, Freitag sued Boeing and the contractor. They defended on the ground that the assurances given Freitag were not written.

DECISION:

Judgment for Freitag. The promises to pay the bills of the subcontractor were made by the defendants primarily for their benefit in order to keep the work progressing so that they, in turn, would not be held liable for failure to complete. Hence, the case came within the primary benefit exception to the written guaranty provision of the statute of frauds. [R.H. Freitag Mfg. Co. v Boeing Airplane Co. 55 Wash 2d 334, 347 P2d 1074 (1959)]

(c) Detrimental Reliance on Oral Contract. The extent to which judicial relief from the statute of frauds will be granted in cases other than land sales and debt guaranties is not clear. The same forces that gave rise to the doctrine of promissory estoppel in connection with the law of consideration are to some extent causing courts to recognize detrimental reliance as excusing noncompliance with the statute of frauds.

FACTS:

Lucas sued the Whittaker Corporation for breaking its oral contract to employ him for two years. Whittaker raised the statute of frauds as a defense. Lucas showed that he had given up his job in Missouri and moved to Colorado in order to take the job with Whittaker. In so doing he gave up his former job after nine years of employment, thereby losing its fringe benefits, including college tuition for eligible dependents; sold his custom-built house in which he and his family had lived for only eight months; and gave up all business and social contacts.

DECISION:

Judgment for Lucas. Equitable principles bar applying the statute of frauds when an "unconscionable injury" will be inflicted if the oral contract is not enforced. Lucas had suffered greater detriment than was involved in the ordinary change of job situation. Whittaker was therefore barred from raising the defense of the statute of frauds. [Lucas v Whitaker Corp. (CA10 Colo) 470 F2d 326 (1972)

The mere fact that the promisee relies on the oral promise is generally not sufficient to entitle the promisee to enforce the oral promise. The promisee must show that because of the reliance on the promise substantial or unconscionable injury would be sustained by the promisee, or the promisor would be unjustly enriched, if the oral promise was not enforced.[13]

[13]Munoz v Kaiser Steel Corp. 156 Cal App 3d 965, 203 Cal Rptr 345 (1984).

B. PAROL EVIDENCE RULE

When the contract is evidenced by a writing, may the contract terms be changed by the testimony of witnesses? The answer depends upon the circumstances surrounding the execution of the writing and the nature of the writing.

§ 17:6.   Exclusion of Parol Evidence.

The general rule is that spoken words, that is, **parol evidence,** will not be allowed to modify or contradict the terms of a written contract which is complete on its face unless there is clear proof that because of fraud, accident, or a mistake, the writing is not in fact the contract or the complete or true contract. This is called the **parol evidence rule.** It excludes words spoken before or at the time the contract was made.[14]

FACTS:

Rincones made a written contract with Windberg to write part of an educational handbook. The contract specified the compensation to be paid. Windberg refused to pay the amount and claimed that the duty to pay was conditional upon receiving funding from the state of California and that as such funding was not received there was no duty to pay.

DECISION:

The written contract called for the payment of a specified amount for doing specified work. There was nothing in the written contract that the obligation to pay was conditional upon the state's providing funding. Proof of such a condition would contradict the obligation imposed by the written contract. Parol evidence was therefore not admissible to prove the existence of an oral condition that would contradict the contract. [Rincones v Windberg (Tex App) 705 SW2d 846 (1986)]

(a) **Reason for the Parol Evidence Rule.** The parol evidence rule is based on the theory that either (1) there never was an oral agreement or (2) if there was, the parties purposely abandoned it when they executed their written contract. The social objective of the parol evidence rule is to give stability to contracts and to prevent the fraudulent assertion of oral terms that never actually existed. Some courts apply the parol evidence rule strictly.

To illustrate the parol evidence rule, assume that L, the landlord who is the owner of several new stores in the same vicinity, discusses leasing one of them to T (tenant). L agrees to give to T the exclusive right to sell soft drinks and agrees to stipulate in the leases with the tenants of other stores that they cannot do so. L and T then execute a detailed written lease for the store. The lease with T makes no provision with respect to an exclusive right of T to sell soft drinks. Thereafter L leases the other stores to A, B, and C, without restricting them as to the sale of soft drinks, which they then begin to sell, causing T to lose money. T sues L, claiming that the latter had broken the contract by which T was to have the exclusive right to sell soft drinks. L

[14]Palmer v Liles (Tex App) 677 SW2d 661 (1984).

defends on the ground that there was no prior oral agreement to that effect. Will the court permit *T* to prove that there was such an oral agreement?

On the facts as stated, if nothing more is shown, the court will not permit such parol evidence to be presented. The operation of this principle can be understood more easily if the actual courtroom procedure is followed. When *T* sues *L*, the first step will be to prove that there is a lease between them. Accordingly, *T* will offer in evidence the written lease between *T* and *L*. *T* will then take the witness stand and begin to testify about an oral agreement giving an exclusive right. At this point, *L*'s attorney will object to the admission of the oral testimony by *T* because it would modify the terms of the written lease. The court will then examine the lease to see if it appears to be complete; and if the court decides that it is, the court will refuse to allow *T* to offer evidence of an oral agreement. The only evidence before the court then will be the written lease. *T* will lose because nothing is in the written lease about an exclusive right to sell soft drinks.

If a written contract appears to be complete, the parol evidence rule prohibits its alteration not only by oral testimony but also by proof of other writings or memorandums made before or at the time the written contract was executed. An exception is made when the written contract refers to and identifies other writings or memorandums and states that they are to be regarded as part of the written contract. In such a case, it is said that the other writings are integrated or incorporated by reference.

(b) Conflict between Oral and Written Contracts. Initially, when there is a conflict between the prior oral contract and the later written contract, the variation is to be regarded as (1) a mistake, which can be corrected by reformation, or (2) an additional term in the written contract, which is not binding because it was not part of the agreement.

Conflicts between written contracts and spoken words frequently arise when an agent or employee gives an explanation that is not what the written contract says.

§ 17:7. Liberalization of Parol Evidence Rule.

The strictness of the parol evidence rule has been relaxed in a number of jurisdictions. A trend is beginning to appear which permits parol evidence as to the intention of the parties when the claimed intention is plausible from the face of the contract even though there is no ambiguity. There is likewise authority that parol evidence is admissible as to matters occurring before the execution of the contract in order to give a better understanding of what the parties meant by their written contract.[15]

---

[15]This is also the view followed by UCC § 2-202(a) which permits terms in a contract for the sale of goods to be "explained or supplemented by a course of dealing or usage of trade...or by course of performance." Such evidence is admissible not because there is an ambiguity but "in order that the true understanding of the parties as to the agreement may be reached." Official Code Comment to § 2-202.

It has also been held that UCC § 1-205 permits proof of trade usage and course of performance with respect to non-Code contracts even though there is no ambiguity. Chase Manhattan Bank v First Marion Bank (CA5 Fla) 437 F2d 1040 (1971).

FACTS:

Olsen Media ran an advertising agency. Energy Sciences, Inc., made a contract with Olsen Media for advertising. The contract stated a monthly compensation to be paid to Olsen and stated further that after six months this amount was "negotiable." The written contract also stated that it contained the entire contract of the parties. In a suit on the contract, evidence was offered to show that "negotiable" meant only "negotiable upwards" and that the compensation could not be lower than the amount stated in the contract.

DECISION:

Parol evidence is admissible to show what the parties meant by the words they used. The fact that the written contract stated that it contained all the terms of the contract did not prevent the admission of parol evidence for this purpose. Parol evidence was therefore admissible to show what was meant by "negotiable." [Olsen Media v Energy Sciences, Inc. 32 Wash App2d 579, 648 P2d 493 (1982)]

The liberalization approach is not followed by all courts and some apply the **four corners rule** under which the court must look for the contract within the four corners of the writing and may not look beyond the paper in the absence of an exception to the parol evidence rule.[16]

§ 17:8.   When the Parol Evidence Rule Does Not Apply.

The parol evidence rule may not apply in certain cases. The most common of these are discussed in the following paragraphs.

(a) **Incomplete Contract.** The parol evidence rule necessarily requires that the written contract sum up or integrate the entire contract. If the written contract is on its face, or is admittedly, not a complete summation, the parties naturally did not intend to abandon the points upon which they agreed but which were not noted in the contract; and parol evidence is admissible to show the actual agreement of the parties.[17]

A contract may appear on its face to be complete and yet not include everything the parties agreed upon. It must be remembered that there is no official standard by which to determine when a contract is complete. All that the court can do is to consider whether all essential terms of the contract are present, that is, whether the contract is sufficiently definite to be enforceable, and whether it contains all provisions which would ordinarily be included in a contract of that nature.

The fact that a contract is silent as to a particular matter does not mean that it is incomplete, for the law may attach a particular legal result (called *implying a term*) when the contract is silent. In such a case, parol evidence which is inconsistent with the term that would be implied cannot be shown. For example, when the contract is silent as to the time of payment, the obligation of making payment concurrently with performance by the

---

[16]Tucker v Richey, _____ Ind App _____, 448 NE2d 1206 (1983).
[17]F. R. Hoar & Sons, Inc. v McElroy Plumbing & Heating Co. (CA5 Miss) 680 F2d 1115 (1982).

other party is implied, and parol evidence is not admissible to show that there was an oral agreement to make payment at a different time.

(b) **Ambiguity.** Parol evidence is admissible to explain ambiguous terms of a contract in order to ascertain the real intent of the parties.[18]

FACTS:

Barden & Robeson Corporation manufactured component parts that were used in building houses. Timmerman was a contractor building houses. He made a contract with Barden & Robeson to purchase certain component parts. The contract stated "Terms: 80%-20%". The buyer later claimed that this made the contract divisible.

DECISION:

Parol evidence would be admitted to show the meaning of the provision. This evidence showed that the parties intended terms of payment, namely, payment of 80% on delivery of the first truckload of parts and 20% on delivery of the second part. The court rejected the contention of the defendant that the term made the contract divisible so that the buyer could choose one part of the contract and reject the balance. [Barden & Robeson Corp. v Timmerman, _____App Div 2d_____, 497 NYS2d 196 (1986)]

If a written contract may have two different meanings, parol evidence may generally be admitted to clarify the meaning. This is particularly true when the contract contains contradictory measurements or descriptions, or when it employs symbols or abbreviations that have no general meaning known to the court.

Parol evidence may also be admitted to show that a word used in a contract has a special trade meaning or a meaning in the particular locality that differs from the common meaning of that word.

The fact that the parties disagree as to the meaning of the contract does not mean that it is ambiguous.

(c) **Fraud, Accident, or Mistake.** A contract apparently complete on its face may have omitted a provision which should have been included. Parol evidence may be admitted to show that a provision was omitted as the result of fraud, accident, or mistake, and to further show what that provision stated.

When one party claims to have been fraudulently induced by the other to enter into the contract, the parol evidence rule does not bar proof that there was fraud.[19]

(d) **Existence of Contract.** Parol evidence is admissible to identify the writing of the parties. When several documents are executed as part of one transaction, parol evidence is admissible to show the relationship of the documents as forming one transaction.

[18]TR Drilling Co., Inc. v Howard (La App) 463 So 2d 923 (1985).
[19]Essex v Getty Oil Co. (Mo App) 661 SW2d 544 (1983).

When it is claimed that there is in fact no contract because of a mutual mistake, parol evidence is admissible to show the existence of such a mistake.[20]

The parol evidence rule does not bar proof that the written contract is in fact not a binding agreement. Thus, it can be shown that there was no consideration for the contract, that the contract was void because it was illegal, or that the contract was voidable because of the incapacity of a party or because of fraud.

(e) **Modification of Contract.** The parol evidence rule prohibits only the contradiction of a complete written contract. It does not prohibit proof that the contract was thereafter modified or terminated.

Written contracts commonly declare that they can only be modified by a writing. In the case of construction contracts, it will ordinarily be stated that no payment will be made for extra work unless there is a written order from the owner or architect calling for such extra work. If the parties proceed in disregard of such a clause requiring a writing, it may be shown by parol evidence that they have done so and the contract will be modified accordingly.

FACTS:

McCarthy, as owner, made a contract with Harrington to build a home. The contract stated that no charges could be made for work in addition to that called for by the contract unless there was a written order for such extra work specifying the charges to be made. During the course of construction, McCarthy orally requested Harrington to make certain additions to the work. This was done without any written order being executed. When the work was finished, McCarthy refused to pay for the extra work on the ground that there were no written orders for such work.

DECISION:

Judgment for Harrington. Although the contract required written orders for extra work, the subsequent conduct of the parties with respect to the extra work that was done constituted a modification of the original contract. The fact that the original contract contained a requirement of written work modifications did not prevent proof that the parties had proceeded in disregard of such requirement, and thereby modified the original contract with respect to the work done. [Harrington v McCarthy, 91 Idaho 307, 420 P2d 790 (1966)]

SUMMARY

An oral agreement can be a contract unless it is the intention of the parties that they should not be bound by the agreement unless a writing is executed by them. If the parties intend to be bound by the oral agreement it is a contract even though it is oral. As an exception to this statement, certain contracts must be evidenced by a writing or they can not be enforced. The statutes that declare this exception are called statutes of frauds and com-

[20]Beynon Building Corp. v National Guard Life Ins. Co. 118 Ill App 3d 754, 74 Ill Dec 216, 455 NE2d 246 (1983).

monly require that a contract be evidenced by writing in the case of (a) an agreement that can not be performed within one year after the agreement is made, (b) an agreement to sell or a sale of any interest in real property, (c) a promise to answer for the debt or default of another, (d) a promise by the executor or administrator of a decedent's estate to pay a claim against the estate from personal funds, (e) a promise made in consideration of marriage, and (f) a contract for the sale of goods for a purchase price over $500. Local statutes may expand the above list to include other types of contracts, such as a contract between a landowner and a real estate agent employed to sell the land.

In order to evidence a contract so as to satisfy a statute of frauds, there must be some permanent record, a writing, of all material terms and this must be signed by the defendant against whom enforcement of the contract or damages for its breach is sought. The signing may be made by printing, stamping, or typewriting or any other means that is intended to identify the particular party. Two or more writings can be combined to form a writing sufficient to satisfy the statute of frauds provided there is an express internal reference in the writings that ties them together.

If the applicable statute of frauds is not satisfied, the oral contract can not be enforced. In order to avoid unjust enrichment, a plaintiff barred from enforcing an oral contract may recover from the other contracting party the reasonable value of the benefits conferred by the plaintiff upon the defendant. In order to prevent the statute of frauds from being used to defraud a party to an oral contract, the courts by decision have made certain exceptions to the statute of frauds. Under the partial performance exception, an oral contract for the sale of land is binding when the buyer has gone into possession and made substantial improvements to the land of such a nature that they can not be compensated for by the payment of money damages. Under the primary or main purpose exception, an oral promise to pay the debt of another can be enforced when the main purpose of the promisor in making such promise is to benefit the promisor rather than to benefit the debtor. Under the detrimental reliance exception, many courts will enforce an oral contract in spite of the statute of frauds when the party seeking performance has relied on the oral contract to such an extent that it would be an unconscionable hardship if the contract were not enforced and this reliance on the oral contract was reasonably foreseeable to the other contracting party.

When there is a written contract, the question arises as to whether that writing is the exclusive statement of the agreement of the parties. If the writing is the complete and final statement of the contract, parol evidence as to matters agreed to before or at the time the writing was signed is not admissible to contradict the writing. This is called the parol evidence rule. Some courts have liberalized the rule so that parol evidence is admitted when it will aid in interpreting what the writing says. In any case, the parol evidence rule does not bar parol evidence when (a) the writing is incomplete; (b) the writing is ambiguous; (c) the writing is not a true statement of the agreement of the parties because of fraud, accident, or mistake; or (d) the existence, (e) modification, or (f) absence of a contract is in controversy. The fact that the parties disagree as to the meaning of a contract or that a court decision is required to settle the point does not make the writing ambiguous. The exception as to mistake permits proof that there is in fact no contract because there is a mutual mistake or that the writing that has been executed does not correctly set forth the terms of the contract that has been in fact agreed to.

QUESTIONS AND CASE PROBLEMS

1. What social forces are affected by the following rule of law? "Parol evidence is not admissible for the purpose of modifying a written contract when that evidence relates to an agreement made before or at the time that the written contract was executed."

2. What is the primary purpose exception to the statute of frauds?

3. In a telephone conversation, Roderick agrees to buy Betty's house. All the details of the transaction were agreed to in the conversation. The next day Betty wrote Roderick a letter stating "This confirms the agreement we made last night that I should sell you my home." Betty refused to go through with the transaction. Roderick sued Betty. Will Roderick recover?

4. Potack made a contract to build a house for Nathan by July 1. After construction was commenced, continuing heavy rains began. Because it was impossible to continue building in the rain, Potack and Nathan orally agreed that Potack could have one extra day in which to complete the work for every day lost because of the bad weather and that in return Potack would reduce the contract price by $100 for every day's delay. The work is not completed until August 1. When Nathan sues Potack for damages for delay, can Potack prove that there were 30 bad weather days and that the oral agreement therefore entitled him to an extension of 30 days?

5. Martin made an oral contract with Cresheim Garage to work as its manager for two years. Cresheim wrote Martin a letter stating that the oral contract had been made and setting forth all its terms. Cresheim later refused to recognize the contract. Martin sued Cresheim for breach of the contract and offered Cresheim's letter in evidence as proof of the contract. Cresheim claimed that the oral contract was not binding because the "contract" was not in writing and its letter referring to the contract was not a contract but only a letter. Was the contract binding?

6. When a nephew buys goods for $100 from a merchant, what is the difference between (a) the uncle's promise to the merchant to pay the bill if the nephew does not, and (b) the uncle's instruction to the merchant to charge the purchase to the uncle?

7. Atari went to work for the Lancaster Insurance Company selling insurance. In order to induce her to do so, the proper representative of the company promised her that she would be promoted to the position of District Manager after she sold one million dollars of insurance. Atari and the representative of the company then signed a detailed contract stating the terms of employment. The contract stated that promotions would be made for cause but that no promotion could be made from one rank to another until after two years of employment in the lower rank. In her first year working for the company, Atari sold one million dollars of insurance. She demanded that she be promoted. Lancaster refused to

promote her on the ground that the employment contract required that two years expire before she could be promoted. Was this defense valid?

8. Lawrence loaned money to Moore. Moore died without repaying the loan. Lawrence claimed that when he mentioned the matter to Moore's widow, she promised to pay the debt. She did not do so and Lawrence sued her on her promise. Does she have any defense? [Moore v Lawrence, 252 Ark 759, 480 SW2d 941]

9. Ramsey Products Corporation desired to have a new factory constructed for it. Ramsey made a written contract with Williams and Associates, architects, to design the building. This contract described the project as being a new manufacturing plant and offices but did not specify the maximum cost or any details of construction. Williams prepared plans for a factory which would cost about one half million dollars to build. This was too much for Ramsey and it abandoned the contract. Williams then sued Ramsey for compensation for services. Ramsey claimed that Williams had not performed the contract because, according to Ramsey, Williams had agreed to prepare plans for a building which would have 25,000 square feet and would cost one quarter million dollars, and that as this had not been done, Williams was not entitled to recover compensation for his services. Williams objected to the admission of the parol evidence as to the size and cost of the proposed factory. Was parol evidence admissible as to the size and cost of the proposed factory? [Williams and Associates v Ramsey Products Corp. 19 NC App 1, 198 SE2d 67]

10. Investors Premium Corporation purchased computer equipment from Burroughs Corporation. It made the purchase because of various statements made by the Burroughs sales representative. A written contract was executed for the purchase of the system. The contract stated that there were no warranties which were not stated in the contract and that the written contract was the complete statement of the obligation of Burroughs. The system did not work properly and Investors claimed that Burroughs was liable because the system did not perform as the salesman had warranted. Is Burroughs liable for breach of the agent's warranty? [Investors Premium Corp. v Burroughs Corp. (DC SC) 389 F Supp 39]

11. Evans made a written contract to buy property from Borkowski. Under the sales contract the buyer was to make payment in certain installments prior to the delivery of the deed. When the buyer could not make payments on time, the parties entered into a new written agreement, the buyer persuading the seller to do so by orally promising him that he would pay interest on late payments. He was late in making the payments and paid the interest under protest. The buyer later sued the seller to recover the interest payments. Was the buyer entitled to recover the interest? [Evans v Borkowski (Fla) 139 So2d 472]

12. An accounting firm sold out its business to a new firm. The sales contract stated that it was the intention of the parties that the new firm should provide service for clients of the old firm. The new firm agreed to pay the old firm 15% of the gross billings for assignments performed by the new firm for a period of 84 months. Later a dispute arose as to whether the 15% of gross billings was limited to the billings of those

who were originally clients of the old firm or whether it also included billings of new clients of the new firm. In a lawsuit over this point, parol evidence was offered to show what the contract covered. Was this evidence admissible? [Rullman v LaFrance, Walker, Jackley & Saville 206 Neb 180, 292 NW2d 19]

13. When will improvements made by a buyer bar the seller from claiming that the purchase contract was not binding because it was oral?

14. Roth made a contract to sell his house to Eric. They signed a written contract but left the purchase price blank because they had agreed that the selling price was to be reduced by the cost of certain necessary repairs that the buyer would be required to make. They later agreed on this amount but the amount was never filled in on the written contract. Is the contract binding?

15. With respect to the applicability of the statute of frauds, compare (a) a promise made by an aunt to her niece to pay the niece's bill owed to the department store; (b) a promise made by the aunt to the department store to pay the amount the aunt owes the store for a television set the aunt purchased as a present for her niece; and (c) a promise made by the aunt to the department store that she would pay her niece's bill if the niece did not do so.

16. Wood was a certified public accountant. She went to work for the accounting firm of Dan P. Holl & Company. There was no written contract of employment and nothing was agreed to with respect of the duration of the employment. After working five years, a dispute arose as to whether Wood had a binding employment agreement. It was claimed that she did not because of the 1-year provision of the statute of frauds. Did the statute of frauds apply? [Wood v Dan P. Holl & Co. 169 Ga App 839, 315 SE2d 51 (1984)]

17. Louise Pulsifer owned a farm. She desired to sell the farm and ran an ad in the local newspaper. Russell Gillespie agreed to purchase the farm. Louise then wrote him a letter stating that she would not sell the farm. He sued her in order to enforce the contract. Louise raised the defense of the statute of frauds. The letter signed by her did not contain any of the terms of the sale. Gillespie, however, claimed that the newspaper ad could be combined with her letter in order to satisfy the statute of frauds. Was he correct? [Gillespie v Pulsifer (Mo App) 655 SW2d 123]

CHAPTER 18

INTERPRETATION OF

CONTRACTS

CHAPTER OBJECTIVES

After studying this chapter you will be able to:

1. Compare the effect of objective and subjective intent of the parties to a contract.
2. Distinguish between conditions precedent and conditions subsequent.
3. State the rules for interpreting ambiguous terms in a contract.
4. State the effect of contradictory terms.
5. Define and illustrate implied terms.
6. Distinguish between joint, several, and joint and several contracts.
7. State what controls the choice of law applicable to an interstate contract.
8. Solve problems involving the interpretation of contracts.

When it has been decided that there is a contract between the parties, the next step is to determine the terms of that contract. Should a contract be interpreted to mean what one of the parties intended it to mean, or should it mean what a reasonable person would believe was intended? Should the contract be held to mean only what it expressly says or can additional terms be implied or read into the contract? What if additional terms are needed to protect one of the parties to the contract from hardship or oppression?

Society has the task of determining just what the contract means and of deciding if society wants to enforce the contract according to its terms. The rules of law that have evolved in finding answers to these questions are the rules governing the interpretation of contracts.

A. RULES OF CONSTRUCTION AND INTERPRETATION

An understanding of the rules discussed in the following paragraphs will help contracting parties avoid many of the difficulties that may arise when a contract is not drafted carefully.

§ 18:1.   Intention of the Parties.

A contract is to be enforced according to its terms. A court cannot remake or rewrite the contract of the parties under the pretense of interpreting it. The court examines the contract to determine what the parties intended. It will then give effect to what the parties intended, as long as it is lawful.

FACTS:

Ernest Rice obtained a divorce from his wife, Ellen. As part of the divorce decree, it was agreed that Ernest would provide support for their son Michael, then eleven years of age, until he reached his "majority." When this decree was entered, twenty-one was the age of majority. Thereafter the legislature reduced the age to eighteen years. When Michael attained the age of eighteen, his father petitioned the court to terminate the support provision. Should the court do so?

DECISION:

Yes. The intention of the parties was that support should be provided as long as the law required the providing of support. As the requirement changed, the obligation of the father under the agreement also changed. The divorce agreement-decree was not to be interpreted as imposing a flat obligation to provide support until Michael attained age twenty-one but only as long as support was required, i.e., up to age eighteen after the age of majority had been reduced. [Rice v Rice, 213 Kan 800, 518 P2d 477 (1974)]

No particular form of words is required and any words manifesting the intent of the parties are sufficient. In the absence of proof that a word has a peculiar meaning or that it was employed by the parties with a particular meaning, a common word is given its ordinary meaning.

A word will not be given its literal meaning when it is clear that the parties did not intend such a meaning. For example, "and" may be substituted for "or," "may," for "shall," and "void" for "voidable," and vice versa, when it is clear that the parties so intended.

(a) **Objective Intent.** When it is stated that the law seeks to enforce the intent of the parties, it is the intent that is outwardly manifested. That is, what would a reasonable third person believe the parties intended? It is this **objective intent** that will be enforced. Conversely, a party can not claim that secretly something else was intended. Such secret or **subjective intent** can not be proven.[1]

[1]Watkins v Petro-Search, Inc. (CA5 Tex) 689 F2d 537 (1982).

FACTS:

Keyworth was employed by Industrial Sales Co. In the course of employment, he was injured by Israelson. Industrial Sales made a contract with Keyworth to pay him $100 per week until he was able to return to normal work but specified that such payments would be paid back to industrial Sales from any recovery that Keyworth would obtain in a lawsuit against Israelson, with payments to be made to Industrial Sales upon the "successful conclusion of the case." Keyworth obtained a recovery in the action against Israelson of $16,000 but refused to make any payment to Industrial Sales because he believed there was not a "successful conclusion of the case." Industrial Sales sued Keyworth.

DECISION:

Judgment for Industrial Sales Co. The fair meaning of the language was that winning the lawsuit was a "successful conclusion of the case." The fact that one of the parties may have a particular belief or intent that it meant winning a particular minimum amount would not be allowed to change the intent of the parties as expressed by the words of the contract. [Keyworth v Industrial Sales Co. 241 Md 453, 217 A2d 253 (1966)]

In these cases, society is balancing the risks involved in enforcing a contract that does not accurately state the intent of the parties with the danger of giving effect to a subjective intent that is falsely asserted. The enforcing of the objectively determined intent appears to society to hold the smaller risk of harm and injury than would opening the door to fraudulent claims that a contract was secretly intended to mean something else. Thus the objectively shown intent controls and secret or subjective intent is ignored.

(b) **Meaning of Words.** Ordinary words are to be interpreted according to their ordinary meaning.

FACTS:

Honey Creek Square, Inc., leased part of its shopping center to Sears, Roebuck & Co. The lease provided for payment of a rent measured as a percentage of net sales with no guaranteed minimum. The lease specified that fees for services were to be excluded in making the computation of net sales. Honey Creek assigned its rights to Washington National Corporation. It claimed that in calculating the rent due, the net proceeds from the sale of goods should be increased by charges made for garment alterations, gift wrapping, bike and automobile work and repair, and service contracts.

DECISION:

Words in a contract are to be given their normal and ordinary meaning unless the contract shows that a different meaning is intended. By the ordinary meaning of words, net sales on which the rental percentage was to be computed involved only transactions in which title to property was transferred for a price. Nothing in the lease showed that a contrary meaning was given by the parties. Likewise, by their ordinary meaning, the disputed items were service charges and did not refer to payments made for the transfer of title to property. Therefore the disputed items were not sales and were properly omitted in determining the base on which the rent was computed. [Washington National Corp. v Sears, Roebuck & Co. _____Ind App_____, 474 NE 2d 116 (1985)]

If technical or trade terms are employed, these are to be interpreted according to the area of technical knowledge or trade from which the terms are taken. If there is a common meaning to a term that meaning will be followed even though the dictionary may give a different meaning.

The prior relationships of the parties may give meaning to the words used by the parties.[2]

(c) **Incorporation by Reference.** The contract may not cover all the terms agreed upon. The missing terms may be found in another document. Frequently the parties executing the contract will state that it embraces or incorporates the other document. Thus a contract for storage will simply state that a storage contract is entered into and will then state that the contract applies to the goods that are listed in the schedule that is attached to the contract and made part of the contract. Likewise a contract for the construction of a building will simply state that the building is to be constructed according to the plans and specifications "which are incorporated herein and made part of this contract." When there is such an **incorporation by reference,** the contract consists of both the original or skeleton document and the detailed statement that is incorporated therein.[3]

§ 18:2.   Whole Contract.

The provisions of a contract must be construed as a whole.[4] This rule is followed even when the contract is partly written and partly oral. Every word of a contract is to be given effect if reasonably possible.

FACTS:

Avis-Rent-A-Car System gave Southwestern Automotive Leasing Corporation (SALCO) a car and truck rental franchise for three Louisiana cities in 1961. The licensing agreement gave each party the right to terminate with or without cause for a certain period of time and further provided that after "five years from the date Licensee first became an Avis System Licensee....Licensor may terminate...only with cause...." SALCO was not successful and by common consent its franchise rights were transferred in 1964 to Gulf Shores Leasing Corp. In 1968, Avis notified Gulf that it was terminating the license held by Gulf without cause. Gulf claimed that Avis could only terminate for cause because five years had run from the date of the original franchise agreement and brought suit to prevent termination.

DECISION:

Gulf could not add on the term of the prior licensee and therefore Gulf's license could be terminated without cause. The contract when read as a whole showed that the five-year period was a probationary or trial period and each licensee was required to stand on its own merits and to show five years of satisfactory work. The years of a former licensor could not be counted, particularly when, as in the case of SALCO, the prior years were not satisfactory. [Gulf Shores Leasing Corp. v Avis Rent-A-Car System, Inc. (CA5 La) 441 F2d 1385 (1971)]

---

[2]See § 18:6 of this book.
[3]Lincoln Welding Works, Inc. v Ramirez, 98 Nev 342, 647 P2d 381 (1982).
[4]Jones v Hinkle (Utah) 611 P2d 733 (1980).

(a) **Divisible Contract.** When a contract contains a number of provisions or performances to be rendered, the question arises as to whether the parties intended merely a group of separate contracts or whether they intended a "package deal" so that complete performance of every provision of the contract was essential.[5]

(b) **What Constitutes the Whole Contract.** The question may arise whether separate papers or particular parts of a paper constitute part of the whole contract.

Terms in a printed letterhead or billhead or on the reverse side of the printed contract form are not part of a contract written thereon unless a reasonable person would regard such terms as part of the contract. An employer's manual that is shown to the job applicant after the signing of an employment contract is not part of that contract. Similarly, provisions in a manufacturer's instruction manual, or in invoices, or on labels that are not seen or called to the attention of a buyer until after a contract of sale has been made are not part of the contract and do not bind the buyer.

§ 18:3.   Conditions.

When the occurrence or non-occurrence of an event affects the obligation of a party to a contract the event is called a **condition.**

(a) **Condition Precedent.** A condition or obligation-triggering event may be described as a **condition precedent** because it precedes the existence of the obligation.

In a fire insurance policy, there is no obligation on the insurer to make any payment until there is a fire loss. The occurrence of such a loss is thus a condition precedent to the duty of the insurer to make payment under the policy. Likewise when an employee is required to give notice to the employer in order to obtain a particular benefit, the giving of notice is a condition precedent to the duty of the employer to provide the benefit.[6]

(b) **Condition Subsequent.** The parties may specify that the contract shall terminate when a particular event occurs or does not occur. Such a provision is a **condition subsequent.** If government approval is required, the parties may specify that the contract shall not bind them if the government approval cannot be obtained.

A contract for the purchase of land may contain a condition subsequent which cancels the contract if the buyer is not able to obtain a zoning permit to use a building for a particular purpose.

(c) **Concurrent Conditions.** In most bilateral contracts, the performances by the parties are **concurrent conditions,** that is, the duty of each party to perform is dependent upon the other party's performing. Thus neither is required to perform until the other performs or tenders performance.[7] Frequently the contract will specify or indicate that one person must perform first. In such case, that performance is a **condition precedent** and the conditions are not concurrent. For example, in a contract to pay a painter

[5]St. John v Barker (Tex App) 638 SW2d 239 (1982).
[6]Sweet v Stormont Vail Regional Medical Center, 231 Kan 604, 647 P2d 1274 (1982).
[7]Pas-teur, Inc. v Energy Sciences, Inc. 11 Mass App 967, 417 NE2d 487 (1981).

$1,000 for painting a house, the painter must perform the painting work before the owner is required to perform the promise of paying for the work. Performance by the painter is thus a condition precedent to the owner's obligation to pay.

§ 18:4.   Contradictory and Ambiguous Terms.

One term in a contract may conflict with another term, or one term may be ambiguous because it has two different meanings.[8] It is then necessary for the court to determine whether there is a contract, and, if so, what the contract really means. When the terms of a contract are contradictory or conflict as to a significant matter, the existence of such conflict prevents there being any contract.

FACTS:

Mohon executed a contract to sell 372.12 acres of land to Moore. One paragraph of the contract stated that the purchase price was $110,000. Another paragraph stated that it was $275.00 an acre, which would produce a total price of $102,333 which would be $7,667 less than the stated price of $110,000. Which amount was binding?

DECISION:

Neither amount. There was no contract because the conflict in the terms could not be reconciled in any way. [Moore v Mohon (Tex Civ App) 514 SW2d 508 (1974)]

In some instances, the conflict between the terms of a contract is eliminated by the introduction of parol evidence or by applying an appropriate rule of construction.

(a) **Nature of Writing.** When a contract is partly printed or typewritten and partly written and the written part conflicts with the printed or typewritten part, the written part prevails. When there is a conflict between a printed part and a typewritten part, the latter prevails. When there is a conflict between an amount or quantity expressed both in words and figures, as on a check, the amount or quantity expressed in words prevails.

FACTS:

Integrated, Inc., entered into a contract with the State of California to construct a building. It then subcontracted the electrical work to Alec Fergusson Electrical Contractors. The subcontract was a printed form with blanks filled in by typewriting. The printed payment clause re-

quired Integrated to pay Fergusson on the 15th day of the month following the submission of invoices by Fergusson. The typewritten part of the contract required Integrated to pay Fergusson "immediately following payment" (by the State) to the general contractor.

[8]Wilke v First Federal Savings & Loan Ass'n, 108 Wis App 2d 650, 323 NW2d 179 (1982).

DECISION:

The typed and printed payment clauses were inconsistent. Therefore, the typewritten clause prevailed. The word "immediately" used therein did not require actual "immediate" action, however, but was satisfied by payment within a reasonable time, having regard to the nature of the circumstances of the case, which necessarily included sufficient time in which to process the payment received from the State before making payment therefrom to the subcontractor. [Integrated, Inc. v Alec Fergusson Electrical Contractors, 250 Cal App 2d 287, 58 Cal Rptr 503 (1967)]

(b) **Strict Construction against Drafting Party.** An ambiguous contract is interpreted strictly against the party who drafted it.[9] Thus, printed forms of a contract, such as insurance policies, which are supplied by the insurer, are interpreted against the insurer and in favor of the insured when two interpretations are reasonably possible. If the contract is clear and unambiguous, it will be enforced according to its terms even though this benefits the party who drafted the contract.

(c) **Ambiguity.** A contract is **ambiguous** when it is uncertain what was the intent of the parties. Disagreement as to the legal effect of the terms used by the parties does not make the contract ambiguous. This is so because the court, by applying the law to their terms can reach a conclusion as to the intent manifested by the contract. In contrast, if the intent would still be uncertain even after rules of law were applied, the contract is ambiguous.

The fact that a particular situation is not provided for by the contract does not make it ambiguous. For example, a summer camp contract was not ambiguous because it did not contain any provision relating to refunds upon cancellation.[10]

Whether a contract is ambiguous can not always be determined merely by looking at the contract. In some cases, the written contract will look perfectly clear and the ambiguity does not become apparent until the contract is applied to the facts or the property concerned.

FACTS:

The Dickinson Elks Club conducted an annual Labor Day golf tournament. Charbonneau Buick-Pontiac offered to give a new car as a prize to anyone making a hole-in-one on hole No.8. The golf course of the club was only nine holes so that in order to play 18 holes, the players would go around the course twice, although they would play from different tees or locations for the second nine holes. On the second time around, what was originally the eighth hole became the seventeenth hole. Grove was a contestant in the tournament. On the first day he scored 3 on the No. 8 hole but on approaching it for the second time as the seventeenth hole, he made a hole-in-one. He claimed the prize car from Charbonneau. The latter claimed that Grove had not won the prize because he did not make the hole-in-one on the eighth hole.

[9]Haener v Ada County Highway District, 108 Idaho 170, 697 P2d 1184 (1985).
[10]Sullivan v Lochearn, Inc. 143 Vt 150, 464 A2d 745 (1983).

DECISION:

Judgment for Grove. The offer made by Charbonneau was ambiguous in that it could refer to the particular cup in the golf course or to the sequence in which the hole-in-one was made. That is, it could refer either to making the hole-in-one as the eighth hole on the first time round the course or to making the hole-in-one in the same cup on either the first time round or on the second time round the course, when it would be the seventeenth hole. As Charbonneau had specified the terms, this ambiguity would be interpreted against it and in favor of Grove. The prize contract was therefore satisfied by making the hole-in-one on either the first or second time round the course. As Grove had done this, he satisfied the terms of the contract and was entitled to the prize. [Grove v Charbonneau Buick-Pontiac, Inc. (ND) 240 NW2d 853 (1976)]

§ 18:5.   Implied Terms.

In some cases the court will imply a term to cover a situation for which the parties failed to provide or when needed to give the contract a construction or meaning that is reasonable.

A term will not be implied in a contract when the court concludes that the silence of the contract on the particular point was intentional.

(a) **Duration of Contract.** When a contract does not state any time for its duration, three alternatives are possible. It could be held that there is no contract at all because an essential term is missing and without the term the agreement is too vague to enforce. It could also be held that as no termination is stated, the contract runs on forever. Neither of these views is adopted by the law.

Instead, when no duration is specified in the contract, courts will imply that the contract is to be performed or will continue for a reasonable time.[11] But either party may terminate the contract by giving notice to the other party.

Note that in effect the court is trying to salvage the transaction and give some effect to the intent of the parties to have a contract. But one should not jump to the conclusion that whenever a term is missing from a contract the word "reasonable" is to be implied. For example, an agreement to sell your house is not a contract when no price is stated and the omission of the price will not be cured by implying that a reasonable price is to be paid.

(b) **Details of Performance.** Details of performance of a contract not expressly stated in the contract will often be implied by the court.[12] Thus, an obligation to pay a specified sum of money is implied to mean payment in legal tender. In a contract to perform work there is an implied promise to use such skill as is necessary for the proper performance of the work. In a "cost plus" contract an undertaking is implied that the costs will be reasonable and proper. When payment is made "as a deposit on account," there is an implied term that if the payment is not used for the purpose stated, the payment will be returned to the person who made the deposit.

[11]Barton v Idaho, 104 Idaho 338, 659 P2d 92 (1983).
[12]Miller v Independent School District No. 56 (Okla) 609 P2d 756 (1980).

A local custom or trade practice, such as that of allowing thirty days' credit to buyers may form part of the contract when it is clear that the parties intended to be governed by this custom or trade practice or when a reasonable person would believe that they had so intended.[13]

When a written contract does not specify the time for performance, a reasonable time is implied.

(c) **Good Faith.** In every contract there is an implied obligation that neither party shall do anything that will have the effect of destroying or injuring the right of the other party to receive the fruits of the contract. This means that in every contract there exists an implied covenant of good faith and fair dealing.

FACTS:
Havel and Kelsey-Hayes Company entered into a licensing agreement by which Kelsey was given an "exclusive license" effective "throughout the world" to use a special process in the manufacturing of parts for jet engines and to grant licenses to others to use this process. Kelsey was to pay a percentage of money received from these activities. A suit was brought to terminate the license on the ground that not enough was being done by Kelsey to exploit or market the license. The defense was raised that the contract said nothing about the efforts required of the licensee.

DECISION:
Judgment for licensor. In view of the fact that every contract contains an implied term requiring the exercise of good faith and in view of the fact that the licensee was given an exclusive world-wide license, there was an implied duty on the licensee to exploit or market the license to sublicensees. The licensee by failing to exploit the license had therefore broken the contract even though there was no express term in the contract that required the licensee to exploit and market the license. [Havel v Kelsey-Hayes Co. 83 App Div 2d 333, 445 NYS 2d 333 (1981)]

(d) **Governmental Approval.** In some situations, the ability to perform a contract will depend upon obtaining a governmental permit or approval. When this is so, the failure to obtain such approval or permit may be made an express condition subsequent so that the contract is discharged by such failure. An implied term generally arises that one party to the contract will cooperate with the other in obtaining any necessary governmental permit or approval.

(e) **Statutory Terms.** Statutes commonly require that certain kinds of contracts contain particular clauses. For example, automobile insurance contracts are often required by statute to contain clauses with respect to no-fault liability and uninsured motorists. When a contract is written that does not contain the required statutory terms, the courts will ordinarily imply the statutory terms and interpret the contract as though it complied with the statute. Similarly, a provision in a contract that would be contrary to required statutory provision will be ignored.[14]

---

[13]Buxton v Harsh (Mo App) 631 SW2d 95 (1982).
[14]Sequoia Insurance Co. v Miller, 202 Cal Rptr 866 (1984).

§ 18:6. Conduct and Custom.

The conduct of the parties and the customs and usages of a particular trade may give meaning to the words of the parties and thus aid in the interpretation of their contract.

(a) **Conduct of the Parties.** The conduct of the parties in carrying out the terms of a contract may be considered in determining just what they meant by the contract. When performance has been repeatedly tendered and accepted without protest, neither party will be permitted to claim that the contract was too indefinite to be binding. For example, when a travel agent made a contract with a hotel to arrange for "junkets" to the hotel, any claim that it was not certain just what was intended must be ignored when some 80 junkets had already been arranged and paid for by the hotel at the contract price without any dispute as to whether the contract obligation was satisfied.[15] Moreover, when the conduct of the parties is inconsistent with the original written contract, proof of such conduct may justify concluding that the parties had orally modified the original agreement.

(b) **Custom and Usage of Trade.** The customs and usages of the trade or commercial activity to which the contract relates may give to the terms of a contract a meaning that the terms would not have in ordinary speech or a meaning where the words of the contract would otherwise appear to have no meaning. For example, when a contract for the construction of a house calls for a "turn-key construction" industry usage is admissible to show that this means a construction in which all the owner need do is "turn the key" in the lock to open the building for use and that all risks are assumed by the contractor.[16]

FACTS:
Beck & Co was a brewery. It gave Gianelli Distributing Company a franchise to distribute Beck's Beer. The franchise agreement specified that it would continue "unless and until terminated at any time by thirty days written notice by either party to the other." Some time thereafter Beck notified Gianelli that the franchise was terminated. Gianelli claimed that the franchise could only be terminated upon proof of reasonable cause for termination. Gianelli offered evidence of trade usage to show that there was a common practice to require cause for termination, and further claimed that such usage should be read into the franchise with Beck.

DECISION:
The franchise contract was not a complete agreement because it did not state whether termination could be for any cause or only for a good cause. Parol evidence of trade custom was therefore admissible on the ground that the parties naturally intended to do business in the way that was customary and that therefore their actual intent was that termination could only be made for good cause. Accordingly, a new trial was required in order to determine whether in fact there was a trade usage as claimed. [Gianelli Distributing Co. v Beck & Co. 215 Cal Rptr 667 (1985)]

---

[15]See Uniform Commercial Code § 2–208(1) as to course of performance in the interpretation of contracts for the sale of goods and UCC § 1–205 as to both Code and non-Code transactions.

[16]Blue v R. L. Glossen Contracting, Inc. 173 Ga App 622, 327 SE2d 582 (1985).

Custom and usage, however, can not override express provisions of a contract that are inconsistent with such customs and usage.

§ 18:7.   Avoidance of Hardship.

As a general rule, a party is bound by a contract even though it proves to be a bad bargain. If possible, a court will interpret a contract to avoid hardship, particularly when the hardship will hurt the weaker of the two parties to the contract.

When there is ambiguity as to the meaning of a contract, a court will avoid the interpretation that gives one contracting party an unreasonable advantage over the other or which causes a forfeiture of a party's interest. When there is an inequality of bargaining power between the contracting parties, courts will sometimes classify the contract as a **contract of adhesion** in that it was offered on a "take-it-or-leave-it" basis by the stronger party, and the court will interpret the contract as providing what appeared reasonable from the standpoint of the weaker bargaining party.

In some instances, if hardship cannot be avoided in this manner, the court may hold that the contract or a particular provision is not binding because it is unconscionable or contrary to public policy. The extent to which this protection is available is uncertain.

When the hardship arises because the contract makes no provision for the situation which has occurred, the court will sometimes imply a term in order to avoid the hardship.

FACTS:

Standard Oil Co. made a nonexclusive jobbing or wholesale dealership contract with Perkins, which limited him to selling Standard's products and required Perkins to maintain certain minimum prices. Standard Oil had the right to approve or disapprove Perkins' customers. In order to be able to perform under his contract, Perkins had to make a substantial money investment, and his only income was from the commissions on the sales of Standard's products. Standard Oil made some sales directly to Perkins' customers. When Perkins protested, Standard Oil pointed out that the contract did not contain any provision making his rights exclusive. Perkins sued Standard Oil to compel it to stop dealing with his customers.

DECISION:

Judgment for Perkins. In view of the expenditure required of Perkins in order to operate his business and to perform his part of the contract and of his dependence upon his customers, the interpretation should be made that Standard Oil would not solicit customers of Perkins, even though the contract did not give him an exclusive dealership within the given geographic area. [Perkins v Standard Oil Co. 235 Or 7, 383 P2d 107 (1963)]

---

§ 18:8.   Joint, Several, and Joint and Several Contracts.

When two or more persons are on either side of a contract, an additional question of interpretation may arise, as it may be necessary to determine whether the contract is (a) joint, (b) several, or (c) joint and several.

(a) **Joint Contracts.** A **joint contract** is one in which two or more persons jointly promise to perform an obligation. If *A*, *B*, and *C* sign a contract stating "we jointly promise" to do a particular act, the obligation is the joint obligation of *A*, *B*, and *C*. In the absence of an express intent to the contrary, a promise by two or more persons is generally presumed to be joint and not several.

Each of two or more joint promisors is liable for the entire obligation, but an action must be brought against all who are living and within the jurisdiction of the court. If one of the promisors dies, the surviving promisors remain bound to perform the contract unless it was personal in character and required the joint action of all the obligors for its performance. If the deceased obligor had received a benefit from the contract, a court of equity will also hold the obligor's estate liable for the performance of the contract.

Generally the release by the promisee of one or more of the joint obligors releases all.

(b) **Several Contracts.** **Several contracts** arise when two or more persons separately agree to perform the same obligation. Such contracts are several even though the separate agreements are set forth in the same paper.

If *A*, *B*, and *C* sign a contract stating "we severally promise" or "each of us promises" to do a particular act or to pay a specified sum of money, the three signers are severally bound to perform or to pay; that is, each signer is individually bound.

As the liability of each obligor of a several contract is by definition separate or distinct, the release of one or more of the obligors by the promisee does not release the others.

(c) **Joint and Several Contracts.** A **joint and several contract** is one in which two or more persons are bound both jointly and severally. If *A*, *B*, and *C* sign a contract stating "we, and each of us, promise" (or "I promise") to pay a specified sum of money, they are jointly and severally bound. The obligee may treat the claim either as a joint claim or as a group of separate claims, and may bring a suit against all at the same time or against one at a time. The plaintiff may also sue any number of the severally liable parties instead of suing them either singly or all at one time.

B. CONFLICT OF LAWS

When a lawsuit is brought on a contract, the court will seek to apply the law under which the contract was made. That is, a California court in many cases will not apply California law to a foreign contract. The principles which determine when a court applies the law of its own state, the **law of the forum,** or some foreign law are called **conflict of laws.**

Because there are fifty state court systems and a federal court system, and a high degree of interstate activity, these conflict of laws questions arise frequently.

§ 18:9.   State Courts.

It is important to distinguish between the state in which the parties are **domiciled** or have their permanent home, the state in which the contract is made, and the state in which the contract is to be performed. The state in which the contract is made is determined by finding the state in which the last act essential to the formation of the contract was performed. Thus, when an acceptance is mailed in one state to an offeror in another state, the state of formation of the contract is the state in which the acceptance is mailed if the acceptance becomes effective at that time.

If acceptance by telephone is otherwise proper, the acceptance takes effect at the place where the acceptance is spoken into the phone. Thus, an employment contract is made in the state in which the job applicant telephoned an acceptance, and consequently, the law of that state governs a claim to workers' compensation, even though the injuries were sustained in another state.

If an action on a contract made in one state is brought in a court of another state, an initial question is whether that court will lend its aid to the enforcement of a foreign (out-of-state) contract. Ordinarily suit may be brought on a foreign contract. But, if there is a strong contrary local policy, recovery may be denied even though the contract was valid in the state where it was made.

The capacity of a natural person to make a contract is governed by the place of contracting; a corporation's capacity to do so is determined by the law of the state of incorporation. The law of the state where the contract is made determines whether it is valid in substance and satisfies requirements as to form. Matters relating to the performance of the contract, excuse or liability for nonperformance, and the measure of damages for nonperformance are generally governed by the law of the state where the contract is to be performed.

When a lawsuit is brought on a contract, the law of the forum determines the procedure and the rules of evidence.

(a) **Specification by the Parties.** It is common for the more important contracts to specify that they shall be governed by the law of a particular state. When this is done, it is generally held that the contract will be enforced in another state and interpreted according to the law of the designated state. This is done even though a contrary result would be reached if governed by the law of the state in which the suit is brought. Whenever a transaction is governed by the Uniform Commercial Code, the parties may agree that their rights and duties shall be governed by the law of any state or nation which "bears a reasonable relation" to the transaction.

(b) **Center of Gravity.** There is a growing acceptance of the rule that a contract should be governed by the law of the state that has the most significant contacts with the transaction, to which state the contract may be said to gravitate.

For example, when the buyer's place of business and the seller's factory are located in state A and the buyer is purchasing to resell to customers in state A, many courts will hold that this is a contract governed by the law of state A in all respects even though it may happen to be a state B contract by virtue of the chance circumstance that the seller's offer was accepted by the buyer in state B. In determining which state has the most significant contacts the court is to consider the place of contracting, negotiating, and performing; the location of the subject matter of the contract; and the domicile, residence, and states of incorporation and principal place of business of the parties.[17]

When all states have the same rule of law, it is not important what rule of conflict of laws is followed. If, however, the law of the states involved is not the same, the choice of the state whose law is to govern will determine how the lawsuit will end.

§ 18:10. Federal Courts.

When the parties to a contract reside in different states and an action is brought on the contract in a federal court because of their different citizenship, the federal court must apply the same rules of conflict of laws that would be applied by the courts of the state in which the federal court is sitting. Thus, a federal court in Chicago deciding a case involving parties from different states must apply the same rule of conflict of laws as would be applied by the state courts in Illinois. The state law must be followed by the federal court in such a case whether or not the federal court agrees with the state law.

SUMMARY

As a contract is based on the agreement of the parties, courts must give effect to the intent of the parties manifested thereby. The intent that is to be enforced is the intent as it reasonably appears to a third person. This objective intent is followed and the subjective or secret intent is ignored because the recognition of secret intention would undermine the stability of contracts and open the door to fraud.

In interpreting a contract, words are to be given their ordinary meaning unless there is some reason, as in the case of trade or technical terms to conclude that the parties gave the words a special meaning. The court must consider the whole contract and not read a particular part out of context. When different writings are executed as part of the same transaction or one writing refers to or incorporates another, all the writings are to be read together as constituting the contract of the parties. In some cases, the reverse is done and a contract is held divisible because it is proper to conclude that the parties were in fact making two or more separate contracts and intended that each contract should stand by itself.

When provisions of a contract are contradictory, the court will try to reconcile or eliminate the conflict but if this can not be done, the conclusion may be reached that there is no contract because the conflict makes the agreement indefinite as to a material matter. In some cases, conflict is solved by considering the form of the conflicting terms and holding that handwriting prevails over typing and printing, and that typing prevails over printing. Ambiguity will be eliminated in some cases by the admission of parol evidence as discussed in Chapter 17 or by interpreting the provision strictly against the party preparing the contract, particularly when that party

---

[17]Boise Cascade Home & Land Corp. v Utilities, Inc. 127 Ill App 3d 14, 82 Ill Dec 177, 468 NE2d 442 (1984).

has significantly greater bargaining power or the contract can be described as an adhesion contract.

In most cases, the parties are held to their contract exactly as it has been written. In other cases, the courts will imply certain terms to preserve the contract against the objection that essential terms are missing or to prevent hardship. As to the former, the law will imply that performance be made within a reasonable time and that details of performance be reasonable when the contract fails to be specific on these points. As to the avoidance of hardship, the law will imply an obligation to act in good faith and a limitation to prevent a franchisor from competing with a franchisee.

When two or more persons are on one side of a contract, it may become necessary to determine whether the contract is joint, in which case all those persons are jointly obligated or jointly entitled; several, in which case each of those persons is individually obligated or entitled; or joint and several, in which case those persons are both jointly and individually liable or entitled.

When a contract has interstate aspects, it is necessary to determine which state's law governs the contract. The rules which govern that decision are called the law of conflict of laws. The parties may specify the jurisdiction whose law is to govern and if that jurisdiction bears a reasonable relationship to the contract it will be given effect by the court. In the absence of such a provision, the older courts will apply the law of the state where the contract was made with respect to most matters and the law of the state where performance is to be made as to matters relating to performance. The modern, or center of gravity view, is to choose that jurisdiction that has the most significant relationship to the parties, the contract, and its performance. When an action is brought in a federal court because it involves citizens of different states (diversity of citizenship), the federal court must apply the conflict of laws principles that would be applied by the courts of the state in which the federal court is sitting.

QUESTIONS AND CASE PROBLEMS

1. What social forces are affected by the rule that a secret intention which is not expressed has no effect?
2. What is a condition precedent?
3. Harrison Builders made a contract to build a house for Kendall on a cost plus 10% profit basis. The cost of the finished house was approximately $100,000. Kendall had expected that it would have been $60,000 and claimed that Harrison was careless and extravagant in piling up costs of $100,000. Harrison asserted that as Kendall did not deny that the costs were $100,000, he could not dispute that they were proper. Is Harrison correct?
4. In letters between the two, Rita contracted to sell "my car" to Viola for $2,000. It is later shown that Rita owned two cars. Rita refused to deliver either car to Viola. Viola sues Rita for breach of contract. Rita raised the defense that the contract is too indefinite to be enforced because it cannot be determined from the writing which car is the subject matter of the contract. Is the contract too indefinite to be enforced?

5. Quinn of Ohio sues Norman of California in the federal district court for the southern district of New York. Quinn claims that the court should apply the conflicts of laws rules of Ohio because he is from Ohio and the plaintiff should have the choice of law. Norman claims that the federal court should apply federal law and not the law of any particular state. Who is correct?

6. The Wendell Saw Company contracted to sell to the Harris Industrial Equipment Company a new power saw if it could be developed and made operational by the Wendell Company. Wendell was not able to make the new saw operate consistently and never delivered it to Harris. Harris sued Wendell for breach of contract. Was Wendell liable?

7. Compare (a) the rule that a contract will be construed strictly against the person preparing it, and (b) the rule that a typewritten provision prevails over a printed provision.

8. McGill and his grandson, Malo, made an agreement by which the former would live with the latter and receive support and maintenance in return for deeding to the grandson the house of the former. After a number of years, the grandfather left the house because of the threats and physical violence of the grandson. There was no complaint of lack of support and maintenance. Had the grandson broken the contract? [McGill v Malo, 23 Conn Supp 447, 184 A2d 517]

9. Compare the effect of (a) a typewritten clause in a signed printed contract that conflicts with the printed provision and (b) a typewritten clause added by an offeree to a printed offer that conflicts with the printed provisions.

10. A obtained a fire insurance policy from the B Insurance Co. One provision of the policy required A to give sixty days' notice of any fire loss. Another provision of the policy stated that no recovery could be had on the policy for any loss of which notice was not given immediately. A had a fire loss and gave notice forty days thereafter. B refused to pay because the notice of the loss had not been given "immediately." Is this defense valid?

11. A contract was made for the sale of a farm. The contract stated that the buyer's deposit would be returned "if for any reason the farm cannot be sold." Thereafter the seller stated that she had changed her mind, and would not sell, and offered to return the deposit. The buyer refused to take the deposit back and brought suit to enforce the contract. The seller defended on the ground that the "any reason" provision extended to anything, including the seller's changing her mind. Was the buyer entitled to recover? [Phillips v Rogers 157 W Va 194, 200 SE2d 676]

12. Gerson Realty Co. rented an apartment to Casaly. The lease stated that it could be renewed on giving notice but declared that "such notice . . . shall be given or served and shall not be deemed to have been duly given or served unless in writing and forwarded by registered mail." Casaly sent a renewal notice by certified mail. Two years after receiving the notice, Gerson claimed that it was not effective because it had not been sent by registered mail. Was this notice effective? [Gerson Realty Inc. v Casaly, 2 Mass App 875, 316 NE2d 767]

13. Harwood rented an apartment in an apartment house complex from Lincoln Square Apartments. Air conditioning was among the services to

be provided by the landlord. The lease stated that the landlord was not liable for "any interruption or curtailment of any service." The central air conditioning system in the apartment house broke down and would not function for 6 weeks in the summer. Harwood rented an air conditioning unit which he placed in his apartment and then sued the landlord for the cost thereof. The landlord denied liability because of the disclaimer clause. Was the landlord right? [Harwood v Lincoln Square Apartments Section 5, Inc. 359 NYS2d 387]

14. Physicians Mutual Insurance Company issued a policy covering the life of Ruby Brown. The policy declared that it did not cover any deaths resulting from "mental disorder, alcoholism, or drug addiction." Ruby was killed when she fell while intoxicated. The insurance company refused to pay because of the quoted provision. Her executor, Savage, sued the insurance company. Did the insurance company have a defense? [Physicians Mut. Ins. Co. v Savage, 156 Ind App 283, 296 NE2d 165]

15. Gonzales agreed to sell his land to Lilley. He read and signed the sales contract. It provided that the purchase price was to be paid in monthly installments but that the entire balance would become immediately due if Lilley would sell the land. Later Gonzales claimed that the provision for payment of the balance when the land was sold did not bind him because he did not understand the provision and never intended to wait for the balance until the land was sold. Was Gonzales bound by the "due on sale" provision?

16. Mary and Michael Pernoud were married and then later divorced. They made a property settlement agreement which provided that they would sell their Canadian real estate and that Mary would receive $30,000 from the proceeds, and that the husband would pay any deficiency if the land was sold for less than that amount. The land was sold for approximately $26,000 Canadian money. This amounted to approximately $22,000 of American money. Mary claimed that Michael was liable to her for $8,000 of American money because the contract required payment in American dollars. Michael claimed that as Canadian land was sold it was Canadian dollars and that he only owed a deficiency of approximately $4,000. Was he correct? [Pernoud v Pernoud (Mo App) 639 SW2d 863]

17. Buice was employed by the Gulf Oil Corporation as a driver. His contract of employment did not state that it was to continue for any specified time. Buice was fired because of excessive drinking. He was treated for alcoholism and was cured. He then applied to Gulf for reinstatement. Gulf refused to reinstate him. Buice then sued Gulf claiming that Gulf had followed the practice of reinstating addiction patients who were cured of their addictions and it was his understanding that this was an implied term of his employment contract. Was Buice entitled to reinstatement? [Buice v Gulf Oil Corp. 172 Ga App 93, 322 SE2d 103]

CHAPTER 19

THIRD PERSONS AND

CONTRACTS

CHAPTER OBJECTIVES

After studying this chapter you will be able to:
1. Distinguish between a third party beneficiary and an incidental beneficiary.
2. Define an assignment of contract rights.
3. State the limitations on the assignability of a right to performance.
4. Describe what constitutes a delegation of duties.
5. State the liability of the parties after a proper delegation of duties has been made.
6. Describe the status of an assignee with respect to defenses and setoffs available against the assignor.
7. State the significance of a notice of assignment.
8. State the liability of an assignor to an assignee.
9. Solve problems involving third party beneficiaries and assignees.

When the economy was agrarian and the modern era of mass selling on credit had not begun, it was logical to regard a contract as a matter that only concerned the contracting parties. It was their private affair and the relationship between them was described as privity of contract. Persons not in privity of contract had no rights with respect to contracts made by other persons. As time went by, society became aware that there were needs that could not be met by this concept of privity of contract. Life insurance would not be possible because the beneficiary, not being in privity of contract, would not have an enforceable claim against the insurance company. Faced with such situations, society modified the rule of law so that third party beneficiaries could sue for breach of a contract to which they were strangers. This decision, however, led to another problem: that of defining third party beneficiaries so as to limit contract rights to those third parties that the original contracting parties sought to benefit. Society chose the policy of drawing a line so that those who are merely incidentally benefited can not sue on a contract to which they are strangers.

The social decision of allowing strangers to get involved in a contract made by others also arose in connection with determining whether a party to a contract could transfer a right to receive money or to receive a performance or to delegate the duties imposed by the contract to another person. Subject to certain practical limitations, society gradually chose to allow the free transfer of rights and the free delegation of duties. Society has done this to provide the economy with greater flexibility in making financial and working arrangements. This has given rise to the body of law governing assignment of rights and delegation of duties.

A. THIRD PARTY BENEFICIARY CONTRACTS

When a contract is intended to benefit a third person, such person is a third party beneficiary and may bring suit on and enforce the contract.

§ 19:1. Definition.

Ordinarily A and B will make a contract that concerns only them. However, they may make a contract by which B promises A that B will make a payment of money to C. That is, the contracting parties intend to benefit C. Because of this intent, if B fails to perform that promise, C, who is not the original promisee, may enforce the contract against B, the promisor. Such an agreement is a **third party beneficiary contract.**[1] A life insurance contract is a third party beneficiary contract, as the insurance company promises the insured to make payment to the beneficiary. Such a contract entitles the beneficiary to sue the insurance company upon the insured's death even though the insurance company never made any agreement directly with the beneficiary.

It is not necessary that the third party beneficiary be identified by name. It is sufficient to identify such beneficiary by class with the result that any member of that class is a third party beneficiary. For example, when a contract between the promoter of an automobile stock car race and the owner of the race track contained a promise to pay specified sums of money to each driver racing a car in certain races, any person driving in one of the designated races was a third party beneficiary and could sue on the contract for the promised compensation.[2]

At times it is difficult to decide whether a stranger to a contract should be called a third party beneficiary, and therefore be entitled to sue on the contract. At other times, the question is easily answered because one purpose dominates the entire transaction.

[1]Laclede Investment Corp v Kaiser (Mo App) 596 SW2d 36 (1980).
[2]Oil Capital Racing Ass'n, Inc. v Tulsa Speedway, Inc. (Okla App) 628 P2d 1176 (1981).

of assignments be in writing or be executed in a particular form. This require-ment is common in respect to statutes limiting the assignment of claims to wages. It is not necessary to use the words "assign" or "transfer." A state-ment that "you will be entitled to" a specific sum of money owed by a named person is sufficient to assign the right to that money.

As no particular words are necessary to create an assignment, an authorization to the obligor to pay a third person is an assignment to such third person. For example, the printed forms supplied by the health insurer which read "I hereby authorize payment directly to the below named dentist of the group insurance benefits otherwise payable to me" constituted an assignment to the dentist of such benefits.[6]

Whether there is consideration or not for the assignment does not affect the validity of the assignment and an assignment can not be challenged by the obligor on the ground that there was no consideration.[7] This is so because an assignment is not a contract. It is a transfer of a property right. An assignment may therefore be made as a gift, although it is usually part of a business transaction.

§ 19:7.   Assignment of Right to Money.

A person entitled to receive money, such as payment for the price of goods or for work done under a contract, may generally assign that right to another person. A claim or cause of action against another person may be assigned. A contractor entitled to receive payment from the owner can assign that right to the bank as security for a loan or can assign it to anyone else.

(a) **Future Rights.** By the modern rule, future and expected rights may be assigned. Thus, the contractor may assign the money which is not yet due under the contract because the building has not yet been constructed. Likewise an author may assign royalties which are expected to be received from contracts which the author expects to enter into in the future. The fact that there is nothing in existence now does not prohibit the assignment of what is expected to be existing in the future.

(b) **Consent to Assignment of Rights.** The party who is subject to the right of the other party may expressly consent to the assignment of the right. A provision that the contract should bind the successors to the parties constitutes consent to future assignments thereof.[8]

(c) **Prohibition of Assignment of Rights.** A contract may prohibit the assignment of any rights arising thereunder. Some courts hold that such a prohibition is binding. This means that an assignment made in violation of the prohibition has no effect. By the modern view, a prohibition against assignment has no effect. Thus an assignment is valid even though prohibited by the contract. By this view, a provision in a construction contract that the contractor may not assign money to become due under the contract without the consent of the other contracting party is not binding and the assignee

---

[6]Smith v Connecticut General Life Ins. Co. 122 Ill App 3d 725. 78 Ill Dec 485, 462 NE2d 604 (1984).
[7]Kennard v McCray (Tex App) 648 SW2d 743 (1983).
[8]Saliterman v Finney (Minn App) 361 NW2d 175 (1985).

may recover the amounts due from the obligor.[9] Under the Uniform Commercial Code, the assignment of accounts receivable can not be prohibited by the parties.[10]

§ 19:8. Assignment of Right to a Performance.

When the right of the obligee under the contract is to receive a performance by the other party, the obligee may assign that right, provided the performance required of the other party will not be materially altered or varied by such assignment. In contrast, if a transfer of a right to a performance would materially affect or alter a duty or the rights of the obligor, an assignment of the rights to the performance is not permitted. When an obligee is entitled to assign a right, it may be done by unilateral act. There is no requirement that the obligor consent or agree. Likewise, the act of assigning does not constitute a breach of the contract, unless the contract specifically declares so.

FACTS:

Oklahoma City made a contract with Hurst, operating under the name of Earth Products Co., giving him the right to remove sand from city property for five years. The contract provided that the city would measure the amount of sand removed and specify the price to be paid per cubic foot, and imposed certain limitations as to location of excavations, depth, and slopes. Hurst assigned the contract to Sand Products, Inc. Oklahoma City claimed that this assignment was a breach of the contract.

DECISION:

The assignment of the contract was not a breach. The contract was of such a nature that it was proper to assign it. By its terms, no special reliance was placed on Hurst, and the limitations as to excavations and slopes could be observed by Sand Products or anyone else and did not involve any special skill. The contract was therefore assignable by Hurst, and the act of assigning did not constitute a breach. [Earth Products Co. v Oklahoma City (Okla) 441 P2d 399 (1968)]

(a) **Assignment Increasing Burden of Performance.** When the assigning of a right would increase the burden of the obligor in performing, an assignment is ordinarily not permitted. To illustrate, if the assignor has the right to buy a certain quantity of a stated article and to take such property from the seller's warehouse, this right can be assigned. If, however, the sales contract stipulated that the seller should deliver to the buyer's premises, and the assignee lived or had a place of business a substantial distance from the assignor's place of business, the assignment would not be given effect. In this case, the seller would be required to give a different performance by providing greater transportation if the assignment were permitted.

---

[9]Aetna Casualty and Surety Co. v Bedford-Stuyvesant Restoration Constr. Corp. 90 App Div 2d 474, 455 NYS2d 265 (1982).
[10]UCC § 9–318(4). Although some cases still follow the contrary pre-Code law. See, for example, Cordis Corp. v Sonics International, Inc. (Fla App) 427 So 2d 782 (1983).

(b) Personal Satisfaction. A similar problem arises when the goods to be furnished must be satisfactory to the personal judgment of the buyer. Since the seller only contracted that the performance would stand or fall according to the buyer's judgment, the buyer may not substitute the personal judgment of an assignee.

(c) Personal Services. An employer cannot assign to another the employer's right to have an employee work. The relationship of employer and employee is so personal that the right cannot be assigned. The performance contracted by the employee was to work for a particular employer at a particular place and at a particular job. To permit an assignee to claim the employee's services would be to change that contract.

(d) Credit Transaction. When a transaction is based on extending credit, the person to whom credit is extended cannot assign any rights under the contract to another. For example, when land is sold on credit the buyer cannot assign the contract unless the seller consents thereto. The making of an assignment is here prohibited because the assignee is a different credit risk. Whether the assignee is a better or worse credit risk is not considered.

§ 19:9. Rights of Assignee.

An assignee stands exactly in the position of the assignor. The assignee's rights are no greater nor less than those of the assignor. If the assigned right to payment is subject to a condition precedent, the assignee is subject to that same condition. For example, when a contractor who is not entitled to receive the balance of money due under the contract until all bills of suppliers of materials have been paid, the assignee to whom the contractor assigns the balance due under the contract is subject to the same condition and can not obtain the money until that condition is satisfied.[11]

§ 19:10. Delegation of Duties.

A **delegation of duties** is a transfer of duties by a party to a contract to another person who is to perform them. Under certain circumstances, a contracting party may obtain someone else to do the work. When the performance is standardized and nonpersonal, so that it is not material who performs, the law will permit the delegation of the performance of the contract. In such cases, however, the contracting party remains liable for the default of the person doing the work just as though no assignment had been made.

FACTS:
The Industrial Construction Co. wanted to raise money to construct a canning factory in Wisconsin. Various persons promised to subscribe the needed amount which they agreed to pay when the construction was completed. The construction company assigned its rights under the agreement to Johnson, who then built the cannery. Vickers, one of the subscribers, refused to pay the amount he had subscribed on the ground that the contract could not be assigned.

[11]Heinrichsdorff v Raat (Colo App) 655 P2d 860 (1982).

DECISION:

Judgment for Vickers. Since the construction of the canning factory called for the skill and experience of the builder and reliance upon the builder by the subscibers, the performance of the contract was a personal matter which could not be delegated by the builder without the consent of the subscribers. As Vickers had not consented to such agreement, Johnson had no rights by virtue of the attempted assignment and could not sue for the subscription. [Johnson v Vickers, 139 Wis 145, 120 NW 837 (1909)]

(a) Intention to Delegate Duties. In the absence of clear language in the assignment stating that duties are or are not delegated, all circumstances must be examined to determine whether there is a delegation. When the total picture is viewed, it may become clear what was intended.

A question of interpretation arises as to whether an assignment of "the contract" is only an assignment of the rights of the assignor or is both an assignment of those rights and a delegation of duties. The trend of authority is to regard such a general assignment as both a transfer of rights and a delegation of duties.

FACTS:

Smith, who owned the Avalon Apartments, sold individual apartments under contracts that required each purchaser to pay $15 a month extra for hot and cold water, heat, refrigeration, taxes, and fire insurance. Smith assigned his interest in the apartment house and under the various contracts to Roberts. When Roberts failed to pay the taxes on the building, the tenants sued to compel her to do so.

DECISION:

Judgment against Roberts. In the absence of a contrary indication, it is presumed that an "assignment" of a contract delegates the performance of the duties as well as transfers the rights. Here there was no indication that a "package" transfer was not intended, and the assignee was therefore obligated to perform in accordance with the contract terms. [Radley v Smith, 6 Utah 2d 314, 313 P2d 465 (1957)]

(b) Delegation of Duties Under the UCC. With respect to contracts for the sale of goods, "an assignment of 'the contract' or of 'all my rights under the contract' or an assignment in similar general terms is an assignment of rights and unless the language or the circumstances (as in an assignment for security) indicate the contrary, it is a delegation of performance of the duties of the assignor and its acceptance by the assignee constitutes a promise . . . to perform those duties. This promise is enforceable by either the assignor or the other party to the original contract."[12]

§ 19:11.   **Continuing Liability of Assignor.**

The making of an assignment does not relieve the assignor of any obligation of the contract. In the absence of a contrary agreement, such as a

[12]UCC § 2–210(4).

novation, an assignor continues to be bound by the obligations of the original contract.[13] Thus, the fact that a buyer assigns the right to goods under a contract does not terminate the buyer's liability to make payment to the seller. Likewise, when an independent contractor is hired to perform a party's obligations under a contract, that party is liable if the independent contractor does not properly perform the contract.

§ 19:12.   Liability of Assignee.

It is necessary to distinguish between the question whether the obligor can assert a particular defense against the assignee and the question whether any person can sue the assignee for failing to perform the contract.

Ordinarily the assignee is not subject to suit by virtue of the fact that the assignment has been made.

§ 19:13. Defenses and Setoffs.

The assignee's rights are no greater than those of the assignor. If the obligor (the other party to the original contract) could successfully defend against a suit brought by the assignor, the obligor will also prevail against the assignee. The fact that the assignee has given value for the assignment does not give the assignee any immunity from defenses which the other party, the obligor, could have asserted against the assignor. The rights acquired by the assignee remain subject to any limitations imposed by the contract.

FACTS:

McCaslin did plastering work in Nitzberg's home. He did not have a license to do the plastering work, and by statute he was barred from suing for the contract price for such work. McCaslin assigned his claim against Nitzberg to Walker, who then sued Nitzberg for the amount due for McCaslin's work.

DECISION:

Judgment for Nitzberg. By virtue of the statute, McCaslin's lack of a license was a defense to recovery on the contract from Nitzberg. Walker, as assignee of McCaslin, had no greater right to sue than McCaslin. [Walker v Nitzberg, 13 Cal App 3d 359, 91 Cal Rptr 526 (1970)]

Modern contract forms commonly provide that the debtor waives or will not assert against an assignee of the contract exemptions and defenses that could have been raised against the assignor. Such waivers are generally valid although consumer protection statutes often prohibit them. Some statutes take a modified position and permit barring a buyer if, when notified of the assignment, the buyer fails to inform the assignee of the defense against the seller.

Assignments of contracts are generally made to raise money, as when an automobile dealer assigns a customer's credit contract to a finance company and receives cash for it. Sometimes they are made when an enterprise

[13]Oregon ex rel v Lester, 45 Or App 389, 608 P2d 588 (1980).

closes down and transfers its business to a new owner. The availability of defenses and setoffs is the same for both cases.

§ 19:14. Notice of Assignment.

An assignment, if otherwise valid, takes effect the moment it is made. It is not necessary that the assignee or the assignor give notice to the other party to the contract that the assignment has been made.

FACTS:

A court order required John Baldassari to make specified payments for the support of his wife and child. His wife needed more money and applied for Pennsylvania welfare payments. In accordance with the law, she assigned to Pennsylvania her right to the support payments from her husband and Pennsylvania then made greater payments to her. Pennsylvania obtained a court order directing John, in accordance with the terms of the assignment from his wife, to make the support order payments directly to the Pennsylvania Department of Public Welfare. John refused to pay on the ground that he had not been notified of the assignment or the hearing directing him to make payment to the assignee.

DECISION:

Judgment for Pennsylvania. The assignment of the right to money was effective as between the wife and Pennsylvania as soon as made and therefore it did not matter that John was not notified of the assignment. Likewise it did not matter that he was not notified of the hearing directing him to pay to the Department of Public Welfare as that order merely identified who was to be paid and stated in words the obligation that was upon John because of the assignment: he was required to pay the assignee. [Pennsylvania v Baldassari, 279 Pa Super 491, 421 A2d 306 (1980)]

It is highly desirable, however, that the other party be notified as soon as possible after the making of the assignment. The notice must identify the particular claim against the defendant.

(a) Priority. If a person assigns the same right to two different assignees, the question arises as to which assignee has obtained the right. By the American rule, the assignee taking the first assignment prevails over the subsequent assignees.

(b) Effect on Defenses and Setoffs. Notice of an assignment prevents the obligor from asserting against the assignee any defense or setoff arising after such notice with respect to a matter not related to the assigned claim.

(c) Discharge. If the obligor is notified that there has been an assignment and that any money due must be paid to the assignee, the obligor's obligation can only be discharged by making payment to the assignee. Before the obligor knows of an assignment and before being notified that payment must be made to the assignee, any payment made by the obligor to the assignor reduces or cancels the debt, even though as between the assignor and the assignee it is the assignee who is entitled to the money. The only remedy of the assignee is to sue the assignor to recover the payments that were made by the obligor.

If the obligor both knows of the assignment and has been notified to make future payments to the assignee, any payment made by the obligor to the assignor has no effect and does not reduce or discharge the debt of the obligor.[14]

The Uniform Consumer Credit Code restates the protection of the consumer-debtor making payment to the assignor without knowledge of the assignment and imposes a penalty for using a contract term that would destroy this protection of the consumer.

FACTS:

Jimmie Machado purchased a mobile home from Crestview Mobile Housing. The contract specified that if it was assigned Machado would pay the balance to the assignee and that any payments "otherwise made shall be at the risk of Purchaser if not received by the assignee." Crestview assigned the contract to the Commercial Credit Corporation. Machado then brought an action to recover the statutory penalty provided by the UCCC, claiming that that Code was violated because that Code provided that payment made to the assignor without knowledge of an assignment would bind the assignee.

DECISION:

The provision of the contract was a violation of the UCCC. The clause in the contract with Machado would make him liable for payments made to the assignor although he did not know that there was an assignment if the assignor did not remit those payments to the assignee. Machado was therefore entitled to recover the penalty authorized by the UCCC. [Machado v Crestview Mobile Housing (Tex App) 650 SW2d 494 (1983)]

---

§ 19:15.   Warranties of Assignor.

When the assignment is made for a consideration, the assignor is regarded as impliedly warranting that the right assigned is valid, that the assignor is the owner of the claim or right assigned, and that the assignor will not interfere with the assignee's enforcement of the obligation. The assignor does not warrant that the other party will pay or perform as required by the contract.

SUMMARY

Ordinarily only the parties to contracts have rights and duties with respect to such contracts. Exceptions are made in the case of third party beneficiary contracts and assignments.

When a contract shows a clear intent to benefit a third person or class of persons, those persons are called third party beneficiaries and may

[14]UCC § 9–318(3). First Fidelity Bank v Matthews, _____ Mont _____, 692 P2d 1255 (1984).

sue for breach of the contract. A third party beneficiary is subject to any limitation or restriction found in the contract and loses all rights when the original contract is terminated by operation of law or the contract reserves the right to change beneficiaries and such a change is made. In contrast with a third party beneficiary, is the incidental beneficiary who benefits from the performance of the contract but the conferring of this benefit was not intended by the contracting parties. An incidental beneficiary can not sue on the contract.

An assignment is a transfer of a right by which the assignor (transferor) transfers a right to the assignee (transferee). In the absence of local statute, there are no formal requirements for an assignment. Any words manifesting the intent to transfer are sufficient to constitute an assignment. No consideration is required. Any right to money may be assigned, whether the assignor is entitled to the money at the time of the assignment or will be entitled or expects to be entitled at some time in the future. A contract term prohibiting the assignment of a right to money is invalid and does not prevent the making of an assignment. The right to make an assignment of money may be prohibited by statute, as in the case of contracts involving the construction of public works.

A right to a performance may also be assigned except when it would increase the burden of performance, or performance under the contract is to be measured by the personal satisfaction of the obligee, or involves the performance of personal services or the credit of the person entitled to the performance.

When a valid assignment is made, the assignee has the same rights and only the same rights as the assignor and is subject to the same defenses and setoffs as the assignor had been.

The performance of duties under a contract may be delegated to another person, except when a personal element of skill or judgment of the original contracting party is involved. The intent to delegate duties may be expressly stated. The intent may also be found in an "assignment" of "the contract", unless the circumstances make it clear that only the right to money was intended to be transferred, as when an automobile dealer assigns "the contract" of the buyer to a finance company. The fact that there has been a delegation of duties does not release the assignor (delegor) from responsibility for performance and the assignor is liable for breach of the contract if the assignee (delegee) does not properly perform the delegated duties. In the absence of an effective delegation or the formation of a third party beneficiary contract, an assignee of rights is not liable to the obligee of the contract for its performance by the assignor. Notice is not required to effect an assignment but it has importance in determining the priority between competing assignees of the same rights, and in terminating the ability of the obligor to assert defenses and setoffs not related to the assigned right. When notice of the assignment is given to the assignee together with a demand that future payments be made to the assignee, the obligor can not discharge liability by payment to the assignor.

When an assignment is made for a consideration, the assignor makes implied warranties that the right assigned is valid, and that the assignor owns that right and will not interfere with its enforcement by the obligee. The assignor does not warrant that the obligor on the assigned right will perform the obligation of the contract.

QUESTIONS AND CASE PROBLEMS

1. What social forces are affected by allowing an obligee to assign the right to obtain payment?
2. Give an example of a third party beneficiary contract.
3. Gilbert owes Jeanette $100. Jeanette gets a job in another city and cannot wait to collect the money from Gilbert. Jeanette gives Barton a letter stating: "To Barton: I hereby give you the right to collect and keep for yourself the $100 owed to me by Gilbert. (signed) Jeanette." Barton shows this letter to Gilbert and requests that Gilbert make payment of the money. Gilbert refuses to do so on the ground that a letter cannot operate as an assignment because it is not sealed and is not sworn to before a notary public. Are these objections valid?
4. Lee contracts to paint Sally's two-story house for $1,000. Sally realizes that she will not have sufficient money so she transfers her rights under this agreement to her neighbor Karen who has a three-story house. Karen notifies Lee that Sally's contract has been assigned to her and demands that Lee paint Karen's house for $1,000. Is Lee required to do so?
5. Assume that Lee agrees to the assignment of the house-painting contract to Karen as stated in No. 4. Thereafter Lee fails to perform the contract to paint Karen's house. Karen sues Sally for damages. Is Sally liable?
6. Jessie borrows $1,000 from Thomas and agrees to repay the money in thirty days. Thomas assigns the right to the $1,000 to the Douglas Finance Company. Douglas sues Jessie. Jessie raises the defense that she had only agreed to pay the money to Thomas and that when she and Thomas had entered into the transaction there was no intention to benefit the Douglas Finance Company. Are these objections valid?
7. Federal Mogul Corporation owned an industrial plant. It made a contract with Universal Construction Company to put a new roof on the plant. Universal made another contract or subcontract with Interstate Roofing to do the actual work. The contract between Federal and Universal stated "nothing contained in the contract document shall create any contractual relation between any subcontractors and the owners." The contract between Universal and Interstate expressly incorporated the terms of the contract between Federal and Universal. The roof put on Federal's plant was defective. Federal sued Interstate on the theory that Federal was the third party beneficiary of the contract between Universal and Interstate. Was it correct? [Federal Mogul Corp. v Universal Construction Co. (Ala Civ App) 376 So2d 716]
8. Classify as beneficiaries of an accident insurance policy obtained by an employer to cover accidents of the employees: (a) the employer, (b) the employee, (c) a hospital providing medical care for an injured employee, and (d) a doctor treating an injured employee for the injury after the employee is discharged from the hospital.
9. When a seller defrauds the buyer and then assigns the seller's claim for the balance due to a bank, what difference does it make if the bank

in taking the assignment (a) knew of the fraud; (b) did not know of the fraud; or (c) acted in good faith and paid full value for the assigned claim?

10. Hudgens purchased a used car from Mack, a dealer. Mack falsely informed Hudgens that the car was in good condition when, in fact, it needed extensive repairs. Mack also refused to live up to his 30-day guarantee when the car was brought back within a few days after the sale. The day following the sale Mack had assigned the contract to Universal C.I.T. Credit Corp. When Hudgens refused to pay on the contract, he was sued by Universal. Hudgens claimed the right to set aside the contract for fraud. Was he entitled to do so? [Universal C.I.T. Credit Corp. v Hudgens, 234 Ark 668, 356 SW2d 658]

11. Lone Star Life Insurance Company agreed to make a long-term loan to Five Forty Three Land, Inc. whenever requested to do so by that corporation. Five Forty Three wanted this loan in order to pay off its short-term debts. The loan was never made as it was never requested by Five Forty Three. That corporation owed the Exchange Bank & Trust Company on a short-term debt. Exchange Bank then sued Lone Star for breach of its promise on the theory that the Exchange Bank was a third party beneficiary of the contract to make the loan. Was the Exchange Bank correct? [Exchange Bank & Trust Co. v Loan Star Life Ins. Co. (Tex Civ App) 546 SW2d 948]

12. The City of New Rochelle Humane Society made a contract with the City of New Rochelle to capture and impound all dogs running at large. Spiegler, a minor, was bitten by some dogs while in the school yard. She sued the School District of New Rochelle and the Humane Society. With respect to the Humane Society, she claimed that she was a third party beneficiary of the contract that the Society had made with the City and could therefore sue it for its failure to capture the dogs by which she had been bitten. Was she entitled to recover? [Spiegler v School District, 39 Misc 2d 946, 242 NYS2d 430]

13. A purchased B's business. A orally agreed to pay the business debts of B. C had sold goods to B for B's store but had not been paid. C sued A. A raised the defense that he was not liable because there was no writing for his promise to pay B's debt and the statute of frauds made an oral promise to pay the debt of another unenforceable. Was this a valid defense?

14. Helen owned a store and a home. She made separate contracts with Henry to put a new roof on each building. Payment was to be made by Helen in installments over a three-month period. When Henry finished the work he immediately assigned the store contract to the First National Bank. He did not assign the house contract because the amount involved was not large. First National promptly notified Helen of the assignment. A week later Helen notified First National that she would not pay on the assignment because both the store roof and the house roof were leaking. Can Helen assert counterclaims for the leaking of each roof?

15. An electric power company made a contract for the construction of a dam to supply water power for the generation of electricity. The dam collapsed. Customers of the power company brought suit against the

contractors who had constructed the dam and various persons who had inspected it, claiming that those persons had improperly performed their duties under their contracts and that the customers of the power company were third party beneficiaries of those contracts. Were the customers of the power company entitled to bring suit on the contract made by the power company with such inspectors and contractors? [Ziegler v Blount Bros. Constr. Co. (Ala) 364 So 2d 1163]

16. The Byron Chamber of Commerce hired Long, an attorney, to petition the local court to put on the next election ballot the question whether the voters wanted to set up a park district. The petition was rejected by the court because the description of the park area was not adequate. Residents and taxpayers who lived in what would be the park area brought a lawsuit against Long on the theory that he had broken a contract of which they were third party beneficiaries. They claimed that they would have received the benefit of the creation of a park district. Were they entitled to recover damages from Long? [Byron Chamber of Commerce, Inc. v Long, 92 Ill App 3d 364, 48 Ill Dec 77, 415 NE2d 1361]

17. The Fourth & Main Company leased a building to Joslin Dry Goods Company. Joslin was required to pay minimum fixed rent and an additional rent on a percentage of sales. Paragraph VIII(a) of the lease required Joslin to "diligently conduct a general retail business" in the rented premises. After some time, Joslin went out of business. J & B Investment Company did business in the neighborhood and would have benefited by increased customer traffic if Joslin had stayed in business. When Fourth & Main sued Joslin, J & B, as a third party beneficiary, asserted a claim against Joslin for damages. Was it entitled to recover? [Fourth & Main Co. v Joslin Dry Goods Co. (Colo App) 648 P2d 178]

CHAPTER 20

DISCHARGE OF

CONTRACTS

CHAPTER OBJECTIVES

After studying this chapter you will be able to:

1. List the ways in which a contract can be discharged.
2. Distinguish between the effect of a rejected tender of payment and a rejected tender of performance.
3. Define when time is of the essence.
4. Compare performance to the satisfaction of the other contracting parties, performance to the satisfaction of a reasonable person, and substantial performance.
5. State when a consumer contract may be rescinded by the consumer.
6. Compare the discharge of a contract by rescission, cancellation, substitution, and novation.
7. State the effect upon a contract of the death or disability of one of the contracting parties.
8. Define the concept of economic frustration.
9. Solve problems relating to the discharge of contracts.

What happens to contracts once they are created? In most cases, they are performed. But, how do we know when the performance is good enough? For example, in a construction contract that specifies a certain type of plumbing pipe, does another equally functional type of pipe satisfy the contract? The courts are frequently called upon to resolve this type of conflict. If society wishes to carry out the intent of the parties as manifested by their contract, there must be a perfect performance and anything less will not be satisfactory. This may work a great hardship when the contract is performed almost perfectly, but not quite. Should protection from oppression and hardship be factors in determining whether the imperfect performance was good enough?

As another problem, can the parties to a contract undo their contract? Or is a contract once entered into a vested and unchangeable obligation?

What effect do external circumstances have upon the contract? If the contract made no provision for an unforeseen event that renders performance impossible, should it be held that a party is not released from liability when such circumstances arise? If society wants to carry out the intent of the parties as manifested by their contract, it will make them adhere to that intent regardless of what happens. But again, the social force of protecting from hardship and oppression raises the question whether society wants to carry out the intent of the parties by enforcing the letter of the contract when such external factors have occurred.

Also facing society is the question of whether a contract can be ended by the operation of law. Again, if the furthering of the intent of the parties is the primary concern of society, it should be held that if the contract was valid when made nothing thereafter could happen to invalidate or discharge it. Opposed to this supremacy of the contract is the social purpose of protecting the general welfare by applying the rules of law that would invalidate the contract.

§ 20:1.   Discharge by Performance.

A contract is usually discharged by the performance of the terms of the agreement. In most cases, the parties perform their promises and the contract ceases to exist or is thereby discharged.

§ 20:2.   Nature of Performance.

Performance may be the doing of an act or the making of payment.

(a) **Tender of Performance.** An offer to perform is known as a **tender**. If performance requires the doing of an act, a tender that is refused will discharge the party offering to perform. If performance requires the payment of a debt, however, a tender that is refused does not discharge the debt. But it stops the running of interest and prevents the collection of court costs if the party is sued, providing the tender is kept open and the money is produced in court.

A **valid tender of payment** consists of an unconditional offer of the exact amount due on the date when due or an amount from which the creditor may take what is due without the necessity of making change. The debtor must offer **legal tender** or, in other words, such form of money as the law recognizes as lawful money and declares to be legal tender for the payment of debts. The offer of a check is not a valid tender of payment, as a check is not legal tender even when it is certified. A tender of part of the debt is not a valid tender. In addition to the amount owed, the debtor must tender all accrued interest and any costs to which the creditor is entitled. If the debtor tenders less than the amount due, the creditor may refuse the offer without affecting the right to collect the amount which is due. If the creditor accepts the smaller amount, the question arises whether it has been accepted as payment on account or as full payment of the balance which was due.

(b) **Payment.** When payment is required by the contract, performance consists of the payment of money or, if accepted by the other party, the delivery of property or the rendering of services.

(1) Application of Payments. If a debtor owes more than one debt to the creditor and pays money, a question may arise as to which debt has been paid. If the debtor specifies the debt to which the payment is to be applied and the creditor accepts the money, the creditor is bound to apply the money as specified. Thus, if the debtor specifies that a payment is to be made for a current purchase, the creditor may not apply the payment to an older balance.

If the debtor does not specify the application to be made, the creditor has the choice of deciding to which debt the payment should be applied. As between secured and unsecured claims, the creditor is free to apply the payment to the unsecured claim. The creditor, however, must apply the payment to a debt that is due as contrasted with one which is not yet due. The creditor cannot apply a payment to a claim that is illegal or invalid; but may apply the payment to a claim which cannot be enforced because it is barred by the statute of limitations and, according to some authorities, to a claim that cannot be enforced for lack of a writing required by the statute of frauds.

(2) No Application Specified. If neither the debtor nor the creditor has made any application of the payment, application will be made by the court. There is a division of authority, however, whether the court is to make such application as will be more favorable to the creditor or the debtor.[1] In some instances, the court will apply the payment to the oldest outstanding debt. Consumer protection statutes commonly require such application to the oldest debt.

(c) Payment by Check. Payment by commercial paper, such as a check, is ordinarily a conditional payment. A check merely suspends the debt until the check is presented for payment.[2] If payment is then made, the debt is discharged; if not paid, the suspension terminates and suit may be brought on either the debt or the check. Frequently payment must be made by a specified date. It is generally held the payment is made on time if it is mailed on or before the final date for payment.

FACTS:

Cooper was purchasing land from Birznieks. Cooper was in possession of the land but was required to pay the purchase price not later than January 30 or get off the land. The attorney for Birznieks told Cooper that payment could be mailed. On January 30, Cooper mailed a letter to Birznieks. The letter contained two checks for the total amount due under the contract. The attorney for Birznieks received the letter on February 1 but refused to recognize it on the ground that payment had not been made in time.

DECISION:

Because of the general custom to regard a check mailed to a creditor as "paying" the bill that is owed, payment was made by Cooper on January 30 when he mailed the checks. Payment was therefore made within the required time even though received after the expiration of the required time. [Birznieks v Cooper, 405 Mich 319, 275 NW2d 221 (1979)]

---

[1]Carter's Insurance Agency, Inc. v Franklin (La App) 428 So 2d 808 (1983) (favoring debtor).

[2]Uniform Commercial Code § 3-802(1)(b).

§ 20:3.   Time of Performance.

When the date or period of time for performance is specified in the contract, performance should be made on that date or within that time period.

(a) **No Time Specified.** When the time for performance is not specified in the contract, an obligation to perform within a reasonable time will be implied. The fact that no time is stated does not impair the contract on the ground that it is indefinite nor does it allow an endless time in which to perform.

(b) **When Time is Essential.** If performance of the contract on or within the exact time specified is vital, it is said that "time is of the essence." Time is of the essence when the contract relates to property that is perishable or that is fluctuating rapidly in value.

An express statement in the contract that time is of the essence is not controlling. When it is obvious that time is not important, such a statement will be ignored by the courts. It is the nature of the subject matter of the contract and the surrounding circumstances rather than the declaration of the parties which control.[3]

(c) **When Time Is Not Essential.** Ordinarily, time is not of the essence, and performance within a reasonable time is sufficient.

In the case of the sale of property, time will not be regarded as of the essence when there has not been any appreciable change in the market value or condition of the property and when the person who delayed does not appear to have done so for the purpose of speculating on a change in market price.

FACTS:

Lane sold a resort to the Cresent Beach Lodge & Resort, Inc. on the installment plan. The contract required Crescent to keep the property insured and specified that the payment of the premiums when due was of the essence. Crescent did not pay the premiums when due but the insurance company extended credit to Crescent and kept the policies in force. Lane sued Crescent to cancel the installment sale contract on the ground that Crescent had breached the contract by failing to pay the insurance on time and that time was of the essence.

DECISION:

There was no breach of the contract because paying the insurance when due was not essential. The essential thing was keeping the insurance protection in force. This had been done because the insurance companies had extended credit for the premiums which were due. No policy was canceled because of nonpayment of premiums nor was any statement made by anyone that there would be a cancellation. Consequently the late payment of the premiums did not cause Lane any loss and therefore was not a breach of the contract. [Lane v Crescent Beach Lodge & Resort (Iowa) 199 NW2d 78 (1972)]

---

[3]Hart v Lyons, 106 Ill App 3d 803, 62 Ill. Dec 697, 436 NE2d 723 (1982).

§ 20:4.   Adequacy of Performance.

When a party renders exactly the performance called for by the contract, no question arises as to whether the contract has been performed. In other cases, there may not have been a perfect performance or a question arises as to whether the performance made satisfies the standard set by the contract.

(a) **Substantial Performance.** Perfect performance of a contract is not required. A party who in good faith has substantially performed the contract may sue to recover the payment specified in the contract. However, because the performance was not perfect, the performing party is subject to a counterclaim for the damages caused the other party. When a building contractor has substantially performed the contract to construct a building, the measure of damages is the cost of repairing or correcting the defects if that can be done at a reasonable cost. If, however, the cost would be unreasonably disproportionate to the importance of the defect, as when a virtual rebuilding of the finished building would be required to make a minor correction, the measure of damages is the difference between the value of the building as completed and the value that the building would have had if the contract had been performed perfectly.[4]

This rule of **substantial performance** applies only when departures from the contract or the defects were not made willfully. A contractor who willfully makes a substantial departure from the contract is in default and cannot recover any payment from the other party to the contract. In large construction contracts when the total value of the partial performance is large compared to the damages sustained through incomplete or imperfect performance, the courts tend to ignore whether or not the breach was intentional on the part of the contractor.

The doctrine of substantial performance does not apply to a condition precedent. Consequently where a lender was obligated to lend a specified amount for the purchase and renovation of an office building, the lender was excused from making such loan when the duty to lend was subject to a condition precedent that a specific amount of office space leases had to be signed, but the required amount was not obtained, as against the claim of the borrower that the substantial performance rule should be applied to hold that there was a sufficient compliance with the rental condition.[5]

(b) **Satisfaction of Promisee or Third Person.** When the agreement requires that the promisor perform an act to the satisfaction, taste, or judgment of the other party on the contract, the courts are divided as to whether the promisor must so perform the contract as to satisfy the promisee or whether it is sufficient that the performance be such as would satisfy a reasonable person under the circumstances. When personal taste is an important element, the courts generally hold that the performance is not sufficient unless the promisee is actually satisfied, although in some instances it is insisted that the dissatisfaction be shown to be in good faith and not merely to avoid paying for the work that has been done. The personal satisfaction of the

[4]Lawing v Interstate Budget Motel, Inc. (Mo App) 655 SW2d 744 (1983).
[5]Brown-Marx Associates, Ltd. v Emigrant Savings Bank (CA11 Ala) 703 F2d 1361 (1983).

promisee is generally required under this rule when one promises to make clothes or to paint a portrait to the satisfaction of the other party.

There is a similar division of authority when the subject matter involves the fitness or mechanical utility of property. With respect to things mechanical and to routine performances, however, the courts are more likely to hold that the promisor has satisfactorily performed if a reasonable person should be satisfied with what was done.

When a building contract requires the contractor to perform the contract to the "satisfaction" of the owner, the owner generally is required to pay if a reasonable person would be satisfied with the work of the contractor.

When performance is to be approved by a third person, the tendency is to apply the reasonable-person test of satisfaction, especially when the third person has wrongfully withheld approval or has become incapacitated.

When work is to be done subject to the approval of an architect, engineer, or other expert, the determination of that expert is ordinarily final and binding upon the parties in the absence of fraud.

FACTS:

Johnson was operating a school bus for School District #12 under a two-year written contract which specified that Johnson "is to have option for next 3 years if a bus is run and his service has been satisfactory." At the end of the two-year period Johnson notified the School District that he had elected to exercise the option, but the School District refused to renew the contract. Johnson sued the School District for breach of the option provision. It raised the defense that it was not satisfied with his services and therefore there was no option to renew.

DECISION:

This was not a defense. When a contract requires "satisfactory" performance, it merely requires performance satisfactory to a reasonable person unless it is clear from the terms or circumstances that "personal" satisfaction is required. Here it should be the "reasonable-person" test since there was no evidence to the contrary. [Johnson v School District #12, 210 Or 585, 312 P2d 591 (1957)]

---

§ 20:5. Guarantee of Performance.

It is common for an obligor to guarantee the performance. Thus, a builder may guarantee for one year that the work will be satisfactory.

The guarantee may be made by a third person. Thus, a surety company may guarantee to the owner that a contractor will perform the contract. In such case, it is clear that the obligation of the surety is in addition to the liability of the contractor and does not take the place of such liability.

§ 20:6. Consumer Protection Rescission.

Contrary to the basic principle of contract law that a contract between competent persons is a binding obligation, consumer protection legislation is introducing into the law a new concept of giving the consumer a chance to think things over and to rescind the contract. Thus, the federal Consumer Credit Protection Act (CCPA) gives the debtor the right to rescind a credit transaction within three days when the transaction would impose a lien upon the debtor's home. A homeowner who mortgages the home to obtain a loan may cancel the transaction for any reason by notifying the lender before midnight of the third full business day after the loan is made.[6]

A Federal Trade Commission Regulation gives the buyer three days in which to avoid a home-solicited sale of goods or services costing more than $25.00.[7]

§ 20:7. Discharge by Unilateral Action.

Ordinarily, a contract cannot be discharged by the action of either party alone. In some cases, the contract will give one or either party the right to cancel the contract by unilateral action, such as by notice to the other party. If the contract does not specify any duration or if it states a duration in such vague terms as "for life," the contract may be terminated by either party at will.[8]

§ 20:8. Discharge by Agreement.

A contract may be terminated by the operation of one of its provisions or by a subsequent agreement.

(a) Provision of Original Contract. The contract may provide that it shall terminate upon the happening of a certain event, such as the destruction of a particular building, or upon the existence of a certain fact, even though the intended performance by one or both parties has not been completed. The contract may specify that one party may terminate the contract upon giving notice to the other.

FACTS:

Ellen and David Rosenbaum left their infant daughter, Lorraine, with Phoebe Szatmari. The contract between them provided that Phoebe would care for the child and that either the parents or Phoebe could terminate the arrangement on four weeks' notice. After several years, Phoebe wrote the parents that she gave notice to terminate the arrangement and that she "offered" them four weeks in which to make other arrangements. The parents replied that they "rejected" the offer and claimed that Phoebe was breaking the contract.

---

[6]If the owner is not informed of this right to cancel, the three-day period does not begin until that information is given. In any case, however, the right to cancel is lost if the owner sells the house or three years elapse after the loan transaction. Consumer Credit Protection Act (CCPA) § 125, 15 USC § 1635 (a), (e), (f).

[7]16 CFR § 429.1. This displaces state laws making similar provision for rescission, such as UCCC § 2.502.

[8]Garber v Harris Trust & Savings Bank, 104 Ill App 3d 675, 60 Ill Dec 410, 432 NE2d 1309 (1982).

DECISION:

The contract between the parties gave both sides the power to terminate at any time upon notice. When this power of termination was exercised by one party the other party could not "reject" the termination. The use of the word "offer" by Phoebe was not a correct use of the term because there was no offer in the true sense, in that the parents could not reject or accept as they chose. The parents, having bound themselves by a contract that gave the other party the power to terminate could only recognize the fact that the contract was terminated and could not insist that the contract was still in force. [Szatmari v Rosenbaum, 490 NYS2d 97 (1985)]

A notice to terminate must be clear and definite. When a contract provides for a continuing performance but does not specify how long it shall continue, it is terminable at the will of either party, with the same consequences as though it had expressly authorized termination upon notice.

(b) **Rescission by Agreement.** The parties to a contract may agree to undo the contract by returning any property or money that had been delivered or paid. It is said that they agree to rescind the contract or that there is a *mutual rescission*. Ordinarily no formality is required for rescission; and an oral rescission, or conduct evidencing such an intent, may terminate a written contract. An oral rescission is not effective, however, in the case of a sale of an interest in land; for, in such case, the purpose of the rescission is to retransfer the interest in land. Accordingly, the retransfer or rescission must satisfy the same formalities of the statute of frauds as are applied to an original transfer.

A mutual rescission works a final discharge of the contract in the absence of an express provision in the rescission agreement providing for the later revival of the original contract. Consequently, when there is a mutual rescission of a sales contract following a fire which destroyed the seller's factory, the contract is not revived by the subsequent rebuilding of the factory.

(c) **Cancellation by Agreement.** The parties may agree to cancel the contract. This ends the contract from that time on. Neither party is under any duty to perform in any way after the cancellation.

FACTS:

Ravenhorst was retained as a mineralogy expert by the Anvil Mineral Mining Corporation. He was to receive compensation as a percentage commission per ton of mineral. After a time he notified the corporation that he wished to terminate the relationship because of ill health. Ravenhorst and Anvil executed a document entitled "Cancellation and Release of Contract." At the time, Anvil owed Ravenhorst approximately $15,000 for compensation which was owing but not paid. After the cancellation contract was signed, Ravenhorst demanded the $15,000.

DECISION:

He was not entitled to the unpaid compensation. There was a cancellation and the original contract under which Ravenhorst was to receive compensation had been terminated. Nothing was said about paying after cancellation of any claim that had existed before the cancellation. The contract did not make any express provision saving a pre-cancellation claim. The courts will not imply such a provision because the intent of the parties, unless otherwise stated, is to be regarded as a mutual wiping of the slate clean. It therefore followed that the plaintiff could not recover commissions earned but unpaid at the time the cancellation agreement was executed. [Anvil Mineral Mining Corp. v Ravenhorst (Miss) 403 So2d 142 (1981)]

Termination by cancellation differs from termination by rescission in that it operates only as to the future. In contrast, mutual rescission both ends the contract as to the future and goes back to the beginning to undo everything that had been done and to put the parties back in the position in which they were before the contract was made. For example, a contract to supply coal to a factory for five years would be canceled when the parties agree that the seller will no longer sell and the factory will no longer buy. In contrast with a rescission, there will be no refunding to the factory of money paid for coal in the past nor any return by the factory to the seller of the coal that had been supplied in the past. The mutual cancellation only wipes the slate clean from the time of the cancellation on. Conversely, the mutual rescission puts everything back the way it was when the contract was made.

(d) **Substitution.** The parties may decide that their contract is not the one they want. They may then replace it with another contract. If they do so, the original contract is discharged by substitution.

It is not necessary that the parties expressly state that they are making a substitution. Whenever they make a new contract that is clearly inconsistent with a former contract, the court will conclude that the earlier contract has been superseded by the later of the two. Since the new contract must in itself be a binding agreement, it must be supported by consideration.

FACTS:

Paul Shires made a contract to build a house for Marion Priem. Disputes arose between them as to whether the house had been properly built. Paul and Marion executed a contract in which it was agreed that Paul would make certain specified repairs which would correct the defects of which Marion complained. These repairs were not made and Marion then sued Paul for breach of the original construction contract.

DECISION:

Suit could not be brought on the original construction contract. The repair contract clearly showed the intention to replace the original contract with the terms of the new repair contract. The original contract was thus discharged by the making of the subsequent contract and the only contract on which Marion could sue was the second or repair contract. [Priem v Shires (Tex App) 697 SW2d 860 (1985)]

The agreement modifying the original contract may be expressed in words or by conduct, but in any event, it is essential that an agreement to modify be found.

(e) **Novation.** One who is entitled to receive performance under a contract may agree to release the person who is bound to perform and to permit another person to render the required performance. The contract or agreement by which one party is released and the other party agrees to render the original performance is called a **novation**. It discharges the original contract by displacing it with the later contract. A subsequent agreement between one of the original contracting parties and a third person can not be a novation because the other original contracting party is not a party to the subsequent agreement.[9]

(f) **Accord and Satisfaction.** In lieu of the performance of an obligation specified by a contract, the parties may agree to a different performance. Such an agreement is called an **accord**. When the accord is performed or executed, there is an **accord and satisfaction**, which discharges the original obligation.

The accord that is the basis for the accord and satisfaction must be a binding agreement, that is, a contract. If it is not a contract, as for example, if it is not supported by consideration, there is no binding accord and the prior contract is not discharged.[10] The making of an accord does not by itself discharge the prior contract. It is not until the terms of the accord are carried out that there is a discharge of the earlier contract.

(g) **Release.** A person who has a contract claim or any other kind of claim against another may agree to give up or release the claim. This may be done by delivering a writing which states that the claim is released. If supported by consideration, or if it comes within a statutory or common-law exception to the requirement of consideration, the release is effective to discharge the obligor from the contract obligation.

(h) **Waiver.** A term of a contract is discharged by **waiver** when one party fails to demand performance by the other party or to object when the other party fails to perform according to the terms of the contract. Unlike rescission, a waiver does not return the parties to their original positions; it leaves the parties where they are at the time.

§ 20:9. Discharge by Impossibility.

Impossibility of performance refers to external or extrinsic conditions as contrasted with the obligor's personal inability to perform. Thus, the fact that a debtor does not have the money to pay and cannot pay a debt does not present a case of impossibility.

Riots, shortages of materials, and similar factors, even though external, usually do not excuse the promisor from performing a contract. The fact that a seller cannot obtain from any supplier the goods which the seller has

[9]Perlick and Company v Lakeview Creditor's Trustee Committee, (WVa) 298 SE2d 228 (1982).
[10]K-Line Builders, Inc. v First Federal Savings & Loan Ass'n, 139 Ariz (App) 209, 677 P2d 1317 (1983).

already contracted to sell to the buyer does not excuse the seller from liability to the buyer, unless the inability to procure the goods was made a condition subsequent to the sales contract. Thus the fact that the road contractor's contemplated gravel source could not be used and it was necessary to transport gravel from a more distant source, making performance more costly, did not discharge the contractor from the obligation to construct a road. As there was nothing in the contract requiring that the gravel be that which was obtained from the unavailable source, no question of impossibility of performance existed.[11]

The fact that it will prove more costly to perform the contract than originally contemplated, or that the obligor has voluntarily gone out of business, does not constitute impossibility which excuses performance. No distinction is made in this connection between the acts of nature, people, or governments.

FACTS:

The Transatlantic Financing Corp. made a contract with the United States to haul a cargo of wheat from the United States to a safe port in Iran. The normal route lay through the Suez Canal. As the result of the nationalization of the Canal by Egypt and the subsequent international crisis which developed, the Canal was closed and it was necessary for Transatlantic to go around Africa to get to the destination. It then sued for additional compensation because of the longer route on the theory that it had been discharged from its obligation to carry to Iran for the amount named in the contract because of "impossibility."

DECISION:

Judgment for United States. Although impossibility does not mean literally impossible, it may be apparent from the contract that the risk of performance becoming commercially impracticable was assumed by one of the parties, in which case such impracticality is necessarily not a defense which that party may raise. As no route was specified and everyone was aware of the problems of international shipping, the unqualified contract to deliver the cargo at a specified point must be interpreted as indicating that the carrier assumed the risk that the shorter route through the Suez Canal might not be available; the carrier thus assumed the risk of "impossibility." [Transatlantic Financing Corp. v United States (CA Dist Col) 363 F2d 312 (1966)]

(a) **Destruction of Particular Subject Matter.** When the parties contract expressly for or with reference to a particular subject matter, the contract is discharged if the subject matter is destroyed through no fault of either party. When a contract calls for the sale of a wheat crop growing on a specific parcel of land, the contract is discharged if that crop is destroyed by blight.

On the other hand, if there is merely a contract to sell a given quantity of a specified grade of wheat, the seller is not discharged when the seller's crop is destroyed by blight. The seller had made an unqualified undertaking

[11]Mat-Su/Blackard/Stephan & Sons v Alaska (Alaska) 647 P2d 1101 (1982).

to deliver wheat of a specified grade. No restrictions or qualifications were imposed as to the source from which the wheat would be obtained. If the seller does not deliver the goods called for by the contract, the contract is broken and the seller is liable for damages.

(b) Change of Law. A contract is discharged when its performance is made illegal by a subsequent change in the law of the state or country in which the contract is to be performed. Thus, a contract to construct a non-fireproof building at a particular place is discharged by the adoption of a zoning law prohibiting such a building within that area. Mere inconvenience or temporary delay caused by the new law, however, does not excuse performance. Likewise, a change of law that merely increases the cost of the promisor is not a "change of law" that discharges the contract. Thus a promisor obligated to construct roads is not discharged from such obligation because the local government adopted new laws governing the construction of road drains and this change increased the cost of construction of the road.[12]

(c) Death or Disability. When the contract obligates a party to perform an act that requires personal skill or which contemplates a personal relationship with the obligee or some other person, the death or disability of the obligor, obligee, or other person (as the case may be) discharges the contract,[13] as when a newspaper cartoonist dies before the expiration of the contract. If the act called for by the contract can be performed by others or by the promisor's personal representative, however, this rule does not apply.

FACTS:
Oneal was a teacher employed by the Colton Consolidated School District. Because of a diabetic condition, his eyesight deteriorated so much that he offered to resign if he would be given pay for a specified number of "sick leave" days. The school district refused to do this and discharged Oneal for nonperformance of his contract. He appealed to remove the discharge from his record.

DECISION:
The action of the school district was improper because the contract had already been discharged by impossibility when Oneal's physical condition made him unable to perform the contract. [Oneal v Colton Consolidated School District, 16 Wash App 2d 488, 557 P2d 11 (1976)]

The death of a person to whom personal services are to be rendered also terminates the contract when the death of that person makes impossible the rendition of the services contemplated. Thus a contract to employ a person as the musical director for a singer terminates when the singer dies.

When the contract calls for the payment of money, the death of either party does not affect the obligation. If the obligor dies, the obligation

[12]Seago v Fellet (Colo App) 676 P2d 1224 (1983).
[13]Bajonski's Estate, 129 Ill App 3d 361, 84 Ill Dec 672, 472 NE2d 809 (1984).

is a liability of the obligor's estate. If the obligee dies, the right to collect the debt is an asset of the obligee's estate. The parties to a contract may agree, however, that the death of either the obligee or the obligor shall terminate the debt. In any case, the creditor can obtain insurance on the life of the debtor.

(d) Act of Other Party. There is in every contract "an implied covenant of good faith and fair dealing" in consequence of which a promisee is under an obligation to do nothing that would interfere with performance by the promisor. When the promisee prevents performance or otherwise makes performance impossible, the promisor is discharged from the contract. Thus, a subcontractor is discharged from any obligation when unable to do the work because the principal contractor refuses to deliver the material, equipment, or money required by the subcontract. When the default of the other party consists of failing to supply goods or services, the duty may rest upon the party claiming a discharge of the contract to show that substitute goods or services could not be obtained elsewhere, either because they were not reasonably available or were not acceptable under the terms of the contract.

When the conduct of the other contracting party does not make performance impossible but merely causes delay or renders performance more expensive, the contract is not discharged; but the injured party is entitled to damages for the loss incurred.

A promisor is not excused from performing under the contract when it is the act of the promisor that has made performance impossible. Consequently, when a data service contracted with a bank to keypunch all its daily operations and to process the cards, the bank was not excused from its obligation under the contract by the fact that it converted to magnetic tapes and installed its own computers. Accordingly the bank could not ignore its contract. It could only terminate the contract with the data service by giving the notice required by the contract.

When one party is to make installment payments as work is done by the other party, the making of the payments as specified is of course the legal obligation of the person required to pay. In many instances, payment is essential to provide the other party with the funds necessary for the continuation of the work.

§ 20:10.   Economic Disappointment.

Some courts hold that a contract is discharged when because of a change of circumstances the performance of the contract has become such an economic disappointment that it would be unjust and oppressive to insist on the performance of the contract.[14]

(a) Commercial Impracticability. When the cost of performance has risen suddenly and so greatly that performance of the contract will result in a substantial loss, some courts hold that the contract is discharged because it is **commercially impracticable** to perform. Although it is possible to perform, it has become such a bad bargain that the courts will not enforce it.

(b) Economic Frustration. Because of a change of circumstance the performance of the contract may have no value to the party entitled to re-

[14]Waegemann v Montgomery Ward & Co., Inc. (CA9 Cal) 713 F2d 452 (1983).

ceive performance. For example, the holder of a franchise may make a contract for the construction of a building that will be used for the purpose of the franchise. Assume that the franchise is terminated before the construction of the building begins, it is obvious that the former franchisee no longer has any use for the building and will want to get out of the contract. Some courts sympathize with the franchisee and hold that the contract with the contractor has been discharged by **economic frustration.**

FACTS:

Nicholson made a contract with Howard to construct a building to meet the specifications of the tenant to whom the building would be rented. The tenant was Honey's International and the building was designed as a bridal salon and could not be used for any other purpose. Honey's went into bankruptcy. When Nicholson found that he had no tenant, he canceled the construction contract. Nicholson claimed that he could cancel the contract because it was discharged by commercial frustration based on the bankruptcy of Honey.

DECISION:

The construction contract was discharged by commercial frustration. The building which was to be constructed could only be used by the particular tenant for whom it was designed. As that tenant had gone into bankruptcy and could not use the building, it would be pointless to construct the useless building. The economic or commercial objective of constructing the building was thus defeated or frustrated by bankruptcy of the tenant. This discharged the contract to construct the building even though it was still physically possible to construct it. [Howard v Nicholson (Mo App) 556 SW2d 477 (1977)]

(c) **The Majority Rule Compared.** The majority or traditional common-law rule refuses to recognize commercial impracticability or economic frustration. By the common-law-rule, the losses and disappointments against which commercial impracticability and economic frustration give protection are merely the risks that one takes in entering into a contract. Moreover, the situations could have been guarded against by including an appropriate condition subsequent in the contract declaring that the contract should be void if a specified event occurred. Or the contract could have provided for a readjustment of compensation when there was a basic change of circumstances. The common-law approach also rejects these two new concepts because they weaken the stability of a contract. The net result of these new concepts is that a contract ceases to be binding when there is a significant change in circumstances. That is, when a contract is most needed to give stability, the courts by these new concepts hold that there is no contract.

The common-law rule is also opposed because the new concepts raise questions of measurement of matters which can not be measured. How much change is needed in order to make a change "significant"?

In spite of the logical and practical objections to the new doctrines, it is likely that they will be given greater recognition by the courts in the future. The expanded recognition to the doctrine of unconscionability is developing a pattern of the judicial monitoring of contracts to prevent injustice. Further indication of a wider recognition of the concept that "extreme" change of circumstances can discharge a contract is found in the fact that the Uniform Commercial Code provides for the discharge of a contract for the sale of goods when a condition that the parties assumed existed or would continue ceases to exist.[15] However, it must be remembered that if a contract clearly places upon one of the parties a particular risk, the contract is not discharged when that risk is realized and loss is sustained. Neither the concept of commercial impracticability nor economic frustration will be applied to cancel out provisions of a contract that allocate the risk of loss.

FACTS:

Twelve railroads coming into Kansas City, Missouri formed the Kansas City Terminal Railway Company. Each of the railroads owned an equal share of the terminal company. By an agreement with the terminal company made in 1909, the railroads agreed to a plan of contributing to the expenses for maintaining the facilities at the terminal owned by the terminal company. By 1969, competing methods of transportation had caused a serious drop in the mail and passenger service of the railroads. One of these, the Atchison, Topeka and Santa Fe Railway Company claimed that because of these changed traffic patterns, the agreement had become unreasonable and was not binding.

DECISION:

The agreement was binding on the railroads as written. There was no ambiguity. The provisions of the clear contract could not be changed by the court merely because transportation conditions proved to be different than had been originally contemplated. [Kansas City Terminal Railway Co. v Atchison, Topeka and Santa Fe Railway Co. (Mo App) 512 SW2d 415 (1974)]

---

§ 20:11.   Temporary Impossibility.

Ordinarily a temporary impossibility has either no effect on the obligation to perform of the party who is affected thereby, or at most suspends the duty to perform so that the obligation to perform is revived upon the termination of the impossibility.[16] If, however, performance at that later date would impose a substantially greater burden upon the obligor, some courts discharge the obligor from the contract.

(a) **Weather.** Acts of God, such as tornadoes, lightning, and sudden floods, usually do not terminate a contract even though they make performance difficult or impossible. Thus, weather conditions constitute a risk that is assumed by a contracting party in the absence of a contrary agreement. Consequently, extra expense sustained by a contractor because of weather

---

[15]UCC § 2–615.

[16]Colorado Coal Furnace Distributors, Inc. v Frill Mfg. Co. (CA10 Wyo) 605 F2d 499 (1979).

conditions is a risk that the contractor assumes in the absence of an express provision for additional compensation in such case.

(b) **Weather Clauses.** Modern contracts commonly contain a "weather" clause, which either expressly grants an extension for delays caused by weather conditions or expressly denies the right to any extension of time or additional compensation because of weather condition difficulties. Some courts hold that abnormal weather conditions excuse what would otherwise be a breach of contract. Thus, nondelivery of equipment has been excused when the early melting of a frozen river made it impossible to deliver.

§ 20:12.   Discharge by Operation of Law.

In certain situations the law provides for the discharge of a contract, such as when the contract has been altered, has been destroyed by the obligee, is subject to bankruptcy proceedings, or is barred by a statute of limitations.

(a) **Alteration.** A written contract, whether under seal or not, may be discharged by alteration.[17] To have this effect, (1) it must be a **material alteration**, that is, it must change the nature of the obligation; (2) it must be made by a party to the contract, because alterations made by a stranger have no effect; (3) it must be made intentionally, and not through accident or mistake; and (4) it must be made without the consent of the other party to the contract. For example, when one party to an advertising contract, without the consent of the other party, added "at a monthly payment basis," thus making the rate of payment higher, the advertiser was discharged from any duty under the contract.

There is no discharge of the contract by alteration when the term added is one which the law would imply, for in such a case the change is not material.

(b) **Destruction of the Contract.** The physical destruction of a written contract may discharge the contract. When the person entitled to performance under a sealed instrument destroys the writing with the intent to terminate the liability of the obligor, the latter's liability is discharged. In any case, the physical destruction of the writing may be evidence of an intention to discharge the obligation by mutual agreement.

FACTS:
J.A. Reed and his wife, Bertha, signed a contract the day before they were married. Several months after their marriage, Reed, with the participation of Bertha and without any objection from her, destroyed the contract by burning it in a stove. After his death, Bertha claimed the contract was still in force.

DECISION:
The contract had been discharged by the physical destruction of the contract with the mutual consent of the parties. [Re Reed's Estate (Mo) 414 SW2d 283 (1967)]

---

[17]The definition and effect of alteration in the case of commercial paper has been modified by UCC § 3–407.

(c) **Merger.** In some instances, contract rights are merged into or absorbed by a greater right. When an action is brought upon a contract and a judgment is obtained by the plaintiff against the defendant, the contract claim is merged into the obligation under the judgment.

(d) **Bankruptcy.** Most insolvent debtors may voluntarily enter into a federal court of bankruptcy or be compelled to do so by creditors. The trustee in bankruptcy then takes possession of the debtor's property and distributes it as far as it will go among the creditors. After this is done, the court grants the debtor a discharge in bankruptcy if it concludes that the debtor has acted honestly and has not attempted to defraud creditors.

Even though all creditors have not been paid in full, the discharge in bankruptcy discharges ordinary contract claims against the debtor.

(e) **Statutes of Limitations.** Statutes provide that after a certain number of years have passed a contract claim is barred. The time limitation provided by state statutes of limitations vary widely. The period usually differs with the type of contract — ranging from a relatively short time for open accounts (ordinary customers' charge accounts) and other sales of goods, 4 years;[18] to a somewhat longer period for written contracts, usually 5 to 10 years; to a maximum period for judgments of record, usually 10 to 20 years.

(f) **Contractual Limitations.** Some contracts, particularly insurance contracts, contain a time limitation within which suit may be brought. This is, in effect, a private statute of limitations created by the agreement of the parties.

A contract may also require that notice of any claim be given within a specified time. A party who fails to give notice within the time specified by the contract is barred from suing thereon.

FACTS:

The State Bank of Viroqua obtained a banker's blanket bond from the Capitol Indemnity Corporation to protect it from loss by forgery. The bond required that the bank give the insurer notice of any loss at "the earliest practicable moment." DeLap borrowed money from the bank by means of paper on which he forged the name of Mellem. This was learned in October, 1969. In October, 1970, an agent of Capitol was discussing the bond with the bank. The bank then realized for the first time that the bond covered the DeLap forgery loss. Fifteen days later the bank notified Captiol of that claim. Capitol denied liability because fo the delay. The bank sued Capitol.

DECISION:

The bank was barred as it had not given notice at the earliest practicable moment after it knew that a loss had been sustained. The failure of the bank to realize sooner that it had a claim under the contract did not excuse it from complying therewith. [State Bank of Viroqua v Capitol Indemnity Corp. 61 Wis 2d 699, 214 NW2d 42 (1974)]

---

[18]UCC § 2–725(1).

§ 20:13.   Discharge by Acceptance of Breach.

There is a **breach of contract** whenever one party or both parties fail to perform the contract. A contract is discharged by breach if, when one party breaks the contract, the other party accepts the contract as ended. When a breach occurs, however, the injured party is not required to treat the contract as discharged. Since the contract bound the defaulting party to perform, the injured party may insist on the observance of the contract and resort to legal remedies. An aggrieved party is not held to have accepted the other party's breach as terminating the contract unless notice has been clearly given that the breach was so accepted.

A breach does not result in the discharge of a contract if the term broken is not sufficiently important. A term of a contract that does not go to the root of the contract is a **subsidiary term.** When there is a failure to perform such a term, the agreement is not terminated, but the defaulting party may be liable for damages for its breach.

In addition to the effect of a breach as such, the occurrence of a breach also excuses the injured party from rendering a performance if the defaulter's performance was a condition precedent to the duty of the injured party to perform. For example, when a seller is required to deliver goods and the buyer is required to pay upon delivery of the goods, the seller's failure to deliver is a breach of the duty to deliver and also excuses the buyer from paying under the contract because the delivery of the goods was a condition precedent to the duty to pay.

(a) **Renunciation.** When a party to a contract declares in advance of the time for performance that the required performance will not be rendered, the other party may (1) ignore this declaration and insist on performance in accordance with the terms of the contract, (2) accept this declaration as an **anticipatory breach** and sue the promisor for damages, or (3) accept the declaration as a breach of the contract and rescind the contract.[19] It is for the injured party to determine what to do when the other party has made a renunciation.

To constitute a renunciation there must be a clear, absolute, unequivocal refusal to perform the contract according to its terms.

(b) **Incapacitating Self.** Another form of anticipatory breach occurs when the promisor makes it impossible to perform the obligation. Under such circumstances, the promisee is entitled to treat the contract as discharged. For example, when one party who is bound by the terms of the contract to deliver specific bonds, stocks, or notes to another party transfers them to a third person instead, the promisee may elect to treat the contract as discharged; or may hold the promisor accountable for nonperformance when the time of performance arrives. The same is true when one agrees to sell specific goods to another person and then sells them to a third person in violation of the original contract.

[19]Hospital Mortgage Group v First Prudential Development Corp. (Fla App) 411 So2d 181 (1982).

SUMMARY

Most contracts are discharged by performance. An offer to perform is called a tender of performance. If a tender of performance is wrongfully refused the duty of the tenderer to perform is terminated. If the performance required was the payment of money, the refusal of a proper tender does not discharge the debt but prevents the creditor from recovering interest or costs if suit is thereafter brought against the tenderer to recover the amount owed. When the performance called for by the contract is the payment of money it must be legal tender which is tendered. In actual practice, it is common to pay and to accept payment by checks or other commercial paper. When the debtor owes the creditor on several accounts and makes a payment, the debtor may specify which account is to be credited with the payment. If the debtor fails to do so, the creditor may make the application. If neither the creditor nor the debtor makes an application of the payment, the court may do so and there is a conflict of authority as to whether the application should be made so as to favor the creditor or the debtor.

When a contract does not state when it is to be performed, it must be performed within a reasonable time. If time for performance is stated in the contract, the contract must be performed at the time specified if such time is essential (is of the essence) although performance within a reasonable time is sufficient if the specified time is not essential.

Ordinarily a contract must be performed exactly in the manner specified by the contract but a less than perfect performance is allowed if it is a substantial performance and if damages are allowed the other party sufficient to compensate for the loss sustained because the performance was not perfect. The other contracting party or a third person may guarantee a perfect performance and such a guarantor is then liable if the performance is less than perfect.

A contract can not be discharged by unilateral action unless authorized by the contract itself or by statute, as in the case of consumer protection rescission.

As a contract arises from an agreement, it may also be terminated by an agreement. This may be a provision in the original contract or a subsequent agreement to rescind the contract. A contract may also be discharged by substitution of a new contract for the original contract; by a novation by making a new contract with a new party; by accord and satisfaction; release; and waiver.

A contract is discharged when it is impossible to perform as in the case of the destruction of the subject matter of the contract, the adoption of a new law that prohibits performance, the death or disability of a party whose personal action was required for performance of the contract, or the act of the other contracting party to the contract. Some courts will also hold that a contract is discharged when its performance is commercially impracticable or there is economic frustration of one of the parties. Although increased cost of performance ordinarily has no effect on a contract, if that increase is grossly disproportionate to the original performance cost, some courts will classify the situation as one of commercial impracticability and hold that the contract is discharged. In the case of economic frustration, the contract can be performed but the performance has ceased to have any significant value to the party who originally contracted to obtain that performance. Temporary impossibility, such as a labor strike or bad weather, has no effect upon a contract although it is common to include protective clauses that excuse delay caused by temporary impossibility. A contract may be discharged by operation of law. This occurs when (1) one of the parties intentionally makes a material alteration to the contract without the consent of the other party, (2) a party destroys a written contract with the intent to end the existence of a contract and release the other contracting party, (3) there is a merger of a contract into a judgment entered in a lawsuit brought upon the contract, (4) the liability arising from the contract is discharged by bankruptcy, or suit on the contract is barred by (5) the applicable statute of limitations, or (6) a time limitation stated in the contract.

QUESTIONS AND CASE PROBLEMS

1. What social forces are affected by the doctrine of economic frustration?
2. Parties to a contract must perform their obligations entirely on the dates specified by the contract and will forfeit all rights if performance is not so made. Appraise this statement.
3. McMullen Contractors made a contract with Richardson to build an apartment house for a specific price. A number of serious apartment house fires broke out in the city and an ordinance was adopted by the City Council increasing the fire precautions which had to be taken in the construction of a new building. Compliance with these new requirements would make the construction of the apartment house for Richardson more expensive than McMullen had originally contemplated. Is McCullen discharged from the contract to build the apartment house?
4. Grattan contracted to build a house and garage for Boris for $50,000. The job was completed according to the specifications in all respects except that Grattan forgot to put a tool shed next to the garage as was required by the contract specifications. Boris refused to pay Grattan. Grattan sued Boris. Boris raised the defense that Grattan was not entitled to any money until the contract was completely performed and that the performance was incomplete because the tool shed had not been constructed. Was Boris correct?
5. Johnson made a contract with Hazel to paint her house for $1,000. Thereafter, Johnson, Hazel, and Plaskey agreed that Plaskey would do the painting and that Johnson would have no further obligation with respect to the painting. Plaskey failed to paint the house and Hazel sued Johnson for damages. Is Johnson liable?
6. Compare (a) the principle that time is generally not of the essence, with (b) the right of a construction contractor to recover for a substantial performance of the contract.
7. A building was being demolished. The demolition contractor made a contract with a brick dealer by which the latter could remove the brick from the demolition area. A dispute arose as to how quickly the brick dealer was required to remove the bricks from the demolition area. The dealer claimed that, as no time was stated in the contract, he could re-

move the bricks any time. Was he correct? [Robinson v Commercial Contractors, Inc. 6 Conn Cir 393, 274 A2d 160]

8. Metalcrafters made a contract to design a new earth-moving vehicle for Lamar Highway Construction Company. Metalcrafters was depending upon the genius of Susan, the head of its research department, to design a new product. Shortly after the contract was made between Metalcrafters and Lamar, Susan was killed in an automobile accident. Metalcrafters was not able to design the product without Susan. Lamar sued Metalcrafters for damages for breach of the contract. Metalcrafters claimed that the contract was discharged by Susan's death. Is it correct?

9. The Tinchers signed a contract to sell land to Creasy. The contract specified that the sales transaction was to be completed in 90 days. At the end of the 90 days, Creasy requested an extension of time. The Tinchers refused to grant an extension and stated that the contract was terminated. Creasy claimed that the 90-day clause was not binding because the contract did not state that time was of the essence. Was the contract terminated? [Creasy v Tincher, 154 W Va 18, 173 SE2d 332]

10. The Powers entered into a home improvement contract with Sims and Levin. The contract declared that the amount due was a lien on the home of the Powers and that they had two days in which to cancel the contract if they changed their minds. Was this cancellation provision valid?

11. Hertz Commercial Leasing Corporation sued Phillips on a leasing contract. The contract was signed "Phillips Ceramic Tile Installation & Boziz Tile Co. of Georgia, Bobby James Phillips Pres." and "Bobby James Phillips—as an individual." Phillips claimed that he was not personally liable on the theory that the words "as an individual" had been added by the plaintiff after the contract had been signed by Phillips and that such addition was an alteration that discharged the contract. Was the contract discharged by alteration? [Phillips v Hertz Commercial Leasing Corp. 138 Ga App 441, 226 SE2d 287]

12. Dickson contracted to build a house for Moran. When it was approximately 25-40% completed, Moran would not let Dickson work any further because he was not following the building plans and specifications and there were many defects. Moran hired another contractor to correct the defects and finish the building, Dickson sued Moran for breach of contract, claiming that he had substantially performed the contract up to the point where he had been discharged. Was Dickson correct? [Dickson v Moran (La App) 344 So 2d 102]

13. Compare a novation and a delegation of duties.

14. A leased a trailer park to B. At the time, sewage was disposed of by a septic tank system which was not connected with the public sewage system. B knew this and the lease declared that B had examined the premises and that A made no representation or guarantee as to the condition of the premises. Some time thereafter, the septic tank system stopped working properly and the county health department notified B that he was required to connect the sewage system with the public sewage system or else close the trailer park. B did not want to pay the additional cost involved in connecting with the public system. B claimed that he was released from the lease and was entitled to a refund of the

deposit which he had made. Was he correct? [Glen R. Sewell Sheet Metal v Loverde, 70 Cal 2d 666, 75 Cal Rptr 889, 451 P2d 721]

15. A farmer made a contract to sell and deliver 10,000 bushels of soybeans. A flood destroyed his entire crop. He claimed that he was discharged from his obligation under the contract. Was he correct?

16. Phillips made a contract with Borgsmiller, Inc. to install acoustical ceilings and insulation in a building that would be constructed by Borgsmiller, Inc. While the building was in course of construction, the corporation sold the building to another corporation, "Grandpa John's Inc." At some point in the performance of his contract, Phillips became aware that the building had been sold but continued performance without any question. When the work was finished Phillips demanded payment of the contract price of $30,000 from Borgsmiller, Inc. The new owner sent a check in the amount of $15,000. No further payment was made to Phillips and he brought suit against Borgsmiller, Inc. and Borgsmiller individually. The defendants claimed that they were not liable because the contract with Borgsmiller, Inc. had been discharged by novation. Were they correct? [Phillips and Arnold, Inc. v Frederick J. Borgsmiller, Inc. 123 Ill App 3d 95, 78 Ill Dec 805, 462 NE2d 924]

CHAPTER 21

BREACH OF CONTRACT

AND REMEDIES

CHAPTER OBJECTIVES

After studying this chapter you will be able to:

1. List and define the kinds of damages that may be recovered when a contract is broken.
2. Describe the requirement of mitigation of damages.
3. State when liquidated damages clauses are valid.
4. State when liability limiting clauses are valid.
5. State when a breach of contract is waived.
6. List the steps that may be used to prevent a waiver of breach of contract.
7. Distinguish between reformation of a contract and interpretation of a contract.
8. State when malpractice liability arises.
9. Solve problems involving remedies for breach of contract.

When a party breaks a contract, society gives the other party, the injured party, a remedy against the defaulter. As seen in Chapter 19, sometimes the right to obtain a remedy for breach has been extended beyond the contracting parties to include third party beneficiaries and assignees.

Assume that the fact situation that constitutes a breach of contract is also a tort, as described in Chapter 10. Can an aggrieved party sue the defaulter for the tort? Society could have taken the position that as the parties had made a contract, their respective rights must stand or fall as contract rights and that any other kind of liability was excluded. In the interest of putting the aggrieved person in as nearly as possible the same position that such person would have held had the contract been performed, the aggrieved person is given the choice of seeking a remedy for breach of contract or for tort.

356

But once society decided to make a tort remedy available it was necessary to decide who could seek such tort remedy. Could third person victims of the default be allowed to sue for the tort involved in the breach of the contract? Unlike the third party beneficiary, there is often nothing in the contract that shows any intent to benefit such victims. Unlike the assignee, there is no relationship between the third person tort victim and a party to the original contract. Society was thus faced with the necessity of deciding whether only a contracting party could sue the other contracting party for a tort or whether anyone who could show injury could sue for such tort. The first choice seemed too narrow and the second seemed far too broad. Somewhere between the two extremes society has been struggling to evolve a dividing line that will allow some third person victims to sue for tortious breach of contract but that will not allow too many to sue.

The subjects of remedies and who may sue are discussed in this Chapter.

A. REMEDIES FOR BREACH OF CONTRACT

There are several remedies for breach of contract, one or more of which may be available to the injured party. The injured party may bring an action for damages, rescind the contract, bring a suit in equity to obtain specific performance, or commence a proceeding to obtain relief from an administrative agency of the government.

§ 21:1.   Damages.

Whenever a breach of contract occurs, the injured party is entitled to bring an action for damages to recover such sum of money as will place the injured party in the same position that would have been attained if the contract had been performed.[1] If the defendant has been negligent in performing the contract, the plaintiff may sue for the damages caused by the negligence. Thus, a person contracting to drill a well for drinking water can be sued for the damage caused by negligently drilling the well so as to cause the water to become contaminated. However, damages representing annoyance or mental anguish ordinarily may not be recovered for breach of contract.

(a) **Direct and Consequential Damages.** The breach of a contract may cause the other party *direct* and *consequential loss*. A **direct loss** is one which necessarily is caused by the breach of contract. A **consequential loss** is one which does not necessarily follow the breach of the contract, but happens to do so in a particular case because of the circumstances of the injured party. For example, if the seller breaks the contract to deliver a truck which operates properly, the buyer sustains the damages of receiving a truck that cannot be used. This is the direct loss. If the buyer of the truck needed the truck to take a harvest of ripe tomatoes to the cannery but was unable to do so because the truck would not operate, the loss of the crop which could not be transported would be the consequential loss sustained by the farmer-buyer.

[1]Downing v Dial (Ind App) 426 NE2d 416 (1981).

In order to recover damages for a particular consequential loss, the plaintiff must show that it was within the defendant's contemplation, that is, it was foreseeable that the kind of loss in question could be sustained by the plaintiff if the contract was broken.

FACTS:

Jerry Birkel was a grain farmer. Hassebrook Farm Service, Inc. made a contract to sell to Jerry and install a grain storage and drying bin. Jerry's old dryer was traded in to the seller. The new equipment did not work properly and Jerry had to pay other persons for drying and storing his grain. Jerry sued Hassebrook for damages and claimed the right to be repaid what he had paid to others for drying and storage.

DECISION:

Jerry was entitled to recover what he had paid others for drying and storage. As Jerry had traded in his old dryer to the seller, it was obvious to the seller that if the new equipment did not work properly, Jerry would be forced to pay for alternative drying and storage in order to prevent the total loss of his crops. The cost of such alternative was therefore within the contemplation of the seller when the contract was made and therefore the buyer could recover such cost as an element of damages for the seller's breach of contract. [Birkel v Hassebrook Farm Service, Inc. 219 Neb 286, 363 NW2d 148 (1985)]

(b) **Measure of Damages.** An injured party who does not sustain an actual loss from the breach of a contract is entitled to a judgment of a small sum, such as $1.00, known as **nominal damages.** A plaintiff who has sustained actual loss is entitled to a sum of money that will, so far as possible, compensate for that loss; such damages are called **compensatory damages.**

The fact that damages cannot be established with mathematical certainty is not a bar to their recovery. All that is required is reasonable certainty and the trier of fact is given a large degree of discretion in determining the damages.

Ordinarily only compensatory damages are recoverable for breach of contract. Damages in excess of actual loss will not be imposed for the purpose of punishing or making an example of the defendant; such damages are known as **punitive damages** or **exemplary damages.** In some consumer situations, the recovery of punitive damages is allowed in order to discourage the defendant from breaking the law with others. For example, in cases in which the plaintiff is a consumer and the seller has acted wrongfully and stubbornly, there is an increasing trend to award punitive damages in order to prevent a repetition of such conduct.

(c) **Mitigation of Damages.** The injured party is under the duty to **mitigate the damages** if reasonably possible. That is, damages must not be permitted to increase if this can be prevented by reasonable efforts. This means that the injured party must generally stop any performance under the contract in order to avoid running up a larger bill. It may require the injured party to buy or rent elsewhere the goods which the wrongdoer was obligated to deliver under the contract. In the case of the breach of an employment contract by the employer, the employee is required to seek other similar employment and the wages earned or which could have been earned from the other similar employment must be deducted from the damages claimed.

(1) *Effect of Failure to Mitigate Damages.* The effect of the requirement of mitigating damages is to limit the recovery by the injured party to the damages which would have been sustained had the injured party mitigated the damages.[2] That is, recovery is limited to the direct loss, and damages for consequential loss are excluded. For example, assume that a commercial hauler makes a contract to buy a truck. Because the seller fails to deliver the truck, the buyer loses a hauling job on which a profit of $500 would have been made. Assume that the hauler could have rented a truck for $50 in time to do the hauling job. The hauler would then be under a duty to rent the truck so that the $500 profit would not be lost. By failing to do this, the hauler permitted the damages to grow from a rental cost of $50 to a loss of profit of $500. When the hauler sues the seller for breach of the sales contract, the rule of mitigation of damages will limit the hauler to recovering only $50 because the additional $450 loss was unnecessarily sustained. If in fact the hauler had rented a truck, the rental of $50 would be recoverable as damages from the seller. Thus, the hauler will only receive $50 damages whether or not a truck is rented in order to mitigate the damages.

(2) *Excuse for Failure to Mitigate Damages.* If there is nothing which the injured party can reasonably do to reduce damages, there is, by definition, no duty to mitigate damages. For example, when a leasing company broke its contract to supply a specified computer and auxiliary equipment by delivering a less desirable computer and the specified computer and equipment could not be obtained elsewhere by the customer, the customer was entitled to recover full damages.

When the cost of mitigating, as by purchasing elsewhere the goods which the seller failed to deliver, is unreasonably great, there is no duty to mitigate damages.

§ 21:2. Liquidated Damages.

The parties may stipulate in their contract that a certain amount shall be paid in case of default. This amount is known as **liquidated damages.** Such a provision will be enforced if the amount specified is not excessive and if the contract is of such a nature that it would be difficult to determine the actual damages.[3] For example, it is ordinarily very difficult, if not impossible, to determine what loss the owner of a building under construction suffers when the contractor is late in completing the building. It is therefore customary to include a liquidated damage clause in a building contract, specifying that the contractor is required to pay a stated sum for each day of delay. Likewise, the contract between a medical corporation and its staff doctors may provide for

---

[2]Grill v Adams, 123 Ill App 3d 913, 79 Ill Dec 342, 463 NE2d 896 (1984).
[3]Robbins v Finlay (Utah) 645 P2d 623 (1982). Uniform Commercial Code § 2–718(1).

liquidated damages for breach at the amount of $35,000. The actual damages that would be sustained by the employer corporation in such case can not be accurately established and the amount stipulated was reasonable, particularly in view of the fact that it would be necessary to train a replacement.[4]

When a liquidated damages clause is held valid, the injured party cannot collect more than the amount specified by the clause; and the defaulting party is bound to pay that much damages once the fact is established that there has been a default.

FACTS:

The Oregon Highway Commission made a contract with the DeLong Corporation for the construction of the major components of a bridge across the Columbia River. The contract specified that $2,000 would be paid for each day's delay. DeLong abandoned the contract. The Highway Commission then had a second contractor finish the work which was finished 476 days after the original completion date. The State then sued DeLong for damages for breach of the contract and for $2,000 for each day's delay. The State claimed that, because of the delay, it lost approximately $1.4 million in bridge tolls, ferry operations, and a bridge subsidy.

DECISION:

Judgment for Oregon for liquidated damages at the rate of $2,000 X 476 days of delay. The actual damages sustained by Oregon could not be determined, but the amount stipulated appeared reasonable in the light of the various losses caused the State by the contractor's delay. Therefore the provision for liquidated damages was binding upon the contractor and entitled the State to recover according to the terms of such provision. [Oregon v DeLong Corp. 9 Or App 550, 495 P2d 1215 (1972)]

If the liquidated damages clause calls for the payment of a sum which is clearly unreasonably large and unrelated to the possible actual damages that might be sustained, the clause will be held void as a **penalty**.

Liquidated damages may be variously measured by the parties. When delay is in mind, it may be a fixed sum, as $100, for each day of delay. When there is a total default, it may be a percentage of the total contract price or the amount of the down payment.

§ 21:3.   Limitation of Liability.

A party to a contract generally may include a provision that there shall be no liability for its breach or that liability shall be limited. An illustration of such clauses is the construction contract provision that the contractor shall not be liable for delays caused by conduct of third persons.

---

[4]Ryan v Orris, 95 App Div 2d 879, 463 NYS2d 883 (1983).

FACTS:

The Otis Elevator Company was about to install an elevator in a high school building. It made a contract with Don Stodola's Well Drilling Company to do the drilling work involved. The contract stated that Don Stodola assumed "no liability" for damage to the building. Because of the alleged negligence of Don Stodola, the building cracked where the elevator was installed. When suit was brought against Don Stodola, he raised the defense that the exculpatory clause barred any suit against him. Otis claimed that the clause could not bar liability for negligence because the clause did not expressly refer to negligence.

DECISION:

Judgment for Don Stodola. An exculpatory clause is to be given the scope intended by the parties. The subcontractor, Don Stodola, declared in the contract that he assumed "no liability" for damage to the building. This clearly included liability based on any theory and therefore the clause covered and excluded liability based on negligence, even though nothing was expressly said about "negligence". [*Otis Elevator Co. v Don Stodola's Well Drilling Co., Inc.* _____Minn App _____, 372 NW2d 77 (1985)]

Generally such provisions are valid, particularly between experienced business persons. Thus, a telephone company may limit its liability to a nominal amount for the omission of a customer's name and number from the yellow page directory where the limitation is conspicuous, the customer is experienced in business, and the omission was merely the result of simple negligence.

There is a growing trend, however, to limit such **exculpatory provisions** or to hold them invalid when it is felt that because of the unequal bargaining power of the contracting parties the surrender of a right to damages for breach by the other is oppressive or unconscionable. When the provision is expanded so as to free the contracting party from liability for that party's own negligence, the provision is sometimes held void as contrary to public policy.[5] This is particularly likely to be the result when the party in question is a public utility, which is under the duty to render the performance or to provide the service in question in a nonnegligent way.

In recent years, the concept has developed that a limitation of liability is invalid when persons in an inferior bargaining position are involved. In any case, a limitation of liability is not binding if obtained by misconduct or deception.

FACTS:

Merten was a student at a horseback riding school run by Nathan. Her contract with the school recited that the school did not have insurance covering horseback riding and that accordingly Merten released the school from all liability for injury sustained while riding in the school. When this form of contract was first used by the school, it in fact did not have any insurance. The school continued to use the same

[5]*Krohnert v Yacht Systems Hawaii, Inc.* (Hawaii App) 664 P2d 738 (1983).

form, however, even though at the time relating to Merten, the school carried insurance providing coverage up to $300,000 per accident. Merten was injured in the riding school and sued Nathan. He defended on the ground that the contract with him released him from all liability.

DECISION:

Judgment for Merten. The representation that there was no insurance was important to her decision to release the school from liability. As the "no insurance" statement was false, the release given on the basis of that statement was not binding. It is contrary to public policy to enforce an exculpatory provision when it was agreed to because of a mistake or deception as to an important matter. [Merten v Nathan, 108 Wis 2d 205, 321 NW2d 173 (1982)]

§ 21:4.   Rescission upon Breach.

When one party commits a material breach of the contract, the other party may rescind the contract because of such breach. In some situations, the right to rescind may be governed or controlled by civil service statutes or similar regulations or by an obligation to submit the matter to arbitration or to a grievance procedure.

An injured party who rescinds after having performed or paid money under the contract may recover the reasonable value of the performance rendered or the money paid. This recovery is not based on the contract which has been rescinded but on a quasi contract which the law implies to prevent the defaulter from keeping the benefit received and thus being unjustly enriched.

The rescinding party must restore the other party to that party's original position. If the rescinding party's own acts make this impossible, the contract cannot be rescinded. Thus, a buyer who has placed a mortgage on property purchased cannot rescind the sales contract because the property cannot be returned to the seller in its original, unmortgaged condition.

Care must be exercised in deciding to rescind a contract. If proper ground for rescission does not exist, the party who rescinds is guilty of repudiating the contract and is liable for damages for its breach.

§ 21:5.   Specific Performance.

Under special circumstances the injured party may seek the equitable remedy of **specific performance** which compels the other party to carry out the terms of a contract. Specific performance is ordinarily granted only if the subject matter of the contract is unique, thereby making a monetary award of damages an inadequate remedy. For example, contracts for the purchase of land will be specifically enforced, as will contracts for the sale of a business and the franchise held by the business.

Specific performance of a contract to sell personal property can generally be obtained only if the article is of unusual age, beauty, unique history, or other distinction, as in the case of heirlooms, original paintings, old editions of books, or relics. In these cases identical articles could not be obtained in the market. Specific performance is also allowed a buyer in the case of a contract to buy shares of stock essential for control of a close corporation when those shares have no fixed or market value and are not quoted in the commercial reports or sold on a stock exchange.[6]

The granting of specific performance is discretionary with the court. This relief will be refused (a) when the contract is not definite; (b) when there is an adequate legal remedy (usually a monetary award); (c) when it works an undue hardship or an injustice on the defaulting party or the consideration is inadequate; (d) when the agreement is illegal, fraudulent, or unconscionable; (e) when the court is unable to supervise the performance of such acts, as when services of a technical nature are to be rendered; or (f) when there has been unreasonable delay in bringing suit.

Ordinarily contracts for the performance of personal services will not be specifically ordered, both because of the difficulty of supervision by the court and because of the restriction of the Thirteenth Amendment of the Federal Constitution prohibiting involuntary servitude except as criminal punishment. In some instances, a court will issue a negative injunction which prohibits the defendant from rendering a similar service for anyone else. This may indirectly have the effect of compelling the defendant to work for the plaintiff.

In order to do complete justice, the court in awarding specific performance can also award damages to compensate for the direct and consequential loss caused by the defendant's refusal to perform the contract.[7]

§ 21:6.   Waiver of Breach.

The fact that one party has broken a contract does not necessarily mean that there will be a lawsuit or a forfeiture of the contract. For practical business reasons, one party may be willing to ignore or **waive** the breach. When it is established that there has been a waiver of a breach, the party waiving the breach cannot take any action on the theory that the contract was broken. The waiver in effect erases the past breach and the contract continues as though the breach had not existed.[8]

Many times a tender of performance will be defective in some respect: there may be delays or the product tendered is not exactly what was ordered. Because the obligee is not really troubled by the defect or because the obligee is in such a position that the defective performance must be accepted as better than none, the obligee will frequently accept the performance, although defective, without making any complaint as to the defect.

FACTS:

Computers and physical equipment used in connection with computers have been given the nickname of "hardware." The programs or instructions on how to use the hardware to produce certain desired results have the nickname of "software." Without the proper software, the hardware is useless. Digital Resources made a contract to supply Seismic and Digital Concepts Inc. with software that it

[6]Brown v Knox, 219 Neb 189, 361 NW2d 540 (1985).
[7]Bregman v Meehan, 125 Misc 2d 332, 479 NYS2d 422 (1984).
[8]Wheeler v Wheeler, 299 NC 633, 263 SE2d 763 (1980).

needed to produce the desired results with its hardware. Digital was ten to twenty-five days late in delivering the software to Seismic. In spite of such lateness, Seismic took the software, used it, and asked Digital to do more work in order to speed up the program. Seismic did not make payment as required by the contract. When Digital brought suit against it, Seismic counterclaimed for damages caused by the delay in the delivery of the software.

DECISION:
Judgment against Seismic. It could not claim damages for delay because it had waived the right to assert the delay by the fact that it took the late delivery and used the software, and even asked the plaintiff to perform additional services. [Seismic & Digital Concepts Inc. v Digital Resources Corp. (Tex Civ App) 590 SW2d 718 (1979)]

---

§ 21:7.   Interpretation and Operation of Waiver of Breach.

A waiver of breach is more often the result of silence or failure to object in timely fashion than it is the result of an express forgiving of a breach. But, whether the waiver is expressly made or arises from conduct or a failure to object, questions may arise as to the scope or extent of the waiver.

(a) **Scope of Waiver.** The waiver of a breach of contract only extends to the matter waived. It does not show any intent to ignore other provisions of the contract. For example, when a contractor is late in completing the construction of a building but the owner waives objection to the lateness and permits the contractor to continue and finish the construction, such waiver as to time does not waive the obligation of the contractor to complete the building according to the plans and specifications. Only the time of performance requirement is waived.

(b) **Reservation of Right.** It may be that a party is willing to accept a defective performance but does not wish to surrender any claim for damages for the breach. For example, the buyer of coal may need a shipment of coal so badly as to be forced to accept it although it is defective, yet at the same time, the buyer does not wish to be required to pay the full purchase price for the defective shipment. To the contrary, the buyer wants to claim a deduction for damages because the shipment was defective. In such a case, the buyer should accept the tendered performance with a **reservation of right.** In the above illustration, the buyer would in effect state that the defective coal was accepted but that the right to damages for nonconformity to the contract was reserved.[9] Frequently the buyer will express the same thought by stating that the coal is accepted without prejudice to a claim for damages for nonconformity or that the shipment is accepted under protest.

The acceptance under reservation described above may be oral. It is preferable for practical reasons that it be in writing. In many cases the practical procedure is to make the declaration orally as soon as possible and then send a confirming letter. When the matter is sufficiently important, it is also desirable to have the wrongdoer countersign or make a written acknowledgment of the reservation letter.

[9]UCC § 1–207.

(c) **Waiver of Breach as Modification of Contract.** When the contract calls for a continuing performance, such as making delivery of goods or the payment of an installment on the first of each month, the acceptance of a late delivery or a late payment may have more significance than merely waiving a claim for damages because of the lateness. Repeated breaches and repeated waivers may show that the parties had modified their original contract. For example, the contract calling for performance on the first of the month may have been modified to permit performance in the first week of the month. When there is a modification of the contract, neither party can go back to the original contract without the consent of the other.

(d) **Anti-Modification Clause.** Modern contracts commonly specify that the terms of a contract shall not be deemed modified by waiver as to any breaches. This means that the original contract remains as agreed to and either party may therefore return to and insist upon compliance with the original contract.

§ 21:8.   Reformation of Contract.

When a written contract does not correctly state what has been agreed to and its correction cannot be obtained by voluntary cooperation, a court will order the correction of the contract when it is clear that a reforming or **reformation** of the contract should be made. In some instances, reforming the contract is the first step in showing that the contract which was actually made has been broken by the defendant. For example, assume that A owns two houses at 510 and 512 North Main Street. Assume that a fire insurance policy is obtained to cover 510 but by mistake the policy refers to 512. Thereafter, 510 is destroyed by fire and the insurance company refuses to pay the loss on the theory that it did not insure 510 but insured 512. At this point, A would ask the court (a) to reform the insurance contract to show that there was in fact insurance on 510, and (b) to award damages to A because of the insurer's breach of its contract as to 510.

Reformation is limited to correcting a mistake in the writing which mistake prevents it from setting forth the actual agreement of the parties. It can not be used to rewrite the contract. Consequently when it is clear that the parties agreed that their contract should be "null and void" when a particular event occurred, a court by reformation can not cancel out the condition subsequent and make the contract binding although by its terms it had become null and void because the specified event had occurred. Likewise if in fact no oral contract was ever formed, as because the offer was not accepted, a reformation action can not be used to create a contract.[10]

B. TORT LIABILITY TO THIRD PERSONS FOR BREACH

Can a third person sue for loss caused by a breach of a contract between other persons?

---

[10]Loeb v Gray, 131 Ill App 3d 793, 86 Ill Dec 775, 475 NE2d 1342 (1985).

§ 21:9.   Tort Liability to
Third Person for Nonperformance.

When a party to a contract fails to perform an obligation imposed thereby, a third person may be harmed. In some cases, the third party may recover damages as a third party beneficiary. If this is not possible, the recovery of damages may be sought on a theory of tort liability.

By the general rule, a total failure to perform a contract does not confer upon a third person a right to sue for tort.

(a) **Discharge of Obligee's Duty.** An exception is made to the general rule when the obligee, that is, the other party to the contract who will receive the benefit of performance, owes a duty to the third person or the general public, and the performance by the contractor would discharge that duty. Here the breach of the duty by the contractor gives rise to a tort liability in favor of the injured third person against the contractor. To illustrate, the operator of an office building owes the duty to third persons of maintaining its elevators in a safe operating condition. In order to discharge this duty, the building management may make a contract with an elevator maintenance contractor. If the latter fails to perform its contract and a third person is injured because of the defective condition of an elevator, the third person may sue the elevator maintenance contractor for the damages sustained.

FACTS:
The U.S.F.&G. Co. issued policies of fire and public liability insurance to the Roosevelt Hotel and agreed to make periodic inspections of the premises for fire hazards and conditions dangerous to guests. Marie Hill and her husband were guests at the hotel. The insurer negligently failed to find a hazard which resulted in a fire that injured Marie Hill and killed her husband. She sued the insurer for damages for her injuries and for the wrongful death of her husband.

DECISION:
U.S.F.&G. Co. was liable to Hill for the harm she sustained and for the wrongful death of her husband. Even though the only contract of the insurer was with the hotel, tort liability arises in favor of guests of the hotel since the insurer should have foreseen that negligence in performing its inspection contract with the hotel would expose the guests to serious danger. [Hill v U.S.F.&G. Co. (CA5 Fla) 428 F2d 112 (1970)]

(b) **Partial Performance.** Confusion exists in the law as to the classification to be made of conduct involved when the contracting party has entered upon the performance of the contract but omits some act or measure in consequence of which harm is sustained by a third person. The problem is the same as that involved in determining whether the negligent actor who omits a particular precaution has "acted" negligently or has been guilty of a negligent "omission." In many of the older cases, the courts denied recovery on the ground that no tort arose when a third person was injured by the breach of a contract between other persons. A modern trend allows recovery by the third person who is caused loss by the breach of a contract between others.

§ 21:10.   Tort Liability to Third Person for Improper Performance.

When one person contracts to perform a service for another person and a defective or improper performance is rendered which causes harm to a third person, such third person may sue the contractor. This is when the performance of the contract would discharge an obligation or duty which is owed to the injured plaintiff by the person dealing with the contractor. By the older rule of the contract law, only the person who had contracted for the services could sue when the services were improperly performed.[11]

FACTS:

The More-Way Development Company contracted with Link to construct a building. DeQuardo, Robinson, Crouch & Associates, Inc., were the architects who designed the building. After the building was constructed, A.E. Investment Corporation rented a part of the building. Because of the negligence of the architects, the building settled. A.E. Investment Corporation was forced to leave the building because of this condition. It then sued the architects for the economic loss sustained thereby. The architects raised the defense that they were not liable to the tenants because they did not have any contact with the tenants.

DECISION:

The absence of a direct contract with the tenant was not a defense. It was foreseeable that if the architects were negligent, their fault could cause loss to persons who were tenants in the building. Because this harm was foreseeable, the architects could be held liable to the tenants even though they had no contract with them. Moreover, the fact that the owner had accepted the building did not shield the architects from liability to third persons who foreseeably would be harmed by any negligence of the architects. [A.E. Investment Corp. v Link Builders, Inc. 62 Wis 2d 479, 214 NW2d 764 (1974)]

By the modern view, it has been held that when the seller of a house is required to give the buyer a certificate of inspection showing the absence of termites, the pest exterminator hired by the seller to make such inspection may be sued by the buyer when in fact there was substantial termite infestation although the exterminator certified that there was none, and the absence of privity of contract between the buyer and the exterminator is not a bar to such action.[12]

When the contractor fails to properly perform a contract for repairs or alterations, there is a conflict of authority as to whether the contractor is liable to a third person who is injured as the result thereof. For example, suppose that an automobile repairer negligently repairs the brakes of an automobile with the result that it does not stop in time when driven by the owner and runs into a pedestrian. Can the pedestrian sue the repairer for tort damages?

By the older view, the injured plaintiff was automatically barred because the plaintiff was not a party to the contract with the repairer. The

[11]H. Rosenblum, Inc. v Adler, 183 NJ Super 417, 444 A2d 66 (1982).
[12]Perloe v Getz Services, Inc. 163 Ga App 397, 294 SE2d 640 (1982).

modern view, however, emphasizes the fact that the person who makes a poor repair of the brakes is launching a dangerous instrumentality on the highway just as much as the manufacturer who constructs an automobile with defective brakes. Both should recognize that their negligence will expose persons on the highway to an unreasonable risk of foreseeable harm. The modern view accordingly holds the negligent repairer liable to the injured third person.

(a) **Assignment of Rights.** In instances in which it is held that a third person can not sue for the improper performance of a contract, the person harmed may frequently recover as an assignee. For example, when the owner of land hired a surveyor to survey the land, then sold it to a buyer, who resold it to another buyer, it was held that a subsequent buyer could not sue the surveyor for negligence in preparing a defective survey, but then held that the owner who hired the surveyor could assign to the subsequent buyer the owner's right under the survey contract so that the subsequent buyer could sue the surveyor as assignee of the owner,[13] with the same net result as though the subsequent buyer had been allowed to sue the surveyor as a third person injured by the surveyor's negligence.

C. MALPRACTICE LIABILITY

When is a professional, such as an attorney, a doctor, or an accountant, liable for harm caused by improper performance? Under what circumstances can third persons sue for harm?

§ 21:11.   What Constitutes Malpractice.

When an accountant, a doctor, or an attorney makes a contract to render services, there is a duty to exercise such skill and care as is common within the community for persons possessing similar skills. If the services are not rendered or not rendered properly, there is a breach of contract which is often described as malpractice.

In most instances, suit will be brought not for breach of contract but for malpractice on the theory that the breach of the contract was tortious. When suit is brought by the client or patient, a malpractice suit rather than a breach of contract suit is often selected by the plaintiff because of the possibility of recovering larger damages and because the statute of limitations runs on a malpractice claim in most instances from the date when the harm was discovered rather than from the date when there was a breach of contract. When suit is brought by a third person, and not by the patient or client, a malpractice or tort theory claim is naturally followed because the plaintiff is neither a party to the original contract nor a third party beneficiary of that contract. When suit for malpractice is brought by a third person, the principles involved are an extension of the principles discussed under § 21:10 as to tort liability to a third person for the improper performance of a contract.

[13]Essex v Ryan (Ind App) 446 NE2d 368 (1983).

§ 21:12. Attorneys.

An attorney is liable to a client for failing to exercise the care and to apply the knowledge that is reasonably expected of attorneys within the community. If the attorney is a general practitioner, the standard is stated in terms of the skill and knowledge of general practitioners. If the attorney is a specialist, as a patent attorney, a bankruptcy attorney, or a corporate securities attorney, the standard is the care and knowledge of such a specialist.

(a) **Particular Applications.** An attorney is liable for improperly abandoning a case, failing to give notice to a governmental unit within the time required for making a claim, failing to bring suit before the claim of the client is barred by the statute of limitations, and negligently investigating the title to real estate purchased by the client.

(b) **Liability to Third Persons.** The majority of states follow the common-law rule that only the client can sue the attorney for malpractice. There is a growing trend which permits third persons harmed by the attorney's negligence to sue the attorney. For example, when a lawyer is hired to draw a will leaving property to particular persons, those persons can sue the lawyer for negligence when the lawyer improperly prepares the will with the result that the third persons do not receive the property intended for them.[14] Courts are more likely to allow such third person recovery where the lawyer's negligence in planning an estate has resulted in greater taxes, where negligence in drafting a will has failed to make proper provision for the third person, or where negligence in making a title search has caused a third person to buy property with a defective title. The fact that in these cases the plaintiff is a person who is more or less within the contemplation of the contracting parties encourages the courts to depart from the privity of contract requirement.

§ 21:13. Medical Doctors.

The malpractice liability of a doctor is governed by the same principles as apply to attorneys. The doctor must follow the standards of practice within the local medical community. If the doctor claims special skill, the standard is then elevated to the exercise of the skill of such a specialist.

(a) **Particular Applications.** A doctor is liable for malpractice when, because of failing to observe the required standards, the doctor fails to properly diagnose the patient's condition, fails to prescribe the proper treatment or medicines, or fails to be attentive to dangerous side effects of the medicine prescribed for the patient. A doctor is liable to a patient for failing to inform the patient of the dangers of a particular treatment or operation, to which the patient consents without being fully informed of the dangers, if the patient then sustains harm because of the undisclosed risks.

(b) **Liability to Third Persons.** Ordinarily the negligence of a doctor does not cause harm to a third person, so that the question of liability to a third person does not arise in the ordinary medical malpractice suit.

[14]Guy v Liederbach, 501 Pa 47, 459 A2d 744 (1983).

There are a few instances, however, in which the right of a third person to recover is well established. If the malpractice of the doctor causes the patient's death, a surviving spouse, child, or parent of the patient may bring an action against the doctor for wrongful death. When the patient does not die but is so seriously disabled that the spouse of the patient has lost the companionship of the patient, at least temporarily, an action may generally be brought by the deprived spouse for the loss of consortium.

A psychotherapist who has reason to believe that a patient will commit a crime against a third person must warn the intended victim and the police and take whatever steps are reasonably necessary to prevent harm.

§ 21:14.   Accountants.

Accountants are liable to their clients when loss is caused the clients because the accountants failed to observe the standards of sound accounting practices and the clients sustain loss or fail to prevent loss because of such malpractice. Basically the concept is the same as is applied to doctors and attorneys.

(a) Particular Applications. An accountant is liable to the client when the accountant negligently fails to detect or fraudulently conceals signs that an employee of the client is embezzling from the client or that the internal audit controls of the client's business are not being observed. An accountant who prepares tax returns and acts as tax manager for the client will be liable when negligently given advice results in additional taxes or penalties being assessed against the client.

(b) Liability to Third Persons. An accountant's liability has been expanded in some situations to include not only the client, but third persons as well.

(1) Common Law. At the beginning of this century, the general American rule was that only the client could sue an accountant for malpractice.[15] In many states, this rule has been abandoned and third persons may sue the accountant when the fraud or negligence of the accountant causes loss to a third party.

When it was foreseen or was within the contemplation of the accountant and the client that a third person would rely on the work of the accountant, there is a greater probability that suit by a third person will be allowed. For example, where the accountant knows that the balance sheet requested by the client is to be shown to a bank from which the client seeks to obtain a loan or to a prospective buyer of the client's business, recovery by the bank or the prospective buyer will probably be allowed because the court does not fear that, in allowing such a third person to sue, it is opening the door to thousands of lawsuits.

---

[15]Ultramares Corp. v Touche, Niven & Co. 255 NY 170, 174 NE 441 (1931). The New York requirement of privity has been slightly relaxed by permitting the third person to sue the accountant for negligence when there have been direct dealings between the third person and the accountant, as when the borrower's accountant and a lender discussed what information was required as to the borrower's financial status in order to obtain a loan. Credit Alliance Corp. v Arthur Andersen & Co. 65 NY2d 536, 483 NE2d 110 (1985).

FACTS:

A certified public accounting partnership of James, Guinn and Head prepared a certified audit report of four corporations, known as the Paschal Enterprises, with knowledge that their report would be used to induce Shatterproof Glass Corporation to lend money to those corporations. The report showed the corporations to be solvent when in fact they were insolvent. Shatterproof relied upon the audit report and loaned approximately one half million dollars to the four corporations and lost almost all of it because the liabilities of the companies were in excess of their assets. Shatterproof claimed that James and the other accountants had been negliegent in preparing the report and sued them to recover the loss on the loan. The accountants raised the defense that they had not been retained by the plaintiff and had instead been retained by Paschal.

DECISION:

The fact that Shatterproof was not the client of the accountants did not bar Shatterproof from suing the accountants for malpractice. To the contrary, the rule to follow is that when an accountant fails to exercise ordinary care in the preparation of statements on which third persons rely, such third persons may recover their loss from the accountant where the reliance of such third persons was foreseeable or expected. [Shatterproof Glass Corporation v James (Tex Civ App) 466 SW2d 873 (1971)]

When accountants make a false financial statement for a corporate client with knowledge that it will be used in selling securities of the corporation to third persons, such third persons may sue the accountant for the damages sustained. Thus, the accountant has been held liable for disguising the true character of a hoped-for profit from the sale and resale of real estate by describing it as "deferred income," although there was little reason to believe that the transaction could ever be completed; because the buyer, who was obligated to pay $5 million for the property, had assets of only $100,000 and the financial statement would have shown a loss instead of a substantial profit if the true character of the transaction had been disclosed. Likewise, it has been held that an accountant negligently preparing a financial statement for a corporate client is liable to purchaser of the stock and lenders of money to the corporation who have relied on the statement prepared by the accountant and sustained loss because of its errors.[16]

Even though reliance on the accountant's work by third persons is foreseeable, many courts refuse to allow a malpractice suit to be brought by a third person whose identity was not known to the accountant. For example, it has been held that where the accountant prepared a financial statement for a contemplated sale to A but the sale was actually made to an unknown B, a malpractice suit could not be brought by B against the accountant.

The fact that an accountant was acting as an independent auditor rather than as an accountant acting for its client has been a factor in some

[16]Citizens State Bank v Timm, Schmidt & Co. 113 Wis 2d 376, 335 NW2d 361 (1983).

cases to impose liability on the accountant to third persons. The rationale is that when the accountant acts as an independent auditor it is reasonable to foresee that third persons, such as investors and lenders, will be relying on the financial statement prepared by the accountant and therefore the accountant if negligent should be held liable to such third persons for the loss caused them, without regard to the absence of privity of contract between the third persons and the accountant.[17]

(2) *Federal Legislation.* The malpractice liability of accountants to third persons has been broadened by the federal regulation of the sale of securities. A person purchasing a security on the basis of false information supplied or certified by an accountant may recover damages from the accountant who fraudulently prepared such information.

An accountant fraudulently certifying to nonexisting values may be held liable to an investor. The accountant may be held liable for failing to detect false entries in the client's records. Under the federal legislation, the accountant has a duty to protect investors from statements which are misleading even though they are true. Thus, liability may be imposed upon an accountant for certifying a statement showing an investment carried at book value when this was much greater than the actual market value. Again, an accountant has been held liable to stockholders for approving information in a statement prepared to show to sellers in which assets were carried at historical or original cost although the current value was greatly in excess. Liability of an accountant to the purchaser of a security may be based on the theory that the accountant aided and abetted the actual perpetrator of a stock fraud.

Liability of an accountant is narrower under the federal law than under state law. Under the federal law, liability cannot be based on negligence. In addition to the falsity of the statements made by the accountant, it must be shown that the accountant acted fraudulently in making the statement or in failing to detect the fraud of others.[18] Because fraudulent intent is required, an accountant is not liable to the purchaser of corporate securities when the accountant was negligent in failing to use appropriate auditing procedures and thereby failed to discover internal accounting practices of the corporate client which prevented the making of an effective audit.[19]

§ 21:15. Architects.

Architects are subject to tort liability for malpractice both with respect to the other contracting party and with respect to third persons harmed by their negligence.

(a) **Particular Applications.** When the negligence of the designing or supervising architect has created an unsafe or defective building, the other contracting party is entitled to recover damages for such negligence. The

---

[17]H. Rosenblum, Inc. v Adler, 93 NJ 324, 461 A2d 138 (1983).

[18]An accountant is liable under the federal statutes for making a fraudulent, false, or deceptive statement in a registration statement which is filed with the Securities and Exchange Commission when a new security is issued, Act of 1933 § 11(a), 15 USC § 77k(a). The accountant is also liable for such statements in any document filed with the Securities and Exchange Commission. Securities and Exchange Commission Act of 1934, § 18, 15 USC § 78r.

[19]Ernst & Ernst v Hochfelder, 425 US 185 (1976).

measure of damage is the same as in the case of the substantial performance of contracts. If the defective condition can be reasonably repaired or corrected, the damage is the cost of such repair. If the cost of repairing would be excessive or require a substantial rebuilding of the building, the measure of damages is the difference between the value of the building as constructed and the value that the building would have had if the contractor had not been negligent.[20]

(b) **Liability to Third Persons.** When the negligence of the architect in the performance of the contract with the owner causes harm to third persons, such third persons can sue the architect for damages when it was reasonably foreseeable that such third persons could be harmed as the result of the negligence of the architect. Thus an architect negligently preparing an inspection report on the condition of the building is liable to the buyer who sustains loss by purchasing the building on the basis that its condition was good, as stated in the report, when, in fact it was not.

Courts are particularly likely to allow suit by the third person when personal injuries are sustained as a result of the architect's negligence which created a very dangerous condition. For example, where the architect negligently designed an airport building so that the jet blast from aircraft could injure persons on the building ramp, the architect was liable to a person injured by a jet blast.[21]

SUMMARY

When a party fails to perform a contract or performs improperly, the other contracting party may sue for damages caused by such person. What may be recovered by the aggrieved person is stated in terms of being direct or consequential damages. Direct damages are those which ordinarily will result from the breach. Consequential damages are those which are in fact caused by the breach but do not ordinarily or necessarily result from every breach of the particular kind of contract. Direct damages may be recovered on proof of causation and amount. Consequential damages can only be recovered if in addition to causation and amount it is shown that they were reasonably within the contemplation of the contracting parties as a probable result of a breach of the contract. The right to recover consequential damages is lost if the aggrieved party could reasonably have taken steps to avoid such damages. That is, the aggrieved person has a duty to mitigate or reduce damages by reasonable means.

In any case, the damages recoverable for breach of contract may be limited to a specific amount by a liquidated damage clause or may be canceled out completely by a limitation of liability clause. A liquidated damage clause is valid when the circumstances are such that the actual damages can not be reasonably determined and the amount specified is not unreasonably disproportionate to the damages that could be caused by a breach of the contract. If both of these conditions are satisfied, the liquidated damage

[20]Rosos Litho Supply Corp. v Hansen, 123 Ill 290 App 3d, 78 Ill Dec 447, 462 NE2d 566 (1984).
[21]Hiatt v Brown (Ind App) 422 NE2d 736 (1981).

clause is valid and the injured party recovers the specified amount and can not recover any greater amount. If both conditions are not satisfied, the liquidated damage clause is held invalid as imposing a penalty and damages are recovered as though the clause never existed. A clause limiting (excluding) liability for harm caused by the conduct of third persons is valid. When the cause of the harm has been the negligence or the willful misconduct of the person protected by the clause, the limitation is frequently held invalid. Limitations of liability are often held invalid when the effect is to allow a contracting party to evade a duty imposed by law or when there is such a bargaining inequality between the parties as to make the limitation appear unconscionable.

In a limited number of situations, the aggrieved party may bring an action for specific performance to compel the other contracting party to perform the acts called for by the contract. Specific performance is always obtainable of a contract to sell land or real estate on the theory that such property has a unique value. With respect to other contracts, specific performance will not be ordered unless it is shown that there was some unique element present so that the aggrieved person would suffer a damage that could not be compensated for by the payment of money damages.

The aggrieved person also has the option of rescinding the contract if (1) the breach has been as to a material term and (2) the aggrieved party returns everything to the way that it was before the contract was made. Rescission and recovery of money damages are alternative remedies except when the contract relates to the sale of goods. In the latter case, the aggrieved party may both rescind and obtain money damages.

Although there has been a breach of the contract, the effect of this breach is nullified if the aggrieved person by word or conduct waives the right to object to the breach. Conversely, an aggrieved party may accept a defective performance without thereby waiving a claim for breach if the party makes a reservation of rights as by stating that the defective performance is accepted without prejudice, under protest, or with reservation of rights.

The continued waiver of a breach of a particular clause may indicate that the parties have modified their contract by abandoning the clause to which the waiver relates. To guard against the unintended modification of a contract by waiver, the contract may contain a clause stating that nothing shall constitute a modification of the contract unless stated in writing. Such a clause, however, may itself be waived.

At times an oral contract is made and then a written contract is executed but contains some error so that the writing is not an accurate statement of the oral contract. If this can be proven to the satisfaction of the court, the written contract may be reformed or corrected by the court to state what was said by the original oral contract.

When a party to a contract fails to perform the contract he can generally not be sued by a third person even though such third person was harmed by the defendant's breach. Contrary to this general rule, the third person is allowed to sue when the defendant failed to do an act that was required of the other contracting party by virtue of a duty owed to the third person or to the general public. In such case, the defendant's failure to perform the duty imposed on the other contracting party makes the defendant liable to the persons to whom such duty was owed and the defendant must compensate them for the loss caused by the non-performance.

When the third person is injured because of the improper way in which the defendant has performed the contract, the older rule denied liability, but the modern view imposes liability. Such "malpractice" liability as to third persons is typically limited to those who would be foreseeably harmed by such improper performance. Malpractice liability to third persons is imposed by the modern view on lawyers, doctors, accountants, and architects. The liability of accountants to third persons is modified by federal law. If the accountant acted fraudulently, the accountant is liable to a person purchasing a security on the basis of false information supplied or certified by an accountant.

QUESTIONS AND CASE PROBLEMS

1. What social forces are affected by the rule as to the mitigation of damages?
2. When must a party to a contract mitigate damages caused by the breach of the contract by the other party?
3. Anthony makes a contract to sell a rare painting to Laura for $100,000. The written contract specifies that if Anthony should fail to perform the contract he will pay to Laura $50,000 as liquidated damages. Anthony fails to deliver the painting and is sued by Laura for $50,000. Can she recover this amount?
4. Hogarth owned a factory which used coal for heat and power. He purchased grade A coal from Kay who owned a coal mine. When one of the truckloads of coal was delivered to Hogarth, it was apparent that there was a large quantity of wood and slate mixed in with the coal. Hogarth would have been within his rights if he had rejected the coal as not conforming to the contract but he needed the coal desperately to keep the furnaces in his factory from going out. He therefore accepted the coal in spite of its defect but expressly stated that he accepted it with a reservation of rights. Kay billed Hogarth for the full price of grade A coal. Hogarth claimed that Kay should reduce the price because of the inferior quality. Kay claimed that Hogarth was not entitled to any reduction. Kay further claimed that Hogarth had had the choice only of rejecting the coal because it was poor or of accepting the coal and paying for it at the contract price. Was Kay correct?
5. Matthew is a certified public accountant. He prepared a balance sheet statement for the Stanley Corporation which Matthew knew would be used by Stanley to obtain a loan from the Third National Bank. In order to satisfy Stanley, Matthew prepared the statement in such a way that the false impression was created that Stanley was a thriving, prosperous corporation. If the statement had been prepared in accordance with standard accounting procedures, it would have shown that Stanley was just about to become insolvent. The Third National Bank, relying on this financial statement, loaned money to Stanley. Shortly thereafter, Stanley went into bankruptcy and the Third National Bank lost virtually the full amount of the loan. The bank sued Matthew for the loss. Matthew as-

serted that he could not be sued by a third person as his only duty was to his client, the Stanley Corporation. Is this a valid defense?

6. *A,* who had contracted to build a house for *B,* departed from the specifications at a number of points. It would cost approximately $1,000 to put the house in the condition called for by the contract. *B* sued *A* for $5,000 for breach of contract and emotional disturbance caused by the breach. Decide.

7. Samari Brothers built an office building for the Pierce Corporation. Pierce rented one of the first floor stores of the building to Byron. Because of defective construction work, there were water leaks into Byron's store. Byron sued Samari for the damage caused to her inventory by such leaks. Samari denied liability on the ground that the building had been approved by the architect and accepted by the Pierce Corporation and therefore a third person, such as Byron, could not bring suit against Samari, as Byron was merely an incidental beneficiary of the contract between Samari and Pierce. Is this a valid defense?

8. Compare the malpractice liability of accountants and doctors.

9. Protein Blenders, Inc., made a contract with Gingerich to buy from him the shares of stock of a small corporation. When the buyer refused to take and pay for the stock, Gingerich sued for specific performance on the contract on the ground that the value of the stock was unknown and could not be readily ascertained because it was not sold on the general market. Was he entitled to specific performance? [Gingerich v Protein Blenders, Inc. 250 Iowa 646, 95 NW2d 522]

10. The buyer of real estate made a down payment. In the contract it was stated that the buyer would be liable for damages in an amount equal to the down payment if the buyer broke the contract. The buyer refused to go through with the contract and demanded his down payment back. The seller refused to return it and claimed that he was entitled to additional damages from the buyer because the damages which he had suffered were greater than the amount of the down payment. Decide. [Waters v Key Colony East, Inc. (Fla App) 345 So2d 367]

11. Kuznicki made a contract for the installation of a fire detection system by Security Safety Corp. for $498. The contract was made one night and canceled at 9:00 a.m. the next morning. Security then claimed one third of the purchase price from Kuznicki by virtue of a provision in the contract that "in the event of cancellation of this agreement . . . the owner agrees to pay 33-1/3 percent of the contract price, as liquidated damages." Was Security Safety entitled to recover the amount claimed? [Security Safety Corp. v Kuznicki, 350 Mass 157, 213 NE2d 866]

12. Stabler was under contract to play professional football for Alabama Football, Inc. The corporation was not able to pay Stabler the amount due him under the contract. He sued for rescission. The club defended on the theory that nonpayment was not a sufficiently substantial breach of the contract to justify rescission. Was the club correct? [Alabama Football, Inc. v Stabler, 294 Ala 551, 319 So2d 678]

13. Melodee Lane Lingerie Co. was a tenant in a building that was protected against fire by a sprinkler and alarm system maintained by the American District Telegraph Co. Because of the latter's fault, the controls on the

system were defective and allowed the discharge of water into the building, which damaged Melodee's property. When Melodee sued A.D.T., it raised the defense that its service contract limited its liability to 10 percent of the annual service charge made to the customer. Was this limitation valid? [Melodee Lane Lingerie Co. v American District Telegraph Co. 18 NY2d 57, 271 NYS2d 937, 218 NE2d 661]

14. A owned a house. In May he made a contract with B, a roofer, to repair the roof on the house by July 1. B never came to repair the roof and heavy rains in the fall damaged the interior of A's house. A sues B for breach of contract and claims damages for the harm done to the interior of the house. Is A entitled to recover such damages?

15. Compare the purpose, effect, and validity of a liquidated damage clause and a limitation of liability clause.

16. Lowell Prentice wanted to sell his farm, house, and land. After negotiation with Charles Classen, who wanted the property to operate a dairy, the price was agreed to as $45,000. Classen signed a contract for the purchase of the land. Under the contract, Classen made an initial deposit of 10% of the purchase price and he was required to pay the balance in specified installments with 8% interest. The contract stated that if the buyer broke the contract, the seller could retain the initial payment of 10% and all improvements that had been made to the property by the buyer. Classen moved into the farmhouse with his family and lived for the next year, during which time he improved the property by adding dairy equipment, a bulk tank, and cement floors in the dairy building. After a year, Classen failed to make necessary payments and Prentice declared him in default. Classen claimed he was entitled to a refund of the initial 10% payment. He claimed that the contract provision allowing Prentice to retain this amount was unconscionable and void. Was he correct? [Prentice v Classen (SD) 355 NW2d 352]

17. Air-Speed, Inc. retained Hansman to obtain insurance to cover workers' compensation payments for its employees. Hansman notified Air-Speed that the insurance had been obtained. In fact it was not because Hansman negligently did not forward the premiums to the insurance company to pay for the insurance. Thomas Rae was an employee of Air-Speed. He was killed in the course of his employment. His wife Christine was appointed as administratrix of his estate. She sued Air-Speed and Hansman for the payments that would have been received under a workers' compensation insurance policy if one had been obtained. Hansman denied liability on the ground that he had not made any contract with Christine to obtain insurance. Was this defense valid? [Rae v Air-Speed, Inc. 386 Mass 167, 435 NE2d 628]

PART 3

PERSONAL PROPERTY AND BAILMENTS

Chapter 22 Personal Property
Chapter 23 Bailments
Chapter 24 Special Bailments and Documents of Title

CHAPTER 22

PERSONAL PROPERTY

CHAPTER OBJECTIVES

After studying this chapter you will be able to:
1. Write a definition of personal property.
2. Differentiate between patents, copyrights, trademarks, and trade secrets.
3. List and explain the various types of gifts.
4. Identify the four forms of multiple ownership of personal property.
5. Set forth the remedies for violations of property rights.

Property includes the rights of any person to possess, use, enjoy, and dispose of a thing or object of value. Property is classified as real property and personal property. **Real property** means land and things permanently affixed to land, such as trees or buildings. **Personal property** includes all other property. This chapter develops the law of personal property, setting forth (1) the basic legal principles of personal property, (2) how title to personal property is acquired, and (3) the law concerning multiple owners of specific personal property.

A. GENERAL PRINCIPLES

In common usage, the term "property" refers to a piece of land or a thing or an object. As a legal concept, however, "property" refers to the rights that an individual may possess in that piece of land or that thing or that object.[1] A right in a thing is property, without regard to whether such right is absolute or conditional, perfect or imperfect, legal or equitable.

[1]Virginia Marine Resources Commission v Forbes, 214 Va 109, 197 SE2d 195 (1973).

381

§ 22:1.   Personal Property.

Personal property consists of: (a) whole or fractional rights in things which are tangible and movable, such as furniture and books; (b) claims and debts, which are called **choses in action;** and (c) intangible proprietary rights, such as trademarks, copyrights, and patents.

The concept of personal property is expanding. For example, courts now generally include gas and water within the definition of "property." Thus persons who tap water mains and gas pipes and so obtain water and gas without paying are guilty of taking property.

The modern techniques of sound and image recording have led to the necessity of giving protection against copying and competition. Federal and state statutes provide for the copyright protection of musical compositions and create crimes of record and tape piracy.[2]

The theft of papers on which computer programs are written is larceny or "theft of property" under a statute which defines "property" as including "all writings, of every description, provided such property possesses any ascertainable value," even though the exact value cannot be determined.

§ 22:2.   Limitations on Ownership.

A person who has all possible rights in and over a thing is said to have **absolute ownership** of it. The term, "absolute," however, is somewhat misleading, for one's rights in respect to the use, enjoyment, and disposal of things are subject to certain restrictions. An owner's property is subject to the government's powers to tax, to regulate under the police power, and to take by eminent domain. It is subject to the creditors of the owner. Above all, the owner may not use property in a way that will unreasonably injure others.

B. ACQUIRING TITLE TO AND PROTECTION OF PERSONAL PROPERTY

Title to personal property may be acquired in different ways. For example, property is commonly purchased, and the purchase and sale of goods is governed by the law of "sales" and covered in Part 4 of this book. Property rights in trademarks, copyrights, and patents are acquired as provided by federal statutes, and the nature and extent of their legal protection will be covered in this chapter. The following methods of acquiring personal property will also be discussed: accession, gifts, lost property, transfer by a nonowner, occupation, and escheat.

§ 22:3.   Trademarks and Servicemarks.

A **mark** is any word, name, symbol, or design, or a combination of these used to identify a product or service.[3] If the mark identifies a product, such as an automobile or soap, it is called a **trademark.** If it identifies a service, such as a restaurant or clothes cleaner, it is called a **servicemark.**

---

[2]PL 92-140, 85 Stat 391, 17 United States Code §§ 1, 5, 20, 101; Pennsylvania, Act of January 10, 1972, PL 872, 18 PS § 1878.1.

[3]15 USC § 1127; Safeway Stores, Inc. v Safeway Discount Drugs, Inc. (CA11 Fla) 675 F2d 1160 (1982). See also Trademark Clarification Act of 1984, PL 98-620, 98 Stat 333.

The owner of a mark may obtain protection from its use by others by registering the mark in accordance with federal law.[4] The critical requirement for registration is that the mark distinguish the goods or service of the applicant from those of others. Under the federal statute, a register, called the Principal Register, is maintained for the recording of such marks. Registration on the Principal Register grants the registrant the exclusive right to use the mark. Challenges may be made to the registrant's rights within five years of registration; but after five years, the rights of the registrant are incontestable.

(a) **Registrable Marks.** Marks which are coined, completely fanciful, or arbitrary are capable of registration on the Principal Register. The mark "Exxon," for example, was coined by the owners. The name "Kodak" is also a creation of the owners of this trademark, has no other meaning in our language, and obviously serves to distinguish the goods of its owners from all others.

A suggestive term may also be registered. Such a term suggests rather than describes some characteristics of the goods to which it applies and requires the consumer to exercise some imagination to reach a conclusion as to the nature of the goods. For example, as a trademark for refrigerators, the term "Penguin" would be suggestive. As a trademark for paperback books, the term "Penguin" is arbitrary and fanciful.

Ordinarily, descriptive terms, surnames, and geographical terms are not registrable on the Principal Register.[5] A descriptive term identifies a characteristic or quality of an article or service, such as color, odor, function, or use.[6] Thus, "Cough Calmers" was held not to be registrable on the Principal Register because it was merely descriptive of the goods normally called cough drops. However, an exception is made where a descriptive or geographic term or a surname has acquired a **secondary meaning**; and such a mark is registrable. A term or terms which have a primary meaning of their own acquire a secondary meaning when, through long use in connection with a particular product, they have come to be known by the public at large as identifying the particular product and its origin.[7] For example, the geographic term, "Philadelphia" has acquired a secondary meaning as applied to cream cheese, and is widely accepted by the public as denoting a particular brand, rather than any cream cheese made in Philadelphia. Factors considered by a court in determining whether a trade mark has acquired secondary meaning are the amount and manner of advertising, volume of sales, and length and manner of use, direct consumer testimony, and consumer surveys.

Generic terms which designate a kind or class of goods, such as "cola" or "rosé wine," are never registrable.

(b) **Injunction Against Improper Use of Mark.** A person who has the right to use a mark may enjoin a competitor from imitating or duplicating the

---

[4]Lanham Act, 15 USC §§ 1050-1127.
[5]A Supplemental Register exists for recording such marks. This recording does not give the registrant any protection but it provides a source to which other persons designing a mark can go to make sure they are not duplicating an existing mark.
[6]Soweco Inc. v Shell Oil Co. (CA5 Tex) 617 F2d 1178 (1980).
[7]Volkswagen v Richard (CA5 Tex) 492 F2d 474 (1974).

mark. The basic question in such litigation is whether the general public is likely to be confused by the mark of the defendant and to wrongly believe that it identifies the plaintiff. If there is this danger of confusion, the court will enjoin the defendant from using the particular mark.

FACTS:

The University of Georgia Athletic Association brought suit against beer wholesaler Bill Laite, for marketing "Battlin' Bulldog Beer," claiming that the cans infringed on its symbol for its athletic teams. The UGAA's symbol, which depicted an English Bulldog wearing a sweater with a "G" and the word "BULLDOGS" emblazoned on it, had been registered as a servicemark. Soon after the beer appeared on the market, the University received telephone calls from friends of the University, who were concerned that Battlin' Bulldog Beer was not the sort of product which should in any way be related to the University of Georgia. The University's suit was based on the theory of false designation of origin in violation of the Lanham Act. Laite contended that there was no likelihood of confusion because his bulldog was different than the University's and his cans bore the disclaimer "Not associated with the University of Georgia."

DECISION:

Judgment for the University. Although not identical, the similarity of the design between the "Battlin Bulldog" and the "University of Georgia Bulldog" supports the determination that there is a likelihood of confusion between the marks. Also significant was the determination that the defendant's intent in designing his mark was to capitalize on the popularity of the UGAA football program to sell his beer. While the defendant did place a disclaimer on the can, it was relatively inconspicuous on an individual can and was not visible on a six-pack. [University of Georgia Athletic Association v Laite (CA 11 Ga) 756 F2d 1535 (1985)]

In some cases, the fact that the products of the plaintiff and the defendant did not compete in the same market was held to entitle the defendant to use a mark which would have been prohibited as confusingly similar if the defendant manufactured the same product as the plaintiff. For example, it has been held that Cadillac as applied to boats is not confusingly similar to Cadillac as applied to automobiles and therefore its use cannot be enjoined.[8]

(c) **Abandonment of Exclusive Rights to Mark.** An owner who has an exclusive right to use a mark may lose that right. If other persons are permitted to use the mark, it loses its exclusive character and is said to pass into the English language and become generic. Examples of formerly enforceable marks which have made this transition into the general language are aspirin, thermos, cellophane, and shredded wheat.

---

[8]General Motors Corporation v Cadillac Marine and Boat Co. 140 USPQ 447 (1964). See also Amstar Corp. v Domino's Pizza Inc. (CA5 Ga) 615 F2d 252 (1980), where the mark Domino as applied to pizza was held not to be confusingly similar to Domino as applied to sugar.

§ 22:4.   Copyrights.

A **copyright** is the exclusive right given by federal statute to the creator of a literary or artistic work to use, reproduce, or display the work. By international treaties, copyrights given under the laws of one nation are generally recognized in another. Works produced in this country for export to foreign countries that have ratified the Universal Copyright Convention may use the internationally accepted copyright symbol © in place of or in addition to the word "copyright" or its abbreviation.

A copyright does not prevent the copying of an idea but only the copying of the way the idea is expressed.[9] That is, the copyright is violated when there is a duplicating of the words or the pictures of the creator but not when there is merely a copying of the idea which those words or pictures express.

(a) **What is Copyrightable.** Copyrights protect literary, musical, dramatic, and artistic work. Protected are books and periodicals; musical and dramatic compositions; choreographic works; maps; works of art, such as paintings, sculptures, and photographs; motion pictures and other audiovisual works; sound recordings; and computer programs, as will be discussed in § 22:7.

(b) **Unpublished Work.** As long as a work is not made public, it has the same protection as though it had been copyrighted. But once it is made public, anyone can use or copy it if it has not been copyrighted.

(c) **Duration of Copyright.** A copyright lasts for the life of the creator of the work and for fifty years after the creator's death.[10] After a copyright has expired, the work is in the public domain and may be used by anyone without cost.

(d) **Limitations on Exclusive Character of Copyright.** A limitation on the exclusive rights of copyright owners exists under the principle of "fair use," which allows for the limited usage of copyrighted material in connection with criticism, news reporting, teaching, and research. Two important factors in judging if the usage is a fair use are: (1) the amount of text used in relation to the copyrighted work as a whole and (2) the effect of the use on the value of the work.[11]

FACTS:

Sony Corporation manufactures video cassette recorders (VCR's) to tape television shows for home viewing, and sells them under the trade name Betamax through retail establishments throughout the country. Universal City Studios and Walt Disney Productions own the copyrights on some of the television programs that are broadcast on public airwaves. Universal and Disney brought an action against Sony and certain large retailers contending that VCR consumers had been recording some of their copyrighted works that had been shown on commercially sponsored television and thereby infringed on these copyrights. These plaintiffs sought damages and an injunction against the manufacture and marketing of VCR's. Sony contended that the noncommercial home use recording of material broadcast over public airwaves was a "fair use" of copyrighted works.

[9]Atari, Inc. v North American Philips Consumer Electronics Corp., (CA7 Ill) 672 F2d 607 (1982).
[10]Copyrights Act of 1976, § 302(a), 17 USC § 302(a).
[11]Copyrights Act of 1976, § 107, 17 USC § 107.

DECISION:

Judgment for Sony. The Studios failed to demonstrate that time-shifting would cause a likelihood of harm to the value of their copyrighted works. The concept of "fair use" requires that the copyright holder demonstrate some likelihood of economic harm before it may condemn a private act of time-shifting as a violation of copyright law. [Sony Corp v Universal Studios, 464 US 417 (1984)]

§ 22:5. Patents.

A **patent** is the exclusive right which the inventor of a device can obtain by filing an application under federal law. The patent gives the inventor an exclusive right to make, use, and sell the thing invented for 17 years. These rights cannot be defeated by the improper combination of components outside the United States for sale in global markets. United States suppliers of components of a patented invention who actively induce the combination of components outside the United States in a manner that would infringe the patent if the activity occurred in the United States are liable as infringers under the Patent Law Amendments Act of 1984.[12] At the end of 17 years the patent expires and cannot be renewed.

If a patent is not obtained or if the patent has expired, anyone may make, use, or sell the invention without permission of the inventor and without making any payment therefor.

(a) **What Is Patentable.** In order to be patentable, the invention must be something which is new and useful and must be something which would not have been obvious to a person of ordinary skill or knowledge in the art or technology to which the invention is related.[13]

It is the thing which is patented: whether it be a machine, a process, or a particular chemical composition of matter. The idea or inspiration, ways of doing business, and scientific principles cannot be patented unless there is some physical thing which is based upon them. Patent law has been interpreted to permit the patenting of human-made life forms.

FACTS:

Chakrabarty was a microbiologist. He found a way of creating a bacteria that would break down crude oil. This could not be done by any bacteria that exists naturally. His discovery had a great potential for cleaning oil spills. When he applied for a patent for this process, the Commissioner of Patents refused to grant it on the ground that what he had done was not a "manufacture" or "composition of matter" within the meaning of the federal statute and because a patent could not be obtained on something that was living. Chakrabarty appealed.

DECISION:

Judgment for Chakrabarty. Discovering a way to produce a living organism that is not found in nature is within the protection of the patent laws. The fact that this kind of invention was not known when the patent laws were first adopted has no effect on the decision because the laws are to be interpreted according to the facts existing when an application for a patent is made. [Diamond v Chakrabarty, 447 US 303 (1980)]

[12]PL 98-622, 98 Stat 3383, 35 USC 361.
[13]35 USC §§ 101, 102, 103, Park-Ohio Industries, Inc. v Letica Corp. (CA6 Mich) 617 F2d 450 (1980).

(b) Contractual Protection of Inventions. Frequently an employee will invent a patentable device during working hours or use the employer's equipment and materials. To protect the employer in such situations, employment contracts commonly provide that any invention relating to the employer's business which is discovered by the employee while still an employee or during the first one or two years after leaving the employment shall be assigned to the employer. Such provisions are generally held valid, although a provision requiring the assignment of all inventions whether or not related to the employer's business has been held contrary to public policy and therefore invalid.

§ 22:6.   Secret Business Information.

A business may have developed a fund of information which is not generally known but which cannot be patented or copyrighted under federal law. As long as such information is kept secret it will be protected under state law relating to trade secrets.

(a) Trade Secrets. A trade secret may consist of any formula, device, or compilation of information which is used in one's business, which is of such a nature that it gives an advantage over competitors who do not have such information. It may be a formula for a chemical compound; a process of manufacturing, treating, or preserving materials; or a list of customers.[14]

(b) Loss of Protection by Publication. When secret business information is made public it loses the protection it had while secret. Such loss of protection by publication occurs when the information is made known without any restrictions. In contrast, there is no loss of protection when secret information is shared or communicated for a special purpose and the person receiving the information knows that it is not to be made public.

§ 22:7.   Protection for Computer Programs.

Computer programs may be protected by copyright law, patent law, trade secrecy laws, and contract law. Difficulties exist, however, in the application of these traditional legal theories to the new technology of computer programming.

(a) Copyrights. Under the Computer Software Copyright Act of 1980[15] computer programs, including program instructions in machine or symbolic languages, now receive the same protection as the other works of authorship covered by the Copyright Act of 1976. Thus, if the owner utilizes the proper copyright notice, the copyright will protect the actual text of the program. It should be remembered that a copyright does not prevent the copying of the basic ideas found in the copyrighted work, but only the way the idea is expressed. Because of the possibility that the underlying ideas of a computer program may be used by competitors, many computer program developers seek protection for their programs through other legal means.

(b) Patents. The extent to which computer programs can be patented is not settled. Many programs are not patentable because they con-

---

[14]Restatement of Torts § 757, comment b; Kewanee Oil Co. v Bicron Corp. 416 US 470 (1974).
[15]PL 96-517, 17 USC §§ 101 and 117.

tain mathematical formulas, and the courts are reluctant to grant a monopoly on a method of solving a mathematical problem since such are the basic tools of scientific work.[16] Patents have been granted for computer programs, however. For example, a method of using a computer to carry out translations from one language to another was held to be patentable.[17] Developers of computer programs often will not attempt to obtain a patent because, once a patent is obtained, the program is available for public inspection at the U.S. Patent Office. Should the program be improperly used by the public, detection of the infringement may be difficult.

(c) **Trade Secrets.** Trade secrecy is widely used in the computer industry to protect computer programs. There are no time limitations on the protection of trade secrets, as exist with patents and copyrights. Also, there is no necessity for filing and disclosure as is required by the patent and copyright laws.

FACTS:

Aries Information Systems, Inc. (Aries), develops and markets computer software. One of Aries principal products is the POBAS III accounting program. Pacific Management Systems Corporation (Pacific) was organized in March 1980 by Scott Dahmer, John Laugan, and Roman Rowan for the purpose of marketing a financial accounting and budgeting system known as FAMIS. Dahmer, Laugan, and Rowan were Aries employees before, during, and shortly after they organized Pacific. As employees, they each gained access to Aries' software materials and had information about Aries' existing and prospective clients. Proprietary notices appeared on every client contract, source code list, and magnetic tape. Dahmer, Laugan, and Rowan each signed an "Employee Confidential Information Agreement" after beginning employment with Aries. Dahmer, Laugan, and Rowan while still employees of Aries submitted a bid on behalf of Pacific to Rock County and were awarded the contract. Pacific's FAMIS software system is substantially identical to Aries' proprietary POBAS III system. Aries sued Pacific to recover damages for misappropriation of its trade secrets.

DECISION:

Judgment for Aries. Aries could assert that POBAS III was a trade secret because it took reasonable efforts to maintain the secrecy of the system. The greatest exposure arose from its own employees, and it took reasonable steps to maintain secrecy by having employees sign confidentiality agreements. These agreements put Dahmer, Laugan, and Rowan on notice that all Aries information was confidential. [Aries Information Systems, Inc. v Pacific Management Systems Corp. (Minn App) 366 NW2d 366 (1985)]

---

[16]Gottschalk v Benson, 409 US 63 (1972); Parker v Flook, 437 US 584 (1978). But see Diamond v Diehr, 450 US 175 (1981), where a computerized process for curing rubber was held to be patentable, even though the process was based on a mathematical formula, since the inventor did not seek to prevent all others from using the formula, but only to prevent the use of the formula in conjunction with the other steps in his rubber curing process.
[17]In re Toma, (CCPA) 575 F2d 872 (1978).

(d) **Contracts.** Where the owner of a computer program desires to sell or lease the program to others, such use is usually controlled by a contract between the owner and customer. Owners also may choose to copyright their programs in order to give notice to third parties who may have innocently received the program.

Owners and developers of computer software commonly utilize noncompetition agreements and nondisclosure agreements as parts of their initial or renewal employment contracts with employees working on research and development in order to protect their computer software from unauthorized disclosures by ex-employees to competitors. A **noncompetition agreement,** reasonable in geographic scope and duration, is an effective deterrent to unauthorized disclosures to competitors because it forecloses employees' freedom to accept employment with competitors. A **nondisclosure agreement** identifies what information the parties consider to be confidential, as opposed to the general skills and knowledge of the business. And, even if the confidential information does not meet the requirements for classification as a trade secret, nevertheless it will be protected as a matter of contract.

§ 22:8.   Semiconductor Chip Protection.

The Semiconductor Chip Protection Act of 1984[18] (SCPA) created a new form of industrial intellectual property, protecting "mask works" and the semiconductor chip products in which they are embodied from chip piracy. **Mask works** refer to the specific form of expression embodied in chip design, including the stencils used in manufacturing semiconductor chip products. A **semiconductor chip product** is a product placed on a piece of semiconductor material in accordance with a predetermined pattern, and intended to perform electronic circuitry functions. This definition includes products such as analog chips, logic function chips such as microprocessors, and memory chips such as RAMs and ROMs.

(a) **Duration and Qualifications for Protection.** The SCPA provides the owners of a mask work fixed in a semiconductor chip product the exclusive right for ten years to reproduce and distribute their products in the United States and to import them into the United States. These rights fully apply to works first commercially exploited after November 8, 1984, the date of the enactment of the law. However, the protection of the act only applies to those works which, when considered as a whole, are not commonplace, staple, or familiar in the semiconductor industry.

(b) **Application Procedure.** The owner of a mask work subject to protection under the SCPA must file an application for a certificate of registration with the Register of Copyrights within two years of the date of the work's first commercial exploitation. Failure to do so within this period will result in forfeiture of all rights under the act. Questions concerning the validity of the works are to be resolved through litigation or arbitration.

(c) **Limitations on Exclusive Rights.** Under the SCPA's reverse engineering exemption, competitors may not only study mask works, but may use the results of that study to design their own semiconductor chip products embodying their own original masks, even if the masks are substantially simi-

---

[18]PL 98-620, 98 Stat 3347, 17 USC 901.

lar (but not substantially identical), so long as their products are the result of substantial study and analysis and not the mere result of plagerism.[19]

Innocent infringers are not liable for infringements occurring before notice of protection is given them and are liable for reasonable royalties on each unit distributed after notice has been given them. However, the continued purchasing of infringing semiconductors after notice has been given can result in penalties up to $250,000.

(d) Remedies. The SCPA provides that the infringer will be liable for actual damages, and will forfeit its profits to the owner. As an alternative the owner may elect to receive statutory damages of up to $250,000 as determined by the court.[20] The court may also order destruction or other disposition of the products and the equipment used to make the products.

§ 22:9.   Accession.

Property may be acquired by **accession**, that is, by means of an addition to or an increase of the thing that is owned, as in the case of produce of land or the young of animals.

§ 22:10.   Gifts.

Title to personal property may be transferred by the voluntary act of the owner without receiving anything in exchange, that is by *gift*. The person making the gift, the **donor**, may do so because of things which the recipient of the gift, the **donee**, has done in the past or which the donee is expected to do in the future, but such matters of inducement are not deemed consideration so as to alter the "free" character of the gift.

(a) Inter Vivos Gifts. The ordinary gift that is made between two living persons is an **inter vivos gift**. For practical purposes, such a gift takes effect upon the donor's expressing an intent to transfer title and making delivery, subject to the right of the donee to disclaim the gift within a reasonable time after learning that it has been made.[21] As there is no consideration for a gift, there is no enforceable contract and an intended donee cannot sue for breach of contract if the donor fails to complete the gift.

(1) Intent. The intent "to make" a gift requires an intent to transfer title at that time. In contrast, an intent to confer a benefit at a future date is not a sufficient intent to create any right in the intended donee. A delivery of property without the intent to make a gift does not transfer title.[22]

(2) Delivery. Ordinarily the delivery required to make a gift will be an actual handing over to the donee of the thing which is given.

FACTS:

Welton handed some bonds to Gallagher. He told Gallagher that there were "no strings attached" and that she should put the bonds in her own safe deposit box. The bonds were payable to bearer and Welton, an experienced businessperson, knew that ownership of such bonds could be transferred by making a physical delivery of them. Some time later, Welton claimed that he still owned the bonds. Gallagher claimed that she owned them by gift.

[19] 17 USC § 906.
[20] 17 USC § 911(c).
[21] Owen v Owen (SD) 351 NW2d 139 (1984).
[22] Re Jacobs' Marriage, 128 Cal App 3d 273, 180 Cal Rptr 234 (1982).

DECISION:

Judgment for Gallagher. When Welton handed her the bonds he made a delivery that satisfied that element of a gift. The fact that ownership of the bonds could be transferred thereby without any indorsement by him combined with the fact that he was experienced in business, indicated that he knew that he would be losing ownership of the bonds by handing them to anyone else. His intent to transfer the ownership by way of a gift was shown by the fact that he told Gallagher that there "were no strings attached" and that she should put the bonds in her safe deposit box. If Welton had not had the intent to make a gift of the bonds, it would have been absurd to state that there were no strings attached or that Gallagher should put the bonds where Welton could not get them. The conduct of Welton thus showed that he intended to make a gift of the bonds to Gallagher. As there was both a delivery and a donative intent, there was a gift of the bonds to Gallagher. Welton no longer owned them. [Welton v Gallagher (Hawaii App) 630 P2d 1077 (1981)]

The delivery of a gift may also be made by a **symbolic delivery**, as by the delivery of means of control of property, such as keys to a lock or ignition keys to an automobile, or by the delivery of papers that are essential to or closely associated with the ownership of the property, such as documents of title or a ship's papers. The delivery of a symbol is effective as a gift if the intent to make a gift is established; this is in contrast to merely giving the recipient of the token temporary access to the property, as for example, until the deliveror comes back from the hospital.

A gift may be made by depositing money in the bank account of an intended donee. If the account is a joint account in the names of two persons, a deposit of money in the account by one person may or may not be a gift to the other. Parol evidence is generally admissible to show whether there was an intention to make a gift.

When a savings account passbook is essential to the withdrawal of money from a savings account, parents do not make a gift to a minor child when they open a savings account in the child's name but keep possession of the passbook.

(3) *Donor's Death.* If the donor dies before doing what is needed to make an effective gift, the gift fails. An agent or the executor or administrator of the donor cannot thereafter perform the missing step on behalf of the donor. For example, in a state where a transfer of title to a motor vehicle could not be made without a transfer of the title certificate, that transfer must be made while the donor is living and cannot be made after the donor's death by the executor of the donor.

(b) **Gifts Causa Mortis.** A **gift causa mortis** is made when the donor, contemplating imminent and impending death, delivers personal property to the donee with the intent that the donee shall own it if the donor dies. This is a conditional gift and the donor is entitled to take the property back (1) if the donor does not die; (2) if the donor revokes the gift before dying; or (3) if the donee dies before the donor.

(c) **Uniform Gifts to Minors Act.** The Uniform Gifts to Minors Act,[23] provides an additional method for making gifts to minors of money

[23] The Uniform Gifts to Minors Act (UGMA) was originally proposed in 1956. It was revised in 1965 and again in 1966. One of these versions, often with minor variations, has been adopted in every state. It has been adopted for the Virgin Islands and the District of Columbia.

and of registered and unregistered securities. Under the Act, a gift of money may be made by an adult to a minor by depositing it with a broker or a bank in an account in the name of the donor or another adult or a bank with trust powers "as a custodian for [*name of minor*] under the [*name of state*] Uniform Gifts to Minors Act." If the gift is a registered security, the donor registers the security in a similar manner. If the security is unregistered, it must be delivered by the donor to another adult or a trust company accompanied by a written statement signed by the donor and the custodian acknowledging receipt of the security.[24]

Under the Uniform Act, the custodian is in effect a guardian of the property for the minor but the custodian may use the property more freely and is not subject to many restrictions applicable to true guardians. When property is held by a custodian for the benefit of a minor under the Uniform Gifts to Minors Act, the custodian has discretionary power to use the property for the "support, maintenance, education, and benefit" of the minor but the custodian may not use the custodial property for the custodian's own personal benefit. The gift is final and irrevocable for tax and all other purposes upon complying with the procedure of the Act.

FACTS:

In 1971 Harry Gordon turned over $40,000 to his son, Murray Gordon. Murray opened two $20,000 custodian bank accounts under the Uniform Gifts to Minors Act for his minor children, Eden and Alexander. Murray was listed as the custodian of both accounts. On January 9, 1976, both accounts were closed, and a single bank check representing the principal of the accounts, was drawn to the order of Harry Gordon. In April of 1976, Murray and his wife, Joan, entered into a separation agreement and were later divorced. Thereafter, Joan, on behalf of her children, Eden and Alexander, brought suit against Murray to recover the funds withdrawn in January of 1976, contending that the deposits in both accounts were irrevocable gifts. Murray contended that the money was his father's and it was never intended as a gift, but was merely a means of avoiding tax liability.

DECISION:

Judgment for Joan on behalf of Eden and Alexander. In order to find that an inter vivos gift has been made, there must be donative intent and delivery. The UGMA expressly deals with "delivery;" and provides that this element of a gift is satisfied by documentary compliance with the procedures of the statute. The issue of "donative intent" is not conclusively resolved by making a determination that there was documentary compliance with the statute. However, documentary compliance with the procedures set forth by the UGMA is highly probative on the issue of intent, and is prima facie evidence that a gift was not only made but intended. The essential element of donative intent refers to the grantor's initial intent at the time of the conveyance, and the donor cannot later change his mind and revoke the transfer. Murray's allegations do not controvert the impressive documentary evidence of donative intent. [Gordon v Gordon, 419 NYS2d 684, 70 App Div 2d 86 (1979)]

(d) Conditional Gifts. A gift may be made on condition, such as "This car is yours when you graduate" or "This car is yours unless you drop

[24]UGMA § 2.

out of school." The former gift is subject to a **condition precedent,** and the latter to a **condition subsequent.** That is, the condition to the first gift must be satisfied before any gift or transfer takes place, while the satisfaction of the second condition operates to destroy or divest a title that had already been transferred. Ordinarily, no condition is recognized unless it is expressly stated; but some courts regard an engagement ring as a conditional gift, particularly if the woman breaks or causes the breaking of the engagement.[25] Other gifts made by the man, the woman, or by friends in contemplation of marriage are not regarded as conditional.

(e) **Anatomical Gifts.** The Uniform Anatomical Gift Act[26] permits persons eighteen years or older to make a gift of their body or any part or organ to take effect upon their death. The gift may be made to a school, a hospital, or organ bank, or to a named patient. Such a gift may also be made, subject to certain restrictions, by the spouse, adult child, parent, adult brother or sister, or guardian of a deceased person.[27] Independently of the Act a living person may make a gift, while living, of part of the person's body, as in the case of a blood transfusion or a kidney transplant.

§ 22:11. Lost Property.

Personal property is *lost* when the owner does not know where it is located but intends to retain title or ownership to it. The person finding lost property does not acquire title but only possession. Ordinarily the finder of lost property is required to surrender the property to the true owner when the latter establishes ownership. Meanwhile the finder is entitled to retain possession as against everyone else.

FACTS:

Anthony Fuentes, a child, was playing in front of his house. He found a bundle of bonds. These were payable to bearer and did not contain the name of the owner. Anthony turned the bonds over to the police but no one ever claimed them. Anthony then claimed the bonds from the police.

DECISION:

Anthony was entitled to the bonds. When no one proved to be the owner of the bonds, the finder was entitled to possession of them. The police therefore had to give the bonds back to Anthony. [Fuentes v Wendt, 436 NYS2d 801 (1981)]

Without a contract with the owner or a statute so providing, the finder of lost property is not entitled to a reward or to compensation for finding or caring for the property.

(a) **Finding in Public Place.** If the lost property is found in a public place, such as a hotel, under such circumstances that to a reasonable person it

[25]In re Marriage of Heinzman, 198 Colo 36, 596 P2d 61 (1979).
[26]This Act has been adopted in every state.
[27]Uniform Anatomical Gift Act (UAGA) §§ 2, 3.

would appear that the property had been intentionally placed there by the owner and that the owner would be likely to recall where the property had been left and to return for it, the finder is not entitled to possession of the property but must give it to the proprietor or manager of the public place to keep it for the owner. This exception does not apply if it appears that the property was not intentionally placed where it was found, because it is not likely that the owner will recall having left it there.

(b) Statutory Change. In some states, statutes have been adopted permitting the finder to sell the property or keep it if the owner does not appear within a stated period of time. In such a case, the finder is required to give notice, as by newspaper publication, in order to attempt to reach the owner.

§ 22:12. Transfer by Nonowner.

Ordinarily a sale or other transfer by one who does not own the property will pass no title. No title is acquired by theft. The thief acquires possession only; and if the thief makes a sale or gift of the property to another, the latter only acquires possession of the property. The true owner may reclaim the property from the thief or from the thief's transferee.[28]

(a) Automobiles. In some states the general rule stated above is fortified by statutes which declare that the title to an automobile cannot be transferred, even by the true owner, without a delivery of a properly indorsed title certificate. The states that follow the common law do not make the holding of a title certificate essential to the ownership of an automobile, although as a matter of police regulation, the owner must obtain such a certificate.

(b) Exceptions. As an exception to the rule that a nonowner cannot transfer title, an agent, who does not own the property, but who is authorized to sell it, may transfer the title of the agent's principal. Likewise, certain relationships create a power to sell and to transfer title, such as a pledge or an entrustment. Likewise an owner of property may be barred or estopped from claiming ownership when the owner has acted to deceive an innocent buyer into believing that someone else was the owner or had authority to sell.

§ 22:13. Occupation of Personal Property.

Title to personal property may be acquired by **occupation**, that is, by taking and retaining possession of the property.

(a) Wild Animals. Wild animals, living in a state of nature, are not owned by any individual. In the absence of restrictions imposed by game laws, the person who acquires dominion or control over a wild animal becomes its owner. What constitutes sufficient dominion or control varies with the nature of the animal and all the surrounding circumstances. If the animal is killed, tied, imprisoned, or otherwise prevented from going at its will, the hunter exercises sufficient dominion or control over the animal and becomes its owner. If the wild animal, subsequent to its capture, should escape and return to its natural state, it resumes the status of a wild animal.[29]

[28] As to the right of the owner to sue for money damages see § 22:15 of this book.
[29] Wiley v Baker (Tex Civ App) 597 SW2d 3 (1980).

As a qualification to the ordinary rule, the exception developed that if an animal is killed or captured on the land of another while the hunter is guilty of trespassing, that is, the hunter is upon the land without the permission of the landowner, the animal, when killed or captured, does not belong to the hunter but to the landowner.

(b) **Abandoned Personal Property.** Personal property is deemed abandoned when the owner relinquishes possession of it with the intention to disclaim title to it. Yesterday's newspaper which is thrown out in the trash is abandoned personal property. Title to abandoned property may be acquired by the first person who obtains possession and control of it. A person becomes the owner at the moment of taking possession of the abandoned personal property.

When the owner of property flees in the face of an approaching peril, property left behind is not abandoned. An abandonment occurs only when the leaving of the property is the voluntary act of the owner.

FACTS:

Menzel fled from Europe upon the approach of enemy armies in World War II, leaving in his apartment certain paintings that were seized by the enemy. After World War II, the paintings were discovered in an art gallery owned by List. Menzel sued List for the paintings. List defended on the ground that Menzel had abandoned the paintings; and therefore title had passed to the person taking possession of them and from such possessor had been transferred lawfully to List.

DECISION:

Judgment for Menzel. There is an abandonment, so as to permit the first occupant to acquire title, only when the act of abandoning is voluntary. When property is left in order to escape from a danger, there is not a voluntary act of abandoning the property and the ownership of the original owner is not lost or affected. Menzel v List, 49 Misc. 2d 300, 267 NYS 2d 804 (1966).

§ 22:14. Escheat.

Difficult questions arise in connection with unclaimed property. In the case of personal property, the practical answer is that the property will probably "disappear" after a period of time, or it may be sold for unpaid charges, as by a carrier, hotel, or warehouse. A growing problem arises with respect to unclaimed corporate dividends, bank deposits, insurance payments, and refunds. Most states have a statute providing for the transfer of title of such unclaimed property to the state government. This transfer of ownership to the government is often called by its feudal name of **escheat**. Many states have adopted the Uniform Disposition of Unclaimed Property Act.[30]

[30]The 1954 version of the Act has been adopted in Arizona, Arkansas, Florida, Idaho, Maryland, New Hampshire, Utah, Vermont, Virginia, Washington, and West Virginia. A 1966 version of the Act has been adopted in Alabama, Arkansas, Georgia, Hawaii, Illinois, Indiana, Louisiana, Maine, Minnesota, Mississippi, Missouri, Montana, Nebraska, Nevada, New Mexico, North Dakota, Oklahoma, Oregon, Rhode Island, South Carolina, South Dakota, Tennessee, and the District of Columbia.

§ 22:15. Remedies for Violation of Property Rights.

The remedy most commonly used by the owner of personal property for violations of property rights is an action for money damages when the property is negligently or willfully harmed, taken, or destroyed by the act of another. When the owner's property is taken under circumstances that would constitute larceny, the owner may sue for the wrong, called **conversion**, and will recover the money value of the property at the time of the unlawful taking, or may recover the property itself by an action at law.

The owner's right to recover damages for conversion may also be asserted against an innocent wrongdoer; that is, a person who in good faith has exercised dominion over the property of the plaintiff. For example, although the buyer of a stolen television set gave value and acted in good faith in the belief that the seller was the owner of the set, the conduct of the innocent buyer in taking possession of the set and exercising control over it is a conversion for which the innocent buyer is liable to the true owner.

If the defendant has infringed copyrights, patents, or marks of the plaintiff, the plaintiff may obtain an injunction ordering the defendant to stop such practices. If the infringement was intentional, the plaintiff may also recover from the defendant any profits obtained by the defendant from such infringement. If the infringement conduct is such as to constitute an unfair trade practice, the plaintiff may obtain a cease and desist order against the defendant from the Federal Trade Commission.

C. MULTIPLE OWNERSHIP OF PERSONAL PROPERTY

When all rights in a particular object of property are held by one person, that property is held in **severalty**. However, two or more persons may hold concurrent rights and interests in the same property. In that case, the property is said to be held in **cotenancy**. The various forms of cotenancy include (1) tenancy in common, (2) joint tenancy, (3) tenancy by entirety, and (4) community property.

§ 22:16. Tenancy in Common.

A **tenancy in common** is a form of ownership by two or more persons. The interest of a tenant in common may be transferred or inherited, in which case the taker becomes a tenant in common with the others. This tenancy is terminated only when there is a partition or division, giving each a specific portion, or when one person acquires all of the interests of the co-owners.

§ 22:17. Joint Tenancy.

A **joint tenancy** is another form of ownership by two or more persons. A joint tenant's interest may be transferred to a third person, but this destroys the joint tenancy. In such a case, the remaining joint tenant becomes a tenant in common with the third person who has acquired the interest of the other joint tenant.

Upon the death of a joint tenant, the remaining tenants take the share of the deceased tenant, and finally the last surviving joint tenant takes the property as a holder in severalty.

FACTS:

Eva opened a joint account in her name and the name of her daughter, Alice. Later Alice withdrew all the money from the account. The next day Eva died. Eva's husband claimed that the money withdrawn by Alice was an asset of Eva's estate.

DECISION:

The money that was withdrawn by Alice belonged to her by survivorship. As there was no evidence of an agency, the money was owned by her and Eva. When Alice withdrew all the money on deposit, it was still owned by her and Eva as joint tenants. When Eva died, Alice became the sole owner by survivorship and therefore the withdrawn money was not part of Eva's estate. [In re Filfiley's Will, 63 Misc2d 1052, 313 NYS2d 793 (1970)]

(a) **Statutory Change.** Statutes in many states have modified the common law by adding a formal requirement to the creation of a joint tenancy with survivorship. At common law, such an estate would be created by a transfer of property to "A and B as joint tenants." Under these statutes, it is necessary to add the words "with right of survivorship," or other similar words, if it is desired to create a right of survivorship. If no words of survivorship are used, the transfer of property to two or more persons will be construed as creating a tenancy in common. Under such a statute, a certificate of deposit issued only in the name of "A or B" does not create a joint tenancy because it does not add words of survivorship.

(b) **Bank Accounts.** The deposit of money in a joint account constitutes a gift of a joint ownership interest in the money when that is the intent of the depositor. The mere fact that money is deposited in a joint account does not in itself establish that there was such a gift, particularly when it can be shown by clear and convincing evidence that the deposits were made in the joint account "solely for the convenience of enabling either of the parties to draw therefrom for family purposes." When the joint account is merely an agency device, the account agent is not entitled to use any part of the account for personal purposes.

FACTS:

The New York Banking Law provides that a presumption arises that a joint tenancy has been created when a bank account is opened in the names of two persons "payable to either or the survivor." While he was still single, Richard Coddington opened a savings account with his mother Amelia. The signature card they signed stated that the account was owned by them as joint tenants with the right of survivorship. No statement as to survivorship was made on the passbook. Richard later married Margaret. On his death, Margaret claimed a share of the account on the ground that it was not a joint tenancy because the passbook did not contain words of survivorship and because the statutory presumption of a joint tenancy was overcome by the fact that Richard had withdrawn substantial sums from the account during his life.

DECISION:

Amelia is entitled to the entire account. The signature card which contained the agreement of the bank and the depositors is controlling, not the passbook. While the passbook did not contain words of survivorship, the signature card contained language which clearly satisfied the statutory form, and therefore the presumption of a joint tenancy applied. Withdrawal of substantial sums of money by Richard at one time, standing alone, is insufficient to overcome the presumption. [Coddington v Coddington, 56 App Div 2d 697, 391 NYS2d 760 (1977)]

§ 22:18. Tenancy by Entirety.

At common law a **tenancy by entirety** or **tenancy by the entireties** was created when property was transferred to both husband and wife. It differs from joint tenancy in that it requires a transfer to husband and wife and also in that the right of survivorship cannot be extinguished and one spouse's interest cannot be transferred to a third person, although in some jurisdictions a spouse's right to share the possession and the profits may be transferred. This form of property holding is popular in common-law jurisdictions because creditors of one of the spouses cannot reach the property while both are living. Only a creditor of both the husband and wife under the same obligation can obtain execution against the property. Moreover, the tenancy by entirety is in effect a substitute for a will since the surviving spouse acquires the complete property interest upon the death of the other. There are usually other reasons, however, why each spouse should make a will.

In many states the granting of an absolute divorce converts a tenancy by the entireties into a tenancy in common.

§ 22:19. Community Property.

In some states property acquired during the period of marriage is the **community property** of the husband and wife. Some statutes provide for the right of survivorship; others provide that half of the property of the deceased husband or wife shall go to the heirs, or permit such half to be disposed of by will. It is commonly provided that property acquired by either spouse during the marriage is prima facie community property, even though title is taken in the spouse's individual name, unless it can be shown that it was obtained with property possessed by that spouse prior to the marriage.

SUMMARY

Personal property consists of whole or fractional ownership rights in things which are tangible and movable as well as rights in things which are intangible and have an economic value.

Property rights in trademarks, copyrights, and patents are acquired as provided in federal statutes. A trademark or servicemark is any word, symbol, or design, or combination of these used to identify a product in the case of a trademark, and a service in the case of a servicemark. Terms for which protection is claimed will fall into one of four categories: (1) generic,

(2) descriptive, (3) suggestive, or (4) arbitrary or fanciful. Generic terms are never registerable. Ordinarily, descriptive terms are not registerable; however, if a descriptive term has acquired a "secondary meaning" it is registerable. Suggestive and arbitrary marks are registerable. If there is likelihood of confusion, a court will enjoin the second user from using a particular mark.

A copyright is the exclusive right given by federal statute to the creator of a literary or artistic work to use, reproduce, or display the work for the life of the creator and fifty years after the creator's death. A patent gives the inventor an exclusive right for seventeen years to make, use and sell an invention which is new and useful and not obvious to those in the business to which the invention is related. Trade secrets which give an owner an advantage over competitors are protected under state law for an unlimited period so long as they are not made public. Computer programs may be protected under the Computer Software Copyright Act, patent law, trade secrecy law, and contract law. Qualifying mask works and the semiconductor chip products in which they are embodied are protected from piracy by the Semiconductor Chip Protection Act for a period of ten years.

Personal property may be acquired by purchase or by production. Personal property may also be acquired by gift where the donor has present intent to make a gift and delivers possession to the donee. Personal property may also be acquired by accession, finding of lost property, and by occupation.

All rights in a particular object of property can be held by one individual, in which case it is said to be held in severalty; or ownership rights may be held concurrently by two or more individuals, in which case it is said to be held in cotenancy. The major forms of cotenancy include (1) tenancy in common, (2) joint tenancy, (3) tenancy by the entireties, and (4) community property.

QUESTIONS AND CASE PROBLEMS

1. What social forces give rise to the rule of law requiring that there be an actual or symbolic delivery in order to make a gift?
2. What qualities must an invention possess in order to be patentable?
3. Compare the protection afforded by a patent and the protection afforded by a trademark registration.
4. How does (a) capturing a wild game animal during the hunting season compare with (b) finding lost property?
5. The Mackey Corporation manufactures furniture polishes. Mackey develops a new polish which it markets under the name of "Super-polish." Mackey wants to register this name as a trademark and prevent anyone else from using it. Can Mackey do so?
6. General Computers Corporation developed a new generation computer at its research and development facility in Bedford, California. Prior to marketing the computer, a competitor, World Data Systems Inc. of Piscataway, New Jersey hired away General's chief research engineer, Tyler Moore. General is worried that World will obtain secret information about the new computer from Moore and consults you. Your inves-

tigation reveals that General did not have a corporate policy of utilizing contracts of employment to protect against disclosure of secret business information and to reasonably restrict employees from working for direct competitors. General did not patent its new computer because of the disclosure requirements necessary to obtain a patent. Is there any legal theory by which General can prohibit Moore from disclosing secret information about the new computer to World?

7. On Christmas day, Anita told her niece that she was giving her a television set for Christmas and that the set would arrive later that week. It arrived on December 27. Was the niece the owner of the set on December 25 or December 27?

8. Ruth and Stella were sisters. They owned a house as joint tenants with right of survivorship. Ruth sold her half interest to Roy. Thereafter, Stella died and Roy claimed the entire property by survivorship. Was he entitled thereto?

9. Mona finds a wallet on the floor of an elevator in the office building in which she works. She posts several notices in the building informing of the finding of the wallet but no one appears to claim it. She waits for six months and then spends the money in the wallet on the belief that she owns it. Thereafter Jason, the person who lost the wallet, brought suit to recover the money and Mona defends that the money was hers since Jason did not claim it within a reasonable time after she posted the notice. Is she correct?

10. Picayune Games, Inc., a small manufacturing company located in New Orleans, Louisiana, developed a computer checker game called "CompuCheck." The program was put on magnetic tape and sold in conjunction with an inexpensive computer for $349.00. No copyright notice appeared on either the tape or the computer since Picayune's marketing manager was confident that the program could not be read as it appeared on the tape. "CompuCheck" was sold very successfully in the South and Midwest for two years. In its third year of sale, just prior to the Christmas selling season, National Computer Games, Inc., a large Midwestern mail-order house, introduced a computer checker game called "King Me" which was sold in conjunction with a computer at a price of $299.00. The program was identical to Picayune's. Picayune, when informed of National's game, initiated application procedures for a copyright on its program with the Register of Copyrights; and on the same day brought suit against National for violation of the Computer Software Copyright Act of 1980, contending that National made and sold an exact copy of "CompuCheck." Picayune's marketing manager was mistaken in the belief that the program could not be read from the tape; and National admits that it simply instructed its home office computer to print the program from Picayune's tape. Picayune contends that National was not misled at any time into thinking that the program was in the public domain, and that a simple phone call could have resolved any question National may have had on Picayune's intention to protect its program. National contends that the widespread distribution of the computer program without the use of the copyright notice constituted a

dedication of Picayune's proprietary interest into the public domain. National states that, as such, it had a right to duplicate the program and sell an identical game. Decide.

11. Carol and Robert, both over 21, became engaged. Robert gave Carol an engagement ring. He was killed in an automobile crash before they were married. His estate demanded that Carol return the ring. Was she entitled to keep it? [Cohen v Bayside Federal Savings and Loan Ass'n, 62 Misc 2d 738, 309 NYS2d 980]

12. Henry Larson delivered a check to his son, Clifford, for $8,500. The check bore the notation "As Loan." Some time later the son asked the father what he should do about the loan. Henry wrote Clifford a note in broken English saying "Keep It No Return." Henry died and the canceled check with the notation "As Loan" was found among his papers. Henry's administratrix sued Clifford for repayment of the loan. Did he have any defense? [Larson's Estate, 71 Wash 2d 349, 428 P2d 558]

13. The plaintiff, Herbert Rosenthal Jewelry Corporation, and the defendant, Kalpakian, manufactured jewelry. The plaintiff obtained a copyright registration of a jeweled pin in the shape of a bee. Kalpakian made a similar pin. Rosenthal sued Kalpakian for infringement of copyright registration. Kalpakian raised the defense that he was only copying the idea and not the way the idea was expressed. Was he liable for infringement of the plaintiff's copyright? [Herbert Rosenthal Jewelry Corp. v Kalpakian (CA9 Cal) 446 F2d 738]

14. Brogden acquired a biblical manuscript in 1945. In 1952 he told his sister Lucy that he wanted Texas A & M University to have this manuscript. He dictated a note so stating and placed it with the manuscript. He made some effort to have an officer of the college come for the manuscript. In 1956 he delivered the manuscript to his sister, stating that he was afraid that someone would steal it. Later in the year he told a third person that he was going to give the manuscript to the university. In 1957 he was declared incompetent. In 1959 the sister delivered the manuscript to the university. In April, 1960, Brogden died, and his heirs, Bailey and others, sued Harrington and other officers of the university to have the title to the manuscript determined. Decide. [Harrington v Bailey (Tex Civ App) 351 SW2d 946]

15. From October, 1965, through July, 1967, Union Carbide Corporation sold certain bulbs for high-intensity reading lamps under its EVEREADY trademark. Carbide's sales of electrical products under the EVEREADY mark exceeded $100,000,000 for every year after 1963; from 1963–67 Carbide spent $50,000,000 in advertising these products. In 1969 the defendant, Ever-Ready, Inc., imported miniature lamp bulbs for high intensity lamps with "Ever-Ready" stamped on their bases. In two surveys conducted by Carbide, 50% of those interviewed associated Carbide products with the marks used by Ever-Ready Inc. Carbide sought an injunction against Ever-Ready's use of the name Ever-Ready on or in connection with the sale of electrical products. No monetary damages were sought. Ever-Ready Inc. defended that Carbide's trademark EVEREADY was descriptive, and therefore the registration of the mark

was improper and invalid. Carbide responded that its mark had acquired secondary meaning. Decide. [Union Carbide Corp. v Ever-Ready Inc. (CA7 Ill) 531 F2d 366.]

16. Anheuser-Busch had been interested in producing a low alcohol beer both because of its need to develop new markets for growth and because of growing public concern over the health aspects of beer consumption and the problem of drunken driving. Other breweries had similar interests and, in fact, two smaller companies, Hudepohl Brewery and Christian Schmidt Brewing Company, had marketed reduced alcohol beers under the brand names of Pace and Break. Anheuser-Busch made an application for registration of the trademark LA and soon thereafter began marketing its low alcohol product under the LA label. Following Anheuser-Busch's introduction of its product, the Stroh Brewery Company introduced "Schaefer LA," also a low alcohol beer. An action to enjoin Stroh's use of LA followed. Anheuser-Busch contends that the term LA was suggestive in that it required some imagination to connect it with the product and, accordingly, was a protectible trademark. Stroh argues that LA is generic or descriptive in nature, since the term is comprised of the initials of the phrase "low alcohol." Decide. [Anheuser-Busch Inc. v The Stroh Brewery Company (CA8 Mo) 750 F2d 631.]

CHAPTER 23

BAILMENTS

CHAPTER OBJECTIVES

After studying this chapter you will be able to:
1. Describe how a bailment is formed.
2. List and distinguish the various classifications of bailments.
3. Contrast the renting of space with the creation of a bailment.
4. Explain the standard of care a bailee is required to exercise over bailed property.
5. State the burden of proof when a bailor sues a bailee for damages to bailed property.
6. Recognize a bailor's implied warranty concerning goods furnished by the bailor.

Many instances arise in which the owner of personal property entrusts it to another. A person checks a coat at a restaurant, delivers a watch to a jeweler for repairs, or loans hedge clippers to a neighbor; or a company rents a car to a tourist for a weekend. The delivery of property to another under such circumstances is a bailment.

A. GENERAL PRINCIPLES

A **bailment** is the legal relation that arises whenever one person delivers possession of personal property to another under an agreement, express or implied, by which the latter is under a duty to return the identical property to the former or to deliver it or dispose of it as agreed. The person who turns over the possession of the property is the **bailor**. The person who accepts possession is the **bailee**.

§ 23:1.   Elements of Bailment.

A bailment is created when the following elements are present:

(a) **Agreement.** The bailment is based upon an agreement. Generally this agreement will contain all the elements of a contract so that the bailment transaction in fact consists of (1) a contract to bail and (2) the actual bailing of the property. Ordinarily there is no requirement that the contract of bailment be in writing. The subject of a bailment may be any personal property of which possession may be given. Real property cannot be bailed.

(b) **Delivery and Acceptance.** The bailment arises when, pursuant to the agreement of the parties, the property is delivered to the bailee and accepted by the bailee as subject to the bailment agreement.[1]

Delivery may be actual, as when the bailor physically hands a book to the bailee, or it may be a **constructive delivery**, as when the bailor points out a package to the bailee who then takes possession of it. In the absence of a prior agreement to the contrary, a valid delivery and acceptance generally requires that the bailee be aware that goods have been placed within the bailee's control.

FACTS:
Berglund was full-time student of Roosevelt University. He was also the editor and photographer of the student newspaper. The University was unaware that Berglund kept his own photographic equipment in the rooms it had assigned to the newspaper. One night this equipment was stolen from the newspaper office. Berglund sued the University on the theory that it had breached its duty as a bailee. He showed that former editors had also left their equipment in the University rooms. The University denied that it was a bailee.

DECISION:
Judgment for the University. There could be no bailment without an agreement express or implied. There was no evidence that the University had any knowledge that the equipment was kept in the newspaper's rooms. Without such knowledge there could not be any bailment agreement and therefore the fact that the equipment had been left in the building did not prove that there had been a delivery of the equipment to the University and an acceptance thereof by the University. Without such knowledge, there was neither a bailment agreement nor an acceptance of the goods as bailee. Consequently, the University was not a bailee. [Berglund v Roosevelt University, 18 IllApp 842, 310 NE2d 773 (1974)]

---

§ 23:2.   Nature of the Parties' Interests.

The bailor and bailee have different legal interests in the bailed property.

(a) **Bailor's Interest.** The bailor is usually the owner, but ownership by the bailor is not required. It is sufficient that the bailor have physical pos-

[1]Merrit v Nationwide Warehouse Co., Ltd. _____ Tenn App _____, 605 SW2d 250 (1980).

session. Thus, an employee may be a bailor in leaving the employer's truck at a garage.

(b) **Bailee's Interest.** The bailee has only possession of the property. Title to the property does not pass to the bailee and the bailee cannot sell the property to a third person unless the bailee is also an agent authorized to make such a sale. If the bailee attempts to sell the property, such sale only transfers possession and the owner may recover the property from the buyer.

The bailor may cause third persons to believe that the bailee is the owner of the bailed property. If the bailor does so, the bailor is estopped to deny that the bailee is the owner as against persons who have relied on the bailor's representations. As a further exception, if the bailee is a dealer in goods of the kind entrusted to the bailee by the bailor, a sale by the bailee to a buyer in the ordinary course of business will pass the bailor's title to the buyer.

§ 23.3.   Classification of Bailments.

Bailments are classified as ordinary and extraordinary (or special). **Extraordinary bailments** are those in which the bailee is under unusual duties and liabilities by law, as in the case of bailments in which a motel or a common carrier is involved. **Ordinary bailments** include all other bailments.

Bailments may or may not provide for compensation to the bailee. Upon that basis they may be classified as **contract bailments** and **gratuitous bailments**. The fact that no charge is made by the bailor does not necessarily make the transaction a gratuitous bailment. If the bailment is made to further a business interest of the bailor, as when something is loaned "free" to a customer, the bailment is not gratuitous.[2]

Bailments may also be classified in terms of benefit as for the (a) sole benefit of the bailor, as when the farmer gratuitously transports another's produce to the city; (b) sole benefit of the bailee, as when a person borrows the automobile of a friend; or (c) benefit of both parties (mutual-benefit bailment), as when one rents a power tool. A mutual-benefit bailment also arises when a prospective buyer of an automobile leaves the automobile to be traded in with the dealer so that the latter may test it and appraise it.

§ 23:4.   Constructive Bailments.

When one person comes into possession of personal property of another without the owner's consent, the law treats the possessor as a bailee and calls the relationship a **constructive bailment**.[3] It is thus held that the finder of lost property is a bailee of that property.

When a city impounds an automobile, a bailment arises as to the vehicle and its contents. A seller who has not yet delivered the goods to the buyer is treated as bailee of the goods if title has pased to the buyer. Similarly, a buyer who is in possession of goods, the title to which has not yet passed from the seller, is a bailee.

[2]Coe Oil Service, Inc. v Hair (La) 283 So2d 734 (1973).
[3]Hertz Corp. v Paloni, 95 NMex App 212, 619 P2d 1256 (1980).

FACTS:

On July 10, 1975 the New York State Police obtained a search warrant which authorized the search and seizure of Cono Terranova's 35 foot Wheeler pleasure craft as part of a homicide investigation. No incriminating evidence was found by the State in its search. Terranova made continuous requests during the summer and fall for the return of his boat to no avail. On November 12, 1975 after his attorney sued for the return of the boat, he found that parts and accessories were either missing, destroyed, or damaged, and the engine was inoperable. Terranova sued the State for the damages to his property. The State denied it was subject to the duties of a bailee.

DECISION:

Judgment for Terranova. Although a true bailment did not exist because there was no agreement between Terranova and the State to bail the property, there was a constructive bailment and therefore the State was subject to the same duties of a bailee. [Terranova v State of New York (Ct Cl) 445 NYS2d 965 (1982)]

§ 23.5.   Renting of Space Distinguished.

When a person rents space in a locker or building under an agreement which gives the renter the exclusive right to use that space, the placing of goods by the renter in that space does not create a bailment. In such a case, putting property into the space does not constitute a delivery of goods into the possession of the owner of the space. On this basis, there is no bailment in a self-service parking lot when the owner of a car parks it, retains the key, and the owner's only contact with any parking lot employee is upon making a payment when leaving the lot. In such situations, the car owner merely rents the space for parking.

The practical consequence of this conclusion is that if the car is damaged or stolen, the car owner cannot recover damages from the parking lot management unless the owner can show some fault on the part of the parking lot. If the transaction were a bailment, the owner of the car would establish a prima facie right to recover by proving the fact of the bailment and that there was a loss.

If the parking lot is a locked enclosure with a guard to whom the patron must surrender a parking ticket received on entering the lot in order to regain possession of the car, a modern trend regards the transaction as a bailment. The theoretical objection to this view is that the lot does not have full dominion and control over the car since it cannot move the car because the patron has retained possession of the keys. At the same time, as the lot has the power to exclude others from the car, it is "realistic" to treat the parking lot as a bailee and hold it to a bailee's standard of care.

§ 23.6.   Bailment of Contents of Container.

It is a question of the intention of the parties, as that appears to a reasonable person, whether the bailing of a container also constitutes a bailment of articles contained in it; that is, whether a bailment of a coat is a bailment of articles in the coat, and so on. When the contained articles are of a class that is reasonably or normally to be found in the container, they may be regarded as bailed in the absence of an express disclaimer. If the articles are not of such a nature and their presence in the container is unknown to the bailee, there is no bailment of such articles. Consequently, although the circumstances were such that the parking of a car constituted a bailment, there was no bailment of valuable drawings and sporting equipment that were on the back seat but which were not visible from the outside of the car. However, there is ordinarily a bailment of whatever is locked in the trunk.

B. RIGHTS AND DUTIES OF THE PARTIES

A bailment creates certain rights and imposes certain duties upon each party. These may be increased or modified by statute, by custom, or by the express agreement of the parties.

§ 23.7.   Duties of the Bailee.

The bailee has certain duties concerning performance, care, maintenance and return of the bailed property. A bailee's lien allows for the retention of goods until charges are paid. Unauthorized use is forbidden.

(a) **Performance.** If the bailment is based upon a contract, the bailee must perform the bailee's part of the contract and is liable to the bailor for ordinary contract damages arising out of the failure to perform the contract.[4] Thus, if the bailment is for repair, the bailee is under the duty to make the repairs properly. The fact that the bailee used due care in attempting to perform the contract does not excuse the bailee from liability for failing to perform the contract.

It is all too common a situation in bailments involving repairs or alterations of personal property for the bailee not to properly perform the bailee's part of a contract with the bailor.

FACTS:

Welge owned a sofa and chair which Baena Brothers agreed to reupholster and to reduce the size of the arms. The work was not done according to the agreement, and the furniture when finished had no value to Welge and was not accepted by him. Baena sued him for the contract price. Welge counterclaimed for the value of the furniture.

DECISION:

Judgment for Welge on the counterclaim. When Baena Brothers made a contract with respect to the furniture, they were required to perform that contract according to ordinary principles of contract law. The concept of due care, which would protect them if the goods were damaged by a third person, act of God, or accident, does not apply when the question is whether the bailee has performed the contract. As there was a failure to perform their contract, Baena Brothers were liable for damages for such breach. [Baena Brothers v Welge, 3 ConnCir 67, 207 A2d 749 (1964)]

[4]Computer Systems v Western Reserve Life (Mass App) 475 NE2d 745 (1985).

(b) Care of Property. The bailee is under a duty to care for the bailed property. If the property is damaged or destroyed, the bailee is liable for the loss (1) if the harm was caused in whole or in part by the bailee's failure to use reasonable care under the circumstances, or (2) if the harm was sustained during the unauthorized use of the property by the bailee. Otherwise the bailor bears the loss. Thus, if the bailee was exercising due care and was making an authorized use of the property, the bailor must bear the loss of or damage to the property caused by an act of a third person, whether willful or negligent; by an accident or occurrence for which no one was at fault; or by an act of God. In this connection, the term, **act of God**, means a natural phenomenon that is not reasonably foreseeable, such as a sudden flood or lightning.

FACTS:

Sky Aviation Corporation rented an airplane to Colt. In flying to his destination, Colt did not make use of weather reports. When he arrived at the destination, there were high winds. He landed, instead of turning back to his point of origin where there were no high winds. In landing, he did not make use of a ground crew man who sought to hold down a wing of the plane while he was taxiing to the tie-down area. The wind flipped the plane over. Sky Aviation sued Colt for the damage to the plane. He defended on the ground that it was an act of God.

DECISION:

Judgment for Sky Aviation. The damage to the plane was not the result of an act of God but of Colt's negligence in attempting to land in the high winds instead of returning to a safe base, in ignoring weather reports in flight, and in failing to use the assistance of the ground crew man. Likewise there was no proof that the winds were so unusual as to constitute an act of God. Colt was therefore a negligent bailee and was liable to the bailor for the damages to the bailed property. [Sky Aviation Corp. v Colt (Wyo) 475 P2d 301 (1970)]

---

(1) Standard of Care. The standard for ordinary bailments is reasonable care under the circumstances, that is, the degree of care which a reasonable person would exercise in the situation in order to prevent the realization of reasonably foreseeable harm. The significant factors in determining what constitutes reasonable care in a bailment are the time and place of making the bailment, the facilities for taking care of the bailed property, the nature of the bailed property, the bailee's knowledge of its nature, and the extent of the bailee's skills and experience in taking care of goods of that kind.

Many courts state the standard of care in terms of the benefit characteristic of the bailment, holding the bailee liable for the slightest negligence when the bailment is for the sole benefit of the bailee and for ordinary negligence when the bailment is for the mutual benefit of the parties. In contrast, if the benefit is for the sole benefit of the bailor, it is said that the bailee is only required to exercise slight care and will only be liable for gross negligence.

(2) *Contract Modification of Liability.* A bailee's liability may be expanded by contract. A provision that the bailee assumes absolute liability for the property is binding, but there is a difference of opinion as to whether a stipulation to return the property "in good condition" or "in as good condition as received" has the effect of imposing such absolute liability.

An ordinary bailee may limit liability, except for willful misconduct, by agreement or contract.[5] However in some states, statutes prohibit certain kinds of paid bailees, such as automobile parking garages, from limiting their liability for negligence.[6]

Also, statutes in some states make it clear that a party cannot contract away its liability for negligent violations of common law standards of care where a public interest is involved.

FACTS:

In June 1978, Bruce Gardner took his 1976 Porsche 911 automobile to be repaired at Downtown Porsche Audi (Downtown). Gardner signed a repair order bearing the disclaimer "not responsible for loss (of) cars... in case of... theft." While it was parked in the repair garage the car was stolen because of Downtown's negligence. Gardner sued Downtown for failing to redeliver his car. Downtown defended that the disclaimer absolved it of liability for its negligence.

DECISION:

Judgment for Gardner. Downtown concedes it was negligent in securing the automobile during the bailment. Because it is in the automobile repair business, which is a business of practical necessity to the people of the state and thus involves the public interest, Downtown cannot exempt itself from liability for ordinary negligence. In addition, California Civil Code [sec] 1668 prohibits a party from contracting away liability for its negligence where a public interest is involved. [Gardner v Downtown Porsche Audi, 225 Cal Rptr 757 (1986)]

By definition, a limitation of liability must be a term of the bailment contract before any question arises as to whether it is binding. Thus, a limitation contained in a receipt mailed by a bailee after receiving a coat for storage is not effective to alter the terms of the bailment as originally made. Likewise, a bailor is not bound by a limitation of liability which was not known at the time the bailment was made.

---

[5]Motors Ins. Corp. v American Garages Inc. 98 Misc 2d 887, 414 NYS2d 841 (9179), applying NY Gen Oblig Law § 5-325 (McKinney).
[6]Blume v Evans Fur Co. (Ill App) 466 NE2d 1366 (1984).

FACTS:

Schroeder parked his car in a parking lot operated by Allright, Inc. The parking stub given him had printed in large, heavy type that the lot closed at 6:00 o'clock. Under this information, and printed in smaller, lighter type was a provision limiting the liability of Allright for theft or loss. A large sign at the lot stated that after 6 p.m. patrons could obtain their car keys at another location. Schroeder's car was stolen from the lot some time after the 6 p.m. closing and he sued Allright for damages. Allright defended on the basis of the limitation of liability provision contained in the parking stub, and the notice given Schroeder that the lot closed at 6:00 p.m.

DECISION:

Judgment for Schroeder. When a bailee attempts to limit liability by printing such a limitation on a claim check, the limitation must be called to the attention of the bailor before it may become part of the bailment contract. The limitation on the claim check was not called to the attention of the bailor, Schroeder, when he left his automobile. Notice that a lot will "close at 6 o'clock p.m." does not give notice that cars left after such time will be at the owner's risk. [Allright Inc. v Schroeder (TexCivApp) 551 SW2d 745 (1977)]

(3) Insurance. In the absence of a statute or contract provision, a bailee is not under any duty to insure for the benefit of the bailor the property entrusted to the bailee.

(c) Maintenance of Property. In the situation of a bailment for hire, such as when a business rents an office copier from a leasing firm, the bailee must bear the expense of repairs that are ordinary and incidental to the use of the machine, in the absence of a contrary contract provision. If, however, the repairs required are of an unusual nature or if the bailment is for a short period of time, the bailor is required to make the repairs unless the need for the repairs arose from the fault of the bailee.

(d) Unauthorized Use. The bailee is liable for conversion, just as though the bailee stole the property, if the bailee uses the property without authority or uses it in any manner to which the bailor had not agreed. Ordinarily the bailee will be required to pay compensatory damages, although punitive damages may be imposed when the improper use was deliberate and the bailee was recklessly indifferent to the effect of the use upon the property.

(e) Return of Property. The bailee is under a duty to return the identical property which is the subject of the bailment or to deliver it as directed by the bailment agreement. An exception exists for **fungible goods,** which are those goods of a homogeneous nature of which any unit is the equivalent of any other like unit. Examples of fungible goods are grain, potatoes (within the same grade), and petroleum (within the same grade). In the case of fungible goods, if the bailee contracts to return an equal amount of the same kind and quality, the transaction is a bailment. If the bailee has the option of paying an amount of money or returning property other than that which was delivered by the bailor, there is generally no bailment, but rather a "sale." Thus, when a farmer delivers wheat to a grain elevator that gives the farmer a receipt which promises to return either a similar amount of wheat or a certain sum of money upon presentment of the receipt, the relationship is generally not a bailment.[7]

The redelivery to the bailor or delivery to a third person must be made in accordance with the terms of the bailment contract as to time, place, and manner. When the agreement between the parties does not control these matters, the customs of the community govern.

(1) Bailee's Lien. By common law or statute, a bailee is given a **lien** or the right to retain possession of the bailed property until the bailee has been paid for any charges for storage or repairs. If the bailee has a lien on the property, the bailee is entitled to keep possession of the property until payment has been made for the claim on which the lien is based. The lien is lost if the property is voluntarily returned to the bailor. If the bailor is guilty of any misconduct in obtaining possession of the property, there is no loss of lien and the bailee may retain possession if possession can be reacquired.[8]

A bailee who is authorized by statute to sell the bailed property to enforce a charge or claim against the bailor must give such notice as is required by the statute. A bailee who sells without giving the required notice is liable for conversion of the property.

(2) Constitutionality of Bailee's Lien. Historically, the bailee's lien was merely a right to retain the goods until paid and a statute which goes no further than to authorize such retention is constitutional. There is authority, however, that when the statute goes beyond this common-law pattern and authorizes a sale of the goods, the statute is unconstitutional if it permits the sale of the property without prior notice and hearing as to the existence of the amount alleged to be due.[9]

§ 23:8.   Burden of Proof.

When the bailor sues the bailee for damages to the bailed property, the bailor has the burden of proving that the bailee was at fault and that such fault was the proximate cause of the loss. A prima facie right of the bailor to recover is established, however, by proof that the property was delivered by the bailor to the bailee and thereafter could not be returned or was returned in a damaged condition. When this is done, the bailee has the burden to prove that the loss or damage was not caused by the bailee's failure to exercise the care required by law or by an unauthorized use of the property.[10]

§ 23:9.   Rights of the Bailor.

The typical commercial bailment is a mutual-benefit bailment. Under such a bailment, the bailor has the right to compensation, commonly called rent, for the use of the bailed property. If the bailor is obligated to render a service to the bailee, such as maintenance of the rented property, the bailor's

[7]In some states statutes declare that the relationship between farmer and the grain elevator is a bailment and not a sale. United States v Haddix & Sons, Inc. (CA6 Mich) 415 F2d 584 (1969).
[8]Smith v Cooper Chevrolet, Inc. _____ Ala _____, 404 So2d 49 (1981).
[9]Hernandez v European Auto Collision, Inc. (CA2 NY) 487 F2d 378 (1973); Whitmore v New Jersey Division of Motor Vehicles, 137 NJ Super 492, 349 A2d 560 (1975).
[10]Smith v Morgan Drive Away, Inc. (Mo App) 613 SW2d 469 (1981).

failure to do so will ordinarily bar the bailor from recovering compensation from the bailee.

(a) **Rights Against the Bailee.** The bailor may sue the bailee for breach of contract if the goods are not redelivered to the bailor or delivered to a third person as specified by the bailment agreement. The bailor may also maintain an action against a bailee for negligence, willful destruction, and unlawful retention or conversion of the goods.

(b) **Rights Against Third Persons.** The bailor may sue third persons damaging or taking the bailed property from the bailee's possession, even though the bailment is for a fixed period that has not yet expired. In such a case, the bailor is said to recover damages for injury to the bailor's **reversionary interest,** that is, the right which the bailor has to regain the property upon the expiration of the period of the bailment.

FACTS:

The "Backstreets Band" entered an engagement contract to perform at the Ramada Inn Lounge in South Bend, Indiana, on June 1. At 11:00 p.m. on May 31, 1981, they unloaded their instruments and took them to the stage area, where Mr. Beal, the manager, let them into the lounge and turned on the lights. The band-leader, Burch, asked Beal to lock up the lounge, and was told that a woman was working in the kitchen, but that the doors would be secured when she left. The next morning, the band discovered some of the instruments were missing. A police investigation disclosed that none of the outer doors were tampered with and that the only unlocked door was 30 feet from the hotel desk where a clerk was supposed to be on duty throughout the night. The band brought suit against Ramada for the value of the missing instruments.

DECISION:

Judgment for the band. A bailment existed in this case since the instruments were delivered into Ramada's exclusive possession and were accepted by Ramada when the manager, Beal, permitted the band to place the instruments in the lounge and said he could secure the area. Since certain of the bailed instruments were not returned by the bailee, a prima facie right of the bailors to recover was established. Ramada, the bailee, failed to establish its lack of negligence. Indeed, the failure to lock the door, and the theft of the instruments within 30 feet of the hotel desk was evidence of negligence on the part of the bailee. [Ramabend v Backstreets Band (Ind App) 482 NE2d 741 (1985)]

---

§ 23:10. Duties of Bailor.

The bailor has certain duties concerning the condition of the property bailed. Sometimes the duty concerning goods furnished by the bailor is described as an implied warranty.

(a) **Condition of the Property.** In a mutual-benefit bailment, as a bailment for hire, the bailor is under a duty to furnish goods reasonably fit for the purpose contemplated by the parties. If the bailee is injured or the bailee's property is damaged because of the defective condition of the bailed property, the bailor may be held liable.[11] If the bailment is for the sole benefit of the bailee the bailor is under a duty to inform the bailee of known defects.

[11]Hall v Skate Escape, Ltd. 171 Ga App 178, 319 SE2d 67 (1984).

If the bailee is harmed by a defect that was known by the bailor, the bailor is liable for damages. If the bailor receives a benefit from the bailment, the bailor must not only inform the bailee of known defects, but must also make a reasonable investigation to discover defects. The bailor is liable for the harm resulting from those defects which would have been disclosed had the bailor made such an examination, in addition to those defects which were known to the bailor.

If the defect would not have been revealed by a reasonable examination, the bailor, regardless of classification of the bailment, is not liable for the harm which results.

In any case, the bailee, if aware of the defective condition of the bailed property, is barred by contributory negligence or assumption of risk, if in spite of that knowledge, the bailee makes use of the property and sustains injury because of its condition.

(b) **Bailor's Implied Warranty.** In many cases, the duty of the bailor is described as an implied warranty that the goods will be reasonably fit for their intended use. Apart from an implied warranty, the bailor may expressly warrant the condition of the property, in which event the bailor will be liable for breach of the warranty to the same extent as though the bailor had made a sale rather than a bailment of the property.

With the increase in car and equipment leasing, there is beginning to appear a new trend in the cases that extends to the bailee and third persons the benefit of an implied warranty by the bailor that the article is fit for its intended use and will remain so, as distinguished from merely that it was reasonably fit, or that it was fit at the beginning of the bailment, or that the property was free from defects known to the bailor or which a reasonable investigation would disclose. The significance of an analysis on the basis of warranty lies in the fact that warranty liability may exist even though the bailor was not negligent.[12]

FACTS:

Contract Packers rented a truck from Hertz Truck Leasing. Packers' employee, Cintrone, was injured while riding in the truck being driven by his helper when the brakes of the truck did not function properly and the truck crashed. Cintrone sued Hertz.

DECISION:

Judgment for Cintrone. As Hertz was in the business of renting trucks, it should have foreseen that persons renting would rely on it to have the trucks in safe condition and would not be making the inspection and repair that an owner could be expected to make of his own car. Hence, there was an implied warranty or guaranty by Hertz that the truck was fit for normal use. That warranty continued for the duration of the truck rental, and the right to sue for its breach ran in favor of third persons, such as employees of the customer of Hertz, and conversely was not limited to suit by the customer. [Cintrone v Hertz Truck Leasing & Rental Service, 45 NJ 434, 212 A2d 769 (1965)]

---

[12]Jones v Keetch 388 Mich 164, 200 NW2d 227 (1972), sustaining right of plaintiff to a new trial on the warranty theory, although the first trial on the theory of negligence had ended with a verdict in favor of the defendant. The commercial lessor may also be liable on the strict tort theory.

§ 23:11.   Liability to Third Persons.

When injuries are sustained by third persons resulting from the use of bailed property liability may, under certain circumstances, be imposed on the bailee or the bailor.

(a) **Liability of Bailee.** When the bailee injures a third person with the bailed property, as when the bailee runs into a third person while driving a rented automobile, the bailee is liable to the third person to the same extent as though the bailee were the owner of the property. When the bailee repairs bailed property, the bailee is liable to a third person who is injured as a result of the negligent way in which the repairs were made.

(b) **Liability of Bailor.** The bailor is ordinarily not liable to a third person injured by the bailee while using the bailed property. In states which follow the common law, a person lending an automobile to another is not liable to the third person injured by such other person when the lender did not know or have reason to know that such other person was not a fit driver.

The bailor is liable, however, to the injured third person: (a) if the bailor has entrusted a dangerous instrumentality to one known to the bailor to be ignorant of its dangerous character; (b) if the bailor has entrusted an instrumentality, such as an automobile, to one known to the bailor to be so incompetent or reckless that injury of third persons is a foreseeable consequence; (c) if the bailor has entrusted property with a defect that causes harm to the third person when the circumstances are such that the bailor would be liable to the bailee if the latter were injured by the defect; or (d) if the bailee is using the bailed article, such as driving an automobile, as the bailor's employee in the course of employment.

(c) **Statutory Change.** A number of states have enacted statutes by which an automobile owner granting permission to another to use the automobile automatically becomes liable for any negligent harm caused by the person to whom the automobile has been entrusted. That is, permissive use imposes liability on the owner or provider for the permittee's negligence. In some states, the statute is limited to cases where the permittee is under a specified age, such as 16 years. Under some statutes, the owner is only liable with respect to harm sustained while the permittee is using the automobile for the specific purpose for which permission was granted.

(d) **Family Purpose Doctrine.** Under what is called the **family purpose doctrine**, some courts hold that when the bailor supplies a car for the use of members of the bailor's family, the bailor is liable for harm caused by a member of the family while negligently driving the car. Other jurisdictions reject this doctrine and refuse to impose liability on the bailor of the automobile unless there is an agency relationship between the bailor and the driver.

SUMMARY

A bailment is the legal relation that exists when personal property is delivered by the bailor into the possession of the bailee, under an agreement, express or implied, that the identical property will be returned or will be delivered in accordance with the agreement. On the creation of a bailment the title remains with the bailor while the bailee has the right of possession. When a person comes into the possession of the personal property of another without the owner's consent, the law refers to the relationship as a constructive bailment.

Bailments may be classified in terms of benefit as for the (a) sole benefit of the bailor, (b) sole benefit of the bailee, or (c) benefit of both parties (mutual-benefit bailment). Many courts state the standard of care required of a bailor in terms of the class of bailment. Thus, if the bailment is for the sole benefit of the bailor, the bailee is only required to exercise slight care and is only liable for gross negligence; when the bailment is for the sole benefit of the bailee, the bailee is liable for the slightest negligence; and when the bailment is for the mutual benefit of the parties, which is the typical commercial bailment, the bailee is liable for ordinary negligence. In some states the courts do not make the above distinctions based on the class of bailment but apply a "reasonable care under the circumstances" standard of care. An ordinary bailee may limit liability, except for willful misconduct or where prohibited by statute, by a provision in the bailment contract. A bailee (1) must perform the bailee's part of the contract; (2) unless otherwise agreed, must bear the repair expenses incidental to the use of a machine in a bailment for hire situation; (3) must return the identical property; and (4) must otherwise fulfill the bailment agreement. The bailee has a lien on the bailed property until paid for storage or repair charges.

In a bailment for hire situation, such as the renting of a motor vehicle or a tool, the bailor is under a duty to furnish goods reasonably fit for the purposes contemplated by the parties, and the bailor may be held liable for damages or injury caused by the defective condition of the bailed property. Should a bailee injure a third person while driving a rental motor vehicle, the bailee is liable to the third person as though the bailee were the owner of the vehicle.

QUESTIONS AND CASE PROBLEMS

1. What social forces are affected by the recognition of a bailment relationship?
2. Mercedes is employed by Park Lane Supply Company to sell its merchandise. In the course of the day she stops and leaves the company car she is driving on a parking lot operated by Simms Garage. The car is stolen from the lot. In a lawsuit brought against Simms on the theory that Simms was a negligent bailee, Simms raises the defense that there was no bailment because Mercedes did not own the car which was left with Simms. Is Simms correct?
3. What is a bailee's lien?
4. Morville went to the store of the Gregory Jewelers, Inc. Morville left with Gregory a very valuable diamond ring to be cleaned. That night Gregory locked the ring in the vault of the store. In the early morning hours of the next day, robbers cut through the roof of the store and dynamited a hole in the side of the vault and stole a number of objects including Morville's ring. Morville sued Gregory for the loss on the the-

ory that Gregory was liable because the loss had occurred and because the loss could have been prevented if the walls of the vault had been thicker and if an armed security guard were on duty in the store twenty-four hours a day. Is Morville correct?

5. Compare a gift with a bailment.

6. Priscilla leaves her car with the Moser Garage so that it can be repaired. The car disappears and cannot be delivered to Priscilla when she returns to the garage. Priscilla sues Moser. Moser claims that it is not liable because Priscilla has not shown that Moser was at fault in any way or responsible for the mysterious disappearance of the car. Is Moser correct?

7. Lillian loaned her automobile to Harry. Harry carelessly drove the automobile and hit Miriam. Miriam sued Lillian for damages. Is Lillian liable?

8. Compare a bailment with a constructive bailment.

9. John Hayes and Lynn Magosian, auditors for Lloyd, Little & Co., a public accounting firm, went to lunch at the Bay View Restaurant in San Francisco. John left his raincoat with a coatroom attendant, while Lynn chose to bring her new raincoat with her to the dining room, where she hung it on a coat hook near her booth. When leaving the restaurant, Lynn discovered that an individual had taken her new, expensive raincoat and left behind a coat of little value. When John sought to claim his raincoat at the coatroom, it could not be found; and the attendant advised that it might have been taken while he was on his break. John and Lynn sue the restaurant claiming that the restaurant was a bailee of the raincoats and had a duty to return them. Are both John and Lynn correct?

10. When Todd departed for college in late August, he left his Boston Whaler motor boat at Terry's Low Tide Marina for land storage during the Fall and Winter months. Terry rented the boat to his customers on a daily basis for the entire month of September. When Todd discovered this he sued Terry for conversion. Terry contends that he has the legal status of bailee, had proper possession of the boat, and that he cannot be held liable for conversion. Decide.

11. Rhodes parked his car on the self-service, park-and-lock lot of Pioneer Parking Lot, Inc. The ticket that he received from the ticket meter stated the following, "NOTICE. THIS CONTRACT LIMITS OUR LIABILITY—READ IT. WE RENT SPACE ONLY. NO BAILMENT IS CREATED. . . ." Rhodes parked the car himself and kept the keys. There was no attendant at the lot. The car was stolen from the lot. Rhodes sued the parking lot on the theory it had breached its duty as a bailee. Was there a bailment? [Rhodes v Pioneer Parking Lot, Inc. (Tenn) 501 SW2d 569.]

12. Lewis put a paper bag containing $3,000 in cash in a railroad station coin-operated locker. After the period of the coin rental expired, a locker company employee opened the locker, removed the money, and because of the amount, surrendered it to the police authorities, as was required by the local law. When Lewis demanded the return of the money from Aderholdt, the police property clerk, the latter required Lewis to prove

his ownership to the funds because there were circumstances leading to the belief that the money had been stolen by Lewis. He sued the police property clerk and the locker company. Was the locker company liable for breach of duty as a bailee? [Lewis v Aderholdt (Dist Col App) 203 A2d 919]

13. Joan took driving lessons at the A-North Shore Driving School. Later the school loaned her an automobile and took her for her state driving test. Crowley was the state examiner. Joan drove into a signal box on the side of the road. Crowley was seriously injured. He sued the driving school. Was it liable? [Crowley v A-North Shore Driving School, 19 Ill App 3d 1035, 313 NE2d 200]

14. Gilchrist took an automobile to a dealer, Winmar J. Ford, Inc., to have the tires rotated. Gilchrist was a refrigerator mechanic and had a special set of tools in the trunk of the car. He did not inform Ford that the tools were in the car. The car was stolen. Ford was sued for the value of the tools. Ford defended on the ground that it was not liable for the value of the tools and that it had never been informed of their value and therefore was not alerted to take special precautions. Was this a valid defense? [Gilchrist v Winmar J. Ford, Inc. 355 NYS2d 261]

15. Morse, who owned a diamond ring valued at $2,000, took the ring to Homer's, Inc., to sell for him. Homer placed the ring in the window display of his store. There was no guard or grating across the opening of the window inside his store. There was a partitioned door that was left unlocked. On two former occasions Homer's store had been robbed. Several weeks after Morse left his ring, armed men robbed the store and took several rings from the store window, including Morse's ring. He sued Homer, who defended on the ground that he was not liable for the criminal acts of others. Decide. [Morse v Homer's, Inc. 295 Mass 606, 4 NE2d 625]

16. Pauline Brooks brought expensive couch and chair covers to Angelo's Cleaners and inquired whether or not they could be safely dry cleaned. Angelo believed in good faith that they could be dry cleaned and so advised Pauline. However, the fabric turned out not to be dry-cleanable by the methods available to Angelo, and the fabrics were ruined. On the reverse side of the cleaning ticket given to Pauline, it stated that Angelo could not and did not warrant his dry cleaning work. Pauline sued Angelo for the replacement value of the covers. Angelo defends that he disclaimed any warranty and was not negligent. Decide. [Brooks v Angelo's Cleaners, 103 App Div 2d 901, 477 NYS2d 923]

17. Kamenir owned the Rosaline Apartments in Akron. The heating boiler quit functioning, pipes froze, and ceilings in the building began to fall in. Kamenir decided that all the tenants would have to vacate and the building be closed, and he orally notified Kayanda that there were "emergency problems in the building and he would have to find another place to live." Kamenir closed the building on December 5, 1981. Plywood was placed over all of the lower windows and balconies, the back door was locked and nailed shut, and the front door closed with a chain and a lock. A sign was posted stating that "all personal items remaining in this building after December 31, 1981 will be considered abandoned...."

When the building was closed, Kayanda had furniture, clothing, and other personal property in his apartment. Kayanda went to Legal Aid for assistance in recovering his property, and an arrangement was made for Kayanda to remove his property, but Kamenir's agent failed to keep that appointment. In February 1982, a second appointment was made, the building was opened for Kayanda, he found the apartment unlocked, the interior a mess, and many items missing. Kayanda sued Kamenir for the losses suffered. Kamenir defended that no bailment existed, and that he disclaimed liability for the period after December 31, 1981. Decide. [Kayanda v Kamenir, 16 Ohio Misc 2d 1, 475 NE2d 519]

CHAPTER 24

SPECIAL BAILMENTS AND

DOCUMENTS OF TITLE

CHAPTER OBJECTIVES

After studying this chapter you will be able to:

1. Differentiate between negotiable and nonnegotiable warehouse receipts.
2. List the three types of carriers of goods.
3. Describe the nature of a common carrier's liability for loss or damage to goods.
4. Explain the effect of a sale on consignment transaction.
5. Describe a hotelkeeper's liability for a guest's property.

Because of the nature of the property involved or because of the circumstances under which possession of that property is transferred, some bailments have a particularly strong effect on the public interest. These bailments are called **special bailments** and include the storage of goods in a warehouse as well as the transportation of goods by a carrier. The warehouses may be general warehouses, refrigerated or cold-storage warehouses, farm-products warehouses, or special-purpose warehouses. The carriers may be motor, rail, or air carriers; they may be water carriers utilizing boats or barges on the coastal waters, the Great Lakes, or the inland waterways; they may even be pipeline companies transporting oil and gas. The storage and transportation of goods as well as the documents used to evidence their ownership are vital to American commerce. For this reason, the law has imposed upon the special bailee a liability more stringent than that imposed upon ordinary bailees. Because of the public interest in protecting the property of travelers, hotelkeepers were absolutely liable for loss or damage to their guests' property at common law. Most states, however, have reduced this liability by statute for the benefit of hotelkeepers, allowing for the limitation of liability where notices inform guests of the existence of a safe where valuables may be deposited.

A. WAREHOUSERS

In contrast with the short-term or casual leaving of property typical of most bailments, some leaving of property is on a longer-term basis and on a larger scale and has become known as warehousing.

§ 24:1.   Definitions.

A **warehouser** is engaged in the business of storing the goods of others for compensation. **Public warehousers** hold themselves out to serve the public generally without discrimination.

A building is not essential to warehousing. Thus, an enterprise which stores boats outdoors on land is engaged in warehousing, since it is "engaged in the business of storing goods for hire."

§ 24:2.   Rights and Duties of Warehousers.

The common-law rights and duties of a warehouser, in the absence of modification by statute, are for the most part the same as those of a bailee in an ordinary mutual-benefit bailment.[1]

FACTS:

The Singer Corporation had been storing air conditioners in Stoda warehouses for several years. In May of 1974, Singer's transportation manager, Guy Bataglia, went to Stoda's "Hoffman Plant" warehouse accompanied by the president of Stoda, Larry Ellis. While looking over the building, Bataglia noticed the sprinkler system and inquired about it. Ellis, who knew the system had been turned off, said the system was active. Singer stored 133 cartons of air conditioning units at the Hoffman Plant as of that day. On July 7, 1974 a fire broke out in the Hoffman Plant, totally destroying Singer's goods. Singer claimed that it was entitled to recover the value of the destroyed air conditioners from Stoda.

DECISION:

Judgment for Singer. The facts showed that Singer had delivered air conditioners but had not received them back from the defendant warehouse. This was sufficient to create a prima facie case of liability. The burden of going forward to show that the warehouse was not negligent was then upon the warehouse. The warehouse had not offered any evidence. The additional evidence offer by the plaintiff merely confirmed the prima facie case. Singer was therefore entitled to recover on the strength of the prima facie case. [Singer Co. v Stoda, 79 App Div 2d 227, 435 NYS2d 508 (1981)]

(a) **Statutory Regulation.** Most states have passed warehouse acts defining the rights and duties of warehousers and imposing regulations as to

[1]Uniform Commercial Code § 7-204; F-M Potatoes, Inc. v Suda (ND) 259 NW2d 487 (1977).

charges and liens, bonds for the protection of patrons, and maintenance of storage facilities in a suitable and safe condition, inspections, and general methods of transacting business.

(b) **Lien of Warehouser.** The public warehouser has a lien against the goods for reasonable storage charges.[2] It is a **specific lien** in that it attaches only to the property with respect to which the charges arose and cannot be asserted against any other property of the same owner in the possession of the warehouser. The warehouser, however, may make a lien carry over to the other goods by noting on the receipt for one lot of goods that a lien is also claimed thereon for charges as to the other goods. The warehouser's lien for storage charges may be enforced by sale after due notice has been given to all persons who claim any interest in the property stored.[3]

FACTS:

When beans are brought to a warehouse for storage, they are cleaned and bagged. The warehouse makes a charge for this processing. Associated Bean Growers brought beans to Chester B. Brown Company for storage. When Associated later sought to withdraw the beans, Brown demanded that it pay a processing fee of $8.00 per one hundred pounds of beans. This was an unreasonable charge. Associated claimed that Brown therefore forfeited its right to any compensation for storage and processing.

DECISION:

Judgment for Brown. The demanding of unreasonable compensation was improper and forfeited Brown's right to hold the beans under a warehouser's lien, UCC § 7-209(4), but it did not forfeit the right to charge reasonable compensation for the services which in fact had been rendered. [Associated Bean Growers v Chester B. Brown Co. 198 Neb 775, 255 NW2d 425 (1977)]

---

§ 24:3. Warehouse Receipts.

A **warehouse receipt** is a written acknowledgment by a warehouser (bailee) that certain property has been received for storage from a named person called a **depositor** (bailor). The warehouse receipt is a memorandum of a contract between the **issuer**, the warehouse which prepares the receipt, and the depositor. It sets forth the terms of the contract for storage. While no particular form is required, the failure to include certain terms within the written or printed provisions of the warehouse receipt may lead to the issuer being held liable for damages to a person injured by the omission. Some of the essential terms are: (a) the location of the warehouse where the goods are stored, (b) date of issuance of the receipt, (c) the number of the receipt,

---

[2]UCC § 7-209(1). The warehouser's lien provision of the UCC is constitutional as a continuation of the common-law lien.

[3]UCC § 7-210. In Svendsen v Smith's Moving and Trucking Co., 76 App Div 2d 504, 431 NYS2d 94 (1980) it was held that this provision of the New York UCC authorizing a warehouse to sell stored property without first affording the customer an opportunity for a hearing violated the constitution of the state of New York. However, the same provision of the New York UCC had previously survived a challenge based on the federal Constitution. Flagg Bros. v Brooks, 436 US 149 (1978).

(d) information on negotiability or nonnegotiability of the receipt, (e) the rate of storage and handling charges, (f) a description of the goods or the packages containing them, and (g) a statement of any liabilities incurred for which the warehouser claims a lien or security interest.[4]

The warehouse receipt is also a **document of title;** that is, a document which in the regular course of business or financing is treated as adequately evidencing that the person in possession of it is entitled to receive, hold, and dispose of the document and the goods it covers.[5] The person lawfully holding this receipt then is entitled to the goods represented by the receipt. A warehouse receipt as a document of title is a symbol representing the goods, which receipt can be bought or sold, and can be used as security to obtain credit from a financial institution.

§ 24:4. Rights of Holders of Warehouse Receipts.

The rights of the holders of warehouse receipts differ depending on whether the receipts are nonnegotiable or negotiable.

(a) Nonnegotiable Warehouse Receipts. A warehouse receipt in which it is stated that the goods received will be delivered to a specified person is a **nonnegotiable warehouse receipt.** A transferee of a nonnegotiable receipt acquires only the title and rights which the transferor had actual authority to transfer.[6] As such, the transferee's rights may be defeated by a good faith purchaser of the goods from the transferor.[7]

(b) Negotiable Warehouse Receipts. A warehouse receipt stating that the goods will be delivered to the "bearer," or "to the order" of any named person is a negotiable warehouse receipt. If such a receipt is duly negotiated, the person to whom it is negotiated may acquire rights superior to those of the transferor.

(1) Negotiation. If the receipt provides for the delivery of the goods "to the bearer," the receipt may be negotiated by delivery of the document. If the receipt provides for delivery of the goods "to the order of" a named individual, the document must be indorsed by that person and delivered.

(2) Due Negotiation. A warehouse receipt is "duly negotiated" when the holder purchases the document in good faith, without notice of any defense to it, for value in the regular course of business or financing.[8] The holder of such a duly negotiated document acquires title to the document and title to the goods.[9] The holder also acquires the direct obligation of the issuer to hold or deliver the goods according to the terms of the warehouse receipt. The holder's rights cannot be defeated by the surrender of the goods by the warehouser to the depositor. Indeed, it is the duty of the warehouser to deliver the goods only to the holder of the negotiable receipt; and to cancel such receipt upon surrendering the goods.[10]

---

[4]UCC § 7-202(2).
[5]UCC § 1-201(15); § 7-102(1)(e).
[6]UCC § 7-504(1).
[7]UCC § 7-504(2)(b).
[8]UCC § 7-501(4).
[9]UCC § 7-502(1).
[10]UCC § 7-403(3).

NORTHERN TRANSFER CO.
880 ENTERPRISE AVE ● CAMDEN, ME 04843
PHONE 1-555-881-7071

NON-NEGOTIABLE WAREHOUSE RECEIPT

NORTHERN TRANSFER CO.
claims a lien for all lawful charges for storage and preservation of the goods; also for all lawful claims for money advanced, interest, insurance, transportation, labor, weighing, coopering and other charges and expenses in relation to such goods, and for the balance on any other accounts that may be due. The property covered by this receipt has NOT been insured by this Company for the benefit of the depositor against fire or any other casualty.

RECEIVED FROM

FOR ACCOUNT OF

THIS IS TO CERTIFY THAT WE HAVE RECEIVED the goods listed hereon in apparent good order, except as noted herein (contents, condition and quality unknown, SUBJECT TO ALL TERMS AND CONDITIONS INCLUDING LIMITATION OF LIABILITY HEREIN AND ON THE REVERSE HEREOF. Such property to be delivered to THE DEPOSITOR upon the payment of all storage, handling and other charges. Advances have been made and liability incurred on these goods as follows:

DOCUMENT NO.

DATE

CUSTOMER NO.

CUST. ORDER NO.

WAREHOUSE NO.

BAY

LOCATION

DELIVERING CARRIER	CARRIER NUMBER	PREPAID/COLLECT	SHIPPERS NUMBER

QUANTITY	SAID TO BE OR CONTAIN (CUSTOMER ITEM NO., WAREHOUSE ITEM NO., LOT NO., DESCRIPTION, ETC.)	WEIGHT	STORAGE	HANDLING
	DAMAGE AND EXCEPTIONS			
	TOTALS			

NORTHERN TRANSFER CO.

BY

NO DELIVERY WILL BE MADE ON THIS RECEIPT EXCEPT ON WRITTEN ORDER.

NONNEGOTIABLE WAREHOUSE RECEIPT

A negotiable warehouse receipt contains a promise to deliver "to depositor *or depositor's order,*" unlike a nonnegotiable warehouse receipt which promises only to deliver to depositor, as shown above.

The rights of a purchaser of a warehouse receipt by due negotiation are not cut off, for example, by the claim that: (a) an original owner was deprived of the receipt in "bearer" form by misrepresentation, fraud, mistake, loss, theft, or conversion; or (b) that a bona fide purchaser bought the goods from the warehouser.

A purchaser of a warehouse receipt who takes by due negotiation does not cut off all prior claims, however. If the person who deposited the goods with the warehouser did not own the goods or did not have power to transfer title to them, the purchaser is subject to the title of the true owner.[11] Accordingly, when goods are stolen and delivered to a warehouse and a warehouse receipt is issued for them, the owner prevails over the purchaser of the receipt by due negotiation.

(c) **Warranties.** The transferor of a negotiable or nonnegotiable warehouse receipt makes certain implied warranties for the protection of the transferee; namely, that the receipt is genuine, that its transfer is rightful and effective, and that the transferor has no knowledge of any facts that impair the validity or worth of the receipt.[12]

§ 24:5. Field Warehousing.

Ordinarily, stored goods are placed in a warehouse belonging to the warehouser. The owner of goods, such as a manufacturer, may keep the goods in the owner's own storage room or building. The warehouser may then take exclusive control over the room or the area in which the goods are stored and issue a receipt for the goods just as though they were in the warehouse. Such a transaction has the same legal effect with respect to other persons and purchasers of the warehouse receipts as though the property were in fact in the warehouse of the warehouser. This practice is called **field warehousing** since the goods are not taken to the warehouse but remain "in the field."

The purpose of field warehousing is to create warehouse receipts which the owner of the goods is able to pledge as security for loans. The owner could, of course, have done this by actually placing the goods in a warehouse, but this would have involved the expense of transportation and storage.

§ 24:6. Limitation of Liability of Warehouser.

A warehouser may limit liability by a provision in the warehouse receipt specifying the maximum amount for which the warehouser can be held liable. This privilege is subject to two qualifications: (a) the customer must be given the choice of storing the goods without such limitation if the customer pays a higher storage rate, and (b) the limitation must be stated as to each item or as to each unit of weight. A limitation is proper when it states that the maximum liability for a piano is $1,000 or that the maximum liability per bushel of wheat is a stated amount. Conversely, there cannot be a blanket limitation of liability, such as "maximum liability $50," when the receipt covers two or more items.

[11]UCC § 7-503(1).
[12]UCC § 7-507. These warranties are in addition to any that may arise between the parties by virtue of the fact that the transferor is selling the goods represented by the receipt to the transferee. See Chapter 25 as to sellers' warranties.

FACTS:

Richard Schewe and others placed personal property in a building occupied by the Winnebago County Fair Association, Inc. The property was destroyed by fire. Prior to placing their property in the building they signed a "Storage Rental Agreement" prepared by the County Fair Association, which stated in part that: "No liability exists for damage or loss to the stored equipment from the perils of fire ...." The individuals brought suit against the County Fair Association to recover damages for the losses on the theory of negligence of a warehouser. Allstate Insurance Company, having paid the fire loss claims, joined in the suit. The County Fair Association defended that the language in the storage agreement relieved it of all liability.

DECISION:

Judgment for the plaintiffs. The agreement language "no liability exists for damage ...from the perils of fire" was ineffective in this case since it did not specifically claim exemption from negligence. Moreover the language of the storage agreement did not contain an agreed monetary limit of liability, which is allowable under § 7-204 of the UCC, but sought a total exemption of all liability for damages, which is not permitted under the UCC. [Allstate v Winnebago County Fair Association, Inc. 131 Ill App 3d 225, 86 Ill Dec 233, 475 NE2d 230 (1985)]

General contract law determines whether a limitation clause is a part of the contract between the warehouser and the customer. A limitation in a warehouse receipt is not part of the contract when the receipt is delivered to the customer a substantial period of time after the goods have been left for storage.

B. COMMON CARRIERS

The purpose of a bailment may be transportation and not storage. In such case, the bailee may be a common carrier.

§ 24:7.   Definitions.

A **carrier** of goods is one who undertakes the transportation of goods, regardless of the method of transportation or the distance covered. The **consignor** or shipper is the person who delivers goods to the carrier for shipment. The **consignee** is the person to whom the goods are shipped and to whom the carrier should deliver the goods.

A carrier may be classified as (a) **a common carrier,** which holds itself out as willing to furnish transportation for compensation without discrimination to all members of the public who apply, assuming that the goods to be carried are proper and the facilities of the carrier are available; (b) **a contract carrier,** which transports goods under individual contracts; or (c) **a private carrier,** such as a truck fleet owned and operated by an industrial firm. The common carrier law applies to the first, the bailment law to the second, and the law of employment to the third.

FACTS:

The J.C. Trucking Co., Inc., was engaged under contracts to transport dress material from New York City to dressmaking establishments in New Haven, Hartford, and Bridgeport, Connecticut, and then to transport the finished dresses back to New York City. Dresses that were being carried to Ace-High Dresses, Inc., were stolen from the trucking company. Ace-High Dresses sued the trucking company and claimed that the latter was liable for the loss as a common carrier.

DECISION:

The trucking company was not liable for the loss as a common carrier since it did not hold itself out to carry for the general public. It was a contract carrier, because it would transport goods only if it had a preexisting contract with a shipper to do so. [Ace-High Dresses v J.C. Trucking Co. 122 Conn 578, 191 A 536 (1937)]

§ 24:8. Bills of Lading.

When the carrier accepts goods for shipment or forwarding, it ordinarily issues to the shipper a **bill of lading** in the case of land or water transportation or an **airbill** for air transportation. This instrument is a document of title and provides rights similar to those provided by a warehouse receipt. A bill of lading is both a receipt for the goods and a memorandum of a contract stating the terms of carriage.[13] Title to the goods may be transferred by transfer of the bill of lading made with that intention.

With respect to intrastate shipments, bills of lading are governed by the Uniform Commercial Code.[14] As to interstate shipments, bills of lading are regulated by the Federal Bills of Lading Act.[15]

(a) Contents of Bill of Lading. The form of the bill of lading is regulated in varying degrees by administrative agencies.[16] For example, the Interstate Commerce Commission requires that negotiable bills of lading must be printed on yellow paper, and nonnegotiable or straight bills of lading must be printed on white paper.[17]

As against the bona fide transferee of the bill of lading, a carrier is bound by the recitals in the bill as to the contents, quantity, or weight of goods.[18] This means that the carrier must produce the goods which are described or pay damages for failing to do so. This rule is not applied if facts appear on the face of the bill that should keep the transferee from relying on the recital.

(b) Negotiation. A bill of lading is a **negotiable bill of lading** when by its terms the goods are to be delivered "to bearer" or "to the order of" a named person.[19] Any other bill of lading, such as one that consigns the goods

[13]Hogan Transfer and Storage Corp. v Waymine, _____ Ind App _____ , 399 NE2d 779 (1980).
[14]UCC, Article 7.
[15]Title 49, United States Code § 81, et seq.
[16]The UCC contains no provision for the regulating of the form of the bill of lading.
[17]Bill of Lading 55 ICC 671.
[18]UCC § 7-301(1).
[19]UCC § 7-104(1)(a).

to a named person is a **nonnegotiable** or **straight bill of lading.** Like transfer-ees of warehouse receipts who take by due negotiation, holders of bills of lading who take by due negotiation ordinarily also acquire the title to the bills and title to the goods represented by them. These rights are not affected by the fact that (1) the original owner had been somehow deprived of the bill in bearer form, (2) that the goods had already been surrendered by the carrier, or (3) had been stopped in transit.[20] The rights are defeated by the true owner, however, when a thief delivers the goods to the carrier and then negotiates the bill of lading.[21]

(c) **Warranties.** By transferring for value a bill of lading, whether negotiable or nonnegotiable, the transferor makes certain implied warranties to the transferee. The transferor impliedly warrants that (1) the bill of lading is genuine, (2) its transfer is rightful and is effective to transfer the goods represented thereby, and (3) the transferor has no knowledge of facts that would impair the validity or worth of the bill of lading.[22]

§ 24:9.   Rights of Common Carrier.

A common carrier of goods has the right to make reasonable and necessary rules for the conduct of its business. It has the right to charge such rates for its services as yield it a fair return on the property devoted to the business of transportation, but the exact rates charged are regulated by the Interstate Commerce Commission in the case of interstate carriers and by state commissions in the case of intrastate carriers. As an incident of the right to charge for its services, a carrier may charge **demurrage**—a charge for the detention of its cars or equipment for an unreasonable length of time by either the consignor or consignee.[23]

As security for unpaid transportation and service charges, a common carrier has a lien on goods that it transports. The carrier's lien also secures demurrage charges, the costs of preservation of the goods, and the costs of sale to enforce the lien.[24] The lien of a carrier is a specific lien. It attaches only to goods shipped under the particular contract, but includes all of the shipment even though it is sent in installments. Thus, when part of the ship-ment is delivered to the consignee, the lien attaches to the portion remaining in possession of the carrier.

§ 24:10.   Duties of Common Carrier.

A common carrier is generally required (a) to receive and carry proper and lawful goods of all persons who offer them for shipment so long as it has room; (b) to furnish facilities that are adequate for the transporta-tion of freight in the usual course of business, and to furnish proper storage

---

[20]UCC § 7-502(2).
[21]UCC § 7-503(1).
[22]UCC § 7-507; Federal Bills of Lading Act (FBLA), 49 USC § 114, 116. When the transfer of the bill of lading is part of a transaction by which the transferor sells the goods repre-sented thereby to the transferee, there will also arise the warranties that are found in other sales of goods. [23]Betsy Ross Foods v A, C & Y Ry. Co. 17 Ohio App 3d 145, 468 NE2d 338 (1983).
[24]UCC § 7-307(1); FBLA, 49 USC § 105.

facilities for goods awaiting shipment or awaiting delivery after shipment;[25] (c) to follow the directions given by the shipper; (d) to load and unload goods delivered to it for shipment (in less-than-carload lots in the case of railroads), but the shipper or consignee may assume this duty by contract or custom; (e) to deliver the goods in accordance with the shipment contract.

Goods must be delivered at the usual place of delivery at the specified destination. When goods are shipped under a negotiable bill of lading, the carrier must not deliver the goods without obtaining possession of the bill properly indorsed. When goods are shipped under a straight bill of lading, the carrier is justified in delivering the goods to the consignee or the consignee's agent without receiving the bill of lading, unless notified by the shipper to deliver the goods to someone else. If the carrier delivers the goods to the wrong person, the carrier is liable for breach of contract and for the tort of conversion.

§ 24:11.   Liabilities of Common Carrier.

When goods are delivered to a common carrier for immediate shipment and while they are in transit, the carrier is absolutely liable for any loss or damage to the goods unless it can prove that it was due solely to one or more of the following excepted causes: (a) act of God, meaning a natural phenomenon that is not reasonably foreseeable; (b) act of public enemy, such as the military forces of an opposing government, as distinguished from ordinary robbers; (c) act of public authority, such as a health officer removing goods from a truck; (d) act of the shipper, such as fraudulent labeling or defective packing; or (e) inherent nature of the goods, such as those naturally tending to spoil or deteriorate.

FACTS:

Frosty Land Foods shipped a load of beef from its plant in Montgomery, Alabama, to Scott Meat Company in Los Angeles via the Refrigerated Transport Co. (RTC), a common carrier. Early Wednesday morning, December 7, at 12:55 a.m., two of RTC's drivers departed from the Frosty Land facility with the load of beef. The bill of lading called for delivery at Scott Meat Company on Friday, December 9, at 6:00 a.m. The RTC drivers arrived in Los Angeles at approximately 3:30 p.m. on Friday, December 9, 1977; and Scott notified the drivers that it could not process the meat at that time. The drivers checked into a motel for the weekend and the load was delivered to Scott on Monday, December 12, 1977. After inspecting 65 of the 308 carcasses, Scott determined that the meat was in "off condition" and refused the shipment. On Tuesday, December 13, 1977, Frosty Land sold the meat, after extensive trimming, at a loss of $13,529. Frosty Land brought suit against RTC for his loss.

DECISION:

Judgment for Frosty Land Foods. The beef was in good condition when given to Refrigerated Transport. It was damaged when delivered by Refrigerated Transport. Refrigerated Transport was a common carrier and upon proof of the in transit loss it became liable for that loss unless it showed that the loss had been due solely to one or more of the excepted causes. The carrier did not establish that the loss was due to such a cause. Therefore the carrier was liable for the loss. [Frosty Land Foods v Refrigerated Transport Co. (CA5 Ala) 613 F2d 1344 (1980)]

---

[25]Exquisite Form Industries v Transporters Ragat (DC Tex) 585 F Supp 473 (1984).

(a) **Carrier's Liability for Delay.** A carrier is liable for losses caused by its failure to deliver goods within a reasonable time. Thus, the carrier is liable for losses arising from a fall in price or a deterioration of the goods caused by its unreasonable delay. The carrier, however, is not liable for every delay. The risk of ordinary delays incidental to transporting goods is assumed by the shipper.

(b) **Liability of Initial and Connecting Carriers.** When goods are carried over the lines of several carriers, the initial and the final carrier, as well as the carrier on whose lines the loss is sustained, may be liable to the shipper or the owner of the goods; but only one payment may be obtained.

(c) **Limitation of Liability of Carrier.** In the absence of a constitutional or statutory prohibition, a carrier generally has the right to limit its liability by contract.[26] A clause limiting the liability of the carrier is not enforceable unless consideration is given for it, usually in the form of a reduced rate, and provided further that the shipper is allowed to ship without limitation of liability if the shipper chooses to pay the higher or ordinary rate.

A carrier may by contract exempt itself from liability for losses not arising from its own negligence, but may not exempt itself from liability for loss due to its own negligence. Thus, a provision which purports to exempt an air carrier from liability for its own negligence in the carriage of live animals as baggage has been held invalid.

(d) **Notice of Claim.** The bill of lading and applicable government regulations may require that a carrier be given notice of any claim for damages or loss of goods within a specified time, generally within nine months.

(e) **C.O.D. Shipment.** A common carrier transporting goods under a C.O.D. (cash on delivery) shipment may not make delivery of the goods without first receiving payment. If it does so, it is liable to the shipper for any loss resulting therefrom. If the carrier accepts a check from the consignee and the check is not honored by the bank on which it is drawn, the carrier is liable to the shipper for the amount thereof.[27]

FACTS:

Swest sent a number of gold and silver shipments C.O.D. to New York on American Airlines, a common carrier, to a person identifying himself as Scott Barter. The first two shipments were accomplished without any problems, with Barter paying by certified personal checks. The last two shipments, also sent C.O.D., and priced on the airbill at $48,200 and $38,160, respectively, were picked up by Barter around midnight on November 11 and November 12.

American accepted payment by what appeared to be certified personal checks but actually the bank certifications were forged. Since the banks were closed at the time the merchandise was picked up, American made no attempt to verify the forged certified checks which were later dishonored. Swest sued American for the amount of the checks. American contends that it had no obligation to make sure that the purported certified checks were genuine and not forgeries.

[26]Star-kist Foods v Chicago, Rock Island & Pacific R.R. (DC Ill) 586 F Supp 252 (1984).

[27]Mountain States Waterbed v O.N.C. Freight System, 44 Colo App 433, 614 P2d 906 (1980).

DECISION:

Judgment for Swest. American had an obligation to verify the checks. When utilizing the C.O.D. method the seller clearly indicates it wants liquid assets, not a contract claim against a distant buyer who may be insolvent, litigious, dishonest, or all three. To hold that a C.O.D. carrier need not verify purported certified checks would undermine the confidence of shippers that they would receive cash or the equivalent in payment for their C.O.D. shipments. [Swest, Inc v American Airlines, Inc (Tex App) 694 SW2d 399 (1985)]

C. FACTORS

Some selling agents are called factors. A **factor** is a special type of bailee who sells goods consigned to the factor as though the factor were the owner of the goods.

§ 24:12. Definitions.

The device of entrusting a person with the possession of property for the purpose of sale is commonly called **selling on consignment.**[28] The owner who consigns the goods for sale is the **consignor.** The person or agent to whom they are consigned is the **consignee**; the consignee may also be known as a commission merchant. A consignee's compensation is known as a **commission** or **factorage.** In a sale on consignment, the property remains the property of the owner or consignor, and the consignee acts as the agent of the owner to pass the owner's title to the buyer.

§ 24:13. Effect of Factor Transaction.

As a factor is by definition authorized by the consignor to sell the goods entrusted to the factor, such a sale will pass the title of the consignor to the purchaser. Before the factor makes the sale, the goods belong to the consignor, but in some instances, creditors of the factor may ignore the consignor and treat the goods as though they belonged to the consignee.[29] If the consignor is not the owner, as when a thief delivers stolen goods to the factor, a sale by the factor is an unlawful conversion.[30] It is constitutional, however, to provide by statute that the factor who sells in good faith in ignorance of the rights of other persons in the goods is protected from liability and cannot be treated as a converter of the goods, as would be the case in the absence of such statutory immunity.

D. HOTELKEEPERS

A hotelkeeper has a bailee's liability with respect to property specifically entrusted to the hotelkeeper's care.

---

[28]Matter of Freidman, 54 App Div 2d 70, 407 NYS2d 999 (1978).
[29]UCC § 2-326.
[30]De Vore v McClure Livestock Commission Co. 207 Kan 499, 485 P2d 1013 (1971).

§ 24:14.   Definitions.

The rules governing the special relationship between a hotelkeeper and guest arose in part because of the special needs of travelers. Thus the legal definitions of "hotelkeeper" and "guest" are meant to exclude lodging of a more permanent character, such as that provided by boardinghouse keepers to boarders.

(a) Hotelkeeper. The term **hotelkeeper** is used by law to refer to an operator of a hotel, motel, tourist home, or to anyone who is regularly engaged in the business of offering living accommodations to all transient persons.[31] In the early law, the hotelkeeper was called an innkeeper or a tavernkeeper.

(b) Guest. The essential element in the definition of a **guest** is that the guest is a transient. The guest need not be a traveler nor come from a distance. A person living within a short distance of a hotel who engages a room at the hotel and remains there overnight is a guest.

A person who enters a hotel at the invitation of a guest or attends a dance or a banquet given at the hotel is not a guest. Similarly, the guest of a registered occupant of a motel room who shares the room with the occupant without the knowledge or consent of the management is not a guest of the motel, since there is no relationship between that person and the motel.

§ 24:15.   Duration of Guest Relationship.

The relationship of guest and hotelkeeper does not begin until a person is received as a guest by the hotelkeeper. The relationship terminates when the guest leaves or when the guest ceases to be a transient, as when the guest arranges for a more or less permanent residence at the hotel. The transition from the status of guest to the status of boarder or lodger must be clearly indicated. It is not established by the mere fact that one remains at the hotel for a long period, even though it runs into months.

FACTS:
Salisbury was a guest at the St. Regis-Sheraton Hotel. He was ready to leave the hotel but wanted to go sightseeing for another day. He checked out of his room and paid the hotel bill. With the consent of the hotel, he left his luggage with the hotel. When he returned he learned that some of the luggage had been stolen. He claimed that the hotel was liable to him as a guest. The hotel asserted that the guest status had ended and that the hotel was merely a bailee of the luggage.

DECISION:
The hotel was still a hotel and Salisbury was still a guest insofar as the luggage was concerned. The holding of luggage temporarily when a guest leaves a hotel is such a normal incident of the hotel-guest relationship that it could not be said that the hotel ceased to have the liability of a hotel with respect to such luggage. Therefore hotel law applied and the hotel was not to be deemed a mere bailee of the luggage. [Salisbury v St. Regis-Sheraton Hotel Corp. (SD NY) 490 F Supp 449 (1980)]

---

[31]A person furnishing the services of a hotelkeeper has the status of such even though the word "hotel" is not used in the business name. Lackman v Department of Labor and Industries, 78 Wash 2d 212, 471 P2d 82 (1970).

§ 24:16.   Hotelkeeper's Liability for Guest's Property.

As to property expressly entrusted to the hotelkeeper's care, the hotelkeeper has a bailee's liability. At common law, the hotelkeeper was an insurer of any other property of a guest.[32] As exceptions to this absolute liability at common law, the hotelkeeper is not liable for loss caused by an act of God, public enemy, act of public authority, the inherent nature of the property, or the fault of the guest.

In most states, statutes limit or provide a method of limiting the common-law liability of a hotelkeeper. The statutes may limit the extent of liability, reduce the liability of a hotelkeeper to that of an ordinary bailee, or permit the hotelkeeper to limit liability by contract or by posting a notice of the limitation. Some statutes relieve the hotelkeeper from liability when directions for depositing valuables with the hotelkeeper are posted on the doors of the rooms occupied and the guest fails to comply with the directions. When a statute permits a hotel receiving valuables for deposit in its safe-deposit box to limit its liability to the amount specified in the agreement signed by the guest, such limitation binds the guest even though the loss was caused by negligence on the part of the hotel. Where a statute modifies the common-law liability of a hotelkeeper, it is critical that the hotelkeeper comply with the statute, for such statutes are strictly construed.[33]

FACTS:

An employee of the plaintiff General Foods Corporation was a paying guest of the Skyways Motor Lodge. Certain airplane parts, the property of General Foods, were stolen from the employee's room. The plaintiff's employee did not see the motel's limitation-of-liability notice which appeared at the bottom of the roomrate sign on the back of the motel door. The notice required that all valuables be left at the office. A state statute which limited hotelkeepers' common-law liability required that notices be placed "in every lodging room" stating the fact that "such safe or vault is provided" for the valuables. General Foods sued Skyways on the theory that the motel had breached its common-law duty as an innkeeper to safeguard a guest's property. A judgment on the issue of liability was granted to General Foods on the ground that Skyways had not complied with the notice requirements of the state statute. Skyways appealed.

DECISION:

Judgment for plaintiff. The state statute, which modifies the common law, must be strictly construed; and in order to gain the statute's protection, an innkeeper must comply meticulously with its requirements. The statute requires notice to guests of the existence of a "secure safe or vault" for valuables. The notice on the hotel room door did not advise the guest of the existence of a secure safe or vault. Therefore Skyways was not entitled to the statute's protection against an innkeeper's absolute liability at common law for the loss of the chattels of its guest. [Skyways Motor Lodge v General Foods Corp. (Del) 403 A2d 722 (1979)]

---

[32]Hanover Ins. Co. v Alamo Hotel (Iowa) 264 NW2d 774 (1978).
[33]Zacharia v Harbor Island Spa, Inc. (CA2 NY) 684 F2d 199 (1982).

§ 24:17.   Hotelkeeper's Lien.

The hotelkeeper has a lien on the baggage of guests for the agreed charges, or if no express agreement was made, for the reasonable value of the accommodations furnished. Statutes permit the hotelkeeper to enforce this lien by selling the goods of the guests at a public sale.[34] The lien of the hotelkeeper is terminated by (a) the guest's payment of the hotel charges, (b) any conversion of the guest's goods by the hotelkeeper, and (c) surrender of the goods to the guest. In the last situation, an exception is made when the goods are given to the guest for temporary use.

§ 24:18.   Boarders or Lodgers.

To those persons who are permanent boarders or lodgers, rather than transient guests, the hotelkeeper owes only the duty of an ordinary bailee of personal property under a mutual-benefit bailment.

A hotelkeeper has no common-law right of lien on property of boarders or lodgers, as distinguished from guests, in the absence of an express agreement creating such a lien. In a number of states, however, legislation giving a lien to a boarding house or a lodging housekeeper has been adopted.

SUMMARY

A warehouser stores the goods of others for compensation, and for the most part has the rights and duties of a bailee in an ordinary mutual benefit bailment. A warehouser issues a warehouse receipt to the depositor of the goods, and this receipt is a document of title which entitles the person in possession of the receipt to receive the goods. The warehouse receipt can be bought or sold, or used as security to obtain financing from banks. A non-negotiable warehouse receipt states that the goods received will be delivered to a specified person. A negotiable warehouse receipt states that the goods will be delivered to the "bearer," or "to the order" of a named person, and if such a receipt is duly negotiated, the transferee may acquire rights superior to the transferor. A warehouser may limit its liability for loss or damage to goods due to its own negligence to an agreed valuation of the property stated in the warehouse receipt, provided the depositor is given the right to store the goods without the limitation at a higher storage rate.

A common carrier is in the business of accepting goods from the public for transportation to a designated destination for compensation. It issues a bill of lading or airbill to the shipper, both of which are documents of title and provide rights similar to those provided by a warehouse receipt. A common carrier is absolutely liable for any loss or damage to the goods unless the carrier can show that the loss was caused by an act of God, an act

---

[34]There is authority that the hotelkeeper's lien may not be exercised unless the guest is given an impartial hearing and that it is unconstitutional as a denial of due process to permit the hotelkeeper to hold or sell the guest's property without such a hearing. Klim v Jones (DC Cal) 315 F Supp 109 (1970). A hotel cannot seize the goods of a guest under a statutory lien law without first affording the guest a hearing as to liability, and the failure to do so deprives the guest of the due process guaranteed by the federal Constitution. New York v Skinner, 33 NYS2d 23, 300 NE2d 716 (1973).

of a public enemy, an act of a public authority, an act of the shipper, or the inherent nature of the goods. The carrier may limit its liability by contract.

A factor is a special type of bailee, who has possession of the owner's property for the purpose of sale. The factor or consignee receives a commission on the sale.

A hotelkeeper is in the business of providing living accommodations to transient persons. These persons are called guests. Subject to exceptions, hotelkeepers were absolutely liable for loss or damage to their guests' property at common law. Most states, however, provide a method of limiting the common-law liability of a hotelkeeper. A hotelkeeper has a lien on the property of the guest for the agreed charges.

QUESTIONS AND CASE PROBLEMS

1. What social forces are involved in the rule of law governing the liability of a common carrier for loss of freight?
2. Gina stored her furniture with the Brady Warehouse & Storage Company for the summer. At the end of the summer, Gina took her furniture away after paying all storage charges. Brady gave her a receipt showing that the storage charges were paid in full. Is this a warehouse receipt?
3. Gowan sent goods by the Southern Mississippi Railroad to Robert in New Orleans. Fulton appeared in the New Orleans freight office of the railroad and stated that he was Robert's employee, and was sent to pick up the shipment. The shipment was given to Fulton without any proof of his authority from Robert. Robert later demanded the goods, and it was then learned that Fulton did not have any authority from Robert and had disappeared with the shipment. Is the railroad liable to Robert?
4. Compare the liens of carriers, warehousers, and hotels in terms of being specific.
5. Jennie is visiting friends in San Francisco. She registered in a motel in the outskirts of the city. One of her friends visits her at the motel. An intense storm springs up and the friend shares Jennie's room overnight. Is the friend a guest of the motel?
6. Ludwig sells 100 television sets to Stewart on consignment. As between Ludwig and Stewart, who owns the television sets while they are in Stewart's store and held as inventory?
7. Compare the limitation of the liability of a warehouser and of a hotel.
8. Compare warehouse receipts and bills of lading as to negotiability.
9. Latham and Loud, sporting goods manufacturers' representatives in Cleveland, Ohio, hijacked a truckload of ice skates from the Bartlett Shoe and Skate Company. Latham and Loud warehoused the skates at Snow's Warehouse, and received a negotiable warehouse receipt. Preston, a lender who had had business dealings with Latham and Loud in the past and believed them to be honest individuals, made a bona fide purchase of the receipt. Bartlett discovered that the skates were at Snow's Warehouse, and informed Snow's of the hijacking. Snow's delivered the skates to Bartlett. Latham and Loud have fled the state. Preston brings an action against Snow's claiming that he was entitled to delivery of the skates, since he acquired the negotiable receipt by due negotiation. Is Preston correct?

10. Welch Brothers Trucking, Inc., a common carrier, made an agreement with B & L Export and Import Co. of San Francisco to transport a shipment of freshly harvested bluefin tuna from Calais, Maine to the Japan Air Lines freight terminal at New York's Kennedy Airport. The "bluefin" had been packed in ice and were to be shipped by Japan Air to Tokyo where fresh bluefin at the peak of their autumnal fattening are used in the traditional Japanese raw fish dish *sashimi* and command very high prices. When transportation charges were not paid by B & L's representative in New York, Welch Brothers refused to release the shipment to Japan Air Lines. B & L's representative in New York explained that he had no check writing authority, but assured Welch that it would be paid and pleaded for the release of the cargo because of its perishable nature. Transportation charges were not paid in the next twelve hour period because the principals of B & L were on a business trip to the Far East and could not be contacted. After waiting the twelve hour period Welch sent a telegram to B & L's offices in San Francisco stating the amount due and that it intended to auction the cargo in twenty-four hours if transportation charges were not paid. Welch also sent telegrams to all fish wholesalers listed in the New York City Yellow Pages seeking bidders after advising that the cargo would be sold at auction in twenty-four hours if the charges were not paid. Welch sold the shipment to the highest bidder at the appointed time for an amount just in excess of the transportation charges plus a demurrage charge for the thirty-six hour waiting period. When the principals of B & L were later informed of what happened, they were outraged and initiated suit against Welch for the profits they would have earned had the cargo been shipped and sold in Japan. Decide.

11. The Birmingham Television Corporation stored television equipment with the Harris Warehouse Company, and received a warehouse receipt. A water main in the city burst, flooding the warehouse and destroying the equipment. Birmingham Corporation sued the water works and the warehouse. The warehouse claimed that it was not liable because the action was not commenced within nine months after notice was given of the damage, as was expressly required by the terms on the back of the warehouse receipt. There was no evidence that the Birmingham Corporation was aware of the requirement printed on the back of the receipt. Is the nine-month limitation effective to bar a suit filed after the expiration of the nine-month period? [Birmingham Television Corp. v Water Works, 292 Ala 147, 290 So2d 636]

12. Evers owned and operated a warehouse. DeCecchis phoned and inquired as to the rates and then brought furniture in for storage. Nothing was said at any time about any limitation of the liability of Evers as a warehouser. A warehouse receipt was mailed to DeCecchis several days later. The receipt contained a clause that limited liability to $50 per package stored. Was the limitation of liability binding on DeCecchis? [DeCecchis v Evers, 54 Del 99, 174 A2d 463]

13. Vanguard Transfer Co. ran a moving and storage business. It obtained an insurance policy from the St. Paul Fire & Marine Insurance Co. covering goods which it had "accepted at the warehouse for storage." Dahl rented a room in Vanguard's building. Both Dahl and Vanguard had

keys to the room. Dahl was charged a flat monthly rental for the room and could keep any property there which he desired. Vanguard did not make any record of the goods which Dahl brought to the warehouse. There was a fire in the warehouse and Dahl's property was destroyed. He sued the insurance company. Was it liable? [Dahl v St. Paul Fire & Marine Insurance Co. 36 Wis 2d 420, 153 NW2d 624]

14. Dovax Fabrics, Inc. had been shipping goods by a common carrier, G & A Delivery Corp., for over a year, during which all of G & A's bills to Dovax bore the notation, "Liability limited to $50 unless value is declared and paid for. . . ." Dovax gave G & A three lots of goods, having a total value of $1,799.95. A truck containing all three was stolen that night, without negligence on the part of G & A. Should Dovax recover from G & A (a) $1,799.95, (b) $150 for three shipments, or (c) nothing? [Dovax Fabrics, Inc. v G & A Delivery Corp. (NY Civ Ct) 4 UCCRS 492]

15. The guest in a motel opened the bedroom window at night and went to sleep. During the night a prowler pried open the screen, entered the room and stole property of the guest. The guest sued the motel. The motel raised the contentions that it was not responsible for property in the possession of the guest and that the guest had been contributorily negligent in opening the window. Could the guest recover damages? [Buck v Hankin, 217 Pa Super 262, 269 A2d 344]

16. On March 30 Emery Air Freight Corp. picked up a shipment of furs from Hopper Furs, Inc. Hopper's chief of security filled in certain items in the airbill. In the box entitled "zip code," he placed the figure "61,045." The "zip code" box is immediately above the "declared value" box. The airbill contained a clause limiting liability to $10 per pound of cargo lost or damaged, unless the shipper makes a declaration of value in excess of the amount and pays a higher fee. A higher fee was not charged in this case; and Gerald Doane signed the airbill for the carrier and took possession of the furs. The furs were lost by Emery in transit, and Hopper sued for the value of the furs, $61,045. Emery's offer to pay $2,150, the $10 per pound rate set forth in the airbill, was rejected. Hopper claims that the amount $61,045, which was mistakenly placed in the zip code box was in fact part of the contract set forth in the airbill; and that Emery upon reviewing the contract must have realized a mistake was made. Decide. [Hopper Furs, Inc. v Emery Air Freight Corporation (CA 8 Mo) 749 F2d 1261]

17. Jose Maria Berga de Lema, a Brazilian resident, arrived in New York City. His luggage consisted of three suitcases, an attache case, and a cylindrical bag. The attache case and the cylindrical bag contained jewels, valued at $300,000. Mr. de Lema went from JFK Airport to the Waldorf Astoria Hotel where he gave the three suitcases to hotel staff in the garage, and then went to the lobby to register. The assistant manager, Mr. Baez, summoned room clerk Mr. Tamburino to assist him. Mr. de Lema stated, "The room clerk asked me if I had a reservation. I said, 'Yes. The name is Jose Berga de Lema.' And I said, 'I want a safety deposit box.' He said, 'Please fill out your registration.'" While de Lema was filling out the reservation form, paying $300 in cash as an advance,

and Tamburino was filling out a receipt for that amount, de Lema had placed the attache case and the cylindrical bag on the floor. A blond woman jostled de Lema, apparently creating a diversion, and when he next looked down, he discovered that the attache case was gone. Mr. de Lema brought suit against the hotel for the value of the jewels stolen in the hotel's lobby. The hotel maintained a safe for valuables and posted notices in the lobby, garage and rooms, as required by the New York law which modifies a hotelkeeper's common-law liability. The notices stated in part that the hotel is not liable for the loss of valuables which a guest neglects to deliver to the hotel for safekeeping. The hotel defends that de Lema neglected to inform it of the presence of the jewels and to deliver the jewels to the hotel. It states that it is not liable. Decide. [De Lema v Waldorf Astoria Hotel, Inc. (SDNY) 588 FSupp 19]

PART 4

SALES

Chapter 25 Nature and Form of Sales
Chapter 26 Risk and Property Rights
Chapter 27 Obligations and Performance
Chapter 28 Warranties and Other Product Liabilities
Chapter 29 Remedies for Breach of Sales Contracts

CHAPTER 25

NATURE AND FORM

OF SALES

CHAPTER OBJECTIVES

After studying this chapter you will be able to:
1. Distinguish between a sale of goods and other transactions relating to goods.
2. List points of difference between general contract law and the law of sales.
3. Define a bulk transfer.
4. State what precautions should be taken by a bulk transferee.
5. State when a contract for the sale of goods must be evidenced by a writing.
6. List and explain the exceptions to the requirement that certain contracts be evidenced by a writing.
7. Solve problems involving the nature and form of contracts for the sale of goods.

The most common business transaction is the sale of goods, such as food, clothing, or books. The law of sales is a combination of the law merchant, the common law of England, and former statutes as modified and codified by Article 2 of the Uniform Commercial Code.

A. NATURE AND LEGALITY

A sale of goods is a present transfer of title to movable personal property for a price. This price may be a payment of money, an exchange of other property, or the performance of services.[1] When a free item is given with the

---

[1] Uniform Commercial Code § 2-304(1). O'Keefe Elevator Co. v Second Ave. Properties, Ltd, 216 Neb 170, 343 NW2d 54 (1984).

purchase of other goods, it is the purchasing of the other goods which is the price for the "free" goods and hence the transaction as to the free goods is a sale.

The parties to a sale are the person who owns the goods and the person to whom the title is transferred. The transferor is the seller or vendor, and the transferee is the buyer or vendee.

§ 25:1.   Subject Matter of Sales.

Goods, the subject matter of a sale under Article 2 of the Uniform Commercial Code, includes any thing movable at the time it is identified as the subject of the transaction.[2] The subject matter may not be (a) investment securities, such as stocks and bonds, the sale of which is regulated by Article 8 of the UCC; (b) choses in action, such as insurance policies and promissory notes since they are assigned or negotiated rather than sold, or which, because of their personal nature, are not transferable in any case; or (c) real estate, such as a house, factory, or farm.

(a) Nature of Goods. Most goods are tangible and solid, such as an automobile or a chair. But goods may also be fluid, as oil or gasoline. Goods may also be intangible, as natural gas and electricity. The Code is applicable to both new and to used and secondhand goods.[3]

(b) Existing and Future Goods. Goods physically existing and owned by the seller at the time of the transaction are called **existing goods**. All other goods are called **future goods**. Future goods include both goods that are physically existing but not owned by the seller and goods that have not yet been manufactured.

A person can make a contract to sell goods at a future date. No sale can be made of future goods. As the "seller" does not have any title to future goods, there can be no transfer of that title now, and hence no sale. For example, an agreement made today that all fish caught on a fishing trip tomorrow shall belong to a particular person does not make that person the owner of any fish today.

When the parties attempt to effect a present sale of future goods, the agreement operates only as a contract to sell the goods. Thus, a farmer purporting to transfer the title today to a future crop would be held subject to a duty to transfer the crop when it came into existence. But the contract itself does not pass the title to the crop.

§ 25:2.   Sale Distinguished.

A sale is an actual present transfer of title. If there is a transfer of a lesser interest than title, the transaction is not a sale.

(a) Bailment. A bailment is not a sale because only possession is transferred to the bailee. The bailor remains the owner. A lease of goods, such as an automobile, is a bailment.

---

[2]It may also include things which are attached to the land, such as those consisting of (a) minerals or buildings or materials forming part of buildings if they are to be removed or severed by the seller, (b) other things attached to the land to be removed by either party. UCC § 2-107.

[3]Rose v Epley Motor Sales, 288 NC 53, 215 SE2d 573 (1975).

Although a bailment is not a sale, there is a trend in the law, to hold the commercial bailor to the same responsibilities as a seller.

(b) Gift. There can be no sale without a price. A **gift** is a gratuitous or free transfer of the title to property.

(c) Contract to Sell. When the parties intend that title to goods will pass at a future time and they make a contract so providing, a **contract to sell** is created.

(d) Option to Purchase. A sale, a present transfer of title, differs from an *option to purchase*. The latter is neither a transfer of title nor a contract to transfer title, but a power to make a contract to sell.

(e) Conditional Sale. A **conditional sale** customarily refers to a "condition precedent" transaction by which title does not vest in the purchaser until payment in full has been made for the property purchased. This was formerly a common type of sale used when personal property was purchased on credit and payment was to be made in installments. In most cases, the conditional sale has been replaced by a secured transaction under Article 9 of the UCC.

(f) Contract for services. A contract for services is an ordinary contract and is not governed by the UCC.[4]

FACTS:

Garmon owned a tract of land. He made a contract with the King Coal Company to mine the coal on his land. King was to deliver the coal to Garmon who would then pay King a specified amount per ton. Garmon claimed that King broke the contract. The decision depended upon whether the contract was a sale of goods.

DECISION:

The contract was not a sale of goods because there was no transfer of title to the coal. The coal belonged to Garmon when it was in the ground. When it was taken from the ground it was still owned by Garmon. Therefore there was no transfer of title from King to Garmon. The contract was merely a contract for services and was covered by general contract law principles and not by the Uniform Commercial Code. [King Coal Company, Inc. v Garmon, _____ Ala _____, 388 So2d 886 (1980)]

If a contract calls for both the rendering of services and the supplying of materials to be used in performing the services, the contract is classified according to its dominant element. If the sale of goods is dominant, it is a sales contract. If the service element is dominant, it is a service contract. For example, the contract of a repairer is a contract for services, even though in making the repairs, parts are supplied to perform the task. The supplying of such parts is not regarded as a sale but is merely incidental to the primary contract of making repairs. In contrast, the purchase of a television set, with

[4]Fruin-Colnon Corp. v Air Door, Inc. 157 Ga App 804, 278 SE2d 708 (1981).

incidental service of installation, is a sale of goods because the purchase of the set is the dominant element.

FACTS:

Meyers was under contract with Henderson to install overhead doors in a factory which Henderson was building. Meyers obtained the disassembled doors from the manufacturer. His contract with Henderson required Meyers to furnish all labor, materials, tools, and equipment to satisfactorily complete the installation of all overhead doors. Meyers sued Henderson five years later for breach of contract. Henderson raised the defense that since the contract was for the sale of goods it was barred by the Code's four-year statute of limitations. Meyers claimed that it was a contract for services and that suit could be brought within six years.

DECISION:

Judgment for Henderson. A hybrid contract which calls for both the sale of goods and the rendering of services is to be classified according to its dominant characteristic. While the overhead doors were useless unless installed, it was the obtaining of the doors which was the dominant element or main objective of the contract and the installation service aspect was merely incidental. Hence the contract was to be classified as a sale of goods. The Code was therefore applicable and the action was barred by the 4-year statute of limitations of UCC [sec] 2-725. [Meyers v Henderson Construction Co. 147 NJ Super 77, 370 A2d 547 (1977)]

§ 25:3. Law of Contracts Applicable.

A sale is a voluntary transaction between two parties. Accordingly, most of the principles that apply to contractual agreements in general are equally applicable to a sale of goods.

FACTS:

Mason, a farmer, wanted to sell wheat to Curtis. He telephoned Curtis and inquired if Curtis wanted to buy the wheat. No definite agreement was made on the telephone. Curtis thereafter sent Mason an order for 9,000 bushels of spring wheat. A few weeks later Curtis sent Mason a "confirmation memorandum" that stated the terms on which Curtis wanted to buy the wheat and further stated that retention of the confirmation constituted agreement of the contract as stated in the confirmation. Mason ignored the order and the confirmation. Curtis sued Mason for breach of contract.

DECISION:

Judgment for Mason. No contract had been made on the telephone. The order sent by Curtis was an offer but it was never accepted by Mason. The later writing sent by Curtis did not create a contract. Curtis' calling the later writing a "confirmation memorandum" was meaningless because there was nothing to confirm. The statement that the failure to reply to the confirmation was an acceptance was also meaningless because an offeror cannot make silence an acceptance. There was therefore no contract because there was no offer and acceptance giving rise to a binding agreement. [D.R. Curtis Co v Mason, 103 Idaho App 476, 649 P2d 1232 (1982)]

Modern marketing practices have modified the strict principles of contract law, and this approach is carried into the UCC. Thus, not only can a sale be made in any manner; but it is sufficient that the parties by their conduct recognize the existence of a contract, even though it cannot be determined when the contract was made, and generally, even though one or more terms are left open.[5]

In most instances, the UCC treats all buyers and sellers alike. In some, it treats merchants differently than it does the occasional or casual buyer or seller. In this way, the UCC recognizes that the merchant is experienced and has a special knowledge of the relevant commercial practices.

(a) **Offer.** Contract law as to offers is applicable to a sales contract with the following exception. A **firm offer** by a merchant cannot be revoked if (1) the offer expresses an intention that it will not be revoked, and is (2) in a writing, (3) signed by the merchant. An express period of irrevocability in the offer, cannot exceed three months. If nothing is said as to the duration of the offer, irrevocability continues only for a reasonable time. This firm offer exception applies without regard to whether the merchant received any consideration to keep the offer open.

(b) **Acceptance.** An offer to buy or sell goods may be accepted in any manner and by any medium which is reasonable under the circumstances.[6] However, if a specific manner or medium is clearly indicated by the terms of the offer or the circumstances of the case, the offer can only be accepted in that manner.

Unless it is expressly specified that an offer to buy or sell goods must be accepted just as made, the offeree may accept an offer and at the same time propose an additional term. Contrary to the general common-law rule, the new term does not reject the original offer. A contract arises on the terms of the original offer and the new term is a counteroffer. If, however, the offer states that it must be accepted exactly as made, the ordinary contract law rules apply. If the additional term is treated as a counteroffer, that term does not become binding until accepted by the original offeror.

In a transaction between merchants, the additional term becomes part of the contract if that term does not materially alter the offer and no objection is made to it. If such an additional term in the seller's form of acknowledgment operates solely to the seller's advantage, however, it is a material term and must be accepted to be effective.

FACTS:
Valley Trout Farms ordered fish food from Rangen. Both parties were merchants. The invoice that was sent with the order stated that a specified charge would be added to any unpaid bills. This was a percentage that was common in the industry. Valley Trout Farms did not pay for the food and did not make any objection to the late charge stated in the invoice. When sued by Rangen, Valley Trout claimed that it had never agreed to the late charge and therefore was not required to pay it.

[5]UCC § 2-204. This provision is limited by requiring that there be "a reasonably certain basis for giving an appropriate remedy."

[6]UCC § 2-206(1). An order or other offer to buy goods that are to be sent promptly or currently can be accepted by the seller by actually shipping the goods.

DECISION:

Judgment for Rangen. The late charge became part of the contract. The adding of such a term was not a material alteration. Since both parties were merchants and the late charge was customary in the trade, the addition of the late charge became part of the contract when it was not objected to. [Rangen, Inc. v Valley Trout Farms, Inc. 104 Idaho 284, 658 P2d 955 (1983)]

The acceptance by the buyer of a term added by the seller to the acceptance of the buyer's offer may be found in an express statement or in conduct. The buyer may state orally or in writing agreement to the additional term. There is an acceptance by conduct if the buyer accepts the goods with knowledge that the term has been added by the seller.

When a term of an acceptance conflicts with a term of an offer, but it is clear that the parties intended to be bound by a contract, the Code recognizes the formation of a contract. The terms which are conflicting cancel out and are ignored. The contract then consists of the terms of the offer and acceptance which agree, together with those terms that the Code or contract law implies into a contract.

(c) **Determination of Price.** The price for goods may be expressly fixed by the contract, or the parties may merely indicate how the price should be determined at a later time.

When persons experienced in a particular industry make a contract without specifying the price to be paid, the price will be determined by the manner which is customary in the industry. Ordinarily, if nothing is said as to price, the buyer is required to pay the reasonable value of the goods, which is generally the market price.

In recent years there has been an increase in use of the "cost plus" formula for determining price. Under this form of agreement, the buyer pays the seller a sum equal to the cost to the seller of obtaining the goods plus a specified percentage of that cost representing the seller's profit.

The contract may expressly provide that one of the parties may determine the price, in which case that party must act in good faith in so doing.[7] Likewise, the contract may specify that the price shall be determined by some standard or by a third person.

(d) **Output and Requirements Contracts.** Somewhat related to the open term concept concerning price is that involved in the output and requirements contracts in which the quantity that is to be sold or purchased is not a specific quantity but is such amount as the seller should produce or the buyer should require. Although this introduces an element of uncertainty, such sales contracts are valid. To prevent oppression, they are subject to two limitations: (1) the parties must act in good faith, and (2) the quantity offered or demanded must not be unreasonably disproportionate to prior output or requirements or to a stated estimate.

When the sales contract is a continuing contract, as one calling for periodic delivery of fuel, but no time is set for the life of the contract,

---

[7]Good faith requires that the party in fact act honestly and, in the case of a merchant, also requires the party to follow reasonable commercial standards of fair dealing which are recognized in the trade. UCC §§ 1-201(19), 2-103(1)(b).

the contract runs for a reasonable time but may be terminated on notice by either party.

(e) **Seals.** A seal on a sales contract or on an offer of sale has no effect. Thus, in determining whether there is consideration or if the statute of limitations is applicable, the fact that there is a seal on the sales contract is ignored.

(f) **Implied Conditions.** The field of implied conditions under contract law is broadened by the UCC to permit the release of a party from any obligation under a sales contract when performance has been made commercially impracticable, as distinguished from impossible: (1) by the occurrence of a contingency, the nonoccurrence of which was a basic assumption on which the contract was made; or (2) by compliance in good faith with any applicable governmental regulation or order. "A severe shortage of raw materials or of supplies due to a contingency such as war, embargo, local crop failure, unforeseen shutdown of major sources of supply or the like, which either causes a marked increase in cost or altogether prevents the seller from securing supplies necessary to his performance, is within the contemplation" of this provision of the Code.[8]

(g) **Modification of Contract.** An agreement to modify a contract for the sale of goods is binding even though the modification is not supported by consideration.[9]

(h) **Parol Evidence Rule.** The parol evidence rule applies to the sale of goods with the slight modification that a writing is not presumed or assumed to represent the entire contract of the parties unless the court specifically decides that it does. If the court so decides, parol evidence is admissible to show what the parties meant by their words but additional terms cannot be added to the writing by parol evidence.

If the court decides that the writing was not intended to represent the entire contract, the writing may be supplemented by parol proof of additional terms as long as such terms are not inconsistent with the original written terms.

(i) **Fraud and Other Defenses.** The defenses that may be raised in a suit on a sales contract are in general the same as those that may be raised in a suit on any other contract. A defrauded party may cancel the transaction and recover what was paid or the goods that were delivered, together with damages for any loss sustained. If title was obtained by the buyer by means of fraud, the title is voidable by an innocent seller.

If the sales contract or any clause in it was unconscionable when made, a court may refuse to enforce it, as discussed in Chapter 16.

(j) **Usage of Trade and Course of Dealing.** Established usages or customs of trade and prior course of conduct or dealings between the parties are to be considered in connection with any sales transaction. If there is no express term excluding or "overruling" the prior pattern of dealings between the parties and the usages of the trade, it is concluded that the parties contracted on the basis of those patterns of doing business. More specifically,

---

[8]UCC § 2-615, Official Comment, point 4.
[9]UCC § 2-209(1).

the patterns of doing business as shown by the prior dealings of the parties and the usages of the trade enter into and form part of their contract, and may be looked to in order to find what was intended by the express provisions and to supply otherwise missing terms.

FACTS:

Raymond International, Inc., was a highway contractor. Blue Rock Industries sold sand to Raymond for use in construction work. The sales contract called for payment on the basis of truck measured cubic yards of sand. Raymond did not pay for the sand. When suit was brought to recover the purchase price, it was claimed that the term "truck measure" was ambiguous. Parol evidence was offered to show that the parties had followed the practice of finding an average weight per cubic yard by dividing the weight of sand in a truck by the cubic yard capacity of the truck and then using this figure as a conversion factor to convert the weight of each truckload of sand into a specified number of cubic yards. Was this evidence admissible?

DECISION:

Yes. The term "truck measure" did not have an exact or clear meaning. Therefore the prior practice of the parties was admissible to show what they meant by that term. [Blue Rock Industries v Raymond International, Inc. _____ Me _____, 325 A2d 66 (1974)]

---

§ 25:4.   Illegal Sales.

At common law, a sale was illegal if the subject matter was itself wrong. A transaction may also be illegal even though the subject matter of the sale is unobjectionable in itself, as when the agreement provides that the goods that are sold shall be employed for some unlawful purpose or when the seller assists in the unlawful act. To illustrate, when the seller falsely labels domestic goods, representing them to be imported, to assist the buyer in perpetrating a fraud upon the buyer's customers, the sale is illegal. The mere fact, however, that the seller has knowledge of the buyer's unlawful purpose does not, under the general rule, make the sale illegal unless the purpose is the commission of a serious crime.

(a) **Illegality Under Statutes.** Practically every state has legislation prohibiting certain sales when they are not conducted according to the requirements of the statutes. Statutes commonly regulate sales by establishing standards as to grading, size, weight, and measure, and by prohibiting adulteration.

Statutes may regulate the sale of "secondhand" goods. Such a statute does not apply to a casual seller, but only applies to one whose regular business consists of selling goods of the kind covered by the statute. States may prohibit the making of sales on Sunday, either generally, or as to particular classes of commodities or stores. The federal Food, Drug, and Cosmetic Act prohibits the interstate shipment of misbranded or adulterated foods, drugs, cosmetics, and therapeutic devices. A product which does not carry adequate use instructions and warnings is deemed "misbranded."

(b) Effect of Illegal Sale. An illegal sale or a contract to sell cannot be enforced. As a general rule, courts will not aid either party in recovering money or property transferred pursuant to an illegal agreement. Here, the ordinary contract-law rule as to "illegality" is applied. However, if a sale is made illegal by statute, a seller who violates the law may be held liable for the damage caused.

FACTS:

The State of Minnesota prohibited the sale of glue to minors in order to protect them from the brain-damaging consequences of glue sniffing. In violation of this statute, Warren sold glue to Ricken, a minor. Zerby, Ricken's minor friend, sniffed the glue and was killed by the fumes. Suit was brought against Warren who raised the defenses of contributory negligence and assumption of risk.

DECISION:

The statutory prohibition was intended to protect minors. Its violation therefore imposed an absolute liability on the violator. Contributory negligence and assumption of risk could not be raised as defenses to this liability. [Zerby v Warren, 297 Minn 134, 210 NW2d 58 (1973)]

---

§ 25:5.   Bulk Transfers.

Whenever a merchant is about to transfer a major part of the merchant's materials, supplies, merchandise, or other inventory, not in the ordinary course of business, advance notice of the transfer should be given to creditors in accordance with Article 6 of the Uniform Commercial Code. The essential characteristic of businesses subject to Article 6 is that they sell from inventory or a stock of goods, as contrasted with businesses that render services.[10] Thus, a beauty salon is ordinarily a service enterprise and is not subject to the bulk transfer article, as contrasted with a store selling cosmetics which is so subject.

(a) Effect of Noncompliance. If the notice required by Article 6 is not given, the creditors of the seller may reach the sold property in the hands of the buyer and also in the hands of any subsequent transferee who knew that there had not been compliance with the UCC or who did not pay value. This is designed to protect the creditors of a merchant from the danger of the merchant's selling all the inventory, pocketing the money, and then disappearing, leaving the creditors unpaid. The protection given to creditors by the bulk transfer legislation is in addition to the protection which they have

---

[10]Allsbrook v Azalea Radiator Serv., Inc. 227 Va 600, 316 SE2d 743 (1984).

against their debtor for fraudulent transfers or conveyances, and the remedies that can be employed in bankruptcy proceedings.

The fact that there has been noncompliance with Article 6 of the UCC regulating bulk transfers, however, does not affect the validity of a bulk sale of goods as between the immediate parties to the transfer, as Article 6 governs only the rights of creditors of the seller.

(b) Liability of Bulk Purchaser. Ordinarily the bulk purchaser who receives the goods does not become liable for the debts of the bulk seller merely because the requirements of Article 6 have not been satisfied. In contrast, if the buyer mixes the transferred goods with other goods so that it is not possible for the creditor to identify the transferred goods which are subject to the creditor's claim, the bulk buyer is personally liable for the debts of the bulk seller.

FACTS:

Costello owned an automobile accessory and appliance business. He purchased goods for his inventory from J & R Motor Supply Corporation. The goods were not paid for at the time when Costello sold his business to Cornelius. Cornelius mixed the Costello inventory with his own so that the two could not be identified. J & R and another creditor claimed that Cornelius was liable for the amount of the bills owed by Costello because the sale of the business had been made without complying with Article 6 of the Uniform Commercial Code.

DECISION:

Cornelius was personally liable. Ordinarily, noncompliance with the bulk transfer article only makes the transferred goods subject to the claims of the transferor's creditors and does not impose personal liability on the transferee. When, however, the transferee mingles existing goods with the transferred goods so that it cannot be determined what goods were the "transferred bulk," the transferee becomes personally liable for the claims of the creditors of the transferor. [Cornelius v J & R Motor Supply Corp. (Ky) 468 SW2d 781 (1971)]

B. FORM OF SALES CONTRACT

A contract for the sale of goods may be oral or written. In some cases, it must be evidenced by a writing or it cannot be enforced in court.

§ 25:6.   Amount.

Whenever the sales price of goods is five hundred dollars or more, the sales contract must be evidenced by a writing.[11]

§ 25:7.   Nature of the Writing Required.

The writing evidencing the sales contract may be either (1) a complete written contract signed by both parties or (2) a memorandum signed by the defendant. In any case, it must meet the following requirements:

[11]UCC § 2-201.

(a) **Terms.** The writing must indicate that there has been a completed transaction as to certain goods. Specifically, it need only indicate that (1) a sale or contract to sell has been made[12] and (2) state the quantity of goods involved. Any other missing terms may be shown by parol evidence.

(b) **Signature.** The writing must be signed by the person who is being sued or by the authorized agent of that person. The signature must be placed on the paper with the intention of authenticating the writing. It may consist of initials or be printed, stamped, or typewritten, as long as made with the necessary intent.

When the transaction is between merchants, an exception is made to the requirement of signing. The failure of a merchant to repudiate a confirming letter sent by another merchant within ten days of receiving such a letter binds the nonsigner just as if the receiving merchant had signed the letter. This makes it necessary for a merchant seller to watch the mail and to act within ten days of receiving a mailed confirmation.

(c) **Purpose of Execution.** A writing can satisfy a statute of frauds although it was not made for that purpose. Accordingly, when the buyer writes in reply to the seller, after a 45-day delay, and merely criticizes the quality of the goods, the letter of the buyer satisfies the statute as it indicates that there was a sale of those goods.

(d) **Particular Writings.** Formal contracts, bills of sale, letters, and telegrams are common forms of writings that satisfy the requirement. Purchase orders, cash register receipts, sales tickets, invoices, and similar papers generally do not satisfy the requirement as to a signature, and sometimes they do not specify any quantity or commodity.

Two or more writings may constitute the "writing" which satisfies the statute of frauds.[13]

§ 25:8.   Effect of Noncompliance.

A sales agreement that does not satisfy the statute of frauds cannot be enforced. However, the oral contract itself is not unlawful and may be voluntarily performed by the parties.[14]

§ 25:9.   When Proof of Oral Contract is Permitted.

The absence of a writing does not always bar proof of a sales contract.

(a) **Nonresellable Goods.** No writing is required when the goods are specially made for the buyer and are of such an unusual nature that they are not suitable for sale in the ordinary course of the seller's business. For example, when 14 steel doors were tailor-made by the seller for the buyer's building, and were not suitable for sale to anyone else in the ordinary course of the seller's business, and could only be sold as scrap, the oral contract of sale could be enforced.

[12]Martco, Inc. v Doran Chevrolet, Inc. (Tex Civ App) 632 SW2d 927 (1982).
[13]West Cent. Packing, Inc. v A. F. Murch Co. 109 Mich App 493, 311 NW2d 404 (1981).
[14]Duffee v Judson, 251 Pa Super 406, 380 A2d 843 (1977).

In order for the nonresellable goods exception to apply, the seller must have made a substantial beginning in manufacturing the goods, or, if a distributor, in procuring them, before notice of repudiation by the buyer is received.

FACTS:

R-P Packaging manufactured cellophane wrapping material which was used by Kern's Bakery in packaging its product. Kern's decided to change its system for the packaging of cookies from a tied bread bag to a tray covered with printed cellophane wrapping. R-P took measurements to determine the appropriate size for the cellophane wrapping and designated appropriate artwork to be printed on the cellophane wrapping. After agreeing that the artwork was satisfactory, Kern entered into a verbal order for the cellophane at a total cost of $13,000. When the printed wrapping material was received, Kern complained that it was too short to fit the trays, and the artwork was not centered. The material, however, conformed exactly to the order placed by Kern. Kern returned the material to R-P by overnight express. R-P sued Kern. Kern claimed that because there was no written contract, the suit was barred by the statute of frauds.

DECISION:

Judgment for R-P Packaging. Oral contracts for the sale of goods are enforceable, even where not evidenced by a writing, if the goods are to be specially manufactured for the buyer, if they are not suitable for sale to others in the course of the seller's business, and if the seller has made a substantial beginning in manufacturing them. The cellophane wrapping material was manufactured to the size required by Kern's containers, was imprinted with Kern's name and unique artwork, and was completely produced by the seller. [Flowers Baking Company v R-P Packaging, Inc. 229 Va 370, 329 SE2d 462 (1985)]

(b) **Receipt and Acceptance.** An oral sales contract may be enforced if it can be shown that the goods were delivered by the seller and were received and accepted by the buyer. Thus, if the buyer purchases and receives goods on credit, the seller may sue for the purchase price even though it is over five hundred dollars and there is no writing, for the reason that the receipt and acceptance of the goods by the buyer took the contract out of the statute of frauds. Both a receipt and an acceptance by the buyer must be shown. If only part of the goods had been received and accepted, the contract may be enforced only insofar as it relates to those goods received and accepted.[15]

(c) **Payment.** An oral contract may be enforced if the buyer has made full payment. In the case of part payment for divisible units of goods, a contract may be enforced only with respect to the goods for which payment has been made and accepted. If part payment is made for indivisible goods,

---

[15]Anthony v Tidwell, _____ Tenn _____, 560 SW2d 908 (1977).

such as an automobile, a part payment avoids the statute of frauds and permits proof of the entire oral contract.

(d) **Admission.** An oral contract may be enforced if the party against whom enforcement is sought admits in pleadings, testimony or otherwise in court that a contract for sale was made. The contract, however, is not enforceable beyond the quantity of goods admitted.[16]

§ 25:10.   Non-Code Local Requirements.

In addition to the UCC requirement as to a writing, other statutes may impose requirements. For example, consumer protection legislation commonly requires the execution of a detailed contract and the giving of a copy thereof to the consumer. The result is that even though the Code requirements have been satisfied, the buyer may still be able to avoid the transaction for noncompliance with the other statutory requirement.

§ 25:11.   Bill of Sale.

Regardless of the requirement of the statute of frauds, the parties may wish to execute a writing as evidence or proof of the sale. Through custom this writing has become known as a **bill of sale;** but it is neither a bill nor a contract. It is merely a receipt or writing signed by the seller reciting the transfer to the buyer of the title to the described property. The only effect of the bill of sale is to bar the seller from later denying the making of the sale. If the seller did not have title to the goods, the bill of sale does not give the buyer any title.

In some states, provision is made for the public recording of bills of sale when goods are left in the seller's possession. Some states require the production of the bill of sale before the title to any automobile will be registered in the name of the purchaser.

Although the bill of sale states that the full purchase price has been paid, the seller may show that in fact it has not been so paid.

SUMMARY

A sale of goods is a present transfer of title to movable personal property for a price. Goods, the subject matter of a sale, include anything movable at the time they are identified as the subject of the transaction. Goods which are not existing goods are known as future goods. There can be no present sale of future goods and any agreement to sell such goods operates as a contract to sell. A bailment is not a sale because no title is transferred. A gift is not a sale since there is no consideration for the gift. A contract for services is an ordinary contract and is not governed by the UCC.

The law of contracts is applicable to a sale of goods. Contract law as to offers is applicable to a sale of goods except for rules concerning an acceptance with new terms which are considered counteroffers. If the transaction is between merchants, the additional terms become part of the contract if those terms do not materially alter the offer and no objection is made to them.

[16]Jackson v Meadows, 153 Ga App 1, 264 SE2d 503 (1980).

The price terms may be expressly fixed by the parties or the parties may indicate how the price terms should be determined later. In output or requirements contracts, the quantity that is to be sold or purchased is not a specific quantity but such contracts are nevertheless valid. A seal has no effect on a contract. A contract relating to a sale of goods may be modified even though the modification is not supported by consideration. The parol evidence rule applies to a sales of goods in much the same manner as to ordinary contracts not for sales of goods with the slight modification that a writing is not presumed to represent the entire contract of the parties unless the court specifically decides that it does. Most contract defenses may be raised in a suit on a sales contract. An illegal sale or a contract to sell cannot be enforced.

Any merchant who transfers a major part of the merchandise or inventory not in the ordinary course of business must comply with the bulk transfer provisions of the UCC.

A sales contract for five hundred dollars or more must be evidenced by a writing unless the goods are nonresellable, or the buyer received and accepted the goods, or the buyer has made either full or part payment, or the party against whom enforcement is sought admits in court pleadings or testimony that a contract for sale was made.

QUESTIONS AND CASE PROBLEMS

1. What social forces are affected by the rule that consideration is not required by a modification of a contract for the sale of goods?
2. On Monday, Nancy sells her sewing machine to Irma. It is agreed that Irma will pay for the sewing machine on the next Friday, payday, and that Nancy will retain title and possession until such payment is made. Is there a sale of the sewing machine on Monday?
3. Ethel wrote to Lasco Dealers inquiring as to the price of a certain freezer. Lasco wrote her a letter signed by its credit manager stating that Ethel could purchase the freezer in question for the next 30 days at the price of $400. Ethel wrote back the next day ordering a freezer at that price. Ethel's letter was received by Lasco the following day but Lasco wrote an answering letter stating that it had changed the price to $450. Ethel claims that Lasco could not change its price. Is Ethel correct?
4. Emily purchases a refrigerator-freezer from the Elton Appliance Shop for $600. The purchase is made over the phone. Thereafter Elton sends Emily a letter thanking her for the purchase of the refrigerator-freezer. Before the refrigerator-freezer is delivered to Emily, she telephones Elton and cancels the purchase. Elton then sues her for damages. She raises the defense of the statute of frauds. Elton produces a copy of the letter that it sent to Emily. Does this letter avoid the defense of the statute of frauds?
5. Danfie Company of New York owns leather hides stored in a warehouse in the south of France. Danfie sells some of these hides to the Haldane Company of Chicago. Danfie and Haldane agree that the price shall be determined by Rumfort who lives in the south of France and is recognized in the trade as an expert in leather. Haldane becomes dissatisfied with the contract and claims that it is not binding because it is too in-

definite because it does not state the price to be paid for the leather. Is Haldane correct?

6. Can a writing satisfy the statute of frauds without a signature of the party being sued or a duly authorized agent?

7. Compare the liability of (a) a transferee of a bulk transfer when the requirements of the Uniform Commercial Code are not satisfied, (b) a person buying goods on credit, and (c) a person buying out an existing business and promising to pay the creditors of the original business.

8. The Tober Foreign Motors, Inc., sold an airplane to Skinner on installments. Later it was agreed that the monthly installments should be reduced in half. Thereafter Tober claimed that the reduction agreement was not binding because it was not supported by consideration. Was this claim correct? [Skinner v Tober Foreign Motors, Inc. 345 Mass 429, 187 NE2d 669]

9. The LTV Aerospace Corporation manufactured all-terrain vehicles for use in Southeast Asia. LTV made an oral contract with Bateman under which he would supply the packing cases needed for their overseas shipment. Bateman made substantial beginnings in the production of packing cases following LTV's specifications. LTV thereafter stopped production of its vehicles and refused to take delivery of any cases. When sued by Bateman for breach of contract, LTV raised the defense that the contract could not be enforced because there was no writing which satisfied the statute of frauds. Was this a valid defense? [LTV Aerospace Corp. v. Bateman (Tex Civ App) 492 SW2d 703]

10. Suburban Gas Heat of Kennewick sold propane gas for domestic consumption. As the result of its negligence in supplying propane gas mixed with water, there was an explosion which caused damage to Kasey. When Kasey sued to enforce the liability of Suburban Gas Heat as a seller, Suburban raised the defense that it was engaged in furnishing a public service and not in the sale of goods. Was Suburban correct? [Kasey v Suburban Gas Heat of Kennewick, Inc. 60 Wash 2d 468, 374 P2d 549]

11. A farmer made a written contract to sell "all cotton produced in 400 acres." The buyer claimed that this required a solid planting of the 400 acres. The seller claimed that it was the custom to plant by "skip row" method in which every two planted rows would be separated by an idle row. The seller claimed that parol evidence was admissible to show that there was a custom to plant in this manner. The buyer claimed that the parol evidence could not be allowed to contradict the writing. Was the parol evidence admissible?

12. Members of the Colonial Club purchased beer from outside the state and ordered it sent to the Colonial Club. The club then kept it in the club refrigerator and served the beer to its respective owners upon demand. The club received no compensation or profit from the transaction. The club was indicted for selling liquor. Was it guilty? [North Carolina v Colonial Club, 154 NC 177, 69 SE 771]

13. Compare the revocability of a firm offer and an ordinary offer.

14. A merchant made an oral contract to sell $1,000 worth of goods to another merchant. The buyer broke the contract and the seller sued for

breach of contract. The buyer raised the defense that suit could not be brought on the oral contract because there was no writing satisfying UCC § 2-201. The seller offered evidence showing that it was customary for merchants in the trade to deal on the basis of oral contracts. Was the seller entitled to recover on the oral contract?

15. A college senior furnished a carpenter a unique design for a bookshelf to be built in her dorm. The carpenter orally agreed to follow the design and build the bookshelf for a total price of $1,000. When the carpenter started the work, the senior informed him that she no longer wished the bookshelf. What are the rights of the carpenter, if any, against the college senior?

16. Lukas ordered goods from the Farbar Tool and Die Corp. The goods were received and accepted by Lucas, but at no time was anything agreed as to the price for the goods. Was there a binding sales contract?

17. A series of oral negotiations took place between the seller and the buyer. The seller eventually sent a confirming memorandum to the buyer stating the terms of the agreement. The buyer received the confirmation and made no objection to the contents. Some weeks later the buyer ordered the goods and took delivery. Upon discovering that the price might be more than was agreed, the buyer refused to pay, asserting that since he never signed a writing the statute of frauds barred the enforcing of the contract. How did the court decide? [Associated Hardware Supply Co. v Big Wheel Distribution Co. 355 F2d 114]

CHAPTER 26

RISK AND PROPERTY

RIGHTS

CHAPTER OBJECTIVES

After studying this chapter you will be able to:
1. State when title and risk of loss pass with respect to goods.
2. Describe when a sale occurs in a self-service store.
3. State the effect of title registration laws upon the transfer of title to an automobile.
4. State who bears the risk of loss when goods are damaged or destroyed.
5. Classify transactions in which the person dealing with the seller may return the goods.
6. State the effect of a sales transaction upon the title to the goods.
7. Solve problems involving risk of loss and title in sales transactions.

In most sales, the buyer receives the proper goods, makes payment, and the transaction is thus completed. However, problems may arise. The parties can foresee these problems and state in their contract what results are desired. If the parties do not do so, the rules in this chapter apply.

§ 26:1. Types of Problems.

Problems involving risk and property rights in sales transactions will often relate to damage to the goods, the claims of creditors of the parties to the sales contract, or the obtaining of insurance by those parties.

(a) **Damage to Goods.** If the goods are damaged or totally destroyed without any fault of either the buyer or the seller, must the seller bear the loss and supply new goods to the buyer? Or is it the buyer's loss, so that the buyer must pay the seller the purchase price even though the goods are damaged or destroyed?[1] The fact that there may be insurance does not avoid this question, for the answer to it determines whose insurer is liable and the extent of that insurer's liability.

(b) Creditors' Claims. Creditors of a delinquent seller may seize the goods as belonging to the seller. The buyer's creditors may seize them on the theory that they belong to the buyer. In such cases the question arises whether the creditors are correct as to who owns the goods. The question of ownership is also important in connection with the consequence of a resale by the buyer, or the liability for or the computation of certain kinds of taxes, and the liability under certain registration and criminal law statutes.[2]

(c) Insurance. Until the buyer has received the goods and the seller has been paid, both the seller and buyer have an economic interest in the sales transaction.[3] The question arises as to whether either or both have enough interest to entitle them to insure the property involved; that is, whether they have an insurable interest.[4]

§ 26:2.   Nature of the Transaction.

The answer to be given to each of the questions noted in the preceding section depends upon the nature of the transaction between the seller and the buyer. Sales transactions may be classified according to the nature of the goods and the terms of the transaction.

(a) Existing and Identified Goods. Existing goods are (1) physically in existence and (2) owned by the seller. When particular goods have been selected by either the buyer or the seller, or both of them, as being the goods called for by the sales contract, the goods are called **identified goods.** Thus when you go into a store, point at a particular item, and tell the clerk "I'll take that one" the sales transaction relates to existing and identified goods.

(b) Future and Unidentified Goods. Goods are **future goods** when they are not yet owned by the seller, or when they are not yet in existence. Before goods have been identified to the contract, they are unidentified. Consequently, when you tell the clerk in the store you want one of the items advertised in the paper, the transaction relates to unidentified goods. Your reference to the newspaper ad described the thing you wanted but it did not identify any particular item as the one the seller was to deliver. Future goods are involved if a store tells you that they are out of the advertised item but can order it from the factory or that the factory is going to make a new run of the item which will arrive next month.

(c) Terms of the Transaction. Ordinarily, the seller is only required to make the goods available to the buyer. If transportation is provided, the seller is normally only required to make shipment and the seller's part of the contract is performed by handing the goods over to a carrier for shipment

---

[1]The subject is regulated by UCC § 2-509.
[2]UCC § 2-401.
[3]See UCC § 2-501(1)(a).
[4]In order to insure property, a person must have such a right or interest in the property that its damage or destruction would cause financial loss. This is called an insurable interest in the property. The ownership of personal property for the purpose of insurance is determined by the UCC.

to the buyer. The terms of the contract, however, may obligate the seller to deliver the goods at a particular place, for example, to make delivery at the destination. The seller's part of the contract is then not completed until the goods are brought to the destination point and there tendered to the buyer. If the transaction calls for sending the goods to the buyer, it is ordinarily required that the seller deliver the goods to a carrier under a proper **contract for shipment** to the buyer. Actual physical **delivery at destination** is only required when the contract expressly so states.

Instead of calling for the actual delivery of goods, the sales transaction may relate to a transfer of the document of title representing the goods. For example, the goods may be stored in a warehouse, and the seller and the buyer have no intention of moving the goods, but intend that there shall be a sale and a delivery of the warehouse receipt that stands for the goods. Here the obligation of the seller is to produce the proper paper as distinguished from the goods themselves. The same is true when the goods are represented by any other document of title, such as a bill of lading issued by a carrier.

§ 26:3.   Existing Goods Identified at Time of Contracting.

This is a transaction relating to existing and identified goods. There is no document of title, such as a warehouse receipt or a bill of lading. In this type of transaction, the title to the goods passes to the buyer at the time the parties agree to the transaction. They may, however, state in the contract that the title shall not pass to the buyer until the full purchase price has been paid.

When the buyer becomes the owner of the goods in the situation here considered, the buyer has an insurable interest in them. In contrast the seller has an insurable interest in the goods before title passes to the buyer. The insurable interest of the seller terminates when title passes to the buyer unless the seller has reserved a security interest to protect any balance due.

As to risk of loss, a distinction must be made between a merchant seller and a nonmerchant seller. If the seller is a merchant, the risk of loss passes to the buyer on receiving the goods from the merchant. If the seller is a nonmerchant, the risk of loss passes when the seller makes the goods available to the buyer. The risk thus remains longer on the merchant seller. Receiving the goods from a merchant means that the buyer takes actual physical possession of the goods.[5]

FACTS:

Ramon Ramos purchased a motorcycle from the Wheel Sports Center. He paid for it in full and was given all papers necessary to register his ownership. Ramos also obtained liability insurance to protect himself from claims from any one he might injure with the motorcycle. However, Ramos did not take the motorcycle, as he was leaving on a vacation, and would get it on his return. Before he returned, there was an electric power blackout in the city. During the blackout, the motorcycle was stolen from the Wheel Sports Center. Ramos sued the Center to get his money back because he never had received the motorcycle. The Center raised the defense that it was not at fault for the loss and that the risk of loss had passed to Ramos.

[5]Spikes v Baier, 6 Kan App2d 45, 626 P2d 816 (1981).

DECISION:

Judgment for Ramos. The seller was a merchant. The risk of loss remained on the seller until the goods were received by the buyer. As receipt by the buyer never took place, the seller bore the risk of loss by the theft. [Ramos v Wheel Sports Center, 409 NYS2d 505, 96 Misc 2d 646 (1978)]

---

§ 26:4.   Goods Represented by Negotiable Document of Title.

Merchants dealing in large quantities of goods will often prefer to deal with negotiable documents of title to the goods instead of making a physical delivery of the goods. In such a transaction, the buyer has an insurable interest in the goods at the time and place of contracting but does not ordinarily become subject to the risk of loss nor acquire the title until delivery of the document is made.[6]

§ 26:5.   Future and Unidentified Goods.

If the goods are either future goods or have not been identified by the time the transaction is agreed to, the rules stated in § 26:3 and § 26:4 do not apply. Instead, the following rules govern the transaction if the parties do not state otherwise.

(a) **Marking for Buyer.** If the buyer sends an order for goods to be manufactured by the seller or to be filled from inventory or by purchases from third persons, one step in the process of filling the order is the seller's act of marking, tagging, labeling, or in some way doing an act for the benefit of the shipping department to indicate that certain goods are the ones to be sent or delivered to the buyer under the order. This act of unilateral identification of the goods is enough to give the buyer a property interest in the goods which entitles the buyer to insure them. Neither risk of loss nor title passes to the buyer at that time, however, but remains with the seller, who, as the continuing owner, also has an insurable interest in the goods. Thus, neither title nor risk of loss passes to the buyer until some later event, such as a shipment or delivery, occurs.

(b) **Contract for Shipment to Buyer.** In this situation, the buyer has placed an order for future goods to be shipped to the buyer, and the contract is performed by the seller by delivering the goods to a carrier for shipment to the buyer. Under such a contract, the risk of loss and the title pass to the buyer when the goods are delivered to the carrier, that is, at the time and place of shipment. After that happens, the seller has no insurable interest unless the seller has reserved a security interest in the goods.

The fact that a shipment of goods is represented by a bill of lading or an airbill issued by the carrier, and that in order to complete the transaction it will be necessary to transfer that bill to the buyer, does not affect these rules or bring the transaction within § 26:4.

---

[6]Express provision is made for the case of a nonnegotiable document and other factual variations. UCC § 2-509(2)(c), § 2-503(4).

(c) **Contract for Delivery at Destination.** When the contract requires the seller to make delivery of future goods at a particular destination point, the buyer acquires a property right and an insurable interest in the goods at the time and place they are marked or shipped; but the risk of loss and the title do not pass until the carrier tenders or makes the goods available at the destination point. The seller retains an insurable interest until that time; and a security interest of the seller in the goods continues until the purchase price has been paid.

A provision in the contract directing the seller to "ship to" the buyer does not convert the contract into a contract calling for delivery at destination.

§ 26:6.   Self-Service Stores.

In the case of goods in a self-service store, the reasonable interpretation of the circumstances is that the store by its act of putting the goods on display on the shelves makes an offer to sell such goods for cash and confers upon a prospective customer a license to carry the goods to the cashier in order to make payment. Most courts hold that there is no transfer of title until the buyer makes payment to the cashier.

A contrary rule adopts the view that "a contract to sell" is formed when the customer "accepts" the seller's offer by taking the item from the shelf.

By another contrary view, a sale actually occurs when the buyer takes the item from the shelf. That is, title passes at that moment to the buyer even though the goods have not yet been paid for. The fact that the buyer can return the item to the shelf is merely a "return" by the buyer by which the buyer transfers back to the seller the title which had already passed to the buyer when the item was removed from the shelf.

FACTS:
Fender was a customer in the Big Star self-service store owned by Colonial Stores, Inc. She placed her selections on the cashier's counter. While lifting a six-pack of Coca Cola from her cart to the counter, one of the bottles exploded and she was injured by the flying glass. She sued Colonial Stores. She claimed that the defendant was liable for breach of warranty. The defendant denied this liability on the ground that there could be no warranty liability until there was a sale and that the Coca Cola had not been sold to Fender because she had not yet paid for the six-pack.

DECISION:
Judgment for Fender. The warranty of merchantability is implied in a contract for the sale of goods and is not limited to transactions that are completed sales, that is, transfer of title. A contract for the sale of goods arose the moment that Fender took the goods from the shelf. This constituted an acceptance of the offer. That the buyer had not paid for the goods or that the buyer could rescind the contract by putting the goods back did not alter the fact that there was a contract for the sale of goods and consequently the warranty of merchantability arose. [Fender v Colonial Stores, Inc. 138 Ga App 138, 225 SE2d 691 (1976)]

§ 26:7.   Automobiles.

Most states provide for the registration of the title to automobiles. These ordinarily provide for the transfer of the title certificate upon the making of a sale of a registered automobile. As between the seller and a buyer, however, the transfer of such a title certificate is not essential. That is, title passes from the seller to the buyer in accordance with the provisions of the Uniform Commercial Code.[7] After it has so passed, the new owner is entitled to obtain a title certificate showing such ownership.

In states that follow the view just stated, the automobile title certificate is merely evidence of the ownership of the automobile. It is not a document of title so that possession or ownership of the title certificate has no importance in determining who is the owner of the automobile.

In contrast to the view that the transfer of title to an automobile is governed by the UCC, some states by statute have declared that the title to an automobile cannot be transferred without an indorsement and delivery of the certificate of title. In those states, the parties must satisfy the requirement of such a statute and it is immaterial that title would otherwise pass under the Uniform Commercial Code.

FACTS:

Kilbourn American Leasing sold an automobile to Mann. He took possession of and paid for the car. Kilbourn did not deliver the title certificate to Mann but obtained a loan from the National Exchange Bank to which it gave the title certificate as collateral. When Kilbourn did not pay back the loan to National, it attempted to take possession of the automobile from Mann. He defended on the ground that title had passed to him, and therefore Kilbourn could not create any security interest therein.

DECISION:

Judgment for Mann. The automobile title certificate statute did not determine when title to the automobile passed. The title certificate did not constitute a document of title. Thus it was immaterial that the buyer never received the title certificate. The title had passed to the buyer in accordance with the provisions of the Uniform Commercial Code. [National Exchange Bank v Mann, 81 Wis 2d 352, 260 NW2d 716 (1978)]

§ 26:8.   Damage or Destruction of Goods.

In the absence of a contrary agreement, damage to or destruction of the goods affects the transaction as follows:

(a) **Damage to Identified Goods Before Risk of Loss Passes.** When goods that were identified at the time the contract was made are damaged or destroyed without the fault of either party before the risk of loss has passed, the contract is avoided if the loss is total. If the loss is partial or if the goods have so deteriorated that they do not conform to the contract, the buyer has the option, after inspection of the goods, (1) to treat the contract as avoided, or (2) to accept the goods subject to an allowance or deduction from the

[7]Bacheller v Employers Mutual Liability Ins. Co. 290 Wis 2d 564, 290 NW2d 872 (1980).

contract price. In either case, the buyer cannot assert any claim against the seller for breach of contract.[8]

(b) Damage to Identified Goods After Risk of Loss Passes. If partial damage or total destruction occurs after the risk of loss has passed to the buyer, it is the buyer's loss. It may be, however, that the buyer will be able to recover the amount of the damages from the person in possession of the goods or from a third person causing the loss.

(c) Damage to Unidentified Goods. As long as the goods are unidentified, no risk or loss passes to the buyer. If any goods are damaged or destroyed during this period, the loss is the seller's. The buyer is still entitled to receive the goods described by the contract. The seller is therefore liable for breach of contract if the proper goods are not delivered.

The only exception arises when the parties have expressly provided in the contract that the destruction of the seller's supply shall release the seller from liability or when it is clear that the parties contracted for the purchase and sale of part of the seller's supply to the exclusion of any other possible source of such goods. In such case, the destruction of or damage to the seller's supply is a condition subsequent which discharges the contract.

(d) Reservation of Title or Possession. When the seller reserves title or possession solely as security to make certain that the buyer will pay the purchase price, the risk of loss is borne by the buyer if the circumstances are such that the loss would be on the buyer in the absence of such a reservation.

§ 26:9.   Effect of Seller's Breach.

When the seller breaches the contract by sending the buyer goods that do not conform to the contract and the buyer rejects the goods, the risk of loss does not pass to the buyer.[9] This means that the risk of loss remains on the seller even though the risk would ordinarily have passed to the buyer. If because of the nature of the transaction, the risk of loss had already passed to the buyer before there was the opportunity to inspect the goods, the buyer's rejection of the goods returns the risk of loss to the seller.

FACTS:
Shook ordered electric cable from Graybar. He was sent the wrong kind of cable. He promptly notified Graybar of the mistake. Graybar did not call for the cable and it remained where it was delivered. Apparently no one could take it back to Graybar because of a truckers' strike. Four months later the cable was stolen from Shook. Graybar demanded payment of the purchase price.

DECISION:
Shook was not liable for the purchase price of the stolen cable. The seller had broken the contract by sending the wrong kind of cable. The risk of loss therefore remained on the seller. Graybar therefore bore the loss by theft taking place after the goods were rejected even though the goods were in the buyer's possession. [Graybar Electric Co. v Shook, 283 NC 213, 195 SE2d 514 (1973)]

---

[8]UCC § 2-613. Carlson v Nelson, 204 Neb 765, 285 NW2d 505 (1979).
[9]United Air Lines, Inc. v Conductron, Corp. 69 Ill App 3d 847, 26 Ill Dec 344, 387 NE2d 1272 (1979).

§ 26:10.   Returnable Goods Transactions.

The parties may agree for the return of conforming goods to the seller. This may be (a) a sale on approval, (b) a sale or return, or (c) a consignment sale. In the first two, the buyer is allowed to return the goods as an added inducement to purchase. The consignment sale is used when the buyer is actually the seller's agent.

The first step is to classify the transaction. A consignment sale is easily recognized because of its agency characteristics. The agreement of the parties may expressly state that the transaction is a sale on approval or a sale and return. If the agreement of the parties is not clear on this point, and the transaction is not an agency or consignment, classification of the transaction is controlled by the use the buyer will make of the goods. It is a **sale on approval** if the goods are purchased for use, that is, by a consumer. It is a **sale or return** if purchased for resale, that is, by a merchant.[10]

If the transaction does not give the buyer the right to return the goods, the buyer cannot return goods that conform to the contract if the seller refuses to take them back.

(a) **Sale on Approval.** In a sale on approval, no sale takes place, meaning there is no transfer of title, until the buyer approves. Title and risk of loss remain with the seller until there is an approval. As the buyer is not the "owner" of the goods before approval, the buyer's creditors cannot reach the goods.

Approval of the buyer may be shown by (a) express words, (b) conduct, or (c) the lapse of time. Use of the goods that is merely a trying out or testing does not constitute approval. Any use which goes beyond trying out or testing, such as repairing or giving away as a present, is inconsistent with the continued ownership of the seller and therefore shows approval by the buyer. The contract may give the buyer a fixed number of days for approval. The expiration of that period of time without any action by the buyer constitutes an approval. If no time is stated in the contract, the lapse of a reasonable time without action by the buyer constitutes an approval. If the buyer gives the seller notice of disapproval, the lapse of time thereafter has no effect.

If the goods are returned by the buyer, the seller bears the risk and expense of the return.[11]

FACTS:

Numismatic sells rare and collector coins by mail throughout the United States. Prewitt, a coin dealer, responded to an advertisement of Numismatic offering coins on approval. Numismatic mailed Prewitt twenty eight gold coins with an invoice value of $61,975. The coins were sent on a fourteen day risk-free basis with no instructions as to the method of returning unwanted coins. Upon receiving the coins, Prewitt instructed his wife to return them via certified mail for the maximum amount of insurance available, $400 for each package. She mailed the coins within the fourteen day period but Numismatic never received them. Prewitt claimed he was not liable for the loss.

[10]UCC § 2-326(1). An "or return" provision is treated as a sales contract for the purpose of applying the statute of frauds, and cannot be established by parol evidence when it would contradict a sales contract indicating an absolute sale. § 2-326(4).
[11]UCC § 2-327(1).

DECISION:

Judgment for Prewitt. Prewitt's return of the coins by mail within fourteen days as provided by the sale on approval contract constituted seasonable notice that the buyer would not accept the proffered sale and therefore the buyer did not assume risk of loss. When goods are returned by the buyer in a sale on approval, the seller bears the risk and expense of the return. [Prewitt v Numismatic Funding Corp. (CA8 Mo) 745 F2d 1175 (1984)]

(b) **Sale or Return.** A sale or return is a completed sale with an option for the buyer to return the goods and thereby sell or transfer back to the seller the title that had already passed to the buyer. As to the original sale, title and risk of loss pass to the buyer as in the case of the ordinary or absolute sale. Until the actual return of the goods is made, the title and risk of loss remain with the buyer. The expense and risk of return is on the buyer.[12]

As long as the goods remain in the buyer's possession, the buyer's creditors may treat the goods as belonging to the buyer. The buyer under a sale or return may return all of the goods or any commercial unit thereof. A *commercial unit* is any article, group of articles, or quantity which commercially is regarded as a separate unit or item, such as a particular machine, a suite of furniture, or a carload lot. In order to exercise the right to return the goods, they must be substantially in their original condition, and the option to return must be exercised within the time specified by the contract or within a reasonable time if none is specified.

(c) **Consignment sale.** By a **consignment** or sale on consignment, the owner of goods sends them to a dealer to sell. As between the owner and the dealer, there is no transfer of title. The relationship is merely an agency relationship. A consignee is of course required to return any goods not sold but this does not make it either a sale on approval or a sale or return. When a sale is made by the consignee to a third person, the title of the consignor passes from the consignor directly to the third person.

At no time is the consignee the owner of the goods. In some instances, however, the creditors of the consignee may treat the goods held by the consignee on consignment as though they belonged to the consignee, thereby ignoring and destroying the consignor's ownership.

§ 26:11. Auction Sales.

When goods are sold at an auction in separate lots, each lot is a separate transaction, and title to each passes independently of the other lots. Title to each lot passes when the auctioneer announces by the fall of the hammer or in any other customary manner that the auction is completed as to that lot,[13] that is, the lot in question has been sold to the bidder.

§ 26:12. Reservation of a Security Interest.

The seller may fear that the buyer will not pay for the goods. The seller could protect against this danger by insisting that the buyer pay cash

[12]UCC § 2-327(2). Seaway Candy, Inc. v Cedar Rapids YMCA (Iowa) 283 NW2d 315 (1979).

[13]UCC § 2-328.

immediately. This may not be practical for geographic or business reasons. The seller may then give credit to the buyer but can obtain protection by retaining a security interest in the goods. When goods are shipped to the buyer, the creditor may create a temporary security interest so that the buyer must make payment before obtaining the goods from the carrier. Between merchants this will be done by various ways of handling the bill of lading issued by the carrier. In the case of a consumer buyer, it is customary for the seller to make the shipment C.O.D. Under the bill of lading or the C.O.D. shipment, the security interest of the seller ends when the goods are delivered to the buyer. If a seller desires a security interest that will continue as long as the purchase price remains unpaid, a secured transaction under Article 9 of the Uniform Commercial Code will be created.

The fact that a seller has a security interest in the goods, by virtue of a C.O.D. provision or any other device, has no effect on the question of whether title or risk of loss has passed to the buyer. These questions are answered just as though there was no security interest. For example, under a shipment contract of future goods from a distant seller, the risk of loss and the title pass to the buyer on delivery to the carrier. The result is the same even though such shipment is made C.O.D.

§ 26:13.   Effect of Sale on Title.

As a general rule, a seller can only sell what the seller owns. If a person in possession of goods is not the owner, as in the case of a finder, thief, or a bailee, a sale by such possessor passes only possession. It is immaterial that the buyer from the possessor had purchased in good faith and had given value. The attempted sale does not pass any title. Consequently, the buyer of stolen goods must surrender them to the true owner and can be sued by the true owner for damages for conversion of the goods. The fact that the negligence of the owner made the theft possible or contributed to the losing of the goods does not bar the owner from recovering the goods or money damages from the thief, the finder, or the purchaser from either of them.[14]

There are instances, however, when either because of the conduct of the owner or the desire of society to protect the bona fide purchaser for value, the law permits a greater title to be transferred than the seller possessed.

(a) **Consignment Sale.** A manufacturer or distributor may send goods to a dealer for sale to the public with the understanding that the manufacturer or distributor is to remain the owner, and the dealer in effect is to act as selling agent. When the dealer maintains a place of business at which the dealer sells goods of the kind in question under a name other than that of the consigning manufacturer or distributor, the creditors of the dealer may reach the goods as though they were owned by the dealer. Such goods are deemed to be on sale or return with title and risk of loss passing to the dealer as in the case of an ordinary sale or return. The consignor can avoid this result by either complying with an applicable law providing for the consignor's interest to be evidenced by a sign, or showing that the person conducting the business

---

[14]Pate v Elliott, 61 Ohio App 2d 144, 400 NE2d 910 (1978) (theft).

is generally known by the creditors to be substantially engaged in selling goods of others, or complying with the filing provisions of Article 9.[15]

(b) **Estoppel.** The owner of property may be estopped from asserting ownership and thus be barred from denying the right of another person to sell the property. A person may purchase something and have the bill of sale made out in the name of a friend to whom possession of the property and the bill of sale are given. This might be done in order to deceive creditors of the true owner or to keep other persons from knowing that the purchase was made. If the friend should sell the property to a bona fide purchaser who relied on the bill of sale as showing that the friend was the owner, the true owner is estopped or barred from denying the friend's apparent ownership and right to sell.

(c) **Powers.** In certain circumstances, persons in possession of someone else's property may sell the property. This arises in the case of pledgees, lienholders, and some finders who, by statute, may have authority to sell the property to enforce their claim or when the owner cannot be found.

(d) **Negotiable Documents of Title.** By statute, certain documents of title, such as bills of lading and warehouse receipts, have been clothed with a degree of negotiability when executed in proper form. By virtue of such provisions, the holder of a negotiable document of title may transfer to a purchaser for value acting in good faith such title as was possessed by the person leaving the property with the issuer of the document. In such cases, it is immaterial that the holder had not acquired the document in a lawful manner.

(e) **Voidable Title.** If the buyer has a voidable title, as when the goods were obtained by fraud, the seller can rescind the sale while the buyer is still the owner. If, however, the buyer resells the property to a bona fide purchaser before the seller has rescinded the transaction, the subsequent purchaser acquires valid title. It is immaterial whether the buyer having the voidable title had obtained title by fraud as to identity, or by larceny by trick, or paid for the goods with a bad check, or that the transaction was a cash sale and the purchase price has not been paid.[16]

If the transferee from the holder of the voidable title is not a good faith purchaser, the title remains voidable and the true owner may reclaim the goods.[17]

(f) **Sale by Entrustee.** If the owner entrusts goods to a merchant who deals in goods of that kind, the latter has the power to transfer the entruster's title to anyone who buys from the entrustee in the ordinary course of business.

It is immaterial why the goods were entrusted to the merchant. Hence the leaving of a watch for repair with a jeweler who sells new and secondhand watches gives the jeweler the power to pass the title of the repair customer to a buyer in the ordinary course of business. Goods in inventory thus have a degree of "negotiability" so that the ordinary buyer, whether a

[15]UCC § 2-326(3).
[16]Ledbetter v Darwin Dobbs Co., Inc. (Ala) 473 SW2d 197 (1985).
[17]Kimberly & European Diamonds, Inc. (CA6 Ky) 684 F2d 363 (1982).

consumer or another merchant, buys the goods free of the ownership interest of the person entrusting the goods to the seller.[18] The entrustee is, of course, liable to the owner for damages caused by the entrustee's sale of the goods and is guilty of some form of statutory offense of embezzlement.

If the entrustee is not a merchant, such as a prospective customer trying out an automobile, there is no transfer of title to the buyer from the entrustee. Likewise, there is no transfer of title when a mere bailee, such as a repairer, who is not a seller of goods of that kind, sells the property of a customer.

If a third person has a claim to the goods that is superior to the entruster, a sale by the entrustee does not destroy that claim but passes the title of the entruster subject to such claim.[19]

FACTS:

Textile Supplies distributed carpets. It employed a salesman named Couch. Garrett sent an order to Textile for carpets. He also sent checks to pay for them. Couch intercepted these checks and sent them back to Garrett with the request to exchange them for other checks payable to Cartersville Textile Sales. This was an assumed name under which Couch secretly sold carpets. As the result of these transactions, carpets were sent by Textile and received by Garrett while Couch intercepted and made off with the money that Textile should have received in payment for the carpets. On discovering the diversion, the manufacturer sued Garrett. Garrett claimed that he had acquired good title to the carpets.

DECISION:

Judgment for Textile. Couch had stolen the carpets from Textile. There was not an entrustment by Textile nor was there any intent that Couch should acquire title. Consequently, neither the entrustment nor the voidable title provisions of the Code were applicable. Therefore, Couch only transferred such title as he possessed. Because he stole the carpets he had no title. Garrett as a transferee also had no title even though he had purchased in good faith and for value. [Textile Supplies, Inc. v Garrett (CA5 Miss) 687 F2d 123 (1982)]

SUMMARY

Problems involving risk and property rights in sales transactions will often relate to damage to the goods, the claims of creditors, and insurance. The eventual solution to these problems often depends upon the nature of the transaction between the seller and the buyer. Sales transactions may be classified according to the nature of the goods and the terms of the transactions.

Existing goods are physically in existence and owned by the seller as distinct from future goods which are not yet owned by the seller or are not yet in existence. The title to existing goods identified at the time of the contract passes to the buyer at the time the parties agree to the transaction. Once

[18]UCC § 2-403(1).
[19]Commercial Credit Equipment Corp. v Bates, 154 Ga App 71, 267 SE2d 469 (1980).

the goods are identified, both the buyer and the seller have an insurable interest in the goods. If the goods are damaged after the sales agreement has been made, a merchant seller bears the loss occurring up until the time the buyer receives the goods. If the seller is not a merchant, the risk of loss passes to the buyer when the goods are tendered or made available to the buyer. In a shipment contract, title and risk of loss pass at the time and place of shipment; in a destination contract, title and risk pass when the goods are made available at the destination. As long as the goods are unidentified, no risk of loss passes to the buyer.

In cases where the risk of loss would ordinarily pass to the buyer, the risk nevertheless remains with the seller if the goods do not conform to the contract. Even when the goods do conform to the contract, the buyer and seller can agree that they may be returned. The nature of their agreement, as a sale on approval, sale or return, or consignment sale, determines who bears the risk of loss.

In an auction sale, title passes when the auctioneer accepts the bidder's offer.

The reservation of a security interest in goods does not affect the question of who bears the risk of loss.

Ordinarily, sellers cannot pass any better title than they possess. In some cases, however, the law permits a greater title to be transferred.

QUESTIONS AND CASE PROBLEMS

1. What social forces are affected by the rule that the buyer has an insurable interest when future goods are marked for shipment to the buyer?
2. When does title pass in the case of goods in a self-service store?
3. Woodrow made a contract to buy ten tons of coal from the Jackson Coal Company. How much coal does Woodrow own?
4. By letter, Felicia in Oklahoma, orders a sewing machine from the Jakoby Sewing Machine Company in Chicago. The order of Felicia is accepted but nothing is said as to whether the sale is for cash or on credit. How can Jakoby be sure that payment is made before Felicia gets possession of the sewing machine?
5. Kirk buys a television set from the Janess Television Store. At the time of the sale, Kirk gives Janess a check for the purchase price and obtains a receipt marked "paid in full." The check is a bad check as it is drawn on an account in which the balance is not sufficient to cover the amount of the check. Kirk knows this but hopes to leave town with the television set before Janess learns that the check is bad. Is Kirk the owner of the television set?
6. Compare the legal classification of (a) goods physically existing and owned by the seller at the time of contracting, (b) goods physically existing but not owned by the seller at the time of contracting, and (c) goods not physically existing at the time of contracting.
7. Wanda ordered a piano from the Jarrett Music Store. The store put a shipping tag on the ordered piano, the tag showing Wanda's name and address. The piano is then put in Jarrett's truck and taken on its way to

Wanda's address. On the way, Jarrett's truck is hit by a heavy trailer and the piano is severely damaged. Jarrett claims that Wanda must bear the loss because the transaction was a contract for the sale of future goods and the risk of loss therefore passed to Wanda when the goods were given to the carrier. Is Jarrett correct?

8. Jamison wants to buy a new truck. Kenton, a dealer, tries to sell him a particular truck. Jamison is not certain that this is the truck he wants. To encourage him to buy, Kenton sells the truck to him on "thirty day approval." Jamison owes the First National Bank on an overdue debt and twenty-five days later the bank has the sheriff seize the truck in order to sell it to pay off the debt owed by Jamison. Both Kenton and Jamison object that the bank cannot do this. Are they correct?

9. *O* owned a television set. *T* stole the set and sold it to *A* who purchased for value and in good faith. *A* resold the set to *B* who also purchased in good faith and for value. *O* sued *B* for the set. *B* raised the defense that he had purchased it in good faith from a seller who had sold in good faith. Was this defense valid? [Johnny Dell, Inc. v New York State Police, 84 Misc 2d 360, 375 NYS2d 545]

10. *B* purchased a used automobile from *A* with a bad check. *B* then took the automobile to an auction in which the automobile was sold to *C*, who had no knowledge of the prior history of the automobile. When *B*'s check was dishonored, *A* brought suit against *C* to reclaim the automobile. Was he entitled to do so? [Greater Louisville Auto Auction, Inc. v Ogle Buick, Inc. (Ky) 387 SW2d 17]

11. Coppola collected coins. He joined a coin club, First Coinvestors, Inc. The club would send coins to its members who were to pay for them or return them within ten days. What was the nature of the transaction? [First Coinvestors, Inc. v Coppola, 88 Misc 2d 495, 388 NYS2d 833]

12. Eastern Supply Co. purchased lawn mowers from the Turf Man Sales Corp. The purchase order stated on its face "Ship direct to 30th & Harcum Way, Pitts., Pa." Turf Man delivered the goods to Helm's Express, Inc. for shipment and delivery to Eastern at the address in question. Did title pass on delivery of the goods to Helm or upon their arrival at the specified address? [In re Eastern Supply Co. 21 (Pa) D&C 2d 128, 107 Pitts Leg J 451]

13. Rowena wrote Marion that she would sell her car to Marion and that if Marion agreed to pay $400 the car was hers. Marion telephoned later that she agreed to pay that amount. The next day Rowena changed her mind and claimed that she still owned the car because she had never transferred the title certificate to Marion. Did Rowena still own the car?

14. A manufacturer of knitwear loaded a trailer with goods ordered by the buyer. The loaded trailer was to be hauled away by a carrier. After the trailer was loaded but before it was taken away, it was damaged by fire. The manufacturer claimed that the buyer must bear the risk of loss because the goods were future goods covered by a shipment contract. Was the manufacturer correct? [A. M. Knitwear Corp. v All America Export-Import Corp. 50 App Div 2d 558, 375 NYS2d 23]

15. Compare the effect upon title of an unauthorized sale made by a repair shop of a customer's television set when (a) the repair shop only makes repairs, and (b) the repair shop also sells new and used television sets.

16. Clinton, who resides in California, ordered a typewriter from the Walker Company. The Walker Company delivered the typewriter to a carrier in New Jersey, arranged for the transportation, mailed an invoice to Clinton, and notified Clinton by telephone that the typewriter had been shipped. The company reserved title to the typewriter for security reasons. The typewriter was destroyed in transit, and Clinton contended that Walker should stand the loss since the title to the typewriter remained in Walker? What will the result be?

17. The Leton Wholesale Company sold and delivered ten executive desks on consignment to Lois, the owner and manager of the Handy Office Supply Company. Lois had severe financial problems and her creditors petitioned the court to allow attachment of her inventory. A marshall seized the entire inventory of the Handy Office Supply Company including the ten executive desks. Explain how the Leton Wholesale Company could have prevented the desks from becoming subject to the claim of the creditors of Lois?

18. Smith operated a marina and sold and repaired boats. Gallagher rented a stall at the marina at which he kept his vessel, the River Queen. Without any authorization, Smith sold the vessel to Courtesy Ford. Gallagher sued Courtesy Ford for the vessel. What result? [Gallagher v Unenrolled Motor Vessel River Queen (CA5 Tex) 475 F2d 117]

CHAPTER 27

OBLIGATIONS AND

PERFORMANCE

CHAPTER OBJECTIVES

After studying this chapter you will be able to:
1. Define the obligation of good faith as applied to merchants and nonmerchants.
2. State what steps can be taken by a party to a sales contract who feels insecure.
3. State the obligations of the buyer to a sales contract.
4. Identify conduct that constitutes an acceptance of goods.
5. Apply the law of assignment to sales contracts.
6. Solve problems involving the obligations and rights of parties to sales transactions.

Each party to a sales contract must perform according to its terms. Each is likewise under the duty to act with good faith in its performance and to do nothing to impair the expectation of the other party that the contract will be performed.

A. GENERAL PRINCIPLES

Contracts for the sale of goods impose certain obligations on the parties to the contracts.

§ 27:1. Obligation of Good Faith.

"Every contract or duty . . . imposes an obligation of good faith in its performance or enforcement."[1] The Uniform Commercial Code defines good

---

[1] Uniform Commercial Code § 1-203. Servbest Foods, Inc. v Emessee Industries, Inc. 82 Ill App 3d 662, 37 Ill Dec 945, 403 NE2d 1 (1980).

faith as meaning "honesty in fact in the conduct or transaction concerned."[2] In the case of a merchant seller or buyer of goods, the Code carries the concept of good faith further and imposes the additional requirement that the merchant seller or buyer observe "reasonable commercial standards of fair dealing in the trade."[3]

FACTS:

Umlas made a contract to buy a new automobile from Acey Oldsmobile. He was allowed to keep his old car until the new car was delivered. The sales contract gave him a trade-in on the old car of $650, but specified that it could be reappraised when it was actually brought in to the dealer. When Umlas brought the trade-in to the dealer, an employee of Acey took it for a test drive and told Acey that it was worth from $300 to $400. Acey stated to Umlas that the trade-in would be appraised at $50. Umlas refused to buy from Acey and purchased from another dealer who appraised the trade-in at $400. Umlas sued Acey for breach of contract. Acey defended on the ground that its conduct was authorized by the reappraisal clause.

DECISION:

Judgment for Umlas. While the contract reserved the right to reappraise the trade-in, this required a good faith reappraisal. From the fact that the reappraised figure was substantially below the value stated by the employee making the test drive, it was clear that the reappraisal had not been made in good faith and it was therefore not binding on the buyer; and the seller remained bound by the original contract and the original appraisal of the trade-in. [Umlas v Acey Oldsmobile, Inc. (NY Civ Ct) 310 NYS2d 147 (1970)]

---

§ 27:2.   Conditions Precedent to Performance.

In the case of a cash sale not requiring the physical moving of the goods, the duties of the seller and buyer are concurrent. Each one has the right to demand that the other perform at the same time. That is, as the seller hands over the goods, the buyer theoretically must hand over the purchase money. If either party refuses to act, the other party has the right to withhold performance. In the case of a shipment contract, there is a time interval between the performance of the parties; the seller will have performed by delivering the goods to the carrier, but the buyer's obligation will not arise until the goods have been received and accepted by the buyer.

§ 27:3.   Repudiation of the Contract.

The seller or the buyer may refuse to perform the contract when the time for performance arises. This is a repudiation of the contract.[4] Likewise, before that time arrives, the one party may inform the other that the contract will never be performed. This repudiation made in advance of the time for performance is called an **anticipatory repudiation.**

[2]UCC § 1-201(19); Chemical Bank of Rochester v Haskell, 51 NY2d 85, 432 NYS2d 478, 411 NE2d 1339 (1980).
[3]UCC § 2-103(1)(b).
[4]Unique Systems, Inc. v Zotos International, Inc. (CA8 Minn) 622 F2d 373 (1980).

FACTS:

A buyer purchased goods on thirty days' credit. The thirty days elapsed but payment was not made. The seller wrote the buyer requesting payment. Thirty more days elapsed and payment was not made. The seller claimed that the buyer had repudiated the contract.

DECISION:

The seller was not correct. The contract had not been repudiated. The failure to perform is not a repudiation. To constitute a repudiation, there must be a clear expression of intent to be not bound by a contract. This is distinct from merely failing to perform the obligation under a contract. [National Ropes, Inc. v National Diving Service, Inc. (CA5 Fla) 513 F2d 53 (1975)]

(a) **Action of Aggrieved Party.** If there is a clear repudiation of the contract and the loss of the repudiated performance substantially impairs the value of the contract to the other party, that other party, the aggrieved party, may request the repudiating party to retract or take back the repudiation. While waiting to see what happens, the aggrieved party may hold up rendering any further performance under the contract. In any case, the aggrieved party may assert that the contract has been broken and utilize any of the remedies available for breach.[5]

If the aggrieved party has acted without sufficient justification, that is, if in fact there was no anticipatory repudiation, the aggrieved party who withholds performance will be the one who is breaking the contract and will be liable for damages for breach.

(b) **Retraction of Anticipatory Repudiation.** Prior to the time when performance is due, the party who made the anticipatory repudiation may retract or take it back. This cannot be done if the other party has (a) canceled the contract because of the repudiation, (b) has materially changed position, as by making other sales or purchases, or (c) has expressly accepted the repudiation as final.

§ 27:4.   Adequate Assurance of Performance.

A party to a sales contract may feel that the other party will not perform the contract. For example, the seller's warehouse is destroyed by fire. The buyer could fear that the seller would not be able to make a delivery scheduled for the following month. Whenever a party to a sales contract has reasonable grounds for being concerned about the future performance of the other party, a written demand may be made upon such other party for assurance that the contract will be performed.

(a) **Form of Assurance.** The person upon whom demand for assurance is made must give "such assurance of due performance as is adequate under the circumstances of the particular case." The exact form of assurance is not specified by the Code. If the party on whom demand is made has an

[5]UCC § 2-610; Diskmakers, Inc. v De Witt Equipment Corp. (CA3 NJ) 555 F2d 1177 (1977).

established reputation, a reaffirmation of the contract obligation and a statement that it will be performed may be sufficient to assure a reasonable person that it will be performed. In contrast, the person's reputation or economic position at the time may be such that mere words and promises would not give any real assurance. In such case, it may be necessary to have a third person or an insurance company guarantee performance, or to put up property as security for performance.

(b) **Failure to Give Assurance.** If adequate assurance is not given, the demanding party may treat the contract as repudiated.[6] The demanding party is then free to make a substitute contract with a third person to replace the repudiated contract.

B. DUTIES OF THE PARTIES

The obligations and performance of the parties to a sales contract may be listed as follows: (1) seller's duty to deliver the goods, (2) buyer's duty to accept the goods, (3) buyer's duty to pay for the goods, and (4) duties of the parties under particular contract terms.

§ 27:5. Seller's Duty to Deliver.

The seller has the duty to deliver the goods in accordance with the terms of the contract. This duty to make "delivery" does not require physical transportation but merely means that the seller must permit the transfer of possession of the goods to the buyer. That is, the seller makes the goods available to the buyer. The delivery is sufficient if it is made in accordance with the terms of the sale or contract to sell.

(a) **Place, Time, and Manner of Delivery.** The terms of the contract determine whether the seller is to send the goods or the buyer is to call for them, or whether the goods must be transported by the seller to the buyer, or whether the transaction is to be completed by the delivery of documents without the movement of the goods. In the absence of a provision in the contract or a contrary course of performance or usage of trade, the place of delivery is the seller's place of business, if the seller has one; otherwise it is the seller's residence. If, however, the subject matter of the contract consists of identified goods that are known by the parties to be in some other place, that place is the place of delivery. Documents of title may be delivered through customary banking channels.[7]

When a method of transportation called for by the contract becomes unavailable or commercially unreasonable, the seller must make delivery by means of a commercially reasonable substitute if available and the buyer must accept such substitute.[8] This provision is applicable when a shipping strike makes impossible the use of the method of transportation specified in the contract of sale.

(b) **Quantity Delivered.** The buyer has the right to insist that all the goods be delivered at one time. If the seller delivers a smaller or larger

[6]UCC § 2-609(4). This assurance must be given within 30 days.
[7]UCC § 2-308.
[8]UCC § 2-514(1).

quantity than that stipulated in the contract, the buyer may refuse to accept the goods.

(c) Cure of Defective Tender. If the seller tenders nonconforming goods, the buyer may reject them. This does not end the transaction because the seller is given a second chance to make a proper or curative tender of conforming goods.[9]

This right is restricted in terms of whether the second tender can be made within the time called for by the contract. If the time for making delivery under the contract has not expired, the seller need only give the buyer seasonable (timely) notice of the intention to make a proper delivery within the time allowed by the contract, and the seller may then do so. If the time for making the delivery has expired, the seller is given an additional reasonable time in which to make a substitute conforming tender if (1) the seller so notifies the buyer and (2) the seller had acted reasonably in making the original tender, believing that it would be acceptable to the buyer.

§ 27:6. Buyer's Duty to Accept Goods.

The buyer must accept goods that conform to the contract. Refusal to do so is a breach of the contract.

(a) Right to Examine Goods. In order to see if the goods in fact conform to the contract, the buyer has the right to examine the goods when tendered by the seller. As an exception to this rule, the buyer must pay for goods sent C.O.D. and has no right to examine the goods until payment is made.

(b) What Constitutes Acceptance of Goods. Acceptance of goods means that the buyer shows in some way that the goods conform to the contract. This may be shown by (a) an express statement of approval, (b) conduct inconsistent with rejection, or (c) lapse of time.[10]

FACTS:

Congress Shops purchased shoes from Banfi for resale. Upon discovering that the shoes did not conform to the specifications in their order, Congress notified Banfi that the shoes were being rejected and that Congress would not pay for them. After rejection, Congress nevertheless placed the shoes in its inventory and offered them for sale. It sold almost half of them the following year. Banfi sued for the price. Congress claimed that it had rejected the goods.

DECISION:

Judgment for Banfi. By retaining and selling the goods, Congress had exercised ownership over them that amounted to an acceptance. Congress had accepted the goods and was liable for the price. [Lorenzo Banfi Di Banfi Renzo & Co. v Congress Shops, Inc. (ND Ill) 568 F Supp 432 (1983)]

---

[9]UCC § 2-508.
[10]UCC § 2-606(1). Danjee, Inc. v Addressograph Multigraph Corp. 44 NC App 626, 262 SE2d 665 (1980).

Thus, a buyer accepts the goods by making continued use of them and by not attempting to return the goods until after 14 months. A buyer, of course, accepts the goods by modifying them because such action is inconsistent with a rejection or the continued ownership of the goods by the seller. Consequently, when the purchaser of a truck installed a hoist and a dump bed on it, such action constituted an acceptance by conduct and the buyer therefore became liable for the contract price of the truck.

§ 27:7.   Buyer's Duty to Pay.

The buyer must pay for goods accepted and must pay the amount stated in the sales contract. The sales contract may require payment in advance or may give the buyer credit by postponing the time for payment.[11]

Unless otherwise agreed, payment by the buyer requires payment in cash.

(a) Payment by Commercial Paper. The seller may accept a check or a promissory note from the buyer. If the check is not paid by the bank, the purchase price remains unpaid. A promissory note gives the buyer credit by postponing the time for payment.

The seller may refuse to accept a check or promissory note. When the seller does so, the seller must give the buyer reasonable time in which to obtain legal tender with which to make payment.

§ 27:8.   Duties under Particular Terms.

A sale may be as simple as a face-to-face exchange of money and goods, but it frequently involves a more complicated pattern, with some element of transportation, generally by a common carrier. This, in turn, generally results in the addition of certain special terms to the sales transaction.

(a) C.I.F. Under a **C.I.F.** contract, the buyer pays the seller a lump sum covering the cost (selling price) of the goods, insurance on them, and freight to the specified destination of the goods. The C.I.F. term imposes upon the seller the obligation of putting the goods in the possession of a proper carrier, of loading and paying for the freight, of procuring the proper insurance, of preparing an invoice of the goods and any other document needed for shipment, and of forwarding all documents to the buyer with commercial promptness.[12]

Under a C.I.F. contract, the buyer bears the risk of loss after the goods have been delivered to the carrier. The buyer must pay for the goods when proper documents representing them are tendered, which in turn means that the buyer is not entitled to inspect the goods before paying for them, unless the contract expressly provides for payment on or after the arrival of the goods.

[11]UCC § 2-310(a). If delivery under the contract is to be made by delivery of a document of title, payment is due at the time and place at which the buyer is to receive the document regardless of where the goods are to be received. § 2-310(c).

[12]UCC § 2-320(1), (2). The term C. & F. or C.F. imposes the same obligations and risks as a C.I.F. term with the exception of the obligation as to insurance. Under a C.F. contract, the seller completes performance by delivery of the goods to the carrier and by proper payment of the freight charges on the shipment, whereupon title and risk of loss pass to the buyer.

FACTS:

Mexican Produce Company sold goods to Sonny Mohamed. The contract was C.I.F. Trinidad. Mexican Produce delivered the goods to a carrier in Puerto Rico, Sea-Land Service, Inc. The goods were damaged in transit. Mexican Produce sued Sea-Land Service, Inc. for the damage.

DECISION:

Judgment for Sea-Land Service, Inc. Under a C.I.F. contract the risk of loss passes to the buyer when the goods are delivered to the carrier. The buyer thus bore the risk of damage while in transit and the seller could not sue for such damages because the seller did not sustain any damage. [Mexican Produce Co. v Sea-Land Service Inc. (DC Puerto Rico) 429 F Supp 552 (1974)]

(b) **F.O.B.** The term **F.O.B.** or "free on board" is a condensed way of saying that the seller has the obligation of (a) putting the goods on board a named vessel, truck or other carrier, or of (b) making tender at a named geographical point. When used to specify a geographical point, it may be F.O.B. the seller's city, the buyer's city, or an intermediate point, such as the Port of New York for goods that are to be sent by land to New York and by water to a foreign country. Under the F.O.B. term (1) risk of loss and (2) title pass to the buyer at the F.O.B. point. This is so even though such transfer would have occurred at a different point if the shipment had not been F.O.B. The seller pays the cost of transporting the goods to the F.O.B. point. The buyer pays transportation costs from that point on.

FACTS:

Custom Built Homes purchased unassembled prefabricated houses from Page-Hill in Minnesota to be delivered by the seller "F.O.B. building site...Kansas." The seller brought the houses to the building site by tractor-trailer, where he would unhitch the trailer and unload the shipment. Kansas taxed Custom Built on the sale.

DECISION:

Judgment for Tax Commission. Under the terms of the contract the seller was required to deliver the goods to the buyer at the building site in Kansas without charge for transportation to that point. As no contrary intention appeared from the contract, the title to the goods passed at the building site. The sale therefore took place in Kansas and was subject to tax there. [Custom Built Homes Co. v Kansas State Commission of Revenue, 184 Kan 31, 334 P2d 808 (1959)]

C. ASSIGNMENT OF SALES CONTRACT

Ordinarily either party may assign a sales contract. The obligations of the parties under the contract are not changed by an assignment.

§ 27:9.   Effect of Assignment.

The duties of the parties are not changed by the making of an assignment. The making of an assignment may be followed by a modification of the original contract. Thus if the buyer makes an assignment, the original contract might be modified to state that the goods shall be delivered to the assignee.

When the seller makes an assignment of the right to payment, the assignee is entitled to the payment made by the buyer. The original contract or a subsequent modification may state that the buyer (a) shall make payments directly to the assignee, or (b) continue to make payments to the assignor-seller. When payments are made to the assignor-seller, the assignment will obligate the assignor-seller to remit such payments to the assignee.

§ 27:10.   Obligation of
Seller's Assignee as to Performance.

Ordinarily an assignment by a seller is merely a way of converting the seller's account receivable or contract right into immediate cash. It is not intended to require the assignee to perform the contract. For example, when the car dealer assigns a contract to the finance company, no one expects the finance company to make repairs to the car.

In contrast, there are situations in which it is intended that the assignee will perform the contract. This can happen when the seller goes out of business and sells the outstanding contracts to a buyer.

§ 27:11.   Defenses of Buyer against Seller's Assignee.

Ordinarily the assignee of the seller is subject to any defense which the buyer would have against the seller. Credit sales contracts commonly provide, however, that the buyer agrees not to assert against the seller's assignee any claim which could be asserted against the seller. This makes the contract much more attractive to the assignee by, giving the assignee greater assurance of being able to collect the amount due under the contract. Such provisions are valid,[13] although greatly restricted in the case of consumer goods.[14]

SUMMARY

Every sales contract imposes an obligation of good faith in its performance or enforcement. Good faith means honesty in fact in the conduct or transaction concerned.

In the case of a cash sale, both the buyer and the seller may demand concurrent performance where no transportation of the goods is required.

If a buyer refuses to perform a contract, it is called a repudiation. A repudiation made in advance of the time for performance is called an anticipatory repudiation. If either party to a contract feels insecure about the performance of the other, that party may demand adequate assurance of

[13]Bankers Trust Co. v Litton Systems, Inc. (CA2 NY) 599 F2d 488 (1979).
[14]See Chapter 8 of this book.

performance and if not given, the demanding party may treat the contract as repudiated.

The seller has the duty to deliver the goods in accordance with the terms of the contract. If the seller tenders nonconforming goods, the buyer may reject them. The buyer has a duty to accept goods that conform to the contract. Refusal to do so is breach of contract. The buyer is deemed to have accepted the goods when the buyer expresses acceptance or does something inconsistent with rejection; the buyer must pay for the goods accepted in accordance with the terms of the contract.

The parties to a sales contract assume certain duties where goods are shipped under particular shipping terms. In a C.I.F. contract the buyer pays the seller the cost of the goods, insurance, and freight to the specified destination. The buyer under a C.I.F. contract bears the risk of loss after the goods have been delivered to the carrier. In an F.O.B., or free on board contract, the seller has the obligation of putting the goods on board a named carrier or making delivery at a particular location. The risk of loss and title to the goods pass to the buyer at the F.O.B. point.

Both the buyer and seller may assign the sales contract. The obligations of the parties under the sales contract are not changed by an assignment. The assignee of the seller is subject to any defense which the buyer would have against the seller unless it is waived in the contract.

QUESTIONS AND CASE PROBLEMS

1. What social forces are involved in the rule of law governing the substitution of a different method of transportation to replace the method specified in the contract of sale?
2. Elkins Appliance Store makes a contract to purchase 100 electric toasters from the Greystone Electric Company, delivery to be made on November 1. A week later Greystone informs Elkins that its factory has been severely damaged by fire and that Greystone is uncertain as to whether it will be able to deliver the toasters by November 1 or at any time. Elkins claims that this statement is an anticipatory repudiation of the contract. Is Elkins correct?
3. The Wolfson Paint Store wants to build up its inventory. It makes a contract to purchase 1,000 cans of paint from the Gordon Paint Factory. A truck from the Gordon Paint Factory delivers 400 cans of paint and the driver tells Wolfson that the balance will come later. Wolfson rejects the 400 cans. Has he broken the contract by so doing?
4. Louise in St. Louis orders by mail from Grant Company in Seattle a set of kitchen knives. They are sent C.O.D. to Louise. In order to be sure that there has been no mistake, Louise wants to examine the knives before she pays the carrier. Can she do so?
5. Compare the making of a curative tender (a) before the expiration of the time for performance, and (b) after the expiration of the time for performance.
6. The Melvin Electric Motor Corporation makes a contract with the Raskob Gear Company for the latter to supply 10,000 sets of reduction gears according to specifications supplied by Melvin. The president of

Melvin reads in the newspaper that there is a strike in the Raskob plant. The president of Melvin telephones the president of Raskob to express concern over whether Raskob will be able to perform the contract. The conversation does not lessen the fears of the president of Melvin and the conversation concludes with Melvin's president demanding assurance from Raskob that performance will be made. The president of Melvin does not hear anything further from Raskob during the next 30 days. Can Melvin treat the contract as repudiated by Raskob?

7. International Minerals and Metals Corporation contracted to sell Weinstein scrap metal to be delivered within 30 days. Later the seller informed the buyer that it could not make delivery within that time. The buyer agreed to an extension of time, but no limiting date was set. Within what time must the seller perform? [International Minerals and Metals Corp. v Weinstein, 236 NC 558, 73 SE2d 472]

8. Carlson ordered equipment from the Ventresca Foundry in St. Louis, Missouri, to be sent "F.O.B. Chicago, Illinois." The equipment was placed on a motor freight truck under a proper shipment contract. The truck was wrecked before it reached Chicago. Ventresca demanded payment of the purchase price from Carlson on the theory that the contract was a shipment contract and that the risk of loss passed to Carlson when the equipment was delivered to the carrier in St. Louis. Was Ventresca correct?

9. The Spaulding & Kimball Co. ordered from the Aetna Chemical Co. 75 cartons of window washers. The buyer received them and sold about a third to its customers. The buyer later refused to pay for them, claiming that the quality was poor. The seller sued for the price, claiming that the goods had been accepted. Decide. [Aetna Chemical Co. v Spaulding & Kimball Co. 98 Vt 51, 126 A 582]

10. A computer manufacturer promoted the sale of a digital computer as a "revolutionary breakthrough." It made a contract to deliver one of these computers to a buyer. It failed to deliver the computer and explained that its failure was caused by unanticipated technological difficulties. Was this an excuse for nonperformance by the seller? [United States v Wegematic Corp. (CA2 NY) 360 F2d 674]

11. A buyer made a contract for equipment which was to be installed in a new building which was being constructed. When the equipment was delivered to the buyer, the buyer refused to accept it on the ground that the architect had made a mistake and the tendered goods could not be used in the new building. The seller sued the buyer for breach of contract. Was the buyer entitled to reject the goods? [R. R. Waites Co. v E. H. Thrift Air Conditioning, Inc. (MoApp) 510 SW2d 759]

12. The Rock Glen Salt Co. agreed to sell to Segal of Massachusetts some bags of salt. It obtained from the Watkins Salt Co., New York, the bags of salt ordered by Segal and 15 barrels of salt ordered by another customer. The bags and barrels of salt were placed in a car and shipped to Boston. The bill of lading for the entire shipment was made out to the seller, and indorsed and sent to Segal, who was notified by the carrier of the arrival of the car. In an action brought by the salt company against Segal to recover the purchase price, he contended that (a) he could accept

the salt in the bags and reject the salt in the barrels or (b) reject the entire shipment. What is your opinion? [Rock Glen Salt Co. v Segal, 229 Mass 115, 118 NE 239]

13. Teeman made a contract to purchase lumber from the Oakhill Mill. The contract called for payment to be made upon delivery to Teeman. When the truck from the Mill arrived to deliver the lumber, Teeman gave the driver a check for the purchase price. The driver refused to take the check, returned to the Mill, and the Mill then notified Teeman that the contract was canceled. Was the Mill entitled to cancel the contract?

14. The buyer accepts the goods when he takes them from the carrier. Appraise this statement.

15. Compare the effect of a C.I.F. and a F.O.B. clause.

16. Lury has a contract for sale with Burns, with whom he has not previously dealt, to make four quarterly deliveries of Product Z on thirty days' credit. Two months after the first delivery under the contract, Burns has not yet paid. May Lurie demand adequate assurance of performance?

17. Rader & Co. of St. John, Newfoundland, contracted to sell to Morano, of Philadelphia, 1,000 drums first quality codfish at fifteen dollars a drum, c.i.f. Philadelphia. The fish were shipped by steamer from St. Johns to Philadelphia. The invoice, negotiable bill of lading, and insurance policy were sent by Rader & Co. to Morano. While en route to Philadelphia, the ship transporting the fish was sunk. Is Morano obligated to pay for the goods?

CHAPTER 28

WARRANTIES AND OTHER

PRODUCT LIABILITIES

CHAPTER OBJECTIVES

After studying this chapter you will be able to:

1. List the theories of product liability.
2. Say who may sue and who may be sued when a defective product causes harm.
3. List and define the implied warranties and distinguish them from express warranties.
4. Explain and distinguish between full warranties and limited warranties under federal law.
5. State what constitutes a breach of warranty.
6. Describe the extent and manner in which implied warranties may be disclaimed by agreement.
7. Solve problems involving product liability.

When goods are defective and cause injury or loss, the person harmed has a claim for product liability.

A. GENERAL PRINCIPLES

The remedy of the harmed person may be governed by the common law, by the Uniform Commercial Code, or by the newly emerging case law.

§ 28:1. Theories of Liability.

Two centuries ago, a buyer was limited to suing a seller for breach of an express guarantee or for negligence or fraud. After the modern era of mass production and distribution developed, these remedies had little value. A guarantee was good, but in the ordinary sales transaction no one stopped to get a guarantee. You never asked the manager of the supermarket to give you a guarantee that the loaf of bread you were buying was fit to eat. Negligence and fraud are generally impossible to prove in a mass production world. How can you prove how a can of soup was prepared months ago? The making of fraudulent statements by the seller is rather rare.

In order to give protection from harm-causing products, the law developed the concept of warranty liability. Warranties are either express or implied and are governed by the Uniform Commercial Code. Within the last few decades, many courts have decided that broader protection was still required and created an additional concept of strict tort liability.

There are accordingly six theories in the law to protect from harm caused by defective products: (1) guarantee; (2) negligence; (3) fraud; (4) express warranty; (5) implied warranty; and (6) strict tort liability. If the plaintiff is a consumer or an employee, there might also be (7) consumer protection liability and (8) employee protection liability. In every case, the plaintiff does not have a choice of all theories. The facts of the case will ordinarily exclude some theories. In other situations, the plaintiff will have the choice of two or more theories.

§ 28:2. Nature of Harm.

When a product is defective, harm may be caused to (1) person, (2) property, or (3) economic or commercial interests. Under (1), the buyer of a truck may be injured when it goes out of control and plunges down the side of a hill. Third persons may also be injured, such as passengers in the truck, bystanders, or the driver of a car hit by the truck. The defective truck may also cause injury to a total stranger who seeks to rescue one of the victims. Property damage under (2) is sustained when the buyer's truck is damaged when it plunges down the slope. The car of the other driver may be damaged or a building into which the runaway truck careens may be damaged. Under (3), commercial and economic interests of the buyer are affected by the fact that the truck is defective. Even if no physical harm is sustained, the fact remains that the truck is not as valuable as it would have been, and the buyer who has paid for the truck on the basis of the value it should have had has sustained an economic loss. If the buyer is required to rent a truck from someone else or loses an opportunity to haul freight for compensation, the fact that the truck was defective also causes economic or commercial loss.

§ 28:3. Who May Sue and Be Sued.

Down to the early part of this century, only the parties to the sales contract could sue each other. Thus a seller could be sued by the buyer but other persons were excluded by the concept that they were not parties to the sales contract. That is, they could not sue because they were not in privity of contract.

This requirement of privity of contract has been widely rejected and the law is moving toward the conclusion that anyone harmed because of an "improper" product may sue whoever is in any way responsible.

(a) **The Plaintiff.** By the modern view, not only the buyer, but also customers and employees of the buyer and even third persons or bystanders may sue because of harm caused by an improper product. The UCC expressly abolishes the requirement of privity when the plaintiff is a member of the buyer's family or household or a guest of the buyer and has sustained personal injury because of the product.[1]

Some states require privity of contract, particularly when the plaintiff does not sustain personal injury or property damage and seeks to recover only economic loss. However, a manufacturer making an express warranty as to a consumer product costing over $15 which was manufactured after July 4, 1975, may be sued for the economic loss sustained by the buyer.

(b) **The Defendant.** The plaintiff who is entitled to sue may sue the seller, a remote seller, a manufacturer, and generally even the manufacturer of the component part of the product which caused the harm.[2] For example, when a person is struck by an automobile because of its defective brakes, the victim may sue the seller and the manufacturer of the car and the maker of the brake assembly or system which the car manufacturer installed in the car.

FACTS:

Shivers purchased a mobile home from Hurley. Because of many defects, the home had a market value of approximately $9,000 less than the contract price. The buyer sued the manufacturer, Nobility Homes of Texas, for this amount. Nobility Homes raised the defense that it had not sold the home to Shivers and that as he was suing only for economic loss the lack of privity barred suit by him.

DECISION:

Judgment for Shivers. Public policy requires that the ultimate purchaser be allowed to sue the manufacturer. "Equity and justice" require that such suit be allowable against the manufacturer even when brought to recover only economic loss. [Nobility Homes of Texas v Shivers (Tex Civ App) 539 SW2d 190 (1976)]

(c) **Direct Sales Contact.** In many instances recovery is allowed by a buyer against a remote manufacturer because there have been direct dealings between them which justify regarding the buyer and the manufacturer as being in privity, as against the contention that the buyer was only in privity with the local dealer from whom the product was bought.[3] When the manufacturer enters into direct negotiations with the ultimate buyer with respect to any phase of the manufacturing or financing of the transaction, the sale will probably be treated as though it were made directly by the manufacturer to the ultimate purchaser even though, for the purpose of record keeping, the transaction is treated as a sale by the manufacturer to the dealer and by that dealer to the ultimate purchaser. Likewise, recovery may be allowed when the

[1]Uniform Commercial Code § 2-318.
[2]Mendelson v General Motors Corp. 432 NYS2d 132 (1980).
[3]Richards v Goerg Boat & Motors, Inc. _____ Ind App _____, 384 NE2d 1084 (1979).

consumer mails to the manufacturer a warranty registration card which the manufacturer packed with the manufactured article.

B. EXPRESS WARRANTIES

A warranty may be express or implied. Both have the same effect and operate as though the defendant had made an express guarantee. An express guarantee is governed by the common law of contracts. Warranties are governed primarily by the Uniform Commercial Code.

§ 28:4.   Definition of Express Warranty.

An **express warranty** is a statement by the defendant relating to the goods that is part of the basis of the bargain. That is, it is part of the basis of the sale. This means that the buyer has purchased the goods on the reasonable assumption that they were as stated by the seller. Thus, a statement by the seller with respect to the quality, capacity, or other characteristic of the goods is an express warranty. To illustrate, the seller may say: "This cloth is all wool," "This paint is for household woodwork," or "This engine can produce 50 horsepower."

A representation that an airplane is a 1983 model is an express warranty. A statement that a product was particularly developed for a special purpose is an express warranty that it will achieve that purpose.[4]

There is no requirement of reliance upon an express warranty as the question is merely whether the statement of the seller became part of the bargain of the parties.

§ 28:5.   Form of Express Warranty.

No particular form of words is necessary to constitute an express warranty. A seller need not state that a warranty is being made nor that one is intended. It is sufficient that the seller assert a fact that becomes a part or term of the bargain or transaction between the parties.

FACTS:

Brian Keith attended a boat show in Long Beach and looked at a number of boats, spoke to sales representatives, and obtained advertising literature. The literature described a sailboat called an Island Trader 41 as a seaworthy vessel. In numerous brochures the vessel was described by defendants as a picture of surefooted seaworthiness and as a carefully well-equipped and very seaworthy live-aboard vessel. Keith purchased the sailboat from defendants for a total price of $75,000. After delivery of the vessel, a dispute arose in regard to its seaworthiness. Keith sued the defendants alleging breach of an express warranty. Defendants claimed no warranty had been made since the words warranty or guaranty had not been used and because none of the defendants had undertaken in writing to preserve the seaworthiness of the vessel.

[4]Swenson v Chevron Chemical Co. (SD) 234 NW2d 38 (1975).

DECISION:

Judgment for Keith. In order to maintain an action for breach of an express warranty, a seller's representation need only be part of the basis of the bargain, inducing the buyer to enter into the bargain. Formal words such as warranty or guaranty are not required. Seller's affirmation in the brochures became part of the basis of the bargain and was relied on as one of the inducements for the purchase. The seller's affirmation that the vessel was seaworthy was a factor inducing Keith to buy the boat. [Keith v Buchanan, (Cal App) 220 Cal Rprt 392 (1985)]

It is not necessary that the seller make an express statement, for the express warranty may be found in conduct. Accordingly, if the buyer asks for a can of outside house paint and the seller hands over a can of paint, the seller's conduct expresses a warranty that the can contains outside house paint.

The seller's statement may be written or printed, as well as oral. The words on the label of a can and in a newspaper ad for "boned chicken" constitute an express warranty that the can contains chicken that is free of bones.

The illustrations in a seller's catalogue are descriptions of the goods and therefore an express warranty arises that the goods will conform to a catalogue illustration.

§ 28:6.   Time of Making Express Warranty.

It is immaterial whether the express warranty is made at the time of or after the sale. No separate consideration is required for the warranty when it is a part of a sale. If a warranty is made after the sale, no consideration is required as it is regarded as a modification of the sales contract.

§ 28:7.   Seller's Opinion or Statement of Value.

"An affirmation merely of the value of goods or a statement purporting to be merely the seller's opinion or commendation of the goods does not create a warranty."[5] A purchaser, as a reasonable person, should not believe such statements implicitly, and therefore cannot hold the seller to them should they prove false. Thus, "sales talk" by a seller that "this is the best piece of cloth in the market" or that glassware "is as good as anyone else's" is merely an opinion which the buyer cannot ordinarily treat as a warranty.

The statements made by the seller of cosmetics that its products were "the future of beauty" and that they were "just the product for you [the plaintiff]" were "sales talk" arising "in the ordinary course of merchandising" and did not constitute warranties.

FACTS:

Chase Resorts, Inc. purchased an automatic sprinkler system from the Johns-Manville Corporation to water its golf course. In inducing the sale, the seller had assured the buyer that the

[5]UCC § 2-313(2).

system would provide "years of trouble-free service." Contrary to this prediction, substantial repairs were required. Chase sued Johns-Manville claiming that there was a breach of a warranty that no repairs would be required.

DECISION:

Judgment for Johns-Manville. The statement as to trouble-free service was merely a matter of opinion and did not constitute an express warranty. This was so because the future need for repairs could not be determined at the time of making the sale, so that it was apparent that the seller was merely making a prophecy or a forecast as to the future. Such an opinion did not constitute an express warranty. [Chase Resorts, Inc. v Johns-Manville Corp. (DC Mo) 476 F Supp 633 (1979)]

It is probable, however, that the UCC will permit an exception to be made, as under the prior law, when the circumstances are such that a reasonable person would rely on such a statement. If the buyer has reason to believe that the seller is possessed of expert knowledge of the conditions of the market and the buyer requests the seller's opinion as an expert, the buyer would be entitled to accept as a fact the seller's statement as to whether a given article was the best obtainable. The statement could be reasonably regarded as forming part of the basis of the bargain. Thus, a statement by a florist that bulbs are of first-grade quality may be a warranty.

§ 28:8.   Warranty of Conformity to Description, Sample, or Model.

When the contract is based in part on the understanding that the seller will supply goods according to a particular description or that the goods will be the same as the sample or a model, the seller is bound by an express warranty that the goods shall conform to the description, sample, or model.[6] Ordinarily a **sample** is a portion of the whole mass that is the subject of the transaction, while a **model** is a replica of the article in question.

§ 28:9.   Federal Regulation of Express Warranties.

A seller who makes an express warranty as to a consumer product costing more than $15 must conform to certain standards imposed by federal statute[7] and by regulations of the Federal Trade Commission.[8] Initially, the seller is not required to make any express warranty but if one is made, it must be stated in ordinary understandable language and must be made available for inspection before purchasing so that the consumer may "comparison shop."

(a) **Full Warranties.** If the seller or the label states that a **full warranty** is made, the seller is obligated to fix or replace a defective product within a reasonable time, without cost to the buyer. If the product cannot be fixed or if a reasonable number of repair attempts are unsuccessful, the buyer has the choice of a cash refund or a free replacement. No unreasonable burden may be placed on a buyer seeking to obtain warranty service. A full warranty runs for its specified life without regard to the ownership of the product.

[6]UCC § 2-313(1)(b), (c).
[7]PL 93-636, 15 USC § 2301 et seq.
[8]16 CFR § 700.1 et seq.

(b) **Limited Warranties.** Any warranty which does not provide the complete protection of a full warranty is a **limited warranty** and must be so described by the seller. For example, a warranty is limited if the buyer must pay any cost, or if only the first buyer is covered by the warranty, or if the warranty only covers part of the product. A warrantor making a full warranty cannot require that the buyer pay the cost of sending the product to or from a warranty service point, or to return the product to such a point if it weighs over 35 pounds, or to return a part for service unless it can be easily removed, or to fill and return a warranty registration card shortly after purchase in order to make the warranty effective. If the warrantor imposes any of these burdens the warranty must be called a limited warranty.

§ 28:10. Effect of Breach of Express Warranty.

If the express warranty is false, there is a breach of the warranty. The warrantor is then liable just as though the truth of the warranty had been guaranteed. It is no defense that the defendant honestly believed that the warranty was true, or had exercised due care in manufacturing or handling the product, or had no reason to believe that the warranty was false.

C. IMPLIED WARRANTIES

Whenever a sale of goods is made, certain warranties are implied unless they are expressly excluded. The scope of these warranties differs in terms of whether the seller is a merchant or a casual seller.

§ 28:11. Definition of Implied Warranty.

An **implied warranty** is one that was not made by the seller but which is implied by the law. In certain instances, the law implies or reads a warranty into a sale although the seller did not make it. That is, the implied warranty arises automatically from the fact that a sale has been made; as compared with express warranties, which arise because they form part of the basis on which the sale has been made.

The fact that express warranties are made does not exclude implied warranties; and when both express and implied warranties exist, they should be construed as consistent with each other and as cumulative if such construction is reasonable. In case it is unreasonable to construe them as consistent and cumulative, an express warranty prevails over an implied warranty as to the subject matter, except in the case of an implied warranty of fitness for a particular purpose. When there is an express warranty as to a particular matter, it is unnecessary to find an implied warranty relating thereto.

§ 28:12. Implied Warranties of all Sellers.

A distinction is made between a merchant seller and the casual seller. There is a greater range of warranties in the case of the merchant seller.

(a) **Warranty of Title.** Every seller, by the mere act of selling, makes a warranty that the seller's title is good and that the transfer is rightful.

A warranty of title may be specifically excluded, or the circumstances may be such as to prevent the warranty from arising. The latter situation is found when the buyer has reason to know that the seller does not claim to hold the title or that the seller is purporting to sell only such right or title as the seller or a third person may have. For example, no warranty of title arises when the seller makes the sale in a representative capacity, such as a sheriff, an auctioneer, or an administrator of a decedent's estate. Likewise, no warranty arises when the seller makes the sale as a pledgee or mortgagee.

FACTS:

American Container Corp. purchased a semitrailer from Hanley Trucking Corp. The semitrailer was seized and impounded by the New Jersey police on the ground that it was stolen, and American was notified that it had 90 days in which to prove its ownership. Within 2 weeks, American notified Hanley of the above facts and declared that it canceled the contract for breach of warranty. American sued Hanley for breach of warranty damages.

DECISION:

Judgment for American. The seizure of the semitrailer by the police cast such a shadow on American's title that regardless of what the outcome would be of a lawsuit to determine ownership, the police seizure was a violation of the seller's implied warranty of title. [American Container Corp. v Hanley Trucking Corp. 111 NJ Super 322, 268 A2d 313 (1970)]

(b) **Warranty Against Encumbrances.** Every seller by the mere act of selling makes a warranty that the goods shall be delivered free from any security interest or any other lien or encumbrance of which the buyer at the time of the sales transaction had no knowledge. Thus, there is a breach of warranty if the automobile sold to the buyer is delivered subject to an outstanding encumbrance that had been placed on it by the original owner and which was unknown to the buyer at the time of the sale.

This warranty refers to the goods only at the time they are delivered to the buyer and is not concerned with an encumbrance which existed before or at the time the sale was made. For example, a seller may not have paid in full for the goods and the original supplier may have a lien on them. The seller may resell the goods while that lien is still on them and the seller's only duty is to pay off the lien before delivering the goods to the buyer.

(c) **Warranty of Fitness for a Particular Purpose.** If the buyer intends to use the goods for a particular or unusual purpose, as contrasted with the ordinary use for which they are customarily sold, the seller makes an implied warranty that the goods will be fit for the purpose when the buyer relies on the seller's skill or judgment to select or furnish suitable goods, and when the seller at the time of contracting knows or has reason to know the buyer's particular purpose and the buyer's reliance on the seller's judgment.[9] For example, where a government representative inquired of the seller whether

---

[9]UCC § 2-315. This warranty applies to every seller, but as a matter of fact it will probably always be a merchant seller who has such skill and judgment so that the Code provision would be applicable.

the seller had a tape suitable for use in the government's NCR 304 computer system, there arose an implied warranty, unless otherwise excluded, that the tape furnished by the seller was fit for that purpose. When the seller knows that the buyer is purchasing an accounting machine in order to produce a payroll on time and with reduced work hours, an implied warranty arises that the machine will perform as desired by the buyer.

When the buyer makes the purchase without relying on the seller's skill and judgment, no warranty of fitness for a particular purpose arises.[10]

FACTS:

The United Geological Survey made a contract with Layne-Atlantic Company to construct an underground well. It contemplated that a particular pipe, "Koppers fiberglass casting," would be used. Koppers recommended that the pipe be .5 inch thick. In order to reduce the cost of construction, UGS specified pipe .3 inch thick. The pipe collapsed. Layne claimed that there was a breach of warranty of fitness for a particular purpose.

DECISION:

There was no such breach because there was no warranty of fitness for a particular purpose because there was no evidence that Layne had relied on the skill and judgment of Koppers in making the purchase. The recommendation to purchase .5 inch thick pipe was rejected. Hence no warranty of fitness for a particular purpose arose. Likewise, the mere fact that the pipe had collapsed did not show that it was not fit and therefore no breach of the warranty of merchantability occurred. [Layne-Atlantic Co. v Koppers Co., Inc. 214 Va 467, 201 SE2d 609 (1974)]

---

§ 28:13.   Additional Implied Warranties of Merchant Seller.

A seller who deals in goods of the kind in question is classified as a **merchant** by the UCC and is held to a higher degree of responsibility for the product than one who is merely making a casual sale.

(a) **Warranty against Infringement.** Unless otherwise agreed, every merchant seller warrants that the goods shall be delivered free of the rightful claim of any third person by way of patent or trademark infringement or the like.

(b) **Warranty of Merchantability or Fitness for Normal Use.** A merchant seller makes an implied warranty of the merchantability of the goods sold.[11] This warranty is in fact a group of warranties, the most important of which is that the goods are fit for the ordinary purposes for which they are sold.

A merchant is not protected from warranty liability by the fact that every possible step was taken to make the product safe. Similarly, it is no defense that the defendant could not have known of or discovered the defective

---

[10]B. W. Feed Co., Inc. v General Equipment Co. 44 Or App 467, 605 P2d 1205 (1980).
[11]Maybank v S. S. Kresge Co. 46 NC App 687, 266 SE2d 409 (1980).

character of the product, for warranty liability is not merely an assurance that the defendant has exercised due care but is an undertaking or guarantee that the product is fit for use.

FACTS:

Frederick purchased a mobile home from Dreyer, a dealer. There were many defects in the home which made it unfit for use. Frederick sued Dreyer for breach of warranty. Dreyer raised the defense that the defects were latent and unknown to him and could not have reasonably been discovered.

DECISION:

Judgment for Frederick. Warranty liability is only concerned with the quality of the product received by the buyer and is not concerned with any fault of the seller. It was therefore immaterial that the defects were unknown to the seller and could not have been reasonably discovered. [Frederick v Dreyer (SD) 257 NW2d 835 (1977)]

---

§ 28:14.   Warranties in Particular Sales.

Particular types of sales may involve special considerations.

(a) Sale on Buyer's Specifications. When the buyer furnishes the seller with exact specifications for the preparation or manufacture of such goods, the same warranties arise as in the case of any other sale of such goods by the particular seller. No warranty of fitness for a particular purpose can arise, however, since it is clear that the buyer is purchasing on the basis of the buyer's own decision and is not relying on the seller's skill and judgment. Likewise, the manufacturer is not liable for loss caused by a design defect.[12]

(b) Sale of Secondhand or Used Goods. As far as the Code is concerned, there is no difference between the warranties arising in the sale of used or secondhand goods and those arising in the sale of new goods.[13] As to ordinary goods, what is "fit for normal use" will be a lower standard for used than for new goods. Some courts still follow their pre-Code law under which no warranties of fitness arose in the sale of used goods.

(c) Sale of Food or Drink. The sale of food or drink, whether to be consumed on or off the seller's premises, is a sale and, when made by a merchant, carries the implied warranty that the food is fit for its ordinary purpose, that is, human consumption.

Thus the seller of canned crabmeat has broken this warranty when the can contains a nail. Does it make any difference if the thing which harms the buyer is a crabshell? Some courts refuse to impose warranty liability if the thing in the food which causes the harm was naturally present, as the crabshell in crabmeat, prune stones in stewed prunes, or bones in canned fish. Other courts reject this natural substance exception. They hold that

---

[12]Wisconsin Electric Power Co. v Zallea Brothers, Inc. (CA7 Wis) 606 F2d 697 (1979).
[13]Perry v Lawson Ford Tractor Co. (Okla) 413 P2d 459 (1980).

there is liability if the seller does not deliver to the buyer goods of the character that the buyer reasonably expected. Thus there is a breach of the implied warranty of fitness for normal use if the buyer reasonably expected the food to be free of harm-causing natural things, such as shells and bones.

FACTS:

Webster ordered a bowl of fish chowder in the Blue Ship Tea Room. She was injured by a fish bone in the chowder. She sued the Tea Room for breach of warranty. It was shown that when chowder is made, the entire unboned fish is cooked.

DECISION:

As the soup was typically made with whole fish, it was apparent that the presence of fish bones in the soup should be foreseen by a reasonable person. Thus, there was no breach of warranty of merchantability. [Webster v Blue Ship Tea Room, 347 Mass 421, 198 NE2d 309 (1964)]

---

§ 28:15. Necessity of Defect.

In order to impose liability for breach of an implied warranty, it is ordinarily necessary to show that there was a defect in the product and that this defect was the cause of the plaintiff's harm. A product may be defective because there is (a) a manufacturing defect, (b) a design defect, (c) inadequate instruction on how to use the product; or (d) inadequate warning against dangers involved in using the product.

If the manufacturer's blueprint shows that there should be two bolts at a particular place and the factory only puts in one bolt, there is a manufacturing defect. If the two bolts are put in but the product breaks because four bolts are required to provide sufficient strength there is no manufacturing defect, but there is a design defect. A product that is properly designed and properly manufactured may be dangerous because the user is not given sufficient instructions on how to use the product. Also a product is defective if there is a danger that is not obvious and there is no warning at all or a warning which does not describe the full danger. For example, a can of adhesive used to cement tiles to a floor is defective when the can merely says that the cement should not be used near an open flame, but does not state that a newly cemented floor would throw off vapor which would stay in the room for several hours and would explode if any spark or flame were present.

Many courts are relaxing the requirement of proving the existence of a specific defect. These courts impose liability when the goods are in fact not fit for their normal purpose, and allow the buyer to prove this by evidence that the goods do not function properly, even though the buyer does not establish the specific defect that made the goods malfunction.[14]

In contrast with the suit for breach of an implied warranty, when the plaintiff sues for breach of an express warranty or a guarantee, it is not necessary to show that there was a defect that caused the breach. It is sufficient

---

[14]Worthey v Specialty Foam Products, Inc. (Mo App) 591 SW2d 145 (1980).

to show that the goods did not conform to the guarantee or to the express warranty. Why they did not, is not material.

D. DISCLAIMER OF WARRANTIES

The seller and the buyer may agree that there shall be no warranties. In some states this is limited in terms of public policy or consumer protection.

§ 28:16.   Validity of Disclaimer.

Warranties may be disclaimed by agreement of the parties, subject to the limitation that such a provision must not be unconscionable.[15]

If a warranty of fitness[16] is excluded or if it is modified in writing, it must be conspicuous in order to make certain that the buyer will be aware of its presence. If the implied warranty of merchantability is excluded, the exclusion clause must expressly mention the word "merchantability" and it must be conspicuous.

(a) **Conspicuousness.** A disclaimer provision is made conspicuous by printing it under a conspicuous heading, but in such case the heading must indicate that there is an exclusion or modification of warranties. Conversely, a heading cannot be relied upon to make such a provision "conspicuous" when the heading is misleading and wrongfully gives the impression that there is a warranty, as a heading stating "Vehicle Warranty," when in fact the provision that follows contains a limitation of warranties. And a disclaimer that is hidden in a mass of printed material handed to the buyer is not conspicuous and is not effective to exclude warranties. Similarly, an inconspicuous disclaimer of warranties under a heading of "notice to retail buyers" has no effect.

When a waiver of warranties fails to be effective because it is not conspicuous, the implied warranties which would arise in the absence of any waiver are operative.

FACTS:

Rothe purchased a 1982 Cadillac Sedan DeVille from Maloney Cadillac. Maloney's contract expressly provided in three separate places that Maloney disclaimed all warranties, express or implied, including any implied warranty of merchantability or fitness for a particular purpose. Two of these provisions were set off in boxes: one employed large bold print; the other used italics. After using the car a short time,

Rothe began to experience serious problems with the operation of the vehicle. Rothe alleged that the automobile had been equipped with an improper crankshaft causing excessive vibrations and improper operation on the road and that the engine was defective in materials and workmanship causing improper acceleration. Rothe sued for damages for breach of implied warranties of merchantability and fitness for a particular purpose. Maloney denied liability.

[15]UCC §§ 2-316(1), 2-302(1). A distinction must be made between holding that the circumstances do not give rise to a warranty, thus precluding warranty liability, and holding that the warranty which would otherwise arise was excluded or surrendered by the contract of the parties.

[16]By the letter of the Code, the text statement is applicable to any warranty of fitness, see UCC § 2-316(2), although by the Official Comment to § 2-316, point 4, it would appear to be only the warranty of fitness for a particular purpose.

DECISION:

Judgment for Maloney Cadillac. The UCC permits both the exclusion or limitation of an implied warranty of merchantability by conspicuous writing which uses the word "merchantability," and the disclaimer of an implied warranty of fitness for a particular purpose provided the disclaimer is conspicuous. The disclaimers in Maloney's contract were conspicuous since the provisions were in bold print and italics. Such disclaimers effectively avoid liability for breach of implied warranty under the UCC. [Rothe v Maloney Cadillac, Inc. (Ill App) 492 NE2d 497 (1986)]

(b) **Unconscionability and Public Policy.** An exclusion of warranties made in the manner specified by the Code is not unconscionable. But there is also authority that when the breach of warranty was the result of negligence of the seller, the disclaimer of warranty liability and a limitation of remedies to refunding the purchase price is not binding because such a limitation is unreasonable, unconscionable, and against sound public policy. In some states, warranty disclaimers are invalid as contrary to public policy or because they are prohibited by consumer protection laws.

If a seller makes any written warranty of a consumer product costing more than $15, the seller is barred from excluding any implied warranty that would be implied under the law of sales.

§ 28:17.   Particular Provisions.

A statement such as "there are no warranties which extend beyond the description on the face hereof" excludes all implied warranties of fitness. Implied warranties are excluded by the statement of "as is," "with all faults," or other language which in normal common speech calls attention to the warranty exclusion and makes it clear that there is no implied warranty.

FACTS:

Hutchinson Homes purchased a mobile home from Guerdon Industries. The invoice contained a clearly typed and underscored statement: "NOTE SOLD AS IS." The home was constructed in two parts. While being transported by the buyer from the seller, the home collapsed. The buyer claimed that there was a breach of warranty and sued for damages.

DECISION:

Judgment for Guerdon Industries. The "as is" clause excluded all implied warranties. [Hutchinson Homes, Inc. v Guerdon Industries, Inc. 143 Ga App 664, 239 SE2d 553. (1977)]

In order for a disclaimer of warranties to be a binding part of an oral sales contract, the disclaimer must be called to the attention of the buyer.

Provisions in a sales contract excluding warranties have only that effect. They do not bar the plaintiff from recovering damages for fraud, negligence, nor strict tort liability.

§ 28:18. Exclusion of
Warranties by Examination of Goods.

There is no implied warranty with respect to defects in goods that an examination should have revealed when the buyer before making the final contract has examined the goods, or model or sample, or has refused to make such examination.

The examination of the goods by the buyer does not exclude the existence of an express warranty unless it can be concluded that the buyer thereby learned of the falsity of the statement claimed to be a warranty, with the consequence that such statement did not in fact form part of the basis of the bargain.

§ 28:19. Post-Sale Disclaimer.

Frequently the statement excluding or modifying warranties appears for the first time in a written contract sent to confirm or memorialize the oral contract made earlier; or it appears in an invoice,[17] a bill, or an instruction manual delivered to the buyer at or after the time the goods are received. Such post-sale disclaimers have no effect on warranties that arose at the time of the sale.

An exclusion of warranties in a manufacturer's manual given to the buyer after the sale is not binding on a buyer because it is not a term of the sales contract.

If the buyer assents to the post-sale disclaimer, however, it is effective as a modification of the sales contract.

§ 28:20. Other Theories of Product Liability.

In addition to suit for breach of an express guarantee, an express warranty, or an implied warranty, a plaintiff in a given product liability case may be able to sue for negligence, fraud, or strict tort liability.

(a) **Negligence.** A person injured because of the defective condition of a product may be entitled to sue the seller or manufacturer for the damages. The injured person must be able to show that the defendant was negligent in the preparation or manufacture of the article or failed to provide proper instructions and warnings as to dangers. An action for negligence rests upon common law tort principles and does not require privity of contract.

(b) **Fraud.** The UCC expressly preserves the pre-Code law as to fraud. Thus, a person defrauded by false statements as to a product obtained from a distributor or manufacturer will generally be able to recover damages for the harm sustained because of such misrepresentations when they were made with knowledge that they were false or with reckless indifference as to whether they were true.

(c) **Strict Tort Liability.** Independently of the UCC, a manufacturer or distributor of a defective product is liable to a person who is injured by the product without regard to whether the person injured is a purchaser, a con-

---

[17]Old Albany Estates, Ltd v Highland Carpet Mills, Inc. (Okla) 604 P2d 849 (1979).

sumer, or a third person such as a bystander.[18] It is no defense that privity of contract does not exist between the injured party and the seller nor that the defect was found in a component part purchased from another manufacturer.[19] This concept is not one of absolute liability; that is, it must first be shown that there was a defect in the product at the time it left the control of the seller. The seller is liable because the product is defective and unreasonably dangerous and has caused harm. It is immaterial whether or not the seller was negligent or whether the user was guilty of contributory negligence. Assumption of risk by the injured party, on the other hand, is a defense available to the seller.[20]

FACTS:

Ace-Chicago Great Dane Corp., a dealer and distributor of trailers, bought a trailer equipped with a refrigeration unit for the purpose of resale. Ace-Chicago sent the trailer to Illinois Auto Central under a manufacturer's warranty, for the repair of a possible leak in the refrigeration unit. Illinois Auto Central, a dealer in the business of selling and servicing such refrigeration units, employed Richard Skarski as a mechanic. Skarski suffered injuries when, in the process of separating the refrigeration unit from the trailer, the unit fell from the trailer, striking him. Skarski sued Ace-Chicago under the theory of products liability, alleging that the refrigeration unit was unreasonably dangerous because it was not properly secured to the trailer and because it did not contain written instructions warning of the danger in removing it from the trailer. Ace-Chicago denied liability contending that it manufactured neither the trailer nor the refrigeration unit and furthermore that the plaintiff, Skarski, was not an ultimate user or consumer of the product.

DECISION:

Judgment for Skarski. Although Ace-Chicago sold trailers and did not manufacture them, it was in the distribution chain and therefore could be liable for resulting injuries. Ace-Chicago was in the business of selling trailers and bought the defective trailer from the manufacturer for the purpose of resale for profit. It placed the defective product into the stream of commerce. In a products liability case, it is not a defense that the injured person is not the purchaser, a consumer, or a bystander, or as here a third person who repaired the product and suffered an injury. [Skarski v Ace-Chicago Great Dane Corp. (Ill App) 485 NE2d 1312 (1985)]

---

§ 28:21. Cumulative Theories of Liability.

The theories of product liability are not mutually exclusive. Thus a given set of facts may give rise to two or more theories of liability.

---

[18]Walker v Clark Equipment Co. (Iowa) 320 NW2d 561 (1982).

[19]The concept of strict tort liability was judicially declared in Greenman v Yuba Power Products, 59 Cal 2d 57, 27 Cal Rptr 697, 377 P2d 897 (1963). This concept has been incorporated in the Restatement of Torts 2d as § 402A.

[20]Pearson v Hevi-Duty Elec. (Tex App) 618 SW2d 784 (1981).

SUMMARY

There are six theories in the law to protect from harm caused by defective products. They are: (a) guarantee, (b) negligence, (c) fraud, (d) express warranty, (e) implied warranty, and (f) strict tort liability.

The requirement of privity of contract, that is, that only the parties to the sales contract could sue each other, has been widely rejected. The law is moving toward the conclusion that anyone harmed because of an improper product may sue whoever is in any way responsible. The requirement of privity has been expressly abolished by the UCC when the plaintiff is a member of the buyer's family or household or a guest of the buyer and has sustained personal injury because of the product.

Warranties may be express or implied and both have the same effect and operate as though the defendant had made an express guarantee.

A warranty made after a sale does not require consideration as it is regarded as a modification of the sales contract.

Certain express warranties are regulated by federal statute and the FTC. These warranties are labeled as full or limited warranties and must conform to certain standards.

A distinction is made between a merchant seller and the casual seller. There is a greater range of warranties in the case of the merchant seller.

A seller makes a warranty of title unless such warranty is excluded. Warranties that the goods shall conform to the description, sample, or model are express warranties, while warranties of fitness for a particular purpose and merchantability are implied warranties.

Warranties may be disclaimed by agreement of the parties, provided the disclaimer is not unconscionable. Disclaimer provisions to exclude warranties must be conspicuous. Post-sale disclaimers have no effect on warranties that arose at the time of the sale.

In addition to warranties, a plaintiff may sue for negligence, fraud or strict liability. Both negligence and strict liability exist independently of the UCC.

The concept of strict liability is not one of absolute liability as the plaintiff must first show that there was a defect in the product at the time it left the control of the seller. No negligence need be established on the part of the manufacturer, nor is contributory negligence of the plaintiff an issue. The seller may show that the injured party assumed the risk.

Theories of product liability are not mutually exclusive and a given set of facts may give rise to two or more theories of product liability.

QUESTIONS AND CASE PROBLEMS

1. What social forces are affected by the abolition of the requirement of privity in product liability suits?
2. Norma purchased a dress from the Borolsky Dress Shop. After she got the dress home, she was doubtful as to the quality of the cloth. When she complained to Borolsky, they assured her that the cloth was 100% wool. Later, Norma proved that the dress was only 60% wool. Can she hold Borolsky liable on the statement that it was 100% wool?

3. The Erie Railroad holds a public auction sale of unclaimed baggage. Mayo purchases a trunk at the sale. Later the police take the trunk from Mayo on the ground that it had been stolen from its true owner. Mayo sued the Erie Railroad on the ground that by selling the trunk it had made an implied warranty that it had the title or the right to sell and that as it did not it must pay Mayo for the loss sustained because of the taking of the trunk by the police. Is Mayo correct?

4. Taylor sold a tractor to Smith. Unknown to Taylor, the tractor was subject to a lien in favor of Long Implement and Tractor Company. The tractor was repossessed by Long, and Smith sued Taylor for the return of the purchase price. Taylor raised the defense that he had acted in good faith without knowledge of the prior lien. Was this defense valid? [Smith v Taylor, 44 NC App 363, 261 SE2d 19]

5. Rose purchases an electric kitchen range from the Shermack Electric Appliance Company. In the instruction manual which is enclosed in the crate in which the range is delivered to Rose's home, there is a statement that Shermack makes no warranty express or implied with respect to the range. The range works properly for two weeks and then ceases to function. When Rose demands her money back from Shermack, it raises the defense that all warranties, including that of fitness for normal use, were excluded by the statement in the manual. Is Shermack correct?

6. Is a seller liable for damages to a buyer caused by the conduct of the buyer or by an accident?

7. Edgmore has a class reunion at his house. There is a substantial amount of food that is left over. He sells the surplus food to his neighbor Hartranft for a fraction of its price. In eating this food, Hartranft is injured from a piece of glass that was contained in a can of salmon. Hartranft sued Edgmore for the injuries sustained. Is Edgmore liable?

8. A buyer purchased a new automobile car wash from a dealer. It washed the cars effectively but it would knock off external accessories such as mirrors and radio antennas. When the buyer complained, the seller stated that the contract made no provision with respect to such matters. Was this a valid defense?

9. Federal law requires that all merchant sellers make certain warranties in addition to those implied by the Uniform Commercial Code. Appraise this statement.

10. A purchased a refrigerator from the B store. The written contract stated that the refrigerator was sold "as is" and that the warranty of merchantability and all warranties of fitness were excluded. This was stated in large capital letters printed just above the line on which A signed her name. The refrigerator worked properly for a few weeks and then stopped. B refused to do anything about it because of the exclusion of the warranties made by the contract. A claimed that this exclusion was not binding because it was unconscionable. Was A correct? [Avery v Aladdin Products Div., Nat. Service Industries, Inc. 128 Ga App 266, 196 SE2d 357]

11. A manufacturer advertised its product in national magazines. The advertisement induced a buyer to purchase the product. The product did not live up to the statements in the advertisement. The buyer claimed that

there was a breach of warranty. The manufacturer contended that the statements in the advertisement were obviously sales talk and therefore could not constitute a warranty. Was this a valid defense? [Westrie Battery Co. v Standard Electric Co. (CA10 Colo) 482 F2d 1307]

12. Joyce worked in a business office. She sold her motorcycle to Goldie. The motorcycle did not run properly. Goldie demanded the return of her money because there had been a breach of the implied warranty that the motorcycle would be fit for normal use. Was Goldie entitled to recover the purchase price on this ground?

13. The defendant, Zogarts, manufactured and sold a practice device for beginning golfers. The statements on the package stated that the device was completely safe and that a player could never be struck by the golf ball of the device. Hauter was hit by the ball when practicing with the device. He sued Zogarts. Zogarts denied liability on the ground that the statements were merely matters of opinion and therefore liability could not be based on them. Was this a valid defense? [Hauter v Zogarts, 14 Cal 104, 120 Cal Rptr 681, 534 P2d 377]

14. The buyer purchased an engine to operate an irrigation pump. The buyer selected the engine from a large number that were standing on the floor of the seller's stockroom. A label on the engine stated that it would produce one hundred horsepower. The buyer needed an engine which would generate at least eighty horsepower. In actual use in the buyer's irrigation system, the pump only generated sixty horsepower. The buyer sued the seller for damages. The seller raised the defense that no warranty of fitness for the buyer's particular purpose of operating an irrigation pump had arisen because the seller did not know of the use to which the buyer intended to put the pump and the buyer had not relied on the seller's skill and judgment in selecting the particular pump. Was the seller liable? [Potter v Ryndall, 22 NC App 129, 205 SE2d 808, cert den 285 NC 661, 207 SE2d 762]

15. Compare a breach of warranty, a breach of an express guarantee, and fraud.

16. Deal, a manufacturer who regularly sells a variety of special types of machines, has on hand a number of machines designed and suitable for the mechanical packaging of certain food products. Deal sold one of the machines to Fonda Co., a packager and wholesaler of food products. Shortly after Fonda Co. began using the machine, it was restrained from further use by legal action of Murdock, who held a valid patent granting the exclusive right to manufacture and sell the machines. What, if any, are the rights of Fonda Co.?

17. Roberts, a certified public accountant, explained to Haynes, a sales agent for a manufacturer of calculating machines, a certain kind of accounting work for which he needed a machine, and asked Haynes to select a machine from his principal's stock and deliver it. Haynes caused his firm to deliver a machine to Roberts, for which Roberts paid cash. Later, Roberts discovered that the machine would not do the required work. What warranty, if any, has been breached?

18. A new Dodge automobile was purchased from a Dodge dealer. Numerous problems existed with the transmission and it had to be replaced a

few times. Soon the purchaser was having other problems with the car. The purchaser sued the Dodge dealer for breach of the implied warranty of merchantability. The dealer argued that he was not liable as he had disclaimed all warranties and furthermore the purchase order signed by the buyer contained a clause on its front stating that the automobile was sold "AS IS." In addition a disclaimer of the warranties of merchantability and fitness was printed in contrasting red type. Decide. [Koperski v Husker Dodge, Inc., 208 Neb 29, 302 NW2d 655]

CHAPTER 29

REMEDIES FOR BREACH OF

SALES CONTRACTS

CHAPTER OBJECTIVES

After studying this chapter you will be able to:
1. List the remedies of the seller upon breach by the buyer.
2. List the remedies of the buyer upon breach by the seller.
3. Distinguish between rejection of defective goods and revocation of acceptance.
4. Determine the validity of clauses limiting damages.
5. Determine when a limited remedy has failed and describe the effect of such failure.
6. Discuss the waiver and preservation of defenses of a buyer.
7. Solve problems involving questions of the remedies of sellers and buyers.

If one of the parties to a sale fails to perform the contract duties, the law makes several remedies available to the other party. In addition, the parties may have included provisions pertaining to remedies in their contract.

A. STATUTE OF LIMITATIONS

Judicial remedies are ordinarily subject to a time limitation which bars resort to the courts after the expiration of a particular period of time. The Uniform Commercial Code supplies the statute of limitations for sales of goods except when suit is brought on a theory of tort, such as negligence, fraud, or strict tort.

§ 29:1. Code Claim.

An action for a breach of a sales contract must be commenced within four years after the cause of action arises, regardless of when the aggrieved party learned that there was a cause of action.[1] In the case of a warranty, the breach occurs when tender of delivery is made to the buyer even though no defect then appears and no harm is sustained until a later date.

(a) **Future Performance Warranty.** When an express warranty is made as to future performance, the statute of limitations does not run from the time of the sale but from the date when the future performance begins.[2]

(b) **Notice of Defect.** In addition to bringing suit within four years under the UCC statute of limitations, the plaintiff who sues the person from whom the goods were purchased for damages claimed because of a breach of the sales contract must have given the seller notice of such breach within a reasonable time after the plaintiff discovered or should have discovered the defect.[3]

FACTS:
Bennett purchased cattle from Jansma. The next day, Bennett realized that the cattle were diseased. Four and a half months later, Bennett gave notice that the cattle were diseased. By that time, about one-half of those affected had died and the other half had recovered. Bennett sued Jansma for breach of the implied warranty of merchantability. Jansma denied liability on the ground that notice had not been given in time.

DECISION:
Judgment for Jansma. Notice of defects must be timely given in order to protect from stale claims. Whether the notice was timely depends upon all the circumstances of the transaction. As the affected cattle were either cured or dead, the notice had not been given in time to examine the cattle and determine their actual condition. The notice therefore had not been timely given and Bennett could not recover for breach of the implied warranty of merchantability. [Bennett v Jansma (SD) 329 NW2d 134 (1983)]

---

§ 29:2. Non-Code Claim.

When the plaintiff sues on a non-Code theory, even though it relates to goods, the UCC statute of limitations does not apply. Thus, when the plaintiff sues on the basis of strict tort liability, the action is subject to the general tort statute of limitations and not the UCC four-year limitation.

B. REMEDIES OF THE SELLER

When a sales contract is broken by the buyer, the seller has a number of remedies available. The more common ones are here discussed.[4]

---

[1]Uniform Commercial Code § 2-725(1),(2).
[2]Jones & Laughlin Steel Corp. v Johns-Manville Sales Corp. (CA3 Pa) 626 F2d 280 (1980).
[3]UCC § 2-607(3)(a).
[4]When the goods purchased by the buyer are being shipped to the buyer or are held in a warehouse, an unpaid seller has a limited right to prevent delivery of the goods to the buyer. UCC § 2-705. If the buyer repudiates the contract while the goods are being manufactured, the seller-manufacturer may stop further production or may continue to complete the manufacturing of the goods. UCC § 2-704(2). An unpaid seller who sold on credit has a limited right to take the goods back if the buyer was insolvent. UCC § 2-702.

§ 29:3. Seller's Lien.

In the absence of an agreement for the extension of credit to the purchaser, the seller has a lien on the goods, that is, the right to retain possession of the goods until the seller is paid for them. Even when the goods are sold on credit, the seller has a lien on the goods if the buyer becomes insolvent or if the credit period expires while the goods are in the seller's possession.

The seller's lien may be lost by (a) waiver, as by a later extension of credit, (b) delivery of the goods to a carrier or other bailee, without a reservation of title or possession, for the purpose of delivery to the buyer, (c) acquisition of the property by the buyer or an agent by lawful means, or (d) payment or tender of the price by the buyer.

§ 29:4. Resale by Seller.

When the buyer has broken the contract by wrongfully rejecting the goods, wrongfully revoking acceptance, failing to pay, or repudiating the contract, the seller may resell the goods or the balance of them in the seller's possession. After the resale, the seller is not liable to the original buyer upon the contract or for any profit obtained on the resale. On the other hand, if the proceeds are less than the contract price, the seller may recover the loss from the original buyer.[5]

Reasonable notice must be given to the original buyer of the intention to make a private sale. Such notice must also be given of a public sale unless the goods are perishable in nature or threaten to decline rapidly in value. Notice of a public sale must also be given to the general public in such manner as is commercially reasonable under the circumstances.

§ 29:5. Cancellation by Seller.

When the buyer wrongfully rejects the goods, wrongfully revokes an acceptance of the goods, repudiates the contract, or fails to make a payment due on or before delivery, the seller may cancel the contract. Such action puts an end to the contract, discharging all obligations on both sides that are still unperformed but the seller retains any remedy with respect to the breach by the buyer. Cancellation revests the seller with title to the goods.

A seller may only cancel the contract if the buyer's breach substantially impairs the value of the contract to the seller.

§ 29:6. Seller's Action for Damages.

If the buyer wrongfully refuses to accept the goods or repudiates the contract, the seller may sue for the damages that the seller sustains. In the ordinary case, the amount of damages is to be measured by the difference between the market price at the time and place of the tender of the goods and the contract price.

If this measure of damages does not place the seller in the position in which the seller would have been placed by the buyer's performance, recovery may be permitted of lost profits, together with an allowance for overhead. The seller may in any case recover, as incidental damages, any

---

[5]UCC § 2-706(1),(6).

commercially reasonable charges, expenses, or commissions, incurred in enforcing that remedy, such as those sustained in the transportation, care, and custody of the goods after the buyer's breach; and in the return or resale of the goods. Such additional damages are recovered in addition to any other damages that may be recovered by the seller.

The seller is not entitled to recover the contract or purchase price except as stated in § 29:7.

§ 29:7.   Seller's Action for the Purchase Price.

The seller may bring an action to recover the purchase price, together with incidental damages as described in connection with the action for damages, if (a) the goods have been accepted and there has not been any rightful revocation of acceptance; (b) conforming goods were damaged or destroyed after the risk of loss passed to the buyer; or (c) the seller has identified proper goods to the contract but, after the buyer's breach, has been or will be unable to resell them at a reasonable price. In consequence of these limitations, the right to sue for the contract price, as distinguished from a suit for damages for breach of contract, is a remedy that is not ordinarily available to the seller.

C. REMEDIES OF THE BUYER

When a sales contract is broken by the seller, the buyer has a number of remedies provided by Article 2 of the Uniform Commercial Code.

§ 29:8.   Rejection of Improper Delivery.

If the goods or the tender made by the seller do not conform to the contract in any respect, the buyer may reject the goods. For example, the buyer may reject a mobile home when it does not contain the capacity of air conditioner specified by the contract.

The buyer may reject a tender which is not perfect, as against the contention that a substantial performance is sufficient.[6]

When the goods tendered consist of different units some of which conform to the contract, the buyer has the choice of (a) rejecting the entire quantity tendered, (b) accepting the entire tender, or (c) accepting any one or more commercial units and rejecting the rest.

The rejection must be made within a reasonable time after the delivery or tender, and the buyer must notify the seller of the choice made.[7]

After rejecting the goods, the buyer may not exercise any right of ownership as to the goods but must hold them awaiting instructions from the seller.

§ 29:9.   Revocation of Acceptance.

The buyer may revoke acceptance of the goods when they do not conform to the contract to such an extent that the defect substantially im-

---

[6]Moulton Cavity & Mold, Inc. v Lyn-Flex Industries, Inc. _____ Me _____, 396 A2d 1024 (1979).

[7]UCC § 2-602(1).

pairs the value of the contract to the buyer. For example, where the buyer purchased an emergency electric power plant but the plant only produced about 65% of the power called for by the contract and this was not sufficient to operate the buyer's equipment, and repeated attempts to improve the system failed, there was such a nonconformity as substantially impaired the value of the contract to the buyer and the buyer was entitled to revoke acceptance.

It is proof of substantial impairment that is required to justify revocation of acceptance. The mere fact that the goods do not conform to the contract does not entitle the buyer to revoke acceptance. On the other hand, it is not necessary that the buyer show that the goods are "worthless."

FACTS:

Black worked at two jobs and needed a car daily for transportation in connection with his work. He purchased an automobile from Don Schmid Motor, Inc. He had to take the car back for repairs five times in the next five months. The repairs did not correct the defects. The accelerator would stick when the car was going over forty miles an hour, a leak in the transmission could not be stopped, and following one repair the air conditioner clutch fell out. Because of the leak in the transmission, Black had to add transmission fluid to the car every day. Because of the repairs, he lost time from work, rented a car one time, and finally bought another car. He then notified Schmid that he revoked his acceptance of the car and demanded his money back.

DECISION:

Judgment for Black. The nature of the defects and the inability to correct them justified his claim that the value of the contract had been substantially impaired. He was therefor entitled to revoke acceptance of the car and recover any part of the purchase price paid by him. [Black v Don Schmid Motor, Inc. 232 Kan 458, 657 P2d 517 (1983)]

The revocation of acceptance does no more than revoke the acceptance. In itself, it does not cancel the contract with the seller. After revoking acceptance, the buyer has the choice of canceling that contract or insisting that the seller deliver conforming goods in place of the goods originally delivered.

§ 29:10. Procedure for Revoking Acceptance.

In order to revoke acceptance of the goods, the buyer must take certain steps.

(a) **Notice of Revocation.** The acceptance of goods cannot be revoked unless the buyer gives the seller a notice of revocation. The revocation of acceptance is effective when the buyer notifies the seller. It is not necessary that the buyer make an actual return of the goods in order to make the revocation effective.

(b) Time for Revocation. The notice of revocation must be given within a reasonable time after the buyer discovers that the goods do not conform or after the buyer should have discovered such nonconformity. A buyer is not required to notify the seller of the revocation of acceptance until the buyer is reasonably certain that the nonconformity of the goods substantially impairs the value of the contract. Thus, the mere fact that the buyer suspects that the goods do not conform and that such nonconformity may substantially impair the value of the contract does not itself require that the buyer immediately give notice to the seller.

A buyer is not barred from revoking acceptance of the goods because the buyer has delayed until attempts of the seller to correct the defects proved unsuccessful. For example, the lapse of even a year does not bar revocation of acceptance where the goods are of a complex nature, such as a computer, and the seller was continuously experimenting and assuring the buyer that the goods would be made to work.

(c) Disposition of Goods after Revocation. After making a revocation of acceptance, the buyer must hold the goods awaiting instructions from the seller. If the buyer has paid the seller in advance, the buyer may retain possession of the goods after revoking acceptance as security for the refund of the money which has been paid. Post-revocation use of the goods does not nullify the prior revocation of acceptance when such use is reasonable under the circumstances.[8]

FACTS:
Brown purchased a mobile home from Mobile Home Sales Management. There were many defects in the home and six weeks after delivery of the home to Brown, he wrote Mobile Home that he revoked acceptance of the home and canceled the contract. Mobile Home refused to return the purchase price. Brown then sued Mobile Home to cancel the contract and recover the purchase price and damages. Mobile Home raised the defense that Brown was not entitled to the relief sought because he had not returned the mobile home and that his continued use of the home while the lawsuit was pending waived any objection that he might have had.

DECISION:
Judgment for Brown. The fact that Brown had continued to use the mobile home did not cause him to lose the rights acquired by revoking the acceptance. This was so because the continued use of the home was commercially reasonable in view of the fact that the seller refused to take the home back and to return the purchase price. [Mobile Home Sales Management Inc. v Brown, 115 Ariz App 11, 562 P2d 1378 (1977)]

---

[8]Johannsen v Minnesota Valley Ford Tractor Co. _____ Minn _____, 304 NW2d 654 (1981).

§ 29:11. Buyer's Action for Damages for Nondelivery.

If the seller fails to deliver as required by the contract or repudiates the contract, or if the buyer properly rejects tendered goods or revokes acceptance as to such goods, the buyer is entitled to sue the seller for damages for breach of contract. The buyer is entitled to recover the difference between the market price at the time the buyer learned of the breach and the contract price.

Within a reasonable time after the seller's breach, the buyer may *cover,* that is, procure the same or similar goods elsewhere.[9] If the buyer acts in good faith, the measure of damages for the seller's nondelivery or repudiation is then the difference between the cost of cover and the contract price.

§ 29:12. Action for Breach of Warranty.

(a) **Notice of Breach.** If the buyer has accepted goods that do not conform to the contract or as to which there is a breach of warranty, the buyer must notify the seller of the breach within a reasonable time after the breach is discovered or should have been discovered. Otherwise the buyer is not entitled to complain.[10]

FACTS:

A grocer purchased canned grapefruit. Thereafter the cans began to swell. Customers complained. Some time later, the State Department of Agriculture examined the cans and declared that they should not be sold as human food. The grocer then destroyed the cans and notified the seller of what had happened. The grocer later sued the seller for breach of the implied warranty of merchantability. Was the grocer entitled to recover damages?

DECISION:

No. The buyer had not given notice to the seller as soon as the defect was discovered or could have been reasonably discovered. This is required by UCC [sec] 2-607(3)(a). Its purpose is to give the seller the opportunity to investigate the matter, reduce or mitigate damages if possible, and make suggestions or take steps to cure the defect. By destroying the goods, the buyer had made it impossible for the seller to investigate or to take corrective measures as to the goods. By waiting until after the destruction of the goods, it is apparent that notice was not given as soon as the buyer knew of the defect. [General Matters, Inc. v Paramount Canning Co. (Fla App) 382 So2d 1262 (1980)]

(b) **Measure of Damages.** If the buyer has given the necessary notice of breach, the buyer may recover damages measured by the loss resulting in the normal course of events from the breach. If suit is brought for breach of warranty, the measure of damages is the difference between the value of the goods as they were when accepted and the value that they would have had if they had been as warranted.

[9]Banner Iron Works, Inc. v Amax Zinc Co. (CA8 Mo) 621 F2d 883 (1980).
[10]Armco Steel Corp. v Isaacson Structural Steel Co. (Alaska) 611 P2d 507 (1980).

In other cases, the buyer may recover the difference between the contract price and the actual value of the goods.

The buyer may also recover as damages the loss directly and naturally resulting from that breach. In other words, the buyer may recover for the loss proximately resulting from the failure to deliver the goods as warranted. Thus a buyer may recover the cost of renting other equipment when the equipment sold by the defendant did not work because of its defective condition. When the buyer resells the goods and then, because of their defective condition, is required to indemnify customers of the buyer, the original buyer may recover such loss from the original seller as consequential damages.

Where the condition which breaches the warranty induces fright which causes illness, the warranty liability includes damages for such illness.

FACTS:

A child ate a slice of bread from a loaf which contained red string and decomposed brown paper. The child's mother was frightened on seeing this because she believed that she herself had eaten some of the same bread and that it contained poison. She became acutely ill. The mother sued the seller for damages for her illness and for her medical expenses.

DECISION:

Judgment for mother. The bread was not fit for use and therefore the warranty of merchantability was broken. The liability for such breach embraced the fright-caused illness and the medical expenses necessitated thereby. [Wisnieski v Great A & P Tea Co. 226 Pa Super 574, 323 A2d 744 (1974)]

A buyer who is entitled to recover damages from the seller may deduct the amount of such damages from any balance remaining due on the purchase price, provided the seller is notified of the buyer's intention to do so.[11]

(c) **Notice of Third Party Action Against Buyer.** The buyer may be sued in consequence of the seller's breach of warranty, as when the buyer's customers sue because of the condition of the goods which the buyer has resold to them. In such a case, it is optional with the buyer whether or not to give the seller notice of the action and to request the seller to defend that action.

The buyer may also be sued by a third person because of patent infringement. In this case, however, the buyer must give notice of the action to the seller. Moreover, the seller can demand control over the defense of that action.[12]

§ 29:13. Cancellation by Buyer.

The buyer may cancel or rescind the contract if the seller fails to deliver the goods or repudiates the contract or if the buyer has rightfully

[11]UCC § 2-717.
[12]UCC § 2-607.

rejected tender of the goods or rightfully revoked acceptance of them. A buyer who cancels the contract is entitled to recover as much of the purchase price as has been paid, including the value of any property given as a trade-in as part of the purchase price. The fact that the buyer cancels the contract does not destroy the buyer's cause of action against the seller for breach of that contract. The buyer may therefore recover from the seller not only any payment made on the purchase price, but, in addition, damages for the breach of the contract. The damages represent the difference between the contract price and the cost of cover.[13]

The right of the buyer to cancel or rescind the sales contract may be lost by a delay in exercising the right. A buyer who with full knowledge of the defects in the goods makes partial payments or performs acts of dominion inconsistent with any intent to cancel cannot thereafter cancel the contract.

§ 29:14.   Buyer's Resale of Goods.

When the buyer has possession of the goods after rightfully rejecting them or after rightfully revoking acceptance, the buyer is treated the same as a seller in possession of goods after the default of a buyer. That is, the aggrieved buyer has a security interest in the goods to protect the claim against the seller and may resell the goods as though the aggrieved buyer were a seller. From the proceeds of the sale, the aggrieved buyer is entitled to deduct any payments made on the price and any expenses reasonably incurred in the inspection, receipt, transportation, care and custody, and resale of the goods.[14]

§ 29:15.   Action for Conversion or Recovery of Goods.

When, as a result of the sales agreement, ownership passes to the buyer and the seller wrongfully refuses or neglects to deliver the goods, the buyer may maintain any action allowed by law to the owner of goods wrongfully converted or withheld. The obligation of the seller to deliver proper goods may be enforced by an order for specific performance when the goods are "unique or in other proper circumstances."[15] Distributors have been granted specific performance against suppliers to deliver the goods covered by supply contracts. Specific performance will not be granted, however, merely because the price of the goods purchased from the seller has gone up. In such a case, the buyer can still purchase the goods in the open market and the fact that it will cost more to cover can be compensated for by allowing the buyer to recover greater damages from the seller.

FACTS:

Stephan's Machine & Tool, Inc., purchased a boring mill from D & H Machinery Consultants. The mill was a specialized type of equipment and was essential to the operation of Stephan's plant. The purchase price was $96,000 and Stephan had to borrow this amount from a bank in order to finance the sale. This loan exhausted Stephan's borrowing capacity. The mill was unfit and D & H agreed to

[13]UCC § 2-712(1), (2).
[14]UCC § 2-715(1).
[15]UCC § 2-716(1).

replace it. D & H did not keep its promise and Stephan sued D & H for specific performance of the contract as modified by the replacement agreement.

DECISION:

Judgment for Stephan's. Under UCC § 2-716, specific performance may be obtained in proper circumstances. The circumstances for such relief were proper in this case,

the equipment was essential to the business operations of Stephan's and it could not be expected that the buyer could go out and buy another machine as it could not pay or borrow to do so. The failure of D & H to keep its promise was causing irreparable harm to Stephan's. The granting of specific performance was therefore proper. [Stephan's Machine & Tool, Inc. v D & H Machinery Consultants, Inc. 65 Ohio App 2d 197, 417 NE2d 579 (1979)]

---

§ 29:16. Remedies for Fraud of Seller.

Independently of the preceding remedies, the buyer has the right to sue the seller for damages for the latter's fraud and to cancel the transaction on that ground.[16] As these remedies for fraud exist independently of the provisions of the UCC, the buyer may assert such remedies even though barred by the UCC from exercising any remedy for a breach of warranty. Likewise a limitation on remedies or exclusion of warranty liability has no effect on the buyer's claim for damages for fraud.

When the seller of an automobile fraudulently turns back the odometer, the defrauded buyer may recover damages either under the Federal Motor Vehicle Information and Cost Savings Act, or under the applicable state law governing liability for fraud. Under the federal statute, the buyer recovers three times the actual damages sustained or $1,500, whichever is greater. Under state law, the buyer may recover damages for the loss actually sustained and may also recover punitive damages.

Suit for fraud is generally not a satisfactory solution for the consumer because of the difficulty of proving the existence of fraud. Furthermore, some courts require clear and convincing proof of fraud. Hence, it is not sufficient in those courts to prove the existence of fraud by a mere preponderance of evidence, although that ordinarily is a sufficient degree of proof in civil litigation.

D. CONTRACT PROVISIONS ON REMEDIES

The UCC permits the parties to modify or limit by their contract the remedies which they otherwise possess.

§ 29:17. Limitation of Damages.

The parties to the sales contract may seek to limit or exclude the recovery of damages in case of breach.

(a) **Liquidation of Damages.** The parties may specify the exact amount of damages which may be recovered in case of breach. Such a **liquidation of damages** is valid if the amount so specified is reasonable in the light of the actual harm that would be caused by the breach, the difficulty of prov-

---

[16]Stephenson v Frazier, _____ Ind App _____, 399 NE2d 794 (1980).

ing the amount of such loss, and the inconvenience and impracticality of suing for damages or enforcing other remedies for breach.

(b) **Exclusion of Damages.** The sales contract may provide that in case of breach no damages may be recovered or that no consequential damages may be recovered. Such total exclusions are prima facie unconscionable, and therefore prima facie not binding, when goods are sold for consumer use and personal injuries are sustained. Thus, a defendant, in such a case, cannot rely on the contract limitation unless the defendant is able to prove that the limitation of liability was commercially reasonable and fair, rather than oppressive and surprising. Moreover, when the seller would be liable to the buyer for damages, the seller cannot exclude liability for personal injuries to members of the buyer's family or household, or to guests of the buyer.

In cases not involving consumer goods and personal injuries, the plaintiff has the burden of proving that a limitation on damages is not binding because unconscionable. When the seller knows that the failure of the product, such as a harvester, to perform will cause serious economic loss, a limitation of damages for breach to the return of the purchase price is void as unconscionable.

A limitation of damages which is hidden in a paragraph which is headed "guarantee" is misleading and unconscionable.[17]

§ 29:18. Down Payments and Deposits.

The buyer may have made a deposit with the seller or an initial or down payment at the time of making the contract. If the contract contains a valid liquidation-of-damages provision and the buyer defaults, the seller must return any part of the down payment or deposit in excess of the amount specified by the liquidated damages clause. In the absence of such a clause, and in the absence of proof of greater damages sustained, the seller's damages are computed as 20 percent of the purchase price or $500, whichever is the smaller. The extent to which the down payment exceeds such amount must be returned to the buyer.

FACTS:
Stanturf wanted a van. He went to Quality Dodge, Inc. and selected a particular van, left his car as a trade-in valued at $1,000, and made a cash payment of $500. He later refused to go through with the sale because he believed that the seller had substituted another van in place of the one he had selected. He demanded the return of his money and the trade-in. Quality Dodge refused to make such return. Stanturf then sued Quality Dodge.

DECISION:
Judgment for Stanturf. The Code gives the defaulting buyer the right to recover back any down payment or deposit to the extent specified by UCC § 2-718. No distinction is made as to whether the buyer had paid with cash or with goods or a combination of both. [Stanturf v Quality Dodge, Inc. 3 Kan App 2d 485, 596 P2d 1247 (1979)]

---

[17]Jutta's Incorporated v Fireco Equipment Co. 150 NJ Super 301, 375 A2d 687 (1977).

§ 29:19. Limitation of Remedies.

The parties may validly limit the remedies that are provided by the Code in the case of breach of contract. Thus a seller may specify that the only remedy of the buyer for breach of warranty shall be the repair or replacement of the goods or that the buyer shall be limited to returning the goods and obtaining a refund of the purchase price. A limitation of remedies need not be conspicuous.

(a) **Construction Favoring Cumulative Remedies.** When the sales contract specifies a remedy to which a party will be entitled, a question arises whether the parties intended that that should be the sole or exclusive remedy. It must be clearly stated that the remedy was to be the exclusive remedy. If it is not clearly stated, the remedy stated will be regarded as being in addition or cumulative to the remedies already existing under the Code.[18]

(b) **Failure of Limited Remedy.** A provision limiting the seller's obligation to the repair of the goods or the replacement of defective parts fails of its essential purpose and is not binding when the seller is unable or refuses to make the goods function properly within a reasonable time, because the buyer is entitled to goods which will be fit to the extent required by the particular warranties which have been made expressly or which are implied. When there is such a failure to correct the defect, the buyer may use any remedy authorized by the Code, just as though the contract had not contained any limitation on remedies.

FACTS:

Osburn purchased a mobile home from Bendix Home Systems, Inc. The "warranty" of the dealer and of the manufacturer stated that the liability for breach of warranty was limited to repairing any defects. The Osburn home had numerous defects. After repeated repairs were made, the home was still defective. Osburn sued the dealer and the manufacturer for breach of warranty. The defendants asserted that their only obligation was to make repairs and that it was immaterial that the repairs did not cure the defect.

DECISION:

Judgment for Osburn. When a buyer's remedies are limited to the seller's making repairs, the purpose of such repairs is to make the goods free from any defects so that the buyer has the goods that were bargained for and in the condition that was contemplated. If the repairs failed to do this, the limited remedy has failed on its purpose and the limitation ceases to be binding on the buyer. The buyer is then free to assert any Code remedy that could have been asserted in the absence of the limitation. [Osburn v Bendix Home Systems, Inc. (Okla) 613 P2d 445 (1980)]

---

§ 29:20. Waiver of Defenses.

A buyer may be barred from objecting to a breach of the contract by the seller because the buyer has waived the right to do so.

---

[18]V. Zappala & Co. v Pyramid Co. 81 App Div 2d 983, 439 NYS2d 765 (1981).

(a) **Express Waiver.** When sales are made on credit, the seller will ordinarily plan to assign the sales contract to a bank or other financer and thereby convert into immediate cash the customer's obligation to pay in the future. To make the transaction more attractive to banks and financers, the credit seller will generally include in the sales contract with each buyer a **waiver of defense** clause. By this clause, the buyer agrees not to assert against the seller's assignee any defense held against the seller. For example, if the television set does not work properly, the buyer agrees to complain only to the seller. The buyer agrees not to complain to the seller's assignee but will continue to pay the assignee just as though everything were satisfactory.

(b) **Implied Waiver.** When the buyer executes a promissory note as part of the credit transaction described above, the buyer automatically waives with respect to the seller's assignee any defense which could not be raised against a holder in due course of the note. This will be considered in greater detail in Chapter 33. What it means in the ordinary situation is that when the buyer signs a promissory note for the balance due, the buyer cannot assert against the finance company or the bank the defense that the buyer never got the goods called for by the contract, that the goods were defective and did not work, or that the contract had been entered into because of the fraudulent misstatements of the seller.

§ 29:21.   Preservation of Defenses.

Consumer protection laws and regulations seek to protect consumers by preserving defenses. In such cases, there is no waiver of defenses as described in § 29:20. If the basis for the defense to a home-solicited sale becomes apparent within time to cancel the sale, it is possible that the consumer may assert the defense by exercising the right of cancellation as described in § 20:6.

(a) **Preservation Notice.** Consumer defenses will be preserved by the Federal Trade Commission regulation requiring that the papers signed by a consumer contain a provision which expressly states that the consumer is reserving any defense arising from the transaction.[19] A third person acquiring such paper is necessarily charged with knowledge of such provision and a defense of the consumer arising from the original transaction may therefore be asserted against such third person.

(b) **Prohibition of Waiver.** When the Federal Trade Commission preservation notice is included in the paper which is received by the third person, it is unnecessary to consider whether a waiver of defenses could be validly made. If the preservation notice is not included, the seller has committed an unfair trade practice but the question then arises of whether the buyer may assert against an assignee a defense which could have been asserted against the seller. The answer to this question depends upon state law. In many states, consumer protection statutes nullify a waiver of defenses by expressly providing that the buyer may assert against the seller's transferee any defense which might have been raised against the seller. Under some

---

[19] 16 CFR § 433.1. It is an unfair or deceptive trade practice to take or receive a consumer credit contract which fails to contain such a preservation notice. See § 32:7 of this text.

statutes, the buyer must give notice of any defense within a specified number of days after being notified of the assignment. Some courts extend consumer protection beyond the scope of the statute by ignoring a time limitation on the giving of notice of defenses and allow consumers to give late notice of defenses.

SUMMARY

The law provides a number of remedies for the breach of a sales contract. Remedies based on UCC theories are subject to a four-year statute of limitations. If the remedy sought is based on a non-UCC theory, the four-year limitation does not apply.

Remedies of the seller may include (1) a lien on the goods until the seller is paid, (2) the right to resell goods, (3) the right to cancel the sales contract, and (4) the right to bring an action for damages or in some cases for the purchase price.

Remedies of the buyer may include (1) rejection of nonconforming goods, (2) revocation of acceptance, (3) an action for damages, (4) an action for breach of warranty, (5) cancellation of the sales contract, (6) the right to resell the goods, and (7) the right to bring an action for conversion.

The parties may be permitted to modify their remedies by contractual provision for liquidated damages, limitations on statutory remedies, or waiver of defenses. Protective legislation restricts this freedom of contract to some extent for the benefit of consumers.

QUESTIONS AND CASE PROBLEMS

1. What social forces are involved in the rule of law allowing the buyer to cover upon the seller's breach?
2. Donna purchased a snowmobile from the Park Manufacturing Company. Three years later it rolled over and injured her. She sued Park two years after her accident, alleging that Park had breached its implied warranty of merchantability on the theory that the snowmobile had rolled over because of a design defect and that this defect showed that the snowmobile was not fit for its normal use. Is Park liable for the injuries sustained by Donna?
3. Gwendolyn purchased a washing machine from the Melvin Appliance Center. She did not notice that on the back of the contract that she signed there was a statement in fine print that in the event of any defects, Melvin's liability was limited to repairing or replacing the defective parts. There was a defective switch in the washing machine. The switch caused the machine to overheat and set fire to the laundry room of Gwendolyn's house. She demanded that Melvin pay her for the damage caused to the laundry room. Melvin offered to repair the washing machine free of charge and insisted that it had no greater liability because of the limitation of liability in the contract. Gwendolyn claimed that the limitation clause was not binding because it was not conspicuous. Is she correct?
4. What is the nature of a liquidation of damages clause?

5. Eleanor purchases a bottle of hair dye from Remson Drug Store. The label gives various warnings to the user and states that the liability of Remson and the manufacturer is limited to a refund of the purchase price. When Eleanor uses the dye, she is severely burned. Chemical tests show that there were certain impurities in the bottle purchased by her. She demands that Remson pay her damages to cover her medical expenses and pain and suffering. Remson refuses to pay Eleanor more than the purchase price on the theory that Eleanor agreed to this when she purchased the bottle of hair dye. Is the limitation on the bottle binding on Eleanor?

6. Ward ordered a $500 television set from Greyline Markets Inc. Greyline wrote Ward an acceptance of his order. The next day Ward found a store selling the same set for $400. He notified Greyline that he was canceling his order of the day before. Greyline insisted that he could not do this and that he must pay $500 for the set. Was Greyline correct?

7. Compare a buyer's rejection of nonconforming goods with the buyer's revocation of acceptance of goods.

8. The goods purchased by the buyer were defective. The seller made repeated attempts to correct the defect. It became apparent that it was impossible to correct the defect. The buyer notified the seller that the buyer was revoking acceptance of the goods. The seller offered to try again to repair the goods. The buyer rejected this offer and repeated that acceptance of the goods was being revoked. The seller claimed that the buyer could not revoke acceptance as long as the seller offered to repair the goods. Was the seller correct? [See Fenton v Contemporary Development Co. 12 Wash App 345, 529 P2d 883]

9. After a sales contract was made, the seller's factory was destroyed by fire. The seller and the buyer then agreed to cancel the contract. Thereafter the seller's factory was rebuilt, and the buyer demanded that the seller perform the contract. Was the seller required to do so? [Goddard v Ishikawajima-Harima Heavy Industries Co. 29 App Div 2d 754, 287 NYS2d 901]

10. The buyer of goods at an auction sale did not pay for and take the goods. The auctioneer sued the buyer for the amount of the buyer's bid. Was the buyer liable for that amount? [French v Sotheby & Co. (Okla) 470 P2d 318]

11. Sue wants to buy a car on credit from Henry Motors. She is afraid, however, that Henry will assign her contract to a finance company and that the finance company will be able to collect the balance due on the car even though the car does not run properly. Sue wants to be able to defend against the finance company by showing that there are defects in the car. Is this possible?

12. Wolosin purchased a vegetable and dairy refrigerator case from the Evans Manufacturing Corp. Evans sued Wolosin for the purchase price. Wolosin raised as a defense a claim for damages for breach of warranty. The sales contract provided that Evans would replace defective parts free of charge for one year and that "this warranty is in lieu of any and all other warranties stated or inferred, and of all other obligations on the part of the manufacturer, which neither assumes nor authorizes anyone to assume for it any other obligations or liability in connection with the

sale of its products." Evans claimed that it was only liable for replacement of parts. Wolosin claimed that the quoted clause was not sufficiently specific to satisfy the requirement of UCC §2-719. Decide. [Evans Mfg. Corp. v Wolosin (Pa) 47 Luzerne County Leg Reg 238]

13. McInnis purchased a tractor and scraper as new equipment of current model from the Western Tractor & Equipment Co. The written contract stated that the seller disclaimed all warranties and that no warranties existed except as were stated in the contract. Actually, the equipment was not the current model but that of the prior year. Likewise, the equipment was not new but had been used for 68 hours as a demonstrator model and then the hour meter had been reset to zero. The buyer sued the seller for damages. The latter defended on the ground that all liability for warranties had been disclaimed. Was this defense valid? [McInnis v Western Tractor & Equipment Co. 63 Wash 2d 652, 388 P2d 562]

14. Bosway Tube and Steel Corporation purchased a machine for making tubes from McKay Machine Company. The machine did not work properly and McKay was unable to repair the machine. Bosway sued for damages. McKay claimed that it was only liable for the cost of repairs, as the contract specified that it had no liability "beyond repairing or replacing it." Was McKay correct?

15. Compare the right of a buyer to a refund of a deposit when (a) the seller has repudiated the contract, and (b) the buyer has repudiated the contract.

16. Keenan rejected nonconforming goods delivered to him by Ross. After such rejection, but before Ross had been allowed a reasonable time to give instructions for the goods' disposition, Keenan arranged a sale of the goods at a substantially reduced price. Ross in the meantime had sold the goods to another of his customers. What rights, if any, does Ross have against Keenan?

17. Peters, the buyer, received merchandise from Hadley, the seller. Upon looking over the goods, Peters noticed that certain of the goods did not conform to the contract. He therefore called Hadley, who stated "We always take care of our customers." Peters then accepted the goods. The nonconformity not being remedied within a reasonable time, Peters informed Hadley that he revoked his acceptance. Hadley refused to take back the goods. Who will prevail?

PART 5

COMMERCIAL PAPER

Chapter 30 Kinds of Paper, Parties, and Negotiability
Chapter 31 Transfer of Commercial Paper
Chapter 32 Rights of Holders and Defenses
Chapter 33 Presentment of Paper for Payment and Acceptance
Chapter 34 Discharge of Commercial Paper
Chapter 35 Checks and Customer-Bank Relationship

C H A P T E R   30

KINDS OF PAPER, PARTIES,

AND NEGOTIABILITY

CHAPTER OBJECTIVES

After studying this chapter you will be able to:

1. Explain the importance and function of commercial paper.
2. Name the parties to commercial paper.
3. Describe the concept of negotiability and distinguish it from assignability.
4. List the essential elements of a negotiable instrument.
5. Identify provisions in commercial paper that affect negotiability.
6. Solve problems involving the negotiability of commercial paper.

Under the law of contracts a promise, when supported by consideration, creates certain legal rights that may be assigned to another person. Even before these common-law rules relating to contracts were developing, another body of law, the law merchant, was creating principles relating to a different type of obligation and the transfer of rights arising therefrom. In the course of time this obligation became the bill of exchange, which today we also know as a draft, a trade acceptance, or, with certain modification, a check. In time, another type of instrument, the promissory note, appeared. Both drafts and promissory notes may have the quality of negotiability. This is a quality that distinguishes them from contracts, because the rights they represent can be transferred in such a way that the transferee may be immune from certain contract defenses. As a group, these instruments are known as commercial paper or negotiable instruments.

A. KINDS OF COMMERCIAL PAPER AND PARTIES

Commercial paper, such as checks and promissory notes, provide a substitute for money and can be used as a means of providing credit.

§ 30:1. Definition.

Commercial paper includes written promises (such as promissory notes) or orders (such as checks or drafts) to pay money that may be transferred by the process of negotiation. Much of the importance of commercial paper lies in the fact that it is more readily transferred than ordinary contract rights and that the transferee of commercial paper may acquire greater rights than would an ordinary assignee. A person who acquires a commercial paper may therefore be subject to less risk.

§ 30:2. Kinds of Commercial Paper.

Commercial paper falls into four categories: (a) promissory notes, (b) drafts or bills of exchange, (c) checks, and (d) certificates of deposit.

(a) **Promissory Notes.** A **negotiable promissory note** is an unconditional promise in writing made by one person to another, signed by the maker, engaging to pay on demand or at a definite time a sum certain in money to order or to bearer.[1]

(b) **Drafts.** A **negotiable draft** or **bill of exchange** is an unconditional order in writing addressed by one person to another, signed by the person giving it, requiring the person to whom it is addressed to pay on demand, or at a definite time, a sum certain in money to order or to bearer.[2] In effect, it is an order by one person upon a second person to pay a sum of money. The person who gives the order is called the **drawer** and is said to draw the bill. The person on whom the order to pay is drawn is the **drawee**. The person to whom payment is to be made is the **payee**. The drawer may also be named as the payee.

The drawee who is ordered to pay the paper is not bound to do so. The drawee, however, may agree to pay the paper, in which case the drawee is called an **acceptor**.

(c) **Checks.** A **check** is a draft drawn on a bank payable on demand.[3] It is an order by a depositor (the drawer) upon a bank (the drawee) to pay a sum of money to the order of another person (the payee). A check is always drawn upon a bank as drawee and is always payable upon demand.

(d) **Certificates of Deposit.** A **certificate of deposit** is an instrument issued by a bank that acknowledges the deposit of a specific sum of money and promises to pay the holder of the certificate that amount, usually with interest, when the certificate is surrendered.[4]

§ 30:3. Parties to Commercial Paper.

A note has two original parties—the maker and the payee; and a draft or a check has three original parties—the drawer, the drawee, and the

[1]Uniform Commercial Code § 3-104(1).
[2]UCC § 3-104(1).
[3]UCC § 104(2)(b).
[4]A certificate of deposit "is an acknowledgment by a bank of receipt of money with an engagement to repay it," as distinguished from a note, which "is a promise other than a certificate of deposit." UCC § 3-104(2)(c), (d).

$ _650 00_	Albany, New York _August 15_ 19 _— —_
Three months	after date _I_ promise to pay to
the order of _Paul Garcia_	
six hundred fifty	Dollars
Payable at _Citizens State Bank_	
with interest at _14_ %	
No. _36_ Due _November 15, 19 —_	_Linda Robinson_

PROMISSORY NOTE

Parties: maker (buyer, borrower, or debtor) — Linda Robinson; payee (seller, lender, or creditor) — Paul Garcia.

$ 200 00	Des Moines, Iowa _March 17,_ 19 _— —_
Sixty days after date	PAY TO THE
ORDER OF _Security National Bank_	
Two hundred	DOLLARS
VALUE RECEIVED AND CHARGE TO ACCOUNT OF	
TO _Susan Miller_	
No. _15_ _Chicago, Illinois_	_David Bowman_

DRAFT (BILL OF EXCHANGE)

Parties: drawer (seller or creditor) — Bowman; drawee (buyer or debtor) — Miller; payee (seller's or creditor's bank) — Security National Bank.

payee. In addition to these original parties, a commercial paper may have one or more of the parties described under (e) through (i) of this section.

(a) **Maker.** The **maker** is the person who writes out and creates a promissory note. If the paper is not a promissory note, this person has a different name, as the drawer of a check.

(b) **Drawer.** The **drawer** is the person who writes out and creates a draft. This includes bills of exchange, trade acceptances, and checks. It is essential to bear in mind the distinction between a maker and a drawer for the reason that the liability of the maker is primary while that of a drawer is secondary.

(c) **Drawee.** The **drawee** is the person to whom the draft is addressed and who is ordered to pay the amount of money specified in the draft.

(d) **Payee.** The **payee** is the person named on the face of the paper to receive payment. In "pay to the order of John Jones," the named person, John Jones, is the payee.

A payee has no rights in the paper until it has been delivered by the drawer or the maker. Likewise, the payee is not liable on the paper in any way until the payee transfers the paper to someone else or receives payment of it.

(e) **Acceptor.** When the drawee has signified in writing on the draft the willingness to make the specified payment, the drawee is called the **acceptor.**

(f) **Indorser.**[5] The owner of commercial paper who signs on the back of the paper is an **indorser.** Thus, if a check is made payable to the order of *P*, *P* may indorse it to *E* to pay a debt that *P* owes *E*. In such a case, *P*, who is the payee of the check is now also an indorser.

(g) **Indorsee.** The person to whom an indorsement is made payable is called an **indorsee.** The indorsee may in turn indorse the instrument; and then is also an indorser.

(h) **Bearer.** The person in physical possession of a commercial paper which is payable to bearer is called a **bearer.**

(i) **Holder.** A **holder** is a person in possession of commercial paper which is payable at that time either to such person, as payee or indorsee, or to bearer.

A person who becomes a holder of the paper in the regular course of ordinary business is called a **holder in due course** and is immune from certain defenses when such favored holder brings suit on the paper. A person becoming the holder of an instrument at any time after it was once held by a holder in due course is described as a **holder through a holder in due course,** and is ordinarily given the same special rights as a holder in due course.

(j) **Accommodation Party.** A person who becomes a party to a commercial paper in order to add strength to the paper for the benefit of another party to the paper is called an **accommodation party.**

(k) Guarantor. A **guarantor** is a person who signs a commercial paper and adds a promise to pay the instrument under certain circumstances. Ordinarily this is done by merely adding "payment guaranteed" or "collection guaranteed" to the signature of the guarantor on the paper.

The addition of "payment guaranteed" or similar words mean that the guarantor will pay the instrument when due. "Collection guaranteed" or similar words mean that the guarantor will not pay the paper until after the holder has sought to collect payment from the maker or acceptor and has been unable to do so.

---

[5]The spelling *endorse* is commonly used in business. The spelling *indorse* is used in the UCC.

FACTS:

Ruth Laudati obtained a student loan from Brown University and signed a promissory note for the repayment of the loan. Her mother, Josephine, guaranteed payment of the note. When the note was not paid, Brown University sued Josephine. She raised the defense that Brown had not sued Ruth.

DECISION:

A guarantor of payment may be sued upon default on the paper and the holder is not required to proceed against any other party before suing the guarantor. [Brown University v Laudati, 113 RI 926, 320 A2d 609 (1974)]

If the meaning of the guaranty is not clear, it is construed as a guaranty of payment. For example, when an indorser adds a statement that the paper is "guaranteed" or adds the word "guarantor" to the indorsement without specifying whether it is payment or collection which is guaranteed, the indorser is deemed to be a guarantor of payment, with the consequence that the holder of the paper may proceed directly against such guarantor without first proceeding against any other party on the paper.

The liability of a guarantor is as extensive as that of the original debtor.

§ 30:4. Liability of Parties.

A person who by the terms of the instrument is absolutely required to pay is primarily liable. For a note, the maker is primarily liable; for a draft, the acceptor (the drawee who has accepted) is primarily liable. A guarantor of payment is primarily liable in any case. Other parties are either secondarily or conditionally liable, as in the case of an indorser, or they are not liable in any capacity. A person who transfers the paper but does not sign it is not liable for its payment.[6]

(a) **Accommodation Parties.** An accommodation party is liable for payment of the paper regardless of whether the paper is signed merely as a matter of friendship or in return for payment. When suit is brought against an accommodation party by a plaintiff who acquired the paper before it was due and who gave value for it, the accommodation party cannot avoid liability on the ground that the plaintiff knew of the accommodation character.

The accommodation party is not liable to the party accommodated.[7] If the accommodation party is required to pay the paper; that party may recover the payment from the person accommodated. Parol evidence may be admitted to show that a party to the paper had signed to accommodate another party.[8]

[6]Pike Burden Printing, Inc. v Pike Burden, Inc. (La App) 396 So2d 361 (1981).
[7]UCC § 3-415(5).
[8]Dalton v George B. Hatley Co. Inc. (Tex App) 634 SW2d 374 (1982).

FACTS:

Community Bank loaned money to Pitrolo Pontiac Co. This company was a corporation through which Paul Pitrolo and his wife ran an automobile dealership. On the note given by Pitrolo Pontiac to the bank to represent the loan, Paul and his wife wrote that they guaranteed payment of the note. The note was not paid and Community Bank sued Paul and his wife. They raised the defenses that they could not be sued because (1) the note was a corporation note and (2) they had not received any consideration for their guaranties.

DECISION:

Judgment for Community Bank. (1) The fact that it was a corporation note was immaterial as the liability of Paul and his wife was to be determined by the capacity in which they signed the paper. As indorsers guaranteeing payment, they were primarily liable for payment of the paper. (2) The fact that they had not received consideration was immaterial. Their undertaking was supported by the consideration they requested: the making of a loan to the corporation. The fact that Paul and his wife received nothing merely emphasized the fact that they were accommodation parties. [Pitrolo v Community Bank & Trust Co. _____ WVa _____, 298 SE2d 853 (1982)]

(b) **Guarantors.** A **guarantor of payment** has primary liability. The guarantor of payment is liable for payment of the paper even though the holder has not sought to obtain payment from any other party and it is immaterial that payment was not demanded from the primary party or that the primary party had sufficient assets to pay the paper.

The **guarantor of collection** is not required to pay the paper until collection has been attempted and has failed, or an attempt to collect would obviously be useless.

B. NEGOTIABILITY

As noted early in this chapter, one of the important qualities of commercial paper is its negotiability. It is this quality of negotiability that makes commercial paper acceptable as a circulating medium of exchange, that is, a substitute for money or credit, in commercial transactions.

§ 30:5.   Requirements of Negotiability.

In order to be negotiable, an instrument must be (a) in writing and (b) signed by the maker or drawer; it must contain (c) a promise or order (d) of an unconditional character (e) to pay in money (f) a sum certain; (g) it must be payable on demand or at a definite time; (h) it must be payable to order or bearer;[9] and (i) a party who is a drawee must be identified with reasonable certainty.

In addition to these formal requirements, the instrument usually must be delivered or issued by the maker or drawer to the payee or the latter's agent with the intent that it be effective and create a legal obligation.

[9]Holsonback v First State Bank (Ala Civ App) 394 So2d 381 (1980).

If an instrument is not negotiable, the rights of the parties are governed by the general body of contract law.[10] If there is any uncertainty as to whether a paper is negotiable it is deemed nonnegotiable.

§ 30:6.   Writing.

A commercial paper must be in writing. "Writing" includes handwriting, typing, printing, and any other method of setting words down in a permanent form. The use of a pencil is not wise because such writing is not as durable as ink and the instrument may be more easily altered. A commercial paper may be partly printed and partly typewritten with a handwritten signature.

As the commercial paper is a writing, the parol evidence rule applies. This rule prohibits modifying the instrument by proving the existence of a conflicting oral agreement alleged to have been made before or at the time of the execution of the commercial paper.

§ 30:7.   Signature.

The instrument must be signed by the maker or drawer. The signature usually appears at the lower right-hand corner of the face of the instrument, but it is immaterial whether the signature is so placed. However, if the signature is placed on the instrument in such a manner that it does not in itself clearly indicate that the signer was the maker, drawer, or acceptor, the signer is held to be only an indorser.

In the absence of a local statute that provides otherwise, the signature may be made by pen or pencil, by typewriter, by print, or by stamp.

The signature itself may consist of the full name or of any symbol adopted for that purpose. It may consist of initials, figures, or a mark. A person signing a trade or an assumed name is liable to the same extent as though the signer's own name had been used.

(a) **Agent.** A signature may be made by the drawer or maker or by an authorized agent.[11] No particular form of authorization to an agent to execute or sign a commercial paper is required.

An agent signing commercial paper should disclose on the paper (1) the identity of the principal, and (2) the fact that the signing is made in a representative capacity. When both are done, an authorized agent is not liable on the paper. The representative capacity of an officer of an organization is sufficiently shown by the signature of the officer preceded or followed by the title of the office and the organization name.

(b) **Nondisclosure of Agency or Principal.** If a person who signs a commercial paper in a representative capacity, such as an agent or an officer of a corporation, executes the paper without disclosing both the identity of the principal and the existence of the representative capacity, the agent

---

[10]First Investment Co. v Andersen (Utah) 621 P2d 683 (1980). Note however, that if the nonnegotiability results from the fact that the instrument is not payable to order or bearer, it is governed by Article 3 of the Code with the limitation that there cannot be a holder in due course of such paper. UCC § 3-805.

[11]UCC § 3-403(1).

appears to be signing the paper as a personal obligation. Under these circumstances, the agent is personally bound by the paper with respect to subsequent holders, regardless of whether the agent had intended to be personally bound or to act in a representative capacity.

However, courts in some jurisdictions have adopted a more liberal rule.

FACTS:

Cook, the treasurer of Arizona Auto Auction, Inc., issued three corporate checks to Central Motors. The checks clearly indicated that the money was payable from the account of Arizona Auto Auction, Inc. Cook signed the checks at the bottom on the signature line under the printed name of the corporation. She did not, however, specifically signify that she was signing in her representative capacity as treasurer. The checks were deposited in the Valley National Bank which attempted to collect them. The checks were dishonored and Valley National sued both the corporation and Cook. Cook argued that she was not personally liable.

DECISION:

Judgment for Cook. While a strict application of the UCC would result in Cook being considered an accommodation party, the court in this case chose to adopt a more liberal, minority position. The court reasoned that it is the common business and banking expectation that where a corporate name is printed on a check, and where the check is drawn against a corporate account, any accompanying signature relating to the corporate drawer will be the signature of an officer authorized to sign the instrument in a representative capacity. Since Cook made no personal guaranty of these checks or any other corporate obligation, she is not personally liable. [Valley National Bank, Sunnymead v Cook, 136 Ariz App 232, 665 P2d 576 (1983)]

---

§ 30:8.   Promise or Order to Pay.

A promissory note must contain a promise to pay money. No particular form of promise is required; the intention as gathered from the face of the instrument controls.[12] If the maker uses such a phrase as "I certify to pay," a promise is implied; but a mere acknowledgment of a debt, such as a writing stating "I.O.U." is not a commercial paper.

A draft or check must contain an order or command to pay money.[13] As in the case of a promise in a note, no particular form of order is required.

§ 30:9.   Unconditional Promise or Order.

The promise or order to pay must be unconditional. For example, when an instrument makes the duty to pay dependent upon the completion of the construction of a building or upon the placement of the building at a particular location, the promise is conditional and the instrument is nonnegotiable. Also, the promise or order is conditional and the instrument is

---

[12]Fejta v Werner Enterprises (La App) 412 So2d 155 (1982).
[13]UCC § 3–104(1)(b).

nonnegotiable if the instrument states that it is subject to another agreement. In such a case, negotiability is destroyed because the terms of payment cannot be determined by looking at the instrument alone.

An order for the payment of money out of a particular fund, such as ten dollars from next week's salary, is conditional.[14] If, however, the instrument is based upon the general credit of the drawer and the reference to a particular fund is merely to indicate a source of reimbursement for the drawee, such as "charge my expense account" the order is considered absolute.[15]

§ 30:10.   Payment in Money.

A commercial paper must call for payment in *money*, that is, any circulating medium of exchange which is legal tender at the place of payment. If the order or promise is not for money, the instrument is not negotiable. For example, an instrument which requires the holder to take stock or goods in place of money is nonnegotiable.

§ 30:11.   Sum Certain.

This means an exact amount. The instrument must not only call for payment in money but also for an exact amount of money. Unless the instrument is definite on its face as to how much is to be paid, there is no way of determining how much the instrument is worth.

Minor variations from the above rule are allowed in certain cases. Thus, commercial paper is not made nonnegotiable because the interest rate changes at maturity or because certain costs and attorney's fees may be recovered by the holder.[16]

§ 30:12.   Time of Payment.

A commercial paper must be payable on demand or at a definite time. If it is payable "when convenient" the instrument is nonnegotiable because the day of payment may never arrive. An instrument payable only upon the happening of a particular event that may never happen is not negotiable. For example, a provision to pay when a person marries is not payable at a definite time since that particular event may never occur. It is immaterial whether the contingency in fact has happened, because from an examination of the instrument alone it still appears to be subject to a condition that may never happen.

(a) **Demand.** An instrument is payable on **demand** when it is expressly specified to be payable "on demand," or at sight or upon presentation, that is, whenever the holder tenders the instrument to the party required to pay and demands payment. Commercial paper is also payable on demand when no time for payment is stated in the instrument.[17]

---

[14]UCC § 3–105(2)(b).
[15]Rogers v Willard (Fla App) 453 So2d 1175 (1984).
[16]UCC § 3-106.
[17]UCC § 3-108.

(b) **Definite Time.** The time of payment is **definite** if it can be determined from the face of the instrument. An instrument satisfies this requirement when it is payable (a) on or before a stated date, (b) at a fixed period after a stated date, (c) at a fixed period after sight, (d) at a definite time subject to any acceleration, (e) at a definite time subject to extension at the option of the holder, (f) at a definite time subject to extension to a further definite date at the option of the maker or acceptor, or (g) at a definite time subject to an extension to a further definite date automatically upon or after the occurrence of a specified act or event.[18]

FACTS:

James T. Balkus died. Shortly after his death, his sister Ann Vesely examined Balkus's personal property and discovered six deposit slips from a savings account maintained by Balkus. On each slip was a handwritten notation: Payable to the order of Ann Balkus Vesely on death, the full amount. Each slip was dated and signed by Balkus. Vesely claimed that the deposit slips are negotiable instruments.

DECISION:

The deposit slips are not negotiable instruments because they fail to meet the requirements that the writing be payable at a definite time. An instrument payable only upon an act or event uncertain as to time of occurrence is not payable at a definite time. Because the payable on death term of the deposit slips makes the instrument payable upon an event uncertain as to the time of occurrence, i.e., the date of Balkus's death, the deposit slips are not payable at a definite time and are therefore not negotiable instruments. [Matter of Estate of Balkus, 128 Wis2d 246, 381 NW2d 593 (1985)]

(c) **Missing or Incorrect Date.** In the event the instrument is not dated, it is regarded as carrying the date of the day on which it was executed and delivered to the payee. If the date is essential to the operation of the instrument, as when the instrument is payable a stated number of days or months "after date," any holder who knows the true date may insert that date.

When a commercial paper is dated, the date is deemed prima facie to be the true date, whether the date was originally inserted or was thereafter added.[19] A commercial paper may be antedated or postdated, provided that it is not done to defraud anyone. The holder acquires title as of the date of delivery without regard to whether this is the date stated in the instrument.

§ 30:13.   Order or Bearer.

A commercial paper must be payable to order or bearer.[20] This requirement is met by such expressions as "Pay to the order of John Jones,"

---

[18]UCC § 3-109(1).

[19]UCC § 3-114(3). If the wrong date is inserted, the true date can be proved unless the holder is a holder in due course or a holder through a holder in due course, in which case the date, even though wrong, cannot be contradicted.

[20]Beyer v First National Bank, 188 Mont 208, 612 P2d 1285 (1980).

"Pay to John Jones or order," "Pay to bearer," and "Pay to John Jones or bearer." The use of the phrase "to the order of John Jones" or to "John Jones or order" is important in showing that the person executing the instrument is indicating that there is no intention to restrict payment of the instrument to John Jones only and that there is no objection to paying anyone to whom John Jones orders the paper to be paid. Similarly, if the person executing the instrument originally states that it will be paid to "bearer" or "to John Jones or bearer," there is no restricting of payment of the paper to the original payee. If the instrument is payable on its face "to John Jones," however, the instrument is not negotiable.

FACTS:

Nation-Wide Check Corp. sold money orders through local agents. A customer would purchase a money order by paying an agent the amount of the desired money order plus a fee. The customer would then sign the money order as the remitter or sender and would fill in the name of the person who was to receive the money following the printed words "Payable to." In a lawsuit between Nation-Wide and Banks, a payee on some of these orders, the question was raised whether these money orders were negotiable.

DECISION:

The money orders were not negotiable because they were payable to a specified or named payee and not to the order of a named payee or bearer. [Nation-Wide Check Corp. v Banks (Dist Col App) 260 A2d 367 (1969)]

(a) **Order Paper.** An instrument is payable to **order** when by its terms it is payable to the order of any person specified therein with reasonable certainty (pay to the order of K. Read), or to a person so described or order (pay to K. Read or order).

(b) **Bearer Paper.** An instrument is **payable to bearer** when by its terms it is payable (1) to bearer or the order of bearer, (2) to a specified person or bearer, or (3) to "cash," or "the order of cash," or any other designation that does not purport to identify a person.

§ 30:14. Effect of Provisions
for Additional Powers or Benefits.

Certain provisions in an instrument that give the holder certain additional powers and benefits may or may not affect negotiability.

(a) **Collateral.** The inclusion of a power to sell collateral security, such as corporate stocks and bonds, upon default does not impair negotiability. An instrument secured by collateral contains as absolute a promise or order as an unsecured instrument. Negotiability is not affected by a promise or power to maintain or protect collateral or to give additional collateral or to make the entire debt due if the additional collateral is not supplied according to the terms of the promise.

(b) Acceleration. A power to accelerate the due date of an instrument upon a default in the payment of interest or of any installment of the principal, or upon the failure to maintain or provide collateral does not affect the negotiability of an instrument. However, a holder's power to accelerate the due date "at will" or when a person "deems himself insecure" must be exercised in good faith.[21]

(c) Requirement of Another Act. A provision authorizing the holder to require an act other than the payment of money, such as the delivery of goods, makes the instrument nonnegotiable.[22]

§ 30:15. Additional Documents.

The fact that a separate document is executed that gives the creditor additional protection, as a mortgage on real estate, or the right to repossess goods sold to the maker of the instrument, does not impair the negotiability of the commercial paper.

As between the parties to the original transaction, the liability on the paper will be controlled by the terms of any other documents. In contrast, subsequent holders of the commercial paper can rely on the face of the paper and are not affected by the terms of any additional separate document.

SUMMARY

Commercial paper is a contract to pay money but special rules are applicable to such paper. A transferee of commercial paper may be immune from certain contract defenses.

There are four categories of commercial paper: (1) promissory notes, (2) drafts or bills of exchange, (3) checks, and (4) certificates of deposit.

A negotiable promissory note is an unconditional promise in writing, made by one person to another, signed by the maker, promising to pay on demand or at a definite time, a sum certain in money, to order or to bearer. A negotiable draft or bill of exchange is an unconditional order in writing, addressed by one person to another, signed by the one giving it, requiring the person to whom it is addressed to pay on demand or at a definite time, a sum certain in money, to order or to bearer. A check is a draft drawn on a bank and payable on demand. A certificate of deposit is an instrument issued by a bank that acknowledges the deposit of a specified sum of money and promises to pay the holder of the certificate that amount, usually with interest, upon surrender of the certificate.

The original parties to a note are the maker and payee. The original parties to a draft are the drawer, the drawee, and the payee. The owner of commercial paper who signs on the back of the paper is called an indorser. The person to whom an indorsement is made payable is called an indorsee. A

[21]UCC § 1-208.
[22]UCC § 3-104(1)(b).

person in physical possession of a commercial paper which is payable to bearer is called a bearer.

A holder in due course is a favored holder of commercial paper. A person taking commercial paper through a holder in due course is known as a holder through a holder in due course and is immune from certain defenses.

The requirements of negotiability are: (1) the instrument must be in writing, (2) signed by the maker or drawer, (3) contain an unconditional promise or order, (4) to pay a sum certain in money, (5) on demand or at a definite time, (6) to order or to bearer. If an instrument is not negotiable, it is governed by the rules of contract law.

QUESTIONS AND CASE PROBLEMS

1. What social forces are affected by the rule of law governing the nature of a signature on commercial paper?
2. Name the four kinds of commercial paper.
3. Dorothy purchased a power mower from Reilly Brothers on credit and gave Reilly a promissory note for the balance due. To induce Reilly to accept this note, Jeanette wrote on the back "guaranteed" and then signed her name. Dorothy promised Jeanette that Jeanette would never be required to pay this note. Dorothy did not pay the note to Reilly and Reilly sued Jeanette. Jeanette claimed that Reilly could not sue her because of Dorothy's promise and that in any case Reilly could not sue Jeanette until Reilly had attempted to collect the money from Dorothy. On the facts stated, is Jeanette liable?
4. Gertrude purchased cloth from Regal Fibres, Inc., on behalf of Twentieth Century Clothing Company, by whom Gertrude was employed. Gertrude informed Regal that she was acting for Twentieth Century and signed a promissory note for the purchase price of the cloth. The note stated "I promise to pay . . ." and was signed "Gertrude." Regal sold the note to the Commercial Finance Company. Commercial sued Gertrude on the note. She claimed that she was not liable because she had acted as agent for Twentieth Century and had so informed Regal Fibres. Is this a valid defense?
5. Adolph gave Sarah a note which promised to pay $10,000 to the order of Sarah when Adolph sold his house. Adolph thereafter sold his house and made a net profit of $40,000. Sarah sued Adolph on the note. Is the note negotiable?
6. Compare the obligation of a party to a contract and the obligation of a party to commercial paper.
7. Barbara executes a promissory note due in 60 days payable to the order of Arthur for $1,000 with 4% interest up to maturity and 6% interest after maturity. Barbara later claims that this note is not negotiable because it does not specify the exact amount of money which is to be paid and therefore does not satisfy the requirement of specifying a "sum certain." Is Barbara correct?
8. Nathan gave Larson the following instrument, dated July 6, 1983: One year after date I promise to pay to the order of Larson one thousand

dollars in United States Savings Bonds payable at Last Mortgage Bank. (signed) Nathan. Does this instrument qualify as a negotiable instrument?

9. Compare the liability of the acceptor of a draft with the liability of the maker of a note.

10. The Charter Bank of Gainesville had in its possession a note containing the following provision: "This note with interest is secured by a mortgage on real estate, of even date herewith, made by the maker hereof in favor of the said payee.... The terms of said mortgage are by this reference made a part hereof." When the bank sued on the note, the defendant raised the defense that the payee was guilty of fraud in obtaining the mortgage. The bank claimed to be a holder in due course. Is the bank a holder in due course? [Holly Hill Acres, Ltd. v Charter Bk. of Gainesville, (Fla App) 314 So2d 209]

11. Money was borrowed from a bank by a corporation. The president of the corporation negotiated the loan and signed the promissory note. On the first line he wrote the name of the corporation. On the second line he signed his own name. The note was negotiated by the lending bank to the Federal Reserve Bank. The note was not paid when due, and the Federal Reserve Bank sued the corporation and the president. The president raised the defense that he was not bound on the note because he did not intend to bind himself and because the money obtained by the loan was used by the corporation. Is the president liable on the note? [See Talley v Blake (La App) 322 So2d 877 (non-Code); Geer v Farquhar, 270 Or 642, 528 P2d 1335.]

12. B wished to pay a bill that he owed to C but did not have sufficient money in his bank. He drew a postdated check on his bank account and gave it to A. A then gave B a check drawn on A's bank account for the amount of B's check. When A was sued on his check by C, A claimed that he was an accommodation party. Was he correct? [Midtown Commercial Corp. v Keiner, 29 App Div 2d 349, 288 NYS2d 122]

13. A note was made by the Mid-South Building & Improvement Co., Inc. Cotten indorsed the note as an accommodation indorser. Later suit was brought on the note by Parker, the holder, against Mid-South Building and Cotten. Cotten raised the defense that when he indorsed the note he was not aware that he could be required to pay the note if it was not paid by Mid-South Building. Was this a valid defense? [Parker v Mid-South Building & Improvement Co. (Ala Civ App) 326 So2d 763]

14. Rinehart issues a check which satisfies all the requirements of negotiability. It is payable to the order of cash. Is the instrument payable to order or to bearer?

15. Is the following instrument negotiable?

> I, Richard Bell, hereby promise to pay to the order of Lorry Motors ten thousand dollars ($10,000) upon the receipt of the final distribution from the estate of my deceased aunt, Rita Dorn. This negotiable instrument is given by me as the down payment on my purchase of a 1986 Buick to be delivered in three weeks.
>
> Richard Bell (signature)

16. Smith has in his possession the following instrument.

September 1, 1986

I, Selma Ray, hereby promise to pay Helen Savit One Thousand Dollars ($1,000) one year after date. This instrument was given for the purchase of Two Hundred (200) shares of Redding Mining Corporation, Interest 6%.

Selma Ray (signature)

Smith purchased the instrument from Helen Savit at a substantial discount. Savit specializes in the sale of counterfeit stock. Selma Ray was one of her innocent victims. Smith is seeking to collect on the instrument. What are the rights of Smith against Ray on the instrument?

17. Master Homecraft Company received a promissory note with a stated face value from Mr. and Mrs. Zimmerman. The note was payment for remodeling of their home. The note contained unused blanks for installment payments. There was no maturity date. Master Homecraft sued the Zimmermans on the note. They argue that they should not be liable on the note because it is impossible to determine from its face the amount due or the date of maturity. Decide. [Master Homecraft Co. v Zimmerman, 208 Pa 401, 22 A2d 440]

CHAPTER 31

TRANSFER OF

COMMERCIAL PAPER

CHAPTER OBJECTIVES

After studying this chapter you will be able to:
1. List the types of indorsements and describe their respective uses.
2. Distinguish the effect of a transfer by assignment from that of a negotiation.
3. Explain the difference between negotiation of order paper and negotiation of bearer paper.
4. Determine the legal effect of forged and authorized indorsements.
5. Be familiar with the forged payee impostor exceptions.
6. List the indorser's warranties and describe their significance.
7. Solve problems involving the transfer of commercial paper.

Commercial paper may be transferred by negotiation or assignment. When the transfer is made by negotiation, the rights of the transferee may rise higher than those of the transferor, depending upon the circumstances attending the negotiation. When the transfer is made by assignment, the assignee has only those rights which the assignor possessed.

A. KINDS OF INDORSEMENTS

Some commercial paper may be transferred without an indorsement. An indorsement is required in other cases. If the transfer is made in the manner required by the Uniform Commercial Code, the transfer is called a negotiation and the transferee becomes a holder. If there is no negotiation, the transferee is merely an assignee.

The person to whom an instrument is payable either on its face or by indorsement or the person in possession of bearer paper may indorse it for the purpose of negotiating it by merely signing it, or may add certain words or statements as part of the indorsement. By definition, an indorsement is written on the back of an instrument.[1]

The transfer of ownership of commercial paper may be made as a gift. In most cases it will be made for value.

§ 31:1. Blank Indorsement.

When the indorser merely signs the paper, the indorsement is called a **blank indorsement** since it does not indicate the person to whom the instrument is to be paid, that is the indorsee. A person who is in possession of paper on which the last indorsement is blank is the holder and may sue thereon without proving ownership of the paper.

The holder of an instrument on which the last indorsement is blank may write above the blank indorsement a statement that the instrument is payable to that particular holder.[2] This is called "completing" the indorsement or "converting" the blank indorsement to a special indorsement by specifying the identity of the indorsee. It protects the holder because the paper cannot be negotiated thereafter without the indorsement and delivery of such holder.

Unless they otherwise agree, indorsers are liable to each other in the order in which they indorse, which is presumed to be the order in which their signatures appear on the paper.

Negotiation by a blank indorsement does four things: (1)it passes the ownership of the instrument; (2)it imposes upon the indorser certain warranties about the instrument; (3)it imposes upon the indorser a secondary liability to pay the amount of the instrument if the maker or drawer fails to do so and the holder of the instrument satisfies certain conditions; and (4)it changes the paper to bearer paper which may be negotiated by transfer of possession alone.

§ 31:2. Special Indorsement.

A **special indorsement** consists of the signature of the indorser and words specifying the person to whom the indorser makes the instrument payable, that is, the indorsee. Common forms of this type of indorsement are "Pay to the order of Robert Hicks, E.S. Flynn" and "Pay to Robert Hicks or order, E.S. Flynn." It is not necessary that the indorsement contain the words "order" or "bearer." Thus, a commercial paper indorsed in the form "Pay to Robert Hicks, E.S. Flynn" continues to be negotiable and may be negotiated further. In contrast, an instrument which on its face reads "Pay to E.S. Flynn" is not negotiable.

As in the case of the blank indorsement, a special indorsement transfers title to the instrument. It also results in the indorser making certain warranties about the instrument and imposes upon the indorser a secondary

[1]Lester v Groves, _____ Ga App _____, 291 SE2d 785 (1982).
[2]UCC §3-204(3).

BLANK INDORSEMENT   SPECIAL INDORSEMENT

liability to pay the amount of the instrument when certain requirements are satisfied. When the paper is so indorsed, it becomes order paper and may only be negotiated by an indorsement and delivery.

§ 31:3.   Qualified Indorsement.

A **qualified indorsement** is one that qualifies the effect of a blank or a special indorsement by disclaiming or destroying the liability of the indorser to answer for the default of the maker or drawee. This may be done by including the words "without recourse" in the body of the indorsement or by using any other words that indicate an intention to destroy the indorser's secondary liability for the default of the maker or drawee.[3]

The qualification of an indorsement does not affect the passage of title or the negotiable character of the paper. It merely disclaims the indorser's secondary liability for payment of the paper.

This form of indorsement is most commonly used when the qualified indorser is known to be a person who has no personal interest in the transaction, as in the case of an agent or an attorney who is merely indorsing to a principal or client a check of a third person made payable to the agent or attorney. Here the transferee recognizes that the transferor is not a party to the transaction and therefore should not be asked to vouch for the payment of the paper.

§ 31:4.   Restrictive Indorsements.

A **restrictive indorsement** specifies the purpose of the indorsement or the use to be made of the paper. An indorsement is restrictive when it includes words showing that the paper is to be deposited, as "for deposit," or is negotiated for collection, or to an agent or trustee, or the negotiation is conditional.[4]

Even though an instrument bears a restrictive indorsement, this indorsement is not effective to prevent further transfer or negotiation even though it expressly prohibits further transfer or negotiation.

If the restriction is in the form of a conditional indorsement, the holder may be a holder in due course subject only to the requirement that the

[3]Florida Coast Bank v Monarch Dodge (Fla App) 430 So2d 607 (1983).
[4]UCC §3-205.

Without recourse *Diana Morris*	*For deposit only* *E.L. Martin*

QUALIFIED INDORSEMENT   RESTRICTIVE INDORSEMENT

maker must pay only if the condition is fulfilled. For example, an instrument payable to the order of P is indorsed by P, "Pay Allen if X ship arrives at port before October 1." Allen indorsed the instrument to Beth. Beth cannot collect from the maker unless the X ship arrives at port before October 1. If the maker pays Beth, he may have to pay again to P, who indorsed restrictively.

A bank may ignore and is not affected by the restrictive indorsement of any person except the holder transferring the instrument to the bank or the person presenting it to the bank for payment. However, a *depositary bank,* that is, the one in which the customer deposits the item, and persons not in the bank collection process must recognize the restrictive indorsement to the extent of applying any value given in a manner consistent with the indorsement.[5]

§ 31:5.   Correction of Name by Indorsement.

Sometimes the name of the payee or indorsee of a commercial paper is improperly spelled. Thus, H.A. Price may receive a paycheck which improperly is payable to the order of "H.O. Price." If this was a clerical error and the check was intended for H. A. Price, the employee may ask the employer to write a new check payable in the proper name.

Instead of doing this, the payee or indorsee whose name is misspelled may indorse the wrong name, the correct name, or both. A person giving or paying value for the instrument may require both.[6]

This correction of name by indorsement may only be used when it was intended that the indorsement should be payable to the person making the corrective indorsement. If there were in fact two employees, one named H.A. Price and the other H.O. Price, it would be illegal as a forgery for one to take the check intended for the other and by indorsing it obtain the benefit of the proceeds of the check.

§ 31:6.   Bank Indorsements.

In order to simplify the transfer of commercial paper from one bank to another in the process of collecting items, "any agreed method which iden-tifies the transferor bank is sufficient for the item's further transfer to another

[5]Marine Midland Bank, N.A. v Prince 457 NYS2d 458, 443 NE2d 932 (1982).
[6]UCC §3-203.

bank."[7] Thus, a bank may indorse with its Federal Reserve System number instead of using its name.

Likewise, when a customer has deposited an instrument with a bank but has failed to indorse it, the bank may make an indorsement for the customer unless the instrument expressly requires the payee's personal indorsement. Furthermore, the mere stamping or marking on the item of any notation showing that it was deposited by the customer or credited to the customer's account is declared to be as effective as an indorsement by the customer would have been.[8]

B. NEGOTIATION OF COMMERCIAL PAPER

Negotiation is the transferring of commercial paper in such a way as to make the transferee the holder of the paper. This in turn is controlled by whether the paper is order paper or bearer paper.

§ 31:7.   Time for Determining Order or Bearer Character of Paper.

The order or bearer character of the paper is determined as of the time when the negotiation is about to take place, without regard to what it was originally or at any intermediate time. Accordingly, when the last indorsement is special, the paper is order paper without regard to whether it was bearer paper originally or at any intermediate time, and the holder cannot treat the paper as bearer paper merely because it had once been bearer paper.

§ 31:8.   Negotiation of Order Paper.

An instrument payable to order may be negotiated only by indorsement by the person to whom it is payable at that time and the delivery of the paper by such person. Indorsement and delivery may also be made by an authorized agent of the person to whom the paper is then payable.

(a) **Multiple Payees and Indorsees.** Ordinarily one person is named as the payee in the instrument, but two or more payees may be named. In that case, the instrument may specify that it is payable to any one or more of them or that it is payable to all jointly. If nothing is specified, the instrument is payable to all of the payees and they are **joint payees.** For example, if the instrument is made payable "to the order of A and B," the two persons named are joint payees. The indorsement of both A and B is required to negotiate the instrument.

If the instrument is payable to **alternate payees** or if it has been negotiated to alternate indorsees, as A or B, it may be indorsed and delivered by either of them.

(b) **Agent or Officer as Payee.** The instrument may be made payable to the order of an officeholder. For example, a check may read "Pay to the order of Receiver of Taxes." Such a check may be received and negotiated by the person who at the time is the Receiver of Taxes. This is a matter of con-

[7]UCC §4-206.
[8]UCC §4-205(1).

venience since the person writing the check is not required to find out the actual name of the Receiver of Taxes at that time.

If the instrument is drawn in favor of a person as "Cashier" or some other fiscal officer of a bank or corporation, it is prima facie payable to the bank or corporation of which such person is an officer, and may be negotiated by the indorsement of either the bank or the corporation, or of the named officer. If drawn in favor of an agent, it may similarly be negotiated by the agent or the agent's principal.[9]

(c) **Missing Indorsement.** Although order paper cannot be negotiated without indorsement, it can be assigned to another without indorsement. In such a case, the transferee has the same rights as the transferor; and if the transferee gave value for the paper, the transferee also has the right to require that the transferor indorse the instrument unqualifiedly and thereby effect a negotiation of the instrument.

When the transferor fails to indorse, the transferee may bring suit as an assignee and it is no defense to the obligor that there was no indorsement.

§ 31:9. Negotiation of Bearer Paper.

Any commercial paper payable to bearer may be negotiated by a mere transfer of possession. Thus, bearer paper is negotiated to a person taking possession of it, without regard to whether this was done with the consent of the owner of the paper.

The paper may be negotiated by a mere transfer of possession not only when the instrument expressly states that it is payable to bearer, but also when the law interprets it as being payable to bearer, as in the case of a check payable to the order of "Cash."

Although bearer paper may be negotiated by such transfer, the one to whom it is delivered may insist that the bearer indorse the paper so as to impose the liability of an indorser. This situation most commonly arises when a check payable to "Cash" is presented to a bank for payment.

§ 31:10. Forged and Unauthorized Indorsements.

A forged or unauthorized indorsement is by definition no indorsement of the person by whom it appears to have been made and, accordingly, the possessor of the paper is not the holder when the indorsement of that person was necessary for effective negotiation of the paper to the possessor.

If payment of commercial paper is made to one claiming under or through a forged indorsement, the payor is ordinarily liable to the person who is the rightful owner of the paper, unless such person is estopped or barred by negligence or other conduct from asserting any claim against the payor.

A forged or unauthorized indorsement may be ratified.[10] In that case, it is effective as though it had been genuine and authorized.

---

[9]UCC §3-117.
[10]American Travel Corp. v Central Carolina Bank & Trust Co. _____ NC App _____, 291 SE2d 892 (1982).

FACTS:

Eutsler forged his brother Richard's indorsement on certified checks and cashed them at the First National Bank. Richard sought to recover the funds from the bank. The bank stated that it would press criminal charges against his brother. Richard asked the bank to delay prosecution of his brother to give him time to collect directly from his brother. His brother promised to repay him the money but vanished some six months later without having paid any money. Richard sued the bank.

DECISION:

Judgment against Richard. Richard had ratified the forgery since he had asked the bank to take no action against his brother, had entered into a repayment agreement with his brother, and had waited too long before attempting to collect from the bank. [Eutsler v First National Bank, Pawhuska (Okla) 639 P2d 1245 (1982)]

§ 31:11. Impostor rule.

Ordinarily when the name of the payee is indorsed on commercial paper by a person who is not the payee nor the agent of the payee such indorsement is not effective to negotiate the paper to the person to whom it is delivered thereafter because the paper has not been indorsed and delivered by the person to whom it was then payable, namely the payee, nor by his authorized agent.

The Code makes exceptions to this general rule in three situations. In these situations, the unauthorized or forged character of the payee's signature is ignored as far as negotiation is concerned and the signature is given the same effect as though it had been authorized by the named payee: (a)an impostor has induced the maker or drawer to issue the instrument to the person whose identity has been assumed by the impostor, or to a confederate, in the name of that payee; (b)the person signing as, or on behalf of, the drawer intends that the named payee shall have no interest in the paper, or (c)an agent or employee of the drawer has given the drawer the named used as the payee, intending that the payee should not have any interest in the paper. These three exceptions are known as the **impostor rule**.[11]

The first situation is present when a person impersonates the holder of a savings account and, by presenting a forged withdrawal slip to the savings bank, gets the bank to issue a check payable to the bank's customer but which it hands to the impersonator in the belief that the impersonator is the customer. The second situation arises when the owner of a checking account, who wishes to conceal the true purpose of taking money from the bank, makes out a check purportedly in payment of a debt which in fact does not exist.

The last situation is illustrated by the case of the employee who fraudulently causes the employer to sign a check made to a customer or another person, whether existing or not, but the employee does not intend to send it

[11]UCC §3-405.

to that person but rather intends to forge the latter's indorsement, to cash the check, and to keep the money.

The impostor rule does not apply when there is a valid check to an actual creditor for a correct amount owed by the drawer and someone thereafter forges the payee's name, even though the forger is an employee of the drawer.

Even when the unauthorized indorsement of the payee's name is effective by virtue of the impostor rule, a person forging the payee's name is subject to civil and criminal liability for making such indorsement.

The impostor rule applies without regard to whether or not the drawee acted with reasonable care.

FACTS:

Two employees of the state of New Mexico fraudulently procured and endorsed a draft drawn against funds of the state made out to the Greater Mesilla Valley Sanitation District. There was no such sanitation district. The employees obtained payment of the draft from the Citizens Bank. Western Casualty, the state's insurer, reimbursed the state for its loss and then brought suit against the bank for negligently paying the draft. The bank claimed it was not liable because employees of the state supplied the fictitious name intending the payee to have no interest in the draft.

DECISION:

Judgment for the bank. The employees supplied the employer with the name of the payee, the fictitious sanitation district, intending the payee to have no interest in the instrument issued. By virtue of the impostor rule, the forged indorsement of the payee's name was effective to negotiate the paper and therefore the bank had acted properly in paying the draft when it was presented for payment. [Western Casualty & Surety Co. v Citizens Bank of Las Cruces (CA10 NM) 676 F2d 1344 (1982)]

---

§ 31:12.   Effect of Incapacity or Misconduct on Negotiation.

A negotiation is effective even though (a) it is made by a minor or any other person lacking capacity; (b) it is an act beyond the powers of a corporation; (c) it is obtained by fraud, duress, or mistake of any kind; (d) or the negotiation is part of an illegal transaction or was made in breach of duty. Under general principles of law apart from the UCC, the transferor in such cases may be able to set aside the negotiation or to obtain some other form of legal relief. If, however, the instrument has in the meantime been acquired by a holder in due course, the negotiation can no longer be set aside.

§ 31:13.   Lost Paper.

The effect of losing commercial paper depends upon who is suing or demanding payment from whom and whether the paper was order paper or bearer paper when it was lost. If the paper is order paper, the finder does not become the holder because the paper, by definition, is not indorsed and delivered by the person to whom it was then payable. The former holder who lost it is still the rightful owner of the paper, although technically not the holder because not in possession of the paper.

When a commercial paper is lost, it may be possible to have a new paper issued in its place. Thus, an employer may issue a new paycheck to replace the check lost by the employee. If the lost paper is a promissory note, it is less likely that the maker will oblige by executing a new promissory note. In any event, the owner of the lost paper may bring suit on it against any party liable thereon.

FACTS:

Sommer delivered a check to Kraft. The bank on which the check was drawn refused to pay it and Kraft sued Sommer. The original check had been lost; however, Kraft had a copy. Sommer claimed that suit could not be brought on the copy and that Kraft was required to reproduce the original.

DECISION:

Kraft could bring suit on the copy without producing the original. The fact that commercial paper is lost, stolen, or destroyed, does not terminate the right of the holder of the paper to recover payment as long as the terms of the paper can be proven. The copy of the check produced by Kraft was sufficient to prove the terms of the original check and therefore payment could be enforced according to its terms. [Kraft v Sommer 54 App Div 598, 387 NYS2d 318 (1976)]

There is of course, the practical difficulty of proving just what the lost paper provided and explaining the loss of the paper. The court may also require that the plaintiff suing on the lost instrument furnish the defendant with security to indemnify the defendant against loss by reason of any claim which might thereafter be made on the lost instrument.[12]

If the paper is in bearer form when it is lost, the finder, as the possessor of bearer paper, is the holder, and is entitled to enforce payment.

C. ASSIGNMENT OF COMMERCIAL PAPER

Although commercial paper may be negotiated, it may also be assigned. The assignment may result from the act of the parties or by operation of law.

§ 31:14.   Assignment by Act of the Parties.

Commercial paper may be assigned in the same manner as any other contract right by the express act of the holder. A commercial paper is also regarded as assigned when a person whose indorsement is required to negotiate the instrument transfers it without indorsing it.

[12]UCC §3-804.

FACTS:

Roberts issued a promissory note payable to the order of Baines. Baines handed this note over to Duxbury. Baines also gave him a separate paper in which Baines stated that the note was being transferred to Duxbury. When Duxbury sued Roberts, he contended that he was not liable because Duxbury was not the holder of the paper.

DECISION:

Judgment for Duxbury. Roberts was correct in contending that Duxbury was not the holder. This was so because the paper was order paper and required the indorsement of Duxbury in order to negotiate the paper so as to make the transferee the holder. This had not been done. Therefore, Baines was not the holder. However, the transaction was effective to transfer or assign to Duxbury whatever rights were held by Baines. Therefore, Duxbury as assignee, could sue Roberts. [Duxbury v Roberts, 388 Mass 385, 446 NE2d 401 (1983)]

When a necessary indorsement is missing, the transferee has only the rights of an assignee. If the transferee acquires the paper for value, the transferee is entitled, however, to require that the transferor indorse the instrument.[13] If the indorsement is obtained, then the transferee is deemed a holder but only as of the time when the indorsement is made.

§ 31:15.   Assignment by Operation of Law.

An assignment by operation of law occurs when by virtue of the law the title of one person to commercial paper is vested in another. For example, if the holder of a commercial paper becomes bankrupt or dies, the title to the instrument vests automatically in the trustee in bankruptcy or in the personal representative of the decedent's estate.

D. WARRANTIES OF TRANSFEROR

When commercial paper is transferred, the transferor ordinarily makes certain implied warranties. When an instrument is transferred in exchange for value, the transaction is similar in some respects to a sale of merchandise. In the case of a sale of merchandise, certain warranties as to title, description, and quality arise, which, if breached, give the buyer a cause of action against the seller. The transferor of commercial paper, by the act of making the transfer, warrants the existence of certain facts. These warranties vary according to whether the instrument is transferred with or without an indorsement and according to the nature of the indorsement.

§ 31:16.   Warranties of Unqualified Indorser.

When the holder of a commercial paper negotiates it by an unqualified indorsement, and receives consideration, the transferor warrants:

[13]UCC §3-201(3).

(1) **Ownership of good title, which in cludes the genuineness of all indorsements necessary to title to the instrument, or authorization to act for one who has such good title.** For example, Rita makes a note payable to the order of Bob. The note is stolen and the thief forges Bob's signature on the back of the note, making it payable to the order of Lawten. Lawten, without knowledge of the forged indorsement, transfers and indorses the note to Selma for value. Selma could not recover from the maker since she did not have good title. Selma, however, can sue Lawten for breach of warranty of good title because a necessary signature (Bob's) was not genuine.

(2) **The act of transferring the instrument is rightful, independent of the question of title or authority to act.** For example, if a payee of a note breaches a contract with the maker to hold the note until certain goods are shipped by transferring the note before the goods are shipped, the transfer is not rightful and the payee becomes liable to the transferee for any loss occasioned by the early transfer of the note.

(3) **The signatures on the instrument are genuine or executed by authorized agents.**

(4) **The instrument has not been materially altered.**

(5) **The indorser has no knowledge of the existence or commencement of any insolvency proceeding against the maker or acceptor of the instrument, or against the drawer of an unaccepted draft or bill of exchange.**

(6) **No defense of any party is good as against the indorser.**

These warranties made by the unqualified indorser pass to the transferee and to any subsequent holder who acquires the instrument in good faith.[14]

When the holder presents a check to the drawee bank for payment, the holder's indorsement of the check does not give rise to any warranty that the account of the drawer in the drawee bank contains funds sufficient to cover the check.

§ 31:17.   Warranties of Other Parties.

Warranties are also made by the indorser who indorses "without recourse" and by one who transfers by delivery only.

(a) **Qualified Indorser.** The warranty liability of the indorser who indorses "without recourse" is the same as the unqualified indorser with one difference. The warranty as to "no defenses" (6)is limited to a warranty that the indorser does not have knowledge of any defense rather than that no defense exists.[15] The warranties of a qualified indorser run to the same persons as those of an unqualified indorser.

(b) **Transferor by Delivery.** The warranties made by one who transfers a commercial paper by delivery are the same as those made by an unqualified indorser except that they run only to the immediate transferee and

---

[14]UCC §3-417(2).
[15]UCC §3-417(3). The qualified indorsement does not exclude other warranties unless it is specified to be "without warranties."

then only if consideration has been given for the transfer.[16] Subsequent holders cannot enforce such warranties against this prior transferor by delivery regardless of the character of such holders.

SUMMARY

Commercial paper may be transferred by negotiation or assignment. If an instrument is negotiated, the rights of the transferee may rise higher than those of the transferor; if an instrument is assigned, the assignee has only those rights which the assignor had.

There are a number of different kinds of indorsements which can be made on commercial paper. When an indorser merely signs the paper, the indorsement is called a blank indorsement. If the last indorsement is a blank indorsement, it changes the paper to bearer paper which may be negotiated by transfer of possession alone. A special indorsement consists of the signature of the indorser and words specifying the person to whom the indorser makes the instrument payable. If the last indorsement is a special indorsement, it changes the paper to order paper and may only be negotiated by an indorsement and delivery. A qualified indorsement destroys the liability of the indorser to answer for the default of the maker or drawee. A restrictive indorsement specifies the purpose of the indorsement or the use to be made of the paper.

Negotiation is the transfer of commercial paper in such a way as to make the transferee the holder of the paper. Order paper is negotiated by an indorsement and a delivery. Bearer paper is negotiated by transfer of possession.

A forged or unauthorized indorsement is no indorsement and the possessor of the paper cannot be a holder. The Code makes exceptions to this general rule in three situations and the indorsement is given the same effect as though it had been authorized by the named payee: (1)an impostor has induced the maker or drawer to issue the instrument to the person whose identity has been assumed by the impostor, (2)the person signing on behalf of the drawer intends that the named payee shall have no interest in the paper, or (3)an agent or employee of the drawer has given the drawer the name used as the payee, intending that the payee should not have any interest in the paper.

A negotiation is effective even though: (1)it is made by a minor, (2)it is an act beyond the powers of a corporation, (3)it is obtained by fraud, or (4)the negotiation is part of an illegal transaction. The transferor may be able to set aside the negotiation.

An indorser who negotiates by an unqualified indorsement and receives consideration makes the following warranties: (1)ownership of good title, (2) transfer is rightful, (3) all the signatures are genuine, (4) the instrument has not been materially altered, (5) the indorser has no knowledge of any insolvency proceeding against the maker or drawer, and (6) no defense of any party is good against the indorser. A transferor indorsing with a qualified indorsement warrants only that the transferor has no knowledge of any defense rather than that no defense exists. A transferor who does not indorse the instrument makes these warranties only to the immediate transferee.

[16]UCC §3-417(2).

QUESTIONS AND CASE PROBLEMS

1. What social forces are affected by the law as to qualified indorsements?

2. As soon as Bertha gets her weekly paycheck, she carefully writes her name on the back so that everyone will know that it is her check. Is Bertha protected by doing this?

3. Allan pays Bestor the $100 which Allan owes Bestor with a check stating "pay to the order of Bestor $100." How can Bestor transfer this check to Wickard in such a way as to make Wickard the holder of the check?

4. Higgins owes the Packard Appliance store $100. He mails a check to Packard. The check is drawn on the First National Bank and states "pay to the order of cash $100." This check is stapled to a letter stating that the $100 is in payment of the debt owed by Higgins. Edward is employed by Packard in the mailroom. Edward removes the letter from its envelope, detaches the check, and disappears and no one knows what becomes of the check until it is presented at the First National Bank by a person identifying himself as Howard. The bank pays this person $100 and debits that amount against the account of Higgins. Higgins protests that this cannot be done because the check was lost and never belonged to Howard. Is Higgins correct?

5. When the holder presents a check to the drawee bank for payment, does an indorsement of the check give rise to any warranty that the account of the drawer in the drawee bank is sufficient to cover the check?

6. Compare the status of the finder of a lost watch and the finder of a lost check.

7. How can a blank indorsement be converted to a special indorsement?

8. Harriet, the assistant to the controller of a general partnership, told the controller that the firm owed Richards $750. Richards was a fictitious person, but relying upon Harriet's statement, the controller signed the partnership's name to a check. Harriet indorsed the check on its back, signing the name "Richards," and cashed it at a liquor store. Hudson Bank charged the partnership's account for the $750 and returned it with the rest of the checks for the month. Subsequently, the fraudulent conduct of Harriet was discovered by the partnership's auditors. Must the Hudson Bank recredit the partnership's account with $750?

9. Mildred paid her rent by indorsing to Parker, her landlord, a check payable to the order of Mildred. The check appeared to have been drawn by McCoy. Actually the signature of McCoy was a forgery. The check is indorsed by Parker with only his name and delivered by him to Ralph, a roofer who had repaired the roof. Ralph delivers the check without any indorsement to the Ruane Supply Company, the supply house from which he purchased the roofing materials. Ruane transfers the check without indorsement to the Metropolitan Manufacturing Company which manufactured the supplies sold to the supply house. Metropolitan presents the check to the bank. The bank refuses to pay the check. Metropolitan demands payment from McCoy. McCoy refuses to pay because the check is a forgery. Metropolitan then sues Ralph for breach of warranty. Is Ralph liable?

10. A check given in settlement of a lawsuit was drawn to the order of "A, attorney for B." Could A negotiate the check? [Maber, Inc. v Factor Cab Corp. 19 App Div 2d 500, 244 NYS2d 768]

11. Benton, as agent for Savidge, received an insurance settlement check from the Metropolitan Life Insurance Co. He indorsed it "For deposit" and deposited it in the Bryn Mawr Trust Company in the account of Savidge. What was the nature and effect of this indorsement? [Savidge v Metropolitan Life Insurance Co. 380 Pa 205, 110 A2d 730]

12. Humphrey drew a check for $100. It was stolen and the payee's name forged as an indorser. The check was then negotiated to Miller who had no knowledge of these facts. Miller indorsed the check to the Citizens Bank. Payment of the check was voided on the ground of the forgery. The Citizens Bank then sued Miller as indorser. Decide. [Citizens Bank of Hattiesburg v Miller, 194 Miss 557, 11 So2d 457]

13. When claims filed with the insurance company were approved for payment, they were given to the claims clerk who would prepare checks to pay those claims and then give the checks to the treasurer to sign. The claims clerk of the insurance company made a number of checks payable to persons who did not have any claims, gave them to the treasurer together with the checks for valid claims, and the treasurer signed all the checks. The claims clerk then removed the false checks, indorsed them with the names of their respective payees, and cashed them at the bank where the insurance company had its account. The bank debited the account of the insurance company with the amount of these checks. The insurance company claimed that the bank could not do this because the indorsements on the checks were forgeries. Is the insurance company correct? [General Acci. Fire & Life Assur. Corp. v Citizens Fidelity Bank & Trust Co. (Ky) 519 SW2d 817.]

14. Vance issued a negotiable promissory note payable to the order of Adams. Adams transferred by delivery this note for value and before maturity to Martha. Was this a proper negotiation by Adams to Martha?

15. Jerry Waters and his wife Patsy were not getting along well. Patsy commenced a divorce proceeding against Jerry. As a result of the proceeding, Patsy received a property settlement. Under the terms of the settlement, it was agreed that a demand note signed by Jerry and payable to the order of Patsy's father should be transferred to Patsy in the future. Her father delivered the note to her but did not indorse the paper or write anything on the note. Upon the death of her father, Patsy sued her former husband on the note. Jerry refused to pay, alleging that she could not sue as she was not the owner of the note. Decide. [Waters v Waters (Tex Civ App) 498 SW2d 236]

16. Fisher wanted to have his house painted. His father wrote out a check to the order of Fisher for $200 as a down payment for the painting. Fisher then made a contract with Denny to paint the house. For the down payment on this contract he took his father's check and indorsed on it "Pay to Denny upon condition of the proper painting of my home at 510 N. Maine St., Jonesville." He then delivered the check to Denny. Could Denny cash the check before he completed the painting work?

17. Anita received a check drawn by Charney and payable to Cash. She transferred the check to Gunter without indorsing it. Charney contended that Gunter held the instrument merely as an assignee. Do you agree?

CHAPTER 32

RIGHTS OF HOLDERS AND

DEFENSES

CHAPTER OBJECTIVES

After studying this chapter you will be able to:
1. Distinguish between an ordinary holder and a favored holder.
2. List the requirements to become a holder in due course.
3. Explain the rights of a holder through a holder in due course.
4. List and explain the limited defenses not available against a holder in due course.
5. List and explain the universal defenses available against all holders.
6. Describe how the rights of a holder in due course have been limited by the Federal Trade Commission.
7. Solve problems involving favored holders.

Commercial paper litigation may arise between the original parties to the instrument or, where commercial paper has been negotiated to a favored holder, may arise between the maker or drawer and a holder in due course. When the original parties are involved, ordinary contract defenses such as failure of consideration may be asserted. When the instrument has left the hands of the payee and has been negotiated to a holder in due course, such holder will take the instrument free from many types of claims which might be asserted by a party to the instrument.

A. KINDS OF HOLDERS

When a commercial paper is negotiated to a person, that person is the holder: either an ordinary holder or a favored holder.

§ 32:1. Ordinary Holders and Assignees.

Any holder has all the rights relating to the paper. The holder, although an ordinary holder, is the only person who may demand payment, or bring suit for the collection of the paper, or give a discharge or release from liability on the paper, or cancel the liability of another party to the paper.

When the holder sues on the paper, it is only required that the holder produce the paper in court and show that the signature of the defendant is genuine. If that is done and there is no evidence of a defense, the holder is entitled to a judgment for the full face amount of the paper.

FACTS:

Halleck executed a promissory note payable to the order of Leopold. Halleck did not pay the note when due and Leopold brought suit on the note. Leopold produced the note in court. Halleck admitted that he had signed the note but claimed that the plaintiff was required to prove that the note had been issued for consideration, and that the plaintiff was in fact the holder.

DECISION:

The plaintiff had made out a prima facie case by producing the paper in court and establishing that it was signed by the defendant. It was not necessary that the plaintiff prove anything else. To the contrary, the defendant had the burden of proving the existence of a defense against the plaintiff's right to recover on the paper. [Leopold v Halleck, 106 Ill App 3d 386, 62 Ill Dec 447, 436 NE2d 29 (1982)].

The holder may generally sue any one or more prior parties on the paper without regard to the order in which such persons signed the paper or the order in which such persons may be liable to each other.

The fact that the holder is merely an ordinary holder has no significance if the defendant does not have any defense.

The assignee of a commercial paper is in the same position and has the same rights as an ordinary holder. It is immaterial whether the person is an assignee by express assignment, by operation of law, or in consequence of the omission of an essential indorsement.

§ 32:2. Favored Holders.

The law gives certain holders of commercial paper a preferred standing by protecting them from certain defenses when they sue to collect payment. This protection is given in order to make commercial paper more attractive by giving the favored holder an immunity not possessed by an ordinary holder or an assignee. The favored holders are known as the **holder in due course**, and a **holder through a holder in due course**.

(a) **Holders in Due Course.** In order to have the preferred status of a holder in due course, a person must first be a holder. This means that the possessor of the paper must have acquired it by proper negotiation. That is, the person in question must be the possessor of bearer paper or must be the possessor of order paper which is then payable to that person as payee or indorsee.[1]

Secondly, the holder must have acquired the paper "in due course." The concept may be better understood if modern terminology is substituted and "due course" is thought of as a regular, normal business routine. That is, the law protects persons taking the commercial paper as part of a regular, normal business routine—in due course.

In addition to being a holder, the holder in due course must meet certain conditions that pertain to (1) value, (2) good faith, (3) ignorance of paper overdue or dishonored, and (4) ignorance of defenses and adverse claims.[2]

(1) Value. Since the law of commercial paper is fundamentally a merchant's or business person's law, it favors only the holders who have given value for the paper. For example, since a legatee under a will does not give value, a person receiving bonds as a legacy is not a holder in due course. When value is given, the courts do not measure or appraise the value given.

A person takes an instrument for value (1) by performing the act for which the instrument was given, such as delivering the goods for which the check was sent in payment; (2) by acquiring a security interest in the paper, as when it has been pledged as security for another obligation; or (3) by taking the instrument in payment of, or as security for a debt.[3]

A promise not yet performed, although sufficient as consideration for a contract, ordinarily does not constitute value to satisfy this requirement for a holder in due course.[4]

A bank does not give value for a deposited check when it credits the depositor's account with the amount of the deposit. The bank gives value to the extent that the depositor withdraws money against that credit.

(2) Good Faith. The element of good faith requires that the taker of commercial paper act honestly in the acquisition of the instrument. Bad faith may sometimes be indicated by the small value given. This does not mean that the transferee must give full value, but it does mean that a gross inadequacy of consideration may be evidence of bad faith. Bad faith is established by proof that the transferee had knowledge of such facts as rendered it improper to acquire the instrument under the circumstances.

If the transferee takes the instrument in good faith, it is immaterial whether the transferor acted in good faith. The fact that a transferee acted carelessly does not establish that it acted in bad faith.[5]

---

[1]Although it is an uncommon occurrence, the original payee may also be a holder in due course provided the necessary elements are satisfied. UCC §3-302(2).

[2]In a few special cases, a purchaser of commercial paper will not be considered a holder in due course even though all the elements of being a holder have been satisfied. This is true when the sales are not of an ordinary commercial nature, such as when paper is acquired by judicial sale, sale of the assets of an estate, or a bulk sale not in the regular course of business of the transferor. UCC §3-302(3).

[3]UCC §3-303. It is also provided that there is a taking for value when another commercial paper is given in exchange or when the taker makes an irrevocable commitment to a third person as by providing a letter of credit, UCC §3-303(c).

[4]Sea Air Support, Inc. v Herrmann, 96 Nev 574, 613 P2d 413 (1980).

[5]Funding Consultants, Inc. v Aetna Casualty and Surety Co. 187 Conn 637, 447 A2d 1163 (1982).

FACTS:

The Angelinis made a contract for substantial home repairs with Lustro Aluminum Products and signed a promissory note for the contract price. The contract specified that payments were not due until 60 days after completion of the work. Ten days later, Lustro transferred the note and the contract to General Investment Corp. General knew from prior dealing with Lustro that the 60 day provision was typical of Lustro's contracts. Lustro's indorsement on the note warranted that the work had been completed. The work in fact was never completed, and the Angelinis raised this defense when sued on the note by General. General, claiming that it was a holder in due course, contended that its failure to have inquired of the Angelinis whether the work was completed was immaterial.

DECISION:

The failure to inquire of the Angelinis constituted bad faith under the circumstances, for it justified the conclusion that General was willfully seeking to avoid learning the facts that an inquiry would have disclosed. Since General knew that payment was not due until 60 days after completion and that the work was substantial, it was bad faith for it to accept the contractor's warranty that the work had been completed when it could have readily obtained a completion certificate from the Angelinis if the work had in fact been completed. [General Investment Corp. v Di Angelini, 58 NJ 396, 278 A2d 193 (1971)]

(3) Ignorance of Paper Overdue or Dishonored. Commercial paper may be negotiated even though (1) it has been dishonored, whether by nonacceptance or nonpayment; or (2) the paper is overdue, whether because of lapse of time or the acceleration of the due date; or (3) it is demand paper that has been outstanding more than a reasonable time. In other words, ownership may still be transferred. Nevertheless, the fact that the paper is circulating at a late date or after it has been dishonored is a suspicious circumstance that is deemed to put the person acquiring the paper on notice that there is some adverse claim or defense. A person who acquires title to the paper under such circumstances therefore cannot be a holder in due course.

(4) Ignorance of Defenses and Adverse Claims. Prior parties on the paper may have defenses which they could raise if sued by the person with whom they dealt. For example, the drawer of a check, if sued by the payee, might have the defense that the merchandise delivered by the payee was defective. In addition to defenses, third persons, whether prior parties or not, may be able to assert that the instrument belongs to them and not to the possessor. A person who acquires the commercial paper with notice or knowledge that any party might have a defense or that there is any adverse claim to the ownership of the instrument cannot be a holder in due course. Thus, the holder of commercial paper cannot be a holder in due course when the holder acquired the paper with knowledge that there had been a failure of consideration with respect to the contract for which the paper had been given.

Knowledge acquired by the taker after acquiring the paper does not prevent the taker from being a holder in due course. Consequently, the fact that the payee, after acquiring the paper, learns of a defense, does not operate retroactively to destroy the payee's character as a holder in due course.

FACTS:

Statham drew a check. The payee indorsed it to the Kemp Motor Sales. Statham then stopped payment on the check on the ground that there was a failure of consideration for the check. Kemp sued Statham on the check. When Statham raised the defense of failure of consideration, Kemp replied that it was a holder in due course. Statham claimed that Kemp could not recover because it learned of his defense before it deposited the check in its bank account.

DECISION:

Kemp was a holder in due course. The knowledge acquired by it after acquiring the check had no effect on its status. The fact that it learned of the defense before it deposited the check in its account or did anything to collect the check was immaterial. [Kemp Motor Sales v Statham, 120 Ga App 515, 171 SE2d 389 (1969)]

Knowledge of certain facts constitutes notice to the person acquiring a commercial paper that there is a defense or an adverse claim. The holder or purchaser of the paper is deemed to have notice of a claim or defense (1)if the instrument is so incomplete, bears such visible evidence of forgery or alteration, or is otherwise so irregular as to call into question its validity, terms, or ownership, or to create an ambiguity as to the party who is required to pay; or (2)if the purchaser has notice that the obligation of any party is voidable in whole or in part, or that all parties to the paper have been discharged.[6] For example, if the subsequent holder knows that a note given for home improvement work in fact covers both the improvements and a loan and that the transaction is usurious because excessive costs were charged for the work to conceal the usurious interest, the subsequent holder is not a holder in due course.

In general, a holder who has knowledge of such facts as would put a reasonable person upon inquiry is deemed to have knowledge of the facts which would be learned if such inquiry were made.

The purchaser of commercial paper does not have notice of a defense which bars such purchaser from being a holder in due course merely because the purchaser knows that the instrument is antedated or postdated; that any person has signed for accommodation; that an incomplete instrument has been completed, unless the purchaser has notice of any improper completion; that there was a negotiation by a fiduciary unless the purchaser had knowledge that the fiduciary is breaching a duty; or that there is a default in payment of interest on the instrument.[7]

FACTS:

An employee of Epicycle cashed his final payroll check at Money Mart Check Cashing Center. Epicycle had issued a stop payment order on the check. Money Mart deposited the check through normal banking channels. The check was returned to Money Mart marked "Payment Stopped." Money Mart brought an

[6]UCC §3-304(1).
[7]UCC §3-304.

action against Epicycle claiming that, as a holder in due course, it was entitled to recover against Epicycle. Epicycle argued that Money Mart could not be a holder in course because it failed to verify the check as good prior to cashing it.

DECISION:
Judgment for Money Mart. Where an instrument is regular on its face there is no duty to inquire as to possible defenses unless the circumstances of which the holder has knowledge are of such a nature that failure to inquire reveals a deliberate desire to evade knowledge because of a fear that investigation would disclose the existence of a defense. There is nothing in using a check-cashing service instead of a bank that would lead to a rule imposing different standards on the two kinds of institutions. [Money Mart Check Cashing Center Inc. v Epicycle Corporation, ____ Colo ____, 667 P2d 1372 (1983)]

(b) Holder Through a Holder in Due Course. Those persons who become holders of the instrument after a holder in due course are given the same protection as the holder in due course provided they are not parties to fraud or illegality that would affect the instrument.

This means that if an instrument is negotiated from A to B to C to D and B is a holder in due course, both C and D will enjoy the same rights as B. If C received the instrument as a gift or with knowledge of failure of consideration or other defense, or if D took the instrument after maturity, they could not themselves be holders in due course. Nevertheless, they are given the same protection as a holder in due course because they took the instrument through such a holder, namely, B. It is not only C, the person taking directly from B, but also D, who is given this extra protection.

B. DEFENSES

The importance of being a holder in due course or a holder through a holder in due course is that those holders are not subject to certain defenses when they demand payment or bring suit upon a commercial paper. These may be described as **limited defenses.** Another class of defenses, **universal defenses,** may be asserted against any plaintiff, whether the party is an assignee, an ordinary holder, a holder in due course, or holder through holder in due course.

§ 32:3. Defenses Available Against an Ordinary Holder.

A holder who is neither a holder in due course nor a holder through a holder in due course is subject to every defense just as though the instrument were not negotiable. Thus an ordinary holder suing on the promissory note of the buyer is subject to the latter's defense of breach of warranty.[8]

§ 32:4. Limited Defenses Not Available Against a Holder in Due Course.

Neither a holder in due course nor one having the rights of such a holder is subject to any of the following defenses.[9] They are limited defenses.

[8]Canam Hambro Systems, Inc. v Horback, 33 Wash App 452, 655 P2d 1182 (1982)
[9]UCC §3-305.

These defenses are also barred with respect to any instrument that is executed to renew or extend the original instrument.

(a) **Ordinary Contract Defenses.** In general terms, the defenses that could be raised against a suit on an ordinary contract cannot be raised against a holder in due course. Such a holder is not subject to defenses based on defects in the underlying contract. Accordingly, the defendant cannot assert against the holder in due course the defense of lack, failure, or illegality of consideration with respect to the transaction between the defendant and the person with whom the defendant dealt.

(b) **Incapacity of Defendant.** The incapacity of the defendant may not be raised against a holder in due course unless by general principles of law that incapacity, such as insanity of a person for whom a guardian has been appointed by a court, makes the instrument a nullity.[10]

(c) **Fraud in the Inducement.** When a person knowingly executes commercial paper and knows its essential terms but is persuaded or induced to execute it because of false statements or representations, such fraud cannot be raised against a holder in due course nor a holder through a holder in due course. As an illustration, M is persuaded to purchase an automobile because of P's statements concerning its condition. M gives P a note, which is negotiated until it reaches H, who is a holder in due course. M meanwhile learns that the car is not as represented and that P's statements were fraudulent. When H demands payment of the note, M cannot refuse to pay on the ground of P's fraud. M must pay the note and then recover the loss from P.

(d) **Prior Payment or Cancellation.** When a commercial paper is paid, the person making the payment should demand the surrender of the instrument. If this is not done, it is possible for the holder to continue to negotiate it. Another person may thus become the holder of the instrument. When the new holder demands payment of the instrument, the defense cannot be raised that payment had been made to a former holder if the new holder is a holder in due course. The fact that the person making the payment obtained a receipt from the former holder does not affect the application of this principle.

When the holder and the party primarily liable have agreed to cancel the instrument but the face of the instrument does not show any sign of cancellation, the defense of cancellation cannot be asserted against a holder in due course. Similarly, an order to stop payment of a check cannot be raised as a defense by the drawer of a check against a holder in due course.

(e) **Nondelivery of an Instrument.** A person may write out a commercial paper or indorse an existing paper and leave it on a desk for future delivery. At that moment, the instrument or the indorsement is not effective because there has been no delivery.

Assume that through the negligence of an employee or through the theft of the instrument, it comes into the hands of another person. If the instrument is in such form that it can be negotiated, as when it is payable to bearer, a subsequent receiver of the instrument may be a holder in due course

[10]UCC §3-305(2)(b)

or a holder through a holder in due course. As against that holder, the person who wrote the instrument or indorsed it cannot defend on the ground that there had been no delivery.

(f) Conditional or Specified Purpose Delivery. As against a favored holder, a person who would be liable on the instrument cannot show that the instrument which is absolute on its face was in fact delivered subject to a condition that had not been performed, or that it was delivered for a particular purpose but was not so used. Assume *A* makes out a check to the order of *B* and hands it to *C* with the understanding that *C* shall not deliver the check to *B* until *B* delivers certain merchandise. If *C* should deliver the check to *B* before the condition is satisfied and *B* then negotiates the check, a holder in due course or a holder through a holder in due course may enforce the instrument.

(g) Duress Consisting of Threats. The defense that a person signed or executed a commercial paper under threats of harm or violence may not be raised as a defense against a holder in due course when the effect of such duress is merely to make the contract voidable at the election of the victim of the duress.

(h) Unauthorized Completion. If a maker or drawer signs a commercial paper and leaves blank the name of the payee, or the amount, or any other term, and then hands the instrument to another to be completed, the defense of an improper completion cannot be raised when payment is demanded or suit brought by a subsequent holder in due course or a holder through a holder in due course. For example, Fulton gave Perry a note duly executed except for the amount. Fulton gave Perry authority to fill in an amount not to exceed $300. Perry filled in the note for $500. If Perry had negotiated the instrument to a holder in due course, the instrument could have been enforced as completed.[11]

FACTS:

Tibbs had a long course of dealings with Virginia Capital Bank and with James Mathews, president of Mathews General Insurance Corporation. Tibbs would purchase business insurance through Mathews and borrow money from the bank to finance the premiums. Tibbs customarily signed, in blank, promissory notes on the bank's forms and delivered them to Mathews. Mathews would fill in the notes for the amount of the premiums after informing Tibbs of the amount and deliver the notes to the bank. The bank would then advance the money for the premiums to Mathews and Tibbs would pay the notes when due. On a recent note, Mathews told Tibbs that the note would cover a premium of $960, and Tibbs signed it in blank as usual. Without Tibbs' knowledge, Mathews filled in the note in the amount of $9,600. Mathews added the indorsement of his corporation, presented the note to the bank, and received the proceeds. Tibbs made some payments on the note, but then realized that they were excessive and refused to make further payments. The bank claimed that as a holder in due course it could collect the full amount.

[11]UCC §3-407(3).

DECISION:

Judgment for the Virginia Bank. When an incomplete instrument has been completed contrary to authority, a holder in due course may enforce it as completed. The bank accepted it in good faith and without any notice of the unauthorized completion. [Virginia Capital Bank v Aetna Casualty & Surety Company (Va) 343 SE2d 81 (1986)]

(i) Theft. As a matter of definition, a holder in due course will not have acquired the paper through theft and any defense of theft therefore must relate to the conduct of a prior party. Assuming that the theft of the paper does not result in a defect in the chain of necessary indorsements, the defense that the instrument has been stolen cannot be raised against a holder in due course.[12]

§ 32:5.   Universal Defenses Available Against All Holders.

Certain defenses are regarded as so basic that the social interest in preserving them outweighs the social interest of giving commercial paper the freepassing qualities of money. Accordingly, such defenses are given universal effect and may be raised against all holders, whether ordinary holders, holders in due course, or holders through a holder in due course. Such defenses are therefore appropriately called universal defenses.

(a) Fraud as to the Nature or Essential Terms of the Paper. The fact that a person signs a commercial paper because fraudulently deceived as to its nature or essential terms is a defense available against all holders. This is the situation when an experienced business person induces an illiterate person to sign a note by falsely representing that it is a contract for repairs or by representing that it is a character reference. This defense, however, cannot be raised when it is the negligence of the defending party that prevented learning the true nature and terms of the instrument.

FACTS:

Estepp borrowed money from the United Bank and Trust Company. He signed a promissory note and in order to induce the bank to make the loan, Estepp had Schaeffer sign as an accommodation maker. Estepp was Schaeffer's supervisor at the country club where they both worked and they were friends. Schaeffer could not read and Estepp told him that the paper which Schaeffer was signing was a character reference. When the note was not paid, the bank sued Schaeffer who raised the defense of fraud. The bank claimed that this defense was not available against it since it did not perpetrate the fraud.

DECISION:

Judgment for Schaeffer. The fraud prevented Schaeffer from knowing what he was signing. This is fraud as to the nature of the instrument and may be raised against any holder without regard to who committed the fraud. Schaeffer was therefore not liable on the note. [Schaeffer v United Bank and Trust Company, 32 Md App 329, 360 A2d 461 (1976)]

---

[12]UCC §3-305(1).

(b) Forgery or Lack of Authority. The defense that a signature was forged or signed without authority may be raised against any holder unless the person whose name was signed has ratified it or is estopped by conduct or negligence from denying it.[13]

The fact that the drawer may have been lax and unbusinesslike in issuing the check to a named payee does not bar raising the defense of forgery.

(c) Duress Depriving Control. When a person executes or indorses a commercial paper in response to a force of such a nature that under general principles of law there is duress which makes the transaction a nullity, rather than merely voidable, such duress may be raised as a defense against any holder.

(d) Incapacity. The fact that the defendant is a minor, who under general principles of contract law may avoid the obligation, is a matter that may be raised against any kind of holder. Other kinds of incapacity may only be raised as a defense if the effect of the incapacity is to make the instrument a nullity.

(e) Illegality. If the law declares that an instrument is void when executed in connection with certain conduct, such as gambling or usury, that defense may be raised against any holder. Similarly, when contracts of a corporate seller are a nullity because its charter has been forfeited for non-payment of taxes, a promissory note given to it by a buyer is void and that defense may be raised as against a holder in due course. If the law merely makes the transaction illegal but does not make the instrument void, the defense cannot be asserted against a holder in due course or a holder through a holder in due course.

FACTS:

Brazil wished to make major improvements on his home. He entered into a contract with a contractor to do the work. The contractor made numerous false representations that he had already purchased material to be used in doing the work. Relying on these false statements, Brazil executed a check to the order of the contractor. On the same day that the contractor received the check, he cashed it at the Citizens National Bank. Brazil soon discovered that no material had been purchased and stopped payment on the check. The bank sued Brazil on the check. He claimed that the check was not binding because the contractor had been guilty of a crime by obtaining the check by means of false pretenses.

DECISION:

Judgment for Citizens National Bank. The bank was a holder in due course. The defense of illegality could only be asserted against it if there was such illegality as made the check void. On the facts of the case, there was merely fraud that made the check voidable. Such fraud did not constitute "illegality" that could be raised against a holder in due course. Brazil was therefore liable for payment of the check. [Citizens National Bank of Quitman v Brazil, 141 Ga App 388, 233 SE2d 482 (1977)]

---

[13]UCC §3-404(1); Eutsler v First Nat. Bank (Okla) 639 P2d 1245 (1982).

(f) **Alteration.** An alteration is a change to an instrument which is both material and fraudulently made. An alteration is material when it changes the contract of any party in any way, as by changing the date, place of payment, rate of interest, or any other term. It also includes any modification that changes the number or the relationship of the parties to the paper, by adding new terms, or by cutting off a part of the paper itself.

An alteration must be made to the instrument itself. An oral or a collateral written agreement between the holder and one of the parties that modifies the obligation of the party is not an "alteration" within the sense just discussed, even though the obligation of a party is changed or altered thereby.

(1) Person Making Alteration. By definition, an **alteration** is a change made by a party to the instrument. A change of the instrument made by a nonparty has no effect, and recovery may be had on the instrument as though the change had not been made, provided it can be proved what the instrument had been in its original form.

(2) Effect of Alteration. The fact that an instrument has been altered may be raised against any holder. Unlike other defenses, however, it is only a partial defense as against a holder in due course. That is, the latter holder may enforce the instrument according to its original terms prior to its alteration.[14]

For example, Ryan signed a negotiable demand note for $500, made payable to Long. A subsequent holder changed the amount from $500 to $700. A later holder in due course presented the note to Ryan for payment. Ryan would still be liable for the original amount, $500. Moreover, if the person sued by the holder in due course has by negligence substantially contributed to making the alteration possible, that defendant is precluded or barred from asserting the defense of alteration.

§ 32:6.   **Adverse Claims to the Paper.**

Distinct from a defense which a defendant may raise against the plaintiff as a reason against paying the instrument is a claim of a third person to be the owner of the paper. Assume that a check was made payable to the order of *B;* that thereafter blank indorsements are made by *B, C,* and *D;* and that *E* in possession of the check appears to be the holder. *B* might then claim and show, if such be the case, that *C* had fraudulently deceived *B* into indorsing the check; and that *B* therefore avoids the indorsement because of such fraud; and that accordingly the check still belongs to *B. B* in such case is making an adverse claim to the instrument.

(a) **Effect of Adverse Claim.** A holder in due course holds commercial paper free and clear from all adverse claims of any other person to the paper, including both equitable and legal interests of third persons, and the right of a former holder to rescind negotiation.[15]

In contrast, such adverse claims may be asserted against a holder who is not a holder in due course, which means that the adverse claimant may bring an action against the holder to obtain the paper as the law generally provides for the recovery of property by the owner from anyone else.

[14]UCC §3-407(3).
[15]UCC §§3-305(1), 3-207(2).

(b) **Defendant's Assertion of Adverse Claim.** Ordinarily a defendant when sued by a holder cannot raise against the holder the defense that the holder's ownership is subject to an adverse claim. This may be done only when the adverse claimant has also become a party to the action or is defending the action on behalf of the defendant.

This limitation is imposed to protect the adverse claimant from a decision in an action to which the adverse claimant was not a party and to prevent opening the door to perjury by giving any defendant the opportunity of beclouding the issues by raising a false claim that a third person has an adverse interest.

§ 32:7.   Avoidance of Holder in Due Course Protection.

In certain situations, the taker of a commercial paper is denied the status of a holder in due course or is denied the protection of a holder in due course.

(a) **Participating Transferee.** The seller of goods on credit frequently assigns the sales contract and buyer's promissory note to the manufacturer who made the goods, or to a finance company or a bank. In such a case, the assignee of the seller will be a holder in due course of the buyer's commercial paper if the paper is properly negotiated and the transferee satisfies all the elements of being a holder in due course. The transferee, however, may take such an active part in the sale to the seller's customer or may be so related to the seller that it is proper to conclude that the transferee was in fact a party to the original transaction and had notice or knowledge of any defense of the buyer against the seller, which conclusion automatically bars holding that the transferee is a holder in due course.

(b) **The Federal Trade Commission Rule.** In 1976, the FTC adopted a rule which to some extent limits the rights of a holder in due course in a **consumer credit transaction.** The rule protects consumers who purchase goods or services for personal, family, or household use.[16] When the buyer is sued by a finance company on the note given to the seller, the buyer may raise any defense that could have been raised against the seller. By the rule any transferee of the seller is put on notice that the transferee is not a holder in due course but an assignee of the seller. The Commission regulation requires that the following notice be included in boldface type at least ten point in size:

NOTICE
ANY HOLDER OF THIS CONSUMER CREDIT CONTRACT IS SUBJECT TO ALL CLAIMS AND DEFENSES WHICH THE DEBTOR COULD ASSERT AGAINST THE SELLER OF GOODS OR SERVICES OBTAINED WITH THE PROCEEDS HEREOF. RECOVERY HEREUNDER BY THE DEBTOR SHALL NOT EXCEED AMOUNTS PAID BY THE DEBTOR HEREUNDER.

---

[16]The regulation does not cover purchases of real estate, securities, or consumer goods or services where the purchase price is more than $25,000.

SUMMARY

A holder of commercial paper can be either an ordinary holder or a favored holder. The ordinary holder has the same rights that an assignee would have. Favored holders are protected from certain defenses when they sue to collect payment. These holders are known as (1)a holder in due course, and (2)a holder through a holder in due course. To have this preferred status, a person must first be a holder, that is, the paper must have been acquired by a proper negotiation. Secondly, the holder must have acquired the paper as part of a regular, normal business routine. Finally the holder must meet certain requirements to be a holder in due course. The holder must take for value, in good faith, without notice of paper overdue or dishonored, and without notice of defenses and adverse claims. Those persons who become holders of the instrument after a holder in due course are given the same protection as the holder in due course provided they are not parties to any fraud or illegality that would affect the instrument.

The importance of being a holder in due course or a holder through a holder in due course is that those holders are not subject to certain defenses when they demand payment or bring suit on commercial paper. These defenses are limited defenses and include ordinary contract defenses, incapacity, fraud in the inducement, prior payment, nondelivery of an instrument, unauthorized completion, and theft of the paper that does not result in a defect in the chain of necessary indorsments. Universal defenses may be asserted against any plaintiff, whether that party is an assignee, an ordinary holder, a holder in due course, or a holder through a holder in due course. Universal defenses include fraud as to the nature of the paper, forgery or lack of authority, infancy, illegality, and alteration. With regard to alteration, it is only a partial defense, as the holder may enforce the instrument according to its original terms. The Federal Trade Commission limits the immunities available to a holder in due course in consumer credit transactions.

QUESTIONS AND CASE PROBLEMS

1. What social forces are affected by the holder in due course rule?
2. Barbara owes Zeigler $100. Barbara draws a check on her bank payable to the order of Zeigler for $100, and delivers the check to Zeigler. The question arises whether Zeigler has taken the check for value. The argument is made that Zeigler did not give anything in return for the check and therefore has not given value. Is this argument correct?
3. Bushnell purchased an automobile from Gable because of the latter's fraudulent statements as to the condition of the car. Bushnell gave Gable a check for the purchase price drawn on the Exchange Bank. Gable cashed the check at the Industrial Bank. When Bushnell learned that he had been defrauded, he stopped payment on the check. Bushnell also informed the Exchange Bank and the Industrial Bank of Gable's misconduct. Industrial Bank claimed that Bushnell was liable to it on the dishonored check. Bushnell claimed that the Industrial Bank was subject to the defense of fraud in the inducement. Industrial Bank denied this on the ground that it was a holder in due course. Bushnell claimed that

Industrial Bank was not a holder in due course because it knew of Gable's fraud. Was Bushnell correct?

4. Dawn gave Cleo a promissory note promising to pay $1,000 to the order of Cleo in thirty days. Cleo transferred this note to Carlos thirty-five days later. When Carlos demanded payment from Dawn, Dawn raised the defense that Cleo did not perform the work for which the note was given as payment in advance. Carlos replied that the defense of Dawn was a matter between Dawn and Cleo only and that Carlos was not concerned with it. Is Carlos correct?

5. What is the underlying reasoning behind making universal defenses available against all holders?

6. Schell makes a contract with Emma to paint her house. To assist Schell in financing the job, Emma gives Schell a part-payment check in advance so that Schell can purchase the paint for the job. Has Schell taken the check for value?

7. Compare (a) an assignee, (b) a holder, (c) a holder in due course, and (d) a holder through a holder in due course with respect to the defense that the defendant is seventeen years of age.

8. How does fraud as a limited defense differ from fraud as a universal defense?

9. Jones, wishing to retire from a business enterprise which he had been conducting for a number of years, sold all the assets of the business to Jackson Corporation. Included among such assets were a number of promissory notes payable to the order of Jones which he had taken from his customers. On maturity of one of such notes, the maker would not pay, alleging failure of consideration (which was a fact). Jackson Corporation sues the maker of the note. Who should succeed?

10. D drew a check to the order of P. It was later claimed that P was not a holder in due course because the check was postdated and because P knew that D was having financial difficulties and that the particular checking account on which this check was drawn had been frequently overdrawn. Do these circumstances prevent P from being a holder in due course? [Citizens Bank, Booneville v National Bank of Commerce (CA 10 Okla) 334 F2d 257; Franklin National Bank v Sidney Gotowner (NY SupCt) 4 UCCRS 953]

11. A and B were negotiating for the sale of land. A paid B in advance with a postdated check. When A and B could not agree on a final contract, A stopped payment of the check. Was B a holder in due course? [Briand v Wild, 110 NH 373, 268 A2d 896]

12. H acquired a check by indorsement. At the time that H acquired the check he knew of all the circumstances surrounding the original issue of the check. If H knew the legal significance of those circumstances, he would have realized that the drawer of the check had a valid defense. Because H did not know the law, he did not realize that the drawer had a defense and took the check in good faith believing that everything was proper. In a subsequent lawsuit on the check, the question arose whether H was a holder in due course. The defendant claimed that H was not because H knew of the defense based on the surrounding circumstances and H's ignorance of the law did not excuse him from the consequence

of that knowledge, because ignorance of the law is no excuse. Is *H* a holder in due course? [Hartford Life Ins. Co. v Title Guarantee Co. 172 App DC 156, 520 F2d 1170.]

13. A customer of a bank purchased a bank money order and paid for it with a forged check. The money order was negotiable and was acquired by *N* who was a holder in due course. When *N* sued the bank on the money order, it raised the defense that its customer had paid with a bad check. Could this defense be raised against *N*? [Bank of Niles v American State Bank, 14 Ill App 3d 729, 303 NE2d 186.]

14. Charney pays his negotiable promissory note made in favor of Sandler fifteen days before the date of maturity. Charney leaves the note in Sandler's possession. Sandler negotiates the note to Dean, a holder in due course. Dean sues Charney on the note. Will Dean be able to recover?

15. Holler sold stolen goods to the Star Provision Company which paid by check, believing that Holler was the owner. The check was subsequently negotiated to Sears, Roebuck & Company, which was a holder in due course. When Sears sued Star for nonpayment of the check, Star raised the defense that the goods had been stolen. Can Sears recover? [Star Provision Company v Sears Roebuck & Co. 93 Ga App 799, 92 SE2d 835]

16. Layton wished to make a gift to his niece of $2,000, but he did not have the cash. Layton therefore executed a demand negotiable promissory note for $2,000 payable to the order of his niece, delivered the note to his niece, and stated: "You can present this note as a claim against my estate if the note is not paid before my death." The niece immediately sold the note to Richard, a holder in due course. Richard presented the note to Layton for payment, and Layton refused payment. What defense is available to Layton?

C H A P T E R 33

PRESENTMENT OF PAPER

FOR PAYMENT AND

ACCEPTANCE

CHAPTER OBJECTIVES

After studying this chapter you will be able to:
1. Distinguish between presentment for payment and presentment for acceptance of both notes and drafts.
2. Explain why presentment for payment and presentment for acceptance is important.
3. Set forth the rules for presentment for payment and presentment for acceptance.
4. Explain the importance of giving notice of dishonor and when such notice is excused.
5. Distinguish between a general acceptance and a draft-varying acceptance.
6. Solve problems related to the presentment of notes and drafts.

A promissory note is a two-party commercial paper, which means that originally there is only a maker and a payee. The maker is liable for payment on the due date specified in the note or on demand if the note is a demand instrument. If the maker dishonors the note when it is presented for payment, the indorsers, if there are any, may become liable for payment of the paper. This chapter considers the rules of law that must be followed in order to enforce the liability of a party to a note. It must be remembered that even though these rules have been satisfied, the plaintiff may lose in a given case if the plaintiff is not the holder, or if the defendant has a defense that may be asserted against the plaintiff.

A. PRESENTMENT OF NOTES FOR PAYMENT

There are specific procedures for presenting a note for payment and for giving notice of dishonor. The procedures for presenting a promissory note for payment and for giving notice of dishonor, which are explained in this chapter, apply also to other types of commercial paper, that is, drafts and checks.

§ 33:1. Liability of Maker.

The liability of a maker of a promissory note is primary. This means that payment may be demanded of the maker and a maker may be sued by the holder as soon as the debt is due, though not before that time.

FACTS:
Burke executed a promissory note. He later informed Bertolet, the holder of the note, that he would not make payment on the note when it became due. Bertolet immediately sued Burke. The defendant moved for summary judgment.

DECISION:
Judgment for Burke. The doctrine of anticipatory repudiation does not apply to commercial paper. Consequently, when paper is due on a specific date, it does not become due at an earlier date merely because the obligor declares that he will default on the day when the paper is due. [Bertolet v Burke (DC Virgin Islands) 295 FSupp 1176 (1969)]

The maker is under the duty to pay the note at the time and at the place named, if any place is specified in the note, unless a defense can be set up that is valid against the holder.

By the very act of signing the promissory note, the maker gives up two possible defenses. The maker thereby admits (1) the existence of the payee named in the instrument, and (2) the payee's capacity at that time to indorse the paper.[1] Thus, even though the payee of a note is a minor or a bankrupt, the maker cannot deny the validity of the title of a subsequent holder of the paper on the ground that the payee lacked capacity to transfer title to the paper.

When a note is issued in payment of a debt, the underlying obligation is suspended until the instrument is due or until presentment for payment in the case of demand paper. If the note is dishonored by nonpayment, the holder may sue either on the note or on the underlying obligation.

§ 33:2. Need for Presentment for Payment.

The holder of a promissory note need not present the paper to the maker for payment in order to hold the latter liable on the note. If the note is payable at a definite time, the maker is under a duty to pay the holder the amount due on the instrument as soon as that date is reached. The liability of

---

[1]Uniform Commercial Code §3-413(3).

the maker continues until barred by the statute of limitations. However, in order to hold an indorser liable on the note, the holder of that note must present it to the maker when due.[2]

§ 33:3.   Presentment for Payment.

When presentment for payment of notes or other commercial paper is required, the following rules apply:

(a) Person Making Presentment. Presentment for payment must be made by the holder of the paper or by one authorized to act and receive payment on behalf of the holder.

(b) Manner of Presentment. Demand for payment in any manner is a sufficient presentment. An actual physical presenting of the paper is not required. The party to whom the demand for payment is made may require, however, that greater formality be observed, such as by requiring (1) reasonable identification of the person making presentment and evidence of authority if that person acts for another; (2) production of the instrument for payment at a place specified in it or, if there be none, at any place reasonable under the circumstances; and (3) a signed receipt on the instrument for any partial or full payment and its surrender upon full payment. If the party presenting the instrument does not comply with such requests at the time of making presentment, the presenting party is allowed a reasonable time within which to do so. If the presenting party does not comply with such reasonable requests, the presentment that was made has no effect.[3]

The presentment must make a clear demand for payment and a mere inquiry as to whether payment would be made in the future is not sufficient.

In addition to a presentment for payment made directly upon the primary party, presentment may be made by sending the paper through the mail to the debtor, or by sending it through a clearinghouse.[4] A collecting bank may also make presentment for payment by sending merely a notice to the nonbank party to whom the demand for payment is made. If the party so notified fails to act within a specified time, such inaction is treated as a dishonor of the note.[5]

(c) On Whom Presentment Is Made. Presentment for payment must be made to the party primarily liable, that is, the maker of the promissory note, or to a person who is authorized to make or refuse payment on behalf of the maker.

The delivery of a check to a data processing center is not a presentment of check to the bank serviced by the center as such a center does not have authority to make or refuse payment.[6]

(d) Place of Making Presentment. Presentment for payment is properly made at the place that is specified in the paper. When a place of payment is not specified, presentment of the instrument is to be made at the place

---

[2]Binford v Lichtenberger Estate, 62 Or App 439, 660 P2d 1077 (1983).
[3]Wilner O'Donnell (Mo App) 637 SW2d 757 (1982).
[4]UCC §3-504(2)(a),(b).
[5]UCC §4-210.
[6]Idah-Best, Inc. v First Security Bank, 99 Idaho 517, 584 P2d 1242 (1978).

of business or the residence of the person from whom payment is to be demanded.

§ 33:4.   Time of Making Presentment.

A note payable at a stated date must be presented for payment on that date. If the time for paying the balance due on the note has been accelerated, presentment must be made within a reasonable time after the default in a scheduled payment of principal or interest. In order to enforce the secondary liability of any party, presentment for payment must be made within a reasonable time after such person became liable on the instrument.

Presentment must be made at a reasonable time, and if made at a bank, must be made during its banking day.

(a) **Computation of Time.** In determining the date of maturity of an instrument, the starting day is excluded and the day of payment is included. Thus, an instrument dated July 3 (which leaves 28 days in July) and payable thirty days from date is due on August 2.

(b) **Instrument Due on Legal or Business Holiday.** When the presentment of the paper is due on a day that is not a full business day, presentment is due on the following full business day. This rule is applied when the due day is not a full business day either because it is a legal holiday or merely because the bank or other person required to make payment on the instrument, as a matter of its business practice, is closed all day or for half a day.

This rule is also applied when the due date is a business holiday for either party, that is, if either the person required to present the instrument or the person who is required to pay upon presentment is not open for a full business day on the due date, the day for presentment is extended to the first day thereafter that is a full business day for both of them.[7]

(c) **Excuse for Delay in Making Presentment.** Failure of the holder to present an instrument for payment at the proper time will be excused when the delay is caused by circumstances beyond the control of the holder. It must not, however, be caused by that person's misconduct, negligence, or fault. Mere inconvenience, such as that arising from inclement weather, is not a valid excuse for delay. When the circumstances that excuse the delay are removed, presentment must be made within a reasonable time thereafter.[8]

(d) **Effect of Delay in Making Presentment.** An unexcused delay in making any necessary presentment for payment discharges an indorser's liability for payment of the paper. If the note is **domiciled**, that is, payable at a bank, the delay may also operate to discharge the maker. The UCC provides as to such paper that "any... maker of a note payable at a bank who because the...payor bank becomes insolvent during the delay is deprived of funds maintained with the...payor bank to cover the instrument may discharge his liability by written assignment to the holder of his rights against the...payor bank in respect of such funds, but such... maker is not otherwise discharged."[9]

[7]UCC §3-503(3).
[8]UCC §3-511(1).
[9]UCC §3-501(1)(b).

§ 33:5. When Presentment for Payment Is Excused or Unnecessary.

Presentment for payment is often not made for various reasons. The requirement for presentment is entirely excused or unnecessary under the following circumstances:

(a) **Waiver.** Presentment for payment is not required if it has been waived by an express or implied agreement of the secondary party in question. A waiver of presentment is binding upon all parties if it appears on the face of the original note. If the waiver is part of an indorsement, however, it binds only that indorser.

(b) **Inability.** Presentment for payment is not required if it cannot be made in spite of the exercise of due diligence, as when presentment is attempted at the place where payment is to be made but neither the person who is to make payment nor anyone authorized to act can be found at that place.[10]

(c) **Death or Insolvency.** Presentment for payment is not required if the maker of the note has died or has gone into insolvency proceedings after issuing the note.

(d) **Refusal to Pay.** The holder is not required to make presentment upon a maker who has already refused to pay the note for any reason other than an objection that proper presentment had not been made.

FACTS:

Belello brought suit on a promissory note made payable to him by Smith. The note stated it was payable "at 501 Louisiana Avenue," the law office of Mr. O'Neil Walsh, Smith's attorney. Belello did not present the note at the address provided in the instrument for payment. He did, however, on the due date call Smith at his place of business, the Baton Rouge Athletic Club, and request payment. Smith responded that "he could not do anything right now and that it was not convenient or possible for him to pay the note." Smith claimed that since the note did not contain a waiver of presentment, it was necessary that presentment be made.

DECISION:

Presentment was not necessary. When payment of the note was demanded by telephone contact with Smith, payment was refused for reasons other than lack of proper presentment. [Smith v Belello, (La App) 431 So2d 80 (1983)]

(e) **Belief or Conduct of Secondary Party.** A party secondarily liable on the instrument cannot demand that presentment be made if that party has

[10]UCC §§3-504(2), 3-511(2)(c).

no reason to expect that the instrument will be paid and no right to require that payment be made.

§ 33:6. Dishonor of Note.

If the maker fails or refuses to pay the note when it is properly presented, the note has been dishonored by nonpayment. The fact that the maker does not make immediate payment of the note when it is presented does not necessarily dishonor the note. The maker has the right to withhold making a payment until a reasonable examination has been made to determine that the note is properly payable to the holder. This examination process, however, cannot delay payment beyond the close of business on the day of presentment.[11]

§ 33:7. Notice of Dishonor.

If commercial paper is dishonored by nonpayment, any secondary party who is not given proper notice thereof is released from liability, unless the giving of notice is excused.[12]

FACTS:

Theta Electronic Laboratories executed a promissory note payable to Thompson and his wife. The note was payable in installments and contained an acceleration clause that if any payment was missed, the entire note became due on demand. The note also contained a confession of judgment clause which allowed the holder to obtain judgment against the maker and indorsers if the maker defaulted without first bringing suit against the parties. The note was indorsed by Exten, Oneil, and James Hane and their wives. The Thompsons assigned the note to John Hane. The maker had been in default prior to the assignment. Eighteen months later Hane demanded payment from Theta which request was refused. Hane then obtained a judgment by confession against Theta and the Extens. The Extens then brought an action to have the judgment set aside.

DECISION:

Judgment for the Extens. They were indorsers and therefore had only a secondary liability. This meant that they could only be required to pay the paper if it had been presented to the primary party when it was due and they were then given notice of the failure to pay the paper before midnight of the third full business day after such failure. As such presentment had not been made and timely notice had not been given to the Extens, they were discharged from liability. [Hane v Exten, 255 Md 668, 259 A2d 290 (1969)]

---

[11]UCC §3-506(2).

[12]UCC §3-501(2)(a). In the case of a "domiciled" note payable at a bank, the maker must be given notice that the note was not paid when presented at the bank and, if notice is not so given, the maker is released to the same extent already noted in connection with the effect of failure to present at the bank. UCC §3-501(2)(b).

(a) **Who May Give Notice.** The notice of dishonor is ordinarily given by the holder who has been refused payment or the holder's agent. An agent making presentment for payment may give notice of the dishonor to the principal, who in turn may give it to the secondary party in question. When any person who is liable on the paper receives notice of its dishonor, that person may in turn give notice to other secondary parties.

(b) **Form of Notice.** Notice may be given in any reasonable manner. It may be oral[13] or written, and it may be sent by mail. It may have any terms as long as it identifies the instrument and states that it has been dishonored. A misdescription that does not mislead the party notified does not nullify or vitiate the notice. Notice may be effected by sending the instrument itself, with a stamp, ticket, or writing attached thereto, stating that payment has been refused or by sending a notice of debit with respect to the paper.

(c) **Time of Notice.** Notice must be given before midnight of the third business day after dishonor. If the notice is given following the receipt of notice of dishonor from another party, it must be given before midnight of the third business day after receiving such notice. When required of a bank, notice of dishonor must be given before midnight of the banking day following the banking day on which the note is dishonored or the bank receives notice of such dishonor.[14] A written notice of dishonor is effective when sent. Hence a notice sent by mail is sufficient even though it is never received, provided it was properly addressed, bore the necessary postage, and was properly mailed.[15]

If notice is not given within the required time and the delay in or the absence of notice is not excused, the person entitled to notice cannot be held liable for the payment of the paper. The fact that the holder was not personally the cause of the delay in giving notice of dishonor does not prevent the discharge of the person not notified.

FACTS:

Greer and Biesel owned a bowling alley. The bowling complex burned and a check from the insurance company was issued to Greer and Biesel. Greer and Biesel indorsed the check which was deposited in Greer's account at the White Oak State Bank. Greer then issued a check to Ford and B & B Billard Supply of Dallas for liens held by them on the alley. The insurance company was insolvent so that the drawee bank dishonored the insurance check on August 3 and notified the White Oak Bank that same day by telephone. The oral notification was followed by written notice of dishonor which was received by the White Oak Bank on August 13. White Oak then notified the indorsers of the dishonor on August 14. White Oak sued the indorsers on the dishonored check. They denied liability because prompt notice of dishonor was not given to them.

---

[13]Bank of Commerce v De Santis, 114 Misc 2d 491, 451 NYS2d 974 (1982).
[14]UCC §§3-508(2), 4-105(1)(h).
[15]UCC §3-504(4).

DECISION:

Judgment for Greer and Biesel. Unless excused, notice of dishonor is necessary to charge any indorser of an item. Notice must be given by a bank before its midnight deadline (the next banking day after the banking day it received the item), and any unexcused delay in giving notice of dishonor discharges an indorser. White Oak Bank received notice by telephone on August 3. Since the bank delayed in giving notice to Greer and Biesel until August 14, they were not liable. [Greer v White Oak State Bank, (Tex App) 673 SW2d 326 (1984)]

§ 33.8. Excuse for Delay or Absence of Notice of Dishonor.

Delay in giving notice of dishonor is excused under the same circumstances as delay in making presentment for payment.[16]

The absence of any notice of dishonor is excused for three of the reasons considered as excusing the absence of presentment; namely (1) waiver, (2) inability to give notice in spite of due diligence, and (3) the fact that the party not notified did not have any reason to believe that the instrument would be paid nor any right to require payment. When an indorser has such knowledge or so participates in the affairs of the primary party that the indorser knows that the commercial paper will not be honored by the primary party, it is not required that the holder go through the useless gesture of making a presentment and of notifying the secondary party.

§ 33:9. Proof of Dishonor.

As the liability of the secondary party depends upon whether certain steps were taken within the proper time, it is important for the holder to be able to prove compliance with the requirements of the law. In order to aid in proving such essential facts, certain documents and records are considered evidence of dishonor and of any notice recited therein. The trier of fact must accept such evidence in the absence of proof to the contrary.[17] These documents and records include (1)protests, (2)bank stamps and memorandums, and (3)bank records.[18]

B. PRESENTMENT OF DRAFTS

Unlike promissory notes, in most cases a draft will involve three original parties. When this is the case, the holder may be required to take an extra step in order to preserve the liability of secondary parties. A note must be presented for payment in order to hold secondary parties liable; under certain circumstances, a draft must be presented for acceptance as well as for payment.

---

[16]UCC §3-511.
[17]UCC §§3-510, 1-201(31).
[18]A protest is a memorandum or certificate executed by a notary public, or certain other public officers, upon satisfactory information, which sets forth that the particular identified instrument has been dishonored. It may also recite that notice of dishonor was given to all parties or to specified parties.

If the drawer is also named as drawee, the paper has the effect of a promissory note. In such a case, the drawer is the primary party and the procedures peculiar to drafts, such as presentment for acceptance, are eliminated.

§ 33:10. Liability of Drawee.

A drawee is not liable for payment of a draft before acceptance. An **acceptance** is the written assent of the drawee to the order of the drawer.

(a) **Before Acceptance.** In the absence of a prior contract to accept the draft, the drawee is not under any duty to do so. The act of refusing to accept the draft does not give the holder any right to sue the drawee on the paper, even though the refusal breaks the contract with the drawer or some other person which obligated the drawee to accept the draft. Neither does the draft operate as an assignment of money, even though the drawee has possession of funds of the drawer.[19]

(b) **After Acceptance.** After the drawee accepts a draft, the drawee is an **acceptor** and is primarily liable for payment of the draft.

§ 33:11. Liability of Drawer.

The drawer has a secondary liability. By executing the draft, the drawer undertakes to pay the amount of the draft to the holder, if, when the instrument is presented to the drawee for acceptance or payment, it is dishonored and proper proceedings are then taken by the holder.

The drawer, however, may insert in the draft a provision to exclude or limit liability as by adding "without recourse."

FACTS:
Gill sold his airplane to Yoes for $8,000. The purchase price was paid by delivering to Gill a draft drawn by Yoes on the Phoenix Savings & Loan Co. to the order of Gill. Yoes had no money in the savings and loan association but had applied to it for a loan. The loan application was rejected; and when the draft was presented on the association, it refused to pay it. Gill then sued Yoes on the draft. Yoes raised the defense that she had nothing to do with the purchase of the airplane and that she did not need one.

DECISION:
Judgment for Gill. Since Yoes had signed the draft as a drawer, she became secondarily liable as a drawer without regard to whether she had any interest in any transaction in which the draft was used as payment. [Gill v Yoes (Okla) 360 P2d 506 (1961)]

---

[19]Holsomback v Akins, 134 Ga App 543, 215 SE2d 306 (1975).

§ 33:12. Liability of Indorser.

The liability of an unqualified indorser of a draft is broader than that of an unqualified indorser of a promissory note. Any unqualified indorser is under a secondary liability for the nonpayment of the instrument when due. In addition, the unqualified indorser of a draft is under a secondary liability for the refusal of the drawee to accept the instrument when it is presented for acceptance.

In order to charge the unqualified indorser of the draft for either nonacceptance or nonpayment, it is necessary to prove that a presentment to the drawee had been properly made and that due notice was given to the indorser of the drawee's failure to accept or pay.

§ 33:13. Necessity of Presentment for Acceptance.

The best way for the holder to find out whether the drawee will pay a time draft when it becomes due is to present it to the drawee for acceptance. If the drawee is not willing to pay the instrument according to its terms, the drawee will reject it, that is, dishonor it by nonacceptance. If willing to pay the draft when it becomes due, the drawee will accept it.

Any draft may be presented to the drawee for acceptance. A presentment for acceptance must be made if (1) it is necessary in order to fix the date of maturity of the draft, such as when the instrument is payable a specified number of days after sight; (2) the draft expressly states that it must be presented for acceptance, or (3) the draft is made payable elsewhere than at the residence or place of business of the drawee.[20]

§ 33:14. Manner of Presenting for Acceptance.

Presentment of a draft for acceptance is made in the same manner as the presentment of a note for payment, with the obvious difference that the presentment is made upon the drawee rather than upon the maker.

It is not necessary that the drawee accept or dishonor the draft immediately upon its presentment. In order to afford an opportunity of determining from records whether the draft should be accepted, the drawee may postpone making a decision, without thereby dishonoring the draft, until the close of the next business day following the presentment of the draft. Likewise, the holder may allow the postponement of acceptance for one additional business day when the holder acts in good faith in the hope of obtaining an acceptance. If the holder agrees to such additional postponement, the liability of the secondary parties is not affected and the draft is not thereby dishonored.[21]

§ 33:15. Kinds of Acceptances.

(a) **General Acceptance.** A **general acceptance** (or simply an "acceptance") is one in which the acceptor agrees without qualification to pay according to the order of the drawer.

---

[20]UCC §3-501(1)(a).

[21]UCC §3-506(1). The time allowed the drawee to determine whether to accept is distinct from any right of re-presentment after dishonor when authorized by the paper. UCC §3-507(4).

(b) Draft-Varying Acceptance. A **draft-varying acceptance** is one in which the acceptor agrees to pay but not exactly in conformity with the order of the draft. An acceptance varies the draft when it changes the time or place of payment, when it agrees to pay only a part of the amount of the draft, or when it sets up a condition that must be satisfied before the acceptance is effective.

A holder who does not wish to take the varying acceptance, may reject it and treat the draft as dishonored by nonacceptance. After giving due notice, the holder can then proceed at once against secondary parties.

If the holder assents to the draft-varying acceptance, however, the holder in effect consents to the execution of a new instrument; and each drawer and indorser is released from liability unless such other party affirmatively assents to the draft-varying acceptance. The fact that a secondary party fails to object is not sufficient to prevent this release from liability.

§ 33:16.   Form of Acceptance.

An acceptance is the drawee's notation on the draft itself that payment will be made as directed thereby. It may be merely a signature, but customarily it will be the word "accepted" and a signature, and generally the date. In any case, however, the acceptance must be written on the draft itself. Usually it is written across the face of the instrument.

An acceptance cannot be oral, nor can it be contained in some other writing. Thus a bank is not bound by its oral promise to pay a draft drawn upon it. The fact that the drawee is not liable on a draft which it has not accepted means only that it is not liable on the draft. The drawee may still be liable to the holder on other contracts or on the basis of other principles of law.

FACTS:

Schenk's Motor Sales had a checking account in the Home Savings Bank. The balance in the account was $3,080.56. Schenk drew a check for $9,700 payable to the order of the General Finance Corporation. The bank certified the check when General Finance Corporation orally promised to accept a draft drawn on General by Schenk that had just been deposited in Schenk's account. The certified check was paid by the bank, but General refused to pay the draft on the ground that its oral acceptance was not binding. The bank sued General for the amount of the certified check.

DECISION:

Judgment for the bank for $6,619.44. General Finance was not liable on the paper because an oral acceptance is not binding. However, General Finance obtained a certified check for $9,700. This was $6,619.44 more than Schenk could have paid General without the bank's certification, as the Schenk bank account was only $3,080.56. In order to prevent the unjust enrichment of General Finance it must repay the bank the excess of $6,619.44 [Home Savings Bank v General Finance Corp. 10 Wis2d 417, 103 NW2d 117 (1968)]

§ 33:17.   Dishonor by Nonacceptance.

When a draft that is presented for acceptance is not accepted within the allowed time, the person presenting it must treat the draft as dishonored by nonacceptance.[22] The failure to do so releases the secondary parties from liability.

When a draft is dishonored by nonacceptance, the holder must give the same notice of dishonor as in the case of dishonor of paper by nonpayment. If the draft on its face appears to be drawn or payable outside of the United States, its territories, and the District of Columbia, it is also necessary to protest the dishonor in order to charge the drawer and the indorsers.

§ 33:18.   Presentment of Draft for Payment.

The requirements and limitations upon the necessity of presentment of a draft for payment are the same as in the case of a promissory note, with the circumstances excusing delay or failure to make presentment of a note likewise excusing delay or failure to make presentment of a draft for payment. The failure to present for payment is likewise excused with respect to a party who has countermanded payment of the draft.

The provisions governing notice of dishonor of a draft by nonpayment are the same as those for a note.[23]

§ 33:19.   Protest of Dishonor.

A protest of dishonor of a draft by nonacceptance or nonpayment is not necessary unless the draft appears on its face to be drawn or payable outside of the United States, its territories, or the District of Columbia. The holder, however, may protest the dishonor of any instrument.

A **waiver of protest** is effective to excuse the absence of an otherwise required protest. A waiver of protest is also a waiver of the requirement of presentment and notice of dishonor as well as of the protest itself even though the protest is not required.

When words of guaranty, such as, "payment guaranteed" or "collection guaranteed," are used, presentment, notice of dishonor, and protest are not necessary to charge the person using such language.[24]

SUMMARY

The maker of a promissory note is primarily liable for its payment. Payment may be demanded from the maker as soon as the debt is due.

Presentment of the paper is not necessary to hold the maker liable on the note. The maker's liability continues until barred by the statute of limitations. To hold an indorser liable, however, the holder of the note must present it to the maker on the due date.

Presentment for payment must be made by the holder of the paper or an authorized agent. A demand for payment in any manner is sufficient. Presentment for payment must be made to the primary party at the place speci-

---

[22]UCC §3-507(1)(a).
[23]UCC §3-501(2), 3-508. See §33:7 of this text.
[24]UCC §3-416(5).

fied in the instrument or if no place is specified, presentment is to be made at the place of business or residence of the person from whom payment is to be demanded. An instrument maturing on a fixed date must be presented on that date unless it is delayed by circumstances beyond the control of the holder. Any unexcused delay in making presentment for payment discharges an indorser's liability for payment.

If the maker fails to pay the note upon proper presentment, the note is said to be dishonored. All secondary parties not given proper notice will be released from liability unless the giving of notice is excused. Notice of dishonor is ordinarily given by the holder who has been refused payment. Such notice may be given in any reasonable manner and may be oral or written. Notice must be given before midnight of the third business day after dishonor. A holder must be able to prove proper notice of dishonor.

A draft involves three original parties and may be presented for acceptance as well as payment. The drawee of the draft is not liable for payment before acceptance. The acceptance is the written agreement of the drawee to the order of the drawer. Absent any prior agreement, the drawee is under no duty to accept and any failure to accept gives no cause of action by the drawer against the drawee. When the drawee does accept, the drawee is known as an acceptor and is primarily liable for payment of the draft. The drawer has a secondary liability. By issuing the draft, the drawer undertakes to pay the amount to the holder if acceptance or payment is refused by the drawee and proper proceedings are then taken by the holder.

A draft is presented to the drawee for acceptance. In the event the drawee decides to accept, the drawee may either give a general acceptance with no qualifications or a draft-varying acceptance which contains some qualification. A holder may reject a draft-varying acceptance and treat the draft as dishonored by nonacceptance. A drawee's acceptance cannot be oral and must be written on the draft itself.

When the draft is not accepted, it is considered dishonored and the holder must give the same notice of dishonor as in the case of dishonor of paper by nonpayment. The same rules that apply to presentment of a promissory note for payment apply to presentment of a draft for payment.

QUESTIONS AND CASE PROBLEMS

1. What social forces are affected by the rule that giving notice of dishonor to a secondary party before midnight of the third business day following dishonor is sufficient?
2. Ragno borrows money from the Main Street Bank and gives a promissory note for the amount of the loan. The note is due in sixty days. Main Street indorses and delivers the note to the Third National Bank. Ragno fails to pay the note when it is due. A month after it is due, the Third National Bank sues the Main Street Bank for the amount of the note. Is it liable?
3. Who may give notice of dishonor?
4. Mona sent the Annheim Dress Shop a check in payment of the balance due in her charge account with the shop. The bank refused to pay the check because Mona did not have sufficient money in the checking ac-

count to cover the check. Annheim sues Mona for the balance due on the charge account. Mona raises the defense that the charge account bill had been discharged by the check. Was she correct?

5. Raidman drew a draft on Houston directing Houston to pay $1,000 to the order of Pauline in 90 days. Pauline took the draft to Houston who explained that he could not pay in 90 days but would agree to pay in 120 days. What are the consequences of Pauline's agreeing to this time schedule?

6. Henri draws a draft on Marchamp directing Marchamp to pay $1,000 on demand to the order of Clara. Marchamp is indebted to Henri for $10,000. When Clara presents the draft of Henri, Marchamp refuses to make any payments to Clara. Clara sues Marchamp. Can she recover?

7. Compare a note and draft both payable at a definite time with respect to the need of presentment for payment with respect to (a) the maker, (b) an acceptor, and (c) an unqualified indorser.

8. State how notice of dishonor may be given.

9. A thirty-day draft showed on its face that it was drawn by Wooster in Toronto, Canada, on Messig in Detroit, Michigan, payable to the order of Smith, also of Detroit. Messig accepted the draft. Thereafter, Smith negotiated the draft to Elsworth, and the latter negotiated the draft to Liston. When Liston presented the draft to Messig on the due date, Messig refused to pay. Liston immediately, by telephone, advised Wooster, Smith, and Elsworth of the dishonor. Later, when Liston sought to hold these three parties, liable, each contended that she was free from liability on the instrument. Discuss the validity of this contention.

10. Four promissory notes were executed by Continental Diamond Mines, Inc. payable to the order of M. Kopp. The notes were thereafter indorsed to M. Kopp, Inc. and then to Rafkin. Rafkin was the holder on the due date. Was it necessary for him to make a presentment of the notes to Continental Diamond Mines in order to hold it liable on the notes? [Rafkin v Continental Diamond Mines, Inc. 33 Misc 2d 156, 228 NYS2d 317]

11. In an action brought by Hughes against a corporation that had indorsed a promissory note, the latter claimed that notice of protest had not been properly given. It was shown that the notice had been left at the company's office during business hours after the holder was unable to find any of the officers of the corporation. Was sufficient notice given? [Hughes v Rankin Realty Co. 108 NJL 185, 158 A 487]

12. Lowe & Myers were contractors doing construction work for the Druid Realty Co. In order to pay for their materials they drew a draft on the realty company directing it to pay $2,000 to the order of the Crane Co. The realty company, through its president, wrote on the instrument that it accepted the instrument and agreed to pay it within 30 days after the completion of the work, provided Crane Company continued to furnish materials to Lowe & Myers. What was the effect of the action by the realty company? [Crane Co. v Druid Realty Co. 137 Md 324, 112 A 621]

13. A indorsed a promissory note on the back. At the top of the back, above all indorsements, there were printed the words "Notice of protest waived." The note was not paid when due. The holder sent A notice that

the note was not paid, but *A* did not receive the notice because it was sent to a former address at which he no longer lived. *A* denied liability because he had not been properly notified. Decide. [Lizza Asphalt Construction Co. v Greenvale Construction Co. (NY Sup Ct) 4 UCCRS 954]

14. Richards presents a time draft for acceptance to Lionel, the drawee. Lionel tells Richards to come back the next business day. Richards refuses and claims the draft has been dishonored. Is Richards correct?

15. Cotton States Mutual Insurance Company made a draft payable to the order of Baum. The draft was payable on acceptance and was drawn on the First National Bank. When Baum presented the draft to First National Bank it refused to accept it. He then sued Cotton States. It raised the defense that it was not liable because the draft was payable on acceptance and the draft had not been accepted. Was this defense valid? [Baum v Cotton States Mut. Ins. Co. 141 Ga App 635, 234 SE2d 178]

16. Stewart holds a negotiable promissory note indorsed to him by Robins. The note was signed by Martha as maker. It failed to indicate where presentment for payment was to be made. Stewart meets Martha at a local tennis match. May he present the note for payment there? If Martha refuses to pay the note, will this be considered a dishonor?

17. Mellen-Wright Lumber Co., the holder of a note, sued McNett, as maker, and Kendall, as indorser. The latter claimed that he had not received notice of the dishonor of the note by the maker. The holder proved that he had sent the following letter, dated June 10, to Kendall:

> Dear Sir: We hold note for $2,000 with interest at 7percent signed by Earl P. McNett and Anna J. McNett, his wife, on which you indorsed guaranteeing payment.
>
> This note will be due June 12 and we are going to ask that you arrange to pay same promptly. We would appreciate this being paid by not later than Friday, June 18.
>
> Kindly advise if you wish to make payment at our office or at one of our local banks.
>
> We are enclosing stamped envelope for reply.

Was Kendall liable? [Mellen-Wright Lumber Co. v McNett, 242 Mich 369, 218 NW 709]

18. De Lise was secondarily liable on a note held by the First Pennsylvania Banking & Trust Co. When sued on the note, De Lise claimed that he was not liable because notice of the maker's default had been given by telephone. Was this a valid defense? [First Pennsylvania Banking & Trust Co. v De Lise, 186 Pa Super 398, 142 A2d 401]

CHAPTER 34

DISCHARGE OF

COMMERCIAL PAPER

CHAPTER OBJECTIVES

After studying this chapter you will be able to:

1. Describe how individual parties may be discharged from liability on an instrument.
2. List and explain the various methods of discharge.
3. Distinguish the discharge of individual parties from the discharge of all parties.
4. Explain the effect of a discharge on a holder in due course.
5. Solve problems involving the discharge of parties to commercial paper.

Each party to commercial paper assumes a liability with respect to such paper. A party may be discharged from such liability, in whole or in part, and in various ways. A party may be discharged either individually or by some act that discharges all parties to the paper at one time. The nature of the transaction or occurrence determines which takes place.

A. DISCHARGE OF INDIVIDUAL PARTIES

A party to a commercial paper, like a party to an ordinary contract, is usually discharged from liability by making payment to the proper person; but the discharge from liability may be effected in a number of other ways.

§ 34:1. Manner of Discharge.

A party is discharged from liability to any other party (1) with whom an express agreement for discharge is made, or (2) with whom a transaction is entered into which under the law of contracts is effective to discharge liability on an ordinary contract for the payment of money.[1] Accordingly, there may be a discharge by accord and satisfaction, a novation, a covenant not to sue, rescission, or the substitution of another instrument. The liability may also be barred by operation of the law as in the case of a discharge in bankruptcy, the operation of the statute of limitations, or by the merger of liability into a judgment in favor of the holder when an action has been brought on the instrument.

§ 34:2.   Discharge by Payment.

The obligation of a particular party on commercial paper is discharged by paying the amount of the instrument to the holder or to the holder's authorized agent. Payment to anyone else is not effective to discharge the liability of the payor.

(a) **Knowledge of Adverse Claim to the Paper.** When the payment of the amount of the paper is made to the holder, the party making payment may know that some other person claims an interest in or ownership of the paper. The knowledge that there is an adverse claimant does not prevent making a payment to the holder, and such payment is still a discharge of the obligation of the party making payment.

(b) **Satisfaction.** The principles governing payment apply to a satisfaction entered into with the holder of the instrument.[2] Instead of paying the holder in full in money, a payment of less than all is accepted as full payment or some service is rendered or property is given by the party discharged.

(c) **Tender of Payment.** A party who is liable may offer to the holder the full payment when or after the instrument is due. If the holder refuses such payment, the party making the tender of payment is not discharged from liability for the amount then due; but the holder cannot thereafter hold that party liable for any interest that accrues after the date of the rejected tender.

(d) **Payment by Secondary Party.** When a party secondarily liable pays, such payment does not discharge the paper or prior parties but merely transfers the rights of the holder to the party making the payment. This is so even though there is no assignment or transfer of the paper from the paid holder to the secondary party making payment. Consequently, the paper is not discharged when paid by an accommodation party.[3]

FACTS:

Howard, who purchased farm equipment on credit from K & S International, signed a promissory note for the balance of the purchase price. K & S transferred the note to a Jonesboro bank. When Howard stopped making payments, K & S paid the bank the balance due on the note. The bank marked the note paid. K & S then sued Howard for the amount they had paid the bank. Howard claimed that he was discharged because the note had been paid and K & S could not sue because the note had not been reassigned to them.

[1]UCC §3-601(2).
[2]UCC §3-601(1).
[3]Anna Nat. Bank v Wingate, 63 Ill App 3d 676, 21 Ill Dec 84, 381 NE2d 19 (1978).

DECISION:

Judgment for K & S. When a secondary party pays the paper, the primary party is not discharged even though the holder of the paper marks the paper as "paid." By virtue of the payment, the secondary party becomes the holder of the paper and is entitled to enforce payment by the primary party even though there is no assignment or transfer of the paper from the paid holder to the secondary party. [K & S International, Inc. v Howard, 249 Ark 901, 462 SW2d 458 (1971)]

---

§ 34:3.   Cancellation.

The holder of an instrument, with or without consideration, may discharge the liability of a particular party by cancellation by a notation on the paper which makes that intent apparent, or by destroying, mutilating, or striking out the party's signature on the paper. Even though this cancels an indorsement necessary to the chain of title of the holder, the holder's title to the paper is not affected, as the paper had already been properly negotiated.

There is no cancellation when the paper is physically destroyed by accident or mistake. In all cases, the party claiming that an apparent cancellation should not take effect has the burden of proof.

FACTS:

Route 156 Service Corporation executed a promissory note to the order of the Guaranty Bank & Trust Company in the amount of $5,000. Dowling, an officer of the corporation, signed the back of the note as an indorser. The principal of the note was to be repaid over a twelve month period, ending on February 15, 1975. The corporation defaulted on the note in November, 1974, at which point $1,795 remained outstanding. In November, the Guaranty Bank debited that amount from an account of a partnership in which Dowling had an interest and returned the note to the corporation bearing the legend "paid in full." Upon realizing that the debit was improper, the bank restored the funds to that account. The note remained unpaid. The bank brought suit against Dowling on the note. Dowling claimed a discharge by reason of cancellation.

DECISION:

Judgment for the Guaranty Bank & Trust Company. The cancellation of a negotiable instrument generally has no effect when it is made by mistake. The bank surrendered the instrument believing that the debit against the partnership account had satisfied the debt. The bank would not have surrendered the note if it did not, in good faith, believe it had in fact been paid. [Guaranty Bank & Trust Company v Dowling, 4 Conn App 376, 49 A2d 1216 (1985)]

The owner of the paper or the owner's agent may make the cancellation or may surrender the paper for cancellation to a party liable thereon. A cancellation is not effective if it is made by a person who is not the owner or the owner's agent. Thus the surrender of a check to the drawer for cancellation has no effect when not made by the payee or the payee's agent. If the paper has not been issued to the payee, it may be canceled or surrendered by the person who prepared it or who caused it to be prepared.

§ 34:4.   Renunciation.

The holder of an instrument, with or without consideration, may discharge the liability of a particular party by renunciation. This is done either (1) by surrendering the instrument to the party to be discharged, or (2) by executing a signed written renunciation which is then delivered to the party to be discharged.[4] There is no renunciation when the written renunciation is not delivered but is retained by the holder.

A renunciation may only be made by the owner of the paper or the owner's authorized agent. When made by any other person, the renunciation has no effect and the person making the renunciation may be liable for the tort of conversion of the paper to any person whose joinder in the renunciation was required. If the requirements of the Code are not satisfied there is no renunciation.

§ 34:5.   Impairment of Right of Recourse.

In most instances, there is at least one party to commercial paper who, if required to pay, will have a right of recourse, or a right to obtain indemnity from some other party. For example, in the least complicated situation, the payee of a note has indorsed it without qualification to the present holder. If the holder obtains payment from the indorsing payee, the latter has a right of recourse against the maker of the note. If the holder, without the indorser's consent, discharges the liability of the maker, extends the time for payment, or agrees not to sue, the indorser is also discharged, because the right of recourse held by the indorser has been impaired thereby.[5]

A creditor may prevent a release of one party to the instrument from discharging other parties to the instrument by expressly reserving the right to proceed against such other parties. Such a reservation of rights preserves the right of recourse of the other parties against the party released notwithstanding the terms of the release.

FACTS:

Kohntopp and Turner signed a promissory note as makers. Hallowell held the note. In consideration of a payment of $2,500 to him made by Kohntopp, Hallowell executed an agreement not "to execute" against Kohntopp. This agreement expressly reserved Hallowell's rights against Turner. Turner did not know of the existence of this agreement and thus did not consent to it. Later Hallowell sued Turner on the note. The defense was raised that the agreement not to execute against Kohntopp operated as a discharge of Turner. From a judgment for Turner, an appeal was taken by Hallowell.

[4] UCC § 3-605(1).
[5] UCC § 3-606(1)(a). Note that this is similar to the situation where a holder refuses to accept a proper tender of payment from the maker, in which case an indorser is discharged.

DECISION:

Judgment for Hallowell. An agreement not to sue a party impairs the security of any other party who upon paying the paper would have the right to sue the released party. As an exception to this, there is no release of the third party when the person releasing expressly reserves the right to proceed against the third party. Hallowell's release of Kohntopp did not release Turner because Hallowell expressly reserved his rights against Turner. The fact that Turner did not know of the releasing agreement nor of the reservation of rights against him had no effect. His consent to the reservation was not required. [Hallowell v Turner, 95 Idaho 392, 509 P2d 1313 (1973)]

---

§ 34:6.   Impairment of Collateral.

When commercial paper is executed, the maker may give property, such as stocks or bonds, to the payee to hold as security for the payment of the instrument. Likewise, any other party liable on the instrument may give collateral as security to the holder for the same purpose. This collateral security benefits all parties who might be liable on the paper because, to the extent that payment is obtained from the security, they are not required to make payment. Conversely, if the collateral security is impaired or harmed in any way that reduces its value, the parties who are liable are harmed since the possibility that they will be required to pay increases. Accordingly, a particular party is discharged if the holder unjustifiably impairs collateral security provided by that party or by any person against whom such party has a right of recourse.

It is customary for the modern promissory note to contain a provision consenting in advance to the extending of the time for payment. Such a provision on the face of the note binds all subsequent holders. They are therefore not discharged by such extensions.[6]

FACTS:

Michael Marshall and his wife borrowed money from the Beneficial Finance Co. The credit manager did not consider them a good credit risk and asked them to obtain a co-signer. Doug Garren agreed to co-sign the note with them. Since Garren was not sure of the credit reputation of the Marshalls, he requested that Beneficial take a security interest in Mr. Marshall's custom built Harley Davidson motorcycle as additional security for the loan. Garren subsequently learned that the Marshalls were attempting to sell the motorcycle and asked Beneficial to protect his interest. Beneficial refused since the Marshalls were then not in default. The Marshalls eventually defaulted on the loan. Beneficial and Marshall reached an agreement that Marshall would sell the motorcycle and pay the amount received to reduce the loan. Marshall eventually vanished and Beneficial received no proceeds from the sale. Beneficial sued Garren who defended on the grounds that the collateral for the loan had been impaired. From a judgement in favor of Garren, Beneficial appealed.

[6]Bay Nat. Bank & Trust Co. v James R. Mason and Mary S. Johnson (Fla App) 349 So 2d 810 (1977).

DECISION:

Judgment for Garren. The creditor lost his security interest in the collateral when Marshall sold the motorcycle. Garren also lost his right of recovery against the collateral upon it sale. Since the sale of the collateral without Garren's express consent constituted an unjustifiable impairment of the collateral which Garren relied upon as additional security for the loan, Garren was released. [Beneficial Finance Company of Norman v Marshall (Okla App) 551 P2d 315 (1976)]

---

§ 34:7. Reacquisition of Paper by Intermediate Party.

Commercial paper is sometimes reacquired by a party who has been an earlier holder. This occurs most commonly when that earlier party pays the then existing holder the amount due, thereby in effect purchasing the paper from the holder. When this occurs, the prior party may cancel all indorsements subsequent to the indorsement which such prior party had made on first indorsing the paper, and then may reissue or further negotiate the paper. Those subsequent indorsers whose indorsements have been canceled are discharged as to the reacquirer and all subsequent holders.[7]

§ 34:8. Alteration.

When an instrument is materially and fraudulently altered by the holder, any party whose obligation on the paper is changed thereby is discharged, unless such party has assented to the alteration or is barred by conduct from asserting a discharge. The effect of the discharge by alteration is limited, however, for a holder in due course may enforce the paper according to its original terms.[8]

FACTS:

Douglas Taylor executed three promissory notes to the Citizen's National Bank in the amount of $48,991 together with 15% interest. After the notes became past due the bank sent Taylor a letter informing him that since the maturity date had passed, the bank was increasing the interest on the notes to 22 1/2%. The three notes had been altered by crossing out the interest figure of 15% in pencil and writing in its place the new rate of 22 1/2%. Taylor was notified of the change in interest rate and later signed an extension of the notes after the alteration took place. The bank sued Taylor to recover on the three notes. Taylor claimed that he had been discharged because the bank had fraudulently altered the interest rate on the notes.

DECISION:

Judgment for the bank. As against any person other than a subsequent holder in due course, alteration by the holder which is both fraudulent and material discharges any party whose contract is thereby changed unless that party assents or is precluded from asserting the defense. The bank was clearly the holder of the notes, and the changes in interest rate from 15% to 22 1/2% were clearly material. The

[7]UCC §3-208.
[8]UCC §3-407.

bank, however, did not fraudulently alter the note. There must be a dishonest and deceitful purpose to acquire more than one was entitled to under the note as signed by the maker. Taylor consented to the change. He was notified of the change in interest rate and later signed an extension of the notes after the alteration had taken place. [Citizen's National Bank of Wilmar v Taylor, _____Minn_____, 368 NW2d 913 (1985)]

§ 34:9.   Discharge for Miscellaneous Causes.

In addition to the discharge of a party as discussed in the preceding sections, the conduct of certain parties with respect to the commercial paper or the enforcement of rights thereunder may release some of the parties to the paper. This occurs (1) when a check has been certified on the application of the holder; (2) when the holder accepts an acceptance that varies the terms of the draft; and (3) when a presentment, notice of dishonor, or protest, when required, is delayed beyond the time permitted or is absent and such delay or absence is not excused.

In addition, federal or local statutes may provide for the discharge of a party by bankruptcy proceedings or by local laws declaring certain obligations not enforceable because they violate particular statutes.

B. DISCHARGE OF ALL PARTIES

In contrast with conduct which discharges individual parties to paper, some types of conduct release everyone from liability.

§ 34:10.   Discharge of Party Primarily Liable.

The primary party on an instrument, that is, the maker of a note or the acceptor of a draft,[9] has no right of recourse against any party to the paper. Conversely, every other party who may be held liable on the paper has a right of recourse against the person primarily liable. If the holder discharges in any way a party who is primarily liable, all parties to the instrument are discharged, as the discharge of the primary party discharges the persons who had a right of recourse against the primary party.[10]

§ 34:11.   Primary Party's Reacquisition of Paper.

When a party primarily liable on the paper reacquires it as owner at any time, whether before or after it is due, the instrument is then held by one who has no right to sue any other party on the paper. Such reacquisition therefore discharges the liability of all intervening parties to the instrument.[11]

C. EFFECT OF DISCHARGE ON HOLDER IN DUE COURSE

An ordinary holder or assignee of paper is subject to any discharge. A holder in due course may or may not be subject to a prior discharge.

[9]An accommodated payee may in some respects also be a primary party since the accommodating party, if required to pay an indorsee, has a right of recourse against such payee.
[10]UCC §3-601(3). In some instances this rule is modified by §3-606.
[11]Litwin v Barrier, 6 Kan App 2d 128, 626 P2d 1232 (1981).

§ 34:12. Discharge of Individual Party.

The fact that a party has been discharged of liability, and even that a new holder of the paper knows of it, does not prevent the new holder from being a holder in due course as to any party remaining liable on the paper.[12] If the holder in due course does not have notice or knowledge of the discharge of a party before acquiring the paper, the holder in due course is not bound by that discharge and may enforce the obligation of the discharged party as though there had been no discharge.[13] To avoid being sued by such a holder in due course, a party obtaining a discharge should have a notation of it made on the paper so that any subsequent holder would necessarily have notice of that fact.

§ 34:13. Discharge of All Parties.

The fact that the liabilities of all parties to a commercial paper have been discharged does not destroy the negotiable character nor the existence of the commercial paper. If it should thereafter be negotiated to a person who qualifies as a holder in due course, the latter may enforce the liability of any party on the paper, although otherwise discharged, of whose discharge the holder in due course had no notice or knowledge.

SUMMARY

A party may be discharged either individually or by some act that has discharged all parties to the paper at one time. A party to a commercial paper is usually discharged by making payment to the proper person. There may be a discharge by accord and satisfaction, a novation, a covenant not to sue, rescission, or the substitution of another instrument. The obligation of a particular party on commercial paper is discharged by paying the amount of the instrument to the holder or to the holder's authorized agent. Payment to anyone else is not effective to discharge the liability of the payor.

The liability of a particular party may be discharged by cancellation. The holder of an instrument with or without consideration may discharge the liability of a particular party by renunciation. An impairment of the right of recourse or an unjustifiable impairment of the collateral by the holder will discharge the liability of a particular party. If an intermediate party reacquires the paper it may result in a discharge of parties. An alteration will discharge any party whose contract is thereby changed. The discharge is limited, however, for a holder in due course may enforce the paper according to its original terms.

A discharge of the party primarily liable discharges all persons who had a right of recourse against the primary party. No discharge of any party is effective against a subsequent holder in due course unless the holder in due course has notice thereof when such holder takes the instrument. An exception is made for insolvency discharges which are effective without notice.

---

[12]UCC §3-305(2)(e).
[13]UCC §3-602. As an exception to this rule, the holder in due course is bound by a prior discharge in insolvency proceedings, such as bankruptcy, whether the holder had notice thereof or not. UCC §3-305(2)(d).

QUESTIONS AND CASE PROBLEMS

1. What social forces are affected by the rule of law that permits the holder of commercial paper to discharge selected parties without discharging the other parties to the paper?

2. Does the knowledge that there is an adverse claimant prevent the making of a payment to the holder which discharges the obligation of the party making payment?

3. Donavan owed the A & B Body Works for repairs to her auto. She gave the Body Works a promissory note payable to its order for the amount which was due. When she found that she could not pay the note when due, she so informed Ray, the son of one of the owners of Body Works. He told her to forget the debt. Later Body Works sued Donavan on the note. She claimed that the note had been discharged by cancellation. Was she correct?

4. Harrison gave the Construction Transport Company a promissory note representing a freight bill owed it. The note was payable in sixty days. The transport company wanted the money sooner and changed the note to make the amount due in thirty days. Harrison refused to pay the note and was sued on the sixty-first day. Is Harrison liable?

5. Stokes, as maker, executed a promissory note. The note was indorsed by the payee and ultimately indorsed to the Arrow Rental Company. Arrow discharged all parties to the note but did not surrender the note to anyone. Thereafter Arrow transferred the note to Klaxon who had no knowledge of the discharge of the parties to the paper. In a suit by Klaxon against the prior parties, it was claimed that the paper was not negotiable because the discharge of the prior parties had terminated or destroyed its negotiable character. Was this correct?

6. On August 15, Janet borrowed $3,000 from Richard, giving Richard in return a negotiable promissory note for $3,000 payable to the order of Richard. The note was due in thirty days. On September 10th, Richard indorsed the note to the Alden Car Co. On September 12th, Alden Car Co. learned that Janet was seriously ill. Alden Car Co. wrote Janet that they were discharging her from liability on the instrument. On the due date, Alden Car Co. asked Richard to pay the note as an indorser, explaining why they did not collect from Janet. Is Richard obligated to pay?

7. A discharge of all parties to commercial paper destroys the negotiable character of the paper. Appraise this statement.

8. Rosemarie purchased a freezer on credit from the Abbot Department Store. She gave Abbot a promissory note for the balance due. Abbot negotiated the note by indorsement to the Central Finance Company. Rosemarie did not pay the note when it was due. Central demanded and obtained payment of the note from Abbot. Abbot then sued Rosemarie on the note. She raised the defense that as the note had been paid once all liability had been discharged and she therefore could not be sued on the note by Abbot. Was she correct?

9. Compare discharge by (a) renunciation and (b) cancellation.

10. Burg executed and delivered a promissory note for $1,060 payable to Liesemer. When the note was due, Burg paid $893 and demanded credit for the remainder of the amount due because of the boarding expense

incurred by Liesemer's daughter. Liesemer gave Burg the note so that he could compute the amount due. Burg refused to give credit for Liesemer's claim and kept the note. When Liesemer brought an action to recover the remainder of the note, it appeared that Burg had written across the face of the note, "Paid February 9th." It was contended that the note had been discharged by cancellation. Do you agree? [Liesemer v Burg, 106 Mich 124, 63 NW 999]

11. As part of a business plan, Schwald executed and delivered a note to Montgomery. The parties then made a new business arrangement, and Montgomery intentionally tore up the note and threw it into the waste-basket. It was subsequently contended that this note had been canceled. Do you agree? [Montgomery v Schwald, 117 Mo App 75, 166 SW 831]

12. *H* was the holder of a promissory note made by *M*. The note was payable in 12 months. After preliminary discussion between the parties in the eleventh month with respect to refinancing, *H* telephoned *M* that he "canceled" the note. The next day, *H* changed his mind and negotiated the note to *C* who satisfied the requirements of being a holder in due course. When *C* demanded payment of *M*, *M* asserted that he was not liable because he had been discharged when *H* canceled the note. Was he correct? [Citizens Fidelity Bank & Trust Co. v Stark (Ky) 431 SW2d 722; Bihlmire v Hahn (DC Wis) 43 FRD 503]

13. Gorman executed and delivered to the First National Bank a negotiable promissory note payable to its order. The note was stolen from the bank. Some time later, Richardson, a former employee of the bank, delivered the note to Gorman in return for Gorman's payment of the balance then due. The note was returned to Gorman marked "paid." First National Bank sued Gorman for the balance of the loan. He raised the defense that the note had been discharged by payment. Decide. [First National Bank v Gorman, 45 Wyo 519, 21 P2d 549]

14. Rochelle executed a promissory note. Nevis was the holder of the note. Nevis renounced his claim against Rochelle on the note. Thereafter, he asserted that his renunciation was not binding because he had not received any consideration for it. Is Rochelle liable on the note?

15. Bates, the maker of a negotiable promissory note payable to bearer paid the note to the holder Charles, knowing that Charles had stolen the note from Doreen. Is Bates discharged of liability?

16. Bond, Lewis, and Fernwood are indorsers, in that order, of a promissory note given by Adams to Bond. Gates, the holder, presents the note to Adams, who fails to pay. Gates notified Bond, Lewis, and Fernwood. In his written notice to Bond, Gates stated "You can be assured that I will not proceed against you in this matter." State what effect, if any, these words would have on the liability of Bond, Lewis, and Fernwood.

17. The Citizens State Bank issued a cashier's check payable to the order of Donovan. He indorsed it to Denny, who did business as the Houston Aircraft Co., and included in the indorsement a recital that it was "in full satisfaction of any and all claims of any character whatever." Denny crossed out this quoted phrase and wrote Donovan and the bank that he had done so. The Houston Aircraft Co. sued the Citizens National Bank on the check. Was the bank liable? [Houston Aircraft v Citizens State Bank (Tex Civ App) 184 SW2d 335]

CHAPTER 35

CHECKS AND CUSTOMER-

BANK RELATIONSHIP

CHAPTER OBJECTIVES

After studying this chapter you will be able to:
1. Discuss the significance of certification.
2. List and explain the duties of the drawee bank.
3. Set forth the methods for and legal effect of stopping payment.
4. State when a check must be presented for payment in order to charge secondary parties.
5. Describe the liability of a bank for improper payment and collection.
6. Discuss the legal effect of forgeries and material alterations.
7. Describe the time limitations for reporting forgeries and alterations.

A. CHECKS

In modern business the overwhelming majority of money obligations are settled by means of checks drawn by the debtor on his own bank and payable to the order of the creditor. By means of checks it is possible to make payment safely and conveniently without the need of safeguarding a shipment of money. The checkbook stub and the canceled check make a written record which may be used at a later date to show that payment was made.

§ 35:1. Nature of a Check.

A **check** is a particular kind of draft. The first three of the following features of a check distinguish it from other drafts or bills of exchange:[1]

---

[1]Checks are governed by both Article 3 of the Uniform Commercial Code relating to commercial paper and Article 4 governing bank deposits and collections.

(1) **The drawee of a check is always a bank.**

(2) **As a practical matter, the check is drawn on the assumption that the bank has on deposit in the drawer's account an amount sufficient to pay the check.** In the case of a draft, there is no assumption that the drawee has any of the drawer's money with which to pay the instrument. Actually, the rights of the parties are not affected by the fact that the depositor does not have funds on deposit with the bank sufficient to pay the check.

If a draft is dishonored, the drawer is civilly liable; but if a check is drawn with intent to defraud the person to whom it is delivered, the drawer is also subject to criminal prosecution in most states under what are known as *bad check laws*. Most states provide that if the check is not made good within a stated period, such as 10 days, it will be presumed that the check was originally issued with the intent to defraud.

(3) **A check is demand paper.** A draft may be payable either on demand or at a future date. The standard form of check does not specify when it is payable, and it is therefore automatically payable on demand. This eliminates the need for an acceptance since the holder of the check will merely present it for payment.

One exception arises when a check is postdated, that is, when the check shows a date later than the actual date of execution and delivery. Here the check is not payable until the date arrives.[2] This, in effect, changes the check to time paper without expressly stating so.

While it is customary for banks to supply depositors with printed forms of checks, a check may be any writing.[3] A card, given to a computer terminal located away from a bank for the purpose of withdrawing money from the bank or making a repayment on a loan, is also a check.[4]

(4) **The delivery of a check is not regarded as an assignment of the money on deposit.** It therefore does not automatically transfer the rights of the depositor against the bank to the holder of the check, and there is no duty on the part of the drawee bank to the holder to pay the holder the amount of the check.[5]

§ 35:2.   Certified Checks.

The drawee bank may certify a check drawn on it, which has the same legal consequence as the acceptance of a draft. The certification must be written on the check and signed by an authorized representative of the bank.

The effect of the certification is to set aside in a special account maintained by the bank as much of the depositor's account as is needed to pay the certified check. With respect to the holder of the check, the certification is an undertaking by the bank that when the check is presented for payment, it will make payment according to the terms of the check without regard to the standing of the depositor's account at that time.

[2]Howells, Inc. v Nelson (Utah) 565 P2d 1147 (1977).
[3]The printed bank check is preferable because it generally carries magnetic ink figures which facilitate sorting and posting.
[4]Illinois v Continental Illinois National Bank (CA7 Ill) 536 F2d 176 (1976).
[5]UCC §3-409(1). Galaxy Boat Mfg. Co. v East End State Bank (Tex App) 641 SW2d 594 (1982).

A check may be certified by a bank upon the request of the drawer or the holder. In the latter case all prior indorsers and the drawer are automatically released from liability.[6] Since the holder could have received payment, as the bank was willing to certify the check, and since the holder did not take the payment but chose to take the certification, the prior secondary parties are released from liability. When the certification is obtained by the drawer, there is no release of the secondary parties.

FACTS:

Menke submitted a bid for construction work to the Board of Education of West Burlington. With his bid, he submitted a check which had been stamped with words stating that the check was certified by the State Central Savings Bank. Under these words was a line for a signature but there was no signature on this line. The Board of Education claimed that the check was not a certified check and rejected Menke's bid. Menke then sued the bank for failing to certify his check. The bank defended on the ground that it had in fact certified the check because the stamp on the check was by itself a certification.

DECISION:

Judgment for Menke. In order to be a certified check, words of certification must be written on the check and this must be signed by an authorized representative of the bank. Without the signature, there is no certification even though the bank had intended to certify the check. [Menke v Board of Education (Iowa) 211 NW2d 601 (1973)]

---

§ 35:3.   Liability of Drawer.

If the check is presented for payment and paid, no liability of the drawer arises. If the bank refuses to make payment, the drawer is then subject to the same liability as in the case of the nonpayment of an ordinary draft. If proper notice of dishonor is not given the drawer of the check,[7] the drawer will be discharged from liability to the same extent as the drawer of an ordinary draft.

§ 35:4.   Duties of Drawee Bank.

It is necessary to distinguish between the status of the drawer with respect to a check and the drawer's relationship with the bank on the contract of deposit.

(a) **Privacy.** The bank owes the depositor the duty of maintaining secrecy concerning information which the bank acquires in connection with the depositor-bank relationship. Law enforcement officers and administrative agencies cannot require the disclosure of information relating to a depositor's account without obtaining the depositor's consent, a search warrant, or fol-

[6]UCC §3-411(1). Sherwin-Williams Co. v Sarrett (Miss) 405 So2d 842 (1981).
[7]Under federal reserve regulations notice of dishonor may be given by telephone. Security Bank and Trust Co. v Federal National Bank (OklaApp) 554 P2d 119 (1976).

lowing the statutory procedures designed to protect from unreasonable invasions of privacy.[8]

(b) **Payment.** A bank is under a general contractual duty to its depositor to pay on demand all checks to the extent of the funds in the depositor's account. When the bank breaches this contract, the bank is liable to the drawer for damages. As in the case of an unaccepted draft, there is ordinarily no duty owed the holder to accept or pay a check.

(c) **Stale Checks.** A bank acting in good faith may pay a check presented more than six months after its date (commonly known as a **stale check**); but, unless the check is certified, it is not required to do so. The fact that a bank may refuse to pay a check which is more than six months old does not mean that it must pay a check which is less than six months old or that it is not required to exercise reasonable care in making payment of any check.

(d) **Payment After Depositor's Death.** The effectiveness of a check ordinarily ceases with the death of the drawer. The death of the drawer, however, does not revoke the agency of the bank until it has knowledge of the death and has had reasonable opportunity to act. Even with such knowledge, the bank may continue for ten days to pay or certify checks drawn by the drawer unless ordered to stop payment by a person claiming an interest in the account.[9]

Even when the bank has the right to make payment after the death of the depositor, it may refuse to do so and its dishonor of the check in such case is not wrongful.

FACTS:

Marlow had a checking account in the Bank of Hartshorne. He drew a check on the account on May 14. He died on May 30. Marlow's daughter, Cirar, informed the bank on May 31 that her father had died. On June 4, the bank paid the check which Marlow had drawn. Cirar sued the bank for the amount of the check.

DECISION:

The bank was not liable. The bank was only notified of Marlow's death. It therefore could continue to pay checks for ten days. No stop order had been given the bank. Had the daughter notified the bank both of Marlow's death and her interest in the account and had also ordered the bank not to pay any checks, the bank could not have paid any check thereafter. In the absence of such a stop payment order, it had ten days after being notified of the death in which it could pay the checks which had been drawn by the deceased depositor. [Cirar v Bank of Hartshorne (Okla) 567 P2d 96 (1977)]

---

[8]Right to Financial Privacy Act of 1978, PL 95-630, 92 Stat 3697, 12 United States Code §3401 et seq.
[9]UCC §4-405.

§ 35:5. Stopping Payment of Check.

The drawer has the power of **stopping payment** of a check by notifying the drawee bank not to pay it when it is presented for payment. This is a useful device when a check is lost or mislaid. A duplicate check can be written, and, to make sure that the payee does not receive payment twice or that an improper person does not receive payment on the first check, payment on the first check can be stopped. Likewise, if payment is made by check and then the payee defaults on the contract so that the drawer would have a claim for breach of contract, payment on the check can be stopped, assuming that the payee has not already cashed it.

It is to the advantage of the payee to require either a certified check or a cashier's check, for with respect to either check, the other party to the transaction cannot stop payment.

(a) Form of Stop Payment Order. The stop payment order may be either oral or written. If oral, however, it is only binding on the bank for 14 calender days unless confirmed in writing within that time. A written stop payment order or confirmation is effective for six months.

(b) Liability to Holder for Stopping Payment. The act of stopping payment may in some cases make the depositor liable to the holder of the check. If the depositor has no proper ground for stopping payment, the depositor is liable to the holder of the check. In any case, the depositor is liable for stopping payment with respect to any holder in due course or other party having the rights of a holder in due course, unless payment was stopped for a reason that may be asserted against such a holder as a defense. The fact that payment of a check has been stopped does not affect its negotiable character.[10]

§ 35:6. Time of Presentment of Check for Payment.

In order to charge a secondary party to demand paper, presentment for payment must generally be made upon the primary party to the instrument within a reasonable time after that secondary party has signed it. Reasonable time is determined by the nature of the instrument, by commercial usage, and by the facts of the particular case.[11]

Failure to make timely presentment discharges all prior indorsers of the instrument. It also discharges the drawer, if the draft was payable at a bank, to the extent that the drawer has lost, through the bank's failure, money which was on deposit at the bank to meet the payment of the instrument.[12]

The UCC establishes two presumptions as to what is a reasonable time in which to present a check for payment.[13] If the check is not certified and is both drawn and payable within the United States, it is presumed as to the drawer that thirty days after the date of the check or the date of its issuance, whichever is later, is the reasonable period in which to make pre-

---

[10]Bigbee v Indiana, 173 Ind App 462, 364 NE2d 149 (1977).
[11]UCC § 3-503(1)(e),(2).
[12]UCC §3-502(1).
[13]A presumption means that the trier of fact must find the existence of the fact presumed in the absence of evidence that supports a contrary conclusion. UCC §1-201(31).

sentment for payment. With respect to the liability of an indorser, seven days after indorsing is presumed to be a reasonable time.[14]

§ 35:7.   Dishonor of Check.

When a check is dishonored by nonpayment, the holder must follow the same procedure of notice to the secondary parties as in the case of a draft or bill of exchange in order to hold them liable for payment. As in the case of any drawer of a draft or bill of exchange who countermands payment, notice of dishonor need not be given to the drawer who has stopped payment on a check. Notice is also excused under any circumstances that would excuse notice in the case of a promissory note. For example, no notice need be given a drawer or an indorser who knows that sufficient funds to cover the check are not on deposit, since such party has no reason to expect that the check will be paid by the bank.[15]

When a check is sent in the course of the collection process to the bank on which it is drawn, that bank must either pay or promptly return the check as unpaid, or send notice of its dishonor, as by returning the check unpaid for "insufficient funds." If the drawee bank does not act before midnight of the business day on which it received the check, it automatically becomes liable for the face of the instrument.[16] Oral notice of dishonor is sufficient.

(a) **Bank's Liability to Drawer of Check.** The contract between the depositor (drawer) and the bank (drawee) obligates the latter to pay in accordance with the orders of its depositor as long as there is sufficient money on deposit to make such payment. If the bank improperly refuses to make payments, it is liable to the drawer for damages sustained by the drawer in consequence of such dishonor.

(b) **Bank's Liability to Holder.** If the check has not been certified, the holder has no claim against the bank for the dishonor of the check, regardless of the fact that the bank had acted in breach of its contract with its depositor. If the bank had certified the check, it is liable to the holder when it dishonors the check as the certification imposes upon the bank a primary liability to pay the face amount of the check.

FACTS:

Hixson owed money to Galyen Petroleum Company. He paid with three checks. The bank refused to cash the three checks because there was not sufficient money in the Hixson account to pay all three. Galyen sued Hixson and the bank.

DECISION:

Judgment for bank. When a bank has not certified a check, the payee can not sue the bank when it refuses to pay the check when presented to it. The check does not operate as an assignment of whatever money there is in the account. Therefore, the bank was not required

[14]UCC §3-503(2).
[15]UCC §3-511(2)(b).
[16]UCC §4-302, 4-104(1)(h).

to pay the payee as much money as there was in the drawer's account. The bank had no liability on the checks because they had not been certified by it. Therefore, the bank was not liable to the payee for the dishonor of the checks. [Galyen Petroleum Co. v Hixson, 213 Neb 683, 331 NW2d 1 (1983)]

Regardless of whether the holder has any right against the bank, the holder may proceed against the secondary parties, the drawer, and any unqualified indorsers.

FACTS:

The Office Furniture Outlet issued to International Furniture a check for $1,000 drawn on its account with First Georgia Bank. International presented the check to the bank and received in exchange a cashier's check for $1,000. International Furniture paid a $2.50 fee for the cashier's check. Office Furniture had stopped payment on its check to International. The bank through its own error, failed to note the stop payment until after the cashier's check had been issued. When the cashier's check was presented for payment, the bank refused to honor it. International brought suit against the bank. The bank claimed that it received no consideration for the cashier's check.

DECISION:

Judgment for the First Georgia Bank. The $2.50 charge was clearly a processing fee and not consideration for the check. Consideration for the $1,000 cashier's check was the $1,000 check issued by Office Furniture Outlet. Once payment was properly stopped on this check, there was no consideration for the cashier's check. Where the instrument is in the hands of the original payee, where no holder in due course is involved, where the payee has not suffered any detriment or changed position because of reliance on the instrument, the bank may properly defend itself on the basis of mistake and want of consideration. [International Furniture Distributors, Inc. v First Georgia Bank, 163 Ga App 765, 294 SE2d 732 (1982)]

§ 35.8. Agency Status of Collecting Bank.

When a person deposits a commercial paper in a bank, the bank is ordinarily thereby made an agent to collect or obtain the payment of the paper. Unless the contrary intent clearly appears, a bank receiving an item is deemed to take it as agent for the depositor rather than as becoming the purchaser of the paper. This presumption is not affected by the form of the indorsement nor by the absence of any indorsement. The bank is also regarded as being merely an agent even though the depositor has the right to make immediate withdrawals against the deposited item.[17] In consequence of the agency status, the depositor remains the owner of the item and is therefore subject to the risks of ownership involved in its collection, in the absence of fault on the part of any collecting bank.[18]

[17] UCC § 4-201(1).
[18] UCC § 4-202.

When a bank cashes a check deposited by its customer or cashes a check drawn by its customer on the strength of a deposited check, it is a holder of the check deposited by its customer and may sue the parties thereon, even though as between the customer and the bank the latter is an agent for collection and has the right to charge back the amount of the deposited check if it cannot be collected. When the bank receives final settlement for an item taken for collection, the agency status ends and the bank is merely a debtor of its customer just as though the customer had made an ordinary cash deposit in the bank.[19]

B. LIABILITY OF BANK FOR IMPROPER PAYMENT AND COLLECTION

The drawee bank may be liable for paying a check contrary to a stop payment order or when there has been a forgery or alteration.

§ 35:9. Payment Over Stop Payment Order.

A bank must be given a reasonable time to put a stop payment order into effect. However, if the bank makes payment of a check after it has been properly notified to stop payment, it is liable to the depositor for the loss the depositor sustains, in the absence of a valid limitation of the bank's liability.[20] The burden of establishing the loss resulting in such case rests upon the depositor.

FACTS:

Tusso sent a check for $600 drawn on the Security National Bank payable to the order of the Adamson Construction Company. He then realized that he had already paid Adamson. At 9:00 a.m. the next morning, he notified the bank to stop payment. Later that morning, the check was brought to the bank, and, at 10:40 a.m., the bank certified the check and charged it to Tusso's account. Tusso sued the bank to recover the amount so charged. The bank claimed that he was required to prove that the bank had been negligent.

DECISION:

The depositor was not required to prove that the bank had been negligent in making payment over the stop payment order. The bank was liable because it had violated the order; the absence of negligence was not a defense. [Tusso v Security National Bank, 349 NYS2d 914 (1973)]

§ 35:10. Payment on Forged Signature of Drawer.

A **forgery** of the signature occurs when the name of the depositor has been signed by another person without authority to do so and with the intent

---

[19] Cooper v Union Bank, 9 Cal3d 123, 107 CalRptr 1, 507 P2d 609 (1973).
[20] A bank cannot contractually limit its liability for paying over a valid stop payment order. UCC § 4-403 Comment 8.

to defraud by making it appear that the check was signed by the depositor. The bank is liable to the depositor (drawer) if it pays a check on which the drawer's signature has been forged since a forgery ordinarily has no effect as a signature. The risk of loss caused by the forged signature of the drawer is thus placed upon the bank without regard to whether the bank could have detected the forgery.[21]

Although the bank has no right to pay a check on which the drawer's signature is forged, the drawer may be barred from objecting that the signature was a forgery. If the drawer's negligence contributed substantially to the forging of the signature, the drawer cannot assert that it was forged when the drawee bank makes payment of the check while acting in good faith and conforming to reasonable commercial standards. For example, if the drawer signs checks with a mechanical writer, reasonable care must be exercised to prevent unauthorized persons from making use of it to forge or "sign" the drawer's name with such device. If the depositor's negligence enables a third person to make such improper use of it, the depositor is barred from objecting to the payment of the check by the bank.

FACTS:

Judy Bode worked for Read & Read as executive secretary. Shortly after being hired, she began forging the signature of Emerson Read on checks drawn on the South Carolina National Bank, making them payable to herself. She also began forging checks on several other checking accounts of businesses owned or managed by Read and his brother. She would either forge Read's signature by signing his name or using a rubber facsimile stamp of Read's signature which Read obtained to enable him to sign checks in a more expeditious manner. It was Bode's responsibility to reconcile the bank statements of all the accounts entrusted to her and no one was given the responsibility to check behind her. Bode destroyed all of the forged checks on receipt of the statements from the bank. No one compared the balance on the statement to the balance in the checkbook nor compared the number of the checks in the statement with the number of checks written in the checkbook. Emerson Read brought an action against the bank for damages. The bank denied liability alleging that Read was negligent.

DECISION:

Judgment for the bank. Read's negligence as a matter of law substantially contributed to the forgeries. He was negligent in failing to maintain proper control over the signature stamp. He allowed the same person who had possession of the checkbook to reconcile the statements with no verification, and he failed to examine the statements. [Read v South Carolina National Bank, ____ SC ____, 335 SE2d 359 (1985)]

---

[21]Perini Corp. v First National Bank (CA5 Ga) 553 F2d 398 (1977).

When a check is presented to the drawee bank for payment, it alone is responsible for determining whether the signature of the drawer, its customer, is a forgery. Prior indorsers do not warrant that the signature of the drawer is genuine; and, if the bank pays money or gives a cashier's check in payment of the depositor's check, it cannot thereafter recover the money paid or defend against payment on the cashier's check on the ground that the drawer's signature had been forged.

§ 35:11.   Payment on Forged or Missing Indorsement.

A drawee bank that honors a depositor's check bearing a forged indorsement must recredit the drawer's account upon the drawer's discovery of the forgery and notification to the bank. Since the bank paid out the money to a person who was not the holder of the instrument, the drawer may bring an action against the bank to recredit the drawer's account and the owner of the instrument may sue the bank for conversion.[22]

A drawee bank is liable for the loss when it pays a check that lacks an essential indorsement. In such a case, the instrument has not been properly presented; and by definition the person presenting the check for payment is not the holder of the instrument and is not entitled to demand or receive payment.

When a person deposits a check but neglects to indorse it, the depositor's bank may make an indorsement on behalf of the depositor unless the check expressly requires the customer's indorsement. But a bank can not add the missing indorsement of a person who is not its customer depositing the item in the customer's account in the bank.[23]

§ 35:12.   Alteration of Check.

If the face of the check has been altered so that the amount to be paid has been increased, the bank is liable to the drawer for the amount of the increase when it makes payment for the greater amount. The bank has the opportunity of examining the check when it is presented for payment and, if it fails to detect the alteration, it is liable for the loss.

The drawer may be barred from claiming that there was an alteration by virtue of conduct with respect to writing the check or conduct after receiving the canceled check from the bank. As to the former, the drawer is barred if the check was carelessly written and the negligence substantially contributed to the making of the material alteration and the bank honored the check in good faith and observed reasonable commercial standards in so doing.[24] For example, the drawer is barred when the check was written with blank spaces so that it was readily possible to change "four" to "four-hundred," and the drawee bank paid out the latter sum without any cause to know that there was an alteration. A careful person will therefore write figures and words close together and run a line through or cross out any blank spaces.

---

[22]UCC §3-419(1)(c).
[23]Krump Construction Co., Inc. v First National Bank (Nev) 655 P2d 524 (1982).
[24]UCC §3-406.

§ 35:13.   Unauthorized Collection of Check.

Although a bank acts as agent for its customer in obtaining payment of a check deposited with it by its customer, it may be liable to a third person when the act of its customer is unauthorized or unlawful with respect to the third person. That is, if the customer has no authority to deposit the check, the bank, in obtaining payment from the drawee of the check and thereafter depositing the proceeds of the check in the account of its customer, may be liable for conversion of the check to the person lawfully entitled to the check and its proceeds.

§ 35:14.   Indemnity Right of Bank.

When a bank is held liable to a drawer or a depositor for a payment or collection which is improper because a signature on the check is a forgery, the bank will in many instances be able to recover its loss from a prior party to the paper who has made either an express or implied warranty that signatures are genuine.

§ 35:15.   Time Limitations.

(a) **Non-Code Statute of Limitations.** A local non-Code statute of limitations will fix the maximum time for asserting a claim against a bank for the breach of the customer-bank deposit contract, an action against any bank for conversion of an item of commercial paper, or an action by one bank against another bank or party to paper to obtain indemnity or contribution.

(b) **Forgery and Alteration Reporting Time.** A depositor has the duty to examine with reasonable care and promptness a bank statement and relevant checks which are paid in good faith and sent to the depositor by the bank, and to discover any unauthorized signature or alteration on the checks. The depositor must notify the bank promptly after discovering either of the foregoing. If the bank exercises ordinary care in paying such a check and suffers a loss because the depositor fails to perform these duties, the depositor cannot assert the unauthorized signature, or the alteration, against the bank.[25]

Regardless of the care or lack of care of either the depositor or the bank, the depositor is precluded from asserting the depositor's unauthorized signature or any alteration if the depositor does not report it within one year from the time the bank statement is received. A forged indorsement must be reported within three years.[26]

(c) **Unauthorized Signature or Alteration By Same Wrongdoer.** Often the same wrongdoer is perpetrating a series of forgeries or alterations. The depositor must warn the bank as soon as possible of the first forgery or altered item so that the bank can protect itself from a repetition of the misconduct. A failure by the depositor to notify the bank within fourteen days after a statement of account with the paid items is sent, causes the depositor

[25]UCC §4-406(2)(a).
[26]UCC §4-406(4).

to bear the loss on additional checks, forged or altered by the same wrong-doer thereafter paid in good faith by the bank.[27]

§ 35:16.   Electronic Fund Transfer Act.

The primary objective of the **Electronic Fund Transfer Act (EFTA)** is to provide a basic framework for individual consumer rights. The term **electronic fund transfer** means any transfer of funds (other than a transaction originated by check, draft, or similar paper instrument) which is initiated through an electronic terminal, telephone or computer or magnetic tape so as to authorize a financial institution to debit or credit an account. The service available from the automated teller machine is a common form of an EFT.

§ 35:17.   Types of Electronic Fund Transfers.

There are presently four common types of EFT systems in use. In some of these systems, the consumer has a card giving the consumer access to the machine. The consumer usually has a private code which prevents others from using the card who may obtain possession of it.

(a) **Automated Teller Machines.** The automated teller machine performs many of the tasks of human bank tellers. Once an individual activates the ATM, it allows the user to deposit and withdraw funds from his or her account, to transfer funds between accounts, to make payments on loan accounts, and to obtain cash advances from bank credit cards.

(b) **Pay by Phone Systems.** This system facilitates the paying of telephone and utility bills without writing checks. The consumer calls the bank and directs the transfer of funds to a designated third party.

(c) **Direct Deposits and Withdrawals.** An employee may authorize an employer to deposit the employee's wages directly to the employee's account. A consumer who has just purchased an automobile on time may elect to have monthly payments withdrawn from the consumer's bank account and paid directly to the seller.

(d) **Point-of-Sale-Terminals.** This allows the business with a terminal to transfer funds from the consumer's account to the store account.

§ 35:18.   Responsibility and Liability of Financial Institution.

The consumer must be furnished with the prescribed terms and conditions of all EFT services in advance, be given periodic statements covering account activity, and any preauthorized EFT from an individual's account must be authorized in writing in advance.

The financial institution is liable to a consumer for all damages proximately caused by its failure to make an EFT in accordance with the terms and conditions of an account, unless the consumer's account has insuf-

[27]UCC §4-406(2)(b).
[28]15 USC §§1693 et seq.

ficient funds, the funds are subject to legal process, the transfer would exceed an established credit limit, or insufficient cash is available in an ATM.

§ 35.19.   Consumer Liability.

A consumer who notifies the issuer of the EFT card within two days after learning of a loss or theft of the card is limited to a maximum liability of $50 for unauthorized use of the card. Failure to notify within this time will increase the consumer's liability for losses to a maximum of $500.

The consumer has a responsibility to examine periodic statements provided by the financial institution. If it is established that a loss would not have occurred but for the failure of the consumer to report within sixty days of the transmittal of the statement any unauthorized transfer, then the loss is borne by the consumer.

SUMMARY

A check is a particular kind of draft; it is drawn on a bank and payable on demand. A delivery of a check is not an assignment of money on deposit with the bank on which it is drawn. It therefore does not automatically transfer the rights of the depositor against the bank to the holder of the check and there is no duty on the part of the drawee bank to the holder to pay the holder the amount of the check.

Certification of a check by the bank has the same legal consequence as the acceptance of a draft—the bank becomes the primary party. Certification may be at the request of the drawee or the holder. Upon certification by the holder, all prior indorsers and the drawer are automatically released from liability. Notice of nonpayment of a check must be given to the drawer of a check. If no notice is given, the drawer will be discharged from liability to the same extent as the drawer of an ordinary draft. The drawee bank owes the depositor certain duties, such as not disclosing information relating to the depositor's account and paying on demand all checks issued by the depositor.

A depositor may stop payment on a check already issued. However, the depositor may become liable to a holder in due course unless such stop payment was for a reason that may be raised against a holder in due course.

Upon dishonor, a holder must follow the same procedure of notice to each of the secondary parties as in the case of a draft in order to hold them liable for payment.

The bank is the agent of the depositor. The bank may become liable for paying a check contrary to a stop payment order or when there has been a forgery or alteration. The bank will not be liable, however, if the drawer's negligence has substantially contributed to the forgery. A bank that pays on a forged indorsement must recredit the drawer's account. A depositor is subject to certain time limitations in order to impose liability upon the bank.

An electronic fund transfer is a transfer of money that is made by using an electric terminal, without a physical transfer of cash, check, or other negotiable paper. The Electronic Fund Transfer Act requires that a financial institution furnish consumers with specific information containing all the terms and conditions of all EFT services. Under certain conditions, the financial institutions will bear the loss for unauthorized transfers. Under other circumstances, the loss will be borne by the consumer.

QUESTIONS AND CASE PROBLEMS

1. What social forces are involved in the common statutory provision that it will be presumed that a check was issued with intent to defraud if the drawer does not pay the amount of the check within ten days after its dishonor?

2. When a bank certifies a check, what does it undertake to do with respect to the holder of the check?

3. Shirley drew a check on her account in the First Central Bank. She later telephoned the bank to stop payment on the check. The bank agreed to do so. Sixteen days thereafter the check was presented to the bank for payment and was paid by the bank. Shirley sued the bank for violating the stop payment order. The bank claimed it was not liable. Is Shirley entitled to recover?

4. Tom had a checking account with the Farmers National Bank. A check was written by an unknown person who forged the signature of Tom as a drawer of the check and then presented the check to the Farmers National bank for payment. The bank paid the check and debited Tom's account with the amount of the check. When Tom received the monthly statement from the bank, he demanded that the bank restore the amount of this debit. Was he correct?

5. A check on the Central Exchange Bank was drawn by Bruce payable to the order of Helen. The check was indorsed by Carlson by writing on the back "pay to Maria (signed) Carlson." Maria cashed the check at the Central Bank. Helen then sued Central. Is it liable?

6. Reed drew a check on the Third Manhattan Bank payable to the order of Mather. He had the check certified by the bank and then mailed it to Mather. Reed died the next day and his executor informed the bank of that fact and ordered the bank to stop payment of the check to Mather because he, the executor, claimed the amount of the check on behalf of Reed's estate. Mather demanded payment from the bank and threatened to sue it. To whom should the bank make payment?

7. Compare (a)an assignment by a depositor of the amount in the depositor's bank account, with (b)a check drawn by a depositor for the full amount of the bank account.

8. Gloria maintains a checking account at the First Bank. On the third day of January, the bank sent to Gloria a statement of her account for December, accompanied by the checks which the bank had paid. One of the checks had her forged signature, which Gloria discovered on the 25th of the month when she prepared a bank reconciliation. Upon this discovery, Gloria immediately notified the bank. On January 21 the bank paid another check forged by the same party who had forged the December item. Who must bear the loss on the forged January check?

9. Contrast the liability of the drawer of a check with that of the drawer of an ordinary draft.

10. Dean bought a car from Cannon. In payment, Dean gave him a check drawn on the South Dorchester Bank of the Eastern Shore Trust Company. The payee, Cannon, cashed the check at the Cambridge Bank of the Eastern Shore Trust Company. The drawee bank refused payment when the check was presented on the ground that Dean had stopped payment because of certain misrepresentations made by Cannon. Will the Eastern Shore Trust Company succeed in an action against Dean for payment? [Dean v Eastern Shore Trust Co., 159 Md 213, 150 A 797]

11. A depositor drew a check and delivered it to the payee. Fourteen months later the check was presented to the drawee bank for payment. The bank did not have any knowledge that anything was wrong and paid the check. The depositor then sued the person receiving the money and the bank. The depositor claimed that the bank could not pay a stale check without asking the depositor whether payment should be made. Was the depositor correct? [Advanced Alloys, Inc. v Sergeant Steel Corp. 340 NYS2d 266]

12. Siniscalchi drew a check on his account in the Valley Bank of New York. About a week later, the holder cashed the check at the bank on a Saturday morning. The following Monday morning, Siniscalchi gave the bank a stop payment order on the check. The Saturday morning transactions had not yet been recorded and neither the bank nor Siniscalchi knew that the check had been cashed. When that fact was learned, the bank debited Siniscalchi's account with the amount of the check. He claimed the bank was liable because the stop payment order had been violated. Was the bank liable? [Siniscalchi v Valley Bank of New York, 359 NYS2d 173]

13. Bogash drew a check on the National Safety Bank and Trust Co. payable to the order of the Fiss Corp. At the request of the corporation, the bank certified the check. The bank later refused to make payment on the check because there was a dispute between Bogash and the corporation as to the amount due to the corporation. The corporation sued the bank on the check. Decide. [Fiss Corp. v National Safety Bank and Trust Co. 191 Misc 397, 77 NYS2d 293]

14. Gracious Homes maintained a checking account with the Crandall Bank. Dawson, owner of Gracious Homes, and his daughter Linda were the only persons authorized to sign checks on behalf of the store. Lawrence, who was the bookkeeper for the store, had forged checks drawn on the Gracious Homes account for almost two years. Lawrence has escaped detection of the forgeries since he has done the bank reconciliation each month. An examination by Linda of the books and records disclosed the forgeries. Gracious Homes brought an action against the Crandall Bank to recover the amount paid out on the forged checks. Will Gracious Homes be successful?

15. Cicci drew a check on his bank, Lincoln National Bank and Trust Co., payable to the order of Santo. He thereafter notified the bank to stop payment. The bank ignored the stop payment order and made payment of the check. Cicci then sued Lincoln National Bank for the amount of the check. The bank raised the defense that Cicci had not shown that he was damaged by the payment of the check. Was this defense

valid? [Cicci v Lincoln National Bank and Trust Co. 46 Misc2d 465, 260 NYS2d 100]

16. Steinbaum executed and delivered a check to the order of the White Way Motors, the name under which DiFranco was doing business. Before the check was paid, Steinbaum stopped payment on the check. DiFranco sued Steinbaum on the check. Decide. [DiFranco v Steinbaum (Mo App) 177 SW2d 697]

17. Stewart's client indorsed to Stewart a check for $185.00 in payment of services rendered. The check was from a corporate account with the Citizens & Southern National Bank. The check was payable to Stewart's client. The bank refused to cash the check even though there were sufficient funds to cover the check. Stewart sued the bank. Decide. [Stewart v Citizens & Southern National Bank, 138 Ga App 209, 225 SE2d 761]

18. Sandra died on April 5. Three days prior to her death, Sandra had issued a check to Galt in payment of a debt. The bank on which the check was drawn paid it to Galt on April 13. The bank had no knowledge of the death of Sandra. Was payment of the check proper?

PART 6

SECURED TRANSACTIONS,

CREDITORS' RIGHTS, AND INSURANCE

Chapter 36 Secured Transactions Under Article 9
Chapter 37 Other Security Devices
Chapter 38 Bankruptcy
Chapter 39 Insurance
Chapter 40 Kinds of Insurance

C H A P T E R 36

SECURED TRANSACTIONS

UNDER ARTICLE 9

CHAPTER OBJECTIVES

After studying this chapter you will be able to:

1. Describe a secured transaction.
2. Explain the requirements for creating a valid security interest.
3. List the four major types of collateral.
4. Distinguish between secured credit sales of consumer goods and secured credit sales of inventory.
5. State the rights of the parties upon the debtor's default.
6. Solve problems involving secured transactions.

A person selling goods on credit or lending money has a right, grounded in contract, to receive from the debtor the amount due under the terms of the agreement. If the debtor defaults, the creditor has the right to sue for damages. However, the creditor may want more protection than that afforded by this right to sue on the debt.

Prior to the UCC there were a number of devices designed to give the lender/seller an interest in specific property of the borrower/buyer that could be used to satisfy any claims of the creditor resulting from the debtor's breach. These devices included: (1) conditional sales, where the seller retained title until the condition of payment in full had been satisfied; (2) bailment leases, where the buyer rented the property and could only acquire title after the payment of sufficient rentals to equal the purchase price; (3) chattel mortgages, where the buyer, upon taking title from the seller, gave the seller a mortgage on the property for the amount of the purchase price; and (4) trust receipts, where the borrower/buyer agreed to hold the goods in trust for the lender.

A. GENERAL PRINCIPLES

Article 9 of the UCC consolidates this fragmented field of security devices into one device called a **secured transaction.**[1] A creditor who complies with the requirements of Article 9 may create a security interest that protects the creditor against the debtor's default by allowing the creditor to recover the goods in the debtor's possession. Any transaction intended to create such an interest (regardless of its form) is subject to the requirements of Article 9.

§ 36:1.   Creation of a Security Interest.

A **security interest** is an interest in personal property or fixtures that secures payment or performance of an obligation.[2] The property in which the interest is held is called the **collateral.** The party holding the interest is termed the **secured party.**[3] The interest may be possessory, where the collateral is in the possession of the secured party; or it may be nonpossessory, where the debtor is in possession of the collateral.

A security interest is said to *attach* at the time it becomes enforceable. There are three prerequisites to the attachment of a security interest: (1) there must be a security agreement; (2) value must be given; and (3) the debtor must have rights in the collateral.[4]

(a) **Security Agreement.** The agreement of the creditor and the debtor that the creditor shall have a security interest in the goods must be evidenced by a written **security agreement** unless the creditor retains a possessory security interest by taking possession of the collateral. The agreement must be signed by the debtor and reasonably describe the collateral.

FACTS:
Gill sold office furniture to Security Corporation Builders and Realtors. In February, Security bought more furniture. To secure the sale the parties entered into a security agreement. The security agreement described the collateral as "Furniture as per attached listing." No listing was attached to the security agreement. The Security Corporation sold the furniture to Fireside Realty. Gill Corporation claimed that it had a security interest in the furniture.

DECISION:
Judgment for Fireside Realty. A security agreement describing collateral as "Furniture as per attached listing," but with no listing attached failed to sufficiently describe the collateral and was not an enforceable security agreement. Since there was no enforceable security agreement, the Gill Corporation did not have a valid security interest in the collateral. [J.K. Gill Company v Fireside Realty Inc. 260 Or 511, 499 P2d 813 (1972)]

(b) **Value.** To be effective for the attaching of a security interest, *value* is given when the secured party loans money to the debtor or agrees

---

[1]This chapter is based on the UCC, including the 1972 amendments, which is set forth in the Appendix. The changes made by the 1972 amendments are confined mainly to Article 9 on secured transactions.
[2]UCC §1-201(37).
[3]UCC §9-105(1).
[4]UCC §9-203.

to loan money to the debtor. In most cases value is any consideration that supports a simple contract.

(c) **Debtor has Rights in the Collateral.** The debtor must have *rights* in the collateral. That is, the debtor must either own or have the right to possession of the collateral.

(d) **Future Transactions.** The security agreement may contemplate future action by extending to goods that are to be acquired and delivered to the buyer at a future date. In general, the security interest does not attach to future goods until the buyer has rights in such goods.[5]

In order to protect consumers, a limit is placed upon the extent to which after-acquired property may be bound by a security interest. In order to be collateral for a consumer obligation, the consumer must acquire the later property within ten days after the creditor gave value to the consumer. That is, the creditor cannot bind all property acquired at any time in the future but only such as is acquired within ten days after the creditor sells the goods or loans the money to the consumer.

(e) **Perfection.** When a security interest in property is superior to other interests and claims to the property, it is said to be **perfected**. Perfection may generally be obtained by filing a financing statement in the proper governmental office. If the collateral is tangible personal property, the creditor has the alternative of perfecting the security interest by taking possession of the collateral. If the collateral is consumer goods neither filing nor taking possession is required to perfect a purchase money security interest in the goods, because such an interest is perfected as soon as it attaches.[6]

§ 36:2. Classification of Collateral.

The Code divides tangible personal property or goods into four different classes: consumer goods, equipment, inventory, and farm products.[7] These goods are classified by the debtor's intended use, not their physical characteristics. For example, a television set in the hands of a manufacturer or retailer would be inventory. However, in the buyer-borrower's hands, it is a consumer good.

(a) **Consumer Goods.** Goods are **consumer goods** if they are used or bought primarily for personal, family, or household use (for example, a television set).

(b) **Equipment Goods.** Goods are **equipment goods** if they are used or bought primarily for use in a business (for example, a musical instrument used by a night club entertainer).

(c) **Inventory Goods.** Goods are **inventory goods** if they are held by the debtor primarily for sale or lease to others (for example, a refrigerator bought by a dealer).

(d) **Farm Products.** Goods are **farm products** if they are crops or livestock or supplies used in farming operations.

[5]UCC §9-204(1),(2).
[6]The perfection based on attachment is more readily lost than that based on filing or possession.
[7]UCC §9-109.

B. SECURED CREDIT SALES OF CONSUMER GOODS

Consumer credit sales are treated differently than secured credit sales of inventory goods. Perfection by filing in a public office is not required for consumer goods. For most consumer transactions, the amount involved would not warrant the filing expense.

§ 36:3. Rights of the Seller of Consumer Goods Independent of Default.

The seller stands in a dual position of being both a seller, having rights under Article 2 of the UCC governing sales, and a secured creditor, having rights under Article 9 of the UCC regulating secured transactions.[8]

The secured credit seller of consumer goods has rights that are effective not only against the buyer, but also against purchasers of the property from the buyer as soon as the security agreement is executed with respect to goods in which the buyer has acquired an interest. From that moment on, the seller's interest is generally effective against third persons[9] and is described as a **perfected security interest.**

(a) **Filing Not Required.** In an ordinary sale of consumer goods under a secured transaction, no filing in any state or government office is required in order to perfect the secured seller's interest. The security agreement will protect the seller against creditors of the buyer and most third parties who thereafter buy the property from the buyer.[10]

(b) **Interstate Security Interests.** The UCC regulates not only transactions within the state, but also the effect to be given security interests in property brought into the state from another state. If the interest of the secured party was perfected in the other state, that interest will be regarded as perfected by the state into which the property is brought. Within the second state, however, it is necessary to file within four months in order to keep the security interest continuously perfected.

If title to the property, such as an automobile, is represented by a title certificate, the law of the state which issued the certificate determines whether an interest is perfected. Accordingly, if the law of the certificate-issuing state requires that a security interest be noted on the title certificate in order to be perfected, that requirement is the exclusive means of perfecting the interest of the secured creditor.[11]

(c) **Repair and Storage Lien.** In most states, persons making repairs to or storing property have a right to assert a lien against the property for the amount of their charges. A question of priority arises when the customer bringing the goods for repair or storage is not the absolute owner and there is an outstanding security interest in the goods. In such a case, the lien for repairs or storage charges has priority over the outstanding security interest.[12]

[8]UCC §9-113.
[9]UCC §9-201.
[10]UCC §9-302(1)(d).
[11]UCC § 9-103(4).
[12]UCC § 9-310.

FACTS:

Gladys Schmidt financed the purchase of a new automobile. She gave the bank a security interest in the automobile and the bank perfected its interest by filing a financing statement. The car was later taken by Gladys to Bergeron Cadillac for repairs. Subsequently she stopped making payments to the bank and the bank sought to repossess the automobile from Bergeron. The dealer refused to surrender the automobile until it was paid for the repairs. The bank claimed it was entitled to the automobile because it had a perfected security interest.

DECISION:

Judgment for Bergeron Cadillac. A person repairing goods, such as an automobile, has a lien on the goods until paid. This lien takes priority over a perfected security interest in the goods held by another creditor unless the repairer's lien is a statutory lien and the statute expressly gives priority to the security interest. The lien of Bergeron was based upon the common law of the state and therefore the statutory exception did not apply. Consequently, Bergeron could retain possession of the automobile under its lien until paid for its services even though the bank had a perfected security interest. [National Bank v Bergeron Cadillac, Inc. 66 Ill2d 140, 361 NE2d 1116 (1977)]

§ 36:4. Rights of the Buyer of Consumer Goods Independent of Default.

The buyer in a secured transaction, like the seller, has a double status under the UCC. By virtue of Article 2, the buyer has certain rights as a buyer, and by virtue of Article 9, the buyer has certain rights as a debtor in a secured transaction.

(a) **Rights as a Buyer.** The buyer has certain rights of ownership in the collateral. It is not material whether technically the buyer is the owner of the title. The buyer may voluntarily transfer whatever interest is owned by the buyer, and the creditors of the buyer may reach that interest by the process of law as fully as though there were no security agreement. Such third persons generally cannot acquire any greater rights than the buyer, and therefore they hold the property subject to the security interest of the seller.

(b) **Rights as a Debtor.** The secured transaction buyer is a debtor to the extent that there is a balance due on the purchase price. In order for the buyer to know just how much is owed and to check what the seller claims is due, the buyer has the right to compel the seller to state what balance is owed and also to specify in which collateral the seller claims a security interest. This is done by the buyer's sending the seller a statement of the amount believed to be due, or a statement of the collateral believed to be subject to the security agreement, with the request that the seller approve or correct the statement. The seller must so indicate; and if there has been an assignment of the contract and the security interest to a third person, the seller must furnish the buyer with the name and address of such successor in interest.

§ 36:5. Protection of Subpurchaser.

When the seller of consumer goods sells on credit, filing of a financing statement is not necessary to protect the seller's security interest in the goods against other creditors of the buyer. A security interest in the goods is perfected, that is, arises by attachment alone, even though the seller gives the buyer possession of the goods. This rule relieves retail merchants who sell many articles on installment plans of the burden of filing and payment of filing fees.

When no financing statement is filed, however, a resale by the consumer to another consumer will destroy the seller's security interest if the second purchaser does not have knowledge of the security interest of the original party and buys for personal, family, or household use.[13] For example, a consumer buys a refrigerator under an installment contract whereby the appliance store retains a security interest in the refrigerator. The appliance store does not file a financing statement, though its interest is perfected by attachment. Some time later, the consumer sells the refrigerator to a neighbor, who is unaware of the prior security interest. The neighbor will take free of the security interest.

FACTS:

On July 2, 1980, Scott executed a security agreement granting to First National Bank a security interest in a 1980 Marquis Mercruiser boat. On July 14, 1980, First National filed a financing statement on the boat in Clark County, the county of Scott's residence. Sometime in May of 1981, Scott sold the boat to Bass. The Bank was not notified actually or constructively of the proposed transfer of the boat from Scott to Bass prior to the transfer. The Bank claims its security interest is superior to any interest of Bass. Bass contends that he is a good faith purchaser, having bought the boat for value and without knowledge of the Bank's prior security interest.

DECISION:

Judgment for First National Bank. In the case of consumer goods, a buyer takes free of a perfected security interest when a financing statement has not been filed if he buys without knowledge of the security interest, for value, and for his own personal, family, or household use. Here, however, the bank filed a financing statement prior to the purchase. Bass purchased the boat in May 1981. The financing statement was filed by the Bank in 1980, clearly prior to Bass' purchase. As to priority between these two claimants, the Bank prevails and is entitled to possession of the boat. [In re Scott, 52 BR 821 (WD KY 1985)]

C. SECURED CREDIT SALES OF INVENTORY

In contrast with one who buys goods for personal use, the buyer may be a merchant or dealer who intends to resell the goods. The goods which such a merchant or dealer buys are classified as **inventory**. The financing of the purchase of inventory may involve a third person, rather than the seller, as creditor. For example, a third person, such as a bank or finance company, may loan the dealer the money with which to make the purchase and to pay the seller in full. In such a case the security interest in the goods may be given by the buyer to the third person and not to the seller. Accordingly, the terms

[13]UCC §9-307(2).

"creditor" and "secured party" may refer to a seller who sells on credit or to a third person who finances the purchase of goods.

In general, the provisions regulating a secured transaction in inventory follow the same pattern as is applicable to the secured credit sale of consumer goods. Variations recognize the differences in the commercial settings of the two transactions.

Initially there must be a security agreement to give rise to the security interest. If perfection of the interest is desired, there must also be a filing of a financing statement or the creditor must hold possession of the collateral.

§ 36:6. Use of Property and Extent of Security Interest.

A secured transaction relating to inventory will generally give the buyer full freedom to deal with the collateral goods as though the buyer were the absolute owner and the goods were not subject to a security interest. Thus, the parties may agree that the buyer-dealer may mingle the goods with existing inventory, resell the goods, take goods back and make exchanges, and so on, without being required to keep any records of just what became of the goods covered by the security agreement, or to replace the goods sold with other goods, or to account for the proceeds from the sale of the original goods.

(a) **After-Acquired Property.** The security agreement may expressly provide that the security interest of the creditor shall bind **after-acquired property,** that is, other goods thereafter acquired by the buyer. The combination of the buyer's freedom to use and dispose of the collateral and the subjecting of after-acquired goods to the interest of the secured creditor permits the latter to have a **floating lien** on a changing or shifting stock of goods of the buyer. Conversely stated, the UCC rejects the common-law concept that the security interest was lost if the collateral was not maintained and accounted for separately and that a floating lien upon the buyer's property was void as a fraud against the latter's creditors.

The security interest in inventory covered as after-acquired property has priority over claims of subsequent creditors and third persons, except buyers in the ordinary course of business and sellers to the debtor holding perfected purchase money security interests in the goods sold to the debtor.

(b) **Proceeds of Collateral.** The secured transaction covers proceeds from the collateral unless such interest is expressly excluded. **Proceeds** includes cash, checks, and accounts receivable arising on a sale of the collateral and also indemnification from an insurer for damage to the collateral.[14]

§ 36:7. Filing of Financing Statement.

Filing is usually required to perfect the creditor's interest in inventory or the proceeds therefrom. An exception is made when a statute requires the security interest to be noted on the title certificate issued for the property. A security interest in a motor vehicle that is inventory is perfected by filing

---

[14]UCC §9-306(1), C.O. Funk & Son Inc. v Sullivan Equipment, Inc., 89 Ill 2d 27, 431 NE2d 370 (1982).

under the Code; but a privately owned vehicle is perfected by a notation on the title registration certificate.

An unperfected security interest is valid as against anyone standing in the position of the debtor or whose rights rise no higher than those of the debtor.

(a) **Financing Statement.** The paper that is filed is a financing statement and is distinct from the security agreement which was executed by the parties to give rise to the secured transaction.[15] The **financing statement** must be signed by the debtor; it must give an address of the secured party from which information concerning the security interest may be obtained; it must give a mailing address of the debtor; and it must contain a statement indicating the types, or describing the items, of collateral.

The financing statement does not set forth the terms of the agreement between the parties. This is done in the security agreement. All that the financing statement does is give notice to the world that the debtor has financed; that is, that the secured creditor who has filed may have a security interest in the collateral described in the statement.

Errors in the financing statement have no effect unless they are seriously misleading. If they are seriously misleading, the filing has no effect and does not perfect the security interest. For example, a description of the collateral in the financing statement as "all personal property" is not sufficient and therefore the filing of the statement does not perfect the security interest.

(b) **Place of Filing.** The Code gives each state the option to provide for the filing of the financing statement under (1) *local filing,* as in the county of residence or place of business of the debtor, (2) *central filing,* as in a particular office in the state capitol, or (3) *dual filing,* a combination of both local and central filing.

(c) **Defective Filing.** When the filing of the statement is defective either because the statement is so erroneous as to be seriously misleading or the filing is made in a wrong county or office, the filing fails to perfect the security interest. This means that other creditors who have liens on the collateral and the trustee in bankruptcy of the debtor have a right to the collateral superior to that of the original secured creditor.

FACTS:

RCA financed the purchase of telephone equipment by Swati, Inc. Pursuant to the contract, RCA reserved title to and took a security interest in the telephone equipment. A financing statement evidencing RCA's security interest was filed. The financing statement did not designate Swati, Inc as the debtor, but listed the debtor's trade name, King's Plaza Motel.

Sometime thereafter, Swati, Inc. filed for bankruptcy. RCA brought suit to prohibit the debtor's use of the property and to allow RCA to foreclose upon the equipment for money owed. Swati, Inc. contends that because RCA filed its financing statement under the debtor's trade name and not its corporate name, RCA failed to prefect its security interest and is therefore merely a general unsecured creditor.

[15]UCC §9-402. However, the security agreement may be filed as a financing statement if it contains the required information.

DECISION:

Judgment for Swati, Inc. A secured party seeking to perfect a security interest in collateral must provide enough information to alert an interested party of a possible prior security interest in that collateral. Here the trade name materially differs from the debtor's name; a financing statement filed thereunder does not give notice to other creditors, making the filing defective. [In Re Swati, Inc. 54 BR 498 (ED 11 1985)]

---

§ 36:8.   Duration and Continuation of Filing.

The filing of the financing statement is effective for 5 years. At the expiration thereof, the perfection of the security interest terminates unless a continuation statement has been filed prior thereto. The **continuation statement** is merely a written declaration by the secured party which identifies the original financing statement by its file number and declares that it is still effective. The filing of the continuation statement continues perfection of the security for a period of 5 years after the last date on which the original filing was effective. The filing of successive continuation statements will continue the perfection indefinitely.[16]

§ 36:9.   Termination of the Buyer's Obligation.

A buyer who has paid the debt in full may make a written demand on the secured party, or the latter's assignee if the security interest has been assigned, to send the buyer a *termination statement* that a security interest is no longer claimed under the specified financing statement. The buyer then may present this statement to the filing officer who marks the record "terminated" and returns to the secured party the various papers which had been filed. Public notice is now given that the secured obligation is discharged and the financing transaction terminated.[17]

§ 36:10.   Protection of Customers of the Buyer.

The customer of the dealer selling from inventory takes the goods free from the security interest of the dealer's supplier. That is, one who buys in the ordinary course of business items of property taken from the original buyer's inventory is free of the secured party's interest, even though the interest was perfected by filing and even though such ultimate customer knew of the secured party's interest.[18] For example, a finance company loans money to a retailer to finance the retailer's inventory of new refrigerators. It takes a security interest in the inventory and files a financing statement. The retailer then sells a refrigerator to a customer. The customer will take the refrigerator free of the finance company's security interest even though the dealer may be in default on its loan to the finance company. If this were not so, buyers would be reluctant to buy goods. The sale to the consumer was obviously contemplated by the parties. The finance company really expected to be paid from the proceeds of the sale of the collateral.

[16]UCC §9-403(3).
[17]UCC §9-404.
[18]UCC §9-307(1), Cessna Finance Corp. v Skyways Enterprises Inc. (Ky) 580 SW2d 491 (1979).

D. SECURED CREDIT SALES OF EQUIPMENT

In general, secured credit sales of equipment are treated the same as secured transactions as to inventory, except that the various provisions relating to resale by the buyer and the creditor's rights in proceeds have no practical application because the buyer does not resell the property but makes the purchase with the intention of keeping and using or operating it.

§ 36:11. Use of Collateral.

For the purpose of secured transactions, a distinction is made as to the purpose for which the buyer procures the goods. If an ultimate consumer purchases primarily for personal, family, or household use, the goods are described as **consumer goods.** The consumer's purchase, however, is described as **equipment** if used or purchased for use primarily in a business, in farming, or in a profession.

§ 36:12. Filing.

In the ordinary sale of consumer goods, filing of a financing statement is not required. In contrast, filing is required to perfect a security interest in equipment.

E. RIGHTS OF PARTIES AFTER DEFAULT

When a debtor defaults on an obligation in a secured transaction, the secured party has certain rights with respect to the enforcement of the claim against the collateral.[19] These rights can be spelled out by the security agreement itself. The Code also provides for procedures that the secured party can follow in the event the security agreement does not itself make provisions for them.

§ 36:13. Secured Seller's Repossession and Resale of Collateral.

Upon the buyer's default, the secured party is entitled to take the collateral or purchased property from the buyer. If this can be done without causing a breach of the peace, the seller may repossess the property without legal proceedings.

The seller who has repossessed the goods may resell them at a private or public sale at any time and place and on any terms, provided this is done in good faith in a manner that is commercially reasonable.[20] The seller must give the debtor reasonable advance notice of a resale unless the goods are perishable, or unless they threaten to decline speedily in value, or unless they are a type customarily sold on a recognized market. The seller's resale destroys all interest of the debtor in the goods.

(a) **Compulsory Resale.** If the buyer has paid 60 percent or more of the cash price of the consumer goods, the seller must resell them within 90 days after repossession, unless the buyer, after default, has signed a written

---

[19]The term "default" is not defined in Article 9. It is up to the parties to a secured transaction to specify in their agreement what constitutes a default.

[20]UCC §9-504.

statement surrendering the right to require the resale. If the seller does not resell within the time specified, the buyer may sue for conversion of the collateral or proceed under the UCC provision applicable to failure to comply with the UCC.[21]

(b) **Notice.** Ordinarily notice must be given of the sale of collateral. The UCC does not specify the form of notice, and any form of notice that is reasonable is sufficient. A letter to the debtor can satisfy this requirement. If a public sale is made, the notice must give the time and place of the sale. If a private sale is made, it is sufficient to give reasonable notice of the time after which the private sale will be made. No notice is required when the collateral is perishable or is threatening to decline rapidly in value or is sold on a recognized market or exchange.

FACTS:

Bondurant purchased secondhand equipment from Beard. Beard obtained a security interest in the equipment and perfected his interest by filing a financing statement. Bondurant returned the equipment for repairs and then refused to take it back. Beard told Bondurant over the phone that the equipment had to be sold and that he would hold Bondurant liable for the difference. Some three months later and without any further notice to Beard, the equipment was sold. Beard then sued Bondurant for the difference in the resale price and the original contract price. Bondurant argued that he had not been given adequate notice of Beards's intention to resell, since he had only been notified by phone and not in writing.

DECISION:

Judgment for Beard. The oral notification was sufficient. Bondurant knew at all times where the collateral was and why it was being sold. In addition, he had three months to find a buyer for the equipment. [Bondurant v Beard Equipment Co. (Fla App) 345 So2d 806 (1977)]

---

§ 36:14.   Debtor's Right of Redemption.

If the debtor acts in time, the debtor may exercise the right to redeem the collateral at any time prior to the time the secured party has disposed of the collateral or entered into a binding contract for resale. To redeem, the debtor must tender the entire obligation that is owed plus any legal costs and expenses incurred by the secured party.[22]

§ 36:15.   Disposition of Collateral by Sale.

Upon the debtor's default, the creditor may sell the collateral at **public** or **private sale** or may lease it to a third party as long as the creditor

[21]UCC §9-507.
[22]UCC §9-506.

acts in a commercially reasonable manner. The proceeds of the sale are applied in the following order: (1) to pay the expenses of the secured party in connection with the default; (2) to pay the debt owed the secured party; and (3) to pay the indebtedness owed other secured parties in the collateral.

SUMMARY

A security interest is an interest in personal property or fixtures that secures payment or performance of an obligation. The property in which the interest is held is called the collateral and the party holding the interest is called the secured party. Attachment establishes the secured party's right to the collateral against the defaulting debtor. To secure protection against claims to the collateral that third parties might assert, the secured party must perfect the security interest.

Tangible collateral is divided into four classes: consumer goods, equipment goods, inventory goods, and farm products. These goods are classified by the debtor's intended use and not by their physical characteristics.

In the ordinary credit sale of consumer goods, no filing in any state or government office is required in order to perfect the secured party's interest. The secured party who does not file will still have priority over other creditors of the buyer, but will not have priority over a subpurchaser of the debtor who buys for personal, family, or household use without knowledge of the security interest. If the secured party wants to be protected against the subpurchaser, a financing statement must be filed.

In the case of inventory goods, unless the secured party holds possession of the collateral, the secured party must file a financing statement. A financing statement must be signed by the debtor, must have the names and addresses of the parties, and must describe the collateral. Inventory financing covers proceeds from the sale of the collateral unless such interest is expressly excluded. Any customer of the dealer selling from inventory will take the goods free from the security interest of the dealer's supplier even though the customer knows that the goods are subject to a perfected security interest. The filing, however, will protect the secured creditor from certain other creditors. A secured credit sale of equipment is treated the same as secured credit sales of inventory except that the buyer does not resell the property.

Upon default, a secured party may repossess the collateral from the buyer if this can be done without a breach of the peace. If the buyer has paid 60% or more of the cash price of the consumer goods, the seller must resell them within 90 days after repossession unless the buyer after default has waived this right in writing. Notice of the sale of the collateral to the debtor is usually required.

QUESTIONS AND CASE PROBLEMS

1. What social forces are affected by the destruction of a security interest in consumer goods when a consumer-debtor resells the goods to another consumer who does not know of the security interest?
2. List three ways for a secured party to perfect a security interest.

3. Natasha purchases on credit a $1,000 freezer from the Silas Household Appliance Store. After she had paid approximately $700, Natasha missed the next monthly installment payment. Silas repossessed the freezer and billed Natasha for the balance of the purchase price of $300. Natasha claimed that the freezer, now in the possession of Silas, was worth much more than the balance due and requested Silas to sell the freezer in order to wipe out the balance of the debt and to leave something over for Natasha. Silas claimed that as Natasha had broken her contract to pay the purchase price, she had no right to say what should be done with the freezer. Was Silas correct?

4. Thompson Home Appliance Store purchased refrigerator-freezers from the Henson Manufacturing Company and financed the purchase by obtaining a loan from the First National Bank. Thompson signed an agreement giving the bank a security interest in its inventory of refrigerator-freezers. Renée purchased a refrigerator-freezer from Thompson on credit. The bank claimed that its security interest extended to the down payment which Renée had made and to the unpaid balance which she owed Thompson. Was the bank correct?

5. Model Tailors desired to enlarge its store. It arranged with the Main Street Bank to lend it $100,000 to be paid out as the construction work progressed and was certified as completed by the building architect. This agreement was set forth in a letter signed by the president of the bank. Is this letter a financing statement?

6. The Start Television Co. sold a portable TV set to an accountant to be used in her home. Classify the TV as collateral with respect to (a) the Television Co., and (b) the accountant.

7. Compare or contrast attachment of a security interest with perfection of a security interest.

8. Selma purchased a typewriter from the Kroll Typewriter Co. for $600. At the time of the purchase, she made an initial payment of $75 and agreed to pay the balance in monthly installments. A security agreement was prepared which complied with the UCC. The agreement, however, was never filed. Selma, at a time when she still owed a balance on the typewriter and without the consent of Kroll, sold the typewriter to a neighbor. The neighbor, who had no knowledge of the security interest, used the typewriter in her home. Will Kroll be able to repossess the typewriter from the neighbor?

9. Compare or contrast a financing statement, a continuation statement and a termination statement.

10. Benson purchased a new Ford Thunderbird automobile. She traded in her old car and used the Magnavox Employees Credit Union to finance the balance. The Credit Union took a security interest in the Ford. Subsequently, the Ford was involved in a number of accidents. It was taken to a dealer for repairs. Benson was unable to pay for the work done. The dealer claimed a lien on the car for services and materials furnished. The Magnavox Employees Credit Union also claimed priority. Which claim has priority? [Magnavox Employees Credit Union v Benson, 165 Ind App 155, 331 NE2d 46]

11. Diodato borrowed money from Canna for the purchase of an automobile. A promissory note was signed by Diodato in favor of Canna for the loan. Diodato also procured a title certificate for the automobile. The title certificate included a typed provision designating Canna as a secured party. First National Bank sued Diodato for money that Diodato owed the bank. A judgment was obtained against Diodato and the bank then attempted to levy execution against the automobile. When the bank learned of Canna's interest and prior claim to the car by reason of the title certificate provision, it attempted to have Canna's lien set aside. What decision? [First National Bank and Trust Co. v Canna, 124 NJ Supp 154, 305 A2d 442]

12. A owned a store. He borrowed from the B Bank and gave the bank a security interest in the "inventory" of the store. The security agreement described the collateral as inventory but did not contain any provision as to after-acquired property. A later went bankrupt and his trustee in bankruptcy claimed the secured transaction did not bind after-acquired property because the security agreement did not expressly state that it did. Was the trustee correct? [Re Fibre Glass Boat Corp. (DC Fla) 324 FSupp 1054, aff'd (CA5 Fla) 448 F2d 781]

13. Hull-Dobbs sold an automobile to Mallicoat and then assigned the sales contract to the Volunteer Finance & Loan Corp. Later Volunteer repossessed the automobile and sold it. When Volunteer sued Mallicoat for the deficiency between the contract price and the proceeds on resale, Mallicoat raised the defense that he had not been properly notified of the resale. The loan manager of the finance company testified that Mallicoat had been sent a registered letter stating that the car would be sold. He did not state whether the letter merely declared in general terms that the car would be sold or specified a date for its resale. He admitted that the letter never was delivered to Mallicoat and was returned to the finance company "unclaimed." The loan manager also testified that the sale was advertised by posters, but on cross examination he admitted that he was not able to state when or where it was thus advertised. It was shown that Volunteer knew where Mallicoat and his father lived and where Mallicoat was employed. Mallicoat claimed that he had not been properly notified. Volunteer asserted that sufficient notice had been given. Was the notice of the resale sufficient? [Mallicoat v Volunteer Finance & Loan Corp. 57 TennApp 106, 415 SW2d 347]

14. A borrowed money from B. He orally agreed that B should have a security interest in certain equipment that was standing in A's yard. There was nothing in writing to show this and no filing of any kind was made. Nine days later, B took possession of the equipment. What kind of interest did B have in the equipment? [Transport Equipment Co. v Guaranty State Bank (CA 10 Kan) 518]

15. Cook sold to Martin a new tractor truck for approximately $13,000 with a down payment of approximately $3,000 and the balance to be paid in 30 monthly installments. The sales agreement provided that upon default in any payment Cook could take "immediate possession of the property . . . without notice or demand. For this purpose vendor may enter upon any premises the property may be." Martin failed to pay the

installments when due, and Cook notified him that the truck would be repossessed. Martin had the tractor truck, attached to a loaded trailer, locked on the premises of a company in Memphis. Martin intended to drive to the West Coast as soon as the trailer was loaded. When Cook located the tractor truck, no one was around. In order to disconnect the trailer from the truck, as Cook had no right to the trailer, Cook removed the wire screen over a ventilator hole by unscrewing it from the outside with his penknife. He next reached through the ventilator hole with a stick and unlocked the door of the tractor truck. He then disconnected the trailer and had the truck towed away. Martin sued Cook for unlawfully repossessing the truck by committing a breach of the peace. Decide. [Martin v Cook, 237 Miss 267, 114 So2d 669]

16. The United Gas Improvement Co. sold gas-burning equipment to McFalls for use in his home. The transaction was a lease under which title was retained by the seller until all the installments were paid. United Gas Improvement did not file the lease or make any other filing. McFalls claimed that United Gas did not have a valid security interest. Decide.

17. Wilson purchased and paid for a drill from Colusa. Prior to delivery of the drill, a creditor of Colusa holding a perfected security interest in Colusa's inventory repossessed the entire inventory including the drill Wilson had purchased. Wilson sued the creditor for conversion. Result? [Wilson v M & W Gear (Ill App) 442 NE2d 670]

18. The Wayne Corporation operates a retail appliance store. Wayne borrowed $2,000 from Kasten to supplement its working capital. At that time it granted to Kasten a security interest in its present and future inventory pursuant to a written security agreement signed by both parties. Kasten filed a financing statement a few days later. In the ordinary course of business, a customer purchased a $600 television set from Wayne. The customer knew of the existence of Kasten's security interest. What rights does Kasten have against Wayne's customer?

CHAPTER 37

OTHER SECURITY DEVICES

CHAPTER OBJECTIVES

After studying this chapter you will be able to:

1. Distinguish a contract of suretyship from a contract of guaranty.
2. Define the parties involved in a contract of suretyship and a contract of guaranty.
3. List and explain the rights of sureties to protect themselves from sustaining a loss.
4. Explain the types of defenses which are available to a surety.
5. Explain the nature of a letter of credit and the liabilities of the various parties to a letter of credit.
6. Solve problems involving security devices.

Subject to certain exceptions, Article 9 of the Uniform Commercial Code regulates all secured transactions dealing with personal property. The secured credit sales of consumer goods, inventory goods, and equipment goods were discussed in Chapter 36. This chapter considers other common forms of secured transactions.

A. SURETYSHIP AND GUARANTY

The relationship by which one person becomes responsible for the debt or undertaking of another person is used most commonly to insure that a debt will be paid or that a contractor will perform the work called for by the contract. A distinction may be made between the two kinds of such agreements. One kind is called a contract or undertaking of **suretyship** and the third person is called a **surety**. The other kind is called a contract or undertaking of **guaranty**, and the third person is called a **guarantor**. In both cases the person who owes the money or is under the original obligation to pay or perform is called the **principal**, the principal debtor, or debtor and the person to whom the debt or obligation is owed is known as the **creditor**.[1]

Suretyship and guaranty undertakings have the common feature of a promise to answer for the debt or default of another; but they have a basic difference. The surety is primarily liable for the debt or obligation of the principal; ordinarily the guarantor is only secondarily liable. This means that the moment the principal is in default, the creditor may demand performance or payment of the surety. The creditor generally cannot do so in the case of the guarantor and must first attempt to collect from the principal. An exception is an **"absolute guaranty"** which creates the same obligation as a suretyship. A guaranty of payment creates an absolute guaranty.

§ 37:1.   Indemnity Contract.

Both suretyship and guaranty differ from an **indemnity contract**, which is an undertaking by one person for a consideration to pay another person a sum of money in the event that the other person sustains a specified loss. A fire insurance policy is a typical example of an indemnity contract.

§ 37:2.   Creation of the Relation.

The suretyship and guaranty relationships are based upon contract. The principles applicable to the capacity, formation, validity, and interpretation of contracts are applicable. Generally the ordinary rules of offer and acceptance apply. Notice of acceptance must usually be given by the creditor to the guarantor.

In most states, the statute of frauds requires that contracts of guaranty be in writing in order to be enforceable, subject to the exception that no writing is required when the promise is made primarily for the promisor's benefit.

In the absence of a special statute, no writing is required for contracts of suretyship or indemnity, because they impose primary liability, and not a secondary liability to answer for the debt or default of another. Special statutes or sound business practice, however, commonly require the use of written contracts for both suretyship and indemnity.

When the contract of guaranty is made at the same time as the original transaction, the consideration for the original promise which is covered by the guaranty is also consideration for the performance of the guarantor. When the guaranty contract is entered into subsequent to the original transaction, it is necessary that there be a new consideration for the promise of the guarantor.

---

[1] Unless otherwise stated, "surety" as used in the text includes guarantor as well as surety, and "guaranty" is limited to a conditional guaranty. The word "principal" is also used by the law to identify the person who employs an agent. The "principal" in suretyship must be distinguished from the agent's "principal."

FACTS:

Reuben Scherbenske was a partner in a construction business. The partnership eventually formed a corporation and all the debts and assets of the partnership were transferred to the corporation. Reuben was a principal shareholder of the corporation. His wife, Iola, worked for the corporation but was neither a shareholder nor a member of the board of directors. She had always worked for her husband in all his business dealings. Reuben and Iola executed a guaranty to First Bank for all the debts of the corporation in the amount of $325,000. The guaranty was executed to induce First Bank to extend credit to the corporation. The guaranty was signed by both Reuben and Iola. When the debt became due, the First Bank sued Reuben and Iola on the guaranty. Iola claimed she was not liable as there was no consideration given by the bank in connection with the guaranty.

DECISION:

Judgment for First Bank. A separate and distinct consideration is not necessary when the guaranty is entered into at the same time or is part of the same transaction as the principal obligation. Iola signed the guaranty in order to induce First Bank to extend credit to the corporation in which her husband held stock and for which she worked. [First Bank of N.D. v Scherbenske (ND) 375 NW2d 156 (1985)]

§ 37:3. Rights of Surety.

Sureties have a number of rights to protect them from sustaining loss, to obtain their discharge because of the conduct of others that would be harmful to them, or to recover money that they were required to pay because of the debtor's breach.

(a) **Exoneration.** If the surety finds its position threatened with danger, as when the debtor is about to leave the state, the surety may call upon the creditor to take action against the debtor. If at that time, the creditor could proceed against the debtor and fails to do so, the surety is released or exonerated from liability to the extent that the surety has been harmed by such failure.

(b) **Subrogation.** When a surety pays a debt that it is obligated to pay, it automatically acquires the claim and the rights of the creditor. This is known as *subrogation*. That is, once the creditor is paid in full, the surety stands in the same position as the creditor and may sue the debtor or enforce any security that was available to the creditor in order to recover the amount it has paid. The effect is the same as if the creditor, on being paid, made an express assignment of all rights to the surety.

(c) **Indemnity.** A surety that has made payment of a claim for which it was liable as surety is entitled to indemnity from the principal, that is, it is entitled to demand from the principal reimbursement of the amount which it has paid.

(d) **Contribution.** If there are two or more sureties, each is liable to the creditor for the full amount of the debt, until the creditor has been paid in full. As between themselves, however, each is only liable for a proportionate share of the debt. Accordingly, if the surety has paid more than its share of the debt, it is entitled to demand that its co-sureties contribute to it in order to share the burden, which in the absence of a contrary agreement, must be borne equally.

§ 37:4. Defenses of the Surety.

The surety's defenses include not only those that may be raised by a party to any contract but also the special defenses that are peculiar to the suretyship relation.

(a) **Ordinary Defenses.** Since the relationship of suretyship is based upon a contract, the surety may raise any defense that a party to an ordinary contract may raise, such as lack of capacity of parties, absence of consideration, fraud or mistake.

Fraud and concealment are common defenses. Since the risk of the principal's default is thrown upon the surety, it is unfair for the creditor to conceal from the surety facts that are material to the surety's risk.

Fraud on the part of the principal that is unknown to the creditor and in which the creditor has not taken part does not ordinarily release the surety.

By common law the creditor was not required to volunteer information to the surety and was not required to disclose that the principal was insolvent. There is a growing modern view which requires the creditor to inform the surety of matters material to the risk when the creditor has reason to believe that the surety does not possess such information.

(b) **Suretyship Defenses.** In addition to the ordinary defenses that can be raised against any contract, the following defenses are peculiar to the suretyship relation:

(1) The original obligation was invalid.

(2) The principal was discharged by payment or some other means.

(3) The original contract was modified without the surety's consent.

FACTS:

3-W Enterprises, Inc., entered into a franchise agreement with Inter-Sport, Inc. The Wilsons executed a guaranty agreement covering the payment of royalties as part of the franchise contract. Sometime thereafter, 3-W Enterprises and Inter-Sport, Inc., modified their agreement by varying some of the original terms and also changing the amount due under the terms of the franchise. 3-W failed to perform their agreement and Inter-Sport, Inc. sued the Wilsons on the guaranty. The Wilsons claimed they were not liable due to the modification.

DECISION:

Judgment for the Wilsons. A material alteration in the contract of guaranty without the consent of the guarantor will discharge a surety or guarantor who has not given assent to the new agreement. [Inter-Sport, Inc. v Wilson (Ark) 661 SW2d 367 (1983)]

B. LETTERS OF CREDIT

A letter of credit is a form of agreement that the issuer of the letter will pay drafts drawn by the creditor. It is thus a form of advance arranging of financing in that it is known in advance how much money may be obtained from the issuer of the letter. It is likewise a security device because the creditor knows that the drafts which the creditor draws will be accepted or paid by the issuer of the letter.

The use of letters of credit arose in international trade. While this continues to be the primary area of use, there is a growing use of letters in domestic sales and in transactions in which the letter of credit takes the place of a surety bond. Thus a letter of credit has been used to assure that a borrower would repay a loan, that a tenant would pay the rent due under a lease, and that a contractor would properly perform a construction contract.[2]

§ 37:5.   Definition.

A **letter of credit** is an engagement by its issuer that it will pay or accept drafts when the conditions specified in the letter are satisfied. The issuer is usually a bank.

Three contracts are involved in most letter-of-credit transactions: (1) the contract between the issuer and the account party for the issuance of the credit; (2) the letter of credit itself; and (3) the underlying agreement, often a contract of sale, between the beneficiary and the account party. The letter of credit is completely independent from the other two contracts.

The issuer of the letter of credit is not a surety that is underwriting payment by its customer. The issuer of the letter is in effect the obligor on a third party beneficiary contract made for the benefit of the beneficiary of the letter.

FACTS:

Berley was a party to a lawsuit. The court required him to file a $40,000 bond. The Travelers Indemnity Company issued the bond but required him to give it a certified check for $40,000 as security. Subsequently Berley obtained a letter of credit for $40,000 from the Flushing National Bank by which the bank agreed to honor drafts drawn upon it by the indemnity company when it incurred liability on the Berley bond. Berley gave this letter of credit to the indemnity company and took back his certified check. Thereafter a claim was made on the Berley bond. The indemnity company then drew a draft upon the bank pursuant to the letter of credit. The bank refused to pay the draft on the ground that the indemnity company had not given any consideration for the letter of credit and that the bank was released from liability because the indemnity company's release of the certified check constituted an impairment of collateral which released the bank as a surety.

DECISION:

Judgment for Travelers Indemnity Company. A letter of credit is binding on the issuer by the mere fact that it has been issued and it is no defense that there was no consideration. Moreover, the letter imposes a primary obligation upon the issuer. The issuer does not have the status of a surety or a guarantor and therefore is not affected by matters which would be defenses in favor of sureties and guarantors. [Travelers Indemnity Company v Flushing National Bank, 396 NYS2d 754 (1977)]

---

[2]Barclays Bank D.C.O. v The Merchantile National Bank (CA5 Ga) 481 F2d 1224 (1973).

§ 37:6.   Parties.

The parties to a letter of credit are (1) the issuer, (2) the customer who makes the arrangements with the issuer, and (3) the beneficiary who will be the drawer of the drafts which will be drawn under the letter of credit. There may also be (4) an advising bank.[3] This will occur when the local issuer of the letter of credit requests its correspondent bank where the beneficiary is located to notify or advise the beneficiary that the letter has been issued.

As an illustration of the above definitions, an American merchant may buy goods from a Spanish merchant. There may be a prior course of dealings between the parties so that the seller is willing to accept the buyer's commercial paper as payment or to accept trade acceptances drawn on the buyer. If the foreign seller is not willing to do this, the American buyer, as customer, may go to a bank, the issuer, and obtain a letter of credit naming the Spanish seller as beneficiary. The American bank's correspondent or advising bank in Spain notifies the Spanish seller that this has been done. The Spanish seller will then draw drafts on the American buyer. By the letter of credit, the issuer is required to accept or pay these drafts.

§ 37:7.   Duration.

A letter of credit continues for any time specified in the letter. Generally a maximum amount is stated in the letter so that the letter is exhausted or used up when drafts aggregating that maximum amount have been accepted or paid by the issuer. A letter of credit may be used in installments as the beneficiary chooses. A letter of credit cannot be revoked or modified by the issuer or the customer without the consent of the beneficiary unless that right is expressly reserved in the letter.

§ 37:8.   Form.

A letter of credit must be in writing and signed by the issuer. If the credit is issued by a bank and requires a documentary draft or a documentary demand for payment or if the credit is issued by a nonbank and requires that the draft or demand for payment be accompanied by a document of title, the instrument will be presumed to be a letter of credit (rather than a contract of guaranty). Otherwise, the instrument must conspicuously state that it is a letter of credit.[4] Consideration is not required to establish or modify a letter of credit.

§ 37:9.   Duty of Issuer.

The issuer is obligated to honor drafts drawn under the letter of credit if the conditions specified in the letter have been satisfied. Generally this means that the bank must assure itself that all specified papers have been submitted. The issuer has no duty to verify that the papers are properly supported by facts or that the underlying transaction has been performed. It is thus immaterial that the goods sold by the seller in fact do not conform to the contract as long as the seller tenders the documents specified by the letter of

---

[3]UCC §5-103(e).
[4]UCC §5-102.

THE NATIONAL BANK OF COMMERCE
St. Louis, MO

To: _____   DATE _____

BRANCH _____

GENTLEMEN,

We open an IRREVOCABLE DOCUMENTARY CREDIT NO

in favor of _____

_____

For account of _____

_____

For an amount not exceeding _____

Valid until _____ Available by beneficiary's draft in duplicate on accountees at _____
_____ drawn to the order of negotiating Bank (without recourse) for 100% of net Invoice value bearing
date, credit number and accompanied by documents (marked X below) at least in duplicate, unless otherwise specified.

☐ Full set of CLEAN ON BOARD OCEAN BILLS OF LADING to order endorsed in blank, marked "freight paid/payable at destination" and notify accreditors.

☐ INSURANCE POLICY OR UNDERWRITERS' CERTIFICATE in duplicate, blank endorsed in currency of credit for at least _____% of invoice value against Marine, War and Strike risks.

☐ PACKING SPECIFICATION in quadruplicate.

☐ INVOICE in sextuplicate in English duly signed by beneficiaries certifying that the goods shipped are in accordance with order / indent/pro-forma Invoice No. _____ dated _____
showing Import Licence No. _____

Documents to cover shipment of:				
From:	To:	Shipment not later than	Partshipment	Transhipment

All bank charges, including postage s for beneficiaries account.

Original draft and one set of documents to be sent to us by registered airmail and the duplicate draft with the remaining documents by subsequent registered air-mail.

REIMBURSEMENT INSTRUCTIONS.

Yours faithfully,
THE NATIONAL BANK OF COMMERCE,

_____   _____
ACCOUNTANT   MANAGER

No. 4355610

LETTER OF CREDIT

While there are few formal requirements for creating a letter of credit, banks often use a standard form, similar to the one pictured here, for convenience.

credit.[5] If the issuer dishonors a draft without justification, it is liable to its customer for breach of contract.

SUMMARY

Suretyship and guaranty undertakings have the common feature of a promise to answer for the debt or default of another. A surety is primarily

[5]Intraworld Industries, Inc. v Girard Trust Bank, 461 Pa 343, 336 A2d 316 (1975).

liable for the debt or obligation of the principal debtor. The guarantor is ordinarily only secondarily liable unless the guarantor has made an absolute guaranty, in which case the guarantor becomes primarily liable. The surety and guaranty relationships are based upon contract. Sureties have a number of rights to protect them. They are: exoneration, subrogation, indemnity, and contribution. In addition to those rights, sureties also have certain defenses. They include ordinary contract defenses as well as some defenses peculiar to the suretyship relationship; such as, that the original contract was invalid, that the principal obligation was discharged, or that the original contract was modified without the surety's consent.

A letter of credit is an agreement that the issuer of the letter will pay drafts drawn on the issuer by the beneficiary of the letter. The issuer of the letter of credit is usually a bank. There are usually three contracts involved in most letter of credit transactions: (1) the contract between the issuer and the account party for the issuance of the letter of credit, (2) the letter of credit itself, and (3) the underlying agreement between the beneficiary and the account party. The parties to a letter of credit are the issuer, the customer (or account party) who makes the arrangement with the issuer, and the beneficiary who will be the drawer of the draft to be drawn under the letter of credit. The letter of credit continues for any time specified in the letter. The letter of credit must be in writing and signed by the issuer. Consideration is not required to establish or modify a letter of credit. If the conditions in the letter of credit have been complied with, the issuer is then obligated to honor drafts drawn under the letter of credit.

QUESTIONS AND CASE PROBLEMS

1. What social forces are affected by the use of a letter of credit?
2. Kiernan Construction Company makes a contract with Viola to build a house for her. The Century Surety Company executes a bond to protect Viola from loss should Kiernan fail to construct the house or pay labor and material bills. Kiernan fails to build the house. Viola sues the Century Surety Company. It raises the defense that Viola must first sue Kiernan. Is it correct?
3. What is the duration of a letter of credit?
4. What is the nature of an indemnity contract?
5. The surety's right of subrogation arises as soon as the surety pays any part of the debt that the surety is obligated to pay. Appraise this statement.
6. Eberstadt owed Terence $500. He gave his note for that amount to Terence. At the same time, an agreement signed by Reid and given to Terence was as follows:
   "I agree to be surety for the payment of Eberstadt's note for $500." On maturity of the note, Eberstadt paid $200 on account and gave a new note for $300 due in three months. Reid was not informed of this transaction. The new note was not paid at maturity. Terence sues Reid. Does Reid have any defense?
7. Marcia pawned certain property with the Banty Loan Co. to secure a loan which was to be repaid in regular installments. After several months of making the regular payments, Marcia offered to pay the loan com-

pany the full amount which would be due it under the terms of the loan and demanded the return of her property. The loan company refused and demanded more money. Marcia sued the loan company. Decide.

8. Vort owed Yarrow the sum of $500. When it appeared that Vort would probably not be able to pay when his obligation came due, Grant orally advised Yarrow, "Don't worry, if you cannot collect from Vort, I will pay you." Vort did not pay the $500 when it became due and Yarrow sued Grant. State any defenses available to Grant.

9. James and Henry are co-sureties on an obligation of Stark to Prior. Stark defaults on his obligation. James, although wealthy, advised Prior that he would pay nothing on his suretyship obligation. Prior then brings legal action against Henry for the entire amount by which Stark was in default. Henry is short of funds, and if he were to pay the amount in its entirety, he would suffer severely in his other business ventures through lack of funds to finance such operations. State what, if any, legal relief is available to Henry.

10. A made a contract to purchase goods from B. In order to assure B that he would be paid, A obtained a letter of credit from the C bank. The letter was irrevocable and provided that C would honor drafts for the purchase price of goods shipped to A upon presentment to the bank of the drafts, the bill of lading showing shipment to A, and the invoice showing the nature and price of the goods shipped. Because of financial difficulties, A did not want to receive the goods under the contract and made an agreement with C that no drafts would be honored pursuant to the letter of credit. B shipped goods to A under the contract and presented drafts, and the proper bills of lading, and invoices to C. C refused to honor the drafts. B sued C. It claimed that it was not liable because the letter of credit which had obligated it to accept the drafts had been terminated by the agreement of its customer. Was this a valid defense?

11. Lambert loaned Heaton $25,000 for six months. Heaton gave a promissory note, payable at the end of six months, in the face amount of $30,000, thereby concealing the fact that usurious interest was charged. Under the local statute, the loan contract was, in fact, void because of the usury. Heaton obtained a bond from the United Bonding Insurance Co., which guaranteed to Lambert that the promissory note would be paid when due. When the note was not paid, Lambert sued Heaton and the bonding company. The latter raised the defense that its obligation was voided because the usurious character of the transaction had not been disclosed to it. Decide. [Lambert v Heaton (FlaApp) 134 So2d 536]

12. The Kitsap County Credit Bureau held against Alderman a claim, the payment of which had been guaranteed by Richards. When Richards was sued on his guaranty, he proved that the claim against Alderman had been settled by compromise upon his paying $100 to the creditor. What result? [Kitsap County Credit Bureau v Richards, 52 Wash 381, 325 P2d 292]

13. Hugill agreed to deliver shingles to the W. I. Carpenter Lumber Co. He furnished a surety bond to secure the faithful performance of the contract on his part. After a breach of the contract by Hugill, the lumber company brought an action to recover its loss from the surety, the

Fidelity & Deposit Co. of Maryland. The surety denied liability on the ground that there was concealment of (1) the price to be paid for the shingles, and (2) the fact that a material advance had been made to the contractor equal to the amount of the profit that he would make by performing the contract. Decide. [W.I. Carpenter Lumber Co. v Hugill, 149 Wash 45, 270 P 94]

14. Donaldson sold plumbing supplies. The St. Paul-Mercury Indemnity Co., as surety for him, executed and delivered a bond to the State of California for the payment of all sales taxes. Donaldson failed to pay, and the company paid the taxes which he owed. The company then sued him for the taxes. What result? [St. Paul-Mercury Indemnity Co. v Donaldson, 225 SC 476, 83 SE2d 159]

15. Stewart, Brown, and James were sureties on a $9,000 promissory note signed by Hunter, as maker, in favor of the Fanton Finance Company. When the note became due, Stewart paid the $9,000 to the Fanton Finance Company. Stewart then brought an action against Brown and James to recover $6,000. Brown and James contend that Stewart must first proceed against Hunter. Decide.

16. First National Bank hired Lenore as a secretary and obtained a surety bond from Belton covering the Bank against losses up to $100,000 resulting from Lenore's improper conduct in the performance of her duties. Both Lenore and the Bank signed the application for the bond. After one year of service Lenore was promoted to the position of teller in the Bank and the original bond remained in effect. Shortly after Lenore's promotion a surprise examination revealed that Lenore had taken advantage of her new position and had stolen $50,000 from the Bank. She was arrested and charged with embezzlement. Lenore had only $5,000 in assets at the time of her arrest. (a) If the Bank demands a payment of $50,000 from Belton, what defense, if any, might Belton raise to deny any obligation to the Bank? (b) If Belton fully reimburses the Bank for its loss, under what theory or theories, if any, may Belton attempt to recover from Lenore?

CHAPTER 38

BANKRUPTCY

CHAPTER OBJECTIVES

After studying this chapter you will be able to:

1. List the requirements for the commencement of a voluntary bankruptcy case and an involuntary bankruptcy case.
2. Describe the rights of the trustee in bankruptcy.
3. Explain the procedure for the administration of the debtor's estate.
4. List the debtor's duties and exemptions.
5. Explain the significance of a discharge in bankruptcy.
6. Describe the steps in a business reorganization and an extended time payment plan.
7. Solve problems involving bankruptcy.

Our society has provided a system by which the honest but financially overburdened debtor can pay into court whatever property the debtor possesses, be relieved of most obligations, and start economic life anew. This is achieved through a proceeding called bankruptcy.

Historically the bankruptcy law was not concerned with benefiting the debtor as much as it was with benefiting the debtor's creditors. In its origin, the law was designed to compel fraudulent debtors to bring their property into court and to pay it to their creditors, thus preventing them from concealing their property or from paying it to only some of their creditors. Today, a bankruptcy proceeding has both features, as can be seen from the fact that a case in bankruptcy may be started by the debtor (a voluntary case) or by creditors (an involuntary case).

A. BANKRUPTCY REFORM ACT OF 1978

Congress under the power granted to it by the Constitution enacted the Bankruptcy Act in 1898. It was subsequently amended by the Chandler Act of 1938. However, the Act of 1978 represents the first comprehensive revision to modernize the bankruptcy laws by making both substantive and procedural changes.

The 1978 Act established a United States Bankruptcy Court as an adjunct to the federal district court in each judicial district, which greatly expanded the jurisdiction of the bankruptcy courts. Under the 1978 Act, the bankruptcy courts could not only hear and decide all bankruptcy cases but were also granted nonexclusive jurisdiction to hear and decide all civil proceedings arising under the bankruptcy law or related to cases under the bankruptcy law. This expansion of bankruptcy court jurisdiction was held by the United States Supreme Court to violate Article III of the U.S. Constitution.[1] It had given bankruptcy judges most of the authority of federal district court judges, but none of their tenure or salary protection.

The Bankruptcy Amendments Act of 1984 restructured the bankruptcy court system limiting the powers of bankruptcy judges. It removed their authority over nonbankruptcy issues. In effect, it vested all jurisdiction over bankruptcy cases in the United States District Courts, which may refer all cases and related proceedings to adjunct bankruptcy courts.[2]

Under the 1978 Act, three kinds of bankruptcy proceedings are available to individuals and businesses:

(1) liquidation, sometimes called a "Chapter 7" bankruptcy;

(2) reorganization, sometimes called a "Chapter 11" bankruptcy; and

(3) extended time payment, sometimes called a "Chapter 13" bankruptcy.

B. LIQUIDATION UNDER CHAPTER 7

In liquidation proceedings, the debtor's nonexempt assets are collected by the trustee representing the creditors, who liquidates the assets and distributes the proceeds to the creditors. The debtor is then discharged from most debts except those that were fraudulently incurred. A liquidation can be voluntary or involuntary.

§ 38:1. Commencement of the Bankruptcy Case.

The principal difference between a voluntary case and an involuntary case lies in the manner in which the proceedings are started.

(a) **Voluntary.** A **voluntary case** is commenced by the debtor's filing a petition with the bankruptcy court. A joint petition may be filed by a hus-

---

[1]Northern Pipeline Constr. Co. v Marathon Pipe Line Co. 458 US 50 (1982).
[2]This chapter is based on the Bankruptcy Act of 1978 and the Bankruptcy Amendments of 1984.

band and wife. The commencement of a voluntary or joint case constitutes an order for relief or determination that the petitioner is bankrupt.[3] Unless the court orders otherwise, a debtor must also file a schedule of current income and current expenditures.

Individuals, partnerships, and corporations except railroads, banks, insurance companies, savings and loan associations, and credit unions, may file a voluntary petition.[4]

(b) **Involuntary.** An **involuntary case** is commenced by the creditors by filing a petition with the bankruptcy court.

An involuntary case may be commenced against any individual, partnership or corporation, except a farmer; or a banking, insurance or non-profit corporation.[5]

§ 38:2.   Number and Claims of Petitioning Creditors.

If there are twelve or more creditors, at least three, whose unsecured claims total $5,000 or more, must sign the involuntary petition. If there are less than twelve such creditors excluding employees or insiders, any creditor whose unsecured claim is at least $5,000 may sign the petition.

If the creditor holds security for the claim, only the amount of the claim in excess of the value of the security is counted. The holder of a claim which is the subject of a bona fide dispute may not be counted as a petitioning creditor.[6]

§ 38:3.   Requirements for Involuntary Case.

If the debtor contests the bankruptcy petition, the court may not order the relief requested unless at least one of the following grounds exists: (1) the debtor is not paying debts as they become due, or (2) within 120 days before the date of the filing of the petition, a custodian has been appointed for the debtor's property. No act or misconduct on the part of the debtor need be shown.[7]

FACTS:

Bank Leumi Trust Company commenced an involuntary case against Sol Arker seeking to have him declared a bankrupt. The bank claimed that Arker was generally not paying his debts since the bank had been unable to collect on a $190,000 judgment that the bank held against Arker. Arker denied that he was generally not paying his debts and asserted further that he had no assets which could be used to satisfy the Bank's claim.

DECISION:

Judgment for Arker. The purpose of an involuntary proceeding is to secure an equitable distribution of the assets of the alleged debtor among all creditors. There will be no order for relief in bankruptcy when the alleged debtor fails to meet liability to only a single creditor. In addition, an order for relief will not be granted where there are no assets to be liquidated for the benefit of the creditors. [In re Arker, 6 BR 632, (ED NY 1980)]

---

[3]11 USC § 301, 302.
[4]11 USC § 109(b).
[5]11 USC § 303(a).
[6]11 USC § 303(b)(1).
[7]11 USC § 303(h)(1) and (2).

§ 38:4.   Rights of Debtor in Involuntary Case.

If an involuntary petition is dismissed other than by consent of all petitioning creditors and the debtor, the court may award costs, reasonable attorney fees, or damages to the debtor. The damages are those that may be caused by the taking of possession of the debtor's property. The debtor may also recover damages against any creditor who filed the petition in bad faith.[8]

§ 38:5.   Trustee in Bankruptcy.

The trustee in bankruptcy is elected by the creditors. An interim trustee will be appointed by the court or the United States Trustee if a trustee is not elected by the creditors.

(a) **Status of the Trustee.** The trustee is deemed to be the successor to and stand in the shoes of the bankrupt. The trustee automatically becomes by operation of law the owner of all the property of the bankrupt in excess of the property to which the bankrupt is entitled under exemption laws. Property inherited by the debtor within six months after the filing of the petition also passes to the trustee.

FACTS:

Marin Seafoods drew a check on the Bank of Marin to pay a bill. Seafoods then went into bankruptcy, was adjudicated bankrupt, and England was elected the trustee in bankruptcy. Thereafter the Bank of Marin paid the holder the amount of the check. England sued the Bank of Marin for making this payment, asserting that the title to Seafoods' bank account passed to him and terminated the right of the bank to honor the check of Seafoods.

DECISION:

Judgment for the bank. The principle that title to the debtor's property passes to the trustee in bankruptcy is subject to an equitable exception in the check-paying case. A drawee bank that honors a bankrupt's check in good faith without notice or knowledge of the bankruptcy is not liable to the trustee in bankruptcy for the amount of such payment. [Bank of Marin v England, 385 US 99 (1966)]

(b) **Rights of the Trustee.** The bankruptcy trustee possesses the rights and the powers of the most favored creditor of the bankrupt. This means that the trustee can avoid (1) transfers by the debtor which a creditor holding a valid claim under state law could have avoided at the commencement of the bankruptcy case, (2) preferences, that is, a transfer of property by the debtor to a creditor, the effect of which enables the creditor to obtain a greater percentage of the creditor's claim than the creditor would have received had the debtor's assets been liquidated in bankruptcy, and (3) statutory liens that became effective against the debtor at the commencement of the bankruptcy.

§ 38:6.   Voidable Transfers.

A debtor may not transfer property to prevent creditors from satisfying their legal claims. The trustee may avoid any such transfer made or

[8] 11 USC § 303(i).

obligation incurred by the debtor within one year of bankruptcy when the debtor's actual intent was to hinder, delay, or defraud creditors by so doing.

The trustee may also avoid certain transfers of property made by a debtor merely because their effect is to make the debtor insolvent or to reduce the debtor's assets to an unreasonably low amount.[9]

(a) **The Insolvent Debtor.** A debtor is considered insolvent when the total fair value of all the debtor's assets does not exceed the debts owed by the debtor. This is commonly called the *balance sheet test* because it is merely a comparison of assets to liabilities without considering whether the debtor will be able to meet future obligations as they become due.

(b) **Preferential Transfers.** A transfer of property by the debtor to a creditor may be set aside and the property recovered by the debtor's trustee in bankruptcy if (1) the transfer was to pay a debt incurred at some earlier time, (2) the transfer was made when the debtor was insolvent and within 90 days before the filing of the bankruptcy petition, and (3) by the transfer the creditor received more than such creditor would have received in a liquidation of the debtor's estate. A debtor is presumed to be insolvent on and during the 90 days immediately preceding the date of the filing of the bankruptcy petition.[10]

Preferences made to **insiders,** that is, the debtor's relatives, partners, directors, and controlling persons, within the previous 12 months of the petition may be set aside.[11]

Certain transfers by a debtor may not be attacked by the trustee as preferences. A transaction for a present consideration, such as a cash sale, is not subject to attack. A payment by a debtor in the ordinary course of business is not subject to attack, such as the payment of a utility bill. A payment by an individual debtor whose debts are primarily consumer debts is not subject to attack if the aggregate value of the transfer is less than $600.[12]

FACTS:

On May 7, 1981, Joseph Jaggers filed a petition under Chapter 7 of the Bankruptcy Act. At the time the petition was filed, he was indebted to the Cove State Bank on a promissory note. The principal amount of the note had originally been in excess of $68,000. Two payments had been made on the note: one on February 23, 1981; and another on March 23, 1981. The trustee in bankruptcy claimed that these payments were preferential transfers.

DECISION:

Judgment for the trustee in bankruptcy. The transfer was to pay a debt incurred at an earlier time. The transfer was made when the debtor was insolvent and within ninety days before the filing of the bankruptcy petition. Jaggers is presumed to be insolvent on and during the ninety days immediately preceding the date of the filing of the bankruptcy petition. Jaggers by making payments to the bank, gave the bank more than they would have received in a liquidation of the debtor's estate. The payments made resulted in a diminution of the estate and thereby constituted a preferential transfer of the property of the estate. [In re Jaggers, 48 BR 33 (WD Tex 1985)]

---

[9] 11 USC § 548.
[10] 11 USC § 547(f).
[11] 11 USC § 547(b)(4)(B).
[12] 11 USC § 547(c)(7).

C. ADMINISTRATION OF DEBTOR'S ESTATE

The Bankruptcy Act regulates the manner in which creditors present their claims and how the assets of the debtor are to be distributed in payment of the claims.

§ 38:7.   Proof of Claim.

A creditor must file a proof of claim. A **proof of claim** is a written statement signed by the creditor or an authorized representative setting forth any claim made against the bankrupt and the basis thereof. It must ordinarily be filed within 90 days after the first meeting of creditors.[13] A creditor is not excused from filing within that time even though the trustee in bankruptcy in fact knew of the existence of the creditor's claim. A claim is **provable** when it belongs to a class which may be asserted in bankruptcy. Any claim for money whether liquidated (certain and not disputed), unliquidated, contingent, unmatured, disputed, legal, or equitable may be proved in bankruptcy.

§ 38:8.   Priority of Claims.

Creditors who hold security for payment, such as a mortgage on the debtor's property or a lien, are not affected by the debtor's bankruptcy and may enforce their security in order to obtain payment of their claims. The unsecured creditors share in the remaining assets of the debtor. Some have priority over others. Any balance remaining after all creditors have been paid is turned over to the bankrupt.

(a) **Priority of Unsecured Claims.** The unsecured debts which have priority and the order of priority are:[14]

(1) Costs and expenses of administration of the bankruptcy case, including fees to trustees, attorneys, and accountants and the reasonable expenses of creditors in recovering property transferred or concealed by the bankrupt.

(2) Claims arising in the ordinary course of a debtor's business or financial affairs after the commencement of the case and before the appointment of a trustee.

(3) Claims for wages, salaries, or commissions, including vacation, severance, or sick leave pay earned within 90 days before the filing of the petition or the date of cessation of the debtor's business, whichever occurs first. The amount of such claims is limited, however, to $2,000 for each person.

(4) Claims arising for contributions to employee benefit plans. The amount is limited by the Act, and services must have been rendered within 180 days before the filing of the petition or when the debtor ceased doing business, whichever occurred first.

(5) Claims by consumer creditors, not to exceed $900 for each claimant, arising from the purchase of consumer goods or services, where such property or services were not delivered or provided.

[13]Bankruptcy Rule 3002(c).
[14]11 USC § 507(1) to (6).

(6) Federal and state income taxes due within three years of the filing of the petition.

D. DEBTOR'S DUTIES AND EXEMPTIONS

The Bankruptcy Act imposes certain duties on the bankrupt and provides for specific exemptions of some of the bankrupt's estate from the claims of creditors.

§ 38:9. Debtor's Duties.

The debtor must file with the court a list of creditors, a schedule of assets and liabilities, and a statement of the debtor's financial affairs. The debtor must also appear for examination under oath at the first meeting of creditors.

§ 38:10. Debtor's Exemptions.

The debtor is permitted to claim certain property of the estate in the trustee's possession and keep it free from claims of creditors. The debtor may elect either the exemptions permitted by the laws of his or her state of domicile or those set forth in the Bankruptcy Code. If a husband and wife file a joint petition, they must elect together to use either the state or federal exemptions. If they cannot agree on which to elect, they will be deemed to have chosen the federal exemptions. The Bankruptcy Code provides for the following exemptions, among others: the debtor's interest in real or personal property used as a residence to the extent of $7,500; the debtor's interest in a motor vehicle to the extent of $1,200; household furnishings of the debtor or the debtor's dependents, not to exceed $200 per item, or $4,000 in aggregate value; payments under a life insurance contract; alimony and child support payments; and awards from personal injury causes of action.[15]

E. DISCHARGE IN BANKRUPTCY

The main objectives of a bankruptcy proceeding are the collection and distribution of the debtor's assets, and the discharge of the debtor from obligations. The decree terminating the bankruptcy proceeding is generally a **discharge** which releases the debtor from debts.

§ 38:11. Denial of Discharge.

The court will refuse to grant a discharge if the debtor has: (1) within one year of the filing of the petition, fraudulently transferred or concealed property with intent to hinder, delay, or defraud creditors; (2) failed to keep proper financial records; (3) made a false oath or account; (4) failed to explain satisfactorily any loss of assets; (5) refused to obey any lawful order of the court, or refused to testify after having been granted immunity; (6) obtained a discharge within the last six years; or (7) filed a written waiver of discharge which is approved by the court.[16]

[15] 11 USC § 522.
[16] 11 USC § 727.

§ 38:12.   Effect of Discharge.

A discharge releases the debtor from the unpaid balance of most debts. However, a discharge does not release a person from: (1) a tax, customs duty, or tax penalty; (2) student loans unless the loan first became due more than five years before bankruptcy or unless excepting the loan from discharge would impose undue hardship upon the debtor; (3) loans obtained by use of a false financial statement, made with intent to deceive, and on which the creditor reasonably relied; (4) debts not duly scheduled in time for allowance; (5) liability for fraud while acting in a fiduciary capacity or by reason of embezzlement or larceny; (6) liability for alimony and child support; (7) liability for willful and malicious injury to property; (8) judgments against the debtor for liability for driving while intoxicated; (9) a consumer debt to a single creditor aggregating more than $500 for luxury goods or services; and (10) cash advances based upon consumer credit exceeding $1,000.[17]

The debt for luxury goods must be incurred within 40 days of the order for relief; the cash advances must be incurred within 20 days of the order for relief.

FACTS:

Jay L. Switzer submitted a written credit application to Scarsdale National Bank for a loan to finance interior decorating expenses. In describing his residence on the application, Switzer checked the box indicating that he owned his home. In fact, prior to the filing of the application with Scarsdale, Switzer had transferred his home to his wife. Subsequently, Switzer applied to Scarsdale for an extension of credit and a new loan. Once again Switzer listed the home in his own name. Eventually Switzer filed for bankruptcy. Scarsdale claimed that the debt owed by the debtor to Scarsdale was nondischargeable.

DECISION:

Judgment for Scarsdale National Bank. The financial statement given by Switzer to Scarsdale to obtain the loan was materially false. It listed the debtor's home as an asset of the debtor whereas Switzer did not own the home because he had previously transferred his interest to his wife. Scarsdale reasonably relied on the statement to its detriment when it approved the loan. [In Re Switzer, 55 BR 991 (ED NY 1986)]

F. REORGANIZATIONS AND PAYMENT PLANS UNDER CHAPTERS 11 AND 13

In addition to liquidation as above described, the Bankruptcy Act permits the parties to restructure the organization and finances of a business so that it may continue to operate. The Act also provides for the adoption of extended time payment plans for individual debtors who owe unsecured debts of less than $100,000 and secured debts of less than $350,000.

In these so-called "rehabilitation" plans, the debtor keeps all the assets (exempt and nonexempt), remains in business, and makes a settlement

[17]11 USC § 523.

that is acceptable to the majority of the creditors, whose decision is binding on the minority.

§ 38:13   Business Reorganizations Under Chapter 11.

Individuals, partnerships, and corporations in business may be reorganized under the Bankruptcy Act. The first step is to file a plan for the reorganization of the debtor. This may be filed by the debtor or any party in interest or committee of creditors.

(a) Contents of Plan. The plan divides ownership interests and debts into those that will be affected by the adoption of the plan and those that will not. It then specifies what will be done to those interests and claims which are affected. For example, where mortgage payments are too high for the income of the enterprise, a possible plan would be to reduce the mortgage payments and give the mortgage holder preferred stock to compensate for the loss sustained.

Persons within a particular class must all be treated the same way. For example, the holders of first mortgage bonds must all be treated the same way.

A plan may also provide for the assumption, rejection, or assignment of executory contracts. Thus, the trustee or debtor may under certain circumstances suspend performance of a contract not yet fully performed. Collective bargaining agreements may be rejected in this manner with the approval of the bankruptcy court.[18]

(b) Confirmation of Plan. When the plan is prepared, it must be approved or *confirmed* by the court. This will be done if the plan has been submitted in good faith and its provisions are reasonable.[19]

After the plan is confirmed, the owners and creditors of the enterprise have only such rights as are specified in the plan and cannot go back to their original positions.

FACTS:

Johns-Manville Corp. filed for business reorganization under Chapter 11. This filing was greeted with great surprise on the part of some of Manville's creditors and other corporations that were being sued along with Manville for injuries caused by asbestos exposure. Manville contended that the pending lawsuits as well as the potential future lawsuits necessitated its filing. Manville's creditors objected to the filing on the grounds that it was not in good faith and that Manville was not insolvent when it filed.

DECISION:

Judgment for Johns-Manville. In determining whether to dismiss a filing, a court is not necessarily required to consider whether the debtor has filed in good faith because that is not a requirement for a plan for reorganization. Good faith is required, however, for the confirmation of a plan. A principal goal of the Bankruptcy Code is to provide open access to the bankruptcy process. Manville's purported motivation in filing, namely, to obtain a breathing spell from a proliferation of asbestos health suits

[18]11 USC § 1113, modifying the holding of the U.S. Supreme Court in NLRB v Bildisco, 104 S Ct 1188 (1984).
[19]11 USC § 1129.

brought against it did not conclusively establish its lack of intent to rehabilitate so as to justify dismissal of its petition. Bankruptcy Code sections containing eligibility requirements for Chapter 7 and 11 debtors relating to voluntary petitions by companies do not contain any insolvency requirements. [In Re Johns-Manville Corp., 36 BR 727 (SD NY 1984)]

---

§ 38:14   Extended Time Payment Plans Under Chapter 13.

An individual debtor who has a regular income may submit a plan for the installment payment of outstanding debts. If approved by the court, the debtor may then pay the debts in the installments specified by the plan even though the creditors had not originally agreed to such installment payments.

(a) **Contents of Plan.** The individual debtor plan is, in effect, a budget of the debtor's future income with respect to outstanding debts. The plan must provide for the eventual payment in full of all claims entitled to priority under the Bankruptcy Act. Creditors holding the same type or class of claim must all be treated the same way.

(b) **Confirmation of Plan.** The plan has no effect until it is approved or *confirmed* by the court. This will be done if the plan was submitted in good faith and is in the best interests of the creditors.[20]

When the plan is confirmed, debts are payable in the manner specified in the plan.

(c) **Discharge of Debtor.** After all the payments called for by the plan have been made, the debtor is given a discharge which releases from liability for all debts except those which would not be discharged by an ordinary bankruptcy discharge.[21]

§ 38:15.   Protection Against Discrimination.

Federal, state, or local law may not discriminate against anyone on the basis of a discharge in bankruptcy.[22]

SUMMARY

Jurisdiction over bankruptcy cases is in the United States District Courts, which may refer all cases and related proceedings to adjunct bankruptcy courts.

Three bankruptcy proceedings are available to individuals and businesses: (1) liquidation, (2) reorganization, and (3) extended time payment.

A liquidation proceeding under Chapter 7 may be either voluntary or involuntary. The voluntary case is commenced by the debtor by filing a petition with the bankruptcy court. An involuntary case is commenced by the creditors by filing a petition with the bankruptcy court. If there are twelve or

[20]11 USC § 1325.
[21]11 USC § 1328. See § 38:12 of this book.
[22]11 USC § 525.

more creditors, at least three, whose unsecured claims total at least $5,000 or more must sign the involuntary petition. If there are less than twelve such creditors, any creditor whose unsecured claim is at least $5,000 may sign the petition. If the debtor contests the bankruptcy petition, it must be shown that the debtor is not paying debts as they become due, or that within 120 days before the date of the filing of the petition a custodian had been appointed for the debtor's property.

The trustee in bankruptcy is elected by the creditors and is the successor to and stands in the place of the bankrupt. The trustee can avoid transfers of property to prevent creditors from satisfying their legal claims. Preferential transfers to creditors and to insiders may be set aside. A transaction for a present consideration such as a cash sale is not a preference.

The Bankruptcy Act regulates the manner in which creditors present their claims and how the assets of the debtor are to be distributed in payment of the claims.

Claims are paid in the following order of priority: (1) secured creditors, (2) administrative expenses, (3) claims arising in the ordinary course of the debtor's business, (4) wage claims limited to $2,000 for each claimant earned within 90 days before the filing of the petition, (5) claims for contributions to employee benefit plans, (6) claims by consumer creditors, (7) taxes, and (8) general creditors. Certain property of the debtor is exempt from the claims of creditors.

The decree terminating the bankruptcy proceedings is generally a discharge which releases the debtor from most debts. If the debtor is a dishonest debtor, no discharge will be given. This is so when the debtor has fraudulently transferred property, failed to keep proper records, or failed to obey a court order, among others. Certain debts such as taxes, student loans, loans obtained by use of a false financial statement, alimony, and debts not duly scheduled are not discharged.

Individuals, partnerships, and corporations in business may be reorganized so that a business may continue to operate. A plan for reorganization must be approved by the court. Individual debtors may adopt extended time payment plans for the payment of debts. A plan for extended time payment must also be confirmed by the court.

Federal, state, or local law may not discriminate against anyone on the basis of a discharge in bankruptcy.

QUESTIONS AND CASE PROBLEMS

1. What social forces are affected by permitting a debtor to avoid paying debts by going into bankruptcy?
2. Compare a release of claims given by a creditor with a discharge in bankruptcy.
3. Compare voluntary and involuntary bankruptcy.
4. Compare the concepts of (a) provable claims; (b) allowance of claims; and (c) the discharge of claims.
5. Barron sold goods on credit to Charles by relying on a false financial statement issued by Charles. Charles later filed for voluntary bankruptcy still owing this debt to Barron. Barron claimed that Charles was not

entitled to a discharge from his debts because of the fraud. Was Barron correct?

6. Ruth commenced a voluntary case with the bankruptcy court. After her assets subject to the claims of creditors were liquidated, her trustee had possession of $2,000 in cash. Various creditors had filed claims for $20,000. Ruth's trustee claimed that the $2,000 should be used to pay the fee of the trustee, the fee of Ruth's accountant, and other administrative expenses of the bankruptcy case. The other creditors claimed that they were entitled to a portion of the $2,000. Were the other creditors correct?

7. Anita knows Brown to be insolvent. She sells Brown her auto for $500 and receives cash in payment for the car. An involuntary bankruptcy case is commenced by the creditors sometime later against Brown. The trustee in bankruptcy attempts to recover the $500 on that ground that it was a preferential transfer. Will the trustee be successful?

8. Smith has twenty creditors. Three creditors with unsecured claims which total $10,000 signed an involuntary petition to have Smith declared bankrupt. Smith has been unable to pay debts as they become due. Smith objects to the petition being filed since the creditors have failed to allege that Smith has engaged in any misconduct. Will the creditors be successful?

9. Which of the following, if any, survive Roger's discharge in bankruptcy.
   a. Wages amounting to $400 to three employees earned within 60 days of the bankruptcy.
   b. A judgment against Rogers for injuries received because of Roger's negligent operation of an automobile.
   c. A judgment against Roger by Landers for breach of contract.
   d. Roger's obligation for alimony and child support.

10. Between March 26, 1979, and May 25, 1979, the debtor, Gulf States Marine, Inc. incurred certain obligations to the creditor, Lake Charles Diesel, Inc. upon an open account. On September 29, 1979, the debtor paid the creditor the sum of $879.75 in full satisfaction of the obligation. The debtor filed its petition for relief in early October. The trustee seeks to recover the sum of $879.75 from the creditor alleging that the payment to the creditor was a voidable preference. The creditor denies that the debtor was insolvent but offers no proof to the contrary. Decide. [In re Gulf States Marine, Inc. Debtor, 6 BCD 79 (WD La)]

11. Putman, as executrix of the estate of Fred Putman, obtained a judgment for $10,000 against the Ocean Shore Railway Co. for negligently causing the death of Putman. She and two others filed a petition in bankruptcy against Folger, who had a statutory liability for the debts of the railway corporation. In opposing the petition, Folger contended that the claim of Mrs. Putman was not a provable debt in bankruptcy. Do you agree? [In re Putman (DC Cal) 193 F 464]

12. Certain creditors filed a petition in bankruptcy against the Percy Ford Co. An adjudication of bankruptcy followed. At the time of the filing of the petition, the National Shawmut Bank held four notes upon which the bankrupt was absolutely liable, but the notes were not then due and payable. The bank contended that the notes constituted provable debts. Do you agree? [In re Percy Ford Co. (DC Mass) 199 F 334]

13. A California statute provided that the license of a contractor could be revoked if the contractor failed to pay debts in full by obtaining a discharge in bankruptcy. Grimes was a licensed contractor. He was adjudicated a bankrupt. Thereafter the state licensing board revoked his contractor's license. He brought an action against the registrar of the board to compel the reissuance of such license. Was he entitled to the license? [Grimes v Hoschler, 12 Cal3d 305, 115 CalRptr 625, 525 P2d 65]

14. Essex is in serious financial difficulty and is unable to meet current unsecured obligations of $40,000 to some 20 creditors who are demanding immediate payment. Essex owes Stevens $5,000 and Stevens has decided to file an involuntary petition against Essex. Can Stevens file the petition?

15. Sonia, a retailer, has the following assets: a shop worth $100,000; accounts receivable amounting to $75,000, which fall due in from four to six months; and $2,000 cash in the bank. Sonia's sole liability is a $20,000 note falling due today, which Sonia is unable to pay. May Sonia be forced into involuntary bankruptcy under the Bankruptcy Act?

16. Samson Industries, Inc. ceased doing business and is in bankruptcy. Among the claimants are five employees seeking unpaid wages. Three of the employees are owed $3,500 and two are owed $1,500. These amounts became due within ninety days preceding the filing of the petition. How much, if anything, will the employees receive?

CHAPTER 39

INSURANCE

CHAPTER OBJECTIVES

After studying this chapter you will be able to:
1. Define insurable interest.
2. Compare the contract of insurance with ordinary contracts.
3. Determine when a contract of insurance is effective.
4. List the ways in which a contract of insurance may be modified.
5. List and explain the time limitations binding an insured.
6. Solve problems involving contracts of insurance.

Insurance is a multimillion dollar industry in the United States. The function of insurance is to distribute the risk of substantial, individual loss over a large group of individuals who are exposed to similar risks. Insurance companies, through actuarial and other data collecting devices, measure the risks of loss from the perils covered and set a premium or price for the insurance protection provided.

Insurance companies perform a wide range of services such as training businesses in loss prevention, investigating and appraising losses, and managing the vast sums of money they collect as premiums. Insurance company investments are often evident in the large, metropolitan office buildings that bear their names. However, the cornerstone upon which the insurance industry is built is the contract.

Insurance is essentially a contract by which one party for a stipulated consideration promises to pay another party a sum of money upon the destruction of, loss of, or injury to something in which the other party has an interest.

§ 39:1.   The Parties.

The promisor in an insurance contract is called the **insurer** or **underwriter**. The person to whom the promise is made is the **insured**, the assured, or the policyholder. The promise of the insurer is generally set forth in a written contract called a **policy**.

As a result of statutory regulation, virtually all insurance policies today are written by corporations, fraternal or benefit societies, and national or state governments.

The insured must have the capacity to make a contract. At common aw, a minor's insurance contract could be avoided. Statutes increasingly change this and make the minor's contract of insurance as binding as though the minor were an adult.

Insurance contracts are ordinarily made through an agent or a broker. The **insurance agent** is an agent of the insurance company, generally working exclusively for one company. For the most part, the ordinary rules of agency law govern the dealings between this agent and the applicant for insurance.

The **insurance broker** is generally an independent contractor who is not employed by any one insurance company. When a broker obtains a policy for a customer, the broker is the agent of the customer for the purpose of that transaction.[1] Under some statutes, the broker is made an agent of the insurer with respect to payments made by the applicant for transmission to the insurer.

§ 39:2.   Insurable Interest.

The insured must have an insurable interest in the subject matter insured. If not, the insurance contract cannot be enforced.

(a) Insurable Interest in Property. A person has an insurable interest in property whenever the destruction of the property will cause a direct pecuniary or money loss to that person.[2]

It is immaterial whether the insured is the owner of the legal or equitable title, a lienholder, or merely a person in possession of the property. Thus, a person who is merely a possessor, such as the innocent purchaser of a stolen automobile, has an insurable interest therein.[3] Likewise, a contractor remodeling a building has an insurable interest in the building to the extent of the money that will be paid under the contract; because the contractor would not be able to receive that money if the building were destroyed by fire.

In the case of property insurance, the insurable interest must exist at the time the loss occurs. Except when expressly required by statute, it is not necessary that the interest exist at the time when the policy or contract of insurance was made.

(b) Insurable Interest in Life. A person who obtains life insurance can generally name anyone as beneficiary regardless of whether that beneficiary has an insurable interest in the life of the insured. If the beneficiary obtains the policy, the beneficiary must have an insurable interest in the life

---

[1]Foster v American Deposit Ins. Co. (La App) 435 So2d 571 (1983).
[2]DeWitt v American Family Mutual Ins. Co. (Sup Ct Mo) 667 SW2d 700 (1984).
[3]Castle Cars, Inc. v United States Fire Ins. Co. 221 Va 773, 273 SE2d 793 (1981).

of the insured. Such an interest exists if the beneficiary can reasonably expect to receive pecuniary gain from the continued life of the other person and, conversely, would suffer financial loss from the latter's death.[4] Thus, it is held that a creditor has an insurable interest in the life of the debtor since the death of the debtor may mean that the creditor will not be paid the amount owed.

FACTS:

Wisley obtained a policy of life insurance from the National Reserve Life Insurance Co. In the policy, he named "Sarah A. Wisley, wife" as beneficiary and named his father, Rufus, as beneficiary "should she not live." Two years later, Wisley and his wife were divorced. She then married Mullenax. Upon the death of Wisley, both Sarah and Rufus claimed the proceeds of the policy. Rufus claimed that Sarah did not have an insurable interest.

DECISION:

Judgment for Sarah. Whether a person has an insurable interest is a matter to be raised by the insurance company. It cannot be raised by one beneficiary seeking to disqualify another beneficiary. In any event, Sarah was entitled to recover because there was no requirement that she have an insurable interest in the life of Wisley since that policy had been obtained by him. A person can insure his own life in favor of anyone he chooses, and in most states the beneficiary is not required to have an insurable interest in the insured life unless the policy is procured and paid for by the beneficiary. [Mullenax v National Reserve Life Insurance Co. 29 Colo App 418, 485 P2d 137 (1971)]

A partnership has an insurable interest in the life of each of the partners, for the death of any one of them will dissolve the firm and cause some degree of loss to the partnership. A business enterprise has an insurable interest in the life of an executive or a key employee because that person's death would inflict a financial loss upon the business to the extent that a replacement was not readily available or could not be found.

In the case of life insurance the insurable interest must exist at the time the policy is obtained. It is immaterial that the interest no longer exists when the loss is actually sustained. Thus, the fact that the insured husband and wife beneficiary are divorced after the life insurance policy was procured does not affect the validity of the policy.

§ 39:3.   The Insurance Contract.

The formation of the contract of insurance is governed by the general principles applicable to contracts.[5] Frequently a question arises as to whether

---

[4]New York Life Ins. Co. v Port City Construction Co. 128 Cal App 3d 482, 180 Cal Rptr 359 (1982).

[5]Employers Mutual Casualty Co. v Pigeon Creek Corp. 1 Ark App 179, 614 SW2d 516 (1981).

advertising material, estimates, and statistical projections constitute a part of the contract.

By statute it is now commonly provided that an insurance policy must be written. In order to avoid deception, many statutes also specify the content of certain policies, in whole or in part, and some specify the size and style of type to be used in printing them. Provisions in a policy in conflict with a statute are generally void.

(a) **The Application as Part of the Contract.** The application for insurance is generally attached to the policy when issued and is made part of the contract of insurance by express stipulation of the policy.

The insured must examine the policy and an attached application. Any false statement in the application binds the insured if the policy and the attached application are retained without objection to such statement.

(b) **Statutory Provisions as Part of the Contract.** When a statute requires that insurance contracts contain certain provisions or cover certain specified losses, a contract of insurance that does not comply with the statute will be interpreted as though it contained all the provisions required by the statute.[6] Moreover, when a statute requires that the insurance contract include any exceptions, limitations, or restrictions, then the insurer may not rely upon an exception, limitation, or restriction not stated in the contract to defeat an insured's claim.

FACTS:

In 1975 Edwin Domke submitted an application for mortgage disability insurance, under an employer group insurance plan, to cover his house. On his application he indicated that he had a hearing impairment and he set forth his medical history. Domke was issued a four-page Certificate of Insurance but he was not given a copy of the group master policy which excluded from coverage "pre-existing conditions." A state law required that each certificate of insurance set forth "any exceptions, limitations and restrictions." In 1977, Domke resigned his employment because of his hearing problem and applied for benefits under the mortgage disability policy. The insurance company denied benefits because the master policy excluded coverage for pre-existing conditions and his hearing impairment was a pre-existing condition.

DECISION:

Judgment for Domke. The Certificate of Insurance issued to Domke by the insurance company constituted the insurance contract. The exclusion of "pre-existing conditions" from coverage is clearly an exception which must be set forth in the certificate for the insurance company to be able to rely on it to defeat the claim. [Domke v F & M Savings Bank & N.C. Life Insurance Company (Minn App) 363 NW2d 898 (1985)]

---

[6]Samson v Transamerica Ins. Co. 30 Cal 3d 220, 178 Cal Rptr 343, 636 P2d 32 (1981).

(c) **Duties of Parties to Insurance Contract.** The insured and the insurer owe each other the obligations imposed by the insurance contract. The duty to act in good faith requires that an applicant for insurance tell the insurer any fact material to the risk.[7] The insurer is under the obligation to make any investigation that is required to determine the facts of the case, to make reasonable efforts to settle any claim asserted against the insured when the insurance provides protection from claims of third persons, and to defend the insured if such claims cannot be settled.[8]

§ 39:4.   When the Insurance Contract Is Effective.

An applicant for insurance may or may not be protected by insurance before the written policy is issued. Four situations may arise:

(1) When the applicant tells a broker to obtain property or liability insurance, the applicant is merely employing the broker as an agent. If the broker procures a policy, the customer is insured. If the broker fails to do so, the customer does not have any insurance, but the broker may be personally liable to the customer for the loss.

(2) The person seeking insurance and the insurer or its agent may orally agree that the applicant will be protected by insurance during the interval between the time the application is received and the time when the insurer either rejects the application, or accepts it and issues a policy. This agreement to protect the applicant by insurance during such an interval is binding even though it is oral. Generally, however, when such a preliminary contract is made, the agent will sign a memorandum stating the essential terms of the policy to be executed. This oral contract and the written memorandum are called *binders*.

An "oral binder" of insurance is a temporary contract which terminates when the written policy contemplated by it is issued.[9] In some states, a maximum duration for an oral contract of insurance is set by statute.

(3) The parties may agree that at a later time a policy will be issued and delivered. In that case the insurance contract is not in effect until the policy is delivered or sent to the applicant. Accordingly, loss sustained after the transaction between the applicant and the insurance agent but before the delivery of the policy is not covered by the policy thereafter delivered.

(4) The parties may agree that a policy of life insurance shall be binding upon the payment of the first premium even though the applicant has not been examined provided the applicant thereafter passes an examination.

(a) **Delivery of Policy.** Ordinarily delivery of the policy is not essential to the existence of a contract of insurance. As an exception, delivery of the policy may be made an express condition to coverage.

(b) **Prepayment of Premiums.** Ordinarily a contract of property insurance exists even though the premium due has not been paid. Thus, it is

---

[7]Topps v Universal Life Ins. Co. (La App) 396 So2d 394 (1981).
[8]Hartford Insurance Group v District Court, (Colo) 625 P2d 1013 (1981).
[9]Terry v Mongin Insurance Agency, 102 Wis 2d 239, 306 NW2d 270 (1981).

possible to effect property and liability insurance in most cases by an oral binder or agreement, as by a telephone call. In the case of life insurance policies, it is common to require both delivery of the policy to the insured while in a condition of good health and the prepayment of the first premium on the policy.

(c) **When Coverage Is Effective.** Distinct from the question of when is there a contract of insurance is the question of when does the coverage of the risk commence under a contract of insurance. Some policies of insurance do not cover the specified risk until after a certain period of time has elapsed after the policy becomes binding. That is, there is a waiting period before the contract of insurance provides protection. In most kinds of insurance, the coverage is immediately effective so that there is no waiting period once the insurer has accepted the application and has thereby created a contract of insurance between the parties.

FACTS:
Metts filled out a printed application form for polio insurance distributed by the Central Standard Life Insurance Co. He mailed the application to the company on May 15. It was received by the company on May 23. On May 21, Metts' son was sticken with polio, of which the insurer was notified on May 28. The company refused to pay on the ground that it had not accepted the application. Metts sued the insurer. He proved that the application which he had received from the insurer stated "immediate first day coverage automatically covers the entire family." He claimed that his family was covered by the policy as soon as he signed and mailed the application to the insurer.

DECISION:
Judgment for Metts. The words "immediate" and "automatically" on the application indicated that the insurer intended to be bound at once. Even if there were any uncertainty as to the meaning, such ambiguity must be interpreted against the insurer. A person in the position of the insured would reasonably interpret the application as meaning that there was protection from the moment the signed application was mailed to the insurer. [Metts v Central Standard Life Insurance Co. 142 Cal App 2d 445, 297 P2d 621 (1956)]

(d) **Machine-Vended Insurance.** When insurance is sold by a vending machine, as in the case of air flight insurance, it becomes effective when the applicant places the application and the premium in the machine and receives a receipt.

§ 39:5.   Modification of Contract.

As is the case with most contracts, a contract of insurance can be modified if both insurer and insured agree to the change. In some cases, the insurer reserves the right in the contract to make unilateral modifications. However, the insurer cannot modify the contract without the consent of the insured when the right to do so is not reserved in the insurance contract.[10]

[10]Krebs v Strange (Miss) 419 So2d 178 (1982).

In order to make changes or corrections to the policy, it is not necessary to issue a new policy. An indorsement on the policy or the execution of a separate *rider* is effective for the purpose of changing the policy.

When a provision of an indorsement conflicts with a provision of the policy, the indorsement controls because it is the later document.

§ 39:6. Interpretation of Insurance Contract.

The contract of insurance is interpreted by the same rules that govern the interpretation of ordinary contracts. Words are to be given their ordinary meaning and interpreted in the light of the nature of the coverage intended. Thus, an employee who had been killed was not regarded as "disabled" within the meaning of a group policy covering employees.

The courts are increasingly recognizing the fact that most persons obtaining insurance are not specially trained, and therefore the contract of insurance is to be read as it would be understood by the average person or by the average person in business, rather than by one with technical knowledge of the law or of insurance.

If there is an ambiguity in the policy, the provision is interpreted against the insurer.[11] In some instances courts will give a liberal interpretation to the policy terms in order to favor the insured or the beneficiary on the basis that the insured did not in fact have a free choice.

FACTS:

R. F. Baurer purchased a White Freightliner tractor and agreed that his son-in-law, Britton, could use it in the trucking business. In return Britton agreed to haul Baurer's hay and cattle, thus saving Baurer approximately $30,000 per year. Baurer insured the vehicle with Mountain West Farm Bureau Insurance Co. The policy contained an exclusionary clause that provided: "We don't insure your [truck] while it is rented or leased to others...This does not apply to the use of your [truck] on a share expense basis." When the vehicle was destroyed, Mountain West refused to pay on the policy contending that the arrangement between Baurer and Britton was a lease of the vehicle which was excluded under the policy. Baurer sued contending that it was a "share expense basis" allowed under the policy.

DECISION:

Judgment for Baurer. Ambiguous language in an insurance policy is construed in a way that is most favorable to the insured, and this rule of interpretation particularly applies to exclusionary clauses. Such a construction of the language in this case would result in an exception for arrangements that involved the sharing of expenses even if they also had some of the characteristics of a lease. Thus, despite the fact that the arrangement between Baurer and Britton had some of the characteristics of a lease, because it involved the sharing of expenses which were incidental to the operation of the vehicle it was allowed by the policy. [Baurer v Mountain West Farm Bureau Ins. (Mont) 695 P2d 1307 (1985)]

---

[11]Northland Ins. Co. v Crites, (Ind) 419 NE2d 164 (1981).

§ 39:7.　Premiums.

Premiums may be paid by check. If the check is not paid, however, the instrument loses its character as payment.

If the premiums are not paid, the policy will ordinarily lapse because of nonpayment, subject to antilapse statutes or provisions.

(a) **Return of Unearned Premiums.** When an insurance policy is canceled before the expiration of the term for which premiums have been paid, the insurer is required to return any unearned premiums.

(b) **Nonforfeiture and Antilapse Provisions.** As to the payment of premiums due on life insurance policies subsequent to the first premium, the policies now in general use provide or a statute may specify that the policy shall not automatically lapse upon the date the next premium is due if payment is not then made. By policy provision or statute, the insured is also allowed a *grace period* of 30 to 31 days, in which to make payment of the premium due. When there is a default in the payment of a premium by the insured, the insurer may be required by statute (1) to issue a paid-up policy in a smaller amount, (2) to provide extended insurance for a period of time, or (3) to pay the cash surrender value of the policy.

§ 39:8.　Extent of Insurer's Liability.

In the case of life and disability insurance, the insurer is required to pay the amount called for by the contract of insurance. When the policy is one to indemnify against loss, the liability of the insurer is to pay only to the extent that the insured sustains loss, subject to a maximum amount stated in the contract. Thus, a fire insurer is liable for only $1,000, even though it has written a $20,000 policy, when the fire loss sustained by the insured is in fact only $1,000. If the loss were $22,000, the liability of the insurer would be limited by the face amount of the policy to only $20,000.

§ 39:9.　Cancellation.

The contract of insurance may expressly declare that it may or may not be canceled by the insurer's unilateral act. By statute or policy provision, the insurer is commonly required to give a specific number of days' written notice of a cancellation.

Property and liability policies generally reserve to the insurer the right to cancel the policy upon giving a specified number of days' notice. In some states antidiscrimination statutes restrict the right of insurers to cancel. An insurance company may not exercise its right to cancel the policy when it does so to punish the insured for having appeared as a witness in a case against it.

Only the insured is entitled to notice of cancellation unless the policy or an indorsement expressly declares otherwise. The mere fact that a creditor is entitled to the proceeds of the insurance policy in the case of loss does not in itself entitle the creditor to notice of a cancellation of the policy.

§ 39:10.　Coverage of Policy.

When an insurance claim is disputed by the insurer, the person bringing suit has the burden of proving that there was a loss, that it occurred while the policy was in force, and that the loss was a kind which was within the coverage or scope of the policy.

A policy will contain *exceptions* to the coverage. This means that the policy is not applicable when an exception applies to the situation. Exceptions to coverage are generally strictly interpreted against the insurer. The insurer has the burden of proving that the facts were such that there was no coverage because an exception applied.[12] There is also a modern trend that holds that although an exception is literally applicable to the situation it will be ignored and coverage sustained when there is no cause and effect relationship between the loss and the conduct that was the violation of the exception.

FACTS:

Collins owned a Piper Colt airplane. He obtained a liability policy covering the plane from the South Carolina Insurance Company. The policy provided that it did not cover loss sustained while the plane was being piloted by a person who did not have a valid pilot's certificate and a valid medical examination certificate. Collins held a valid pilot's certificate but his medical examination certificate had expired three months before. Collins was piloting the plane when it crashed and he was killed. The insurer denied liability because Collins did not have a valid medical certificate. It was stipulated by both parties that the crash was in no way caused by the absence of the medical certificate.

DECISION:

Judgment for the estate of Collins. In order to defeat recovery under policies excluding or limiting where death or injury results from failure on the part of the insured to comply with a condition of the policy, there must be shown, in addition to the violation of the condition, some causative connection between such act and the death or injury. [South Carolina Insurance Company v Collins, 237 SE2d 358 (1977)]

---

§ 39:11.   Defenses of the Insurer.

The insurer may raise any defense that would be valid in an action upon a contract. Some defenses that do not apply to an action on an ordinary contract may also be raised.

In a given case, the insurer may be barred from raising a particular defense because it has waived that defense or is estopped from asserting it.[13]

§ 39:12.   Insurer Bad Faith.

Where it is the insurer's duty to defend the insured and the insurer wrongfully refuses to do so, the insurer is guilty of breach of contract and is liable for all consequential damages resulting from the breach. An insured can recover for an excess judgment rendered against the insured where it is proven that the insurer was guilty of negligence or bad faith in failing to defend the action or settle the matter within policy limits.[14]

[12]Rutgena Distributora, Inc. v United States Fidelity and Guaranty Co., 94 Ill App 3d 753, 419 NE2d 59 (1981).
[13]Johnson v Phenix Mutual Fire Ins. Co. (NH) 445 A2d 1097 (1982).
[14]Hodges v State Farm (DC SC) 488 F Supp 1057 (1980).

In some states laws have been enacted making an insurer liable for a statutory penalty and attorneys' fees in case of a failure or delay, in bad faith, to pay a valid claim within a specified period of time. A "bad faith" refusal is generally considered to be any frivolous or unfounded refusal to comply with the demand of a policyholder to pay according to the policy. Penalties are improper where the insurer has any reasonable ground to contest the claim or where there is a bona fide question of fact.[15]

§ 39:13. Time Limitations on Insured.

The insured is subject to a number of time limitations in making a claim against the insurer. If the insured does not satisfy all time limitations, the insurer is not liable.

(a) **Notification of Claim.** The insured is generally required to give the insurer prompt or immediate notice of any claim that arises under the policy. Notice that is given within a reasonable time is ordinarily sufficient, even though the policy requires "immediate" notice or notice "as soon as practicable."[16]

(b) **Proof of Loss.** Within a stated number of days after an occurrence within the coverage of the policy, the insured must file a formal written statement of the claim that is made against the insurer. This written claim is called a *proof of loss.*

(c) **Contract Limitation on Time for Suit.** The policy or contract of insurance will ordinarily state that suit must be brought on the policy within a specified period of time.[17]

(d) **Statute of Limitations.** Without regard to any time limitation in the contract between the parties, the general statute of limitations applicable to contract actions will set a time limit after the expiration of which no suit may be brought on the policy.[18]

Typically the period allowed by the statute of limitations is longer than the period specified in the contract or policy of insurance.

§ 39:14. Subrogation of Insurer.

In some instances, the insured has a claim against a third person for the harm covered by the insurance policy. For example, the insured who has an automobile collision insurance policy who is in a collision may have a claim against the other driver. If the insurer pays the insured the full amount of the insured's claim, the insurer is then subrogated to the insured's claim against the third person who caused the harm. This means that the insurer acquires the claim of the insured against the third person just as though the insured had assigned the claim to the insurer. When the insurer is subrogated to the insured's claim, the insurer may enforce that claim against the third person.[19] The insurer is entitled to keep from the money recovered from the third person an amount equal to the payment made by the insurer to the insured, together with interest and costs.

[15]Fortson v Cotton States Mutual Insurance Co. (Ga App) 308 SE2d 382 (1983).
[16]Allstate Ins. Co. v Moon, 89 App Div 2d 804, 453 NYS2d 467 (1982).
[17]Herring v Middle George Mutual Ins. Co. 149 Ga App 585, 254 SE2d 904 (1979).
[18]Hearn v Rickenbacker (Mich App) 364 NW2d 371 (1985).
[19]Bowen v Waters, 170 Ga App 65, 316 SE2d 497 (1984).

SUMMARY

Insurance is a contract, called a policy, by which a provision is made by the insurer, in consideration of premium payments made by the insured, to pay the insured or beneficiary a sum of money if the insured sustains a specified loss. These contracts are made through an insurance agent, who is an agent for the insurance company, or through an insurance broker, who is the agent of the insured when obtaining a policy for the insured.

The person purchasing an insurance contract must have an insurable interest in the subject matter insured, be it life or property. An insurable interest in property exists when the damage or destruction of the property will cause a direct monetary loss to the insurer. An insurable interest in the life of the insured exists, if the purchaser would suffer a financial loss from the insured's death, as of the time the policy is obtained.

The insurer may agree to protect the applicant during the interval while the insurance application is being processed through an oral binder (a temporary contract, which terminates when the written policy contemplated is issued).

Changes to an insurance policy may be made by executing a rider or adding an indorsement to the policy.

If premiums are not paid, the policy will ordinarily lapse, subject to anti-lapse statutes which may provide for a thirty day grace period in which to make the payment or, in the case of some forms of life insurance, the insurer may be required by statute (1) to issue a paid-up policy in a smaller amount, (2) to provide extended insurance for a period of time, or (3) to pay the cash surrender value of the policy.

The insurer may expressly reserve the right to cancel a policy upon giving a specified number of days written notice.

Insurance policies commonly contain exceptions to coverage, which exceptions are generally strictly construed against the insurer.

The insured must comply with a number of "time limitations" in making a claim; such as, promptly notifying the insurer of any claim that may arise, submitting a proof of loss statement within the time set forth in the policy, and bringing any court actions based on the policy within a specified time period.

Where the insurer pays a claim under a policy, the insurer is then subrogated to the insured's claim against the third party and may enforce the insured's claim against the third party.

QUESTIONS AND CASE PROBLEMS

1. What social forces are affected by imposing the requirement of insurable interest?
2. Viola told Litchfield to obtain a policy of insurance on Viola's house. Litchfield was in the business of obtaining policies of insurance for members of the general public. He obtained a policy of insurance for Viola from the Century Indemnity Company. She paid Litchfield the money due for the premium on the policy but he never sent the money to Century which then canceled Viola's policy. She claimed that it could not do this because she had paid Litchfield. Was she correct?
3. How may a contract of insurance be modified?

4. Helen owned and operated the Center City Slacks Shop. She obtained a policy of fire insurance from the Phoenix Insurance Company on the inventory in her store. The policy was renewed year after year. Several years later, there was a fire in which the inventory in Helen's store was destroyed. Phoenix refused to pay on the policy on the ground that all the dresses which were in the inventory at the time when the insurance was obtained had been sold and that at the time of the fire all the dresses in the inventory were new and therefore not covered by the policy. Was Phoenix correct?

5. Schellinger obtained a policy of insurance on his life from the Simpson Insurance Company. In order to obtain the policy he made false statements as to his prior medical history. The company learned of this and brought a suit a few months later to cancel the policy for fraud. Schellinger claimed that the policy once issued could not be set aside even if he was guilty of fraud because the policy exceptions did not include fraud as one of the situations in which the insurer would not be liable. Was he correct?

6. Compare (a) a contract of insurance, and (b) an ordinary contract.

7. What time limits may bar an insured from recovering on the policy questioned?

8. Lucinda purchased an automobile. She did not have a driver's license. She insured the car against collision. The insurance policy declared that it was void if loss was sustained while the car was being operated in violation of law. Lucinda was driving the car out of a public garage when the overhead door fell and struck and damaged her car. No one could explain why the door fell. Lucinda had her car repaired and then claimed that the insurance company should pay the repair bill. It refused to do so on the ground that the policy was void because Lucinda had been operating the car in violation of the law requiring an operator's license. Was this defense valid?

9. Lisle applied for life insurance with the Federal Life & Casualty Co. Both Lisle and his wife made false, fraudulent statements to the insurer in connection with the application. The insurer's physician examined Lisle twice but did not ascertain anything that revealed the falsity of those statements. After the insured's death about a year later, the insurer denied liability on the ground of fraud. Lisle's widow claimed that the insurer could not raise the question of fraud since it had examined the insured before accepting his application. Was the insurer liable? [Federal Life & Casualty Co. v Lisle, 140 Ohio 2d 269, 172 NE2d 919]

10. James Butler purchased a stolen automobile without knowing that it had been stolen. He insured it with Farmers Insurance Company. The policy covered loss by accidental means. The automobile was seized by the local police and returned to its true owner. Butler then sued on his insurance policy, claiming that there had been a loss by accidental means. The insurer raised the defense that Butler did not have an insurable interest in the automobile because it was a stolen car. Was this defense valid? [Butler v Farmers Insurance Co. 126 Ariz 377, 616 P2d 46]

11. On October 29, Griffin sent an application for life insurance and the first premium to the Insurance Company of North America. In the appli-

cation, her son, Carlisle Moore, was named as beneficiary. On November 25 of the same year, Griffin died. On November 26, the company rejected the application and notified the broker who took the application, who in turn notified Moore by letter dated November 30. Moore sued the company for breach of contract. Decide. [Moore v Insurance Co. of North America, 49 Ill App 2d 287, 200 NE2d 1]

12. Rebecca Foster obtained a policy of life insurance from the United Insurance Co. insuring the life of Lucille McClurkin and naming herself as beneficiary. Lucille did not live with Rebecca, and Rebecca did not inform Lucille of the existence of the policy. Rebecca paid the premiums on the policy, and on the death of Lucille sued the United Insurance Co. for the amount of the insurance. At the trial, Rebecca testified vaguely that her father had told her that Lucille was her second cousin on his side of the family. Was Rebecca entitled to recover on the policy? [Foster v United Insurance Co. 250 SC 423, 158 SE2d 201]

13. Moore's wife applied for accident insurance on her husband. She paid the premium due. Unknown to her, the application was rejected. However, when she inquired of the agent as to the status of the application, the agent said that he had had no word. When she inquired some time later, the agent said he thought that the policy had come in and, if it had not, she would be notified in a few days. She heard nothing. Two weeks later her husband was killed accidentally. After his death the insurance company informed her that the application had been rejected. She sued the insurance company. Decide. [Moore v Palmetto State Life Insurance Co. 222 SC 492, 73 SE2d 688]

14. A policy of insurance had the words "double indemnity" across the top imprinted with a rubber stamp. Nothing was said in the policy about double indemnity. When loss was sustained, the beneficiary claimed that he was entitled to double indemnity. Was he correct?

15. Elvira's only possession was her home. It was insured against fire with the Ajax Indemnity Company. Because of Elvira's advanced age, her neighbor, Helen, did most of her household chores. Elvira transferred the title to her home to Helen in appreciation of her work and in consideration of one dollar paid by Helen. Elvira continued to live in the house. Some time thereafter, the house was damaged by fire. Elvira demanded payment of the fire loss from the Ajax Indemnity Company. It denied liability on the theory that as Helen was the owner, Elvira did not have an insurable interest in the house. Was Ajax correct?

16. Mike Edwards insured his car against theft with the State Farm Mutual Automobile Insurance Company. He later sold the car to Steven Davis who paid for the car with a bad check that the bank refused to pay because of "insufficient funds." Neither Steven nor the car were ever seen again. Mike claimed that his insurance company was liable for the loss on the ground that the policy covered "theft" and there had been a theft of his car. The insurance company answered that Edwards had been defrauded by the use of the bad check but that this was not a "theft" of the car. [Edwards v State Farm Automobile Ins. Co. (Iowa), 296 NW2d 804]

17. Assistant manager trainee R. G. Smith suspected Ms. Bowen of shoplift-
    ing at Broad & Marshall Department Store, and after getting permission
    from the store manager to follow her, he observed Ms. Bowen driving
    out of the store's parking lot. Smith followed her in his car and forced
    her into a ditch, where her car overturned and was destroyed. Ms. Bowen
    received the fair market value for her car from her insurance company,
    General National Mutual (GNM), and executed a subrogation agree-
    ment in connection with this payment. Ms. Bowen is planning on bring-
    ing suit against Smith and the store for actual and punitive damages for
    the injury and indignity suffered. GNM brought suit against Smith and
    the store for damage to the car. They defend that GNM is not the proper
    party plaintiff. Decide.

CHAPTER 40

KINDS OF INSURANCE

CHAPTER OBJECTIVES

After studying this chapter you will be able to:

1. Determine the liability of an insurer given the nature of the policy, the coverage, and the loss.
2. Define extended coverage and vandalism coverage.
3. Compare the insurance coverage under provisions for automobile liability, uninsured motorist, and no fault coverage.
4. List and define the different kinds of life insurance.
5. Explain the effect of an incontestable clause.
6. List the ways in which an insured can convert a life insurance policy into money.
7. Solve problems relating to fire, automobile, and life insurance.

Both businesses and individuals are exposed to the risk of loss of property due to damage, destruction, or theft as well as the risk of economic losses due to legal liability for individual actions and the actions of employees. Employers and employees seek protection against the risk of economic losses due to employees' sicknesses or accidents, and employers seek protection against the risks involved in the unforeseeable events which may cause the interruption of their businesses. Individuals seek to protect their families' financial security in the case of their own untimely deaths, while businesses seek to protect against economic harm to their businesses by the death of key employees. The insurance industry offers a wide range of insurance plans to provide protection suited to the wide range of needs faced by businesses and individuals.

Businesses today have specialized risk managers who identify the risks to which individual businesses are exposed, measure those risks, and purchase insurance to cover those risks (or decide to self-insure in whole or in part). Individuals have a wide range of insurance options, including multi-peril homeowners' policies.

Insurance policies tend to group themselves into a few categories in terms of the nature of the interest protected. Fire, automobile, and life insurance will be considered in this chapter.

A. FIRE INSURANCE

A **fire insurance policy** is a contract to indemnify the insured for destruction of or damage to property caused by fire. In almost every state the New York standard fire insurance form is the standard policy.

§ 40:1.   Nature of Contract.

In order for fire loss to be covered by fire insurance, there must be an actual, hostile fire and that fire must be the immediate or proximate cause of the loss.

(a) **Actual, Hostile Fire.** The hostile character is easily determined when the fire is caused by accident, such as a short circuit in electric wiring; but it is often difficult to determine if the fire is intentional, as when it is being used for heating or cooking. A **hostile fire** in the latter case is one which to some extent becomes uncontrollable, burns with excessive heat, or escapes from the place where it is intended to be.[1] To illustrate, when soot is ignited and causes a fire in the chimney, the fire is hostile. On the other hand, a loss caused by the smoke or heat of a fire in its ordinary container, which has not broken out or become uncontrollable, results from a **friendly fire**, and is not covered by the policy.

FACTS:
Youse owned a ring that was insured with the Employers Fire Insurance Co. against loss, including "all direct loss or damage by fire." The ring was accidentally thrown by Youse into a trash burner and was damaged when the trash was burned. He sued the insurer.

DECISION:
Judgment for insurer. A fire policy only covers loss caused by a hostile fire. The fire was not hostile in that it burned in the area in which it was intended to burn. [Youse v Employers Fire Insurance Co. 172 Kan 111, 238 P2d 472 (1951)]

By endorsement, the coverage may be and frequently is extended to include loss by a friendly fire.

Damage by heat alone is not covered, but damage from heat or smoke caused by a hostile fire is covered.

[1]Schulze and Burch Biscuit Co. v American Protection Ins. Co. 96 Ill App 3d 350, 421 NE2d 331 (1981).

(b) Immediate or Proximate Cause. In addition to direct destruction or damage by fire, a fire may set in motion a chain of events that damages property. When there is a reasonable connection between a fire and the ultimate loss sustained, the insurer is liable for the loss.

The New York standard form of fire insurance policy excludes loss or damage caused directly or indirectly by enemy attack by armed forces, invasion, insurrection, rebellion, revolution, civil war, or usurped power, or by order of any civil authority; or by neglect of the insured to use all reasonable means to save and preserve the property at and after a fire or when the property is endangered by fire in neighboring premises; or by theft.

§ 40:2.   Determination of Insurer's Liability.

Basically the insurer is liable for the actual amount of the loss sustained. This liability is limited, however, by the maximum amount stated in the policy or the amount of damages sustained by total destruction of the property, whichever is less.

(a) Amount of Loss. The amount of a total loss, in the absence of statute or agreement to the contrary, is the actual cash value of the property at the time of the loss. If the insurer and the insured cannot agree, policies commonly provide for the determination of the amount of loss by appraisers or arbitrators.

(b) Total Loss. A **total loss** does not necessarily mean that the property has been completely destroyed. The loss is regarded as being total if the unconsumed portion is of no value for the purposes for which the property was utilized at the time of the insurance. Consequently, the mere fact that some of the walls and the roof remained after the fire did not prove that the loss was not total.

(c) Replacement by Insurer. Frequently the insurer will stipulate in the policy that it has the right to replace or restore the property to its former condition in lieu of paying the insured the cash value of the loss.[2]

(d) Coinsurance. A **coinsurance clause** requires the insured to maintain insurance on the covered property up to a certain amount or a certain percent of the value, generally 80%. Under such a provision, if the policyholder insures the property for less than the required amount, the insurer is liable only for the proportionate share of the amount of insurance required to be carried. To illustrate, suppose the owner of a building with a value of $200,000 insures it against loss to the extent of $120,000, and the policy contains a coinsurance clause requiring that insurance of 80% of the value of the property be carried. Assume that a $80,000 loss is then sustained. The insured would not receive $80,000 from the insurer but only three-fourths of that amount, which is $60,000, because the amount of the insurance carried ($120,000) is only three-fourths of the amount required ($160,000, that is, 80% of $200,000).

The use of a coinsurance clause is not permitted in all states. In some states, it is prohibited or is permitted only with the consent of the insured.

[2]Allstate Ins. Co. v Kleveno, 81 App Div 2d 648. 438 NYS2d 384 (1981).

§ 40:3.　Assignment of Fire Insurance Policy.

Fire insurance is a personal contract, and in the absence of statute or contractual authorization it cannot be assigned before a loss is sustained without the consent of the insurer. In addition, it is commonly provided that the policy shall be void if an assignment to give a purchaser of the property the protection of the policy is attempted. Such a forefeiture clause applies only when the insured attempts to transfer total ownership of the policy. It does not apply to an assignment as security for a loan to the insured.

§ 40:4.　Mortgage Clause.

If the insured property is subject to a mortgage, either or both the mortgagor and mortgagee may take out policies of fire insurance to protect their respective interests in the property. Each has an insurable interest therein. In the absence of a contrary stipulation, the policy taken out by either covers only that insured's own interest. That is, the mortgagor's policy protects only the value of the mortgagor's right to redemption or the value of the property in excess of the mortgage, while the policy of the mortgagee covers only the debt. Neither can claim the benefit of insurance money paid to the other.

It is common, however, for the mortgagee to insist as a condition of making the loan that the mortgagor obtain and pay the premiums on a policy covering the full value of the property and providing that in case of loss the insurance money shall be paid to the mortgagor and the mortgagee as their respective interests may appear. As the amount of the mortgage debt is reduced, the interest of the mortgagee in the property becomes less and the share of insurance proceeds that the mortgagee would receive accordingly becomes less. Such a mortgage clause has the advantage of protecting both the mortgagor and mortgagee by one policy and of providing a flexible method of insuring each of them.[3]

§ 40:5.　Extended Coverage.

The term **extended coverage** generally refers to protection of property against loss from windstorm, hail, riot, civil commotion, aircraft damage, vehicle damage, smoke damage, and most explosions. A "homeowner's policy" commonly protects against these perils and other perils which may occur due to home ownership, including protection in the case of personal injury to others on the homeowner's property. Personal property floaters may also be added to this policy, to protect against the loss or theft of items of special value such as jewelry, paintings, and fur coats.

A special form of extended coverage may be obtained to protect property from vandalism. **Vandalism** is the intentional senseless or malicious destruction or damaging of property.

[3]495 Corp. v New Jersey Insurance Underwriting Association, 86 NJ 159, 430 A2d 203 (1981).

FACTS:

Stack had a policy of insurance with the Hanover Insurance Company against vandalism. A large deer crashed through a glass door of his house, damaged the interior, and then left by crashing through a window. Stack claimed that the insurance company was liable for this damage.

DECISION:

Judgment for the insurance company. The damage by the animal was not vandalism because the animal acted instinctively and lacked the capacity for malicious intent essential to vandalism. [Stack v Hanover Ins. Co. (Ala Civ App), 329 So2d 561 (1976)]

If vandals burn a building, fire insurance would provide coverage. Likewise, if the harm occurred as part of a riot, the standard extended coverage would afford protection.

§ 40:6.   Other Provisions.

Fire insurance policies commonly prohibit the insured from doing certain acts that may increase the risk involved and provide that the policy is void if the insured commits the prohibited acts.

It is commonly provided that false statements made by the insured when they are known to be false shall avoid the policy.[4] Under such a provision a fraudulent misstatement of the value of the property avoids the policy.

The insured may take out more than one policy on the same property, in the absence of a provision in any of the policies to the contrary; but in the event of loss, recovery cannot be greater than the total loss sustained. Such a loss is prorated among the insurers.

An insurer is not liable when the damage or destruction of the property was intentionally caused by the insured.[5] The fact that the insured negligently caused a fire is not a defense to the insurer, even when there is a stipulation that the insured shall not change or increase the hazard insured against.

Provisions in a policy of fire insurance relating to the use and occupancy of the property are generally strictly construed because they relate to the hazards involved.

FACTS:

Miller owned a house. He insured it against fire with Lloyd's of London. In the policy, the house was described as "owner occupied." In fact it was not occupied by Miller but by various tenants to whom Miller successively rented the house. The policy also stated that if the house became vacant or was unoccupied for more than 60 days the insurer would be notified. Miller's tenant moved away and the house remained vacant. Miller began making repairs to the empty house from time to time, but the house remained unoccupied for more than 60 days. A fire occurred. Miller claimed that

[4]Morgan v Cincinnati Ins. Co. 411 Mich 267, 307 NW2d 53 (1981).
[5]Neises v Solomon State Bank, 236 Kan 767, 696 P2d 372 (1985).

Lloyd's was liable for the loss. It denied liability because of the falsity of the statement of being "owner occupied" and because there had been a vacancy in excess of 60 days. Miller sued Lloyd's.

DECISION:

Judgment for Lloyd's. Exceptions in a fire policy are strictly construed. The house was not "owner occupied" as stated merely because the owner was from time to time in the build-ing making repairs. To the contrary, the house was vacant and unoccupied. The fact that the building was not occupied by its owner was significant because the owner would be careful to protect the building. Futhermore, the fact that the building was not occupied by anyone increased the risk to the building because unauthorized persons might enter and start fires and, in any case, no one would be on the premises to see and report the beginning of a fire. [Miller v Underwriters at Lloyd's, London (La App) 398 So2d 654 (1981)]

§ 40:7. Cancellation.

It is common to provide by statute or by the terms of the policy that under certain circumstances the policy may be terminated or canceled by the act of one party alone. When this is done, the provisions of the statute and the policy must be strictly followed in order to make the cancellation effective.

B. AUTOMOBILE INSURANCE

Associations of insurers, such as the National Bureau of Casualty Underwriters and the National Automobile Underwriters Association, have proposed standard forms of automobile insurance policies that have been approved by their members in virtually all the states.

§ 40:8. Nature of Contract.

In the case of insurance to compensate the insured driver or car owner for damages to the insured's own car (**collision insurance**) it is immaterial whether the insured's negligence caused or contributed to the harm sustained. In the case of insurance that protects the insured driver or owner from claims of others (**liability insurance**), no liability of the insurer for a claim arises unless the insured was negligent in the operation of the automobile. To some extent this has been altered by no fault insurance as discussed in §40:13.

§ 40:9. Financial Responsibility Laws.

In a few states and under some no fault insurance statutes, liability insurance must be obtained before a driver's license will be issued. In most states **financial responsibility** laws require that if a driver is involved in an accident, proof of financial responsibility must be furnished. Under some laws this means that the driver must deposit security sufficient to pay any judgment that may be entered with respect to that accident. Under other statutes, it is sufficient that the driver produce a liability policy in a specified amount as to future accidents.

The security form of statute may not protect the victim of the first accident. If the driver is unwilling or unable to deposit the required security, the driver's license is forfeited; but this does not provide any payment to the victim of the first accident. By definition, the second type of law does not protect the victim of the first accident. Moreover, the efficiency of financial responsibility laws has been reduced by the decision that the United States Constitution requires that there be a hearing to establish the probable liability of a driver to the victim before the driver's license can be suspended or revoked.[6] The requirement of such a hearing has the effect of delaying and making cumbersome what was formerly a relatively simple and swift administrative remedy.

§ 40:10.   Liability Insurance.

The owner or operator of a motor vehicle may obtain **liability insurance** for protection from claims made by third persons for damage to their property (property damage liability) or person (bodily injury liability) arising from the use or operation of an automobile. When the insurer pays under such a policy, it is liable to pay for the same items as the insured would be required to pay, but for not more than the maximum amount stated in the policy.

If the insurer is liable for the damage caused a third person or such person's property, it is likewise liable for cost of repairs, loss by destruction of the property, loss of services, and other damages for which the insured would be liable, subject to the policy maximum.

(a) **Ownership of Automobile.** Basically, liability insurance protects the insured with respect to an "owned" automobile. Whether a given automobile is owned by the insured is determined by Article 2 of the Uniform Commercial Code, and it is immaterial whether the steps required by a motor vehicle statute have been taken to transfer the title.

(b) **Use and Operation.** The terms "use" and "operation" as found in a liability policy are liberally interpreted to include events in which there is some involvement of the automobile even though not for the purpose of transportation. For example, the insured "uses" the automobile when packages are being loaded into it.

FACTS:

Evelyn Watkins obtained insurance to protect her from liability arising out of the "ownership, maintenance and use" of her automobile. Her friend, Charlie McNeill, could not start his car. He phoned Evelyn who had Edward Hill take her car to the place where McNeill was stalled. The battery of the Watkins car was then connected to the battery of the McNeill car in order to give the battery a quick charge. McNeill took some of the caps off of his battery. Hill was standing nearby and lit a match. This caused the battery of the McNeill car to explode. McNeill was seriously injured by the explosion. He claimed that he was entitled to recover damages on the Watkins policy. The insurer denied liability on the ground that McNeill had not been injured as the result of

[6]Bell v Burson, 402 US 535 (1971).

the "ownership, maintenance or use" of the Watkins car.

DECISION:

The policy covered the loss because there was a "use" within the meaning of the policy. "Ownership, maintenance and use" clauses do not limit recovery solely to injuries that are caused by direct physical contact with the insured vehicle; nor is it necessary that the damages be directly sustained or inflicted by the operation of the motor vehicle. The use of the Watkins vehicle was clearly a use which was or should have been contemplated and anticipated by the insurance carrier and the owner of the vehicle. It is not unusual that an insured might on occasion use his vehicle to charge the battery of another vehicle. At the time the explosion took place, the Watkins vehicle was still being used in an activity permitted by her policy. The loss that occurred while the automobile was still used was therefore covered by the policy. [McNeill v Maryland Insurance Guaranty Association, 48 Md App 411, 427 A2d 1056 (1981)]

(c) Person Operating. Liability policies ordinarily protect the owner of the auto from liability when it is operated by another person with the permission of the insured, as in the case of an employee or agent of the owner.

Liability insurance may also protect an insured individual or the insured's spouse against liability incurred while operating another person's automobile. This is referred to as **D.O.C.** (drive-other-car) **coverage,** or **temporary replacement coverage.**

(1) Members of Household of Insured. Automobile liability policies variously extend coverage to members of the insured's household or residence. Such terms are generally liberally construed to reach the conclusion that a given relative is a member of the insured's "household" or "residence."

(2) Other Driver. The automobile liability policy protects the insured when driving. If someone else is driving with the insured's permission, the policy protects both the original insured and such other driver.[7] This **omnibus or other driver clause** is generally liberally interpreted so that permission is often found in acquiescence in the other driver's use or in the insured's failing to object or to prevent such use. In the absence of an express prohibition by the insured against the permittee's lending the car to another, a permission by A given to B to use the car generally includes an implied permission to B to permit C to drive, in which case the liability of the insurer is the same as though A or B were driving.[8]

The buyer of an automobile does not come within the scope of an omnibus clause because the buyer's operation of the automobile is not based upon the permission of the seller but upon the buyer's ownership of the automobile. To avoid litigation, policies commonly expressly exclude buyers from the scope of the omnibus clause.

---

[7]DeWitt v Young, 229 Kan 474, 625 P2d 478 (1981).
[8]Some courts interpret the omnibus clause more strictly and refuse to recognize a second permittee when the original insured did not expressly authorize such relending or where the use made by the second permittee was not the same use which the insured contemplated would be made by the first permittee.

(d) **Exclusions.** A liability policy does not cover every harm sustained. Such policies may exclude claims of employees of the owner or claims under the workers' compensation laws, liability for harm intentionally caused by the insured,[9] or liability for claims when the insured admits to the injured third person that the insured is liable and agrees to pay the claim.

In the case of commercial vehicles the insurer may stipulate that it shall only be bound by the policy "provided: (a) the regular and frequent use of the automobile is confined to the area within a fifty mile radius of the limits of the city or town where the automobile is principally garaged..., (b) no regular or frequent trips are made by the automobile to any locations beyond such radius."

(e) **Cancellation.** Automobile liability policies generally contain a provision authorizing the insurer to cancel the policy before a loss is sustained upon giving the insured a stated number of days' notice.[10]

(f) **Notice and Cooperation.** A liability policy generally provides that the insurer is not liable unless the insured (1) gives the insurer prompt notice of any serious accident or claim or lawsuit brought against the insured, (2) furnishes the insurance company with all details of the occurrence, and (3) cooperates with the insurer in the preparation of the defense against a lawsuit brought on the policy and participates at the trial. Notice and cooperation under such a policy are conditions precedent to the liability of the insurer.

These requirements are subject to modification in terms of "reasonableness." Thus, the insured is not required to report a trivial accident when there was no reason to believe that the injured person was going to proceed further with the matter. The notice to the insurer need only be given within a reasonable time after the occurrence, and "reasonable" is determined in the light of all the surrounding circumstances.

(g) **Duty to Defend.** A liability insurer has the duty to defend any suit brought against its insured on a claim which, if valid, would come within the policy coverage. The liability insurer cannot refuse to defend the insured on the ground that it does not believe the claim of the third person. Consequently, when the third person's complaint against the insured states a claim within the coverage of the policy, a liability insurer cannot refuse to defend on the ground that its investigation shows that the claim is without merit.

If the insurer wrongly refuses to defend and the third person recovers a judgment against the insured even though it exceeds the policy maximum, the insurer is liable to the insured for the full amount of the judgment. Under statutes in some states, the insurer may also be required to pay the insured the litigation costs and attorney's fees when the insurer refuses in bad faith to settle or defend the action.

§ 40:11. Collision and Upset Insurance.

Liability insurance does not indemnify the owner for damage to the insured's own property. In order to obtain this protection for an auto,

---

[9]Globe American Cas. Co. v Lyons, 131 Ariz App 337, 641 P2d 251 (1982).
[10]Harris v Criterion Ins. Co. 222 Va 496, 281 SE2d 878 (1981).

its owner must obtain property insurance to cover damage from collision and upset.

The term "collision" is generally liberally interpreted so that there is insurance coverage whenever there is an unintended striking of another object even though the object is not an automobile or is not moving. For example, there is a collision when a wheel comes off of the automobile and the automobile falls to the ground.

The phrase "struck by automobile" is likewise liberally interpreted so that there is coverage when the insured ran a motor scooter into an automobile, as against the contention that "struck by automobile" required that the automobile run into the insured.

FACTS:
Vallot was driving his farm tractor on the highway. It was struck from the rear by a truck, overturned, exploded, and burned. Vallot was killed and a death claim was made against All American Insurance Company. The death of Vallot was covered by the company's policy if Vallot had died from "being struck or run over by" the truck. The insurance company claimed that the policy was not applicable because Vallot had not been struck, in that the farm tractor had been struck and Vallot's death occurred when the overturned tractor exploded and burned. The insurance company also claimed that it was necessary that the insured be both struck and run over by another vehicle.

DECISION:
Judgment against the insurance company. Vallot was struck by the truck even though the actual contact was with the tractor in which he was riding. The policy did not limit coverage to being a pedestrian. Furthermore, "struck" and "run over" were stated as alternatives and not as synonymous terms. Therefore it was sufficient to establish death caused either by being struck or by being run over and both were not required. [Vallot v All American Insurance Co. (La App) 302 So2d 625 (1974)]

(a) **Exclusions.** The insurer against collision is not required to pay in every case. It is commonly provided that the insurer is not liable when the automobile is used by a person who is violating the law. It may also be stipulated that liability is avoided if the auto is subject to a lien or encumbrance that has not been disclosed. It is common to exclude damages, resulting from collision, for the loss of the use of the auto, for depreciation, or for loss of personal property in the auto.

(b) **Notice and Cooperation.** As in the case of public liability insurance, the auto owner is under a duty to give notice, to inform, and to cooperate with the insurer. The owner must also give the insurer an opportunity to examine the automobile to determine the extent of damage before making repairs.

§ 40:12. Uninsured Motorist.

Statutes and liability policies commonly provide for special coverage when the insured sustains loss because of an uninsured motorist.[11] Since the **uninsured motorist coverage** is a liability coverage, there is no liability of the insurer in the absence of establishing that the uninsured motorist was negligent and would be held liable if sued by the insured. Consequently, collision and accident insurance provide greater protection in that under such coverage the insurer is bound by its contract without regard to whether anyone could be held liable to the insured.

Uninsured motorist coverage generally includes the hit-and-run driver who leaves the scene of the collision before being identified. Policies commonly require that the collision be reported to the police or other appropriate authorities within 24 hours and that diligent effort be made to locate the hit-and-run driver. These restrictions are imposed in order to guard against the fraud of reporting the other car as "unknown" when its driver was in fact known, or against the fraud of having a one-car accident and then falsely claiming that the damage was the result of a collision with a hit-and-run driver.

This coverage differs from other insurance that the insured could obtain in that only personal injury claims are covered and generally only up to $10,000. Contact with the uninsured or unidentified vehicle is required, so that there is no uninsured motorist coverage when the insured runs off the road to avoid a collision and sustains injury thereby, or when the insured is injured upon striking oil or an object dropped from the uninsured vehicle.

§ 40:13. No Fault Insurance.

A state statute may require that every automobile liability policy provide for **no fault coverage.**

(a) **Harm to the Insured.** No fault coverage means that when the insured is injured while using the insured automobile, the insurer will make a payment without regard to whose fault caused the harm.[12] In effect, this is insurance for medical expense and loss of wages that runs in favor of the holder of the liability policy and is in addition to or in lieu of the coverage which the policy provides with respect to liability to other persons.

The no fault insurance statutes generally do not provide for payment for pain and suffering. Under some statutes recovery is allowed for pain and suffering if the medical expenses exceed $500 or if certain specified injuries have been sustained by the insured.

(b) **Other Party Injury.** If another person is harmed, such as a pedestrian or other driver, no fault insurance statutes generally provide for a similar kind of payment to such third person by that person's auto insurer or by the insurer of the car inflicting the injury.

(c) **Suit Against Party at Fault.** No fault insurance laws bar the claimant from suing the party at fault for ordinary claims. If the automobile

[11]Guess v Gulf Ins. Co. 96 N Mex 27, 627 P2d 869 (1981).
[12]Troutman v Tabb, 285 Pa Super 353, 427 A2d 673 (1981).

collision results in a permanent serious disablement or disfigurement, or death, or if the medical bills and lost wages of the plaintiff exceed a specified amount, suit may be brought against the party who was at fault. A person who is entitled to sue the at-fault party may collect the maximum amount of no fault insurance and then sue the at-fault party for the total damages, just as though no payment had been received from the insurer. However, if the injured party recovers the total amount from the at-fault party, the injured party must ordinarily repay the insurance company the amount which had been received from it under the no fault coverage.

(d) **Arbitration.** Disputes under no fault insurance are sometimes determined by arbitration. In addition, some states require the arbitration of small claims of any nature.

(e) **Constitutionality.** No fault insurance is generally held constitutional, as against the contention that it violates the guarantees of equal protection and due process. It has been sustained as a carefully studied plan to provide a new remedy to meet the problems caused by the automobile: rising cost of insurance, overloading of courts, and delay in making payment to the injured person.[13]

§ 40:14.   Theft Insurance.

The owner of an automobile can secure theft insurance which will protect from loss through theft and from a damage to the auto caused by a theft.

FACTS:

The Muttontown Golf & Country Club insured six electric golf carts against "larceny." Without the permission of the club, the carts were taken out of the shed in which they were stored overnight and apparently used to bump into one another. In the morning they were found scattered over the golf course in a badly damaged condition. At the time when the policy was obtained, "larceny" was defined so as to include the unauthorized joyriding use that had been made of the carts. After the policy became effective but before the loss was sustained, the larceny statute was amended so that unauthorized use was no longer "larceny" but was made simply a "misdemeanor." When the club made claim on the insurance policy, the insurer raised the defense that there had not been any "larceny."

DECISION:

Judgment for the Country Club. While the unauthorized use that had been made did not constitute larceny when the loss was sustained, it was "larceny" by virtue of the earlier statute at the time when the policy was obtained. "Considerations of equity and fair dealing" require the conclusion that the words in the insurance contract should be interpreted according to their meaning at the time when the contract was made, in the absence of an express provision that the contract should change as the statutory definitions might change. [Muttontown Golf & Country Club, Inc. v Firemen's Insurance Co. 320 NYS2d 369 (1971)]

---

[13]Pinnick v Cleary, 360 Mass 1, 271 NE2d 592 (1971).

An automobile theft policy does not ordinarily protect against loss of contents. It is common to exclude liability for equipment or personal property taken from the auto, but additional insurance protecting from such theft can be secured. It is common also to exclude liability for loss sustained while a passenger auto is used for commercial transportation or is rented to another.

§ 40:15.   Fire, Lightning, and Transportation Insurance.

In this type of insurance the insurer agrees to pay for any loss arising out of damage to or the destruction of a motor vehicle or its equipment caused by fire originating in any manner, by lightning, or by the stranding, sinking, burning, collision, or derailment of any conveyance in or upon which the automobile or the truck is being transported. This type of policy is commonly combined with a policy against theft and pilferage and is usually subject to the same exclusions.

§ 40:16.   Comprehensive Insurance.

In many automobile insurance policies, comprehensive material damage coverage, which protects the policyholder against virtually all such risks except collision or upset, replaces fire and theft insurance. The exclusions for this kind of insurance include wear and tear, freezing, mechanical breakdown, and loss of personal effects.

C. LIFE INSURANCE

A contract of **life insurance** requires the insurer to pay a stipulated sum of money upon the death of the insured. It is not a contract of indemnity since the insurer does not undertake to indemnify the beneficiary for the financial loss sustained as the result of the death of the insured.

§ 40:17.   Kinds of Life Insurance Policies.

Life insurance policies may be classified in terms of their duration and extent of coverage and of the pattern of payment of premiums.

(a) **Ordinary Life Insurance.** Ordinary life insurance may be subclassified as (1) **straight life insurance,** which requires payment of premiums throughout the life of the insured; (2) **limited payment insurance,** requiring the payment of premiums during a limited period, such as ten, twenty, or thirty years, or until the death of the insured if that should occur before the end of the specified period; (3) **endowment insurance,** under which the insurer undertakes to pay a stipulated sum when the insured reaches a specified age, or upon death if that occurs sooner; and (4) **term insurance,** under which the insurer undertakes to pay a stipulated sum only in the event of the death of the insured during a specified period, such as one, two, five, or ten years.

Somewhat similar to policies of endowment insurance are **annuity policies** and **retirement income insurance** under which the insured either pays a lump sum to the insurer and thereafter receives fixed annual payments, or pays periodic premiums to the insurer until a certain date and then receives fixed annual payments.

(b) **Group Insurance. Group life insurance** is insurance of the lives of employees of a particular employer or persons engaged in a particular business or profession. Such policies are usually either term policies or straight life insurance.

(c) **Double Indemnity.** Many life insurance companies undertake to pay double the amount of the policy, called **double indemnity,** if death is caused by an accident and occurs within ninety days after the accident.[14] A comparatively small, additional premium is charged for this special protection.

(d) **Disability Insurance.** In consideration of the payment of an additional premium, many life insurance companies also provide insurance against total permanent disability of the insured. **Disability** is usually defined in a life insurance policy as any "incapacity resulting from bodily injury or disease to engage in any occupation for remuneration or profit." The policy generally provides that a disability which has continued for a stated minimum period, such as four to six months, will be regarded as a **total permanent disability.**

(e) **Exclusions.** Life insurance policies frequently provide that death shall not be within the protection of the policy or that a double indemnity provision shall not be applicable when death is caused by (1) suicide, (2) narcotics, (3) the intentional act of another, (4) execution for a crime, (5) war activities, or (6) operation of aircraft.

FACTS:
Jerome Evans bought a life insurance policy from National Insurance Co. with a death benefit of $10,000. At the same time he bought an Additional Indemnity Agreement (Agreement) which provided an additional $10,000 in benefits if death resulted from "external, violent and accidental means." On February 23, 1979, Thomas Cox shot and killed Evans after an argument in a tavern. National paid the Evanses, the named beneficiaries, the face amount of the life insurance policy, $10,000, but refused to pay the additional $10,000. The Agreement provided benefits only for death resulting from "external, violent and accidental means" and expressly excluded death resulting from the intentional act of another. The Evanses sued National for the additional $10,000 in benefits.

DECISION:
Judgment for National. An insurance company is free to determine by its contract what risks it is undertaking to insure, provided the policy provisions do not violate statutes or public policy. Thus a plainly expressed "intentional act" exclusion in a life insurance policy is enforceable. Since the evidence clearly supported the conclusion that Cox intended to shoot Evans, the "intentional act" exclusion applies and the additional benefits are not recoverable by the Evanses. [Evans v National Life Accident Ins. Co. (Ind App) 467 NE2d 1216 (1984)]

---

§ 40:18.   The Beneficiary.

The person to whom the proceeds of a life insurance policy are payable upon the death of the insured is called the **beneficiary.** The bene-

[14]Valley National Bank v J.C. Penney Ins. Co. 129 Ariz App 108, 628 P2d 991 (1981).

ficiary may be a third person, or the estate of the insured. There may be more than one beneficiary.

The beneficiary named in the policy may be barred from claiming the proceeds of the policy. There may be a prior settlement agreement by which it was agreed that the beneficiary would not claim the insurance. Likewise, it is generally provided by statute or stated by court decision that a beneficiary who has feloniously killed the insured is not entitled to receive the proceeds of the policy.[15]

(a) **Primary and Contingent Beneficiaries.** It is desirable to name a primary and a contingent beneficiary. Thus, A may make insurance payable to B, but provide that if B dies before A, the insurance shall be payable to C. In such case, B is the **primary beneficiary,** and C is the **contingent beneficiary** because C takes the proceeds as beneficiary only upon the contingency that B dies before A.

(b) **Change of Beneficiary.** The customary policy provides that the insured reserves the right to change the beneficiary without the latter's consent. When the policy contains such a provision, the beneficiary cannot object to a change that destroys all of that beneficiary's rights under the policy and that names another person as beneficiary.

The insurance policy will ordinarily state that in order to change the beneficiary, the insurer must be so instructed in writing by the insured and the policy must then be endorsed by the company with the change of the beneficiary. These provisions are generally liberally construed. If the insured has notified the insurer but dies before the endorsement of the change by the company, the change of beneficiary is effective. If, however, the insured has not taken any steps to comply with the policy requirements, a change of beneficiary is not effective, even though a change was intended.

FACTS:

Lesley Puricelli was the estranged wife of the insured, Michael Puricelli. She was named as beneficiary in his life insurance policy. Two days before his death, he executed change of beneficiary forms naming his parents as the new beneficiaries. He gave these forms to his insurance agent. The agent neglected to send the forms to the insurer until two days after Michael's death. Lesley and the parents all claim the proceeds of the life insurance policy.

DECISION:

Judgment for parents. Michael intended to change the beneficiary and substantially complied with the policy requirement for such a change. All that remained to be done was the ministerial act of transmitting the change of beneficiary forms to the insurer. A court of equity regards that as done which ought to have been done. Since the forms had been executed and delivered to the agent with instructions to pass them on to the insurer, the insurer is obligated to pay the proceeds to the parents. [Woodman Accident and Life Co. v Puricelli (Mo App) 669 SW2d 64 (1984)]

[15]State Farm Life Ins. Co. v Smith, 66 Ill 2d 591, 363 NE2d 785 (1977).

§ 40:19. Incontestable Clause.

Statutes commonly require the inclusion of an incontestable clause in life insurance policies. Ordinarily this clause states that after the lapse of two years the policy cannot be contested by the insurance company. The insurer is free to contest the validity of the policy at any time during the contestable period; but once the period has expired, it must pay the stipulated sum upon the death of the insured and cannot claim that in obtaining the policy the insured had been guilty of misrepresentation, fraud, or any other conduct that would entitle it to avoid the contract of insurance.

§ 40:20. Surrender of Policy and Alternatives.

The insured may give up or **surrender** the policy of insurance or may use it to raise money in several ways.

(a) **Cash Surrender Value.** By modern statute or policy provision, it is commonly provided that if the life insurance policy has been in force a stated number of years, usually two or three, the insured may surrender the policy and the insurer will then make a payment of the cash value of the policy to the insured. Term policies do not have a cash surrender value.

Each year a certain percentage of the premiums is set aside by the insurer to hold as a reserve against the date when payment must be made under the policy. If the policy is surrendered or canceled, the potential liability of the reserve fund is removed and part of the fund can then be released as a payment to the insured. The longer the policy has been in existence, the larger is the cash surrender value.

(b) **Loan on Policy.** The insured can generally obtain funds by borrowing from the insurer. The modern policy contains a definite scale of maximum amounts that can be borrowed depending upon the age of the policy. The insurer is able to make such loans because it has the security of the cash surrender value if the loan is not repaid; or if the insured dies without making repayment, it may deduct the debt from the proceeds payable to the beneficiary.

The loan value of a policy is usually the same amount as the cash surrender value. The policy holder, as a borrower, must pay interest to the insurance company on the loan.

(c) **Paid-Up Policy.** Under modern statutes or common forms of policies, an insured who can no longer afford the expense of insurance, may request the insurer to issue a new policy of paid-up insurance. The insured in effect takes out a new but smaller paid-up policy through the transfer of the reserve value of the old policy. In some states, when a policy lapses for nonpayment of premiums, the insurer must automatically issue a paid-up policy on the basis of the reserve value of the lapsed policy.

(d) **Extended Insurance.** Instead of a paid-up policy for a smaller amount, it is generally possible under modern statutes and policies for the insured to obtain term insurance that provides the original amount of protection. This remains effective until the reserve value of the original policy has been consumed.

(e) **Reinstatement of Lapsed Policy.** When a premium on a policy is not paid within the required period or within the grace period, the insured generally may reinstate the policy within a reasonable time thereafter as long as the insured is still an insurable risk and provided all premiums that were in arrears are paid.

§ 40:21.   Settlement Options.

Although an ordinary life insurance policy will provide for the payment of a specified amount upon the death of the insured, the insured generally may designate one or several plans of distribution of this fund. These plans of distribution are called *settlement options*. When the insured has designated a particular option, the beneficiary generally cannot change it after the insured's death. Sometimes the policy reserves to the beneficiary the right to change the settlement option.

§ 40:22.   Rights of Creditors.

Can creditors complain when a debtor obtains a policy of life insurance? To the extent that the debtor is paying premiums to the insurance company, there is less money with which to pay the creditors. Can the creditors reach the cash surrender value of the policy during the insured's life or the proceeds of the policy upon the insured's death?

If the insured makes the policy payable to the estate of the insured, the proceeds become part of the general assets of the insured's estate upon death, and, in the absence of statute, are subject to claims of the insured's creditors. If the insured is solvent at all times when premiums are paid, the creditors cannot reach the policy in payment of their claims, and the beneficiary is entitled to the entire proceeds of the policy.

Between these two extremes are a variety of situations. The insured may have been insolvent during part or all of the life of the policy; or the obtaining of the insurance policy or the assignment of it or the changing of the beneficiary may have been done to defraud the creditors.

SUMMARY

In order for a fire loss to be covered by fire insurance there must be an actual, hostile fire and that fire must be the immediate cause of the loss. The insurer is liable for the actual amount of the loss sustained up to the maximum amount stated in the policy. An exception exists where the policy contains a coinsurance clause requiring the insured to maintain insurance up to a certain percentage of the value of the property. To the extent this is not done, the insured is deemed a coinsurer with the insurer and the insurer is liable for only its proportional share of the amount of insurance required to be carried. A fire insurance policy usually cannot be assigned without the consent of the insurer. It is common for lenders to insist as a condition of making a mortgage loan on real estate that the mortgagor obtain and pay the premiums on a fire insurance policy on the full value of the property, and in case of loss that the insurance money be paid to the mortgagor and mortgagee as their respective interests may appear. Extended coverage generally refers to protection against losses due to wind, hail, riot, aircraft, vehicular damage and smoke damage. Where the insurer cancels a policy, the provisions of the policy or applicable statute must be strictly followed in order for the cancellation to be effective.

The owner or operator of a motor vehicle may purchase "liability insurance" for protection from claims made by third persons for their bodily injuries or the damage to their property caused by the operation or use of the motor vehicle. The owner may also purchase insurance to cover the damage to the owner's property, regardless of whether the owner was at fault. This type of insurance is called collision insurance. Special limited coverage insurance is required by law in most states to cover personal injuries caused by uninsured motorists. A state statute may require "no fault" coverage, which means that when the insured is injured while using the insured automobile the insurer will make payment without regard to whose fault caused the harm. No fault laws bar suits against the party at fault for ordinary claims. However in serious matters, as defined by law, suits may be brought against the party at fault. The insured may purchase theft and fire insurance, or "comprehensive" coverage, which protects against all risks including fire and theft, except collision or certain other exclusions.

A life insurance policy requires the insurer to pay a stipulated sum of money to a named beneficiary upon the death of the insured. It may be a straight life policy, a limited payment policy, an endowment policy, or as is most common today, a term insurance policy. State law commonly requires the inclusion of an incontestability clause, whereupon at the conclusion of a two year period, the insured cannot contest the validity of the policy based on misstatements or misrepresentations of the insured in the application for insurance and must pay the claim. Various settlement options exist.

QUESTIONS AND CASE PROBLEMS

1. What social forces are affected by the concept of no fault insurance?
2. Hernandez owned and operated a grocery store. He obtained a policy of fire insurance on the store and contents from the Casandra Casualty Company. The oil furnace which heated the store became clogged and heavy smoke poured into the store. Much of the food in the store absorbed the smoke with the result that the contaminated food had to be thrown away. Hernandez sued Casandra for the loss. Is he entitled to recover?
3. Explain the terms "use" and "operation" as found in automobile liability policies.
4. Manfred obtains an insurance policy by fraud. Six months later the insurance company sues to cancel the policy on the ground of the fraud. He claims that it cannot do so because the policy contains an incontestable clause. Is he correct?
5. Jay obtained a policy of insurance on his life which named Lila, his wife, as beneficiary. When their daughter, Betty, became of age, she asked her parents to change this policy to make her a co-beneficiary with her mother. The parents objected on the ground that this would require obtaining a new policy and that the premium rates on a new policy would

be higher because Jay was now much older than when the original policy had been obtained. Are the parents correct?

6. Compare the nature of and extent of coverage of (a) life insurance, (b) fire insurance, and (c) automobile liability insurance.

7. The words "total loss" as used in a fire insurance policy mean a total physical destruction of the insured property so that nothing remains after the fire. Appraise this statement.

8. Caroline drives her car off of the road to avoid a collision with an oncoming truck. In so doing, she hits a tree. The truck and its driver cannot be located or identified. Caroline sues her own insurer claiming that it is liable to her for the damage to the car under its uninsured motorist coverage. Is the insurer liable?

9. Joan owns an automobile. She carries public liability insurance. The policy contains an omnibus clause. Joan is discussing selling her car to Carlos. With her consent, he drives the car in the morning to test it out. At noon he tells Joan he will take the car but that he cannot pay for it until the end of the week. Joan tells Carlos that he can drive the car and that she will trust him to come back with the money. Carlos drives away and later that afternoon runs into Thomas. Thomas sues Joan's insurance company on the theory that Carlos was driving with her permission and therefore was covered by the omnibus clause of Joan's insurance policy. Is Thomas correct?

10. Turner had a policy of life insurance issued by the Equitable Life Assurance Society. His wife was the beneficiary. When she died, Turner changed the beneficiary to Olsen. Thereafter he began drinking heavily and was committed two times to institutions for alcoholism. About two years after he was released the second time, he changed the beneficiary of the policy to Hawkins. When Turner died, Olsen sued Hawkins and the insurance company for the proceeds of the policy, claiming that the change of beneficiary was not valid on the theory that Turner lacked capacity to change the beneficiary. In addition to Turner's confinement to institutions for alcoholism, it was shown that on a number of instances he had been arrested for minor offenses committed while intoxicated, and there was evidence that he was childish and forgetful. Was Olsen entitled to the proceeds of the policy? [Olsen v Hawkins, 90 Idaho 28, 408 P2d 462]

11. Marshall Produce Co. insured its milk and egg processing plant against fire with the St. Paul Fire & Marine Insurance Co. Smoke from a fire near its plant was absorbed by its egg powder. Cans of the powder delivered to the United States Government were rejected as contaminated. Marshall Produce sued the insurance company for a total loss. The insurer contended that there had been no fire involving the insured property and no total loss. Decide. [Marshall Produce Co. v St. Paul Fire & Marine Insurance Co. 256 Minn 404, 98 NW2d 280]

12. George Rogers insured his life with the National Producers Life Insurance Company. Ten years later he committed suicide. The insurance company denied liability because the policy stated that death by suicide was excepted. The beneficiary of the policy claimed that the insurer could not raise this defense because the two years specified by the

two-year incontestability clause had expired. She sued the insurance company. Was she entitled to recover? [National Producers Life Ins. Co. v Rogers, 8 Ariz App 53, 442 P2d 876]

13. A father told his son that the son could have the father's car but that the son must not drive it. The son had a friend drive the car. The friend ran into another car. The insurer denied liability on the ground that the father had not given permission to the friend to drive the car and that therefore the friend was not an "other driver" within the protection of the omnibus clause. Decide. [Esmond v Liscio, 209 Pa Super 200, 224 A2d 793]

14. Leverette had a policy insuring his pickup truck with the Aetna Casualty & Surety Company. The policy covered harm sustained through the operation, maintenance, or use of a motor vehicle. Leverette was driving his truck on the highway. He stopped his truck so that he could pick plums from a tree growing by the side of the road. In order to reach the higher plums, he stood on the side panel of the truck. He fell and was injured. He then sued the insurer, claiming that his injury was sustained through the use of the truck. Was his injury covered by the policy? [Leverette v Aetna Casualty & Surety Co. 157 Ga App 175, 276 SE2d 859]

15. Allen's tank truck was insured against "explosion" with the Manhattan Fire and Marine Insurance Company. For an unknown reason, the sides of the tank collapsed inward. Allen claimed that this was an explosion within the protection of the policy. Was he correct?

16. Amador Pena had three insurance policies on his life. He wrote a will in which he specified that the proceeds from the insurance policies should go to his children instead of to Leticia Pena Salinas and other beneficiaries named in the policies. He died the next day. The insurance companies paid the proceeds of the policies to the named beneficiaries. The executor of Pena's estate sued Salinas and the other beneficiaries for the insurance money. Decide. [Pena v Salinas (Tex Civ App) 536 SW2d 671]

17. Spector owned a small automobile repair garage in rural Kansas valued at $40,000. He purchased fire insurance coverage against loss to the extent of $24,000, with the policy containing an 80% coinsurance clause. A fire destroyed a portion of his parts room, causing a loss of $16,000. Spector believes he is entitled to be fully compensated for this loss since it is less than the $24,000 of fire protection which he purchased and paid for. Is Spector correct?

PART 7

AGENCY AND EMPLOYMENT

Chapter 41 Agency — Creation and Termination
Chapter 42 Principal and Agent
Chapter 43 Third Persons in Agency
Chapter 44 Employment

CHAPTER 41

AGENCY—CREATION

AND TERMINATION

CHAPTER OBJECTIVES

After studying this chapter you will be able to:
1. List the four ways in which an agency relationship may be created.
2. Explain and illustrate who may be a principal and who may be an agent.
3. State the three classifications of agents.
4. Differentiate between an agent and an independent contractor.
5. List the six ways an agency may be terminated by an act of one or both of the parties to the agency agreement.
6. List the six ways an agency may be terminated by operation of law.

One of the most common legal relationships is that of agency. By virtue of the agency device, one person can make contracts at numerous different places with many different parties at the same time. A principal or employer can sometimes be held liable in tort when an agent or employee injures a third person while performing business-related tasks directed by the principal or employer. Thus, disputes based on contract law and tort law may arise out of transactions or work done for others. And the rights and liabilities of the parties to the dispute may turn on not only the point of contract or tort law, but also on whether or not an agency relationship existed.

A. NATURE OF THE AGENCY RELATIONSHIP

Agency is a relation based upon an express or implied agreement by which one person, the **agent**, is authorized to act under the control of and for another, the **principal**, in negotiating and making contracts with third persons.[1] The acts of the agent obligate the principal to third persons and give the principal rights against third persons.

Agency is based upon the consent of the parties, and, for that reason, is called a consensual relation. If consideration is present, the relationship is also contractual. The law sometimes imposes an agency relationship.

The term "agency" is frequently used with other meanings. It is sometimes used to denote the fact that one has the right to sell certain products, such as when a dealer is said to possess an automobile agency. In other instances, the term is used to mean an exclusive right to sell certain articles within a given territory. In these cases, however, the dealer is not an agent in the sense of representing the manufacturer.[2] Courts are sometimes called upon to determine if an agency relationship existed although the term "agent" had not been used.

FACTS:
Anita Beck Bosiger, president of Anita Beck Cards & Such Inc. (Beck) and Shirley Hutton, a national sales director for Mary Kay Cosmetics, agreed that Beck would manufacture calendars and stationery to be sold at Mary Kay conventions. To finance the project Hutton gave $20,000 to Beck. They prepared and signed a document to reflect the quantity and prices of goods shipped from Beck to the Dallas convention for sale under Hutton's supervision, which document stated "commission is 15% on all but calendars." Also the unsold goods were shipped back to Beck's business at Beck's expense. The undertaking proved to be a substantial failure. Hutton sued Beck for the return of the $20,000 claiming that she was Beck's agent and the money had been a loan. Beck claimed that the money was the downpayment on the actual purchase of the goods by Hutton.

DECISION:
Judgment for Hutton. While Hutton and Beck never used the term "agent," the events relating to the Dallas convention support Hutton's contention that she was acting as an agent for Beck. Beck's role appeared to be a proprietary one, with the signed document indicating that Hutton was to receive a commission on all goods sold except calendars. Further, the unsold goods were shipped back to Beck's plant in Minnesota at Beck's expense. [Hutton v Anita Beck Cards and Such, Inc. (Minn App) 366 NW 2d 358 (1985)]

---

§ 41:1.   Agent Distinguished.

Because the agency relation creates certain rights and liabilities not present in other relations, it is important to be able to distinguish the agency relation from other similar relations.

---

[1]Restatement, Agency, 2d § 1; Botticello v Stefanovicz, 177 Conn 22, 411 A2d 16 (1979). When the question is the tax liability of an enterprise (see Boise Cascade Corp. v Washington, 3 Wash App 78, 473 P2d 429 (1970)), the definition of agency may be different than when the question is contract or tort liability, which are the areas of law considered in this part.
[2]Pioneer Hi-Bred International, Inc. v Talley (Tex Civ App) 493 SW2d 602 (1973).

(a) **Employees and Independent Contractors.** Control and authority are characteristics that distinguish ordinary employees and independent contractors from agents.

(1) Employees. An agent is distinguished from an ordinary employee, who is not hired to represent the employer in dealings with third persons. It is possible, however, for the same person to be both an agent and an employee. For example, the driver of a milk delivery truck is an agent, as well as an employee, in making contracts between the milk company and its customers, but is only an employee with respect to the work of delivering milk.

(2) Independent Contractors. An agent or employee differs from an **independent contractor** in that the principal or employer has control over and can direct the agent or an employee but does not have control over the performance of the work by an independent contractor.

FACTS:

The Drury Construction Company was remodeling the office building of the Olympic Savings & Loan Association. The contract between them described the work but did not give the Association any control over the doing of the work by Drury. Drury put up a fence barricade around the construction work. A section of the fence fell over and injured Blodgett, a pedestrian. She sued Drury and the Association to recover for her damages. The Association raised the defense that it was not liable for any harm caused by the negligence of Drury as it was an independent contractor. Blodgett claimed that the Association was liable on the theory that Drury was the agent of the Association because Drury was remodeling the building for the Association and was paid by it. Was Drury an independent contractor?

DECISION:

Yes. Drury was an independent contractor. The Association did not have any control over Drury's performance of the contract. Therefore, Drury was not the agent of the Association because control by the principal over the contract is an essential element of an agency. [Blodgett v Olympic Savings and Loan Association, 32 Wash App 2d 116, 646 P2d 139 (1982)]

A person who appears to be an independent contractor may in fact be so controlled by the other party that the contractor is regarded as an agent of or employee of the controlling person.[3]

The separate identity of an independent contractor may be concealed so that the public believes that it is dealing with the principal. When this occurs the principal is liable for the negligence of the independent contractor.

A person may be an independent contractor generally but an agent with respect to a particular transaction. Thus, an "agency" or a "broker" rendering personal services to customers is ordinarily an independent con-

[3]Blumhardt v Harting (SD) 283 NW2d 229 (1979).

tractor but will be the agent of a customer when the rendition of a service involves making a contract on behalf of the customer with a third person.

(b) Real Estate Brokers. A real estate broker is generally not an agent with authority to make a contract with a third person which will bind the broker's client. Typically, the broker's authority is limited to locating a seller or buyer and bringing the parties together but does not extend to making a contract. Even when the third person and the broker sign a "contract," it is generally only an offer by the third person which does not become a binding contract until accepted by the client of the broker.

(c) Bailees. When personal property is delivered to another under an agreement that the property will be returned to the deliveror or transferred to a third person, a bailment arises. The person to whom the property is delivered, the bailee, is not an agent because the bailee has no authority to act for or make any contract on behalf of the bailor.

Situations commonly arise, however, in which the same person is both an agent and a bailee. A salesperson who is loaned a company car, is a bailee with respect to the car; but with respect to making sales contracts, is an agent.

(d) Required Act. The mere fact that one person requires another person to do an act does not make the latter person the agent of the former. For example, when a bank directs a borrower to obtain the signature of another person in order to obtain a bank loan, the borrower is not the agent of the bank in contacting the other person and procuring the required signature.[4]

§ 41:2.   Purpose of Agency.

An agency may be created to perform almost any act which the principal could lawfully do. The object of the agency must not be criminal, nor may it be contrary to public policy. However, some acts must be performed in person and cannot be entrusted or delegated to an agent. Voting, swearing to the truth of documents, testifying in court, and making a will are instances where personal action is required. In the preparation of a document, however, it is proper to employ someone else to prepare the paper which is then signed or sworn to by the employing party. Various forms that are required by statute, such as applications for licenses and tax returns, will in some instances expressly authorize the execution of such forms by an agent as long as the identities of both principal and agent and the latter's representative capacity are clearly shown.

§ 41:3.   Who May Be a Principal.

Any person who is competent to act may act through an agent. The appointment of an agent by a person lacking capacity is generally void or voidable to the same extent that a contract made by such person would be. Thus, a minor may act through an agent, and a resulting contract will be voidable to the same extent as though made by the minor.

Groups of persons may also appoint agents to act for them.

[4]First National Bank v Caro Construction Co., Inc. 211 Kan 678, 508 P2d 516 (1973).

§ 41:4. Who May Be an Agent.

Since a contract made by an agent is in law the contract of the principal, it is immaterial whether or not the agent has legal capacity to make a contract. It is therefore permissible to employ as agents persons who are aliens, minors, and others who are under a natural or legal disability.

While ordinarily an agent is one person acting for another, an agent may be a partnership or a corporation.

§ 41:5. Classification of Agents.

A **general agent** is authorized by the principal to transact all affairs in connection with a particular kind of business or trade, or to transact all business at a certain place. To illustrate, a person who is appointed as manager by the owner of a store is a general agent.

A **special agent** is authorized by the principal to handle a definite business transaction or to do a specific act. One who is authorized by another to purchase a particular house is a special agent.

A **universal agent** is authorized by the principal to do all acts that can be delegated lawfully to a representative. This form of agency arises when a person absent in the military service gives another person a "blanket" power of attorney to do anything that must be done during such absence.

§ 41:6. Agency Coupled with an Interest.

An agent has an **interest in the authority** when consideration has been given or paid for the right to exercise the authority. To illustrate, when a lender, in return for making a loan of money, is given, as security, authority to collect rents due to the borrower and to apply those rents to the payment of the debt, the lender becomes the borrower's agent with an interest in the authority given to collect the rents.[5]

An agent has an **interest in the subject matter** when for a consideration the agent is given an interest in the property with which the agent is dealing. Hence, when the agent is authorized to sell property of the principal and is given a lien on such property as security for a debt owed to the agent by the principal, the agent has an interest in the subject matter.

B. CREATING THE AGENCY

An agency may arise by appointment, conduct, ratification, or operation of law.

§ 41:7. Authorization by Appointment.

The usual method of creating an agency is by express authorization; that is, a person is appointed to act for or on behalf of another.

In most instances the authorization of the agent may be oral. Some appointments, however, must be made in a particular way. A majority of the

---

[5]Halloran-Judge Trust Co. v Heath, 70 Utah 124, 258 P 342 (1927). When personal property or rights to money are involved, the creditor should require the creation of a secured transaction, as Article 9 of the Uniform Commercial Code will then give the creditor greater protection.

states, by statute, require the appointment of an agent to be in writing when the agency is created to acquire or dispose of any interest in land. A written authorization of agency is called a **power of attorney** and an agent acting under a power of attorney is referred to as an **attorney-in-fact.**

Ordinarily no agency arises from the fact that two people are married to each other or that they are co-owners of property. Consequently, when a check was made payable to the order of husband and wife, it was necessary for each to indorse the check because there was no agency by which the husband could indorse the wife's name and deposit the money in the husband's own bank account.

§ 41:8. Authorization by Conduct.

Conduct consistent with the existence of an agency relation may be sufficient to bind the principal.

(a) **Principal's Conduct as to Agent.**   Since agency is created by the consent of the parties, any conduct of the principal, including words, that gives a person reason to believe that the principal consents to that person's acting as agent for the principal is sufficient to create an agency. Likewise, if one person, knowingly and without objection, permits another to act as agent, the law will find in such conduct an expression of authorization to the agent, and the principal will not be permitted to deny that the agent was in fact authorized. Thus if the owner of a hotel allows another person to assume the duties of hotel clerk, that person may infer from the owner's conduct an authority to act as the hotel clerk.

(b) **Principal's Conduct as to Third Persons.**   The principal may have such dealings with third persons as to cause them to believe that the "agent" has authority. Thus, if the owner of a store places another person in charge, third persons may assume that the person in charge is the agent for the owner in that respect. The "agent" then appears to be authorized and is said to have *apparent authority,* and the principal is estopped or prevented from contradicting the appearance that has been created.[6]

When a franchisor permits the franchisee to do business under the name of the franchisor, the latter is estopped from denying that the franchisee has authority to make customary contracts, such as a contract for advertising, and to bind the franchisor by such contracts.

The term "apparent authority" is used when there is only the appearance of authority but no actual authority and that appearance of authority was created by the principal.[7] This apparent authority extends to all acts that a person of ordinary prudence, familiar with business usages, and the particular business, would be justified in assuming that the agent has authority to perform.

The mere placing of property in the possession of another does not give that person either actual or apparent authority to sell the property.[8]

[6]Foote & Davis, Inc. v Arnold Craven, Inc., 72 NC App 591, 324 SE2d 889 (1985).
[7]Springfield Television, Inc. v Gary (Mo App) 628 SW2d 398 (1982).
[8]Krick v First National Bank of Blue Island, 8 Ill App 3d 663, 290 NE2d 661 (1972). Note that under Uniform Commercial Code, § 2–403, an entrustee who deals in goods of that kind has the power but not the right to transfer the entruster's title to a person buying in good faith in the ordinary course of business.

It is essential to the concept of apparent authority that the third person reasonably believe that the agent has authority. If the basis for such belief is not reasonable, no apparent authority arises.

FACTS:

Guy Hunt was a Republican candidate for governor. Jim Hooley, who served at various times as paid campaign manager and as a paid consultant to Hunt, made a fund-raising proposal to Hunt, which consisted of a mass mailing of literature requesting contributions to be used in the campaign. Hunt expressly told Hooley that the campaign could not afford to finance this particular fund-raising plan, and that loans and the proceeds from the fund raising would have to cover all expenses connected with the plan. Hooley raised some $15,000 in loans and deposited these funds in a special account. Mailing brochures were designed and proofs shown to Hunt, who testified he read and approved them. At the bottom of the brochures, the following appeared: "Pd, Pol. Adv. by Guy Hunt Campaign." Hooley then contacted Oscar Davis, telling Davis he represented the Guy Hunt Campaign. Davis, who had previously done printing for the campaign, printed and mailed the materials. The fund-raising plan did not produce enough contributions to pay Davis and he sued Hunt for the balance due. Hunt refused to pay, contending that Hooley did not have authority to obtain credit in Hunt's name. Hunt contended that he expressly informed Hooley that the loans and proceeds would have to cover all expenses, and that the fund-raising venture was to be separate and apart from the campaign.

DECISION:

Judgment for Davis. Hooley had apparent authority to bind Hunt. Hooley was at all times paid a salary by the Hunt campaign. The brochures themselves indicated that they were to be paid for by the Hunt campaign. Further, Davis had printed other materials for the Hunt campaign, and he was not informed that the venture at issue was to be separate and apart from the campaign. The third person, Davis, was justified in relying upon the apparent scope of Hooley's authority. Likewise, apparent authority existed based on the acquiescence by the principal, Hunt. Hunt either knowingly or passively permitted Hooley to act on his behalf when Hunt approved the brochures which showed that such brochures were to be paid for by the Hunt campaign. [Hunt v Davis (Ala Civ App) 387 So2d 209 (1980)]

(c) **Acquiescence by Principal.** The conduct of the principal that gives rise to the agent's authority may be acquiescence in or failing to object to acts done by the purported or apparent agent over a period of time.[9] For example, a person collecting payments on a note and remitting the proper amounts to the holder of the note will be regarded as the latter's agent for collection when this conduct has been followed over a period of years without objection.

[9]Vacura v Haar's Equipment Co. (Minn) 364 NW2d 387 (1985).

§ 41:9. Agency by Ratification.

An agent may attempt on behalf of the principal to do an act which was not authorized. Or a person who is not the agent of another may attempt to act as such an agent. Generally, in such case, the principal for whom the agent claimed to act has the choice of ignoring the transaction or of ratifying it. Ordinarily any unauthorized act may be ratified.

(a) **Intention to Ratify.** Initially, ratification is a question of intention. Just as in the case of authorization, where there is a question of whether or not the principal authorized the agent, so there is a question of whether or not the principal intended to approve or ratify the action of the unauthorized agent.[10]

FACTS:
In August of 1981 Joel Copley renewed his multiperil insurance policy for his appliance store and contents with Pekin Insurance Co. Copley subsequently bought a multiperil insurance policy for his store from Federated Insurance. When its agent, DeFrates, delivered the policy to Copley's store on November 18, 1981, Copley was not present. However, DeFrates was informed that Copley was concerned about getting a refund on the premium paid to Pekin. DeFrates, acting without authorization, then went to the Pekin agency and told them to cancel Copley's policy and to refund Copley's premium. DeFrates returned to Copley's store and told Copley what he had done. On December 15, 1981, prior to receiving any refund of the premium from Pekin, Copley's store was destroyed by fire. Copley brought suit against Pekin for payment on the policy, contending that DeFrates had no authority from him to cancel his insurance with Pekin. Federated Insurance also sued Pekin for contribution to the payment of the fire loss.

DECISION:
Judgment for Pekin. While DeFrates did not have authority to request Pekin to cancel the policy, Copley's failure to object, after learning of DeFrates' actions, constituted a ratification of the request to cancel. In other words, Copley adopted the request as his own. [Copley v Pekin Insurance Co. (Ill App) 474 NE2d 57 (1985)]

The intention to ratify may be expressed in words or it may be found in conduct indicating an intention to ratify, such as paying for goods ordered by the agent or performing the contract which the agent had made and accepting payments for such performance.

If the conditions of ratification are satisfied, a principal ratifies an agent's act when, with knowledge of the act, the principal accepts or retains

[10]Miles v Plumbing Services of Houston, Inc. (Tex Civ App) 668 SW2d 509 (1984).

the benefit of the act, or brings an action to enforce legal rights based upon the act or defends an action by asserting the existence of a right based on the unauthorized transaction, or fails to repudiate the agent's act within a reasonable time. The receipt, acceptance, and deposit of a check by the principal with knowledge that it arises from an unauthorized transaction is a common illustration of ratification of the unauthorized transaction by conduct.

(b) **Conditions for Ratification.** In addition to the intent to ratify, expressed in some instances with certain formality, the following conditions must be satisfied in order that the intention take effect as a ratification:

1. The agent must have purported to act on behalf of or as agent for the identified principal.[11]
2. The principal must have been capable of authorizing the act both at the time of the act and at the time when it was ratified.
3. The principal must ratify the act before the third person withdraws.
4. The act to be ratified must generally be legal.
5. The principal must have full knowledge of all material facts.[12] If the agent conceals a material fact, the ratification of the principal that is made in ignorance of such fact is not binding. Of course, there can be no ratification when the principal does not know of the making of the contract by the alleged agent. Consequently, when the owner's agent and a contractor make unauthorized major changes to an installation contract without knowledge of the owner, the fact that the owner had no knowledge of the matter bars any claim of ratification of the agent's act.

FACTS:

Phyllis Thropp opened a margin trading account with Bache broker R. Gregory placing in his care securities valued at $40,000. Mrs. Thropp was not a sophisticated investor; and she expected Mr. Gregory to manage her account and make investment decisions on her behalf. Subsequently her husband Jack, a friend of the broker, forged his wife's signature on a completely blank power of attorney form and sent it to the broker. Jack Thropp then ordered Gregory to sell his wife's securities for cash, and ordered Bache to issue seven checks in his wife's name, which he later forged and cashed. Mrs. Thropp and her husband saw the broker socially and her frequent questions about her account brought vague answers about the condition of the market, but he never mentioned the numerous sales for cash. In December, 1972

Mrs. Thropp questioned Gregory why a letter from Bache would be addressed to Jack and why her account balance seemed so low. The broker refused to discuss the matter and told her to talk to Mr. Thropp. Mr. Thropp confessed that he had stolen the $40,000 to pay gambling debts; and assured her that the broker was not involved in depleting her account. Mrs. Thropp being seven months pregnant at the time took no action. In 1975 she filed for a divorce; and in a deposition from the broker relating to the divorce she learned that he may have mishandled her account. The evidence showed that the broker had disregarded the firm's rules. A firm assistant manager testified that a broker would not be authorized to take directions to trade in an account from one who held a power of attorney similar to the document forged by Thropp. Mrs. Thropp brought suit against Bache,

---

[11]Jones v Nunley, 274 Or 591, 547 P2d 616 (1976).
[12]Floyd v Jay County Rural Elec. Membership Corp. ___ Ind App ___, 405 NE2d 630 (1980).

claiming as her agent Bache had a duty to use the skills and diligence necessary to protect her interest, and that it had breached this duty. Bache, among other points, contended that Mrs. Thropp ratified the actions of Mr. Thropp and Bache.

DECISION:
Judgment for Mrs. Thropp. To establish ratification, one must show action by the principal, taken with full knowledge of the facts, which manifests her intention to adopt the unauthorized transaction. The evidence reveals that Mrs. Thropp did not learn of the broker's involvement until 1975, thus it cannot be said she ratified Bache's actions. Nor can it be said that she ratified her husband's forgeries. The fact that she remained his wife for two years after finding out his misconduct is not the sort of "action" ratification requires. The stock brokerage firm was negligent in handling Mrs. Thropp's account and it is liable for the damages which resulted. [Thropp v Bache Halsey Stuart Shields, Inc. (CA 6 Ohio) 650 F2d 817 (1981)]

It is not always necessary, however, to show that the principal had actual knowledge; for knowledge will be imputed if a principal knows of such other facts as would put a prudent person on inquiry, or if that knowledge can be inferred from the knowledge of other facts or from a course of business. Knowledge is likewise not an essential factor when the principal does not care to know the details and is willing to ratify the contract regardless of such lack of knowledge.

(c) **Form of Ratification.** An agreement that is binding although oral may be ratified orally or by conduct. If a contract can not be enforced if not evidenced by a writing, it is generally held that a ratification of the contract must be in writing.[13]

(d) **Effect of Ratification.** When an unauthorized act is ratified, the effect is the same as though the act had been originally authorized. Ordinarily this means that the principal and the third party are bound by the contract made by the agent. Conversely, when the principal ratifies the act of the unauthorized person, such ratification releases that person from the liability which would otherwise be imposed for having acted without authority.

§ 41:10. Agency by Operation of Law.

In certain instances, the courts, influenced by necessity or social desirability, create or find an agency when there is none. For example, a wife may purchase necessaries and charge them to her husband's account when the husband does not supply them. Here the social policy is the furtherance of the welfare of the neglected wife.

As another example of agency by operation of law, a minor may purchase necessaries upon the father's credit when the latter fails to supply them. If the minor is already adequately supplied by the father, the mother cannot make additional purchases or contracts and charge the father, even though this could have been done if the minor had not been already adequately provided for by the father.

[13]Monti v Tangora, 99 Ill App 3d 575, 54 Ill Dec 732, 425 NE2d 597 (1981).

An emergency power of an agent to act under unusual circumstances not covered by the agent's authority is recognized when the agent is unable to communicate with the principal and failure to act would cause the principal substantial loss.

§ 41:11. Proving the Agency Relationship.

The burden of proving the existence of an agency relationship rests upon the person who seeks to benefit by such proof. The third person who desires to bind the principal because of the act of an alleged agent has the burden of proving that the latter person was in fact the authorized agent of the principal and possessed the authority to do the act in question. For example, when the buyer asserts that there has been a breach of an express warranty made by the seller's agent, the buyer must establish that there was an actual or apparent authority to make the warranty. In the absence of sufficient proof, the jury must find that there is no agency. The authority of the agent may be established by circumstantial evidence.

C. TERMINATION OF AGENCY

An agency may be terminated by the act of one or both of the parties to the agency agreement, or by operation of law. When the authority of an agent is terminated, the agent loses all right to act for the principal.

§ 41:12. Termination by Act of Parties.

In most cases, either party to an agency relationship has the power to terminate that relationship at any time. In some cases, however, the terminating party may be liable to the other party for damages.

(a) **Expiration of Agency Contract.** The ordinary agency may expire by the terms of the contract creating it. Thus, the contract may provide that it shall last for a stated period, as five years, or until a particular date arrives, or until the happening of a particular event, such as the sale of certain property. In such a case, the agency is automatically terminated when the specified date arrives or the event on which it is to end occurs.

When it is provided that the agency shall last for a stated period of time, it terminates upon the expiration of that period without regard to whether the acts contemplated by the creation of the agency have been performed. If no period is stated, the agency continues for a reasonable time, but it may be terminated at the will of either party.

(b) **Agreement.** Since the agency relation is based upon consent, it can be terminated by the consent of the principal and agent.

(c) **Option of a Party.** An agency agreement may provide that upon the giving of notice or the payment of a specified sum of money, one party may terminate the relationship.

(d) **Revocation by Principal.** The relationship between principal and agent is terminated whenever the principal discharges the agent even though the agency was stated to be "irrevocable." If the agency was not created for a specified time but was to exist only at will, or if the agent has been guilty of misconduct, the principal may discharge the agent without liability. The intent to revoke must be clearly and unequivocally expressed.

FACTS:

Kinmon owned a summer home which he wanted to sell at auction. He employed the J.P. King Auction Company to make the sale. Kinmon complained about the efforts made by King. King sold the property to the highest bidder for $35,000. Kinmon had expected twice that much and refused to convey title to the buyer or to pay commissions to King. King sued Kinmon to collect the commissions. Kinmon raised the defense that he had revoked King's authority to sell the property.

DECISION:

Judgment for King. His authority had not been revoked by Kinmon. The mere expression of dissatisfaction with the work of an agent does not constitute a revocation of his authority. The intent to revoke must be clearly and unequivocally expressed. As there was no such clear expression, the authority of the agent continued and he was therefore entitled to compensation for his services. [Kinmon v J.P. King Auction Co., Inc. 290 Ala 323, 276 So2d 569 (1973)

Any conduct which manifests an intent to revoke the authority is sufficient, as when the principal takes back from the agent the property which had been entrusted to the agent for the purpose of the agency or retains another agent to do what the original agent had been authorized to do. When the agency is based upon a contract to employ the agent for a specified period of time, the principal is liable to the agent for damages if the principal wrongfully discharges the agent. The fact that the principal is liable for damages does not, however, prevent the principal from terminating the agency by discharging the agent. In such a case, it is said that the principal has the power to terminate the agency by discharging the agent but does not have the right to do so.

(e) **Renunciation by Agent.** The agency relationship is terminated if the agent refuses to continue to act as agent when the agent abandons the object of the agency and acts in self-interest in committing a fraud upon the principal.

If the relationship is an agency at will, the agent has the right, as well as the power, to renounce or abandon the agency at any time. In addition, the agent has the right of renunciation of the relationship in any case if the principal was guilty of making wrongful demands or of other misconduct.

If, however, the agency is based upon a contract calling for the continuation of the relationship for a specified or determinable period, that is, until a particular date arrives or a certain event occurs, the agent has no right to abandon or renounce the relationship when the principal is not guilty of wrong.

When the renunciation by the agent is wrongful, the agent is liable to the principal for the damages that the principal sustains.

(f) **Rescission.** The agency contract may be terminated by rescission to the same extent that any other contract may be so terminated.[14]

§ 41:13.   Termination by Operation of Law.

The agency relationship is a personal one and anything that renders one of the parties incapable of performing will result in the termination of the relationship by operation of law.

(a) **Death.** The death of either the principal or agent ordinarily terminates the authority of an agent automatically, even though the death is unknown to the other. Some state statutes provide that the death of the principal is not a revocation until the agent has notice nor as to third persons who deal with the agent in good faith and are ignorant of the death. Generally, however, these statutes are limited to principals who are members of the armed forces.

FACTS:
The owner of paintings left them with a dealer under an arrangement by which the dealer would sell the paintings and would then deduct a specified percentage as commissions and send the balance of the purchase price to the owner. The owner of the paintings died. The owner's widow, as the representative of his estate, sued the dealer to get the paintings back. Was the widow entitled to recover the paintings?

DECISION:
Yes. The relationship between the owner and the dealer was an agency. When the owner died, the agency was terminated by operation of law, and therefore his estate, represented by his widow, was entitled to the return of the paintings. [Friedmans's Estate, 397 NYS2d 561 (1977)]

In an attorney-client relationship the death of the client does not terminate the agency if the client had expressly agreed that the attorney should conduct the proceeding to its conclusion.[15]

(b) **Insanity.** The insanity of either the principal or agent ordinarily terminates the agent's authority. If the incapacity of the principal is only temporary, the agent's authority may be merely suspended rather than terminated.

(c) **Bankruptcy.** Bankruptcy of the principal or agent usually terminates the relationship. It is generally held, however, that the bankruptcy of an agent does not terminate the agent's power to deal with goods of the principal held by the agent.

Insolvency, as distinguished from a formal adjudication of bankruptcy, usually does not terminate the agency. In most states, accordingly,

[14]Cutcliffe v Chestnut, 122 Ga App 195, 176 SE2d 607 (1970).
[15]Vincent v Vincent, 16 Wash App 213, 554 P2d 374 (1976).

the authority of an agent is not terminated by the appointment of a receiver for the principal.

(d) **Impossibility.** The authority of an agent is terminated when it is impossible to perform the agency for any reason, such as the destruction of the subject matter of the agency, the death or loss of capacity of the third person with whom the agent is to contract, or a change in law that makes it impossible to perform the agency lawfully.

(e) **War.** When the country of the principal is at war with that of the agent, the authority of the agent is usually terminated or at least suspended until peace is restored. When the war has the effect of making performance impossible, the agency is, of course, terminated. For example, the authority of an agent who is a nonresident enemy alien to sue is terminated, because such an alien is not permitted to sue.

(f) **Unusual Events or Changes of Circumstances.** The authority of an agent is also terminated by the occurrence of an unusual event or a change in value or business conditions of such a nature that the agent should reasonably infer that the principal would not desire the agent to continue to act under the changed circumstances. For example, an agent employed to sell land at a specified price should regard the authority to sell at that price as terminated when the value of the land increases greatly because of the discovery of oil on the land.

§ 41:14.   Termination of Agency Coupled with an Interest.

An agency coupled with an interest is an exception to the general rule as to the termination of an agency. Such an agency cannot be revoked by the principal before the expiration of the interest and is not terminated by the death or insanity of either the principal or the agent.

§ 41:15.   Effect of Termination of Authority.

If the agency is revoked by the principal, the authority to act for the principal is not terminated until notice of revocation is given to or received by the agent. As between the principal and the agent, the right of the agent to bind the principal to third persons generally ends immediately upon the termination of the agent's authority. Such termination is effective without the giving of notice to third persons.

When the agency is terminated by the act of the principal, notice must be given to third persons. If such notice is not given, the agent may have the power to make contracts that will bind the principal and third persons. This rule is predicated on the theory that a known agent will have the appearance of still being the agent unless notice to the contrary is given to third persons.

FACTS:

Record owned a farm that was operated by his agent, Berry, who lived on the farm. The latter hired Wagner to bale the hay in 1953 and told him to bill Record for this work. Wagner did so and was paid by Record. By the summer of 1954, the agency had been terminated by Record but Berry remained in possession as tenant of the farm and nothing appeared changed. In 1954 Berry asked Wagner to bale the hay the same as in the prior year and bill Record for the work. He did so, but Record refused to pay on the ground that Berry was not then his agent. Wagner sued him.

DECISION:

Judgment for Wagner. As the agency of Berry had been terminated by the voluntary action of the principal, it was necessary that notice of termination be given to third persons who had dealt with the agent. Since this had not been done, the agent continued to appear to have authority to bind the principal, and he therefore could do so in spite of the actual termination of the authority. [Record v Wagner, 100 NH 419, 128 A2d 921 (1957)]

When the law requires the giving of notice in order to end the power of the agent to bind the principal, individual notice must be given or mailed to all persons who had prior dealings with the agent or the principal. Notice to the general public can be given by publishing a statement that the agency had been terminated in a newspaper of general circulation in the affected geographical area.

If a notice is actually received, the power of the agent is terminated without regard to whether the method of giving notice was proper. Conversely, if proper notice is given, it is immaterial that it does not actually come to the attention of the party notified. Thus a member of the general public cannot claim that the principal is bound on the ground that the third person did not see the newspaper notice stating that the agent's authority had been terminated.

SUMMARY

An agency relation is created by an express or implied agreement whereby one person, the agent, is authorized to act on behalf of and subject to the control of another person, the principal. Where an agency relationship exists, the acts of the agent obligate the principal to a third person, and give the principal rights against the third person. An agent differs from an independent contractor in that the principal, who controls the acts of an agent, does not have control over the details of performance of work by the independent contractor.

A general agent is authorized by the principal to transact all business affairs of the principal at a certain place. A special agent is authorized by the principal to handle a specific business transaction. A universal agent is authorized to do all acts that can be lawfully delegated to a representative.

The usual method of creating an agency is by express authorization. However, an agency relationship may be found to exist where the principal causes or permits a third person to reasonably believe that an agency relationship exists. The "agent" appears to be authorized and is said to have apparent authority.

An unauthorized transaction by an agent for a principal may be ratified by the principal, where the principal, with knowledge of all material facts, accepts the benefits of the act.

The duration of the agency relationship is commonly stated in the contract creating the relationship. In most cases, either party has the power to terminate the agency relationship at any time. However, the terminating party may be liable for damages to the other if the termination is in violation of the agency contract. When a principal terminates an agent's authority, it is not effective until the notice is received by the agent. Since a known agent will have the appearance of still being an agent, notice must be given to third persons of the termination, and the agent may have the power to bind the principal and third persons until that notice is given. An agency is terminated by operation of law on (1) the death of the principal or agent; (2) insanity of the principal or agent; (3) bankruptcy of the principal or agent; (4) impossibility of performance, such as the destruction of the subject matter; (5) war; and (6) the occurrence of unusual events or changes of circumstances. An agency coupled with an interest is an exception to the above stated rules on termination and cannot be revoked by the principal prior to the expiration of the interest.

QUESTIONS AND CASE PROBLEMS

1. What social forces are affected by allowing an agent to make a contract which will bind the agent's principal and a third person?
2. How does an agent differ from an independent contractor?
3. Compare authorization of an agent by (a) appointment and (b) ratification.
4. Elberson came to Suzanne's house and showed her order blanks bearing the name of Elco Corporation. Elberson told Suzanne that he was the agent for the Elco Corporation, solicited an order from Suzanne for merchandise manufactured by Elco, and accepted a deposit from Suzanne. Elberson in fact was not the agent of Elco and the forms which Elberson showed Suzanne were "counterfeit" forms that Elberson had printed. Suzanne sued Elco on the ground that Elberson appeared to be the agent of Elco and therefore had apparent authority to bind Elco to Suzanne. Was this correct?
5. Angela claims that she worked for the Globe Plant Company as Globe's agent and is entitled to a commission on a large order called in by a customer from Springfield, Vermont. Globe denies that Angela was the agent of Globe. Angela claims that Globe has the burden of proving that Angela was not the agent of Globe. Is Angela correct?
6. Crawford is the agent for Elaine. Elaine mails Crawford a letter informing him that he is discharged. Crawford makes a contract as agent for Elaine prior to receipt of the letter. Was Crawford Elaine's agent when he made this contract so as to bind Elaine?
7. Kohler saw a painting which he believed Hannah would want to buy. The painting was owned by Pogue. Kohler made a contract to purchase the painting from Pogue without saying anything about Hannah. When

Kohler informed Hannah of the contract, she approved and said that she ratified the contract. Could she do so?

8. Compare (a) the termination of an agency with (b) the discharge of a contract.

9. Ken Jones, the number one ranked prizefighter in his weight class, signed a two-year contract with Howard Stayword, with Stayword being obligated to represent and promote Jones in all business and professional matters, including the arrangement of fights. For these services, Jones contracted to pay Stayword ten percent of gross earnings. After a year, when Stayword proved unsuccessful in arranging a title match with the champion, Jones fired Stayword. During the following year Jones earned $4,000,000. Stayword sued Jones for $400,000. Jones defended that a principal has the absolute power at any time to terminate an agency relationship by discharging the agent, and as such he is not liable to Stayword. Is Jones correct?

10. Paul Strich did business as an optician in Duluth, Minnesota. Paul used only the products of the Plymouth Optical Company, a national manufacturer of optical products and supplies, with numerous retail outlets and some franchise arrangements in areas other than Duluth. In order to increase business, Paul renovated his office and changed the sign on his office to read "Plymouth Optical Co." Paul did business in this manner for more than three years—advertised under that name, paid bills with checks bearing the name of Plymouth Optical Co., and listed himself in the telephone and city directories by that name. Plymouth immediately became aware of what Paul had done. However, since Paul used only Plymouth products, it saw no advantage at that time in prohibiting Paul from using the name and losing him as a customer, since Plymouth did not have any franchisee in Duluth. Paul contracted with the Duluth Tribune for advertising making the contract in the name of Plymouth Optical Co. When the advertising bill was not paid the Duluth Tribune sued Plymouth Optical Company for payment. Plymouth defended that it never authorized Paul to do business under the name, nor had it authorized him to make a contract with the newspaper. Decide.

11. A husband and wife owned a house as tenants in common without the right of survivorship. They insured the building against fire. The property was destroyed by fire. The insurance company paid the full amount of the proceeds to the husband on the basis of a release which he signed with his name and the name of the wife. She had not expressly authorized him to do this. Thereafter the wife sued the insurance company for one half of the amount paid by the insurer. It raised the defense that it had made full payment to the husband. Was this a valid defense? [Gray v Holyoke Mutual Fire Ins. Co. 293 Ala 291, 302 So2d 104]

12. Through his agent, Davis, Fieschko executed a written agreement to sell his real estate to Herlich. The agreement had been negotiated by Dykstra as Herlich's agent. The contract for the purchase of the land was signed by Dykstra as the agent for Herlich. Thereafter Herlich sent a check for the down payment to Davis. The check did not contain any reference to the sale or the terms of the sale. Herlich did not go through with the sale

and, when sued for breach of the contract, he argued that he was not bound by the contract since he had not signed it and Dykstra had not been authorized in writing to sign it. Fieschko claimed that Herlich had ratified the contract when he sent the check for the down payment. Decide. [Fieschko v Herlich, 32 Ill App 2d 280, 177 NE2d 376]

13. Perry was a building contractor. Rothrock made a contract with Perry to build a house for Rothrock on his land. Perry contracted with Maxwell to provide labor and materials for flooring and walls of the house. Maxwell was not paid. He sued Perry and Rothrock for the amount due him. Maxwell claimed that Rothrock was liable because Perry was his agent. Was Maxwell correct? [Maxwell v Perry, 22 NC 58, 205 SE2d 350]

14. Martin and his wife owned farmland, which they listed for sale with Schneider, a real estate broker. Schneider agreed to sell the land to Heinrich. When the Martins later refused to sell the land, Heinrich sued for specific performance claiming that the Martins were bound by the written contract made by their agent Schneider, and that based on the written listing agreement given to Schneider by the Martins, Schneider had authority to sell the land for the Martins. Is Heinrich correct? [Heinrich v Martin (ND) 134 NW2d 786]

15. Walker owned a trailer that he wished to sell. He took it to the business premises of Pacific Mobile Homes. The only person on the premises at that time and several other times when Walker was there was Stewart, who identified himself as a salesman of Pacific and who agreed to take possession of Walker's trailer and to attempt to sell it for him. Stewart made out some forms of Pacific Mobile Homes and thereafter wrote some letters on the letterhead of Pacific to Walker. Walker's trailer was sold, but the salesman disappeared with most of the money. Walker sued Pacific for the proceeds of the sale. It denied liability on the ground that Stewart lacked authority to make any sales agreement and that all salesmen of Pacific were expressly forbidden to take used trailers to try to sell them for their owners. Is this defense valid? [Walker v Pacific Mobile Homes, 68 Wash 2d 347, 413 P2d 3]

16. Hill purchased furniture from Grant Furniture. When she complained that it was damaged, she was told that they would send someone to fix the damage. An independent contractor, Newman, was sent to fix the furniture. He identified himself as the man from Grant's. The lacquer he put on the furniture exploded and caused serious injury to Hill. She sued both Newman and Grant. Grant claimed that Newman was an independent contractor and that it was therefore not liable for his conduct. Was Grant correct? [Hill v Newman, 126 NJ Super 557, 316 A2d 8]

17. Mrs. Bird, a woman of means, was living in deplorable conditions. Because of her bizarre behavior, neighbors contacted her cousin Logan Ledbetter, who in turn had Mrs. Bird examined by Dr. Phillips, a psychiatrist. Dr. Phillips determined that Mrs. Bird was suffering from "an organic brain syndrome, chronic, probably secondary to cerebral arteriosclerosis," that "her mental function was very impaired," and that in his opinion Mrs. Bird was "mentally incompetent at the time of the examination." Ledbetter planned to deal with the situation by selling off

a number of valuable real estate holdings owned by Mrs. Bird and using the proceeds to pay for proper care for Mrs. Bird. Soon thereafter Mrs. Bird executed a power of attorney designating Logan Ledbetter as her attorney-in-fact; and Ledbetter entered into a contract to sell a large parcel of land to Andleman Associates. Mrs. Bird's niece, Barbara, who disliked Ledbetter, filed a petition seeking to have Mrs. Bird declared incompetent and herself named guardian of her estate. The court appointed Barbara as guardian, and she refused to allow the sale of the land to Andleman. In the complicated lawsuit that resulted, Ledbetter and Andleman contended that Ledbetter acted in good faith and had a properly executed power of attorney, and therefore his signing the sales contract with Andleman was binding on Mrs. Bird (the principal). Atkins (the real estate agent who produced the ready, willing, and able buyer) sought his 10% commission under the listing agreement signed by Ledbetter as agent for Mrs. Bird. Barbara contended that the power of attorney was void and that Ledbetter owed the real estate commission since he breached his implied warranty that he had a principal with capacity. Decide.

CHAPTER 42

PRINCIPAL AND AGENT

CHAPTER OBJECTIVES

After studying this chapter you will be able to:

1. Differentiate between express authority, incidental authority, customary authority, and apparent authority.
2. Explain the effect of the proper exercise of authority by an agent.
3. Describe the duty of a third person to ascertain the extent of an agent's authority.
4. Describe and illustrate when an agent may and may not delegate authority to another.
5. Explain the duties and liabilities of an agent to the principal during and after the agency.
6. Explain the duties and liabilites of a principal to the agent during and after the agency.

The principal, the inactive participant in a transaction, may, under certain circumstances, be held liable by courts for the dealings of the agent, the active participant in a transaction. Clearly the principal should be liable for the acts of the agent when the principal has given the agent express authority to so act. Should the principal be bound by an agent where the agent acts beyond authority or where the agent misrepresents authority? The principal may be held liable on one of the "authority" theories set forth in this chapter, if justice requires it. The courts are concerned with protecting the property of the principal; but also the courts recognize that third persons have to be able to rely on the reasonable appearance of authority of agents if our commercial markets are going to function effectively.

The nature of the agency relationship is better understood when the duties and liabilities of the agent and principal to each other are studied. For example, agents owe a duty of loyalty to their principal and should an agent act contrary to the interest of the principal and make a secret profit, the courts will allow the principal to recover the profit from the agent.

A. AGENT'S AUTHORITY

The fact that one person is the agent of another does not dispose of all questions. It is necessary to determine the scope of the agent's authority.

§ 42:1.   Scope of Agent's Authority.

The scope of an agent's authority may be determined from the express words of the principal to the agent, or may be implied from the principal's words or deeds, or the customs of the trade or business.

(a) Express Authority. If the principal tells the agent to perform a certain act, the agent has **express authority** to do so. Express authority can be indicated by conduct as well as by words. Accordingly, when the agent informs the principal of intended plans and the principal makes no objection to them, authorization may be indicated by such silence.

(b) Incidental Authority. An agent has implied **incidental authority** to perform any act reasonably necessary to execute the express authority given to the agent. To illustrate, if the principal authorizes the agent to purchase goods without furnishing funds to the agent to pay for them, the agent has implied incidental authority to purchase the goods on credit.

(c) Customary Authority. An agent has implied **customary authority** to do any act which, according to the custom of the community, usually accompanies the transaction for which the agent is authorized to act. For example, an agent who has express authority to receive payments from third persons has implied authority to issue receipts.

One authorized to act as a general manager has the power to make any contract necessary for the usual and ordinary conduct of business. Likewise, an agent authorized to obtain advertising may contract for television time because the use of television as an advertising medium is customary. Authorization to contract for television time can also be regarded as incidental to a general, unrestricted authorization to advertise.[1]

(d) Apparent Authority. A person has apparent authority as an agent when the principal by words or conduct leads a third person reasonably to believe that such person has that authority and the third person relies on that appearance.[2]

---

[1]Columbia Broadcasting System v Stokely-Van Camp, Inc. (CA2 NY) 522 F2d 369 (1975).
[2]Associated Creditors' Agency v Davis, 13 Cal 3d 374, 118 Cal Rptr 772, 530 P2d 1084 (1975).

FACTS:

Trident Construction Corporation's principal source of business was governmental contracts. To secure a government contract, Trident was required to submit a bid bond, which guaranteed that the lowest bidder would accept the government's offer. Trident purchased its bid bonds from Reliance Insurance Company through the Simkiss Agency. After doing business in this manner for some time, Trident decided to bid on the Willow Grove project, which required a $1.1 million bid bond. Simkiss issued the bond to Trident and then rescinded it, causing Trident to lose the contract. Prior to the Willow Grove project Simkiss had issued a bid bond for $800,000 for another project in the name of Reliance. Trident sued Reliance claiming that Reliance and its agent Simkiss wrongfully rescinded the bond. Reliance defended saying Simkiss had no authority to issue or rescind bonds over $400,000 for a single job, and therefore it had no liability.

DECISION:

Judgment for Trident Construction Corp. Apparent authority exists when the principal has led a third party to believe that an agent has authority to act for the principal. Under the agency agreement with Reliance, Simkiss did not have actual authority to execute bid bonds in excess of $400,000 to Trident. However, prior to the Willow Grove project, Simkiss had issued a Reliance bid bond for $800,000 to Trident. The failure of Reliance to disavow this bond made it appear that Simkiss had authority to write bonds without regard to amount. Simkiss thus had apparent authority to write the Willow Grove bond and its actions bound Reliance. [Trident Corp v Reliance Ins. Co. (Pa Super) 504 A2d 285 (1986)]

§ 42.2.   Effect of Proper Exercise of Authority.

When an agent with authority properly makes a contract with a third person that purports to bind the principal, there is by definition a binding contract between the principal and the third person. The agent is not a party to this contract. Consequently, when the owner of goods is the principal, the owner's agent is not liable for breach of warranty with respect to the goods "sold" by the agent because the owner-principal, not the agent, was the "seller" in the sales transaction.[3]

§ 42:3.   Duty to Ascertain Extent of Agent's Authority.

A third person who deals with a person claiming to be an agent cannot rely on the statements made by the agent concerning the extent of authority. If the agent is not authorized to perform the act or is not even the agent of the principal, the transaction between the alleged agent and the third person will have no legal effect between the principal and the third person.

Third persons who deal with an agent whose authority is limited to a special purpose, are bound at their peril to find out the extent of the agent's authority. An attorney is such an agent; and unless the client holds the attorney out as having greater authority than usual, the attorney has no authority to settle a claim without approval from a client.

[3]Wright Waterproofing Co. v Allied Polymers (Tex Civ App) 602 SW2d 67 (1980).

FACTS:

Miotk retained attorney John D. Logsdon to represent her in a personal injury action against Rudy. Logsdon filed suit on behalf of Miotk, and later entered negotiations with Rudy's attorney to settle the case. As an offer of settlement, Rudy's attorney sent Mr. Logsdon a check made out to "Irene Miotk and John D. Logsdon, her attorney" along with a release for Ms. Miotk to sign. Logsdon failed to return the signed release by the day the case was set for trial, but he advised Rudy's attorney that the settlement was "on." The court contacted Logsdon who told the court that the settlement was agreed to; and the court approved the settlement and dismissed the case. Unknown to all parties and the court, Logsdon had apparently forged Irene Miotk's indorsement to the check, and had retained the proceeds. Miotk hired new counsel, who filed a motion to set aside the dismissal of her action. In an accompanying affidavit, Miotk stated that she at no time authorized the settlement of the case; nor was she ever offered any sum of money by Logsdon. Rudy contended that Logsdon had apparent authority to settle the case.

DECISION:

Judgment for Miotk. Those who deal with an agent whose authority is limited to special purposes, such as an attorney, are bound at their peril to know the extent of the agent's authority. An attorney has no authority to settle the case, since Ms. Miotk did not authorize the settlement. There was no evidence of Logsdon's apparent authority to settle Ms. Miotk's case other than Logsdon's employment as the plaintiff's attorney. This is insufficient evidence to establish apparent authority. [Miotk v Rudy, 227 Kan 296, 605 P2d 587 (1980)]

(a) **Agent's Acts Adverse to Principal.** The third person who deals with an agent is required to take notice of any acts that are clearly adverse to the interest of the principal. Thus, if the agent is obviously making use of funds of the principal for the agent's personal benefit, persons dealing with the agent should recognize that the agent may be acting without authority and that they are dealing with the agent at their peril.

The only certain way that third persons can protect themselves is to inquire of the principal whether the agent is in fact the agent of the principal and has the necessary authority. If the principal states that the agent has the authority, the principal cannot later deny this authorization unless the subject matter is such that an authorization must be in writing in order to be binding.

(b) **Death of Third Person.** The extent of the agent's authority becomes particularly significant when the third person dies after the transaction with the agent but before any action has been taken by the principal. If the agent had authority to contract on behalf of the principal, the agent's agreement with the third person would give rise immediately to a binding contract and the third person's subsequent death would ordinarily not affect that contract. In contrast, if the agent did not have authority to contract but only to transmit an offer from the third person, the death of the third person before the principal had accepted the offer would work a revocation of the offer and the principal could not create a contract by purporting to accept after the death of the third person.

§ 42:4.   Limitations of Agent's Authority.

A person who has knowledge of a limitation on the agent's authority cannot disregard that limitation. When the third person knows that the authority of the agent depends upon whether financing has been obtained, the principal is not bound by the act of the agent if the financing in fact was not obtained. If the authority of the agent is based on a writing and the third person knows that there is such a writing, the third person is charged with knowledge of the limitations contained in it.

FACTS:

Rausch owned the Black Acres Farm. It was subject to a first mortgage. Rausch wanted to refinance the mortgage debt, and sent an agent to the Citizens State Bank with authority to make a new loan and to pledge stock as security for the new loan if a second mortgage was obtained on the farm. This existence of the mortgage was known to the bank. The second mortgage was not obtained but the agent and the bank made a new loan agreement, part of which obligated Rausch to deliver certain shares of stock to the bank as security. The bank sued Rausch and his wife to compel them to deliver the stock to it under the second loan agreement.

DECISION:

Judgment for the Rauschs. When the third person knows that the authority of an agent depends upon whether financing has been obtained, the principal of the agent is not bound by the act of the agent if the financing is not obtained. As the bank knew of the condition, it acted with knowledge of the limitation on the authority of the agent and the principal of the agent was therefore not bound. [Citizens State Bank v Rausch, 9 Ill App3d 1004, 293 NE2d 678 (1973)]

(a) **Apparent Limitations.** In some situations, it will be apparent to third persons that they are dealing with an agent whose authority is limited. When third persons know that they are dealing with an officer of a private corporation or a representative of a governmental agency, they should recognize that such person will ordinarily not have unlimited authority[4] and that a contract made with the officer might not be binding unless ratified by the principal.

(b) **Secret Limitations.** If the principal has clothed an agent with authority to perform certain acts but the principal gives secret instructions that limit the agent's authority, the third person is allowed to take the author-

---

[4]Weil and Associates v Urban Renewal Agency, 206 Kan 405, 479 P2d 875 (1971).

ity of the agent at its face value and is not bound by the secret limitations of which the third person has no knowledge.

§ 42:5.   Delegation of Authority by Agent.

As a general rule, an agent cannot delegate to another the authority obtained from the principal. In other words, unless the principal expressly or impliedly consents, an agent cannot appoint *subagents* to carry out the agent's duties. The reason for this rule is that since an agent is usually selected because of some personal qualifications, it would be unfair and possibly injurious to the principal if the authority to act could be shifted by the agent to another. This is particularly true when the agent was originally appointed for the performance of a task requiring discretion or judgment. For example, an agent who is appointed to adjust claims against an insurance company cannot delegate the performance of that duty to another.

FACTS:

Bucholtz made reservations through the Sirotkin Travel Agency for a three-day trip to Las Vegas. The reservations were in fact not made by the agency and Bucholtz sued the agency for damages for breach of its contract. The agency raised the defense that the mistake was the fault of another travel agency or "wholesaler" through which the agency made reservations on behalf of its client.

DECISION:

Judgment for Bucholtz. The travel agency had no authority to delegate its responsibility to another. It was immaterial whether such other was a subagent or an independent contractor. The travel agency was liable to its customer, Bucholtz, for the nonperformance that occurred, without regard as to who was at fault. [Bucholtz v Sirotkin Travel, Ltd. 343 NYS2d 438 (1973)]

Agents, however, may authorize others to perform their work for them in the following instances:

(a) When the acts to be done involve only mechanical or ministerial duties. Thus, an agent to make application for hail insurance on wheat may delegate to another the clerical act of writing the application. And it may be shown that there is customary authority for a clerk in the office of the insurance agent to sign the agent's name so as to have the effect of a signing by the agent and be binding upon the insurance company, the agent's principal.[5]

(b) When a well-known custom recognizes such appointment. To illustrate, if one is authorized to buy or sell a grain elevator, one may do so through a broker when that is the customary method.

(c) When the appointment is justified by necessity or sudden emergency and it is impractical to communicate with the principal, and the appointment of a subagent is reasonably necessary for the protection of the interests of the principal entrusted to the agent.

[5]United Bonding Insurance Co. v Banco Suizo-Panameno (CA5 Fla) 422 F2d 1142 (1970).

(**d**) When it is contemplated by the parties that subagents would be employed. For example, a bank may now generally use subagents to receive payments of notes that have been left for collection since the parties contemplate that this will be done. Also, the authority to appoint subagents can be inferred where the principal knows or has reason to know that the agent employs subagents. Thus, an agent may grant subagents power to bind a principal fire insurance company, where the agent had a long standing practice of appointing subagents and this was known to the principal.[6]

B. DUTIES AND LIABILITIES OF PRINCIPAL AND AGENT

The creation of the principal-agent relationship gives rise not only to powers but also to duties and liabilities.

§ 42:6.   Duties and Liabilities of Agent During Agency.

While the agency relationship exists, the agent owes certain duties to the principal.

(**a**) **Loyalty.** An agent must be loyal or faithful to the principal. The agent must not obtain any secret profit or benefit from the agency.[7] If the principal is seeking to buy or rent property, the agent cannot secretly obtain the property and then sell or lease it to the principal at a profit.

An agent who owns property cannot sell it to the principal without disclosing that ownership to the principal. If this is not done, the principal may avoid the contract even though the agent's conduct did not cause the principal any financial loss. Or the principal can approve the transaction and sue the agent for any secret profit obtained by the agent.

An agent cannot act as agent for both parties to a transaction unless both know of the dual capacity and agree to it. If the agent does so act without the consent of both parties, the transaction is voidable at the election of any principal who did not know of the agent's double status.

An agent must not accept secret gifts or commissions from third persons in connection with the agency. If the agent does so, the principal may sue the agent for those gifts or commissions. Such practices are condemned because the judgment of the agent may be influenced by the receipt of gifts or commissions.

It is a violation of an agent's duty of loyalty to make and retain secret profits.

An agent is, of course, prohibited from aiding the competitors of a principal or disclosing to them information relating to the business of the principal. It is also a breach of duty for the agent knowingly to deceive a principal.

---

[6]Bloom v Wolfe, 37 Colo App 407, 547 P2d 934 (1976).
[7]Johnson v First Nat'l Bank of Rome, 253 Ga 233, 319 SE2d 440 (1984).

FACTS:

Bankerd and his wife, Virginia, owned, as tenants by the entirety, a home in Maryland. They resided there until 1966, when Mrs. Bankerd moved out as a result of marital problems. Bankerd continued to live in the house until July 1968, when he "left for the west." Mrs. Bankerd thereupon resumed residency and assumed all expenses for the home. Before Bankerd's departure, he executed a power of attorney to King. The power of attorney was later updated to authorize King to sell the property "on such terms as to him seem best." In 1977 Mrs. Bankerd asked King to exercise the power of attorney and to transfer Bankerd's interest in the property to her so she could sell the property and retire. King wrote to Bankerd on three occasions at various addresses, but was unsuccessful in reaching him. King believed Bankerd "didn't give a damn" about the property and that Bankerd had abandoned his interest in the property. King therefore conveyed Bankerd's interest in the property to Mrs. Bankerd. Mrs. Bankerd paid no consideration for the transfer and King received no compensation. Later, Bankerd sued King claiming that King had breached his duty of loyalty in connection with the conveyance of the property. King defended that under the broad language of the power of attorney, he had acted within his authority.

DECISION:

Judgment for Bankerd. An agent is under a duty of loyalty to his principal and must have only his principal's purposes in mind. The language of the power of attorney did not authorize King to make a gift of the principal's property, as King contended. While the needs of Mrs. Bankerd were a serious matter, King had an obligation to act solely in Bankerd's best interests. [King v Bankerd, 303 Md 98, 492 A2d 608 (1985)]

(b) **Obedience and Performance.** An agent is under a duty to obey all lawful instructions. The agent is required to perform the services specified for the period and in the way specified. An agent who does not is liable to the principal for any harm caused. For example, if an agent is instructed to take cash payments only but accepts a check in payment, the agent is liable for the loss caused the principal when the check is dishonored by nonpayment. Likewise, when an insurance broker undertakes to obtain a policy of insurance for a principal that will provide a specified coverage but fails to obtain a policy with the proper coverage, the broker, as agent of the principal, is liable to the principal for the loss thereby caused.

If the agent violates instructions, it is immaterial that the agent acted in good faith or intended to benefit the principal. It is the fact that the agent violated the instructions and thereby caused the principal a loss which imposes a liability on the agent. In determining whether the agent has obeyed instructions, they must be interpreted in a way that a reasonable person would interpret them.

(c) **Reasonable Care.** It is the duty of an agent to act with the care that a reasonable person would exercise under the circumstances. In addition, if the agent possesses a special skill, as in the case of a broker or an attorney, the agent must exercise that skill.

(d) **Accounting.** An agent must account to the principal for all property or money belonging to the principal that comes into the agent's possession. The agent should, within a reasonable time, give notice of collections made and render an accurate account of all receipts and expenditures. The agency agreement may state at what intervals or on what dates such accountings are to be made.

An agent should keep the principal's property and money separate and distinct from that of the agent. If property of the agent is mingled with property of the principal so that the two cannot be identified or separated, the principal may claim all of the commingled mass. Furthermore, when funds of the principal and the agent are mixed, any loss that occurs must be borne by the agent.

(e) **Information.** It is the duty of an agent to keep the principal informed of all facts relating to the agency which are relevant to protecting the principal's interests.[8] In consequence, a principal's promise to pay a bonus to an agent for information secured by the agent in the course of duty is not enforceable because the principal was entitled to that information anyway. The promise of the principal is unenforceable because it is not supported by consideration.

FACTS:

Gail and Marie Sudberry contracted to purchase a parcel of real estate from Allan D. Lowke. Both parties selected the Abstract and Title Corporation of Florida (Title Company) as closing agent. The contract provided for the assumption of an existing mortgage with a 9½ per cent interest rate; and it also provided that if the lender (mortgagee) had the option to increase the interest rate upon conveyance of the realty, the buyers had the option to cancel and rescind the contract. The Title Company received the appropriate mortgage information from the lender, which indicated that the lender had the option of increasing the interest rate and would in fact increase the rate to its then current rate of 11%. The Title Company did not notify the Sudberrys of the contemplated increase, and the transaction was closed. After the closing when the Sudberrys found out about the increase in the interest rate, they sought damages from the Title Co.

DECISION:

Judgment for the Sudberrys. The increase in the interest rate was a material fact because it meant that the buyer would be paying more money. The parties to the sales transaction regarded this as important because the buyers were given the right to cancel the sales contract if the interest rate was increased. The Title Company's failure to inform the Sudberrys of

[8]Restatement, Agency 2d § 381; Owen v Shelton, 221 Va 1047, 277 SE2d 189 (1981).

the increase caused them to lose the opportunity to cancel the contract. The Title Company stood as a fiduciary with respect to the Sudberrys and had the duty of an agent to inform them of all material facts. It had not done so, and therefore it was liable for the loss caused by the increase in the interest rate. [Sudberry v Abstract and Title Corporation of Florida (Fla App) 403 So2d 1117 (1981)]

---

§ 42:7. Duties and Liabilities of
Agent after Termination of Agency.

When the agency relationship ends, the duties of the agent continue only to the extent necessary to perform prior obligations. For example, the agent must return to the former principal any property which had been entrusted to the agent for the purpose of the agency. With the exception of such "winding up" duties, the agency relationship is terminated and the former agent can deal with the principal as freely as with a stranger.

FACTS:

The United States Department of the Interior conducted a monthly lottery of oil leases on United States land. In order to take part in the lottery, it was necessary to select the land on which to bid, file various papers, and take other steps. The Central Southwest Oil Corporation was in the business of doing this work for a monthly fee on behalf of members of the general public. Edrel Clinkenbeard retained the corporation to act for him. After about a year, he won a lease which he then sold to the corporation because Tom Allen, the corporation president, told him the lease was not particularly valuable. The president knew that oil had been discovered on neighboring land, that there were producing oil wells in the vicinity, and knew the prices that had been paid for other neighboring leases. Allen did not tell any of this to Clinkenbeard and Clinkenbeard sold the oil lease to the corporation for a fraction of its true value. When Clinkenbeard learned the truth, he sued to rescind the sale of the lease. The trial court rescinded the sale on the theory that the corporation was under a fiduciary duty to Clinkenbeard at the time of the sale and had breached that duty by failing to disclose to him all information relevant to the value of the lease. The corporation appealed.

DECISION:

Judgment for Central Southwest Oil. The agency relationship between the parties was created to select federal lands on which to bid, to enter bids, and to notify the plaintiff of the results. Thus, at the moment Allen notified Clinkenbeard that he had won a lease the agency relationship terminated since all that Central had agreed to do had been done. When the parties thereafter negotiated the sale of the lease, no fiduciary duty existed since this transaction took place after the termination of the agency. While this conclusion may seem harsh in light of the fact that Clinkenbeard's subjective trust of Allen may have continued beyond, or even have been augmented by Allen's notification that he had won a lease, there is a need for definiteness in the rules governing fiduciary relationships. Such relationships impose certain duties while they exist, and it is imperative that the affected parties be able to determine the duration of an agency. [Clinkenbeard v Central Southwest Oil Corp. (CA5 Tex) 526 F2d 649 (1976)]

§ 42:8.   Enforcement of Liability of Agent.

When the agent's breach of duty causes harm to the principal, the amount of the loss may be deducted from any compensation due the agent or may be recovered in an ordinary lawsuit.

When the agent handles money for the principal, the contract of employment may provide that the amount of any shortages in the agent's account may be deducted from the compensation to which the agent would otherwise be entitled.

If the agent has made a secret profit, the principal may recover that profit from the agent. In addition, the agent may forfeit the right to all compensation, without regard to whether the principal had been benefited by some of the actions of the agent and without regard to whether the principal had actually been harmed.

§ 42:9.   Duties and Liabilities of Principal to Agent.

The principal is under certain duties to the agent. The principal must perform the contract, compensate the agent for services, make reimbursement for proper expenditures, and under certain circumstances must indemnify the agent for loss.

(a) Employment According to Terms of Contract. When the contract is for a specified time, the principal is under the obligation to permit the agent to act as such for the term of the contract, in the absence of any just cause or contract provision which permits the principal to terminate the agency sooner. If the principal gives the agent an exclusive right to act as such, the principal cannot give anyone else the authority to act as agent nor may the principal do the act to which the exclusive agent's authority relates. If the principal or another agent does so, the exclusive agent is entitled to full compensation as though the act had been performed by the exclusive agent.

(b) Compensation. The principal must pay the agent the compensation agreed upon. If the parties have not fixed the amount of the compensation by their agreement but intended that the agent should be paid, the agent may recover the customary compensation for such services. If there is no established compensation, the agent may recover the reasonable value of the services rendered.[9]

(1) Repeating Transactions. In certain industries third persons make repeated transactions with the principal. In such cases the agent who made the original contract with the third person commonly receives a certain compensation or percentage of commissions on all subsequent renewal or additional contracts. In the insurance business, for example, the insurance agent obtaining the policyholder for the insurer receives a substantial portion of the first year's premium and then receives a smaller percentage of the premiums paid by the policyholder in the following years.

Whether an agent or an agent's estate is entitled to receive compensation on repeating transactions, either after the termination of the agent's employment or after the agent's death, depends upon the terms of the agency

---

[9]Flynn v LaVay (Dist Col App) 431 A2d 543 (1981).

contract. Frequently it is provided that the right to receive compensation on repeating transactions terminates upon the termination of the agent's authority or employment by the principal.

(2) Post-Agency Transactions. An agent is not entitled to compensation in connection with transactions, such as sales or renewals of insurance policies, occurring after the termination of the agency, even though the post-agency transactions are the result of the agent's former activities. Some contracts between a principal and an agent expressly state whether the agent has the right to post-termination compensation, however.

(c) **Reimbursement.** The principal is under a duty to reimburse the agent for all disbursements made at the request of the principal and for all expenses necessarily incurred in the lawful discharge of the agency for the benefit of the principal. The agent cannot recover, however, for expenses caused by the agent's own misconduct or negligence. By way of illustration, if the agent transfers title to the wrong person, the agent cannot recover from the principal the expense incurred in correcting the error.

(d) **Indemnity.** It is the duty of the principal to indemnify the agent for any losses or damages suffered on account of the agency which were not caused by the agent's fault.

When the loss sustained is not the result of obedience to the principal's instructions but of the agent's misconduct, or of an obviously illegal act, the principal is not liable for indemnification.

SUMMARY

The scope of an agent's authority is important, since an agent acting with authority has the power to bind the principal. The scope of an agent's authority may be determined from the express words of the principal to the agent and such is called express authority. An agent has "incidental authority" to perform any act reasonably necessary to execute the express authority given the agent. An agent's authority may be implied so as to enable the agent to perform any act in accordance with the general customs or usages in the business or industry. This authority is often referred to as customary authority. An individual is cloaked with apparent authority where the principal, by words or conduct, leads a third person reasonably to believe that the individual has the authority of an agent. The effect of a proper exercise of authority by an agent is to bind the principal and third person to a contract; the agent, not being a party to the contract, is not liable in any respect under the contract. A third person dealing with a person claiming to be an agent, has a duty to ascertain the extent of the agent's authority and has a duty to take notice of any acts that are clearly adverse to the principal's interests. A third person who has knowledge of actual or apparent limitations on an agent's authority is bound by those limitations. A third person is not bound by secret limitations and may take the authority of the agent at face value.

An agent cannot appoint subagents to do the agent's duties unless (1) the duties are ministerial; (2) to do so is a well established custom in the industry in question; (3) to do so is justified by emergency conditions; or (4) it was contemplated by the parties that subagents would be employed.

While the agency relationship exists, the agent owes the principal the duties of (1) being loyal; (2) obeying all lawful instructions; (3) exercising reasonable care; (4) accounting for all property or money belonging to the principal; and (5) informing the principal of all facts relating to the agency which are relevant to the principal's interests. The duties of an agent continue after termination of the agency only to the extent necessary to perform prior obligations, such as return of the former principal's property. After termination of the agency, the agent may deal with the principal as freely as with a stranger.

The principal has certain duties to the agent, including fulfilling all terms of their employment contract, paying the agreed compensation for services of the agent, reimbursing the agent for proper expenditures, and, under certain circumstances, indemnifying the agent for losses suffered on account of the agency through no fault of the agent.

QUESTIONS AND CASE PROBLEMS

1. What social forces are affected by the rule that a third person must ascertain the extent of an agent's authority?

2. Pamela was the authorized agent of Nanette. She so informed Sydney and made a contract with him on behalf of Nanette to purchase Sydney's automobile. Thereafter Sydney failed to deliver the automobile to Nanette. Pamela sued Sydney for breach of contract. Can Pamela recover?

3. Can a person act as agent for both parties to a transaction?

4. Compare (a) secret limitations on authority of an agent with (b) apparent authority of an agent.

5. Robert gave Doris an exclusive agency to sell his house. Robert thereafter made a contract selling his house to Emmett. Later, Emmett wished to cancel the transaction. Emmett claimed that the contract is void because Robert had given Doris an exclusive agency to sell the house and therefore could not sell the house himself. Is Emmett correct?

6. Vivian retains Russell to sell her car for the best price obtainable. Without informing Vivian that he is so doing, Russell purchases the car in the name of his brother. When Vivian learns of this, she sues to avoid the sale. Russell defends by proving that the car was purchased for its fair value and that a higher price could not have been obtained. Should this evidence be admitted?

7. After an agency has been terminated, the agent is not entitled to further compensation. Appraise this statement.

8. Martha Christiansen owns women's apparel stores bearing her name in New Seabury, Massachusetts; Lake Placid, New York; Palm Beach, Florida; and Palm Springs, California. At a meeting with her four store managers she discussed styles she thought appropriate for the forthcoming season; advised them as always to use their best judgment in the goods they purchased for each of their respective stores; and cautioned "but no blue jeans." Later Jane Farley, the manager of the Lake Placid store, purchased a line of high quality blue denim outfits (designer jeans with jacket and vest options) from Women's Wear, Inc. for the summer

season. The outfits did not sell. Martha refused to pay for them, contending that she told all of her managers "no blue jeans," and that if it comes to a lawsuit, she would fly in three managers to testify that Jane Farley had absolutely no authority to purchase denim outfits and was, in fact, expressly forbidden to do so. Women's Wear sued Martha, and the three managers testified for Martha. Is the fact that Martha had explicitly forbidden Farley to purchase the outfits in question sufficient to relieve her from liability for the purchases made by Farley?

9. The Taylors were depositors of the Equitable Trust Company of Maryland. Equitable issued them a treasurer's check for $20,000. Mr. Vittetoe, a loan officer of the bank, received a long-distance telephone call from a person who identified himself as Mr. Taylor and requested that the $20,000 represented by the treasurer's check be transferred to the account of Jody Associates at Irving Trust Company in New York. Mr. Vittetoe did not know Mr. Taylor personally and replied that written instructions from Taylor would be required. Some time later, Frank Terranova appeared at the bank and stated that he was Taylor's agent, surrendered the treasurer's check which had not been indorsed, and requested that the money represented thereby be transferred to the account of Jody Associates in the Irving Trust Company. Terranova also presented a letter which he had signed in his own name, addressed to Mr. Vittetoe, in which was repeated the request to transfer the $20,000. Equitable verified Mr. Terranova's signature by checking his driver's license and a major credit card and thereafter made the transfer as requested. Taylor denied that Terranova had the authority to request such transfer and sued Equitable for damages. The bank contends that it was entitled to reply on the written instructions submitted to the bank by Terranova. Decide.

10. Regional Broadcasters of Michigan, Inc. owned and operated radio station WTRU. Moreschini supplied advertising material to WTRU under contract made with the station manager. When Moreschini sued Regional Broadcasters, it raised the defense that the manager had been instructed not to make any contracts on behalf of the station. Was Regional bound? [Moreschini v Regional Broadcasters, 373 Mich 496, 129 NW2d 859]

11. Hihn and Eastland, doing business in California, were authorized to sell certain land in Texas. They in turn employed Maney, of Texas, to sell the land. He made the sale and then sued them for the commissions due him on the sale. Did Hihn and Eastland have authority to employ Maney to make the sale? [Eastland v Maney, 36 Tex Civ App 147, 81 SW 574]

12. McKinney requested E. M. Christmas, a real estate broker, to sell McKinney's property. A sale to a purchaser was effected with the contract calling for monthly installment payments by the purchaser, which payments were to be collected by the broker. When the purchaser stopped making the payments, McKinney was not notified of that fact but one of the broker's employees bought out the purchaser's contract. The broker continued making payments to McKinney as though they were being made by the purchaser. Later Christmas, the broker, resold the land to another buyer at a substantial profit. McKinney sued

Christmas for this profit. Decide. [McKinney v Christmas, 143 Colo 361, 353 P2d 373]

13. Wiles ran a taxi business. Mullinax, an insurance broker, agreed to obtain and keep Wiles continuously covered with workers' compensation insurance. This was done for a number of years, with Mullinax renewing the policy whenever it expired. The insurance company which had issued the policy to Wiles canceled it, and Mullinax attempted to obtain a policy from other companies. He was unable to do so but did not inform Wiles of his difficulties nor of the fact that Wiles was not covered by insurance. An employee of Wiles was killed, and a workers' compensation claim for his death was successfully made. Wiles then learned for the first time that there was no insurance to cover his claim. Wiles sued Mullinax for the amount of the workers' compensation claim. Decide. [Wiles v Mullinax, 267 NC 392, 148 SE2d 229]

14. An attorney received a check payable to the order of the attorney's client. The attorney indorsed the client's name and cashed the check at the bank on which it was drawn. The client then sued the bank for the amount which had been paid the attorney. The bank raised the defense that the attorney had authority to sign for the client and to receive payment on the client's behalf. Was this a valid defense? [Aetna Casualty & Surety Co. v Traders Nat. Bank & Trust Co. (Mo App) 514 SW2d 860]

15. Kribbs owned real estate that had been rented through his agent, Jackson, at a monthly rental of $275. When this lease terminated, Jackson and a third person, Solomon, made an agreement that if the latter obtained a new tenant for a rental of $500 a month, Jackson would pay Solomon $100 a month. The latter obtained a new tenant who paid a monthly rental of $550. Jackson continued to send Kribbs $275 a month, less his commissions and janitor and utility costs; paid Solomon $100 a month; and kept the balance of the rental for himself. When Kribbs learned of these facts three years later, he sued Jackson for the money he had kept for himself and that which he had paid Solomon. Jackson defended that Kribbs accepted and was satisfied with the $275 per month; and that the additional funds were the sole result of Jackson's own entrepreneurship, which funds should accrue solely to Jackson's benefit. Decide. [Kribbs v Jackson, 387 Pa 611, 129 A2d 490]

16. DSG is in the government food service contracting business. Fredrick Anderson was employed by DSG to survey contracts in preparation for bids. Edward Mitura served as manager of DSG's Fort Riley, Kansas, contract. In early November 1982, the food service contract at Fort Campbell, Kentucky, became available for bidding. On November 8, Anderson and Mitura toured the Fort Campbell facility with other prospective bidders, and Mitura informed Anderson of his intention to bid personally on the contract. Anderson hired an accountant Larry Golden concerning the cost per hour to be utilized in a bid and it was determined to be $7.78. Anderson provided Mitura with this figure and Mitura paid Golden's bill. On November 16, DSG submitted a bid. DSG was not notified by Anderson that Mitura was going to submit a bid. On November 22, Mitura, through his wife, submitted a bid. On November 23, Mitura notified DSG that he had submitted a bid on the Fort

Campbell contract and quit his job. On November 24, the bids were opened and Mitura's bid turned out to be the lowest. On December 12, Anderson resigned from DSG to work with Mitura; and the Fort Campbell contract was subsequently awarded to Mitura. DSG sued Mitura and Anderson for breach of their fiduciary duty to DSG by competing with it while employed by DSG. Mitura and Anderson contend that they were free to compete with their former employer once their employment relationship was terminated. They point out that their contract at Fort Campbell did not start until well after both had terminated their work for DSG. Decide. [DSG Corp v Anderson (CA6 Ky) 754 F2d 678]

CHAPTER 43

THIRD PERSONS IN

AGENCY

CHAPTER OBJECTIVES

After studying this chapter you will be able to:

1. Describe how to execute a contract as an agent on behalf of a principal.
2. Recognize when an agent will have personal liability to a third person on a contract.
3. Describe the effect of a payment made by a third person to an authorized agent.
4. Explain and illustrate the doctrine of *respondeat superior*.
5. Contrast the liability of an owner for a tort committed by an independent contractor with the liability of an employer for a tort committed by an employee.
6. Differentiate between the authority of a soliciting agent and a contracting agent.

In agency transactions, the third person has certain rights and liabilities with respect to the agent and the principal. Many of these rights and liabilities are contractual in nature. However, the agency transaction can also produce tort and criminal liability for the agent, and under certain circumstances for the principal as well.

A. LIABILITY OF AGENT TO THIRD PERSON

The liability of the agent to the third person depends upon the manner in which the transaction was conducted and the nature of the agent's acts.

718

§ 43:1.   Action of
Authorized Agent of Disclosed Principal.

If an agent makes a contract with a third person on behalf of a disclosed principal and has proper authority to do so and if the contract is executed properly, the agent has no personal liability on the contract. Whether the principal performs the contract or not, the agent cannot be held liable by the third party. Thus an insurance agency arranging for the insuring of a customer with a named company is not liable on the policy which the company issues to the insured. If the agent lacks authority, however, or if certain other circumstances exist, the agent may be liable.

In speaking of an agent's action as authorized or unauthorized, it must be remembered that "authorized" includes action which though originally unauthorized was subsequently ratified by the principal.[1] Once there is an effective ratification, the original action of the agent is no longer treated as unauthorized.

§ 43:2.   Unauthorized Action.

If a person makes a contract as agent for another but lacks authority to do so, the contract does not bind the principal. When a person purports to act as agent for a principal, an implied warranty arises that such person has authority to do so.[2] If the agent lacks authority there is a breach of this warranty and if the agent's act causes loss to the third person, that third person may generally hold the agent liable for the loss. It is no defense for the agent in such case that the agent acted in good faith or misunderstood the scope of authority. The purported agent is not liable for conduct in excess of authority when the third person knows that the agent is acting beyond the authority given by the principal.

FACTS:

Craig Industries Inc. was in the business of manufacturing charcoal at its two plants. D. C. Craig, the corporation's president, contracted in the name of the corporation to sell the two plants to Husky Industries. Craig did not have authority from the board of directors to make the contract, and later the board of directors voted not to accept the contract. Husky Industries sued D. C. Craig on the theory that he, as agent for the corporation, exceeded his authority and should be held personally liable for damages.

DECISION:

Judgment for Husky Industries. An agent who purports to contract in the name of a principal without or in excess of authority to do so is personally liable to the other contracting party for the agent's breach of implied warranty of authority. This liability is implied unless the agent manifests that no warranty of authority is made, or the other contracting party knows the agent is not authorized. There was no discussion by the contracting parties concerning a limitation of D. C. Craig's warranty of authority to contract for the corporation and Husky Industries was not aware that D. C. Craig was not authorized to make the contract. [Husky Industries v Craig, (Mo App) 618 SW2d 458 (1981)]

---

[1]Benner v Farm Bureau Mut. Ins. Co. 96 Idaho 311, 528 P2d 193 (1974).
[2]Moore v Lewis, 51 Ill 3d 388, 366 NE2d 594 (1977).

An agent with a written authorization may avoid liability on the implied warranty of authority by showing the written authorization to the third person and permitting the third person to determine the scope of the agent's authority.

§ 43:3.   No Principal with Capacity.

A person purporting to act as agent impliedly warrants that there is an existing principal and that the principal has legal capacity. If there is no principal or if the principal lacks capacity, the person acting as an agent is liable for any loss caused the third person.

The agent can avoid liability on the implied warranty of the existence of a principal with capacity by making known to the third person all material, pertinent facts or by obtaining the agreement of the third person that the agent shall not be liable.

§ 43:4.   Disclosure of Principal.

There are three degrees to which the existence and identity of the principal may be disclosed or not disclosed. An agent's liability as a party to a contract with a third person is affected by the degree of disclosure.

(a) **Disclosed Principal.** When the agent makes known the identity of the principal and the fact that the agent is acting on behalf of that principal, the principal is called a **disclosed principal.** The third person dealing with an agent of a disclosed principal ordinarily intends to make a contract with the principal and not with the agent. Consequently the agent is not a party to and is not bound by the contract which is made.[3]

(b) **Partially Disclosed Principal.** When the agent makes known the existence of an unknown principal but not the principal's identity, the principal is a **partially disclosed principal.** As the third party does not know the identity of the principal, the third person is making the contract with the agent and the agent is therefore a party to the contract.

FACTS:

Joel Patterson and his wife were the sole shareholders of "VVFM, Inc." which owned two stores, "Village Variety Food Mart" and "Village Variety." Patterson informed the salesman from Detroit Pure Milk, who delivered dairy products to the stores, that the stores were owned by a corporation, but did not tell him the name of the corporation. None of the checks used to pay Detroit Milk were in the name of VVFM, Inc., nor did either store have a sign indicating ownership by VVFM, Inc. Detroit Milk sued Patterson for $13,316.29 which was owed for dairy products delivered to the stores. Patterson argued that he was not personally liable; rather the corporation which owned the stores was liable.

DECISION:

Judgment for Detroit Milk. In contracting for dairy products Patterson was acting as an agent for the corporation. While he did inform the salesman that there was a corporation,

[3]Thilman & Co. v Esposito, 87 Ill App 3d 289, 42 Ill Dec 305, 408 NE2d 1014 (1980).

he did not give him the name of the corporation. Patterson was thus an agent for a partially disclosed principal and was a party to and person-

ally liable on the contract. [Detroit Pure Milk Co. v Patterson, 138 Mich App 475, 360 NW2d 221 (1984)]

(c) **Undisclosed Principal.** When the third person is not told or does not know that the agent is acting as an agent for anyone else, the unknown principal is called an **undisclosed principal.**[4] In such case, the third person is making the contract with the agent and the agent is a party to that contract. For example, an agent selling the goods of an undisclosed principal is the "seller" in the sales contract and is liable for breach of the implied warranty of title if the principal in fact was not the owner of the goods sold by the agent.

§ 43:5. Wrongful Receipt of Money.

If an agent obtains a payment of money from the third person by use of illegal methods, the agent is liable to the third person.

If the third person makes an overpayment to the agent or a payment when none is due, the agent is also usually liable to the third person for the amount of such overpayment or payment. If the agent has acted in good faith and does not know that the payment was improperly made, however, the agent is liable to the third person only so long as the agent has possession or control of the overpayment. If the agent has remitted the overpayment to the principal before its return is demanded by the third person, the agent is not liable to the third person. In the latter case, the third person's right of action, if one exists, is only against the principal. But payment to the principal does not relieve the agent of liability when the agent knows that the payment was not proper.

§ 43:6. Assumption of Liability.

Agents may intentionally make themselves liable upon contracts with third persons.[5] This situation frequently occurs when the agent is a well-established local brokerage house or other agency and the principal is located out of town and is not known locally.

In some situations, the agent will make a contract which will be personally binding. If the principal is not disclosed, the agent is necessarily the other contracting party and is bound by the contract. Even when the principal is disclosed, the agent may be personally bound if it was the intention of the parties that the agent was assuming a personal obligation, even though this was done in order to further the business of the principal.

§ 43:7. Execution of Contract.

A simple contract that would appear to be the contract of the agent only can be shown by oral testimony, if believed, to have been intended as a

---

[4]Maxwill's Elec. Inc. v Hegeman-Harris Co. of Canada, 18 Wash App 358, 567 P2d 1149 (1977).
[5]Forbes Homes Inc. v Trimpi (NC App) 320 SE2d 328 (1984).

contract between the principal and the third party. If the intention is established, it will be permitted to contradict the face of the written contract, and the contract as thus modified will be enforced.

FACTS:

During the early morning hours of January 10, 1981, Beverly Baumann accompanied her mother to Memorial Hospital, where her mother was placed in intensive care for heart problems. Baumann was approached by a nurse and signed various documents, including one which authorized the hospital to release medical information and to receive directly the mother's insurance benefits. This form stated, "I understand I am financially responsible to the hospital for charges not covered by this authorization." Baumann's mother died during the course of her hospitalization. Thereafter, the hospital sued Baumann to recover $19,013.42 in unpaid hospital charges based upon the form signed by her which the hospital called a "guarantee of payment." Baumann contended that she signed the document as an agent for her mother and was thus not personally liable.

DECISION:

Judgment for Baumann. She acted as an agent for a disclosed principal, her mother. Unless the contract is clear to the contrary, an agent has no personal liability on a contract executed for a disclosed principal. [Memorial Hospital v Baumann, 475 NYS2d 636 (1984)]

To avoid any question of interpretation, James Craig, an agent for B. G. Gray, should execute an instrument by signing either "*B. G. Gray, by James Craig,*" that is, "*Principal, by Agent*" or "*B. G. Gray, per James Craig,*" that is, "*Principal, per Agent.*" Such a signing is in law a signing by *Gray,* and the agent is therefore not a party to the contract.[6] The signing of the principal's name by an authorized agent without indicating the agent's name or identity is likewise in law the signature of the principal.

If the instrument is ambiguous as to whether the agent has signed in a representative or an individual capacity, parol evidence is admissible, as between the original parties to the transaction, to establish the character in which the agent was acting. If the body of the contract states an obligation that clearly refers only to the principal, the agent is not bound by the contract even though it is signed in the agent's individual name without indicating any agency.

If an agent executes a sealed instrument in those states in which a seal retains its common-law force and does so without disclosing the agency or the principal's identity, the agent is bound and cannot show that the

[6]Barnes v Sadler, 95 NMex 334, 622 P2d 239 (1981).

parties did not intend this result.[7] Because of the formal character of the writing, the liability of the parties is determined from the face of the instrument alone and it cannot be modified or contradicted by proof of matters not set forth in the writing.

§ 43:8.   Failure to Obtain Commitment of Principal.

In some situations, the agent is in effect an intermediary or go-between who has the duty to the third person to see to it that the principal is bound to the third person. For example, when an agent of an insurance company who has authority to write policies of insurance tells a policyholder whose fire policy has been canceled that the agent will look into the matter and that the insured should forget about it unless notified by the agent, the latter is under an obligation to make reasonable efforts to obtain the reinstatement of the policy or to notify the insured that it was not possible to do so. The agent is liable to the insured for the latter's fire loss if the agent does not obtain the reinstatement of the policy and fails to so inform the insured.

§ 43:9.   Torts and Crimes.

Agents are liable for harm caused third persons by the agent's fraudulent, intentional, or negligent acts. The fact that they were acting as agents at the time or that they had acted in good faith under the directions of a principal does not relieve them of liability if their conduct would impose liability upon them were they acting for themselves. With respect to liability for torts and crimes, no distinction is made as to whether the person causing harm is an agent or an employee.

FACTS:

Ralls was an employee of the Arkansas State Highway Department. While repairing a state highway he negligently backed a state truck onto the highway, causing a collision with Mittlesteadt's car. Mittlesteadt sued Ralls. He raised the defense that as he was acting on behalf of the state, he was not liable for his negligence.

DECISION:

The fact that an employee or agent is acting on behalf of someone else does not excuse or exonerate the agent or employee from liability for torts committed by the agent or employee. Ralls was therefore liable for his negligence even though it occurred within the scope of his employment by the state. [Ralls v Mittlesteadt, 268 Ark 471, 596 SW2d 349 (1980)]

If an agent commits a crime, such as stealing from the third person or shooting the third person, the agent is liable for the crime without regard to the fact of acting as an agent, and without regard to whether the agent acted in self-interest or sought to advance the interest of the principal.

[7]Tooke v Thom (Fla App) 281 So2d 34 (1973). As to the signing of commercial paper by an agent, see § 30:7(a) of this book.

B. LIABILITY OF THIRD PERSON TO AGENT

A third party may be liable to the agent because of the manner in which the transaction was conducted or because of acts causing harm to the agent.

§ 43:10.   Action of Authorized Agent of Disclosed Principal.

Ordinarily the third person is not liable to the agent for a breach of contract that the agent has made with the third person on behalf of a disclosed principal. In certain instances, however, the third person may be liable to the agent.

§ 43:11.   Undisclosed and Partially Dis closed Principal.

If the agent executed the contract without informing the third person or without the third party's knowing both of the existence of the agency and the identity of the principal, the agent may sue the third party for breach of contract.

In such instances, if the contract is a simple contract, the principal may also sue the third person even though the third person thought the contract was only with the agent. In states in which the seal has lost its common-law significance, this same rule is applied to sealed contracts. In all such cases, the right of the principal to sue the third person is superior to the agent's right to do so.

In contrast with the foregoing, if the contract is a commercial paper or a sealed contract in a state which gives the seal its common-law force, the undisclosed principal, not appearing on the instrument as a party, may not bring an action to enforce the contract.

§ 43:12.   Agent Intending to Be Bound.

If the third person knew that the agent was acting as an agent but nevertheless the parties intended that the agent should be personally bound by the contract, the agent may sue the third person for breach of contract.

§ 43:13.   Execution of Contract.

The principles that determine when an agent is liable to the third person because of the way in which a written contract was executed apply equally in determining when the third person is liable to the agent because of the way in which the contract is executed. If the agent could be sued by the third person, the third person can be sued by the agent. Thus, if the agent executes a sealed instrument in the agent's own name, only the agent can sue the third person on that instrument in a common-law state. The same rule applies if the contract is in the form of a commercial paper.

§ 43:14.   Agent as Transferee.

The agent may sue the third person for breach of the latter's obligation to the principal when the principal has assigned or otherwise transferred a claim or right to the agent, whether absolutely for the agent's own benefit or for the purpose of collecting the money and remitting it to the principal.

C. LIABILITY OF PRINCIPAL TO THIRD PERSON

The principal is liable to the third person for the properly authorized and executed contracts of the agent and, in certain circumstances, for the agent's unauthorized contracts.

§ 43:15. Agent's Contracts.

The liability of a principal to a third person on a contract made by an agent depends upon the extent of disclosure of the principal and the form of the contract that is executed.

(a) Simple Contract Where Principal Disclosed. When a disclosed principal with contractual capacity authorizes or ratifies an agent's transaction with a third person, and when the agent properly executes a contract with the third person as an agency transaction, a binding contract exists between the principal and the third person. The principal and the third person may each sue the other in the event of a breach of the contract. The agent is not a party to the contract and is not liable for its performance and cannot sue for its breach.[8]

The liability of a disclosed principal to a third person is not discharged by the fact that the principal gives the agent money with which to pay the third person. Consequently, the liability of a buyer for the purchase price of goods is not terminated by the fact that the buyer paid the buyer's agent the purchase price to remit to the seller.

(b) Simple Contract Where Principal Undisclosed. An undisclosed principal is liable for a simple contract made by an authorized agent. While the third person initially contracted with the agent alone, the third person upon learning of the existence of the undisclosed principal, may sue that principal. However, the right to sue the undisclosed principal on a simple contract is subject to two limitations. The third person cannot sue the principal if in good faith the principal has settled the account with the agent with respect to the contract. Some states refuse to apply this limitation, however, unless the third person has led the principal to reasonably believe that the account between the agent and the third person has been settled. Also, the third person cannot sue the principal when satisfaction of the claim has already been obtained from the agent.

(c) Simple Contract Where Principal Partially Disclosed. A partially disclosed principal is liable for a simple contract made by an authorized agent. The right of the third person is concurrent as against either the agent or the principal.[9]

---

[8]Eppler, Guerin & Turner, Inc. v Kasmir (Tex Civ App) 685 SW2d 737 (1985).
[9]James C. Smith & Associates, Inc. v Everett, 1 Ohio App 3d 118, 439 NE2d 932 (1981).

(d) Contract under Seal and Commercial Paper. If a contract is under seal in a state which preserves its common-law force, an undisclosed principal cannot sue or be sued. In a state in which the seal no longer has its common-law force, the fact that the contract made by the agent is under seal does not prohibit the third person from suing the undisclosed principal.[10]

An undisclosed principal whose name or description does not appear on commercial paper is not liable as a party thereto.[11] Thus, an undisclosed principal is not liable on commercial paper executed by an agent in the agent's own name.

§ 43:16. Payment to Agent.

When the third person makes payment to an authorized agent, such payment is deemed made to the principal. The principal must give the third person full credit for the payment made to the agent, even though in fact the agent never remits or delivers the payment to the principal, as long as the third person made the payment in good faith and had no reason to know that the agent would be guilty of misconduct.[12]

As apparent authority has the same legal consequence as actual authority, a payment made to a person with apparent authority to receive the payment is deemed a payment to the apparent principal. When payment by a debtor is made to a person who is not the actual or apparent agent of the creditor, such payment does not discharge the debt unless that person in fact pays the money over to the creditor.

FACTS:

E. I. duPont de Nemours & Co. licensed Enjay Chemical Company, now Exxon, and Johnson & Johnson, to use certain chemical processes, in return for which royalty payments by check were to be made to duPont. By agreement between the companies, the royalty payments to be made to duPont were to be made by check sent to a specified duPont employee, C.H.D., in its Control Division. These checks were sent during the next 9 years. C.H.D. altered some of them so that he was named thereon as the payee and then cashed them and used the money for his own purposes. Liberty Mutual Insurance Company, which insured the fidelity of duPont's employees, and duPont sued Enjay and Johnson & Johnson on the basis that they still owed the money represented by the checks which C.H.D. had converted.

DECISION:

Judgment for Enjay and Johnson & Johnson. Payment to an authorized agent has the legal effect of payment to the principal regardless of whether the agent thereafter remits the payment to the principal or embezzles it. C.H.D. was the agent authorized to receive the royalty checks. Therefore the defendants had effectively paid the royalties when they sent C.H.D. the checks. His misconduct thereafter did not revive the debts which were paid by sending him the checks. [Liberty Mutual Insurance Co. v Enjay Chemical Co. (now Exxon) (Del Super) 316 A2d 219 (1974)]

---

[10]Nalbandian v Hanson Restaurant & Lounge, Inc. 369 Mass 150, 338 NE2d 335 (1975).

[11]UCC §§ 3–401, 3–403.

[12]This general rule of law is restated in some states by § 2 of the Uniform Fiduciaries Act, which is expressly extended by § 1 thereof to agents, partners, and corporate offficers. Similar statutory provisions are found in a number of other states.

§ 43:17.   Agent's Statements.

A principal is bound by a statement made by an agent while transacting business within the scope of authority. This means that the principal cannot thereafter contradict the statement of the agent and show that it is not true. Statements or declarations of an agent, in order to bind the principal, must be made at the time of performing the act to which they relate or shortly thereafter.

§ 43:18.   Agent's Knowledge.

The principal is bound by knowledge or notice of any fact that is acquired by an agent while acting within the scope of actual or apparent authority.[13]

FACTS:
Trahan, who was in prison on a narcotics charge, wished to apply for a funeral expense insurance policy. His father communicated with an agent of the First National Life Insurance Co. The father signed the application, and the agent falsely acknowledged on the application that Trahan had signed it in his presence. Trahan was killed in prison. When the Miguez Funeral Home sought payment on the policy, the insurer refused to pay on the ground that it had not been signed by Trahan.

DECISION:
The insurance agent was the agent of the insurance company. The agent knew the facts, and the insurer was charged with the knowledge of its agent. The insurance company, therefore, was estopped from denying that the application had been signed by Trahan as its agent had stated. [Adam Miguez Funeral Home v First National Life Insurance Co. (LaApp) 234 So2d 496 (1970)]

Conversely, if the subject matter is outside the scope of the agent's authority, the agent is under no duty to inform the principal of the knowledge and the principal is not bound thereby. For example, when the agent is authorized and employed only to collect rents, the agent's knowledge of the dangerous condition of the premises is not imputed to the landlord-principal, as the reporting of such information is not part of the agent's collection duties. When a commercial paper is indorsed to the principal and the agent acting for the principal has a knowledge of a matter which would be a defense to the paper, such knowledge of the agent is imputed to the principal and bars the principal from being a holder in due course. When a fact is known to the agent of the seller, the sale is deemed made by the seller with knowledge of that fact. For example, where the agent recommending and selling weed eradicator to the buyer knew that it would be used in a drainage ditch in the Mississippi River delta, a warranty of fitness for that particular purpose arose because the seller was deemed to know what the agent knew. Likewise, when an employee knows that there has been a pollution of water

---

[13]Baldinger Baking Co. v Stepan (Minn App) 354 NW2d 569 (1984).

contrary to law, such knowledge is imputed to the corporate employer, even though no officer or director had in fact any knowledge thereof.[14]

The rule that the agent's knowledge is imputed to the principal is extended in some cases to knowledge gained prior to the creation of the agency relationship. The notice and knowledge in any case must be based on reliable information. Thus, when the agent hears only rumors, the principal is not charged with notice.

(a) **Exceptions.** The principal is not charged with knowledge of an agent under the following circumstances: (1) when the agent is under a duty to another person to conceal such knowledge; (2) when the agent is acting adversely to the principal's interest; or (3) when the third party acts in collusion with the agent for the purpose of cheating the principal. In such cases, it is not likely that the agent would communicate knowledge to the principal. The principal is therefore not bound by the knowledge of the agent.

(b) **Communication to Principal.** As a consequence of regarding the principal as possessing the knowledge of the agent, when the law requires that a third person communicate with the principal, that duty may be satisfied by communicating with the agent. Thus, an offeree effectively communicates the acceptance of an offer to the offeror when the offeree makes such communication to the offeror's agent, and an offeror effectively communicates the revocation of an offer to the offeree by communicating the revocation to the offeree's agent.

D. LIABILITY OF PRINCIPAL FOR TORTS AND CRIMES OF AGENT

Under certain circumstances the principal may be liable to the third person for the torts or crimes of the agent or employee.

§ 43:19. Vicarious Liability for Torts and Crimes.

Assume that an agent or an employee causes harm to a third person. Is the principal or employer liable for this conduct? If the conduct constitutes a crime, can the principal or employer be criminally prosecuted? The answer is that in many instances the principal or employer is liable civilly and may be prosecuted criminally. That is, the principal or employer is liable although personally free from fault and not guilty of any wrong. This concept of imposing liability for the fault of another is known as **vicarious liability.**

The situation arises both when an employer has an employee and a principal has an agent who commits the wrong. The rules of law governing the vicarious liability of the principal and the employer are the same. In the interest of simplicity, this section will be stated in terms of employees acting in the course of employment. It is to be remembered that these rules are equally applicable to agents acting within the scope of their authority. As a practical matter, some situations will only arise with agents. For example, the vicarious liability of a seller for the misrepresentations made by a salesperson will only arise when the seller appointed an agent to sell. In contrast, both

---

[14]Apex Oil Co. v United States (CA8 Mo) 530 F2d 1291 (1976).

the employee hired to drive a truck and the agent being sent to visit a customer could negligently run over a third person. In many situations, a person employed by another is both an employee and an agent and the tort is committed within the phase of "employee" work.

The rule of law imposing vicarious liability upon an innocent employer for the wrong of an employee is also known as the doctrine of **respondeat superior.** In modern times, this doctrine can be justified on the ground that the business should pay for the harm caused in the doing of the business, that the employer will be more careful in the selection of employees if made responsible for their actions, and that the employer may readily obtain liability insurance to protect against claims of third persons.

(a) **Nature of Act.** The wrongful act committed by the employee may be a negligent act, an intentional act, a fraudulent act, or a violation of a governmental regulation. It may give rise only to civil liability of the employer or it may also subject the employer to prosecution for crime.

(1) Negligent Act. Historically, the act for which liability would be imposed under the doctrine of respondeat superior was a negligent act committed within the scope of employment.

(2) Intentional Act. Under the common law, a master was not liable for an intentional tort committed by a servant. The modern law holds that an employer is liable for an intertional tort committed by an employee for the purpose of furthering the employer's business.[15] Thus an employer is not liable for an intentional, unprovoked assault committed by an employee upon a third person or customer of the employer because of a personal grudge or for no reason, but the employer will be held liable by the modern view when the employee's assault was committed in the belief that the employee was thereby advancing the employer's interest.[16] For example, when an employee is hired to retake property, as in the case of an employee of a finance company hired to repossess automobiles on which installments have not been paid, the employer is generally liable for the unlawful force used by the employee in retaking the property or in committing an assault upon a debtor.

(3) Fraud. The modern decisions hold the employer liable for fraudulent acts or misrepresentations. The rule is commonly applied to a principal-agent relationship. To illustrate, when an agent makes fraudulent statements in selling stock, the principal is liable for the buyer's loss. In states which follow the common-law rule of no liability for intentional torts, the principal is not liable for the agent's fraud when the principal did not authorize or know of the fraud of the agent.

(4) Governmental Regulation. The principal may be liable because of the agent's violation of a governmental regulation. Such regulations are most common in the areas of business and of protection of the environment. In such case, the employer may be held liable for a penalty imposed by the government. In some cases, the breach of the regulation will impose liability

---

[15]Bourk v Iseman Mobile Homes (SD) 316 NW2d 343 (1982).

[16]Restatement, 2d Agency § 231; Bremen State Bank v Hartford Accident & Indemnity Co. (CA7 Ill) 427 F2d 425 (1970). Some courts follow the older rule that the employer is never liable for a willful or malicious act by an employee regardless of its purpose.

upon the principal in favor of a third person who is injured in consequence of the violation.

(b) **Scope of Employment.** The mere fact that a tort or crime is committed by an employee does not necessarily impose vicarious liability upon the employer. It must also be shown that the employee was acting within the scope of the authority if an agent, or of the course of employment if an employee. If the agent or employee was not so acting, there is no vicarious liability.

FACTS:

Sanford Prudden was employed by Golden West Broadcasters, Inc. owners of Los Angeles television station KTLA. On Saturday, March 8, 1974, he was assigned to "remote" work at Palm Springs, California, as Senior Stage Supervisor, and was responsible to set up cameras and supporting equipment for telecast of a California Angels spring training baseball game scheduled for Sunday, March 9, 1974. While at Palm Springs, in addition to his regular hourly wages he was paid a "per diem" by Golden West and these funds could be spent as the employee saw fit. He worked from 7:00 A.M. to 3:30 P.M. on Saturday. That evening he chose to go to the bar at the Gene Autry Hotel. He drove himself and other employees to this establishment in a station wagon supplied him by Golden West. During the several hours at the bar Prudden spent some time with his former wife, Barbara Matson. Dean Ball, a patron of the bar, objected to Prudden's treatment of Barbara Matson. Ball invited Prudden outside, where a fight ensued and Ball was injured. After the fight Prudden was observed driving away from the scene in a station wagon with a KTLA inscription painted on its side. Ball sued Golden West for damages on the theory of *respondeat superior*, claiming that Prudden was acting in the scope of his employment at the time of the fight.

DECISION:

Judgment for Golden West. At the time of the fight, Prudden, an hourly employee, was not at work or being paid by his employer, and was not under his employer's control. The law extends an employer's liability to situations beyond actual control over an employee to include risks inherent in or created by the employer. However, the contention that there is an employer created risk in the nature of a stage supervisor's job that such an employee while off duty would get into a fight and injure a member of the public is untenable and would impose the liability of an insurer on the employer for every willful tortious act of an employee committed while off duty. [Golden West Broadcasters v Ball, 114 Cal App 3d 947, 171 Cal Rptr 95 (1981)]

(c) **Employee of the United States.** The Federal Tort Claims Act declares that the United States shall be liable vicariously whenever a federal employee driving a motor vehicle in the course of employment causes harm under such circumstances that a private employer would be liable. Contrary to the general rule, the statute exempts the employee driver from liability.

§ 43:20.   Other Theories of Liability.

If an employee is not acting within the course of employment, the employer cannot be held liable on the theory of respondeat superior. This does not mean, however, that the employer will necessarily not be liable. In some cases, the employer will be liable without regard to the nature of the act or whether the employee was acting in the course of employment. For example, the employer may be held liable as a bailor for lending an automobile to a bailee-employee.

An employer is liable for the tortious and criminal consequences of acts expressly authorized. For example, if the employer instructs an employee to highjack a competitor's truck, the employer is both civilly and criminally liable without giving any consideration to the question of whether such activity was within the course of employment of the employee. An employer is also liable upon giving defective equipment to an employee when the defect causes harm or upon giving control of proper equipment to an unfit employee when, because of the latter's lack of qualifications, harm is caused a third person.

§ 43:21.   Agent's Crimes.

The principal is liable for the crimes of the agent committed at the principal's direction. When not authorized, however, the principal is ordinarily not liable for the crime of an agent merely because it was committed while otherwise acting within the scope of the latter's authority or employment.

Some states impose liability on the principal when the agent has in the course of employment violated liquor sales laws, pure food laws, or laws regulating prices or prohibiting false weights. Thus, by some courts, a principal may be held criminally responsible for the sale by an agent of liquor to a minor in violation of the liquor law, even though the sale was not known to the principal and violated instructions given to the agent.

§ 43:22.   Owner's Liability for
Acts of an Independent Contractor.

If the work is done by an independent contractor rather than by an employee, the owner is not liable for harm caused by the contractor to third persons or their property nor is the owner bound by the contracts made by the independent contractor. Likewise, the owner is ordinarily not liable for harm caused third persons by the negligence of the employees of the independent contractor.

(a) **Exceptions to Owner's Immunity.** There is, however, a trend toward imposing liability on the owner when the work undertaken by the independent contractor is inherently dangerous. That is, the law is taking the position that if the owner wishes to engage in a particular activity, the owner must be responsible for the harm it causes and cannot be insulated from such liability by the device of hiring an independent contractor to do the work.

In such cases, the courts regard the activity as having such a high potential of harm that the owner is not permitted to delegate to another the duty to protect the public from harm.

FACTS:

General Motors Corporation (GM) contracted with J.S. Alberici Construction Company, an independent contractor, for the construction of an additon to GM's plant on GM's premises. James Donovan was an employee of Alberici. Donovan was working on the unfinished roof of the addition when a plywood panel gave way under him and he fell approximately 28 feet. Donovan sued GM for damages for the injuries suffered from the fall, claiming that GM was liable under the "inherent danger" doctrine. GM contended that ordinary construction work is not inherently dangerous.

DECISION:

Judgment for Donovan. Under the inherent danger doctrine, one contracting with an independent contractor is liable for any harm resulting from the activity if the specific work contracted for is inherently dangerous. The question of whether the specific work involved is inherently dangerous is generally a question of fact for the jury. A reasonable jury could find inherent danger in the roof construction work being performed by Donovan at a height of 28 feet. [Donovan v General Motors (CA8 Mo) 762 F2d 701 (1985)]

Regardless of the nature of the activity, the owner may be liable for the torts and contracts of the independent contractor when the owner controls the conduct of the independent contractor. For example, when the franchisor exercises a high degree of control over the franchisee, the relationship will be recognized as an agency relationship and the franchisor is bound by the action of the franchisee.

When the immunity based on the use of an independent contractor would make it possible for the person using the contractor to defraud others, it will be held that the employer is liable for the acts of the independent contractor and the immunity rule will be ignored.

(b) Undisclosed Independent Contractor. In some situations, the owner appears to be doing the act in question because the existence of the independent contractor is not disclosed or apparent. This happens most commonly when a franchisee does business under the name of the franchisor; when a concessionaire, such as a restaurant in a hotel, appears to be the hotel restaurant, although in fact it is operated by an independent concessionaire; or when the buyer of a business continues to run the business in the name of the seller. In such cases of an undisclosed independent contractor, it is generally held that the ostensible owner, that is, the franchisor, the grantor of the concession, or the seller is liable for the torts and contracts[17] of the undisclosed independent contractor.

[17]Sheraton Corp. v Kingsford Packing Co. 162 Ind App 470, 319 NE2d 852 (1974).

§ 43:23.   Enforcement of Claim by Third Person.

A lawsuit by a third person may be brought against the agent or the principal if each is liable. In most states and in the federal courts, the plaintiff may sue either or both in one action when both are liable. When both are sued, the plaintiff may obtain a judgment against both although the plaintiff will only be allowed to collect the full amount of the judgment once.

E. TRANSACTIONS WITH SALES PERSONNEL

Many transactions with sales personnel do not result in a contract with the third person with whom the salesperson deals.

§ 43:24.   Soliciting Agent.

The giving of an order to a salesperson ordinarily does not give rise to a contract, because ordinarily a salesperson is an agent whose authority is limited to soliciting offers from third persons and transmitting them to the principal for acceptance or rejection. Such an agent does not have authority to make a contract which will bind the principal to the third person, and the employer of the salesperson is not bound by a contract until the employer accepts the order.

(a) **Reasons for Limitation on Authority of Sales Personnel.** The limitation on the authority of the salesperson is commonly based upon the fact that credit may be involved in the transaction, and the employer of the salesperson does not wish to permit its soliciting agent to make decisions as to the sufficiency of the credit standing of the buyer but wishes all of these matters to be handled by the credit management department of the home office.

To avoid difficulties, it is common to limit the authority of a salesperson to that of merely a soliciting agent accepting and transmitting orders to the employer. To make this clear to buyers, order forms signed by the customer, who is given a copy, generally state that the salesperson's authority is limited in this manner and that there is no "contract" with the employer until the order is approved by the home office.

(b) **Withdrawal of Customer.** From the fact that the customer giving a salesperson an order does not ordinarily have a binding contract with the employer of the salesperson until the employer approves the order, it necessarily follows that the customer is not bound by any contract until the employer approves the order. Prior to that time, the "buyer" may withdraw from the transaction. Withdrawal under such circumstances is not a breach of contract, for, by definition, there is no contract to be broken. Likewise, if the buyer had given the salesperson any money deposit, down payment, or part payment on the purchase price, the customer on withdrawing from the transaction, is entitled to a refund of the payment which had been made.

§ 43:25.   Contrast with Contracting Agent.

In contrast with the consequences when the salesperson is only a soliciting agent, if the person with whom the buyer deals has authority to make contracts, there is, by definition, a binding contract between the principal and the customer from the moment that the agent agrees with the customer, that is, when the agent accepts the customer's order. Should the customer seek to withdraw from the contract thereafter, the customer must base such action on a ground which justifies the unilateral repudiation or rejection of the contract. If the customer has no such justification, the action of withdrawing is a breach of contract and the customer is liable for the seller's resulting damages. If the buyer has made any downpayment, prepayment, or deposit, the seller may deduct damages from the amount thereof before refunding any excess to the buyer. When the transaction relates to the sale of goods, the seller is entitled to retain from such advance payment either $500 or 20% of the purchase price, whichever is less, unless the seller can show that greater damages were in fact sustained.[18]

SUMMARY

An agent of a disclosed principal who makes a contract within the scope of authority with a third person has no personal liability on the contract. It is the principal and third person who may each sue the other in the event of a breach. A person purporting to act as an agent for a principal impliedly warrants that there is an existing principal with legal capacity, and that the principal has authorized the agent to act; and the person acting as an agent is liable for any loss caused the third person for breach of any of these warranties. An agent of a partially disclosed or an undisclosed principal is a party to the contract with the third person, may enforce the contract against the third person, and is liable for its breach. Agents are liable for harm caused third persons by their fraudulent, malicious, or negligent acts. To avoid problems of interpretation an agent should execute a contract "Principal, by Agent."

An undisclosed or partially disclosed principal is liable to a third person on a simple contract made by an authorized agent, unless the principal has made a good faith settlement of the account with the agent or where satisfaction of the claim has been obtained from the agent. When a third person makes payment to an authorized agent, it is deemed paid to the principal.

A principal or employer is vicariously liable for the torts of an agent or employee committed within the scope of employment based on the doctrine of respondeat superior. However, a principal is not liable for the crimes of an agent merely because they were committed while otherwise acting within the scope of employment; rather, it is usually necessary to show that the principal authorized or directed the criminal conduct. An owner is not liable for torts caused by an independent contractor to third persons or their property unless the work undertaken by the independent contractor is especially hazardous in nature or the owner exercises a high degree of control over the details of performance by the contractor.

A salesperson is ordinarily an agent whose authority is limited to soliciting offers (orders) from third persons and transmitting them to the principal. The principal is not bound until the principal accepts the order, and the customer may withdraw its offer at any time prior to acceptance.

[18]UCC § 2–718(2)(b). See § 20:6 of this book as to consumer protection rescission.

QUESTIONS AND CASE PROBLEMS

1. What social forces are affected by the rule that an agent receiving an overpayment is not liable for the amount thereof when the payment was received in ignorance of the mistake and has been remitted to the principal?

2. Wilson tells Carolyn that he is acting as agent for the Oberfeld Corporation and makes a contract with her on behalf of Oberfeld. Oberfeld later repudiates the contract on the ground, which is true, that Wilson had no authority to make the contract. Carolyn then sues Wilson for damages. Wilson raises the defense that it was true that he was acting as agent for Oberfeld, that he honestly believed that he had authority to do so, and that he did not guarantee that he had authority. Is Wilson liable to Carolyn?

3. Leonard makes a contract with Norma without informing her that he is acting on behalf of Hermes Plastics Company. Leonard has authority to make the contract. Hermes fails to perform the contract. Norma sues Hermes for breach of the contract. Hermes raises the defense that Norma cannot sue on the contract because the only contract she made was with Leonard. Is this a valid defense?

4. Compare a third party beneficiary contract with a contract made by an agent on behalf of an undisclosed principal.

5. Irvin was the rental collection agent for the Sandro Apartment House. The state antipollution board began a proceeding against the apartment house alleging that its furnace emissions were polluting the air. The board telephoned Irvin of the time and place of the board's hearing. Irvin simply forgot to inform Sandro, the owner of the apartment house, of the hearing. The board issued an order adverse to Sandro. In later proceedings before the board, Sandro claimed that he had never been notified of the prior hearing. The board proved that a message had been telephoned to Irvin. Did this constitute notice to Sandro?

6. What is the justification for the doctrine of respondeat superior?

7. Gambale made a contract with Carmen to purchase an automobile for Anna, the principal of Gambale. Gambale did not disclose his agency to Carmen and signed in his own name both the contract and a promissory note for the unpaid balance. Thereafter Carmen learned of the existence of the agency and when payment was not made sued Anna. Can Carmen sue Anna (1) on the contract, and (2) on the promissory note?

8. Compare the liability of an agent's undisclosed principal to a third person on (a) a promissory note, (b) a sealed contract, and (c) an oral contract.

9. Mills Electric Company signed a contract with S&S Horticulture Architects, a two-person landscaping partnership operated by Sullivan and Smyth, to maintain the grounds and flowers at the Mills Electric Company plant in Jacksonville, Florida. Mills checked references of S&S and found S&S to be highly reputable. The contract set forth that S&S would select the flowers as per season; and would determine when to maintain the lawns, so long as the lawns were properly maintained. The contract called for payments to be made to S&S on the first workday of each month; and the contract stipulated that "nothing herein shall make S&S

an agent of the company." The contract also required that S&S personnel wear uniforms identifying that they were employed by S&S. S&S had other accounts, but the large Mills Electric plant took up most of their time. While working on a terraced area near the visitors' entrance to the plant, Sullivan lost control of his large commercial mower, and the mower struck Gillespie, a plant visitor, causing serious injury to him. A witness heard Sullivan apologizing to Gillespie, saying "running that mower on the terrace is a two-man job." Gillespie brought suit against Mills Electric Co. contending Mills should be held vicariously liable for the negligence of Sullivan. Will Mills be held liable on this theory?

10. Anthony Perkins was admitted to Children's Hospital by a private pediatric surgeon, Dr. Green. On the evening of July 18, 1984 Dr. Green performed a tracheotomy to correct a congenital condition in the infant's windpipe. Thereafter Dr. Green examined Anthony in the intensive care unit, where he had been taken after the surgery, and gave instructions as to his treatment. Dr. Green left the hospital at 11:00 p.m., and Anthony came within the exclusive care of the nurses and residents employed by the hospital. At about 3:55 a.m., Anthony stopped breathing, and during the five-to-seven minutes which elapsed before hospital personnel were able to restore his breathing and heartbeat, he suffered irreversible brain damage. Anthony and his parents brought suit against Children's for negligent post-operative care rendered by the hospital's residents. Expert testimony revealed that the residents who were employed and paid by the hospital had been negligent in failing to employ adequate medical procedures in light of the symptoms which Anthony exhibited for almost two hours before the crisis occurred and in the resuscitation efforts employed after its onset. Children's contends that the residents were under the direction and control of Dr. Green so that he, rather than Children's, was responsible for their negligence. Decide.

11. An agent received in the mail stock certificates intended for his principal. The agent forged on the certificates an indorsement from the original owner of the certificates to himself. In a lawsuit by the owner of the certificates against the principal, the owner claimed that the principal must be held to have known what the agent had done. Was he correct? [Hartford Accident & Indemnity Co. v Walston & Co. 21 NY2d 219, 287 NYS2d 58, 234 NE2d 230; adhered to 22 NY2d 672, 291 NYS2d 366, 238 NE2d 754]

12. Weisz purchased a painting at an auction sale in the Parke-Burnett Galleries. It was later shown that the painting was a forgery. When Weisz sued Parke-Burnett for breach of warranty, it raised the defense that it was making the sale for the owner and therefore any warranty suit must be brought against the owner. Was it correct? [Weisz v Parke-Burnett Galleries, Inc. (NYCivCt) 325 NYS2d 576]

13. Video Independent Theaters advertised in newspapers published by the Oklahoma Publishing Company. The Publishing Company would send periodic statements of the amounts due from Video to the advertising agency Ken Guergens and Associates. The latter would then add its fee to the amount due the Publishing Company and would bill Video for the

aggregate amount. On receiving payment by Video, Guergens was to deduct its fee and then transmit the balance to the Publishing Company. Guergens kept the entire amount paid by Video. The Publishing Company sued Video which claimed that it had paid the bill to Guergens. Was this a defense? [Oklahoma Publishing Company v Video Independent Theaters, Inc. (Okla) 522 P2d 1029]

14. Moritz was a guest at the Pines Hotel. While she was sitting in the lobby, Brown, a hotel employee, dropped a heavy vacuum cleaner on her knee. When she complained, he insulted her and hit her with his fist, and knocked her unconscious. She sued the hotel for damages. Was the hotel liable? [Moritz v Pines Hotel, Inc. 53 AppDiv2d 1020, 383 NYS2d 704]

15. Phillips was employed as an automobile salesman by an automobile dealer, City Motor Company. He had a driver's license. City Motor loaned Phillips a demonstrator car. While Phillips was driving the car from a restaurant to his home, he collided with a third person. The latter sued City Motor in the District Court claiming that City Motor had been negligent in failing to obtain a copy of the driving record of Phillips from the state police before entrusting him with the automobile and claiming that City Motor benefited by having its demonstrator automobile driven on the public streets. Was City Motor liable? [Montana ex rel City Motor Co. v District Court, 166 Mont 52, 530 P2d 486]

16. The Bay State Harness Horse Racing and Breeding Association conducted horse races. Music was supplied for the patrons by an independent contractor hired by the Association. Some of the music played was subject to a copyright held by Famous Music Corporation. The playing of that music was a violation of the copyright unless royalties were paid to Famous Music. None were paid and Famous Music sued the Association. It raised the defense that the violation had been committed by an independent contractor, which was specifically instructed not to play Famous Music copyright material. Decide. [Famous Music Corporation v Bay State Harness Horse Racing and Breeding Association, Inc. (CA1 Mass) 554 F2d 1213]

17. On September 24, 1984, Bernie and Joanne Van Rossem made arrangements for a honeymoon trip to Jamaica with the Penney Travel Service, paying on that date $2,059 to Penney in advance of the scheduled departure date of November 10, 1984. On their wedding day, they received a telephone call from Penney Travel advising them that Lotus Tours, the wholesaler through which Penney had booked their travel reservations, had gone bankrupt. And, they were further informed that Lotus had paid their airfare prior to bankruptcy, but that their reservation at the Sandles Resort had not been paid by Lotus Tours. The Van Rossems booked new reservations at "Couples" resort where they paid $1,312 for substitute accommodations. The Van Rossems were not told at any time prior to their wedding day of the fact that Penney was acting as agent for the wholesaler Lotus. Penney Travel contends that it is well known by the public that travel agents act as agents for wholesalers in the travel business. Penney can show conclusively that the $2,059 received from the Van Rossems was forwarded to Lotus Travel as of October 4, 1984, and

that they had not received any commission because of the bankruptcy. The Van Rossems brought suit against Penney Travel for the cost of the substitute accommodations. What theory or theories could the Van Rossems rely on? What defense would Penney Travel raise? Decide. [Van Rossem v Penney Travel Service, 488 NYS 2d 597]

CHAPTER 44

EMPLOYMENT

CHAPTER OBJECTIVES

After studying this chapter you will be able to:
1. Explain the contractual nature of the employment relationship.
2. List the four ways in which "ERISA" provides protection for the pension interests of employees.
3. Set forth the eligibility requirements for unemployment compensation.
4. Explain how the Occupational Safety and Health Act is designed to reach the goal of assuring safe and heatful working conditions.
5. List the three types of benefits provided by Workers' Compensation statutes.

The law of employment is structured on the law of contracts. It is the role of the employer and an individual or group of employees to contract on terms for wages, hours, working conditions, and the duration of the employment relationship. The employment relationship is also regulated by statutes known as labor legislation, which deal with problems not adequately addressed or resolved by employers and employees in their contracts. For example, labor laws deal with fair hiring practices, termination of employment for union activities, compensation for injured employees, compensation for the unemployed, the protection of the pension interests of employees, and the protection of the health and safety of employees.

A. THE EMPLOYMENT RELATIONSHIP

The relationship of an employer and an employee exists when, pursuant to an express or implied agreement of the parties, one person, the

employee, undertakes to perform services or to do work under the direction and control of another, the **employer.** In the older cases this was described as the master-servant relationship.[1]

§ 44.1.   Nature of Relationship.

An employee without agency authority is hired only to work under the control of the employer, as contrasted with (a) an agent, who is to negotiate or make contracts with third persons on behalf of and under the control of a principal, and with (b) an independent contractor, who is to perform a contract independent of, or free from, control by the other party.[2]

FACTS:

Harris and two other registered barbers operated the Golden Shear Barber Shop. They supplied all the capital which had been required to open the shop. Some time later Olsen, an apprentice barber, joined them at the Golden Shear. Each of the four barbers was to pay $35 a week into a common fund which was used to pay the rent, utilities, purchase additional equipment, and make alterations. Periodically an account was given to each of the four as to the payments made from this fund. A state law required that an apprentice barber be under the supervision of a registered barber. Each of the four barbers had his own clientele, set his own prices, purchased his own materials, kept his own receipts, and fixed his own hours of work. The state department of employment determined that Olsen was employed by the three registered barbers and required them to pay an unemployment insurance tax for Olsen. They appealed.

DECISION:

Judgment against the state department. The independence of each barber showed that the arrangement was merely a space-sharing plan and not an employment relationship. The fact that the state law required that an apprentice barber be under the supervision of a registered barber did not cause the apprentice to have the status of employee of the registered barber when in fact the employment relationship did not exist. [Golden Shear Barber Shop v Morgan, 258 Ore 105, 481 P2d 624 (1971)]

---

§ 44.2.   Creation of Employment Relationship.

The relationship of employer and employee can be created only with the consent of both parties. Generally the agreement of the parties is a contract, and it is therefore subject to all of the principles applicable to contracts. The contract will ordinarily be express but may be implied, as when the

---

[1]The concept of a servant is not identical to that of employee as the servant was regarded as a chattel or thing owned by the master, whereas an employee is a free person who works pursuant to a contract of employment. Frank Horton & Co., Inc. v Diggs (Mo App) 544 SW2d 313 (1976).

[2]Living Inc. v Redinger (Tex CivApp) 667 SW2d 846 (1984).

employer accepts the rendering of services which a reasonable person would recognize as being rendered with the expectation of receiving compensation.

(a) **Individual Employment Contracts.** As in contracts generally, both parties must assent to the terms of the employment contract. The parties are free to make a contract on any terms they wish. Historically, wages constituted the sole reward of labor. Today, additional benefits are usually granted employees either by virtue of the contract of employment or by a federal or state statutory provision.

(b) **Collective Bargaining Contracts.** Collective bargaining contracts govern the rights and obligations of employers and employees in many private and public sector employment relations. Under collective bargaining, representatives of the employees bargain with a single employer or a group of employers for an agreement on wages, hours, and working conditions for the employees. The agreement worked out by the representatives of the employees, usually union officials, is generally subject to a ratification vote by the employees. Terms usually found in collective bargaining contracts are: (1) identification of the work belonging exclusively to designated classes of employees; (2) wage and benefits clauses; (3) promotion and lay-off clauses, which are generally tied in part to seniority; (4) a management's rights clause, and (5) a grievance procedure by which persons contending the contract was violated or that they were disciplined or discharged without "just cause" may ultimately have their cases decided by impartial labor arbitrators.

When there is a collective bargaining contract, the "contract of employment" in effect may consist of two contracts: (1) the collective bargaining contract made by the employees' representative with the employer, and (2) the individual employment contract made by each employee with the employer. Although the individual contracts are distinct, they must conform to the basic plan or terms established by the collective bargaining contract. Examples of employment situations which may involve two contracts are those involving professional athletes and those involving actors and writers working in the entertainment industries, including television, motion pictures and the theater.

§ 44:3. Duration and Termination of Employment Contract.

In many instances, the employment contract will not state any time or duration. In such case, it may be terminated at any time by either party. In contrast, the employment contract may expressly state that it shall last for a specified period of time, as a contract to work as general manager for five years. In some instances, a definite duration may be implied from the circumstances.

Ordinarily a contract of employment may be terminated in the same manner as any other contract. If it is to run for a definite period of time, the employer cannot terminate the contract at an earlier date without justification for so doing. If the employment contract does not have a definite duration, it is terminable at will. Under the employment at will doctrine, the employer has historically been allowed to terminate the employment contract at any time for any reason or no reason.[3] Recently, judicial and in some instances legislative intervention has had an impact on the application of the employment at will doctrine in numerous states. Court decisions in a number of jurisdiction have carved out exceptions to the employment at will doctrine when the discharge violates an established public policy, such as discharging an employee in retaliation for insisting that the employer comply with the state's food and drug act[4] or discharging an employee for filing a workers' compensation claim.

FACTS:

Michael Hauck claimed he was discharged by his employer, Sabine Pilot Service, Inc., because he refused his employer's direction to perform the illegal act of pumping the bilges of his employer's vessel into the waterways. Hauck was an employee at will. Hauck brought a wrongful discharge action against Sabine.

DECISION:

Judgment for Hauck. Employment for an indefinite term may be terminated at will and without cause. Public policy as expressed in the criminal laws of the state and the United States, requires a narrow exception to this employment at will doctrine, whereby an employer cannot discharge an employee for refusal to perform an illegal act. [Sabine Pilot Service Inc v Hauck (Tex) 687 SW2d 733 (1985)]

Some courts have required "good faith and fair dealing" in the employment relationship and have held that a termination of an "at will" employee is improper where done with the intent to benefit the employer financially at the expense of the employee, as by terminating an employee to save the payment of commissions or to save the payment of pension benefits.[5]

Courts have begun to construe statements by employers concerning continued employment, which previously had been viewed as having no binding effect as a part of the employment contract requiring good cause for the discharge of an "at will" employee. Also, written personnel policies used as guidelines for the employer's supervisors have been interpreted as being contractual provisions restricting the employer's right to discharge "at will" employees without proof of good or just cause.[6]

Courts that have refused to recognize any exception to the employment at will doctrine have declined to do so because of the belief that such a significant change in the law is best left to the legislative branch of government.[7]

If an employment contract provides that an employee can only be fired for "good cause" or "just cause," a lesser standard for discharge will not be allowed by a court.

[3]Elder v Ivey, 171 Ga App 496, 320 SE2d 217 (1984).
[4]Sheets v Teddy's Frosted Foods, 179 Conn 471, 427 A2d 385 (1980).
[5]Siles v Travenol Laboratories, Inc. 13 Mass App 354, 433 NE2d 103 (1982).
[6]Toussaint v Blue Cross and Blue Shield, 408 Mich 579, 292 NW2d 880 (1980).
[7]Murphy v American Home Products Corp. 461 NY2d 232 (1983).

FACTS:

Yvonne Rabago-Alvarez left her job to work for Vanda, a division of Dart Industries, Inc., under the assurance that her job was permanent as long as her work was satisfactory. Sometime thereafter, Yvonne's supervisor was replaced by a James Rebal. A short time later, Rebal took some customers and Yvonne to witness live, adult entertainment. Yvonne refused to stay and walked out, making Rebal very angry. From this point on, Rebal continually picked on her for matters not relating to the performance of her duties and eventually fired her "for her lack of administrative management." She sued Dart Industries for damages for breach of the employment contract. Dart Industries claimed that it was in good faith dissatisfied with the work of Yvonne.

DECISION:

Judgment for Yvonne. Under the contract to employ her as long as her work was satisfactory, it was necessary to show that there was just cause to discharge her. No cause relating to the duties of her employment was shown by the employer. Even if the contract were interpreted as requiring performance satisfactory to the employer personally, a discharge could not be made unless there was dissatisfaction in good faith with the performance of the duties of her employment. The evidence showed that it was merely a personal dislike for Yvonne. Firing her because of that dislike constituted a breach of contract of employment. [Rabago-Alverez v Dart Industries, Inc. 55 Cal App 3d 91, 127 CalRptr 222 (1976)]

(a) **Federal Laws.** The National Labor Relations Act prohibits dismissal for union activities. Title VII of the amended Civil Rights Act of 1964 prohibits terminating a contract of employment for a reason amounting to discrimination because of race, color, sex, religion, or national origin. The Age Discrimination in Employment Act protects employees from discrimination and discharge based on age.[8] The Rehabilitation Act[9] protects handicapped persons who with reasonable accommodation can perform the essential functions of the job in question from termination by federal contractors.

(b) **Justifiable Discharge.** An employer may be justified in discharging an employee because of the employee's (1) nonperformance of duties, (2) misrepresentation or fraud in obtaining the employment, (3) disobedience to proper directions, (4) disloyalty, (5) theft or other dishonesty, (6) possession or use of drugs or intoxicants, (7) wrongful misconduct, or (8) incompetency.

FACTS:

Mrs. Fisher was hired by the St. Mary's school as a teacher for a ten-month term. In November, two months after she began work, she suffered a cerebral hemorrage and had to undergo surgery. In early March she informed the school that she would not be available to teach until some time in April. The school then advised Mrs. Fisher that her employment was being terminated. Mrs. Fisher sued the school for breach of contract.

[8]29 USC §§ 621–34.
[9]29 USC §§ 701–794.

DECISION:

Judgment for the school. Contracts for personal services are discharged by the death or incapacity of the person who is to render the services. Therefore an employer is justified in terminating an employment contract when the employee is ill to such an extent as to be material to the performance of the contract. If Fisher returned to work in April, she would have been absent for almost five months out of a ten-month contract. This was so substantial a period of absence that it was material and justified the employer's terminating the employment contract. The school, therefore, did not breach the contract. [Fisher v Church of St. Mary (Wyo) 497 P2d 882 (1972)]

In some states, a "service letter" statute requires an employer upon request to furnish a discharged employee with a letter stating the reason for the discharge.[10]

(c) **Remedies.** An employee who has been wrongfully discharged may bring against the employer an action to recover (1) wages, (2) damages for breach of contract or (3) damages representing the value of services already performed. In certain instances, the employee may also bring (4) an action to compel the employer to specifically perform the employment contract, or (5) a proceeding under federal or state labor relations or anti-discrimination statute, seeking reinstatement with back pay and the reinstatement of full seniority rights.

§ 44:4.   **Duties of the Employee.**

The duties of an employee are determined primarily by the contract of employment with the employer. The law also implies certain obligations.

(a) **Services.** Employees are under the duty to perform or hold themselves in readiness to perform such services as may be required by the contract of employment. If employees hold themselves in readiness to comply with their employer's directions, they have discharged this obligation and they will not forfeit the right to compensation because the employer has withheld directions and has thus kept them idle.

Employees impliedly agree to serve their employer honestly and faithfully. They also impliedly agree to serve the employer exclusively during the hours of employment. The employee may do other work, however, if the time and nature of such other employment are not inconsistent with the duties owed to the first employer and if the contract of employment with the first employer does not contain any provision against it.

An employee must obey reasonable regulations and requirements adopted by the employer.

Employees impliedly purport that, in performing their duties, they will exercise due care and ordinary diligence in view of the nature of the work. When skill is required, employees need exercise only ordinary skill, unless the employees have held themselves out as possessing special skills.

---

[10]Eimer v Texaco, Inc. (CA8 Mo) 518 F2d 807 (1975).

(b) **Trade Secrets.** An employee may be given confidential trade secrets by the employer. In such case, the employee must not disclose such knowledge to others. An agreement by the employee to refrain from disclosing trade secrets is binding. Even in the absence of such an agreement, an employee is prohibited from disclosing the trade secrets of the employer. If the employee violates this obligation, the employer may enjoin the use of the information by the employee and by any person to whom it is disclosed by the employee.[11]

Former employees who are competing with their former employer may be enjoined from utilizing information as to suppliers and customers which they obtained while employees, where such information is of vital importance to the employer's business. Such relief is denied if the information is not important or not secret.

(c) **Inventions.** In the absence of an express or implied agreement to the contrary, the inventions of an employee belong to the employee even though the latter used the time and property of the employer in their discovery, provided that the employee had not been employed for the express purpose of inventing the things or processes which were discovered.

FACTS:

Bandag, Inc. was in the business of recapping used automobile tires. Morenings was employed as its chief chemist. In the course of his work, he discovered a new process for bonding treads to tires that were being recapped. He was not employed to discover such a process, and no agreement had ever been made with Bandag as to the ownership of any discoveries made by Morenings. Bandag sued Morenings, claiming that, as employer, it was entitled to the ownership of the process which had been developed in the course of Morenings' employment.

DECISION:

Judgment for Morenings. The employer has the burden of proving that it is entitled to the invention or process discovered by an employee in the course of employment. As Morenings was not employed for the purpose of discovering the process and as there was no provision in the contract of employment giving the employer the right to such discovery, the employer had no right to it. [Bandag, Inc. v Morenings, 259 Iowa 998, 146 NW2d 916 (1966)]

If the invention is discovered during working hours and with the employer's materials and equipment the employer has the right, called a *shop right,* to use the invention without charge in the running of the employer's business. If the employee has obtained a patent for the invention, the employee must grant the employer a nonexclusive license to use the invention without the payment of any royalty. The shop right of the employer does not give the right to make and sell machines that embody the employee's

---

[11]Henry Hope X-Ray Products, Inc. v Marron Carrel, Inc. (CA9 Ariz) 674 F2d 1336 (1982).

invention; it only entitles the employer to use the invention without cost in the operation of the employer's plant.

In contrast, when an employee is employed to secure certain results from experiments to be conducted in the course of employment, the inventions so discovered belong to the employer on the ground that there is a trust relationship or that there is an implied agreement by the employee to make an assignment of the inventions to the employer.

§ 44.5   Rights of the Employee.

The rights of an employee are determined primarily by the contract of employment. As in the case of duties, the law also implies certain rights.

(a) **Compensation.** The rights of an employee with respect to compensation are governed in general by the same principles that apply to the compensation of an agent. In the absence of an agreement to the contrary, when an employee is discharged, whether for cause or not, the employer must pay wages down to the expiration of the last pay period. The express terms of employment or collective bargaining contracts, or custom, frequently provide for payment of wages for fractional terminal periods, and they may even require a severance pay equal to the compensation for a full period of employment. Provisions relating to deferred compensation under a profit sharing trust for employees are liberally construed in favor of employees.[12]

(b) **Employee's Lien or Preference.** Most states protect an employee's claim for compensation either by a lien or preference over other claimants of payment out of proceeds from the sale of the employer's property. These statutes vary widely in their terms. They are usually called *laborers'* or *mechanics' lien laws.* Sometimes the statutes limit their protection to workers of a particular class, such as plasterers, or bricklayers. Compensation for the use of materials or machinery is ordinarily not protected by such statutes.

§ 44:6.   Pension Plans.

Many employers have established pension plans to benefit their employees after they retire.

(a) **Federal Regulation of Pension Plans.** The Employees Retirement Income Security Act (ERISA)[13], was adopted in 1974 to provide protection for the pension interests of employees.

(1) Fiduciary Standards and Reporting. Persons administering a pension fund must handle it so as to protect the interest of the employees. The fact that an employer contributed all or part of the money does not entitle the employer to use the fund as though it were still owned by the employer. Persons administering pension plans must make detailed reports to the Secretary of Labor.

---

[12]An employee temporarily leaving an employer to serve in the military forces of the United States is entitled to have the time served in the military forces counted as years of service for the employer in computing the pension benefits of the employee. Alabama Power Co. v Davis, 431 US 581 (1977).

[13]PL 93–406, 88 Stat 829, 29 USC §§ 1001–1381. A number of subsequent acts have also affected private pensions, notably the Tax Equity and Fiscal Responsibility Act of 1982 and the Tax Reform Act of 1984.

(2) Vesting. Vesting refers to the right of an employee to pension benefits paid into a pension plan in the employee's name by the employer. Prior to ERISA many pension plans did not vest accrued benefits until 20 to 25 years of service by an employee. Thus an employee who was forced to terminate service after 18 years would not receive any pension rights or benefits whatsoever. Under ERISA employers implementing pension plans must select one of three vesting schedules ranging from 100 percent vesting after 10 years of service to partial or graduated vesting starting at an earlier date.

In the past, it was common for pension plans to contain "break-in-service" clauses whereby employees who left their employment for a period longer than one year for any reason other than an on-the-job injury lost valuable pension eligibility rights. Under the Retirement Equity Act of 1984,[14] which was designed to provide greater pension equity for women, an individual can leave the workforce for up to five consecutive years and still retain eligibility for pension benefits. Also, under the Retirement Equity Act the spouse of a plan participant must give consent to any election to waive the survivor annuity option required by the Act.

(3) Funding. ERISA requires that contributions be made by employers to their pension funds on a basis which is actuarially determined so that the pension fund will be sufficiently large to make the payments which will be required of it. The Treasury Department is authorized to issue regulations, opinions, variances, and waivers pertaining to funding.[15]

(4) Termination Insurance. The Act establishes an insurance plan to protect employees when the employer goes out of business. To provide this protection, the statute creates a Pension Benefit Guaranty Corporation (PBGC). In effect, this corporation guarantees that the employee will receive benefits in much the same pattern as the Federal Deposit Insurance Corporation protects bank depositors. The PBGC is financed by small payments made by employers for every employee covered by a pension plan.

(5) Enforcement. The Act authorizes the Secretary of Labor and employees to bring court actions to compel the observance of the statutory requirements.

§ 44:7.   Attachment and Garnishment of Wages.

It is generally provided that a creditor may require a third person who owes money to a debtor of the creditor to pay such amount to the creditor to satisfy the creditor's claim against the debtor. That is, if *A* has a valid claim for $100 against *B,* and *C* owes *B* $100, *A* can require *C* to pay the $100 to *A,* which thereby satisfies both *C*'s debt to *B* and *B*'s debt to *A.* The necessary legal procedure generally requires the third person to pay the money into court or to the sheriff rather than directly to the original creditor. The original creditor may also, by this process, reach tangible property belonging to the debtor which is in the custody or possession of a third person. This procedure is commonly called **attachment** and the third person is called a **garnishee.**

---

[14]PL 98–397, 98 Stat 1426.
[15]Reorganization Plan No. 4 of 1978, 43 Fed Reg 47713, made effective December 28, 1978, by Executive Order No. 12108, 44 Fed Reg 1065, 29 USC § 1001 (1978).

Under the federal Truth in Lending Act (Title I of the Federal Consumer Credit Protection Act), only a certain portion of an employee's pay can be garnisheed. Ordinarily, the amount that may be garnisheed may not exceed (a) 25 percent of the employee's weekly take-home pay or (b) the amount by which the weekly take-home pay exceeds 30 times the federal minimum hourly wage, whichever is less.[16] The federal statute also prohibits an employer from discharging an employee because wages have been garnisheed for any one indebtedness. The federal statute does not prevent the discharge of an employee because of several garnishments based on different debts.[17]

B. UNEMPLOYMENT BENEFITS

Generally, when employees are without work through no fault of their own, they are eligible for unemployment compensation benefits.

§ 44:8.   Unemployment Compensation.

Unemployment compensation today is provided primarily through a federal-state system under the unemployment insurance provisions of the Social Security Act of 1935. All of the states have laws which provide similar benefits and the state agencies are loosely coordinated under the federal act. Agricultural employees, domestic employees, and state and local government employees are not covered by this federal-state system. Federal programs of unemployment compensation exist for federal civilian workers and ex-service personnel. A separate federal unemployment program applies to railroad workers.

§ 44:9.   Benefits and Eligibility.

The states are largely free to prescribe the amount and duration of benefits, and the conditions required for eligibility for benefits. In most states, the unemployed person must be available for placement in a similar job and be willing to take such employment at a comparable rate of pay.

FACTS:

Robert Evjen was a full-time employee for Boise Cascade. At the same time, he was a full-time student at the Chemeta Community College. He was laid off as part of a general economy move by the employer. He applied for unemployment compensation. The referee found that Evjen never missed work in order to go to classes, that Evjen could not afford to go to school without working, and that in case of any conflict between work and school, work came first.

[16]Consumer Credit Protection Act § 303. Under the Uniform Consumer Credit Code, where adopted, this second alternative has been increased to 40 times the federal hourly minimum pay. UCCC § 5.105(2)(b). Prejudgment attachment of wages without notice and hearing is invalid. Sniadach v Family Finance Corp. 395 US 337 (1969).

[17]Cheatham v Virginia Alcoholic Beverage Control Board (CA4 Va) 501 F2d 1346 (1974).

DECISION:

Judgment for Evjen. In order to obtain unemployment benefits an unemployed individual must prove, among other things, that he is "available for work" and is unable to obtain suitable work. A student's unavailability for work during school hours is contrary to the concept of "available for work," which requires availability for all shifts of suitable work. However Robert Evjen's uncontroverted testimony that his education was secondary to his employment and that his work came first was sufficient to overcome either an inference or presumption of nonavailability. [Evjen v Employment Agency, 22 Or App 372, 539 P2d 662 (1975)]

If an employee quits a job without cause, or is fired for misconduct, or becomes unemployed because of a labor dispute in which the employee actively takes part, the employee is ordinarily disqualified from receiving unemployment compensation benefits.[18]

C. EMPLOYEES HEALTH AND SAFETY

The Occupational Safety and Health Act of 1970 was passed in order to assure so far as possible every working man and woman safe and healthful working conditions and to preserve the country's human resources.[19] The Act provides for (1) establishing safety and health standards, and for (2) effective enforcement of these standards and the other employer duties required by the Act.

§ 44:10.   Standards.

The Secretary of Labor has been granted broad authority under the Act to promulgate occupational safety and health standards. Except in emergency situations, publication in the Federal Register and public hearings are required before the Secretary can issue a new standard. Thereafter, any person adversely affected may challenge the validity of the standard in a United States Court of Appeals. The Secretary's standards will be upheld if they are reasonable and supported by substantial evidence. However, the Secretary does not have unbridled discretion to adopt costly standards to create an absolutely risk-free work place. Rather the Secretary must demonstrate a need for a new standard by showing that it is reasonably necessary to protect employees against a "significant risk" of material health impairment.[20] The cost of compliance with new standards may run into billions of dollars. The Secretary is not required to do a cost-benefit analysis for a new standard. However, the Secretary must show that the standard is economically feasible.[21]

[18]Only New York provides for payment of unemployment compensation to employees out of work because of participation in a strike. New York has concluded that the community interest in the security of persons directly affected by a strike outweighs the interest in avoiding any impact on a particular labor dispute. New York Telephone Co. v. New York Department of Labor, 440 US 519 (1979).

[19]29 USC §§ 651 et seq.

[20]Industrial Union Department, AFL-CIO v American Petroleum Institute, 448 US 607 (1980).

[21]American Textile Manufacturers Institute v Donovan, 452 US 490 (1981).

§ 44:11. Employer Duties.

Employers have a "general duty" to furnish to each employee a place of employment which is free from recognized hazards that are likely to cause death or serious physical injuries.[22]

Employers are required by the Act to maintain records of occupational illness and injuries if they result in death, loss of consciousness, medical treatment other than first aid, or one or more lost workdays. Such records have proven to be a valuable aid in recognizing areas of risk, and have been especially helpful in identifying the presence of occupational illnesses.

§ 44:12. Enforcement.

The Occupational Safety and Health Administration (OSHA), an agency within the Department of Labor, is the primary administrative agency under the Act, having authority to conduct inspections and to seek enforcement action where there has been noncompliance. Worksite inspections are conducted when employer records indicate incidents involving fatalities or serious injuries. Also, worksite inspections may result from employee complaints. Employees making such complaints are protected by the Act from possible employer retaliation.[23] Employers have the right to require that an OSHA inspector secure a warrant prior to inspection of the employer's plant.[24]

If OSHA issues a citation against an employer, the employer may challenge it before the Occupational Safety and Health Review Commission. The Commission is fully independent of OSHA; its sole function is to adjudicate contested enforcement actions. Judicial review of a Commission ruling is obtained before the United States Court of Appeals.

The Secretary of Labor is empowered to seek injunctive and other appropriate relief in a United States district court against an employer who discriminates against an employee for testifying or exercising "any right" under the Act.

FACTS:

Virgil Deemer and Thomas Cornwell, employees at the Whirlpool Corporation's plant in Marion, Ohio, refused to comply with a supervisor's order that they perform maintenance work on certain mesh screens located some 20 feet above the plant floor. Twelve days before this incident a fellow employee had fallen to his death from the screens. After refusal the men were ordered to punch out and leave the plant. They were not paid for the remaining six hours of their shift and written reprimands for insubordination were placed in their employment files. Section 11(C)(1) of the Occupational Safety and Health Act provides that no employer shall discharge or in any manner discriminate against an employee because the employee filed a complaint with OSHA, testified in any OSHA proceeding, or exercised any right afforded by the Act. A regulation issued by the Secretary of Labor under the Act provides that if an employee with no reasonable alternative refuses in good faith to expose himself to a dangerous condition, he will be protected

[22]29 USC § 654(a).
[23]29 USC § 66(C).
[24]Marshall v Barlow's, Inc. 436 US 307 (1978).

against subsequent discrimination. The Secretary of Labor filed suit in U.S. District Court against Whirlpool, contending that Whirlpool's actions against Deemer and Cornwell constituted "discrimination" under the Secretary's regulation and Section 11(C)(1) of the Act. Whirlpool contended that the regulation encouraged workers to engage in "self-help" and unlawfully permitted a "strike with pay."

DECISION:

Judgment against Whirlpool. The Occupational Safety and Health Act's "general duty" clause requires an employer to furnish a work place free from hazards that are likely to cause death or serious injury to employees. OSHA inspectors cannot be present around the clock in every work place to enforce this clause. Thus, in the unusual circumstances faced by Deemer and Cornwell, when in good faith and without reasonable alternatives they refused to expose themselves to the dangerous work on the mesh screens, the Secretary's regulation protects them against subsequent discrimination by the employer for the refusal. The Secretary's regulation is consistent with the Act's "general duty" clause, and the employer violated this regulation when it placed reprimands in the personnel files of Deemer and Cornwell. [Whirlpool v Marshall, 445 US 1 (1980)]

---

§ 44:13. State "Right to Know" Legislation.

Laws which guarantee individual workers the "right to know" if there are hazardous substances in their workplaces have been enacted by many states in recent years. These laws commonly require an employer to make known to an employee's physician the chemical composition of certain substances in the workplace in connection with the diagnosis and treatment of an employee by the physician. Further, local fire and public health officials as well as local neighborhood residents are granted the right to know if local employers are working with hazardous substances that could pose health or safety problems.

D. COMPENSATION FOR EMPLOYEES' INJURIES

For most kinds of employment, workers' compensation statutes govern.[25] They provide that the injured employee is entitled to compensation for accidents occurring in the course of employment from a risk involved in that employment.

§ 44:14. Common-Law Status of Employer.

In some employment situations, the common-law principles apply. This is so because workers' compensation statutes commonly do not apply to employers with less than a minimum number of employees, or to agricultural, domestic or casual employment. It is necessary, therefore, to consider the duties and defenses of employers apart from workers' compensation statutes.

(a) **Duties.** The employer is under the common-law duty to furnish an employee with a reasonably safe place in which to work, reasonably safe

---

[25]Every state has some form of workers' compensation legislation, though the statutes vary widely from state to state. Some statutes apply only to employees engaged in manual or mechanical labor, some extend coverage to virtually all employees. Employer participation is voluntary to certain degrees in eighteen states.

tools and appliances, and a sufficient number of competent fellow employees for the work involved; and to warn the employee of any unusual dangers peculiar to the employer's business.

(b) Defenses. At common law, the employer is not liable to an injured employee if the employee was harmed by the act of a fellow employee; or if harmed by an ordinary hazard of the work because the employee assumed such risks. If the employee was guilty of contributory negligence, regardless of the employer's negligence, the employer is not liable to an injured employee at common law.

§ 44:15. Statutory Changes.

The rising incidence of industrial accidents due to the increasing use of more powerful machinery and the growth of the industrial labor population led to a demand for statutory modification of common-law rules relating to liability of employers for industrial accidents.

(a) Modification of Employer's Common-Law Defenses. One type of change by statute was to modify the defenses which an employer could assert when sued by an employee for damages. For example, under the Federal Employer's Liability Act (FELA) covering railroad workers, the injured employee must still bring an action in court and prove the negligence of the employer or other employees, but the burden of proving the case is made lighter by limitations on employers' defenses. Under the FELA, contributory negligence is a defense only in mitigation of damages; assumption of the risk is not a defense.[26]

(b) Workers' Compensation. A more sweeping development was made by the adoption of workers' compensation statutes in every state. In addition, civil employees of the United States are covered by the Federal Employees' Compensation Act. Where an employee is covered by a workers' compensation statute, and the injury is job-connected, the employee's remedy is limited to that provided in the workers' compensation statute.

FACTS:
Robert Halliman was employed as a teacher by the Los Angeles Unified School District at Milliken Junior High School when a minor student Louis "R." intentionally threw a rock at him, hitting him on the head and seriously injuring him. The same student had committed previous assaults on the school grounds, including an assault earlier that same day. Halliman and his wife brought suit against the Los Angeles Unified School District seeking damages. He contended that the defendant had the power and ability to prevent the student's misconduct by appropriate disciplinary action but did not do so, ignoring its duty to protect students and teachers. The School District filed a motion for a summary judgment on the ground that the Workers' Compensation Act provided the exclusive remedy for Halliman's injury.

[26]Federal Employer's Liability Act, 45 USC §§ 1 et seq.

DECISION:

Judgment for the School District. The State's Workers' Compensation Act provides the exclusive remedy for Halliman's injuries caused by a student's unprovoked assault while this teacher was acting within the scope of his employment; and it bars a civil law suit for damages against the employer. [Halliman v Los Angeles Unified School District, 163 Cal App 3d 46, 209 Cal Rptr 175 (1984)]

For injuries arising within the course of the employee's work from a risk involved in that work, the workers' compensation statutes usually provide: (1) immediate medical benefits, (2) prompt periodic wage replacement, very often computed as a percentage of weekly wages (ranging from 50% to 80% of the injured employee's wage), and (3) a death benefit of a limited amount. In such cases, compensation is paid without regard to whether the employer or the employee was negligent. However, generally no compensation is allowed for a willful, self-inflicted injury or one sustained while intoxicated.

There has been a gradual widening of the workers' compensation statutes, so that compensation today is generally recoverable for both accident-inflicted injuries and occupational diseases. In some states compensation for occupational diseases is limited to those specified in the statute by name, such as silicosis, lead poisoning, or injury to health from radioactivity. In other states, any disease arising from an occupation is compensable.

Workers' compensation preceedings are brought before a special administrative agency or workers' compensation board. In contrast, a common-law action for damages or an action for damages under an employer's liability statute is brought in a court of law.

SUMMARY

The relationship of employer and employee is created by the agreement of the parties and is subject to all of the principles applicable to contracts. Where the employment contract sets forth a specific duration, the employer cannot terminate the contract at an earlier date, unless just cause exists. Where no definite time period exists, the individual is an "at will" employee. In those states where the "employment at will" doctrine applies, an employer can terminate the contract of an at-will employee at any time for any reason or no reason. Courts in a number of jurisdictions however have carved out exceptions to this doctrine where the discharge violates public policy, or is contrary to good faith and fair dealings in the employment relationship. Also federal laws prohibit termination of covered employees because of their union activities or because of their race, color, sex, religion, national origin, age, or handicap. However, employers may terminate employees covered by these federal laws for just cause.

The Employees Retirement Income Security Act (ERISA) was enacted to provide protection of the pension interests of employees by requiring: (1) high standards of those administering the funds; (2) reasonable vesting of benefits; (3) adequate funding; and (4) an insurance program to guarantee payments of earned benefits.

Unemployment compensation benefits are provided to persons for a limited period of time where they are out of work through no fault of their own, and are available for placement in a similar job at a comparable rate of pay.

In order to assure every working person safe and healthful working conditions the Occupational Safety and Health Act provides for (1) the establishment of safety and health standards and (2) the effective enforcement of these standards. "Right-to-know" laws have been enacted by many states which require employers to inform their employees of any hazardous substances present in the work place.

Workers' compensation laws provide for the prompt payment of compensation and medical benefits to persons injured in the course of employment without regard to fault. The injured employee's remedy is generally limited to that provided by the workers' compensation statute.

QUESTIONS AND CASE PROBLEMS

1. What social forces are affected by the shop right rule applicable to inventions of an employee?

2. Compare the protection of trade secrets and the protection given an unpublished literary or artistic work (common-law copyright).

3. What remedies does an employee who has been wrongfully discharged have against an employer?

4. Susan was employed by Harbison Corporation. In the course of her employment, she acquired information from Harbison over the years. She left the employment of Harbison and then set up her own business and started to use the information which she had learned while working for Harbison. Harbison brought a suit against Susan to obtain an injunction to prevent this use of the information. Susan defended on the ground that there was no restrictive covenant in the contract of employment prohibiting her from utilizing anything which she learned and therefore she was free to use it as she chose. Was she correct?

5. Fred went to work for the Bauer Generator Company. He worked in the shipping department and was injured when the floor of the loading platform broke under his weight. Examination showed that the floor had rotted through because of years of exposure to weather. Fred sued Bauer for damages. Bauer raised the defense that there was no statute regulating the condition of loading platforms. Is Bauer liable?

6. Compare (a) an employee and (b) an independent contractor.

7. Chesnick manufactured soap. Chesnick wanted to learn what the public wanted in soap. He prepared a questionnaire and made a contract with Ludlow to interview 1,000 people and ask them the questions on the questionnaire. Ludlow was instructed not to reveal the identity of Chesnick and to submit to Chesnick a written report on each interview. Was Ludlow an employee, an agent, or an independent contractor?

8. Juan Ortiz was regularly employed by Donegan Productions Co. as an actor on an afternoon television series. A dispute arose as to Donegan's

financial obligations to Juan. Donegan claimed that the dispute must be resolved solely on the basis of the written individual employment contract which Juan and Donegan Productions had signed and that the past practice, usages of the profession, and an existing collective bargaining contract with AFTRA (American Federation of Television and Radio Artists) were not relevant. Is Donegan Productions correct?

9. Ralph Richards was employed as the sole crane operator of the Gale Corporation. He also held the part-time union position of shop steward for the plant. On May 15 Richards complained to OSHA concerning what he contended were seven existing violations of the Occupational Safety and Health Act, which alleged violations were brought to his attention by members of the bargaining unit. On May 21, he stated to the Company's General Manager at a negotiating session that "if we don't have a new contract by the time the present one expires on June 15, we will strike." On May 22 an OSHA inspector arrived at the plant and Richards told his supervisor that "I blew the whistle." On May 23 the Company rented and later purchased two large electric fork trucks, which were utilized to do the work formerly performed by the crane; and it abolished the crane operator's job. Under the existing collective bargaining contract, the Company had the right to lay off for lack of work. The contract also provided for arbitration and prohibited discipline or discharge without "just cause." On May 23 Richards was notified that he was being laid off "for lack of work" within his classification of crane operator. He was also advised that the Company was not planning on using the crane in the future, and that if he was smart, he would get another job. Richards claims that his layoff was in violation of the National Labor Relations Act, the Occupational Safety and Health Act, and the collective bargaining agreement. Is he correct?

10. Samuel Sullivan, president of the Truck Drivers and Helpers International Union also holds the position of president of the Union's Pension Fund. The fund consists of both employer and employee contributions, which are forwarded quarterly to the fund's offices in New York City. Sullivan ordered Mark Gilbert, the treasurer of the fund, not to give out any information to anyone at any time concerning the fund, because it is Union money and the Union is entitled to take care of its own internal affairs. Is Sullivan correct?

11. A Louisana statute requires that when an employee hired for a fixed term is fired without cause, the employer must pay him the full "salary" for the contract term. Brasher was employed by Chenille, Inc, by the year and fired by it without cause. Had he worked the full year, Chenille would have made a contribution on his behalf to a retirement fund or pension plan. Brasher claimed that such a contribution was part of his "salary" and therefore that the statute required Chenille to make that contribution. Was he correct? [Brasher v Chenille (LaApp) 251 So2d 824]

12. Faunce was employed by the Boost Co., which manufactured a soft drink. After some years he left its employ and began manufacturing a different soft drink. The company claimed that he was using trade secrets learned while he was in its employ and sought to enjoin him. It was

proved that the soft drink made by the defendant was not the same as that made by the plaintiff; that the difference between one soft drink and another was primarily due to the one percent of the volume that represented flavoring; and that the drink made by the defendant could be made by anyone in the soft drink business on the basis of general knowledge of the trade. Was Boost entitled to an injunction? [Boost Co. v Faunce, 17 NJ Super 458, 86 A2d 283]

13. Buffo was employed by the Baltimore & Ohio Railroad Co. With a number of other workers he was removing old brakes from railroad cars and replacing them with new brakes. In the course of the work, rivet heads and scrap from the brakes accumulated on the tracks under the cars, but these were removed only occasionally when the men had time. Buffo, while holding an air hammer in both arms, was crawling under a car when his foot slipped on scrap on the ground, which caused him to strike and injure his knee. He sued the railroad for damages under the Federal Employers' Liability Act. Decide. [Buffo v Baltimore & Ohio Railroad Co. 364 Pa 437, 72 A2d 593]

14. Baugh was employed by the Lummus Cotton Gin Co. The contract of employment stated that his employment was "conditional on... conduct and service being satisfactory to us, we to be the sole judge...." After some time the company discharged Baugh solely because it could not afford to employ him any longer. Baugh sued the company. Was it liable for breach of contract? [Lummus Cotton Gin Co. v Baugh, 29 Ga App 498, 116 SE 51]

15. Moore was an electronics engineer employed by the United States. While traveling under a work assignment from one air base to another, he ran into and injured Romitti, who then sued the United States. The United States raised the defense that Moore was not acting within the course of his employment while driving to the new job assignment. Was this defense valid? [United States v Romitti (CA9 Cal) 363 F2d 662]

16. Cream was an officer and employee of Leo Silfen, Inc. He was discharged and then went into business for himself, conducting a business similar to that of his former employer. He obtained commercial lists of users of his products from enterprises publishing mailing and commercial lists. Out of the persons he solicited from these lists, forty-seven happened to be customers of Silfen. Silfen brought an action to enjoin Cream from soliciting its customers. Cream showed that Silfen had approximately 1,100 customers. Decide. [Leo Silfen, Inc. v Cream, 29 NY2d 387, 328 NYS2d 423, 278 NE2d 636]

17. Michael Kittell, while operating a saw at the Vermont Weatherboard Company plant, was seriously injured when a splinter flew into his eye and penetrated his head. Kittell sued Vermont Weatherboard seeking damages on a common-law theory. His complaint alleged that he suffered severe injuries due solely to the employer's wanton and willful acts and omissions. The complaint stated that he was an inexperienced worker set to work without instructions or warning on a saw from which the employer had stripped away all safety devices. Vermont Weatherboard made a motion to dismiss the complaint on the ground that Workers' Compensation Act provided the exclusive remedy for his injury. Decide. [Kittell v Vermont Weatherboard, Inc. 138 Vt 439, 417 A2d 926]

PART 8

BUSINESS ORGANIZATIONS

Chapter 45 Forms of Business Organizations
Chapter 46 Creation and Termination of Partnerships
Chapter 47 Powers and Duties of Partners
Chapter 48 Nature, Creation, and Termination of Corporations
Chapter 49 Corporate Powers
Chapter 50 Corporate Stock and Shareholders
Chapter 51 Management of Corporations

CHAPTER 45

FORMS OF BUSINESS

ORGANIZATIONS

CHAPTER OBJECTIVES

After studying this chapter you will be able to:

1. List the advantages and disadvantages of the three principal forms of business.
2. Describe and explain the reasons for the FTC disclosure requirements.
3. Recognize what actions of a limited partner will cause the loss of protection from limited liability.
4. Distinguish a joint venture from a partnership.
5. Compare an unincorporated association to a cooperative.

Business ventures may be conducted under various forms of organization. The principal forms of business organizations are: (1) **individual** or **sole proprietorships**, (2) **partnerships**, and (3) **corporations**. The selection of the form of business organization is often determined by tax considerations, with extent of liability for business debts and the extent of control of the management of the business being other important factors.

Certain forms of special venture organizations have also evolved to meet modern business and investment needs. These include franchises, as well as limited partnerships, joint ventures, cooperatives, and unincorporated associations.

A. PRINCIPAL FORMS OF BUSINESS ORGANIZATIONS

The law of business organizations may be better understood if major advantages and disadvantages of proprietorships, partnerships, and corporations are first considered.

759

§ 45:1.   Individual Proprietorships.

A **sole** or **individual proprietorship** is a form of business ownership in which one individual owns a business, and may either be the sole worker of the business or may employ as many individuals as needed to run the business. Individual proprietorships are commonly used in retail establishments, service businesses, and agriculture.

(a) **Advantages.** The proprietor or owner is not required to expend limited resources on organizational fees. The proprietor, as the sole owner, controls all of the decisions and receives all of the profits. The proprietor's net earnings are not subject to the corporate income tax, but are taxed as personal income.

(b) **Disadvantages.** The proprietor is subject to unlimited personal liability for the debts of the business, and the proprietor cannot effectively limit this risk. The investment capital in the business is limited by the resources of the sole proprietor, which very often impedes the growth of the business. With all contracts of the business being made by the owner or in the owner's name by agents of the owner, the authority to make contracts terminates upon the death of the owner, and the business is subject to disintegration.

§ 45:2.   Partnerships.

While the individual proprietorship relies solely on the capital investment and business skill of the sole owner, a **partnership** involves the pooling of capital resources and the business or professional talents of two or more individuals with the goal of making a profit. Law firms, medical associates, and architecture and engineering firms may operate under the partnership form, although there is a trend for such professional firms to incorporate in order to share in the federal tax benefits available to employees of corporations, such as pension, profit-sharing, sick pay, and other like benefits. A wide range of retail and service businesses currently operate as partnerships.

(a) **Advantages.** The partnership form of business organization allows individuals to pool resources and then initiate and conduct their business without the requirement of a formal organizational structure and without the expense of organizational fees. As will be seen, partnership agreements are often informal and may be unwritten.

(b) **Disadvantages.** Some major disadvantages of a partnership are: the unlimited personal liability of each partner; the uncertain duration of the business because the partnership is dissolved by the death of a partner; and loss of income tax advantages available under the corporate form which allow limited earnings to be retained in the business (a partner pays personal income taxes on the partner's proportionate share of the partnership income whether or not it is actually distributed from the business).

§ 45:3.   Corporations.

Business corporations exist primarily to make a profit. They are created by government grant, and the statute regulating the creation of corporations requires a corporate structure consisting of shareholders, directors, and officers. The shareholders, as the owners of the business, elect a board of directors who are responsible for the management of the business. The directors employ officers, who serve as the agents of the business and run the day-to-day operations of the business. Corporations range in size from incorporated one-owner enterprises to large multinational corporations.

(a) **Advantages.** The major advantage to the shareholder or investor is that the shareholder's risk of loss from the business is limited to the amount of capital the shareholder invested in the business. This factor, coupled with the free transferability of corporate shares, makes the corporate form of business organization an acceptable mechanism for many investors to contribute the capital assets needed to finance modern large business enterprises. Indeed, as the capital needs of the business expand, the corporate form becomes more attractive. A corporation is a separate legal entity capable of holding property, contracting, suing, and being sued in its own name. It may be established with a perpetual life, and unlike the death of a partner, the death of a shareholder has no legal effect on the entity.

A corporation is also a separate taxable entity, and allows for certain tax savings under certain circumstances to the owners of the corporation. Tax advantages also exist in the area of executive compensation for corporate employees.

(b) **Disadvantages.** A corporation is required to pay corporate income taxes. Shareholders, when they receive a distribution of profits for the corporation, are required to pay personal income taxes on the amount received. This is a form of double taxation which may weigh against incorporation.

The limited liability of shareholders may result in a limitation of credit available to the corporation. Also, incorporation involves the expenditure of funds for organizational and operational expenses. Documents necessary for the formation of a corporation, which are required by state law, must be prepared and certain filing fees paid. State corporation laws may also require the filing of an annual report and other reports.

B. SPECIALIZED FORMS OF BUSINESS ORGANIZATION

Specialized forms of business organizations exist to meet modern business and investment needs. Thus a fast food enterprise may choose to expand its business by the use of franchises, whereby it is paid royalties from the gross receipts of restaurants owned and operated by franchisees. Or, two construction companies may form a joint venture to construct a major project, where individually the companies lack sufficient resources to undertake the project. Each enterprise seeks to utilize the form of structure or organization which will permit the attainment of its desired goals in the most efficient manner, while protecting the enterprise and the participants from the risks that may arise.

§ 45:4.   Franchises.

The use of franchises has expanded rapidly in recent years as a method of controlling and financing operations by the franchisor and as a method of investment and participation by the franchisee.

(a) Definitions. A **franchise** has been defined by the Federal Trade Commission as "an arrangement in which the owner of a trademark, tradename, or copyright licenses others, under specified conditions or limitations, to use the trademark, tradename, or copyright in purveying goods or services." The **franchisor** is the party granting the franchise, and the **franchisee** is the person to whom the franchise is given.

(b) The Franchisor and the Franchisee. Theoretically the relationship between the franchisor and the franchisee is an arm's-length relationship between two independent contractors, their respective rights being determined by the contract existing between them.

(1) Duration and Termination. The franchise may last for as long as the parties agree. Commonly it runs for a short period of time, such as a year, so that the franchise holder is well aware that in order to stay in business the terms of the franchise contract must be followed.

Franchise contracts generally specify the causes for which the franchisor may terminate the franchise, such as the franchisee's death, bankruptcy, failure to make payments, or failure to meet sales quotas. Franchise contracts frequently contain an arbitration provision under which a neutral party is to make a final and binding determination on whether or not a breach of the contract had occurred sufficient to justify cancellation of the franchise. The arbitration provision may provide that the franchisor can appoint a trustee to run the business of the franchisee while the arbitration proceedings are pending.

Holders of automobile dealership franchises are protected from bad faith termination of their dealerships by the federal Automobile Dealers' Franchise Act.[1] When an automobile manufacturer makes arbitrary and unreasonable demands and thereafter terminates the dealer's franchise for failure to comply with the demands, the manufacturer is liable for the damages caused thereby. However, a manufacturer is justified in terminating an automobile dealership for failing to maintain the required sales quota where the manufacturer has given the dealer repeated warnings, the quota is reasonable, and the quota has been reduced to reflect local economic conditions.[2]

FACTS:

H. C. Blackwell Co. held a franchise from the Kenworth Truck Co. to sell its trucks. After twelve years the franchise was about to expire. Kenworth notified Blackwell that the franchise would not be renewed unless Blackwell sold more trucks and improved its building and bookkeeping systems in the next 90 days.

Blackwell spent $90,000 in attempting to meet the demands of Kenworth but could not do so because a year was required to make the specified changes. Kenworth refused to renew the franchise. Blackwell sued Kenworth for damages under the Federal Automobile Dealers Franchise Act. Blackwell claimed that Kenworth had refused to renew in bad faith.

[1] 15 USC § 1222. Several states have similar statutes.
[2] Clifford Jacobs Motors, Inc. v Chrysler Corp. (DC Ohio) 357 FSupp 564 (1973).

DECISION:

Judgment for Blackwell. The statute requires that a franchisor act in good faith in terminating or refusing to renew a franchise. Kenworth had acted in bad faith when it demanded that Blackwell do things in 90 days that would take a year to do. The making of such an "impossible" demand as the price for renewal showed bad faith. [Blackwell v Kenworth Truck Co. (CA5 Ala) 620 F2d 104 (1980)]

When the relationship between the franchisor and the franchisee is created primarily for the sale of products manufactured by the franchisor, the rights of the parties are governed by the law of sales of Article 2 of the Uniform Commercial Code. Also, it should be remembered from Chapter 4, Government Regulation, that vertical price fixing agreements between a franchisor-manufacturer and its franchisee-distributors, are a violation of the federal antitrust laws. Thus where a manufacturer of winches terminated one of the distributorships for discounting prices contrary to the manufacturer's resale price maintenance policy, the manufacturer was found to be in violation of section one of the Sherman Act and was required to pay three times the actual damages caused by the termination.[3]

(2) Regulation. There continue to be statutory reform movements, both at the federal and at the state levels, to provide general protection for the franchise holder. Protective regulation of franchisees generally relates to problems of fraud in the sale of the franchise and protecting the franchisee from unreasonable demands and termination by the franchisor.

The Petroleum Marketing Products Act (PMPA) gives a gasoline franchisee the opportunity to continue in business by purchasing the entire premises used in selling motor fuel when the franchisor determines to sell the property and not to renew a lease.

FACTS:

Don Roberts operated an Amoco service station franchise in Des Moines, Iowa, for fifteen years. Under the franchise agreement, he leased the service station premises from Amoco. On August 6, 1981, Amoco sent Roberts a letter notifying him that it did not intend to renew his lease when it expired on January 31, 1982, because Amoco intended to sell the premises. On September 4, 1981, Amoco sent Roberts an offer to sell the premises for $66,500. The offer specifically excluded "the gasoline pumps, dispensers, storage tanks, and piping or other equipment" from the sale. Roberts then filed suit against Amoco, alleging that Amoco's conduct violated the Petroleum Marketing Practices Act (PMPA) in that Amoco had failed to make a bona fide offer to sell the service station premises.

DECISION:

Judgment for Roberts. When Congress under the PMPA, required the franchisor to make a bona fide offer to sell the leased premises to its franchisee it intended that the franchisor must include the property used in selling and distributing gasoline such as the pumps, storage tanks, and dispensers. Amoco's offer was thus made in bad faith and was in violation of the PMPA. [Roberts v Amoco Oil Co. (CA8 Iowa) 740 F2d 602 (1985)]

---

[3]Pierce v Ramsey Winch Co. (CA5 Tex) CCH Bus Fran Rptr ¶ 8318 (1985).

In order to protect a prospective franchisee from deception, a Federal Trade Commission regulation requires that the franchisor give a prospective franchisee a disclosure statement ten days before the franchisee signs a contract or pays any money for a franchise. The disclosure statement provides detailed information relating to the franchisor's finances, experience, size of operation, and involvement in litigation. The statement must set forth any restrictions imposed on the franchisee; any costs which must be paid initially or in the future; and the provisions for termination, cancellation, and renewal of the franchise. False statements as to sales, income, or profits are prohibited. Violation of the regulation is subject to a fine of $10,000.

(c) **The Franchisor and Third Persons.** In theory, the franchisor is not liable to a third person dealing with or affected by the franchise holder. This freedom from liability is one of the reasons franchisors grant franchises. If the negligence of the franchisee causes harm to a third person, the franchisor should not be liable, because the franchisee is an independent contractor. However, franchisors continue to be subject to lawsuits based on the wrongful conduct of their franchisees on apparent authority theories. Where plaintiffs have succeeded against franchisors, they have alleged and proven conduct or representations by the franchisor of control over the franchisee, and reliance on such by the plaintiffs. In a recent case against the Shell Oil Company for damages for an injury caused by an employee of a franchisee, the plaintiff succeeded before the court, relying on the following policy precedent:

> Public policy may require that an oil company ostensibly holding itself out to the public as the owner and operator of a service station and advertising special care and good service should bear the responsibility for seeing that the station's services are dispensed reasonably and appropriately.[4]

In another case against Shell Oil Company by a customer injured at a "Shell" gas station, the court rejected the plaintiff's apparent authority argument, noting that the oil company did not own or operate the station, but merely sold petroleum products to the station.[5]

In order to insulate themselves from liability franchisors often require that individual franchisees take steps to publicly maintain their own individual identity as a business, including informing the public that the franchisee owns, supervises, and controls its own operations. Thus a gasoline service station may post a sign stating that it is "dealer owned and operated;" or a real estate franchisee may list on its business sign the franchise name and the name of the local owner, such as "Century 21, L & K Realty Co."

When the franchisee makes a contract with a third person, the franchisor is not liable on the contract as the franchisee is not the agent of the franchisor and does not have any authority to bind the franchisor by contract.

(1) Actual control. A franchisor is liable to third persons when the franchisor exercises such actual control over the operations of the franchisee

---

[4]Shadel v Shell Oil Co., CCH Bus Fran Rptr, ¶ 8211 at p 14, 623 (NJ Sup Ct 1984).
[5]Albright v Parr, CCH Bus Fran Rptr, ¶ 8228 (Ill Ct of App 1984).

that the latter is not to be regarded as an independent contractor but rather as an employee or agent of the franchisor.[6]

(2) Product Liability. When the franchise involves the resale of goods manufactured or obtained by the franchisor and supplied to the franchisee, there is a growing likelihood that if the product causes harm to the franchisee's customer the franchisor will be liable to the customer on theories of warranty.[7]

(d) The Franchisee and Third Persons. When the franchise holder has any contract relationship or contact with a third person, the contract or tort liability of the franchisee is the same as though there were no franchise. For example, if the franchise is to operate a restaurant, the franchise holder is liable to a customer for breach of an implied warranty of the fitness of the food for human consumption to the same extent as though the franchise holder were running an independent restaurant. If the franchise holder negligently causes harm to a third person, as by running over that person with a truck used in the enterprise, the conclusion is the same and the tort liability of the franchise holder is determined by the principles which would be applicable if no franchise existed. The franchise holder is liable on a contract made in the franchise holder's own name. The fact that there is a franchise does not add to or subtract from the liability which the franchisee would have in the same situation had there been no franchise.

§ 45:5. Limited Partnership.

A common form of modified partnership is the limited partnership. This form of partnership is solely a creature of statute; either the Uniform Limited Partnership Act (ULPA), or the Revised Uniform Limited Partnership Act (RULPA).[8]

In a **limited partnership** certain members contribute capital without liability for firm debts beyond the loss of their investment. These members are known as limited partners. The partners who manage the business and are personally liable for the firm debts are **general partners.** A limited partnership can be formed by "one or more general partners and one or more limited partners."[9]

Unlike a general partnership, this special form can be created only by executing a certificate setting forth the essential details of the partnership and the relative rights of the partners. The certificate, when executed, must be recorded in the office of the official in charge of public records, such as the Recorder of Deeds, of the county in which the principal place of business of the partnership is located. When there is no proper filing of the limited partnership certificate, the participants have the status and liability of general partners in a general partnership.

---

[6]Murphy v Holiday Inns, Inc. 216 Va 490, 219 SE2d 874 (1975).

[7]UCC §§ 2–313, 2–314.

[8]The RULPA has been adopted by Alabama, Arizona, Arkansas, California, Colorado, Connecticut, Delaware, Idaho, Iowa, Kansas, Maryland, Massachusetts, Michigan, Minnesota, Missouri, Montana, Nebraska, Nevada, New Jersey, North Dakota, Ohio, Oklahoma, Oregon, Rhode Island, South Carolina, Virginia, Washington, West Virginia, and Wyoming. The ULPA has been adopted in all of the remaining states except Louisiana, and is in force in the District of Columbia and the Virgin Islands.

[9]Uniform Limited Partnership Act, § 1.

Under the ULPA the limited partner contributes cash or property, but not services. However, under the Revised Act, the limited partner may contribute services. With certain exceptions, the limited partner's name cannot appear in the firm name. The limited partner's rights are limited to receiving a share of the profits and the return of capital upon dissolution; the limited partner cannot exercise any control over the business. If improper use is made of the limited partner's name, giving the public the impression of being an active partner, or if the limited partner exercises any control over the business, the limited partner loses the protection of limited liability and becomes liable without limit as a general partner.

FACTS:

Hacienda Farms, Limited, was organized as a limited partnership with Ricardo de Escamilla as the general partner and James L. Russell and H. W. Andrews as limited partners. The partnership raised vegetables and truck crops which were marketed principally through a produce concern controlled by Mr. Andrews. All three individuals decided which crops were to be planted. The general partner had no power to withdraw money from the partnership's two bank accounts without the signature of one of the limited partners. After operating for some seven and one half months under these procedures, the limited partners required the general partner to resign as farm manager, which he did. Six weeks later the partnership went into bankruptcy. Laurance Holzman, as trustee in bankruptcy, brought an action against Russell and Andrews, claiming that they had become liable to the creditors of the partnership as general partners because they had taken part in the control of the partnership business. From judgment against them, Russell and Andrews appealed.

DECISION:

Judgment for the trustee in bankruptcy, Holzman. The limited partners Russell and Andrews, took part in the control of the business of the partnership and thus became liable as general partners. Russell and Andrews were active in dictating the crops to be planted. The banking procedures of the partnership were such that the general partner had no power to withdraw money from firm accounts without the signature of either Russell or Andrews. And, Russell and Andrews required the general partner to resign as manager and they selected his successor. [Holzman v De Escamilla, 86 Cal App 2d 858, 195 P2d 833 (1948)]

Participation in the affairs of the business by the limited partners can only give rise to a liability to creditors of the partnership. The general partner cannot claim that such participation makes the limited partners bound to share in the losses of the enterprise.

A limited partner may bring an action on behalf of the limited partnership against outsiders for economic injury to the firm, when the general partners refuse to do so. Also, the limited partners may utilize judicial proceedings against the general partners to protect their interests, where it can be shown that the conduct of the general partners is fraudulent as to the limited partners.

The dissolution and winding up of limited partnerships is governed by the same principles applicable to general partnerships. In many respects, the ULPA follows the general pattern of the UPA, and a general partner in a limited partnership has the same rights and liabilities as a partner in a general partnership.[10]

§ 45:6.   Joint Venture.

A **joint venture**, or joint adventure, is a relationship in which two or more persons combine their labor or property for a single business undertaking and share profits and losses equally, or as otherwise agreed. Where several contractors pool all their assets in order to construct one tunnel, the relationship is a joint venture.

FACTS:
Three corporations and two individuals pooled their equipment, services, and assets for the performance of a contract to construct a tunnel. When Wheatley brought suit against them, he claimed that they were a joint venture.

DECISION:
The corporations and individuals had formed a joint venture since they had pooled everything and had limited their associating to the performance of the one tunnel construction contract. [Wheatley v Halvorson, 213 Or 228, 323 P2d 49 (1958)]

A joint venture is similar in many respects to a partnership, but it differs primarily in that the joint venture typically relates to the prosecution of a single enterprise or transaction, although its accomplishment may require several years, while a partnership is generally a continuing business or activity. This is not an exact definition because a partnership may be expressly created for a single transaction. Because this distinction is so insubstantial, many courts hold that a joint venture is subject to the same principles of law as partnerships.[11] Thus, the duties owed by the joint venturers to each other are the same as in the case of partnerships, with the result that when the joint venturers agree to acquire and develop a certain tract of land but some of the venturers secretly purchase the land in their own names, the other joint venturers are entitled to damages for this breach of the duty of loyalty.

It is essential that there be a community of interest or purpose and that each coadventurer have an equal right to control the operations or activities of the undertaking.[12] The actual control of the operations may be

[10]North Peachtree I–285 Properties, Ltd. v Hicks, 136 Ga App 426, 221 SE2d 607 (1975).
[11]Burruss v Green Auction & Realty Co. Inc., 228 Va 6, 319 SE2d 725 (1984).
[12]Milberg Factors Inc. v Hurwitz-Nordlight Joint Venture (Tex Civ App) 676 SW2d 613 (1984).

entrusted to one of the joint venturers. Thus, the fact that one joint adventurer is placed in control of the farming and livestock operations of the undertaking and appears to be the owner of the land does not destroy the joint adventure relationship.

(a) **Duration of Joint Venture.** When a joint venture agreement states the time for which the venture is to last, such specification will be given effect. In the absence of a fixed duration provision, a joint venture is ordinarily terminable at the will of any participant,[13] except that when the joint venture clearly relates to a particular transaction, such as the construction of a specified bridge, the joint venture ordinarily lasts until the particular transaction or project is completed or becomes impossible to complete.

The term "joint venture" is descriptive of a relationship rather than of a structure or organization. Thus two joint venturers may organize a corporation for the purpose of carrying out their joint venture of constructing an apartment building. The relationship between the two is a joint venture even though the organization or structure employed is a corporation.

(b) **Liability to Third Persons.** The conclusion that persons are joint venturers often becomes important when a suit is brought by or against a third person for personal injuries or property damage. If there is a joint venture, the fault or negligence of one venturer will be imputed to the other venturer so that the other venturer may lose the lawsuit because of the misconduct of the coadventurer.

§ 45:7.   Unincorporated Association.

An **unincorporated association** is a combination of two or more persons for the furtherance of a common nonprofit purpose. No particular form of organization is required, and any conduct or agreement indicating an attempt to associate or work together for a common purpose is sufficient. Social clubs, fraternal associations, and political parties are common examples of unincorporated associations.

The authority of an unincorporated association over its members is governed by ordinary principles of contract law, and an association cannot expel a member for a ground which is not expressly authorized by the contract between the association and the member.[14]

Except when otherwise provided by statute, an unincorporated association does not have any legal existence, such as has a corporation, apart from the members who compose it. Thus, an unincorporated association cannot sue or be sued in its own name.

Generally the members of an unincorporated association are not liable for the debts or liabilities of the association by the mere fact that they are members. It is generally required to show that they authorized or ratified the act in question. If either authorization or ratification by a particular member can be shown, that member is unlimitedly liable as in the case of a general partner.

[13]Marmis v Solot Co. 117 Ariz 499, 573 P2d 899 (1977).
[14]Cunningham v Independent Soap & Chemical Workers, 207 Kan 812, 486 P2d 1316 (1971), (holding labor union without authority to expel members for crossing picket line and working during strike).

FACTS:

Golden Spike Little League was an unincorporated association of persons who joined together to promote a little league baseball team in Ogden, Utah. They sent one of their members to arrange for credit at Smith & Edwards, a local sporting goods store. After getting credit, various members went to the store and picked up and signed for different items of baseball equipment and uniforms, at a total cost of $3900. When Mr. Smith, the owner requested payment, the members arranged a fund-raising activity which produced only $149. Smith sued the Golden Spike Little League as an entity and the members who had picked up and signed for the equipment individually. The individual defendants denied that they had any personal liability, contending that only the Golden Spike Little League could be held responsible.

DECISION:

Judgment for Smith against the individual members. No basis exists for the suit against the unincorporated association known as the Golden Spike Little League because such an association is not a legal entity upon which liability can be imposed. But when individuals enter into a contract with another, or authorize or ratify that contract, they render themselves personally liable, even if they purported to make a contract for an unsuable unincorporated association. [Smith & Edwards v Golden Spike Little League (Utah) 577 P 2d 132 (1978)]

---

§ 45:8.   Cooperative.

A **cooperative** consists of a group of two or more independent persons or enterprises which cooperate with respect to a common objective or function. Thus, farmers may pool their farm products and sell them as a group. Consumers may likewise pool their orders and purchase goods in bulk.

(a) **Incorporated Cooperative.** Statutes commonly provide for the special incorporation of cooperative enterprises. Such statutes often provide that any excess of payments over cost of operation shall be refunded to each participant member in direct proportion to the volume of business which the member has done with the cooperative. This contrasts with the payment of a dividend by an ordinary business corporation in which the payment of dividends is proportional to the number of shares held by the shareholder and is unrelated to the extent of the shareholder's business activities with the enterprise.

(b) **Antitrust Law Exemption.** As the agreement by the members of sellers' cooperatives that all products shall be sold at a common price is an agreement to fix prices, the sellers' cooperative is basically an agreement in restraint of trade and a violation of antitrust laws. The Capper-Volstead Act of 1922 expressly exempts normal selling activities of farmers' and dairy farmers' cooperatives from the operation of the federal Sherman Antitrust Act as long as the cooperatives do not conspire with outsiders to fix prices.

SUMMARY

The three principal forms of business organizations are sole proprietorships, partnerships, and corporations. An individual proprietorship is a form of business organization in which one person owns the business, controls all decisions, receives all profits, and is unlimitedly liable for all losses, if any. A partnership involves the pooling of capital resources and talents of two or more persons with the goal of making a profit; the partners are subject to unlimited personal liability. A business corporation exists to make a profit, being created by government grant, with its shareholders electing a board of directors who are responsible to manage the business. A shareholder's liability is limited to the capital the shareholder invested in the business. The corporation may be established with a perpetual life.

The selection of the form of organization is often determined by tax considerations, the financial risk involved and the importance of limited liability, and the extent of control of management desired.

A franchise is an arrangement in which the owner of a trademark, tradename, or copyright licenses others to use such mark or copyright in the selling of goods or services. In order to protect against fraud, the FTC requires that franchisors provide prospective franchisees with a disclosure statement ten days prior to any transaction. The Automobile Dealers' Franchise Act and the Petroleum Marketing Products Act are national laws which provide covered franchisees with protection from bad faith terminations. State laws also provide protection to franchisees in a wide range of businesses. In theory the franchisor is not liable in any way to third persons dealing with the franchisee. However litigation against franchisors for the torts of franchisees is common, with plaintiffs commonly alleging apparent authority. These suits are successful only where the plaintiffs can demonstrate actual or apparent control over the operations of the franchisee by the franchisor.

A limited partnership consists of one or more limited partners who contribute capital without liability for losses beyond their investment, and one or more general partners, who manage the business and have unlimited personal liability. Created by statute, a certificate and public filing are required. A joint venture is a legal entity in which two or more persons combine their labor or property for a single business undertaking and share profits and losses as agreed. An unincorporated association is a combination of two or more persons for the pursuit of a common, nonprofit purpose. A cooperative consists of two or more persons or enterprises, such as farmers, who cooperate with respect to a common objective, such as the distribution of farm products.

QUESTIONS AND CASE PROBLEMS

1. What social forces are affected by the federal Automobile Dealers' Franchise Act?
2. Herbert buys Magda brand television sets directly from the factory and resells them to retail customers. He sells so many of the Magda sets that he does not carry any other make of set. Herbert advertises in the local newspaper as being "your Magda dealer." In a dispute with the factory over entitlement to a large commercial Magda sign given to all Magda

franchisees, Herbert claims that he is a franchisee because he is selling under the Magda name. Is he correct?

3. When is a franchisor held liable to a third person dealing with or affected by the franchisee?

4. Elizabeth, Josephine, and Florence entered into an agreement to purchase a tract of land, build houses on it, sell the houses, and then divide the net profit. What kind of business organization was intended?

5. Jerome, Sheila, Gary, and Ella agreed to purchase a tract of land and make it available for use as a free playground for neighborhood children. They call the enterprise the Meadowbrook Playground. One of the playground swings was improperly hung by Jerome and Gary and a child is injured. Suit is brought for injuries against the Meadowbrook Playground. Can damages be recovered?

6. Compare a limited and a general partnership with respect to (a) formality of creation, and (b) dissolution and winding up.

7. Compare a franchise and a contract.

8. Lauter and Domenick form a partnership. They find that they need more money. They induce Gerard to invest $50,000. He agrees to do so provided he is a limited partner. Lauter and Domenick agree to this and Gerard contributes $50,000. Is Gerard a limited partner?

9. Professor Kerry Rhodes invented a filter for use in microwave telecommunications. She desired to participate in the earnings which she anticipated would result from the manufacture and sale of her invention. Hal Jones, president of a venture capital firm, advised Kerry of the tax advantages of a limited partnership, including the advantage of no liability for the firm's debts beyond the loss of her investment should the venture fail. A limited partnership was created in accordance with state law, and the certificate was properly filed. Henry Nickerson was named as the general partner, and Rhodes and Jones, both of whom contributed cash, were named as the limited partners in the certificate. Initially Rhodes and Jones advised Nickerson "to run all final employment candidates by us for a look see;" and only one candidate was "rejected" by them. When it was established at a weekly luncheon meeting of the three individuals that start-up expenses were greatly exceeding what had been anticipated, it was agreed that as a control feature all firm checks over $1000 would require two signatures, one being Nickerson's and the other being that of either Rhodes or Jones. Later Rhodes found out at a professional meeting that a competitor had developed a new lightweight filter which had technical advantages superior to Rhodes' filter and she and Jones agreed to notify Nickerson to halt production and to lay off employees until Rhodes could improve the filter. The firm ran out of funds and could not pay its suppliers. General Suppliers Corp. sues Nickerson, Rhodes, and Jones as general partners for the money owed it for supplies delivered to the firm. Rhodes and Jones contend that as limited partners they are not liable beyond their investment. Decide.

10. Goodward, a newly hired newspaper reporter for the Cape Cod News, learned that the local cranberry growers had made an agreement under which they pooled their cranberry crops each year and sold the crops at what they determined to be a fair price. Goodward believes that such an

agreement is in restraint of trade and a violation of the antitrust laws. Is he correct?

11. Food Caterers, Inc. of East Hartford Connecticut, obtained a franchise from Chicken Delight, Inc. to use that name at its store and agreed to the product standards and controls specified by the franchisor. The franchise contract required the franchisee to maintain a free delivery service in order to deliver hot, freshly prepared food to customers. The franchisee used a delivery truck which bore no sign or name. Its employee Carfiro drove the truck in making a delivery of food. He negligently struck and killed McLaughlin. The victim's estate sued Chicken Delight on the theory that Carfiro was its agent because he was doing the work which Chicken Delight required to be done and which benefited Chicken Delight. Was Carfiro the agent of Chicken Delight? [McLaughlin's Estate v Chicken Delight, Inc. 164 Conn 317, 321 A2d 456]

12. A limited partnership owned and operated a marina under the name of West River Marina, Ltd. Radack was the general partner. McCully and others were limited partners. The partnership did not pay its debts and a foreclosure action was brought against it. McCully and other limited partners petitioned the court for permission to intervene in the foreclosure action on the theory that the action was a sham which was planned by Radack and others as a way of wiping out the interests of the limited partners and thus acquiring the property for themselves. Radack and the others objected to the intervention on the ground that limited partners have no voice in the management of a limited partnership and therefore could not take part in litigation. Should the intervention be allowed? [McCully v Radack, 27 Md App 350, 340 A2d 374]

13. Nissan was the distributor of Datsuns in the United States. Randy's Datsun and two other dealers held dealer franchises for the Salt Lake City area and were in competition with each other. The other two dealers complained to Nissan that Randy's was cutting prices. Nissan warned Randy to maintain higher prices and attempted to persuade Randy to move outside the city. Randy refused because the last dealer to go there had gone bankrupt. A shortage of Datsuns arose and Nissan allocated the limited supply by a formula which had the effect of reducing the supply to Randy's and increasing the supply to the other two dealers. Thereafter Nissan notified Randy's that it would not renew the franchise agreement with Randy's. Randy's sued Nissan for damages for bad faith termination of the franchise in violation of the federal Automobile Dealers' Franchise Act. Was Nissan liable? [Randy's v Nissan Motor Corp. (CA 10 Utah) 533 F2d 510]

14. Woods Mill was a limited partnership formed for the construction of an apartment complex. Financial difficulties arose and some of the limited partners discussed the economic problems with their general partner. One of the limited partners visited the construction site and complained as to the manner in which the work was being done. Thereafter the building contractor defaulted. The limited partners were sued for the breach of the contract on the theory that they had so participated in the business that they were liable as general partners. Were they liable? [Trans-Am Builders Inc. v Woods Mill Ltd. 133 Ga App 411, 210 SE2d 866]

15. Brenner was in the scrap iron business. Almost daily Plitt loaned Brenner money with which to purchase scrap iron. The agreement of the parties was that when the scrap was sold, Plitt would be repaid and would receive an additional sum as compensation for making the loan. The loans were to be repaid in any case, without regard to whether Brenner made a profit. A dispute arose as to the relationship between the two men. Plitt claimed that it was a joint venture. Decide. [Brenner v Plitt, 182 Md 348, 34 A2d 853]

16. Donald Salisbury, William Roberts and others purchased property from Laurel Chapman, a partner of Chapman Realty, a franchisee of Realty World Inc. They made payments directly to Laurel Chapman at the Realty World office, who was supposed to make payments on the property's mortgage. Chapman, however, did not make the payments, and absconded with the funds. Salisbury and Roberts sued the franchisor, Realty World, contending that Realty World was liable for the wrongful acts of the apparent agent Chapman. Realty World and Chapman Realty are parties to a franchise agreement which states that the parties are franchisor/franchisee and it contained a clause which required Chapman to prominently display a certificate in the office setting forth Chapman's status as an independent franchisee. Chapman displayed such a sign, but the plaintiffs do not recall seeing it. Chapman Realty hires, supervises, and sets the compensation for all of its employees. The plaintiffs point out that Chapman Realty used the service mark "Realty World" on its signs both outside and inside its offices. They point out that a Realty World manual sets forth the general standards by which franchisees must run their businesses, and that such is clear control over the franchise. They contend that all things considered Realty World held out Chapman Realty as having authority to bind Realty World. Realty World disagrees stating both are independent businesses. Decide. [Salisbury v Chapman and Realty World, Inc. 124 Ill App 3d 1057, 65 NE2d 127.]

17. Freeland Thorson operated a real estate agency in Idaho and Tiny Bellamy operated a real estate agency in Oregon. Bellamy obtained an exclusive listing to sell certain land and at the bottom of the listing he included the statement that "this is a cooperative listing with F. Thorson of Wieser, Idaho"; Bellamy also informed the seller that he intended to work with Thorson on the sale and to share the commission with him. Thorson and Bellamy discussed how the commission would be divided if the property sold, but did not reach agreement on these points. Bellamy actively sought a buyer during the period, and Thorson did not. Thorson's sole effort in the sale of the property consisted of visiting the home of a Mrs. Mosden to obtain her signature on a document to clear title. Bellamy refused to share the commission with Thorson, and Thorson brought suit on the theory that a joint venture existed and that he was entitled to half of the commission. Bellamy defended that no joint venture existed; and that Thorson's performance was so inadequate as to preclude him from sharing in the commission. Decide. [Thorson v Bellamy (Or App) 653 P2d 1048.]

CHAPTER 46

CREATION AND

TERMINATION OF

PARTNERSHIPS

CHAPTER OBJECTIVES

After studying this chapter you will be able to:
1. Describe the characteristics of a partnership.
2. Differentiate between general and special partnerships and trading and nontrading partnerships.
3. List the seven guides which aid in determining whether the parties have created a partnership.
4. Describe how a partnership may be dissolved by the acts of the partners, by order of a court, and by operation of law.
5. Explain the effect of a dissolution of a partnership.
6. Describe the extent of a partner's authority during the winding up of a parnership's business.

Modern partnership law shows traces of Roman Law, the law merchant, and the common law of England. A codification of partnership law is found in the Uniform Partnership Act (UPA), which Act has been adopted by forty-nine states.[1]

Partnerships are created by agreement; however, the agreements are often informal and may be unwritten. The UPA contains a set of rules on the creation of partnerships which deal with the wide range of issues that may develop from such an informal formation process.

Dissolution of a partnership may result from the acts of the partners; or may be by operation of law, as in the death of a partner, or by court decree,

[1]This Act has been adopted in all states except Louisiana; and it is in force in the District of Columbia, Guam, and the Virgin Islands.

where the dissension among the partners is so serious that continuation of the business is impracticable. The UPA contains a comprehensive body of rules for the dissolution and termination of the partnership.

A. NATURE AND CREATION

A discussion of the creation of partnerships must be prefaced with a discussion of the nature of the partnership relation, including the characteristics of a partnership, the various classifications of partnerships and partners, and the nature of partnership property.

§ 46:1.   Definition.

A **partnership** is a legal relationship created by the voluntary "association of two or more persons to carry on as co-owners a business for profit."[2] The persons so associated are called **partners**. While each partner is the agent of the partnership, a partner is not regarded as an "employee" of the partnership.

FACTS:

W. M. Ford and James D. Mitcham were partners engaged in construction. Ford was killed at work. His widow made a claim for workers' compensation. Mitcham opposed the claim on the ground that Ford was a partner and not an employee.

DECISION:

Judgment for Mitcham. While a working partner does work, a partner is not an employee. The essential element of an employment relationship is the right of the employer to control the employee. Although a partner is required to act in a proper manner, a partner is not subject to the control of the partnership in the same sense as an employee and therefore is not an "employee" of the partnership for the purpose of workers' compensation. [Ford v Mitcham (Ala Civ App) 298 So2d 34 (1974)]

---

§ 46:2.   Characteristics of a Partnership.

A partnership can be described in terms of its characteristics:

(a) A partnership is a voluntary consensual relationship; it is not imposed by law. Because of the intimate and confidential nature of the partnership relation, courts do not attempt to thrust a partner upon anyone.
(b) A partnership usually involves contributions by the members of capital, labor, or skill, or a combination of these.
(c) The parties are associated as co-owners and principals to transact the business of the firm.

[2] Uniform Partnership Act, § 6(1); Miller v City Bank and Trust Co., 82 Mich App 120, 266 NW2d 687 (1978).

(d) A partnership is organized for the pecuniary profit of its members. If profit is not its object, the group will commonly be an unincorporated association.

The trend of the law is to treat a partnership as a separate legal person, although historically and technically it is merely a group of individuals with each partner being the owner of a fractional interest in the common enterprise. The Uniform Partnership Act does not make the partnership a separate entity and therefore suit cannot be brought by the firm in its firm name,[3] in the absence of a special statute or procedural rule so providing. Some courts regard a partnership as distinct from the individual partners so that a partnership cannot claim the benefit of a personal immunity possessed by an individual partner.

As a partnership is based upon the agreement of the parties, the characteristics and attributes of the partnership relationship are initially a matter of the application of general principles of contract law, upon which the principles of partnership are superimposed.

FACTS:

Burt Marshall and Blanche Olsen were partners in an investment company dealing in the acquisition and lease of land for billboard advertising. Marshall had an 80% interest in the partnership and Olsen a 20% interest in the partnership. Blanche Olsen died on October 29, 1971, and Seattle-First National Bank was named executor of her estate. The partnership agreement contained a buy-sell provision that required the surviving partner to purchase the interest of the deceased partner. The agreement also stipulated a procedure for establishing the market value of the deceased partner's interest in the partnership. Seattle-First sued Marshall to compel him to purchase Olsen's interest at a price of $164,649 which was determined in accordance with the procedures set forth in the partnership agreement. Marshall objected that this price was too high and that it should be discounted by sales costs and capital gains taxes to be paid upon the sale of the partnership interest as is usually done in the sale of other interests.

DECISION:

Judgment for the estate of Blanche Olsen. Because the partnership agreement setting forth the method of valuing a deceased partner's interest makes no allowance for discount factors, Marshall's contention must be rejected even though discounts might be appropriate in the sale of other interests. The agreement is the heart of the partnership and its mandates must be enforced as written. [Seattle-First National Bank v Marshall, 31 Wash App 339, 641 P2d 1194 (1982)]

---

[3]Allgeier v Martin and Associates (Mo App) 508 SW2d 524 (1974).

§ 46:3.   Purposes of a Partnership.

A partnership, whether it relates to the conduct of a business or a profession, may be formed for any lawful purpose. A partnership cannot be formed to carry out immoral or illegal acts, or acts that are contrary to public policy.

§ 46:4.   Classification of Partnerships.

Ordinary partnerships are classified as general and special partnerships, and as trading and nontrading partnerships. The ordinary partnership is distinguished from the statutory limited partnership.[4]

(a) **General and Special Partnerships.** A **general partnership** is created for the general conduct of a particular kind of business, such as a hardware business or a manufacturing business. A **special partnership** is formed for a single transaction, such as the purchase and resale of a certain building.

(b) **Trading and Nontrading Partnerships.** A **trading partnership** is organized for the purpose of buying and selling, such as a firm engaged in the retail grocery business. A **nontrading partnership** is one organized for a purpose other than engaging in commerce, such as the practice of law or medicine.

§ 46:5.   Firm Name.

In the absence of a statutory requirement, a partnership need not have a firm name, although it is customary to have one. The partners may, as a general rule, adopt any firm name they desire. They may use a fictitious name or even the name of a stranger. There are, however, certain limitations upon the adoption of a firm name:

(a) The name cannot be the same as or be deceptively similar to the name of another firm for the purpose of attracting its patrons.
(b) Some states prohibit the use of the words "and company" unless they indicate an additional partner.
(c) Most states require the registration of a fictitious partnership name. For example, Ken and Steve Swain transact business under a partnership name "The Berkshire Dairy Farm." Since such a name does not reveal the names of the partners, a certificate stating the names and addresses of the partners must be filed at the public office designated by state law, usually a city or town clerk's office.

§ 46:6.   Classification of Partners.

(a) **General partners** are those who publicly and actively engage in the transaction of firm business.

[4]See Chapter 45.

(b) **Nominal partners** hold themselves out as partners or permit others to hold them out as such. They are not in fact partners, but in some instances they may be held liable as partners.

(c) **Silent partners** are those who, although they may be known to the public as partners, take no active part in the business.

(d) **Secret partners** are those who take an active part in the management of the firm but who are not known to the public as partners.

(e) **Dormant partners** are ones who take no active part in transacting the business and who remain unknown to the public.

§ 46:7.   Who May Be Partners.

In the absence of statutory provisions to the contrary, persons who are competent to contract may form a partnership. A minor may become a partner, but may avoid the contract of partnership and withdraw.

In general, the capacity of an insane person to be a partner is similar to that of a minor, except that an adjudication of insanity usually makes subsequent agreements void rather than merely voidable. An enemy alien may not be a partner, but other aliens may enter into the relationship. A corporation, unless expressly authorized by statute or its certificate of incorporation, may not act as a partner. The modern statutory trend, however, is to permit corporations to become partners.

§ 46:8.   Creation of Partnership.

A partnership is a voluntary association and exists because the parties agree to be in partnership.[5] If there is no agreement, there is no partnership. If the parties agree that the legal relationship between them shall be such that they in fact operate a business for profit as co-owners, a partnership is created even though the parties may not have labeled their new relationship a "partnership." The law is concerned with the substance of what is done rather than the name. Conversely, a partnership does not arise if the parties do not agree to the elements of a partnership, even though they call it a partnership.

The manner in which an enterprise is described in a tax return or an application for a license is significant in determining whether it is a partnership as against a person making the return or the application. The mere fact that the enterprise is described as a partnership is not controlling or binding, however, as to a person named as a partner in the return or in the application if that person did not know of its preparation, did not sign it, and did not know what it said. When the parties are in fact employer and employee, there is no partnership even though the employer files a partnership form of income tax return.

§ 46:9.   Partnership Agreement.

As a general rule, partnership agreements need not be in writing. A partnership agreement must be in writing, however, if it is within the provision of the statute of frauds that a contract which cannot be performed within one year must be in writing. In some situations the agreement may

---

[5]Shain Investment Co., Inc. v Cohen, 15 Mass App 4, 443 NE2d 126 (1982).

PARTNERSHIP AGREEMENT

It's generally a good idea to spell out the rights and duties of partners in a written partnership agreement.

come under the provision of the statute that requires a transfer of interest in land to be in writing. Generally, however, the agreement need not be written solely because the partnership is formed to engage in the business of buying and selling real estate.

Even when unnecessary, it is always desirable to have the partnership agreement in writing to avoid subsequent controversies as to mutual rights and duties. The formal document that is prepared to evidence the contract of the parties is termed a **partnership agreement, articles of partnership,** or **articles of copartnership.** The partnership agreement will govern the partnership during its existence and may also contain provisions relating to dissolution.[6]

§ 46:10.   Determining Existence of Partnership.

Whether a partnership exists is basically a matter of proving the intention of the parties.

As in the case of agency, the burden of proving the existence of a partnership is upon the person who claims that one exists.

When the parties have not clearly indicated the nature of their relationship, the law has developed the following guides to aid in determining whether the parties have created a partnership:

(a) **Control.** The presence or absence of control of a business enterprise is significant in determining whether there is a partnership and whether a particular person is a partner.

(b) **Sharing Profits and Losses.** The fact that the parties share profits and losses is strong evidence of a partnership.[7]

(c) **Sharing Profits.** An agreement that does not provide for sharing losses but does provide for sharing profits is evidence that the parties are partners, as it is assumed that they will also share losses. Sharing profits is prima facie evidence of a partnership; but a partnership is not to be inferred when profits are received in payment of (1) a debt, (2) wages, (3) rent, (4) an annuity to a deceased partner's surviving spouse or representative, (5) interest, or (6) payment for the goodwill of the business. The fact that one doctor receives one half of the net income does not establish that that doctor is a partner of another doctor where the doctor was guaranteed a minimum annual amount and the federal income tax and social security contributions were deducted from the payments to the doctor, thus indicating that the relationship was employer and employee.[8] If there is no evidence of the reason for receiving the profits, a partnership of the parties involved exists.

FACTS:

Bowen owned and operated the Havana Club in a rented building. He owned all the physical assets of the business. He made an agreement with Cutler, the bartender, that she would operate the club, purchase supplies, pay bills, keep the books, and hire and fire employees. Cutler and Bowen were each to receive $100 a week and to divide the net profits. A partnership form of income tax return was filed for the business. At a later date, the Redevelopment Agency took the building in which the Havana Club was operated. The Club went out of business because it could not find a new location. The Redevelopment Agency paid the Club $10,000 damages for disruption of business. Cutler sued Bowen for one half of the sum paid by the Redevelopment Agency on

[6]Bohn v Bohn Implement Co. (ND) 325 NW2d 281 (1982).
[7]Boyarsky v Froccaro, 479 NYS2d 606 (1984).
[8]UPA § 7(4).

the theory that they had been a partnership. Bowen claimed that he was the sole owner of the business because he was the owner of the physical assets.

DECISION:

Judgment for Cutler. There was a partnership in which one partner contributed assets and the other contributed services. The two divided the profits of the business equally. Tax returns were filed for a partnership. The enterprise was therefore a partnership and not a business solely owned by Bowen, the contributor of the physical assets. [Cutler v Bowen (Utah) 543 P2d 1349 (1975)]

(d) Gross Returns. The sharing of gross returns is itself very slight, if any, evidence of partnership. To illustrate, in a case in which one party owned a show that was exhibited upon land owned by another under an agreement to divide the gross proceeds, no partnership was proven because there was no co-ownership or community of interest in the business. Similarly, it was not established that there was a partnership when it was shown that a farmer rented an airplane to a pilot to do aerial chemical spraying under an agreement by which the pilot would pay the farmer, as compensation for the use of the plane, a share of the fees which the pilot received.

(e) Co-Ownership. Neither the co-ownership of property nor the sharing of profits or rents from property which two or more persons own creates a partnership. Thus, the fact that a person acquires a 49 percent interest in a trailer park does not establish that such person is a partner. This in itself does not establish that the co-owners are together conducting the trailer park business for profit. Conversely, the mere fact that there is a sharing of the income from property by joint owners does not establish that they are partners.

(f) Contribution of Property. The fact that all persons have not contributed capital to the enterprise does not establish that the enterprise is not a partnership. A partnership may be formed even though some of its members furnish only skill or labor.

(g) Fixed Payment. When a person who performs continuing services for another receives a fixed payment for such services, not dependent upon the existence of profit and not affected by losses, that person is not a partner.

§ 46:11.   Partners as to Third Persons.

In some instances, persons who are in fact not partners may be held accountable to third persons as though they were partners. This liability arises when they conduct themselves in such a manner that others are reasonably led to believe that they are partners and to act in reliance on that belief to their injury.[9] A person who is held liable as a partner under such circumstances is termed a nominal partner, a partner by estoppel, or an ostensible partner.

Partnership liability may arise by estoppel when a person who in fact is not a partner is described as a partner in a document filed with the govern-

[9]UPA § 16(1): Johnson v Slusser, 33 Wash App 439, 655 P2d 261 (1982).

ment, provided the person so described has in some way participated in the filing of the document and the person claiming the benefit of the estoppel had knowledge of that document and relied on the statement. For example, suppose that the partnership of *A* and *B*, in registering its fictitious name, names *A*, *B*, and *C* as partners and the registration certificate is signed by all of them. If a creditor who sees this registration statement extends credit to the firm in reliance in part on the fact that *C* is a partner, *C* has a partner's liability insofar as that creditor is concerned.

Conversely, no estoppel arises when the creditor does not know of the existence of the registration certificate and consequently does not rely thereon in extending credit to the partnership. Likewise, such liability does not arise when *C* does not know of the certificate.

§ 46:12.   Partnership Property.

In general, partnership property consists of all the property contributed by the partners or acquired for the firm or with its funds.[10] There is usually no limitation upon the kind and amount of property that a partnership may acquire. The firm may own real as well as personal property, unless it is prohibited from doing so by statute or by the partnership agreement.

The parties may agree that real estate owned by one of the partners should become partnership property. When this intent exists, the particular property constitutes partnership property even though it is still in the name of the original owner.

The determining factor as to whether specific property constitutes partnership property or the individual property of one of the partners is the intention of the partners. The partners' intent may be determined from the actions of the parties, such as the source and accounting treatment of the purchase money for the property in question, and the use to which the property was put.

FACTS:

Robert and William Palmer conducted a large cattle selling partnership called "Palmer Brothers." On Robert's death, William claimed that he was entitled to the funds in the checking account as the surviving joint tenant. The account had been opened by Robert and William as a joint tenancy in 1947, and the Palmer Brothers partnership paid all the expenses of operating the ranch (including purchasing and feeding live stock, trucking, and taxes) from this account and deposited all proceeds from the sale of cattle into the account. Robert's wife, Constance, his sole heir at law, claims that the checking account should be accounted for as partnerhsip property in the winding up and dissolution of the partnership.

DECISION:

Judgment against William. The checking account was the only account used by the partnership for its cattle business, to pay the expenses in operating this business and to receive all proceeds from the sale of cattle. The funds were thus partnership funds and must be accounted for as such in the winding up and dissolution of the partnerhsip, notwithstanding the joint tenancy form of the account. [Matter of the Estate of Robert Palmer (Mont) 708 P2d 242 (1985)]

---

[10]UPA § 8. Rider's Estate, 487 Pa 373, 409 A2d 397 (1979).

§ 46:13. Tenancy in Partnership.

Partners hold title to firm property by **tenancy in partnership.**[11] The characteristics of such a tenancy are:

(a) Each partner has an equal right to use firm property for partnership purposes in the absence of a contrary agreement.

(b) A partner possesses no interest in any specific item of partnership property that can be voluntarily sold, assigned, or mortgaged by a partner.[12]

(c) A creditor of a partner cannot proceed against any specific items of partnership property.[13] The creditor can only proceed against the partner's interest in the partnership. This is done by applying to a court for a **charging order.** By this procedure, the share of any profits that would be paid to the debtor-partner is paid to a receiver on behalf of the creditor or the court may direct the sale of the interest of the debtor-partner in the partnership.

(d) On the death of a partner, the partnership property vests in the surviving partners for partnership purposes and is not subject to the rights of the surviving spouse of the deceased partner.

§ 46:14. Assignment of Partner's Interest.

Although a partner cannot transfer specific items of partnership property, in the absence of authority to so act on behalf of the partnership, a partner's interest in the partnership may be voluntarily assigned by the partners.[14] The assignee does not become a partner without the consent of the other partners. Without this consent, the assignee is only entitled to receive the assignor's share of the profits during the continuance of the partnership and the assignor's interest upon the dissolution of the firm. The assignee has no right to participate in the management of the partnership; nor does the assignee have a right to inspect the books of the partnership.

B. DISSOLUTION AND TERMINATION

Partnerships may be dissolved by the acts of the partners, by order of a court, or by operation of law. Dissolution changes the legal status of both the partnership and the individual partners.

§ 46:15. Effect of Dissolution.

Dissolution ends the right of the partnership to exist as a going concern, but it does not end the existence of the partnership.[15] It is followed by a winding-up period, upon the conclusion of which the partnership's legal existence is terminated.

Dissolution reduces the authority of the partners. From the moment of dissolution, the partners lose authority to act for the firm, "except so far as may be necessary to wind up partnership affairs or to complete transactions begun but not then finished."[16] The vested rights of the partners are not

---

[11]UPA § 25(1): Smoot v Smoot (Tex Civ App) 568 SW2d 177 (1978).
[12]Putnam v Shoaf (Tenn App) 620 SW2d 510 (1981).
[13]UPA § 25(2)(c).
[14]UPA § 27.
[15]Simmons v Quick-Stop Food Mart, Inc. 307 NC 33, 296 SE2d 275 (1982).
[16]UPA § 33.

extinguished by dissolving the firm, and the existing liabilities remain. Thus, when the partnership is dissolved by the death of a partner, the estate of the deceased partner is liable to the same extent as the deceased partner.

§ 46:16. Dissolution by Act of Parties.

(a) **Agreement.** A partnership may be dissolved in accordance with the terms of the original agreement of the parties, as by the expiration of the period for which the relation was to continue or by the performance of the object for which it was organized.[17] The relation may also be dissolved by subsequent agreement, as when the partners agree to dissolve the firm before the lapse of the time specified in the articles of partnership or before the attainment of the object for which the firm was created.

(b) **Expulsion.** A partnership is dissolved by the expulsion of any partner from the business in accordance with such a power conferred by the agreement between the partners.

(c) **Alienation of Interest.** Neither a voluntary sale of a partner's interest nor an involuntary sale for the benefit of creditors works a dissolution of the partnership.

(d) **Withdrawal.** A partner has the power to withdraw from the partnership at any time; but if the withdrawal violates the partnership agreement, the withdrawing partner becomes liable to the copartners for damages for breach of contract. When the relationship is for no definite purpose or time, a partner may withdraw without liability at any time. Postemployment restrictive provisions are commonly found in partnership agreements, particularly in the accounting, legal, and medical professions and in marketing organizations.

§ 46:17. Dissolution by Operation of Law.

(a) **Death.** An ordinary partnership is dissolved immediately upon the death of any partner, even when the agreement provides for the continuance of the business. Thus, when the executor of a deceased partner carries on the business with the remaining partner, there is legally a new firm.

(b) **Bankruptcy.** Bankruptcy of the firm or of one of the partners causes the dissolution of the firm; insolvency alone does not.

(c) **Illegality.** A partnership is dissolved "by an event which makes it unlawful for the business of the partnership to be carried on or for the members to carry it on in partnership." To illustrate, when it is made unlawful by statute for judges to engage in the practice of law, a law firm is dissolved when one of its members becomes a judge.

(d) **War.** A partnership is ordinarily dissolved when there is war between the governments to which the different partners owe allegiance.

§ 46:18. Dissolution by Decree of Court.

When a partnership is to continue for a specified time, there are several situations in which one partner is permitted to obtain its dissolution

---

[17]UPA § 31(1)(a).

through a decree of court. A court will not order the dissolution for trifling causes or temporary grievances that do not involve a permanent harm or injury to the partnership.

The filing of a complaint seeking a judicial dissolution does not in itself cause a dissolution of the partnership as it is the decree of court which has that effect.

A partner may obtain a decree of dissolution for any of the following reasons:

(a) **Insanity.** A partner has been judicially declared insane or of unsound mind.

(b) **Incapacity.** One of the partners has become incapable of performing the terms of the partnership agreement.

(c) **Misconduct.** One of the partners has been guilty of conduct that substantially tends to affect prejudicially the continuance of the business. The habitual drunkenness of a partner is a sufficient cause for judicial dissolution.

(d) **Impracticability.** One of the partners persistently or willfully acts in such a way that it is not reasonably practicable to carry on the partnership business. Dissolution will be granted where dissensions are so serious and persistent as to make continuance impracticable, or where all confidence and cooperation between the parties have been destroyed.

FACTS:

Gus Jebeles and his brother-in-law Gus Costellos entered into an oral partnership agreement on September 2, 1977 to conduct a business under the name of "Dino's Hot Dogs" at a location on the Montgomery Highway. Jebeles, who had an expertise in this type of business, arranged for the lease and furnished the logo used by the partnership. From the start, Costellos devoted full-time to the business, and Jebeles devoted relatively little time to the business. Marital difficulties developed between Jebeles and his wife, who was Costellos' sister. Divorce proceedings began in January of 1979; and at that time Costellos ceased to remit any funds to Jebeles and changed the locks on the doors of the premises. Jebeles filed suit seeking a dissolution of the partnership and an accounting of all profits. The court refused to dissolve the partnership in order to preserve the valuable lease to the business premises and the future profits of the business; and instead ordered that the partnership continue with Costellos as the sole active partner and Jebeles as a silent partner. The trial court also ordered an accounting. Both parties appealed from the court's decree.

DECISION:

The trial court erred by refusing to dissolve the partnership. Cause for dissolution existed simply because Jebeles desired a dissolution. Under UPA [sec] 31 (1)(b) dissolution is caused by the express will of any partner when no definite term is specified in the partnership agreement and Jebeles and Costellos had not agreed on a definite duration for their partnership. Under UPA [sec] 43, Jebeles' right to an accounting accrues at the date of dissolution. The trial court was in error in ordering an accounting without dissolving the partnership and in establishing and imposing a new partnership agreement on the parties. [Jebeles v Costellos, _____ Ala _____, 391 So2d 1024 (1980)]

(e) **Lack of Success.** The partnership cannot continue in business except at a loss.

(f) **Equitable Circumstances.** A decree of dissolution will be granted under any other circumstances that equitably call for a dissolution. Such a situation exists when one partner has been induced by fraud to enter into the partnership.

§ 46:19.   Notice of Dissolution.

The statement that dissolution terminates the authority of the partners to act for the firm requires some modification. Under some circumstances, one partner may continue to possess the power to make a binding contract.

(a) **Notice to Partners.** When the firm is dissolved by the act of a partner, notice must be given to the other partners unless that partner's act clearly showed an intent to withdraw from or to dissolve the firm. If the withdrawing partner acted without notice to the other partners, such partner is bound as between them upon contracts created for the firm. "Where the dissolution is caused by the act, death, or bankruptcy of a partner, each partner is liable to his copartners for his share of any liability created by any partner acting for the partnership as if the partnership had not been dissolved unless (1) the dissolution being by act of any partner, the partner acting for the partnership had knowledge of the dissolution, or (2) the dissolution being by the death or bankruptcy of a partner, the partner acting for the partnership had knowledge or notice of the death or bankruptcy."[18]

(b) **Notice to Third Persons.** When dissolution is caused by the act of a partner or of the partners, notice must be given to third parties. A notice should expressly state that the partnership has been dissolved. Circumstances from which a termination may be inferred are generally not sufficient notice. Thus, the fact that the partnership checks added "Inc." after the partnership name is not sufficient notice that the partnership does not exist and that the business has been incorporated.

FACTS:

Paul Babich ran a business under the name of "House of Paul." The latter became a partnership between Babich, Dyson, and Schnepp but continued under the same name. The partners arranged for printing of advertising material with Philipp Lithographing Co., making contracts on three separate occasions for such printing. During the course of these dealings, the "House of Paul" became a corporation. When the printing bills were not paid in full, Philipp sued the partners as individuals. They claimed they were not liable because the corporation had made the contracts.

DECISION:

Whether or not the "House of Paul" was a corporation with respect to a particular contract was not important because no notice had been given of its change from a partnership to a corporation. Having done business with the persons originally as a partnership, the plaintiff could hold the firm and the individual persons liable as partners until notice to the contrary was given to the plaintiff. [Philipp Lithographing Co. v Babich, 27 Wis 2d 645, 135 NW2d 343 (1965)]

---

[18]UPA § 34.

Actual notice of dissolution must be given to persons who have dealt with the firm. To persons who have had no dealings with the firm, a publication of the fact is sufficient. Such notice may be by newspaper publication, by posting a placard in a public place, or by any similar method. Failure to give proper notice continues the power of each partner to bind the others in respect to third persons on contracts within the scope of the business.

When dissolution has been caused by operation of law, notice to third persons is not required. As between the partners, however, the UPA requires knowledge or notice of dissolution by death and bankruptcy. And it has been held that when the third party dealing with the partnership is not informed of the death of a partner, the surviving partners and the firm are bound by a notice sent by the third person to the deceased partner.

§ 46:20.   Winding up Partnership Affairs.

In the absence of an express agreement permitting continuation of the business by the surviving partners, they must wind up the business and account for the share of any partner who has withdrawn, been expelled, or has died.[19] If the remaining partners continue the business and use the partner's distributive share in so doing, that partner is entitled to that share, together with interest or the profit earned thereon.

Although the partners have no authority after dissolution to create new obligations, they retain authority to do acts necessary to wind up the business.

FACTS:
The Stoddard family, father, mother, and son, were a partnership which published a newspaper, the *Walnut Kernel*. The parents died and the son kept running the paper. King performed accounting services for the paper. When he was not paid, he sued the son and the executors of the estates of the deceased partners, the parents, claiming that his bill was a partnership liability for which each was liable. The executors defended on the ground that the son as surviving partner did not have authority to employ an accountant but was only authorized to wind up the partnership business. To this defense, it was answered that the newspaper was continued in order to preserve its asset value as a going concern so that it could be sold, and that the running of the paper was therefore part of the winding up process, which, if true, would give the surviving partner the authority to employ the accountant.

DECISION:
The accountant was not entitled to recover the value of his services because the son had no authority to continue the publishing of the newspaper indefinitely. The operation of the paper by the son was not a winding up of the estate but was merely a continuing of the business as usual. [King v Stoddard, 28 Cal App 3d 708, 104 Cal Rptr 903 (1972)]

---

[19]Ross v Walsh (Tex Civ App) 629 SW2d 823 (1982).

When dissolution is obtained by court decree, the court may appoint a receiver to conduct the winding up of the partnership business. This may be done in the usual manner or the receiver may sell the business as a going concern to those partners who wish to continue its operation.

With a few exceptions, all partners have the right to participate in the winding up of the business.[20]

When the firm is dissolved by the death of one partner; the partnership property vests in the surviving partners for the purpose of administration. They must collect and preserve the assets, pay the debts, and with reasonable promptness make an accounting to the representative of the deceased partner's estate. In connection with these duties, the law requires the highest degree of integrity. A partner cannot purchase any of the partnership property without the consent of the other partners.

§ 46:21. Distribution of Assets.

Creditors of the firm have first claim on the assets of the partnership. Difficulty arises when there is a contest between the creditors of the firm and the creditors of the individual partners. The general rule is that firm creditors have first claim on assets of the firm, and the individual creditors share in the remaining assets, if there are any.

Conversely, creditors of the individual partners have priority in the distribution of the individual assets; the claims of the firm creditors may be satisfied out of the individual partner's assets only after claims of the individual creditors are settled.

After the firm's liabilities to nonpartners have been paid, the assets of the partnership are distributed as follows: (1) each partner is entitled to a refund of advances made to or for the firm; (2) contributions to the capital of the firm are then returned; (3) the remaining assets, if any, are divided equally as profits among the partners unless there is some other agreement. If the partnership has sustained a loss, the partners share it equally in the absence of a contrary agreement.

FACTS:

On August 23, 1973, Friedman, The "O" Street Carpet Shop, Inc. and Langness formed a partnership known as NFL Associates. "O" Street Carpet's net contribution to capital was $5005. Langness contributed $14,000 in cash. Friedman contributed his legal services, upon which no value was placed by the articles of partnership. The articles stated that Friedman was entitled to 10% of the profits. The articles provided that Langness was to receive payments of $116.66 per month. The partnership's accountant treated the payments to Langness as a return to Langness of her capital. In October of

1978, the partnership sold the rental property owned by the partnership and the partnership was wound up, whereupon Friedman claimed that he was entitled to 10% of the partnership capital upon dissolution. Langness claimed that Friedman was not entitled to a capital distribution and that the monthly payments to her should not have been treated as a return of capital.

DECISION:

Judgment for Langness. A partner who contributes only services to the partnership is

[20]UPA § 37.

not deemed to have made a capital contribution. Thus Friedman was not entitled to be credited with 10 percent of the partnerhsip capital upon dissolution. The monthly checks to Langness of $116.66 must be considered as capital withdrawals, reducing Langness' capital contribution. [Langness v "O" Street Carpet, Inc. (Neb) 353 NW2d 709 (1984)]

Distribution of partnership assets must be made on the basis of actual value when it is clear that the book values are merely nominal or arbitrary amounts.[21]

A provision in a partnership agreement that on the death of a partner the interest of that partner shall pass to that partner's surviving spouse is valid and takes effect as against the contention that it is not valid because it does not satisfy the requirements applicable to wills.

§ 46:22.   Continuation of Partnership Business.

As a practical matter, the business of the partnership is commonly continued after dissolution and winding up. In all cases, however, there is a technical dissolution, winding up, and a termination of the life of the original partnership. If the business continues, either with the surviving partners, or with them and additional partners, it is a new partnership. Again, as a practical matter, the liquidation of the old partnership may in effect be merely a matter of bookkeeping entries with all parties in interest recontributing or relending to the new business any payment to which they would be entitled from the liquidation of the original partnership.

SUMMARY

A partnership is a legal relationship created by the voluntary association of two or more persons to carry on as co-owners a business for profit. General partners are those who are publicly and actively engaged in the transaction of firm business. Nominal partners hold themselves out as partners or permit others to hold them out as such. Secret partners are those who take an active part in the management of the firm but who are not known to the public as partners. A partnership agreement governs the partnership during its existence and may also contain provisions relating to dissolution. The agreement need not be in writing, however. Proof of the existence of a partnership may be found from the presence of an individual's actual control in the running of the business, and the fact that the parties share profits and losses. The sharing of gross returns, as opposed to profits, is very slight evidence of a partnership. Partners hold title to firm property by tenancy in partnership. A creditor of a partner cannot proceed against any specific item of partnership property, but must obtain a charging order to obtain the debtor-partner's share of the profits. An assignee of a partner's interest does not become a partner without the consent of the other partner, and is entitled only to a share of the profits and the assignor's interest upon dissolution.

Dissolution ends the right of the partnership to exist as a going concern and is followed by a winding-up period and the distribution of assets.

[21]Mahan v Mahan, 107 Ariz 517, 489 P2d 1197 (1971).

A partnership may be dissolved by the parties themselves in accordance with the terms of the partnership agreement, by expulsion of a partner, or by withdrawal of a partner. Dissolution by operation of law principally occurs on the death of a partner, or the bankruptcy of the firm or one of the partners. A court may order dissolution of a partnership on the petition of a partner because of the insanity, incapacity, or major misconduct of a partner. Lack of success is also a basis for dissolution as well as impracticability or other circumstances that equitably call for dissolution. Notice of dissolution of the partnership must be given, except dissolution by operation of law, with actual notice being given to those who have dealt with the firm as a partnership. All partners generally have a right to participate in the winding up of the business. After the firm's liabilities to non partners have been paid, the assets are distributed among the partners as follows: (1) refund of advances, (2) return of contributions to capital, and (3) remaining assets are divided in accordance with the partnership agreement or, if no agreement is expressed, the net assets are divided equally among the partners.

QUESTIONS AND CASE PROBLEMS

1. What social forces are affected by the rule that distribution of partnership assets must be made on the basis of actual value when it is clear that the book values are merely nominal or arbitrary amounts?
2. Michael and Bernard form a business to sell automobiles. They lose money steadily and finally go out of business. In the liquidation of the business, Michael claims that their relationship was a partnership. Bernard claims that is was not a partnership because there was no profit. Is Bernard correct?
3. Renata and Viola form a partnership. Renata dies. The husband and son of Renata claim a one half interest of the partnership assets. Are they entitled to it?
4. What is the effect of dissolution on a partnership?
5. In proving that *A* and *B* are partners, compare the effect of proof that they (a) share gross returns, (b) are co-owners of property used in or by a business, or (c) share profits.
6. Ray, Tyler, and Mark form a partnership. Ray and Tyler contribute property and cash. Mark contributes only services. Tyler dies and the partnership is liquidated. After all debts are paid there is not sufficient surplus to pay back Tyler's estate and Ray for the property and cash originally contributed by Ray and Tyler. Mark claims that the balance should be divided equally between Ray, Tyler's estate, and Mark. Is he correct?
7. Shirley owns a business. She employs Teresa in the business. Shirley files an income tax return using a partnership form and naming Shirley and Teresa as the partners. Teresa did not sign the return or have knowledge of the return. Carter later sues Teresa on the theory that Teresa is a partner. Is the tax return admissible as evidence that Teresa is a partner?
8. Compare the requirement of notice to third persons when (a) an agency is terminated, and (b) a partnership is dissolved.
9. Baxter, Bigelow, Owens, and Dailey were partners in a New York City advertising agency. Owens, who was in poor health and desirous of

retiring, advised the partners that she had assigned her full and complete interest in the partnership to her son Bartholomew, a highly qualified person with ten years of experience in the advertising business. Baxter, Bigelow, and Dailey refused to allow Bartholomew to attend management meetings and refused his request to inspect the books. Bartholomew points out that his mother had invested as much in the firm as any other partner. He believes, as assignee of his mother's full and complete partnership interest, that he is entitled to (a) inspect the books as he sees fit and (b) participate fully in the management of the firm. Is Bartholomew correct?

10. Amy Gargulo and Paula Frisken operated "Kiddies Korner", an infants' and childrens' (to age 6) clothing store, in Gainesville, Florida as a partnership. They operated the business very successfully for three years, with both Paula and Amy doing the buying and Paula keeping the books and paying the bills. Amy and Paula decided to expand the business when an adjoining store became vacant, and they incorporated the business for protection against the business risks involved in the expansion. Children's Apparel Inc. was a major supplier to the business before the expansion and allowed very liberal payment terms. Business did not increase after the expansion as anticipated and when a nationally known manufacturer of children's apparel opened a factory outlet nearby, the business could no longer pay its bills. Children's Apparel, Inc., which supplied most of the store's stock after expansion, sued Amy and Paula as partners for past due bills on expansion stock simply because it did not know Amy and Paula had incorporated. Amy and Paula defend that the business was incorporated and therefore they may not be held personally liable for business debts occurring after incorporation. Are Amy and Paula correct?

11. Bates and Huffman formed a partnership to run a shoe business. In a lawsuit between the partners, Huffman claimed that the partnership agreement was void because Bates was a minor. Was he correct? [Huffman v Bates (Mo App) 348 SW2d 363]

12. Williams owned and operated a bakery business. His two sons were employed in the business and from time to time received a share of the profits as a bonus. The father and one of the sons died. The administrator of the son's estate, the First National Bank, then sued the estate of the father for an accounting, claiming that the father and the two sons were a partnership and that the deceased son's estate was therefore entitled to a one-third share. Decide. [First National Bank v Williams, 142 Or 648, 20 P2d 222]

13. A suit was brought by the heirs of members of a partnership to determine the right to the proceeds of sale of certain real estate. The real estate had been purchased by the partnership with partnership money and in the partnership name. The real estate was not used in the partnership business but was held only for investment purposes. It was claimed by the heirs that this real estate was not subject to the provisions of the Uniform Partnership Act governing tenancy by partnership because it was not used in the business. Were they correct? [Brown v Brown, 45 Tenn App 78, 320 SW2d 721]

14. Langdon, Hurdle, and Hoffman formed a partnership to practice medi-

cine. The agreement provided that if any partner withdrew from the firm within five years he could not practice within a specified geographic area for a specified time. Five years and one day later, Hoffman withdrew from the partnership. Langdon and Hurdle brought suit against Hoffman claiming that Hoffman was liable for damages for withdrawing from the partnership. Decide. [Langdon v Hurdle 17 NC App 530, 195 SE2d 71]

15. Simpson and Balaban, as partners, owned and operated the Desert Cab Company. Simpson died. The administrator of his estate obtained a court order authorizing the sale of Simpson's interest in the partnership and in the physical assets of the partnership. Was this order proper? [Balaban v Bank of Nevada, 86 Nev 826, 477 P2d 860]

CHAPTER 47

POWERS AND DUTIES

OF PARTNERS

CHAPTER OBJECTIVES

After studying this chapter you will be able to:

1. Differentiate between express authority and customary authority of a partner to act for a firm.
2. Identify the situations which indicate the existence of limitations on a partner's authority.
3. Set forth the seven prohibited transactions which a partner cannot undertake unless expressly authorized to do so.
4. Identify the duties of partners to one another.
5. State the rights of partners as owners of the business.
6. Explain the nature and extent of a partner's liability for the debts of the firm.

The powers and duties of partners may, to a large extent, be governed by a partnership agreement in those situations where the parties had the foresight to reach a written accord on how the partnership should deal with the various types of decisions incident to the running of the partnership's business. In all situations not covered by a partnership agreement, partnership law applies.

A partner's authority to act for the firm is similar to that of an agent's authority to act for a principal; but, unlike an agent, a partner is a co-owner who has rights in the partnership property and liability for partnership losses. As a result of each partner's power to make decisions that may bind the firm, high standards of fair dealing are necessary between the partners, and such high standards of conduct affect the duties, rights, and liabilities of the partners.

A. AUTHORITY OF PARTNERS

The scope of a partner's authority is determined by the partnership agreement and by the nature of the partnership relation.

§ 47:1.   Authority of Majority of Partners.

When there are more than two partners in a firm, the decision of the majority prevails in matters involving the manner in which the ordinary functions of the business will be conducted. To illustrate, a majority of the partners of a firm decide to increase the firm's advertising and enter into a contract for that purpose. The transaction is valid and binds the firm and all of the partners.

The act of the majority is not binding if it contravenes the partnership agreement. For such matters, unanimous action is required.[1] Thus, the majority of the members cannot change the nature of the business against the protests of the minority.

When there are two or any other even number of partners, there is the possibility of an even division on a matter that requires majority approval. In such a case no action can be taken, and the partnership is deadlocked. When the partners are evenly divided on any question, one partner has no authority to act. If the division is over a basic issue and the partners persist in the deadlock so that it is impossible to continue the business, any one of the partners may petition the court to order the dissolution of the firm.

FACTS:

Summers and Dooley formed a partnership to collect trash. Summers became unable to work, and he hired a third man to do his work and paid him out of his personal funds. Summers suggested to Dooley that the third man be paid from the partnership funds but Dooley refused to do so. Finally Summers sued Dooley for reimbursement for the money he had spent to pay the third man.

DECISION:

Judgment for Dooley. Summers had no authority to employ the third man at the expense of the firm. As the partners were evenly divided on the question of such employment, Summers had no authority to act. [Summers v Dooley, 94 Idaho 87, 481 P2d 318 (1971)]

---

§ 47:2.   Express Authority of Individual Partners.

An individual partner may have express authority to do certain acts, either because the partnership agreement so declares or because a sufficient number of partners have agreed thereto.

A partner's authority to act for the firm is similar to that of an agent to act for a principal. Thus, in addition to express authority, a partner has the authority to do those acts which are customary for a member of a part-

---

[1]Uniform Partnership Act, § 18(h).

nership conducting the particular business of the partnership.[2] As in the case of an agent, the acts of a partner in excess of authority do not ordinarily bind the partnership.

§ 47:3.   Customary Authority of Individual Partners.

A partner, by virtue of being a co-manager of the business, customarily has certain powers necessary and proper to carry out that business. In the absence of express limitation, the law will therefore imply that a partner has such powers. The scope of such powers varies with the nature of the partnership and also with the business customs and usages of the area in which the partnership operates.

The following are the more common of the customary or implied powers of individual partners:

(a) **Contracts.** A partner may make any contract necessary to the transaction of the firm business.[3]

When a plaintiff sues on a promissory note or other contract executed by a partner who does not possess express authority to enter into such transaction, the plaintiff has the burden of proving that the making of the contract or the giving of commercial paper was "usual" for a business of the character of the partnership.

(b) **Sales.** A partner may sell the firm's goods in the regular course of business and make the usual warranties incidental to such sales. This authority, however, is limited to the goods held for sale by the partnership.

(c) **Purchases.** A partner may purchase any kind of property within the scope of the business, and for this purpose may pledge the credit of the firm. This authority is not affected by the fact that the partner subsequently misuses or keeps the property instead of turning it over to the firm.

(d) **Loans.** A partner in a trading firm may borrow money for partnership purposes. In doing so, the partner may execute commercial paper in the firm name or give security, such as a mortgage or a pledge of the personal property of the firm. If the third person acts in good faith, the transaction is binding even though the partner misappropriates the money. A partner in a non-trading partnership does not ordinarily possess the power to borrow in the name of the firm.

(e) **Insurance.** A partner may insure the firm property, cancel a policy of insurance, or make proof of loss and accept a settlement for the loss.

(f) **Employment.** A partner may hire such employees and agents as are necessary to carry out the purpose of the enterprise.

(g) **Claims against Firm.** A partner has the authority to compromise, adjust, and pay bona fide claims against the partnership. A partner may pay debts out of the firm funds or may pay them by transfering firm property.

(h) **Claims of Firm.** A partner may adjust, receive payment of, and release debts and other claims of the firm. In so doing, a partner may take

[2]Ball v Carlson (Colo App) 641 P2d 303 (1981).
[3]Barnes v Campbell Chain Co., Inc. 47 NC App 488, 267 SE2d 388 (1980).

money or commercial paper but, as a general rule, cannot accept goods in payment. One who makes a proper payment is protected even though the partner to whom the payment is made embezzles the money or fails to account to the firm for the payment.

(i) **Admissions.** A partner may bind the firm by admissions or statements that are adverse to the interests of the partnership if they are made in regard to firm affairs and in pursuance of firm business. For example, when a buyer takes a purchase back to the partnership's store, the admission by the partner then in the store that the product was defective binds the firm.

(j) **Notice.** A partner may receive notice of matters affecting the partnership affairs, and such notice, in the absence of fraud, is binding on the other partners.[4]

§ 47:4.   Limitations on Authority.

The partners may agree to limit the normal powers of each partner. When a partner, contrary to such an agreement, negotiates a contract for the firm with a third person, the firm is bound if the third person was unaware of the agreement. In such a case, the partner violating the agreement is liable to the other partners for any loss caused by the breach of the limitation. If the third person knew of the limitation, however, the firm would not be bound.[5]

A third person cannot assume that the partner has all the authority which the partner purports to have. If there is anything that would put a reasonable person on notice that the partner's powers are limited, the third person is bound by that limitation.

The third person must be on the alert for the following situations in particular, as they warn that the partner with whom the third person deals either has restricted authority or no authority at all:

(a) **Nature of Business.** A third person must take notice of limitations arising out of the nature of the business. A partnership may be organized for a particular kind of business, trade, or profession, and third persons are presumed to know the limitations commonly imposed on partners in such an enterprise. Thus, an act of a partner that would ordinarily bind a commercial firm, such as the issuance of a note, would not bind a partnership engaged in a profession. A partner in a trading partnership has much greater powers than one in a nontrading firm.

(b) **Scope of Business.** A third person must recognize and act in accordance with limitations that arise from the scope of the business. A partner cannot bind the firm to a third person in a transaction not within the scope of the firm's business unless the partner had express authority to do so. Thus, when a partner in a dental firm speculates in land or when a partner in a firm dealing in automobiles buys television sets for resale, the third person, in the absence of estoppel or express authority, cannot hold the other partners liable on such a contract. The scope of the business is a question of fact to be determined by the jury from the circumstances of each case. In general,

[4]Grayson v Wolfsey, Rosen, Kweskin & Kuriansky, 40 Conn Supp 1, 478 A2d 629 (1984).

[5]UPA § 9(4).

it means the activities commonly recognized as a part of a given business at a given place and time. The usual scope, however, may be enlarged by agreement or by conduct.

(c) **Termination of Partnership.** A third person must watch for the termination of the partnership relation, either when the partnership is terminated under conditions requiring no notice or when notice of the termination has been properly given.

(d) **Adverse Interest.** A third person must take notice of an act of a partner that is obviously against the interest of the firm. To illustrate, if a partner issues a promissory note in the firm name and delivers it to a creditor in payment of a personal obligation, the creditor risks nonpayment because such an act may be a fraud upon the firm.

§ 47:5.   Prohibited Transactions.

There are certain transactions into which a partner cannot enter on behalf of the partnership unless the partner is expressly authorized to do so. A third person entering into such a transaction does so at the risk that the partner has not been so authorized.[6]

The following are prohibited transactions:

(a) **Cessation of Business.** A partner cannot bind the firm by a contract that would make it impossible for the firm to conduct its usual business.

(b) **Suretyship.** A partner has no implied authority to bind the firm by contracts of surety, guaranty, or indemnity for purposes other than the firm business.

(c) **Arbitration.** A partner cannot submit controversies of the firm to arbitration "unless authorized by the other partners or unless they have abandoned the business."[7]

(d) **Confession of Judgment.** A partner cannot confess judgment against the firm upon one of its obligations, because all partners should have an opportunity to defend in court, except when the other partners consent or when they have abandoned the business.

(e) **Assignment for Creditors.** A partner cannot ordinarily make a general assignment of firm property for the benefit of creditors, unless authorized by the other partners or unless they have abandoned the business.

(f) **Personal Obligations.** A partner cannot discharge personal obligations or claims of the firm by interchanging them in any way.[8]

(g) **Sealed Instruments.** Instruments under seal are binding upon the firm when they are made in the usual course of business. In a minority of the states, however, a partner cannot bind copartners by an instrument under seal.

[6]UPA § 9(3).
[7]UPA § 9(3)(e).
[8]Slingerland v Hurley (Fla App) 288 So2d 587 (1980).

B. DUTIES, RIGHTS, REMEDIES, AND LIABILITIES OF PARTNERS

The duties, rights, remedies, and liabilities between the partners are influenced, to a large extent, by the high standards of fair dealing necessary for the successful operation of the partnership form of business.

§ 47:6. Duties of Partners.

In many respects, the duties of a partner are the same as those of an agent.

(a) **Loyalty and Good Faith.** Each partner must act in the highest good faith toward the others and one must not take any advantage over the others by the slightest misrepresentation or concealment. Each partner owes a duty of loyalty to the firm which requires a partner's devotion to the firm's business and bars the making of any secret profit at the expense of the firm, the use of the firm's property for personal benefit, or the exploitation for personal gain of a business opportunity of the partnership.[9] A partner's duties to the firm must be observed above the furtherance of the partner's own personal interest. To illustrate, when one partner renewed a lease of the building occupied by the firm but the lease was renewed in the name of that partner alone, that partner was compelled to hold the lease for the firm on the ground that the failure to renew the lease in the name of the firm was a breach of the duties of good faith and loyalty owed to the firm.

A partner, in the absence of an agreement to the contrary, is required to give undivided time and energy to the furtherance of the business of the partnership. In any case, a partner cannot promote a competing business. If the partner does so, the partner is liable for damages sustained by the partnership.

FACTS:

The Whittier Leasing Company was a partnership formed to purchase equipment and lease it to the Whittier Hospital. Nine of the partners formed a new partnership, the Friendly Hills Leasing Company. Thereafter, all leasing was made by Friendly to the hospital. The partners of Whittier Leasing who had not joined Friendly brought an action against the partners who had formed Friendly and sought in that action to (1) obtain a dissolution of Whittier Leasing, and (2) recover the profits made by Friendly from the Whittier Hospital leases.

DECISION:

Judgment for the plaintiffs. The Whittier Leasing partners who competed with Whittier Leasing violated the obligation of loyalty that every partner owes to the partnership. This breach of duty was so serious that they would be ordered to give up the profit that they had made from the Whittier Hospital leases. In addition, the court would order the dissolution of the partnership because it was impracticable to expect that the parties could thereafter continue to work with the harmony and faith in each other that are essential to a successful partnership. [Olivet v Frischling, 104 Cal App 3d 831, 164 Cal Rptr 87 (1980)]

---

[9]Phillips v Kula 200 Wick Realty, Inc. (Hawaii App) 629 P2d 119 (1981).

The obligation of a partner to refrain from competing with the partnership continues after the termination of the partnership if the partnership agreement contains a valid anticompetitive covenant.[10] In the absence of any such restriction, or if the restriction agreed upon is held invalid, a partner is free to compete with the remaining partners, even though they continue the partnership business.

(b) **Obedience.** Each partner is under the obligation to perform all duties and to obey all restrictions imposed by the partnership agreement or by the vote of the requisite number of partners. Consequently, each partner must observe any limitation imposed by a majority of the partners with respect to the ordinary details of the partnership business. If a majority of the partners operating a retail store decide that no sales shall be made on credit, a partner who is placed in charge of the store must obey this limitation. If a third person does not know of the limitation, the managing partner will have the power to make a binding sale on credit to such person. If the third person does not pay the bill and the firm thereby suffers loss, the partner who violated the "no-credit" limitation is liable to the firm for the loss caused by such disobedience.

(c) **Reasonable Care.** A partner must use reasonable care in transacting the business of the firm and is liable for any loss resulting from a failure to do so. A partner is not liable, however, for honest mistakes or errors of judgment.

(d) **Information.** A partner has the duty to inform the partnership of matters relating to the partnership and must "render on demand true and full information of all things affecting the partnership to any partner or the legal representative of any deceased partner or partner under legal disability."[11]

The obligation to inform embraces matters relating to the purchase by one partner of the interest of another and to matters relating to the liquidation of the partnership.

(e) **Accounting.** A partner transacting any business for the firm must make and keep, or turn over to the proper person, correct records thereof.

If the partners have delegated to one of the partners the task of keeping the books and accounts for all the business of the firm, the record keeper must keep proper records. If they are disputed, the record keeper has the burden of proving their accuracy, which means that if it is not shown that the records are correct, the record keeper will be held liable.

When an action is brought to compel a partner to account, the court may require the making of an audit by a disinterested third person.

When a partnership is organized for an illegal purpose or for conducting a lawful business in an unlawful manner, a wrongdoing partner cannot obtain an accounting by the partnership. For example, where the members of an engineering partnership did not have the license required for engineering work, one of the partners, an unlicensed engineer, could not require the other partners to account.

---

[10]Wright v Belt, 6 Kan App 2d 854, 636 P2d 188 (1981).
[11]UPA § 20.

§ 47:7.   Rights of Partners as Owners.

Each partner, in the absence of a contrary agreement, has the following rights, which stem from the fact that the partner is a co-owner of the partnership business.

(a) **Management.** Each partner has a right to take an equal part in transacting the business of the firm. It is immaterial that one partner contributed more than another or that one contributed only services.

As an incident of the right to manage the partnership, each partner has the right to possession of the partnership property for the purposes of the partnership.

(b) **Inspection of Books.** All partners are equally entitled to inspect the books of the firm. "The partnership books shall be kept, subject to any agreement between the partners, at the principal place of business of the partnership, and every partner shall at all times have access to and may inspect and copy any of them."[12]

(c) **Share of Profits.** Each partner is entitled to a share of the profits. The partners may provide, if they so wish, that profits shall be shared in unequal proportions. In the absence of such a provision in the partnership agreement, each partner is entitled to an equal share of the profits without regard to the amount of capital contributed or services performed for the partnership.

The right to profits is regarded as personal property regardless of the nature of the partnership business. Upon the death of a partner, the right to a share of the profits and an accounting passes to the dead partner's executor or administrator.

(d) **Compensation.** In the absence of a contrary agreement, a partner is not entitled to compensation for services performed for the partnership.[13] This is so even though the services are unusual or more extensive than the services rendered by other partners. Consequently when one partner becomes seriously ill and the other partners transact all of the firm's business, they are not entitled to compensation for these services, because the sickness of a partner is considered a risk assumed in the relation. No agreement can be implied that the active partners are to be compensated, even though the services rendered by them are such that ordinarily they would be rendered in the expectation of receiving compensation. As an exception, "a surviving partner is entitled to reasonable compensation for services performed in winding up the partnership affairs."[14]

To illustrate the effect of an agreement of the partners, they may agree that one of the partners shall devote full time as manager of the business and that a salary shall be paid for such services in addition to the managing partner's share of the profits.

(e) **Repayment of Loans.** A partner is entitled to the return of any money advanced to or for the firm. These amounts, however, must be sepa-

[12]UPA § 19.
[13]Altman v Altman (CA3 Pa) 653 F2d 755 (1981).
[14]UPA § 18(f).

rate and distinct from original or additional contributions to the capital of the firm.

(f) **Payment of Interest.** In the absence of an agreement to the contrary, contributions to capital do not draw interest. The theory is that the profits constitute sufficient compensation. Advances by a partner in the form of loans are treated as if they were made by a stranger and bear interest from the date the advance is made.

(g) **Contribution and Indemnity.** A partner who pays more than a proportionate share of the debts of the firm has a right to contribution from the other partners. Under this principle, if an employee of a partnership negligently injures a third person while acting within the scope of employment and the injured party collects damages from one partner, the latter may enforce contribution from the other partners in order to divide the loss equally between them.

The partnership must indemnify every partner for payments made and personal liabilities reasonably incurred in the ordinary and proper conduct of its business or for the preservation of its business or property. A partner has no right, however, to indemnity or reimbursement if the partner has (1) acted in bad faith, (2) negligently caused the necessity for payment, or (3) previously agreed to bear the expense alone.

(h) **Distribution of Capital.** Every partner is entitled to receive a share of the firm property upon dissolution after the payment of all creditors and the repayment of loans made to the firm by partners.[15] Unless otherwise stated in the partnership agreement, all partners are entitled to the return of their capital contributions.

After such distribution is made, each partner is the sole owner of the fractional part distributed to that partner, rather than a co-owner of all the property as during the existence of the partnership.

§ 47:8.   Liability of Partners and Partnership as to Particular Acts.

The liability of a partnership and of the partners for the acts of individual partners and of employees is governed by the same principles as apply to the liability of an employer or a principal for the acts of an employee or agent.

(a) **Contracts.** All members of the firm are liable on contracts made by a partner for the partnership and in its name if they were made within the scope of the partner's real or apparent authority. This is true even though the partners may be unknown to the third person. Thus, a dormant partner, when discovered, can be held liable with the others.

When a partner, acting on behalf of the partnership, makes an authorized, simple contract but does so in the partner's own name, the firm and the other partners are liable as undisclosed principals.

When a partner with necessary authority executes commercial paper in the name of the firm, the firm and every partner is bound thereby, even

[15]Mandell v Centrum Frontier Corp. 86 Ill App 3d 437, 41 Ill Dec 323, 407 NE2d 821 (1980).

though the individual partners did not sign the paper. If a partner signs commercial paper in the partner's own name, the partnership and the other partners cannot sue or be sued thereon as undisclosed principals. While partnership law determines the authority of a partner to enter into transactions on behalf of the firm, the Uniform Commercial Code governs how commercial paper is to be executed by a partner.

When a borrowing partner gives the lender a promissory note for the partner's personal obligation, the partnership and the other partners cannot be liable thereon, even though the borrowing partner used the money for the benefit of the partnership.

The fact that a partner has either express or implied authority to bind the partnership does not in itself establish that a contract made by the partner is a partnership contract, as distinguished from the individual contract of the partner. As in the case of agency situations generally, a contract between the third person and the principal, here the partnership, does not arise when that is not the intention of the parties. Consequently, where a third person and a partner make a contract intending to bind the partner individually, rather than the partnership, no contract liability of the partnership is created. Care must be taken to distinguish this situation from that in which the partnership is not disclosed and in which the third person has the intention of dealing with the partner only, as in such cases the partnership and the other partners may be bound or have rights under the rules governing undisclosed principals who act through authorized agents.

(b) Torts. All partners are liable for torts, such as fraud, trespass, negligence, and assaults' committed by one partner while transacting firm business.[16] Accordingly, a partnership formed to manage real estate is liable for a battery inflicted by one partner upon a tenant in collecting the rent. Each partner in a partnership formed for the general practice of medicine is liable for an injury to a patient resulting from lack of skill or negligence of any one of the partners.

FACTS:

Zemelman and others did business as a partnership under the name of Art Seating Company. The partnership obtained a fire insurance policy from the Boston Insurance Company. There was a fire loss and a claim was filed under the policy. The claim was prepared by one of the partners, Irving Zemelman. The insurance company asserted that false statements were made by Zemelman and consequently the insurer was not liable on the policy because the policy contained an express provision stating that it was void if a false claim was made. The partnership replied that it was not bound by any fraudulent statement of Zemelman, as the making of fraudulent statements was not within the scope of his authority.

DECISION:

Judgment for the insurance company. When a partner is guilty of fraud in dealing with a third person, the partnership is liable for the consequences of the fraud even though the commission of such fraud was not within the scope of the partner's authority. [Zemelman v Boston Insurance Co. 4 Cal App 3d 15, 84 Cal Rptr 206 (1970)]

---

[16]UPA § 13.

(c) **Crimes.** The partners of a firm and the partnership itself are liable for certain crimes committed by a partner in the course of the business, such as selling goods without obtaining a necessary vendor's license or selling in violation of a statute prohibiting sale. A partnership, as distinct from the individual partners, may be fined for committing the crime of violating the federal law establishing regulations for the safe transportation in interstate commerce of explosives and other dangerous articles.[17] If carrying on the firm business does not necessarily involve the commission of the act constituting a crime, the firm and the partners not participating in the commission of the crime or authorizing its commission generally are not criminally liable. This exception is not recognized in some cases, such as the making of prohibited sales to minors or sales of adulterated products.

§ 47:9.   Nature of Partner's Liability.

By virtue of the Uniform Partnership Act, partners are jointly liable on all firm contracts. They are jointly and severally liable for all torts committed by an employee or one of the partners in the scope of the partnership business. When partners are liable for the wrongful injury caused a third person, the latter may sue all or any number of the members of the firm.

FACTS:

Daniel Zuckerman, a minor, and Elaine Zuckerman, his mother, brought a medical malpractice action against Dr. Joseph Antenucci and Dr. Jose Pena. Although the summons did not state that the two defendants were partners, the undisputed evidence at the trial established that relationship, and that the alleged acts of malpractice were done in the course of partnership business. The jury returned a verdict finding that Dr. Pena was guilty of malpractice, but that Dr. Antenucci was not guilty of malpractice. The amount of the verdict was $4,000,000. Dr. Antenucci contends that he should not be held liable on a partnership theory for the act of his partner when the plaintiffs had not named the partnership entity on the summons and when the summons did not designate him as a partner.

DECISION:

Judgment against Dr. Antenucci. A partner is jointly and severally liable for torts chargeable to the partnership. Jurisdiction over Dr. Antenucci individually is sufficient for a judgment against him based on a tort committed by his partner. [Zuckerman v Antenucci, 478 NYS2d 578 (1984)]

---

§ 47:10   Extent of Partner's Liability.

Each member of the firm is individually and unlimitedly liable for the debts of the partnership regardless of the member's investment or interest in the firm.

[17]United States v A&P Trucking Co. 358 US 121 (1958).

FACTS:

Leland McElmurry was one of three partners of MHS Enterprises, a Michigan partnership. Commonwealth Capital Investment Corporation sued the partnership and obtained a judgment of $1,137,285 against it. The partnership could not pay the judgment. Commonwealth then sued McElmurry for the entire debt on the theory that as a partner of MHS he was liable for its debts.

DECISION:

UPA [sec] 15 provides that all partners are jointly liable for the debts and obligations of the partnership. And, where no partnership assets remain to satisfy the judgment, as in this case, the judgment creditor properly sought general partner McElmurry's individual assets to satisfy the entire debt. Under UPA [sec] 18(a) McElmurry has the right to contribution from the other partners should they have assets. [Commonwealth Capital Investment Corporation v McElmurry, 102 Mich App 536, 302 NW2d 222 (1981)]

(a) **Liability for Breach of Duty.** When a partner violates a duty owed to the partnership, the partner's liability is determined by the general principles of law applicable to such conduct.

When one partner commits a fraud upon another partner, the injured partner may recover both compensatory and exemplary damages from the wrongdoing partner.

(b) **Liability of New Partners.** A person admitted as a partner into an existing partnership is limitedly liable for all the obligations of the partnership arising before such admission. This is a limited liability in that the pre-admission claim may be satisfied only out of partnership property and does not extend to the individual property of the newly admitted partner.[18] The incoming partner does not become personally liable for pre-admission claims unless the incoming partner expressly promises to pay such claims.

(c) **Effect of Dissolution on Partner's Liability.** A partner remains liable after dissolution of the partnership unless expressly released by the creditors or unless all claims against the partnership have been satisfied. The dissolution of the partnership does not of itself discharge the existing liability of any partner. The individual property of a deceased partner is liable for the obligations of the partnership which were incurred while the deceased partner was alive, but the individual creditors of the deceased partner have priority over the partnership creditors with respect to such property.[19]

§ 47:11.   Enforcement of Partner's Liability.

The manner in which the civil liability of a partner may be enforced depends upon the form of the lawsuit brought by the creditor. The firm may have been sued in the name of all the individual partners doing business as the partnership, as "Plaintiff v *A, B,* and *C,* doing business as the Ajax Ware-

---

[18]UPA § 17; see also UPA § 41(1), (7).
[19]UPA § 36.

house." In such a case, those partners named are bound by the judgment against the firm if they have been properly served in the suit. Partners either not named or not served are generally not bound by the judgment.

When a judgment is obtained against a partner, it may be enforced against the non-partnership assets of that partner in the same way as a judgment would be enforced against any judgment debtor. The creditor may enforce judgment against the partner's interest in the partnership only by obtaining a charging order against that interest.

If the judgment binds an individual partner, the creditor may enforce the judgment against the partner before, at the same time, or after the creditor seeks to enforce the judgment against the firm or other partners who are also bound by the judgment. If a partner is not bound by a judgment, the creditor must bring another lawsuit against the partner in which the creditor establishes that the defendant is a partner in the particular partnership and that a judgment was entered against the partnership for a partnership liability. When this is established, a judgment is entered in favor of the creditor against the particular partner. The creditor may then have execution on this judgment against the property of the partner.

SUMMARY

Where there are more than two partners in a firm, the decisions of the majority prevail on ordinary matters relating to the firm's business, unless they are contrary to the partnership agreement. A partner's authority to act for the firm is similar to that of an agent to act for a principal. A partner may have express authority to act as set forth in the partnership agreement or as agreed to by a sufficient number of partners. A partner has the customary or implied power to make contracts to transact the firm's business; to sell the firm's goods in the regular course of business; to make purchases within the scope of the business; and, in a trading partnership, to borrow money for firm purposes. Further, a partner may purchase insurance, hire employees, and adjust claims for and against the firm. A partner may not, however, bind the firm by a contract that would make it impossible for the firm to conduct its business. Additional prohibited transactions by an individual partner involve suretyship contracts, agreements to submit matters to arbitration, confessions of judgment, assignments for creditors, and interchanging personal obligations with those of the firm.

A partner's duties are in many respects the same as those of an agent, including the duty of loyalty and good faith, obedience, reasonable care, full information on all matters affecting the firm, and keeping proper and correct records. Absent a contrary agreement, each partner has the right to take an equal part in the management of the business, to inspect the books, to share in the profits and, after payment of all of the firm's debts and the return of capital, to share in the firm's property or surplus upon dissolution.

Partners are subject to unlimited personal liability to partnership claimants. Partners are jointly liable on all firm contracts. They are jointly and severally liable for all torts committed by one of the partners or a firm employee within the scope of the partnership's business. A partner remains liable after dissolution, unless expressly released by creditors. Absent assumption, an incoming partner is not personally liable for existing partnership debts.

QUESTIONS AND CASE PROBLEMS

1. What social forces are affected by the rule governing the authority of a majority of the partners?
2. The Acorn Hardware Store is owned and operated by a partnership consisting of five partners. They disagree as to whether they should have the building repainted. How many partners must agree to repaint?
3. Mark, Sylvia, and Lucy form and operate an automobile dealership as a partnership. Mark sells one of the automobiles of the partnership to Frances at a price below dealer cost, thinking that a profit could be made in servicing the vehicle. Sylvia and Lucy seek to avoid the sale to Frances on the ground that Mark was never authorized to make the sale to Frances. Is the sale binding on the partnership?
4. Compare the right of a partner to engage in a business which competes with the firm (a) while still a partner, and (b) after leaving the partnership.
5. Ross, Henry, and Albert are partners. Ross and Henry each contributed $60,000 to the partnership. Albert contributed $30,000. At the end of the fiscal year, there are distributable profits totaling $150,000. Ross claims $60,000 as his share of the profits. Is he entitled thereto?
6. What is the effect of dissolution on a partner's liability?
7. Brenda and Stephen are partners owning and operating a paint store. Stephen opens another store in his own name. This second store competes with the partnership store. Brenda objects to Stephen's running his own store. Stephen replies that he can do so because there is nothing in the partnership agreement which prohibits such activity. Is Stephen entitled to run his own store in competition with the partnership store?
8. Compare the effect of a secret limitation on the authority of (a) an agent, and (b) a partner.
9. Elrod and Hansford were partners under the name of Walter Elrod & Co. Hansford purchased on credit from the firm of Dawson Blakemore & Co. certain merchandise for the firm. Before the sale, Elrod had notified Dawson Blakemore & Co. that he would not be bound to pay for any purchase for the firm made on credit by Hansford. Thereafter Dawson Blakemore & Co. brought an action against the members of Walter Elrod & Co. to recover the price of the goods. Elrod contended that he was not bound by the contract made by Hansford. Decide. [Dawson Blakemore & Co. v Elrod, 105 Ky 624, 49 SW 465]
10. Mason and Phyllis Ledbetter operated a business in Northbrook, Illinois as a partnership. Called Ledbetters' Nurseries, it specialized in the sale of garden lilies. The grounds of the nurseries were cultivated with the numerous species of garden lilies, and hundreds of people toured the Ledbetters' gardens each day. After a tour Mrs. Shelia Clark invited Mason to Chicago to discuss the possible sale of the facilities at a "top notch price". Mason felt he could not refuse the high offer made by Mrs. Clark on a take-it-or-leave-it basis, and he signed a contract to sell the entire facilities, including all flowers and the business name to

Mrs. Clark. When Phyllis refused to go along with the contract, Mrs. Clark brought suit against the Ledbetters' Nurseries partnership seeking to obtain a decree of specific performance of the sales contract. Decide.

11. O'Bryan, Sullivan, and Davis were partners engaged in operating freight steamers on the Yukon River. Sullivan purchased in the firm name and received from Merrill certain lumber for the construction of firm warehouses at terminal points for the storage of freight. In an action on the contract of sale brought by Merrill against the members of the firm, it was contended that some of the partners had no power to bind the firm on this kind of contract. Do you agree with this contention? [Merrill v O'Bryan, 48 Wash 415, 93 P 917]

12. Holmes and Clay are partners in a medical partnership. Each had invested $25,000 in the practice; and the total market value of all firm assets was $50,000. Marsh, a former patient of Holmes, sued Holmes and Clay for malpractice because of surgery performed by Holmes. Marsh's suit was successful, and a judgment was entered for $150,000 against the two partners. Holmes had suffered a prior financial setback, and he did not have funds or property other than partnership assets to pay the judgment. Arrangements were made by Holmes and Clay to pay $50,000 utilizing the firm assets. Marsh now seeks to collect $100,000 from Clay. Clay objects that it is absurd to seek payment from him out of his own personal assets, when he was not at fault, and indeed was not even at the hospital on the day the surgery was performed. Is Clay liable to Marsh for the unpaid balance of judgment?

13. The Port Richey Shopping Village was owned and operated by a partnership. Myrick and his wife were two of the partners. They owed money to the Second National Bank. The Second National Bank obtained a judgment against the Myricks which directed the sheriff to sell the Myricks' interest in the shopping village. Myrick and his wife filed a motion to prevent the sale. Will they succeed? [Myrick v Second National Bank (Fla App) 335 So2d 343]

14. Wilke, President of the Commercial Bank of Webster City, Iowa, and Wright entered into a farming and stock-raising partnership. The business was conducted under the name of Wilke and Wright Farm Co. The agreement stipulated that Wilke was "to have control and management of said business." Thereafter, Wright sold some partnership cattle to Gross and Gidley, cattle buyers, who resold the cattle to Simon. In an action brought against Simon to recover the cattle, Wilke alleged that Wright had no authority to sell them. Decide. [Wilke v Simon, 46 SD 422, 193 NW 666]

15. The St. John Transportation Co., a corporation, made a contract with the partnership of Bilyeu & Herstel, contractors, by which the latter was to construct a ferryboat. Herstel, a member of the firm of contractors, executed a contract in the firm name with Benbow for certain materials and labor in connection with the construction of the ferryboat. In an action brought by Benbow to enforce a lien against the ferryboat, called the James Johns, it was contended that all members of the firm were bound by the contract made by Herstel. Do you agree? [Benbow v The James Johns, 56 Or 554, 108 P 634]

16. William and Charlotte Davis operated the Davis Nursing Home as a partnership. William made a contract to sell the home and all its assets and goodwill to Feingold. Charlotte refused to recognize the contract. Feingold sued William and Charlotte to obtain a decree of specific performance of the sales contract. Decide. [Feingold v Davis, 444 Pa 339, 282 A2d 291]

17. William and Woodson Johnson, partners in a dairy, purchased their feed from Edwards Feed Mill. Woodson made a purchase of feed in his own name and executed a promissory note for its payment in his own name. Edwards sued both partners on the note on the theory that Williams was also liable since the partnership had received the benefit of the purchase. Decide. [Edwards Feed Mill v Johnson (Tex Civ App) 302 SW2d 151]

CHAPTER 48

NATURE, CREATION, AND

TERMINATION OF

CORPORATIONS

CHAPTER OBJECTIVES

After studying this chapter you will be able to:
1. Classify corporations according to nature, state of incorporation, and functions performed.
2. Decide when the corporate entity will be ignored.
3. List the steps to be taken in forming a corporation.
4. Compare corporations de jure, de facto, and corporations by estoppel.
5. List and describe the ways in which corporate existence may be terminated.
6. Compare consolidations, mergers, and conglomerates.
7. Solve problems involving the creation and termination of corporations.

The corporation is one of the most important forms of business organization. To the large-scale enterprise the corporate form makes financing easier by dividing its ownership into many small units that can be sold to a wide economic range of investors. In addition to assisting financing operations, the corporate device offers a limited liability to the owners and a perpetual succession not affected by the death of any particular owner or by the transfer of the shares of any particular owner.

A. NATURE AND CLASSES

A corporation is a legal person that is created by governmental action. A number of different types of corporations may be created.

§ 48:1.   The Corporation as a Legal Person.

A corporation is an artificial legal being, created by government grant and endowed with certain powers. That is, the corporation exists in the eyes of the law as a person, separate and distinct from the people who own the corporation.[1]

This concept means that property of the corporation is not owned by the persons who own shares in the corporation, but by the corporation. Debts of the corporation are debts of this artificial person and not of the people running the corporation or owning shares of stock in it. The corporation can sue and be sued in its own name with respect to corporate rights and liabilities, but the shareholders cannot sue or be sued as to those rights and liabilities.

FACTS:

Hereford Realty, Inc. had a checking account in the Liberty Bank & Trust Co. The bank improperly refused to pay a check drawn by Hereford on the corporate account. Kesner, the treasurer of Hereford, personally sued the bank for wrongful dishonor of the check.

DECISION:

Judgment for the bank. The right to sue for wrongful dishonor of a check is limited to the customer whose check has been dishonored. The corporation is an entity separate and distinct from its officers and shareholders. Hereford Realty was the customer of the bank, and only Hereford had the right to sue for the dishonor of its check. Kesner had no right as an individual to sue for the dishonor. [Kesner v Liberty Bank & Trust Co. 7 Mass App 934, 390 NE2d 259 (1979)]

A corporation is formed by obtaining approval of a **certificate of incorporation, articles of incorporation,** or a **charter** from the state or national government.[2] The persons who developed the idea of forming a corporation and who induce others to join in the enterprise are called **promoters.** The persons who make the application for the certificate of incorporation are called **incorporators.**

§ 48:2.   Classifications of Corporations.

Corporations may be classified in terms of their relationship to the public, the source of their authority, and the nature of their activities.

---

[1]Macaluso v Jenkins, 96 Ill App 3d 254, 51 Ill Dec 743, 420 NE2d 251 (1981).

[2]"Charter," "certificate of incorporation," and "articles of incorporation" are all terms used to refer to the documents which serve as evidence of a government's grant of corporate existence and powers. Most state incorporation statutes now provide for a certificate of incorporation issued by the secretary of state, but a newly revised Model Business Corporation Act has done away with the certificate of incorporation in an attempt to reduce the volume of paperwork handled by the secretary of state. Under the RMBCA, corporate existence begins when articles of incorporation are filed with the secretary of state. An indorsed copy of the articles together with a fee receipt or acknowledgment replace the certificate of incorporation. See RMBCA §§ 1.25 and 2.03 and footnote 5 in this chapter.

(a) **Public, Private, and Quasi-Public Corporations.** A **public corporation** is one established for governmental purposes and for the administration of public affairs. A city is a public or municipal corporation acting under authority granted to it by the state.

A **private corporation** is one established by private interests, whether for charitable and benevolent purposes or for purposes of finance, industry, and commerce. Private corporations are often called "public" in business circles when the stock is sold to the public.

A **quasi public corporation,** which is also known as a public service corporation or a public utility, is a private corporation furnishing services upon which the public is particularly dependent, such as a railroad, gas, or electric company.

(b) **Public Authorities.** In the twentieth century, the public is increasingly demanding that government perform services. Some of these are performed directly by government. Others are performed by separate corporations or **authorities** that are created by government. For example, a city parking facility may be organized as a separate **municipal parking authority.** A public low cost housing project may be operated as an independent **housing authority.**

(c) **Domestic and Foreign Corporations.** If a corporation has been created under the law of a particular state or nation, it is called a **domestic corporation** with respect to that state or nation. Any other corporation going into that state or nation is called a **foreign corporation.** Thus a corporation holding a Texas charter is a domestic corporation in Texas but a foreign corporation in all other states and nations.

(d) **Special Service Corporations.** Corporations formed for transportation, banking, insurance, savings and loan operations, and similar specialized functions, are subject to separate codes or statutes with regard to their organization. In addition, federal and state laws and administrative agencies regulate in detail the manner in which their business is conducted.

(e) **Close Corporations.** A corporation whose shares are held by a single shareholder or a closely knit group of shareholders is known as a **close corporation.** The shares are not traded publicly. Many such corporations are small firms which in the past would have operated as proprietorships or partnerships but are incorporated either to obtain the advantages of limited liability or a tax benefit, or both.

Statutes have in many states liberalized the corporation law when close corporations are involved, as by permitting their incorporation by a smaller number of persons, allowing them to have a one-person board of directors, and eliminating the requirement of formal meetings.[3]

(f) **Professional Corporations.** A corporation may be organized for the purpose of conducting a profession.

(g) **Nonprofit Corporations.** A **nonprofit corporation** (or an eleemosynary corporation) is one that is organized for charitable or benevolent

[3]This distinction between large and small corporations is part of the same current of legal development that in the Uniform Commercial Code has given rise to the distinction between the merchant seller or buyer on the one hand, and the casual seller or buyer, on the other.

ARTICLES OF INCORPORATION

OF

SYNTRON, INC.

The undersigned, desiring to form a corporation for profit under the provisions of Title XVII. of the Revised Code of Ohio, hereby certifies:

FIRST: The name of said corporation shall be SYNTRON, INC.

SECOND: The place in the State of Ohio where its principal office is to be located is in the City of Columbus, County of Franklin.

THIRD: The purpose for which it is formed is:

To carry on or undertake any business, activities, or transactions in the State of Ohio, in any other State of the United States, or in any foreign country, which a corporation may lawfully carry on or undertake under the General Corporation Law of Ohio and under the laws of such other state or foreign country.

The corporation reserves the right, by action of its shareholders or otherwise, to amend these Articles, to reorganize, to sell, lease or otherwise dispose of all or substantially all of its property or assets, and to consolidate or merge with another corporation, and no dissenting shareholder shall, in any such case, or in any other case, have the right to be paid the fair cash value of his or her shares.

FOURTH: The number of shares which the corporation is authorized to have outstanding is one hundred (100), all of which shall be common shares without par value.

Said shares may be issued pursuant to subscriptions taken by the incorporator, for such amount of consideration as may be specified by the incorporator, and after organization, shares without par value now or hereafter authorized, may be issued or agreed to be issued from time to time for such amount or amounts of consideration as may be fixed from time to time by the Board of Directors. The Board of Directors in its discretion may fix different amounts and kinds of consideration for the issuance of shares without par value, whether issued at the same time or different times, and may determine that only a part or portion of the amount or amounts of a consideration for which as fixed by the incorporator, or by the Board of Directors, has been paid or delivered, shall be fully paid and non-assessable. The above stock is being authorized and shall be issued so as to qualify such stock under the provisions of present Section 1244 of the Internal Revenue Code of 1954, and shall be offered and sold at an aggregate price not to exceed Four Hundred Thousand Dollars ($400,000.00). All such qualifying provisions of said section shall be applicable.

...ital with which the corporation will ...dollars ($10,000.00).

...ors is hereby authorized to fix and ...of working capital of the corporation. ...any, what part of its surplus, ...be used or disposed of or declared ...rs, and without action by the ...h surplus or any part thereof at ...he purchase or acquisition of ...ates for shares, bonds, debentures, ...evidences of indebtedness of the ...he corporation, to such extent ...on such terms, as the Board of

...the corporation of any class ...of right, to subscribe for ...r hereafter authorized, or to ...convertible into or exchangeable ...ch shall be attached or ...entitling the holder thereof to ...se shares, except such rights to subscription ...any, at such price or prices and upon such terms and ...as the Board of Directors in its discretion from time to ...me may determine.

EIGHTH: Notwithstanding any provisions of the Revised Code of Ohio, now or hereafter in force, requiring for any purpose the vote or consent of the holders of shares entitling them to exercise two-thirds or any other proportion of the voting power of the corporation or of any class or classes of shares thereof, such action, unless otherwise expressly required by statute, may be taken by the vote or consent of the holders of shares entitling them to exercise a majority of the voting power of the corporation or of such class or classes.

IN WITNESS WHEREOF, I have hereunto subscribed my name this 9th day of September, 1983.

Susan K. Means

Susan K. Means, Incorporator

ARTICLES OF INCORPORATION

Articles of Incorporation must contain information required by a state's general incorporation statutes.

purposes, such as certain hospitals, homes, and universities.[4] Special procedure for incorporation is sometimes prescribed, with provision being made for a detailed examination and hearing as to the purpose, function, and methods of raising money for the enterprise.

[4]The Committee on Corporate Laws of the American Bar Association has prepared a Model Non-Profit Corporation Act as a comparison to the Model Business Association Act. The Non-Profit Corporation Act has formed the basis for nonprofit corporation statutes in Alabama, Iowa, Nebraska, North Carolina, North Dakota, Ohio, Oregon, Texas, Virginia, Washington, Wisconsin, and the District of Columbia.

§ 48:3.   Corporations and Governments.

Problems between governments and corporations arise with respect to the power of governments to create and regulate corporations.

(a) **Power to Create.** Since by definition a corporation is created by government grant, the right to be a corporation must be obtained from the proper government. The federal government may create corporations whenever appropriate to carry out the powers granted to it.

FACTS:

Maryland enacted a law that imposed a tax on bank notes issued by any bank not chartered by the state legislature. McCulloch, the cashier of the Baltimore branch of the United States Bank, issued bank notes on which this tax had not been paid. Suit was brought by the State of Maryland against McCulloch to recover the statutory penalties imposed for the violation of the law.

DECISION:

Congress, as a means of carrying out its express powers, had the implied authority to create a national bank; and such a bank could not be subjected to state taxation. [McCulloch v Maryland, 4 Wheat (US) 316 (1819)]

Generally a state by virtue of its police power may create any kind of corporation for any purpose. Most states have a **general corporation code** that lists certain requirements, and anyone who satisfies the requirements and files the necessary papers with the government may automatically become a corporation. The American Bar Association has proposed a Model Business Corporation Act (ABA MBCA) to assist legislative bodies in the modernization of state corporation laws.[5] Statutory language similar to that contained in 1969 version of the MBCA has been adopted in whole or in part by some thirty-five states. A 1984 revision of the Model Act (RMBCA) represents the first complete revision of the Model Act in more than thirty years. It is important to remember that jurisdictions following the Model Act have made numerous modifications to the Act to reflect their differing views in the balancing of the interests of public corporations, shareholders, and management. Caution must therefore be exercised in making generalizations about Model Act jurisdictions. There is no uniform corporation act.

(b) **Power to Regulate.** The extent of the power of governments to regulate corporations is affected by whether a corporation is given the rights of a person and of a citizen.

(1) The Corporation as a Person. The Constitution of the United States prohibits the national government and the state governments from depriving any "person" of life, liberty, or property without due process of

---

[5]The Revised Model Business Corporation Act (1984) was approved by the Committee on Corporate Laws of the Section of Corporation, Banking and Business Law of the American Bar Association. The 1984 Act is presented in an Appendix to this book. Model Act citations are to the 1984 Revised Model Business Corporation (RMBCA) unless specifically designated otherwise.

law. Many state constitutions contain a similar limitation upon their respective state governments. A corporation is regarded as a 'person" within the meaning of such provisions.

The federal Constitution prohibits a state from denying to any "person" within its jurisdiction the equal protection of the laws. No such express limitation is placed upon the federal government, although the due process clause binding the federal government is liberally interpreted so that it prohibits substantial inequality of treatment.

(2) The Corporation as a Citizen. For certain purposes, such as determining the right to bring a lawsuit in a federal court, a corporation is today deemed a "citizen" of any state in which it has been incorporated and of the state where it has its principal place of business, without regard to the actual citizenship of the individual persons owning the stock of the corporation. Thus, the corporation incorporated in New York is a New York corporation even though its shareholders are citizens of many other states. Likewise, a Delaware corporation having its principal place of business in New York is deemed a citizen of New York as well as Delaware.[6] An environmental protection law authorizing any "citizen" to bring suit to prevent pollution permits a corporation to bring such a suit.

The federal Constitution prohibits states from abridging "the privileges or immunities of citizens of the United States." A corporation, however, is not regarded as a "citizen" within this clause. Thus, with one exception, a foreign corporation has no constitutional right to do business in another state if that other state wishes to exclude it. For example, Pennsylvania can deny a New York corporation the right to come into Pennsylvania to do business. As a practical matter, most states do not exclude foreign corporations but seize upon this power as justifying special regulation or taxation. On this basis it is commonly provided that a foreign corporation must register or even take out a domestic charter, file copies of its charter, pay certain taxes, or appoint a resident agent before it can do business within the state.

§ 48:4.   Ignoring the Corporate Entity.

Ordinarily each corporation will be regarded and treated as a separate legal person and the law will not look behind a corporation to see who owns or controls it.

The fact that two corporations have identical shareholders does not justify a court in regarding the two corporations as being one. Likewise the fact that there is a close working relationship between two corporations does not in itself constitute any basis for ignoring their separate corporate entities when they in fact are separately run enterprises.[7]

(a) Prevention of Fraud or Illegality. When the corporation is formed to perpetrate a fraud or to conceal illegality, a court will ordinarily ignore the corporate entity, or as it is figuratively called, "pierce the corporate veil."[8] For example, a buyer under a requirements contract remains liable even though the buyer incorporates the business in the effort to avoid the contract obligation.

[6]28 United States Code § 1332(c).
[7]Extra Energy Coal Co. v Diamond, ____ Ind ____, 467 NE2d 439 (1984).
[8]Nebraska Engineering Co. v Gerstner, 212 Neb 440, 323 NW2d 84 (1982).

When a person engages in business and uses the corporation as a mask by which to hide from a person being defrauded, the law will ignore the separate corporate entity and will hold the wrongdoer liable for the acts of the corporation on the theory that it is the *alter ego* of the wrongdoer.

(b) **Prevention of Injustice.** Disregarding the corporate entity is not limited to cases of actual fraud or illegality. The corporate entity may also be disregarded to prevent injustice or inequitable consequences.[9]

FACTS:

Jordon and Walter Kaiser organized a corporation called The Chicago Aces Tennis Team, Inc. In the name of the corporation, they made a contract with Susan Stap to play professional tennis. She was never paid the money called for by the contract and she sued the Kaiser brothers. They raised the defense that they could not be sued because Susan's contract was with the corporation. She claimed that the corporate entity should be ignored and that the brothers should be held liable on the contract of the corporation. She based this claim on the fact that the brothers owned 100% of the stock of the corporation and had contributed 100% of the capital of a partnership that was a majority shareholder in another corporation that owned the facilities used by The Chicago Aces corporation. She further claimed that the Kaiser brothers had handled the funds of the partnership and The Chicago Aces in disregard of the separate identity of the corporation.

DECISION:

The Kaiser brothers were liable on the corporate contract because the corporate entity would be ignored. The close relationship between the brothers and the corporation and their control over the corporation and the use of its funds showed that the corporation was merely a mask for their operations and that it would be a fraud to allow the corporation to insulate the brothers from liability for their acts. [Stap v Chicago Aces Tennis Team, Inc. 63 Ill App 3d 23, 20 Ill Dec 230, 379 NE2d 1298 (1978)]

(c) **Functional Reality.** When a corporation is in effect merely a department of a large enterprise, as when a large manufacturer incorporates its marketing department, it is likely that the separate corporate character of the incorporated department will be ignored.

FACTS:

A Dodge truck was manufactured by the Chrysler Corp. and sold by it to its wholly owned subsidiary, Chrysler Motors, which in turn sold it to its wholly owned subsidiary,

Dodge Trucks, Inc., a retail truck dealer. The latter changed the front axle and neglected to tighten the steering assembly properly after making the change. The truck was then sold to Clark Motor Co., which sold it to Welborn.

---

[9]Kwick Set Components, Inc. v Davidson Industries, Inc. (Ala) 411 So2d 134 (1982).

Vaughn was injured when the Dodge truck went out of control because of the defect. He sued Chrysler Corp. It defended on the ground that the truck was not defective when it left the factory and that the defect had been generated by the act of an independent corporation in making an alteration which was both unauthorized by and unknown to Chrysler.

DECISION:

Judgment for Vaughn. Consumer protection requires that there be liability for defective products and the manufacturer cannot escape this liability on the grounds that it had been caused by a particular branch of the complicated corporate structure that the manufacturer had created for the distribution of its products. [Vaughn v Chrysler Corp. (CA10 Okla) 442 F2d 619 (1971)]

(d) Obtaining Advantages of Corporate Existence. The court will not go behind the corporate identity merely because the corporation has been formed to obtain tax savings or to obtain limited liability for its shareholders.[10] Likewise, the corporate entity will not be ignored merely because the corporation does not have sufficient assets to pay the claims against it.

The fact that recognizing the corporate entity has the effect of preventing creditors of the corporation from reaching assets which would otherwise be held by the shareholders, in whose hands they would be subject to the claims of the creditors, is not in itself a ground for refusing to recognize the corporate entity. It is immaterial that one individual is the only shareholder in the corporation.

B. CREATION OF THE CORPORATION

All states have general laws governing the creation of corporations by persons who comply with the provisions of the statutes.

§ 48:5. Promoters.

Corporations frequently come into existence as the result of the activities of one or more persons known as **promoters**, although there is no legal requirement for the services of a promoter in the formation of a corporation.

The promoter brings together persons interested in the enterprise, aids in obtaining subscriptions to stock, and sets in motion the machinery which leads to the formation of the corporation itself.

A corporation is not liable on a contract made by its promoter for its benefit unless it takes some affirmative action to adopt such contract. Such action may be express words of adoption, or the adoption of the contract may be inferred from the corporation's accepting the benefits thereof. A corporation may also become bound by such contracts by assignment or by novation.[11]

The promoter is personally liable for all contracts made in behalf of the corporation before its existence unless exempted by the terms of the agreement or by the circumstances surrounding it. When a promoter makes

[10]Kline v Kline, 104 Mich App 700, 305 NW2d 297 (1981).
[11]Jacobson v Stern, 96 Nev 56, 605 P2d 198 (1980).

a contract on behalf of a corporation to be formed thereafter, the promoter is liable thereon if the corporation is not formed, in the absence of an agreement that the promoter should not be so liable.

FACTS:

Quaker Hill made a contract for the sale of plants to the "Denver Memorial Nursery, Inc." The contract was signed by Parr as Denver's president. Quaker Hill knew that the corporation was not yet formed and the contract so stated, but Quaker Hill had insisted that the contract be executed in this manner rather than wait until the corporation was organized. The corporation was never formed, and Quaker Hill sued Parr and other promoters of the corporation.

DECISION:

Judgment against Quaker Hill. A promoter is ordinarily liable on a contract made on behalf of a corporation not yet formed. This rule does not apply, however, where, as here, the third person knows that the corporation is not in existence and enters into the agreement with the intention that the promoter shall not be liable thereon. [Quaker Hill v Parr, 148 Colo 45, 364 P2d 1056 (1961)]

A promoter is liable for all torts committed in connection with the promoter's activities. The corporation is not ordinarily liable for the torts of the promoter, but it may become liable by its conduct after incorporation. Thus, when a corporation, with actual or implied notice of the fraud of the promoter, assumes the promoter's contract, it is liable for the promoter's fraud which induced the other party to enter into the contract.

A promoter stands in a fiduciary relation to the corporation and to stock subscribers, and cannot make secret profits at their expense. Accordingly, if a promoter makes a secret profit on a sale of land to the corporation, the promoter must account to the corporation for this profit; that is, the promoter must surrender the profit to it. The promoter may be held guilty of embezzlement if the promoter converts property that should have gone to the corporation.

The corporation is not liable in most states for the expenses and services of the promoter unless it subsequently promises to pay for them or unless its charter or a statute imposes such liability upon it.

§ 48:6.   Incorporation.

One or more natural persons, or a domestic or a foreign corporation, may act as incorporators of a corporation by signing and filing articles of incorporation with the designated government official.[12] These articles are filed in duplicate. The designated official (usually the secretary of state) upon being satisfied that the articles conform to the statutory requirements, stamps "filed" and the date on each copy. The official then retains one copy and returns the other copy along with a filing fee receipt to the corporation.[13]

[12]RMBCA § 2:01.
[13]RMBCA § 1.25.

Statutes may require the incorporators to give some form of public notice, as by advertising in a newspaper, of the intention to form the corporation.

§ 48:7.   Application for Incorporation.

The instrument by which a private corporation is formed in most jurisdictions is called the **articles of incorporation.** The instrument sets forth certain information about the new corporation. The articles of incorporation must contain (1) the name of the corporation, (2) the number of shares the corporation is authorized to issue, (3) the street address of the corporation's initial registered office and the name of its initial registered agent, and (4) the name and address of each incorporator.[14] The articles of incorporation may contain optional provisions such as the purpose or purposes for which the corporation is organized, but if it contains no "purpose clause," the corporation will automatically have the purpose of engaging in any lawful business.[15] Also, if no reference is made to the period of duration of the corporation in the articles of incorporation, it will automatically have perpetual duration.[16]

§ 48:8.   The Certificate of Incorporation.

While most state incorporation statutes now provide for a "certificate of incorporation" issued by the secretary of state, the Revised Model Business Corporation Act has eliminated the certificate of incorporation in an effort to reduce the volume of paper work handled by the secretary of state. Under the Revised Act, corporate existence begins when the articles are filed with the secretary of state.[17] Under the older practice still followed by many states, corporate existence begins upon the issuance of the certificate of incorporation by the secretary of state.

§ 48:9.   Proper and Defective Incorporation.

If the legal procedure for incorporation has been followed, the corporation has a perfect legal right to exist. It is then called a **corporation de jure,** meaning that it is a corporation by virtue of law.[18]

Assume that there is some defect in the corporation which is formed. If the defect is not a material one, the law usually will overlook the defect and hold that the corporation is a corporation de jure.

The RMBCA abolishes objections to irregularities and defects in incorporating. It provides that the "secretary of state's filing of the articles of incorporation is conclusive proof that the incorporators satisified all conditions precedent to incorporation...."[19] Many state statutes follow this pattern. Such an approach is based upon the practical consideration that when countless people are purchasing shares of stock and entering into business transactions with thousands of corporations, it becomes an absurdity to

[14]RMBCA § 2:02.
[15]RMBCA § 3:01.
[16]RMBCA § 3:02.
[17]RMBCA § 2:03(a).
[18]Kansas v Construction Enterprises, Inc. 6 Kan App 2d 627, 631 P2d 1240 (1981).
[19]RMBCA § 2.03(b).

expect that anyone is going to make the detailed search that would be required to determine whether a given corporation is a de jure corporation.[20]

(a) **De Facto Corporation.** The defect in the incorporation may be so substantial that the law cannot ignore it and will not accept the corporation as a de jure corporation. Yet there may be sufficient compliance so that the law will recognize that there is a corporation. When this occurs, the association is called a de facto corporation.

Although there is conflict among the authorities, the traditional elements of a de facto corporation are: (1) a valid law exists under which the corporation could have been properly incorporated; (2) an attempt to organize the corporation has been made in good faith; (3) a genuine attempt to organize in compliance with the requirements of the statute has been made; and (4) there has been a use of the corporate powers.

(b) **Partnership v Corporation by Estoppel.** The defect in incorporation may be so great that the law will not accept the association as a de facto corporation. In such a case, in the absence of a statute making the incorporation conclusive, there is no corporation. If the individuals proceed to run the business in spite of such irregularity, they may be held liable as partners.[21]

The partnership liability rule is sometimes not applied when the third person dealt with the business as though it were a corporation. In such instances, it is stated that the third person is estopped from denying that the "corporation" with which the business was transacted has legal existence. In effect, there is a corporation by estoppel with respect to that creditor.

Several jurisdictions which follow the 1969 MBCA have expressly retained the doctrines of corporation by estoppel and de facto corporations.[22] However courts interpreting the language of the 1969 MBCA have determined that the de facto corporation doctrine and the corporation by estoppel doctrine no longer exist.

FACTS:

On January 27, 1982 Joe Walker purchased a wheel loader machine from the Thompson & Green Machinery Co. (T-G). Mr. Walker signed a promissory note for $37,886.30 on behalf of "Music City Sawmill, Inc. by Joe Walker, President." When Sawmill was unable to make payments on the loader, the machine was returned to T-G. T-G brought suit against Sawmill and thereafter discovered that Sawmill had not been incorporated on January 27, 1982 when the machine was purchased, but rather had been incorporated on the next day. T-G then sued Walker individually. The lawsuit was Walker's first notice that Sawmill was not incorporated on the date of the sale. Walker defended

---

[20]This trend and the reasons therefore may be compared to those involved in the concept of the negotiability of commercial paper. Note the similar protection from defenses given to the person purchasing shares for value and without notice. Uniform Commercial Code § 8–202.

[21]In a minority of states the court will not hold the individuals liable as partners, but will hold liable the person who committed the act on behalf of the business on the theory that such person was an agent who acted without authority and is therefore liable for breach of the implied warranties of the existence of a principal possessing capacity and of proper authorization.

[22]See Ga. Bus. Corp. Code § 22–5103; Minn. Bus. Corp. Act § 301:08.

that T-G dealt with Sawmill as a corporation and did not intend to bind him personally on the note, and therefore was estopped to deny Sawmill's corporate existence.

DECISION:

Judgment for Thompson and Green Machinery Co. Section 146 of the 1969 MBCA mandates that all persons who assume to act as a corporation without authority shall be liable for debts which result from these actions. The language of this statute is clear and unambiguous and contains no good faith exceptions. The doctrine of corporation by estoppel was abolished by the enactment of Section 146. Walker thus cannot rely on this doctrine and he is individually liable for the debt. [Thompson & Green Machinery Co. v Music City Lumber Co. (Tenn App) 683 SW2d 340 (1984)]

The 1984 Model Act contains a more flexible standard than the 1969 version, imposing liability for preincorporation debts only on persons who act as or on behalf of a corporation "knowing" that no corporation exists.[23]

§ 48:10.   Insolvency, Bankruptcy, and Reorganization.

When a corporation has financial troubles that are so serious that it is insolvent, the best thing may be to go through bankruptcy or reorganization proceedings.

(a) **Insolvency.** The insolvency of a corporation does not in itself terminate the corporate existence. Statutes in some states, however, provide that when the corporation is insolvent, creditors may commence proceedings to dissolve the corporation. Sometimes the statute merely dissolves the corporation as to creditors. This situation is sometimes called a **de facto dissolution** or **quasi dissolution.**

(b) **Bankruptcy.** When a corporation is adjudicated bankrupt, a sale of all its assets will be ordered. This leaves the corporation without any assets with which to do business unless there should be a surplus above the amount required to pay off the debts of the corporation. The bankruptcy proceeding does not, however, terminate the legal existence of the corporation.

(c) **Reorganization.** When a reorganization of a corporation occurs under the federal bankruptcy laws, the corporate existence is not terminated. If the reorganization is successful, the result is the same as though the corporation merely exchanged obligations and securities. Under state law, however, reorganization proceedings generally result in formation of a new corporation.

§ 48:11.   Administrative Dissolution.

Under the Revised Model Act the secretary of state may commence proceedings to administratively dissolve a corporation if (1) the corporation does not pay franchise taxes within 60 days after they are due, (2) the corporation does not file its annual report within 60 days after it is due,

[23]RMBCA § 2.04.

or (3) the corporation is without a registered agent or registered office for 60 days or more.[24]

§ 48:12.   Judicial Dissolution.

In some states, provision is made for the judicial dissolution of a corporation when its management is deadlocked and the deadlock cannot be broken by the shareholders.[25] In some states, a "custodian" may be appointed for a corporation when the shareholders are unable to break a deadlock in the board of directors and irreparable harm is threatened or sustained by the corporation because of the deadlock.

D. CONSOLIDATIONS, MERGERS, AND CONGLOMERATES

Two or more corporations may be combined to form a new structure or enterprise. This may be a consolidation, a merger, or the formation of a conglomerate.

§ 48:13.   Definitions.

The form through which the combination is accomplished will affect the identity of the resulting corporation.

(a) **Consolidation.** In a **consolidation** of two or more corporations, their separate existences cease and a new corporation with the property and the assets of the old corporations comes into being.

When a consolidation is effected, the new corporation ordinarily succeeds to the rights, powers, and immunities of its component parts. Limitations, however, may be prescribed by certificate of incorporation, constitution, or statute.

(b) **Merger. Merger** differs from consolidation in that, when two corporations merge, one absorbs the other. One corporation preserves its original charter and identity and continues to exist, and the other disappears and its corporate existence terminates.

Usually if a stockholder dissents from a proposed consolidation or merger, or if a stockholder fails to convert existing shares into stock of the new or continuing corporation, the dissenting stockholder or the corporation may make application to the courts to appraise the value of the stock held. The new or continuing corporation is then required to pay the value of the stock to the stockholder, and the stockholder is required to transfer the stock to the new or continuing corporation. In effect, the court orders the new or continuing corporation to buy the stock from the dissenting stockholder.

Complex series of transactions are often involved in the elimination of the ownership interests of minority shareholders. It is known as a "two-step merger": (1) an outside investor purchases control of the majority shares of the target corporation by tender offer or through private negotia-

[24]RMBCA § 14:20.
[25]RMBCA § 14:30(2)(i).

tions; (2) this newly acquired control is used to arrange for the target and a second corporation controlled by the outside investor to merge, with one condition being the "freeze-out" of the minority shareholders of the target corporation by the forced cancellation of their shares, generally through a cash purchase.

FACTS:

Madison Associates purchased control of the majority of shares of 79 Realty Corp from the Kimmelmans and the Zauders, who then resigned as directors. The Alpert group, which owned the remaining 26% of 79 Realty refused to sell their shares. Partners of Madison Associates replaced the Kimmelmans and Zauders as directors of 79 Realty Corp, and as controlling directors, they approved a plan to merge 79 Realty Corp with the Williams Street Corp., which was owned by Madison Associates. A shareholders' meeting was called; and the merger was approved by two-thirds of the shareholders. The Alpert group's shares were then forcibly canceled, with the price paid for these shares determined at their fair market value. The Alpert group brought suit contending the merger was unlawful because the sole purpose was to benefit the Madison Associates, which group had a clear conflict of interest.

DECISION:

Judgment for Madison Associates. State law allows for the merger of two corporations into a single corporation as long as certain procedures are followed, such as obtaining approval of the merger by a two-thirds vote of shareholders. Madison met all required procedures. Even a freeze-out merger which involves the removal of minority shareholders by a forced cancellation of their shares by a cash purchase is allowed, provided it advances a general corporate interest. The merger in this case was valid since it advanced the bona fide business purpose of obtaining increased capital. [Alpert v 28 Williams Street Corp. 63 NY2d 557, 473 NE2d 19 (1984)]

(c) Conglomerate. **Conglomerate** is the term describing the relationship of a parent corporation to subsidiary corporations engaged in diversified fields of activity unrelated to the field of activity of the parent corporation. For example, a wire manufacturing corporation that owns all the stock of a newspaper corporation and of a drug manufacturing corporation would be described as a conglomerate. In contrast, if the wire manufacturing company owned a mill to produce the metal used in making the wire and owned a mine which produced the ore that was used by the mill, the relationship would probably be described as an *integrated industry* rather than as a conglomerate. This is merely a matter of usage, rather than of legal definition. Likewise, when the parent company is not engaged in production or the rendering of services, it is customary to call it a holding company.

Without regard to whether the enterprise is a holding company, or whether the group of businesses constitute a conglomerate or an integrated industry, each part is a distinct corporation to which the ordinary corporation law applies. In some instances additional principles apply because of the nature of the relationship existing between the several corporations involved. In some instances the entity of one of the corporations in the conglomerate group may be ignored.

§ 48:14.   Legality.

Consolidations, mergers, and asset acquisitions between enterprises are often prohibited by federal antitrust legislation on the ground that the effect is to lessen competition in interstate commerce. A business corporation may not merge with a charitable corporation because this would divert the assets of the respective corporations to purposes not intended by their shareholders.

§ 48:15.   Liability of Enterprise.

When corporations are combined in any way, the question arises of who is liable for the debts and obligations of the original corporations.

(a) **Liability of Successor Enterprise.** Generally the enterprise engaging in or continuing the business after a merger or consolidation will be subject to the contract obligations and debts of the original corporations.[26]

The corporation which absorbs another corporation by merger is generally liable for the contract of the corporation which was absorbed, and it is no defense that the third party does not have any contract with the absorbing corporation.

FACTS:

Gaswint was employed by an Oregon corporation, Amigo Motor Homes, Inc. The stock of the corporation was acquired by Black Diamond Enterprises, Inc. Some time thereafter Gaswint was discharged. He sued Case, a corporate officer and the two corporations for damages for breach of contract. Black Diamond asserted that it was not liable to the plaintiff because it had never made any contract with him. A local statute declared that when one corporation took over the business of another, the surviving corporation would be liable for the debts of the original corporation.

DECISION:

The statute imposing liability on the surviving corporation made Black Diamond liable for any claim for which Amigo would have been liable. This liability was based on statute, and therefore it was immaterial that there was no express agreement by Black Diamond to pay the claims. [Gaswint v Case, 265 Or 248, 509 P2d 19 (1973)]

In contrast with the situation of a merger or consolidation, a successor corporation that merely purchases the assets of the former business does not become liable for the obligations of the former business.[27]

[26]Bernard v Kee Manufacturing Co. (Fla App) 394 So2d 552 (1981).
[27]Manh Hung Nguyen v Johnson Machine & Press Corp. 104 Ill App 3d 1141, 60 Ill Dec 866, 433 NE2d 1104 (1982).

(b) **Liability of Component Enterprise.** An existing business may be acquired by another corporation under a variety of circumstances. How does the acquisition affect the rights and liabilities of the business that is acquired? For example, when corporation *A* buys out corporation *B*, what becomes of the rights and liabilities of corporation *B*?

When there is a formal consolidation or merger, statutes commonly provide expressly for the transfer of rights and liabilities to the surviving corporation or the new corporation. The contract of sale or agreement between corporation *A* and corporation *B* will ordinarily expressly assign *B*'s rights to *A* and contain an assumption by *A* of the liabilities of *B*.

SUMMARY

A corporation is an artificial legal being created by government action which exists as a separate and distinct entity and is endowed with certain powers. In most states the corporation comes into existence when the secretary of state issues a certificate of incorporation. The most common forms of corporations are private business corporations whose stock is sold to the "public" (publicly held), and close corporations, which are business firms whose shares are not traded publicly. Corporations may be formed for purposes other than conducting a business, such as nonprofit corporations for charitable purposes, and municipal corporations and public authorities for governmental purposes.

Ordinarily each corporation will be treated as a separate legal person, and the law will not look beyond the corporate identity merely because it has been formed to obtain tax savings or limited liability. The fact that two corporations have the same shareholders does not justify disregarding the separate corporate entities. However when a corporation is formed to perpetrate a fraud, a court will ignore the corporate form or "pierce the corporate veil". The corporate form will also be ignored to prevent injustice, or because of the functional reality that the two corporations in question are one.

A promoter is the person who brings together the persons interested in the enterprise, and sets in motion all that must be done to form a corporation. A corporation is not liable on contracts made by its promoter for the corporation unless it adopts the contracts; and the promoter is personally liable for contracts made for the corporation before its existence. A promoter stands in a fiduciary relation to the corporation and share subscribers.

A corporation is a legal being created by law. The procedures for incorporation are set forth in the statutes of each state. The corporation comes into existence upon issuance of the certificate of incorporation. It is then called a *corporation de jure*. Where all statutory procedures for incorporation have not been complied with, after a good faith attempt to incorporate under the state statute has been made, a *de facto* corporation may be found to exist. Or, where sufficient compliance for a *de facto* corporation does not exist, a third person may be estopped from denying the legal existence of the "corporation" with which it did business (corporation by estoppel). However the 1969 MBCA has been construed as having abolished the *de facto* and estoppel doctrines.

A corporation may be dissolved or terminated by agreement, reorganization proceedings, or forfeiture of its charter. Two or more corporations may be combined to form a new enterprise. This may be a consolidation with a new corporation coming into existence, or a merger where one absorbs the other.

QUESTIONS AND CASE PROBLEMS

1. What social forces are affected by the recognition of a corporation as a distinct legal entity?
2. The Karnak Chemical Company is incorporated in Utah. It wishes to do business in Oklahoma but is required to pay a tax assessed by Oklahoma against foreign corporations. Stephen owns shares in Karnak. He claims that it is not subject to the Oklahoma tax because Karnak is an American corporation and therefore is a domestic corporation to all states. Is he correct?
3. Daisy sued the Mobile Construction Company. Philip was the only shareholder of the corporation. Daisy obtained a judgment against the corporation. Philip then dissolved the corporation and took over all its assets. He agreed to pay all outstanding debts of the corporation except the judgment in favor of Daisy. She sued Philip on the ground that he was liable for the judgment against the corporation. He claimed that the judgment was only the liability of the corporation and that he was not liable because he was merely a shareholder and had not assumed the liability for the judgment. Is Philip liable on the judgment?
4. Florence promoted a new corporation, the Kaskey Print Shop. She made contracts in the name of Kaskey with third persons. Thereafter Kaskey was formed but soon went out of business. Suit was brought against Florence on the contracts which she had made for Kaskey. She claimed that she was not liable because she had made them on behalf of the corporation. Is she liable on the contracts?
5. What are common grounds for forfeiture of the corporate charter?
6. Acting under the statute of the state in which they practice medicine, Patricia, Judy, and Elizabeth form a professional corporation to engage in the practice of medicine. The statement is later made that their corporation is a close corporation. This is denied on the ground that it is a professional corporation. How would you describe the corporation?
7. Compare consolidations, mergers, and conglomerates.
8. Norman was organizing a new corporation: the Collins Home Construction Company. Fairchild knew that the corporation was not yet formed but made a contract by which he agreed to sell certain goods to Collins. The corporation was later organized and ratified the contract that Norman had made with Fairchild. Fairchild, however, did not perform the contract and was sued by Collins. Fairchild raised the defense that he had never made any contract with Collins and that a corporation that did not exist could not have made a contract. Were these defenses valid?
9. Tilton and others formed a voluntary association called the Ottumwa Temperance Reform Club. Tilton and others were chosen to act as an

executive committee. The committee made a contract with the Ottumwa Gas-Light Co. on behalf of the club. An action was later brought by the utility company to recover for the gas supplied. The members of the committee claimed that they were not individually liable because the club was a corporation. Was the group a corporation? [Lewis v Tilton, 64 Iowa 220, 19 NW 911]

10. An action was brought by Alabama Tank Lines and other carriers against the Martin Truck Line, claiming that the truck line was operating without the necessary certificate of the state Public Service Commission. It was shown that Martin Truck Line had obtained a certificate at a time when all of its stock was owned by Thornbury, Cook, and Edwards. The stock was thereafter sold to Houghland and Page. No approval of the transfer of stock to them was obtained from the Public Service Commission. Was Martin Truck Line entitled to continue to do business under the certificate that had been originally issued? [Martin Truck Line v Alabama Tank Lines, 261 Ala 163, 73 So2d 756]

11. The Branmar Theatre Co., a family corporation, leased a theater from Branmar, Inc. The lease prohibited it from assigning the lease. The holders of the stock of Branmar Theatre Co. sold their stock to the Schwartzes. The lessor, Branmar, Inc., claimed that this was a prohibited assignment and threatened to cancel the lease. Branmar Theatre Co. thereafter brought an action for a declaratory judgment to enjoin the cancellation of the lease. Should the court enjoin the cancellation of the lease? [Branmar Theatre Co. v Branmar, Inc. (Del Ch) 264 A2d 526]

12. Mulley was a promoter of a corporation not yet formed, Collier County Developers, Inc. He made a contract as promoter with Vodopich for services in selling certain real estate. Vodopich later sued Mulley for breach of the contract. Mulley claimed that he was not liable because Vodopich knew that the corporation had not yet been formed. Was he correct? [Vodopich v Collier County Developers, Inc. (Fla App) 319 So2d 43]

13. A made a contract with B on behalf of X Corporation. B knew that X Corporation was not yet formed. Thereafter X Corporation was properly organized, but B refused to perform its contract on the ground that X had not been in existence when the contract was made. Was this a valid defense?

14. Is the guarantor of the debt of a corporation discharged from liability when the debtor corporation merges into another corporation? Discuss.

15. Adams and two other persons were promoters for a new corporation, the Aldrehn Theaters Co. The promoters retained Kridelbaugh to perform legal services in connection with the incorporation of the new business and promised to pay him $1,500. The corporation was incorporated through Kridelbaugh's services, and the promoters became its only directors. Kridelbaugh attended a meeting of the board of directors at which he was told that he should obtain a permit for the corporation to sell stock because the directors wished to pay him for his prior services. The promoters failed to pay Kridelbaugh, and he sued the corporation. Was the corporation liable? [Kridelbaugh v Aldrehn Theaters Co. 195 Iowa 147, 191 NW 803]

16. On August 19, 1980, the plaintiff, Joan Ioviero, injured her hand when she slipped and fell while leaving the dining room at the Hotel Excelsior in Venice, Italy, which hotel is owned by the Italian corporation "Ciga-hotels, S.p.A." In 1973 a firm called "Ciga Hotels, Inc." was incorporated, in New York. Its certificate of incorporation was amended in 1979, changing its name to "Landia International Services, Inc." This New York corporation was employed by the Italian corporation, Ciga-hotels, S.p.A. to provide sales and promotional services in the United States and Canada. Ms. Ioviero seeks to hold the New York corporation liable for her hand injury at the Venice hotel. She points to the similarity of the first corporate name used by the New York firm to the name Ciga-hotels, S.p.A., and the fact the New York firm represents the interests of the Italian firm in the U.S., as clear evidence that the two firms are the same single legal entity. She asks that the court disregard the separate corporate entities. The New York corporation moves that the case be dismissed because it is duly incorporated in New York and does not own the Excelsior Hotel in which Ms. Ioviero was injured. Decide. [Ioviero v CigaHotel, Inc. aka Landia I.S. Inc. 475 NYS2d 880].

17. Spiro was the president, treasurer, director, and majority shareholder of Piccadilly Land Corporation, making all decisions for the business. Prior to December 2, 1974, Spiro represented to Ricardo and Sandra De Santis that Piccadilly was actively engaged in the construction of homes and that its financial status was sound. Relying on these representations, which proved to be untrue, the DeSantises entered into a written agreement with Piccadilly on December 2, 1974, which provided that Piccadilly would build a home for the DeSantises according to certain plans and specifications. Pursuant to the agreement, they made an $8,000 down payment. After performing some site work, Piccadilly ceased work on the home. The down payment was not returned since Piccadilly was insolvent at the time the written agreement was signed. The DeSantises filed suit against Spiro personally for breach of contract and fraud, claiming that the court should pierce the corporate veil. Spiro contends that the agreement in question was made with Piccadilly Land Corp., a duly incorporated corporation, and that corporate law provides him the privilege of limited liability. He contends that limited liability is not lost because a firm has the misfortune of becoming insolvent. Decide. [DeSantis v Piccadilly Land Corp (Conn App) 487 A2d 1110]

CHAPTER 49

CORPORATE POWERS

CHAPTER OBJECTIVES

After studying this chapter you will be able to:
1. List ten powers commonly possessed by corporations.
2. Describe the scope and status of corporate bylaws.
3. Compare treasury stock with ordinary common stock.
4. Distinguish between illegal contracts and ultra vires contracts.
5. State the extent to which liability arises because of an ultra vires contract.
6. Solve problems involving powers of corporations.

By common law and by virtue of the statute under which it is incorporated, a corporation has certain powers. Some of the powers possessed by a corporation are the same as those powers held by a natural person, such as the right to own property. Others are distinct powers not possessed by natural persons, such as the power of perpetual succession.

The articles of incorporation often contain a comprehensive and complicated "powers clause" setting forth in detail the corporation's powers. Where a corporation acts beyond the limits of its powers, the act is ultra vires. Modern statutes grant broad corporate powers to lessen the likelihood that a corporation will act beyond its powers.

§ 49:1. Nature and Limitations of Corporate Powers.

A corporation has implied power to make any contract needed to conduct its business and accomplish its corporate purposes.[1]

---

[1]Bergy Brothers, Inc. v Zeeland Feeder Pig, Inc. 96 Mich App 111, 292 NW2d 493 (1980).

All corporations do not have the same powers. For example, those that operate banks, insurance companies, savings and loan associations, and railroads generally have special powers.

Except for limitations in the federal Constitution or the state's own constitution, a state may grant to a corporation any powers that it chooses. The Revised Model Act contains a broadly phrased general provision on corporate powers granting the corporation "the same powers as an individual to do all things necessary or convenient to carry out its business and affairs."[2] Many state statutes also contain broad catchall grants of powers.

FACTS:

The Philadelphia Electric Company was incorporated "for the purpose of supplying heating, lighting, and power by electricity to the public." The company supplied electricity but in addition began to sell to its customers household electrical appliances. The Attorney General claimed that the sale of appliances was not authorized by the company's charter's provision to produce and sell electricity. He brought a lawsuit to forfeit the charter of the Philadelphia Electric Company, on the theory that it was acting beyond the scope of its charter.

DECISION:

Judgment for Philadelphia Electric Company. The fact that the company was authorized to produce and supply electricity did not mean that it could do nothing more. To the contrary, it was reasonable for the company to promote the sale of its electricity by expanding the number of users of electricity, which it was doing by having more people own electrical appliances. The sale of such appliances was therefore within the scope of the corporate charter. [Pennsylvania v Philadelphia Electric Co. 300 Pa 577, 151 A 344 (1930)]

In some states, a corporation may not exercise its power until an organizational meeting has been held.[3]

§ 49:2.   Particular Powers.

Modern corporation codes give corporations a wide range of powers.

(a) Perpetual Succession. One of the distinctive features of a corporation is its perpetual succession or continuous life—the power to continue as a unit forever or for a stated period of time regardless of changes in stock ownership. If no period is fixed for its duration, the corporation will exist indefinitely unless it is legally dissolved. When the period is limited, the corporation may in many states extend the period by meeting additional requirements of the statute.

(b) Corporate Name. A corporation must have a name to identify it. As a general rule, it may select any name for this purpose.

Most states require that the corporate name contain some word indicating the corporate character[4] and that it shall not be the same as or decep-

---

[2]RMBCA § 3.02.
[3]Bostetter v Freestate Land Corp. 48 Md App 142, 426 A2d 404 (1981).
[4]RMBCA § 4.01(a) declares that the corporate name must contain the word "corporation," "company," "incorporated," "limited," or an abbreviation of one of such words.

tively similar to the name of another corporation. Some statutes likewise prohibit the use of a name which is likely to mislead the public. The Revised Model Act states that the corporate name "may not contain language stating or implying that the corporation is organized for a purpose other than that permitted by . . . its articles of incorporation."[5]

(c) **Corporate Seal.** A corporation may have a distinctive seal. However, a corporation need not use a seal in the transaction of business unless it is required by statute to use a seal or unless a natural person in transacting that business would be required to use a seal. Likewise a corporation may use a seal different than the official corporate seal unless the use of that official seal is required for the particular document that is being executed.

(d) **Bylaws.** Bylaws are the rules and regulations enacted by a corporation to govern the affairs of the corporation and its shareholders, directors, and officers. The shareholders of a corporation have inherent power to make bylaws to supplement the charter of the corporation, but the right to do so is commonly expressed by statute.

Bylaws are adopted by the action of the shareholders, but some statutes provide for the adoption of bylaws by the directors unless otherwise provided. Action by the state or an amendment of the corporation charter is not required to make the bylaws effective.

The bylaws are subordinate to the general law of the state, including the statute under which the corporation is formed, as well as to the charter of the corporation.[6] Bylaws that conflict with such superior authority or which are in themselves unreasonable are invalid. Bylaws that are valid are binding upon all shareholders regardless of whether they know of the existence of those bylaws or were among the majority which consented to their adoption. Bylaws are not binding upon third persons, however, unless they have notice or knowledge of them.

(e) **Stock.** A corporation may issue stock and certificates representing such stock.

(f) **Borrowing Money.** Corporations have the implied power to borrow money in carrying out their authorized business purposes. For example, a fire insurance company may borrow money to pay losses due on its policies. Statutes commonly prohibit corporations from raising the defense of usury.

(g) **Execution of Commercial Paper.** The power to issue or indorse commercial paper, or to accept drafts, is implied when the corporation has the power to borrow money and when such means are appropriate and ordinarily used to further the authorized objectives of the corporation.

(h) **Bonds.** A corporation having the power to borrow money has the implied power to issue various types of bonds.

The bonds issued by a corporation are subject to Article 8 of the Uniform Commercial Code. If the bonds satisfy the requirements of UCC § 3-104,

[5]RMBCA § 4.01(a)(2).
[6]Roach v Bynum, (Ala) 403 So2d 187 (1981).

they are governed by Article 3 of the Code on commercial paper as far as negotiation is concerned.

Ordinarily conditions inserted in the corporate bonds for the protection of the bondholders have the effect of making the bonds nonnegotiable and therefore not within the scope of Article 3 of the Uniform Commercial Code, and only Article 8 applies to them.

(i) **Transferring Property.** The corporate property may be leased, assigned for the benefit of creditors, or sold. In many states, however, a solvent corporation may not transfer all of its property except with the consent of all or a substantial majority of its shareholders. In any case, the sale must be for a fair price.

The power to sell and transfer corporate property includes the power to assign accounts receivable and contracts with customers and to negotiate commercial paper received by the corporation.

FACTS:

The Silverbrook Cemetery Company sold bronze grave markers. The Wilmington Memorial Company also sold bronze grave markers and claimed that the cemetery company did not have authority to make such sales. The charter of the cemetery company gave it power to sell "personal estate of every kind" and a general power to make all contracts and do all acts necessary for the conducting of the cemetery. Wilmington Memorial brought an action for a declaratory judgment against the cemetery. The cemetery moved for summary judgment.

DECISION:

Judgment for the cemetery. Its charter gave it the authority to sell personal property of any kind. Memorializing the dead by grave markers was closely related to burying and therefore the sale of grave markers could be considered to be contracts necessary for the conducting of the cemetery. The cemetery therefore had authority to sell grave markers. [Wilmington Memorial Co., Inc. v Silverbrook Cemetery Co. (Del Ch) 287 A2d 405 (1972)]

A corporation, having power to incur debts, may mortgage or pledge its property as security for those debts. This rule does not apply to franchises of public service companies, such as street transit systems and gas and electric companies.

(j) **Acquisition of Property.** Although the power to acquire and hold property is usually given in the charter, a corporation always has the implied power to acquire and hold such property as is reasonably necessary for carrying out its express powers. In some states, the power of a corporation to hold property is restricted as to the method of acquiring it, or is limited as to the quantity or the value of the property or the period of time for which it may be held. Restrictions on holding real estate are also imposed upon corporations by the constitutions of some states.

FACTS:

The State of Oklahoma sued the International Paper Company for the statutory penalty for unlawfully owning rural land in violation of the state constitutional provision that no corporation should own rural land "except such as shall be necessary and proper for carrying on the business for which it was chartered." The paper company claimed that the rural land it owned was being reforested by it. It was shown that the reforested area would not develop a crop of timber for 40 to 70 years.

DECISION:

Judgment for International Paper Company. The concept of "necessary and proper" does not mean absolutely necessary, and is satisfied if the conduct in question is proper, useful, and conducive to the accomplishment of the corporation's objectives. The acquisition of the rural land which the paper company was reforesting was a reasonable step to insure a continuous supply of wood pulp necessary for making paper. In view of the scarcity of wood and the time required to grow a crop of timber, the acquisition of the timberland by the corporation was reasonable and therefore was not prohibited by the Oklahoma constitution. [Oklahoma v International Paper Co. (Okla) 342 P2d 565 (1959)]

(1) Investments. Modern corporation codes generally provide that a corporation may acquire the stock of other corporations.

(2) Holding Companies. A corporation owning stock of another corporation may own such a percentage of the stock of the other company that it controls the latter's operations. In such a case, the first company is commonly called a **holding company.** Sometimes a holding company is organized solely for the purpose of controlling other companies called **operating** or **subsidiary companies.**

(k) Acquisition of Own Stock. Generally a corporation may purchase its own stock if it is solvent at the time and the purchase does not impair capital.[7] In a few states corporations are denied implied power to purchase their own stock, but they are permitted to receive it as a gift, in payment of a debt, or as security for a debt.

Stock which is reacquired by the corporation that issued it is commonly called **treasury stock.** Ordinarily the treasury stock is regarded as still being issued or outstanding stock.[8] As such, the shares are not subject to the rule that original shares cannot be issued for less than par. They can be sold by the corporation at any price.

The Revised Model Act eliminates the concept of par value and the technical distinctions between original shares and treasury shares which exist in conventional statutes. Thus under the Revised Model Act, authorized but unissued shares may be issued on the same basis as treasury shares.[9]

[7]See RMBCA § 6.31(a) subject to the limitations of § 6.40.
[8]When a corporation reacquires its own shares, it has the choice of "retiring" them and thus restoring them to the status of authorized but unissued shares or to treat them as still issued and available for transfer. It is the latter which are described as treasury shares.
[9]See Official Comments to RMBCA §§ 6.21 and 6.31.

Although treasury stock retains the character of outstanding stock, it has an inactive status while it is held by the corporation. Thus, the treasury shares cannot be voted nor can dividends be declared on them.

(l) **Business in Another State.** A corporation has the inherent power and generally is expressly authorized to engage in business in other states. This grant of power by the incorporating state does not exempt the corporation, however, from satisfying the restrictions imposed by the foreign state in which it seeks to do business.

(m) **Participation in Enterprise.** Corporations may generally participate in an enterprise to the same extent as individuals. They may enter into joint ventures. The modern statutory trend is to permit a corporation to be a member of a partnership. A corporation may be a limited partner. The Revised Model Act authorizes a corporation "to be a promoter, partner, member, associate, or manager of any partnership, joint venture, trust, or other entity."[10]

(n) **Employee Benefit and Aid.** The Revised Model Act empowers a corporation "to pay pensions and establish pension plans, pension trusts, profit sharing plans, stock bonus plans, stock option plans, and other incentive plans for any or all of its current or former directors, officers, and employees."[11]

(o) **Charitable Contributions.** The Revised Model Act authorizes a corporation without any limitation "to make donations for the public welfare or for charitable, scientific, or educational purposes." In some states limitation is imposed upon the amount that can be donated for charitable purposes.

§ 49:3.   Ultra Vires Acts.

When a corporation acts in excess of or beyond the scope of the powers granted by its charter and the statute under which it was organized, the corporation's act is described as **ultra vires.** Such an act is improper because it is a violation of the obligation of the corporation to the state. It is also improper with respect to shareholders and creditors of the corporation because corporate funds have been diverted to unauthorized uses.

In the past, corporations were formed by obtaining a grant of a charter from the king or state legislature. Thus a charter would be granted to build a turnpike or to run a bank. Typically, the application for a charter would concentrate on the main point and specifically grant the powers needed to attain the objective of the corporation. There was no general listing of corporate powers. In this century corporate existence begins by fulfilling the clerical matter of filing articles of incorporation that conform to the statute adopted by the legislature. Typically, this statute will state that every corporation formed under the statute will have certain powers unless the articles of incorporation expressly exclude some of the listed powers, and then follows a list of every possible power that is needed to run a business. In some states, the legislature makes a blanket grant of all the power that a

[10]RMBCA § 3.02(9).
[11]RMBCA § 3.02(12).

natural person running the business would possess.[12] The net result is that the modern corporation possesses such a broad scope of powers that it is difficult to find an action that is ultra vires. If a mining corporation would begin manufacturing television sets, there may be an ultra vires transaction but this obviously rarely happens. The modern business corporation is rarely involved in ultra vires activity.

(a) **Ultra Vires Acts and Illegality Distinguished.** Although it is not lawful for a corporation to perform ultra vires acts, the objection to the commission of such acts is distinct from the objection of illegality. In the case of illegality, the act would be wrong regardless of the nature of the person or the association committing it. The fact that an act is ultra vires merely means that this particular corporation does not have permission from the government to do the act. Thus, it would ordinarily be beyond the powers of a business corporation, and therefore ultra vires, to engage in a charitable enterprise, such as the building of a church or college. But the activity would hardly be termed illegal.

FACTS:
   The Ladd Estate Company brought suit on a promissory note signed by Wheatley and guaranteed by Westover Tower, Inc. Westover claimed that its guaranty of the note was not binding because Wheatley was a director of the corporation when the guaranty was made and the guaranty was therefore ultra vires and illegal as it violated a statute prohibiting loans to directors.

DECISION:
   Judgment for Ladd. The guaranty of a loan is not a loan. The corporation had not made a loan and the statute against loans did not apply. The corporation was therefore liable on the guaranty. [Ladd Estate Co. v Wheatley, 246 Or 627, 426 P2d 878 (1967)]

(b) **Effect of Ultra Vires Contracts.** There is some conflict in the law as to the effect of an ultra vires contract. Under the modern statutory trend, ultra vires cannot be raised to attack the validity of any act, contract, or transfer of property,[13] except as noted under § 49:3(c) in this book.

   In most states if the ultra vires contract has been completely performed, neither party can rescind the contract on the ground that it was originally ultra vires. Conversely, if neither party to the ultra vires contract has performed, the court will neither enforce the contract nor hold either party liable for a breach of the contract.

(c) **Remedies for Ultra Vires Acts.** In all states (1) a shareholder may obtain an injunction to stop the board of directors or other persons involved

---

[12]Note the broad powers granted under the RMBCA § 3.02; see also Cal. Corp. Code §§ 202(b), 207, 208 for all purpose clause granting "all of the powers of a natural person in carrying out its business activities."

[13]RMBCA § 3.04; Re Terminal Moving and Storage Co. (CA8 Ark) 631 F2d 547 (1980).

from entering into an ultra vires transaction; (2) the corporation, or a shareholder acting on behalf of the corporation, may sue the persons who made or approved the contract in order to recover damages for the loss caused the corporation by the ultra vires act; and (3) an action may be brought by the attorney general of the state to revoke the charter on the ground of its serious or repeated violation.[14]

FACTS:

The Ohio Central Credit Union, Inc. (OCCU) made a loan to the Hamfab Credit Union (HCU). In borrowing this money HCU violated a state statute which prohibited a credit union from borrowing in excess of 25% of its unimpaired capital and surplus. Some time later, HCU became insolvent and Wagner was appointed the liquidator. Wagner admitted HCU's debt to OCCU but refused to pay it because the loan was made in excess of the 25% statutory limit, and was therefore ultra vires. A state statute abolished the defense of ultra vires as between corporations.

DECISION:

Judgment for OCCU. The state statute restricts a credit union as a borrower, rather than as a lender. HCU's act of borrowing in excess of 25% of the statutory limit was ultra vires. But OCCU's lending was not ultra vires. Moreover, another state statute abolished the use of ultra vires as a defense in an action between two corporations. Thus Wagner could not use the defense of ultra vires to withhold payment of the debt. [Ohio Central Credit Union v Wagner, 67 Ohio App2d 138, 426 NE2d 198 (1980)]

SUMMARY

A corporation has implied power to make any contract needed to conduct its business and to accomplish its corporate purposes. The powers granted to corporations in Model Act jurisdictions are set forth in the RMBCA. Special service corporations such as banks, insurance companies, and railroads are subject to separate statutes with regard to their organization and powers. A corporation has the power to continue as a unit forever or for a stated period of time, regardless of changes in the ownership of the stock. It may issue stocks and bonds, borrow money, execute commercial paper, transfer and acquire property, acquire its own stock if it is solvent and the purchase does not impair capital, and make charitable contributions. A corporation has the inherent power to do business in other states. A corporation also may participate in a business enterprise to the same extent as an individual, that is, it may be a partner in a partnership or it may enter a joint venture or other enterprise.

An ultra vires act occurs when a corporation acts beyond the scope of the powers granted by its charter and the statute under which it was organized. Because of the modern trend towards granting broader powers to corporations, it is unlikely that a modern corporation would act beyond the scope of its powers. Also the modern statutory trend has been to restrict

[14]RMBCA § 3.04(b).

the use of the ultra vires doctrine. As a result the doctrine's importance has been reduced. In all states a shareholder may obtain an injunction against the corporation to stop an ultra vires transaction, and the corporation may recover damages from the persons who made the ultra vires contract. The state also has the right to bring an action to revoke the charter because of ultra vires activity.

QUESTIONS AND CASE PROBLEMS

1. What social forces are affected by the rule of law permitting corporations to issue certificates representing shares of stock?

2. Do all corporations have the same powers?

3. The Nicholson Corporation wrote a letter to Bertha offering to sell her an automobile. She wrote back accepting the offer. Later she changed her mind. Nicholson sued her for the purchase price. She raised the defense that there was no binding contract because the corporation had not put the corporate seal on the letter which contained the offer. Was this a valid defense?

4. The Mackelree Corporation owns 100 shares of its own stock. At a hotly contested shareholders' election, the board of directors votes these 100 shares. This provides the deciding margin and the directors are reelected by a margin of 23 votes. Leon, who owns 10 shares of the corporate stock, had voted against reelecting the directors. Can he successfully challenge their reelection?

5. Porter Electronics was a corporation. Its board of directors purchased a yacht for use by the executives of the corporation. Jill owned stock in Porter Electronics. She brought a suit on behalf of the corporation and other shareholders against the directors to recover for the corporation the loss sustained by the purchase of the yacht. The directors raised the defense that no suit could be brought because the ultra vires contract had been performed. Is this a valid defense?

6. Carleson Builders, Inc., was incorporated for the purpose of building private homes. The corporation began to expand into the construction of industrial buildings and airports. Reese, who owns a small number of shares of Carleson Builders complains to the district attorney that the corporation is acting illegally. Is he correct?

7. Compare the power of a corporation to (a) give a promissory note to represent a loan to the corporation, and (b) be an accommodation indorser on a note given in payment for the issue of its own corporate stock.

8. The Central Mutual Auto Insurance Co. was a Michigan corporation. A foreign corporation, the Central Mutual Insurance Co., was granted a license to do business in Michigan. Central Mutual Auto Insurance Co. brought an action to prevent the foreign corporation from doing business within Michigan under that name. Decide. [Central Mutual Auto Insurance Co. v Central Mutual Insurance Co. 275 Mich 554, 267 NW 733]

9. In an action by the Federal Savings State Bank as the holder of a note against Grimes, the maker of the note, the authority of the corporate payee, the Industrial Mutual Life Insurance Co., to accept the note from

the maker was questioned. It was argued that the corporate payee possessed the power because there was no statute expressly prohibiting the exercise of that power. Was this argument valid? [Federal Savings State Bank v Grimes, 156 Kan 55, 131 P2d 894]

10. The Orion Hotel purchased an expensive touring car to meet guests at the nearby airport. The car did not run properly. The hotel sued the seller for breach of warranty. The seller raised the defense that there could not be any liability for breach of warranty because there was no lawful sales contract on the theory that a hotel corporation had no right to purchase an expensive means of transportation and that accordingly the contract was ultra vires and void. Was this defense valid?

11. A husband, H, borrowed money from bank B. B promised to insure the loan so that if H died before the debt was repaid, the proceeds of the insurance policy would pay off the debt. B failed to obtain the insurance, and H died owing a balance on the debt. H's widow sued the bank to cancel the balance remaining on the theory that if B had obtained the insurance as it had promised to do, there would not be any balance. B defended on the ground that it could not have obtained the insurance because it would have been ultra vires for it to have done so. Was this defense valid?

12. The good faith of a director is a defense when sued for loss caused by an ultra vires act because there is no liability unless the director had the intent to defraud. Is this statement correct?

13. An employee of the Archer Pancoast Co., a corporation, was killed as the result of falling through a hatchway in a building occupied by the company as a factory. Hoffman, superintendent of the factory, called Noll, an undertaker, and arranged for the funeral. Hoffman agreed to pay Noll $100 for his services. After performing the work, Noll brought an action against the Archer Pancoast Co. to recover the agreed sum. The defendant raised the defense that the contract with Noll was ultra vires. Decide. [Noll v Archer Pancoast Co. 60 App Div 414, 69 NYS 1007]

14. Porter owned stock in the Plymouth Gold Mining Company, a corporation. Porter made a contract with the corporation to sell his stock to the corporation. He later refused to perform the contract. The corporation sued him for breach of contract. He raised the defense that there was no valid contract because the corporate charter did not expressly give the corporation the power to purchase its own stock from stockholders. Was this defense valid? [Porter v Plymouth Gold Mining Co. 29 Mont 347, 74 P 983]

15. Connecticut General Life Insurance Co. is a Connecticut insurance company which obtained a license to write life insurance policies in New York. It thereafter proposed to acquire 80 percent or more of the common stock of the National Fire Insurance Co. of Hartford, a fire and casualty insurance company licensed to write policies in New York. The New York State Superintendent of Insurance brought an action for a declaratory judgment to have the Connecticut company prohibited from writing life policies in New York if it acquired such stock because, through its subsidiary, it would then also be writing fire and casualty insurance in New York. Was the Superintendent correct? [Connecticut

General Life Insurance Co. v Superintendent of Insurance, 10 NY2d 42, 217 NYS2d 39, 176 NE2d 631]

16. In 1903 Santa Fe Pacific Railroad conveyed all of its railroad operating properties to the Atchison, Topeka & Santa Fe Railway Company. Thereafter the Santa Fe Pacific Railroad Co. continued to own large areas of land in Arizona, which it leased to individuals for cattle grazing. During 1945 and 1946 it sold much of its land holdings to its former grazing lessees, retaining rights to "all minerals." Helium gas was discovered on this property, and Santa Fe Pacific leased its mineral interests in the land to Kerr McGee, which explored for and produced the helium gas. Spurlock, a rancher who had purchased his surface estate from the original 1945 and 1946 purchasers, sued Santa Fe Pacific and Kerr McGee for conversion of the gas and to quiet title. Spurlock contended that Santa Fe Pacific's continued ownership of the land and its conveyances to Spurlock's predecessors were ultra vires acts due to the de facto dissolution of the corporation by its inactivity as a railroad since 1903. Santa Fe Pacific contends that Spurlock's position is erroneous. Can a dissolved corporation perform an ultra vires act? [Spurlock v Santa Fe Pacific Railroad Co., 143 Ariz App 469, 694 P2d 299]

17. Total Automation, a corporation, had a checking account in the Illinois National Bank. Total owed money to the bank's travel department. The bank deducted the amount of the travel bill from the checking account balance. Creditors of Total brought an action on its behalf against the bank, claiming that the bank had no right to set off the agency debt because it was ultra vires for a national bank to operate a travel department. Decide. [Total Automation v Illinois National Bank & Trust Co. 40 Ill App 3d 266, 351 NE2d 879]

CHAPTER 50

CORPORATE STOCK AND

SHAREHOLDERS

CHAPTER OBJECTIVES

After studying this chapter you will be able to:

1. Distinguish between subscriptions for stock and transfers of stock.
2. Describe the mechanics of transferring stock.
3. Describe the rights of shareholders.
4. Identify exceptions to the limited liability of shareholders.
5. Describe the federal regulation of corporate securities.
6. Solve problems involving corporate shares and shareholders.

The ownership of a corporation is divided among the shareholders, and the ownership is evidenced by the holders' shares of stock. Shares of stock may be acquired by subscription of shares when they are originally issued or by transfer of existing shares from a shareholder or from the corporation.

After the stock market crash of 1929 Congress investigated the buying and selling practices which existed in the securities markets, and determined that federal regulation was necessary to prevent the fraudulent, deceptive, and manipulative practices it found to exist. Various federal statutes administered by the Securities and Exchange Commission were then enacted to regulate the sale of securities for the benefit of investors.

Shareholders have certain rights, including the right to vote in the election of directors and the right to receive dividends as they are declared. Shareholders are ordinarily exempt from liability for the acts of the corporation.

A. CORPORATE STOCK

The ownership of a fractional part of a corporation is evidenced by the share or stock of the shareholder or stockholder. "Share" and "stock" mean the same.

§ 50:1.   Nature of Stock.

Membership in a corporation is usually based upon ownership of one or more shares of stock of the corporation. Each share represents a fractional interest in the total property possessed by the corporation. The shareholder does not own or have an interest in any specific property of the corporation; the corporation is the owner of all of its property.

(a) **Capital and Capital Stock. Capital** refers to the net assets of the corporation. Shares which have been issued to holders are said to be **outstanding. Capital stock** refers to the value received by the corporation for its outstanding stock.

(b) **Valuation of Stock.** Corporate stock may have a specified **par value**. This means that the person subscribing to the stock and acquiring it from the corporation must pay that amount. When stock is issued by the corporation for a price greater than the par value, some statutes provide that only the par value amount is to be treated as stated capital, the excess being allocated to surplus.

Shares may be issued with no par value. In such a case no amount is stated in the certificate, and the amount that the subscriber pays the corporation is determined by the board of directors. The Revised Model Business Corporation Act eliminates the concept of par value.

The value found by dividing the value of the corporate assets by the number of shares outstanding is the **book value** of the shares. The **market value** of a share of stock is the price at which that stock can be voluntarily bought or sold.

§ 50:2.   Certificate of Stock.

The corporation ordinarily issues a **certificate of stock** or share certificate as evidence of the shareholder's ownership of stock. The issuance of such certificates is not essential either to the existence of a corporation or to the ownership of its stock.[1] However, it is an almost universal practice since it is a convenient method of proving ownership and since it makes transfer of ownership easier.

§ 50:3.   Kinds of Stock.

The stock of a corporation may be divided into two or more classes.

---

[1]Krosnar v Schmidt Krosnar McNaughton Garret Co. 282 Pa Super 526, 423 A2d 370 (1980). Amendments to Article 8 of the Uniform Commercial Code adopted in 1977 give corporations the option of providing for the ownership of shares not represented by certificates. In substance, ownership is established by information stored in a data bank, but no share certificates are issued. These 1977 amendments have been adopted in Arkansas, California, Colorado, Connecticut, Delaware, Idaho, Massachusetts, Minnesota, Montana, Nevada, New York, North Dakota, Ohio, Oklahoma, Oregon, Texas, Virginia, West Virginia, and Wyoming. The certificated share system described in this chapter is the prevailing system at the present time.

(a) **Preferences. Common stock** is ordinary stock that has no preferences. Each share usually entitles the holder to one vote and to a share of the profits in the form of dividends when declared, and to participate in the distribution of capital upon dissolution of the corporation. **Preferred stock** has a priority over common stock. The priority may be with respect to dividends. Preferred stock may also have a priority over common stock in the distribution of capital upon dissolution of the corporation. Preferred stock is ordinarily nonvoting.

(1) Cumulative Preferred Stock. Ordinarily the right to receive dividends is dependent upon the declaration of dividends by the board of directors for that particular period of time. If there is no fund from which the dividends may be declared or if the directors do not declare them from an available fund, the shareholder has no right to dividends. The fact that a shareholder has not received dividends for the current year does not in itself give the right to accumulate or carry over into the next year a claim for those dividends.

In the absence of a statement that the right to dividends is noncumulative, it is frequently held that preferred stock has the right to cumulate dividends, particularly with respect to each year in which there was a surplus available for dividend declaration.

(2) Participating Preferred Stock. Sometimes the preferred stock is given the right of participation. After the common shares receive dividends or a capital distribution equal to that first received by the preferred stock, both kinds share equally in the balance.

(b) **Duration of Shares.** Ordinarily shares continue to exist for the life of the corporation. Under modern statutes, however, any kind of shares, whether common or preferred, may be made terminable at an earlier date.

(1) Redeemable Shares. A corporation may at its election accept the surrender of **redeemable shares** and pay the shareholder the par value of the shares or such amount as is stated in the redemption agreement. Redeemed shares ordinarily cease to exist after redemption, as distinguished from being owned by the corporation as treasury stock.

(2) Convertible Shares. **Convertible shares** entitle the shareholder to exchange owned shares for a different type of share or for bonds of the corporation.

(c) **Fractional Shares.** Modern statutes expressly authorize a corporation to issue fractional shares or to issue scrip or certificates representing such fractional shares that can be sold or combined for the acquisition of whole shares.

B. ACQUISITION OF SHARES

Shares of stock may be acquired by (1) subscription, either before or after the corporation is organized, or (2) transfer of existing shares from a shareholder or from the corporation.

§ 50:4. Statute of Frauds.

A contract for the sale of corporate shares must be evidenced by a writing or it cannot be enforced.[2] The writing must show that there has been

[2]Uniform Commercial Code, § 8-319(a).

a contract for the sale of a stated quantity of described securities at a defined or stated price. The writing must be signed in the manner required of a writing for the sale of goods. No writing is required for instructions between a customer and a broker.

§ 50:5. Subscription.

A **stock subscription** is a contract or an agreement to buy a specific number and kind of shares when they are issued. As in the case of any other contract, the agreement to subscribe to shares of a corporation is subject to avoidance for fraud.

(a) Subscription before Incorporation. In many states a preincorporation subscription of shares is regarded as an offer to the corporation. By this view it is necessary for the corporation to accept the subscription offer either expressly or by conduct. A few states hold that such subscriptions automatically become binding contracts when the organization has been completed.

In some states the preincorporation subscription is irrevocable for a stated period. The RMBCA provides that "a subscription for shares entered into before incorporation is irrevocable for six months unless the subscription agreement provides a longer or shorter period or all the subscribers agree to revocation."[3]

(b) Subscription after Incorporation. Subscriptions may be made after incorporation. In that event, the transaction is like any other contract with the corporation. The offer of the subscription may come from the subscriber or from the corporation. In either case there must be an acceptance. Upon acceptance the subscriber immediately becomes a shareholder with all the rights, privileges, and liabilities of a shareholder even though the subscriber has not paid any of the purchase price. The transaction, however, may only be a contract for the future issue of shares rather than a present subscription.

§ 50:6. Transfer of Shares.

In the absence of a valid restriction, a shareholder may transfer shares to anyone.

(a) Restrictions on Transfer. Restrictions on the transfer of stock are valid provided they are not unreasonable. In order to prevent its stock from going into the hands of strangers, it is lawful to require that the corporation or other stockholders be given the first right to purchase stock before a shareholder may sell it to an outsider. A provision giving a corporation the right to purchase a shareholder's shares upon death is valid.

FACTS:

The stock of the West End Development Company was subject to a transfer restriction which required that any shareholder selling shares must first offer every other shareholder the right to purchase a proportion of the shares being sold, the proportion being the same as the percentage of the outstanding shares which the

[3]RMBCA § 6.20(a).

other shareholder already owned. This restriction was stated in the articles of incorporation but was not stated on the stock certificates of the corporation. The Taylors owned stock in the company. They sold their stock to Vroom, an officer of the corporation, without first offering any stock to the other shareholders as required by the restriction. The other shareholders brought an action against Vroom to recover from him the percentages of the shares to which they would have been entitled had the Taylors followed the transfer restriction.

DECISION:

Judgment for the shareholders. A transfer restriction is not binding unless it is conspicuously noted on the share certificates or is known by the transferee. The restriction was not noted on the certificates. However, Vroom as an officer of the corporation was charged with knowledge of what was stated in the articles of incorporation. In the eyes of the law, he therefore knew of the existence of the restriction and was subject to it. Consequently, he was required to recognize the superior rights of the other shareholders to their proportion of the shares. [Irwin v West End Development Co. (CA 10 Colo) 481 F2d 34 (1973)]

A restriction upon the right to transfer is not valid as against the purchaser of the certificate unless the restriction is conspicuously noted on the certificate or unless the transferee has actual knowledge of the restriction.

In any case, a restriction on the transfer of stock is strictly interpreted.[4] For example, a restriction on the sale of stock is not applicable to a "gift" of stock made in accordance with the Gifts to Minors Act.

(b) **Interest Transferred.** The transfer of shares may be absolute, that is, it may divest all ownership and make the transferee the full owner, or it may be merely for security, as when stock is pledged to secure the repayment of a loan.

§ 50:7. Mechanics of Transfer.

The ownership of shares is transferred by the delivery of the certificate of stock indorsed by its owner in blank, or to a specified person; or by the delivery of the certificate by such person accompanied by a separate assignment or power of attorney executed by the owner.[5]

A delivery from the owner of the shares directly to the transferee is not required. It can be made to an intermediary. When there is no delivery of the share certificate to anyone, however, there is no transfer of ownership of the shares.

FACTS:

LaVern Millin owned 3,700 shares of stock in the Western Printing & Lithographing Co. He went with his son, James, to the local bank and told the vice president that he wanted the stock transferred to his son. LaVern signed

[4]Castonguay v Castonguay, (Minn) 306 NW2d 143 (1981).
[5]UCC § 8-309. The second alternative of a delivery of an unindorsed certificate is designed to keep the certificate "clean," as when the transfer is for a temporary or special purpose as in the case of a pledge of the certificate as security for a loan.

his name on the transfer form on the back of each certificate, the vice president signed each certificate as a guarantor of LaVern's signature, and the certificates were sent to Western with a covering letter requesting that a new certificate be issued in the name of the son, James, and sent directly to him. Thereafter it was claimed that the transaction had no effect because the share certificates were not delivered by the father to his son.

DECISION:
The transaction was effective to constitute a delivery of the stock certificates. A delivery to the transferee personally is not required. Under the circumstances it was clear that the delivery was made to the corporation, as agent, to act for the son in issuing him new shares. [Kintzinger v Millin, 254 Iowa 173, 117 NW2d 68 (1962)]

A physical transfer of the certificate without a necessary indorsement is effective as between the parties because indorsement is only necessary to make a transferee a "bona fide" purchaser as against third parties. Thus a gift of shares is binding even though the above rules have not been satisfied.[6]

The owner of a security can prove continued ownership of a security by showing that what appears to be a proper indorsement on the security is actually unauthorized. Upon so doing, the owner recovers the security from the transferee of the security. The owner may not do so, however, if (1) the owner has ratified the unauthorized indorsement or (2) the security was obtained by a purchaser for value without notice of any adverse claim who in good faith surrendered the indorsed security to the issuer or its transfer agent and received a new, re-issued, or re-registered security.

In the latter case, the remedy of the true owner is restricted to the issuer and its transfer agent. The owner may hold them liable for money damages for improper registration. As an alternative, the owner may require the issuance of a replacement security unless this would result in the overissue of outstanding stock, in which case the issuer must purchase a like security for the owner or pay the owner the value of the original security.

In general, the transfer agent stands in the same position as the corporation with respect to its stock and must make a formal transfer whenever the corporation would itself be required to recognize a transfer. When a corporation or its transfer agent wrongfully refuses to register a transfer of shares of stock, the new owner of the shares may bring suit for damages sustained and in some states may sue for the value of the shares on the theory of conversion.

§ 50:8.   Effect of Transfer.

The transfer of existing shares of stock raises questions as to the validity and effect of the transfer as between the parties to the transfer and between them and the corporation.

(a) Validity of Transfer. As a transfer of shares is a transfer of ownership, the transfer must in general satisfy the requirements governing any other transfer of property or agreement to transfer property. As between

[6]Ross' Estate (Utah) 626 P2d 489 (1981).

the parties, a transfer may be set aside for any ground that would warrant similar relief under property law. If the transfer of stock has been obtained by duress, the transferor may obtain a rescission of the transfer.

(b) **Negotiability.** Under the common law, the transferee of shares of stock had no greater right than the transferor because the certificate and the shares represented by the certificate were nonnegotiable. By statute, the common-law rule has been changed by imparting negotiability to the certificate. Just as various defenses cannot be asserted against the holder in due course of a commercial paper, it is provided that similar defenses cannot be raised against the person acquiring the certificate in good faith and for value. As against such a person, the defenses cannot be raised that the transferor did not own the shares, or did not have authority to deliver the certificate, or that the transfer was made in violation of a restriction upon transfer not known to such person and not noted conspicuously on the certificate.

The fact that corporate stock has the quality of negotiability does not make it commercial paper within Article 3 of the Uniform Commercial Code. Shares of stock are classified under the UCC as investment securities; and Article 8, as supplemented by the non-Code law which has not been displaced, is the source of the law governing the rights of the parties to the transaction involving such securities. Nevertheless, courts may look to Article 3 for guidance when a question regarding an investment security cannot be resolved on the basis of the language in Article 8 alone.

(c) **Secured Transaction.** Corporate stock is frequently delivered to a creditor as security for a debt owed by the shareholder. Thus, a debtor borrowing money from a bank may deliver shares of stock to the bank as collateral security for the repayment of the loan, or a broker's customer purchasing stock on margin may leave the stock in the possession of the broker as security for the payment of any balance due. The delivery of the security to the creditor gives rise to a perfected security interest without any filing by the creditor. In itself, the pledge does not make the pledgee of the corporate stock the owner of the stock.

(d) **Effect of Transfer on Corporation.** Until there is a transfer on its books, the corporation is entitled to treat as the owner the person whose name is on the books. The corporation may properly refuse to recognize the transferee when the corporation is given notice or has knowledge that the transfer is void or in breach of trust. In such a case, the corporation properly refuses to register a transfer until the rights of the parties have been determined.

The corporation may also refuse to register the transfer of shares when the outstanding certificate is not surrendered to it, in the absence of satisfactory proof that it has been lost, destroyed, or stolen.

§ 50:9.   Lost, Destroyed, and Stolen Securities.

The owner of a lost, destroyed, or stolen security is entitled to a replacement security if the owner files a sufficient indemnity bond and requests the new security within a reasonable time before the issuer has notice that the original certificate has been acquired by a bona fide purchaser. If after the issue of the new security, a bona fide purchaser appears with the original security, the corporation must register a transfer of the security to that person and accept such person as the owner of the shares.[7]

§ 50:10.   Protection of the Public.

State and federal laws have been adopted to protect investors.

(a) **State Regulation.** In order to protect the public from the sale of fraudulent securities, many states have adopted regulations called **blue sky laws.** The term "blue sky" derives from the purpose of such laws which is the preventing of the sale of speculative schemes which have no more value than a small area of "blue sky." The state statutes vary in detail. They commonly contain (1) an antifraud provision prohibiting fraudulent practices and imposing criminal penalties for violations; (2) broker-dealer licensing provisions regulating the persons engaged in the securities business; and (3) the registration of securities including disclosure requirements with a designated governmental official.

State blue sky laws are subject to the very important limitation that they can apply only to intrastate transactions and cannot apply to sales made in interstate commerce.

A Uniform Securities Act,[8] covering the above three categories of regulations, exists to provide guidance to states in updating their securities laws. This act contains alternative regulations, which can be adopted by states with different regulatory philosophies.

(b) **Federal Regulation.** The stock market crash of 1929 and the great depression which followed led to the enactment of legislation to regulate the securities industry. Six federal securities regulation laws were passed in the period between 1933 and 1940. The two principal laws which provide the basic framework for the federal regulation of the sale of securities in interstate commerce are the Securities Act of 1933 and the Securities Exchange Act of 1934. The 1933 Act deals with the original distribution of securities by the issuing corporations, while the 1934 Act is concerned with the secondary distribution of securities in the national securities markets and in the over-the-counter markets.

Four other federal laws deal with more specific aspects of the securities industry. The Public Utility Holding Company Act of 1935[9] provides comprehensive regulation of holding companies and their subsidiaries in the interstate gas and electric utilities businesses. The Trust Indenture Act of 1939[10] was enacted to protect the interests of the holders of bonds and other debt securities offered to the public in interstate commerce through the required appointments of independent institutional trustees. The Investment Company Act of 1940[11] provides for the registration and comprehensive regulation of mutual funds and all other investment companies. The Investment Advisors Act of 1940[12] requires registration with the Securities and

[7]UCC § 8–405.
[8]7B Uniform Laws Annotated 515.
[9]15 USC §§ 79-792-6.
[10]15 USC §§ 77aaa to 77bbb.
[11]15 USC §§ 80a-1 to 80a-52.
[12]15 USC §§ 80b-1 to 80-b21.

Exchange Commission of all persons engaged in the business of providing investment advice in interstate commerce.

§ 50:11.   Securities Act of 1933.

The 1933 Act deals with the original distribution of securities. It prohibits the offer or sale of securities to the public in interstate commerce before a **registration statement** containing disclosure of specific financial information regarding the security, the issuer, and the underwriter has been filed with the Securities and Exchange Commission (SEC). The seller must also provide a **prospectus** to each potential purchaser of the securities setting forth the key information contained in the registration statement. The object is to provide the interested investor with detailed information about the security and the enterprise. The SEC does not approve or disapprove the securities as being good or bad investments but only reviews the form and content of the registration statement and the prospectus to assure full disclosure. The requirements of advance disclosure to the public through the filing of the registration statement with the SEC and the sending of a prospectus to each potential purchaser are commonly referred to as the **registration requirements** of the 1933 Act.

(a) **Applicability.** The Act applies not only to the issuing of stocks and bonds but also to any conceivable type of interest or instrument with investment characteristics.

(b) **Registration Exemptions.** Certain private and limited offerings of securities are exempt from the registration requirements of the Act.[13] Under SEC Regulation D offerings of any amount made solely to "accredited investors," such as banks, insurance companies, investment companies, or directors and executive officers of the issuing corporation, are exempt from the registration requirements of the Act. These accredited investors generally have access to the kinds of information disclosed in a registration statement and prospectus.

(1) *Rule 505 exemption.* SEC Rule 505, promulgated under Regulation D, exempts from registration offerings of less than $5,000,000 to less than 35 nonaccredited purchasers (not offerees) over a 12-month period. No limit exists on the number of accredited investors who may participate. No general solicitation or general advertising is permitted under Rule 505. If any prospective investors are nonaccredited, the issuer must furnish all investors with specific information on the issuer, its business, and the securities offered for sale.

(2) *Rule 504 exemption.* Under SEC Rule 504 of Regulation D an issuer is permitted to sell securities for an aggregate price up to $500,000 in a one-year period to any number of investors without furnishing any explanation to the purchasers. This rule was fashioned to provide an exception for small offerings by small issuers.

(3) *Rule 506 exemption.* As opposed to Rules 505 and 504 which exempt offerings limited to $5,000,000 and $500,000 respectively, SEC Rule 506, the so-called "private placement" exemption, has no limitation on the amount which may be raised by the offering. As in Rule 505, specific in-

[13]17 CFR §§ 239.501 to 506 (1982).

formation must be provided to all buyers if any buyers are nonaccredited investors; and the number of nonaccredited investors is limited to less than thirty-five. Further, the rule requires that the issuer shall reasonably believe that each nonaccredited investor has sufficient experience in investments as to be capable of evaluating the merits and risks of the investment.

(4) Restrictions. Securities acquired under a Regulation D exemption from registration are considered **restricted securities,** and their resale may require registration. Rules requiring registration of Regulation D Securities prior to resale are promulgated to insure that investors purchase these securities as an investment rather than for public distribution. And when there is no attempt to make public distributions, investors ordinarily fit within one of several exemptions to registration upon resale.

(c) Liability. The Securities Act of 1933 imposes civil liability under Section 11 for filing materially false or misleading statements in a registration statement, and for the omission of any required material fact. Any investor who sustains a loss because of the false statements or omissions on the registration statement may sue to recover damages under Section 11. An issuing company has virtually no defense in such an action if there has been a false statement and a loss. However, individual defendants, such as accountants who helped prepare portions of the registration statement, may defend by proving they acted in good faith and with "due diligence."

Section 12 of the Act applies to those who "offer or sell" securities and employ any device or scheme to defraud or obtain money by means of untrue statements of material facts; and this section makes such individuals or firms liable to purchasers for damages sustained.[14]

Section 24 of the 1933 Act imposes criminal penalties for anyone who "willfully" makes untrue statements of material facts or omits required material facts in a registration statement. Section 17 of the Securities Act makes it unlawful for any person to employ any device, scheme, or artifice to defraud in the offer or sale of securities. Law firms and public accounting firms who prepare fraudulent registration statements in conjunction with clients may be subject to civil liability as "aiders and abettors" under Section 12(2) of the Act, and criminal liability under Section 17(a) of the Act. Even though a security is exempt from registration, the civil and criminal liability discussed above still apply if interstate commerce or the mails are involved in the offer or sale of the security.

§ 50:12.   Securities Exchange Act of 1934.

The 1934 Act, as stated previously, deals with the secondary distribution of securities. It was designed to prevent fraudulent and manipulative practices on the security exchanges and in over-the-counter markets. The Act also seeks to provide for fair and honest markets for securities by requiring disclosure of information to buyers and sellers of the securities. The Act also controls credit in these markets.

(a) Registration Requirements. Exchanges, brokers, and dealers who deal in the securities traded in interstate commerce or on any national security exchange must register with the SEC unless exempted by it.

[14]Securities Act of 1933, § 12(2)

Companies whose securities are listed on a national securities exchange, or unlisted companies that have assets in excess of $3 million and 500 or more shareholders, are subject to the reporting requirements of the Act.[15]

Form 10-K is the principal annual report form used by commercial and industrial companies required to file under the 1934 Act. The reports require nonfinancial information about the registrant's activities during the year, such as the nature of the firm's business, the property or businesses it owns, and a statement concerning legal proceedings by or against the company. The report requires the submission of financial statements, with management's analysis of the financial condition of the company, and a report and analysis of the performance of corporate shares. It requires a listing of all directors and executive officers and disclosure of executive compensation information.

Registrants who are required to file 10-K reports must also file quarterly reports, which are principally concerned with financial information relevant to the quarterly period.

Annual shareholder reports are required by the SEC to be submitted to shareholders in any proxy solicitation on behalf of management and contain essentially the same information provided in the 10-K report.

(b) Anti-Fraud Provision. Section 10(b) of the 1934 Act makes it unlawful for any person to use any manipulative or deceptive device in contravention of SEC rules.[16] Under the authority of Section 10(b) of the 1934 Act, the SEC has promulgated Rule 10b-5. This rule is the principal anti-fraud rule relating to the secondary distribution of securities. The rule states:

> It shall be unlawful for any person, directly or indirectly, by use of any means or instrumentality of interstate commerce, or of the mails or of any facility of any national securities exchange,
>
> (a) To employ any device, scheme, or artifice to defraud.
>
> (b) To make any untrue statement of a material fact or to omit to state a material fact necessary in order to make the statements made, in the light of the circumstances under which they were made, not misleading, or
>
> (c) To engage in any act, practice, or course of business which operates or would operate as a fraud or deceit upon any person, in connection with the purchase or sale of any security.[17]

Rule 10b-5 applies to all securities, whether registered or not as long as use is made of the mails, interstate commerce, or a national stock exchange. Under this rule, a civil action for damages may be brought by any injured party who purchased or sold securities because of false, misleading, or undisclosed information.[18] Criminal penalties may also be imposed for willful violation of the Act or SEC Regulations promulgated under the Act.

It is not unusual for there to be some overlap between the provisions of the 1933 Act and the 1934 Act. Thus purchasers of registered securities who allege they were defrauded by misrepresentations in a registration

---

[15]SEC Release No. 34-18647 (April 15, 1982).
[16]15 USC § 78j(b).
[17]17 CFR § 240, 10b-5 (1982).
[18]Blue Chip Stamps v Manor Drug Store, 421 US 723 (1975).

statement filed under the 1933 Act, may bring an action under the "catchall" anti-fraud provision of Section 10(b) of the 1934 Act and SEC Rule 10b-5, notwithstanding the express remedy for misstatements in registration statements provided by Section 11 of the 1933 Act.[19]

(c) **Insider Information.** Prior to 1984, the SEC and the courts relied on Rule 10b-5 as the legal basis for imposing sanctions for trading on **insider information.** Under the Insider Trading Sanctions Act of 1984, which amended the 1934 Act, the SEC may now bring an action against an individual purchasing or selling a security while in possession of material, inside information and the court may impose a civil penalty of up to three times the profit gained or loss avoided as a result of the unlawful sale.[20]

An insider is liable for inside trading where the insider fails to disclose material nonpublic information before trading on it and thus makes a secret profit. A **"tippee,"** that is, an individual who receives information from an insider, is subject to the insider's fiduciary duty to shareholders where the insider has breached the fiduciary duty to shareholders by improperly disclosing the information to the tippee and the tippee knows or should know there has been a breach. Such a breach occurs when an insider benefits personally from his or her disclosure.

FACTS:

On March 6, Dirks, an investment analyst, received information from Secrist, a former officer of Equity Funding of America, alleging that the assets of Equity Funding were vastly overstated as the result of fraudulent corporate practices. Upon investigation by Dirks certain corporation employees corroborated the charges of fraud. Neither Dirks nor his firm owned or traded any Equity Funding stock, but throughout his investigation he openly discussed the information he had obtained with a number of clients and investors, which induced them to sell Equity Funding stock in excess of $16 million. On March 27, the NYSE halted trading of Equity Funding stock and a subsequent investigation revealed the vast fraud that had taken place. The SEC, investigating Dirks' role in the exposure of the fraud, found that Dirks had aided and abetted violations of the Securities Act of 1933, the Securities Exchange Act of 1934, and SEC Rule 10b-5 by repeating the allegations of fraud to members of the investment community who later sold their Equity Funding stock. Dirks appealed.

DECISION:

Judgment for Dirks. Secrist, the insider, did not violate any fiduciary duty to shareholders when he disclosed information about the fraudulent practices to the tipee, Dirks. Secrist received no monetary or personal benefit for the information but was motivated by the desire to expose the fraud. Since the insider did not breach his fiduciary duty when he gave nonpublic information to Dirks, Dirks breached no duty when he passed the information on to investors [Dirks v SEC, 463 US 646 (1983)]

---

[19]Herman & MacLean v Huddleston, 459 US 375 (1983).
[20]PL 98-376, 58 Stat 1264, 15 USC § 780.

Investors who lack inside information possessed by the insider and have sold their stock at a loss, may recover damages from any insider who has made use of the undisclosed information in a civil action based on Rule 10b-5.

(d) Disclosure of Ownership and Short-Swing Profit. Corporate directors and officers owning registered securities of their corporation and any shareholder owning more than ten percent of any class of the issuer's securities must file a statement as to such ownership with the SEC.

If such a person sells at a profit any of such securities in less than six months after their purchase, the profit is called a short-swing profit. The corporation may sue the director, officer, or stockholder for the short-swing profit and may recover that profit even though there was no fraudulent intent in acquiring or selling the securities.[21]

§ 50:13.   Tender Offers.

A corporation or group of investors may seek to acquire control of another corporation by making a general offer to all shareholders of the target corporation to purchase their shares for cash at a specified price, subject to a minimum or maximum number of shares that the offeror will accept. Such is called a **cash tender offer.** The offer to purchase is usually contingent on the tender of a fixed number of shares sufficient to assure takeover; and the bid price is set at a premium over the prevailing market price.

The Williams Act, which amended the 1934 Act,[22] was passed in order to ensure that public shareholders who are confronted with a cash tender offer will not be required to respond without adequate information. Under Section 14(d) of the Williams Act a person making a tender offer must ordinarily file appropriate SEC forms providing information about the background and identity of the person filing, the source of funds used to make purchases of stock, the amount of stock beneficially owned, the purpose of the purchases, any plan the purchaser proposes to implement if it gains control over the target corporation, and any contracts or understandings that it has with other persons concerning the target corporation.[23]

Section 14(e) of the Williams Act is the anti-fraud section of the Act and prohibits fraudulent, deceptive, or manipulative practices. SEC Rule 14e-1 requires any tender offer to remain open for a minimum of twenty business days from the date it is first published or given to security holders. The SEC believes that tender offers which do not stay open for a reasonable length of time increase the likelihood of hasty, ill-considered decision making on the basis of inadequate or incomplete information as well as the possibility for fraudulent, deceptive or manipulative acts or practices by a bidder and others.

The courts are not inclined to subject every tender offer to close judicial scrutiny, which could generally inhibit shareholders from taking advantage of favorable offerings. Fairness or unfairness of the offer may not be the

---

[21]Securities Exchange Act of 1934, § 16(a, b).

[22]90-439, 82 Stat 454, 15 USC §§ 78m(d)-(e).

[23]Section 14(d) requires a filing by any person making a tender offer that, if successful, would result in the acquisition of five percent of any class of an equity security required to be registered under the Exchange Act.

basis of a Section 14(e) action, but rather it is essential to allege and prove misrepresentation.[24]

C. RIGHTS OF SHAREHOLDERS

The control of the shareholders over the corporation is indirect. Periodically, ordinarily once a year, the shareholders elect directors and through this means can control the corporation. At other times, however, the shareholders have no right or power to control the corporate activity so long as it is conducted within lawful channels.

§ 50:14.   Ownership Rights.

Ownership rights in a corporation are generally represented by shares of stock and are generally freely transferable.

(a) **Certificates of stock.** A shareholder generally has the right to have a properly executed certificate as evidence of ownership of shares.[25]

(b) **Transfer of Shares.** Subject to certain valid restrictions, a shareholder has the right to transfer the shares, and may sell the shares at any price or transfer them as a gift.

§ 50:15.   Right to Vote.

The right to vote means the right to vote at shareholders' meetings for the election of directors and on such other special matters as must be passed upon by the shareholders. As an illustration of the latter, a proposal to change the capital structure of the corporation or a proposal to sell all or substantially all the assets of the corporation must be approved by the shareholders.

(a) **Who May Vote.** Ordinarily only those common shareholders in whose name the stock appears on the books of the corporation are entitled to vote. Generally the directors may fix a date for determining the shareholders who may vote.[26]

(b) **Number of Votes.** Absent a provision to the contrary each shareholder is entitled to one vote for each share owned on each matter to be voted. This is called **straight voting,** and it is the normal method for shareholder voting on corporate matters. However, in the case of voting to elect directors only, cumulative voting is mandatory in nearly half of the states, being imposed by either constitution or statute; and it is permissive by law in other states, where cumulative voting rights are provided for in the articles of incorporation or bylaws. **Cumulative voting** is a form of voting which is designed to give proportional representation on the board of directors to minority shareholders. Under a cumulative voting plan, each shareholder has as many votes as the number of shares owned multiplied by the number of

---

[24]Data Probe Acquisition Corp. v Datatab, Inc. (CA2 NY), 722 F2d 1 (1983).

[25]As to shares without certificates under the 1977 version of the Uniform Commercial Code, see footnote 2 of this chapter.

[26]RMBCA § 7.07.

directors to be elected. Minority shareholders may then cast all of their votes for a candidate who will represent their interests on the board of directors. Under straight voting, minority shareholders would always be outvoted.

(c) **Voting by Proxy.** A shareholder has the right to authorize another to vote the shares owned by the shareholder. This is known as **voting by proxy.** In the absence of restrictions to the contrary, any person, even one not a shareholder, may act as a proxy. Ordinarily authority to act as a proxy may be conferred by an informal written instrument.[27] The corporation law of a particular state may expressly require that a proxy be signed.

(d) **Voting Agreements and Trusts.** Shareholders, as a general rule, are allowed to enter into an agreement by which they concentrate their voting strength for the purpose of controlling the management.

A **voting trust** exists when by agreement a group of shareholders, or all of the shareholders, transfer their shares in trust to one or more persons as trustees who are authorized to vote the stock during the life of the trust agreement. In general, such agreements have been upheld if their object is lawful. In some jurisdictions such trusts cannot run beyond a specific number of years. There are some signs of a relaxation as to this matter. Several states have abandoned any time limitations, several have extended the time limitation, and many states provide for an extension or renewal of the agreement.

§ 50:16.   Preemptive Offer of Shares.

If the capital stock of a corporation is increased, shareholders ordinarily have the preemptive right to subscribe to such percentage of the new shares as their old shares bore to the former total of capital stock. This right is given in order to enable shareholders to maintain their relative interests in the corporation.

The existence of a preemptive right may make impossible the concluding of a transaction in which the corporation is to transfer a block of stock as consideration. Moreover, practical difficulties arise as to how stock should be allocated among shareholders of different classes.

The Revised Model Act provides that shareholders do not have preemptive rights unless the articles of incorporation so provide.[28] Where the corporation elects to have preemptive rights by so stating in its articles of incorporation, the Revised Model Act sets forth rules dealing with most of the problems involving preemptive rights.[29] Under this model provision there is no preemptive right with respect to the transfer of a block of stock as consideration. Also the model provision deals with how stock should be allocated among shareholders of different classes.

§ 50:17.   Inspection of Books.

A shareholder has the right to inspect the books of the shareholder's corporation. The request for inspection must be made in good faith, for

---

[27]See, for example, the regulations of the Securities and Exchange Commission, Rule X-14A-4.

[28]RMBCA § 6.30(a).

[29]RMBCA § 6.30(b).

proper motives, and at a reasonable time and place. The Revised Model Act authorizes inspection of corporate records "if the demand is made in good faith and for proper purpose."[30]

The purpose of inspection must be reasonably related to the shareholder's interest as a shareholder. A shareholder is entitled to inspect the records to determine the financial condition of the corporation, the quality of its management, and any matters relating to rights or interests in the corporate business, such as the value of stock.

FACTS:

Ronald Naquin, an employee of Air Engineered Systems & Services, Inc. (Air Engineered), owned one third of its outstanding shares. After six years he was fired and an offer was made to buy out his interest in Air Engineered at a price that Naquin thought inadequate. He then formed a competing business and made a written request to examine the corporate records of Air Engineered, which was denied. Naquin filed suit to require Air Engineered to allow him to examine the books. Air Engineered raised the defense that he was a competitor seeking to gain unfair competitive advantage.

DECISION:

Judgment for Naquin. Since Air Engineered was attempting to buy him out at a price he thought inadequate, Naquin had the right to examine the corporation's financial records so that he could determine the true value of his shares. Naquin as a six-year employee already knew who Air Engineered's customers were and could gain no unfair advantage as asserted by Air Engineered. [Naquin v Air Engineered Systems & Services, Inc. (La App) 463 So2d 992 (1985)]

A shareholder is entitled to inspect the books to obtain information needed for a lawsuit against the corporation or its directors or officers; to organize the other shareholders into an "opposition" party to remove the board of directors at the next election; or to buy the shares of other shareholders.

Inspection has frequently been refused when it was sought merely from idle curiosity or for "speculative purposes." Inspection has sometimes been denied on the ground that it was merely sought to obtain a mailing list of persons who would be solicited to buy products of another enterprise. Inspection has also been refused where the object of the shareholder was to advance political or social beliefs without regard to the welfare of the corporation.

Many cases deny the right of inspection when it would be harmful to the corporation or is sought only for the purpose of annoying, harassing, or causing vexation, or for the purpose of aiding competitors of the corporation. In contrast, the right of inspection is so broadly recognized in some states that the fact that the shareholder may possibly make an improper use of the information obtained does not bar inspection.

[30]RMBCA § 16.02(c).

(a) **Form of Books.** There are generally no legal requirements as to the form of corporate books and records. The Revised Model Act recognizes that corporate books and records may be stored in modern data storage systems. "A corporation shall maintain its records in written form or in any other form capable of conversion into written form within a reasonable time."[31]

(b) **Financial Statements.** In recognition of the widespread practice of corporations' preparing formal financial statements, the Revised Model Act requires a corporation to furnish annual financial statements, which include a balance sheet as of the end of the fiscal year, an income statement for that year, and a statement of changes in shareholders' equity for that year.[32] A number of states have similar provisions.

§ 50:18.   Dividends.

A shareholder has the right to receive a proportion of dividends as they are declared, subject to the relative rights of other shareholders to preferences, accumulation of dividends, and participation. However, there is no absolute right to receive dividends.

(a) **Funds Available for Declaration of Dividends.** Statutes commonly provide that no dividends may be declared unless there is a "surplus" for their payment. This surplus is generally calculated as the amount of the corporate assets in excess of all outstanding liabilities and paid-in capital of the corporation.

As an exception to these rules, a wasting assets corporation may pay dividends out of current net profits without regard to the preservation of the corporate assets. **Wasting assets corporations** include those enterprises that are designed to exhaust or use up the assets of the corporation (as by extracting oil, coal, iron, and other ores), as compared with a manufacturing plant where the object is to preserve the plant as well as to continue to manufacture. A wasting assets corporation may also be formed for the purpose of buying and liquidating a bankrupt's stock of merchandise.

In some states statutes provide that dividends may be declared from current net profits, without regard to the existence of a deficit from former years, or from surplus.

(b) **Discretion of Directors.** Assuming that a fund is available for the declaration of dividends, it is then a matter primarily within the discretion of the board of directors whether a dividend shall be declared. The fact that there is a surplus which could be used for dividends does not determine that they must be declared. This rule is not affected by the nature of the shares. Thus, the fact that the shareholders hold cumulative preferred shares does not give them any right to demand a declaration of dividends or to interfere with an honest exercise of discretion by the directors.

In general, a court will refuse to substitute its judgment for the judgment of the directors of the corporation and will interfere with their decision

[31]RMBCA § 16.01(d).
[32]RMBCA § 16.20.

as to dividend declaration only when it is shown that their conduct is harmful to the welfare of the corporation or its shareholders.[33] The courts, however, will compel the declaration of a dividend when it is apparent that the directors have amassed a surplus beyond any practical business need.

(c) **Form of Dividends.** Customarily, a dividend is paid in money; but it may be paid in property, such as a product manufactured by the corporation, in shares of other corporations held by the corporation, or in shares of the corporation itself.

(d) **Effect of Transfer of Shares.** In determining who is entitled to dividends, it is immaterial when the surplus from which the distribution is made was earned. As between the transferor and the transferee, if the dividend is in cash or property other than the shares of the corporation declaring the dividend, the person who was the owner on the date the dividend was declared is entitled to the dividend. Thus, if a cash dividend is declared before a transfer is made, the transferor is entitled to it. If the transfer was made before the declaration date, the transferee is entitled to it. In applying this rule, it is immaterial when distribution of the dividend is made.

The rule that the date of declaration determines the right to a cash dividend is subject to modification by the corporation. The board of directors in declaring the dividend may state that it will be payable to those who will be the holders of record on a later specified date.

If the dividend consists of shares in the corporation declaring the dividend, ownership is determined by the date of distribution. Whichever party is the owner of the shares when the stock dividend is distributed is entitled to the stock dividend. The reason for this variation from the cash dividend rule lies in the fact that the declaration of a stock dividend has the effect of diluting the existing corporate assets among a large number of shares. The value of the holding represented by each share is accordingly diminished. Unless the person who owns the stock on the distribution date receives a proportionate share of the stock dividend, the net effect will be to lessen that person's holding.

The transferor and transferee may enter into any agreement they choose with respect to dividends.

These rules determine the right to dividends as between transferor and transferee. Regardless of what those rights may be, the corporation is generally entitled to continue to recognize the transferor as a shareholder until it has been notified that a transfer has been made and the corporate records are accordingly changed. If the corporation, believing that the transferor is still the owner of the shares, sends the transferor a dividend to which the transferee is entitled, the transferee cannot sue the corporation. In that case, the remedy of the transferee is to sue the transferor for the dividend that the latter has received.

§ 50:19.   Capital Distribution.

Upon the dissolution of the corporation, the shareholders are entitled to receive any balance of the corporate assets that remains after the payment

---

[33]Gabelli & Co. v Liggett Group, Inc. (Del Supr) 479 A2d 276 (1984).

of all creditors. Certain classes of stock may have a preference or priority in this distribution.

§ 50:20. Shareholders' Actions.

When the corporation has the right to sue its directors or officers or third persons for damages caused by them to the corporation or for breach of contract, one or more shareholders may bring such action if the corporation refuses to do so. This is a **derivative** (secondary) **action** in that the shareholder enforces only the cause of action of the corporation, and any money recovery is paid into the corporate treasury.[34]

In a derivative action, when a corporation has failed to enforce a right, a shareholder bringing such a suit must show that a demand was made on the directors to enforce the right in question and the directors refused to do so. The Investment Company Act of 1940 (ICA) authorizes shareholders to sue investment advisors to recover excessive fees paid advisors by the corporation. The shareholders may bring such action without any prior demand on the directors of the corporation.[35]

An action cannot be brought by minority shareholders, however, if the action of the corporate directors or officers has been ratified by a majority of the shareholders acting in good faith and if the matter is of such a nature that had such majority originally authorized the acts of the directors or officers, there would not have been any wrong.

Shareholders may also intervene or join in an action brought against the corporation when the corporation refuses to defend the action against it or is not doing so in good faith. Otherwise the shareholders may take no part in an action by or against the corporation.

Shareholders in a deadlocked corporation may bring an action to obtain a dissolution of the corporation.

FACTS:

Marvin and Betty Goldstein were shareholders of the Missouri Machinery and Engineering Company. They owned one half of its stock. The other half was owned by James and Eileen Studley. The two families held all the corporate offices. They could not agree on how the corporation should be run. Sales dropped sharply. The shareholders could not agree as to data needed for filing a federal tax return. The Goldsteins brought a derivative action to obtain the appointment of a receiver for the corporation and to liquidate the corporaion.

DECISION:

Liquidation would be ordered and a receiver appointed to carry out the liquidation. This was necessary because the continued attempt to operate the business was hopeless, sales had dropped, and the board of directors and the shareholders were evenly and hopelessly deadlocked. [Goldstein v Studley (MoApp) 452 SW2d 75 (1970)]

---

[34]Zapata Corporation v Maldonado (Del) 430 A2d 779 (1981).
[35]Daily Income Fund, Inc. v Fox, 104 SCt 831 (1984).

D. LIABILITIES OF SHAREHOLDERS

The shareholder is ordinarily protected from liability for the acts of the corporation. Some exceptions are made by statute.

§ 50:21. Limited Liability.

The liability of a shareholder is generally limited. This means that the shareholder is not personally responsible for the debts and liabilities of the corporation. The capital contributed by the shareholders may be exhausted by the claims of creditors, but there is no personal liability for any unpaid balance.

§ 50:22. Exceptions to Limited Liability.

Liability may be imposed upon a shareholder as though there were no corporation when either the court ignores the corporate entity because of the particular circumstances of the case, or when the corporation is so defectively organized that it is deemed not to exist.

(a) **Wage Claims.** Statutes sometimes provide that the shareholders shall be unlimitedly liable for the wage claims of corporate employees. This principle has been abandoned in some states in recent years or has been confined to the major shareholders of corporations of which the stock is not sold publicly.

(b) **Unpaid Subscriptions.** Most states prohibit the issuance of par value shares for less than par or except for "money, labor done, or property actually received." Whenever shares issued by a corporation are not fully paid for, the original subscriber receiving the shares or any transferee who does not give value, or who knows that the shares were not fully paid, may be liable for the unpaid balance if the corporation is insolvent and the money is required to pay the creditors.[36]

If the corporation has issued the shares as fully paid, or has given them as a bonus, or has agreed to release the subscriber for the unpaid balance, the corporation cannot recover that balance. The fact that the corporation is thus barred does not prevent the creditors of the corporation from bringing an action to compel payment of the balance. The same rules are applied when stock is issued as fully paid in return for property or services which were overvalued so that the stock is not actually paid for in full. There is a conflict of authority, however, as to whether the shareholder is liable from the mere fact that the property or service given for the shares was in fact overvalued by the directors or whether in addition it must be shown that the directors had acted in bad faith in making the erroneous valuation. The trend of modern statutes is to prohibit disputing the valuation placed by the corporation on services or property in the absence of proof of fraud.

If a statute makes void the shares issued for less than par, they may be canceled upon suit of the corporation.

(c) **Unauthorized Dividends.** If dividends are improperly paid out of capital, the shareholders generally are liable to creditors to the extent of such depletion of capital. In some states the liability of the shareholder de-

---

[36]Frasier v Trans-western Land Corp. 210 Neb 681, 316 NW2d 612 (1982).

pends on whether the corporation was insolvent at the time, whether debts were existing at the time, and whether the shareholders had notice of the source of the dividend.

§ 50:23.   The Professional Corporation.

The liability of a shareholder in a professional corporation is limited to the same degree as that of a shareholder in an ordinary business corporation.[37] Several fact situations may arise.

(a) **Act of Shareholder in Creating Liability.** The statutes which authorize the formation of professional corporations usually require that share ownership be limited to duly licensed professionals. If a shareholder in a professional corporation, such as a corporation of physicians, negligently drives the professional corporation's automobile in going to attend a patient, or is personally obligated on a contract made for the corporation, or is guilty of malpractice, the physician-shareholder is liable without limit for the liability that has been created. This is the same rule of law that applies in the case of the ordinary business corporation. Professional corporation statutes generally repeat the rule with respect to malpractice liability by stating that the liability of a shareholder for malpractice is not affected by the fact of incorporation.

(b) **Malpractice Liability of an Associate.** The liability of a shareholder in a professional corporation for the malpractice of an associate varies from state to state depending on the language of the professional corporation statute in effect and court decisions under the statute.[38] If the statute provides for limited liability as in a business corporation, then where doctors A, B, and C are a professional corporation, B will not be liable for the malpractice of C. If the statute provides for vicarious personal liability as in a partnership, and doctors A, B, and C are a professional corporation, each will be unlimitedly liable for any malpractice liability incurred by the other. Often the statutory reference to malpractice liability is not very clear and the courts are called upon to resolve the question of the liability of a shareholder-professional for the malpractice of an associate.

FACTS:

Birt was a patient in the hospital. The doctor who treated him was a shareholder of a professional corporation organized under the Indiana Medical Professional Corporation Act. Birt claimed that the doctor who treated him was guilty of malpractice. Birt then sued the doctor. He also sued the professional corporation, and all the officers, directors, and shareholders of the professional corporation. These other defendants asserted that they were not liable because the corporate entity shielded them. The plaintiff claimed that the corporation was not a shield because in fact all the persons were rendering medical services and should therefore be held liable as in a partnership. The

---

[37]Pennsylvania v Upper Providence Township Municipal Authority, 55 Pa Cmnwth Ct 398, 423 A2d 769 (1980).

[38]ABA Model Professional Corporation Supplement (1984) § 34 offers three alternative positions as to liability of shareholders: (1) limited liability as in a business corporation, (2) vicarious personal liability as in a partnership, and (3) personal liability limited in amount conditioned upon financial responsibility in the form of insurance or a surety bond.

statute did not expressly regulate the matter beyond declaring that it did not change the law between a person supplying medical services and the patient.

DECISION:

Judgment against Birt as to the other defendants. These other defendants had not rendered services to the plaintiff. The fact that they were part of a corporation did not impose vicarious liability upon them for the conduct of anyone else. Nothing in the statute required imposing such liability. A partnership liability would not be imposed upon them, as claimed by the plaintiff, when the legislature had not declared that such liability would exist and, to the contrary, had expressly authorized the formation of the corporation. The corporate entity therefore protected all persons connected with the corporation from malpractice liability rendered by an employee of the corporation. [Birt v St. Mary Mercy Hospital 175 Ind App 32, 370 NE2d 379 (1977)]

SUMMARY

The ownership of a corporation is evidenced by a holder's shares of stock, which have been issued by the corporation. Common stock is ordinary stock which has no preferences, but entitles the holder to (1) participate in the control of the corporation by having the right to exercise one vote per share of record, (2) share in the profits in the form of dividends and (3) participate upon dissolution in the distribution of net assets, after the satisfaction of all creditors including bond holders. Other classes of stock exist, such as preferred stock, which has a priority over common stock as to dividends and distributions of net assets upon dissolution. Shares may be acquired by subscription of an original issue or by transfer of existing shares.

State "blue sky" laws, which apply only to intrastate transactions, protect the public from the sale of fraudulent securities. The two principal laws providing the basic framework for federal regulation of the sale of securities in interstate commerce are the Securities Act of 1933, which deals with the original distribution of securities by the issuing corporations, and the Securities Exchange Act of 1934, which is concerned with the secondary distribution of securities on the security exchanges. These acts are administered by the Securities and Exchange Commission. Except for certain private and limited offerings, the 1933 Act requires that a registration statement be filed with the SEC and a prospectus be provided to each potential purchaser. Criminal and civil penalties exist for fraudulent statements made in this process. The 1934 Act provides reporting requirements for companies whose securities are listed on a national exchange, or unlisted companies that have assets in excess of $3 million and 500 or more shareholders. Rule 10b-5 is the principal antifraud rule under the 1934 Act. Trading on "inside information" is unlawful and may subject those so involved to a civil penalty of three times the profit made on the improperly disclosed information. Cash tender offers are regulated by the SEC under authority of the Williams Act, which amended the 1934 Act.

Shareholders control the corporation, but this control is indirect. Through their voting rights they elect directors, and through this means can control the corporation. Preemptive rights allow shareholders to maintain their voting percentage and control when the corporation issues additional shares of stock. Shareholders have the right to inspect the books of the corporation, unless it would be harmful to the corporation. Shareholders also have the right to receive dividends at the discretion of the directors. Shareholders may bring a derivative action on behalf of the corporation for damages to the corporation if, upon demand, the corporation refuses to do so. Shareholders are ordinarily protected from liability for the acts of the corporation.

QUESTIONS AND CASE PROBLEMS

1. What social forces are affected by the rule requiring that a transfer restriction be known to the transferee or conspicuously noted on the share certificate?

2. What is the distinction between capital and capital stock?

3. Brinckley owns redeemable shares of stock of the Garrett-Denver Company. When the market value of the shares declined, Brinckley requested that the corporation exchange the shares for bonds of the corporation. The corporation refused to do so, and Brinckley sued to compel the conversion. Is he entitled thereto?

4. Judith purchased 10% of the stock of the Heritage Cosmetics Company in October, and another 10% in January of the following year. The next month, she was elected president of the company. In April, she sold three fourths of her stock at a profit of $50,000. Later that year, the corporation sued her for the $50,000. She defended on the ground that she had sold her own stock and therefore could keep the profit. Is she correct?

5. Barbara, Joel, and Edna each own less than 5% of the stock of the Enrico Storm Door Corporation. Individually their holdings are too small to be significant in any stockholders' election. Barbara suggests that they and other small shareholders combine their votes and that they do this by transferring their shares to trustees who will vote the aggregate of their shares as a block. Joel agrees with the idea but says he is afraid that this is an illegal conspiracy. Is he correct?

6. Compare the effect of an oral contract (a) by A to sell 100 shares of X corporation stock to B, and (b) by stockbroker C to sell A's stock in the X corporation when the market price reaches $10.00 a share.

7. Hildegarde owns 100 shares of stock of the Kline-Linquist Corporation. She sells her stock to Paul and delivers to him: (1) her stock certificate for 100 shares, and (2) a written, signed assignment of the 100 shares to Paul. The assignment form printed on the back of the share certificate is left blank and is not signed. Paul refuses to take the certificate and the assignment on the ground that Hildegarde must fill in and sign the assignment form on the stock certificate in order to make the transfer of stock effective. Is he correct?

8. Siebrecht organized a corporation called the Siebrecht Realty Co. and then transferred his building to the corporation in exchange for its stock. The corporation rented different parts of the building to different tenants. Elenkrieg, an employee of one of the tenants, fell and was injured because of the defective condition of a stairway. She sued Siebrecht individually on the ground that the corporation had been formed by him for the purpose of securing limited liability. Decide. [Elenkrieg v Siebrecht, 238 NY 254, 144 NE 519]

9. Dixon requested to inspect the books of G. S. & M. Company. The objection was raised that he did not own 5% or more of the corporate stock. If this is true, is Dixon barred from inspecting the books?

10. Monroe owned 100 shares of stock in the Apex Corporation. On the certificates for the stock the following notation was conspicuously printed: "No shareholder shall transfer any shares of this corporation without first offering such shares for purchase by the other shareholders." Monroe died owning these shares. He died without a will and his entire estate was inherited by his wife, Valenta. Some of the shareholders of Apex claimed that Valenta was not the owner of Monroe's shares because those shares had never been offered to them for purchase. Were they correct?

11. A owned corporate stock. He told B that he was going to give the stock to B and handed the stock certificate to B. B requested that A indorse the certificate. A refused to do so. Who was the owner of the stock? [Smith v Augustine, 82 Misc 2d 326, 368 NYS2d 675]

12. Shares of stock represent debts owed by the corporation to the shareholders. Is this statement correct?

13. K owned shares of stock in the J corporation. He left the shares of stock lying on top of a desk in his office. Many people continually passed through the office and one day K realized that someone had taken the shares of stock from the top of his desk. K applied to the J corporation for the issuance of a duplicate stock certificate. The corporation refused to issue a duplicate on the ground that it was K's own fault that the original certificate had been stolen. K claimed that he was entitled to a new certificate even though he had been at fault. Was he correct? [Ibanez v Farmers Underwriters Ass'n 14 Cal 3d 390, 121 Cal Rptr 256, 534 P2d 1336.]

14. Corporation A wished to employ B. Negotiations were conducted by telephone. In order to induce B to accept employment, the proper representative of corporation A promised B that, in addition to a money salary, B would receive a specified number of shares of stock of corporation A for each year of employment. B went to work for corporation A and received his money salary but three years went by with no stock being delivered to him. B then sued A corporation to compel it to issue the stock. It raised the defense that the agreement to give B stock could not be enforced because it was not evidenced by a writing as required by UCC §8-319. Was this a valid defense? [Bingham v Wells, Rich, Greene, Inc. 34 App Div 2d 924, 311 NYS2d 508; Butcher v United States Invest. Corp. 236 Pa Super 8, 344 A2d 583.]

15. Linhart owned shares of stock in the First National Bank. She borrowed money from the bank and pledged the stock as security. She thereafter decided to transfer 70 head of cattle and the shares of stock to her son. She could not deliver the share certificate to him because it was held by the bank. She therefore executed a bill of sale reciting the transfer of the cattle and the stock to the son. She gave him the bill of sale and he had the bill recorded. After her death, the son brought an action to determine the ownership of the stock. Was the son the owner of the shares? [Pederson v Branter (Mo App) 502 SW2d 25]

16. Texas International Speedway, Inc. (TIS), filed a registration statement and prospectus with the Securities and Exchange Commission offering a total of $4,398,900 in securities to the public. The proceeds of the sale were to be used to finance the construction of an automobile speedway. The entire issue was sold on the offering date. TIS did not meet with success, however, and the corporation filed a petition for bankruptcy. Huddleston and Bradley instituted a class action in the United States District Court on behalf of themselves and other purchasers of TIS securities. The complaint alleged violations of Section 10(b) of the 1934 Act. They sued most of the participants in the offering, including the accounting firm, Herman & MacLean, which had issued an opinion concerning certain financial statements and a pro forma balance sheet that were contained in the registration statement and prospectus. They claimed that the defendants had engaged in a fraudulent scheme to misrepresent or conceal material facts regarding the financial condition of TIS, including the costs incurred in building the speedway. Herman & MacLean defended that the case should be dismissed because Section 11 of the 1933 Act provides an express remedy for a misrepresentation in a registration statement, and therefore an action under Section 10(b) of the 1934 Act is precluded. Decide. [Herman & MacLean v Huddleston, 459 US 375, 103 SCt 683.]

CHAPTER 51

MANAGEMENT OF

CORPORATIONS

CHAPTER OBJECTIVES

After studying this chapter you will be able to:

1. Name the persons entitled to manage a corporation and describe their powers.
2. State the requirements as to meetings of shareholders and directors.
3. Describe and illustrate the liability of corporate officers and directors to the corporation.
4. Describe and illustrate the liability of corporate officers and directors to third persons.
5. State the criminal liability of officers and directors of a corporation.
6. State when an officer, director, or employee of a corporation may obtain indemnification from the corporation.
7. Solve problems involving questions of corporate management.

A corporation is managed, directly or indirectly, by its shareholders, board of directors, and officers.

Shareholders' management functions are very limited and usually take the form of voting at shareholders' meetings to elect directors whose management philosophies and interests best coincide with their own. In this sense they indirectly determine the management policies of the business. Also, they may vote at shareholders' meetings to amend bylaws, approve shareholder resolutions, or vote on so-called extraordinary corporate matters such as the sale of corporate assets outside the regular course of the corporation's business or the merger or dissolution of the corporation.

The management of the corporation is vested in the board of directors. Normally officers are appointed by the directors, and are responsible for the day-to-day operation of the business.

In the large corporation it is common to find that the owners (the shareholders) are not to any appreciable extent the managers (directors and officers); while in a closely held corporation the owners commonly serve on the board of directors and hold corporate offices.

§ 51:1.   Meetings of Shareholders.

To have legal effect, action by the shareholders must be taken at a regular or special meeting. The time and place of regular or stated meetings are usually prescribed by the articles of incorporation or bylaws. Notice to shareholders of such meetings is ordinarily not required, but it is usually given as a matter of good business practice. Some statutes require that notice be given of all meetings, and generally notice must be given specifying the subject matter when the meeting is of an unusual character. Unless otherwise prescribed, special meetings are called by the directors. It is sometimes provided that a special meeting may be called by a certain percentage of shareholders.[1] Notice of the day, hour, and the place of a special meeting must be given to all shareholders. The notice must also include a statement of the nature of the business to be transacted. No other business may be transacted at such a meeting.

(a) **Quorum.** A valid meeting requires the presence of a quorum of the voting shareholders. In order to constitute a quorum, usually a specified number of shareholders or a number authorized to vote a stated proportion of the voting stock must attend. If a quorum is present, a majority of those present may act with respect to any matter, unless there is an express requirement of a greater affirmative vote.

When a meeting opens with a quorum, the quorum generally is not thereafter broken if shareholders leave the meeting and those remaining are not sufficient to constitute a quorum.

(b) **No Meeting Action.** A number of statutes provide for corporate action by shareholders without holding a meeting. The Revised Model Act provides that "action required or permitted by this Act to be taken at a shareholder's meeting may be taken without a meeting if the action is taken by all shareholders entitled to vote on the action."[2] The action must be evidenced by a written consent, describing the action taken, signed by all the shareholders entitled to vote on the action, and delivered to the corporation for inclusion in the minutes. Such provisions give flexibility of operation, which is needed by the small or close corporation.

§ 51:2.   Directors.

The management of a corporation is usually under the guidance of a board of directors elected by the shareholders. Most states now permit the

---

[1]New York Business Corporation Law § 603.
[2]RMBCA § 7.04 (a).

number of directors to be fixed by the bylaws. Many specify that the board of directors shall consist of not less than three directors. A few authorize one or more directors.[3] Professional corporation legislation often authorizes or is interpreted as authorizing a one- or two-person board of directors.

(a) **Qualifications.** Eligibility for membership on a board of directors is determined by statute, articles of incorporation, or bylaws. In the absence of a contrary provision, any person is eligible for membership, including a nonresident, a minor, or even a person who is not a shareholder.

Bylaws may require that a director own stock in the corporation, although ordinarily this requirement is not imposed.

(b) **Powers of Directors.** The board of directors has authority to manage the corporation. The court will not interfere with the board's discretion in the absence of illegal conduct or fraud harming the rights of creditors, shareholders, or the corporation.[4]

The board of directors may enter into any contract or transaction necessary to carry out the business for which the corporation was formed. The board may appoint officers and other agents to act for the company; or it may appoint several of its own members as an executive committee to act for the board between board meetings.

Broad delegation of authority to a single officer may, however, run the risk of being treated as an unlawful abdication of the board's management function.

FACTS:

In 1981 the Boston Athletic Association (BAA), a nonprofit corporation created to present the annual Boston Marathon, authorized William Cloney, President of the BAA, to negotiate contracts for it. Cloney executed a contract with attorney Marshall Medoff, giving Medoff exclusive power to promote the Marathon, with the BAA transferring to him all rights to use the Marathon name and logos. The contract's financial terms were extremely favorable to Medoff who could renew it from year to year, while the BAA had no way to end the contract. When the BAA's board learned of the contract they declared that it was beyond the authorization vested in Cloney. The board brought an action to have the contract set aside. Medoff defended that Cloney had authority to make the contract and therefore the contract bound the corporation.

DECISION:

Judgment for the BAA. It is the obligation of the board to direct the corporation. Consistent with this obligation a board may delegate general managerial functions to corporate officers. But certain powers cannot be delegated. The contract made with Medoff surrendered virtually complete control of the Marathon to Medoff. The board in this case improperly delegated to Cloney the authority to make such a contract, which totally encumbered the BAA's corporate purpose, that of the presentation of the Marathon. Authority to make such a contract was beyond the power of the board to delegate. [Boston Athletic Association v International Marathon, Inc. 392 Mass 356, 467 NE2d 58 (1984)]

---

[3]Delaware Ann § 141 (b). See also ABA MBCA § 36.
[4]Iwasaki v Iwasaki Bros., Inc. 58 Or App 543, 649 P2d 598 (1982).

(c) Conflict of Interests. A director is disqualified from taking part in corporate action with respect to a matter in which the director has a conflicting interest. Since it cannot be known how the other directors would have acted if they had known of the conflict of interest, the corporation generally may avoid any transaction because of the director's disqualification.

A number of states provide by statute that the conflict of interest of a director does not impair the transaction or contract entered into or authorized by the board of directors if the disqualified director disclosed the interest and the contract or transaction is fair and reasonable with respect to the corporation.

§ 51:3.   Meetings of Directors.

Theoretically, action by directors can only be taken at a proper meeting of the board. Bylaws sometimes require the meeting to be held at a particular place. Most states expressly provide that the directors may meet either in or outside of the state of incorporation. Directors who participate without objection in a meeting irregularly held as to place or time other than as specified in the bylaws cannot object later. Generally a director is not allowed to vote by proxy.

Most states permit action to be taken by the board of directors without the holding of an actual meeting. It is commonly provided when such action is taken that it be set forth in writing and signed by all the directors.

§ 51:4.   Liability of Directors.

In dealing with the corporation, the directors act in a fiduciary capacity, as it is to their care that the stockholders have entrusted the control of the corporate property and the management of the business.[5]

Directors must perform their duties in good faith, in a manner each director reasonably believes to be in the best interests of the corporation, and with such care as an ordinarily prudent person in a like position would use under similar circumstances. A director is liable for the illegal payment of dividends, the illegal purchase by the corporation of its own shares, and illegal distributions of the assets of the corporation upon liquidation.[6]

In performing their duties, directors may in good faith rely on information prepared by others such as officers or employees of the corporation, lawyers, accountants, or a committee of the board upon which the directors do not serve.

Directors who have acted in good faith and have exercised reasonable care will not be liable for losses resulting from their management of the corporation.[7]

Directors of a corporation are not personally liable for wrongs committed by the corporation merely by virtue of the fact that they are directors. It must be shown that they have authorized or ratified the improper conduct or have in some way participated therein.

---

[5]Tillis v United Parts, Inc. (Fla App) 395 So2d 518 (1981).
[6]RMBCA § 8.33.
[7]Midwest Management Corp v Stephans (Iowa) 353 NW2d 76 (1984).

If a director signs a contract on behalf of the corporation without authority to do so, the director is liable to the same extent as an ordinary unauthorized agent.[8]

(a) **Director's Liability for Conflict of Interests.** When a director violates the rule prohibiting conflicting interests, the corporation may recover any secret profit made by the director. The ordinary rule of agency law as to loyalty determines liability.

(b) **Action against Director.** Actions against directors should be brought by the corporation. If the corporation fails to act, as is the case when the directors alleged to be liable control the corporation, one or more shareholders may bring the action in a representative capacity for the corporation.

(c) **Removal of Director.** Ordinarily directors are removed by the vote of the shareholders. In some states the board of directors may remove a director and elect a successor on the ground that the director removed (1) did not accept office; (2) failed to satisfy the qualifications for office; (3) was continuously absent from the state without a leave of absence granted by the board, generally for a period of six months or more; (4) was adjudicated as bankrupt; (5) was convicted of a felony; (6) was unable to perform the duties of director because of any illness or disability, generally for a period of six months or more; or (7) has been judicially declared of unsound mind.[9]

The Revised Model Act provides for removal of directors "with or without cause" by a majority vote of the shareholders, unless the articles of incorporation provide that directors may be removed only for cause.[10]

§ 51:5.   Officers of the Corporation.

Corporations will generally have a president, at least one vice-president, a secretary, and a treasurer. The duties of these officers are generally set forth in the corporation's bylaws. Commonly included is the duty of the secretary to keep minutes of the proceedings of shareholders and directors. Corporation codes generally expressly permit the same person to be both secretary and treasurer. In larger corporations there will often be a recording secretary and a corresponding secretary.

Sometimes the officers are elected by the shareholders but usually they are appointed by the board of directors. The Revised Model Act follows the general pattern of providing for the appointment of officers by the board of directors.[11] Ordinarily no particular formality need be observed in making such appointments. There are seldom particular qualifications required of officers. Unless prohibited, a director may hold an executive office.

§ 51:6.   Powers of Officers.

The officers of a corporation are its agents. Consequently, their powers are controlled by the law of agency.[12] As in the case of any other

---

[8]Woods v Commercial Contractors, Inc. (Ala.) 384 So2d 1076 (1980).
[9]See California Corporations Code § 807, recognizing grounds (1), (2), (5), and (7).
[10]RMBCA § 8.08(a).
[11]RMBCA § 8.40(a).
[12]Kuehn v Kuehn, (Colo App), 642 P2d (1982).

agency, the third person has the burden of proving that a particular officer has the authority which such officer purports to have.

The fact that the officer or employee acting on behalf of the corporation is a major shareholder does not give the officer or employee any greater agency powers. Moreover, the person dealing with the officer or employee is charged with knowledge of any limitation on authority contained in the recorded corporate charter.

FACTS:

Barth Incorporated, owned an apartment complex. The charter of the corporation was locally recorded and stated that the property of the corporation could not be sold without the consent of the preferred stockholders. The only preferred shareholder of Barth was the federal housing commissioner. Florence Barth was a major shareholder and manager of the apartments. Following the death of her husband, the other major shareholder, Florence made a contract to sell the apartment complex to Newberry. She believed that she had the authority to do so. The contract was never performed and Newberry brought suit for specific performance against her and the corporation.

DECISION:

Judgment for Barth, Incorporated. The articles of incorporation or charter of a corporation create the corporation and define its powers. Third persons dealing with the corporation or its agent are treated as knowing what is stated in the charter. Newberry therefore was regarded as knowing that no sale of the property could be made without the consent of the preferred stockholder. The fact that Florence was a major stockholder and the manager of the corporation did not give her any power to make a contract which the corporation itself could not make. As the preferred stockholder had not consented to the sale, the corporation was not bound by any contract to Newberry. [Newberry v Barth, Inc. (Iowa) 252 NW2d 711 (1977)]

When the nature of the transaction is unusual, that unusual nature should alert a third person to the necessity of specific authorization from the corporation.[13]

(a) **President.** It is sometimes held that in the absence of some limitation upon authority, the president of a corporation has by virtue of that office the authority to act as agent on behalf of the corporation within the scope of the business in which the corporation is empowered to engage. It has also been held, however, that the president has such broad powers only when the president is the general manager of the corporation, and then such powers stem from the office of general manager and not from that of president. In any event, the president does not have authority by virtue of that office to make a contract which because of its unusual character would require action by the board of directors.[14] The president, therefore, cannot make a contract to fix long-term or unusual contracts of employment, to

---

[13]Kanavos v Hancock Bank & Trust Co. 14 Mass App 326, 439 NE2d 311 (1982).
[14]Molasky Enterprises, Inc. v Carps, Inc. (Mo App) 615 SW2d 83 (1981).

bind the corporation as a guarantor, to release a claim of the corporation, or to promise that the corporation will later repurchase shares when issued to a subscriber.

It is ordinarily held that the president of a business ccrporation is not authorized to execute commercial paper in the name of the corporation although the president may do so when authorized by the board of directors to borrow money for the corporation.

(b) Other Officers and Employees. The authority of corporate employees and other officers, such as secretary or treasurer, is generally limited to the duties of their offices. The authority may, however, be extended by the conduct of the corporation, in accordance with the general principles governing apparent authority based on the conduct of the principal. An unauthorized act may, of course, be ratified. The authority of the general manager of the corporation is determined by principles of ordinary agency law.

§ 51:7.   Liability of Officers.

The relation of the officers to the corporation, like that of the directors, is fiduciary in nature. For this reason, the officers are liable for secret profits made in connection with or at the expense of the business of the corporation.

If an officer diverts a corporate opportunity, the corporation may recover from the officer the profit of which the corporation has been thus deprived.

FACTS:

Klinicki and Lundgren incorporated Berlinair, Inc., in Oregon, with Klinicki owning one-third of the stock and Lundgren controlling the remaining stock. Lundgren was president, and responsible for developing business. Klinicki was vice-president in charge of operations. A year after they had formed Berlinair, Lundgren learned that a consortium of Berlin travel agents, BFR, might be offering a valuable contract for flights to warmer climates. Without telling Klinicki about this opportunity or offering the opportunity to Berlinair, Lundgren formed a new corporation Air Berlin Charter Co. (ABC) and sought and was awarded the BFR contract. Upon learning of Lundgren's activities, Klinicki brought a derivative action against Lundgren for diverting a corporate opportunity of Berlinair. Lundgren defended that there was no diversion of a corporate opportunity because Berlinair did not have the financial ability to undertake the contract.

DECISION:

Judgment for Berlinair. Before an officer may take a corporate opportunity, the officer must first offer the opportunity and disclose all material facts regarding the opportunity to the corporation. No exception is made on the ground that the corporation, although solvent, does not have the financial resources to make use of the opportunity. Lundgren did not offer the contract with BRF to Berlinair. He thus improperly diverted the corporate opportunity and he is liable to Berlinair for the loss of profits. [Klinicki v Lundgren (Ore) 695 P2d 906 (1985)]

The advent of the age of computers has not changed the basic principles of determining the liability of corporate officers but gives rise to new situations to which the old principles will be applied. When computers are used, management may be liable for failure to exercise proper care in their use. Management may also be liable for failing to utilize computers.

Under some state statutes regulating the sale of corporate securities, an officer taking part in a sale which violates the statute is liable without regard to knowledge or lack of knowledge that the sale violated the statute. When the corporation has violated a statute designed to protect health or environment, corporate officers may be held liable for having failed to prevent the violation.

Officers are liable for willful or negligent acts that cause a loss to the corporation.On the other hand, they are not liable for mere errors in judgment committed while exercising their discretion, provided they have acted with reasonable prudence and care.

§ 51:8.   Agents and Employees of Corporation.

The authority, rights, and liabilities of an agent of a corporation are governed by the same rules applicable when the principal is a natural person. The authority of corporate employees also is governed by general agency principles.

The fact that a person is acting on behalf of a corporation does not shield from the liability that would be imposed for such acts if done on behalf of a natural person.[15]

§ 51:9.   Indemnification of
Officers, Directors, Employees, and Agents.

While performing what they believe to be their duty, officers, directors, employees, and agents of corporations may commit acts for which they are later sued or criminally prosecuted. The Model Act broadly authorizes the corporation to indemnify such persons if they acted in good faith and in a manner reasonably believed to be in or not opposed to the interests of the corporation and had no reason to believe that their conduct was unlawful.

In some states statutory provision is made requiring the corporation to indemnify directors and officers for reasonable expenses incurred by them in defending unwarranted suits brought against them by shareholders. Such statutes have been adopted to induce responsible persons to accept positions of corporate responsiblity.

§ 51.10.   Liability of Management to Third Persons.

Ordinarily the management of a corporation, meaning its directors, officers, and executive employees, is not liable to third persons for the effect upon such third persons of their management or advice. The liability of a director or officer for misconduct ordinarily is a liability which may be enforced only by the corporation or by shareholders bringing a derivative action on behalf of the corporation. Ordinarily, directors or officers are not

---

[15]National Acceptance Co. v Pintura Corp. 94 Ill App 3d 703, 50 Ill Dec 120, 418 NE2d 1114 (1981).

liable to a third person for loss caused by the negligent performance of their duties as directors or officers, even though because of such negligence the corporation is in turn liable to the third person to whom the corporation owed the duty to use care or was under a contract obligation to render a particular service.

Officers and managers of a corporation are not liable for the economic consequence of their advice upon third persons, even though they caused the corporation to refuse to deal with or to break its contract with such third persons; as long as the officers and managers acted in good faith to advance the interests of the corporation.

FACTS:

Larry Phillips was hired as Executive Secretary of the Montana Education Association (MEA) for two years. Six months later he was fired. He then sued MEA for breach of contract and sued the directors and some of the other employees of MEA on the theory that they had caused MEA to break the contract with him and were therefore guilty of the tort of maliciously interfering with his contract with MEA. The evidence showed that the individual defendants had induced the corporation to break the contract with Phillips but that this had been done in order to further the welfare of the corporation.

DECISION:

· Judgment for Phillips as to the corporation. Judgment against Phillips as to the individual defendants. When a corporation breaks a contract it is liable for breach of the contract regardless of why it broke the contract. The fact that officers or employees had induced the corporation to break its contract with a third person does not give the third person the right to sue them. Such liability arises only if the directors or officers had induced the breach of the contract in order to harm the third person or to further their personal interest. No such liability arises when the directors or officers had acted solely in order to benefit the corporation. Phillips did not produce any evidence to show that the individual defendants had acted to hurt him or to benefit themselves. The individual defendants therefore were not liable. Only the corporation was liable for the breach of the corporate contract. [Phillips v Montana Education Association, 187 Mont 419, 610 P2d 154 (1980)]

---

§ 51.11. Criminal Liablity.

Officers and directors, as in the case of agents generally, are personally responsible for any crimes committed by them even when they act in behalf of the corporation. At the local level they may be criminally responsible for violation of ordinances relating to sanitation, safety, and hours of closing. At the state level they may be criminally liable for conducting a business without obtaining necessary licenses or after the corporate certificate of incorporation was forfeited for failing to file reports or pay taxes. At the national level they may be prosecuted for violation of the federal antitrust laws.

Some statutes designed to regulate corporate activity provide specifically for fines and imprisonment of corporate officers and other individuals responsible for corporate violations. For example, the president of a national food chain corporation has been held criminally liable under the federal Food, Drug, and Cosmetic Act on the ground that food in the corporation's warehouse had been exposed to rodent contamination.[16] Also, the Foreign Corrupt Practices Act makes it a crime to bribe a foreign official or political candidate to use influence to obtain business for an American corporation. The American corporation is subject to a fine and officers and other individuals are subject to fine and imprisonment.[17]

A corporation itself may be convicted of a crime involving specific intent, like theft by swindle or forgery, where it is shown beyond a reasonable doubt, (1) that the agent was acting at least in part in furtherance of the corporation's business interests and (2) that corporate management authorized, tolerated, or ratified the criminal activity.

FACTS:
Christy Pontiac, a corporation, was indicted for theft by swindle and forgery involving the GM cash rebate program in effect in 1981. Hesli, a middle management employee of Christy Pontiac, had forged the cash rebate applications for two cars, so that the rebate money was paid to Christy Pontiac instead of to its customers. When confronted by a customer who should have received a rebate, the president of the dealership attempted to negotiate a settlement and did not contact GM headquarters until after an investigation was begun by the state attorney general. Christy Pontiac argued that it could not be held liable for a specific intent crime since only "natural" persons, as opposed to corporations, can form such intent.

DECISION:
Judgment against the corporation. Christy Pontiac, not Hesli, received the GM rebate money, so it is clear that Hesli was acting in furtherance of the corporation's interests. When one of the buyers complained to the president, James Christy, he attempted to negotiate a settlement and did not contact GM headquarters. The rebate money was obtained, accepted, and kept by Christy Pontiac until somebody "blew the whistle." This evidence established that the theft by swindle and the forgeries constituted the acts of the corporation. [State v Christy Pontiac-GMC, Inc. (Minn) 354 NW2d 17 (1984)]

---

§ 51:12.   Corporate Debts and Taxes.

As the corporation is a separate legal person, debts and taxes owed by the corporation are ordinarily the obligations of the corporation only. Consequently, neither directors nor officers are individually liable for the corporate debts or taxes, even though it may have been their acts which gave rise to the debts or their neglect which resulted in the failure to pay the taxes.

In some states civil liability for corporate debts is imposed upon the officers and directors of the corporation when it improperly engages in busi-

[16]United States v Park, 421 US 658 (1975).
[17]PL 95-213, 91 Stat 1494, 15 USC § 78m et seq.

ness. Some states make the directors and officers personally liable for taxes that the corporation has neglected to pay.

§ 51:13. Protection of Shareholders.

Various devices and limitations have developed to protect shareholders both from misconduct by management and from the action of the majority of the shareholders. Shareholders may protect themselves by voting at the next annual election for new directors, and also officers, if the latter are elected; or they may take special remedial action at a special meeting of shareholders called for that purpose. In any case, the objecting shareholders may bring a legal action when the management misconduct complained of constitutes a legal wrong.

§ 51:14. Irregular Procedure.

There is a strong judicial tendency to ignore a procedural error or irregularity when the circumstances are such that it can be concluded that all or substantially all of the shareholders have agreed to or waived any objection to the procedure which was followed.[18] A third person sued by the corporation cannot challenge the right of the corporation to sue on the ground that corporate procedure requirements have not been observed.

When the corporation has received the benefit of a transaction, it will be estopped from claiming that there was some irregularity in the corporate procedure followed. As in the case of agency generally, a corporation may ratify acts of its officers or directors that were unauthorized.

§ 51:15. Liability of Corporation for Acts of Management.

A corporation is liable to third persons for the acts of its officers, employees, and agents to the same extent as a natural person is liable for the acts of others.[19] This means that the ordinary rules of agency law determine the extent to which the corporation is liable to a third person for a contract made or a tort committed by management personnel, employees, and agents.[20]

SUMMARY

To have legal effect shareholder action must be taken at a regular meeting as specified in the bylaws or at a special meeting after due notice to shareholders. Also, the presence of a quorum of the voting shareholders is required.

Management of a corporation is under the control of a board of directors. The courts will not interfere with the board's discretion in the absence of unusual conduct such as fraud. A director is disqualified from taking part in corporate action where the director has a conflict of interest. Action by directors is usually taken at a properly called meeting of the board. Directors

---

[18]Leslie, Semple & Garrison, 81 App Div 2d 950, 439 NYS2d 707 (1981).
[19]Mercury Motors Express, Inc. v Smith, (Fla), 393 So2d 545 (1981).
[20]Jenson v Alaska Valuation Service, Inc. (Alaska) 688 P2d 161 (1984).

act in a fiduciary capacity in dealing with the corporation. Directors who act in good faith and have exercised reasonable care are not liable for losses resulting from their management decisions. Ordinarily directors are removed by shareholders.

Officers of a corporation, including a president, vice president, secretary, and treasurer, are selected and removed by the board of directors. Officers are agents of the corporation and their powers are governed by the law of agency. Their relations with the corporation are fiduciary in nature, and they are liable for any secret profits and for diverting corporate opportunities to their own advantage.

Directors and officers, as in the case of agents generally, are personally responsible for any crimes they commit when they act on behalf of the corporation. The corporation itself may be prosecuted for crimes and is subject to fines if convicted.

The ordinary rules of agency law determine the extent to which a corporation is liable for a contract made or tort committed by a corporate agent or employee.

QUESTIONS AND CASE PROBLEMS

1. What social forces are affected by the rule that a person dealing with a corporation officer is charged with knowledge of any limitation on the officer's authority contained in the recorded corporate charter?
2. What constitutes a quorum at a meeting of shareholders?
3. Roxanne owned 10 of the 1,000 outstanding shares of Stony Point Urban Renewal, Inc. She disagreed with the future planning of the board of directors. Should she bring a lawsuit against the directors?
4. Watson is the secretary of the Industro-Tech Corporation. Some of the directors desire to oust him from office because he has failed to keep accurate minutes of the corporate meetings. He defends on the ground that this is no great wrong because no one reads the minutes anyway. Should Watson be removed as secretary?
5. Clara is the sales manager of Carmody Cosmetics, Inc. She plans and directs the advertising campaigns of the company. In a criminal prosecution brought by the attorney general of the state it is held that the ads of the corporation violate the state consumer protection law. By that statute, such violation is a crime. Clara claims that she is not guilty of a crime because the advertising was run by the corporation. Is she correct?
6. Veronica owns 10% of the stock of the Vulcan Press Company, Inc. She makes a sale of some of its presses to Carton. The contract is not performed by Vulcan. Carton sues Vulcan and claims that it is bound by the contract made on its behalf by Veronica. Is Carton correct?
7. Directors must always own stock of the corporation in order to insure that they will be attentive to their duties. Appraise this statement.
8. Discuss the power of a corporation president to employ a sales manager and to agree that the manager should be paid a stated amount per year plus a percentage of any increase in the dollar volume of sales that would take place.

9. Klockner and Combellick were directors and officers of K.M.S., a corporation engaged in the business of auctioning automobiles. The corporation sold some automobiles for Keser and gave him a check in payment of the proceeds. At the time the check was issued, Klockner and Combellick knew that the account of the corporation was overdrawn. When the check was dishonored by the bank, Keser sued them. They defended on the ground that the delivering of the bad check was the act of the corporation and that they were not liable for the wrong done by the corporation. Were Klockner and Combellick liable? [Klockner v Keser, 29 Colo App 475, 488 P2d 1135]

10. Ponder was the president of the Long Beach Motel Hotel Corporation. He requested a quotation from General Electric on air conditioners for the hotel. He was sent a quotation, on the basis of which he sent in a purchase order on behalf of the corporation. General Electric rejected this order made in the name of the corporation and in effect stated that it would only sell to Ponder personally. A new purchase order was sent to Ponder which showed him individually as the buyer. He signed his name but then added "Pres." When General Electric sued him for the purchase price, he claimed that he had signed on behalf of the corporation and that General Electric knew that it was dealing with the corporation. Was he bound by the contract? [General Electric Co. v Ponder (La App) 234 So2d 786]

11. Henry is treasurer of the Danbar Corporation. He wants to purchase an expensive car for his own use and pay for it with a corporate check. The dealer asks Henry if he has the authority to do this. Henry replies that he controls the money of the corporation and therefore can say when and how it should be spent. Is he correct?

12. Cholfin and his wife were two of the three directors of the Allied Freightways Corporation. Cholfin ran the business, and his wife and the other director took no active part in its management. Cholfin unlawfully used $16,587.25 of the corporate funds to pay his own debts and $3,086.39 of the corporate funds to pay those of his wife. Allied Freightways brought suit to recover from the Cholfins the money improperly spent from the corporation. Allied Freightways claimed that each of the defendants was liable for the full amount of all improper expenditures. Was this correct? [Allied Freightways v Cholfin, 325 Mass 630, 91 NE2d 765]

13. A director of a corporation cannot loan money to the corporation because that will create the danger of a conflict of interests between the director's status as a director and the status as a creditor. Appraise this statement.

14. AT&T had contracts with five subsidiary corporations by which AT&T furnished certain services for each subsidiary and each subsidiary was under contract to pay AT&T compensation of 2 1/2 percent of gross revenues of the subsidiary. Kutik owned shares in AT&T. He brought a lawsuit against Taylor and other directors of AT&T and the five subsidiaries. Kutik claimed that in the preceding six years AT&T had only collected 1% instead of 2 1/2% from each of the subsidiaries. Were the directors liable? [Kutik v Taylor, 364 NYS2d 387]

15. Anthony Yee was the president of the Waipahu Auto Exchange, a corporation. As part of his corporate duties, he arranged financing for the company. The Federal Services Finance Corporation drew twelve checks payable to the order of the Waipahu Auto Exchange. These were then indorsed by its president: "Waipahu Auto Exchange, Limited, by Anthony Yee, President," and were cashed at two different banks. The Bishop National Bank of Hawaii, on which the checks were drawn, charged its depositor, Federal Services, with the amount of these checks. Federal Services then sued Bishop National Bank to restore to its account the amount of these twelve checks on the theory that Bishop National Bank had improperly made payment on the checks because Anthony Yee had no authority to cash them. Did Yee have authority to indorse and cash the checks? [Federal Services Finance Corp. v Bishop National Bank of Hawaii (CA9 Haw) 190 F2d 442]

16. E. P. Fournier Co. is a closely held corporation engaged in the sale of new and used automobiles. The board of directors hired Paul Fournier and agreed that he "shall act as general manager with full authority to hire, approve sales, and contribute to policy decisions affecting the interests of the corporation." On the same date Roland Fournier was hired by the board to act as assistant general manager. Paul was president and treasurer of the corporation and Roland was vice-president and secretary. Paul and Roland had a dispute about the roles of their respective sons who were also employed in the business. Soon thereafter Paul informed Roland that "his services with the company were no longer required" and removed two vehicles from Roland's garage which were owned by the corporation but used by Roland. Roland sued the corporation for back pay and benefits, claiming that Paul did not have authority to terminate him unilaterally without authorization from the board of directors. Paul defends that his employment agreement with the board clearly delegated to him all of the board's authority to manage the business, including the power to remove Roland. Decide. [Fournier v Fournier, (RI) 479 A2d 708]

17. Rudolph Redmont was the president of Abbott Thinlite Corporation. He left that corporation and ran the Circle Corporation in competition with his former employer. In so doing, it was claimed that he diverted contracts from his former employer to his company, having gained the advantage of the specific information of the deals in progress while employed by Abbott. The former employer sued Redmont and Circle Corporation to recover lost profits. Redmont defends that all of the contracts in question were made after he left Abbott, at which time his fiduciary duty to Abbott had ceased. Decide. [Abbott Redmont Thinlite Corp. v Redmont (CA2 NY) 475 F2d 85]

PART 9

REAL PROPERTY

Chapter 52 Nature and Ownership of Real Property
Chapter 53 Leases

CHAPTER 52

NATURE AND OWNERSHIP

OF REAL PROPERTY

CHAPTER OBJECTIVES

After studying this chapter you will be able to:
1. List the classes of real property.
2. Distinguish between liens, licenses, and easements.
3. List and illustrate the forms of co-ownership of real property.
4. Define a deed and describe its operation.
5. Describe and illustrate the warranties of the grantor and the grantee of real estate.
6. Describe the characteristics and effect of a mortgage.
7. Solve problems involving questions of real property law.

The law of real property is technical and to a large extent uses a vocabulary drawn from the days of feudalism. Much of the earlier law of real property is no longer of practical importance in the modern business world. The following discussion is therefore a simplified presentation of the subject.

A. NATURE OF REAL PROPERTY

Real property has special characteristics of permanence and uniqueness that have strongly influenced the rules that society has developed to resolve disputes concerning real property.

§ 52:1. Definitions.

Real property includes (a) land, (b) buildings and fixtures, and (c) rights in the land of another.

(a) **Land. Land** means more than the surface of the earth. It embraces the soil and all things of a permanent nature affixed to the ground, such as herbs, grass, or trees, and other growing, natural products. The term also includes the waters upon the ground and things that are embedded beneath the surface. For example, coal, oil, and marble embedded beneath the surface form part of the land.

Technically, land is considered as extending downward to the earth's center and upward indefinitely. The Uniform Aeronautics Act states that the owner of the land owns the space above, subject to the right of aircraft in flight which does not interfere with the use of the land and is not dangerous to persons or property lawfully on the land.[1]

(b) **Buildings and Fixtures.** A **building** includes any structure placed on or beneath the surface of land, without regard to its purpose or use. A **fixture** is personal property that has been attached to the earth or placed in a building in such a way or under such circumstances that it is deemed part of the real property.

(c) **Rights in Land of Another.** These rights include easements, such as the right to cross another's land, and **profits**, such as the right to take coal from another's land.

§ 52:2.   Easements.

An **easement** is not only a right in the land of another, but it is a right that belongs to the land which is benefited. The benefited land is called the **dominant tenement,** and the land which is subject to the easement is called the **servient tenement.**

An easement is an interest in land and therefore an oral promise to create an easement is not binding because of the statute of frauds.

(a) **Creation of Easement.** An easement may be created in several ways.

(1) An easement may be created by deed.

(2) An easement may be created by implication when one conveys part of the land that has been used as a dominant estate in relation to the part retained. To illustrate, if water or drain pipes run from the part conveyed through the part retained, there is an implied right to have such use continued. In order for an easement to be implied in such a case, the use must be apparent, continuous, and reasonably necessary.

(3) An easement may also be created by implication when it is necessary to the use of the land conveyed. This ordinarily arises when one subdivides land and sells a portion to which no entry can be made, except over the land retained or over the land of a stranger. The grantee's right to use the land retained by the grantor for the purpose of going to and from the land conveyed is known as a **way of necessity.**[2]

---

[1]The Uniform Aeronautics Act (UAA) has been adopted in Arizona, Delaware, Georgia, Hawaii, Idaho, Indiana, Maryland, Minnesota, Missouri, Montana, Nevada, New Jersey, North Carolina, North Dakota, Pennsylvania, South Carolina, South Dakota, Tennessee, Utah, Vermont, and Wisconsin, but was withdrawn by the Commissioners on Uniform State Laws in 1943.

[2]Helms v Tullis, __ Ala __, 398 So2d 253 (1981).

(4) An easement may be created by estoppel, as when the grantor states that the plot conveyed is bounded by a street. If in such case, the grantor owns the adjoining land, the public cannot be denied the right to use the area which the owner has described as a street.

(5) An easement may be created by prescription by adverse use for a statutory period. [3] No easement is acquired if the use of the land is with the permission of the owner. This adverse use by which an easement is acquired is similar to the adverse possession by which title is acquired as is discussed in § 52:28.

(b) **Termination of Easement.** Once an easement has been granted, it cannot be destroyed by the act of the grantor. A "revocation" attempted without the easement owner's consent has no effect.

An easement may be lost by nonuse when there are surrounding circumstances which show an intent to abandon the easement. For example, where a surface transit system had an easement to maintain trolley tracks, it could be found that there was an abandonment of the easement when the tracks were removed and all surface transportation was discontinued. Likewise, where the owner of the easement planted a flowerbed on the land across the end of the path of the easement, the intent to abandon the easement was evident.

§ 52:3.   Licenses.

A **license** is a personal, revocable privilege to do an act or series of acts upon the land of another. Unlike an easement, a license is not an interest in land. The person allowed to come into the house to use the phone has a license. The advertising company that has permission to paint a sign on the side of a building also has a license.

A license may be terminated at the will of the licensor and continues only as long as the licensor is the owner of the land.

FACTS:
Bunn and his wife claimed that they had an easement to enter and use the swimming pool on neighboring land. A contract between the former owners of the Bunn's property and the adjacent apartment complex contained a provision that the use of the apartment swimming pool would be available to the purchaser and family. No reference to the pool was made in the contract between the former owners and the Bunns nor was there any reference thereto in the deed conveying the property to the Bunns.

DECISION:
Judgment against the Bunns. The only right to use the swimming pool had been given to the original purchaser and family. No express statement was made in either the contract with or the deed to the original purchaser stating that subsequent owners could also use the swimming pool. The right to use the swimming pool given the first purchaser was therefore merely a license and was not transferred to a purchaser of the land. [Bunn v Offutt, 216 Va 681, 222 SE2d 522 (1976)]

---

[3] Auxier v Holmes (Mo App) 605 SW2d 804 (1980).

§ 52:4.   Liens.

Real property may be subject to liens that arise by the voluntary act of the owner of the land, such as the lien of a mortgage which is created when the owner voluntarily borrows money and the land is made security for the repayment of the debt. Liens may also arise involuntarily as in the case of tax liens, judgment liens, and mechanics' liens. In the case of taxes and judgments, the liens provide a means for enforcing the obligations of the owner of the land to pay the taxes or the judgment.

Mechanics' liens give persons furnishing labor and materials in the improvement of real estate the right to proceed against the real estate for the collection of the amounts due them.

§ 52:5.   Duration and Extent of Ownership.

The interest held by a person in real property may be defined in terms of the period of time for which such person will remain the owner, as (1) a fee simple estate or (2) a life estate. These estates are termed **freehold estates.** In addition, either of these estates may be subject to a condition or may expire or terminate upon the happening of a specified contingency. Although a person may own property for a specified number of years this interest is not regarded as a freehold estate, but is a **leasehold estate** and is subject to special rules of law.

(a) **Fee Simple Estate.** An **estate in fee, a fee simple** or a **fee simple absolute,** lasts forever. The owner of such fee has the absolute and entire interest in the land. The important characteristics of this estate are as follows: (1) it is alienable during life; (2) it is alienable by will; (3) it descends to heirs generally if not devised (transferred by will); (4) it is subject to rights of the owner's surviving spouse; and (5) it is liable for debts of the owner before or after death.

(b) **Life Estate.** A **life estate** (or life tenancy), as its name indicates, lasts only during the life of a person, ordinarily its owner. Upon the owner's death, no interest remains to pass to heirs or by will.

B. FIXTURES

By the concept of fixtures, personal property changes to real property and third persons and creditors may acquire rights therein.

§ 52:6.   Definition.

A **fixture** is personal property that is attached to the earth or placed in a building in such a way or under such circumstances that it is deemed part of the real property.

A person buys a refrigerator, an air conditioner, or a furnace, or some other item that is used in a building, and then has the item installed. The question whether the item is a fixture and therefore part of the building can arise in a variety of situations. (1) The real estate tax assessor assesses the building and adds in the value of the item on the theory that it is part of the building. (2) The buyer of the item owns the building and then sells the building, and the buyer of the building claims that the item stays with the building. (3) The buyer places the mortgage on the building, and the mortgagee claims that the item is bound by the mortgage. (4) The buyer is a tenant in the building in which the item is installed and the landlord claims that the item must stay in the building when the tenant leaves. (5) The buyer does not pay in full for the item, and the seller of the item has a security interest that the seller asserts against the buyer of the item or against the landlord of the building in which the buyer installs the item. The seller of the item may also be asserting a claim against the mortgagee of the building or against the buyer of the building.

The determination of the rights of these parties depends upon the common law of fixtures, as occasionally modified by statute.

§ 52:7.   Tests of a Fixture.

In the absence of an agreement between the parties, the courts apply three tests to determine whether the personal property has become a fixture:

(a) **Annexation.** Generally the personal property becomes a fixture if it is so attached to the realty that it cannot be removed without materially damaging the realty or destroying the personal property itself. If the property is so affixed as to lose its specific identity, such as bricks in a wall, it becomes part of the realty. Where railroad tracks are so placed as to be immovable, they are to be deemed fixtures.

(b) **Adaptation.** Personal property especially adapted or suited to the use made of the building may constitute a fixture.

(c) **Intent.** The true test is the intention of the person affixing the property at the time it was affixed.[4]

In the absence of direct proof of such intent, it is necessary to resort to the nature of the property, the method of its attachment, and all the surrounding circumstances to determine what the intent was.

FACTS:

In 1958, a supermarket was constructed and owned by Jacobs Realty Corporation. The market contained five large walk-in coolers or refrigerators. Title to the market was thereafter transferred to the Premonstratensian Fathers and was insured against fire by Badger Mutual Insurance Company. The building was severely damaged by fire and the insurer paid approximately $80,000 for the building damage. The Fathers claimed an additional $20,000 for the destruction of the coolers. The insurer refused to pay this amount and asserted that the coolers were not owned by the Fathers.

DECISION:

The coolers were fixtures because it was the intent of the affixer that they be permanently attached to the building. Moreover, there was such physical attachment to the building and such adaptation to use as to lead to the conclusion that the coolers had become fixtures. They were therefore owned by the Fathers as part of the building. [and were covered by fire insurance on the building. [Premonstratensian Fathers v Badger Mutual Insurance Co. 46 Wis 2d 362, 175 NW2d 337 (1970)]

---

[4]Norwalk Vault Co. v Mountain Grove Cemetery Ass'n, 180 Conn 680, 433 A2d 979 (1980).

The fact that machinery installed in a plant would be very difficult and expensive to move and so delicate that the moving would cause damage and unbalancing is significant in reaching the conclusion that the owner of the plant had installed the equipment as a permanent addition and thus had the intent which would make the equipment become fixtures. When the floors in a large apartment house are of concrete which is covered with a thin sheet of plywood to which is stapled wall to wall carpeting, the carpeting consitutes a fixture which cannot be removed from the building, as removal would probably destroy the carpeting, it having been cut to size, and the carpeting being necessary to make the building livable as an apartment.

§ 52:8.   Movable Machinery and Equipment.

Machinery and equipment that is movable is ordinarily held not to constitute fixtures, even though, in order to move it, it is necessary to unbolt it from the floor or to disconnect electrical wires or water pipes.

It is ordinarily held that refrigerators and freezers, and gas and electric ranges are not fixtures and do not lose their character as personal property when they are readily removable upon disconnecting pipes or unplugging wires. A portable window air conditioner which rests on a rack which is fixed to the window sill by two screws and is connected directly to the building only by an electric cord plug is not a fixture.

The mere fact that an item may be "unplugged," however, does not establish that it is not a fixture. For example, a computer and its related hardware constituted "fixtures" when there was such a mass of wires and cables under the floor that the installation gave the impression of permanence.

§ 52:9.   Trade Fixtures.

Equipment which is attached to a rented building by a tenant for use in trade or business is ordinarily removable by the tenant upon permanently leaving the premises. Such equipment is commonly called a **trade fixture**.[5]

C. LIABILITY TO THIRD PERSONS FOR CONDITION OF REAL PROPERTY

In the case of real estate, liability is ordinarily based upon occupancy. That is, the person in possession may be liable for harm to the third person caused by a condition of the premises, even though the occupier is not the owner but is merely a tenant renting the premises.

§ 52:10.   Status-of-Plaintiff Common-Law Rule.

Under the common law, liability to a person injured on real estate was controlled by the status of the injured person, that is, whether the person injured was a trespasser, a licensee, or an invitee. A different duty was owed by the occupier of land to each of these three categories.[6]

---

[5]B. Kreisman & Co. v First Arlington National Bank, 91 Ill App 3d 47, 47 Ill Dec 757, 415 NE2d 1070 (1981).
[6]Huyck v Hecla Mining Co. 101 Idaho 299, 612 P2d 142 (1980).

(a) **Trespassers.** As to **trespassers**, the occupier ordinarily owes only the duty of refraining from causing intentional harm once the presence of the trespasser is known; but the occupier is not under any duty to warn of dangers or to make the premises safe to protect the trespasser from harm. The most significant exception to this rule arises in the case of small children who, although trespassers, are generally afforded greater protection through the **attractive nuisance doctrine.** For example, the owner of a private residential swimming pool was liable for the drowning of a 5-year-old trespasser when the owner did not maintain adequate fencing around the pool, since the placing of such fencing would not have imposed a great burden.

(b) **Licensees.** As to **licensees**, who are on the premises with the permission of the occupier, the latter owes the duty of warning of nonobvious dangers that are known to the occupier. For example, a host must warn a guest of the known danger. Consequently where a sliding glass door was "invisible" when the patio lights were on and the house lights were off, the host must warn guests of the presence of the glass and is liable when the guest is injured in shattering the glass when reaching for a phone which was in fact on the other side of the glass.

In contrast, the occupier owes no duty to the licensee to take any steps to learn of the presence of unknown dangers.

FACTS:
Glen Harrod, age 12, had gone over to the house of his friend Aaron Grider, also age 12 to have dinner and attend a movie. Saccomen, the boys' football coach, was waiting for them at the house to take them to the movie. After dinner the three boys went to Aaron's room while Mrs. Grider performed chores in the kitchen. While goofing around in the bedroom, Saccomen picked up a BB gun believing it to be empty, and discharged it in the direction of Glenn. A BB struck Glenn in the armpit. He was taken to the hospital, kept overnight and discharged. Glenn's parents later filed suit against Mrs. Grider and Saccomen alleging various acts of negligence. Saccomen pleaded guilty. Mrs. Grider denied liability claiming the only duty she owed Glenn was the duty owed a social guest-licensee and that she had not breached that duty.

DECISION:
Judgment for Grider. A host is held to owe a social guest only the duty not to injure him by wilful, wanton, or gross negligence. The measure of duty of a person undertaking control and supervision of a child to exercise reasonable care for the safety of the child is to be gauged by the standard of the average reasonable parent; such person is not an insurer of the safety of the child and has no duty to foresee and guard against every possible hazard. [Harrod v Grider, (Tex App) 701 SW2d 937 (1985)]

(c) **Invitees.** As to **invitees**, whose presence is sought to further the economic interest of the occupier, such as customers, there is a duty to take reasonable steps to discover any danger and a duty to warn the invitee or to correct the danger. For example, a store must make a reasonable inspection of the premises to determine that there is nothing on the floor that would be dangerous, such as a slippery substance that might cause a patron to fall, and must either correct the condition or appropriately rope off the danger area or give suitable warning. If the occupier of the premises fails to conform to the degree of care described and harm results to an invitee on the premises, the occupier is liable for such harm.

In most states the courts have expanded the concept of invitees beyond the category of those persons whose presence will economically benefit the occupier so that it includes members of the public who are invited when it is apparent that such persons cannot be reasonably expected to make an inspection of the premises before making use of them and that they would not be making repairs to correct any dangerous condition. Some courts have also made inroads into the prior law by treating a recurring licensee, such as a letter carrier, as an invitee.

FACTS:

Wilson, a business invitee, stopped at the National Food Store in Ocean Springs to shop. Her bagged purchases were placed in a shopping cart belonging to National Food Store. As she proceeded toward her car with the cart full of groceries, the front wheel of the cart hit a pothole in the parking lot causing it to overturn. When she held on to the cart in an attempt to keep it from falling, she injured her back as the cart pulled her to the ground. Wilson sued the National Food Store on the ground of negligence. National claimed it was not liable to a third party for injuries received on property leased by National Food Stores from Chrisler Properties, the lessor.

DECISION:

Judgment for Wilson. Since the lessee occupied and controlled the premises, there was a duty on the lessee to repair the dangerous condition or to warn invitees coming onto the premises. National had possession and did exercise control of the parking lot in that National had errected a cart control there and its employees went onto the lot at least twelve times each day to gather the carts. It invited customers to park in the lot and in front of the store. Its presence and activities on the lot put it in the position to know of dangers and thereby gave rise to a duty to at least warn its invitees of those dangers. [Wilson v Allday (Miss) 487 So2d 793 (1986)]

---

§ 52:11. Negligence Rule.

Several courts have begun a strong new trend in ignoring these common-law distinctions and holding the occupier liable according to ordinary negligence standards; that is, when the occupier as a reasonable person should foresee from the circumstances that harm would be caused a third person, the occupier has the duty to take reasonable steps to prevent such harm, without regard to whether the potential victim would be traditionally classified as a trespasser, a licensee, or an invitee.[7]

---

[7]Rowland v Christian, 69 Cal 2d 108, 70 Cal Rptr 97, 443 P2d 561 (1968).

FACTS:

Ice Caves Mountain, Inc. operated a scenic park as a tourist attraction. One of the patrons fell into a crevice. Among the people coming to the patron's rescue were Miller and Basso. These two were riding on a motorcycle driven by Miller. When they arrived at the Ice Caves, they were told not to go to the scene of the accident. They nevertheless proceeded and took part in the rescue operation without any objection from those in charge. In returning from the rescue scene, the motorcycle hit some holes in the motor trail, went out of control, and threw both riders onto rocks. Basso sued Miller and Ice Caves. Basso claimed that Ice Caves owed him a duty to warn of the dangers of the road. Ice Caves claimed that Basso was merely a licensee and therefore there was no duty to warn him of any dangers.

DECISION:

Whether a duty was owed to warn of dangers depended upon whether the circumstances were such that a reasonable person would foresee that harm was likely to follow if no warning was given. The court refused to follow the common law rule by which the duty of the defendant was measured by whether the plaintiff was classified as an invitee, a licensee, or a trespasser. It was therefore necessary for a jury to determine whether the circumstances were such that a reasonable person in the position of Ice Caves would have foreseen harm to those using the road. If such harm was foreseeable, there was a duty to warn, regardless of whether Basso was an invitee, a licensee, or a trespasser. [Basso v Miller, 40 NY2d 233, 386 NY2d 564 (1976)]

§ 52:12.   Intermediate Rule.

Some courts have taken an intermediate position and have merely abolished the distinction between licensees and invitees so that the occupier owes the same duty of care to all lawful visitors; and whether one is a licensee or an invitee is merely a circumstance to be considered by the jury in applying the ordinary rule of negligence.

In some states, the distinction between licensees and invitees has been retained in name but destroyed in fact by requiring an occupier to warn the licensee of unknown dangers of which the occupier in the exercise of reasonable care should have known, or by classifying a licensee as an invitee.[8]

D. CO-OWNERSHIP OF REAL PROPERTY

All interests in particular real property may be held in severalty, that is by one person alone. As explained in Chapter 22, ownership in severalty also exists when title is held in the form of "A or B."

§ 52:13.   Multiple Ownership.

Several persons may have concurrent interests in the same real property. The forms of multiple ownership for real property are the same as those for personal property.[9]

[8]Caroff v Liberty Lumber Co. 146 NJ Super 353, 369 A2d 983 (1977) (holding that a public officer, such as a police officer or health inspector, who enters premises in the performance of official duties, has the same status as a business invitee when injured because of a condition of the premises).

[9]See Chapter 22.

When co-owners sell property, they hold the proceeds of sale by the same type of tenancy as they held the original property.

§ 52:14. Condominiums.

A **condominium** is a combination of co-ownership and individual ownership. For example, persons owning an office building or an apartment house by condominium are co-owners of the land and of the halls, lobby, elevators, stairways and exits; yards, gardens, and surrounding land; incinerator, laundry rooms, and other areas used in common; but each apartment or office in the building is individually owned by its occupant.

(a) Control and Expense. In some states, the owners of the various units in the condominium have equal voice in the management and share an equal part of its expenses. In others, control and liablty for expenses are shared by a unit owner in the same ratio that the value of the unit bears to the value of the entire condominium project. In all states, the unit owners have an equal right to use the common areas.

The owner of each condominium unit makes such repairs as are required by the owner's deed or contract of ownership, and the owner is prohibited from making any major change which would impair or damage the safety or value of an adjoining unit.

(b) Collection of Expenses from Unit Owner. When a unit owner fails to pay the owner's share of taxes, operating expenses, and repairs, it is commonly provided that a lien may be entered against that owner's unit for the amount which is due.

(c) Tort Liability. Most condominium projects fail to make provision as to the liability of unit owners for a tort occurring in the common areas. A few states expressly provide that when a third person is injured in the common areas a suit may only be brought against the condominium association and any judgment recovered is a charge against the association to be paid off as a common expense. When the condomimium association is incorporated, the same result should be obtained by applying ordinary principles of corporation law under which liability for torts occurring on the premises of the corporation are not the liability of the individual shareholders.

(d) Cooperatives Distinguished. Ownership in a condominium is to be distinguished from ownership in a **cooperative**. An apartment cooperative will typically be a corporation renting apartments to persons who are also owners of stock of the corporation. The apartment complex is owned only by the corporation and the only "ownership" interests of the stockholders are as tenants of their respective apartments or offices.

§ 52:15. Advantages of Condominium Ownership.

The owner of a condominium unit has the benefits of limited liability, greater tax deductions, and the ownership of property that can be transferred or sold.

(a) Freedom from Enterprise Liability. The ownership of a unit is not liable personally for an enterprise liability nor may the unit of the owner be taken to pay for such a liability.

(b) **Transferability of Unit.** The condominium unit is property which the unit owner can transfer as freely as any other kind of property.

(c) **Tax Deductions.** A deduction for a share of the mortgage interest and property taxes paid may be claimed by the unit owners on their individual income tax returns. Over a period of time, the unit owner can thus effect a tax savings which in effect will lower the cost of the condominium unit.

E. TRANSFER OF REAL PROPERTY BY DEED

Although many of the technical limitations of the feudal and earlier common-law days have disappeared, much of the law relating to the modern deed orginated in those days.

§ 52:16. Definitions.

A **deed** is an instrument or writing by which an owner or **grantor** transfers or conveys an interest in land to a new owner called a **grantee** or transferee.

Unlike a contract, no consideration is required to make a deed effective.[10] Although consideration is not required to make a valid deed or transfer of title by deed, the absence of consideration may be evidence to show that the transfer is made by the owner in fraud of creditors who may then be able to set aside the transfer.

Real property, as in the case of personal property, may either be sold or given as a gift. However, a deed is necessary to transfer title to land, even though it is a gift.

§ 52:17. Classification of Deeds.

Deeds may be classified in terms of the interest conveyed as (1) a **quitclaim deed,** which transfers merely whatever interest, if any, the grantor may have in the property, without specifying that interest in any way, and (2) a **warranty deed,** which purports to transfer a specified interest and which warrants or guarantees that such interest is transferred.

A deed may also be classified as a common-law deed or a statutory deed. The **common-law deed** is a long form that sets forth the details of the transaction. The statutory deed in substance merely recites that a named person is making a certain conveyance to a named grantee.

§ 52:18. Execution of Deeds.

Ordinarily a deed must be signed, by signature or mark, or sealed by the grantor. In order to have the deed recorded, statutes generally require that two or more witnesses sign the deed and that the grantor then acknowledge the deed before a notary public or other officer. In the interest of legibility, it is frequently required that the signature of the parties be followed by their printed or typewritten names.

In many states the statute that authorizes a short or simplified form of deed also declares that no seal is required to make effective a writing which purports to convey an interest in land.

[10]Robinson v Thompson, 192 Neb 428, 222 NW2d 123 (1974).

A deed must be executed and delivered by a person having capacity. It may be set aside by the grantor on the ground of the fraud of the grantee provided that innocent third persons have not acquired rights in the land.

The deed remains binding as between the grantor and the grantee even though it has not been acknowledged or recorded.

§ 52:19.   Delivery of Deeds.

A deed has no effect and title does not pass until the deed has been delivered. Delivery is a matter of intent as shown by words and conduct,[11] no particular form of ceremony is required. The essential intent in delivering a deed is not merely that the grantor intends to hand over physical control and possession of the paper on which the deed is written, but that the grantor intends thereby to transfer the ownership of the property described in the deed. That is, the grantor must deliver the deed with the intent that it should take effect as a deed and convey an interest in the property.

FACTS:

Jennie Shroyer executed a deed transferring her farm to Wayne and Wesley, the sons of her deceased brother. By her will, Jennie left the same farm to Jessie, the widow of her deceased brother. An action was brought after Jennie's death to determine who owned Jennie's farm. The evidence showed that, after Jennie had executed the deed, it was acknowledged before a notary public and shown to Wayne, who looked at it and returned it to Jennie. Thereafter, she remained in possession of the land and acted in all respects as though she still owned it. However, Jennie told other persons that the boys were the owners of the farm and she was merely holding the deed for safekeeping. The unrecorded deed was found among Jennie's papers after her death. An action was brought by Jessie to cancel the deed on the ground that it was not effective because it had never been delivered.

DECISION:

The fact that the deed was found among the papers of the grantor at the time of her death and that it had never been recorded raised a presumption that it had never been delivered. This placed upon the grantee in the deed the burden of proving that the deed in fact was delivered. This was not done and therefore it must be concluded that the deed had never been delivered. Jennie's conduct was consistent with this conclusion. Her continued use of the farm as her own indicated that it was her intention that the farm should belong to her grantees after her death. The deed was never effective as a deed and the land passed under Jennie's will at her death. [Shroyer v Shroyer (Mo) 425 SW2d 214 (1968)]

A deed is ordinarily made effective by handing it to the grantee with the intention that the grantee should thenceforth be the owner of the property described in the deed. A delivery may also be made by placing the deed, addressed to the grantee, in the mail or by giving it to a third person with directions to hand it to the grantee.

[11]Smith v Smith (Tex Civ App) 607 SW2d 617 (1980).

When a deed is delivered to a third person for the purpose of delivery to the grantee upon the happening of some event or contingency, the transaction is called a **delivery in escrow.** No title passes until the fulfillment of the condition or the happening of the event or contingency.

An effective delivery of a deed may be made symbolically as by delivering to the grantee the key to a locked box and informing the grantee that the deed to the property is in the box.

§ 52:20.   Acceptance of Deeds.

Generally there must be an acceptance by the grantee. In all cases an acceptance is presumed. However, the grantee may disclaim the transfer if the grantee acts within a reasonable time after learning that the transfer has been made.

§ 52:21.   Recording of Deeds.

If the owner of lands desires to do so, the deed may be recorded in the office of a public official sometimes called a recorder or commissioner of deeds. The recording is not required to make the deed effective to pass title but it is done so that the public will know that the grantee is the present owner and thereby prevent the former owner from making any other transaction relating to the property. The recording statutes provide that a person purchasing land from the last holder of record will take title free of any unrecorded claim to the land of which the purchaser does not have notice or knowledge.

The fact that a deed is recorded charges everyone with knowledge of its existence even though they in fact do not know of it because they have neglected to examine the record. The recording of a deed, however, is only such notice if the deed was properly executed. Likewise, the grantee of land cannot claim any protection by virtue of the recording of a deed when (1) a claim is made by one whose title is superior to that of the owner of record; (2) the grantee had notice or knowledge of the adverse claim when title was acquired; (3) a person acting under a hostile claim was then in possession of the land; (4) the grantee received the land as a gift; or (5) the transfer to the grantee was fraudulent.

§ 52:22.   Additional Protection of Buyers.

Apart from the protection given to buyers and third persons by the recorded title to property, a buyer may generally also be protected by procuring title insurance or an **abstract of title,** which is a summarized report of the title to the property as shown by the records, together with a report of all judgments, mortgages, and similar claims against the property that have been recorded.

§ 52:23.   Cancellation of Deeds.

A deed, although delivered, acknowledged, and recorded may be set aside or canceled by the grantor upon proof of such circumstances as would warrant the setting aside of a contract. For example, when a conveyance is made in consideration of a promise to support the grantor, the failure of the grantee to perform will ordinarily justify cancellation of the deed.

§ 52:24.   Grantor's Warranties.

The warranties of the grantor relate to the title transferred by the grantor and to the fitness of the property for use.

(a) **Warranties of Title.** In the common-law deed the grantor may expressly warrant or make certain covenants as to the title conveyed. The statutes authorizing a short form of deed provide that unless otherwise stated in the deed, the grantor shall be presumed to have made certain warranties of title.

The more important of the covenants or warranties of title which the grantor may make are: (1) **covenant of seisin,** or guarantee that the grantor owns the exact estate conveyed; (2) **covenant of right to convey,** or guarantee that the grantor, if not the owner, as in the case of an agent, has the right or authority to make the conveyance; (3) **covenant against encumbrances,** or guarantee that the land is not subject to any right or interest of a third person, such as a lien or easement; (4) **covenant for quiet enjoyment,** or covenant by the grantor that the grantee's possession of the land shall not be disturbed either by the grantor, in the case of a limited covenant, or by the grantor or any person claiming title under the grantor, in the case of a general covenant; and (5) **covenant for further assurances,** or promise that the grantor will execute any additional documents that may be required to perfect the title of the grantee.

(b) **Fitness for Use.** In the absence of an express warranty in the deed, no warranty as to fitness arises under the common law in the sale or conveyance of real estate. Thus, by the common law there is no implied warranty that a house is reasonably fit for habitation, even though it is a new house sold by the builder.[12]

In accord with a modern trend, however, courts in most of the states hold that when a builder or real estate developer sells a new house to a home buyer, an implied warranty that the house and foundation are fit for occupancy or use arises without regard to whether the house was purchased before, during, or after completion of construction. This warranty will not be implied against the first buyer when the house is resold, but there is authority that the second buyer may sue the original contractor for breach of the implied warranty, as against the contention that lack of privity of contract barred suit.[13]

FACTS:
    Fred Hunt Company was a building contractor. It purchased a tract of land on which it built a house that it sold to the Dentons in December 1978. They sold it to the American Foundation Life Insurance Company which in

---

[12]The buyer of a house should give notice to the seller of any defects within a reasonable time after the buyer learns or should have learned of the defects. Pollard v Saxe & Yolles Development Co. 12 Cal 3d 374, 115 Cal Rptr 648, 525 P2d 88 (1974) (extending the concept of UCC § 2–607(3), although recognizing that it was applicable only to the sale of goods).

[13]Barnes v MacBrown and Co., Inc. 264 Ind 227, 342 NE2d 619 (1976).

June 1979 sold the property to J. T. Blagg and his wife Kathye. Shortly after the Blaggs moved into the house they smelled a strong odor coming from the carpeting. The Blaggs sued Fred Hunt claiming he was liable for breach of the implied warranty of habitability. Hunt denied liability claiming the builder-vendor only impliedly warranted the home to the first purchaser.

DECISION:

Judgment for the Blaggs. The original homebuyer has been able to place reliance on the builder-vendor's implied warranty. These same basic concepts should be extended to subsequent purchasers of real estate. The defect became apparent within a reasonable time after the purchase. The builder-vendor's implied warranty of fitness for habitability runs not only in favor of the first owner, but extends to subsequent purchasers for a reasonable time where there is no substantial change or alteration in the condition of the building from the original sale. This warranty, however, is limited to latent defects which are not discoverable by subsequent purchasers upon reasonable inspection. [Blagg v Fred Hunt Company (Ark) 612 SW2d 321 (1981)]

---

§ 52:25. Grantee's Covenants.

In a deed the grantee may agree to do or to refrain from doing certain acts. Such an agreement becomes a binding contract between the grantor and the grantee. The grantor may sue the grantee for its breach. When the covenant of the grantee relates directly to the property conveyed, such as an agreement to maintain fences on the property or that the property shall be used only for residential purposes, it is said not only that the covenant is binding between the grantor and the grantee but also that it **runs with the land.** This means that anyone acquiring the grantee's land from the grantee is also bound by the covenant of the grantee, even though this subsequent owner had not made any such agreement with anyone.

The right to enforce the covenant also runs with the land owned by the grantor to whom the promise was made. Thus, if A owns adjoining tracts of land and conveys one of them to B and B covenants to maintain the surface drainage on the land so that it will not flood A's land, the benefit of this covenant will run with the land retained by A. If A sells the remaining tract of land to C, B is bound to perform the covenant so as to benefit the neighboring tract even though it is now owned by C.

A covenant which provides that the grantee shall refrain from certain conduct is termed a **restrictive** (or negative) **covenant.** It runs with the land in the same manner as a covenant that calls for the performance of an act, that is, an **affirmative covenant.**

FACTS:

A real estate developer conveyed separate lots to Hannaford and the Dotsons. The deeds specified that "no lot owner shall erect a dwelling...that has less than 1150 square feet inside living area." The Dotsons permitted the father of Mrs. Dotson and his wife to keep their mobile home on their lot. The father and his wife slept in the mobile home and had their meals in the Dotson home. The mobile home had only 500 feet of inside living area. Hannaford sued to stop the use of the mobile home on the Dotson lot, claiming that it violated the restrictive covenant.

DECISION:

A restrictive covenant is to be interpreted in favor of the grantee. The mobile home was not attached in any way to the land and therefore was not "erected" on the lot. Consequently the covenant did not apply to the mobile home in question. [Dotson v Hannaford, 226 Ga 732, 177 SE2d 376 (1970)]

§ 52:26. Scope of Grantee's Restrictive Covenants.

A **restrictive covenant** may impose both a limitation on the kind of structure that can be erected on the land and the use which may be made.

(a) **General Building Scheme.** When a tract of land is developed and individual lots or homes are sold to separate purchasers, it is common to use the same restrictive covenants in all deeds in order to impose uniform restrictions and patterns on the property. Any person acquiring a lot within the tract is bound by the restrictions if they are in the deed or a prior recorded deed, or the grantee has notice or knowledge of such restrictions. Any person owning one of the lots in the tract may bring suit against another lot owner to enforce the restrictive covenant. The effect is to create a zoning code based upon the agreement of the parties in their deeds, as distinguished from one based upon government regulation.

(b) **Restraints on Alienation.** The covenants of the grantee may restrict the sale or transfer of the property. It is lawful to provide that the grantor shall have the option to purchase the property, or that if the grantee offers to sell it to anyone, the grantor will be given an opportunity to match the price that a third person is willing to pay. Restrictions on the grantee's right to sell the property are not enforceable when the restriction discriminates against potential buyers because of race, color, creed, or national origin.

F. OTHER METHODS OF TRANSFERRING REAL PROPERTY

Title to real property can also be acquired by eminent domain and by adverse possession.

§ 52:27. Eminent Domain.

By **eminent domain** property is taken from its private owner and the title is acquired by the taking government or public authority. Two important questions arise: namely, whether there is a taking of property, and whether the property is taken for a public use. In respect to the first, it is not necessary that the owner be physically deprived of the property. It is sufficient that the normal use of the property has been impaired or lost. As to the second, it is not necessary that the public at large actually use the property. It is sufficient that it is appropriated for the public benefit.

§ 52:28. Adverse Possession.

Title to land may be acquired by holding it adversely to the true owner for a certain period of time. In such a case, the possessor gains title by

adverse possession. If such possession is maintained, the possessor automatically becomes the owner of the property, even though the possessor admittedly had no lawful claim to the land.

In order to acquire title in this manner, possession must be (1) actual, (2) visible and notorious, (3) exclusive, (4) hostile, and (5) continuous for a required period of time.[14]

Commonly the period of time is 21 years but statutes may provide 10 to 20 years. Occupation of land in the mistaken belief that one is the owner is a "hostile" possession.

FACTS:

Bradt believed his back yard ran all the way to a fence. Actually there was a strip on Bradt's side of the fence which belonged to his neighbor, Giovannone. Bradt never intended to take land away from anyone. Bradt later brought an action against Giovannone to determine who owned the strip on Bradt's side of the fence.

DECISION:

The strip was owned by Bradt by adverse possession, even though such possession was based on a mistake and he had not intended to deprive anyone of the land. Bradt in fact possessed the strip of land to the exclusion of the rest of the world and did so in the belief that he was its owner, which was therefore a possession adverse to everyone else. [Bradt v Giovannone, 35 App Div 2d 322, 315 NYS2d 961 (1970)]

G. MORTGAGES

An agreement that creates an interest in real property as security for an obligation and which is to cease upon the performance of the obligation is a **mortgage.** The person whose interest in the property is given as security is the **mortgagor.** The person who receives the security is the **mortgagee.**

§ 52:29.   Characteristics of a Mortgage.

There are three outstanding characteristics of a mortgage: (1) the termination of the mortgagee's interest upon the performance of the obligation secured by the mortgage; (2) the right of the mortgagee to enforce the mortgage by foreclosure upon the mortgagor's failure to perform; and (3) the mortgagor's right to redeem or regain the property. In any case, however, the intention of the parties determines whether there is a mortgage.

FACTS:

Donohoe owed money to Osborne. In order to pay the debt, he conveyed a tract of land to Osborne and the parties agreed that the debt was canceled. The deed contained a clause

that Osborne and the parties agreed that the debt was canceled. The deed contained a clause that Osborne would reconvey the land to Donohoe if the amount of the canceled debt were paid. In a suit against Landoe, Osborne's execu-

[14]Wojahn v Johnson, __ Minn __, 297 NW2d 298 (1980).

tor, Donohoe claimed that the deed was merely a mortgage.

DECISION:

The debt of Donohoe had been canceled when he executed the deed. Since there was no debt, there could be no mortgage. The instrument was therefore a deed. [Donohoe v Landoe, 126 Mont 351, 251 P2d 567 (1953)]

---

§ 52:30.   Property Subject to Mortgage.

In general, any form of property that may be sold or conveyed may be mortgaged. It is immaterial whether the right is a present right or a future interest, or merely a right in the land of another. It is not necessary that the mortgagor have complete or absolute ownership in the property. The mortgagor may mortgage any interest, legal or equitable, divided or undivided.

§ 52:31.   Form of Mortgage.

As a mortgage upon real property transfers an interest in the property, it must be in writing by virtue of the statute of frauds.

As a general rule, no particular form of language is required, provided the language used expresses the intent of the parties to create a mortgage. In many states, the substance of a mortgage is practically indentical to that of a deed with the exception that a mortgage contains a defeasance clause, a description of the obligation secured, and sometimes a covenant to pay or perform the obligation. The **defeasance clause** states that the mortgage shall cease to have any effect when the obligation is performed, as when the debt of the mortgagor is paid. In many states, statutes provide a standardized form of mortgage that may be used.

§ 52:32.   Recording or Filing of Mortgage.

An unrecorded mortgage is valid and binding between the parties to it. The heirs or donees of a mortgagor cannot defend against the mortgage on the ground that it has not been recorded. Recording statutes in most states, however, provide that purchasers or creditors who give value and act in good faith in ignorance of an unrecorded mortgage may enforce their respective rights against the property without regard to the existence of the unrecorded mortgage. Accordingly, the purchaser of the land in good faith for value from the mortgagor holds the land free of the unrecorded mortgage, and the mortgagee's only remedy is against the mortgagor on the debt due the mortgagee. The mortgagee can proceed against the transferee only if the mortgagee can prove that the transferee of the land did not purchase it in good faith, for value, and in ignorance of the unrecorded mortgage.

§ 52:33.   Repairs and Improvements.

In the absence of an agreement to the contrary, a mortgagor is under no duty to make improvements or to restore or repair parts of the premises that are destroyed or damaged through no fault of the mortgagor.

A mortgagee, when in possession, must make reasonable and necessary repairs in order to preserve the property and is entitled to reimbursement for such repairs. Ordinarily, however, the mortgagee may not charge to the mortgagor expenditures for valuable or enduring improvements.

§ 52:34. Taxes, Assessments, and Insurance.

The duty to pay taxes and assessments rests upon the mortgagor. In the absence of an agreement, neither party is under a duty to insure the mortgaged property. Both parties, however, may insure their respective interests. It is common practice for the mortgagor to obtain a single policy of insurance on the property payable to the mortgagee and the mortgagor as their interests may appear.

§ 52:35. Impairment of Security.

The mortgagor is liable to the mortgagee for any damage to the property, caused by the mortgagor's fault, that impairs the security of the mortgage by materially reducing the value of the property. Both the mortgagor and the mortgagee have a right of action against a third person who wrongfully injures the property.

FACTS:

The mortgagor removed dirt and gravel from his land and sold it to the Berns Construction Co. The mortgagee claimed that he could not do so because that impaired the value of the land. The mortgagor claimed that he could do so because, as mortgagor, he was still the owner and could use the land to make money.

DECISION:

The mortgagor could not remove anything from the land when it would result in a permanent loss to the land. The earth once removed was gone forever. This was improper regardless of what was left or the actual value of what was taken. This contrasts with the growing of things on the land, as such things may be removed by the mortgagor and sold. [Berns Construction Co. v Highley (CA7 Ind) 332 F2d 240 (1964)]

---

§ 52:36. Transfer of Interest.

Questions arise as to transfers by the mortgagor and the mortgagee of their respective interests and of the liability of a transferee of the mortgagor.

(a) **Transfer by Mortgagor.** The mortgagor may ordinarily transfer the land without the consent of the mortgagee. Such a transfer passes only the interest of the mortgagor and does not divest or impair the mortgage if properly recorded.

The transfer of the property by the mortgagor does not affect the liability of the mortgagor to the mortgagee. Unless the latter has agreed to substitute the mortgagor's grantee for the mortgagor, the latter remains liable for the mortgage debt as though no transfer had been made.

(b) **Liability of Mortgagor's Transferee.** The purchaser of mortgaged property does not become personally liable for the mortgage debt unless the purchaser expressly assumes that debt. Such an assumption of the debt does not release the mortgagor from liability to the mortgagee unless the mortgagee agrees to such substitution of parties.

(c) **Transfer by Mortgagee.** In most states, a mortgage may be transferred or assigned by the mortgagee.

§ 52:37.   Rights of Mortgagee after Default.

Upon the mortgagor's default, the mortgagee in some states is entitled to obtain possession of the property and collect the rents[15] or to have a receiver appointed for that purpose. In all states, the mortgagee may enforce the mortgage by **foreclosure** or sue to enforce the mortgage debt.

Generally it is provided that upon any default under the terms of the mortgage agreement, the mortgagee has the right to declare that the entire mortgage debt is due even though the default related only to an installment or to the doing of some act, such as maintaining insurance on the property or producing receipts for taxes.

A sale on the foreclosure of the mortgage destroys the mortgage, and the property passes to the buyer at the sale free of the mortgage. But the extinction of the mortgage by foreclosure does not destroy the debt that was secured by the mortgage. The mortgagor remains liable for any unpaid balance or deficiency, although by statute, the mortgagor is generally given credit for the fair value of the property if it was purchased by the mortgagee.

§ 52:38.   Rights of Mortgagor After Default.

After default the mortgagor may seek to stop or stay foreclosure or to redeem the mortgaged land.

(a) **Stay of Foreclosure.** In certain cases, authorized by statute, a **stay** (or delay) **of foreclosure** may be obtained by the mortgagor to prevent undue hardship.

(b) **Redemption.** The **right of redemption** means the right of the mortgagor to free the property of the mortgage lien after default. By statute in many states, the right may be exercised during a certain time following foreclosure and sale of the mortgaged land.

SUMMARY

Real property includes land, buildings and fixtures, and rights in the land of another such as easements.

The interest held by a person in real property may be defined in terms of the period of time for which such person will remain the owner and may be a fee simple estate or a life estate. These estates are known as freehold estates.

---

[15]Pine Lawn Bank and Trust Co. v M. H. & H. Inc. (Mo App) 607 SW2d 696 (1980).

Property that was once personal property may be attached in such a way to the real property that it is deemed part of the real property. In such a case it is called a fixture. To determine whether property has in fact become a fixture, the courts look to: the method of attachment, how the property has been adapted to the realty, and the intent of the person attaching the property.

The liability of an occupier of land for injury to third persons on the premises is dependent upon the status of the third persons as trespassers, licensees, or invitees. Many jurisdictions are ignoring these common law distinctions, however, in favor of an ordinary negligence standard.

Real property may be the subject of multiple ownership. The forms of multiple ownership are the same as for personal property. In addition, there are special forms of coownership for real property, such as condominiums and cooperatives.

A deed is an instrument transferring an interest in land by a grantor to a grantee. A deed can be a quitclaim deed, a warranty deed, or a statutory deed. A deed to be effective must be signed or sealed by the grantor and delivered to the grantee. Recording the deed is not required to make the deed effective to pass title but provides notice to the public that the grantee is the present owner. The warranties of the grantor relate to the title transferred by the grantor and to the fitness of the property for use. Absent any express warranty in the deed, no warranty of fitness arises under the common law in the sale or the conveyance of real estate. A substantial number of states today hold that when the builder or real estate developer sells a new home to a home buyer, an implied warranty of habitability arises. Title to real estate may also be acquired by eminent domain and adverse possession.

An agreement that creates an interest in real property as security for an obligation and which ends upon the performance of the obligation is a mortgage. A mortgage must be in writing under the statute of frauds. If the mortgage is unrecorded, it is valid between the parties. The mortgage should be recorded to put good faith purchasers on notice of the mortgage. A purchaser of the mortgaged property does not become liable for the mortgaged debt unless such purchaser assumes the mortgage. The mortgagor still remains liable unless the mortgagee agrees to a substitution of parties. If the mortgagor defaults, the mortgagee may enforce the mortgage by foreclosure. Such foreclosure may be delayed because of undue hardship.

QUESTIONS AND CASE PROBLEMS

1. What social forces are affected by recognizing the right of aircraft to fly over land at such a height that the flight does not interfere with the use of the land and is not dangerous to persons or property on the land?
2. Edward makes a contract to sell his house to Frank. They sign a written contract which states that Edward is obligated to convey a fee simple estate. Edward claims that the contract should be reformed because it does not state the intention of the parties that Frank was to convey the complete ownership of the land. Is Edward correct?
3. Price sued Whisnant for cutting and removing trees from certain land. Price claimed title to the land by adverse possession. He proved that for

over twenty years he had from time to time entered on the land and cut and removed trees. Was Price the owner of the land by adverse possession? [Price v Whisnant, 236 NC 381, 72 SE2d 851]

4. Cindy owned and operated a jewelry store. She moved the store into a new building in which she rented space for five years. She moved her showcases, chairs, lighting fixtures, and other equipment from her original store to the newly rented store. When the lease expired at the end of the five years, Cindy moved out and was about to take the showcases, chairs, lighting fixtures, and other equipment with her. The landlord objected and claimed that those items had become fixtures and therefore Cindy was required to leave them when she left. Was the landlord correct?

5. Lucille signed, sealed, and delivered to her niece, Reba, a deed by which Lucille conveyed her house to Reba. After Lucille's death, her son, Julius, claimed that the house belonged to him and that the deed was not valid because it had never been acknowledged before a notary public and had never been recorded. Is he correct?

6. Compare (a) an easement, (b) a profit, and (c) a fixture.

7. Compare the status of an apartment "owner" in (a) a condominium and (b) a cooperative.

8. What is the most important difference between a license and an easement?

9. Bradham and others, trustees of the Mount Olivet Church, brought an action to cancel a mortgage on the church property that had been executed by Davis and others as trustees of the church and given to Robinson as mortgagee. It was found by the court that the church was not indebted to the mortgagee for any amount. Should the mortgage be canceled? [Bradham v Robinson, 236 NC 589, 73 SE2d 555]

10. Miller executed a deed to real estate naming Mary Zieg as grantee. He placed the deed in an envelope on which was written, "To be filed at my death," and put the envelope and deed in a safe deposit box in the National Bank. The box had been rented in the names of Miller and Mary Zieg. After his death Mary removed the deed from the safe deposit box. Moseley, as executor under Miller's will, brought an action against Mary to declare the deed void. Decide. [Moseley v Zieg, 180 Neb 810, 146 NW2d 72]

11. Henry Lile owned a house. When the land on which it was situated was condemned for a highway, he removed the house to the land of his daughter, Sarah Crick. In the course of construction work, blasting damaged the house and Sarah Crick sued the contractors, Terry & Wright. They claimed that Henry should be joined in the action as a plaintiff and that Sarah could not sue by herself because it was Henry's house. Were the defendants correct? [Terry & Wright v Crick (Ky) 418 SW2d 217]

12. Malone and Roper owned adjoining lots. There was a short driveway from Roper's garage to the highway. This driveway ran along the boundary of Roper's land. Roper allowed Malone to use Roper's driveway as there was no driveway on the land of Malone. Roper sold his house to Girard. Girard wanted to add some rooms on the driveway side

of his house, shutting off the existing driveway and moving the driveway to the other side of the house. If the driveway was moved in this manner, it could not be used by Malone. Malone claimed that Girard could not close the existing driveway. Was he correct?

13. Sears Roebuck and Co. supplied the Seven Palms Motor Inn with window drapes and rods and matching bedspreads. When payment was not made, it claimed that these were fixtures for which a mechanic's lien could be asserted. Were they fixtures?

14. Larry Wiersema was building a house for himself in the country. He made a contract with Workman Plumbing, Heating & Cooling, Inc. to do most of the plumbing and heating work in the new house. This included the installation of a septic tank. Workman performed the contract correctly but, because of the peculiar kind of clay surrounding the house, the drainage from the septic tank system was very poor and the basement of Larry's house was frequently flooded. He sued Workman for breach of the implied warranty of habitability. Was Workman liable? [Wiersema v Workman Plumbing, Heating & Cooling, Inc. 87 Ill App 3d 535, 42 Ill Dec 664, 409 NE2d 159]

15. Davis Store Fixtures sold certain equipment on credit to Head, who installed it in a building which was later owned by the Cadillac Club. When payment was not made, Davis sought to repossess the equipment. If the equipment constituted fixtures, this could not be done. The equipment consisted of a bar for serving drinks, a bench, and a drainboard. The first two were attached to the floor or wall with screws, and the drainboard was connected to water and drainage pipes. Did the equipment constitute fixtures?

16. Lyle, Inc., a Montana corporation, purchased certain land in Florida from Albert but neglected to record the deed. Sometime thereafter, Albert sold the same property to Harrison, a resident of Florida, who purchased in good faith and recorded his deed. In a suit by Lyle against Harrison to resolve the title question, who will succeed?

17. Rider moved onto Laura's undeveloped land without permission. Sometime thereafter, Laura learned from friends that Rider was there. Laura told Rider that he could remain there indefinitely without paying rent if he would keep the land clear of underbrush and trespassers. Rider agreed and did so for some fifteen years which was the statutory period in the state for obtaining title by adverse possession. Rider eventually alleged he had title by adverse possession. Was Rider correct?

18. Smikahl sold to Hansen a tract of land on which there were two houses and four trailer lots equipped with concrete patios and necessary connections for utility lines. The tract purchased by Hansen was completely surrounded by the land owned by Smikahl and third persons. In order to get onto the highway, it was necessary to cross the Smikahl tract. Several years later, Smikahl put a barbed wire fence around his land. Hansen sued to prevent obstruction to travel between his land and the highway over the Smikahl land. Smikahl defended on the ground that no such right of travel had been given to Hansen. Was he correct? [Hansen v Smikahl, 173 Neb 309, 113 NW2d 210]

CHAPTER 53

LEASES

CHAPTER OBJECTIVES

After studying this chapter you will be able to:
1. Define a lease and list its essential elements.
2. List the ways in which a lease may be terminated.
3. List and explain the rights and duties of the parties to a lease.
4. Describe the remedies of a landlord for breach by the tenant.
5. Describe the liability of the landlord for injury on the premises sustained by the tenant and by a third person.
6. Define and distinguish between assignments of a lease and a sublease.
7. Solve problems involving questions as to leases.

By a lease, one person has for a time the possession and benefit of real property owned by another.

A. CREATION AND TERMINATION

Leases are governed by the common law of property as modified by judicial decisions and statutes.[1]

§ 53:1. Definition and Nature.

The agreement by which one person holds possession of the real property owned by another is a **lease**.

[1]A uniform act, the Uniform Residential Landlord and Tenant Act (URLTA), has been adopted in Alaska, Arizona, Florida, Hawaii, Iowa, Kansas, Kentucky, Montana, Nebraska, New Mexico, Oregon, Tennessee, and Virginia.

The person who owns the real property and permits the occupation of the premises is known as the **lessor** or **landlord**. The **lessee** or **tenant** is the one who occupies the property. A **lease** establishes the relationship of landlord and tenant.

Basically a lease parallels a bailment in which there is an agreement to make the bailment and a subsequent transfer of possession to carry out that agreement. In the case of a lease, there is the lease contract and the interest thereafter acquired by the tenant when possession is delivered under the lease contract. The common law looked at the transfer of possession and regarded the lease as merely the creation of an interest in land. The modern law looks at the contract and regards the lease as the same as the renting of an automobile. With this new approach, typical contract law concepts of unconscionability, mitigation of damages, and the implication of warranties are brought into the law of leases.

§ 53:2. Creation of the Lease Relationship.

The relationship of landlord and tenant is created by an express or implied contract. An oral lease is valid at common law, but statutes in most states require written leases for certain tenancies. Many states provide that a lease for a term exceeding three years must be in writing. Statutes in other states require written leases when the term exceeds one year.

(a) **Antidiscrimination.** Statutes in many states prohibit an owner who rents property for profit from discriminating against prospective tenants on the basis of race, color, religion, or national origin. Enforcement of such statutes is generally entrusted to an administrative agency.

(b) **Covenants and Conditions.** Some obligations of the parties in the lease are described as covenants. Thus, a promise by the tenant to make repairs is called a **covenant to repair**. Sometimes it is provided that the lease shall be forfeited or terminated upon a breach of a promise, and that provision is then called a **condition** rather than a covenant.

(c) **Other Agreements.** The lease may be the only agreement between the parties. In contrast, there may also be a separate guaranty or a letter of credit to protect the landlord from breach by the tenant. The tenant, in addition to holding under the lease may also hold a franchise from the lessor.

(d) **Unconscionability.** At common law, the parties to a lease had a relatively uncontrolled freedom to include such terms as they chose. As the lease is increasingly treated as a contract, some states require that leases conform to the concept of conscionability and follow the pattern of UCC § 2–302.[2] A provision in a residential lease stating that curtailment of services by the landlord would not constitute an eviction unless caused willfully or by gross negligence and that such interruption would not entitle the tenant to any compensation is unconscionable and does not bar the tenant from suing for breach of the warranty of habitability. Similarly, a provision in a lease declaring that the landlord would not be responsible for interruptions in

---

[2]Flam v Herrmann, 90 Misc 2d 434, 395 NYS2d 136 (1977); URLTA § 1.303.

the various services provided tenants will not protect the landlord when the air conditioning system was out of operation for six weeks in midsummer.

§ 53:3. Essential Elements.

The following elements are necessary to the establishment of the relation of landlord and tenant:

(a) The occupying of the land must be with the express or implied consent of the landlord.
(b) The tenant must occupy the premises in subordination to the rights of the landlord.
(c) A reversionary interest in the land must remain in the landlord. That is, the landlord must be entitled to retake the possession of the land upon the expiration of the lease.
(d) The tenant must have an estate of present possession in the land. This means a right to be in possession of the land now.

§ 53:4. Classification of Tenancies.

Tenancies are classified as to duration, as tenancies for years, from year to year, at will, and by sufferance.

(a) Tenancy for Years. A **tenancy for years** is one under which the tenant has an estate of definite duration. The term "for years" is used to describe such a tenancy even though the duration of the tenancy is for only one year or for less than a year.

(b) Tenancy from Year to Year. A **tenancy from year to year** is one under which a tenant, holding an estate in land for an indefinite duration, pays an annual, monthly, or weekly rent. A distinguishing feature of this tenancy is the fact that it does not terminate at the end of a year, month, or week except upon proper notice.

In almost all states a tenancy from year to year is implied if the tenant holds over after a tenancy for years with the consent of the landlord, as shown by an express statement or by conduct such as continuing to accept rent.[3] The lease will frequently state that a holding over shall give rise to a tenancy from year to year unless written notice to the contrary be given.

(c) Tenancy at Will. When land is held for an indefinite period, which may be terminated at any time by the landlord or the tenant, a **tenancy at will** exists. A person who enters into possession of land for an indefinite period with the owner's permission but without any agreement as to rent is a tenant at will.

Statutes in some states and decisions in others require advance notice of termination of this type of tenancy.

(d) Tenancy by Sufferance. When a tenant holds over without permission of the landlord, the latter may treat the tenant as a trespasser or as

---

[3]In some jurisdictions, when rent is accepted from a tenant holding over after the expiration of the term of the lease and there is no agreement to the contrary, there results only a periodic tenancy from month to month rather than a tenancy from year to year. S.D.G. v Inventory Control Co. 178 NJ Super 411, 429 A2d 394 (1981).

a tenant. Until the landlord elects to do one or the other, a **tenancy by sufferance** exists.

§ 53:5. Termination of Lease.

A lease is generally not terminated by the death, insanity, or bankruptcy of either party, except in the case of a tenancy at will. Provisions in a lease giving the landlord the right to terminate the lease under certain conditions are generally strictly construed.

Leases may be terminated in the following ways:

(a) **Termination by Notice.** A lease may give the landlord the power to terminate it by giving notice to the tenant. In states which follow the common law, it is immaterial why the landlord terminates the lease by notice.

(b) **Expiration of Term in a Tenancy for Years.** When a tenancy for years exists, the relation of landlord and tenant ceases upon the expiration of the term, without any requirement that one party give the other any notice of termination. Express notice to end the term may be required of either or both parties by provisions of the lease, except when a statute prohibits the landlord from imposing such a requirement.

(c) **Notice in a Tenancy from Year to Year.** In the absence of an agreement of the parties, notice is now usually governed by statute. Thirty or sixty days' notice is generally required to end a tenancy from year to year. As to tenancies for periods of less than a year, the provisions of the statutes commonly require notice of only one week.

(d) **Release.** The relation of landlord and tenant is terminated if the landlord makes a release or conveyance of the landlord's interest in the land to the tenant.

(e) **Merger.** If the tenant acquires the landlord's interest in any manner, as by inheritance or purchase, the leasehold interest is said to disappear by merger into the title to the land now held by the former tenant.

The lease may give the tenant an option to purchase the property at any time or upon the expiration of the term of the lease, or may provide that the lessor should offer to sell to the tenant before offering to sell the property to anyone else.[4]

(f) **Surrender.** A surrender or giving up of the tenant's estate to the landlord terminates the tenancy if the surrender is accepted by the landlord.[5] A surrender may be made expressly or impliedly. An express surrender must, under the statute of frauds, be in writing and be signed by the person making the surrender or by an authorized agent.

(g) **Forfeiture.** The landlord may terminate the lease by forfeiting the relation because of the tenant's misconduct or breach of a condition, if a term of the lease or a statute so provides. In the absence of such a provision, the landlord may only claim damages for the breach. Terminating the relationship by forfeiture is not favored by the courts.

[4]Moore v Dodge (Tex Civ App) 603 SW2d 236 (1980).
[5]Roosen v Schaffer, 127 Ariz App 346, 621 P2d 33 (1980).

(h) **Destruction of Property.** If a lot and building on it are leased, either an express provision in the lease or a statute generally releases the tenant from liability when the building is destroyed, or reduces the amount of rent in proportion to the loss sustained. Such statutes do not impose upon the landlord any duty to repair or restore the property to its former condition.

When the lease covers rooms or an apartment in a building, a destruction of the leased premises terminates the lease.

(i) **Fraud.** As a lease is based on a contract, a lease may be avoided when the circumstances are such that a contract could be avoided for fraud.

(j) **Transfer of the Tenant.** Residential leases commonly contain a provision for termination upon the tenant's being transferred by his employer to another city or the tenant's being called into military service. Since such provisions are often strictly construed against the tenant, he should exercise care to see that the provision is sufficiently broad to cover the situations that may arise.

FACTS:

A tenant executed a lease which recited "It is further agreed that the Lessee is a member of the Peace Corps and is subject to transfer; in the event of such transfer from the city, Lessee shall be released from the agreement by delivering to Lessor written orders of said transfer along with a 30-day notice to vacate...." Some time later, the tenant was assigned to the A.I.D., a government agency distinct from the Peace Corps, and was transferred to India. Was the tenant released from the lease?

DECISION:

No. The tenant was not transferred as a member of the Peace Corps but took employment with a different government agency. The tenant's going to India therefore did not come within the termination clause of the lease. [Satin v Buckley (Dist Col App) 246 A2d 778 (1968)]

---

§ 53:6.   Notice of Termination.

When notice of termination is required, no particular words are necessary to constitute a sufficient notice, provided the words used clearly indicate the intention of the party. The notice, whether given by the landlord or the tenant, must be definite. Statutes sometimes require that the notice be in writing. In the absence of such a provision, however, oral notice is generally held to be sufficient.

FACTS:

The Bhar Realty Corp. rented an apartment to Becker on a month-to-month lease. Later the corporation gave Becker written notice that the "monthly tenancy is hereby terminated" as of a certain date and that the tenant could renew the tenancy by paying a specified increased rental from that date on. Becker claimed that the notice did not terminate the lease because there was no demand for possession of the property.

DECISION:

Judgment for Realty Corp. A notice to terminate a lease need only state that it is termi-nated as of a specific date. It need not demand possession of the premises but may offer the making of a new lease on different terms, as was done. [Bhar Realty Corp. v Becker, 49 NJSuper 585, 140 A2d 756 (1958)]

---

§ 53:7.   Renewal of Lease.

When a lease terminates for any reason, it is ordinarily a matter for the landlord and the tenant to enter into a new agreement if they wish to extend or renew the lease. The power to renew the lease may be stated nega-tively by declaring that the lease runs indefinitely, as from year to year, sub-ject to being terminated by either party by giving written notice a specified number of days or months before the termination date.

FACTS:

In June, 1966, Forester leased an apart-ment to Kilbourne for one year. The lease stated "the lease is renewable at the end of the year pe-riod." Kilbourne renewed the lease for the year 1967-1968. She again gave notice of renewal for the year 1968-1969 but Forester refused to rec-ognize such renewal and brought an action to recover possession of the premises.

DECISION:

Judgment for Forester. The statement that the lease was renewable at the end of the year period meant exactly that. Hence, it could only be renewed once at the termination of the original term and could not be renewed a sec-ond or subsequent time. [Kilbourne v Forester (MoApp) 464 SW2d 770 (1971)]

The lease may require the tenant to give written notice of the inten-tion to renew the lease. In such case, there is no renewal if the tenant does not give the required notice, but merely remains in the premises after the expiration of the original term.[6]

B. RIGHTS AND DUTIES OF PARTIES

The rights and duties of the landlord and tenant are based upon prin-ciples of real estate law and contract law. With the rising tide of consumer protectionism, the tendency is increasing to treat the relationship as merely a contract and to govern the rights and duties of the parties by general princi-ples of contract law.

[6]Ahmed v Scott, 65 Ohio App 2d 271, 418 NE2d 406 (1979).

§ 53:8. Possession.

Possession involves both the right to acquire possession at the beginning of the lease and the right to retain possession until the lease is ended.

(a) **Tenant's Right to Acquire Possession.** By making a lease, the lessor impliedly covenants to give possession of the premises to the tenant at the agreed time. If the landlord rents a building which is being constructed, there is an implied covenant that it will be ready for occupancy at the commencement of the term of the lease.

(b) **Tenant's Right to Retain Possession.** After the tenant has entered into possession, the tenant has the exclusive possession and control of the premises as long as the lease continues and so long as there is no default under the lease, unless the lease otherwise provides. Thus, the tenant can refuse to allow the lessor to enter the property for the purpose of showing it to prospective customers, although today most leases expressly give this right to the landlord.

If the landlord interferes with this possession by evicting the tenant, the landlord commits a wrong for which the tenant is afforded legal redress. An **eviction** occurs when the tenant is deprived of the possession, use, and enjoyment of the premises by the interference of the lessor or the lessor's agent. If the landlord wrongfully deprives the tenant of the use of one room when the tenant is entitled to use an entire apartment or building, there is a **partial eviction.**

(c) **Covenant for Quiet Enjoyment.** Most written leases today contain an express promise by the landlord to respect the possession of the tenant, called a **covenant for quiet enjoyment.** Such a provision protects the tenant from interference with possession by the landlord or the landlord's agent, but it does not impose liability upon the landlord for the unlawful acts of third persons.[7] Thus, such a covenant does not require the landlord to protect a tenant from damages by a rioting mob.

(d) **Constructive Eviction.** An eviction may be actual or constructive. It is a **constructive eviction** when some act or omission of the landlord substantially deprives the tenant of the use and enjoyment of the premises.

It is essential in a constructive eviction that the landlord intended to deprive the tenant of the use and enjoyment of the premises. This intent may, however, be inferred from conduct. A tenant cannot claim a constructive eviction by a particular condition unless the tenant in fact has left the premises because of that condition. If the tenant continues to occupy the premises for more than a reasonable time after the acts claimed to constitute a constructive eviction, a waiver arises and the tenant cannot thereafter abandon the premises and claim to have been evicted.[8]

---

[7]Rittenbert v Donohoe Construction Co. (Dist Col App) 426 A2d 338 (1981).

[8]Some states prohibit a landlord of residential property from "willfully" turning off the utilities of a tenant for the purpose of evicting the tenant. Kinney v Vaccari, 23 Cal 3d 348, 165 Cal Rptr 787, 612 P2d 877 (1980) (imposing civil penalty of $100 a day for every day utilities are shut off). Such conduct is also a violation of URLTA §§ 2.104, 4.105.

§ 53:9. Use of Premises.

The lease generally specifies the use to which the tenant may put the property and authorizes the landlord to adopt regulations with respect to the use of the premises that are binding upon the tenant as long as they are reasonable, lawful, and not in conflict with the terms of the lease. In the absence of express or implied restrictions, a tenant is entitled to use the premises for any lawful purpose for which they are adapted or for which they are ordinarily employed or in a manner contemplated by the parties in executing the lease. A provision specifying the use to be made of the property is strictly construed against the tenant.

(a) **Change of Use.** The modern lease will in substance make a change of use a condition subsequent so that if the tenant uses the property for any purpose other than the one specified, the landlord has the option of declaring the lease terminated.

(b) **Continued Use of Property.** With the increased danger of damage to the premises by vandalism or fire when the building is vacant and because of the common insurance provision making a fire insurance policy void when a vacancy continues for a specified time, the modern lease will ordinarily require the tenant to give the landlord notice of nonuse or vacancy of the premises.

(c) **Rules.** The modern lease generally contains a blanket agreement by the tenant to abide by the provisions of rules and regulations adopted by the landlord. These rules are generally binding on the tenant whether they exist at the time the lease was made or were thereafter adopted.

(d) **Restriction of Animals.** A restriction in a lease prohibiting the keeping of pets is valid.

§ 53:10. Rent.

The tenant is under a duty to pay rent as compensation to the landlord. The amount of rent agreed to by the parties may be subject to governmental limitations establishing maximum amounts that can be charged.

The time of payment of rent is ordinarily fixed by the lease. When the lease does not control, rent generally is not due until the end of the term. Statutes or custom, however, may require rent to be paid in advance when the agreement of the parties does not regulate the point. Rent that is payable in crops is generally payable at the end of the term.

If the lease is assigned, the assignee is liable to the landlord for the rent. The assignment, however, does not in itself discharge the tenant from the duty to pay the rent. The landlord thus may bring an action for the rent against either the original tenant or the assignee, or both, but is entitled to only one satisfaction. A sublessee ordinarily is not liable to the original lessor for rent, unless that liability has been expressly assumed or is imposed by statute.

(a) **Rent Escalation.** When property is rented for a long term, it is common to include some provision for the automatic increase of the rent at periodic intervals. Such a provision is often tied to increases in the cost of living or in the landlord's operating costs. Such a provision is called an **escalation** clause.

FACTS:

George Backer Management owned an office building. Acme Quilting wished to rent office space in the building. There was long and careful negotiation over the terms of the lease. The lease when finally agreed to contained a rent escalation caluse providing for the increase of rent when the wage scale fixed by the Realty Advisory Board (RAB) rose. After the lease was executed, the wage scale was increased by RAB. George Backer did not belong to the group that was bound by the RAB wage scale and in fact paid its employees below the RAB scale. Nevertheless George Backer demanded that Acme pay additional rent based on the RAB scale. Acme refused to pay the increase in the rent. George Backer sued Acme for the amount of the increase in the rent.

DECISION:

Acme was bound by the promise to pay the increased rent. The lease had been carefully negotiated and the escalation clause was common. Therefore there was no element of surprise. The lease had been voluntarily entered into and the escalation provision was therefore binding upon the parties. Whether the rent increase was more than Acme had expected was immaterial because Acme had agreed to adjust the rent and had expressly agreed that it should be increased according to the RAB scale. [George Backer Management Corp. v Acme Quilting Co., Inc. 413 NYS2d 135, 46 NY2d 211, 385 NE2d 1062 (1978)]

---

§ 53:11.   Repairs and Condition of Premises.

In the absence of an agreement to the contrary, the tenant has the duty to make those repairs that are necessary to prevent waste and decay of the premises, and is liable for **permissive waste** on failing to do so. When the landlord leases only a portion of the premises, or leases the premises to different tenants, the landlord is under a duty to make repairs to connecting parts, such as halls, basements, elevators, and stairways, which are under the landlord's control. When the landlord makes repairs, reasonable care must be exercised to make them in a proper manner; but the landlord is not automatically liable as an insurer if the tenant is injured after the landlord has made the repairs. The tenant is ordinarily liable for any damage to the premises caused by willful or negligent act of the tenant.[9]

(a) **Inspection of Premises.** Most states deny the landlord the right to enter the leased premises to inspect them for waste and need for repairs except when the right is expressly reserved in the lease. It is customary for leases of apartments and commercial property to reserve to the landlord the right to enter to inspect the premises and to make repairs.

[9]New Hampshire Ins. Co. v Hewins, 6 Kan App 2d 259, 627 P2d 1159 (1981); URLTA § 3.101.

(b) **Housing Laws.** Various laws protect tenants, as by requiring landlords to observe specified safety, health, and fire prevention standards. Some statutes require that a landlord who leases a building for dwelling purposes must keep it in a condition fit for habitation. Leases commonly require the tenant to obey local ordinances and laws relating to the care and use of the premises. If compliance with a law requires the making of repairs, such a provision imposes upon the tenant the duty to make the repairs necessary to comply with the law.

(c) **Warranty of Habitability.** At common law a landlord was not bound by a warranty that the premises were fit for use unless the lease contained an express warranty to that effect. Most jurisdictions now reject this view and imply in residential leases of furnished and unfurnished property a warranty that the premises are habitable. If the landlord breaches this warranty, the tenant is entitled to damages. These damages may be set off against the rent which is due, or if no rent is due, the tenant may bring an independent lawsuit to recover damages from the landlord.[10]

FACTS:

King leased a single-family dwelling to Moorehead. He brought an action against her to recover the premises because of nonpayment of rent and in order to collect the unpaid rent. Moorehead raised the defense that the house was not habitable and that it violated the housing code.

DECISION:

Judgment for Moorehead. A lease is not only a transfer of possession of land to the lessee but it is also a contract between the lessor and the lessee. As part of the lessor's obligation under that contract, a warranty is implied that the property shall be habitable or fit for its intended use. The duty of the lessee to pay rent is dependent upon the lessor's providing a habitable dwelling. If the lessor fails to do so, the tenant is not required to pay rent. Therefore Moorehead had not failed in her obligation to pay rent and the lessor was not entitled to regain possession on the theory that the rent had not been paid. [King v Moorehead (Mo App) 495 SW2d 65 (1973)]

(d) **Abatement and Escrow Payment of Rent.** In order to protect tenants from unsound living conditions, statutes sometimes provide that a tenant is not required to pay rent as long as the premises are not fit to live in. As a compromise, some statutes require the tenant to continue to pay the rent but require that it be paid into an escrow or agency account from which it is paid to the landlord only on proof that the necessary repairs have been made to the premises.

---

[10]Knight v Hallsthammar, 171 Cal Rptr 707, 623 P2d 268 (1981).

FACTS:

The C. F. Seabrook Co. rented a house to Beck. She paid the rent for several months and then stopped because of numerous defects in the house. Seabrook sued her for the rent. The trial judge reduced her rent to $75 a month. Seabrook claimed that this reduction was excessive because it amounted to 77% of the rent that had been agreed to and that all of the defects did not relate to habitability.

DECISION:

A landlord renting a property for a residence impliedly warrants that the premises are fit for being lived in. This warranty of habitability is broken when in fact the premises are not fit to live in. When such is the case, it would be manifestly unjust to allow the landlord to collect the full rent. In such case, the amount of the rent should be reduced to an amount representing the fair value of the premises in their actual condition. In making this computation, deduction should be made only for those conditions that are of such a serious nature as to impair the habitability of the premises. The case was therefore sent back to the trial judge to recompute the amount of the reduction that should be made of the rent by limiting consideration to those defects that affected habitability. [C. F. Seabrook Co. v Beck, 174 NJ Super 577, 417 A2d 89 (1980)]

§ 53:12. Improvements.

In the absence of special agreement, neither the tenant nor the landlord is under the duty to make improvements, as contrasted with repairs. Either party may, however, make a covenant for improvements, in which case a failure to perform will result in liability in an action for damages for breach of contract brought by the other party. In the absence of an agreement to the contrary, improvements that are attached to the land become part of the realty and belong to the landlord.

§ 53:13. Taxes and Assessments.

In the absence of an agreement to the contrary, the landlord, and not the tenant, is usually under a duty to pay taxes or assessments. The lease may provide for an increase in rent if taxes on the rented property are increased.[11]

If taxes or assessments are increased because of improvements made by the tenant the landlord is liable for such increases if the improvements remain with the property. If the improvements can be removed by the tenant, the amount of the increase must be paid by the tenant.

§ 53:14. Tenant's Deposit.

A landlord may require a tenant to make a deposit to protect the landlord from any default on the part of the tenant.

[11] J. C. Penny Co., Inc. v 1700 Broadway Co. 104 Misc. 2d 787, 429 NYS2d 369 (1980).

(a) **Custody.** In some states, protection is given the tenant who is required to make a payment to the landlord as a "deposit" to insure compliance with the lease. It is sometimes provided that the landlord holds such payment as a trust fund and must inform the tenant of any bank in which the money is deposited, and be subject to a penalty if the money is used before the tenant has breached the lease.

(b) **Refund.** Once paid by the tenant, it frequently happens that the landlord will keep the entire deposit, even though it is in excess of any claim against the tenant, and tenants will not bring suit because the amount involved is too small to justify an action. Tenant protection statutes sometimes remedy this situation by requiring the landlord to refund any part of the deposit in excess of the amount actually needed to compensate for the breach by the tenant.

§ 53:15. Protection from Retaliation.

There is a modern trend to protect tenants from retaliation by the landlord to take revenge because the tenants have exercised their lawful rights or have reported the landlord for violating a housing and sanitation code.[12] The retaliation of the lessor may take the form of refusing to renew a lease or evicting the tenant.

§ 53:16. Remedies of Landlord.

The landlord may bring an ordinary lawsuit to collect the rent and in some states may seize and hold the property of the tenant for nonpayment of rent.

(a) **Landlord's Lien.** In the absence of an agreement or statute so providing, the landlord does not have a lien upon the personal property or crops of the tenant for money due for rent. The parties may create by express or implied contract a lien in favor of the landlord for rent, and also for advances, taxes, or damages for failure to make repairs.

In the absence of a statutory provision, the lien of the landlord is superior to the claims of all other persons, except prior lienors and bona fide purchasers without notice.

(b) **Suit for Rent.** Whether or not the landlord has a lien for unpaid rent, the landlord may sue the tenant on the latter's obligation to pay rent as specified in the lease, or if payment of rent is not specified, the landlord may enforce a quasi-contractual obligation to pay the reasonable value of the use and occupation of the property. In some jurisdictions, the landlord is permitted to bring a combined action to recover the possession of the land and the overdue rent at the same time.

(c) **Distress.** The common law devised a speedy remedy to aid the landlord in collecting rent. It permitted seizure of personal property found on the premises and allowed the landlord to hold such property until the arrears of rent were paid. This right was known as **distress.** It was not an

---

[12]Mobil Oil Corp. v Handly, 76 Cal App 3d 956, 143 Cal Rptr 321 (1978). URLTA § 5.101.

action against the tenant for rent but merely a right to retain the property as security until the rent was paid. Statutes have generally either abolished or greatly modified the remedy of distress.[13]

(d) Recovery of Possession. The lease commonly provides that upon the breach of any of its provisions by the tenant, such as the failure to pay rent, the lease shall terminate or the landlord may exercise the option to declare the lease terminated. When the lease is terminated for any reason, the landlord then has the right to evict the tenant and retake possession of the property.

At common law, the landlord, when entitled to possession, could regain it without resorting to legal proceedings. This **right of reentry** is available in many states even when the employment of force is necessary. Other states deny the right to use force.

Modern cases hold that a landlord cannot lock out a tenant for overdue rent and must employ legal process to regain possession even though the lease expressly gives the landlord the right to self-help.

The landlord may resort to legal process to evict the tenant in order to enforce the right to possession of the premises. The action of ejectment is ordinarily used. In addition to the common-law remedies, statutes in many states provide a summary remedy to recover possession that is much more efficient than the slow common-law remedies.

(e) Landlord's Duty to Mitigate Damages. If the tenant leaves the premises before the expiration of the lease, is the landlord under any duty to rerent the premises in order to reduce the rent or damages for which the departing tenant will be liable? By the common law and majority rule, a tenant owns an estate in land and if the tenant abandons it there is no duty on the landlord to seek to find a new tenant for the premises. A growing minority view places greater emphasis on the contractual aspects of a lease, so that when the tenant abandons the property and thereby defaults or breaks the contract, the landlord is under the duty to seek to mitigate the damages caused by the tenant's breach and must make reasonable effort to rerent the property.

FACTS:

Kridel rented an apartment from Sommer for two years. Kridel never moved into the apartment. Sommer did not attempt to lease the Kridel apartment to anyone else. At the end of the two years, Sommer sued Kridel for two years' rent. Kridel claimed that Sommer could not recover the full amount of the rent, on the theory that Sommer should have attempted to lease the apartment to someone else.

DECISION:

Judgment for Kridel. When a tenant breaks a lease, the landlord should make reasonable efforts to rent the tenant's apartment to someone else. If the property was so rented, the landlord's loss would be reduced by the amount received as rent from the substitute tenant. This would reduce the amount that the first tenant was required to pay as rent under the original lease. Sommer was therefore under

[13]It is abolished by the URLTA § 4.205(b). Callen v Sherman's, Inc. 182 NJ Super 438, 442 A2d 626 (1982).

the obligation to make reasonable efforts to rerent Kridel's apartment in order to reduce or mitigate the damages that Kridel's breach had caused. [Sommer v Kridel, 74 NJ 446, 378 A2d 767 (1977)]

C. LIABILITY FOR INJURY ON PREMISES

When the tenant, a member of the tenant's family, or a third person is injured by a condition of the premises, the question arises as to who is liable for the damages sustained by the injured person.

§ 53:17. Landlord's Liability to Tenant.

In the absence of a covenant to keep the premises in repair, the landlord is ordinarily not liable to the tenant for the latter's personal injuries caused by the defective condition of the premises that are placed under the control of the tenant by the lease. Likewise, the landlord is not liable for the harm caused by an obvious condition that was known to the tenant at the time the lease was made. For example, a landlord is not liable for the fatal burning of a tenant whose clothing was set on fire by an open-faced radiant gas heater.

The landlord is liable to the tenant for injuries caused by latent or nonapparent defects of which the landlord has knowledge.[14] A new trend is beginning to appear which makes foreseeability of harm the test of the landlord's liability rather than the mechanical test of whether the landlord had control of the part of the premises involved.

In a number of states, by decision or statute, a landlord is liable to a tenant or a child or guest of the tenant where there is a defect which makes the premises dangerously defective, even though the landlord did not have any knowledge of the defect. Other states refuse to apply this strict tort liability concept.

(a) **Crimes of Third Persons.** Ordinarily the landlord is not liable to the tenant for crimes committed on the premises by third persons, as when a third person enters the premises and commits larceny or murder. The landlord is not required to establish any security system to protect the tenant from crimes of third persons.

In contrast, when the criminal acts of third persons are reasonably foreseeable, the landlord may be held liable for the harm thereby caused a tenant. Consequently, when a tenant has repeatedly reported that the deadlock on the apartment door was broken, the landlord is liable for the tenant's loss when a thief enters through the door, because such criminal conduct was foreseeable. Likewise, when the landlord of a large apartment complex does not take reasonable steps to prevent repeated criminal acts the landlord is liable to the tenant for the harm caused by the foreseeable criminal act of a third person.[15]

[14]Alvarez v DeAguirre (Fla App) 395 So2d 213 (1981).
[15]Ten Associates v McCutchen (Fla App) 398 So2d 860 (1981).

FACTS:

C. S., a tenant in an apartment complex owned and operated by Sophir, was sexually assaulted in the parking lot provided for tenants. She alleged that the manager of the complex had actual knowledge of an earlier sexual assault and that the defendant should have warned the plaintiff of that assault. The tenant further alleged that the landlord was negligent for failure to provide proper lighting for security purposes. The landlord denied liability.

DECISION:

Judgment for Sophir. Landlords are not insurers that a tenant will be protected at all times. There is no duty to warn of known dangers. The ordinary reasonable person is aware or should be aware that open parking lots provide an optimum place for crime to occur. Finally, there is no guarantee that if the duty to warn was imposed, a crime would be averted. To impose liability over the mere possibility of a crime occurring is folly. [C.S. v Sophir (Neb App) 368 NW2d 444 (1985)]

(b) **Limitation of Liability.** A provision in a lease excusing or exonerating the landlord from liability is generally valid, regardless of the cause of the tenant's loss. A number of courts, however, have restricted the landlord's power to limit liability in the case of residential as distinguished from commercial, leasing; so that a provision in a residential lease that the landlord shall not be liable for damage caused by water, snow, or ice is void. A modern trend holds that clauses limiting liability of the landlord are void with respect to harm caused by the negligence of the landlord when the tenant is a residential tenant generally or is a tenant of a government low-cost housing project.

Third persons on the premises, even though with the consent of the tenant, are generally not bound by such a clause and may therefore sue the landlord when they sustain injuries. Thus, it has been held that members of the tenant's family, employees, and guests, are not bound where they do not sign the lease; although there is authority to the contrary.

(c) **Indemnification of Landlord.** The modern lease commonly contains a provision declaring that the tenant will indemnify the landlord for any liability of the landlord to a third person which arises in connection with the rented premises.

§ 53:18.   **Landlord's Liability to Third Persons.**

The landlord is ordinarily not liable to third persons injured because of the condition of any part of the rented premises that is in the possession of a tenant by virtue of a lease.[16]

If the landlord retains control over a portion of the premises, such as hallways or stairways, however, liability exists for injuries to third persons caused by failure to exercise proper care in connection with that part of the premises. The modern trend of cases imposes liability on the landlord when a third person is harmed by a condition that the landlord had contracted with the tenant to correct or had contracted to keep the premises in repair.

[16]Gilbreath v J. H. Greenwalt, 88 Ill App 3d 265, 43 Ill Dec 533, 410 NE2d 539 (1980).

FACTS:

James Ferro was injured while entering an outdoor patio lounge, a part of the Ivanhoe Hotel situated on the Virginia Beach ocean front. He was beaten brutally by a bouncer employed by the lessee of the premises. Harbour Enterprises owned the property which included the patio lounge where alcoholic beverages were served during the vacation season. Harbour leased the premises to Bur-Mi-Hut, Ltd. Harbour was licensed by the Virginia Alcoholic Beverage Control Commission to dispense beer, wine, and mixed beverages in the restaurant and patio. Bur-Mi-Hut agreed to obtain its own license before opening but failed to do so. The previous license issued to Harbour remained hanging on the wall at the time of the incident. Ferro sued both Harbour and Bur-Mi-Hut for damages for personal injury. Bur-Mi-Hut admitted liability. Ferro claimed that Harbour as the holder of the liquor license, was vicariously liable for the acts of the tenant's employee.

DECISION:

Judgment for Harbour Enterprises. A landlord is not generally liable to third persons for the negligent or wilful acts of a tenant or tenant's employees. The owner has surrendered control to the lessee. The relationship between the landlord and tenant is not the same as that existing between principal and agent. The tenant's breach of its promise to obtain its own license did not subject the landlord to liability for the tortious acts of the tenant's employee and is irrelevant in determining civil liability for damages. [Harbour Enterprises, Inc. v Ferro (Va) 340 SE2d 818 (1986)]

§ 53:19. Tenant's Liability to Third Persons.

A tenant in complete possession has control of the property and is therefore liable when the tenant's failure to use due care under the circumstances causes harm to (1) licensees, such as a person allowed to use a telephone, and (2) invitees, such as customers entering a store. With respect to both classes, the liability is the same as an owner in possession of property. It is likewise immaterial whether the property is used for residential or business purposes, provided the tenant has control of the area where the injury occurs.

The liability of the tenant to third persons is not affected by the fact that the landlord may have contracted in the lease to make repairs, which, if made, would have avoided the injury. The tenant can be protected, however, in the same manner that the landlord can, by procuring public liability insurance for indemnity against loss from claims of third persons.

D. TRANSFER OF RIGHTS

Both the landlord and the tenant have property and contract rights with respect to the lease. When either makes a transfer of them, questions arise as to the rights and liabilities of the transferee.

§ 53:20. Transfer of Landlord's Reversionary Interest.

The reversionary interest of the landlord may be transferred voluntarily by the landlord, or involuntarily by a judicial or execution sale. The tenant then becomes the tenant of the new owner of the reversionary interest, and the new owner is bound by the terms of the lease.

When the landlord assigns the reversion, the assignee is, in the absence of an agreement to the contrary, entitled to subsequent accruals of rent. The rent may, however, be reserved in an assignment or a reversion. The landlord also has the right to assign the lease independent of the reversion, or to assign the rent independent of the lease.

Upon the transfer of the lessor's reversionary interest, the transferee, the new landlord, becomes bound by the obligations stated in the lease, such as a covenant to repair.

§ 53:21.   Tenant's Assignment of Lease and Sublease.

An **assignment of a lease** is a transfer by the tenant of the tenant's entire interest in the premises to a third person. A tenancy for years may be assigned by the tenant unless the latter is restricted from so doing by the terms of the lease or by a statute. A **sublease** is a transfer of any part of the premises by the tenant to a third person, the **sublessee**, for a period less than the term of the lease.

Whether the transaction between the tenant and the third person is a sublease or an assignment is determined by the effect of the transaction. If the entire interest of the tenant is transferred to the third person, the transaction is an assignment of the lease, without regard to whether the parties have described the transaction as a sublease or as an assignment. In contrast, if there is some interest left over after the interest of the third person expires, the relationship is a sublease.

(a) **Limitations on Rights.** The lease may contain provisions denying the right to assign or sublet or imposing specified restrictions on the privilege of assigning or subletting. Such restrictions enable the landlord to obtain protection from new tenants who would damage the property or be financially irresponsible.

Restrictions in the lease are construed liberally in favor of the tenant. An ineffectual attempt to assign or sublet does not violate a provision prohibiting such acts. This is equally true when the tenant merely permits someone else to use the premises.

(b) **Effect of Assignment or Sublease.** An express covenant or promise by the sublessee is necessary to impose liability on the sublessee for the obligations of the lease. In contrast, when the lease is assigned, the assignee becomes bound by the terms of the lease upon taking possession of the property. In any case, the rights of a sublessee and of an assignee can rise no higher than the rights of the original lessee under the lease.[17]

Neither the act of subletting nor the landlord's agreement to it releases the original tenant from liability under the terms of the original lease.

When a lease is assigned, the original tenant remains liable for the rent which becomes due thereafter. If the assignee renews or extends the lease by virtue of an option contained therein, the original tenant is likewise liable for the rent for such extended period in the absence of a contrary

[17]Gulden v Newberry Wrecker Service, Inc. 154 Ga App 130, 267 SE2d 763 (1980).

agreement or novation by which the landlord agrees that the assignee shall be deemed substituted as tenant and the original tenant shall be released from further liability.

It is customary and desirable for the tenant to require the sublessee to covenant or promise to perform all obligations under the original lease and to indemnify the tenant for any loss caused by the default of the sublessee. An express covenant or promise by the sublessee is necessary to impose such liability. The fact that the sublease is made "subject" to the terms of the original lease merely recognizes the superiority of the original lease but does not impose any duty upon the sublessee to perform the tenant's obligation under the original lease. If the sublessee promises to assume the obligations of the original lease, the landlord, as a third party beneficiary, may sue the sublessee for breach of the provisions of the original lease.

SUMMARY

The agreement between a lessor and a lessee by which one person holds possession of real property owned by another is a lease. Statutes in many states prohibit discrimination by an owner who rents property and require that the lease, like contracts under the UCC, may not be unconscionable. Tenancies are classified as to duration, as tenancies for years, from year to year, at will, and by sufferance. A lease is generally not terminated by the death, insanity, or bankruptcy of either party except for a tenancy at will. Leases usually are terminated by notice, release, merger, surrender, forfeiture, destruction of the property, and because of fraud. A tenant has the right to acquire possession at the beginning of the lease and has the right to retain possession until the lease is ended. Evictions may be either actual or constructive. The tenant is under a duty to pay rent as compensation for the landlord. In the event the lease is assigned, the assignee is liable to the landlord for the rent. Such an assignment, however, does not discharge the tenant from the duty to pay rent. In a sublease, the sublessee ordinarily is not liable to the original lessor for rent unless that liability has been assumed or is imposed by statute. In long term leases, rent escalation clauses are often included.

The tenant must make repairs to the premises absent agreement to the contrary. A warranty of habitability was not implied at common law. Many states now reject this view and imply in residential leases a warranty that the premises are fit for habitation.

A landlord is usually only liable to the tenant for injuries caused by latent or nonapparent defects of which the landlord had knowledge. Some states apply a strict tort liability holding the landlord liable to a tenant or a child or guest of the tenant where there is a defect which makes the premises dangerously defective, even though the landlord does not have any knowledge of the defect. The landlord is not liable to the tenant for crimes of third persons unless they are reasonably foreseeable.

An assignment of a lease by the tenant is a transfer of the tenant's entire interest in the property to a third person; a sublease is a transfer of any part of the premises to a third person for less than the term of the lease. A lease may prohibit both. In the event of an assignment, the assignee becomes bound by the terms of the lease upon taking possession of the property; a sublessee is not liable for the lease obligations unless there is a promise by the sublessee to assume such obligations.

QUESTIONS AND CASE PROBLEMS

1. What social forces are affected by the rule governing the duty of a landlord to relet premises wrongfully abandoned by a tenant?
2. Jacqueline rented a house from Harvey for two years. At the end of the two years, she remained in the house and offered to pay the next month's rent. Harvey refused to take the rent, told Jacqueline to leave, and stated that she was a trespasser and could be thrown out. She claimed that she was not a trespasser because she had lawfully entered the premises under the lease. Was she correct?
3. Melvin rented an apartment from Robert. The lease contains a covenant for quiet enjoyment. The neighbors of Melvin were very noisy. He complained to Robert about the noise and asserted that the noise constituted a breach of the covenant for quiet enjoyment. Was he correct?
4. Must a landlord mitigate damages when a tenant breaches a lease?
5. Maralyn rented a farm from Reeves for 20 years. She rented the south part of the land to Bruce for 5 years. Was Bruce an assignee or a sublessee?
6. Compare (a) an actual eviction of the tenant, (b) a constructive eviction of the tenant, and (c) a breach of the warranty of habitability.
7. To what extent is a tenant liable for increased taxes assessed against the landlord because of improvements made by the tenant?
8. Clay owned a tract of land. Clay permitted Hartney to live in a cabin on the land. Nothing was said as to the length of time that it could be used by Hartney. Nothing was said as to paying anything for the use of the cabin. Hartney died. The next day Clay closed up the cabin and put Hartney's possessions outside the door. Paddock was appointed the executor of Hartney's will. Paddock claimed the right to use the cabin. Was he entitled to do so?
9. Phillips Petroleum, Inc. leased a service station to Prather. McWilliam was a customer at the service station. A rusted window fell from the wall, injuring her. She sued Phillips Petroleum. Was Phillips liable? [McWilliam v Phillips Petroleum, Inc. 269 Or 526, 525 P2d 1011]
10. Matilda rented an apartment in the Melrose Apartments. A number of crimes were committed in the apartment house. Matilda notified Melrose that it was required to hire additional security guards in order to protect the lessees in the apartment house from crimes. Was Matilda correct?
11. Stockham owned certain real estate. For a consideration he gave to the Borough Bill Posting Co. the exclusive privilege of erecting and using a signboard to be located on the land for bill posting purposes. He reserved the right, in case the property was sold or required for building purposes, to cancel all privileges upon returning to the company a pro rata amount of the consideration. In an action brought by Stockham against the company, it was contended that a landlord-tenant relationship had been created. Do you agree?

12. The Old Dover Tavern, Inc., rented a building from Amershadian to conduct a "business under the style and trade name of 'Old Dover Tavern, Inc.' engaging in the serving and selling [of] cigars, tobacco and all kinds of drinks and beverages of any name, nature and description." Thereafter, the tenant claimed that it was entitled to sell cold foods, such as sandwiches, on the theory that such sale was "incidental to the sale of beverages." The Corporation brought an action to establish that it was so entitled. Was it? [Old Dover Tavern, Inc. v Amershadian, 2 Mass App 882, 318 NE2d 191]

13. Cantanese leased a drugstore building from Saputa. Cantanese moved his store from the rented store to another location but continued to pay the rent to Saputa. Saputa, fearing that he was losing his tenant, entered the premises without the permission of Cantanese and made extensive alterations to the premises to suit two physicians who had agreed to rent the premises from Saputa. Cantanese informed Saputa that he regarded the making of the unauthorized repairs as ground for canceling the lease. Saputa then claimed that Cantanese was liable for the difference between the rent that Cantanese had agreed to pay and the rent that the doctors would pay for the remainder of the term of the Cantanese lease. Was Cantanese liable for such rent? [Saputa v Cantanese (La App) 182 So2d 826]

14. Sargent rented a second floor apartment in an apartment house owned by Ross. Anna, the four-year-old daughter of Sargent, fell from an outdoor stairway and was killed. Suit was brought for her death against Ross. She defended on the ground that she did not have control over the stairway and therefore was not liable for its condition. Was this defense valid? [Sargent v Ross, 113 NH 388, 308 A2d 528]

15. Joy White rented an apartment in an apartment house operated by Ridgleawood, Inc. After some discussion, she gave her apartment over to Allan and took a more expensive apartment in the same apartment house. Ridgleawood accepted rent from both White and Allan for the respective apartments. When Allan damaged his apartment, Ridgleawood sued White on the ground she was liable for the conduct of her assignee. Was she liable? [Ridgleawood, Inc. v White (Tex Civ App) 380 SW2d 766]

16. Lester obtained a twenty-year leasehold interest in an office building owned by Tess. Tess died a few months later. Her heirs claimed that her death terminated the lease. Decide.

17. Green rented an apartment from Stockton Realty. The building was a three story building which had a washroom and clothesline on the roof for use by the tenants. The clothesline ran very near the skylight. There was no guardrail between the clothesline and the skylight. Mrs. Green's friend, who was fourteen years old was helping her remove clothes from the line. Her friend tripped on some object and fell against the skylight. The glass was too weak to support her weight and she fell to the floor below sustaining serious injuries. Is the landlord responsible for damages for the injury sustained? Decide. [Reiman v Moore, 42 Cal2d 130, 180 P2d 452]

P A R T 10

ESTATES

Chapter 54 Decedents' Estates
Chapter 55 Trusts

CHAPTER 54

DECEDENTS' ESTATES

CHAPTER OBJECTIVES

After studying this chapter you will be able to:
1. Define testamentary capacity and testamentary intent.
2. Distinguish between signing, attesting, and publishing a will.
3. List the ways in which a will may be modified or revoked.
4. Describe briefly the probate and contest of a will.
5. List the special types of wills.
6. Describe the order of distribution by intestacy.
7. Solve problems involving testate and intestate distribution.

Public policy dictates that when an individual dies, the cost of proper burial, and other expenses that may arise in connection with death, be paid; that the just debts contracted before death be settled; that the property owned at the time of death be taken care of and applied to the payment of expenses and the debts mentioned; and that the remainder, if any, be distributed among those properly entitled to receive it.

The law of decedents' estates is governed by the statutes and the court decisions in the several states. The general principles and the procedures that will be discussed herein may be considered as typical. The statutory provisions of a particular jurisdiction, however, may differ more or less from the principles and the procedures considered. A step toward national uniformity has been taken by the American Bar Association and the National Conference of Commissioners on Uniform Laws by approving a Uniform Probate Code (UPC) and submitting it to the states for adoption.[1]

[1]The Uniform Probate Code has been adopted in Alaska, Arizona, Colorado, Florida, Hawaii, Idaho, Maine, Michigan, Minnesota, Montana, Nebraska, New Mexico, North Dakota, and Utah. A number of minor amendments have since been made. Kentucky has adopted only Article VII, Part I, of the UPC.

A. WILLS

After all of the debts of a decedent are paid, distribution is made of any balance of the estate to those entitled to receive it. If the decedent made a valid will, it determines which persons are entitled to receive the property. If the decedent did not make a valid will, the distribution is determined by the intestate law.

§ 54:1. Definitions.

Testate distribution describes the distribution that is made when the decedent leaves a valid will. A **will** is ordinarily a writing that provides for a distribution of property upon the death of the writer but which confers no rights prior to that time. A man who makes a will is called a **testator**; a woman, a **testatrix**.

The person to whom property is left by a will is a **beneficiary**. A gift of personal property by will is a **legacy** or **bequest,** in which case the beneficiary may also be called a **legatee**. A gift of real property by will is a **devise**, in which case the beneficiary may be called a **devisee**.

§ 54:2. Parties to Will.

Each state has a right to prescribe the qualifications of persons who wish to make a will. While there are some variations among the states, the following is typical.

(a) Testator. Generally the right to make a will is limited to persons 18 and older. The testator must always have **testamentary capacity**.[2] In order to have testamentary capacity, a person must have sufficient mental capacity to understand that the writing which is being executed is a will, that is, that it disposes of the person's property after death, and must also have a reasonable appreciation of the identity of relatives and friends and of the nature and extent of the property which may exist at death.

The excessive and continued use of alcohol, producing mental deterioration, may be sufficient to justify the conclusion that the decedent lacked testamentary capacity.

FACTS:
Gentry, the testator, was an ex-serviceman with a history of frequent hospitalization for mental illness. While confined at a veterans hospital because of such illness, Gentry executed a will naming his mother as the sole beneficiary of his estate. This disinherited Gentry's daughter who was his only child. She contested the validity of the will on the ground that her father lacked testamentary capacity to make the will because he was institutionalized for mental incompetence and was receiving extensive medication. The evidence showed that at the time that Gentry had made the will he understood what he was doing and the effect of his actions.

DECISION:
The will was valid. The fact that a person is institutionalized because of mental illness or is under medication does not conclusively

[2]Kleeb's Estate, 41 Neb 763, 320 NW2d 459 (1982).

establish that the person lacked testamentary capacity. The evidence showed that Gentry made his will in a lucid interval when he in fact knew that he was making a will and he understood that it was disposing of his property upon his death. He therefore had testamentary capacity and the will was valid. [Gentry's Estate, 32 Or App 45, 573 P2d 322 (1978)]

(b) **Beneficiary.** Generally there is no restriction with respect to the capacity of the beneficiary. However, when part of a decedent's estate passes to a minor, it is ordinarily necessary to appoint a guardian to administer such interest for the minor. Two common exceptions are: (1) If there is a will which directs that any share payable to a minor be held by a particular person as trustee for the minor, the minor's interest will be so held and a guardian is not required. (2) Statutes often provide that if the estate or interest of the minor is not large, it may be paid directly to the minor or to the parent or person by whom the minor is maintained.

§ 54:3. Testamentary Intent.

There cannot be a will unless the testator manifests an intention to make a provision that will be effective only upon death. This is called a **testamentary intent.**[3] Ordinarily this is an intention that certain persons shall become the owners of certain property upon the death of the testator. But a writing also manifests a testamentary intent when the testator only designates an executor and does not make any disposition of property.

§ 54:4. Form.

Since the privilege of disposing of property by will is purely statutory, the will must be executed in the manner and with the formalities required by state statutes. Unless statutory requirements are met, the will is invalid and the testator is considered to have died intestate. In such a case the decedent's property will be distributed according to the laws of intestacy of the particular state.

(a) **Writing.** Ordinarily, a will must be in writing. Some state statutes, however, permit oral wills made by soldiers and sailors.

(b) **Signature.** A written will must be signed by the testator. In the absence of a provision of the statute stating that the will must be signed "in writing," a rubber stamp signature has been held sufficient. It is common, however, to require a written signature.

Generally a will must be signed at the bottom or end. The purpose of this requirement is to prevent unscrupulous persons from taking a will that has been validly signed and writing or typing additional provisions in the space below the signature.

(c) **Attestation and Publication. Attestation** is the act of witnessing the execution of a will.[4] Generally it includes signing the will as a witness,

---

[3]Preston v Preston (Tex Civ App) 617 SW2d 841 (1981).
[4]Weaver v Grant (Ala) 394 So2d 15 (1981).

after a clause which recites that the witness has observed either the execution of the will or the testator's acknowledgment of the writing as the testator's will. This clause is commonly called an **attestation clause.** Statutes often require that attestation be made by the witnesses in the presence of the testator and in the presence of each other.

FACTS:

Louis Grossen wrote his will in 1974. One of the witnesses, Scott Hill, was only sixteen years of age. The law at that time did not specify any minimum age required for witnesses to a will. In 1977, the Uniform Probate Code was adopted. It provided that a written will was valid if when made it complied with the law of the place where the will was executed. It also required that witnesses to wills be eighteen years of age. Grossen died in 1981. His heirs claimed that his will was invalid because Hill was underage as a witness.

DECISION:

The will was valid. The provision that a will was valid under the new Probate Code if valid by the law of the place where the will was executed extended to the time that the will was executed. When Grossen made his will, Hill was a proper witness, and therefore the will was valid as of that time and was likewise valid under the Uniform Probate Code thereafter adopted. [Grossen's Estate (Utah) 657 P2d 1345 (1983)]

Publication is the act of the testator of informing the attesting witnesses that the document which is signed before them or is shown to them is the testator's will. The law varies between states as to the necessity of publication.

In some states witnesses are not required. In others, either two or three are required.

(d) Date. There is generally no requirement that a will be dated. It is advisable, however, to date a will, for when there are several wills, the most recent prevails with respect to conflicting provisions.

§ 54:5. Modification of Will.

A will may be modified by executing a codicil. A **codicil** is a separate writing that amends a will. The will, except as changed by the codicil, remains the same. The result is as though the testator rewrote the will, substituting the provisions of the codicil for those provisions of the will that are inconsistent with the codicil. A codicil must be executed with all the formality of a will and is treated in all other respects the same as a will.

A will cannot be modified merely by crossing out a clause and writing in what the testator wishes. Such an interlineation is not operative unless it is executed with the same formality required of a will, or in some states unless the will is republished in its interlineated form.

§ 54:6.   Revocation of Will.

At any time during the testator's life, the testator may revoke the will made or make changes in its terms. It may be revoked by act of the testator or by operation of law.

(a) **Revocation by Act of Testator.** A will is revoked when the testator destroys, burns, or tears the will, or crosses out the provisions of the will with the intention to revoke it. The revocation may be in whole or in part.

FACTS:

Feir executed a will in 1979. In late 1980, Feir sent a typed letter to his attorney advising that he was voiding the will executed in 1979. The letter was signed by Feir and notarized. Feir died sometime thereafter. The original of the will and a copy of the typed letter were found in his safe deposit box. Feir's sister contends that he died intestate. His attorney, as executor of the original will, contends that the letter did not revoke the will.

DECISION:

The will was not revoked. Revocation of a will requires burning, tearing, cancellation, obliteration, or destruction by the testator with the intent and for the purpose of revoking it. The letter sent by the testator did not destroy the will itself and thus was not a revocation by the act of the testator even though the letter expressed such intent. [In re Estate Of Feir (Ariz App) 701 P2d 3 (1985)]

A testator must have the same degree of mental capacity to revoke a will as is required to make a will.

(b) **Revocation by Operation of Law.** In certain instances statutes provide that a change of circumstances has the effect of a revocation. Thus it may be provided that when a person marries after executing a will, the will is revoked or is presumed revoked, unless it was made in contemplation of marriage or unless it provided for the future spouse. In some states the revocation is not total but only to the extent of allowing the spouse to take such share of the estate as that to which the spouse would have been entitled had there been no will.

It is also commonly provided that the birth or adoption of a child after the execution of a will works a revocation or partial revocation of the will as to that child. In the case of a partial revocation, the child is entitled to receive the same share as though the testator had died intestate.

The divorce of the testator does not in itself work a revocation, but the majority of courts hold that if a property settlement is carried out on the basis of the divorce, a prior will of the testator is revoked, at least to the extent of the legacy given to the divorced spouse.

§ 54:7.   Probate of Will.

Probate is the act by which the proper court or official accepts a will and declares that the instrument satisfies the statutory requirements as the will of the testator. Until a will is probated, it has no legal effect.

When witnesses have signed a will, generally they must appear and state that they saw the testator sign the will. If those witnesses cannot be found, have died, or are outside the jurisdiction, the will may be probated nevertheless. When no witnesses are required, it is customary to require two or more persons to identify the signature of the testator at time of probate.

After the probate witnesses have made their statements under oath, the officer or court will ordinarily admit the will to probate in the absence of any particular circumstances indicating that the writing should not be probated. A certificate or decree which officially declares that the will is the will of the testator and has been admitted to probate is then issued.

Any qualified person wishing to object to the probate of the will on the ground that it is not a proper will may appear before the official or court prior to the entry of the decree of probate or may petition after probate to have the probate of the will set aside.

§ 54:8.   Will Contest.

The probate of a will may be refused or set aside on the ground that the will is not the free expression of the intention of the testator. It may be attacked on the ground of (1) lack of mental capacity to execute a will, (2) undue influence, duress, fraud, or mistake existing at the time of the execution of the will that induced or led to its execution, or (3) forgery. With the exception of mental capacity, these concepts mean the same as they do in contract law.

If it is found that any one of these elements exists, the probate of the will is refused or set aside. The decedent's estate is then distributed as if there had been no will unless an earlier will can be probated.

FACTS:

Jeanette Wall worked for D. J. Sharron for many years. Sharron executed a will leaving his entire estate to Jeanette. He re-executed the will sometime thereafter with the same provisions. Sharron's children contested the will. They offered evidence that Sharron was a very sick man, physically as well as mentally and that Wall was active in Sharron's business as well as his personal life. They offered no evidence that Wall had any involvement in the procurement of the original or the re-executed will.

DECISION:

Judgment for Wall. It is true that there was a confidential relationship between Wall and Sharron, and that the influence of Wall was dominant and controlling as his business manager. However, there was no improper activity on the part of Wall in procuring the execution of the will. Since the children could present no evidence of improper activity, Jeanette Wall is entitled to the entire estate. [Wall v Hodges (Ala App) 465 So2d 359 (1984)]

---

§ 54:9.   Special Types of Wills.

A **holographic will** is one that is written by the testator entirely by hand. In many states no distinction is made between a holographic and other wills. In other states the general body of the law of wills applies, but certain variations are established. Thus it may be required that a holographic be dated.

A **nuncupative will** is an oral will made and declared by the testator in the presence of witnesses to be a will. Generally it can be made only with respect to personal property during the last illness of the testator.

It is commonly provided that a nuncupative will cannot be probated unless the witnesses reduce it to writing and sign the writing within a certain period of time after the declaring of the will.

Soldiers and sailors generally may make an oral or a written will of their personal estates without complying with the formalities required of other wills. It is sufficient that testamentary intent be shown.

A will made by a soldier or sailor is not revoked by the termination of the testator's period of service. It remains in force on returning to civilian life, and it can only be revoked in the same manner as any other will.

B. DISTRIBUTION UNDER THE WILL

If the decedent died leaving a valid will, the last phase of the administration of the estate by the decedent's personal representative is the distribution of property remaining after the payment of all debts and taxes, in accordance with the provisions of the will.

§ 54:10.   Legacies.

The testator will ordinarily bequeath to named persons certain sums of money, called **general legacies** because no particular money is specified; or identified property, called **specific legacies** or **specific devises.** Thus the testator may say, "$1,000 to A; $1,000 to B; my auto to C."The first two bequests are general, the third is specific. After such bequests, the testator may make a bequest of everything remaining, called a **residuary bequest,** such as "the balance of my estate to D."

(a) **Abatement of Legacies.** Assume in the preceding example that after all debts are paid, there remains only $1,500 and the auto. What disposition is to be made? Legacies abate or bear loss in the following order: (1) residuary, (2) general, (3) specific. The law also holds that legacies of the same class abate proportionately. Accordingly, in the hypothetical case, C, the specific legatee, would receive the auto; A and B, the general legatees, would each receive $750, and D, the residuary legatee would not receive anything.

(b) **Ademption of Property.** When specifically bequeathed property is sold or given away by the testator prior to death, the bequest is considered **adeemed** or canceled and the specific legatee is not entitled to receive any property or money. Ademption has the same consequence as though the testator had formally canceled the bequest.

(c) **Antilapse Statutes.** If the beneficiary named in the testator's will has died before the testator, and the testator did not make any alternate provision applicable in such case, the gift ordinarily does not lapse because **antilapse** statutes commonly provide that the gift to the deceased beneficiary shall not lapse but that the children or heirs of that beneficiary may take the legacy in the place of the deceased beneficiary.[5]

FACTS:

Murray wrote a will by which he left all his property to his sisters Mary and Isabel. He further provided "in the event of the prior decease of Isabel, her share is to go to Mary. In the event of the prior decease [of] Mary, her share is to go to Isabel." Mary died in 1971 and was survived by a son. Isabel died in 1973 and was survived by a son. Murray died thereafter. The applicable antilapse statute provided that the share of a legatee dying before a testator should not lapse but should pass under the legatee's will or to the legatee's heirs. The sons of the two sisters claimed that the gifts to the named sisters had lapsed and that Murray's estate therefore passed to them.

DECISION:

Each son was entitled to his mother's share. The fact that Murray provided for a gift over to the surviving daughter in the event of her dying before him showed that he did not wish that any part of his estate should pass by intestacy. This intent, combined with the intent of the antilapse statute, could be carried out by holding that when both daughters died before Murray the son of each daughter should take the share that his mother would have received had she survived Murray. The sons were therefore each entitled to one half of Murray's estate. [Murray v Willett, 36 Md App 551, 373 A2d 1303 (1977)]

An antilapse statute does not apply if the testator specifies a disposition which should be made of the gift if the original legatee has died.

§ 54:11.   Election to Take Against the Will.

In order to protect the husband or wife of a testator, the surviving spouse may generally ignore the provisions of a will and elect to take against the will. In such a case the surviving spouse receives the share of the estate which that spouse would have received had the testator died without leaving a will, or a fractional share specified by statute.

The right to take against the will is generally barred by certain kinds of misconduct of the surviving spouse. Thus, if the spouse is guilty of such desertion or nonsupport as would have justified the decedent in obtaining a divorce, the surviving spouse usually cannot elect to take against the will.

§ 54:12.   Disinheritance.

With two exceptions,[6] any person may be disinherited or excluded from sharing in the estate of a decedent.[7] A person who would inherit if there were no will is excluded from receiving any part of a decedent's estate if the decedent has left a will giving everything to other persons.

---

[5]Malecki's Estate, 79 App Div 2d 799, 435 NYS2d 112 (1980).

[6]The exceptions to this rule are based (a) upon the election of a spouse to take against the will and (b) in certain cases upon the partial revocation of a will by a subsequent marriage, birth, or adoption.

[7]Brown v Drake, 275 SC 299, 270 SE2d 130 (1980).

§ 54:13.   Construction of Will.

The will of a decedent is to be interpreted according to the ordinary or plain meaning evidenced by its words. The court will strive to give effect to every provision of the will in order to avoid concluding that any part of the decedent's estate was not disposed of by the will.[8]

C. INTESTACY

If the decedent does not effectively dispose of all property by will or does not have a will, the decedent's property is distributed to certain relatives. Since such persons acquire or succeed to the rights of the decedent and since the circumstances under which they do so is the absence of an effective will, it is said that they acquire title by **intestate succession.**

The right of intestate succession or inheritance is not a basic right of the citizen or an inalienable right but exists only because the state legislature so provides. It is within the power of the state legislature to modify or destroy the right to inherit property.

§ 54:14.   Plan of Intestate Distribution.

Although wide variations exist among the statutory provisions of the states, a common pattern of intestate distribution can be observed:

(a) **Spouses.** The surviving spouse of the decedent, whether husband or wife, shares in the estate. Generally the amount received is a fraction which varies with the number of children and other heirs. If no blood relatives survive, the spouse is generally entitled to take the entire estate. Otherwise the surviving spouse ordinarily receives a one-half or one-third share of the estate.

(b) **Lineals. Lineals** or **lineal descendants** are blood descendants of the decedent. That portion of the estate which is not distributed to the surviving spouse is generally distributed to lineals.

(c) **Parents.** If the estate has not been fully distributed by this time, the remainder is commonly distributed to the decedent's parents.

(d) **Collateral Heirs.** These are persons who are not descendants of the decedent but who are related through a common ancestor. Generally brothers and sisters and their descendants share any part of the estate that has not already been distributed.

Statutes vary as to how far distribution will be made to the descendants of brothers and sisters. Under some statutes a degree of relationship is specified, such as first cousins, and no person more remotely related to the decedent is permitted to share in the estate. If the entire estate is not distributed within the permitted degree of relationship, the property that has not been distributed is given to the state government. This right of the state to take the property is the **right of escheat.** Under some statutes the right of escheat arises only when there is no relative of the decedent, however remotely related.

[8]Silverthorn v Jennings (Tex Civ App) 620 SW2d 894 (1981).

(e) **Distribution Per Capita and Per Stirpes.** The fact that different generations of distributees may be entitled to receive the estate creates a problem of determining the proportions in which distribution is to be made. When all the distributees stand in the same degree of relationship to the decedent, **distribution** is made **per capita**, each receiving the same share. Thus, if the decedent is survived by three children, *A*, *B*, and *C*, each of them is entitled to receive one third of the estate.

If the distributees stand in different degrees of relationship, distribution is made in as many equal parts as there are family lines or stirpes represented in the nearest generation. Parents take to the exclusion of their children or subsequent descendants; and when members of the nearest generation have died, their descendants take by way of representation. This is called **distribution per stirpes** or **stirpital distribution.**

(f) **Murder of Decedent.** Statutes generally provide that a person who murders the decedent cannot inherit from the victim by intestacy. In the absence of such a statute, some courts hold that the inheritance cannot be denied, while others refuse to allow inheritance under such circumstances.

(g) **Death of Distributee after Decedent.** The persons entitled to distribution of a decedent's estate are determined as of the date of death. If a distributee dies thereafter, the rights of the distributee are not lost but pass from the original decedent's estate to the deceased distributee's estate.

(h) **Simultaneous Death.** The Uniform Simultaneous Death Act[9] provides that where survivorship cannot be established, "the property of each person shall be disposed of as if he had survived the other."[10]

D. ADMINISTRATION OF DECEDENTS' ESTATES

A decedent's estate consists of the assets that a person owns at death. It must be determined who is entitled to receive that property. If the decedent owed debts, those debts must be paid first. After that, any balance is to be distributed according to the terms of any will, or by the intestate law if the decedent did not leave a will.

§ 54:15.   Definitions.

The decedent has the privilege of naming in the will the person who will administer the estate. A man named in a will to administer the estate of the decedent is an **executor**, a woman, an **executrix**. If the decedent failed to name an executor or did not leave a will, the law permits another person, usually a close relative, to obtain the appointment of someone to wind up the estate. This person is an **administrator** or **administratrix**.

In certain special instances a temporary administrator may be appointed. Thus, if there is a will contest, an **administrator pendente lite** may be appointed; that is, an administrator who serves during the litigation for the purpose of preserving the estate.

---

[9]This Act has been adopted for the District of Columbia and the Panama Canal Zone and in every state except Louisiana and Ohio.

[10]Special provision is made in the case of beneficiaries, joint tenants, tenants by entireties, community property, and insurance policies.

Administrators and executors are often referred to generally as **personal representatives** of the decedents since they represent the decedents or stand in their place.

§ 54:16.   When Administration is not Necessary.

No administration is required when the decedent did not own any property at the time of death or when all the property owned was jointly owned with another person who acquired the decedent's interest by right of survivorship. Thus, if all of the property of a husband and wife is held as tenants by the entireties, no administration is required upon the death of either of them because the other automatically acquires the entire estate free of any debts or liabilities of the decedent.

In some states special statutes provide for a simplified administration when the decedent leaves only a small estate, commonly under $1,000 to $5,000.

§ 54:17.   Appointment of Personal Representative.

Both executors and administrators must be appointed to act as such by a court or officer designated by law. The appointment is made by granting to the personal representative **letters testamentary,** in the case of an executor, or **letters of administration,** in the case of an administrator. For the appointment of a personal representative, an application or petition is filed with the court or officer setting forth the details of the decedent's death, stating that the decedent, if a resident of the state, lived within the county or, if a nonresident, that property of the decedent is within the county, and reciting the facts which justify the appointment of the personal representative.

(a) **Person Entitled to Act as Personal Representative.** If the decedent has named an executor, that person has the right to act as personal representative or to decline to do so. If no executor has been named, an administrator is appointed.

The right to act as administrator is regulated by statutes, which generally give the right to administer to the surviving spouse; but if there is no surviving spouse or if the spouse declines, the right is given to the next of kin.

FACTS:

R. Walker died. His entire estate was to go to his brother, W. Walker. This brother selected the Southern Trust Co. as administrator, and letters of administration were granted to it. An aunt and first cousin of the decedent petitioned to vacate the appointment and to appoint the first cousin as administrator. The applicable Tennessee statute provided that administration should be granted to the widow of a decedent or, if none, then to the "next of kin." Who was entitled to administer?

DECISION:

"Next of kin" in the statute defining the right to administer a decedent's estate is limited to persons who receive a share of the estate. As the brother W. Walker would receive the entire estate, the aunt and first cousin were not "next of kin" within the statute. The administrator nominated by W. Walker, being the nominee of the "next of kin," was therefore properly appointed. [Tudor v Southern Trust Co. 193 Tenn 331, 246 SW2d 33 (1952)]

(b) **Oath and Bond.** A personal representative who is appointed, is required to take an oath and to file a bond that the estate will be properly administered according to law. In some states an executor is not required to furnish a bond if a resident of the state and in sound financial condition or if the testator has expressly directed that no bond be required.

§ 54:18.   Proof of Claims against the Estate.

The statutes vary widely with respect to the presentation of claims against a decedent's estate. In very general terms the statutes provide for some form of public notice of the grant of letters, as by advertisement. Creditors are then required to give notice of their claims within a period specified either by statute or a court order, as within six months. In most states the failure to present the claim within the specified time bars the claim.

FACTS:

An airplane piloted by Benkert crashed. The crash killed the pilot and his passenger, Milton Glass. The pilot's wife was appointed administratrix of his estate. She gave notice of her appointment by means of newspaper publication, informing the public that anyone with a claim against Benkert or his estate should file that claim with her within six months after the date the notice was first published. The filing of claims within such period was required by statute. More than six months after the publication date, a claim was filed with her on behalf of the children of Milton Glass by which the children sought to recover damages for the death of their father. Benkert's administratrix asserted that the claim of the children of Glass was barred because it had not been filed with her within the statutory six-month period. The children of Glass contended that the six-months' limitation was not binding on them because they were minors.

DECISION:

The children of Glass were barred by the six-month limitation. The public policy favored the early settlement of estates and therefore the time limitation applied to everyone regardless of age. A contrary interpretation would hold all estates open until every minor had attained majority. [Glass v Benkert, 18 Cal App 3d 322, 95 CalRptr 735 (1971)]

(a) **Nature of Claims.** Claims against an estate can be grouped into one of four classifications. The classification of a particular claim will affect the order in which it is satisfied.

(1) Funeral Expenses. In most jurisdictions a personal representative either cannot or will not be appointed before the burial of the decedent. Accordingly, it is the surviving spouse or the next of kin who has the responsibility of arranging for the burial of the decedent.

(2) Administration Expenses. The estate is charged with the expenses of its administration. These include the cost of the personal representative's bond, if any; the fee charged by the court or clerk for the grant of the letters to the personal representative; the cost of advertising and giving notice when required; the cost of filing the account; the cost of any particular services, such as bringing suit against third persons; and the compensation of the personal representative and the estate's attorney.

(3) Family Allowance. Most states make some provision for the immediate necessities of a decedent's family during the period of administration. The widow, or the children, and in some instances the husband of a decedent, are generally entitled to receive a certain portion of the estate for this purpose. In some states the granting of this allowance lies within the discretion of the court; while in others it is a matter of right. It most commonly takes the form of a specified sum of money, although in some states it is the right to take certain specified articles of property or to live in the house of the decedent for a specified time. It is immaterial whether the decedent left a will or, if there is a will, whether the claimant receives anything under the decedent's will.

The right of a spouse to receive this allowance is generally barred by conduct on the claimant's part that would have entitled the decedent to obtain a divorce. Thus a wife who is guilty of deserting her husband is not entitled, upon his death, to receive the family allowance from his estate.

The family allowance is ordinarily not subject to the claim of creditors. This means that the person entitled to the allowance may receive it even though there will not be enough to pay creditors after the allowance has been deducted.

(4) Debts and Liabilities of the Decedent. Generally any debt or liability of the decedent existing at the time of death may be asserted against the estate.

(b) Priority of Claims. When the estate of a decedent is insolvent, that is, when it is not sufficiently large to pay all debts and taxes, the law generally provides that certain claims shall be paid first. Although there is great variation of detail, the most common pattern of priority provides for the payment of claims against the estate in the following order: (1) funeral expenses; (2) administration expenses; (3) family allowance; (4) claims due the United States;[11] (5) expenses of the last illness; (6) debts due state, county, and city governments; (7) claims for wages; (8) lien claims; (9) all other debts.

Assuming a state in which the priorities are as stated, the effect is that the decedent's estate is first used to pay claims listed in (1). If any balance remains, claims (2) are paid. If any balance remains, claims (3) are paid, and so on. If there are several claimants within a particular class, but not enough money to pay each in full, they share proportionately the balance remaining and creditors in lower priorities receive nothing.

§ 54:19. Powers and Duties of Personal Representative.

The powers and duties of the personal representative relate to the collection of the assets of the estate; the care and preservation of the assets;

[11]31 USC § 191.

the management of the estate; the prosecution and defense of lawsuits to which the estate is a party; the payment of debts of the decedent, administration expenses, federal estate taxes and state taxes; accounting to the extent required by law; and distributing the estate to those entitled to it. Apart from special powers that a decedent may confer upon an executor, the powers of an executor and administrator are the same.

(a) **Performance.** A personal representative is under the duty to administer the estate according to law. An executor must also comply with directions contained in the will.

(b) **Due Care and Loyalty.** A personal representative has the duty of exercising due care and loyalty.

(c) **Possession and Preservation of Estate.** The personal representative has the task of collecting the assets of the estate and subsequently of distributing them to the persons entitled to them. An executor or administrator has the duty to defend the estate against adverse claims.

It is customary for the personal representative to deposit cash of the estate in a bank. In some states this is specifically required by statute. The deposit in any case must be made in the representative's name as representative, that is, as *John Jones, Administrator of the Estate of Henry Brown, Deceased,* or in the name of the estate, as *Estate of Henry Brown, Deceased.* In either case checks on the account would be signed by John Jones as administrator of the named estate.

(d) **Payment of Debts.** The personal representative has the duty to pay the debts of the decedent, taxes, and the expenses of administering the estate.

FACTS:

Julia Kirkpatrick was the administratrix of her husband's estate. He had owned an automobile valued at $2,150, which was subject to a loan of $1,347.15. In order to prevent the loss of the auto, she personally borrowed $802.85 which she paid on the loan and refinanced the debt. At the audit of her account, she claimed credit for making the payment of $802.85. Objection was made to the claim on the ground that no verified statement of the claim had been presented and that court approval for the refinancing transaction had not been obtained.

DECISION:

Judgment for Julia. A personal representative may pay a proper claim that is admittedly due even though verified proof of the claim is not presented. The absence of prior court approval did not make the transaction illegal, because the personal representative may spend money in good faith in a prudent manner to protect the interests of the estate. [Kirkpatrick's Estate, 109 Cal App 2d 709, 241 P2d 555 (1952)]

(e) **Inventory and Appraisal.** The personal representative must make a list or inventory of the assets of the decedent's estate. With this inventory must be an appraisal of the value of the various items so that the value of each bequest or distributive share and the total value of the estate can be determined.

Generally the inventory and the appraisal are restricted to personal property, although some statutes require the listing of real estate as well. A number of states allow the omission of certain types of personal property, such as clothing, Bibles, and school books.

(f) **Monument or Tombstone.** The personal representative has the duty to erect a tombstone or monument on the grave of the decedent.

(g) **Investments.** Since the function of the personal representative is to distribute the estate, the representative ordinarily has no authority to make investments. Sometimes the duty to do so will be implied when, because of litigation or the nature of the assets, there will be a long delay in the distribution of the estate.

(h) **Administration of Real Estate.** Whether the administrator has any duty or power with respect to real estate of the decedent depends upon the law of the particular state. At common law only the personal property of a decedent was administered by a personal representative. Real estate of the decedent vested upon death in heirs or devisees.

In most states this rule has been modified to the extent that where it is necessary to pay debts of the decedent, the personal representative may take control of the real estate and rent or sell it for that purpose. In some states the distinction between real and personal property is abolished, and the personal representative has the same administrative control over real estate of the decedent as over personal property.

In the absence of a statutory provision, generally the personal assets of the decedent must be consumed in the payment of debts before the real estate can be touched for that purpose.

Whether the personal representative is under a duty to insure the real estate depends upon whether, under the circumstances, a reasonable person would obtain insurance.

(i) **Continuation of Business.** In the absence of statute or an express direction in the will, an executor does not have the right to continue the business of the decedent.

(j) **Determination of Proper Distributees.** It is the duty of the personal representative to ascertain by the exercise of reasonable diligence the proper persons to whom distribution is to be made. For example, if an estate is to be divided among the brothers of the decedent, the personal representative should ascertain as far as can reasonably be done the identity and whereabouts of all of the brothers. Or if a spouse is disqualified from sharing in the estate, the personal representative must make that fact known to the court.

After the rights of the parties who are entitled to the estate have been determined, the personal representative is under the duty to make distribution in accordance with those rights.

(k) **Accounting.** A personal representative is under the same duty to account as an agent.

(l) **Liability of Personal Representative.** If misconduct of the executor or the administrator or failure to act causes loss to the estate, such representative may be required to indemnify the estate for the amount of the loss which has been caused.[12] The decree or order imposing liability is commonly called a **surcharge**.

§ 54:20. Termination of Authority of Personal Representative.

The termination of the authority of a personal representative ordinarily has no retroactive effect. The validity of transactions completed before the termination of authority is not affected.

(a) **Discharge of the Representative.** After the administration of the estate is completed, the personal representative applies to the court to be discharged. Once a discharge is entered, authority to act is terminated.

(b) **Revocation of Grant of Letters.** The letters may have been erroneously granted. The letters will, in such a case, be revoked.

Letters will also be revoked when they have been granted in the wrong county, or when the person appointed was not qualified. Thus, letters of administration granted to the decedent's apparent widow will be revoked when it is shown that she had not been the decedent's wife.

Letters of administration will be revoked when it is later found that the decedent left a will and the will is admitted to probate. Conversely, letters testamentary will be revoked when the will is set aside as being invalid.

(c) **Resignation.** In most states the personal representative can resign if permission of the court is obtained. This request will ordinarily be granted if a good cause for resignation is shown and the estate will not be prejudiced thereby.

(d) **Removal.** In most states, statutes have been adopted which specify the grounds for the removal of a personal representative. In general, these include any delinquency, misconduct, or personal incapacity of a nature sufficiently serious as to interfere with the administration of the estate. Thus a personal representative may be removed for failure to file required papers, or for fraud, misappropriation of funds of the estate, or a loss of personal competence or fitness to act as administrator. A personal representative may also be removed for representing an interest adverse to the estate.

SUMMARY

A will is a disposition of property to take effect on death. A man who makes a will is called the testator, a woman, the testatrix. The person to whom property is left by will is a beneficiary. A legacy is a gift of personal property by will is known as a devise.

A testator must have testamentary capacity to make a will and must manifest some intention that the will be effective only upon death.

The will must ordinarily be in writing and must be signed by the testator and witnessed. Some states require publication, that is, some declaration that the document which is signed before the witnesses is the testator's will.

[12]Corbin's Estate (Fla App) 391 So2d 731 (1980).

A will may be modified by a codicil or revoked by either the act of the testator or by operation of law.

Probate is the act by which a proper court official accepts a will. Probate of a will may be refused or set aside on grounds that the will is not the free expression of the testator.

A holographic will is one written entirely in the handwriting of the testator. A nuncupative will is an oral will.

If there is a valid will, the last phase of administration of the estate is the distribution of property after the payment of all debts and taxes. General legacies are bequests of money, while specific legacies or specific devises are gifts of identified personal or real property. Legacies abate in the following order: residuary, general, and specific. If a beneficiary named in the will has died before the testator and no alternate provision has been made for such beneficiary, antilapse statutes provide that the gift will not lapse. In that event, the children or heirs of the beneficiary may take the legacy in the place of the deceased beneficiary.

If the decedent does not dispose of all property by will or does not have a will, the property will be distributed according to state intestacy statutes. A surviving spouse may generally elect to take the statutory allocation instead of that provided in the will.

The estate of the testator will be administered by the person appointed in the will (the executor) or if there is no will by a person appointed by the court (an administrator). Creditors who have claims against the estate are required to give notice of their claim to the personal representative, otherwise the claim will be barred. When the estate is insolvent, claims are generally paid in the following order of priority: funeral expenses; administration expenses; family allowance; claims due to the United States; expenses of the last illness; debts due state, county, and city governments; claims for wages; lien claims; and all other debts.

The personal representative must administer the estate according to law. If the misconduct of the executor or administrator or failure to act causes loss to the estate, such representative may be required to indemnify the estate for the amount of the loss.

QUESTIONS AND CASE PROBLEMS

1. What social forces are affected by allowing a person to give property after death by means of leaving a will?
2. Jean repeatedly told her best friend, Dinah, and their neighbors, that Jean would leave her house to Dinah when she died. Jean died without having written any will. Dinah claimed the house and the neighbors testified in court that Jean had repeatedly declared that she would leave the house to Dinah. Is Dinah entitled to the house?
3. Michael wrote his lawyer that he wanted the lawyer to prepare a will which would leave his property in the manner then set forth in the letter. Michael signed and mailed this letter but died before the letter was received by his attorney. On receiving the letter, the attorney offered the letter for probate as the will of Michael. Should it be probated?

4. Iona wrote her will. The following year she wrote another will which expressly revoked the earlier will. Later, while cleaning house, she came across the second will. She mistakenly thought that it was the first will and tore it up because the first will had been revoked. Iona died shortly thereafter. The beneficiaries named in the second will claimed that the second will should be probated. The beneficiaries named in the first will claimed that the second will had been revoked when it was torn up. Had the second will been revoked?

5. Gary died without any will or known relatives. During the last years of Gary's life, his neighbors had continually assisted him and taken care of him. The neighbors agreed that the proper thing to do since there were no relatives was for the neighbors to divide the property which was in Gary's house. Are they correct?

6. Compare attestation and publication as it relates to the formalities for proper execution of a will.

7. What is the purpose of a codicil?

8. Lucille, by the terms of her will, gave and bequeathed her sterling silverware to her son, William, and the balance or residue of her estate to her daughter, Linda. Prior to the death of Lucille, she sold the sterling silverware and deposited the proceeds from the sale in the Eastern Bank. After the death of Lucille, William petitioned the court to award him the proceeds of the sterling silverware. What will the result be?

9. Contrast letters testamentary with letters of administration.

10. Logsdon, who had three children, disliked one of them without any reason. In his will he left only a small amount to the child he disliked and gave the bulk of his estate to the remaining two. Upon his death, the disliked child claimed that the will was void and had been obtained by undue influence. Do you agree? [Logsdon v Logsdon, 412 Ill 19, 104 NE2d 622]

11. Field executed a will. Upon her death the will was found in her safe deposit box, but the part of the will containing the fifth bequest was torn from the will. This torn fragment was also found in the box. There was no evidence that anyone other than Field had ever opened the box. A proceeding was brought to determine whether the will was entitled to be probated. Decide. [Flora v Hughes, 312 Ky 478, 228 SW2d 27]

12. Anna Miller wrote a will 11 pages long and enclosed it in an envelope, which she sealed. She then wrote on the envelope, My last will & testament," and signed her name below this statement. This was the only place where she signed her name on any of the papers. Could this writing be admitted to probate as her will? [Miller's Executor v Shannon (Ky) 299 SW2d 103]

13. A bequeathed the balance of her estate to B and C "if they both be living at the time of my demise and if one shall have predeceased me then all of my estate to the one remaining." Both B and C died before A. B was survived by a daughter, D. C was not survived by any children or grandchildren. A was survived by E, a nephew, the child of a deceased brother. E and D each claimed the estate of A. The claim of D was based on the antilapse statute. The claim of E was based on the fact that he was the closest living relative of A. Who was entitled to A's estate? [Kerr's Estate (CA Dist Col) 433 F2d 479]

14. Plate was about to sign his will. He began writing his name. He made one stroke of the pen on the paper and then laid the pen down stating, "I can't sign it now." The will was offered for probate. Decide.

15. E. J. White wrote by hand and signed the following: "To Whom It May concern. If anything should happen to me, I want all My Property & otherthing & Bonds divided between Marvin, Arlene & my sisters. Eight Thousand to Earl's children, the House 311 North 25 Ave. to Marvin, sell the property. I will finish this later." No change or addition was ever made to this writing. She died seven years later. This writing was offered for probate as her will. Objection was made to the probate on the ground that the last sentence showed that the writing had not been made with testamentary intent. Was this objection valid? [Maines v Davis (Miss) 227 So2d 844]

16. Probate of the will of Vivian Lingenfelter was opposed. It was shown that the testatrix was sick, highly nervous, and extremely jealous and that she committed suicide a week after executing the will. In support of the will, it was shown that she understood the will when she discussed it with an attorney; that her husband was seriously ill when she wrote the will; that he died the following day; and that she grieved his death. A proceeding was brought to determine whether the will was entitled to probate. Decide. [Lingenfelter's Estate, 38 Cal2d 571, 241 P2d 990]

17. Brock made a will in which he bequeathed a legacy of $10,000 to his wife Mary. There then followed a clause stating "it is my express wish that no part of my estate shall go to my son Stewart." No further gift or testamentary provision was made in the will. When Brock died, Mary and Stewart survived him, and his net estate amounted to $30,000. Stewart claims that he is entitled to a share of $20,000. Is he correct?

18. Land duly subscribed and published his will in the presence of two witnesses whom he requested to sign. They signed as witnesses but were not informed of the contents of the will. Has the will been validly executed?

CHAPTER 55

TRUSTS

CHAPTER OBJECTIVES

After studying this chapter you will be able to:
1. Explain the nature of a trust.
2. List the requirements to create a trust.
3. State the duties of a trustee.
4. List the remedies for breach of trust.
5. Explain how a trust may be terminated.
6. Distinguish between tentative trusts, charitable trusts, and implied trusts.
7. Solve problems involving the creation of trusts.

A **trust** is a legal device by which property is held by one person for the benefit of another. It may consist of either real or personal property. Legal problems in the area of trusts invariably require a determination as to the nature of the relationship which has been created by the trust and the rights and obligations of the parties with respect to such relationship.

§ 55:1. Definitions.

The owner of the property who creates the trust is the **settlor**, the word being taken from the old legal language of "settling the property in trust." The settlor is sometimes called the donor or trustor. The person to whom the property is transferred in trust is the **trustee**. The person for whose benefit the trustee holds the property is the **beneficiary** (or **cestui que trust**).

Property held in trust is sometimes called the **trust corpus, trust fund, trust estate,** or **trust res.** A distinction is made between the **principal**, or the property in trust, and the **income** which is earned by the principal and distributed by the trustee.

946

Although an express trust is ordinarily created by a transfer of property, the settlor may retain the property as trustee for the beneficiary. The fact that there is a duty to make a payment does not create a trust.[1]

If the trust is created to take effect within the lifetime of the settlor, it is a **living trust** or an **inter vivos trust**. If the trust is provided for in the settlor's will and is to become effective only when the will takes effect after death, the trust is called a **testamentary trust**.

§ 55:2.   Creation of Trusts.

The requirements to create a trust are not uniform. The following, however, are typical of what is or is not required.

(a) **Consideration.** Since a trust is a transfer of property, consideration is not required, although the absence of consideration may show that the trust is a transfer in fraud of creditors.

(b) **Legality.** A trust may generally be created for any lawful purpose. A trust is invalid when it is for an unlawful purpose or is in fraud of creditors.

(c) **Capacity of Beneficiary.** The capacity of the beneficiary of the trust to hold property or to contract is immaterial. Many trusts are created because the beneficiary lacks legal or actual capacity to manage the property.

(d) **Formality.** In creating a trust, it is common practice to execute a writing, called a **trust agreement** or **deed of trust**. No particular form of language is necessary to create a trust so long as the property, the trust purpose, and the beneficiaries are designated. If an inter vivos trust relates to an interest in land, the statute of frauds requires that the trust be evidenced by a writing setting forth the details of the trust. A writing signed by the trustee which refers to a deed from the trustor can satisfy this requirement. When the trust depends upon a transfer of title to land, there must be a valid transfer of the title to the trustee.

FACTS:

T. K. Laursen executed a deed which purported to convey his Lincoln County property to his son Orville. On the day the deed was executed, Orville Laursen executed an affidavit acknowledging a transfer of property from T. K. Laursen and agreeing that the property would be held in trust for his father, and that his father was to receive all rents and profits from the property, and that the property would be reconveyed upon trustor's request or death. This document was delivered to T. K.'s attorney. Because of the father's mental and physical condition, a conservator was appointed to manage his affairs. The conservator sued Orville to re-cover title to the property. Orville contended that no trust existed.

DECISION:

Judgment for the conservator. Orville is a trustee. The affidavit delivered to the attorney proves that Orville accepted the deed from his father with the intent of holding the property for the benefit of his father. He promised to convey the property to his father on request or, should his father die, to his estate. These promises show Orville's intent to act as trustee for his father's property. [McCaffrey v Laursen (Mont App) 697 P2d 103 (1985)]

---

[1]Spicer v Wright, 215 Va 520, 211 SE2d 79 (1975).

A trust in personal property may be declared orally without any writing. If a trust is created by the will of the settlor, there must be a writing which meets the requirements of a will. The same is true when the trust is not intended to come into existence until the death of the settlor.

In the absence of a specific requirement of the statute of frauds as to land or the statute of wills, any conduct or writing which shows an intent to create a trust will be given effect.

(e) **Intention.** An intention to impose a duty on the trustee with respect to specific property must be expressed. It is not necessary, however, that the word "trust" or "trustee" be used. The settlor will ordinarily name a trustee, but failure to do so is not fatal to the trust because a trustee will be appointed by the court.

(f) **Active Duty.** A trust does not exist unless an active duty is placed upon the trustee to manage the property in some manner or to exercise discretion or judgment. A bare direction to hold the property in trust without any direction as to its use or distribution is not sufficient for an active duty. Thus, when a decedent transferred $5,000 to a trustee to be held in trust for A, no trust was created. In such a case, the intended beneficiary is entitled to receive the property outright as though the decedent had not attempted to create a trust.

(g) **Identity of Beneficiary.** Every trust must have a beneficiary. In a private trust the beneficiaries must be identified by name, description, or designation of the class to which the beneficiaries belong. In a charitable trust it is sufficient that the beneficiaries be members of the public at large or a general class of the public.

Trusts for religious masses, for the maintenance of grave monuments, or for the care of particular animals are technically invalid because there is no human, identified beneficiary; but such trusts are nevertheless enforced because of the social interests that are involved.

(h) **Acceptance of Trust.** As the performance of a trust imposes duties upon the trustee, a trustee may renounce or reject the trust, but acceptance will be presumed in the absence of a disclaimer. A renunciation, however, does not affect the validity of the trust because a court will appoint a substitute trustee if the settlor does not do so.

§ 55:3.   Nature of Beneficiary's Interest.

The effect of a transfer in trust is to divide the property so that the legal title is given to the trustee and the **equitable title** or beneficial interest is given to the beneficiary. The beneficiary may ordinarily transfer or assign such interest in the trust, and the beneficiary's creditors may reach that interest in satisfaction of their claims. An exception arises when the settlor has restricted the trust in such a way that the beneficiary cannot assign nor creditors reach the interest, creating what is commonly called a **spendthrift trust.**[2]

[2]Erickson v Bank of Cal, 25 Wash App 337, 623 P2d 721 (1981).

§ 55:4.   Powers of Trustee.

A trustee can exercise only those powers that are given by law or the trust instrument or those which the court will construe as being impliedly given. Modern trusts commonly give the trustee discretion to make decisions on matters that could not be foreseen by the settlor. For example, the trustee may be authorized to expend principal as well as income when in the trustee's opinion it is necesary for the education or medical care of a beneficiary. The trustee must exercise discretion in a reasonable manner.

§ 55:5.   Duties of Trustee.

The duty of a trustee is to administer the trust. The trustee who accepts the appointment must take all the necessary steps to carry out the trust in a proper manner.

(a) **Performance.** A trustee is under the duty to carry out the trust according to its terms and is personally liable for any loss sustained from an unjustified failure to perform such duties. A trustee cannot delegate the performance of personal duties.[3]

(b) **Due Care.** The trustee is under a duty to use reasonable skill, prudence, and diligence in the performance of trust duties. More simply stated, the trustee must use the care which would be exercised by a reasonable person under the circumstances.

(c) **Loyalty.** A trustee is not permitted to profit personally from the position as trustee, other than to receive the compensation allowed by contract or law.

(d) **Possession and Preservation of Trust Property.** The trustee is under a duty to take possession of trust property and to preserve it from loss or damage. If the property includes accounts receivable or outstanding debts, the trustee is under the duty to collect them.

(e) **Defense of Trust.** The trustee must defend the trust when its validity is disputed in court.

(f) **Production of Income.** Either by express or implied direction, the trustee is required to invest the money or property in enterprises or transactions that will yield an income to the estate.[4]

A trustee is generally permitted to invest in bonds of the United States, or of instrumentalities of the United States; bonds of states, cities, and counties, subject to certain restrictions: first mortgages on real estate when the mortgage does not represent more than a specified percentage of the value of the land; and mortgage bonds of certain types of corporations. Most states now permit a trustee to invest in corporate stocks. Court approval is generally required for investments in real estate.

---

[3]U.A. of Joliet v First Nat'l Bank of Joliet, 93 Ill App3d 890, 417 NE2d 1077 (1981).
[4]Witmer v Blair (Mo App) 588 SW2d 222 (1979).

(g) Accounting and Information. A trustee must keep accurate records so that it can be determined whether the trust has been properly administered. Upon request by a beneficiary, the trustee must furnish information with respect to the trust. Periodically, or at certain times, as determined by the law in each state, a trustee must file an account in court at which time the court passes upon the stewardship of the trust.

§ 55:6.   Remedies for Breach of Trust.

A breach of trust may occur in a variety of ways, which in turn affects the remedies available. These remedies include:

(a) money judgment against trustee for loss caused

(b) injunction or order to compel the trustee to do or refrain from doing an act

(c) criminal prosecution of the trustee for misconduct

(d) tracing and recovery of trust property which has been converted by the trustee,[5] unless the property had been acquired by a bona fide purchaser who gave value and purchased without notice of the breach of trust

(e) judgment against surety on the trustee's bond for loss caused the trust by the trustee's default

(f) removal of the trustee for misconduct, and

(g) suit against third persons who participated in a breach of trust.

§ 55:7.   Termination of Trust.

A trust may be terminated (1) in accordance with its terms,[6] (2) because of the impossibility of attaining the object of the trust; (3) by revocation by the settlor, when allowed by the terms of the trust; (4) by merger of all interests in the same person; and (5) upon the request of all the beneficiaries when there is no express purpose that requires continuation of the trust.

§ 55:8.   Tentative Trusts.

The law has developed a peculiar trust theory to govern a bank deposit made by *A* in an account marked "*A*, in trust for *B*." In the absence of any evidence showing an intention to create a formal trust by this method of deposit, a true trust is not created. Such a deposit is regarded as creating a **tentative trust** which the depositor and the depositor's creditors are permitted to treat as though there were no trust; but if the depositor dies, any money that remains in the account after creditors are paid belongs to the person named as the beneficiary. Some states refuse to recognize tentative trusts, while others have expressly authorized them by statute, or by judicial decision.

[5]General Association of D.S.D.A., Inc. v. General Association of D.S.D.A. (Tex Civ App) 410 SW2d 256 (1966).

[6]Work v National Bank & Trust Company, 260 Iowa 898, 151 NW2d 490 (1967).

FACTS:

Charles Wright opened a savings account in the Farmers State Bank. The account was marked "Charles Wright, Pay on Death to Mary Lowe." It was not intended that Mary should have any right to withdraw money from the account while Charles was alive. Charles thereafter died. By his will, he left his entire estate to his sons. Nothing was said in the will about the bank account. Both Mary and the sons claimed the balance on deposit in the account.

DECISION:

Judgment for Mary. By depositing the money in the bank in a "pay on death" account, Charles had created a valid tentative trust in her favor. The trust could have been revoked by Charles, and his creditors could reach the money on deposit; but once Charles died and no claims were made by creditors, the balance in the account passed to Mary, the named death beneficiary. [Wright's Estate, 17 Ill App3d 894, 308 NE2d 319 (1974)]

§ 55:9. Charitable Trusts.

Often a wealthy donor wishes to benefit society. This may be accomplished by the use of **charitable trusts.** They are administered and created in much the same manner as any other private trust.

(a) **Purpose. Charitable trusts** may be created for any purpose that advances the public welfare. These include trusts to; (1) maintain or propagate religion, religious education, and missionary work; (2) further health and relieve human suffering by establishing institutions or by direct aid of food, clothing, shelter, and medical care to the needy; (3) found or maintain educational institutions, museums, libraries, or aid students or teachers; (4) care for and maintain public cemeteries; (5) erect monuments to public persons or national heroes; (6) construct and maintain public buildings or improvements, such as an irrigation system or a playground; (7) further patriotism; and (8) prevent cruelty to animals.

(b) **Cy Pres Doctrine.** In the absence of a contrary provision in the trust agreement, the law will not permit a charitable trust to end even though the original purpose has been accomplished or can no longer be achieved, or because the beneficiary no longer exists. In such a case the courts apply the **cy pres doctrine,** an abbreviation of the Norman French words "cy pres comme possible" or "as near as possible." By this doctrine the court directs that the trust fund be held for another purpose that will be as near as possible to that intended by the settlor.[7]

If, however, it is clear that the settlor intended the trust to be performed exactly as specified or not at all, the trust fails when it is not possible to follow directions.

(c) **Limitations.** In most aspects a charitable trust is the same as a private trust. In some states additional limitations are imposed. Thus a maximum amount may be set on the property that a charitable corporation may

[7]Trammel v Elliott, 230 Ga 841, 199 SE2d 194 (1973).

own. In some states a decedent is limited as to the amount of property which can be left to charity when the decedent is survived by near relatives. When an absolute gift is made to a charity, the charity generally must hold it in trust for the purposes of the charity.

§ 55:10.   Implied Trusts.

In certain instances trusts are implied in order to carry out the presumed intention of the parties or to protect the former owner of property from the fraud of the present owner. When the court implies a trust to carry out the presumed intent of the parties, the trust is called a **resulting trust;** when it implies a trust to correct or prevent a wrong, it is called a **constructive trust.**[8]

(a) **Purchase Money Resulting Trust.** The most common resulting trust arises when a person pays for the purchase of property but title to the property is taken in the name of another person. It is then presumed that the titleholder was intended to hold as trustee for the benefit of the person paying the money. To give effect to this presumption, a resulting trust is generally imposed upon the property and the titleholder. This means that the titleholder cannot use the property but must dispose of it as directed by the person paying the money. This presumption is not conclusive and may be overcome by evidence showing that it was the intention of the person paying the money to lend the money to the person taking title or to make a gift of the property. If the person paying the money is the husband or parent of the person taking title, there is a presumption that the payment was made as a gift, in which case a resulting trust does not arise unless the presumption of a gift is overcome by contrary evidence.

(b) **Constructive Trust of Improperly Acquired Property.** When a person has acquired title to property by unlawful or unfair means or in breach of a duty as an agent or trustee, the law will make such person hold it as constructive trustee for the person who has been unjustly deprived of the property. Thus if an agent privately purchases property that was to be purchased for the principal, the latter may hold the agent as constructive trustee of that property.

FACTS:

Shaw and his wife faced possible foreclosure on their home by First Federal Loan. Klein, their close friend and management consultant for their firm, made the following proposal. The Shaws would deed their house to him. He would assume the payments to First Federal Loan and lease the house back to the Shaws. Klein promised to reconvey the house to them when they got back on their feet. Klein's proposal was accepted and title was transferred to him. Later, Klein refused to reconvey the house and the Shaws brought an action against Klein alleging that Klein held title as a constructive trustee for the benefit of the Shaws.

[8]Leonard v Courts, 221 Va 582, 272 SE2d 190 (1980).

DECISION:

Judgment for the Shaws. There was a confidential relationship between Klein and the Shaws based upon their friendship and as a business advisor to their firm. A betrayal of a confidential relationship is deemed fraudulent. A constructive trust will be created by courts of equity whenever title to property is found in one who in fairness ought not to retain it. Klein is treated as if he had been an express trustee from the date of the wrongful holding and is required to reconvey the property to the Shaws. [Klein v Shaw (Idaho App) 706 P2d 1348 (1985)]

SUMMARY

A trust is a legal device by which property is held by one person for the benefit of another. The settlor creates the trust and the person for whose benefit the trustee holds the property is the beneficiary. Property held in trust is called the trust corpus, trust fund, trust estate, or res.

A trust is usually created by a writing called a trust agreement or deed of trust. No particular form or language is required. A trust will not exist unless an active duty is placed upon the trustee to manage the property in some manner. Acceptance of duties under a trust is presumed.

Legal title to trust property is given to the trustee while equitable title is held by the beneficiary. A beneficiary may transfer an interest in the trust except in a spendthrift trust.

The trustee can only exercise those powers that are given by law or the trust instrument. The trustee must administer the trust and carry out the trust in a proper manner. A trustee may be sued for breach of the terms of the trust agreement. A trust comes to an end when its terms so provide or when it becomes impossible to attain the object of the trust.

Many states refuse to recognize tentative trusts while others have expressly authorized them.

A charitable trust is created where a donor wishes to benefit society. By the cy pres doctrine, the law will not permit a charitable trust to end though the original purpose can no longer be attained.

A trust to carry out the presumed intention of the parties is called a resulting trust, while a trust established to correct a wrong is called a constructive trust.

QUESTIONS AND CASE PROBLEMS

1. What social forces are affected by the rule of law authorizing the enforcement or application of constructive trusts?
2. Dolores states in her will "I leave $10,000 to the First National Bank in trust for my niece, Clara." After the death of Dolores, the will is probated. Is the trust for Clara valid?
3. Robert is trustee under the will of his uncle. As trustee, he is holding $400,000. Because of the uncertainty of the stock market and the rising cost of living, Robert is uncertain as to how he should invest the money. He deposits it all in a checking account in the name of the trust estate. The checking account does not pay any interest. The beneficiaries of the

trust complain that Robert will be liable to the trust for failing to earn income for the trust. Are they correct?

4. Rowena wrote a will which made a bequest of $1,000,000 in trust to pay the income to the Ulan Free Public Library. She also stated that if for any reason the library ceased to exist or moved from the city, the money should be paid to her sister, Josephine, or, if the latter were deceased, to the lineal descendants of Josephine. Rowena died. Two years later Josephine died. Ten years later the Ulan Library moved to another city. A new library was formed by the "Friends of Learning." It rented the building formerly occupied by the Ulan Library and notified the trustee of Rowena's will that it claimed the money from the library bequest by virtue of the cy pres doctrine. Josephine's son, Milton, claimed the money. Decide.

5. What is the difference between an inter vivos trust and a testamentary trust?

6. State three ways a trust may be terminated.

7. What is the purpose of the cy pres doctrine?

8. Rachael conveyed certain land to Roland in trust for her daughter, Mary. Roland refused to accept the trust. What effect does this refusal have on the rights of her daughter, Mary?

9. Gerald was the agent of Victor. Gerald was authorized to purchase a certain tract of land for Victor. Gerald purchased the land but took title to the land in his own name instead of the name of Victor. When Victor learned of this, he fired Gerald and demanded that Gerald convey the land to him. Gerald refused to do so and Victor brought a lawsuit in which he claimed that Gerald held the land for him as constructive trustee and requested the court to order Gerald to convey the land to him. Gerald raised the defenses that he had never agreed to be a trustee on behalf of Victor and that he did not owe Victor any obligation as he was no longer Victor's agent. Are these defenses valid?

10. By her will, Owsley left money to Bell as trustee to hold as a scholarship fund to pay tuition for worthy students attending "Carthage College, Carthage, Illinois." After her death, Carthage College moved to Wisconsin. Another college in Carthage, Illinois claimed that the trust fund should be held for its benefit under the cy pres doctrine. Was it correct? [Bell v Carthage College, 103 IllApp2d 289, 243 NE2d 23]

11. Burton wrote a will of 3 sentences. In the first she named her brother as the "executor and trustee" of her estate. In the next sentence she left her property to her brother. In the last sentence she stated "My Brother knows my wishes and will carry them out to the best of his ability." After her death, the brother claimed her entire estate for himself. The heirs claimed that there was no trust and that the estate should therefore pass to them. Was the brother correct? [Burton v Irwin, 212 Va 104, 181 SE2d 624]

12. By her will, Hendricks provided: "I give, devise, and bequeath (the balance of my estate) to the City of Brookfield, Missouri, for the sole purpose of building and equipping and maintaining a city hospital...." The city claimed that this was an absolute gift to the city subject to a

condition as to its use. Do you agree? [Ramsey v City of Brookfield, 361 Mo 857, 237 SW2d 143]

13. The Pioneer Trust and Savings Bank was trustee of certain land for the benefit of Harmon. Under the terms of the trust, Harmon could require the trustee to sell the land as he directed. Schneider wrote Pioneer Trust, offering to buy the land. Harmon made a written notation on the letter that he accepted the offer and sent it back to Schneider. Schneider withdrew his offer and claimed that there was no contract. Harmon claimed that Schneider was bound by a contract. Decide. [Schneider v Pioneer Trust and Savings Bank, 26 IllApp2d 463, 168 NE2d 808]

14. Fry was made trustee of approximately 880 acres of oil and gas land. The trust agreement gave him authority to execute "leases" of the land. He executed a lease of 80 acres to McCormick. Later Fry sued to set aside the lease on the ground that he had no authority to lease a portion of the property. Decide. [Fry v McCormick, 170 Kan 741, 228 P2d 727]

15. Moulton executed and delivered a deed transferring property in trust to pay the income to his grandchild, Henry, and others for life, subject to spendthrift-trust limitations. Later, Henry was divorced and, as part of the property settlement with his wife, assigned to her a share of his interest in the income from the trust. The trustee refused to recognize the assignment. An action was brought to determine the validity of the assignment. Decide.

16. By his will, Biles directed that the balance of his estate be given to such charitable organization or organizations as his executors should select. Objection was made that this gave the executors authority to apply the cy pres doctrine. Was this correct? [Biles v Martin (Ala) 259 So2d 258]

17. Lauren obtains a conveyance of property owned by Tomas, an illiterate person, by falsely representing that a document Tomas was to sign was a tax form. It was in fact a deed. What type of trust, if any, arises in this situation.

18. Turner conveyed certain land to Charles in trust for his son Peter. Charles refused to accept the trust. What effect, if any, does this have on the rights of Peter?

APPENDICES

HOW TO FIND THE LAW

In order to determine what the law on a particular question or issue is, it may be necessary to examine (1) compilations of constitutions, treaties, statutes, executive orders, proclamations, and administrative regulations; (2) reports of state and federal court decisions; (3) digests of opinions; (4) treatises on the law; and (5) looseleaf services.

COMPILATIONS

In the consideration of a legal problem in business it is necessary to determine whether the matter is affected or controlled by the Constitution, national or state; by a national treaty; by an Act of Congress or a state legislature, or by a city ordinance; by a decree or proclamation of the President of the United States, a governor, or a mayor; or by a regulation of a federal, state, or local administrative agency.

Each body or person that makes laws, regulations, or ordinances usually will compile and publish at the end of each year or session all of the matter that it has adopted. In addition to the periodical or annual volumes, it is common to compile all the treaties, statutes, regulations, or ordinances in separate volumes. To illustrate, the federal Anti-Injunction Act may be cited as the Act of March 23, 1932, 47 Stat 70, 29 USC Sections 101 et seq. This means that this law was enacted on March 23, 1932, and that this law can be found at page 70 in Volume 47 of the reports that contain all of the statutes adopted by the Congress.

The second part of the citation, 29 USC Sections 101 et seq., means that in the collection of all of the federal statutes, which is known as the United States Code, the full text of the statute can be found in the sections of the 29th title beginning with Section 101.

COURT DECISIONS

For complicated or important legal cases or when an appeal is to be taken, a court will generally write an *opinion*, which explains why the court made the decision. Appellate courts as a rule write opinions. The great majority of these decisions, particularly in the case of the appellate courts, are collected and printed. In order to avoid confusion, the opinions of each court will ordinarily be printed in a separate set of reports, either by official reporters or private publishers.

In the reference "Pennoyer v Neff, 95 US 714, 24 LEd 565," the first part states the names of the parties. It does not necessarily tell who was the plaintiff and who was the defendant. When an action is begun in a lower court, the first name is that of the plaintiff and the second name that of the defendant. When the case is appealed, generally the name of the person taking the appeal appears on the records of the higher court as the first one and that of the adverse party as the second. Sometimes, therefore, the original order of the names of the parties is reversed.

The balance of the reference consists of two citations. The first citation, 95 US 714, means that the opinion which the court filed in the case of Pennoyer and Neff may be found on page 714 of the 95th volume of a series of books in which are printed officially the opinions of the United

States Supreme Court. Sometimes the same opinion is printed in two different sets of volumes. In the example, 24 LEd 565 means that in the 24th volume of another set of books, called *Lawyer's Edition*, of the United States Supreme Court Reports, the same opinion begins on page 565.

In opinions by a state court there are also generally two citations, as in the case of "Morrow v Corbin, 122 Tex 553, 62 SW2d 641." This means that the opinion in the lawsuit between Morrow and Corbin may be found in the 122d volume of the reports of the highest court of Texas, beginning on page 553; and also in Volume 62 of the *Southwestern Reporter*, Second Series, at page 641.

The West Publishing Company publishes a set of sectional reporters covering the entire United States. They are called sectional because each reporter, instead of being limited to a particular court or a particular state, covers the decisions of the courts of a particular section of the country. Thus the decisions of the courts of Arkansas, Kentucky, Missouri, Tennessee, and Texas are printed by the West Publishing company as a group in a sectional reporter called the *Southwestern Reporter*.[1] Because of the large number of decisions involved, generally only the opinions of the state appellate courts are printed. A number of states[2] have discontinued publication of the opinions of their courts, and those opinions are now found only in the West reporters.

The reason for the "Second Series" in the Southwestern citation is that when there were 300 volumes in the original series, instead of calling the next volume 301, the publisher called it Volume 1, Second Series. Thus 62 SW2d Series

really means the 362d volume of the *Southwestern Reporter*. Six to eight volumes appear in a year for each geographic section.

In addition to these state reporters, the West Publishing Company publishes a *Federal Supplement*, which primarily reports the opinions of the Federal District Courts; the *Federal Reporter*, which primarily reports the decisions of the United States Courts of Appeals; and the *Supreme Court Reporter*, which reports the decisions of the United States Supreme Court. The Supreme Court decisions are also reported in a separate set called the *Lawyers' Edition*, published by the Lawyers Co-operative Publishing Company.

The reports published by the West Publishing Company and Lawyers Co-operative Publishing Company are unofficial reports, while those bearing the name or abbreviation of the United States or of a state, such as "95 US 714" or "122 Tex 553" are official reports. This means that in the case of the latter, the particular court, such as the United States Supreme Court, has officially authorized that its decisions be printed and that by federal statute such official printing is made. In the case of the unofficial reporters, the publisher prints the decisions of a court on its own initiative. Such opinions are part of the public domain and not subject to any copyright or similar restriction.

DIGESTS OF OPINIONS

The reports of court decisions are useful only if one has the citation, that is, the name and volume number of the book and the page number of the opinion one is seeking. For this reason, digests of the decisions have been prepared. These digests organize the entire field of law under major headings, which are then arranged in alphabetic order. Under each heading, such as "Contracts," the subject is divided into the different questions that can arise with respect to that field. A master outline is thus created on the subject. This outline includes short paragraphs describing what each case holds and giving its citation.

TREATISES AND RESTATEMENTS

Very helpful in finding a case or a statute are the treatises on the law. These may be special

[1] The sectional reporters are: Atlantic—A. (Connecticut, Delaware, District of Columbia, Maine, Maryland, New Hampshire, New Jersey, Pennsylvania, Rhode Island, Vermont); Northeastern—N.E. (Illinois, Indiana, Massachusetts, New York, Ohio); Northwestern—N.W. (Iowa, Michigan, Minnesota, Nebraska, North Dakota, South Dakota, Wisconsin); Pacific—P. (Alaska, Arizona, California, Colorado, Hawaii, Idaho, Kansas, Montana, Nevada, New Mexico, Oklahoma, Oregon, Utah, Washington, Wyoming); Southeastern—S.E. (Georgia, North Carolina, South Carolina, Virginia, West Virginia); Southwestern—S.W. (Arkansas, Kentucky, Missouri, Tennessee, Texas); and Southern—So. (Alabama, Florida, Louisiana, Mississippi). There is also a special New York State reporter known as the New York Supplement and a special California State reporter known as the California Reporter.

[2] See, for example, Alaska, Florida, Iowa, Kentucky, Louisiana, Maine, Mississippi, Missouri, North Dakota, Oklahoma, Texas, and Wyoming.

books, each written by an author on a particular subject, such as *Williston on Contracts, Bogert on Trusts, Fletcher on Corporations,* or they may be general encyclopedias, as in the case of *American Jurisprudence, American Jurisprudence, Second,* and *Corpus Juris Secundum.*

Another type of treatise is found in the restatements of the law prepared by the American Law Institute. Each restatement consists of one or more volumes devoted to a particular phase of the law, such as the *Restatement of the Law of Contracts, Restatement of the Law of Agency,* and *Restatement of the Law of Property.* In each restatement the American Law Institute, acting through special committees of judges, lawyers, and professors of law, has set forth what the law is; and in many areas where there is no law or the present rule is regarded as unsatisfactory, the restatement specifies what the Institute deems to be the desirable rule.

LOOSE-LEAF SERVICES

A number of private publishers, notably Commerce Clearing House and Prentice-Hall, publish loose-leaf books devoted to particular branches of the law. Periodically the publisher sends to the purchaser a number of pages that set forth any decision, regulation, or statute made or adopted since the prior set of pages was prepared. Such services are unofficial.

THE CONSTITUTION
OF THE UNITED STATES

We the people of the United States, in order to form a more perfect union, establish justice, insure domestic tranquillity, provide for the common defense, promote the general welfare, and secure the blessings of liberty to ourselves and our posterity, do ordain and establish this Constitution for the United States of America.

Article I

Section 1.   All legislative powers herein granted shall be vested in a Congress of the United States, which shall consist of a Senate and House of Representatives.

Section 2.   1. The House of Representatives shall be composed of members chosen every second year by the people of the several States, and the electors in each State shall have the qualifications requisite for electors of the most numerous branch of the State legislature.

2. No person shall be a representative who shall not have attained to the age of twenty-five years, and been seven years a citizen of the United States, and who shall not, when elected, be an inhabitant of that State in which he shall be chosen.

3. Representatives and direct taxes[1] shall be apportioned among the several States which may be included within this Union, according to their respective numbers, which shall be determined by adding to the whole number of free persons, including those bound to service for a term of years, and excluding Indians not taxed, *three fifths of all other persons.*[2] The actual enumeration shall be made within three years after the first meeting of the Congress of the United States, and within every subsequent term of ten years, in such manner as they shall by law direct. The number of representatives shall not exceed one for every thirty thousand, but each State shall have at least one representative; and until such enumeration shall be made, the State of New Hampshire shall be entitled to choose three, Massachusetts eight, Rhode Island and Providence Plantations one, Connecticut five, New York six,

New Jersey four, Pennsylvania eight, Delaware one, Maryland six, Virginia ten, North Carolina five, South Carolina five, and Georgia three.

4. When vacancies happen in the representation from any State, the executive authority thereof shall issue writs of election to fill such vacancies.

5. The House of Representatives shall choose their speaker and other officers; and shall have the sole power of impeachment.

Section 3.   1. The Senate of the United States shall be composed of two senators from each State, *chosen by the legislature thereof,*[1] for six years; and each senator shall have one vote.

2. Immediately after they shall be assembled in consequence of the first election, they shall be divided as equally as may be into three classes. The seats of the senators of the first class shall be vacated at the expiration of the second year, of the second class at the expiration of the fourth year, and of the third class at the expiration of the sixth year, so that one third may be chosen every second year; and if vacancies happen by resignation, or otherwise, during the recess of the legislature of any State, the executive thereof may make temporary appointments until the next meeting of the legislature, which shall then fill such vacancies.[3]

3. No person shall be a senator who shall not have attained to the age of thirty years, and been nine years a citizen of the United States, and who shall not, when elected, be an inhabitant of that State for which he shall be chosen.

4. The Vice President of the United States shall be President of the Senate, but shall have no vote, unless they be equally divided.

5. The Senate shall choose their other officers, and

---

[1]   See the 16th Amendment.
[2]   See the 14th Amendment.

[3]   See the 17th Amendment.

also a president *pro tempore*, in the absence of the Vice President, or when he shall exercise the office of the President of the United States.

6. The Senate shall have the sole power to try all impeachments. When sitting for that purpose, they shall be on oath or affirmation. When the President of the United States is tried, the chief justice shall preside: and no person shall be convicted without the concurrence of two thirds of the members present.

7. Judgment in cases of impeachment shall not extend further than to removal from office, and disqualifications to hold and enjoy any office of honor, trust or profit under the United States: but the party convicted shall nevertheless be liable and subject to indictment, trial, judgment and punishment, according to law.

Section 4. 1. The times, places, and manner of holding elections for senators and representatives, shall be prescribed in each State by the legislature thereof; but the Congress may at any time by law make or alter such regulations, except as to the places of choosing senators.

2. The Congress shall assemble at least once in every year, and such meeting shall be on the first Monday in December, unless they shall by law appoint a different day.

Section 5. 1. Each House shall be the judge of the elections, returns and qualifications of its own members, and a majority of each shall constitute a quorum to do business; but a smaller number may adjourn from day to day, and may be authorized to compel the attendance of absent members, in such manner, and under such penalties as each House may provide.

2. Each House may determine the rules of its proceedings, punish its members for disorderly behavior, and, with the concurrence of two thirds, expel a member.

3. Each House shall keep a journal of its proceedings, and from time to time publish the same, excepting such parts as may in their judgment require secrecy; and the yeas and nays of the members of either House on any question shall, at the desire of one fifth of those present, be entered on the journal.

4. Neither House, during the session of Congress, shall, without the consent of the other, adjourn for more than three days, nor to any other place than that in which the two Houses shall be sitting.

Section 6. 1. The senators and representatives shall receive a compensation for their services, to be ascertained by law, and paid out of the Treasury of the United States. They shall in all cases, except treason, felony, and breach of the peace, be privileged from arrest during their attendance at the session of their respective Houses, and in going to and returning from the same; and for any speech or debate in either House, they shall not be questioned in any other place.

2. No senator or representative shall, during the time for which he was elected, be appointed to any civil office under the authority of the United States, which shall have been created, or the emoluments whereof shall have been increased during such time; and no person holding any office under the United States shall be a member of either House during his continuance in office.

Section 7. 1. All bills for raising revenue shall originate in the House of Representatives; but the Senate may propose or concur with amendments as on other bills.

2. Every bill which shall have passed the House of Representatives and the Senate, shall, before it becomes a law, be presented to the President of the United States; if he approves he shall sign it, but if not he shall return it, with his objections to that House in which it shall have originated, who shall enter the objections at large on their journal, and proceed to reconsider it. If after such reconsideration two thirds of that House shall agree to pass the bill, it shall be sent, together with the objections, to the other House, by which it shall likewise be reconsidered, and if approved by two thirds of that House, it shall become a law. But in all such cases the votes of both Houses shall be determined by yeas and nays, and the names of the persons voting for and against the bill shall be entered on the journal of each House respectively. If any bill shall not be returned by the President within ten days (Sundays excepted) after it shall have been presented to him, the same shall be a law, in like manner as if he had signed it, unless the Congress by their adjournment prevent its return, in which case it shall not be a law.

3. Every order, resolution, or vote to which the concurrence of the Senate and the House of Representatives may be necessary (except on a question of adjournment) shall be presented to the President of the United States; and before the same shall take effect, shall be approved by him, or being disapproved by him, shall be repassed by two thirds of the Senate and House of Representatives, according to the rules and limitations prescribed in the case of a bill.

Section 8. The Congress shall have the power

1. To lay and collect taxes, duties, imposts, and excises, to pay the debts and provide for the common defense and general welfare of the United States; but all duties, imposts, and excises shall be uniform throughout the United States;

2. To borrow money on the credit of the United States;

3. To regulate commerce with foreign nations, and among the several States, and with the Indian tribes;

4. To establish a uniform rule of naturalization, and uniform laws on the subject of bankruptcies throughout the United States;

5. To coin money, regulate the value thereof, and of foreign coin, and fix the standard of weights and measures;

6. To provide for the punishment of counterfeiting the securities and current coin of the United States;

7. To establish post offices and post roads;

8. To promote the progress of science and useful arts, by securing for limited times to authors and inventors the exclusive right to their respective writings and discoveries;

9. To constitute tribunals inferior to the Supreme Court;

10. To define and punish piracies and felonies committed on the high seas, and offenses against the law of nations;

11. To declare war, grant letters of marque and reprisal, and make rules concerning captures on land and water;

12. To raise and support armies, but no appropriation of money to that use shall be for a longer term than two years;

13. To provide and maintain a navy;

14. To make rules for the government and regulation of the land and naval forces;

15. To provide for calling forth the militia to execute the laws of the Union, suppress insurrections and repel invasions;

16. To provide for organizing, arming, and disciplining the militia, and for governing such part of them as may be employed in the service of the United States, reserving to the States respectively, the appointment of the officers, and the authority of training the militia according to the discipline prescribed by Congress.

17. To exercise exclusive legislation in all cases whatsoever, over such district (not exceeding ten miles square) as may, by cession of particular States, and the acceptance of Congress, become the seat of the government of the United States, and to exercise like authority over all places purchased by the consent of the legislature of the State in which the same shall be, for the erection of forts, magazines, arsenals, dockyards, and other needful buildings; and

18. To make all laws which shall be necessary and proper for carrying into execution the foregoing powers, and all other powers vested by this Constitution in the government of the United States, or in any department or officer thereof.

Section 9.   1. The migration or importation of such persons as any of the States now existing shall think proper to admit, shall not be prohibited by the Congress prior to the year one thousand eight hundred and eight, but a tax or duty may be imposed on such importation, not exceeding ten dollars for each person.

2. The privilege of the writ of *habeas corpus* shall not be suspended, unless when in cases of rebellion or invasion the public safety may require it.

3. No bill of attainder or *ex post facto* law shall be passed.

4. No capitation, or other direct, tax shall be laid, unless in proportion to the census or enumeration hereinbefore directed to be taken.[4]

---

[4]   See the 16th Amendment.

5. No tax or duty shall be laid on articles exported from any State.

6. No preference shall be given by any regulation of commerce or revenue to the ports of one State over those of another: nor shall vessels bound to, or from, one State be obliged to enter, clear, or pay duties in another.

7. No money shall be drawn from the treasury, but in consequence of appropriations made by law; and a regular statement and account of the receipts and expenditures of all public money shall be published from time to time.

8. No title of nobility shall be granted by the United States: and no person holding any office of profit or trust under them, shall, without the consent of the Congress, accept of any present, emolument, office, or title, of any kind whatever, from any king, prince, or foreign State.

Section 10.   1. No State shall enter into any treaty, alliance, or confederation; grant letters of marque and reprisal; coin money; emit bills of credit; make anything but gold and silver coin a tender in payment of debts; pass any bill of attainder, *ex post facto* law, or law impairing the obligation of contracts, or grant any title of nobility.

2. No State shall, without the consent of the Congress, lay any imposts or duties on imports or exports, except what may be absolutely necessary for executing its inspection laws: and the net produce of all duties and imposts laid by any State on imports or exports, shall be for the use of the treasury of the United States; and all such laws shall be subject to the revision and control of the Congress.

3. No State shall, without the consent of the Congress, lay any duty of tonnage, keep troops, or ships of war in time of peace, enter into any agreement or compact with another State, or with a foreign power, or engage in war, unless actually invaded, or in such imminent danger as will not admit of delay.

Article II

Section 1.   1. The executive power shall be vested in a President of the United States of America. He shall hold his office during the term of four years, and, together with the Vice President, chosen for the same term, be elected as follows:

2. Each State shall appoint, in such manner as the legislature thereof may direct, a number of electors, equal to the whole number of senators and representatives to which the State may be entitled in the Congress: but no senator or representative, or person holding an office of trust or profit under the United States, shall be appointed an elector.

The electors shall meet in their respective States, and vote by ballot for two persons, of whom one at least shall not be an inhabitant of the same State with themselves. And they shall make a list of all the persons voted for, and of the number of votes for each; which list they shall sign and certify, and transmit sealed to the seat of the government of the United States, directed to the president of the Senate. The president of the Senate shall, in the presence of the Senate and House of Representatives, open all the certificates, and the votes shall then be counted. The person having the greatest number of votes shall be the President, if such number be a majority of the whole number of electors appointed; and if there be more than one who have such majority, and have an equal number of votes, then the House of Representatives shall immediately choose by ballot one of them for President; and if no person have a majority, then from the five highest on the list the said House shall in like manner choose the President. But in choosing the President, the votes shall be taken by States, the representation from each State having one vote; a quorum for this purpose shall consist of a member or members from two thirds of the States, and a majority of all the States shall be necessary to a choice. In every case, after the choice of the President, the person having the greatest number of votes of the electors shall be the Vice President. But if there should remain two or more who have equal votes, the Senate shall choose from them by ballot the Vice President.[5]

3. The Congress may determine the time of choosing the electors, and the day on which they shall give their votes; which day shall be the same throughout the United States.

4. No person except a natural born citizen, or a citizen of the United States, at the time of the adoption of this Constitution, shall be eligible to the office of President; neither shall any person be eligible to that office who shall not have attained to the age of thirty-five years, and been fourteen years a resident within the United States.

5. In case of the removal of the President from office, or of his death, resignation, or inability to discharge the powers and duties of the said office, the same shall devolve on the Vice President, and the Congress may by law provide for the case of removal, death, resignation, or inability, both of the President and Vice President, declaring what officer shall then act as President, and such officer shall act accordingly, until the disability be removed, or a President shall be elected.

6. The President shall, at stated times, receive for his services a compensation, which shall neither be increased nor diminished during the period for which he shall have been elected, and he shall not receive within that period any other emolument from the United States, or any of them.

7. Before he enter on the execution of his office, he shall take the following oath or affirmation: — "I do solemnly swear (or affirm) that I will faithfully execute the office of President of the United States, and will to the best of my ability, preserve, protect and defend the Constitution of the United States."

Section 2. 1. The President shall be commander in chief of the army and navy of the United States, and of the militia of the several States, when called into the actual service of the United States; he may require the opinion, in writing, of the principal officer in each of the executive departments, upon any subject relating to the duties of their respective office, and he shall have power to grant reprieves and pardons for offenses against the United States, except in cases of impeachment.

2. He shall have power, by and with the advice and consent of the Senate, to make treaties, provided two thirds of the senators present concur; and he shall nominate, and by and with the advice and consent of the Senate, shall appoint ambassadors, other public ministers and consuls, judges of the Supreme Court, and all other officers of the United States, whose appointments are not herein otherwise provided for, and which shall be established by law: but the Congress may by law vest the appointment of such inferior officers, as they think proper, in the President alone, in the courts of law, or in the heads of departments.

3. The President shall have power to fill up all vacancies that may happen during the recess of the Senate, by granting commissions which shall expire at the end of their next session.

Section 3. He shall from time to time give to the Congress information of the state of the Union, and recommend to their consideration such measures as he shall judge necessary and expedient; he may, on extraordinary occasions, convene both Houses, or either of them, and in case of disagreement between them with respect to the time of adjournment, he may adjourn them to such time as he shall think proper; he shall receive ambassadors and other public ministers; he shall take care that the laws be faithfully executed, and shall commission all the officers of the United States.

Section 4. The President, Vice President, and all civil officers of the United States, shall be removed from office on impeachment for, and conviction of, treason, bribery, or other high crimes and misdemeanors.

Article III

Section 1. The judicial power of the United States shall be vested in one Supreme Court, and in such inferior courts as the Congress may from time to time ordain and establish. The judges, both of the Supreme and inferior courts, shall hold their offices during good behavior, and shall, at stated times, receive for their services, a compensation, which shall not be diminished during their continuance in office.

Section 2. 1. The judicial power shall extend to all cases, in law and equity, arising under this Consti-

[5] Superseded by the 12th Amendment.

tution, the laws of the United States, and treaties made, or which shall be made, under their authority; — to all cases affecting ambassadors, other public ministers and consuls; — to all cases of admiralty and maritime jurisdiction; — to controversies to which the United States shall be a party; — to controversies between two or more States; between a State and citizens of another State;[6] — between citizens of different States; — between citizens of the same State claiming lands under grants of different States, and between a State, or the citizens thereof, and foreign States citizens or subjects.

2. In all cases affecting ambassadors, other public ministers and consuls, and those in which a State shall be party, the Supreme Court shall have original jurisdiction. In all the other cases before mentioned, the Supreme Court shall have appellate jurisdiction, both as to law and to fact, with such exceptions, and under such regulations as the Congress shall make.

3. The trial of all crimes, except in cases of impeachment, shall be by jury; and such trial shall be held in the State where the said crimes shall have been committed; but when not committed within any State, the trial shall be at such place or places as the Congress may by law have directed.

Section 3. 1. Treason against the United States shall consist only in levying war against them, or in adhering to their enemies, giving them aid and comfort. No person shall be convicted of treason unless on the testimony of two witnesses to the same overt act, or on confession in open court.

2. The Congress shall have power to declare the punishment of treason, but no attainder of treason shall work corruption of blood, or forfeiture except during the life of the person attained.

Article IV

Section 1. Full faith and credit shall be given in each State to the public acts, records, and judicial proceedings of every other State. And the Congress may by general laws prescribe the manner in which such acts, records and proceedings shall be proved, and the effect thereof.

Section 2. 1. The citizens of each State shall be entitled to all privileges and immunities of citizens in the several States.[7]

2. A person charged in any State with treason, felony, or other crime, who shall flee from justice, and be found in another State, shall on demand of the executive authority of the State from which he fled, be delivered up to be removed to the State having jurisdiction of the crime.

3. No person held to service or labor in one State under the laws thereof, escaping into another, shall in consequence of any law or regulation therein, be discharged from such service or labor, but shall be delivered up on claim of the party to whom such service or labor may be due.[8]

Section 3. 1. New States may be admitted by the Congress into this Union; but no new State shall be formed or erected within the jurisdiction of any other State, nor any State be formed by the junction of two or more States, or parts of States, without the consent of the legislatures of the States concerned as well as of the Congress.

2. The Congress shall have power to dispose of and make all needful rules and regulations respecting the territory or other property belonging to the United States; and nothing in this Constitution shall be so construed as to prejudice any claims of the United States, or of any particular State.

Section 4. The United States shall guarantee to every State in this Union a republican form of government, and shall protect each of them against invasion; and on application of the legislature, or of the executive (when the legislature cannot be convened) against domestic violence.

Article V

The Congress, whenever two thirds of both Houses shall deem it necessary, shall propose amendments to this Constitution, or, on the application of the legislature of two thirds of the several States, shall call a convention for proposing amendments, which in either case, shall be valid to all intents and purposes, as part of this Constitution when ratified by the legislatures of three fourths of the several States, or by conventions in three fourths thereof, as the one or the other mode of ratification may be proposed by the Congress; Provided that no amendment which may be made prior to the year one thousand eight hundred and eight shall in any manner affect the first and fourth clauses in the ninth section of the first article; and that no State, without its consent, shall be deprived of its equal suffrage in the Senate.

Article VI

1. All debts contracted and engagements entered into, before the adoption of this Constitution, shall be as valid against the United States under this Constitution, as under the Confederation.[9]

2. This Constitution, and the laws of the United States which shall be made in pursuance thereof; and all treaties made, or which shall be made, under the authority of the United States, shall be the supreme law of the land; and the Judges in every State shall be bound thereby, anything in the Constitution or laws of any State to the contrary notwithstanding.

---

6 See the 11th Amendment.
7 See the 14th Amendment, Sec. 1.

8 See the 13th Amendment.
9 See the 14th Amendment, Sec. 4.

3. The senators and representatives before mentioned, and the members of the several State legislatures, and all executive and judicial officers, both of the United States and of the several States, shall be bound by oath or affirmation to support this Constitution; but no religious test shall ever be required as a qualification to any office or public trust under the United States.

Article VII

The ratification of the conventions of nine States shall be sufficient for the establishment of this Constitution between the States so ratifying the same.

Done in Convention by the unanimous consent of the States present the seventeenth day of September in the year of our Lord one thousand seven hundred and eighty-seven, and of the independence of the United States of America the twelfth. In witness whereof we have hereunto subscribed our names.

AMENDMENTS

First Ten Amendments passed by Congress Sept. 25, 1789. Ratified by three-fourths of the States December 15, 1791.

Article I

Congress shall make no law respecting an establishment of religion, or prohibiting the free exercise thereof; or abridging the freedom of speech, or of the press; or the right of the people peaceably to assemble, and to petition the government for a redress of grievances.

Article II

A well regulated militia, being necessary to the security of a free State, the right of the people to keep and bear arms, shall not be infringed.

Article III

No soldier shall, in time of peace be quartered in any house, without the consent of the owner, nor in time of war, but in a manner to be prescribed by law.

Article IV

The right of the people to be secure in their persons, houses, papers, and effects, against unreasonable searches and seizures, shall not be violated, and no warrants shall issue, but upon probable cause, supported by oath or affirmation, and particularly describing the place to be searched, and the persons or things to be seized.

Article V

No person shall be held to answer for a capital, or otherwise infamous crime, unless on a presentment or indictment of a grand jury, except in cases arising in the land or naval forces, or in the militia, when in actual service in time of war or public danger; nor shall any person be subject for the same offense to be twice put in jeopardy of life or limb; nor shall be compelled in any criminal case to be a witness against himself, nor be deprived of life, liberty, or property, without due process of law; nor shall private property be taken for public use without just compensation.

Article VI

In all criminal prosecutions, the accused shall enjoy the right to a speedy and public trial, by an impartial jury of the State and district wherein the crime shall have been committed, which district shall have been previously ascertained by law, and to be informed of the nature and cause of the accusation; to be confronted with the witnesses against him; to have compulsory process for obtaining witnesses in his favor, and to have the assistance of counsel for his defense.

Article VII

In suits at common law, where the value in controversy shall exceed twenty dollars, the right of trial by jury shall be preserved, and no fact tried by a jury shall be otherwise reexamined in any court of the United States, than according to the rules of the common law.

Article VIII

Excessive bail shall not be required, nor excessive fines imposed, nor cruel and unusual punishments inflicted.

Article IX

The enumeration in the Constitution of certain rights shall not be construed to deny or disparage others retained by the people.

Article X

The powers not delegated to the United States by the Constitution, nor prohibited by it to the States, are reserved to the States respectively, or to the people.

Article XI

Passed by Congress March 5, 1794. Ratified January 8, 1798.

The judicial power of the United States shall not be construed to extend to any suit in law or equity, commenced or prosecuted against one of the United States by citizens of another State, or by citizens or subjects of any foreign State.

Article XII

Passed by Congress December 12, 1803. Ratified September 25, 1804.

The electors shall meet in their respective States, and vote by ballot for President and Vice President, one of whom, at least, shall not be an inhabitant of the same State with themselves; they shall name in their ballots the person voted for as President, and in distinct ballots, the person voted for as Vice President, and they shall make distinct lists of all persons voted for as President and of all persons voted for as Vice President, and of the number of votes for each, which lists they shall sign and certify, and transmit sealed to the seat of the government of the United States, directed to the President of the Senate; — The President of the Senate shall, in the presence of the Senate and House of Representatives, open all the certificates and the votes shall then be counted; — The person having the greatest number of votes for President, shall be the President, if such number be a majority of the whole number of electors appointed; and if no person have such majority, then from the persons having the highest numbers not exceeding three on the list of those voted for as President, the House of Representatives shall choose immediately, by ballot, the President. But in choosing the President, the votes shall be taken by States, the representation from each State having one vote; a quorum for this purpose shall consist of a member or members from two thirds of the States, and a majority of all the States shall be necessary to a choice. And if the House of Representatives shall not choose a President whenever the right of choice shall devolve upon them, before the fourth day of March next following, then the Vice President shall act as President, as in the case of the death or other constitutional disability of the President. The person having the greatest number of votes as Vice President shall be the Vice President, if such number be a majority of the whole number of electors appointed, and if no person have a majority, then from the two highest numbers on the list, the Senate shall choose the Vice President; a quorum for the purpose shall consist of two thirds of the whole number of Senators, and a majority of the whole number shall be necessary to a choice. But no person constitutionally ineligible to the office of President shall be eligible to that of Vice President of the United States.

Article XIII

Passed by Congress February 1, 1865. Ratified December 18, 1865.

Section 1. Neither slavery nor involuntary servitude, except as punishment for crime whereof the party shall have been duly convicted, shall exist within the United States, or any place subject to their jurisdiction.

Section 2. Congress shall have power to enforce this article by appropriate legislation.

Article XIV

Passed by Congress June 16, 1866. Ratified July 23, 1868.

Section 1. All persons born or naturalized in the United States, and subject to the jurisdiction thereof, are citizens of the United States and of the State wherein they reside. No State shall make or enforce any law which shall abridge the privileges or immunities of citizens of the United States; nor shall any State deprive any person of life, liberty, or property, without due process of law; nor deny to any person within its jurisdiction the equal protection of the laws.

Section 2. Representatives shall be apportioned among the several States according to their respective numbers, counting the whole number of persons in each State, excluding Indians not taxed. But when the right to vote at any election for the choice of electors for President and Vice President of the United States, representatives in Congress, the executive and judicial officers of a State, or the members of the legislature thereof, is denied to any of the male inhabitants of such State, being twenty-one years of age, and citizens of the United States, or in any way abridged, except for participation in rebellion, or other crime, the basis of representation therein shall be reduced in the proportion which the number of such male citizens shall bear to the whole number of male citizens twenty-one years of age in such State.

Section 3. No person shall be a senator or representative in Congress, or elector of President and Vice President, or hold any office, civil or military, under the United States, or under any State, who having previously taken an oath, as a member of Congress, or as an officer of the United States, or as a member of any State legislature, or as an executive or judicial officer of any State, to support the Constitution of the United States, shall have engaged in insurrection or rebellion against the same, or given aid or comfort to the enemies thereof. But Congress may by a vote of two thirds of each House, remove such disability.

Section 4. The validity of the public debt of the United States, authorized by law, including debts incurred for payment of pensions and bounties for services in suppressing insurrection or rebellion, shall not be questioned. But neither the United States nor any State shall assume or pay any debt or obligation incurred in aid of insurrection or rebellion against the United States, or any claim for the loss or emancipation of any slave; but all such debts, obligations, and claims shall be held illegal and void.

Section 5. The Congress shall have power to enforce, by appropriate legislation, the provisions of this article.

Article XV

Passed by Congress February 27, 1869. Ratified March 30, 1870.

Section 1. The right of citizens of the United States

to vote shall not be denied or abridged by the United States or by any State on account of race, color, or previous condition of servitude.

Section 2. The Congress shall have power to enforce this article by appropriate legislation.

Article XVI

Passed by Congress July 12, 1909. Ratified February 25, 1913.

The Congress shall have power to lay and collect taxes on incomes, from whatever source derived, without apportionment among the several States, and without regard to any census or enumeration.

Article XVII

Passed by Congress May 16, 1912. Ratified May 31, 1913.

The Senate of the United States shall be composed of two senators from each state, elected by the people thereof, for six years; and each senator shall have one vote. The electors in each State shall have the qualifications requisite for electors of the most numerous branch of the State legislature.

When vacancies happen in the representation of any State in the Senate, the executive authority of such State shall issue writs of election to fill such vacancies: *Provided,* That the legislature of any State may empower the executive thereof to make temporary appointments until the people fill the vacancies by election as the legislature may direct.

This amendment shall not be so construed as to affect the election or term of any senator chosen before it becomes valid as part of the Constitution.

Article XVIII

Passed by Congress December 17, 1917. Ratified January 29, 1919.

After one year from the ratification of this article, the manufacture, sale, or transportation of intoxicating liquors within, the importation thereof into, or the exportation thereof from the United States and all territory subject to the jurisdiction thereof for beverage purposes is hereby prohibited.

The Congress and the several States shall have concurrent power to enforce this article by appropriate legislation.

This article shall be inoperative unless it shall have been ratified as an amendment to the Constitution by the legislatures of the several States, as provided in the Constitution, within seven years from the date of the submission hereof to the states by Congress.

Article XIX

Passed by Congress June 5, 1919. Ratified August 26, 1920.

The right of citizens of the United States to vote shall not be denied or abridged by the United States or by any State on account of sex.

The Congress shall have power by appropriate legislation to enforce the provisions of this article.

Article XX

Passed by Congress March 3, 1932. Ratified January 23, 1933.

Section 1. The terms of the President and Vice President shall end at noon on the 20th day of January, and the terms of Senators and Representatives at noon on the 3d day of January, of the years in which such terms would have ended if this article had not been ratified; and the terms of their successors shall then begin.

Section 2. The Congress shall assemble at least once in every year, and such meeting shall begin at noon on the 3d day of January, unless they shall by law appoint a different day.

Section 3. If, at the time fixed for the beginning of the term of the President, the President-elect shall have died, the Vice President-elect shall become President. If a President shall not have been chosen before the time fixed for the beginning of his term, or if the President-elect shall have failed to qualify, then the Vice President-elect shall act as President until a President shall have qualified; and the Congress may by law provide for the case wherein neither a President-elect nor a Vice President-elect shall have qualified, declaring who shall then act as President, or the manner in which one who is to act shall be selected, and such person shall act accordingly until a President or Vice President shall have qualified.

Section 4. The Congress may by law provide for the case of the death of any of the persons from whom the House of Representatives may choose a President whenever the right of choice shall have devolved upon them, and for the case of the death of any of the persons from whom the Senate may choose a Vice President whenever the right of choice shall have devolved upon them.

Section 5. Sections 1 and 2 shall take effect on the 15th day of October following the ratification of this article.

Section 6. This article shall be inoperative unless it shall have been ratified as an amendment to the Constitution by the legislatures of three-fourths of the several States within seven years from the date of its submission.

Article XXI

Passed by Congress February 20, 1933. Ratified December 5, 1933.

Section 1. The Eighteenth Article of amendment to the Constitution of the United States is hereby repealed.

Section 2. The transportation or importation into any State, Territory, or possession of the United States for delivery or use therein of intoxicating liquors in violation of the laws thereof, is hereby prohibited.

Section 3.   This article shall be inoperative unless it shall have been ratified as an amendment to the Constitution by conventions in the several States, as provided in the Constitution, within seven years from the date of the submission thereof to the States by the Congress.

Article XXII

Passed by Congress March 24, 1947. Ratified February 26, 1951.

Section 1.   No person shall be elected to the office of the President more than twice, and no person who has held the office of President, or acted as President, for more than two years of a term to which some other person was elected President shall be elected to the office of the President more than once. But this article shall not apply to any person holding the office of President when this article was proposed by the Congress, and shall not prevent any person who may be holding the office of President, or acting as President, during the term within which this article becomes operative from holding the office of President or acting as President during the remainder of such term.

Section 2.   This article shall be inoperative unless it shall have been ratified as an amendment to the Constitution by the legislatures of three-fourths of the several States within seven years from the date of its submission to the States by the Congress.

Amendment XXIII

Passed by Congress June 16, 1960. Ratified April 3, 1961.

Section 1   The District constituting the seat of Government of the United States shall appoint in such manner as the Congress may direct:

A number of electors of President and Vice President equal to the whole number of Senators and Representatives in Congress to which the District would be entitled if it were a State, but in no event more than the least populous State; they shall be in addition to those appointed by the States, but they shall be considered, for the purposes of the election of President and Vice President, to be electors appointed by a State; and they shall meet in the District and perform such duties as provided by the twelfth article of amendment.

Section 2   The Congress shall have power to enforce this article by appropriate legislation.

Amendment XXIV

Passed by Congress August 27, 1962. Ratified February 4, 1964.

Section 1   The right of citizens of the United States to vote in any primary or other election for President or Vice President, for electors for President or Vice President, or for Senator or Representative in Congress, shall not be denied or abridged by the United States or any State by reason of failure to pay any poll tax or other tax.

Section 2   The Congress shall have power to enforce this article by appropriate legislation.

Amendment XXV

Passed by Congress July 6, 1965. Ratified February 23, 1967.

Section 1   In case of the removal of the President from office or of his death or resignation, the Vice President shall become President.

Section 2   Whenever there is a vacancy in the office of the Vice President, the President shall nominate a Vice President who shall take office upon confirmation by a majority vote of both Houses of Congress.

Section 3   Whenever the President transmits to the President pro tempore of the Senate and the Speaker of the House of Representatives has written declaration that he is unable to discharge the powers and duties of his office, and until he transmits to them a written declaration to the contrary, such powers and duties shall be discharged by the Vice President as Acting President.

Section 4   Whenever the Vice President and a majority of either the principal officers of the executive departments or of such other body as Congress may by law provide, transmit to the President pro tempore of the Senate and the Speaker of the House of Representatives their written declaration that the President is unable to discharge the powers and duties of his office, the Vice President shall immediately assume the powers and duties of the office as Acting President.

Thereafter, when the President transmits to the President pro tempore of the Senate and the Speaker of the House of Representatives his written declaration that no inability exists, he shall resume the powers and duties of his office unless the Vice President and a majority of either the principal officers of the executive department or of such other body as Congress may by law provide, transmit within four days to the President pro tempore of the Senate and the Speaker of the House of Representatives their written declaration that the President is unable to discharge the powers and duties of his office. Thereupon Congress shall decide the issue, assembling within forty-eight hours for that purpose if not in session. If the Congress, within twenty-one days after receipt of the latter written declaration, or, if Congress is not in session, within twenty-one days after Congress is required to assemble, determines by two-thirds vote of both Houses that the President is unable to discharge the powers and duties of his office, the Vice President shall continue to discharge the same as Acting President; otherwise, the President shall resume the powers and duties of his office.

Amendment XXVI

Passed by Congress March 23, 1971. Ratified July 5, 1971.

Section 1   The right of citizens of the United States, who are eighteen years of age or older, to vote shall not be denied or abridged by the United States or by any State on account of age.

UNIFORM COMMERCIAL CODE

TITLE

AN ACT

To be known as the Uniform Commercial Code, Relating to Certain Commercial Trans-actions in or regarding Personal Property and Contracts and other Documents concerning them, including Sales, Commercial Paper, Bank Deposits and Collections, Letters of Credit, Bulk Transfers, Warehouse Receipts, Bills of Lading, other Documents of Title, Investment Securities, and Secured Transactions, including certain Sales of Accounts, Chattel Paper, and Contract Rights; Providing for Public Notice to Third Parties in Certain Circumstances; Regulating Procedure, Evidence and Damages in Certain Court Actions Involving such Transactions, Contracts or Documents; to Make Uniform the Law with Respect Thereto; and Repealing Inconsistent Legislation.

ARTICLE 1

GENERAL PROVISIONS

Part 1

SHORT TITLE, CONSTRUCTION, APPLICATION AND SUBJECT MATTER OF THE ACT

§ 1—101. Short Title

This Act shall be known and may be cited as Uniform Commercial Code.

§ 1—102. Purposes; Rules of Construction; Variation by Agreement

(1) This Act shall be liberally construed and applied to promote its underlying purposes and policies.

(2) Underlying purposes and policies of this Act are

    (a) to simplify, clarify and modernize the law governing commercial transactions;

    (b) to permit the continued expansion of commercial practices through custom, usage and agreement of the parties;

    (c) to make uniform the law among the various jurisdictions.

(3) The effect of provisions of this Act may be varied by agreement, except as otherwise provided in this Act and except that the obligations of good faith, diligence, reasonableness and care prescribed by this Act may not be disclaimed by agreement, but the parties may by agreement determine the standards by which the performance of such obligations is to be measured if such standards are not manifestly unreasonable.

(4) The presence in certain provisions of this Act of the words "unless otherwise agreed" or words of similar import does not imply

that the effect of other provisions may not be varied by agreement under subsection (3).

(5) In this Act unless the context otherwise requires
   (a) words in the singular number include the plural, and in the plural include the singular;
   (b) words of the masculine gender include the feminine and the neuter, and when the sense so indicates, words of the neuter gender may refer to any gender.

§ 1—103. Supplementary General Principles of Law Applicable

Unless displaced by the particular provisions of this Act, the principles of law and equity, including the law merchant and the law relative to capacity to contract, principal and agent, estoppel, fraud, misrepresentation, duress, coercion, mistake, bankruptcy, or other validating or invalidating cause shall supplement its provisions.

§ 1—104. Construction Against Implicit Repeal

This Act being a general act intended as a unified coverage of its subject matter, no part of it shall be deemed to be impliedly repealed by subsequent legislation if such construction can reasonably be avoided.

§ 1—105. Territorial Application of the Act; Parties' Power to Choose Applicable Law

(1) Except as provided hereafter in this section, when a transaction bears a reasonable relation to this state and also to another state or nation, the parties may agree that the law either of this state or of such other state or nation shall govern their rights and duties. Failing such agreement, this Act applies to transactions bearing an appropriate relation to this state.

(2) Where one of the following provisions of this Act specifies the applicable law, that provision governs and a contrary agreement is effective only to the extent permitted by the law (including the conflict of laws rules) so specified:

   Rights of creditors against sold goods. Section 2—402.
   Applicability of the Article on Bank Deposits and Collections. Section 4—102.
   Bulk transfers subject to the Article on Bulk Transfers. Section 6—102.
   Applicability of the Article on Investment Securities. Section 8—106.
   Perfection provisions of the Article on Secured Transactions. Section 9—103.

§ 1—106. Remedies to Be Liberally Administered

(1) The remedies provided by this Act shall be liberally administered to the end that the aggrieved party may be put in as good a position as if the other party had fully performed, but neither consequential or special nor penal damages may be had except as specifically provided in this Act or by other rule of law.

(2) Any right or obligation declared by this Act is enforceable by action unless the provision declaring it specifies a different and limited effect.

§ 1—107. Waiver or Renunciation of Claim or Right After Breach

Any claim or right arising out of an alleged breach can be discharged in whole or in part without consideration by a written waiver or renunciation signed and delivered by the aggrieved party.

§ 1—108. Severability

If any provision or clause of this Act or application thereof to any person or circumstances is held invalid, such invalidity shall not affect other provisions or applications of the Act which can be given effect without the invalid provision or application, and to this end the provisions of this Act are declared to be severable.

§ 1—109. Section Captions

Section captions are parts of this Act.

Part 2

GENERAL DEFINITIONS AND PRINCIPLES OF INTERPRETATION

§ 1—201. General Definitions

Subject to additional definitions contained in the subsequent Articles of this Act which are applicable to specific Articles or Parts thereof, and unless the context otherwise requires, in this Act:

(1) "Action" in the sense of a judicial proceeding includes recoupment, counterclaim, set-off, suit in equity and any other proceedings in which rights are determined.

(2) "Aggrieved party" means a party entitled to resort to a remedy.

(3) "Agreement" means the bargain of the parties in fact as found in their language or by implication from other circumstances including course of dealing or usage of trade or course of performance as provided in this Act (Sections 1—205 and 2—208). Whether an agreement has legal consequences is determined by the provisions of this Act, if applicable; otherwise by the law of contracts (Section 1—103). (Compare "Contract.")

(4) "Bank" means any person engaged in the business of banking.

(5) "Bearer" means the person in possession of an instrument, document of title, or certificated security payable to bearer or indorsed in blank.

(6) "Bill of lading" means a document evidencing the receipt of goods for shipment issued by a person engaged in the business of transporting or forwarding goods, and includes an airbill. "Airbill" means

a document serving for air transportation as a bill of lading does for marine or rail transportation, and includes an air consignment note or air waybill.

(7) "Branch" includes a separately incorporated foreign branch of a bank.

(8) "Burden of establishing" a fact means the burden of persuading the triers of fact that the existence of the fact is more probable than its nonexistence.

(9) "Buyer in ordinary course of business" means a person who in good faith and without knowledge that the sale to him is in violation of the ownership rights or security interest of a third party in the goods buys in ordinary course from a person in the business of selling goods of that kind but does not include a pawnbroker. All persons who sell minerals or the like (including oil and gas) at wellhead or minehead shall be deemed to be persons in the business of selling goods of that kind. "Buying" may be for cash or by exchange of other property or on secured or unsecured credit and includes receiving goods or documents of title under a preexisting contract for sale but does not include a transfer in bulk or as security for or in total or partial satisfaction of a money debt.

(10) "Conspicuous": A term or clause is conspicuous when it is so written that a reasonable person against whom it is to operate ought to have noticed it. A printed heading in capitals (as: NON-NEGOTIABLE BILL OF LADING) is conspicuous. Language in the body of a form is "conspicuous" if it is in larger or other contrasting type or color. But in a telegram any stated term is "conspicuous." Whether a term or clause is "conspicuous" or not is for decision by the court.

(11) "Contract" means the total legal obligation which results from the parties' agreement as affected by this Act and any other applicable rules of law. (Compare "Agreement.")

(12) "Creditor" includes a general creditor, a secured creditor, a lien creditor and any representative of creditors, including an assignee for the benefit of creditors, a trustee in bankruptcy, a receiver in equity and an executor or administrator of an insolvent debtor's or assignor's estate.

(13) "Defendant" includes a person in the position of defendant in a cross-action or counterclaim.

(14) "Delivery" with respect to instruments, documents of title, chattel paper or certificated securities means voluntary transfer of possession.

(15) "Document of title" includes bill of lading, dock warrant, dock receipt, warehouse receipt or order for the delivery of goods, and also any other document which in the regular course of business or financing is treated as adequately evidencing that the person in possession of it is entitled to receive, hold and dispose of the document and the goods it covers. To be a document of title a document must purport to be issued by or addressed to a bailee and purport to cover goods in the bailee's possession which are either identified or are fungible portions of an identified mass.

(16) "Fault" means wrongful act, omission or breach.

(17) "Fungible" with respect to goods or securities means goods or securities of which any unit is, by nature or usage of trade, the equivalent of any other like unit. Goods which are not fungible shall be deemed fungible for the purposes of this Act to the extent that under a particular agreement or document unlike units are treated as equivalents.

(18) "Genuine" means free of forgery or counterfeiting.

(19) "Good faith" means honesty in fact in the conduct or transaction concerned.

(20) "Holder" means a person who is in possession of a document of title or an instrument or a certificated investment security drawn, issued or indorsed to him or to his order or to bearer or in blank.

(21) To "honor" is to pay or to accept and pay, or where a credit so engages, to purchase or discount a draft complying with the terms of the credit.

(22) "Insolvency proceedings" includes any assignment for the benefit of creditors or other proceedings intended to liquidate or rehabilitate the estate of the person involved.

(23) A person is "insolvent" who either has ceased to pay his debts in the ordinary course of business or cannot pay his debts as they become due or is insolvent within the meaning of the federal bankruptcy law.

(24) "Money" means a medium of exchange authorized or adopted by a domestic or foreign government as a part of its currency.

(25) A person has "notice" of a fact when
    (a) he has actual knowledge of it; or
    (b) he has received a notice or notification of it; or
    (c) from all the facts and circumstances known to him at the time in question he has reason to know that it exists.

A person "knows" or has "knowledge" of a fact when he has actual knowledge of it. "Discover" or "learn" or a word or phrase of similar import refers to knowledge rather than to reason to know. The time and circumstances under which a notice or notification may cease to be effective are not determined by this Act.

(26) A person "notifies" or "gives" a notice or notification to another by taking such steps as may be reasonably required to inform the other in ordinary course whether or not such other actually comes to know of it. A person "receives" a notice or notification when
    (a) it comes to his attention; or
    (b) it is duly delivered at the place of business through which the contract was made or at any other place held out by

him as the place for receipt of such communications.

(27) Notice, knowledge or a notice or notification received by an organization is effective for a particular transaction from the time when it is brought to the attention of the individual conducting that transaction, and in any event from the time when it would have been brought to his attention if the organization had exercised due diligence. An organization exercises due diligence if it maintains reasonable routines for communicating significant information to the person conducting the transaction and there is reasonable compliance with the routines. Due diligence does not require an individual acting for the organization to communicate information unless such communication is part of his regular duties or unless he has reason to know of the transaction and that the transaction would be materially affected by the information.

(28) "Organization" includes a corporation, government or governmental subdivision or agency, business trust, estate, trust, partnership or association, two or more persons having a joint or common interest, or any other legal or commercial entity.

(29) "Party," as distinct from "third party," means a person who has engaged in a transaction or made an agreement within this Act.

(30) "Person" includes an individual or an organization (See Section 1—102).

(31) "Presumption" or "presumed" means that the trier of fact must find the existence of the fact presumed unless and until evidence is introduced which would support a finding of its nonexistence.

(32) "Purchase" includes taking by sale, discount, negotiation, mortgage, pledge, lien, issue or reissue, gift or any other voluntary transaction creating an interest in property.

(33) "Purchaser" means a person who takes by purchase.

(34) "Remedy" means any remedial right to which an aggrieved party is entitled with or without resort to a tribunal.

(35) "Representative" includes an agent, an officer of a corporation or association, and a trustee, executor or administrator of an estate, or any other person empowered to act for another.

(36) "Rights" includes remedies.

(37) "Security interest" means an interest in personal property or fixtures which secures payment or performance of an obligation. The retention or reservation of title by a seller of goods notwithstanding shipment or delivery to the buyer (Section 2—401) is limited in effect to a reservation of a "security interest." The term also includes any interest of a buyer of accounts or chattel paper which is subject to Article 9. The special property interest of a buyer of goods on identification of such goods to a contract for sale under Section 2—401 is not a "security interest," but a buyer

may also acquire a "security interest" by complying with Article 9. Unless a lease or consignment is intended as security, reservation of title thereunder is not a "security interest" but a consignment is in any event subject to the provisions on consignment sales (Section 2—326). Whether a lease is intended as security is to be determined by the facts of each case; however, (a) the inclusion of an option to purchase does not of itself make the lease one intended for security, and (b) an agreement that upon compliance with the terms of the lease the lessee shall become or has the option to become the owner of the property for no additional consideration or for a nominal consideration does make the lease one intended for security.

(38) "Send" in connection with any writing or notice means to deposit in the mail or deliver for transmission by any other usual means of communication with postage or cost of transmission provided for and properly addressed and in the case of an instrument to an address specified thereon or otherwise agreed, or if there be none to any address reasonable under the circumstances. The receipt of any writing or notice within the time at which it would have arrived if properly sent has the effect of a proper sending.

(39) "Signed" includes any symbol executed or adopted by a party with present intention to authenticate a writing.

(40) "Surety" includes guarantor.

(41) "Telegram" includes a message transmitted by radio, teletype, cable, any mechanical method of transmission, or the like.

(42) "Term" means that portion of an agreement which relates to a particular matter.

(43) "Unauthorized" signature or indorsement means one made without actual, implied or apparent authority and includes a forgery.

(44) "Value." Except as otherwise provided with respect to negotiable instruments and bank collections (Sections 3—303, 4—208 and 4—209) a person gives "value" for rights if he acquires them

(a) in return for a binding commitment to extend credit or for the extension of immediately available credit whether or not drawn upon and whether or not a charge-back is provided for in the event of difficulties in collection; or

(b) as security for or in total or partial satisfaction of a preexisting claim; or

(c) by accepting delivery pursuant to a preexisting contract for purchase; or

(d) generally, in return for any consideration sufficient to support a simple contract.

(45) "Warehouse receipt" means a receipt issued by a person engaged in the business of storing goods for hire.

(46) "Written" or "writing" includes printing,

typewriting or any other intentional reduction to tangible form.

§ 1—202. Prima Facie Evidence by Third Party Documents

A document in due form purporting to be a bill of lading, policy or certificate of insurance, official weigher's or inspector's certificate, consular invoice, or any other document authorized or required by the contract to be issued by a third party shall be prima facie evidence of its own authenticity and genuineness and of the facts stated in the document by the third party.

§ 1—203. Obligation of Good Faith

Every contract or duty within this Act imposes an obligation of good faith in its performance or enforcement.

§ 1—204. Time; Reasonable Time; "Seasonably"

(1) Whenever this Act requires any action to be taken within a reasonable time, any time which is not manifestly unreasonable may be fixed by agreement.

(2) What is a reasonable time for taking any action depends on the nature, purpose and circumstances of such action.

(3) An action is taken "seasonably" when it is taken at or within the time agreed or, if no time is agreed, at or within a reasonable time.

§ 1—205. Course of Dealing and Usage of Trade

(1) A course of dealing is a sequence of previous conduct between the parties to a particular transaction which is fairly to be regarded as establishing a common basis of understanding for interpreting their expressions and other conduct.

(2) A usage of trade is any practice or method of dealing having such regularity of observance in a place, vocation or trade as to justify an expectation that it will be observed with respect to the transaction in question. The existence and scope of such a usage are to be proved as facts. If it is established that such a usage is embodied in a written trade code or similar writing the interpretation of the writing is for the court.

(3) A course of dealing between parties and any usage of trade in the vocation or trade in which they are engaged or of which they are or should be aware give particular meaning to and supplement or qualify terms of an agreement.

(4) The express terms of an agreement and an applicable course of dealing or usage of trade shall be construed wherever reasonable as consistent with each other; but when such construction is unreasonable, express terms control both course of dealing and usage of trade and course of dealing controls usage of trade.

(5) An applicable usage of trade in the place where any part of performance is to occur shall be used in interpreting the agreement as to that part of the performance.

(6) Evidence of a relevant usage of trade offered by one party is not admissible unless and until he has given the other party such notice as the court finds sufficient to prevent unfair surprise to the latter.

§ 1—206. Statute of Frauds for Kinds of Personal Property Not Otherwise Covered

(1) Except in the cases described in subsection (2) of this section, a contract for the sale of personal property is not enforceable by way of action or defense beyond five thousand dollars in amount or value of remedy unless there is some writing which indicates that a contract for sale has been made between the parties at a defined or stated price, reasonably identifies the subject matter, and is signed by the party against whom enforcement is sought or by his authorized agent.

(2) Subsection (1) of this section does not apply to contracts for the sale of goods (Section 2—201) nor of securities (Section 8—319) nor to security agreements (Section 9—203).

§ 1—207. Performance or Acceptance Under Reservation of Rights

A party who with explicit reservation of rights performs or promises performance or assents to performance in a manner demanded or offered by the other party does not thereby prejudice the rights reserved. Such words as "without prejudice," "under protest" or the like are sufficient.

§ 1—208. Option to Accelerate at Will

A term providing that one party or his successor in interest may accelerate payment or performance or require collateral or additional collateral "at will" or "when he deems himself insecure" or in words of similar import shall be construed to mean that he shall have power to do so only if he in good faith believes that the prospect of payment or performance is impaired. The burden of establishing lack of good faith is on the party against whom the power has been exercised.

§ 1—209. Subordinated Obligations

An obligation may be issued as subordinated to payment of another obligation of the person obligated, or a creditor may subordinate his right to payment of an obligation by agreement with either the person obligated or another creditor of the person obligated. Such a subordination does not create a security interest as against either the common debtor or a subordinated creditor. This section shall be construed as declaring the law as it existed prior to the enactment of this section and not as modifying it.

ARTICLE 2

SALES

Part 1

Short Title, General Construction and Subject Matter

§ 2—101. Short Title

This Article shall be known and may be cited as Uniform Commercial Code—Sales.

§ 2—102. Scope; Certain Security and Other Transactions Excluded From This Article

Unless the context otherwise requires, this Article applies to transactions in goods; it does not apply to any transaction which although in the form of an unconditional contract to sell or present sale is intended to operate only as a security transaction nor does this Article impair or repeal any statute regulating sales to consumers, farmers or other specified classes of buyers.

§ 2—103. Definitions and Index of Definitions

(1) In this Article, unless the context otherwise requires,

    (a) "Buyer" means a person who buys or contracts to buy goods.

    (b) "Good faith" in the case of a merchant means honesty in fact and the observance of reasonable commercial standards of fair dealing in the trade.

    (c) "Receipt" of goods means taking physical possession of them.

    (d) "Seller" means a person who sells or contracts to sell goods.

(2) Other definitions applying to this Article or to specified Parts thereof, and the sections in which they appear are:

"Acceptance." Section 2—606.
"Banker's credit." Section 2—325.
"Between merchants." Section 2—104.
"Cancellation." Section 2—106(4).
"Confirmed credit." Section 2—325.
"Conforming to contract." Section 2—106.
"Contract for sale." Section 2—106.
"Cover." Section 2—712.
"Entrusting." Section 2—403.
"Financing agency." Section 2—104.
"Future goods." Section 2—105.
"Goods." Section 2—105.
"Identification." Section 2—501.
"Installment contract." Section 2—612.
"Letter of Credit." Section 2—325.
"Lot." Section 2—105.
"Merchant." Section 2—104.
"Overseas." Section 2—323.
"Person in position of seller." Section 2—707.

"Present sale." Section 2—106.
"Sale." Section 2—106.
"Sale on approval." Section 2—326.
"Sale or return." Section 2—326.
"Termination." Section 2—106.

(3) The following definitions in other Articles apply to this Article:

"Check." Section 3—104.
"Consignee." Section 7—102.
"Consignor." Section 7—102.
"Consumer goods." Section 9—109.
"Dishonor." Section 3—507.
"Draft." Section 3—104.

(4) In addition Article 1 contains general definitions and principles of construction and interpretation applicable throughout this Article.

§ 2—104. Definitions: "Merchant"; "Between Merchants"; "Financing Agency"

(1) "Merchant" means a person who deals in goods of the kind or otherwise by his occupation holds himself out as having knowledge or skill peculiar to the practices or goods involved in the transaction or to whom such knowledge or skill may be attributed by his employment of an agent or broker or other intermediary who by his occupation holds himself out as having such knowledge or skill.

(2) "Financing agency" means a bank, finance company or other person who in the ordinary course of business makes advances against goods or documents of title or who by arrangement with either the seller or the buyer intervenes in ordinary course to make or collect payment due or claimed under the contract for sale, as by purchasing or paying the seller's draft or making advances against it or by merely taking it for collection whether or not documents of title accompany the draft. "Financing agency" includes also a bank or other person who similarly intervenes between persons who are in the position of seller and buyer in respect to the goods (Section 2—707).

(3) "Between merchants" means in any transaction with respect to which both parties are chargeable with the knowledge or skill of merchants.

§ 2—105. Definitions: Transferability; "Goods"; "Future" Goods; "Lot"; "Commercial Unit"

(1) "Goods" means all things (including specially manufactured goods) which are movable at the time of identification to the contract for sale other than the money in which the price is to be paid, investment securities (Article 8) and things in action. "Goods" also includes the unborn young of animals and growing crops and other identified things attached to realty as

described in the section on goods to be severed from realty (Section 2—107).

(2) Goods must be both existing and identified before any interest in them can pass. Goods which are not both existing and identified are "future" goods. A purported present sale of future goods or of any interest therein operates as a contract to sell.

(3) There may be a sale of a part interest in existing identified goods.

(4) An undivided share in an identified bulk of fungible goods is sufficiently identified to be sold although the quantity of the bulk is not determined. Any agreed proportion of such a bulk or any quantity thereof agreed upon by number, weight or other measure may to the extent of the seller's interest in the bulk be sold to the buyer who then becomes an owner in common.

(5) "Lot" means a parcel or a single article which is the subject matter of a separate sale or delivery, whether or not it is sufficient to perform the contract.

(6) "Commercial unit" means such a unit of goods as by commercial usage is a single whole for purposes of sale and division of which materially impairs its character or value on the market or in use. A commercial unit may be a single article (as a machine) or a set of articles (as a suite of furniture or an assortment of sizes) or a quantity (as a bale, gross, or carload) or any other unit treated in use or in the relevant market as a single whole.

§ 2—106. Definitions: "Contract"; "Agreement"; "Contract for Sale"; "Sale"; "Present Sale"; "Conforming" to Contract; "Termination"; "Cancellation"

(1) In this Article unless the context otherwise requires, "contract" and "agreement" are limited to those relating to the present or future sale of goods. "Contract for sale" includes both a present sale of goods and a contract to sell goods at a future time. A "sale" consists in the passing of title from the seller to the buyer for a price (Section 2—401). A "present sale" means a sale which is accomplished by the making of the contract.

(2) Goods or conduct, including any part of a performance, are "conforming" or conform to the contract when they are in accordance with the obligations under the contract.

(3) "Termination" occurs when either party pursuant to a power created by agreement or law puts an end to the contract otherwise than for its breach. On "termination" all obligations which are still executory on both sides are discharged by any right based on prior breach or performance survives.

(4) "Cancellation" occurs when either party puts an end to the contract for breach by the other and its effect is the same as that of "termination" except that

the cancelling party also retains any remedy for breach of the whole contract or any unperformed balance.

§ 2—107. Goods to Be Severed From Realty: Recording

(1) A contract for the sale of minerals or the like (including oil and gas) or a structure or its materials to be removed from realty is a contract for the sale of goods within this Article if they are to be severed by the seller, but until severance a purported present sale thereof which is not effective as a transfer of an interest in land is effective only as a contract to sell.

(2) A contract for the sale apart from the land of growing crops or other things attached to realty and capable of severance without material harm thereto but not described in subsection (1) or of timber to be cut is a contract for the sale of goods within this Article whether the subject matter is to be severed by the buyer or by the seller even though it forms part of the realty at the time of contracting, and the parties can by identification effect a present sale before severance.

(3) The provisions of this section are subject to any third party rights provided by the law relating to realty records, and the contract for sale may be executed and recorded as a document transferring an interest in land and shall then constitute notice to third parties of the buyer's rights under the contract for sale.

Part 2

Form, Formation and Readjustment of Contract

§ 2—201. Formal Requirements; Statute of Frauds

(1) Except as otherwise provided in this section, a contract for the sale of goods for the price of $500 or more is not enforceable by way of action or defense unless there is some writing sufficient to indicate that a contract for sale has been made between the parties and signed by the party against whom enforcement is sought or by his authorized agent or broker. A writing is not insufficient because it omits or incorrectly states a term agreed upon but the contract is not enforceable under this paragraph beyond the quantity of goods shown in such writing.

(2) Between merchants, if within a reasonable time a writing in confirmation of the contract and sufficient against the sender is received and the party receiving it has reason to know its contents, it satisfies the requirements of subsection (1) against such party unless written notice of objection to its contents is given within 10 days after it is received.

(3) A contract which does not satisfy the requirements of subsection (1) but which is valid in other respects is enforceable

    (a) if the goods are to be specially manufactured for the buyer and are not suitable for sale to others in the ordinary course of the seller's business and the seller, before notice of repudiation is received and under circumstances which reasonably indicate that the goods are for the buyer, has made either a substantial beginning of their manufacture or commitments for their procurement; or

(b) if the party against whom enforcement is sought admits in his pleading, testimony or otherwise in court that a contract for sale was made, but the contract is not enforceable under this provision beyond the quantity of goods admitted; or

(c) with respect to goods for which payment has been made and accepted or which have been received and accepted (Sec. 2—606).

§ 2—202. Final Written Expression: Parol or Extrinsic Evidence

Terms with respect to which the confirmatory memoranda of the parties agree or which are otherwise set forth in a writing intended by the parties as a final expression of their agreement with respect to such terms as are included therein may not be contradicted by evidence of any prior agreement or of a contemporaneous oral agreement but may be explained or supplemented

(a) by course of dealing or usage of trade (Section 1—205) or by course of performance (Section 2—208); and

(b) by evidence of consistent additional terms unless the court finds the writing to have been intended also as a complete and exclusive statement of the terms of the agreement.

§ 2—203. Seals Inoperative

The affixing of a seal to a writing evidencing a contract for sale or an offer to buy or sell goods does not constitute the writing a sealed instrument and the law with respect to sealed instruments does not apply to such a contract or offer.

§ 2—204. Formation in General

(1) A contract for sale of goods may be made in any manner sufficient to show agreement, including conduct by both parties which recognizes the existence of such a contract.

(2) An agreement sufficient to constitute a contract for sale may be found even though the moment of its making is undetermined.

(3) Even though one or more terms are left open a contract for sale does not fail for indefiniteness if the parties have intended to make a contract and there is a reasonably certain basis for giving an appropriate remedy.

§ 2—205. Firm Offers

An offer by a merchant to buy or sell goods in a signed writing which by its terms gives assurance that it will be held open is not revocable, for lack of consideration, during the time stated or if no time is stated for a reasonable time, but in no event may such period of irrevocability exceed three months; but any such term of assurance on a form supplied by the offeree must be separately signed by the offeror.

§ 2—206. Offer and Acceptance in Formation of Contract

(1) Unless otherwise unambiguously indicated by the language or circumstances

(a) an offer to make a contract shall be construed as inviting acceptance in any manner and by any medium reasonable in the circumstances;

(b) an order or other offer to buy goods for prompt or current shipment shall be construed as inviting acceptance either by a prompt promise to ship or by the prompt or current shipment of conforming or non-conforming goods, but such a shipment of non-conforming goods does not constitute an acceptance if the seller seasonably notifies the buyer that the shipment is offered only as an accommodation to the buyer.

(2) Where the beginning of a requested performance is a reasonable mode of acceptance, an offeror who is not notified of acceptance within a reasonable time may treat the offer as having lapsed before acceptance.

§ 2—207. Additional Terms in Acceptance or Confirmation

(1) A definite and seasonable expression of acceptance or a written confirmation which is sent within a reasonable time operates as an acceptance even though it states terms additional to or different from those offered or agreed upon, unless acceptance is expressly made conditional on assent to the additional or different terms.

(2) The additional terms are to be construed as proposals for addition to the contract. Between merchants such terms become part of the contract unless:

(a) the offer expressly limits acceptance to the terms of the offer;

(b) they materially alter it; or

(c) notification of objection to them has already been given or is given within a reasonable time after notice of them is received.

(3) Conduct by both parties which recognizes the existence of a contract is sufficient to establish a contract for sale although the writings of the parties do not otherwise establish a contract. In such case the terms of the particular contract consist of those terms on which the writings of the parties agree, together with any supplementary terms incorporated under any other provisions of this Act.

§ 2 — 208. Course of Performance or Practical Construction

(1) Where the contract for sale involves repeated occasions for performance by either party with knowledge of the nature of the performance and opportunity for objection to it by the other, any course of performance accepted or acquiesced in without objection shall be relevant to determine the meaning of the agreement.

(2) The express terms of the agreement and any such course of performance, as well as any course of dealing and usage of trade, shall be construed whenever reasonable as consistent with each other; but when such construction is unreasonable, express terms shall control course of performance and course of performance shall control both course of dealing and usage of trade (Section 1 — 205).

(3) Subject to the provisions of the next section on modification and waiver, such course of performance shall be relevant to show a waiver or modification of any term inconsistent with such course of performance.

§ 2 — 209. Modification, Rescission and Waiver

(1) An agreement modifying a contract within this Article needs no consideration to be binding.

(2) A signed agreement which excludes modification or rescission except by a signed writing cannot be otherwise modified or rescinded, but except as between merchants such a requirement on a form supplied by the merchant must be separately signed by the other party.

(3) The requirements of the statute of frauds section of this Article (Section 2 — 201) must be satisfied if the contract as modified is within its provisions.

(4) Although an attempt at modification or rescission does not satisfy the requirements of subsection (2) or (3) it can operate as a waiver.

(5) A party who has made a waiver affecting an executory portion of the contract may retract the waiver by reasonable notification received by the other party that strict performance will be required of any term waived, unless the retraction would be unjust in view of a material change of position in reliance on the waiver.

§ 2 — 210. Delegation of Performance; Assignment of Rights

(1) A party may perform his duty through a delegate unless otherwise agreed or unless the other party has a substantial interest in having his original promisor perform or control the acts required by the contract. No delegation of performance relieves the party delegating of any duty to perform or any liability for breach.

(2) Unless otherwise agreed, all rights of either seller or buyer can be assigned except where the assignment would materially change the duty of the other party, or increase materially the burden or risk imposed on him by his contract, or impair materially his chance of obtaining return performance. A right to damages for breach of the whole contract or a right arising out of the assignor's due performance of his entire obligation can be assigned despite agreement otherwise.

(3) Unless the circumstances indicate the contrary, a prohibition of assignment of "the contract" is to be construed as barring only the delegation to the assignee of the assignor's performance.

(4) An assignment of "the contract" or of "all my rights under the contract" or an assignment in similar general terms is an assignment of rights and, unless the language or the circumstances (as in an assignment for security) indicate the contrary, it is a delegation of performance of the duties of the assignor, and its acceptance by the assignee constitutes a promise by him to perform those duties. This promise is enforceable by either the assignor or the other party to the original contract.

(5) The other party may treat any assignment which delegates performance as creating reasonable grounds for insecurity and may without prejudice to his rights against the assignor demand assurances from the assignee (Section 2 — 609).

Part 3

General Obligation and Construction of Contract

§ 2 — 301. General Obligations of Parties

The obligation of the seller is to transfer and deliver and that of the buyer is to accept and pay in accordance with the contract.

§ 2 — 302. Unconscionable Contract or Clause

(1) If the court as a matter of law finds the contract or any clause of the contract to have been unconscionable at the time it was made, the court may refuse to enforce the contract, or it may enforce the remainder of the contract without the unconscionable clause, or it may so limit the application of any unconscionable clause as to avoid any unconscionable result.

(2) When it is claimed or appears to the court that the contract or any clause thereof may be unconscionable, the parties shall be afforded a reasonable opportunity to present evidence as to its commercial setting, purpose and effect to aid the court in making the determination.

§ 2 — 303. Allocation or Division of Risks

Where this Article allocates a risk or a burden as between the parties "unless otherwise agreed," the agreement may not only shift the allocation but may also divide the risk or burden.

§ 2 — 304. Price Payable in Money, Goods, Realty, or Otherwise

(1) The price can be made payable in money or otherwise. If it is payable in whole or in part in goods each party is a seller of the goods which he is to transfer.

(2) Even though all or part of the price is payable in an interest in realty the transfer of the goods and the seller's obligations with reference to them are subject to this Article, but not the transfer of the interest in realty or the transferor's obligations in connection therewith.

§ 2 — 305. Open Price Term

(1) The parties, if they so intend, can conclude a contract for sale even though the price is not settled. In such a case, the price is a reasonable price at the time for delivery if

    (a) nothing is said as to price; or
    (b) the price is left to be agreed by the parties and they fail to agree; or
    (c) the price is to be fixed in terms of some agreed market or other standard as set or recorded by a third person or agency and it is not so set or recorded.

(2) A price to be fixed by the seller or by the buyer means a price for him to fix in good faith.

(3) When a price left to be fixed otherwise than by agreement of the parties fails to be fixed through fault of one party, the other may at his option treat the contract as cancelled or himself fix a reasonable price.

(4) Where, however, the parties intend not to be bound unless the price be fixed or agreed and it is not fixed or agreed, there is no contract. In such a case, the buyer must return any goods already received or if unable so to do must pay their reasonable value at the time of delivery and the seller must return any portion of the price paid on account.

§ 2 — 306. Output, Requirements and Exclusive Dealings

(1) A term which measures the quantity by the output of the seller or the requirements of the buyer means such actual output or requirements as may occur in good faith, except that no quantity unreasonably disproportionate to any stated estimate or in the absence of a stated estimate to any normal or otherwise comparable prior output or requirements may be tendered or demanded.

(2) A lawful agreement by either the seller or the buyer for exclusive dealing in the kind of goods concerned imposes, unless otherwise agreed, an obligation by the seller to use best efforts to supply the goods and by the buyer to use best efforts to promote their sale.

§ 2 — 307. Delivery in Single Lot or Several Lots

Unless otherwise agreed all goods called for by a contract for sale must be tendered in a single delivery and payment is due only on such tender; but where the circumstances give either party the right to make or demand delivery in lots, the price if it can be apportioned may be demanded for each lot.

§ 2 — 308. Absence of Specified Place for Delivery

Unless otherwise agreed

    (a) the place for delivery of goods is the seller's place of business or, if he has none, his residence; but
    (b) in a contract for sale of identified goods which to the knowledge of the parties at the time of contracting are in some other place, that place is the place for their delivery; and
    (c) documents of title may be delivered through customary banking channels.

§ 2 — 309. Absence of Specific Time Provisions; Notice of Termination

(1) The time for shipment or delivery or any other action under a contract if not provided in this Article or agreed upon shall be a reasonable time.

(2) Where the contract provides for successive performances but is indefinite in duration, it is valid for a reasonable time; but unless otherwise agreed may be terminated at any time by either party.

(3) Termination of a contract by one party, except on the happening of an agreed event, requires that reasonable notification be received by the other party and an agreement dispensing with notification is invalid if its operation would be unconscionable.

§ 2 — 310. Open Time for Payment or Running of Credit; Authority to Ship Under Reservation

Unless otherwise agreed

    (a) payment is due at the time and place at which the buyer is to receive the goods even though the place of shipment is the place of delivery; and
    (b) if the seller is authorized to send the goods, he may ship them under reservation, and may tender the documents of title, but the buyer may inspect the goods after their arrival before payment is due unless such inspection is inconsistent with the terms of the contract (Section 2 — 513); and
    (c) if delivery is authorized and made by way of documents of title otherwise than by subsection (b), then payment is due at the time and place at which the buyer is to receive the documents regardless of where the goods are to be received; and
    (d) where the seller is required or authorized to ship the goods on credit, the credit period runs from the time of shipment but postdating the invoice or delaying its dispatch will correspondingly delay the starting of the credit period.

§ 2—311. Options and Cooperation Respecting Performance

(1) An agreement for sale which is otherwise sufficiently definite (subsection (3) of Section 2—204) to be a contract is not made invalid by the fact that it leaves particulars of performance to be specified by one of the parties. Any such specification must be made in good faith and within limits set by commercial reasonableness.

(2) Unless otherwise agreed, specifications relating to assortment of the goods are at the buyer's option and, except as otherwise provided in subsections (1) (c) and (3) of Section 2—319, specifications or arrangements relating to shipment are at the seller's option.

(3) Where such specification would materially affect the other party's performance but is not seasonably made or where one party's cooperation is necessary to the agreed performance of the other but is not seasonably forthcoming, the other party in addition to all other remedies

    (a) is excused for any resulting delay in his own performance; and

    (b) may also either proceed to perform in any reasonable manner or after the time for a material part of his own performance treat the failure to specify or to cooperate as a breach by failure to deliver or accept the goods.

§ 2—312. Warranty of Title and Against Infringement; Buyer's Obligation Against Infringement

(1) Subject to subsection (2), there is in a contract for sale a warranty by the seller that

    (a) the title conveyed shall be good, and its transfer rightful; and

    (b) the goods shall be delivered free from any security interest or other lien or encumbrance of which the buyer at the time of contracting has no knowledge.

(2) A warranty under subsection (1) will be excluded or modified only by specific language or by circumstances which give the buyer reason to know that the person selling does not claim title in himself or that he is purporting to sell only such right or title as he or a third person may have.

(3) Unless otherwise agreed a seller who is a merchant regularly dealing in goods of the kind warrants that the goods shall be delivered free of the rightful claim of any third person by way of infringement or the like but a buyer who furnishes specifications to the seller must hold the seller harmless against any such claim which arises out of compliance with the specifications.

§ 2—313. Express Warranties by Affirmation, Promise, Description, Sample

(1) Express warranties by the seller are created as follows:

    (a) Any affirmation of fact or promise made by the seller to the buyer which relates to the goods and becomes part of the basis of the bargain creates an express warranty that the goods shall conform to the affirmation or promise.

    (b) Any description of the goods which is made part of the basis of the bargain creates an express warranty that the goods shall conform to the description.

    (c) Any sample or model which is made part of the basis of the bargain creates an express warranty that the whole of the goods shall conform to the sample or model.

(2) It is not necessary to the creation of an express warranty that the seller use formal words such as "warrant" or "guarantee" or that he have a specific intention to make a warranty, but an affirmation merely of the value of the goods or a statement purporting to be merely the seller's opinion or commendation of the goods does not create a warranty.

§ 2—314. Implied Warranty; Merchantability; Usage of Trade

(1) Unless excluded or modified (Section 2—316), a warranty that the goods shall be merchantable is implied in a contract for their sale if the seller is a merchant with respect to goods of that kind. Under this section, the serving for value of food or drink to be consumed either on the premises or elsewhere is a sale.

(2) Goods to be merchantable must be at least such as

    (a) pass without objection in the trade under the contract description; and

    (b) in the case of fungible goods, are of fair average quality within the description; and

    (c) are fit for the ordinary purposes for which such goods are used; and

    (d) run, within the variations permitted by the agreement, of even kind, quality and quantity within each unit and among all units involved; and

    (e) are adequately contained, packaged, and labeled as the agreement may require; and

    (f) conform to the promises or affirmations of fact made on the container or label if any.

(3) Unless excluded or modified (Section 2—316), other implied warranties may arise from course of dealing or usage of trade.

§ 2—315. Implied Warranty: Fitness for Particular Purpose

Where the seller at the time of contracting has reason to know any particular purpose for which the goods are required and that the buyer is relying on the seller's skill or judgment to select or furnish suitable goods, there is unless excluded or modified under the next section an implied warranty that the goods shall be fit for such purpose.

§ 2—316. Exclusion or Modification of Warranties

(1) Words or conduct relevant to the creation of an express warranty and words or conduct tending to negate or limit warranty shall be construed wherever reasonable as consistent with each other; but, subject to the provisions of this Article on parol or extrinsic evidence (Section 2—202), negation or limitation is inoperative to the extent that such construction is unreasonable.

(2) Subject to subsection (3), to exclude or modify the implied warranty of merchantability or any part of it, the language must mention merchantability and in case of a writing must be conspicuous, and to exclude or modify any implied warranty of fitness the exclusion must be by a writing and conspicuous. Language to exclude all implied warranties of fitness is sufficient if it states, for example, that "There are no warranties which extend beyond the description on the face hereof."

(3) Notwithstanding subsection (2)

(a) unless the circumstances indicate otherwise, all implied warranties are excluded by expressions like "as is," "with all faults" or other language which in common understanding calls the buyer's attention to the exclusion of warranties and makes plain that there is no implied warranty; and

(b) when the buyer before entering into the contract has examined goods or the sample or model as fully as he desired or has refused to examine the goods, there is no implied warranty with regard to defects which an examination ought in the circumstances to have revealed to him; and

(c) an implied warranty can also be excluded or modified by course of dealing or course of performance or usage of trade.

(4) Remedies for breach of warranty can be limited in accordance with the provisions of this Article on liquidation or limitation of damages and on contractual modification of remedy (Sections 2—718 and 2—719).

§ 2—317. Cumulation and Conflict of Warranties Express or Implied

Warranties whether express or implied shall be construed as consistent with each other and as cumulative, but if such construction is unreasonable the intention of the parties shall determine which warranty is dominant. In ascertaining that intention the following rules apply:

(a) Exact or technical specifications displace an inconsistent sample or model or general language of description.

(b) A sample from an existing bulk displaces inconsistent general language of description.

(c) Express warranties displace inconsistent implied warranties other than an implied warranty of fitness for a particular purpose.

§ 2—318. Third Party Beneficiaries of Warranties Express or Implied

Note: *If this Act is introduced in the Congress of the United States this section should be omitted. (States to select one alternative.)*

Alternative A

A seller's warranty whether express or implied extends to any natural person who is in the family or household of his buyer or who is a guest in his home if it is reasonable to expect that such person may use, consume or be affected by the goods and who is injured in person by breach of the warranty. A seller may not exclude or limit the operation of this section.

Alternative B

A seller's warranty whether express or implied extends to any natural person who may reasonably be expected to use, consume or be affected by the goods and who is injured in person by breach of the warranty. A seller may not exclude or limit the operation of this section.

Alternative C

A seller's warranty whether express or implied extends to any person who may reasonably be expected to use, consume or be affected by the goods and who is injured by breach of the warranty. A seller may not exclude or limit the operation of this section with respect to injury to the person of an individual to whom the warranty extends.

§ 2—319. F.O.B. and F.A.S. Terms

(1) Unless otherwise agreed, the term F.O.B. (which means "free on board") at a named place, even though used only in connection with the stated price, is a delivery term under which

(a) when the term is F.O.B. the place of shipment, the seller must at that place ship the goods in the manner provided in this Article (Section 2—504) and bear the expense and risk of putting them into the possession of the carrier; or

(b) when the term is F.O.B. the place of destination, the seller must at his own expense and risk transport the goods to that place and there tender delivery of them in the manner provided in this Article (Section 2—503);

(c) when under either (a) or (b) the term is also F.O.B. vessel, car or other vehicle, the seller must in addition at his own expense and risk load the goods on board. If the term is F.O.B. vessel, the buyer must name the vessel and, in an appropriate case, the seller must comply with the provisions of this Article on the form of bill of lading (Section 2—323).

(2) Unless otherwise agreed, the term F.A.S. vessel (which means "free alongside") at a named port, even though used only in connection with the stated price, is a delivery term under which the seller must

    (a) at his own expense and risk deliver the goods alongside the vessel in the manner usual in that port or on a dock designated and provided by the buyer; and

    (b) obtain and tender a receipt for the goods in exchange for which the carrier is under a duty to issue a bill of lading.

(3) Unless otherwise agreed in any case falling within subsection (1) (a) or (c) or subsection (2) the buyer must seasonably give any needed instructions for making delivery, including, when the term is F.A.S. or F.O.B., the loading berth of the vessel and, in an appropriate case, its name and sailing date. The seller may treat the failure of needed instructions as a failure of cooperation under this Article (Section 2—311). He may also at his option move the goods in any reasonable manner preparatory to delivery or shipment.

(4) Under the term F.O.B. vessel or F.A.S., unless otherwise agreed, the buyer must make payment against tender of the required documents and the seller may not tender nor the buyer demand delivery of the goods in substitution for the documents.

§ 2—320. C.I.F. and C. & F. Terms

(1) The term C.I.F. means that the price includes in a lump sum the cost of the goods and the insurance and freight to the named destination. The term C. & F. or C.F. means that the price so includes cost and freight to the named destination.

(2) Unless otherwise agreed and even though used only in connection with the stated price and destination, the term C.I.F. destination or its equivalent requires the seller at his own expense and risk to

    (a) put the goods into the possession of a carrier at the port for shipment and obtain a negotiable bill or bills of lading covering the entire transportation to the named destination; and

    (b) load the goods and obtain a receipt from the carrier (which may be contained in the bill of lading) showing that the freight has been paid or provided for; and

    (c) obtain a policy or certificate of insurance, including any war risk insurance, of a kind and on terms then current at the port of shipment in the usual amount, in the currency of the contract, shown to cover the same goods covered by the bill of lading and providing for payment of loss to the order of the buyer or for the account of whom it may concern; but the seller may add to the price the amount of the premium for any such war risk insurance; and

    (d) prepare an invoice of the goods and procure any other documents required to effect shipment or to comply with the contract; and

    (e) forward and tender with commercial promptness all the documents in due form and with any indorsement necessary to perfect the buyer's rights.

(3) Unless otherwise agreed, the term C. & F. or its equivalent has the same effect and imposes upon the seller the same obligations and risks as a C.I.F. term except the obligation as to insurance.

(4) Under the term C.I.F. or C. & F., unless otherwise agreed the buyer must make payment against tender of the required documents and the seller may not tender nor the buyer demand delivery of the goods in substitution for the documents.

§ 2—321. C.I.F. or C. & F.: "Net Landed Weights"; "Payment on Arrival"; Waranty of Condition on Arrival

Under a contract containing a term C.I.F. or C. & F.

(1) Where the price is based on or is to be adjusted according to "net landed weights," "delivered weights," "out turn" quantity or quality of the like, unless otherwise agreed the seller must reasonably estimate the price. The payment due on tender of the documents called for by the contract is the amount so estimated, but after final adjustment of the price a settlement must be made with commercial promptness.

(2) An agreement described in subsection (1) or any warranty of quality or condition of the goods on arrival places upon the seller the risk of ordinary deterioration, shrinkage and the like in transportation but has no effect on the place or time of identification to the contract for sale or delivery or on the passing of the risk of loss.

(3) Unless otherwise agreed, where the contract provides for payment on or after arrival of the goods the seller must before payment allow such preliminary inspection as is feasible; but if the goods are lost, delivery of the documents and payment are due when the goods should have arrived.

§ 2—322. Delivery "Ex-Ship"

(1) Unless otherwise agreed, a term for delivery of goods "ex-ship" (which means from the carrying vessel) or in equivalent language is not restricted to a particular ship and requires delivery from a ship which has reached a place at the named port of destination where goods of the kind are usually discharged.

(2) Under such a term, unless otherwise agreed

    (a) the seller must discharge all liens arising out of the carriage and furnish the buyer with a direction which puts the carrier under a duty to deliver the goods; and

    (b) the risk of loss does not pass to the buyer until the goods leave the ship's tackle or are otherwise properly unloaded.

§ 2—323. Form of Bill of Lading Required in Overseas Shipment; "Overseas"

(1) Where the contract contemplates overseas shipment and contains a term C.I.F. or C. & F. or F.O.B. vessel, the seller unless otherwise agreed must obtain a negotiable bill of lading stating that the goods have been loaded on board or, in the case of a term C.I.F. or C. & F., received for shipment.

(2) Where in a case within subsection (1) a bill of lading has been issued in a set of parts, unless otherwise agreed, if the documents are not to be sent from abroad the buyer may demand tender of the full set; otherwise only one part of the bill of lading need be tendered. Even if the agreement expressly requires a full set

(a) due tender of a single part is acceptable within the provisions of this Article on cure of improper delivery (subsection (1) of Section 2—508); and

(b) even though the full set is demanded, if the documents are sent from abroad the person tendering an incomplete set may nevertheless require payment upon furnishing an indemnity which the buyer in good faith deems adequate.

(3) A shipment by water or by air or a contract contemplating such shipment is "overseas" insofar as by usage of trade or agreement it is subject to the commercial, financing or shipping practices characteristic of international deep water commerce.

§ 2—324. "No Arrival, No Sale" Term

Under a term "no arrival, no sale" or terms of like meaning, unless otherwise agreed,

(a) the seller must properly ship conforming goods and if they arrive by any means he must tender them on arrival, but he assumes no obligation that the goods will arrive unless he has caused the non-arrival; and

(b) where without fault of the seller the goods are in part lost or have so deteriorated as no longer to conform to the contract or arrive after the contract time, the buyer may proceed as if there had been casualty to identified goods (Section 2—613).

§ 2—325. "Letter of Credit" Term; "Confirmed Credit"

(1) Failure of the buyer seasonably to furnish an agreed letter of credit is a breach of the contract for sale.

(2) The delivery to seller of a proper letter of credit suspends the buyer's obligation to pay. If the letter of credit is dishonored, the seller may on seasonable notification to the buyer require payment directly from him.

(3) Unless otherwise agreed, the term "letter of credit" or "banker's credit" in a contract for sale means an irrevocable credit issued by a financing agency of good repute and, where the shipment is overseas, of good international repute. The term "confirmed credit" means that the credit must also carry the direct obligation of such an agency which does business in the seller's financial market.

§ 2—326. Sale on Approval and Sale or Return; Consignment Sales and Rights of Creditors

(1) Unless otherwise agreed, if delivered goods may be returned by the buyer even though they conform to the contract, the transaction is

(a) a "sale on approval" if the goods are delivered primarily for use, and

(b) a "sale or return" if the goods are delivered primarily for resale.

(2) Except as provided in subsection (3), goods held on approval are not subject to the claims of the buyer's creditors until acceptance; goods held on sale or return are subject to such claims while in the buyer's possession.

(3) Where goods are delivered to a person for sale and such person maintains a place of business at which he deals in goods of the kind involved, under a name other than the name of the person making delivery, then with respect to claims of creditors of the person conducting the business the goods are deemed to be on sale or return. The provisions of this subsection are applicable even though an agreement purports to reserve title to the person making delivery until payment or resale or uses such words as "on consignment" or "on memorandum." However, this subsection is not applicable if the person making delivery

(a) complies with an applicable law providing for a consignor's interest or the like to be evidenced by a sign, or

(b) establishes that the person conducting the business is generally known by his creditors to be substantially engaged in selling the goods of others, or

(c) complies with the filing provisions of the Article on secured Transactions (Article 9).

(4) Any "or return" term of a contract for sale is to be treated as a separate contract for sale within the statute of frauds section of this Article (Section 2—201) and as contradicting the sale aspect of the contract within the provisions of this Article on parol or extrinsic evidence (Section 2—202).

§ 2—327. Special Incidents of Sale on Approval and Sale or Return

(1) Under a sale on approval, unless otherwise agreed

(a) although the goods are identified to the contract, the risk of loss and the title do not pass to the buyer until acceptance; and

(b) use of the goods consistent with the purpose of trial is not acceptance but failure seasonably to notify the seller of election to return the goods is acceptance, and if the goods conform to the contract acceptance of any part is acceptance of the whole; and

(c) after due notification of election to return, the return is at the seller's risk and expense but a merchant buyer must follow any reasonable instructions.

(2) Under a sale or return, unless otherwise agreed

(a) the option to return extends to the whole or any commercial unit of the goods while in substantially their original condition, but must be exercised seasonably; and

(b) the return is at the buyer's risk and expense.

§ 2—328. Sale by Auction

(1) In a sale by auction, if goods are put up in lots each lot is the subject of a separate sale.

(2) A sale by auction is complete when the auctioneer so announces by the fall of the hammer or in other customary manner. Where a bid is made while the hammer is falling in acceptance of a prior bid, the auctioneer may in his discretion reopen the bidding or declare the goods sold under the bid on which the hammer was falling.

(3) Such a sale is with reserve unless the goods are in explicit terms put up without reserve. In an auction with reserve, the auctioneer may withdraw the goods at any time until he announces completion of the sale. In an auction without reserve, after the auctioneer calls for bids on an article or lot, that article or lot cannot be withdrawn unless no bid is made within a reasonable time. In either case a bidder may retract his bid until the auctioneer's announcement of completion of the sale, but a bidder's retraction does not revive any previous bid.

(4) If the auctioneer knowingly receives a bid on the seller's behalf or the seller makes or procures such a bid, and notice has not been given that liberty for such bidding is reserved, the buyer may at his option avoid the sale or take the goods at the price of the last good faith bid prior to the completion of the sale. This subsection shall not apply to any bid at a forced sale.

Part 4

Title, Creditors and Good Faith Purchasers

§ 2—401. Passing of Title; Reservation for Security; Limited Application of This Section

Each provision of this Article with regard to the rights, obligations and remedies of the seller, the buyer, purchasers or other third parties applies irrespective of title to the goods except where the provision refers to such title. Insofar as situations are not covered by the other provisions of this Article and matters concerning title become material the following rules apply:

(1) Title to goods cannot pass under a contract for sale prior to their identification to the contract (Section 2—501), and unless otherwise explicitly agreed the buyer acquires by their identification a special property as limited by this Act. Any retention or reservation by the seller of the title (property) in goods shipped or delivered to the buyer is limited in effect to a reservation of a security interest. Subject to these provisions and to the provisions of the Article on Secured Transactions (Article 9), title to goods passes from the seller to the buyer in any manner and on any conditions explicitly agreed on by the parties.

(2) Unless otherwise explicitly agreed, title passes to the buyer at the time and place at which the seller completes his performance with reference to the physical delivery of the goods, despite any reservation of security interest and even though a document of title is to be delivered at a different time or place; and in particular and despite any reservation of a security interest by the bill of lading

(a) if the contract requires or authorizes the seller to send the goods to the buyer but does not require him to deliver them at destination, title passes to the buyer at the time and place of shipment; but

(b) if the contract requires delivery at destination, title passes on tender there.

(3) Unless otherwise explicitly agreed, where delivery is to be made without moving the goods,

(a) if the seller is to deliver a document of title, title passes at the time when and the place where he delivers such documents; or

(b) if the goods are at the time of contracting already identified and no documents are to be delivered, title passes at the time and place of contracting.

(4) A rejection or other refusal by the buyer to receive or retain the goods, whether or not justified, or a justified revocation of acceptance revests title to the goods in the seller. Such revesting occurs by operation of law and is not a "sale."

§ 2—402. Rights of Seller's Creditors Against Sold Goods

(1) Except as provided in subsections (2) and (3), rights of unsecured creditors of the seller with respect to goods which have been identified to a contract for sale are subject to the buyer's rights to recover the goods under this Article (Sections 2—502 and 2—716).

(2) A creditor of the seller may treat a sale or an identification of goods to a contract for sale as void if as against him a retention of possession by the seller is fraudulent under any rule of law of the state where the goods are situated, except that retention of possession

in good faith and current course of trade by a merchant-seller for a commercially reasonable time after a sale or identification is not fraudulent.

(3) Nothing in this Article shall be deemed to impair the rights of creditors of the seller

(a) under the provisions of the Article on Secured Transactions (Article 9); or

(b) where identification to the contract or delivery is made not in current course of trade but in satisfaction of or as security for a preexisting claim for money, security or the like and is made under circumstances which under any rule of law of the state where the goods are situated would apart from this Article constitute the transaction a fraudulent transfer or voidable preference.

§ 2—403. Power to Transfer; Good Faith Purchase of Goods; "Entrusting"

(1) A purchaser of goods acquires all title which his transferor had or had power to transfer except that a purchaser of a limited interest acquires rights only to the extent of the interest purchased. A person with voidable title has power to transfer a good title to a good faith purchaser for value. When goods have been delivered under a transaction of purchase, the purchaser has such power even though

(a) the transferor was deceived as to the identity of the purchaser, or

(b) the delivery was in exchange for a check which is later dishonored, or

(c) it was agreed that the transaction was to be a "cash sale" or

(d) the delivery was procured through fraud punishable as larcenous under the criminal law.

(2) Any entrusting of possession of goods to a merchant who deals in goods of that kind gives him power to transfer all rights of the entruster to a buyer in ordinary course of business.

(3) "Entrusting" includes any delivery and any acquiescence in retention of possession regardless of any condition expressed between the parties to the delivery or acquiescence and regardless of whether the procurement of the entrusting or the possessor's disposition of the goods have been such as to be larcenous under the criminal law.

(4) The rights of other purchasers of goods and of lien creditors are governed by the Articles on Secured Transactions (Article 9), Bulk Transfers (Article 6) and Documents of Title (Article 7).

Part 5
Performance

§ 2—501. Insurable Interest in Goods; Manner of Identification of Goods

(1) The buyer obtains a special property and an insurable interest in goods by identification of existing goods as goods to which the contract refers even though the goods so identified are non-conforming and he has an option to return or reject them. Such identification can be made at any time and in any manner explicitly agreed to by the parties. In the absence of explicit agreement, identification occurs

(a) when the contract is made, if it is for the sale of goods already existing and identified;

(b) if the contract is for the sale of future goods other than those described in paragraph (c), when goods are shipped, marked or otherwise designated by the seller as goods to which the contract refers;

(c) when the crops are planted or otherwise become growing crops or the young are conceived, if the contract is for the sale of unborn young to be born within twelve months after contracting or for the sale of crops to be harvested within twelve months or the next normal harvest season after contracting whichever is longer.

(2) The seller retains an insurable interest in goods so long as title to or any security interest in the goods remains in him; and where the identification is by the seller alone, he may until default or insolvency or notification to the buyer that the identification is final substitute other goods for those identified.

(3) Nothing in this section impairs any insurable interest recognized under any other statute or rule of law.

§ 2—502. Buyer's Right to Goods on Seller's Insolvency

(1) Subject to subsection (2), and even though the goods have not been shipped, a buyer who has paid a part or all of the price of goods in which he has a special property under the provisions of the immediately preceding section may, on making and keeping good a tender of any unpaid portion of their price, recover them from the seller if the seller becomes insolvent within ten days after receipt of the first installment on their price.

(2) If the identification creating his special property has been made by the buyer, he acquires the right to recover the goods only if they conform to the contract for sale.

§ 2—503. Manner of Seller's Tender of Delivery

(1) Tender of delivery requires that the seller put and hold conforming goods at the buyer's disposition and give the buyer any notification reasonably necessary to enable him to take delivery. The manner, time and place for tender are determined by the agreement and this Article, and in particular

(a) tender must be at a reasonable hour, and, if it is of goods, they must be kept available for the period reasonably necessary to enable the buyer to take possession; but

(b) unless otherwise agreed, the buyer must furnish facilities reasonably suited to the receipt of the goods.

(2) Where the case is within the next section respecting shipment, tender requires that the seller comply with its provisions.

(3) Where the seller is required to deliver at a particular destination, tender requires that he comply with subsection (1) and also, in any appropriate case, tender documents as described in subsections (4) and (5) of this section.

(4) Where goods are in the possession of a bailee and are to be delivered without being moved

(a) tender requires that the seller either tender a negotiable document of title covering such goods or procure acknowledgment by the bailee of the buyer's right to possession of the goods; but

(b) tender to the buyer of a nonnegotiable document of title or of a written direction to the bailee to deliver is sufficient tender unless the buyer seasonably objects, and receipt by the bailee of notification of the buyer's rights fixes those rights as against the bailee and all third persons; but risk of loss of the goods and of any failure by the bailee to honor the nonnegotiable document of title or to obey the direction remains on the seller until the buyer has had a reasonable time to present the document or direction, and a refusal by the bailee to honor the document or to obey the direction defeats the tender.

(5) Where the contract requires the seller to deliver documents

(a) he must tender all such documents in correct form, except as provided in this Article with respect to bills of lading in a set (subsection (2) of Section 2—323); and

(b) tender through customary banking channels is sufficient and dishonor of a draft accompanying the documents constitutes nonacceptance or rejection.

§ 2—504. Shipment by Seller

Where the seller is required or authorized to send the goods to the buyer and the contract does not require him to deliver them at a particular destination, then, unless otherwise agreed, he must

(a) put the goods in the possession of such a carrier and make such a contract for their transportation as may be reasonable having regard to the nature of the goods and other circumstances of the case; and

(b) obtain and promptly deliver or tender in due form any document necessary to enable the buyer to obtain possession of the goods or otherwise required by the agreement or by usage of trade; and

(c) promptly notify the buyer of the shipment.

Failure to notify the buyer under paragraph (c) or to make a proper contract under paragraph (a) is a ground for rejection only if material delay or loss ensues.

§ 2—505. Seller's Shipment Under Reservation

(1) Where the seller has identified goods to the contract by or before shipment

(a) his procurement of a negotiable bill of lading to his own order or otherwise reserves in him a security interest in the goods. His procurement of the bill to the order of a financing agency or of the buyer indicates in addition only the seller's expectation of transferring that interest to the person named.

(b) a nonnegotiable bill of lading to himself or his nominee reserves possession of the goods as security but except in a case of conditional delivery (subsection (2) of Section 2—507) a nonnegotiable bill of lading naming the buyer as consignee reserves no security interest even though the seller retains possession of the bill of lading.

(2) When shipment by the seller with reservation of a security interest is in violation of the contract for sale it constitutes an improper contract for transportation within the preceding section but impairs neither the rights given to the buyer by shipment and identification of the goods to the contract nor the seller's powers as a holder of a negotiable document.

§ 2—506. Rights of Financing Agency

(1) A financing agency by paying or purchasing for value a draft which relates to a shipment of goods acquires to the extent of the payment or purchase, and in addition to its own rights under the draft and any document of title securing it, any rights of the shipper in the goods, including the right to stop delivery and the shipper's right to have the draft honored by the buyer.

(2) The right to reimbursement of a financing agency which has in good faith honored or purchased the draft under commitment to or authority from the buyer is not impaired by subsequent discovery of defects with reference to any relevant document which was apparently regular on its face.

§ 2—507. Effect of Seller's Tender; Delivery on Condition

(1) Tender of delivery is a condition to the buyer's duty to accept the goods and, unless otherwise agreed, to his duty to pay for them. Tender entitles the seller to acceptance of the goods and to payment according to the contract.

(2) Where payment is due and demanded on the delivery to the buyer of goods or documents of title, his

right as against the seller to retain or dispose of them is conditional upon his making the payment due.

§ 2—508. Cure by Seller of Improper Tender or Delivery; Replacement

(1) Where any tender or delivery by the seller is rejected because non-conforming and the time for performance has not yet expired, the seller may seasonably notify the buyer of his intention to cure and may then within the contract time make a conforming delivery.

(2) Where the buyer rejects a non-conforming tender which the seller had reasonable grounds to believe would be acceptable with or without money allowance, the seller may if he seasonably notifies the buyer have a further reasonable time to substitute a conforming tender.

§ 2—509. Risk of Loss in the Absence of Breach

(1) Where the contract requires or authorizes the seller to ship the goods by carrier

    (a) if it does not require him to deliver them at a particular desitnation, the risk of loss passes to the buyer when the goods are duly delivered to the carrier even though the shipment is under reservation (Section 2—505); but

    (b) if it does require him to deliver them at a particular destination and the goods are there duly tendered while in the possession of the carrier, the risk of loss passes to the buyer when the goods are there duly so tendered as to enable the buyer to take delivery.

(2) Where the goods are held by a bailee to be delivered without being moved, the risk of loss passes to the buyer

    (a) on his receipt of a negotiable document of title covering the goods; or

    (b) on acknowledgment by the bailee of the buyer's right to possession of the goods; or

    (c) after his receipt of a nonnegotiable document of title or other written direction to deliver, as provided in subsection (4)(b) of Section 2—503.

(3) In any case not within subsection (1) or (2), the risk of loss passes to the buyer on his receipt of the goods if the seller is a merchant; otherwise the risk passes to the buyer on tender of delivery.

(4) The provisions of this section are subject to contrary agreement of the parties and to the provisions of this Article on sale on approval (Section 2—327) and on effect of breach on risk of loss (Section 2—510).

§ 2—510. Effect of Breach on Risk of Loss

(1) Where a tender or delivery of goods so fails to conform to the contract as to give a right of rejection, the risk of their loss remains on the seller until cure or acceptance.

(2) Where the buyer rightfully revokes acceptance, he may to the extent of any deficiency in his effective insurance coverage treat the risk of loss as having rested on the seller from the beginning.

(3) Where the buyer, as to conforming goods already identified to the contract for sale, repudiates or is otherwise in breach before risk of their loss has passed to him, the seller may to the extent of any deficiency in his effective insurance coverage treat the risk of loss as resting on the buyer for a commercially reasonable time.

§ 2—511. Tender of Payment by Buyer; Payment by Check

(1) Unless otherwise agreed, tender of payment is a condition to the seller's duty to tender and complete any delivery.

(2) Tender of payment is sufficient when made by any means or in any manner current in the ordinary course of business unless the seller demands payment in legal tender and gives any extension of time reasonably necessary to procure it.

(3) Subject to the provisions of this Act on the effect of an instrument on an obligation (Section 3—802), payment by check is conditional and is defeated as between the parties by dishonor of the check on due presentment.

§ 2—512. Payment by Buyer Before Inspection

(1) Where the contract requires payment before inspection, non-conformity of the goods does not excuse the buyer from so making payment unless

    (a) the non-comformity appears without inspection; or

    (b) despite tender of the required documents, the circumstances would justify injunction against honor under the provisions of this Act (Section 5–114).

(2) Payment pursuant to subsection (1) does not constitute an acceptance of goods or impair the buyer's right to inspect or any of his remedies.

§ 2—513. Buyer's Right to Inspection of Goods

(1) Unless otherwise agreed and subject to subsection (3), where goods are tendered or delivered or identified to the contract for sale, the buyer has a right before payment or acceptance to inspect them at any reasonable place and time and in any reasonable manner. When the seller is required or authorized to send the goods to the buyer, the inspection may be after their arrival.

(2) Expenses of inspection must be borne by the buyer but may be recovered from the seller if the goods do not conform and are rejected.

(3) Unless otherwise agreed and subject to the provisions of this Article on C.I.F. contracts (subsection (3) of Section 2—321), the buyer is not entitled to inspect the goods before payment of the price when the contract provides

(a) for delivery "C.O.D." or on other like terms; or

(b) for payment against documents of title, except where such payment is due only after the goods are to become available for inspection.

(4) A place or method of inspection fixed by the parties is presumed to be exclusive but, unless otherwise expressly agreed, it does not postpone identification or shift the place for delivery or for passing the risk of loss. If compliance becomes impossible, inspection shall be as provided in this section unless the place or method fixed was clearly intended as an indispensable condition, failure of which avoids the contract.

§ 2—514. When Documents Deliverable on Acceptance; When on Payment

Unless otherwise agreed, documents against which a draft is drawn are to be delivered to the drawee on acceptance of the draft if it is payable more than three days after presentment; otherwise, only on payment.

§ 2—515. Preserving Evidence of Goods in Dispute

In furtherance of the adjustment of any claim or dispute

(a) either party on reasonable notification to the other, and for the purpose of ascertaining the facts and preserving evidence, has the right to inspect, test and sample the goods including such of them as may be in the possession or control of the other; and

(b) the parties may agree to a third party inspection or survey to determine the conformity or condition of the goods and may agree that the findings shall be binding upon them in any subsequent litigation or adjustment.

Part 6

Breach, Repudiation and Excuse

§ 2—601. Buyer's Rights on Improper Delivery

Subject to the provisions of this Article on breach in installment contracts (Section 2—612) and unless otherwise agreed under the sections on contractual limitations of remedy (Sections 2—718 and 2—719), if the goods or the tender of delivery fail in any respect to conform to the contract, the buyer may

(a) reject the whole; or

(b) accept the whole; or

(c) accept any commercial unit or units and reject the rest.

§ 2—602. Manner and Effect of Rightful Rejection

(1) Rejection of goods must be within a reason-able time after their delivery or tender. It is ineffective unless the buyer seasonably notifies the seller.

(2) Subject to the provisions of the two following sections on rejected goods (Sections 2—603 and 2—604),

(a) after rejection any exercise of ownership by the buyer with respect to any commercial unit is wrongful as against the seller; and

(b) if the buyer has before rejection taken physical possession of goods in which he does not have a security interest under the provisions of this Article (subsection (3) of Section 2—711), he is under a duty after rejection to hold them with reasonable care at the seller's disposition for a time sufficient to permit the seller to remove them; but

(c) the buyer has no further obligations with regard to goods rightfully rejected.

(3) The seller's rights with respect to goods wrongfully rejected are governed by the provisions of this Article on Seller's remedies in general (Section 2—703).

§ 2—603. Merchant Buyer's Duties as to Rightfully Rejected Goods

(1) Subject to any security interest in the buyer (subsection (3) of Section 2—711), when the seller has no agent or place of business at the market of rejection, a merchant buyer is under a duty after rejection of goods in his possession or control to follow any reasonable instructions received from the seller with respect to the goods and in the absence of such instructions to make reasonable efforts to sell them for the seller's account if they are perishable or threaten to decline in value speedily. Instructions are not reasonable if on demand indemnity for expenses is not forthcoming.

(2) When the buyer sells goods under subsection (1), he is entitled to reimbursement from the seller or out of the proceeds for reasonable expenses of caring for and selling them, and if the expenses include no selling commission then to such commission as is usual in the trade or, if there is none, to a reasonable sum not exceeding ten per cent on the gross proceeds.

(3) In complying with this section, the buyer is held only to good faith and good faith conduct hereunder is neither acceptance nor conversion nor the basis of an action for damages.

§ 2—604. Buyer's Options as to Salvage or Rightfully Rejected Goods

Subject to the provisions of the immediately preceding section on perishables, if the seller gives no instructions within a reasonable time after notification of rejection the buyer may store the rejected goods for the seller's account or reship them to him or resell them for the seller's account with reimbursement as provided in the preceding section. Such action is not acceptance or conversion.

§ 2 — 605. Waiver of Buyer's Objections by Failure to Particularize

(1) The buyer's failure to state in connection with rejection a particular defect which is ascertainable by reasonable inspection precludes him from relying on the unstated defect to justify rejection or to establish breach

  (a) where the seller could have cured it if stated seasonably; or
  (b) between merchants when the seller has after rejection made a request in writing for a full and final written statement of all defects on which the buyer proposes to rely.

(2) Payment against documents made without reservation of rights precludes recovery of the payment for defects apparent on the face of the documents.

§ 2 — 606. What Constitutes Acceptance of Goods

(1) Acceptance of goods occurs when the buyer
  (a) after a reasonable opportunity to inspect the goods signifies to the seller that the goods are conforming or that he will take or retain them in spite of their non-conformity; or
  (b) fails to make an effective rejection (subsection (1) of Section 2 — 602), but such acceptance does not occur until the buyer has had a reasonable opportunity to inspect them; or
  (c) does any act inconsistent with the seller's ownership; but if such act is wrongful as against the seller it is an acceptance only if ratified by him.

(2) Acceptance of a part of any commercial unit is acceptance of that entire unit.

§ 2 — 607. Effect of Acceptance; Notice of Breach; Burden of Establishing Breach After Acceptance; Notice of Claim or Litigation to Person Answerable Over

(1) The buyer must pay at the contract rate for any goods accepted.

(2) Acceptance of goods by the buyer precludes rejection of the goods accepted and if made with knowledge of a non-conformity cannot be revoked because of it unless the acceptance was on the reasonable assumption that the non-conformity would be seasonably cured but acceptance does not of itself impair any other remedy provided by this Article for non-conformity.

(3) Where a tender has been accepted
  (a) the buyer must within a reasonable time after he discovers or should have discovered any breach notify the seller of breach or be barred from any remedy; and

  (b) if the claim is one for infringement or the like (subsection (3) of Section 2 — 312) and the buyer is sued as a result of such a breach, he must so notify the seller within a reasonable time after he receives notice of the litigation or be barred from any remedy over for liability established by the litigation.

(4) The burden is on the buyer to establish any breach with respect to the goods accepted.

(5) Where the buyer is sued for breach of a warranty or other obligation for which his seller is answerable over
  (a) he may give his seller written notice of the litigation. If the notice states that the seller may come in and defend and that if the seller does not do so he will be bound in any action against him by his buyer by any determination of fact common to the two litigations, then unless the seller after seasonable receipt of the notice does come in and defend he is so bound.
  (b) if the claim is one for infringement or the like (subsection (3) of Section 2 — 312), the original seller may demand in writing that his buyer turn over to him control of the litigation including settlement or else be barred from any remedy over and if he also agrees to bear all expense and to satisfy any adverse judgment, then unless the buyer after seasonable receipt of the demand does turn over control the buyer is so barred.

(6) The provisions of subsections (3), (4) and (5) apply to any obligation of a buyer to hold the seller harmless against infringement or the like (subsection (3) of Section 2 — 312).

§ 2 — 608. Revocation of Acceptance in Whole or in Part

(1) The buyer may revoke his acceptance of a lot or commercial unit whose non-conformity substantially impairs its value to him if he has accepted it
  (a) on the reasonable assumption that its non-conformity would be cured and it has not been seasonably cured; or
  (b) without discovery of such non-conformity if his acceptance was reasonably induced either by the difficulty of discovery before acceptance or by the seller's assurances.

(2) Revocation of acceptance must occur within a reasonable time after the buyer discovers or should have discovered the ground for it and before any substantial change in condition of the goods which is not caused by their own defects. It is not effective until the buyer notifies the seller of it.

(3) A buyer who so revokes has the same rights and duties with regard to the goods involved as if he had rejected them.

§ 2—609. Right to Adequate Assurance of Performance

(1) A contract for sale imposes an obligation on each party that the other's expectation of receiving due performance will not be impaired. When reasonable grounds for insecurity arise with respect to the performance of either party, the other may in writing demand adequate assurance of due performance and until he receives such assurance may, if commercially reasonable, suspend any performance for which he has not already received the agreed return.

(2) Between merchants, the reasonableness of grounds for insecurity and the adequacy of any assurance offered shall be determined according to commercial standards.

(3) Acceptance of any improper delivery or payment does not prejudice the aggrieved party's right to demand adequate assurance of future performance.

(4) After receipt of a justified demand, failure to provide within a reasonable time, not exceeding thirty days, such assurance of due performance as is adequate under the circumstances of the particular case is a repudiation of the contract.

§ 2—610. Anticipatory Repudiation

When either party repudiates the contract with respect to a performance not yet due, the loss of which will substantially impair the value of the contract to the other, the aggrieved party may

    (a) for a commercially reasonable time await performance by the repudiating party; or

    (b) resort to any remedy for breach (Section 2—703 or Section 2—711), even though he has notified the repudiating party that he would await the latter's performance and has urged retraction; and

    (c) in either case suspend his own performance or proceed in accordance with the provisions of this Article on the seller's right to identify goods to the contract notwithstanding breach or to salvage unfinished goods (Section 2—704).

§ 2—611. Retraction of Anticipatory Repudiation

(1) Until the repudiating party's next performance is due, he can retract his repudiation unless the aggrieved party has since the repudiation cancelled or materially changed his position or otherwise indicated that he considers the repudiation final.

(2) Retraction may be by any method which clearly indicates to the aggrieved party that the repudiating party intends to perform, but must include any assurance justifiably demanded under the provisions of this Article (Section 2—609).

(3) Retraction reinstates the repudiating party's rights under the contract with due excuse and allowance to the aggrieved party for any delay occasioned by the repudiation.

§ 2—612. "Installment Contract"; Breach

(1) An "installment contract" is one which requires or authorizes the delivery of goods in separate lots to be separately accepted, even though the contract contains a clause "each delivery is a separate contract" or its equivalent.

(2) The buyer may reject any installment which is non-conforming if the non-conformity substantially impairs the value of that installment and cannot be cured or if the non-conformity is a defect in the required documents; but if the non-conformity does not fall within subsection (3) and the seller gives adequate assurance of its cure, the buyer must accept that installment.

(3) Whenever non-conformity or default with respect to one or more installments substantially impairs the value of the whole contract, there is a breach of the whole. But the aggrieved party reinstates the contract if he accepts a non-conforming installment without seasonably notifying of cancellation or if he brings an action with respect only to past installments or demands performance as to future installments.

§ 2—613. Casualty to Identified Goods

Where the contract requires for its performance goods identified when the contract is made, and the goods suffer casualty without fault of either party before the risk of loss passes to the buyer, or in a proper case under a "no arrival, no sale" term (Section 2—324) then

    (a) if the loss is total the contract is avoided; and

    (b) if the loss is partial or the goods have so deteriorated as no longer to conform to the contract the buyer may nevertheless demand inspection and at his option either treat the contract as avoided or accept the goods with due allowance from the contract price for the deterioration or the deficiency in quantity but without further right against the seller.

§ 2—614. Substituted Performance

(1) Where without fault of either party the agreed berthing, loading, or unloading facilities fail or an agreed type of carrier becomes unavailable or the agreed manner of delivery otherwise becomes commercially impracticable but a commercially reasonable substitute is available, such substitute performance must be tendered and accepted.

(2) If the agreed means or manner of payment fails because of domestic or foreign governmental regulation, the seller may withhold or stop delivery unless the buyer provides a means or manner of payment which is commercially a substantial equivalent. If delivery has already been taken, payment by the means or in the manner provided by the regulation discharges the buyer's obligation unless the regulation is discriminatory, oppressive or predatory.

§ 2—615. Excuse by Failure of Presupposed Conditions

Except so far as a seller may have assumed a greater obligation and subject to the preceding section on substituted performance:

(a) Delay in delivery or nondelivery in whole or in part by a seller who complies with paragraphs (b) and (c) is not a breach of his duty under a contract for sale if performance as agreed has been made impracticable by the occurrence of a contingency the non-occurrence of which was a basic assumption on which the contract was made or by compliance in good faith with any applicable foreign or domestic governmental regulation or order whether or not it later proves to be invalid.

(b) Where the causes mentioned in paragraph (a) affect only a part of the seller's capacity to perform, he must allocate production and deliveries among his customers but may at his option include regular customers not then under contract as well as his own requirements for further manufacture. He may so allocate in any manner which is fair and reasonable.

(c) The seller must notify the buyer seasonably that there will be delay or nondelivery and, when allocation is required under paragraph (b), of the estimated quota thus made available for the buyer.

§ 2—616. Procedure on Notice Claiming Excuse

(1) Where the buyer receives notification of a material or indefinite delay or an allocation justified under the preceding section, he may by written notification to the seller as to any delivery concerned; and where the prospective deficiency substantially impairs the value of the whole contract under the provisions of this Article relating to breach of installment contracts (Section 2—612), then also as to the whole,

(a) terminate and thereby discharge any unexecuted portion of the contract; or

(b) modify the contract by agreeing to take his available quota in substitution.

(2) If, after receipt of such notification from the seller, the buyer fails so to modify the contract within a reasonable time not exceeding thirty days, the contract lapses with respect to any deliveries affected.

(3) The provisions of this section may not be negated by agreement except insofar as the seller has assumed a greater obligation under the preceding section.

Part 7

Remedies

§ 2—701. Remedies for Breach of Collateral Contracts Not Impaired

Remedies for breach of any obligation or promise collateral or ancillary to a contract for sale are not impaired by the provisions of this Article.

§ 2—702. Seller's Remedies on Discovery of Buyer's Insolvency

(1) Where the seller discovers the buyer to be insolvent, he may refuse delivery except for cash including payment for all goods theretofore delivered under the contract, and stop delivery under this Article (Section 2—705).

(2) Where the seller discovers that the buyer has received goods on credit while insolvent, he may reclaim the goods upon demand made within ten days after the receipt, but if misrepresentation of solvency has been made to the particular seller in writing within three months before delivery the ten day limitation does not apply. Except as provided in this subsection, the seller may not base a right to reclaim goods on the buyer's fraudulent or innocent misrepresentation of solvency or of intent to pay.

(3) The seller's right to reclaim under subsection (2) is subject to the rights of a buyer in ordinary course or other good faith purchaser under this Article (Section 2—403). Successful reclamation of goods excludes all other remedies with respect to them.

§ 2—703. Seller's Remedies in General

Where the buyer wrongfully rejects or revokes acceptance of goods or fails to make a payment due on or before delivery or repudiates with respect to a part or the whole, then with respect to any goods directly affected and, if the breach is of the whole contract (Section 2—612), then also with respect to the whole undelivered balance, the aggrieved seller may

(a) withhold delivery of such goods;

(b) stop delivery by any bailee as hereafter provided (Section 2—705);

(c) proceed under the next section respecting goods still unidentified to the contract;

(d) resell and recover damages as hereafter provided (Section 2—706);

(e) recover damages for non-acceptance (Section 2—708) or in a proper case the price (Section 2—709);

(f) cancel.

§ 2—704. Seller's Right to Identify Goods to the Contract Notwithstanding Breach or to Salvage Unfinished Goods

(1) An aggrieved seller under the preceding section may

(a) identify to the contract conforming goods not already identified if at the time he learned of the breach they are in his possession or control;

(b) treat as the subject of resale goods which have demonstrably been intended for the particular contract even though those goods are unfinished.

(2) Where the goods are unfinished an aggrieved seller may, in the exercise of reasonable commercial judgment for the purposes of avoiding loss and of effective realization, either complete the manufacture and wholly identify the goods to the contract or cease manufacture and resell for scrap or salvage value or proceed in any other reasonable manner.

§ 2—705. Seller's Stoppage of Delivery in Transit or Otherwise

(1) The seller may stop delivery of goods in the possession of a carrier or other bailee when he discovers the buyer to be insolvent (Section 2—702) and may stop delivery of carload, truckload, planeload or larger shipments of express or freight when the buyer repudiates or fails to make a payment due before delivery or if for any other reason the seller has a right to withhold or reclaim the goods.

(2) As against such buyer, the seller may stop delivery until

(a) receipt of the goods by the buyer; or

(b) acknowledgment to the buyer by any bailee of the goods except a carrier that the bailee holds the goods for the buyer; or

(c) such acknowledgment to the buyer by a carrier by reshipment or as warehouseman; or

(d) negotiation to the buyer of any negotiable document of title covering the goods.

(3) (a) To stop delivery the seller must so notify as to enable the bailee by reasonable diligence to prevent delivery of the goods.

(b) After such notification the bailee must hold and deliver the goods according to the directions of the seller, but the seller is liable to the bailee for any ensuing charges or damages.

(c) If a negotiable document of title has been issued for goods, the bailee is not obliged to obey a notification to stop until surrender of the document.

(d) A carrier who has issued a nonnegotiable bill of lading is not obliged to obey a notification to stop received from a person other than the consignor.

§ 2—706. Seller's Resale Including Contract for Resale

(1) Under the conditions stated in Section 2—703 on seller's remedies, the seller may resell the goods concerned or the undelivered balance thereof. Where the resale is made in good faith and in a commercially reasonable manner, the seller may recover the difference between the resale price and the contract price together with any incidental damages allowed under the provisions of this Article (Section 2—710), but less expenses saved in consequence of the buyer's breach.

(2) Except as otherwise provided in subsection (3) or unless otherwise agreed, resale may be at public or private sale including sale by way of one or more contracts to sell or of identification to an existing contract of the seller. Sale may be as a unit or in parcels and at any time and place and on any terms but every aspect of the sale including the method, manner, time, place and terms must be commercially reasonable. The resale must be reasonably identified as referring to the broken contract, but it is not necessary that the goods be in existence or that any or all of them have been identified to the contract before the breach.

(3) Where the resale is at private sale, the seller must give the buyer reasonable notification of his intention to resell.

(4) Where the resale is at public sale

(a) only identified goods can be sold except where there is a recognized market for a public sale of futures in goods of the kind; and

(b) it must be made at a usual place or market for public sale if one is reasonably available and except in the case of goods which are perishable or threaten to decline in value speedily the seller must give the buyer reasonable notice of the time and place of the resale; and

(c) if the goods are not to be within the view of those attending the sale, the notification of sale must state the place where the goods are located and provide for their reasonable inspection by prospective bidders; and

(d) the seller may buy.

(5) A purchaser who buys in good faith at a resale takes the goods free of any rights of the original buyer even though the seller fails to comply with one or more of the requirements of this section.

(6) The seller is not accountable to the buyer for any profit made on any resale. A person in the position of a seller (Section 2—707) or a buyer who has rightfully rejected or justifiably revoked acceptance must account for any excess over the amount of his security interest, as hereinafter defined (subsection (3) of Section 2—711.)

§ 2—707. "Person in the Position of a Seller"

(1) A "person in the position of a seller"

includes, as against a principal, an agent who has paid or become responsible for the price of goods on behalf of his principal or anyone who otherwise holds a security interest or other right in goods similar to that of a seller.

(2) A person in the position of a seller may as provided in this Article withhold or stop delivery (Section 2—705) and resell (Section 2—706) and recover incidental damages (Section 2—710).

§ 2—708. Seller's Damages for Nonacceptance or Repudiation

(1) Subject to subsection (2) and to the provisions of this Article with respect to proof of market price (Section 2—723), the measure of damages for nonacceptance or repudiation by the buyer is the difference between the market price at the time and place for tender and the unpaid contract price together with any incidental damages provided in this Article (Section 2—710), but less expenses saved in consequence of the buyer's breach.

(2) If the measure of damages provided in subsection (1) is inadequate to put the seller in as good a position as performance would have done, then the measure of damages is the profit (including reasonable overhead) which the seller would have made from full performance by the buyer, together with any incidental damages provided in this Article (Section 2—710), due allowance for costs reasonably incurred and due credit for payments or proceeds of resale.

§ 2—709. Action for the Price

(1) When the buyer fails to pay the price as it becomes due, the seller may recover, together with any incidental damages under the next section, the price
   (a) of goods accepted or of conforming goods lost or damaged within a commercially reasonable time after risk of their loss has passed to the buyer; and
   (b) of goods identified to the contract if the seller is unable after reasonable effort to resell them at a reasonable price or the circumstances reasonably indicate that such effort will be unavailing.

(2) Where the seller sues for the price, he must hold for the buyer any goods which have been identified to the contract and are still in his control except that if resale becomes possible he may resell them at any time prior to the collection of the judgment. The net proceeds of any such resale must be credited to the buyer and payment of the judgment entitles him to any goods not resold.

(3) After the buyer has wrongfully rejected or revoked acceptance of the goods or has failed to make a payment due or has repudiated (Section 2—610), a seller who is held not entitled to the price under this section shall nevertheless be awarded damages for nonacceptance under the preceding section.

§ 2—710. Seller's Incidental Damages

Incidental damages to an aggrieved seller include any commercially reasonable charges, expenses or commissions incurred in stopping delivery, in the transportation, care and custody of goods after the buyer's breach, in connection with return or resale of the goods or otherwise resulting from the breach.

§ 2—711. Buyer's Remedies in General; Buyer's Security Interest in Rejected Goods

(1) Where the seller fails to make delivery or repudiates or the buyer rightfully rejects or justifiably revokes acceptance, then with respect to any goods involved, and with respect to the whole if the breach goes to the whole contract (Section 2—612), the buyer may cancel and whether or not he has done so may in addition to recovering so much of the price as has been paid
   (a) "cover" and have damages under the next section as to all the goods affected whether or not they have been identified to the contract; or
   (b) recover damages for nondelivery as provided in this Article (Section 2—713).

(2) Where the seller fails to deliver or repudiates, the buyer may also
   (a) if the goods have been identified recover them as provided in this Article (Section 2—502); or
   (b) in a proper case obtain specific performance or replevy the goods as provided in this Article (Section 2—716).

(3) On rightful rejection or justifiable revocation of acceptance, a buyer has a security interest in goods in his possession or control for any payments made on their price and any expenses reasonably incurred in their inspection, receipt, transportation, care and custody and may hold such goods and resell them in like manner as an aggrieved seller (Section 2—706).

§ 2—712. "Cover"; Buyer's Procurement of Substitute Goods

(1) After a breach within the preceding section, the buyer may "cover" by making in good faith and without unreasonable delay any reasonable purchase of or contract to purchase goods in substitution for those due from the seller.

(2) The buyer may recover from the seller as damages the difference between the cost of cover and the contract price together with any incidental or consequential damages as hereinafter defined (Section 2—715), but less expenses saved in consequence of the seller's breach.

(3) Failure of the buyer to effect cover within this section does not bar him from any other remedy.

§ 2—713. Buyer's Damages for Nondelivery or Repudiation

(1) Subject to the provisions of this Article with respect to proof of market price (Section 2—723), the

measure of damages for nondelivery or repudiation by the seller is the difference between the market price at the time when the buyer learned of the breach and the contract price together with any incidental and consequential damages provided in this Article (Section 2—715), but less expenses saved in consequence of the seller's breach.

(2) Market price is to be determined as of the place for tender or, in cases of rejection after arrival or revocation of acceptance, as of the place of arrival.

§ 2—714. Buyer's Damages for Breach in Regard to Accepted Goods

(1) Where the buyer has accepted goods and given notification (subsection (3) of Section 2—607), he may recover as damages for any non-conformity of tender the loss resulting in the ordinary course of events from the seller's breach as determined in any manner which is reasonable.

(2) The measure of damages for breach of warranty is the difference at the time and place of acceptance between the value of the goods accepted and the value they would have had if they had been as warranted, unless special circumstances show proximate damages of a different amount.

(3) In a proper case any incidental and consequential damages under the next section may also be recovered.

§ 2—715. Buyer's Incidental and Consequential Damages

(1) Incidental damages resulting from the seller's breach include expenses reasonably incurred in inspection, receipt, transportation and care and custody of goods rightfully rejected, any commercially reasonable charges, expenses or commissions in connection with effecting cover and any other reasonable expense incident to the delay or other breach.

(2) Consequential damages resulting from the seller's breach include

    (a) any loss resulting from general or particular requirements and needs of which the seller at the time of contracting had reason to know and which could not reasonably be prevented by cover or otherwise; and

    (b) injury to person or property proximately resulting from any breach of warranty.

§ 2—716. Buyer's Right to Specific Performance or Replevin

(1) Specific performance may be decreed where the goods are unique or in other proper circumstances.

(2) The decree for specific performance may include such terms and conditions as to payment of the price, damages, or other relief as the court may deem just.

(3) The buyer has a right of replevin for goods identified to the contract if after reasonable effort he is unable to effect cover for such goods or the circumstances reasonably indicate that such effort will be unavailing or if the goods have been shipped under reservation and satisfaction of the security interest in them has been made or tendered.

§ 2—717. Deduction of Damages From the Price

The buyer on notifying the seller of his intention to do so may deduct all or any part of the damages resulting from any breach of the contract from any part of the price still due under the same contract.

§ 2—718. Liquidation or Limitation of Damages; Deposits

(1) Damages for breach by either party may be liquidated in the agreement but only at an amount which is reasonable in the light of the anticipated or actual harm caused by the breach, the difficulties of proof of loss, and the inconvenience or nonfeasibility of otherwise obtaining an adequate remedy. A term fixing unreasonably large liquidated damages is void as a penalty.

(2) Where the seller justifiably withholds delivery of goods because of the buyer's breach, the buyer is entitled to restitution of any amount by which the sum of his payments exceeds

    (a) the amount to which the seller is entitled by virtue of terms liquidating the seller's damages in accordance with subsection (1), or

    (b) in the absence of such terms, twenty percent of the value of the total performance for which the buyer is obligated under the contract or $500, whichever is smaller.

(3) The buyer's right to restitution under subsection (2) is subject to offset to the extent that the seller establishes

    (a) a right to recover damages under the provisions of this Article other than subsection (1), and

    (b) the amount or value of any benefits received by the buyer directly or indirectly by reason of the contract.

(4) Where a seller has received payment in goods, their reasonable value or the proceeds of their resale shall be treated as payments for the purposes of subsection (2); but if the seller has notice of the buyer's breach before reselling goods received in part performance, his resale is subject to the conditions laid down in this Article on resale by an aggrieved seller (Section 2—706).

§ 2—719. Contractual Modification or Limitation of Remedy

(1) Subject to the provisions of subsections (2) and (3) of this section and of the preceding section on liquidation and limitation of damages,

    (a) the agreement may provide for remedies in addition to or in substitution for those provided in this Article and may limit or alter the measure of damages recoverable under this Article, as by limiting the buyer's remedies to return of the goods and repayment of the price or to repair and replacement of non-conforming goods or parts; and

(b) resort to a remedy as provided is optional unless the remedy is expressly agreed to be exclusive, in which case it is the sole remedy.

(2) Where circumstances cause an exclusive or limited remedy to fail of its essential purpose, remedy may be had as provided in this Act.

(3) Consequential damages may be limited or excluded unless the limitation or exclusion is unconscionable. Limitation of consequential damages for injury to the person in the case of consumer goods is prima facie unconscionable but limitation of damages where the loss is commercial is not.

§ 2—720. Effect of "Cancellation" or "Rescission" on Claims for Antecedent Breach

Unless the contrary intention clearly appears, expressions of "cancellation" or "rescission" of the contract or the like shall not be construed as a renunciation or discharge of any claim in damages for an antecedent breach.

§ 2—721. Remedies for Fraud

Remedies for material misrepresentation or fraud include all remedies available under this Article for non-fraudulent breach. Neither rescission or a claim for rescission of the contract for sale nor rejection or return of the goods shall bar or be deemed inconsistent with a claim for damages or other remedy.

§ 2—722. Who Can Sue Third Parties for Injury to Goods

Where a third party so deals with goods which have been identified to a contract for sale as to cause actionable injury to a party to that contract

(a) a right of action against the third party is in either party to the contract for sale who has title to or a security interest or a special property or an insurable interest in the goods; and if the goods have been destroyed or converted, a right of action is also in the party who either bore the risk of loss under the contract for sale or has since the injury assumed that risk as against the other;

(b) if at the time of the injury the party plaintiff did not bear the risk of loss as against the other party to the contract for sale and there is no arrangement between them for disposition of the recovery, his suit or settlement is, subject to his own interest, as a fiduciary for the other party to the contract;

(c) either party may with the consent of the other sue for the benefit of whom it may concern.

§ 2—723. Proof of Market Price: Time and Place

(1) If an action based on anticipatory repudiation comes to trial before the time for performance with respect to some or all of the goods, any damages based on market price (Section 2—708 or Section 2—713) shall be determined according to the price of such goods prevailing at the time when the aggrieved party learned of the repudiation.

(2) If evidence of a price prevailing at the times or places described in this Article is not readily available, the price prevailing within any reasonable time before or after the time described or at any other place which in commercial judgment or under usage of trade would serve as a reasonable substitute for the one described may be used, making any proper allowance for the cost of transporting the goods to or from such other place.

(3) Evidence of a relevant price prevailing at a time or place other than the one described in this Article offered by one party is not admissible unless and until he has given the other party such notice as the court finds sufficient to prevent unfair surprise.

§ 2—724. Admissibility of Market Quotations

Whenever the prevailing price or value of any goods regularly bought and sold in any established commodity market is in issue, reports in official publications or trade journals or in newspapers or periodicals of general circulation published as the reports of such market shall be admissible in evidence. The circumstances of the preparation of such a report may be shown to affect its weight but not its admissibility.

§ 2—725. Statute of Limitations in Contracts for Sale

(1) An action for breach of any contract for sale must be commenced within four years after the cause of action has accrued. By the original agreement, the parties may reduce the period of limitation to not less than one year but may not extend it.

(2) A cause of action accrues when the breach occurs, regardless of the aggrieved party's lack of knowledge of the breach. A breach of warranty occurs when tender of delivery is made, except that where a warranty explicitly extends to future performance of the goods and discovery of the breach must await the time of such performance the cause of action accrues when the breach is or should have been discovered.

(3) Where an action commenced within the time limited by subsection (1) is so terminated as to leave available a remedy by another action for the same breach, such other action may be commenced after the

expiration of the time limited and within six months after the termination of the first action unless the termination resulted from voluntary discontinuance or from dismissal for failure or neglect to prosecute.

(4) This section does not alter the law on tolling of the statute of limitations nor does it apply to causes of action which have accrued before this Act becomes effective.

ARTICLE 3

COMMERCIAL PAPER

Part 1

Short Title, Form and Interpretation

§ 3—101. Short Title

This Article shall be known and may be cited as Uniform Commercial Code—Commercial Paper.

§ 3—102. Definitions and Index of Definitions

(1) In this Article unless the context otherwise requires

    (a) "Issue" means the first delivery of an instrument to a holder or a remitter.

    (b) An "order" is a direction to pay and must be more than an authorization or request. It must identify the person to pay with reasonable certainty. It may be addressed to one or more such persons jointly or in the alternative but not in succession.

    (c) A "promise" is an undertaking to pay and must be more than an acknowledgment of an obligation.

    (d) "Secondary party" means a drawer or indorser.

    (e) "Instrument" means a negotiable instrument.

(2) Other definitions applying to this Article and the sections in which they appear are:

"Acceptance." Section 3—410.
"Accommodation party." Section 3—415.
"Alteration." Section 3—407.
"Certificate of deposit." Section 3—104.
"Certification." Section 3—411.
"Check." Section 3—104.
"Definite time." Section 3—109.
"Dishonor." Section 3—507.
"Draft." Section 3—104.
"Holder in due course." Section 3—302.
"Negotiation." Section 3—202.
"Note." Section 3—104.
"Notice of dishonor." Section 3—508.
"On demand." Section 3—108.
"Presentment." Section 3—504.
"Protest." Section 3—509.

"Restrictive Indorsement." Section 3—205.
"Signature." Section 3—401.

(3) The following definitions in other Articles apply to this Article:

"Account." Section 4—104.
"Banking Day." Section 4—104.
"Clearing house." Section 4—104.
"Collecting bank." Section 4—105.
"Customer." Section 4—104.
"Depositary Bank." Section 4—105.
"Documentary Draft." Section 4—104.
"Intermediary Bank." Section 4—105.
"Item." Section 4—104.
"Midnight deadline." Section 4—104.
"Payor bank." Section 4—105.

(4) In addition Article 1 contains general definitions and principles of construction and interpretation applicable throughout this Article.

§ 3—103. Limitations on Scope of Article

(1) This Article does not apply to money, documents of title or investment securities.

(2) The provisions of this Article are subject to the provisions of the Article on Bank Deposits and Collections (Article 4) and Secured Transactions (Article 9).

§ 3—104. Form of Negotiable Instruments; "Draft"; "Check"; "Certificate of Deposit"; "Note"

(1) Any writing to be a negotiable instrument within this Article must

    (a) be signed by the maker or drawer; and

    (b) contain an unconditional promise or order to pay a sum certain in money and no other promise, order, obligation or power given by the maker or drawer except as authorized by this Article; and

    (c) be payable on demand or at a definite time; and

    (d) be payable to order or to bearer.

(2) A writing which complies with the requirements of this section is

    (a) a "draft" ("bill of exchange") if it is an order;

(b) a "check" if it is a draft drawn on a bank and payable on demand;

(c) a "certificate of deposit" if it is an acknowledgment by a bank of receipt of money with an engagement to repay it;

(d) a "note" if it is a promise other than a certificate of deposit.

(3) As used in other Articles of this Act, and as the context may require, the terms "draft," "check," "certificate of deposit" and "note" may refer to instruments which are not negotiable within this Article as well as to instruments which are so negotiable.

§ 3 — 105.   When Promise or Order Unconditional

(1) A promise or order otherwise unconditional is not made conditional by the fact that the instrument

(a) is subject to implied or constructive conditions; or

(b) states its consideration, whether performed or promised, or the transaction which gave rise to the instrument, or that the promise or order is made or the instrument matures in accordance with or "as per" such transaction; or

(c) refers to or states that it arises out of a separate agreement or refers to a separate agreement for rights as to prepayment or acceleration; or

(d) states that it is drawn under a letter of credit; or

(e) states that it is secured, whether by mortgage, reservation of title or otherwise; or

(f) indicates a particular account to be debited or any other fund or source from which reimbursement is expected; or

(g) is limited to payment out of a particular fund or the proceeds of a particular source, if the instrument is issued by a government or governmental agency or unit; or

(h) is limited to payment out of the entire assets of a partnership, unincorporated association, trust or estate by or on behalf of which the instrument is issued.

(2) A promise or order is not unconditional if the instrument

(a) states that it is subject to or governed by any other agreement; or

(b) states that it is to be paid only out of a particular fund or source except as provided in this section.

§ 3 — 106.   Sum Certain

(1) The sum payable is a sum certain even though it is to be paid

(a) with stated interest or by stated installments; or

(b) with stated different rates of interest before and after default or a specified date; or

(c) with a stated discount or addition if paid before or after the date fixed for payment; or

(d) with exchange or less exchange, whether at a fixed rate or at the current rate; or

(e) with costs of collection or an attorney's fee or both upon default.

(2) Nothing in this section shall validate any term which is otherwise illegal.

§ 3 — 107.   Money

(1) An instrument is payable in money if the medium of exchange in which it is payable is money at the time the instrument is made. An instrument payable in "currency" or "current funds" is payable in money.

(2) A promise or order to pay a sum stated in a foreign currency is for a sum certain in money and, unless a different medium of payment is specified in the instrument, may be satisfied by payment of that number of dollars which the stated foreign currency will purchase at the buying sight rate for that currency on the day on which the instrument is payable or, if payable on demand, on the day of demand. If such an instrument specifies a foreign currency as the medium of payment the instrument is payable in that currency.

§ 3 — 108.   Payable on Demand

Instruments payable on demand include those payable at sight or on presentation and those in which no time for payment is stated.

§ 3 — 109.   Definite Time

(1) An instrument is payable at a definite time if by its terms it is payable

(a) on or before a stated date or at a fixed period after a stated date; or

(b) at a fixed period after sight; or

(c) at a definite time subject to any acceleration; or

(d) at a definite time subject to extension at the option of the holder, or to extension to a further definite time at the option of the maker or acceptor or automatically upon or after a specified act or event.

(2) An instrument which by its terms is otherwise payable only upon an act or event uncertain as to time of occurrence is not payable at a definite time even though the act or event has occurred.

§ 3 — 110.   Payable to Order

(1) An instrument is payable to order when by its terms it is payable to the order or assigns of any person therein specified with reasonable certainty, or to him or his order, or when it is conspicuously designated on its face as "exchange" or the like and names a payee. It may be payable to the order of

(a) the maker or drawer; or

(b) the drawee; or

(c) a payee who is not maker, drawer or drawee; or

(d) two or more payees together or in the alternative; or

(e) an estate, trust or fund, in which case it is payable to the order of the representative of such estate, trust or fund or his successors; or

(f) an office, or an officer by his title as such in which case it is payable to the principal but the incumbent of the office or his successors may act as if he or they were the holder; or

(g) a partnership or unincorporated association, in which case it is payable to the partnership or association and may be indorsed or transferred by any person thereto authorized.

(2) An instrument not payable to order is not made so payable by such words as "payable upon return of this instrument properly indorsed."

(3) An instrument made payable both to order and to bearer is payable to order unless the bearer words are handwritten or typewritten.

§ 3 — 111. Payable to Bearer

An instrument is payable to bearer when by its terms it is payable to

(a) bearer or the order of bearer; or

(b) a specified person or bearer; or

(c) "cash" or the order of "cash," or any other indication which does not purport to designate a specific payee.

§ 3 — 112. Terms and Omissions Not Affecting Negotiability

(1) The negotiability of an instrument is not affected by

(a) the omission of a statement of any consideration or of the place where the instrument is drawn or payable; or

(b) a statement that collateral has been given to secure obligations either on the instrument or otherwise of an obligor on the instrument or that in case of default on those obligations the holder may realize on or dispose of the collateral; or

(c) a promise or power to maintain or protect collateral or to give additional collateral; or

(d) a term authorizing a confession of judgment on the instrument if it is not paid when due; or

(e) a term purporting to waive the benefit of any law intended for the advantage or protection of any obligor; or

(f) a term in a draft providing that the payee by indorsing or cashing it acknowledges full satisfaction of an obligation of the drawer; or

(g) a statement in a draft drawn in a set of parts (Section 3 — 801) to the effect that the order is effective only if no other part has been honored.

(2) Nothing in this section shall validate any term which is otherwise illegal.

§ 3 — 113. Seal

An instrument otherwise negotiable is within this Article even though it is under a seal.

§ 3 — 114. Date, Antedating, Postdating

(1) The negotiability of an instrument is not affected by the fact that it is undated, antedated or postdated.

(2) Where an instrument is antedated or postdated, the time when it is payable is determined by the stated date if the instrument is payable on demand or at a fixed period after date.

(3) Where the instrument or any signature thereon is dated, the date is presumed to be correct.

§ 3 — 115. Incomplete Instruments

(1) When a paper, whose contents at the time of signing show that it is intended to become an instrument, is signed while still incomplete in any necessary respect, it cannot be enforced until completed; but when it is completed in accordance with authority given, it is effective as completed.

(2) If the completion is unauthorized, the rules as to material alteration apply (Section 3 — 407), even though the paper was not delivered by the maker or drawer; but the burden of establishing that any completion is unauthorized is on the party so asserting.

§ 3 — 116. Instruments Payable to Two or More Persons

An instrument payable to the order of two or more persons,

(a) if in the alternative, is payable to any one of them and may be negotiated, discharged or enforced by any of them who has possession of it;

(b) if not in the alternative, is payable to all of them and may be negotiated, discharged or enforced only by all of them.

§ 3 — 117. Instruments Payable With Words of Description

An instrument made payable to a named person with the addition of words describing him

(a) as agent or officer of a specified person is payable to his principal but the agent or officer may act as if he were the holder;

(b) as any other fiduciary for a specified person or purpose is payable to the payee and may be negotiated, discharged or enforced by him;

(c) in any other manner is payable to the payee unconditionally and the additional words are without effect on subsequent parties.

§ 3 — 118. Ambiguous Terms and Rules of Construction

The following rules apply to every instrument:

(a) Where there is doubt whether the instrument is a draft or a note, the holder may treat it as either. A draft drawn on the drawer is effective as a note.

(b) Handwritten terms control typewritten and printed terms, and typewritten control printed.

(c) Words control figures except that if the words are ambiguous figures control.

(d) Unless otherwise specified, a provision for interest means interest at the judgment rate at the place of payment from the date of the instrument, or if it is undated from the date of issue.

(e) Unless the instrument otherwise specifies, two or more persons who sign as maker, acceptor or drawer or indorser and as a part of the same transaction are jointly and severally liable even though the instrument contains such words as "I promise to pay."

(f) Unless otherwise specified, consent to extension authorizes a single extension for not longer than the original period. A consent to extension, expressed in the instrument, is binding on secondary parties and accommodation makers. A holder may not exercise his option to extend an instrument over the objection of a maker or acceptor or other party who in accordance with Section 3 — 604 tenders full payment when the instrument is due.

§ 3 — 119. Other Writings Affecting Instrument

(1) As between the obligor and his immediate obligee or any transferee, the terms of an instrument may be modified or affected by any other written agreement executed as a part of the same transaction, except that a holder in due course is not affected by any limitation of his rights arising out of the separate written agreement if he had no notice of the limitation when he took the instrument.

(2) A separate agreement does not affect the negotiability of an instrument.

§ 3 — 120. Instruments "Payable Through" Bank

An instrument which states that it is "payable through" a bank or the like designates that bank as a collecting bank to make presentment but does not of itself authorize the bank to pay the instrument.

§ 3 — 121. Instruments Payable at Bank

Note: *If this Act is introduced in the Congress of the United States this section should be omitted. (States to select either alternative)*

Alternative A —

A note or acceptance which states that it is payable at a bank is the equivalent of a draft drawn on the bank payable when it falls due out of any funds of the maker or acceptor in current account or otherwise available for such payment.

Alternative B —

A note or acceptance which states that it is payable at a bank is not of itself an order or authorization to the bank to pay it.

§ 3 — 122. Accrual of Cause of Action

(1) A cause of action against a maker or an acceptor accrues,

(a) in the case of a time instrument, on the day after maturity;

(b) in the case of a demand instrument, upon its date or, if no date is stated, on the date of issue.

(2) A cause of action against the obligor of a demand or time certificate of deposit accrues upon demand, but demand on a time certificate may not be made until on or after the date of maturity.

(3) A cause of action against a drawer of a draft or an indorser of any instrument accrues upon demand following dishonor of the instrument. Notice of dishonor is a demand.

(4) Unless an instrument provides otherwise, interest runs at the rate provided by law for a judgment

(a) in the case of a maker, acceptor or other primary obligor of a demand instrument, from the date of demand;

(b) in all other cases from the date of accrual of the cause of action.

Part 2

Transfer and Negotiation

§ 3 — 201. Transfer: Right to Indorsement

(1) Transfer of an instrument vests in the transferee such rights as the transferor has therein, except that a transferee who has himself been a party to any fraud or illegality affecting the instrument or who as a prior holder had notice of a defense or claim against it cannot improve his position by taking from a later holder in due course.

(2) A transfer of a security interest in an instrument vests the foregoing rights in the transferee to the extent of the interest transferred.

(3) Unless otherwise agreed, any transfer for value of an instrument not then payable to bearer gives the transferee the specifically enforceable right to have the unqualified indorsement of the transferor. Negotiation takes effect only when the indorsement is made and until that time there is no presumption that the transferee is the owner.

§ 3 — 202. Negotiation

(1) Negotiation is the transfer of an instrument in such form that the transferee becomes a holder. If the instrument is payable to order, it is negotiated by delivery with any necessary indorsement; if payable to bearer, it is negotiated by delivery.

(2) An indorsement must be written by or on behalf of the holder and on the instrument or on a paper so firmly affixed thereto as to become a part thereof.

(3) An indorsement is effective for negotiation only when it conveys the entire instrument or any unpaid residue. If it purports to be of less, it operates only as a partial assignment.

(4) Words of assignment, condition, waiver, guaranty, limitation or disclaimer of liability and the like accompanying an indorsement do not affect its character as an indorsement.

§ 3 — 203. Wrong or Misspelled Name

Where an instrument is made payable to a person under a misspelled name or one other than his own, he may indorse in that name or his own or both; but signature in both names may be required by a person paying or giving value for the instrument.

§ 3 — 204. Special Indorsement; Blank Indorsement

(1) A special indorsement specifies the person to whom or to whose order it makes the instrument payable. Any instrument specially indorsed becomes payable to the order of the special indorsee and may be further negotiated only by his indorsement.

(2) An indorsement in blank specifies no particular indorsee and may consist of a mere signature. An instrument payable to order and indorsed in blank becomes payable to bearer and may be negotiated by delivery alone until specially indorsed.

(3) The holder may convert a blank indorsement into a special indorsement by writing over the signature of the indorser in blank any contract consistent with the character of the indorsement.

§ 3 — 205. Restrictive Indorsements

An indorsement is restrictive which either

(a) is conditional; or

(b) purports to prohibit further transfer of the instrument; or

(c) includes the words "for collection," "for deposit," "pay any bank," or like terms signifying a purpose of deposit or collection; or

(d) otherwise states that it is for the benefit or use of the indorser or of another person.

§ 3 — 206. Effect of Restrictive Indorsement

(1) No restrictive indorsement prevents further transfer or negotiation of the instrument.

(2) An intermediary bank, or a payor bank which is not the depositary bank, is neither given notice nor otherwise affected by a restrictive indorsement of any person except the bank's immediate transferor or the person presenting for payment.

(3) Except for an intermediary bank, any transferee under an indorsement which is conditional or includes the words "for collection," "for deposit," "pay any bank," or like terms (subparagraphs (a) and (c) of Section 3 — 205) must pay or apply any value given by him for or on the security of the instrument consistently with the indorsement and to the extent that he does so he becomes a holder for value. In addition, such transferee is a holder in due course if he otherwise complies with the requirements of Section 3 — 302 on what constitutes a holder in due course.

(4) The first taker under an indorsement for the benefit of the indorser or another person (subparagraph (d) of Section 3 — 205) must pay or apply any value given by him for or on the security of the instrument consistently with the indorsement and, to the extent that he does so, he becomes a holder for value. In addition, such taker is a holder in due course if he otherwise complies with the requirements of Section 3 — 302 on what constitutes a holder in due course. A later holder for value is neither given notice nor otherwise affected by such restrictive indorsement unless he has knowledge that a fiduciary or other person has negotiated the instrument in any transaction for his own benefit or otherwise in breach of duty (subsection (2) of Section 3 — 304).

§ 3 — 207. Negotiation Effective Although It May Be Rescinded

(1) Negotiation is effective to transfer the instrument although the negotiation is

(a) made by an infant, a corporation exceeding its powers, or any other person without capacity; or

(b) obtained by fraud, duress or mistake of any kind; or

(c) part of an illegal transaction; or

(d) made in breach of duty.

(2) Except as against a subsequent holder in due course, such negotiation is in an appropriate case subject to rescission, the declaration of a constructive trust or any other remedy permitted by law.

§ 3 — 208. Reacquisition

Where an instrument is returned to or reacquired by a prior party, he may cancel any indorsement which is not necessary to his title and reissue or further negotiate the instrument; but any intervening party is discharged as against the reacquiring party and subsequent holders not in due course and, if his indorsement has been cancelled, is discharged as against subsequent holders in due course as well.

Part 3

Rights of a Holder

§ 3—301. Rights of a Holder

The holder of an instrument whether or not he is the owner may transfer or negotiate it and, except as otherwise provided in Section 3—603 on payment or satisfaction, discharge it or enforce payment in his own name.

§ 3—302. Holder in Due Course

(1) A holder in due course is a holder who takes the instrument
    (a) for value; and
    (b) in good faith; and
    (c) without notice that it is overdue or has been dishonored or of any defense against or claim to it on the part of any person.
(2) A payee may be a holder in due course.
(3) A holder does not become a holder in due course of an instrument:
    (a) by purchase of it at judicial sale or by taking it under legal process; or
    (b) by acquiring it in taking over an estate; or
    (c) by purchasing it as part of a bulk transaction not in regular course of business of the transferor.
(4) A purchaser of a limited interest can be a holder in due course only to the extent of the interest purchased.

§ 3—303. Taking for Value

A holder takes the instrument for value
    (a) to the extent that the agreed consideration has been performed or that he acquires a security interest in or a lien on the instrument otherwise than by legal process; or
    (b) when he takes the instrument in payment of or as security for an antecedent claim against any person whether or not the claim is due; or
    (c) when he gives a negotiable instrument for it or makes an irrevocable commitment to a third person.

§ 3—304. Notice to Purchaser

(1) The purchaser has notice of a claim or defense if
    (a) the instrument is so incomplete, bears such visible evidence of forgery or alteration, or is otherwise so irregular as to call into question its validity, terms or ownership or to create an ambiguity as to the party to pay; or
    (b) the purchaser has notice that the obligation of any party is voidable in whole or in part, or that all parties have been discharged.
(2) The purchaser has notice of a claim against the instrument when he has knowledge that a fiduciary has negotiated the instrument in payment of or as security for his own debt or in any transaction for his own benefit or otherwise in breach of duty.
(3) The purchaser has notice that an instrument is overdue if he has reason to know
    (a) that any part of the principal amount is overdue or that there is an uncured default in payment of another instrument of the same series; or
    (b) that acceleration of the instrument has been made; or
    (c) that he is taking a demand instrument after demand has been made or more than a reasonable length of time after its issue. A reasonable time for a check drawn and payable within the states and territories of the United States and the District of Columbia is presumed to be thirty days.
(4) Knowledge of the following facts does not of itself give the purchaser notice of a defense or claim
    (a) that the instrument is antedated or postdated;
    (b) that it was issued or negotiated in return for an executory promise or accompanied by a separate agreement, unless the purchaser has notice that a defense or claim has arisen from the terms thereof;
    (c) that any party has signed for accommodation;
    (d) that an incomplete instrument has been completed, unless the purchaser has notice of any improper completion;
    (e) that any person negotiating the instrument is or was a fiduciary;
    (f) that there has been default in payment of interest on the instrument or in payment of any other instrument, except one of the same series.
(5) The filing or recording of a document does not of itself constitute notice within the provisions of this Article to a person who would otherwise be a holder in due course.
(6) To be effective, notice must be received at such time and in such manner as to give a reasonable opportunity to act on it.

§ 3—305. Rights of a Holder in Due Course

To the extent that a holder is a holder in due course, he takes the instrument free from
    (1) all claims to it on the part of any person; and
    (2) all defenses of any party to the instrument with whom the holder has not dealt except
        (a) infancy, to the extent that it is a defense to a simple contract; and
        (b) such other incapacity, or duress, or illegality of the transaction, as renders the obligation of the party a nullity; and
        (c) such misrepresentation as has induced the party to sign the instrument with neither knowledge nor reasonable opportunity to

obtain knowledge of its character or its essential terms; and

(d) discharge in insolvency proceedings; and

(e) any other discharge of which the holder has notice when he takes the instrument.

§ 3—306. Rights of One Not Holder in Due Course

Unless he has the rights of a holder in due course, any person takes the instrument subject to

(a) all valid claims to it on the part of any person; and

(b) all defenses of any party which would be available in an action on a simple contract; and

(c) the defenses of want or failure of consideration, nonperformance of any condition precedent, nondelivery, or delivery for a special purpose (Section 3—408); and

(d) the defense that he, or a person through whom he holds the instrument, acquired it by theft, or that payment or satisfaction to such holder would be inconsistent with the terms of a restrictive indorsement. The claim of any third person to the instrument is not otherwise available as a defense to any party liable thereon unless the third person himself defends the action for such party.

§ 3—307. Burden of Establishing Signatures, Defenses and Due Course

(1) Unless specifically denied in the pleadings, each signature on an instrument is admitted. When the effectiveness of a signature is put in issue

(a) the burden of establishing it is on the party claiming under the signature; but

(b) the signature is presumed to be genuine or authorized except where the action is to enforce the obligation of a purported signer who has died or become incompetent before proof is required.

(2) When signatures are admitted or established, production of the instrument entitles a holder to recover on it unless the defendant establishes a defense.

(3) After it is shown that a defense exists, a person claiming the rights of a holder in due course has the burden of establishing that he or some person under whom he claims is in all respects a holder in due course.

Part 4

Liability of Parties

§ 3—401. Signature

(1) No person is liable on an instrument unless his signature appears thereon.

(2) A signature is made by use of any name, including any trade or assumed name, upon an instru-

ment, or by any word or mark used in lieu of a written signature.

§ 3—402. Signature in Ambiguous Capacity

Unless the instrument clearly indicates that a signature is made in some other capacity, it is an indorsement.

§ 3—403. Signature by Authorized Representative

(1) A signature may be made by an agent or other representative, and his authority to make it may be established as in other cases of representation. No particular form of appointment is necessary to establish such authority.

(2) An authorized representative who signs his own name to an instrument

(a) is personally obligated if the instrument neither names the person represented nor shows that the representative signed in a representative capacity;

(b) except as otherwise established between the immediate parties, is personally obligated if the instrument names the person represented but does not show that the representative signed in a representative capacity, or if the instrument does not name the person represented but does show that the representative signed in a representative capacity.

(3) Except as otherwise established, the name of an organization preceded or followed by the name and office of an authorized individual is a signature made in a representative capacity.

§ 3—404. Unauthorized Signatures

(1) Any unauthorized signature is wholly inoperative as that of the person whose name is signed unless he ratifies it or is precluded from denying it; but it operates as the signature of the unauthorized signer in favor of any person who in good faith pays the instrument or takes it for value.

(2) Any unauthorized signature may be ratified for all purposes of this Article. Such ratification does not of itself affect any rights of the person ratifying against the actual signer.

§ 3—405. Impostors; Signature in Name of Payee

(1) An indorsement by any person in the name of a named payee is effective if

(a) an impostor by use of the mails or otherwise has induced the maker or drawer to issue the instrument to him or his confederate in the name of the payee; or

(b) a person signing as or on behalf of a maker or drawer intends the payee to have no interest in the instrument; or

(c) an agent or employee of the maker or drawer has supplied him with the name of the payee intending the latter to have no such interest.

(2) Nothing in this section shall affect the criminal or civil liability of the person so indorsing.

§ 3—406. Negligence Contributing to Alteration or Unauthorized Signature

Any person who by his negligence substantially contributes to a material alteration of the instrument or to the making of an unauthorized signature is precluded from asserting the alteration or lack of authority against a holder in due course or against a drawee or other payor who pays the instrument in good faith and in accordance with the reasonable commercial standards of the drawee's or payor's business.

§ 3—407. Alteration

(1) Any alteration of an instrument is material which changes the contract of any party thereto in any respect, including any such change in
    (a) the number or relations of the parties; or
    (b) an incomplete instrument, by completing it otherwise than as authorized; or
    (c) the writing as signed, by adding to it or by removing any part of it.

(2) As against any person other than a subsequent holder in due course.
    (a) alteration by the holder which is both fraudulent and material discharges any party whose contract is thereby changed unless that party assents or is precluded from asserting the defense;
    (b) no other alteration discharges any party and the instrument may be enforced according to its original tenor, or as to incomplete instruments, according to the authority given.

(3) A subsequent holder in due course may in all cases enforce the instrument according to its original tenor, and when an incomplete instrument has been completed, he may enforce it as completed.

§ 3—408. Consideration

Want or failure of consideration is a defense as against any person not having the rights of a holder in due course (Section 3—305), except that no consideration is necessary for an instrument or obligation thereon given in payment of or as security for an antecedent obligation of any kind. Nothing in this section shall be taken to displace any statute outside this Act under which a promise is enforceable notwithstanding lack or failure of consideration. Partial failure of consideration is a defense pro tanto whether or not the failure is in an ascertained or liquidated amount.

§ 3—409. Draft Not an Assignment

(1) A check or other draft does not of itself operate as an assignment of any funds in the hands of the drawee available for its payment, and the drawee is not liable on the instrument until he accepts it.

(2) Nothing in this section shall affect any liability in contract, tort or otherwise arising from any letter of credit or other obligation or representation which is not an acceptance.

§ 3—410. Definition and Operation of Acceptance

(1) Acceptance is the drawee's signed engagement to honor the draft as presented. It must be written on the draft, and may consist of his signature alone. It becomes operative when completed by delivery or notification.

(2) A draft may be accepted although it has not been signed by the drawer or is otherwise incomplete or is overdue or has been dishonored.

(3) Where the draft is payable at a fixed period after sight and the acceptor fails to date his acceptance, the holder may complete it by supplying a date in good faith.

§ 3—411. Certification of a Check

(1) Certification of a check is acceptance. Where a holder procures certification, the drawer and all prior indorsers are discharged.

(2) Unless otherwise agreed, a bank has no obligation to certify a check.

(3) A bank may certify a check before returning it for lack of proper indorsement. If it does so, the drawer is discharged.

§ 3—412. Acceptance Varying Draft

(1) Where the drawee's proffered acceptance in any manner varies the draft as presented, the holder may refuse the acceptance and treat the draft as dishonored in which case the drawee is entitled to have his acceptance cancelled.

(2) The terms of the draft are not varied by an acceptance to pay at any particular bank or place in the United States, unless the acceptance states that the draft is to be paid only at such bank or place.

(3) Where the holder assents to an acceptance varying the terms of the draft, each drawer and indorser who does not affirmatively assent is discharged.

§ 3—413. Contract of Maker, Drawer and Acceptor

(1) The maker or acceptor engages that he will pay the instrument according to its tenor at the time of his engagement or as completed pursuant to Section 3—115 on incomplete instruments.

(2) The drawer engages that upon dishonor of the draft and any necessary notice of dishonor or protest he will pay the amount of the draft to the holder or to any indorser who takes it up. The drawer may disclaim this liability by drawing without recourse.

(3) By making, drawing or accepting, the party admits as against all subsequent parties including the drawee the existence of the payee and his then capacity to indorse.

§ 3—414. Contract of Indorser; Order of Liability

(1) Unless the indorsement otherwise specifies (as by such words as "without recourse"), every indorser engages that upon dishonor and any necessary notice of dishonor and protest he will pay the instrument according to its tenor at the time of his indorsement to the holder or to any subsequent indorser who takes it up, even though the indorser who takes it up was not obligated to do so.

(2) Unless they otherwise agree, indorsers are liable to one another in the order in which they indorse, which is presumed to be the order in which their signatures appear on the instrument.

§ 3—415. Contract of Accommodation Party

(1) An accommodation party is one who signs the instrument in any capacity for the purpose of lending his name to another party to it.

(2) When the instrument has been taken for value before it is due, the accommodation party is liable in the capacity in which he has signed even though the taker knows of the accommodation.

(3) As against a holder in due course and without notice of the accommodation, oral proof of the accommodation is not admissible to give the accommodation party the benefit of discharges dependent on his character as such. In other cases, the accommodation character may be shown by oral proof.

(4) An indorsement which shows that it is not in the chain of title is notice of its accommodation character.

(5) An accommodation party is not liable to the party accommodated, and if he pays the instrument has a right of recourse on the instrument against such party.

§ 3—416. Contract of Guarantor

(1) "Payment guaranteed" or equivalent words added to a signature mean that the signer engages that if the instrument is not paid when due he will pay it according to its tenor without resort by the holder to any other party.

(2) "Collection guaranteed" or equivalent words added to a signature mean that the signer engages that if the instrument is not paid when due he will pay it according to its tenor, but only after the holder has reduced his claim against the maker or acceptor to judgment and execution has been returned unsatisfied, or after the maker or acceptor has become insolvent or it is otherwise apparent that it is useless to proceed against him.

(3) Words of guaranty which do not otherwise specify guarantee payment.

(4) No words of guaranty added to the signature of a sole maker or acceptor affect his liability on the instrument. Such words added to the signature of one of two or more makers or acceptors create a presumption that the signature is for the accommodation of the others.

(5) When words of guaranty are used, presentment, notice of dishonor and protest are not necessary to charge the user.

(6) Any guaranty written on the instrument is enforceable notwithstanding any statute of frauds.

§ 3—417. Warranties on Presentment and Transfer

(1) Any person who obtains payment or acceptance and any prior transferor warrants to a person who in good faith pays or accepts that

(a) he has a good title to the instrument or is authorized to obtain payment or acceptance on behalf of one who has a good title; and

(b) he has no knowledge that the signature of the maker or drawer is unauthorized, except that this warranty is not given by a holder in due course acting in good faith

    (i) to a maker with respect to the maker's own signature; or

    (ii) to a drawer with respect to the drawer's own signature, whether or not the drawer is also the drawee; or

    (iii) to an acceptor of a draft if the holder in due course took the draft after the acceptance or obtained the acceptance without knowledge that the drawer's signature was unauthorized; and

(c) the instrument has not been materially altered, except that this warranty is not given by a holder in due course acting in good faith

    (i) to the maker of a note; or

    (ii) to the drawer of a draft whether or not the drawer is also the drawee; or

    (iii) to the acceptor of a draft with respect to an alteration made prior to the acceptance if the holder in due course took the draft after the acceptance, even though the acceptance provided "payable as originally drawn" or equivalent terms; or

    (iv) to the acceptor of a draft with respect to an alteration made after the acceptance.

(2) Any person who transfers an instrument and receives consideration warrants to his transferee and if the transfer is by indorsement to any subsequent holder who takes the instrument in good faith that

(a) he has a good title to the instrument or is authorized to obtain payment or acceptance on behalf of one who has a good title and the transfer is otherwise rightful; and

(b) all signatures are genuine or authorized; and

(c) the instrument has not been materially altered; and

(d) no defense of any party is good against him; and

(e) he has no knowledge of any insolvency proceeding instituted with respect to the maker or acceptor or the drawer of an unaccepted instrument.

(3) By transferring "without recourse," the transferor limits the obligation stated in subsection (2) (d) to a warranty that he has no knowledge of such a defense.

(4) A selling agent or broker who does not disclose the fact that he is acting only as such gives the warranties provided in this section, but if he makes such disclosure warrants only his good faith and authority.

§ 3 — 418.   Finality of Payment or Acceptance

Except for recovery of bank payments as provided in the Article on Bank Deposits and Collections (Article 4) and except for liability for breach of warranty on presentment under the preceding section, payment or acceptance of any instrument is final in favor of a holder in due course, or a person who has in good faith changed his position in reliance on the payment.

§ 3 — 419.   Conversion of Instrument; Innocent Representative

(1) An instrument is converted when

(a) a drawee to whom it is delivered for acceptance refuses to return it on demand; or

(b) any person to whom it is delivered for payment refuses on demand either to pay or to return it; or

(c) it is paid on a forged indorsement.

(2) In an action against a drawee under subsection (1), the measure of the drawee's liability is the face amount of the instrument. In any other action under subsection (1), the measure of liability is presumed to be the face amount of the instrument.

(3) Subject to the provisions of this Act concerning restrictive indorsements, a representative, including a depositary or collecting bank, who has in good faith and in accordance with the reasonable commercial standards applicable to the business of such representative dealt with an instrument or its proceeds on behalf of one who was not the true owner, is not liable in conversion or otherwise to the true owner beyond the amount of any proceeds remaining in his hands.

(4) An intermediary bank or payor bank which is not a depositary bank is not liable in conversion solely by reason of the fact that proceeds of an item indorsed restrictively (Sections 3 — 205 and 3 — 206) are not paid or applied consistently with the restrictive indorsement of an indorser other than its immediate transferor.

Part 5

Presentment, Notice of Dishonor and Protest

§ 3 — 501.   When Presentment, Notice of Dishonor, and Protest Necessary or Permissible

(1) Unless excused (Section 3 — 511), presentment is necessary to charge secondary parties as follows:

(a) presentment for acceptance is necessary to charge the drawer and indorsers of a draft where the draft so provides, or is payable elsewhere than at the residence or place of business of the drawee, or its date of payment depends upon such presentment. The holder may at his option present for acceptance any other draft payable at a stated date;

(b) presentment for payment is necessary to charge any indorser;

(c) in the case of any drawer, the acceptor of a draft payable at a bank or the maker of a note payable at a bank, presentment for payment is necessary, but failure to make presentment discharges such drawer, acceptor, or maker only as stated in Section 3 — 502(1) (b).

(2) Unless excused (Section 3 — 511)

(a) notice of any dishonor is necessary to charge any indorser;

(b) in the case of any drawer, the acceptor of a draft payable at a bank or the maker of a note payable at a bank, notice of any dishonor is necessary, but failure to give such notice discharges such drawer, acceptor or maker only as stated in Section 3 — 502(1) (b).

(3) Unless excused (Section 3 — 511), protest of any dishonor is necessary to charge the drawer and indorsers of any draft which on its face appears to be drawn or payable outside of the states, territories, dependencies and possessions of the Unites States, the District of Columbia and the Commonwealth of Puerto Rico. The holder may at his option make protest of any dishonor of any other instrument and in the case of a foreign draft may on insolvency of the acceptor before maturity make protest for better security.

(4) Notwithstanding any provision of this section, neither presentment nor notice of dishonor nor protest is necessary to charge an indorser who has indorsed an instrument after maturity.

§ 3 — 502.   Unexcused Delay; Discharge

(1) Where without excuse any necessary presentment or notice of dishonor is delayed beyond the time when it is due

(a) any indorser is discharged; and

(b) any drawer or the acceptor of a draft payable at a bank or the maker of a note payable at a bank who because the drawee or payor bank becomes insolvent during the delay is deprived of funds maintained with the drawee or payor bank to cover the instrument may discharge his liability by written assignment to the holder of his rights against the drawee or payor bank in respect of such funds, but such drawer, acceptor or maker is not otherwise discharged.

(2) Where without excuse a necessary protest is delayed beyond the time when it is due, any drawer or indorser is discharged.

§ 3—503. Time of Presentment

(1) Unless a different time is expressed in the instrument, the time for any presentment is determined as follows:
   (a) where an instrument is payable at or a fixed period after a stated date, any presentment for acceptance must be made on or before the date it is payable;
   (b) where an instrument is payable after sight, it must either be presented for acceptance or negotiated within a reasonable time after date or issue whichever is later;
   (c) where an instrument shows the date on which it is payable, presentment for payment is due on that date;
   (d) where an instrument is accelerated, presentment for payment is due within a reasonable time after the acceleration;
   (e) with respect to the liability of any secondary party, presentment for acceptance or payment of any other instrument is due within a reasonable time after such party becomes liable thereon.

(2) A reasonable time for presentment is determined by the nature of the instrument, any usage of banking or trade and the facts of the particular case. In the case of an uncertified check which is drawn and payable within the United States and which is not a draft drawn by a bank, the following are presumed to be reasonable periods within which to present for payment or to initiate bank collection:
   (a) with respect to the liability of the drawer, thirty days after date or issue whichever is later; and
   (b) with respect to the liability of an indorser, seven days after his indorsement.

(3) Where any presentment is due on a day which is not a full business day for either the person making presentment or the party to pay or accept, presentment is due on the next following day which is a full business day for both parties.

(4) Presentment to be sufficient must be made at a reasonable hour, and, if at a bank, during its banking day.

§ 3—504. How Presentment Made

(1) Presentment is a demand for acceptance or payment made upon the maker, acceptor, drawee or other payor by or on behalf of the holder.

(2) Presentment may be made
   (a) by mail, in which event the time of presentment is determined by the time of receipt of the mail; or
   (b) through a clearing house; or
   (c) at the place of acceptance or payment specified in the instrument or, if there be none, at the place of business or residence of the party to accept or pay. If neither the party to accept or pay nor anyone authorized to act for him is present or accessible at such place, presentment is excused.

(3) It may be made
   (a) to any one of two or more makers, acceptors, drawees or other payors; or
   (b) to any person who has authority to make or refuse the acceptance or payment.

(4) A draft accepted or a note made payable at a bank in the United States must be presented at such bank.

(5) In the cases described in Section 4—210 presentment may be made in the manner and with the result stated in that section.

§ 3—505. Rights of Party to Whom Presentment Is Made

(1) The party to whom presentment is made may without dishonor require
   (a) exhibition of the instrument; and
   (b) reasonable identification of the person making presentment and evidence of his authority to make it if made for another; and
   (c) that the instrument be produced for acceptance or payment at a place specified in it, or if there be none at any place reasonable in the circumstances; and
   (d) a signed receipt on the instrument for any partial or full payment and its surrender upon full payment.

(2) Failure to comply with any such requirement invalidates the presentment, but the person presenting has a reasonable time in which to comply and the time for acceptance or payment runs from the time of compliance.

§ 3—506. Time Allowed for Acceptance or Payment

(1) Acceptance may be deferred without dishonor until the close of the next business day following presentment. The holder may also in a good faith effort to obtain acceptance, and without either dishonor

of the instrument or discharge of secondary parties, allow postponement of acceptance for an additional business day.

(2) Except as a longer time is allowed in the case of documentary drafts drawn under a letter of credit, and unless an earlier time is agreed to by the party to pay, payment of an instrument may be deferred without dishonor pending reasonable examination to determine whether it is properly payable, but payment must be made in any event before the close of business on the day of presentment.

§ 3—507. Dishonor; Holder's Right of Recourse; Term Allowing Re-Presentment

(1) An instrument is dishonored when

(a) a necessary or optional presentment is duly made and due acceptance or payment is refused or cannot be obtained within the prescribed time or in case of bank collections the instrument is seasonably returned by the midnight deadline (Section 4—301); or

(b) presentment is excused and the instrument is not duly accepted or paid.

(2) Subject to any necessary notice of dishonor and protest, the holder has upon dishonor an immediate right of recourse against the drawers and indorsers.

(3) Return of an instrument for lack of proper indorsement is not dishonor.

(4) A term in a draft or an indorsement thereof allowing a stated time for re-presentment in the event of any dishonor of the draft by nonacceptance if a time draft or by nonpayment if a sight draft gives the holder as against any secondary party bound by the term an option to waive the dishonor without affecting the liability of the secondary party and he may present again up to the end of the stated time.

§ 3—508. Notice of Dishonor

(1) Notice of dishonor may be given to any person who may be liable on the instrument by or on behalf of the holder or any party who has himself received notice, or any other party who can be compelled to pay the instrument. In addition, an agent or bank in whose hands the instrument is dishonored may give notice to his principal or customer or to another agent or bank from which the instrument was received.

(2) Any necessary notice must be given by a bank before its midnight deadline and by any other person before midnight of the third business day after dishonor or receipt of notice of dishonor.

(3) Notice may be given in any reasonable manner. It may be oral or written and in any terms which identify the instrument and state that it has been dishonored. A misdescription which does not mislead the party notified does not vitiate the notice. Sending the instrument bearing a stamp, ticket or writing stating that acceptance or payment has been refused or sending a notice of debit with respect to the instrument is sufficient.

(4) Written notice is given when sent although it is not received.

(5) Notice to one partner is notice to each although the firm has been dissolved.

(6) When any party is in insolvency proceedings instituted after the issue of the instrument, notice may be given either to the party or to the representative of his estate.

(7) When any party is dead or incompetent, notice may be sent to his last known address or given to his personal representative.

(8) Notice operates for the benefit of all parties who have rights on the instrument against the party notified.

§ 3—509. Protest; Noting for Protest

(1) A protest is a certificate of dishonor made under the hand and seal of a United States consul or vice consul or a notary public or other person authorized to certify dishonor by the law of the place where dishonor occurs. It may be made upon information satisfactory to such person.

(2) The protest must identify the instrument and certify either that due presentment has been made or the reason why it is excused and that the instrument has been dishonored by nonacceptance or nonpayment.

(3) The protest may also certify that notice of dishonor has been given to all parties or to specified parties.

(4) Subject to subsection (5), any necessary protest is due by the time that notice of dishonor is due.

(5) If, before protest is due, an instrument has been noted for protest by the officer to make protest, the protest may be made at any time thereafter as of the date of the noting.

§ 3—510. Evidence of Dishonor and Notice of Dishonor

The following are admissible as evidence and create a presumption of dishonor and of any notice of dishonor therein shown:

(a) a document regular in form as provided in the preceding section which purports to be a protest;

(b) the purported stamp or writing of the drawee, payor bank or presenting bank on the instrument or accompanying it stating that acceptance or payment has been refused for reasons consistent with dishonor;

(c) any book or record of the drawee, payor bank, or any collecting bank kept in the usual course of business which shows dishonor, even though there is no evidence of who made the entry.

§ 3—511. Waived or Excused Presentment, Protest or Notice of Dishonor or Delay Therein

(1) Delay in presentment, protest or notice of dishonor is excused when the party is without notice

that it is due or when the delay is caused by circumstances beyond his control and he exercises reasonable diligence after the cause of the delay ceases to operate.

(2) Presentment or notice or protest as the case may be is entirely excused when

    (a) the party to be charged has waived it expressly or by implication either before or after it is due; or

    (b) such party has himself dishonored the instrument or has countermanded payment or otherwise has no reason to expect or right to require that the instrument be accepted or paid; or

    (c) by reasonable diligence the presentment or protest cannot be made or the notice given.

(3) Presentment is also entirely excused when

    (a) the maker, acceptor or drawee of any instrument except a documentary draft is dead or in insolvency proceedings instituted after the issue of the instrument; or

    (b) acceptance or payment is refused but not for want of proper presentment.

(4) Where a draft has been dishonored by non-acceptance, a later presentment for payment and any notice of dishonor and protest for nonpayment are excused unless in the meantime the instrument has been accepted.

(5) A waiver of protest is also a waiver of presentment and of notice of dishonor even though protest is not required.

(6) Where a waiver of presentment or notice or protest is embodied in the instrument itself, it is binding upon all parties; but where it is written above the signature of an indorser, it binds him only.

Part 6

Discharge

§ 3 — 601.   Discharge of Parties

(1) The extent of the discharge of any party from liability on an instrument is governed by the sections on

    (a) payment or satisfaction (Section 3 — 603); or

    (b) tender of payment (Section 3 — 604); or

    (c) cancellation or renunciation (Section 3 — 605); or

    (d) impairment of right of recourse or of collateral (Section 3 — 606); or

    (e) reacquisition of the instrument by a prior party (Section 3 — 208); or

    (f) fraudulent and material alteration (Section 3 — 407); or

    (g) certification of a check (Section 3 — 411); or

    (h) acceptance varying a draft (Section 3 — 412); or

    (i) unexcused delay in presentment or notice of dishonor or protest (Section 3 — 502).

(2) Any party is also discharged from his liability on an instrument to another party by any other act or agreement with such party which would discharge his simple contract for the payment of money.

(3) The liability of all parties is discharged when any party who has himself no right of action or recourse on the instrument

    (a) reacquires the instrument in his own right; or

    (b) is discharged under any provision of this Article, except as otherwise provided with respect to discharge for impairment of recourse or of collateral (Section 3 — 606).

§ 3 — 602.   Effect of Discharge Against Holder in Due Course

No discharge of any party provided by this Article is effective against a subsequent holder in due course unless he has notice thereof when he takes the instrument.

§ 3 — 603.   Payment or Satisfaction

(1) The liability of any party is discharged to the extent of his payment or satisfaction to the holder even though it is made with knowledge of a claim of another person to the instrument unless prior to such payment or satisfaction the person making the claim either supplies indemnity deemed adequate by the party seeking the discharge or enjoins payment or satisfaction by order of a court of competent jurisdiction in an action in which the adverse claimant and the holder are parties. This subsection does not, however, result in the discharge of the liability

    (a) of a party who in bad faith pays or satisfies a holder who acquired the instrument by theft or who (unless having the rights of a holder in due course) holds through one who so acquired it; or

    (b) of a party (other than an intermediary bank or a payor bank which is not a depositary bank) who pays or satisfies the holder of an instrument which has been restrictively indorsed in a manner not consistent with the terms of such restrictive indorsement.

(2) Payment or satisfaction may be made with the consent of the holder by any person including a stranger to the instrument. Surrender of the instrument to such a person gives him the rights of a transferee (Section 3 — 201).

§ 3 — 604.   Tender of Payment

(1) Any party making tender of full payment to a holder when or after it is due is discharged to the extent

of all subsequent liability for interest, costs and attorney's fees.

(2) The holder's refusal of such tender wholly discharges any party who has a right of recourse against the party making the tender.

(3) Where the maker or acceptor of an instrument payable otherwise than on demand is able and ready to pay at every place of payment specified in the instrument when it is due, it is equivalent to tender.

§ 3 — 605. Cancellation and Renunciation

(1) The holder of an instrument may even without consideration discharge any party

(a) in any manner apparent on the face of the instrument or the indorsement, as by intentionally cancelling the instrument or the party's signature by destruction or mutilation, or by striking out the party's signature; or

(b) by renouncing his rights by a writing signed and delivered or by surrender of the instrument to the party to be discharged.

(2) Neither cancellation nor renunciation without surrender of the instrument affects the title thereto.

§ 3 — 606. Impairment of Recourse or of Collateral

(1) The holder discharges any party to the instrument to the extent that, without such party's consent, the holder

(a) without express reservation of rights releases or agrees not to sue any person against whom the party has to the knowledge of the holder a right of recourse or agrees to suspend the right to enforce against such person the instrument or collateral or otherwise discharges such person, except that failure or delay in effecting any required presentment, protest or notice of dishonor with respect to any such person does not discharge any party as to whom presentment, protest or notice of dishonor is effective or unnecessary; or

(b) unjustifiably impairs any collateral for the instrument given by or on behalf of the party or any person against whom he has a right of recourse.

(2) By express reservation of rights against a party with a right of recourse, the holder preserves

(a) all his rights against such party as of the time when the instrument was originally due; and

(b) the right of the party to pay the instrument as of that time; and

(c) all rights of such party to recourse against others.

Part 7

Advice of International Sight Draft

§ 3 — 701. Letter of Advice of International Sight Draft

(1) A "letter of advice" is a drawer's communication to the drawee that a described draft has been drawn.

(2) Unless otherwise agreed, when a bank receives from another bank a letter of advice of an international sight draft the drawee bank may immediately debit the drawer's account and stop the running of interest pro tanto. Such a debit and any resulting credit to any account covering outstanding drafts leaves in the drawer full power to stop payment or otherwise dispose of the amount and creates no trust or interest in favor of the holder.

(3) Unless otherwise agreed and except where a draft is drawn under a credit issued by the drawee, the drawee of an international sight draft owes the drawer no duty to pay an unadvised draft but if it does so and the draft is genuine, may appropriately debit the drawer's account.

Part 8

Miscellaneous

§ 3 — 801. Drafts in a Set

(1) Where a draft is drawn in a set of parts, each of which is numbered and expressed to be an order only if no other part has been honored, the whole of the parts constitutes one draft but a taker of any part may become a holder in due course of the draft.

(2) Any person who negotiates, indorses or accepts a single part of a draft drawn in a set thereby becomes liable to any holder in due course of that part as if it were the whole set, but as between different holders in due course to whom different parts have been negotiated, the holder whose title first accrues has all rights to the draft and its proceeds.

(3) As against the drawee, the first presented part of a draft drawn in a set is the part entitled to payment, or if a time draft to acceptance and payment. Acceptance of any subsequently presented part renders the drawee liable thereon under subsection (2). With respect both to a holder and to the drawer, payment of a subsequently presented part of a draft payable at sight has the same effect as payment of a check notwithstanding an effective stop order (Section 4 — 407).

(4) Except as otherwise provided in this section, where any part of a draft in a set is discharged by payment or otherwise the whole draft is discharged.

§ 3 — 802. Effect of Instrument on Obligation for Which It Is Given

(1) Unless otherwise agreed, where an instrument is taken for an underlying obligation

(a) the obligation is pro tanto discharged if a bank is drawer, maker or acceptor of the instrument and there is no recourse on the instrument against the underlying obligor; and

(b) in any other case the obligation is suspended pro tanto until the instrument is due or, if it is payable on demand, until its presentment. If the instrument is dishonored, action may be maintained on either the instrument or the obligation; discharge of the underlying obligor on the instrument also discharges him on the obligation.

(2) The taking in good faith of a check which is not postdated does not of itself so extend the time on the original obligation as to discharge a surety.

§ 3—803. Notice to Third Party

Where a defendant is sued for breach of an obligation for which a third person is answerable over under this Article, he may give the third person written notice of the litigation, and the person notified may then give similar notice to any other person who is answerable over to him under this Article. If the notice states that the person notified may come in and defend and that if the person notified does not do so, he will in any action against him by the person giving the notice be bound by any determination of fact common to the two litigations, then unless after seasonable receipt of the notice, the person notified does come in and defend he is so bound.

§ 3—804. Lost, Destroyed or Stolen Instruments

The owner of an instrument which is lost, whether by destruction, theft or otherwise, may maintain an action in his own name and recover from any party liable thereon upon due proof of his ownership, the facts which prevent his production of the instrument and its terms. The court may require security indemnifying the defendant against loss by reason of further claims on the instrument.

§ 3—805. Instruments Not Payable to Order or to Bearer

This Article applies to any instrument whose terms do not preclude transfer which is otherwise negotiable within this Article but which is not payable to order or to bearer, except that there can be no holder in due course of such an instrument.

ARTICLE 4

BANK DEPOSITS AND COLLECTIONS

Part 1

General Provisions and Definitions

§ 4—101. Short Title

This Article shall be known and may be cited as Uniform Commercial Code—Bank Deposits and Collections.

§ 4—102. Applicability

(1) To the extent that items within this Article are also within the scope of Articles 3 and 8, they are subject to the provisions of those Articles. In the event of conflict the provisions of this Article govern those of Article 3 but the provisions of Article 8 govern those of this Article.

(2) The liability of a bank for action or nonaction with respect to any item handled by it for purposes of presentment, payment or collection is governed by the law of the place where the bank is located. In the case of action or nonaction by or at a branch or separate office of a bank, its liability is governed by the law of the place where the branch or separate office is located.

§ 4—103. Variation by Agreement; Measure of Damages; Certain Action Constituting Ordinary Care

(1) The effect of the provisions of this Article may be varied by agreement except that no agreement can disclaim a bank's responsibility for its own lack of good faith or failure to exercise ordinary care or can limit the measure of damages for such lack or failure; but the parties may by agreement determine the standards by which such responsibility is to be measured if such standards are not manifestly unreasonable.

(2) Federal Reserve regulations and operating letters, clearing house rules, and the like, have the effect of agreements under subsection (1), whether or not specifically assented to by all parties interested in items handled.

(3) Action or nonaction approved by this Article or pursuant to Federal Reserve regulations or operating letters constitutes the exercise of ordinary care and, in the absence of special instructions, action or nonaction consistent with clearing house rules and the like or with a general banking usage not disapproved by this Article, prima facie constitutes the exercise of ordinary care.

(4) The specification or approval of certain procedures by this Article does not constitute disapproval of other procedures which may be reasonable under the circumstances.

(5) The measure of damages for failure to exercise ordinary care in handling an item is the amount of the item reduced by an amount which could not have been realized by the use of ordinary care, and where

there is bad faith it includes other damages, if any, suffered by the party as a proximate consequence.

§ 4–104. Definitions and Index of Definitions

(1) In this Article unless the context otherwise requires

(a) "Account" means any account with a bank and includes a checking, time, interest or savings account;

(b) "Afternoon" means the period of a day between noon and midnight;

(c) "Banking day" means that part of any day on which a bank is open to the public for carrying on substantially all of its banking functions;

(d) "Clearing house" means any association of banks or other payors regularly clearing items;

(e) "Customer" means any person having an account with a bank or for whom a bank has agreed to collect items and includes a bank carrying an account with another bank;

(f) "Documentary draft" means any negotiable or nonnegotiable draft with accompanying documents, securities or other papers to be delivered against honor of the draft;

(g) "Item" means any instrument for the payment of money even though it is not negotiable but does not include money;

(h) "Midnight deadline" with respect to a bank is midnight on its next banking day following the banking day on which it receives the relevant item or notice or from which the time for taking action commences to run, whichever is later;

(i) "Property payable" includes the availability of funds for payment at the time of decision to pay or dishonor;

(j) "Settle" means to pay in cash, by clearing house settlement, in a charge or credit or by remittance, or otherwise as instructed. A settlement may be either provisional or final;

(k) "Suspends payments" with respect to a bank means that it has been closed by order of the supervisory authorities, that a public officer has been appointed to take it over or that it ceases or refuses to make payments in the ordinary course of business.

(2) Other definitions applying to this Article and the sections in which they appear are:

"Collecting bank" Section 4—105.
"Depositary bank" Section 4—105.
"Intermediary bank" Section 4—105.
"Payor bank" Section 4—105.
"Presenting bank" Section 4—105.
"Remitting bank" Section 4—105.

The following definitions in other Articles apply to this Article:

"Acceptance" Section 3—410.
"Certificate of Deposit" Section 3—104.
"Certification" Section 3—411.
"Check" Section 3—104.
"Draft" Section 3—104.
"Holder in due course" Section 3—302.
"Notice of dishonor" Section 3—508.
"Presentment" Section 3—504.
"Protest" Section 3—509.
"Secondary party" Section 3—102.

(4) In addition Article 1 contains general definitions and principles of construction and interpretation applicable throughout this Article.

§ 4—105. "Depositary Bank"; "Intermediary Bank"; "Collecting Bank"; "Payor Bank"; "Presenting Bank"; "Remitting Bank"

In this Article unless the context otherwise requires:

(a) "Depositary bank" means the first bank to which an item is transferred for collection even though it is also the payor bank;

(b) "Payor bank" means a bank by which an item is payable as drawn or accepted;

(c) "Intermediary bank" means any bank to which an item is transferred in course of collection except the depositary or payor bank;

(d) "Collecting bank" means any bank handling the item for collection except the payor bank;

(e) "Presenting bank" means any bank presenting an item except a payor bank;

(f) "Remitting bank" means any payor or intermediary bank remitting for an item.

§ 4—106. Separate Office of a Bank

A branch or separate office of a bank [maintaining its own deposit ledgers] is a separate bank for the purpose of computing the time within which and determining the place at or to which action may be taken or notices or orders shall be given under this Article and under Article 3.

Note: *The brackets are to make it optional with the several states whether to require a branch to maintain its own deposit ledgers in order to be considered to be a separate bank for certain purposes under Article 4. In some states, "maintaining its own deposit ledgers" is a satisfactory test. In others, branch banking practices are such that this test would not be suitable.*

§ 4—107. Time of Receipt of Items

(1) For the purpose of allowing time to process items, prove balances and make the necessary entries on its books to determine its position for the day, a bank may fix an afternoon hour of 2 p.m. or later as a cutoff hour for the handling of money and items and the making of entries on its books.

(2) Any item or deposit of money received on any day after a cutoff hour so fixed or after the close of the banking day may be treated as being received at the opening of the next banking day.

§ 4—108. Delays

(1) Unless otherwise instructed, a collecting bank in a good faith effort to secure payment may, in the case of specific items and with or without the approval of any person involved, waive, modify or extend time limits imposed or permitted by this Act for a period not in excess of an additional banking day without discharge of secondary parties and without liability to its transferor or any prior party.

(2) Delay by a collecting bank or payor bank beyond time limits prescribed or permitted by this Act or by instructions is excused if caused by interruption of communication facilities, suspension of payments by another bank, war, emergency conditions or other circumstances beyond the control of the bank provided it exercises such diligence as the circumstances require.

§ 4—109. Process of Posting

The "process of posting" means the usual procedure followed by a payor bank in determining to pay an item and in recording the payment including one or more of the following or other steps as determined by the bank:

(a) verification of any signature;
(b) ascertaining that sufficient funds are available;
(c) affixing a "paid" or other stamp;
(d) entering a charge or entry to a customer's account;
(e) correcting or reversing an entry or erroneous action with respect to the item.

Part 2

Collection of Items: Depositary and Collecting Banks

§ 4—201. Presumption and Duration of Agency Status of Collecting Banks and Provisional Status of Credits; Applicability of Article; Item Indorsed "Pay Any Bank"

(1) Unless a contrary intent clearly appears and prior to the time that a settlement given by a collecting bank for an item is or becomes final (subsection (3) of Section 4—211 and Sections 4—212 and 4—213), the bank is an agent or subagent of the owner of the item and any settlement given for the item is provisional. This provision applies regardless of the form of indorsement or lack of indorsement and even though credit given for the item is subject to immediate withdrawal as of right or is in fact withdrawn; but the continuance of ownership of an item by its owner and any rights of the owner to proceeds of the item are subject to rights of a collecting bank such as those resulting

from outstanding advances on the item and valid rights of setoff. When an item is handled by banks for purposes of presentment, payment and collection, the relevant provisions of this Article apply even though action of parties clearly establishes that a particular bank has purchased the item and is the owner of it.

(2) After an item has been indorsed with the words "pay any bank" or the like, only a bank may acquire the rights of a holder

(a) until the item has been returned to the customer initiating collection; or
(b) until the item has been specifically indorsed by a bank to a person who is not a bank.

§ 4—202. Responsibility for Collection; When Action Seasonable

(1) A collecting bank must use ordinary care in

(a) presenting an item or sending it for presentment; and
(b) sending notice of dishonor or nonpayment or returning an item other than a documentary draft to the bank's transferor [or directly to the depositary bank under subsection (2) of Section 4—212] *(see note to Section 4—212)* after learning that the item has not been paid or accepted, as the case may be; and
(c) settling for an item when the bank receives final settlement; and
(d) making or providing for any necessary protest; and
(e) notifying its transferor of any loss or delay in transit within a reasonable time after discovery thereof.

(2) A collecting bank taking proper action before its midnight deadline following receipt of an item, notice or payment acts seasonably; taking proper action within a reasonably longer time may be seasonable but the bank has the burden of so establishing.

(3) Subject to subsection (1) (a), a bank is not liable for the insolvency, neglect, misconduct, mistake or default of another bank or person or for loss or destruction of an item in transit or in the possession of others.

§ 4—203. Effect of Instructions

Subject to the provisions of Article 3 concerning conversion of instruments (Section 3—419) and the provisions of both Article 3 and this Article concerning restrictive indorsements, only a collecting bank's transferor can give instructions which affect the bank or constitute notice to it; and a collecting bank is not liable to prior parties for any action taken pursuant to such instructions or in accordance with any agreement with its transferor.

§ 4—204. Methods of Sending and Presenting; Sending Direct to Payor Bank

(1) A collecting bank must send items by reason-

ably prompt method taking into consideration any relevant instructions, the nature of the item, the number of such items on hand, and the cost of collection involved and the method generally used by it or others to present such items.

(2) A collecting bank may send

(a) any item direct to the payor bank;

(b) any item to any nonbank payor if authorized by its transferor; and

(c) any item other than documentary drafts to any nonbank payor, if authorized by Federal Reserve regulation or operating letter, clearing house rule or the like.

(3) Presentment may be made by a presenting bank at a place where the payor bank has requested that presentment be made.

§ 4—205. Supplying Missing Indorsement; No Notice from Prior Indorsement

(1) A depositary bank which has taken an item for collection may supply any indorsement of the customer which is necessary to title unless the item contains the words "payee's indorsement required" or the like. In the absence of such a requirement, a statement placed on the item by the depositary bank to the effect that the item was deposited by a customer or credited to his account is effective as the customer's indorsement of.

(2) An intermediary bank, or payor bank which is not a depositary bank, is neither given notice nor otherwise affected by a restrictive indorsement of any person except the bank's immediate transferor.

§ 4—206. Transfer Between Banks

Any agreed method which identifies the transferor bank is sufficient for the item's further transfer to another bank.

§ 4—207. Warranties of Customer and Collecting Bank on Transfer or Presentment of Items; Time for Claims

(1) Each customer or collecting bank who obtains payment or acceptance of an item and each prior customer and collecting bank warrants to the payor bank or other payor who in good faith pays or accepts the item that

(a) he has a good title to the item or is authorized to obtain payment or acceptance on behalf of one who has a good title; and

(b) he has no knowledge that the signature of the maker or drawer is unauthorized, except that this warranty is not given by any customer or collecting bank that is a holder in due course and acts in good faith

(i) to a maker, with respect to the maker's own signature; or

(ii) to a drawer, with respect to the drawer's own signature, whether or not the drawer is also the drawee; or

(iii) to an acceptor of an item, if the holder in due course took the item after the acceptance or obtained the acceptance without knowledge that the drawer's signature was unauthorized; and

(c) the item has not been materially altered, except that this warranty is not given by any customer or collecting bank that is a holder in due course and acts in good faith

(i) to the maker of a note; or

(ii) to the drawer of a draft whether or not the drawer is also the drawee; or

(iii) to the acceptor of an item with respect to an alteration made prior to the acceptance if the holder in due course took the item after the acceptance, even though the acceptance provided "payable as originally drawn" or equivalent terms; or

(iv) to the acceptor of an item with respect to an alteration made after the acceptance.

(2) Each customer and collecting bank who transfers an item and receives a settlement or other consideration for it warrants to his transferee and to any subsequent collecting bank who takes the item in good faith that

(a) he has a good title to the item or is authorized to obtain payment or acceptance on behalf of one who has a good title and the transfer is otherwise rightful; and

(b) all signatures are genuine or authorized; and

(c) the item has not been materially altered; and

(d) no defense of any party is good against him; and

(e) he has no knowledge of any insolvency proceeding instituted with respect to the maker or acceptor or the drawer of an unaccepted item.

In addition, each customer and collecting bank so transferring an item and receiving a settlement or other consideration engages that upon dishonor and any necessary notice of dishonor and protest he will take up the item.

(3) The warranties and the engagement to honor set forth in the two preceding subsections arise notwithstanding the absence of indorsement or words of guaranty or warranty in the transfer or presentment and a collecting bank remains liable for their breach despite remittance to its transferor. Damages for breach of such warranties or engagement to honor shall not exceed the consideration received by the customer or collecting bank responsible plus finance charges and expenses related to the item, if any.

(4) Unless a claim for breach of warranty under this section is made within a reasonable time after the person claiming learns of the breach, the person liable

is discharged to the extent of any loss caused by the delay in making claim.

§ 4—208. Security Interest of Collecting Bank in Items, Accompanying Documents and Proceeds

(1) A bank has a security interest in an item and any accompanying documents or the proceeds of either

   (a) in case of an item deposited in an account, to the extent to which credit given for the item has been withdrawn or applied;

   (b) in case of an item for which it has given credit available for withdrawal as of right, to the extent of the credit given whether or not the credit is drawn upon and whether or not there is a right of charge-back; or

   (c) if it makes an advance on or against the item.

(2) When credit which has been given for several items received at one time or pursuant to a single agreement is withdrawn or applied in part, the security interest remains upon all the items, any accompanying documents or the proceeds of either. For the purpose of this section, credits first given are first withdrawn.

(3) Receipt by a collecting bank of a final settlement for an item is a realization on its security interest in the item, accompanying documents and proceeds. To the extent and so long as the bank does not receive final settlement for the item or give up possession of the item or accompanying documents for purposes other than collection, the security interest continues and is subject to the provisions of Article 9 except that

   (a) no security agreement is necessary to make the security interest enforceable (subsection (1) (b) of Section 9—203); and

   (b) no filing is required to perfect the security interest; and

   (c) the security interest has priority over conflicting perfected security interests in the item, accompanying documents or proceeds.

§ 4—209. When Bank Gives Value for Purposes of Holder in Due Course

For purposes of determining its status as a holder in due course, the bank has given value to the extent that it has a security interest in an item provided that the bank otherwise complies with the requirements of Section 3—302 on what constitutes a holder in due course.

§ 4—210. Presentment by Notice of Item Not Payable by, Through or at a Bank; Liability of Secondary Parties

(1) Unless otherwise instructed, a collecting bank may present an item not payable by, through or at a bank by sending to the party to accept or pay a written notice that the bank holds the item for acceptance or payment. The notice must be sent in time to be received on or before the day when presentment is due, and the bank must meet any requirement of the party to accept or pay under Section 3—505 by the close of the bank's next banking day after it knows of the requirement.

(2) Where presentment is made by notice and neither honor nor request for compliance with a requirement under Section 3—505 is received by the close of business on the day after maturity or in the case of demand items by the close of business on the third banking day after notice was sent, the presenting bank may treat the item as dishonored and charge any secondary party by sending him notice of the facts.

§ 4—211. Media of Remittance; Provisional and Final Settlement in Remittance Cases

(1) A collecting bank may take in settlement of an item

   (a) a check of the remitting bank or of another bank on any bank except the remitting bank; or

   (b) a cashier's check or similar primary obligation of a remitting bank which is a member of or clears through a member of the same clearing house or group as the collecting bank; or

   (c) appropriate authority to charge an account of the remitting bank or of another bank with the collecting bank; or

   (d) if the item is drawn upon or payable by a person other than a bank, a cashier's check, certified check or other bank check or obligation.

(2) If before its midnight deadline the collecting bank properly dishonors a remittance check or authorization to charge on itself or presents or forwards for collection a remittance instrument of or on another bank which is of a kind approved by subsection (1) or has not been authorized by it, the collecting bank is not liable to prior parties in the event of the dishonor of such check, instrument or authorization.

(3) A settlement for an item by means of a remittance instrument or authorization to charge is or becomes a final settlement as to both the person making and the person receiving the settlement

   (a) if the remittance instrument or authorization to charge is of a kind approved by subsection (1) or has not been authorized by the person receiving the settlement and in either case the person receiving the settlement acts seasonably before its midnight deadline in presenting, forwarding for collection or paying the instrument or authorization,—at the time the remittance instrument or authorization is finally paid by the payor by which it is payable;

   (b) if the person receiving the settlement has authorized remittance by a nonbank check or obligation or by a cashier's check or similar primary obligation of or a check upon the payor or other remitting bank which is not of a kind approved by subsection (1) (b),—at the time of the receipt of such remittance check or obligation; or

(c) if in a case not covered by sub-paragraphs (a) or (b) the person receiving the settlement fails to seasonably present, forward for collection, pay or return remittance instrument or authorization to it to charge before its midnight deadline, — at such midnight deadline.

§ 4—212. Right of Charge-Back or Refund

(1) If a collecting bank has made provisional settlement with its customer for an item and itself fails by reason of dishonor, suspension of payments by a bank or otherwise to receive a settlement for the item which is or becomes final, the bank may revoke the settlement given by it, charge back the amount of any credit given for the item to its customer's account or obtain refund from its customer whether or not it is able to return the items, if by its midnight deadline or within a longer reasonable time after it learns the facts it returns the item or sends notification of the facts. These rights to revoke, charge-back and obtain refund terminate if and when a settlement for the item received by the bank is or becomes final (subsection (3) of Section 4—211 and subsections (2) and (3) of Section 4—213).

[(2) Within the time and manner prescribed by this section and Section 4—301, an intermediary or payor bank, as the case may be, may return an unpaid item directly to the depositary bank and may send for collection a draft on the depositary bank and obtain reimbursement. In such case, if the depositary bank has received provisional settlement for the item, it must reimburse the bank drawing the draft and any provisional credits for the item between banks shall become and remain final.]

Note: *Direct returns is recognized as an innovation that is not yet established bank practice, and therefore, Paragraph 2 has been bracketed. Some lawyers have doubts whether it should be included in legislation or left to development by agreement.*

(3) A depositary bank which is also the payor may charge-back the amount of an item to its customer's account or obtain refund in accordance with the section governing return of an item received by a payor bank for credit on its books. (Section 4—301)

(4) The right to charge-back is not affected by

(a) prior use of the credit given for the item; or

(b) failure by any bank to exercise ordinary care with respect to the item but any bank so failing remains liable.

(5) A failure to charge-back or claim refund does not affect other rights of the bank against the customer or any other party.

(6) If credit is given in dollars, as the equivalent of the value of an item payable in a foreign currency, the dollar amount of any charge-back or refund shall be calculated on the basis of the buying sight rate for the foreign currency prevailing on the day when the per-

son entitled to the charge-back or refund learns that it will not receive payment in ordinary course.

§ 4—213. Final Payment of Item for Payor Bank; When Provisional Debits and Credits Become Final; When Certain Credits Become Available for Withdrawal

(1) An item is finally paid by a payor bank when the bank has done any of the following, whichever happens first:

(a) paid the item in cash; or

(b) settled for the item without reserving a right to revoke the settlement and without having such right under statute, clearing house rule or agreement; or

(c) completed the process of posting the item to the indicated account of the drawer, maker or other person to be charged therewith; or

(d) made a provisional settlement for the item and failed to revoke the settlement in the time and manner permitted by statute, clearing house rule or agreement.

Upon a final payment under subparagraphs (b), (c) or (d), the payor bank shall be accountable for the amount of the item.

(2) If provisional settlement for an item between the presenting and payor banks is made through a clearing house or by debits or credits in an account between them, then to the extent that provisional debits or credits for the item are entered in accounts between the presenting and payor banks or between the presenting and successive prior collecting banks seriatim, they become final upon final payment of the item by the payor bank.

(3) If a collecting bank receives a settlement for an item which is or becomes final (subsection (3) of Section 4—211, subsection (2) of Section 4—213), the bank is accountable to its customer for the amount of the item and any provisional credit given for the item in an account with its customer becomes final.

(4) Subject to any right of the bank to apply the credit to an obligation of the customer, credit given by a bank for an item in an account with its customer becomes available for withdrawal as of right

(a) in any case where the bank has received a provisional settlement for the item, — when such settlement becomes final and the bank has had a reasonable time to learn that the settlement is final;

(b) in any case where the bank is both a depositary bank and a payor bank and the item is finally paid, — at the opening of the bank's second banking day following receipt of the item.

(5) A deposit of money in a bank is final when made but, subject to any right of the bank to apply the deposit to an obligation of the customer, the deposit becomes available for withdrawal as of right at the

opening of the bank's next banking day following receipt of the deposit.

§ 4—214. Insolvency and Preference

(1) Any item in or coming into the possession of a payor or collecting bank which suspends payment and which item is not finally paid shall be returned by the receiver, trustee or agent in charge of the closed bank to the presenting bank or the closed bank's customer.

(2) If a payor bank finally pays an item and suspends payments without making a settlement for the item with its customer or the presenting bank which settlement is or becomes final, the owner of the item has a preferred claim against the payor bank.

(3) If a payor bank gives or a collecting bank gives or receives a provisional settlement for an item and thereafter suspends payments, the suspension does not prevent or interfere with the settlement becoming final if such finality occurs automatically upon the lapse of certain time or the happening of certain events (subsection (3) of Section 4—211, subsections (1) (d), (2) and (3) of Section 4—213).

(4) If a collecting bank receives from subsequent parties settlement for an item which settlement is or becomes final and suspends payments without making a settlement for the item with its customer which is or becomes final, the owner of the item has a preferred claim against such collecting bank.

Part 3

Collection of Items: Payor Banks

§ 4—301. Deferred Posting; Recovery of Payment by Return of Items; Time of Dishonor

(1) Where an authorized settlement for a demand item (other than a documentary draft) received by a payor bank otherwise than for immediate payment over the counter has been made before midnight of the banking day of receipt, the payor bank may revoke the settlement and recover any payment if before it has made final payment (subsection (1) of Section 4—213) and before its midnight deadline it

    (a) returns the item; or

    (b) sends written notice of dishonor or nonpayment if the item is held for protest or is otherwise unavailable for return.

(2) If a demand item is received by a payor bank for credit on its books, it may return such item or send notice of dishonor and may revoke any credit given or recover the amount thereof withdrawn by its customer, if it acts within the time limit and in the manner specified in the preceding subsection.

(3) Unless previous notice of dishonor has been sent, an item is dishonored at the time when for purposes of dishonor it is returned or notice sent in accordance with this section.

(4) An item is returned:

    (a) as to an item received through a clearing house, when it is delivered to the presenting or last collecting bank or to the clearing house or is sent or delivered in accordance with its rules; or

    (b) in all other cases, when it is sent or delivered to the bank's customer or transferor or pursuant to his instructions.

§ 4—302. Payor Bank's Responsibility for Late Return of Item

In the absence of a valid defense such as breach of a presentment warranty (subsection (1) of Section 4—207), settlement effected or the like, if an item is presented on and received by a payor bank the bank is accountable for the amount of

    (a) a demand item other than a documentary draft whether properly payable or not if the bank, in any case where it is not also the depositary bank, retains the item beyond midnight of the banking day of receipt without settling for it or, regardless of whether it is also the depositary bank, does not pay or return the item or send notice of dishonor until after its midnight deadline; or

    (b) any other properly payable item unless within the time allowed for acceptance or payment of that item the bank either accepts or pays the item or returns it and accompanying documents.

§ 4—303. When Items Subject to Notice, Stop-Order, Legal Process or Setoff; Order in Which Items May Be Charged or Certified

(1) Any knowledge, notice or stop-order received by, legal process served upon or setoff exercised by a payor bank, whether or not effective under other rules of law to terminate, suspend or modify the bank's right or duty to pay an item or to charge its customer's account for the item, comes too late to so terminate, suspend or modify such right or duty if the knowledge, notice, stop-order or legal process is received or served and a reasonable time for the bank to act thereon expires or the setoff is exercised after the bank has done any of the following:

    (a) accepted or certified the item;

    (b) paid the item in cash;

    (c) settled for the item without reserving a right to revoke the settlement and without having such right under statute, clearing house rule or agreement;

    (d) completed the process of posting the item to the indicated account of the drawer, maker or other person to be charged therewith or otherwise has evidenced by examination of such indicated account and by action its decision to pay the item; or

    (e) become accountable for the amount of the item under subsection (1) (d) of

Section 4—213 and Section 4—302 dealing with the payor bank's responsibility for late return of items.

(2) Subject to the provisions of subsection (1), items may be accepted, paid, certified or charged to the indicated account of its customer in any order convenient to the bank.

Part 4

Relationship Between Payor Bank and Its Customer

§ 4—401. When Bank May Charge Customer's Account

(1) As against its customer, a bank may charge against his account any item which is otherwise properly payable from that account even though the charge creates an overdraft.

(2) A bank which in good faith makes payment to a holder may charge the indicated account of its customer according to

(a) the original tenor of his altered item; or
(b) the tenor of his completed item, even though the bank knows the item has been completed unless the bank has notice that the completion was improper.

§ 4—402. Bank's Liability to Customer for Wrongful Dishonor

A payor bank is liable to its customer for damages proximately caused by the wrongful dishonor of an item. When the dishonor occurs through mistake, liability is limited to actual damages proved. If so proximately caused and proved, damages may include damages for an arrest or prosecution of the customer or other consequential damages. Whether any consequential damages are proximately caused by the wrongful dishonor is a question of fact to be determined in each case.

§ 4—403. Customer's Right to Stop Payment; Burden of Proof of Loss

(1) A customer may by order to his bank stop payment of any item payable for his account but the order must be received at such time and in such manner as to afford the bank a reasonable opportunity to act on it prior to any action by the bank with respect to the item described in Section 4—303.

(2) An oral order is binding upon the bank only for fourteen calendar days unless confirmed in writing within that period. A written order is effective for only six months unless renewed in writing.

(3) The burden of establishing the fact and amount of loss resulting from the payment of an item

contrary to a binding stop payment order is on the customer.

§ 4—404. Bank Not Obligated to Pay Check More Than Six Months Old

A bank is under no obligation to a customer having a checking account to pay a check, other than a certified check, which is presented more than six months after its date, but it may charge its customer's account for a payment made thereafter in good faith.

§ 4—405. Death or Incompetence of Customer

(1) A payor or collecting bank's authority to accept, pay or collect an item or to account for proceeds of its collection if otherwise effective is not rendered ineffective by incompetence of a customer of either bank existing at the time the item is issued or its collection is undertaken if the bank does not know of an adjudication of incompetence. Neither death nor incompetence of a customer revokes such authority to accept, pay, collect or account until the bank knows of the fact of death or of an adjudication of incompetence and has reasonable opportunity to act on it.

(2) Even with knowledge a bank may for 10 days after the date of death pay or certify checks drawn on or prior to that date unless ordered to stop payment by a person claiming an interest in the account.

§ 4—406. Customer's Duty to Discover and Report Unauthorized Signature or Alteration

(1) When a bank sends to its customer a statement of account accompanied by items paid in good faith in support of the debit entries or holds the statement and items pursuant to a request or instructions of its customer or otherwise in a reasonable manner makes the statement and items available to the customer, the customer must exercise reasonable care and promptness to examine the statement and items to discover his unauthorized signature or any alteration on an item and must notify the bank promptly after discovery thereof.

(2) If the bank establishes that the customer failed with respect to an item to comply with the duties imposed on the customer by subsection (1), the customer is precluded from asserting against the bank

(a) his unauthorized signature or any alteration on the item if the bank also establishes that it suffered a loss by reason of such failure; and
(b) an unauthorized signature or alteration by the same wrongdoer on any other item paid in good faith by the bank after the first item and statement was available to the customer for a reasonable period not exceeding fourteen calendar days and before the bank receives notification from

the customer of any such unauthorized signature or alteration.

(3) The preclusion under subsection (2) does not apply if the customer establishes lack of ordinary care on the part of the bank in paying the item(s).

(4) Without regard to care or lack of care of either the customer or the bank, a customer who does not within one year from the time the statement and items are made available to the customer (subsection (1)) discover and report his unauthorized signature or any alteration on the face or back of the item or does not within 3 years from that time discover and report any unauthorized indorsement is precluded from asserting against the bank such unauthorized signature or indorsement or such alteration.

(5) If under this section a payor bank has a valid defense against a claim of a customer upon or resulting from payment of an item and waives or fails upon request to assert the defense, the bank may not assert against any collecting bank or other prior party presenting or transferring the item a claim based upon the unauthorized signature or alteration giving rise to the customer's claim.

§ 4—407. Payor Bank's Right to Subrogation on Improper Payment

If a payor bank has paid an item over the stop payment order of the drawer or maker or otherwise under circumstances giving a basis for objection by the drawer or maker, to prevent unjust enrichment and only to the extent necessary to prevent loss to the bank by reason of its payment of the item, the payor bank shall be subrogated to the rights

(a) of any holder in due course on the item against the drawer or maker; and
(b) of the payee or any other holder of the item against the drawer or maker either on the item or under the transaction out of which the item arose; and
(c) of the drawer or maker against the payee or any other holder of the item with respect to the transaction out of which the item arose.

Part 5

Collection of Documentary Drafts

§ 4—501. Handling of Documentary Drafts; Duty to Send for Presentment and to Notify Customer of Dishonor

A bank which takes a documentary draft for collection must present or send the draft and accompanying documents for presentment and, upon learning that the draft has not been paid or accepted in due course, must seasonably notify its customer of

such fact even though it may have discounted or bought the draft or extended credit available for withdrawal as of right.

§ 4—502. Presentment of "On Arrival" Drafts

When a draft or the relevant instructions require presentment "on arrival," "when goods arrive" or the like, the collecting bank need not present until in its judgment a reasonable time for arrival of the goods has expired. Refusal to pay or accept because the goods have not arrived is not dishonor; the bank must notify its transferor of such refusal but need not present the draft again until it is instructed to do so or learns of the arrival of the goods.

§ 4—503. Responsibility of Presenting Bank for Documents and Goods; Report of Reasons for Dishonor; Referee in Case of Need

Unless otherwise instructed and except as provided in Article 5, a bank presenting a documentary draft

(a) must deliver the documents to the drawee on acceptance of the draft if it is payable more than three days after presentment; otherwise, only on payment; and
(b) upon dishonor, either in the case of presentment for acceptance or presentment for payment, may seek and follow instructions from any referee in case of need designated in the draft or if the presenting bank does not choose to utilize his services it must use diligence and good faith to ascertain the reason for dishonor, must notify its transferor of the dishonor and of the results of its effort to ascertain the reasons therefor and must request instructions.

But the presenting bank is under no obligation with respect to goods represented by the documents except to follow any reasonable instructions seasonably received; it has a right to reimbursement for any expense incurred in following instructions and to prepayment of or indemnity for such expenses.

§ 4—504. Privilege of Presenting Bank to Deal With Goods; Security Interest for Expenses

(1) A presenting bank which, following the dishonor of a documentary draft, has seasonably requested instructions but does not receive them within a reasonable time may store, sell, or otherwise deal with the goods in any reasonable manner.

(2) For its reasonable expenses incurred by action under subsection (1), the presenting bank has a lien upon the goods or their proceeds, which may be foreclosed in the same manner as an unpaid seller's lien.

ARTICLE 5

LETTERS OF CREDIT

§ 5 — 101.   Short Title

This Article shall be known and may be cited as Uniform Commercial Code — Letters of Credit.

§ 5 — 102.   Scope

(1) This Article applies

    (a) to a credit issued by a bank, if the credit requires a documentary draft or a documentary demand for payment; and

    (b) to a credit issued by a person other than a bank, if the credit requires that the draft or demand for payment be accompanied by a document of title; and

    (c) to a credit issued by a bank or other person, if the credit is not within subparagraphs (a) or (b) but conspicuously states that it is a letter of credit or is conspicuously so entitled.

(2) Unless the engagement meets the requirements of subsection (1), this Article does not apply to engagements to make advances or to honor drafts or demands for payment, to authorities to pay or purchase to guarantees or to general agreements.

(3) This Article deals with some but not all of the rules and concepts of letters of credit as such rules or concepts have developed prior to this act or may hereafter develop. The fact that this Article states a rule does not by itself require, imply or negate application of the same or a converse rule to a situation not provided for or to a person not specified by this Article.

§ 5 — 103.   Definitions

(1) In this Article unless the context otherwise requires

    (a) "Credit" or "letter of credit" means an engagement by a bank or other person, made at the request of a customer and of a kind within the scope of this Article (Section 5 — 102), that the issuer will honor drafts or other demands for payment upon compliance with the conditions specified in the credit. A credit may be either revocable or irrevocable. The engagement may be either an agreement to honor or a statement that the bank or other person is authorized to honor.

    (b) A "documentary draft" or a "documentary demand for payment" is one honor of which is conditioned upon the presentation of a document or documents. "Document" means any paper including document of title, security, invoice, certificate, notice of default and the like.

    (c) An "issuer" is a bank or other person issuing a credit.

    (d) A "beneficiary" of a credit is a person who is entitled under its terms to draw or demand payment.

    (e) An "advising bank" is a bank which gives notification of the issuance of a credit by another bank.

    (f) A "confirming bank" is a bank which engages either that it will itself honor a credit already issued by another bank or that such a credit will be honored by the issuer or a third bank.

    (g) A "customer" is a buyer or other person who causes an issuer to issue a credit. The term also includes a bank which procures issuance or confirmation on behalf of that bank's customer.

(2) Other definitions applying to this Article and the sections in which they appear are:

    "Notation of Credit." Section 5 — 108.

    "Presenter." Section 5 — 112(3).

(3) Definitions in other Articles applying to this Article and the sections in which they appear are:

    "Accept" or "Acceptance." Section 3 — 410.

    "Contract for sale." Section 2 — 106.

    "Draft." Section 3 — 104.

    "Holder in due course." Section 3 — 302.

    "Midnight deadline." Section 4 — 104.

    "Security." Section 8 — 102.

(4) In addition, Article 1 contains general definitions and principles of construction and interpretation applicable throughout this Article.

§ 5 — 104.   Formal Requirements; Signing

(1) Except as otherwise required in subsection (1) (c) of Section 5 — 102 on scope, no particular form of phrasing is required for a credit. A credit must be in writing and signed by the issuer, and a confirmation must be in writing and signed by the confirming bank. A modification of the terms of a credit or confirmation must be signed by the issuer or confirming bank.

(2) A telegram may be a sufficient signed writing if it identifies its sender by an authorized authentication. The authentication may be in code and the authorized naming of the issuer in an advice of credit is a sufficient signing.

§ 5 — 105.   Consideration

No consideration is necessary to establish a credit or to enlarge or otherwise modify its terms.

§ 5 — 106.   Time and Effect of Establishment of Credit

(1) Unless otherwise agreed, a credit is established

(a) as regards the customer, as soon as a letter of credit is sent to him or the letter of credit or an authorized written advice of its issuance is sent to the beneficiary; and

(b) as regards the beneficiary, when he receives a letter of credit or an authorized written advice of its issuance.

(2) Unless otherwise agreed, once an irrevocable credit is established as regards the customer, it can be modified or revoked only with the consent of the customer; and once it is established as regards the beneficiary, it can be modified or revoked only with his consent.

(3) Unless otherwise agreed after a revocable credit is established, it may be modified or revoked by the issuer without notice to or consent from the customer or beneficiary.

(4) Notwithstanding any modification or revocation of a revocable credit, any person authorized to honor or negotiate under the terms of the original credit is entitled to reimbursement for or honor of any draft or demand for payment duly honored or negotiated before receipt of notice of the modification or revocation and the issuer in turn is entitled to reimbursement from its customer.

§ 5 — 107. Advice of Credit; Confirmation; Error in Statement of Terms

(1) Unless otherwise specified, an advising bank by advising a credit issued by another bank does not assume any obligation to honor drafts drawn or demands for payment made under the credit, but it does assume obligation for the accuracy of its own statement.

(2) A confirming bank by confirming a credit becomes directly obligated on the credit to the extent of its confirmation as though it were its issuer and acquires the rights of an issuer.

(3) Even though an advising bank incorrectly advises the terms of a credit it has been authorized to advise, the credit is established as against the issuer to the extent of its original terms.

(4) Unless otherwise specified, the customer bears as against the issuer all risks of transmission and reasonable translation or interpretation of any message relating to a credit.

§ 5 — 108. "Notation Credit"; Exhaustion of Credit

(1) A credit which specifies that any person purchasing or paying drafts drawn or demands for payment made under it must note the amount of the draft or demand on the letter or advice of credit is a "notation credit."

(2) Under a notation credit

(a) a person paying the beneficiary or purchasing a draft or demand for payment from him acquires a right to honor only if

the appropriate notation is made; and by transferring or forwarding for honor the documents under the credit, such a person warrants to the issuer that the notation has been made; and

(b) unless the credit or a signed statement that an appropriate notation has been made accompanies the draft or demand for payment, the issuer may delay honor until evidence of notation has been procured which is satisfactory to it; but its obligation and that of its customer continue for a reasonable time not exceeding thirty days to obtain such evidence.

(3) If the credit is not a notation credit

(a) the issuer may honor complying drafts or demands for payment presented to it in the order in which they are presented and is discharged pro tanto by honor of any such draft or demand;

(b) as between competing good faith purchasers of complying drafts or demands, the person first purchasing has priority over a subsequent purchaser even though the later purchased draft or demand has been first honored.

§ 5 — 109. Issuer's Obligation to Its Customer

(1) An issuer's obligation to its customer includes good faith and observance of any general banking usage but, unless otherwise agreed, does not include liability or responsibility

(a) for performance of the underlying contract for sale or other transaction between the customer and the beneficiary; or

(b) for any act or omission of any person other than itself or its own branch or for loss or destruction of a draft, demand or document in transit or in the possession of others; or

(c) based on knowledge or lack of knowledge of any usage of any particular trade.

(2) An issuer must examine documents with care so as to ascertain that on their face they appear to comply with the terms of the credit but, unless otherwise agreed, assumes no liability or responsibility for the genuineness, falsification or effect of any document which appears on such examination to be regular on its face.

(3) A nonbank issuer is not bound by any banking usage of which it has no knowledge.

§ 5 — 110. Availability of Credit in Portions; Presenter's Reservation of Lien or Claim

(1) Unless otherwise specified, a credit may be used in portions in the discretion of the beneficiary.

(2) Unless otherwise specified, a person by presenting a documentary draft or demand for payment under a credit relinquishes upon its honor all

claims to the documents and a person by transferring such draft or demand or causing such presentment authorizes such relinquishment. An explicit reservation of claim makes the draft or demand non-complying.

§ 5 — 111. Warranties on Transfer and Presentment

(1) Unless otherwise agreed, the beneficiary, by transferring or presenting a documentary draft or demand for payment, warrants to all interested parties that the necessary conditions of the credit have been complied with. This is in addition to any warranties arising under Articles 3, 4, 7 and 8.

(2) Unless otherwise agreed, a negotiating, advising, confirming, collecting or issuing bank presenting or transferring a draft or demand for payment under a credit warrants only the matters warranted by a collecting bank under Article 4 and any such bank transferring a document warrants only the matters warranted by an intermediary under Articles 7 and 8.

§ 5 — 112. Time Allowed for Honor or Rejection; Withholding Honor or Rejection by Consent; "Presenter"

(1) A bank to which a documentary draft or demand for payment is presented under a credit may without dishonor of the draft, demand or credit

(a) defer honor until the close of the third banking day following receipt of the documents; and

(b) further defer honor if the presenter has expressly or impliedly consented thereto.

Failure to honor within the time here specified constitutes dishonor of the draft or demand and of the credit [except as otherwise provided in subsection (4) of Section 5 — 114 on conditional payment].

Note: *The bracketed language in the last sentence of subsection (1) should be included only if the optional provisions of Section 5 — 114(4) and (5) are included.*

(2) Upon dishonor the bank may unless otherwise instructed fulfill its duty to return the draft or demand and the documents by holding them at the disposal of the presenter and sending him an advice to that effect.

(3) "Presenter" means any person presenting a draft or demand for payment for honor under a credit even though that person is a confirming bank or other correspondent which is acting under an issuer's authorization.

§ 5 — 113. Indemnities

(1) A bank seeking to obtain (whether for itself or another) honor, negotiation or reimbursement under a credit may give an indemnity to induce such honor, negotiation or reimbursement.

(2) An indemnity agreement inducing honor, negotiation or reimbursement

(a) unless otherwise explicitly agreed applies to defects in the documents but not in the goods; and

(b) unless a longer time is explicitly agreed expires at the end of ten business days following receipt of the documents by the ultimate customer unless notice of objection is sent before such expiration date. The ultimate customer may send notice of objection to the person from whom he received the documents and any bank receiving such notice is under a duty to send notice to its transferor before its midnight deadline.

§ 5 — 114. Issuer's Duty and Privilege to Honor; Right to Reimbursement

(1) An issuer must honor a draft or demand for payment which complies with the terms of the relevant credit regardless of whether the goods or documents conform to the underlying contract for sale or other contract between the customer and the beneficiary. The issuer is not excused from honor of such a draft or demand by reason of an additional general term that all documents must be satisfactory to the issuer, but an issuer may require that specified documents must be satisfactory to it.

(2) Unless otherwise agreed, when documents appear on their face to comply with the terms of a credit but a required document does not in fact conform to the warranties made on negotiation or transfer of a document of title (Section 7 — 507) or of a certificated security (Section 8 — 306) or is forged or fraudulent or there is fraud in the transaction

(a) the issuer must honor the draft or demand for payment, if honor is demanded by a negotiating bank or other holder of the draft or demand which has taken the draft or demand under the credit and under circumstances which would make it a holder in due course (Section 3 — 302) and in an appropriate case would make it a person to whom a document of title has been duly negotiated (Section 7 — 502) or a bona fide purchaser of a certificated security (Section 8 — 302); and

(b) in all other cases, as against its customer, an issuer acting in good faith may honor the draft or demand for payment despite notification from the customer of fraud, forgery or other defect not apparent on the face of the documents but a court of appropriate jurisdiction may enjoin such honor.

(3) Unless otherwise agreed, an issuer which has duly honored a draft or demand for payment is entitled to immediate reimbursement of any payment made under the credit and to be put in effectively available funds not later than the day before maturity of any acceptance made under the credit.

[(4) When a credit provides for payment by the issuer on receipt of notice that the required documents are in the possession of a correspondent or other agent of the issuer

    (a) any payment made on receipt of such notice is conditional; and

    (b) the issuer may reject documents which do not comply with the credit, if it does so within three banking days following its receipt of the documents; and

    (c) in the event of such rejection, the issuer is entitled by charge-back or otherwise to return of the payment made.]

[(5) In the case covered by subsection (4), failure to reject documents within the time specified in subparagraph (b) constitutes acceptance of the documents and makes the payment final in favor of the beneficiary.]

Note: *Subsections (4) and (5) are bracketed as optional. If they are included the bracketed language in the last sentence of Section 5—112(1) should also be included.*

§ 5—115. Remedy for Improper Dishonor or Anticipatory Repudiation

(1) When an issuer wrongfully dishonors a draft or demand for payment presented under a credit, the person entitled to honor has, with respect to any documents, the rights of a person in the position of a seller (Section 2—707) and may recover from the issuer the face amount of the draft or demand, together with incidental damages under Section 2—710 on seller's incidental damages and interest but less any amount realized by resale or other use or disposition of the subject matter of the transaction. In the event no resale or other utilization is made the documents, goods or other subject matter involved in the transaction must be turned over to the issuer on payment of judgment.

(2) When an issuer wrongfully cancels or otherwise repudiates a credit before presentment of a draft or demand for payment drawn under it, the beneficiary has the rights of a seller after anticipatory repudiation by the buyer under Section 2—610 if he learns of the repudiation in time reasonably to avoid procurement of the required documents. Otherwise the beneficiary has an immediate right of action for wrongful dishonor.

§ 5—116. Transfer and Assignment

(1) The right to draw under a credit can be transferred or assigned only when the credit is expressly designated as transferable or assignable.

    (2) Even though the credit specifically states that it is nontransferable or nonassignable, the beneficiary may, before performance of the conditions of the credit, assign his right to proceeds. Such an assignment is an assignment of an account under Article 9 on Secured Transactions and is governed by that Article except that

    (a) the assignment is ineffective until the letter of credit or advice of credit is delivered to the assignee which delivery constitutes perfection of the security interest under Article 9; and

    (b) the issuer may honor drafts or demands for payment drawn under the credit until it receives a notification of the assignment signed by the beneficiary which reasonably identifies the credit involved in the assignment and contains a request to pay the assignee; and

    (c) after what reasonably appears to be such a notification has been received the issuer may without dishonor refuse to accept or pay even to a person otherwise entitled to honor until the letter of credit or advice of credit is exhibited to the issuer.

(3) Except where the beneficiary has effectively assigned his right to draw or his right to proceeds, nothing in this section limits his right to transfer or negotiate drafts or demands drawn under the credit.

§ 5—117. Insolvency of Bank Holding Funds for Documentary Credit

    (1) Where an issuer or an advising or confirming bank or a bank which has for a customer procured issuance of a credit by another bank becomes insolvent before final payment under the credit and the credit is one to which this Article is made applicable by paragraphs (a) or (b) of Section 5—102(1) on scope, the receipt or allocation of funds or collateral to secure or meet obligations under the credit shall have the following results:

    (a) to the extent of any funds or collateral turned over after or before the insolvency as indemnity against or specifically for the purpose of payment of drafts or demands for payment drawn under the designated credit, the drafts or demands are entitled to payment in preference over depositors or other general creditors of the issuer or bank; and

    (b) on expiration of the credit or surrender of the beneficiary's rights under it unused any person who has given such funds or collateral is similarly entitled to return thereof; and

    (c) a charge to a general or current account with a bank if specifically consented to for the purpose of indemnity against or payment of drafts or demands for payment drawn under the designated credit falls under the same rules as if the funds had been drawn out in cash and then turned over with specific instructions.

(2) After honor or reimbursement under this section, the customer or other person for whose account the insolvent bank has acted is entitled to receive the documents involved.

ARTICLE 6

BULK TRANSFERS

§ 6 — 101.   Short Title

This Article shall be known and may be cited as Uniform Commercial Code — Bulk Transfers.

§ 6 — 102.   "Bulk Transfers"; Transfers of Equipment; Enterprises Subject to This Article; Bulk Transfers Subject to This Article

(1) A "bulk transfer" is any transfer in bulk and not in the ordinary course of the transferor's business of a major part of the materials, supplies, merchandise or other inventory (Section 9 — 109) of an enterprise subject to this Article.

(2) A transfer of a substantial part of the equipment (Section 9 — 109) of such an enterprise is a bulk transfer if it is made in connection with a bulk transfer of inventory, but not otherwise.

(3) The enterprises subject to this Article are all those whose principal business is the sale of merchandise from stock, including those who manufacture what they sell.

(4) Except as limited by the following section, all bulk transfers of goods located within this state are subject to this Article.

§ 6 — 103.   Transfers Excepted From This Article

The following transfers are not subject to this Article:

(1) Those made to give security for the performance of an obligation;

(2) General assignments for the benefit of all the creditors of the transferor, and subsequent transfers by the assignee thereunder;

(3) Transfers in settlement or realization of a lien or other security interests;

(4) Sales by executors, administrators, receivers, trustees in bankruptcy, or any public officer under judicial process;

(5) Sales made in the course of judicial or administrative proceedings for the dissolution or reorganization of a corporation and of which notice is sent to the creditors of the corporation pursuant to order of the court or administrative agency;

(6) Transfers to a person maintaining a known place of business in this State who becomes bound to pay the debts of the transferor in full and gives public notice of that fact, and who is solvent after becoming so bound;

(7) A transfer to a new business enterprise organized to take over and continue the business, if public notice of the transaction is given and the new enterprise assumes the debts of the transferor and he receives nothing from the transaction except an interest in the new enterprise junior to the claims of creditors;

(8) Transfers of property which is exempt from execution.

Public notice under subsection (6) or subsection (7) may be given by publishing once a week for two consecutive weeks in a newspaper of general circulation where the transferor had its principal place of business in this state an advertisement including the names and addresses of the transferor and transferee and the effective date of the transfer.

§ 6 — 104.   Schedule of Property, List of Creditors

(1) Except as provided with respect to auction sales (Section 6 — 108), a bulk transfer subject to this Article is ineffective against any creditor of the transferor unless:

(a) The transferee requires the transferor to furnish a list of his existing creditors prepared as stated in this section; and

(b) The parties prepare a schedule of the property transferred sufficient to identify it; and

(c) The transferee preserves the list and schedule for six months next following the transfer and permits inspection of either or both and copying therefrom at all reasonable hours by any creditor of the transferor, or files the list and schedule in (a public office to be here identified).

(2) The list of creditors must be signed and sworn to or affirmed by the transferor or his agent. It must contain the names and business addresses of all creditors of the transferor, with the amounts when known, and also the names of all persons who are known to the transferor to assert claims against him even though such claims are disputed. If the transferor is the obligor of an outstanding issue of bonds, debentures or the like as to which there is an indenture trustee, the list of creditors need include only the name and address of the indenture trustee and the aggregate outstanding principal amount of the issue.

(3) Responsibility for the completeness and accuracy of the list of creditors rests on the transferor, and the transfer is not rendered ineffective by errors or omissions therein unless the transferee is shown to have had knowledge.

§ 6 — 105.   Notice to Creditors

In addition to the requirements of the preceding section, any bulk transfer subject to this Article, except one made by auction sale (Section 6 — 108), is ineffective against any creditor of the transferor unless at least ten days before he takes possession of the goods or pays for them, whichever happens first, the transferee gives notice of the transfer in the manner and to the persons hereafter provided (Section 6 — 107).

[§ 6 — 106.   Application of the Proceeds

In addition to the requirements of the two preceding sections:

(1) Upon every bulk transfer subject to this Article for which new consideration becomes payable except those made by sale at aucttion, it is the duty of the transferee to assure that such consideration is applied so far as necessary to pay those debts of the transferor which are either shown on the list furnished by the transferor (Section 6—104) or filed in writing in the place stated in the notice (Section 6—107) within thirty days after the mailing of such notice. This duty of the transferee runs to all the holders of such debts, and may be enforced by any of them for the benefit of all.

(2) If any of said debts are in dispute, the necessary sum may be withheld from distribution until the dispute is settled or adjudicated.

(3) If the consideration payable is not enough to pay all of the said debts in full, distribution shall be made pro rata.]

Note: *This section is bracketed to indicate division of opinion as to whether or not it is a wise provision, and to suggest that this is a point on which State enactments may differ without serious damage to the principle of uniformity.*

In any State where this section is omitted, the following parts of sections, also bracketed in the text, should also be omitted, namely:
Section 6—107(2)(e).
    6—108(3)(c).
    6—109(2).
In any State where this section is enacted, these other provisions should be also.

Optional Subsection (4)

[(4) The transferee may within ten days after he takes possession of the goods pay the consideration into the (specify court) in the county where the transferor had its principal place of business in this state and thereafter may discharge his duty under this section by giving notice by registered or certified mail to all the persons to whom the duty runs that the consideration has been paid into that court and that they should file their claims there. On motion of any interested party, the court may order the distribution of the consideration to the persons entitled to it.]

Note: *Optional subsection (4) is recommended for those states which do not have a general statute providing for payment of money into court.*

§ 6—107.   The Notice

(1) The notice to creditors (Section 6—105) shall state:
(a) that a bulk transfer is about to be made; and
(b) the names and business addresses of the transferor and transferee, and all other business names and addresses used by the transferor within three years last past so far as known to the transferee; and
(c) whether or not all the debts of the transferor are to be paid in full as they fall due as a result of the transaction, and if so, the

address to which creditors should send their bills.
(2) If the debts of the transferor are not to be paid in full as they fall due or if the transferee is in doubt on that point, then the notice shall state further:
(a) the location and general description of the property to be transferred and the estimated total of the transferor's debts;
(b) the address where the schedule of property and list of creditors (Section 6—104) may be inspected;
(c) whether the transfer is to pay existing debts and if so, the amount of such debts and to whom owing;
(d) whether the transfer is for new consideration and if so, the amount of such consideration and the time and place of payment; [and]
[(e) if for new consideration, the time and place where creditors of the transferor are to file their claims.]

(3) The notice in any case shall be delivered personally or sent by registered or certified mail to all the persons shown on the list of creditors furnished by the transferor (Section 6—104) and to all other persons who are known to the transferee to hold or assert claims against the transferor.

Note: *The words in brackets are optional. See Note under § 6—106.*

§ 6—108.   Auction Sales; "Auctioneer"

(1) A bulk transfer is subject to this Article even though it is by sale at auction, but only in the manner and with the results stated in this section.

(2) The transferor shall furnish a list of his creditors and assist in the preparation of a schedule of the property to be sold, both prepared as before stated (Section 6—104).

(3) The person or persons other than the transferor who direct, control or are responsible for the auction are collectively called the "auctioneer." The auctioneer shall:
(a) receive and retain the list of creditors and prepare and retain the schedule of property for the period stated in this Article (Section 6—104);
(b) give notice of the auction personally or by registered or certified mail at least ten days before it occurs to all persons shown on the list of creditors and to all other persons who are known to him to hold or assert claims against the transferor; [and]
[(c) assure that the net proceeds of the auction are applied as provided in this Article (Section 6—106).]

(4) Failure of the auctioneer to perform any of these duties does not affect the validity of the sale or the title of the purchasers; but if the auctioneer knows that the auction constitutes a bulk transfer, such failure

renders the auctioneer liable to the creditors of the transferor as a class for the sums owing to them from the transferor up to but not exceeding the net proceeds of the auction. If the auctioneer consists of several persons their liability is joint and several.

Note: *The words in brackets are optional. See Note under § 6—106.*

§ 6—109. What Creditors Protected; [Credit for Payment to Particular Creditors]

(1) The creditors of the transferor mentioned in this Article are those holding claims based on transactions or events occurring before the bulk transfer, but creditors who become such after notice to creditors is given (Sections 6—105 and 6—107) are not entitled to notice.

[(2) Against the aggregate obligation imposed by the provisions of this Article concerning the application of the proceeds (Section 6—106 and subsection (3) (c) of 6—108), the transferee or auctioneer is entitled to credit for sums paid to particular creditors of the transferor, not exceeding the sums believed in good faith at the time of the payment to be properly payable to such creditors.]

Note: *The words in brackets are optional. See Note under § 6—106.*

§ 6—110. Subsequent Transfers

When the title of a transferee to property is subject to a defect by reason of his noncompliance with the requirements of this Article, then:

(1) a purchaser of any of such property from such transferee who pays no value or who takes with notice of such noncompliance takes subject to such defect, but

(2) a purchaser for value in good faith and without such notice takes free of such defect.

§ 6—111. Limitation of Actions and Levies

No action under this Article shall be brought nor levy made more than six months after the date on which the transferee took possession of the goods unless the transfer has been concealed. If the transfer has been concealed, actions may be brought or levies made within six months after its discovery.

Note to Article 6: *Section 6—106 is bracketed to indicate division of opinion as to whether or not it is a wise provision, and to suggest that this a point on which State enactments may differ without serious damage to the principle of uniformity.*

In any State where Section 6—106 is not enacted, the following parts of sections, also bracketed in the text, should also be omitted, namely:

Sec. 6—107(2) (e).
      6—108(3) (c).
      6—109(2).

In any State where Section 6—106 is enacted, these other provisions should be also.

ARTICLE 7

WAREHOUSE RECEIPTS, BILLS OF LADING AND OTHER DOCUMENTS OF TITLE

Part 1

General

§ 7—101. Short Title

This Article shall be known and may be cited as Uniform Commercial Code—Documents of Title.

§ 7—102. Definitions and Index of Definitions

(1) In this Article, unless the context otherwise requires:

(a) "Bailee" means the person who by a warehouse receipt, bill of lading or other document of title acknowledges possession of goods and contracts to deliver them.

(b) "Consignee" means the person named in a bill to whom or to whose order the bill promises delivery.

(c) "Consignor" means the person named in a bill as the person from whom the goods have been received for shipment.

(d) "Delivery order" means a written order to deliver goods directed to a warehouseman, carrier or other person who in the ordinary course of business issues warehouse receipts or bills of lading.

(e) "Document" means document of title as defined in the general definitions in Article 1 (Section 1—201).

(f) "Goods" means all things which are treated as movable for the purposes of a contract of storage or transportation.

(g) "Issuer" means a bailee who issues a document except that in relation to an unaccepted delivery order it means the person who orders the possessor of goods to deliver. Issuer includes any person for whom an agent or employee purports to act in issuing a document if the agent or employee has real or apparent authority to issue documents, notwithstanding that the issuer received no goods or that the goods were misdescribed or that in any other respect the agent or employee violated his instructions.

(h) "Warehouseman" is a person engaged in the business of storing goods for hire.

(2) Other definitions applying to this Article or to specified Parts thereof, and the sections in which they appear are:

"Duly negotiate." Section 7—501.

"Person entitled under the document."
Section 7—403(4).

(3) Definitions in other Articles applying to this Article and the sections in which they appear are:

"Contract for sale." Section 2—106.

"Overseas." Section 2—323.

"Receipt" of goods. Section 2—103.

(4) In addition, Article 1 contains general definitions and principles of construction and interpretation applicable throughout this Article.

§ 7—103. Relation of Article to Treaty, Statute, Tariff, Classification or Regulation

To the extent that any treaty or statute of the United States, regulatory statute of this State or tariff, classification or regulation filed or issued pursuant thereto is applicable, the provisions of this Article are subject thereto.

§ 7—104. Negotiable and Nonnegotiable Warehouse Receipt, Bill of Lading or Other Document of Title

(1) A warehouse receipt, bill of lading or other document of title is negotiable

(a) if by its terms the goods are to be delivered to bearer or to the order of a named person; or

(b) where recognized in overseas trade, if it runs to a named person or assigns.

(2) Any other document is nonnegotiable. A bill of lading in which it is stated that the goods are consigned to a named person is not made negotiable by a provision that the goods are to be delivered only against a written order signed by the same or another named person.

§ 7—105. Construction Against Negative Implication

The omission from either Part 2 or Part 3 of this Article of a provision corresponding to a provision made in the other Part does not imply that a corresponding rule of law is not applicable.

Part 2

Warehouse Receipts: Special Provisions

§ 7—201. Who May Issue a Warehouse Receipt; Storage Under Government Bond

(1) A warehouse receipt may be issued by any warehouseman.

(2) Where goods including distilled spirits and agricultural commodities are stored under a statute requiring a bond against withdrawal or a license for the issuance of receipts in the nature of warehouse receipts, a receipt issued for the goods has like effect as a warehouse receipt even though issued by a person who is the owner of the goods and is not a warehouseman.

§ 7—202. Form of Warehouse Receipt; Essential Terms; Optional Terms

(1) A warehouse receipt need not be in any particular form.

(2) Unless a warehouse receipt embodies within its written or printed terms each of the following, the warehouseman is liable for damages caused by the omission to a person injured thereby:

(a) the location of the warehouse where the goods are stored;

(b) the date of issue of the receipt;

(c) the consecutive number of the receipt;

(d) a statement whether the goods received will be delivered to the bearer, to a specified person, or to a specified person or his order;

(e) the rate of storage and handling charges, except that where goods are stored under a field warehousing arrangement a statement of that fact is sufficient on a nonnegotiable receipt;

(f) a description of the goods or of the packages containing them;

(g) the signature of the warehouseman, which may be made by his authorized agent;

(h) if the receipt is issued for goods of which the warehouseman is owner, either solely or jointly or in common with others, the fact of such ownership; and

(i) a statement of the amount of advances made and of liabilities incurred for which the warehouseman claims a lien or security interest (Section 7—209). If the precise amount of such advances made or of such liabilities incurred is, at the time of the issue of the receipt, unknown to the warehouseman or to his agent who issues it, a statement of the fact that advances have been made or liabilities incurred and the purpose thereof is sufficient.

(3) A warehouseman may insert in his receipt any other terms which are not contrary to the provisions of this Act and do not impair his obligation of delivery (Section 7—403) or his duty of care (Section 7—204). Any contrary provisions shall be ineffective.

§ 7—203. Liability for Non-Receipt or Misdescription

A party to or purchaser for value in good faith of a document of title other than a bill of lading relying in either case upon the description therein of the goods may recover from the issuer damages caused by the non-receipt or misdescription of the goods, except to the extent that the document conspicuously indicates that the issuer does not know whether any part or all of the goods in fact were received or conform to the description, as where the description is in terms of marks or labels or kind, quantity or condition, or the receipt or description is qualified by "contents, condition and quality unknown," "said to contain" or the like, if such indication be true, or the party or purchaser otherwise has notice.

§ 7—204. Duty of Care; Contractual Limitation of Warehouseman's Liability

(1) A warehouseman is liable for damages for loss of or injury to the goods caused by his failure to exercise such care in regard to them as a reasonably careful man would exercise under like circumstances but, unless otherwise agreed, he is not liable for damages which could not have been avoided by the exercise of such care.

(2) Damages may be limited by a term in the warehouse receipt or storage agreement limiting the amount of liability in case of loss or damage, and setting forth a specific liability per article or item, or value per unit of weight, beyond which the warehouseman shall not be liable; provided, however, that such liability may on written request of the bailor at the time of signing such storage agreement or within a reasonable time after receipt of the warehouse receipt be increased on part or all of the goods thereunder, in which event increased rates may be charged based on such increased valuation, but that no such increase shall be permitted contrary to a lawful limitation of liability contained in the warehouseman's tariff, if any. No such limitation is effective with respect to the warehouseman's liability for conversion to his own use.

(3) Reasonable provisions as to the time and manner of presenting claims and instituting actions based on the bailment may be included in the warehouse receipt or tariff.

(4) This section does not impair or repeal...

Note: *Insert in subsection (4) a reference to any statute which imposes a higher responsibility upon the warehouseman or invalidates contractual limitations which would be permissible under this Article.*

§ 7—205. Title Under Warehouse Receipt Defeated in Certain Cases

A buyer in the ordinary course of business of fungible goods sold and delivered by a warehouseman who is also in the business of buying and selling such goods takes free of any claim under a warehouse receipt even though it has been duly negotiated.

§ 7—206. Termination of Storage at Warehouseman's Option

(1) A warehouseman may, on notifying the person on whose account the goods are held and any other person known to claim an interest in the goods, require payment of any charges and removal of the goods from the warehouse at the termination of the period of storage fixed by the document, or, if no period is fixed, within a stated period not less than thirty days after the notification. If the goods are not removed before the date specified in the notification, the warehouseman may sell them in accordance with the provisions of the section on enforcement of a warehouseman's lien (Section 7—210).

(2) If a warehouseman in good faith believes that the goods are about to deteriorate or decline in value to less than the amount of his lien within the time prescribed in subsection (1) for notification, advertisement and sale, the warehouseman may specify in the notification any reasonable shorter time for removal of the goods and in case the goods are not removed, may sell them at public sale held not less than one week after a single advertisement or posting.

(3) If as a result of a quality or condition of the goods of which the warehouseman had no notice at the time of deposit, the goods are a hazard to other property or to the warehouse or to persons, the warehouseman may sell the goods at public or private sale without advertisement on reasonable notification to all persons known to claim an interest in the goods. If the warehouseman after a reasonable effort is unable to sell the goods, he may dispose of them in any lawful manner and shall incur no liability by reason of such disposition.

(4) The warehouseman must deliver the goods to any person entitled to them under this Article upon due demand made at any time prior to sale or other disposition under this section.

(5) The warehouseman may satisfy his lien from the proceeds of any sale or disposition under this section but must hold the balance for delivery on the demand of any person to whom he would have been bound to deliver the goods.

§ 7—207. Goods Must Be Kept Separate; Fungible Goods

(1) Unless the warehouse receipt otherwise provides, a warehouseman must keep separate the goods covered by each receipt so as to permit at all times identification and delivery of those goods, except that different lots of fungible goods may be commingled.

(2) Fungible goods so commingled are owned in common by the persons entitled thereto, and the warehouseman is severally liable to each owner for that owner's share. Where because of overissue a mass of fungible goods is insufficient to meet all the receipts which the warehouseman has issued against it, the persons entitled include all holders to whom overissued receipts have been duly negotiated.

§ 7—208. Altered Warehouse Receipts

Where a blank in a negotiable warehouse receipt has been filled in without authority, a purchaser for value and without notice of the want of authority may treat the insertion as authorized. Any other unauthorized alteration leaves any receipt enforceable against the issuer according to its original tenor.

§ 7 — 209. Lien of Warehouseman

(1) A warehouseman has a lien against the bailor on the goods covered by a warehouse receipt or on the proceeds thereof in his possession for charges for storage or transportation (including demurrage and terminal charges), insurance, labor, or charges present or future in relation to the goods, and for expenses necessary for preservation of the goods or reasonably incurred in their sale pursuant to law. If the person on whose account the goods are held is liable for like charges or expenses in relation to other goods whenever deposited and it is stated in the receipt that a lien is claimed for charges and expenses in relation to other goods, the warehouseman also has a lien against him for such charges and expenses whether or not the other goods have been delivered by the warehouseman. But against a person to whom a negotiable warehouse receipt is duly negotiated, a warehouseman's lien is limited to charges in an amount or at a rate specified on the receipt or if no charges are so specified then to a reasonable charge for storage of the goods covered by the receipt subsequent to the date of the receipt.

(2) The warehouseman may also reserve a security interest against the bailor for a maximum amount specified on the receipt for charges other than those specified in subsection (1), such as for money advanced and interest. Such a security interest is governed by the Article on Secured Transactions (Article 9).

(3) (a) A warehouseman's lien for charges and expenses under subsection (1) or a security interest under subsection (2) is also effective against any person who so entrusted the bailor with possession of the goods that a pledge of them by him to a good faith purchaser for value would have been valid but is not effective against a person as to whom the document confers no right in the goods covered by it under Section 7 — 503.

(b) A warehouseman's lien on household goods for charges and expenses in relation to the goods under subsection (1) is also effective against all persons if the depositor was the legal possessor of the goods at the time of deposit. "Household goods" means furniture, furnishings and personal effects used by the depositor in a dwelling.

(4) A warehouseman loses his lien on any goods which he voluntarily delivers or which he unjustifiably refuses to deliver.

§ 7 — 210.   Enforcement of Warehouseman's Lien

(1) Except as provided in subsection (2), a warehouseman's lien may be enforced by public or private sale of the goods in block or in parcels, at any time or place and on any terms which are commercially reasonable, after notifying all persons known to claim an interest in the goods. Such notification must include a statement of the amount due, the nature of the proposed sale and the time and place of any public sale. The fact that a better price could have been obtained by a sale at a different time or in a different method from that selected by the warehouseman is not of itself sufficient to establish that the sale was not made in a commercially reasonable manner. If the warehouseman either sells the goods in the usual manner in any recognized market therefor, or if he sells at the price current in such market at the time of his sale, or if he has otherwise sold in conformity with commercially reasonable practices among dealers in the type of goods sold, he has sold in a commercially reasonable manner. A sale of more goods than apparently necessary to be offered to insure satisfaction of the obligation is not commercially reasonable except in cases covered by the preceding sentence.

(2) A warehouseman's lien on goods other than goods stored by a merchant in the course of his business may be enforced only as follows:

(a) All persons known to claim an interest in the goods must be notified.

(b) The notification must be delivered in person or sent by registered or certified letter to the last known address of any person to be notified.

(c) The notification must include an itemized statement of the claim, a description of the goods subject to the lien, a demand for payment within a specified time not less than ten days after receipt of the notification, and a conspicuous statement that unless the claim is paid within that time the goods will be advertised for sale and sold by auction at a specified time and place.

(d) The sale must conform to the terms of the notification.

(e) The sale must be held at the nearest suitable place to that where the goods are held or stored.

(f) After the expiration of the time given in the notification, an advertisement of the sale must be published once a week for two weeks consecutively in a newspaper of general circulation where the sale is to be held. The advertisement must include a description of the goods, the name of the person on whose account they are being held, and the time and place of the sale. The sale must take place at least fifteen days after the first publication. If there is no newspaper of general circulation where the sale is to be held, the advertisement must be posted at least ten days before the sale in not less than six conspicuous places in the neighborhood of the proposed sale.

(3) Before any sale pursuant to this section, any person claiming a right in the goods may pay the amount necessary to satisfy the lien and the reasonable expenses incurred under this section. In that event, the goods must not be sold but must be retained by the warehouseman subject to the terms of the receipt and this Article.

(4) The warehouseman may buy at any public sale pursuant to this section.

(5) A purchaser in good faith of goods sold to enforce a warehouseman's lien takes the goods free of any rights of persons against whom the lien was valid, despite noncompliance by the warehouseman with the requirements of this section.

(6) The warehouseman may satisfy his lien from the proceeds of any sale pursuant to this section but must hold the balance, if any, for delivery on demand to any person to whom he would have been bound to deliver the goods.

(7) The rights provided by this section shall be in addition to all other rights allowed by law to a creditor against his debtor.

(8) Where a lien is on goods stored by a merchant in the course of his business, the lien may be enforced in accordance with either subsection (1) or (2).

(9) The warehouseman is liable for damages caused by failure to comply with the requirements for sale under this section and, in case of willful violation, is liable for conversion.

Part 3

Bills of Lading: Special Provisions

§ 7—301. Liability for Non-Receipt or Misdescription; "Said to Contain"; "Shipper's Load and Count"; Improper Handling

(1) A consignee of a nonnegotiable bill who has given value in good faith or a holder to whom a negotiable bill has been duly negotiated relying in either case upon the description therein of the goods, or upon the date therein shown, may recover from the issuer damages caused by the misdating of the bill or the nonreceipt or misdescription of the goods, except to the extent that the document indicates that the issuer does not know whether any part or all of the goods in fact were received or conform to the description, as where the description is in terms of marks or labels or kind, quantity, or condition or the receipt or description is

qualified by "contents or condition of contents of packages unknown," "said to contain," "shipper's weight, load and count" or the like, if such indication be true.

(2) When goods are loaded by an issuer who is a common carrier, the issuer must count the packages of goods if package freight and ascertain the kind and quantity if bulk freight. In such cases, "shipper's weight, load and count" or other words indicating that the description was made by the shipper are ineffective except as to freight concealed by packages.

(3) When bulk freight is loaded by a shipper who makes available to the issuer adequate facilities for weighing such freight, an issuer who is a common carrier must ascertain the kind and quantity within a reasonable time after receiving the written request of the shipper to do so. In such cases, "shipper's weight" or other words of like purport are ineffective.

(4) The issuer may by inserting in the bill the words "shipper's weight, load and count" or other words of like purport indicate that the goods were loaded by the shipper; and if such statement be true, the issuer shall not be liable for damages caused by the improper loading. But their omission does not imply liability for such damages.

(5) The shipper shall be deemed to have guaranteed to the issuer the accuracy at the time of shipment of the description, marks, labels, number, kind, quantity, condition and weight, as furnished by him; and the shipper shall indemnify the issuer against damage caused by inaccuracies in such particulars. The right of the issuer to such indemnity shall in no way limit his responsibility and liability under the contract of carriage to any person other than the shipper.

§ 7—302. Through Bills of Lading and Similar Documents

(1) The issuer of a through bill of lading or other document embodying an undertaking to be performed in part by persons acting as its agents or by connecting carriers is liable to anyone entitled to recover on the document for any breach by such other persons or by a connecting carrier of its obligation under the document but, to the extent that the bill covers an undertaking to be performed overseas or in territory not contiguous to the continental United States or an undertaking including matters other than transportation, this liability may be varied by agreement of the parties.

(2) Where goods covered by a through bill of lading or other document embodying an undertaking to be performed in part by persons other than the issuer are received by any such person, he is subject with respect to his own performance while the goods are in his possession to the obligation of the issuer. His obligation is discharged by delivery of the goods to another such person pursuant to the document, and does not include liability for breach by any other such persons or by the issuer.

(3) The issuer of such through bill of lading or other document shall be entitled to recover from the connecting carrier or such other person in possession of the goods when the breach of the obligation under the document occurred, the amount it may be required to pay to anyone entitled to recover on the document therefor, as may be evidenced by any receipt, judgment, or transcript thereof, and the amount of any expense reasonably incurred by it in defending any action brought by anyone entitled to recover on the document therefor.

§ 7—303. Diversion; Reconsignment; Change of Instructions

(1) Unless the bill of lading otherwise provides, the carrier may deliver the goods to a person or destination other than that stated in the bill or may otherwise dispose of the goods on instructions from

(a) the holder of a negotiable bill; or

(b) the consignor on a nonnegotiable bill notwithstanding contrary instructions from the consignee; or

(c) the consignee on a nonnegotiable bill in the absence of contrary instructions from the consignor, if the goods have arrived at the billed destination or if the consignee is in possession of the bill; or

(d) the consignee on a nonnegotiable bill if he is entitled as against the consignor to dispose of them.

(2) Unless such instructions are noted on a negotiable bill of lading, a person to whom the bill is duly negotiated can hold the bailee according to the original terms.

§ 7—304. Bills of Lading in a Set

(1) Except where customary in overseas transportation, a bill of lading must not be issued in a set of parts. The issuer is liable for damages caused by violation of this subsection.

(2) Where a bill of lading is lawfully drawn in a set of parts, each of which is numbered and expressed to be valid only if the goods have not been delivered against any other part, the whole of the parts constitute one bill.

(3) Where a bill of lading is lawfully issued in a set of parts and different parts are negotiated to different persons, the title of the holder to whom the first due negotiation is made prevails as to both the document and the goods, even though any later holder may have received the goods from the carrier in good faith and discharged the carrier's obligation by surrender of his part.

(4) Any person who negotiates or transfers a single part of a bill of lading drawn in a set is liable to holders of that part as if it were the whole set.

(5) The bailee is obliged to deliver in accordance with Part 4 of this Article against the first presented part of a bill of lading lawfully drawn in a set. Such delivery discharges the bailee's obligation on the whole bill.

§ 7—305. Destination Bills

(1) Instead of issuing a bill of lading to the consignor at the place of shipment, a carrier may at the request of the consignor procure the bill to be issued at destination or at any other place designated in the request.

(2) Upon request of anyone entitled as against the carrier to control the goods while in transit and on surrender of any outstanding bill of lading or other receipt covering such goods, the issuer may procure a substitute bill to be issued at any place designated in the request.

§ 7—306. Altered Bills of Lading

An unauthorized alteration or filling in of a blank in a bill of lading leaves the bill enforceable according to its original tenor.

§ 7—307. Lien of Carrier

(1) A carrier has a lien on the goods covered by a bill of lading for charges subsequent to the date of its receipt of the goods for storage or transportation (including demurrage and terminal charges) and for expenses necessary for preservation of the goods incident to their transportation or reasonably incurred in their sale pursuant to law. But against a purchaser for value of a negotiable bill of lading, a carrier's lien is limited to charges stated in the bill or the applicable tariffs, or if no charges are stated then to a reasonable charge.

(2) A lien for charges and expenses under subsection (1) on goods which the carrier was required by law to receive for transportation is effective against the consignor or any person entitled to the goods unless the carrier had notice that the consignor lacked authority to subject the goods to such charges and expenses. Any other lien under subsection (1) is effective against the consignor and any person who permitted the bailor to have control or possession of the goods unless the carrier had notice that the bailor lacked such authority.

(3) A carrier loses his lien on any goods which he voluntarily delivers or which he unjustifiably refuses to deliver.

§ 7—308. Enforcement of Carrier's Lien

(1) A carrier's lien may be enforced by public or private sale of the goods, in block or in parcels, at any time or place and on any terms which are commercially reasonable, after notifying all persons known to claim an interest in the goods. Such notification must include a statement of the amount due, the nature of the proposed sale and the time and place of any public sale. The fact that a better price could have been obtained by a sale at a different time or in a different method from

that selected by the carrier is not of itself sufficient to establish that the sale was not made in a commercially reasonable manner. If the carrier either sells the goods in the usual manner in any recognized market therefor or if he sells at the price current in such market at the time of his sale or if he has otherwise sold in conformity with commercially reasonable practices among dealers in the type of goods sold, he has sold in a commercially reasonable manner. A sale of more goods than apparently necessary to be offered to ensure satisfaction of the obligation is not commercially reasonable except in cases covered by the preceding sentence.

(2) Before any sale pursuant to this section, any person claiming a right in the goods may pay the amount necessary to satisfy the lien and the reasonable expenses incurred under this section. In that event the goods must not be sold, but must be retained by the carrier subject to the terms of the bill and this Article.

(3) The carrier may buy at any public sale pursuant to this section.

(4) A purchaser in good faith of goods sold to enforce a carrier's lien takes the goods free of any rights of persons against whom the lien was valid, despite noncompliance by the carrier with the requirements of this section.

(5) The carrier may satisfy his lien from the proceeds of any sale pursuant to this section but must hold the balance, if any, for delivery on demand to any person to whom he would have been bound to deliver the goods.

(6) The rights provided by this section shall be in addition to all other rights allowed by law to a creditor against his debtor.

(7) A carrier's lien may be enforced in accordance with either subsection (1) or the procedure set forth in subsection (2) of Section 7—210.

(8) The carrier is liable for damages caused by failure to comply with the requirements for sale under this section and in case of willful violation is liable for conversion.

§ 7—309.   Duty of Care; Contractual Limitation of Carrier's Liability

(1) A carrier who issues a bill of lading, whether negotiable or nonnegotiable, must exercise the degree of care in relation to the goods which a reasonably careful man would exercise under like circumstances. This subsection does not repeal or change any law or rule of law which imposes liability upon a common carrier for damages not caused by its negligence.

(2) Damages may be limited by a provision that the carrier's liability shall not exceed a value stated in the document if the carrier's rates are dependent upon value and the consignor by the carrier's tariff is afforded an opportunity to declare a higher value or a value as lawfully provided in the tariff, or, where no tariff is filed, he is otherwise advised of such opportunity; but no such limitation is effective with respect to the carrier's liability for conversion to its own use.

(3) Reasonable provisions as to the time and manner of presenting claims and instituting actions based on the shipment may be included in a bill of lading or tariff.

Part 4

Warehouse Receipts and Bills of Lading: General Obligations

§ 7—401.   Irregularities in Issue of Receipt or Bill or Conduct or Issuer

The obligations imposed by this Article on an issuer apply to a document of title regardless of the fact that

(a) the document may not comply with the requirements of this Article or of any other law or regulation regarding its issue, form or content; or

(b) the issuer may have violated laws regulating the conduct of his business; or

(c) the goods covered by the document were owned by the bailee at the time the document was issued; or

(d) the person issuing the document does not come within the definition of warehouseman, if it purports to be a warehouse receipt.

§ 7—402.   Duplicate Receipt or Bill; Overissue

Neither a duplicate nor any other document of title purporting to cover goods already represented by an outstanding document of the same issuer confers any right in the goods, except as provided in the case of bills in a set, overissue of documents for fungible goods and substitutes for lost, stolen or destroyed documents. But the issuer is liable for damages caused by his overissue or failure to identify a duplicate document as such by conspicuous notation on its face.

§ 7—403.   Obligation of Warehouseman or Carrier to Deliver; Excuse

(1) The bailee must deliver the goods to a person entitled under the document who complies with subsections (2) and (3), unless and to the extent that the bailee establishes any of the following.

(a) delivery of the goods to a person whose receipt was rightful as against the claimant;

(b) damage to or delay, loss or destruction of the goods for which the bailee is not liable [, but the burden of establishing negligence in such cases is on the person entitled under the document];

Note: *The brackets in (1)(b) indicate that State enactments may differ on this point without serious damage to the principle of uniformity.*

(c) previous sale or other disposition of the goods in lawful enforcement of a lien or on warehouseman's lawful termination of storage;

(d) the exercise by a seller of his right to stop delivery pursuant to the provisions of the Article on Sales (Section 2—705);

(e) a diversion, reconsignment or other disposition pursuant to the provisions of this Article (Section 7—303) or tariff regulating such right;

(f) release, satisfaction or any other fact affording a personal defense against the claimant;

(g) any other lawful excuse.

(2) A person claiming goods covered by a document of title must satisfy the bailee's lien where the bailee so requests or where the bailee is prohibited by law from delivering the goods until the charges are paid.

(3) Unless the person claiming is one against whom the document confers no right under Sec. 7—503(1), he must surrender for cancellation or notation of partial deliveries any outstanding negotiable document covering the goods, and the bailee must cancel the document or conspicuously note the partial delivery thereon or be liable to any person to whom the document is duly negotiated.

(4) "Person entitled under the document" means holder in the case of a negotiable document, or the person to whom delivery is to be made by the terms of or pursuant to written instructions under a nonnegotiable document.

§ 7—404. No Liability for Good Faith Delivery Pursuant to Receipt or Bill

A bailee who in good faith, including observance of reasonable commercial standards, has received goods and delivered or otherwise disposed of them according to the terms of the document of title or pursuant to this Article is not liable therefor. This rule applies even though the person from whom he received the goods had no authority to procure the document or to dispose of the goods and even though the person to whom he delivered the goods had no authority to receive them.

Part 5

Warehouse Receipts and Bills of Lading: Negotiation and Transfer

§ 7—501. Form of Negotiation and Requirements of "Due Negotiation"

(1) A negotiable document of title running to the order of a named person is negotiated by his indorsement and delivery. After his indorsement in blank or to bearer, any person can negotiate it by delivery alone.

(2) (a) A negotiable document of title is also negotiated by delivery alone when by its original terms it runs to bearer.

(b) When a document running to the order of a named person is delivered to him, the effect is the same as if the document had been negotiated.

(3) Negotiation of a negotiable document of title after it has been indorsed to a specified person requires indorsement by the special indorsee as well as delivery.

(4) A negotiable document of title is "duly negotiated" when it is negotiated in the manner stated in this section to a holder who purchases it in good faith without notice of any defense against or claim to it on the part of any person and for value, unless it is established that the negotiation is not in the regular course of business or financing or involves receiving the document in settlement or payment of a money obligation.

(5) Indorsement of a nonnegotiable document neither makes it negotiable nor adds to the transferee's rights.

(6) The naming in a negotiable bill of a person to be notified of the arrival of the goods does not limit the negotiability of the bill nor constitute notice to a purchaser thereof of any interest of such person in the goods.

§ 7—502. Rights Acquired by Due Negotiation

(1) Subject to the following section and to the provisions of Section 7—205 on fungible goods, a holder to whom a negotiable document of title has been duly negotiated acquires thereby:

(a) title to the document;

(b) title to the goods;

(c) all rights accruing under the law of agency or estoppel, including rights to goods delivered to the bailee after the document was issued; and

(d) the direct obligation of the issuer to hold or deliver the goods according to the terms of the document free of any defense or claim by him except those arising under the terms of the document or under this Article. In the case of a delivery order, the bailee's obligation accrues only upon acceptance and the obligation acquired by the holder is that the issuer and any indorser will procure the acceptance of the bailee.

(2) Subject to the following section, title and rights so acquired are not defeated by any stoppage of the goods represented by the document or by surrender of such goods by the bailee, and are not impaired even though the negotiation or any prior negotiation constituted a breach of duty or even though any person has been deprived of possession of the

document by misrepresentation, fraud, accident, mistake, duress, loss, theft or conversion, or even though a previous sale or other transfer of the goods or document has been made to a third person.

§ 7—503.   Document of Title to Goods Defeated in Certain Cases

(1) A document of title confers no right in goods against a person who before issuance of the document had a legal interest or a perfected security interest in them and who neither

(a) delivered or entrusted them or any document of title covering them to the bailor or his nominee with actual or apparent authority to ship, store or sell or with power to obtain delivery under this Article (Section 7—403) or with power of disposition under this Act (Sections 2—403 and 9–307) or other statute or rule of law; nor

(b) acquiesced in the procurement by the bailor or his nominee of any document of title.

(2) Title to goods based upon an unaccepted delivery order is subject to the rights of anyone to whom a negotiable warehouse receipt or bill of lading covering the goods has been duly negotiated. Such a title may be defeated under the next section to the same extent as the rights of the issuer or a transferee from the issuer.

(3) Title to goods based upon a bill of lading issued to a freight forwarder is subject to the rights of anyone to whom a bill issued by the freight forwarder is duly negotiated; but delivery by the carrier in accordance with Part 4 of this Article pursuant to its own bill of lading discharges the carrier's obligation to deliver.

§ 7—504.   Rights Acquired in the Absence of Due Negotiation; Effect of Diversion; Seller's Stoppage of Delivery

(1) A transferee of a document, whether negotiable or nonnegotiable, to whom the document has been delivered but not duly negotiated, acquires the title and rights which his transferor had or had actual authority to convey.

(2) In the case of a nonnegotiable document, until but not after the bailee receives notification of the transfer, the rights of the transferee may be defeated

(a) by those creditors of the transferor who could treat the sale as void under Section 2—402; or

(b) by a buyer from the transferor in ordinary course of business if the bailee has delivered the goods to the buyer or received notification of his rights; or

(c) as against the bailee by good faith dealings of the bailee with the transferor.

(3) A diversion or other change of shipping instructions by the consignor in a nonnegotiable bill of lading which causes the bailee not to deliver to the consignee defeats the consignee's title to the goods if they have been delivered to a buyer in ordinary course of business and in any event defeats the consignee's rights against the bailee.

(4) Delivery pursuant to a nonnegotiable document may be stopped by a seller under Section 2—705, and subject to the requirement of due notification there provided. A bailee honoring the seller's instructions is entitled to be indemnified by the seller against any resulting loss or expense.

§ 7—505.   Indorser Not a Guarantor for Other Parties

The indorsement of a document of title issued by a bailee does not make the indorser liable for any default by the bailee or by previous indorsers.

§ 7—506.   Delivery Without Indorsement: Right to Compel Indorsement

The transferee of a negotiable document of title has a specifically enforceable right to have his transferor supply any necessary indorsement, but the transfer becomes a negotiation only as of the time the indorsement is supplied.

§ 7—507.   Warranties on Negotiation or Transfer of Receipt or Bill

Where a person negotiates or transfers a document of title for value otherwise than as a mere intermediary under the next following section, then unless otherwise agreed he warrants to his immediate purchaser only, in addition to any warranty made in selling the goods,

(a) that the document is genuine; and

(b) that he has no knowledge of any fact which would impair its validity or worth; and

(c) that his negotiation or transfer is rightful and fully effective with respect to the title to the document and the goods it represents.

§ 7—508.   Warranties of Collecting Bank as to Documents

A collecting bank or other intermediary known to be entrusted with documents on behalf of another or with collection of a draft or other claim against delivery of documents warrants by such delivery of the documents only its own good faith and authority. This rule applies even though the intermediary has purchased or made advances against the claim or draft to be collected.

§ 7—509.   Receipt or Bill: When Adequate Compliance With Commercial Contract

The question whether a document is adequate to fulfill the obligations of a contract for sale or the conditions of a credit is governed by the Articles on Sales (Article 2) and on Letters of Credit (Article 5).

Part 6

Warehouse Receipts and Bills of Lading: Miscellaneous Provisions

§ 7 — 601.   Lost and Missing Documents

(1) If a document has been lost, stolen or destroyed, a court may order delivery of the goods or issuance of a substitute document and the bailee may without liability to any person comply with such order. If the document was negotiable, the claimant must post security approved by the court to indemnify any person who may suffer loss as a result of non-surrender of the document. If the document was not negotiable, such security may be required at the discretion of the court. The court may also in its discretion order payment of the bailee's reasonable costs and counsel fees.

(2) A bailee who without court order delivers goods to a person claiming under a missing negotiable document is liable to any person injured thereby, and if the delivery is not in good faith becomes liable for conversion. Delivery in good faith is not conversion if made in accordance with a filed classification or tariff or, where no classification or tariff is filed, if the claimant posts security with the bailee in an amount at least double the value of the goods at the time of posting to indemnify any person injured by the delivery who files a notice of claim within one year after the delivery.

§ 7 — 602.   Attachment of Goods Covered by a Negotiable Document

Except where the document was originally issued upon delivery of the goods by a person who had no power to dispose of them, no lien attaches by virtue of any judicial process to goods in the possession of a bailee for which a negotiable document of title is outstanding unless the document be first surrendered to the bailee or its negotiation enjoined, and the bailee shall not be compelled to deliver the goods pursuant to process until the document is surrendered to him or impounded by the court. One who purchases the document for value without notice of the process or injunction takes free of the lien imposed by judicial process.

§ 7 — 603.   Conflicting Claims; Interpleader

If more than one person claims title or possession of the goods, the bailee is excused from delivery until he has had a reasonable time to ascertain the validity of the adverse claims or to bring an action to compel all claimants to interplead and may compel such interpleader, either in defending an action for non-delivery of the goods, or by original action, whichever is appropriate.

ARTICLE 8

INVESTMENT SECURITIES

Part 1

Short Title and General Matters

§ 8 — 101.   Short Title

This Article shall be known and may be cited as Uniform Commercial Code — Investment Securities.

§ 8 — 102.   Definitions and Index of Definitions

(1) In this Article, unless the context otherwise requires:

(a) A "certificated security" is a share, participation, or other interest in property of or an enterprise of the issuer or an obligation of the issuer which is

  (i) represented by an instrument issued in bearer or registered form;

  (ii) of a type commonly dealt in on securities exchanges or markets or commonly recognized in any area in which it is issued or dealt in as a medium for investment; and

  (iii) either one of a class or series or by its terms divisible into a class or series of shares, participations, interests, or obligations.

(b) An "uncertificated security" is a share, participation, or other interest in property or an enterprise of the issuer or an obligation of the issuer which is

  (i) not represented by an instrument and the transfer of which is registered upon books maintained for that purpose by or on behalf of the issuer;

  (ii) of a type commonly dealt in on securities exchanges or markets; and

  (iii) either one of a class or series or by its terms divisible into a class or series of shares, participations, interests, or obligations.

(c) A "security" is either a certificated or an uncertificated security. If a security is certificated, the terms "security" and "certificated security" may mean either the intangible interest, the instrument representing that interest, or both, as the context requires. A writing that is a certificated security is governed by this Article and not by Article 3, even though it also meets the requirements of that Article. This Article does not apply to money. If a certificated security has been retained by or surrendered to the issuer or its transfer agent for reasons other than registration of transfer, other temporary purpose, payment, exchange, or acquisition by the issuer, that security shall be treated as an uncertificated security for purposes of this Article.

(d) A certificated security is in "registered form" if

    (i) it specifies a person entitled to the security or the rights it represents; and

    (ii) its transfer may be registered upon books maintained for that purpose by or on behalf of the issuer, or the security so states.

(e) A certificated security is in "bearer form" if it runs to bearer according to its terms and not by reason of any indorsement.

(2) A "subsequent purchaser" is a person who takes other than by original issue.

(3) A "clearing corporation" is a corporation registered as a "clearing agency" under the federal securities laws or a corporation:

(a) at least 90 percent of whose capital stock is held by or for one or more organizations, none of which, other than a national securities exchange or association, holds in excess of 20 percent of the capital stock of the corporation, and each of which is

    (i) subject to supervision or regulation pursuant to the provisions of federal or state banking laws or state insurance laws,

    (ii) a broker or dealer or investment company registered under the federal securities laws, or

    (iii) a national securities exchange or association registered under the federal securities laws; and

(b) any remaining capital stock of which is held by individuals who have purchased it at or prior to the time of their taking office as directors of the corporation and who have purchased only so much of the capital stock as is necessary to permit them to qualify as directors.

(4) A "custodian bank" is a bank or trust company that is supervised and examined by state or federal authority having supervision over banks and is acting as custodian for a clearing corporation.

(5) Other definitions applying to this Article or to specified Parts thereof and the sections in which they appear are:

"Adverse claim." Section 8—302.

"Bona fide purchaser." Section 8—302.
"Broker." Section 8—303.
"Debtor." Section 9—105.
"Financial intermediary." Section 8—313.
"Guarantee of the
  signature." Section 8—402.
"Initial transaction
  statement." Section 8—408.
"Instruction." Section 8—308.
"Intermediary bank." Section 4—105.
"Issuer." Section 8—201.
"Overissue." Section 8—104.
"Secured Party." Section 9—105.
"Security Agreement." Section 9—105.

(6) In addition, Article 1 contains general definitions and principles of construction and interpretation applicable throughout this Article.

§ 8—103. Issuer's Lien

A lien upon a security in favor of an issuer thereof is valid against a purchaser only if:

(a) the security is certificated and the right of the issuer to the lien is noted conspicuously thereon; or

(b) the security is uncertificated and a notation of the right of the issuer to the lien is contained in the initial transaction statement sent to the purchaser or, if his interest is transferred to him other than by registration of transfer, pledge, or release, the initial transaction statement sent to the registered owner or the registered pledgee.

§ 8—104. Effect of Overissue; "Overissue"

(1) The provisions of this Article which validate a security or compel its issue or reissue do not apply to the extent that validation, issue, or reissue would result in overissue; but if:

(a) an identical security which does not constitute an overissue is reasonably available for purchase, the person entitled to issue or validation may compel the issuer to purchase the security for him and either to deliver a certificated security or to register the transfer of an uncertificated security to him, against surrender of any certificated security he holds; or

(b) a security is not so available for purchase, the person entitled to issue or validation may recover from the issuer the price he or the last purchaser for value paid for it with interest from the date of his demand.

(2) "Overissue" means the issue of securities in excess of the amount the issuer has corporate power to issue.

§ 8—105. Certificated Securities Negotiable; Statements and Instructions Not Negotiable; Presumptions

(1) Certificated securities governed by this Article are negotiable instruments.

(2) Statements (Section 8—408), notices, or the like, sent by the issuer of uncertificated securities and instructions (Section 8—308) are neither negotiable instruments nor certificated securities.

(3) In any action on a security:

(a) unless specifically denied in the pleadings, each signature on a certificated security, in a necessary indorsement, on an initial transaction statement, or on an instruction, is admitted;

(b) if the effectiveness of a signature is put in issue, the burden of establishing it is on the party claiming under the signature, but the signature is presumed to be genuine or authorized;

(c) if signatures on a certificated security are admitted or established, production of the security entitles a holder to recover on it unless the defendant establishes a defense or a defect going to the validity of the security;

(d) if signatures on an initial transaction statement are admitted or established, the facts stated in the statement are presumed to be true as of the time of its issuance; and

(e) after it is shown that a defense or defect exists, the plaintiff has the burden of establishing that he or some person under whom he claims is a person against whom the defense or defect is ineffective (Section 8—202).

§ 8—106. Applicability

The law (including the conflict of laws rules) of the jurisdiction of organization of the issuer governs the validity of a security, the effectiveness of registration by the issuer, and the rights and duties of the issuer with respect to:

(a) registration of transfer of a certificated security;

(b) registration of transfer, pledge, or release of an uncertificated security; and,

(c) sending of statements of uncertificated securities.

§ 8—107. Securities Transferable; Action for Price

(1) Unless otherwise agreed and subject to any applicable law or regulation respecting short sales, a person obligated to transfer securities may transfer any certificated security of the specified issue in bearer form or registered in the name of the transferee, or indorsed to him or in blank, or he may transfer an equivalent uncertificated security to the transferee or a person designated by the transferee.

(2) If the buyer fails to pay the price as it comes due under a contract of sale, the seller may recover the price of:

(a) certificated securities accepted by the buyer;

(b) uncertificated securities that have been transferred to the buyer or a person designated by the buyer; and

(c) other securities if efforts at their resale would be unduly burdensome or if there is no readily available market for their resale.

§ 8—108. Registration of Pledge and Release of Uncertificated Securities

A security interest in an uncertificated security may be evidenced by the registration of pledge to the secured party or a person designated by him. There can be no more than one registered pledge of an uncertificated security at any time. The registered owner of an uncertificated security is the person in whose name the security is registered, even if the security is subject to a registered pledge. The rights of a registered pledgee of an uncertificated security under this Article are terminated by the registration of release.

Part 2

Issue—Issuer

§ 8—201. "Issuer"

(1) With respect to obligations on or defenses to a security, "issuer" includes a person who:

(a) places or authorizes the placing of his name on a certificated security (otherwise than as authenticating trustee, registrar, transfer agent, or the like) to evidence that it represents a share, participation, or other interest in his property or in an enterprise, or to evidence his duty to perform an obligation represented by the certificated security;

(b) creates shares, participations, or other interests in his property or in an enterprise or undertakes obligations, which shares, participations, interests, or obligations are uncertificated securities;

(c) directly or indirectly creates fractional interests in his rights or property, which fractional interests are represented by certificated securities; or

(d) becomes responsible for or in place of any other person described as an issuer in this section.

(2) With respect to obligations on or defenses to a security, a guarantor is an issuer to the extent of his guaranty, whether or not his obligation is noted on a certificated security or on statements of uncertificated securities sent pursuant to Section 8—408.

(3) With respect to registration of transfer, pledge, or release (Part 4 of this Article), "issuer" means a person on whose behalf transfer books are maintained.

§ 8—202.   Issuer's Responsibility and Defenses; Notice of Defect or Defense

(1) Even against a purchaser for value and without notice, the terms of a security include:

(a) if the security is certificated, those stated on the security;

(b) if the security is uncertificated, those contained in the initial transaction statement sent to such purchaser or, if his interest is transferred to him other than by registration of transfer, pledge, or release, the initial transaction statement sent to the registered owner or registered pledgee; and

(c) those made part of the security by reference, on the certificated security or in the initial transaction statement, to another instrument, indenture, or document or to a constitution, statute, ordinance, rule, regulation, order or the like, to the extent that the terms referred to do not conflict with the terms stated on the certificated security or contained in the statement. A reference under this paragraph does not of itself charge a purchaser for value with notice of a defect going to the validity of the security, even though the certificated security or statement expressly states that a person accepting it admits notice.

(2) A certificated security in the hands of a purchaser for value or an uncertificated security as to which an initial transaction statement has been sent to a purchaser for value, other than a security issued by a government or governmental agency or unit, even though issued with a defect going to its validity, is valid with respect to the purchaser if he is without notice of the particular defect unless the defect involves a violation of constitutional provisions, in which case the security is valid with respect to a subsequent purchaser for value and without notice of the defect. This subsection applies to an issuer that is a government or governmental agency or unit only if either there has been substantial compliance with the legal requirements governing the issue or the issuer has received a substantial consideration for the issue as a whole or for the particular security and a stated purpose of the issue is one for which the issuer has power to borrow money or issue the security.

(3) Except as provided in the case of certain unauthorized signatures (Section 8—205), lack of genuineness of a certificated security or an initial transaction statement is a complete defense, even against a purchaser for value and without notice.

(4) All other defenses of the issuer of a certificated or uncertificated security, including nondelivery and conditional delivery of a certificated security, are ineffective against a purchaser for value who has taken without notice of the particular defense.

(5) Nothing in this section shall be construed to affect the right of a party to a "when, as and if issued" or a "when distributed" contract to cancel the contract in the event of a material change in the character of the security that is the subject of the contract or in the plan or arrangement pursuant to which the security is to be issued or distributed.

§ 8—203.   Staleness as Notice of Defects or Defenses

(1) After an act or event creating a right to immediate performance of the principal obligation represented by a certificated security or that sets a date on or after which the security is to be presented or surrendered for redemption or exchange, a purchaser is charged with notice of any defect in its issue or defense of the issuer if:

(a) the act or event is one requiring the payment of money, the delivery of certificated securities, the registration of transfer of uncertificated securities, or any of these on presentation or surrender of the certificated security, the funds or securities are available on the date set for payment or exchange, and he takes the security more than one year after that date; and

(b) the act or event is not covered by paragraph (a) and he takes the security more than 2 years after the date set for surrender or presentation or the date on which performance became due.

(2) A call that has been revoked is not within subsection (1).

§ 8—204.   Effect of Issuer's Restrictions on Transfer

A restriction on transfer of a security imposed by the issuer, even if otherwise lawful, is ineffective against any person without actual knowledge of it unless:

(a) the security is certificated and the restriction is noted conspicuously thereon; or

(b) the security is uncertificated and a notation of the restriction is contained in the initial transaction statement sent to the person or, if his interest is transferred to him other than by registration of transfer, pledge, or release, the initial transaction statement sent to the registered owner or the registered pledgee.

§ 8—205.   Effect of Unauthorized Signature on Certificated Security or Initial Transaction Statement

An unauthorized signature placed on a certificated security prior to or in the course of issue or placed on an initial transaction statement is ineffective, but the signature is effective in favor of a purchaser for value of the certificated security or a purchaser for value of an uncertificated security to whom the initial transaction statement has been sent, if the purchaser is without notice of the lack of authority and the signing has been done by:

(a) an authenticating trustee, registrar, transfer agent, or other person entrusted by the issuer with the signing of the security, or similar securities, or of initial transaction statements or the immediate preparation for signing of any of them; or

(b) an employee of the issuer, or of any of the foregoing, entrusted with responsible handling of the security or initial transaction statement.

§ 8 — 206. Completion or Alteration of Certificated Security or Initial Transaction Statement

(1) If a certificated security contains the signatures necessary to its issue or transfer but is incomplete in any other respect:

(a) any person may complete it by filling in the blanks as authorized; and

(b) even though the blanks are incorrectly filled in, the security as completed is enforceable by a purchaser who took it for value and without notice of the incorrectness.

(2) A complete certificated security that has been improperly altered, even though fraudulently, remains enforceable, but only according to its original terms.

(3) If an initial transaction statement contains the signatures necessary to its validity, but is incomplete in any other respect:

(a) any person may complete it by filling in the blanks as authorized; and

(b) even though the blanks are incorrectly filled in, the statement as completed is effective in favor of the person to whom it is sent if he purchased the security referred to therein for value and without notice of the incorrectness.

(4) A complete initial transaction statement that has been improperly altered, even though fraudulently, is effective in favor of a purchaser to whom it has been sent, but only according to its original terms.

§ 8 — 207. Rights and Duties of Issuer With Respect to Registered Owners and Registered Pledgees

(1) Prior to due presentment for registration of transfer of a certificated security in registered form, the issuer or indenture trustee may treat the registered owner as the person exclusively entitled to vote, to receive notifications, and otherwise to exercise all the rights and powers of an owner.

(2) Subject to the provisions of subsections (3), (4), and (6), the issuer or indenture trustee may treat the registered owner of an uncertificated security as the person exclusively entitled to vote, to receive

notifications, and otherwise to exercise all the rights and powers of an owner.

(3) The registered owner of an uncertificated security that is subject to a registered pledge is not entitled to registration of transfer prior to the due presentment to the issuer of a release instruction. The exercise of conversion rights with respect to a convertible uncertificated security is a transfer within the meaning of this section.

(4) Upon due presentment of a transfer instruction from the registered pledgee of an uncertificated security, the issuer shall:

(a) register the transfer of the security to the new owner free of pledge, if the instruction specifies a new owner (who may be the registered pledgee) and does not specify a pledgee;

(b) register the transfer of the security to the new owner subject to the interest of the existing pledgee, if the instruction specifies a new owner and the existing pledgee; or

(c) register the release of the security from the existing pledge and register the pledge of the security to the other pledgee, if the instruction specifies the existing owner and another pledgee.

(5) Continuity of perfection of a security interest is not broken by registration of transfer under subsection (4) (b) or by registration of release and pledge under subsection (4) (c), if the security interest is assigned.

(6) If an uncertificated security is subject to a registered pledge:

(a) any uncertificated securities issued in exchange for or distributed with respect to the pledged security shall be registered subject to the pledge;

(b) any certificated securities issued in exchange for or distributed with respect to the pledged security shall be delivered to the registered pledgee; and

(c) any money paid in exchange for or in redemption of part or all of the security shall be paid to the registered pledgee.

(7) Nothing in this Article shall be construed to affect the liability of the registered owner of a security for calls, assessments, or the like.

§ 8 — 208. Effect of Signature of Authenticating Trustee, Registrar, or Transfer Agent

(1) A person placing his signature upon a certificated security or an initial transaction statement as authenticating trustee, registrar, transfer agent, or the like, warrants to a purchaser for value of the certificated security or a purchaser for value of an uncertificated security to whom the initial transaction statement has been sent, if the purchaser is without notice of the particular defect, that:

(a) the certificated security or initial transaction statement is genuine;

(b) his own participation in the issue or registration of the transfer, pledge, or release of the security is within his capacity and within the scope of the authority received by him from the issuer; and

(c) he has reasonable grounds to believe the security is in the form and within the amount the issuer is authorized to issue.

(2) Unless otherwise agreed, a person by so placing his signature does not assume responsibility for the validity of the security in other respects.

Part 3

Transfer

§ 8—301.   Rights Acquired by Purchaser

(1) Upon transfer of a security to a purchaser (Section 8—313), the purchaser acquires the rights in the security which his transferor had or had actual authority to convey unless the purchaser's rights are limited by Section 8—302(4).

(2) A transferee of a limited interest acquires rights only to the extent of the interest transferred. The creation or release of a security interest in a security is the transfer of a limited interest in that security.

§ 8—302.   "Bona Fide Purchaser"; "Adverse Claim"; Title Acquired by Bona Fide Purchaser

(1) A "bona fide purchaser" is a purchaser for value in good faith and without notice of any adverse claim:

(a) who takes delivery of a certificated security in bearer form or in registered form, issued or indorsed to him or in blank;

(b) to whom the transfer, pledge, or release of an uncertificated security is registered on the books of the issuer; or

(c) to whom a security is transferred under the provisions of paragraph (c), (d), (i), or (g) of Section 8—313(1).

(2) "Adverse claim" includes a claim that a transfer was or would be wrongful or that a particular adverse person is the owner of or has an interest in the security.

(3) A bona fide purchaser in addition to acquiring the rights of a purchaser (Section 8—301) also acquires his interest in the security free of any adverse claim.

(4) Notwithstanding Section 8—301(1), the transferee of a particular certificated security who has been a party to any fraud or illegality affecting the security, or who as a prior holder of that certificated security had notice of an adverse claim, cannot improve his position by taking from a bona fide purchaser.

§ 8—303.   "Broker"

"Broker" means a person engaged for all or part of his time in the business of buying and selling securities, who in the transaction concerned acts for, buys a security from, or sells a security to, a customer. Nothing in this Article determines the capacity in which a person acts for purposes of any other statute or rule to which the person is subject.

§ 8—304.   Notice to Purchaser of Adverse Claims

(1) A purchaser (including a broker for the seller or buyer, but excluding an intermediary bank) of a certificated security is charged with notice of adverse claims if:

(a) the security, whether in bearer or registered form, has been indorsed "for collection" or "for surrender" or for some other purpose not involving transfer; or

(b) the security is in bearer form and has on it an unambiguous statement that it is the property of a person other than the transferor. The mere writing of a name on a security is not such a statement.

(2) A purchaser (including a broker for the seller or buyer, but excluding an intermediary bank) to whom the transfer, pledge, or release of an uncertificated security is registered is charged with notice of adverse claims as to which the issuer has a duty under Section 8—403(4) at the time of registration and which are noted in the initial transaction statement sent to the purchaser or, if his interest is transferred to him other than by registration of transfer, pledge, or release, the initial transaction statement sent to the registered owner or the registered pledgee.

(3) The fact that the purchaser (including a broker for the seller or buyer) of a certificated or uncertificated security has notice that the security is held for a third person or is registered in the name of or indorsed by a fiduciary does not create a duty of inquiry into the rightfulness of the transfer or constitute constructive notice of adverse claims. However, if the purchaser (excluding an intermediary bank) has knowledge that the proceeds are being used or the transaction is for the individual benefit of the fiduciary or otherwise in breach of duty, the purchaser is charged with notice of adverse claims.

§ 8—305.   Staleness as Notice of Adverse Claims

An act or event that creates a right to immediate performance of the principal obligation represented by a certificated security or sets a date on or after which a certificated security is to be presented or surrendered for redemption or exchange does not itself constitute any notice of adverse claims except in the case of a transfer;

(a) after one year from any date set for presentment or surrender for redemption or exchange; or

(b) after 6 months from any date set for payment of money against presentation or surrender of the security if funds are available for payment on that date.

§ 8—306. Warranties on Presentment and Transfer of Certificated Securities; Warranties of Originators of Instructions

(1) A person who presents a certificated security for registration of transfer or for payment or exchange warrants to the issuer that he is entitled to the registration, payment, or exchange. But, a purchaser for value and without notice of adverse claims who receives a new, reissued, or re-registered certificated security on registration of transfer or receives an initial transaction statement confirming the registration of transfer of an equivalent uncertificated security to him warrants only that he has no knowledge of any unauthorized signature (Section 8—311) in a necessary indorsement.

(2) A person by transferring a certificated security to a purchaser for value warrants only that:

(a) his transfer is effective and rightful;

(b) the security is genuine and has not been materially altered; and

(c) he knows of no fact which might impair the validity of the security.

(3) If a certificated security is delivered by an intermediary known to be entrusted with delivery of the security on behalf of another or with collection of a draft or other claim against delivery, the intermediary by delivery warrants only his own good faith and authority, even though he has purchased or made advances against the claim to be collected against the delivery.

(4) A pledgee or other holder for security who redelivers a certificated security received, or after payment and on order of the debtor delivers that security to a third person, makes only the warranties of an intermediary under subsection (3).

(5) A person who originates an instruction warrants to the issuer that:

(a) he is an appropriate person to originate the instruction; and

(b) at the time the instruction is presented to the issuer he will be entitled to the registration of transfer, pledge, or release.

(6) A person who originates an instruction warrants to any person specially guaranteeing his signature (subsection 8—312(3)) that:

(a) he is an appropriate person to originate the instruction; and

(b) at the time the instruction is presented to the issuer

(i) he will be entitled to the registration of transfer, pledge, or release; and

(ii) the transfer, pledge, or release requested in the instruction will be registered by the issuer free from all liens, security interests, restrictions, and claims other than those specified in the instruction.

(7) A person who originates an instruction warrants to a purchaser for value and to any person guaranteeing the instruction (Section 8—312(6)) that:

(a) he is an appropriate person to originate the instruction;

(b) the uncertificated security referred to therein is valid; and

(c) at the time the instruction is presented to the issuer

(i) the transferor will be entitled to the registration of transfer, pledge, or release;

(ii) the transfer, pledge, or release requested in the instruction will be registered by the issuer free from all liens, security interests, restrictions, and claims other than those specified in the instruction; and

(iii) the requested transfer, pledge, or release will be rightful.

(8) If a security party is the registered pledgee or the registered owner of an uncertificated security, a person who originates an instruction of release or transfer to the debtor or, after payment and on order of the debtor, a transfer instruction to a third person, warrants to the debtor or the third person only that he is an appropriate person to originate the instruction and, at the time the instruction is presented to the issuer, the transferor will be entitled to the registration of release or transfer. If a transfer instruction to a third person who is a purchaser for value is originated on order of the debtor, the debtor makes to the purchaser the warranties of paragraphs (b), (c)(ii) and (c)(iii) of subsection (7).

(9) A person who transfers an uncertificated security to a purchaser for value and does not originate an instruction in connection with the transfer warrants only that:

(a) his transfer is effective and rightful; and

(b) the uncertificated security is valid.

(10) A broker gives to his customer and to the issuer and a purchaser the applicable warranties provided in this section and has the rights and privileges of a purchaser under this section. The warranties of and in favor of the broker, acting as an agent are in addition to applicable warranties given by and in favor of his customer.

§ 8—307. Effect of Delivery Without Indorsement; Right to Compel Indorsement

If a certificated security in registered form has been delivered to a purchaser without a necessary indorsement he may become a bona fide purchaser only as of the time the indorsement is supplied; but against the transferor, the transfer is complete upon delivery and the purchaser has a specifically enforceable right to have any necessary indorsement supplied.

§ 8—308. Indorsements; Instructions

(1) An indorsement of a certificated security in

registered form is made when an appropriate person signs on it or on a separate document an assignment or transfer of the security or a power to assign or transfer it or his signature is written without more upon the back of the security.

(2) An indorsement may be in blank or special. An indorsement in blank includes an indorsement to bearer. A special indorsement specifies to whom the security is to be transferred, or who has power to transfer it. A holder may convert a blank indorsement into a special indorsement.

(3) An indorsement purporting to be only of part of a certificated security representing units intended by the issuer to be separately transferable is effective to the extent of the indorsement.

(4) An "instruction" is an order to the issuer of an uncertificated security requesting that the transfer, pledge, or release from pledge of the uncertificated security specified therein be registered.

(5) An instruction originated by an appropriate person is:

(a) a writing signed by an appropriate person; or

(b) a communication to the issuer in any form agreed upon in a writing signed by the issuer and an appropriate person.

If an instruction has been originated by an appropriate person but is incomplete in any other respect, any person may complete it as authorized and the issuer may rely on it as completed even though it has been completed incorrectly.

(6) "An appropriate person" in subsection (1) means the person specified by the certificated security or by special indorsement to be entitled to the security.

(7) "An appropriate person" in subsection (5) means:

(a) for an instruction to transfer or pledge an uncertificated security which is then not subject to a registered pledge, the registered owner; or

(b) for an instruction to transfer or release an uncertificated security which is then subject to a registered pledge, the registered pledgee.

(8) In addition to the persons designated in subsections (6) and (7), "an appropriate person" in subsections (1) and (5) includes:

(a) if the person designated is described as a fiduciary but is no longer serving in the described capacity, either that person or his successor;

(b) if the persons designated are described as more than one person as fiduciaries and one or more are no longer serving in the described capacity, the remaining fiduciary or fiduciaries, whether or not a successor has been appointed or qualified;

(c) if the person designated is an individual and is without capacity to act by virtue of

death, incompetence, infancy, or otherwise, his executor, administrator, guardian, or like fiduciary;

(d) if the persons designated are described as more than one person as tenants by the entirety or with right of survivorship and by reason of death all cannot sign, the survivor or survivors;

(e) a person having power to sign under applicable law or controlling instrument; and

(f) to the extent that the person designated or any of the foregoing persons may act through an agent, his authorized agent.

(9) Unless otherwise agreed, the indorser of a certificated security by his indorsement or the originator of an instruction by his origination assumes no obligation that the security will be honored by the issuer but only the obligations provided in Section 8—306.

(10) Whether the person signing is appropriate is determined as of the date of signing and an indorsement made by or an instruction originated by him does not become unauthorized for the purposes of this Article by virtue of any subsequent change of circumstances.

(11) Failure of a fiduciary to comply with a controlling instrument or with the law of the state having jurisdiction of the fiduciary relationship, including any law requiring the fiduciary to obtain court approval of the transfer, pledge, or release, does not render his indorsement or an instruction originated by him unauthorized for the purposes of this Article.

§ 8—309. Effect of Indorsement Without Delivery

An indorsement of a certificated security, whether special or in blank, does not constitute a transfer until delivery of the certificated security on which it appears or, if the indorsement is on a separate document, until delivery of both the document and the certificated security.

§ 8—310. Indorsement of Certificated Security in Bearer Form

An indorsement of a certificated security in bearer form may give notice of adverse claims (Section 8—304) but does not otherwise affect any right to registration the holder possesses.

§ 8—311. Effect of Unauthorized Indorsement or Instruction

Unless the owner or pledgee has ratified an unauthorized indorsement or instruction or is otherwise precluded from asserting its effectiveness:

(a) he may assert its ineffectiveness against the issuer or any purchaser, other than a purchaser for value and without notice of adverse claims, who has in good faith received a new, reissued, or re-registered certificated security on registration of transfer or received an initial transaction statement confirming the registration of transfer, pledge, or release of an equivalent uncertificated security to him; and

(b) an issuer who registers the transfer of a certificated security upon the unauthorized indorsement or who registers the transfer, pledge, or release of an uncertificated security upon the unauthorized instruction is subject to liability for improper registration (Section 8—404).

§ 8—312. Effect of Guaranteeing Signature, Indorsement or Instruction

(1) Any person guaranteeing a signature of an indorser of a certificated security warrants that at the time of signing:

(a) the signature was genuine;

(b) the signer was an appropriate person to indorse (Section 8—308); and

(c) the signer had legal capacity to sign.

(2) Any person guaranteeing a signature of the originator of an instruction warrants that at the time of signing:

(a) the signature was genuine;

(b) the signer was an appropriate person to originate the instruction (Section 8—308) if the person specified in the instruction as the registered owner or registered pledgee of the uncertificated security was, in fact, the registered owner or registered pledgee of the security, as to which fact the signature guarantor makes no warranty;

(c) the signer had legal capacity to sign; and

(d) the taxpayer identification number, if any, appearing on the instruction as that of the registered owner or registered pledgee was the taxpayer identification number of the signer or of the owner or pledgee for whom the signer was acting.

(3) Any person specially guaranteeing the signature of the originator of an instruction makes not only the warranties of a signature guarantor (subsection (2)) but also warrants that at the time the instruction is presented to the issuer:

(a) the person specified in the instruction as the registered owner or registered pledgee of the uncertificated security will be the registered owner or registered pledgee; and

(b) the transfer, pledge, or release of the uncertificated security requested in the instruction will be registered by the issuer free from all liens, security interests, restrictions, and claims other than those specified in the instruction.

(4) The guarantor under subsections (1) and (2) or the special guarantor under subsection (3) does not

otherwise warrant the rightfulness of the particular transfer, pledge, or release.

(5) Any person guaranteeing an indorsement of a certificated security makes not only the warranties of a signature guarantor under subsection (1) but also warrants the rightfulness of the particular transfer in all respects.

(6) Any person guaranteeing an instruction requesting the transfer, pledge, or release of an uncertificated security makes not only the warranties of a special signature guarantor under subsection (3) but also warrants the rightfulness of the particular transfer, pledge, or release in all respects.

(7) No issuer may require a special guarantee of signature (subsection (3)), a guarantee of indorsement (subsection (5)), or a guarantee of instruction (subsection (6)) as a condition to registration of transfer, pledge, or release.

(8) The foregoing warranties are made to any person taking or dealing with the security in reliance on the guarantee, and the guarantor is liable to the person for any loss resulting from breach of the warranties.

§ 8—313. When Transfer to Purchaser Occurs; Financial Intermediary as Bona Fide Purchaser; "Financial Intermediary"

(1) Transfer of a security or a limited interest (including a security interest) therein to a purchaser occurs only:

(a) at the time he or a person designated by him acquires possession of a certificated security;

(b) at the time the transfer, pledge, or release of an uncertificated security is registered to him or a person designated by him;

(c) at the time his financial intermediary acquires possession of a certificated security specially indorsed to or issued in the name of the purchaser;

(d) at the time a financial intermediary, not a clearing corporation, sends him confirmation of the purchase and also by book entry or otherwise identifies as belonging to the purchaser

(i) a specific certificated security in the financial intermediary's possession;

(ii) a quantity of securities that constitute or are part of a fungible bulk of certificated securities in the financial intermediary's possession or of uncertificated securities registered in the name of the financial intermediary; or

(iii) a quantity of securities that constitute or are part of a fungible bulk of securities shown on the account of the financial intermediary on the books of another financial intermediary;

(e) with respect to an identified certificated security to be delivered while still in the possession of a third person, not a financial intermediary, at the time that person acknowledges that he holds for the purchaser;

(f) with respect to a specific uncertificated security the pledge or transfer of which has been registered to a third person, not a financial intermediary, at the time that person acknowledges that he holds for the purchaser;

(g) at the time appropriate entries to the account of the purchaser or a person designated by him on the books of a clearing corporation are made under Section 8—320;

(h) with respect to the transfer of a security interest where the debtor has signed a security agreement containing a description of the security, at the time a written notification, which, in the case of the creation of the security interest, is signed by the debtor (which may be a copy of the security agreement) or which, in the case of the release or assignment of the security interest created pursuant to this paragraph, is signed by the secured party, is received by

   (i) a financial intermediary on whose books the interest of the transferor in the security appears;

   (ii) a third person, not a financial intermediary, in possession of the security, if it is certificated;

   (iii) a third person, not a financial intermediary, who is the registered owner of the security, if it is uncertificated and not subject to a registered pledge; or

   (iv) a third person, not a financial intermediary, who is the registered pledgee of the security, if it is uncertificated and subject to a registered pledge;

(i) with respect to the transfer of a security interest where the transferor has signed a security agreement containing a description of the security, at the time new value is given by the secured party: or

(j) with respect to the transfer of a security interest where the secured party is a financial intermediary and the security has already been transferred to the financial intermediary under paragraphs (a), (b), (c), (d), or (g), at the time the transferor has signed a security agreement containing a description of the security and value is given by the secured party.

(2) The purchaser is the owner of a security held for him by a financial intermediary, but cannot be a bona fide purchaser of a security so held except in the circumstances specified in paragraphs (c), (d)(i), and (g) of subsection (1). If a security so held is part of a fungible bulk, as in the circumstances specified in paragraphs (d)(ii) and (d)(iii) of subsection (1), the purchaser is the owner of aproportionate property interest in the fungible bulk.

(3) Notice of an adverse claim received by the financial intermediary or by the purchaser after the financial intermediary takes delivery of a certificated security as a holder for value or after the transfer, pledge, or release of an uncertificated security has been registered free of the claim to a financial intermediary who has given value is not effective either as to the financial intermediary or as to the purchaser. However, as between the financial intermediary and ,the purchaser the purchaser may demand transfer of an equivalent security as to which no notice of adverse claim has been received.

(4) A "financial intermediary" is a bank, broker, clearing corporation, or other person (or the nominee of any of them) which in the ordinary course of its business maintains security accounts for its customers and is acting in that capacity. A financial intermediary may have a security interest in securities held in account for its customer.

§ 8—314. Duty to Transfer, When Completed

(1) Unless otherwise agreed, if a sale of a security is made on an exchange or otherwise through brokers:

(a) the selling customer fulfills his duty to transfer at the time he:

   (i) places a certificated security in the possession of the selling broker or a person designated by the broker;

   (ii) causes an uncertificated security to be registered in the name of the selling broker or a person designated by the broker;

   (iii) if requested, causes an acknowledgment to be made to the selling broker that a certificated or uncertificated security is held for the broker; or

   (iv) places in the possession of the selling broker or of a person designated by the broker a transfer instruction for an uncertificated security, providing the issuer does not refuse to register the requested transfer if the instruction is presented to the issuer for registration within 30 days thereafter; and

(b) the selling broker, including a correspondent broker acting for a selling customer, fulfills his duty to transfer at the time he:

   (i) places a certificated security in the possession of the buying broker or a person designated by the buying broker;

(ii) causes an uncertificated security to be registered in the name of the buying broker or a person designated by the buying broker;

(iii) places in the possession of the buying broker or of a person designated by the buying broker a transfer instruction for an uncertificated security, providing the issuer does not refuse to register the requested transfer if the instruction is presented to the issuer for registration within 30 days thereafter; or

(iv) effects clearance of the sale in accordance with the rules of the exchange on which the transaction took place.

(2) Except as provided in this section or unless otherwise agreed, a transferor's duty to transfer a security under a contract of purchase is not fulfilled until he:

(a) places a certificated security in form to be negotiated by the purchaser in the possession of the purchaser or of a person designated by the purchaser;

(b) causes an uncertificated security to be registered in the name of the purchaser or a person designated by the purchaser; or

(c) if the purchaser requests, causes an acknowledgment to be made to the purchaser that a certificated or uncertificated security is held for the purchaser.

(3) Unless made on an exchange, a sale to a broker purchasing for his own account is within subsection (2) and not within subsection (1).

§ 8—315. Action Against Transferee Based Upon Wrongful Transfer

(1) Any person against whom the transfer of a security is wrongful for any reason, including his incapacity, as against anyone except a bona fide purchaser, may:

(a) reclaim possession of the certificated security wrongfully transferred;

(b) obtain possession of any new certificated security representing all or part of the same rights;

(c) compel the origination of an instruction to transfer to him or a person designated by him an uncertificated security constituting all or part of the same rights; or

(d) have damages.

(2) If the transfer is wrongful because of an unauthorized indorsement of a certificated security, the owner may also reclaim or obtain possession of the security or a new certificated security, even from a bona fide purchaser, if the ineffectiveness of the purported indorsement can be asserted against him under the provisions of this Article on unauthorized indorsements (Section 8—311).

(3) The right to obtain or reclaim possession of a certificated security or to compel the origination of a transfer instruction may be specifically enforced and the transfer of a certificated or uncertificated security enjoined and a certificated security impounded pending the litigation.

§ 8—316. Purchaser's Right to Requisites for Registration of Transfer, Pledge, or Release on Books

Unless otherwise agreed, the transferor of a certificated security or the transferor, pledgor, or pledgee of an uncertificated security on due demand must supply his purchaser with any proof of his authority to transfer, pledge, or release or with any other requisite necessary to obtain registration of the transfer, pledge, or release of the security; but if the transfer, pledge, or release is not for value, a transferor, pledgor, or pledgee need not do so unless the purchaser furnishes the necessary expenses. Failure within a reasonable time to comply with a demand made gives the purchaser the right to reject or rescind the transfer, pledge, or release.

§ 8—317. Creditors' Rights

(1) Subject to the exceptions in subsections (3) and (4), no attachment or levy upon a certificated security or any share or other interest represented thereby which is outstanding is valid until the security is actually seized by the officer making the attachment or levy, but a certificated security which has been surrendered to the issuer may be reached by a creditor by legal process at the issuer's chief executive office in the United States.

(2) An uncertificated security registered in the name of the debtor may not be reached by a creditor except by legal process at the issuer's chief executive office in the United States.

(3) The interest of a debtor in a certificated security that is in the possession of a secured party not a financial intermediary or in an uncertificated security registered in the name of a secured party not a financial intermediary (or in the name of a nominee of the secured party) may be reached by a creditor by legal process upon the secured party.

(4) The interest of a debtor in a certificated security that is in the possession of or registered in the name of a financial intermediary or in an uncertificated security registered in the name of a financial intermediary may be reached by a creditor by legal process upon the financial intermediary on whose books the interest of the debtor appears.

(5) Unless otherwise provided by law, a creditor's lien upon the interest of a debtor in a security obtained pursuant to subsection (3) or (4) is not a restraint on the transfer of the security, free of the lien, to a third party for new value; but in the event of a transfer, the lien applies to the proceeds of the transfer in the hands of the secured party or financial intermediary, subject to any claims having priority.

(6) A creditor whose debtor is the owner of a security is entitled to aid from courts of appropriate jurisdiction, by injunction or otherwise, in reaching the

security or in satisfying the claim by means allowed at law or in equity in regard to property that cannot readily be reached by ordinary legal process.

§ 8 — 318. No Conversion by Good Faith Conduct

An agent or bailee who in good faith (including observance of reasonable commercial standards if he is in the business of buying, selling, or otherwise dealing with securities) has received certificated securities and sold, pledged, or delivered them or has sold or caused the transfer or pledge of uncertificated securities over which he had control according to the instructions of his principal, is not liable for conversion or for participation in breach of fiduciary duty although the principal had no right so to deal with the securities.

§ 8 — 319. Statute of Frauds

A contract for the sale of securities is not enforceable by way of action or defense unless:

(a) there is some writing signed by the party against whom enforcement is sought or by his authorized agent or broker, sufficient to indicate that a contract has been made for sale of a stated quantity of described securities at a defined or stated price;

(b) delivery of a certificated security or transfer instruction has been accepted, or transfer of an uncertificated security has been registered and the transferee has failed to send written objection to the issuer within 10 days after receipt of the initial transaction statement confirming the registration, or payment has been made, but the contract is enforceable under this provision only to the extent of the delivery, registration, or payment;

(c) within a reasonable time a writing in confirmation of the sale or purchase and sufficient against the sender under paragraph (a) has been received by the party against whom enforcement is sought and he has failed to send written objection to its contents within 10 days after its receipt; or

(d) the party against whom enforcement is sought admits in his pleading, testimony, or otherwise in court that a contract was made for the sale of a stated quantity of described securities at a defined or stated price.

§ 8 — 320. Transfer or Pledge Within Central Depository System

(1) In addition to other methods, a transfer, pledge, or release of a security or any interest therein may be effected by the making of appropriate entries on the books of a clearing corporation reducing the account of the transferor, pledgor, or pledgee and increasing the account of the transferee, pledgee, or pledgor by the amount of the obligation or the number of shares or rights transferred, pledged, or released, if the security is shown on the account of a transferor, pledgor, or pledgee on the books of the clearing corporation; is subject to the control of the clearing corporation; and

(a) if certificated,

(i) is in the custody of the clearing corporation, another clearing corporation, a custodian bank, or a nominee of any of them; and

(ii) is in bearer form or indorsed in blank by an appropriate person or registered in the name of the clearing corporation, a custodian bank, or a nominee of any of them; or

(b) if uncertificated, is registered in the name of the clearing corporation, another clearing corporation, a custodian bank, or a nominee of any of them.

(2) Under this section entries may be made with respect to like securities or interests therein as a part of a fungible bulk and may refer merely to a quantity of a particular security without reference to the name of the registered owner, certificate or bond number, or the like, and, in appropriate cases, may be on a net basis taking into account other transfers, pledges, or releasee of the same security.

(3) A transfer under this section is effective (Section 8 — 313) and the purchaser acquires the rights of the transferor (Section 8 — 301). A pledge or release under this section is the transfer of a limited interest. If a pledge or the creation of a security interest is intended, the security interest is perfected at the time when both value is given by the pledgee and the appropriate entries are made (Section 8 — 321). A transferee or pledgee under this section may be a bona fide purchaser (Section 8 — 302).

(4) A transfer or pledge under this section is not a registration of transfer under Part 4.

(5) That entries made on the books of the clearing corporation as provided in subsection (1) are not appropriate does not affect the validity of effect of the entries or the liabilities or obligations of the clearing corporation to any person adversely affected thereby.

§ 8 — 321. Enforceability, Attachment, Perfection and Termination of Security Interests

(1) A security interest in a security is enforceable and can attach only if it is transferred to the secured party or a person designated by him pursuant to a provision of Section 8 — 313(1).

(2) A security interest so transferred pursuant to agreement by a transferor who has rights in the security to a transferee who has given value is a perfected security interest, but a security interest that has been transferred solely under paragraph (i) of Section

8—313(1) becomes unperfected after 21 days unless, within that time, the requirements for transfer under any other provision of Section 8—313(1) are satisfied.

(3) A security interest in a security is subject to the provisions of Article 9, but:

(a) no filing is required to perfect the security interest; and

(b) no written security agreement signed by the debtor is necessary to make the security interest enforceable, except as provided in paragraph (h), (i), or (j) of Section 8—313(1). The secured party has the rights and duties provided under Section 9—207, to the extent they are applicable, whether or not the security is certificated, and, if certificated, whether or not it is in his possession.

(4) Unless otherwise agreed, a security interest in a security is terminated by transfer to the debtor or a person designated by him pursuant to a provision of Section 8—313(1). If a security is thus transferred, the security interest, if not terminated, becomes unperfected unless the security is certificated and is delivered to the debtor for the purpose of ultimate sale or exchange or presentation, collection, renewal, or registration of transfer. In that case, the security interest becomes unperfected after 21 days unless, within that time, the security (or securities for which it has been exchanged) is transferred to the secured party or a person designated by him pursuant to a provision of Section 8—313(1).

Part 4
Registration

§ 8—401. Duty of Issuer to Register Transfer, Pledge, or Release

(1) If a certificated security in registered form is presented to the issuer with a request to register transfer or an instruction is presented to the issuer with a request to register transfer, pledge, or release, the issuer shall register the transfer, pledge, or release as requested if:

(a) the security is indorsed or the instruction was originated by the appropriate person or persons (Section 8—308);

(b) reasonable assurance is given that those indorsements or instructions are genuine and effective (Section 8—402);

(c) the issuer has no duty as to adverse claims or has discharged the duty (Section 8—403);

(b) any applicable law relating to the collection of taxes has been complied with; and

(e) the transfer, pledge, or release is in fact rightful or is to a bona fide purchaser.

(2) If an issuer is under a duty to register a transfer, pledge, or release of a security, the issuer is also liable to the person presenting a certificated security or an instruction for registration or his principal for loss resulting from any unreasonable delay in registration or from failure or refusal to register the transfer, pledge, or release.

§ 8—402. Assurance that Indorsements and Instructions Are Effective

(1) The issuer may require the following assurance that each necessary indorsement of a certificated security or each instruction (Section 8—308) is genuine and effective:

(a) in all cases, a guarantee of the signature (Section 8—312(1) or (2)) of the person indorsing a certificated security or originating an instruction including, in the case of an instruction, a warranty of the taxpayer identification number or, in the absence thereof, other reasonable assurance of identity;

(b) if the indorsement is made or the instruction is originated by an agent, appropriate assurance of authority to sign;

(c) if the indorsement is made or the instruction is originated by a fiduciary, appropriate evidence of appointment or incumbency;

(d) if there is more than one fiduciary, reasonable assurance that all who are required to sign have done so; and

(e) if the indorsement is made or the instruction is originated by a person not covered by any of the foregoing, assurance appropriate to the case corresponding as nearly as may be to the foregoing.

(2) A "guarantee of the signature" in subsection (1) means a guarantee signed by or on behalf of a person reasonably believed by the issuer to be responsible. The issuer may adopt standards with respect to responsibility if they are not manifestly unreasonable.

(3) "Appropriate evidence of appointment or incumbency" in subsection (1) means:

(a) in the case of a fiduciary appointed or qualified by a court, a certificate issued by or under the direction or supervision of that court or an officer thereof and dated within 60 days before the date of presentation for transfer, pledge, or release; or

(b) in any other case, a copy of a document showing the appointment or a certificate issued by or on behalf of a person reasonably believed by the issuer to be responsible or, in the absence of that document or certificate, other evidence reasonably deemed by the issuer to be appropriate. The issuer may adopt standards with respect to the evidence if they are not manifestly unreasonable. The issuer is not charged with notice of the contents of any document obtained pursuant to this paragraph (b) except to the extent that the contents relate directly to the appointment or incumbency.

(4) The issuer may elect to require reasonable assurance beyond that specified in this section, but if it does so and, for a purpose other than that specified in subsection (3) (b), both requires and obtains a copy of a will, trust, indenture, articles of co-partnership, by-laws, or other controlling instrument, it is charged with notice of all matters contained therein affecting the transfer, pledge, or release.

§ 8—403. Issuer's Duty as to Adverse Claims

(1) An issuer to whom a certificated security is presented for registration shall inquire into adverse claims if:

(a) a written notification of an adverse claim is received at a time and in a manner affording the issuer a reasonable opportunity to act on it prior to the issuance of a new, reissued, or re-registered certificated security, and the notification identifies the claimant, the registered owner, and the issue of which the security is a part, and provides an address for communications directed to the claimant; or

(b) the issuer is charged with notice of an adverse claim from a controlling instrument it has elected to require under Section 8—402(4).

(2) The issuer may discharge any duty of inquiry by any reasonable means, including notifying an adverse claimant by registered or certified mail at the address furnished by him or, if there be no such address, at his residence or regular place of business that the certificated security has been presented for registration of transfer by a named person, and that the transfer will be registered unless within 30 days from the date of mailing the notification, either:

(a) an appropriate restraining order, injunction, or other process issues from a court of competent jurisdiction; or

(b) there is filed with the issuer an indemnity bond, sufficient in the issuer's judgment to protect the issuer and any transfer agent, registrar, or other agent of the issuer involved from any loss it or they may suffer by complying with the adverse claim.

(3) Unless an issuer is charged with notice of an adverse claim from a controlling instrument which it has elected to require under Section 8—402(4) or receives notification of an adverse claim under sub-

section (1), if a certificated security presented for registration is indorsed by the appropriate person or persons the issuer is under no duty to inquire into adverse claims. In particular:

(a) an issuer registering a certificated security in the name of a person who is a fiduciary or who is described as a fiduciary is not bound to inquire into the existence, extent, or correct description of the fiduciary relationship; and thereafter the issuer may assume without inquiry that the newly registered owner continues to be the fiduciary until the issuer receives written notice that the fiduciary is no longer acting as such with respect to the particular security;

(b) an issuer registering transfer on an indorsement by a fiduciary is not bound to inquire whether the transfer is made in compliance with a controlling instrument or with the law of the state having jurisdiction of the fiduciary relationship, including any law requiring the fiduciary to obtain court approval of the transfer; and

(c) the issuer is not charged with notice of the contents of any court record or file or other recorded or unrecorded document even though the document is in its possession and even though the transfer is made on the indorsement of a fiduciary to the fiduciary himself or to his nominee.

(4) An issuer is under no duty as to adverse claims with respect to an uncertificated security except:

(a) claims embodied in a restraining order, injunction, or other legal process served upon the issuer if the process was served at a time and in a manner affording the issuer a reasonable opportunity to act on it in accordance with the requirements of subsection (5);

(b) claims of which the issuer has received a written notification from the registered owner or the registered pledgee if the notification was received at a time and in a manner affording the issuer a reasonable opportunity to act on it in accordance with the requirements of subsection (5);

(c) claims (including restrictions on transfer not imposed by the issuer) to which the registration of transfer to the present registered owner was subject and were so noted in the initial transaction statement sent to him; and

(d) claims as to which an issuer is charged with notice from a controlling instrument it has elected to require under Section 8—402(4).

(5) If the issuer of an uncertificated security is under a duty as to an adverse claim, he discharges that duty by:

(a) including a notation of the claim in any statements sent with respect to the security under Sections 8—408(3), (6), and (7); and

(b) refusing to register the transfer or pledge of the security unless the nature of the claim does not preclude transfer or pledge subject thereto.

(6) If the transfer or pledge of the security is registered subject to an adverse claim, a notation of the claim must be included in the initial transaction statement and all subsequent statements sent to the transferee and pledgee under Section 8—408.

(7) Notwithstanding subsections (4) and (5), if an uncertificated security was subject to a registered pledge at the time the issuer first came under a duty as to a particular adverse claim, the issuer has no duty as to that claim if transfer of the security is requested by the registered pledgee or an appropriate person acting for the registered pledgee unless:

(a) the claim was embodied in legal process which expressly provides otherwise;

(b) the claim was asserted in a written notification from the registered pledgee;

(c) the claim was one as to which the issuer was charged with notice from a controlling instrument it required under Section 8—402(4) in connection with the pledgee's request for transfer; or

(d) the transfer requested is to the registered owner.

§ 8—404. Liability and Non-Liability for Registration

(1) Except as provided in any law relating to the collection of taxes, the issuer is not liable to the owner, pledgee, or any other person suffering loss as a result of the registration of a transfer, pledge, or release of a security if:

(a) there were on or with a certificated security the necessary indorsements or the issuer had received an instruction originated by an appropriate person (Section 8—308); and

(b) the issuer had no duty as to adverse claims or has discharged the duty (Section 8—403).

(2) If an issuer has registered a transfer of a certificated security to a person not entitled to it, the issuer on demand shall deliver a like security to the true owner unless:

(a) the registration was pursuant to subsection (1);

(b) the owner is precluded from asserting any claim for registering the transfer under Section 8—405(1); or

(c) the delivery would result in overissue, in which case the issuer's liability is governed by Section 8—104.

(3) If an issuer has improperly registered a transfer, pledge, or release of an uncertificated security, the issuer on demand from the injured party shall restore the records as to the injured party to the condition that would have obtained if the improper registration had not been made unless:

(a) the registration was pursuant to subsection (1); or

(b) the registration would result in overissue, in which case the issuer's liability is governed by Section 8—104.

§ 8—405. Lost, Destroyed, and Stolen Certificated Securities

(1) If a certificated security has been lost, apparently destroyed, or wrongfully taken, and the owner fails to notify the issuer of that fact within a reasonable time after he has notice of it and the issuer registers a transfer of the security before receiving notification, the owner is precluded from asserting against the issuer any claim for registering the transfer under Section 8—404 or any claim to a new security under this section.

(2) If the owner of a certificated security claims that the security has been lost, destroyed, or wrongfully taken, the issuer shall issue a new certificated security or, at the option of the issuer, an equivalent uncertificated security in place of the original security if the owner:

(a) so requests before the issuer has notice that the security has been acquired by a bona fide purchaser;

(b) files with the issuer a sufficient indemnity bond; and

(c) satisfies any other reasonable requirements imposed by the issuer.

(3) If, after the issue of a new certificated or uncertificated security, a bona fide purchaser of the original certificated security presents it for registration of transfer, the issuer shall register the transfer unless registration would result in overissue, in which event the issuer's liability is governed by Section 8—104. In addition to any rights on the indemnity bond, the issuer may recover the new certificated security from the person to whom it was issued or any person taking under him except a bona fide purchaser or may cancel the uncertificated security unless a bona fide purchaser or any person taking under a bona fide purchaser is then the registered owner or registered pledgee thereof.

§ 8—406. Duty of Authenticating Trustee, Transfer Agent, or Registrar

(1) If a person acts as authenticating trustee, transfer agent, registrar, or other agent for an issuer in the registration of transfers of its certificated securities or in the registration of transfers, pledges, and releases of its uncertificated securities, in the issue of new securities, or in the cancellation of surrendered securities:

(a) he is under a duty to the issuer to exercise good faith and due diligence in performing his functions; and

(b) with regard to the particular functions he performs, he has the same obligation to the holder or owner of a certificated security or to the owner or pledgee of an uncertificated security and has the same rights and privileges as the issuer has in regard to those functions.

(2) Notice to an authenticating trustee, transfer agent, registrar or other agent is notice to the issuer with respect to the functions performed by the agent.

§ 8 — 407. Exchangeability of Securities

(1) No issuer is subject to the requirements of this section unless it regularly maintains a system for issuing the class of securities involved under which both certificated and uncertificated securities are regularly issued to the category of owners, which includes the person in whose name the new security is to be registered.

(2) Upon surrender of a certificated security with all necessary indorsements and presentation of a written request by the person surrendering the security, the issuer, if he has no duty as to adverse claims or has discharged the duty (Section 8 — 403), shall issue to the person or a person designated by him an equivalent uncertificated security subject to all liens, restrictions, and claims that were noted on the certificated security.

(3) Upon receipt of a transfer instruction originated by an appropriate person who so requests, the issuer of an uncertificated security shall cancel the uncertificated security and issue an equivalent certificated security on which must be noted conspicuously any liens and restrictions of the issuer and any adverse claims (as to which the issuer has a duty under Section 8 — 403(4)) to which the uncertificated security was subject. The certificated security shall be registered in the name of and delivered to:

(a) the registered owner, if the uncertificated security was not subject to a registered pledge; or

(b) the registered pledgee, if the uncertificated security was subject to a registered pledge.

§ 8 — 408. Statements of Uncertificated Securities

(1) Within 2 business days after the transfer of an uncertificated security has been registered, the issuer shall send to the new registered owner and, if the security has been transferred subject to a registered pledge, to the registered pledgee a written statement containing:

(a) a description of the issue of which the uncertificated security is a part;

(b) the number of shares or units transferred;

(c) the name and address and any taxpayer identification number of the new regis-

tered owner and, if the security has been transferred subject to a registered pledge, the name and address and any taxpayer identification number of the registered pledgee;

(d) a notation of any liens and restrictions of the issuer and any adverse claims (as to which the issuer has a duty under Section 8 — 403(4)) to which the uncertificated security is or may be subject at the time of registration or a statement that there are none of those liens, restrictions, or adverse claims; and

(e) the date the transfer was registered.

(2) Within 2 business days after the pledge of an uncertificated security has been registered, the issuer shall send to the registered owner and the registered pledgee a written statement containing:

(a) a description of the issue of which the uncertificated security is a part;

(b) the number of shares or units pledged;

(c) the name and address and any taxpayer identification number of the registered owner and the registered pledgee;

(d) a notation of any liens and restrictions of the issuer and any adverse claims (as to which the issuer has a duty under Section 8 — 403(4) to which the uncertificated security is or may be subject at the time of registration or a statement that there are none of those liens, restrictions, or adverse claims; and

(e) the date the pledge was registered.

(3) Within 2 business days after the release from pledge of an uncertificated security has been registered, the issuer shall send to the registered owner and the pledgee whose interest was released a written statement containing:

(a) a description of the issue of which the uncertificated security is a part;

(b) the number of shares or units released from pledge;

(c) the name and address and any taxpayer identification number of the registered owner and the pledgee whose interest was released;

(d) a notation of any liens and restrictions of the issuer and any adverse claims (as to which the issuer has a duty under Section 8 — 403(4)) to which the uncertificated security is or may be subject at the time of registration or a statement that there are none of those liens, restrictions, or adverse claims; and

(e) the date the release was registered.

(4) An "initial transaction statement" is the statement sent to:

(a) the new registered owner and, if applicable, to the registered pledgee pursuant to subsection (1);

(b) the registered pledgee pursuant to subsection (2); or

(c) the registered owner pursuant to subsection (3).

Each initial transaction statement shall be signed by or on behalf of the issuer and must be identified as "Initial Transaction Statement."

(5) Within 2 business days after the transfer of an uncertificated security has been registered, the issuer shall send to the former registered owner and the former registered pledgee, if any, a written statement containing:

(a) a description of the issue of which the uncertificated security is a part;

(b) the number of shares or units transferred;

(c) the name and address and any taxpayer identification number of the former registered owner and of any former registered pledgee; and

(d) the date the transfer was registered.

(6) At periodic intervals no less frequent than annually and at any time upon the reasonable written request of the registered owner, the issuer shall send to the registered owner of each uncertificated security a dated written statement containing:

(a) a description of the issue of which the uncertificated security is a part;

(b) the name and address and any taxpayer identification number of the registered owner;

(c) the number of shares or units of the uncertificated security registered in the name of the registered owner on the date of the statement;

(d) the name and address and any taxpayer identification number of any registered pledgee and the number of shares or units subject to the pledge; and

(e) a notation of any liens and restrictions of the issuer and any adverse claims (as

to which the issuer has a duty under Section 8 — 403(4)) to which the uncertificated security is or may be subject or a statement that there are none of those liens, restrictions, or adverse claims.

(7) At periodic intervals no less frequent than annually and at any time upon the reasonable written request of the registered pledgee, the issuer shall send to the registered pledgee of each uncertificated security a dated written statement containing:

(a) a description of the issue of which the uncertificated security is a part;

(b) the name and address and any taxpayer identification number of the registered owner;

(c) the name and address and any taxpayer identification number of the registered pledgee;

(d) the number of shares or units subject to the pledge; and

(e) a notation of any liens and restrictions of the issuer and any adverse claims (as to which the issuer has a duty under Section 8 — 403(4)) to which the uncertificated security is or may be subject or a statement that there are none of those liens, restrictions, or adverse claims.

(8) If the issuer sends the statements described in subsections (6) and (7) at periodic intervals no less frequent than quarterly, the issuer is not obliged to send additional statements upon request unless the owner or pledgee requesting them pays to the issuer the reasonable cost of furnishing them.

(9) Each statement sent pursuant to this section must bear a conspicuous legend reading substantially as follows: "This statement is merely a record of the rights of the addressee as of the time of its issuance. Delivery of this statement, of itself, confers no rights on the recipient. This statement is neither a negotiable instrument nor a security."

ARTICLE 9

SECURED TRANSACTIONS; SALES OF ACCOUNTS AND CHATTEL PAPER

Part 1

Short Title, Applicability and Definitions

§ 9 — 101. Short Title

This Article shall be known and may be cited as Uniform Commercial Code — Secured Transactions.

§ 9 — 102. Policy and Subject Matter of Article

(1) Except as otherwise provided in Section 9 — 104 on excluded transactions, this Article applies

(a) to any transaction (regardless of its form) which is intended to create a security interest in personal property or fixtures including goods, documents, instruments, general intangibles, chattel paper or accounts; and also

(b) to any sale of accounts or chattel paper.

(2) This Article applies to security interests created by contract including pledge, assignment, chattel mortgage, chattel trust, trust deed, factor's lien, equipment trust, conditional sale, trust receipt, other lien or title retention contract and lease or consignment in-

tended as security. This Article does not apply to statutory liens except as provided in Section 9—310.

(3) The application of this Article to a security interest in a secured obligation is not affected by the fact that the obligation is itself secured by a transaction or interest to which this Article does not apply.

Note: *The adoption of this article should be accompanied by the repeal of existing statutes dealing with conditional sales, trust receipts, factor's liens where the factor is given a nonpossessory lien, chattel mortgages, crop mortgages, mortgages on railroad equipment, assignment of accounts and generally statutes regulating security interests in personal property.*

Where the state has a retail installment selling act or small loan act, that legislation should be carefully examined to determine what changes in those acts are needed to conform them to this Article. This Article primarily sets out rules defining rights of a secured party against persons dealing with the debtor; it does not prescribe regulations and controls which may be necessary to curb abuses arising in the small loan business or in the financing of consumer purchases on credit. Accordingly there is no intention to repeal existing regulatory acts in those fields by enactment or re-enactment of Article 9. See Section 9—203(4) and the Note thereto.

§ 9—103. Perfection of Security Interests in Multiple State Transactions

(1) Documents, instruments and ordinary goods.

(a) This subsection applies to documents and instruments and to goods other than those covered by a certificate of title described in subsection (2), mobile goods described in subsection (3), and minerals described in subsection (5).

(b) Except as otherwise provided in this subsection, perfection and the effect of perfection or non-perfection of a security interest in collateral are governed by the law of the jurisdiction where the collateral is when the last event occurs on which is based the assertion that the security interest is perfected or unperfected.

(c) If the parties to a transaction creating a purchase money security interest in goods in one jurisdiction understand at the time that the security interest attaches that the goods will be kept in another jurisdiction, then the law of the other jurisdiction governs the perfection and the effect of perfection or non-perfection of the security interest from the time it attaches until thirty days after the debtor receives possession of the goods and thereafter if the goods are taken to the other jurisdiction before the end of the thirty-day period.

(d) When collateral is brought into and kept in this state while subject to a security interest perfected under the law of the jurisdiction from which the collateral was removed, the security interest remains perfected, but if action is required by Part 3 of this Article to perfect the security interest,

(i) if the action is not taken before the expiration of the period of perfection in the other jurisdiction or the end of four months after the collateral is brought into this state, whichever period first expires, the security interest becomes unperfected at the end of that period and is thereafter deemed to have been unperfected as against a person who became a purchaser after removal;

(ii) if the action is taken before the expiration of the period specified in subparagraph (i), the security interest continues perfected thereafter;

(iii) for the purpose of priority over a buyer of consumer goods (subsection (2) of Section 9—307), the period of the effectiveness of a filing in the jurisdiction from which the collateral is removed is governed by the rules with respect to perfection in subparagraphs (i) and (ii).

(2) Certificate of title.

(a) This subsection applies to goods covered by a certificate of title issued under a statute of this state or of another jurisdiction under the law of which indication of a security interest on the certificate is required as a condition of perfection.

(b) Except as otherwise provided in this subsection, perfection and the effect of perfection or non-perfection of the security interest are governed by the law (including the conflict of laws rules) of the jurisdiction issuing the certificate until four months after the goods are removed from that jurisdiction and thereafter until the goods are registered in another jurisdiction, but in any event not beyond surrender of the certificate. After the expiration of that period, the goods are not covered by the certificate of title within the meaning of this section.

(c) Except with respect to the rights of a buyer described in the next paragraph, a security interest, perfected in another jurisdiction otherwise than by notation on a certificate of title, in goods brought into this state and thereafter covered by a certificate of title issued by this state is subject to the rules stated in paragraph (d) of subsection (1).

(d) If goods are brought into this state while a security interest therein is perfected in any manner under the law of the jurisdiction from which the goods are removed and a certificate of title is issued by this state and the certificate does not show that the goods are subject to the security interest or that they may be subject to security interests not shown on the certificate, the security interest is subordinate to the rights of a buyer of the goods who is not in the business of selling goods of that kind to the extent that he gives value and receives delivery of the goods after issuance of the certificate and without knowledge of the security interest.

(3) Accounts, general intangibles and mobile goods.

(a) This subsection applies to accounts (other than an account described in subsection (5) on minerals) and general intangibles (other than uncertificated securities) and to goods which are mobile and which are of a type normally used in more than one jurisdiction, such as motor vehicles, trailers, rolling stock, airplanes, shipping containers, road building and construction machinery and commercial harvesting machinery and the like, if the goods are equipment or are inventory leased or held for lease by the debtor to others, and are not covered by a certificate of title described in subsection (2).

(b) The law (including the conflict of laws rules) of the jurisdiction in which the debtor is located governs the perfection and the effect of perfection or non-perfection of the security interest.

(c) If, however, the debtor is located in a jurisdiction which is not a part of the United States, and which does not provide for perfection of the security interest by filing or recording in that jurisdiction, the law of the jurisdiction in the United States in which the debtor has its major executive office in the United States governs the perfection and the effect of perfection or non-perfection of the security interest through filing. In the alternative, if the debtor is located in a jurisdiction which is not a part of the United States or Canada and the collateral is accounts or general intangibles for money due or to become due, the security interest may be perfected by notification to the account debtor. As used in this paragraph, "United States" includes its territories and possessions and the Commonwealth of Puerto Rico.

(d) A debtor shall be deemed located at his place of business if he has one, at his chief executive office if he has more than one place of business, otherwise at his residence. If, however, the debtor is a foreign air carrier under the Federal Aviation Act of 1958, as amended, it shall be deemed located at the designated office of the agent upon whom service of process may be made on behalf of the foreign air carrier.

(e) A security interest perfected under the law of the jurisdiction of the location of the debtor is perfected until the expiration of four months after a change of the debtor's location to another jurisdiction, or until perfection would have ceased by the law of the first jurisdiction, whichever period first expires. Unless perfected in the new jurisdiction before the end of that period, it becomes unperfected thereafter and is deemed to have been unperfected as against a person who became a purchaser after the change.

(4) Chattel paper.

The rules stated for goods in subsection (1) apply to a possessory security interest in chattel paper. The rules stated for accounts in subsection (3) apply to a non-possessory security interest in chattel paper, but the security interest may not be perfected by notification to the account debtor.

(5) Minerals.

Perfection and the effect of perfection or non-perfection of a security interest which is created by a debtor who has an interest in minerals or the like (including oil and gas) before extraction and which attaches thereto as extracted, or which attaches to an account resulting from the sale thereof at the wellhead or minehead are governed by the law (including the conflict of laws rules) of the jurisdiction wherein the wellhead or minehead is located.

(6) Uncertificated securities.

The law (including the conflict of laws rules) of the jurisdiction of organization of the issuer governs the perfection and the effect of perfection or non-perfection of a security interest in uncertificated securities.

§ 9—104. Transactions Excluded from Article

This Article does not apply

(a) to a security interest subject to any statute of the United States, to the extent that such statute governs the rights of parties to and third parties affected by transactions in particular types of property; or

(b) to a landlord's lien; or

(c) to a lien given by statute or other rule of law for services or materials except as provided in Section 9—310 on priority of such liens; or

(d) to a transfer of a claim for wages, salary or other compensation of an employee; or

(e) to a transfer by a government or governmental subdivision or agency; or

(f) to a sale of accounts or chattel paper as part of a sale of the business out of which they arose, or an assignment of accounts or chattel paper which is for the purpose of collection only, or a transfer of a right to payment under a contract to an assignee who is also to do the performance under the contract or a transfer of a single account to an assignee in whole or partial satisfaction of a preexisting indebtedness; or

(g) to a transfer of an interest in or claim in or under any policy of insurance, except as provided with respect to proceeds (Section 9—306) and priorities in proceeds (Section 9—312); or

(h) to a right represented by a judgment (other than a judgment taken on a right to payment which was collateral); or

(i) to any right of setoff; or

(j) except to the extent that provision is made for fixtures in Section 9—313, to the creation or transfer of an interest in or lien on real estate, including a lease or rents thereunder; or

(k) to a transfer in whole or in part of any claim arising out of tort; or

(l) to a transfer of an interest in any deposit account (subsection (1) of Section 9—105), except as provided with respect to proceeds (Section 9—306) and priorities in proceeds (Section 9—312).

§ 9—105. Definitions and Index of Definitions

(1) In this Article unless the context otherwise requires:

(a) "Account debtor" means the person who is obligated on an account, chattel paper or general intangible;

(b) "Chattel paper" means a writing or writings which evidence both a monetary obligation and a security interest in or a lease of specific goods, but a charter or other contract involving the use or hire of a vessel is not chattel paper. When a transaction is evidenced both by such a security agreement or a lease and by an instrument or a series of instruments, the group of writings taken together constitutes chattel paper;

(c) "Collateral" means the property subject to a security interest, and includes accounts and chattel paper which have been sold;

(d) "Debtor" means the person who owes payment or other performance of the obligation secured, whether or not he owns or has rights in the collateral, and includes the seller of accounts or chattel paper. Where the debtor and the owner of the collateral are not the same person, the term "debtor" means the owner of the collateral in any provision of the article dealing with the collateral, the obligor in any provision dealing with the obligation, and may include both where the context so requires;

(e) "Deposit account" means a demand, time, savings, passbook or like account maintained with a bank, savings and loan association, credit union or like organization, other than an account evidenced by a certificate of deposit;

(f) "Document" means document of title as defined in the general definitions of Article 1 (Section 1—201), and a receipt of the kind described in subsection (2) of Section 7—201;

(g) "Encumbrance" includes real estate mortgages and other liens on real estate and all other rights in real estate that are not ownership interests;

(h) "Goods" includes all things which are movable at the time the security interest attaches or which are fixtures (Section 9—313), but does not include money, documents, instruments, accounts, chattel paper, general intangibles, or minerals or the like (including oil and gas) before extraction. "Goods" also includes standing timber which is to be cut and removed under a conveyance or contract for sale, the unborn young of animals, and growing crops;

(i) "Instrument" means a negotiable instrument (defined in Section 3—104), or a certificated security (defined in Section 8—102) or any other writing which evidences a right to the payment of money and is not itself a security agreement or lease and is of a type which is in ordinary course of business transferred by delivery with any necessary indorsement or assignment;

(j) "Mortgage" means a consensual interest created by a real estate mortgage, a trust deed on real estate, or the like;

(k) An advance is made "pursuant to commitment" if the secured party has bound himself to make it, whether or not a subsequent event of default or other event not within his control has relieved or may relieve him from his obligation;

(l) "Security agreement" means an agreement which creates or provides for a security interest;

(m) "Secured party" means a lender, seller or other person in whose favor there is a security interest, including a person to whom accounts or chattel paper have been sold. When the holders of obligations issued under an indenture of trust, equipment trust agreement or the like are represented by a trustee or other person, the representative is the secured party;

(n) "Transmitting utility" means any person primarily engaged in the railroad, street railway or trolley bus business, the electric or electronics communications transmission business, the transmission of goods by pipeline, or the transmission or the production and transmission of electricity, steam, gas or water, or the provision of sewer service.

(2) Other definitions applying to this Article and the sections in which they appear are:

"Account."	Section 9—106.
"Attach."	Section 9—203.
"Construction mortgage."	Section 9—313(1).
"Consumer goods."	Section 9—109(1).
"Equipment."	Section 9—109(2).
"Farm products."	Section 9—109(3).
"Fixture."	Section 9—313(1).
"Fixture filing."	Section 9—313(1).
"General intangibles."	Section 9—106.
"Inventory."	Section 9—109(4).
"Lien creditor."	Section 9—301(3).
"Proceeds."	Section 9—306(1).
"Purchase money security interest."	Section 9—107.
"United States."	Section 9—103.

(3) The following definitions in other Articles apply to this Article:

"Check."	Section 3—104.
"Contract for sale."	Section 2—106.
"Holder in due course."	Section 3—302.
"Note."	Section 3—104.
"Sale."	Section 2—106.

(4) In addition Article 1 contains general definitions and principles of construction and interpretation applicable throughout this Article.

§ 9—106. Definitions: "Account"; "General Intangibles"

"Account" means any right to payment for goods sold or leased or for services rendered which is not evidenced by an instrument or chattel paper, whether or not it has been earned by performance. "General intangibles" means any personal property (including things in action) other than goods, accounts, chattel paper, documents, instruments, and money. All rights to payment earned or unearned under a charter or other contract involving the use or hire of a vessel and all rights incident to the charter or contract are accounts.

§ 9—107. Definitions: "Purchase Money Security Interest"

A security interest is a "purchase money security interest" to the extent that it is

(a) taken or retained by the seller of the collateral to secure all or part of its price; or

(b) taken by a person who, by making advances or incurring an obligation, gives value to enable the debtor to acquire rights in or the use of collateral, if such value is in fact so used.

§ 9—108. When After-Acquired Collateral Not Security for Antecedent Debt

Where a secured party makes an advance, incurs an obligation, releases a perfected security interest, or otherwise gives new value which is to be secured in whole or in part by after-acquired property, his security interest in the after-acquired collateral shall be deemed to be taken for new value and not as security for an antecedent debt if the debtor acquires his rights in such collateral either in the ordinary course of his business or under a contract of purchase made pursuant to the security agreement within a reasonable time after new value is given.

§ 9—109. Classification of Goods; "Consumer Goods"; "Farm Products"; "Inventory"

Goods are

(1) "consumer goods" if they are used or bought for use primarily for personal, family or household purposes;

(2) "equipment" if they are used or bought for use primarily in business (including farming or a profession) or by a debtor who is a non-profit organization or a governmental subdivision or agency or if the goods are not included in the definitions of inventory, farm products or consumer goods;

(3) "farm products" if they are crops or livestock or supplies used or produced in farming operations or if they are products of crops or livestock in their unmanufactured states (such as ginned cotton, woolclip, maple syrup, milk and eggs) and if they are in the possession of a debtor engaged in raising, fattening, grazing or other farming operations. If goods are farm products, they are neither equipment nor inventory;

(4) "inventory" if they are held by a person who holds them for sale or lease or to be furnished under

contracts of service or if he has so furnished them, or if they are raw materials, work in process or materials used or consumed in a business. Inventory of a person is not to be classified as his equipment.

§ 9 — 110. Sufficiency of Description

For the purposes of this Article, any description of personal property or real estate is sufficient whether or not it is specific if it reasonably identifies what is described.

§ 9 — 111. Applicability of Bulk Transfer Laws

The creation of a security interest is not a bulk transfer under Article 6 (see Section 6 — 103).

§ 9 — 112. Where Collateral Is Not Owned by Debtor

Unless otherwise agreed, when a secured party knows that collateral is owned by a person who is not the debtor, the owner of the collateral is entitled to receive from the secured party any surplus under Section 9 — 502(2) or under Section 9 — 504(1), and is not liable for the debt or for any deficiency after resale, and he has the same right as the debtor

    (a) to receive statements under Section 9 — 208;

    (b) to receive notice of and to object to a secured party's proposal to retain the collateral in satisfaction of the indebtedness under Section 9 — 505;

    (c) to redeem the collateral under Section 9 — 506;

    (d) to obtain injunctive or other relief under Section 9 — 507(1); and

    (e) to recover losses caused to him under Section 9 — 208(2).

§ 9 — 113. Security Interests Arising Under Article on Sales

A security interest arising solely under the Article on Sales (Article 2) is subject to the provisions of this Article except that to the extent that and so long as the debtor does not have or does not lawfully obtain possession of the goods

    (a) no security agreement is necessary to make the security interest enforceable; and

    (b) no filing is required to perfect the security interest; and

    (c) the rights of the secured party on default by the debtor are governed by the Article on Sales (Article 2).

§ 9 — 114. Consignment

(1) A person who delivers goods under a consignment which is not a security interest and who would be required to file under this Article by paragraph (3) (c) of Section 2 — 326 has priority over a secured party who is or becomes a creditor of the consignee and who would have a perfected security interest in the goods if they were the property of the

consignee, and also has priority with respect to identifiable cash proceeds received on or before delivery of the goods to a buyer, if

    (a) the consignor complies with the filing provision of the Article on Sales with respect to consignments (paragraph (3) (c) of Section 2 — 326) before the consignee receives possession of the goods; and

    (b) the consignor gives notification in writing to the holder of the security interest, if the holder has filed a financing statement covering the same types of goods before the date of the filing made by the consignor; and

    (c) the holder of the security interest receives the notification within five years before the consignee receives possession of the goods; and

    (d) the notification states that the consignor expects to deliver goods on consignment to the consignee, describing the goods by item or type.

(2) In the case of a consignment which is not a security interest and in which the requirements of the preceding subsection have not been met, a person who delivers goods to another is subordinate to a person who would have a perfected security interest in the goods if they were the property of the debtor.

Part 2

Validity of Security Agreement and Rights of Parties Thereto

§ 9 — 201. General Validity of Security Agreement

Except as otherwise provided by this Act, a security agreement is effective according to its terms between the parties, against purchasers of the collateral and against creditors. Nothing in this Article validates any charge or practice illegal under any statute or regulation thereunder governing usury, small loans, retail installment sales, or the like, or extends the application of any such statute or regulation to any transaction not otherwise subject thereto.

§ 9 — 202. Title to Collateral Immaterial

Each provision of this Article wtih regard to rights, obligations and remedies applies whether title to collateral is in the secured party or in the debtor.

§ 9 — 203. Attachment and Enforceability of Security Interest; Proceeds; Formal Requisites

(1) Subject to the provisions of Section 4 — 208 on the security interest of a collecting bank, Section 8 — 321 on security interests in securities and Section 9 — 113 on a security interest arising under the Article of Sales, a security interest is not enforceable against the debtor or third parties with respect to the collateral and does not attach unless

(a) the collateral is in the possession of the secured party pursuant to agreement, or the debtor has signed a security agreement which contains a description of the collateral and in addition, when the security interest covers crops growing or to be grown or timber to be cut, a description of the land concerned; and

(b) value has been given; and

(c) the debtor has rights in the collateral.

(2) A security interest attaches when it becomes enforceable against the debtor with respect to the collateral. Attachment occurs as soon as all of the events specified in subsection (1) have taken place unless explicit agreement postpones the time of attaching.

(3) Unless otherwise agreed, a security agreement gives the secured party the rights to proceeds provided by Section 9—306.

(4) A transaction, although subject to this Article, is also subject to............*, and in the case of conflict between the provisions of this Article and any such statute, the provisions of such statute control. Failure to comply with any applicable statute has only the effect which is specified therein.

Note: *At * in subsection (4) insert reference to any local statute regulating small loans, retail installment sales and the like.*

The foregoing subsection (4) is designed to make it clear that certain transactions, although subject to this Article, must also comply with other applicable legislation.

This Article is designed to regulate all the "security" aspects of transactions within its scope. There is, however, much regulatory legislation, particularly in the consumer field, which supplements this Article and should not be repealed by its enactment. Examples are small loan acts, retail installment selling acts and the like. Such acts may provide for licensing and rate regulation and may prescribe particular forms of contract. Such provisions should remain in force despite the enactment of this Article. On the other hand if a retail installment selling act contains provisions on filing, rights on default, etc., such provisions should be repealed as inconsistent with this Article except that inconsistent provisions as to deficiencies, penalties, etc., in the Uniform Consumer Credit Code and other recent related legislation should remain because those statutes were drafted after the substantial enactment of the Article and with the intention of modifying certain provisions of this Article as to consumer credit.

§ 9—204. After-Acquired Property; Future Advances

(1) Except as provided in subsection (2), a security agreement may provide that any or all obligations covered by the security agreement are to be secured by after-acquired collateral.

(2) No security interest attaches under an after-acquired property clause to consumer goods other than accessions (Section 9—314) when given as additional security unless the debtor acquires rights in them within ten days after the secured party gives value.

(3) Obligations covered by a security agreement may include future advances or other value whether or not the advances or value are given pursuant to commitment (subsection (1) of Section 9—105).

§ 9—205. Use or Disposition of Collateral Without Accounting Permissible

A security interest is not invalid or fraudulent against creditors by reason of liberty in the debtor to use, commingle or dispose of all or part of the collateral (including returned or repossessed goods) or to collect or compromise accounts or chattel paper, or to accept the return of goods or make repossessions, or to use, commingle or dispose of proceeds or by reason of the failure of the secured party to require the debtor to account for proceeds or replace collateral. This section does not relax the requirements of possession where perfection of a security interest depends upon possession of the collateral by the secured party or by a bailee.

§ 9—206. Agreement Not to Assert Defenses Against Assignee; Modification of Sales Warranties Where Security Agreement Exists

(1) Subject to any statute or decision which establishes a different rule for buyers or lessees of consumer goods, an agreement by a buyer or lessee that he will not assert against an assignee any claim or defense which he may have against the seller or lessor is enforceable by an assignee who takes his assignment for value, in good faith and without notice of a claim or defense, except as to defenses of a type which may be asserted against a holder in due course of a negotiable instrument under the Article on Commercial Paper (Article 3). A buyer who as part of one transaction signs both a negotiable instrument and a security agreement makes such an agreement.

(2) When a seller retains a purchase money security interest in goods, the Article on Sales (Article 2) governs the sale and any disclaimer, limitation or modification of the seller's warranties.

§ 9—207. Rights and Duties When Collateral is in Secured Party's Possession

(1) A secured party must use reasonable care in the custody and preservation of collateral in his possession. In the case of an instrument or chattel paper, reasonable care includes taking necessary steps to preserve rights against prior parties unless otherwise agreed.

(2) Unless otherwise agreed, when collateral is in the secured party's possession

(a) reasonable expenses (including the cost of any insurance and payment of taxes or other charges) incurred in the custody, preservation, use or operation of the collateral are chargeable to the debtor and are secured by the collateral;

    (b) the risk of accidental loss or damage is on the debtor to the extent of any deficiency in any effective insurance coverage;

    (c) the secured party may hold as additional security any increase or profits (except money) received from the collateral, but money so received, unless remitted to the debtor, shall be applied in reduction of the secured obligation;

    (d) the secured party must keep the collateral identifiable but fungible collateral may be commingled;

    (e) the secured party may repledge the collateral upon terms which do not impair the debtor's right to redeem it.

(3) A secured party is liable for any loss caused by his failure to meet any obligation imposed by the preceding subsections but does not lose his security interest.

(4) A secured party may use or operate the collateral for the purpose of preserving the collateral or its value or pursuant to the order of a court of appropriate jurisdiction or, except in the case of consumer goods, in the manner and to the extent provided in the security agreement.

§ 9—208. Request for Statement of Account or List of Collateral

(1) A debtor may sign a statement indicating what he believes to be the aggregate amount of unpaid indebtedness as of a specified date and may send it to the secured party with a request that the statement be approved or corrected and returned to the debtor. When the security agreement or any other record kept by the secured party identifies the collateral, a debtor may similarly request the secured party to approve or correct a list of the collateral.

(2) The secured party must comply with such a request within two weeks after receipt by sending a written correction or approval. If the secured party claims a security interest in all of a particular type of collateral owned by the debtor, he may indicate that fact in his reply and need not approve or correct an itemized list of such collateral. If the secured party without reasonable excuse fails to comply, he is liable for any loss caused to the debtor thereby; and if the debtor has properly included in his request a good faith statement of the obligation or a list of the collateral or both, the secured party may claim a security interest only as shown in the statement against persons misled by his failure to comply. If he no longer has an interest in the obligation or collateral at the time the request is received, he must disclose the name and address of any successor in interest known to him; and he is liable for any loss caused to the debtor as a result of failure to disclose. A successor in interest is not subject to this section until a request is received by him.

(3) A debtor is entitled to such a statement once every six months without charge. The secured party may require payment of a charge not exceeding $10 for each additional statement furnished.

Part 3

Rights of Third Parties; Perfected and Unperfected Security Interests; Rules of Priority

§ 9—301. Persons Who Take Priority Over Unperfected Security Interests; Rights of "Lien Creditor"

(1) Except as otherwise provided in subsection (2), an unperfected security interest is subordinate to the rights of

    (a) persons entitled to priority under Section 9—312;

    (b) a person who becomes a lien creditor before the security interest is perfected;

    (c) in the case of goods, instruments, documents, and chattel paper, a person who is not a secured party and who is a transferee in bulk or other buyer not in ordinary course of business or is a buyer of farm products in ordinary course of business, to the extent that he gives value and receives delivery of the collateral without knowledge of the security interest and before it is perfected;

    (d) in the case of accounts and general intangibles, a person who is not a secured party and who is a transferee, to the extent that he gives value without knowledge of the security interest and before it is perfected.

(2) If the secured party files with respect to a purchase money security interest before or within ten days after the debtor receives possession of the collateral, he takes priority over the rights of a transferee in bulk or of a lien creditor which arise between the time the security interest attaches and the time of filing.

(3) A "lien creditor" means a creditor who has acquired a lien on the property involved by attachment, levy or the like and includes an assignee for benefit of creditors from the time of assignment, and a trustee in bankruptcy from the date of the filing of the petition or a receiver in equity from the time of appointment.

(4) A person who becomes a lien creditor while a security interest is perfected takes subject to the security interest only to the extent that it secures advances made before he becomes a lien creditor or within 45 days thereafter or made without knowledge of the lien or pursuant to a commitment entered into without knowledge of the lien.

§ 9—302. When Filing Is Required to Perfect Security Interest; Security Interests to Which Filing Provisions of This Article Do Not Apply

(1) A financing statement must be filed to perfect all security interests except the following:

(a) a security interest in collateral in possession of the secured party under Section 9—305;

(b) a security interest temporarily perfected in instruments or documents without delivery under Section 9—304 or in proceeds for a 10 day period under Section 9—306;

(c) a security interest created by an assignment of a beneficial interest in a trust or a decedent's estate;

(d) a purchase money security interest in consumer goods; but filing is required for a motor vehicle required to be registered; and fixture filing is required for priority over conflicting interests in fixtures to the extent provided in Section 9—313;

(e) an assignment of accounts which does not alone or in conjunction with other assignments to the same assignee transfer a significant part of the outstanding accounts of the assignor;

(f) a security interest of a collecting bank (Section 4—208) or in securities (Section 8—321) or arising under the Article on Sales (see Section 9—313) or covered in subsection (3) of this section;

(g) an assignment for the benefit of all the creditors of the transferor, and subsequent transfers by the assignee thereunder.

(2) If a secured party assigns a perfected security interest, no filing under this Article is required in order to continue the perfected status of the security interest against creditors of and transferees from the original debtor.

(3) The filing of a financing statement otherwise required by this Article is not necessary or effective to perfect a security interest in property subject to

(a) a statute or treaty of the United States which provides for a national or international registration or a national or international certificate of title or which specifies a place of filing different from that specified in this Article for filing of the security interest; or

(b) the following statutes of this state; [list any certificate of title statute covering automobiles, trailers, mobile homes, boats, farm tractors, or the like, and any central filing statute*.]; but during any period in which collateral is inventory held for sale by a person who is in the business of selling goods of that kind, the filing provisions of this Article (Part 4) apply to a security interest in that collateral created by him as debtor; or

(c) a certificate of title statute of another jurisdiction under the law of which indication of a security interest on the certificate is required as a condition of perfection (subsection (2) of Section 9—103).

(4) Compliance with a statute or treaty described in subsection (3) is equivalent to the filing of a financing statement under this Article, and a security interest in property subject to the statute or treaty can be perfected only by compliance therewith except as provided in Section 9—103 on multiple state transactions. Duration and renewal of perfection of a security interest perfected by compliance with the statute or treaty are governed by the provisions of the statute or treaty; in other respects the security interest is subject to this Article.

*Note: *It is recommended that the provisions of certificate of title acts for perfection of security interests by notation on the certificates should be amended to exclude coverge of inventory held for sale.*

§ 9—303. When Security Interest Is Perfected; Continuity of Perfection

(1) A security interest is perfected when it has attached and when all of the applicable steps required for perfection have been taken. Such steps are specified in Section 9—302, 9—304, 9—305 and 9—306. If such steps are taken before the security interest attaches, it is perfected at the time when it attaches.

(2) If a security interest is originally perfected in any way permitted under this Article and is subsequently perfected in some other way under this Article, without an intermediate period when it was unperfected, the security interest shall be deemed to be perfected continuously for the purposes of this Article.

§ 9—304. Perfection of Security Interest in Instruments, Documents, and Goods Covered by Documents; Perfection by Permissive Filing; Temporary Perfection Without Filing or Transfer of Possession

(1) A security interest in chattel paper or negotiable documents may be perfected by filing. A security interest in money or instruments (other than certificated securities or instruments which constitute part of chattel paper) can be perfected only by the secured party's taking possession, except as provided in subsections (4) and (5) of this section and subsections (2) and (3) of Section 9—306 on proceeds.

(2) During the period that goods are in the possession of the issuer of a negotiable document therefor, a security interest in the goods is perfected by perfecting a security interest in the document, and any security interest in the goods otherwise perfected during such period is subject thereto.

(3) A security interest in goods in the possession of a bailee other than one who has issued a negotiable document therefor is perfected by issuance of a document in the name of the secured party or by the bailee's receipt of notification of the secured party's interest or by filing as to the goods.

(4) A security interest in instruments (other than certified securities) or negotiable documents is perfected without filing or the taking of possession for a period of 21 days from the time it attaches to the extent that it arises for new value given under a written security agreement.

(5) A security interest remains perfected for a period of 21 days without filing where a secured party having a perfected security interest in an instrument (other than a certificated security), a negotiable document or goods in possession of a bailee other than one who has issued a negotiable document therefor

    (a) makes available to the debtor the goods or documents representing the goods for the purpose of ultimate sale or exchange or for the purpose of loading, unloading, storing, shipping, transshipping, manufacturing, processing or otherwise dealing with them in a manner preliminary to their sale or exchange, but priority between conflicting security interests in the goods is subject to subsection (3) of Section 9—312; or

    (b) delivers the instrument to the debtor for the purpose of ultimate sale or exchange or of presentation, collection, renewal or registration of transfer.

(6) After the 21 day period in subsections (4) and (5), perfection depends upon compliance with applicable provisions of this Article.

§ 9—305. When Possession by Secured Party Perfects Security Interest Without Filing

A security interest in letters of credit and advices of credit (subsection (2) (a) of Section 5—116), goods, instruments (other than certificated securities), money, negotiable documents or chattel paper may be perfected by the secured party's taking possession of the collateral. If such collateral other than goods covered by a negotiable document is held by a bailee, the secured party is deemed to have possession from the time the bailee receives notification of the secured party's interest. A security interest is perfected by possession from the time possession is taken without relation back and continues only so long as possession is retained, unless otherwise specified in this Article. The security interest may be otherwise perfected as provided in this Article before or after the period of possession by the secured party.

§ 9—306. "Proceeds"; Secured Party's Rights on Disposition of Collateral

(1) "Proceeds" includes whatever is received upon the sale, exchange, collection or other disposition of collateral or proceeds. Insurance payable by reason of loss or damage to the collateral is proceeds, except to the extent that it is payable to a person other than a party to the security agreement. Money, checks, deposit accounts, and the like are "cash proceeds." All other proceeds are "noncash proceeds."

(2) Except where this Article otherwise provides, a security interest continues in collateral notwithstanding sale, exchange or other disposition thereof unless the disposition was authorized by the secured party in the security agreement or otherwise, and also continues in any identifiable proceeds including collections received by the debtor.

(3) The security interest in proceeds is a continuously perfected security interest if the interest in the original collateral was perfected, but it ceases to be a perfected security interest and becomes unperfected ten days after receipt of the proceeds by the debtor unless

    (a) a filed financing statement covers the original collateral and the proceeds are collateral in which a security interest may be perfected by filing in the office or offices where the financing statement has been filed and, if the proceeds are acquired with cash proceeds, the description of collateral in the financing statement indicates the types of property constituting the proceeds; or

    (b) a filed financing statement covers the original collateral and the proceeds are identifiable cash proceeds; or

    (c) the security interest in the proceeds is perfected before the expiration of the ten day period.

Except as provided in this section, a security interest in proceeds can be perfected only by the methods or under the circumstances permitted in this Article for original collateral of the same type.

(4) In the event of insolvency proceedings instituted by or against a debtor, a secured party with a perfected security interest in proceeds has a perfected security interest only in the following proceeds:

    (a) in identifiable noncash proceeds and in separate deposit accounts containing only proceeds;

    (b) in identifiable cash proceeds in the form of money which is neither commingled with other money nor deposited in a deposit account prior to the insolvency proceedings;

    (c) in identifiable cash proceeds in the form of checks and the like which are not deposited in a deposit account prior to the insolvency proceedings; and

    (d) in all cash and deposit accounts of the debtor in which proceeds have been commingled with other funds, but the perfected security interest under this paragraph (d) is

(i) subject to any right to setoff; and

(ii) limited to an amount not greater than the amount of any cash proceeds received by the debtor within ten days before the institution of the insolvency proceedings, less the sum of (I) the payments to the secured party on account of cash proceeds received by the debtor during such period and (II) the cash proceeds received by the debtor during such period to which the secured party is entitled under paragraphs (a) through (c) of this subsection (4).

(5) If a sale of goods results in an account or chattel paper which is transferred by the seller to a secured party and if the goods are returned to or are repossessed by the seller or the secured party, the following rules determine priorities:

(a) If the goods were collateral at the time of sale, for an indebtedness of the seller which is still unpaid, the original security interest attaches again to the goods and continues as a perfected security interest if it was perfected at the time when the goods were sold. If the security interest was originally perfected by a filing which is still effective, nothing further is required to continue the perfected status; in any other case, the secured party must take possession of the returned or repossessed goods or must file.

(b) An unpaid transferee of the chattel paper has a security interest in the goods against the transferor. Such security interest is prior to a security interest asserted under paragraph (a) to the extent that the transferee of the chattel paper was entitled to priority under Section 9—308.

(c) An unpaid transferee of the account has a security interest in the goods against the transferor. Such security interest is subordinate to a security interest asserted under paragraph (a).

(d) A security interest of an unpaid transferee asserted under paragraph (b) or (c) must be perfected for protection against creditors of the transferor and purchasers of the returned or repossessed goods.

§ 9—307. Protection of Buyers of Goods

(1) A buyer in ordinary course of business (subsection (9) of Section 1—201), other than a person buying farm products from a person engaged in farming operations, takes free of a security interest created by his seller even though the security interest is perfected and even though the buyer knows of its existence.

(2) In the case of consumer goods, a buyer takes free of a security interest even though perfected if he buys without knowledge of the security interest, for

value and for his own personal, family or household purposes unless prior to the purchase the secured party has filed a financing statement covering such goods.

(3) A buyer other than a buyer in ordinary course of business (subsection (1) of this section) takes free of a security interest to the extent that it secures future advances made after the secured party acquires knowledge of the purchase, or more than 45 days after the purchase, whichever first occurs, unless made pursuant to a commitment entered into without knowledge of the purchase and before the expiration of the 45 day period.

§ 9—308. Purchase of Chattel Paper and Instruments

A purchaser of chattel paper or an instrument who gives new value and takes possession of it in the ordinary course of his business has priority over a security interest in the chattel paper or instrument

(a) which is perfected under Section 9—304 (permissive filing and temporary perfection) or under Section 9—306 (perfection as to proceeds) if he acts without knowledge that the specific paper or instrument is subject to a security interest; or

(b) which is claimed merely as proceeds of inventory subject to a security interest (Section 9—306) even though he knows that the specific paper or instrument is subject to the security interest.

§ 9—309. Protection of Purchasers of Instruments, Documents and Securities

Nothing in this Article limits the rights of a holder in due course of a negotiable instrument (Section 3—302) or a holder to whom a negotiable document of title has been duly negotiated (Section 7—501) or a bona fide purchaser of a security (Section 8—302), and such holders or purchasers take priority over an earlier security interest even though perfected. Filing under this Article does not constitute notice of the security interest to such holders or purchasers.

§ 9—310. Priority of Certain Liens Arising by Operation of Law

When a person in the ordinary course of his business furnishes services or materials with respect to goods subject to a security interest, a lien upon goods in the possession of such person given by statute or rule of law for such materials or services takes priority over a perfected security interest unless the lien is statutory and the statute expressly provides otherwise.

§ 9—311. Alienability of Debtor's Rights: Judicial Process

The debtor's rights in collateral may be voluntarily or involuntarily transferred (by way of sale, creation of a security interest, attachment, levy, garnishment or other judicial process) notwithstanding a provision in the security agreement prohibiting any transfer or making the transfer constitute a default.

§ 9—312. Priorities Among Conflicting Security Interests in the Same Collateral

(1) The rules of priority stated in other sections of this Part and in the following sections shall govern when applicable: Section 4—208 with respect to the security interests of collecting banks in items being collected, accompanying documents and proceeds; Section 9—103 on security interests related to other jurisdictions; Section 9—114 on consignments.

(2) A perfected security interest in crops for new value given to enable the debtor to produce the crops during the production season, and given not more than three months before the crops become growing crops by planting or otherwise, takes priority over an earlier perfected security interest to the extent that such earlier interest secures obligations due more than six months before the crops become growing crops by planting or otherwise, even though the person giving new value had knowledge of the earlier security interest.

(3) A perfected purchase money security interest in inventory has priority over a conflicting security interest in the same inventory and also has priority in identifiable cash proceeds received on or before the delivery of the inventory to a buyer if

    (a) the purchase money security interest is perfected at the time the debtor receives possession of the inventory; and

    (b) the purchase money secured party gives notification in writing to the holder of the conflicting security interest if the holder had filed a financing statement covering the same types of inventory (i) before the date of the filing made by the purchase money secured party, or (ii) before the beginning of the 21 day period where the purchase money security interest is temporarily perfected without filing or possession (subsection (5) of Section 9—304); and

    (c) the holder of the conflicting security interest receives the notification within five years before the debtor receives possession of the inventory; and

    (d) the notification states that the person giving the notice has or expects to acquire a purchase money security interest in inventory of the debtor, describing such inventory by item or type.

(4) A purchase money security interest in collateral other than inventory has priority over a conflicting security interest in the same collateral or its proceeds if the purchase money security interest is perfected at the time the debtor receives possession of the collateral or within ten days thereafter.

(5) In all cases not governed by other rules stated in this section (including cases of purchase money security interests which do not qualify for the special priorities set forth in subsections (3) and (4) of this sec-

tion), priority between conflicting security interests in the same collateral shall be determined according to the following rules:

    (a) Conflicting security interests rank according to priority in time of filing or perfection. Priority dates from the time a filing is first made covering the collateral or the time the security interest is first perfected, whichever is earlier, provided that there is no period thereafter when there is neither filing nor perfection.

    (b) So long as conflicting security interests are unperfected, the first to attach has priority.

(6) For the purposes of subsection (5), a date of filing or perfection as to collateral is also a date of filing or perfection as to proceeds.

(7) If future advances are made while a security interest is perfected by filing or the taking of possession, or under Section 8—321 on securities, the security interest has the same priority for the purposes of subsection (5) with respect to the future advances as it does with respect to the first advance. If a commitment is made before or while the security interest is so perfected, the security interest has the same priority with respect to advances made pursuant thereto. In other cases, a perfected security interest has priority from the date the advance is made.

§ 9—313. Priority of Security Interests in Fixtures

(1) In this section and in the provisions of Part 4 of this Article referring to fixture filing, unless the context otherwise requires

    (a) goods are "fixtures" when they become so related to particular real estate that an interest in them arises under a real estate law

    (b) a "fixture filing" is the filing in the office where a mortgage on the real estate would be filed or recorded of a financing statement covering goods which are or are to become fixtures and conforming to the requirements of subsection (5) of Section 9—402

    (c) a mortgage is a "construction mortgage" to the extent that it secures an obligation incurred for the construction of an improvement on land including the acquisition cost of the land, if the recorded writing so indicates.

(2) A security interest under this Article may be created in goods which are fixtures or may continue in goods which become fixtures, but no security interest exists under this Article in ordinary building materials incorporated into an improvement on land.

(3) This Article does not prevent creation of an encumbrance upon fixtures pursuant to real estate law.

(4) A perfected security interest in fixtures has

priority over the conflicting interest of an encumbrancer or owner of the real estate where

    (a) the security interest is a purchase money security interest, the interest of the encumbrancer or owner arises before the goods become fixtures, the security interest is perfected by a fixture filing before the goods become fixtures or within ten days thereafter, and the debtor has an interest of record in the real estate or is in possession of the real estate; or

    (b) the security interest is perfected by a fixture filing before the interest of the encumbrancer or owner is of record, the security interest has priority over any conflicting interest of a predecessor in title of the encumbrancer or owner, and the debtor has an interest of record in the real estate or is in possession of the real estate; or

    (c) the fixtures are readily removable factory or office machines or readily removable replacements of domestic appliances which are consumer goods, and before the goods become fixtures the security interest is perfected by any method permitted by this Article; or

    (d) the conflicting interest is a lien on the real estate obtained by legal or equitable proceedings after the security interest was perfected by any method permitted by this Article.

(5) A security interest in fixtures, whether or not perfected, has priority over the conflicting interest of an encumbrancer or owner of the real estate where

    (a) the encumbrancer or owner has consented in writing to the security interest or has disclaimed an interest in the goods as fixtures; or

    (b) the debtor has a right to remove the goods as against the encumbrancer or owner. If the debtor's right terminates, the priority of the security interest continues for a reasonable time.

(6) Notwithstanding paragraph (a) of subsection (4) but otherwise subject to subsections (4) and (5), a security interest in fixtures is subordinate to a construction mortgage recorded before the goods become fixtures if the goods become fixtures before the completion of the construction. To the extent that it is given to refinance a construction mortgage, a mortgage has this priority to the same extent as the construction mortgage.

(7) In cases not within the preceding subsections, a security interest in fixtures is subordinate to the conflicting interest of an encumbrancer or owner of the related real estate who is not the debtor.

(8) When the secured party has priority over all owners and encumbrancers of the real estate, he may, on default, subject to the provisions of Part 5, remove his collateral from the real estate but he must reimburse any encumbrancer or owner of the real estate who is not the debtor, and who has not otherwise agreed, for the cost of repair of any physical injury, but not for any diminution in value of the real estate caused by the absence of the goods removed or by any necessity of replacing them. A person entitled to reimbursement may refuse permission to remove until the secured party gives adequate security for the performance of this obligation.

§ 9—314.   Accessions

(1) A security interest in goods which attaches before they are installed in or affixed to other goods takes priority as to the goods installed or affixed (called in this section "accessions") over the claims of all persons to the whole except as stated in subsection (3) and subject to Section 9—315(1).

(2) A security interest which attaches to goods after they become part of a whole is valid against all persons subsequently acquiring interests in the whole except as stated in subsection (3) but is invalid against any person with an interest in the whole at the time the security interest attaches to the goods who has not in writing consented to the security interest or disclaimed an interest in the goods as part of the whole.

(3) The security interests described in subsections (1) and (2) do not take priority over

    (a) a subsequent purchaser for value of any interest in the whole; or

    (b) a creditor with a lien on the whole subsequently obtained by judicial proceedings; or

    (c) a creditor with a prior perfected security interest in the whole to the extent that he makes subsequent advances.

If in the subsequent purchase is made, the lien by judicial proceedings obtained or the subsequent advance under the prior perfected security interest is made or contracted for without knowledge of the security interest and before it is perfected. A purchaser of the whole at a foreclosure sale other than the holder of a perfected security interest purchasing at his own foreclosure sale is a subsequent purchaser within this section.

(4) When under subsections (1) or (2) and (3), a secured party has an interest in accessions which has priority over the claims of all persons who have interests in the whole, he may, on default, subject to the provisions of Part 5, remove his collateral from the whole but he must reimburse any encumbrancer or owner of the whole who is not the debtor and who has not otherwise agreed for the cost of repair of any physical injury but not for any diminution in value of the whole caused by the absence of the goods removed or by any necessity for replacing them. A person entitled to reimbursement may refuse permission to remove

until the secured party gives adequate security for the performance of this obligation.

§ 9—315. Priority When Goods Are Commingled or Processed

(1) If a security interest in goods was perfected and subsequently the goods or a part thereof have become part of a product or mass, the security interest continues in the product or mass if

(a) the goods are so manufactured, processed, assembled or commingled that their identity is lost in the product or mass; or

(b) a financing statement covering the original goods also covers the product into which the goods have been manufactured, processed or assembled.

In a case to which paragraph (b) applies, no separate security interest in that part of the original goods which has been manufactured, processed or assembled into the product may be claimed under Section 9—314.

(2) When under subsection (1) more than one security interest attaches to the product or mass, they rank equally according to the ratio that the cost of the goods to which each interest originally attached bears to the cost of the total product or mass.

§ 9—316. Priority Subject to Subordination

Nothing in this Article prevents subordination by agreement by any person entitled to priority.

§ 9—317. Secured Party Not Obligated on Contract of Debtor

The mere existence of a security interest or authority given to the debtor to dispose of or use collateral does not impose contract or tort liability upon the secured party for the debtor's acts or omissions.

§ 9—318. Defenses Against Assignee; Modification of Contract After Notification of Assignment; Term Prohibiting Assignment Ineffective; Identification and Proof of Assignment

(1) Unless an account debtor has made an enforceable agreement not to assert defenses or claims arising out of a sale as provided in Section 9—206, the rights of an assignee are subject to

(a) all the terms of the contract between the account debtor and assignor and any defense or claim arising therefrom; and

(b) any other defense or claim of the account debtor against the assignor which accrues before the account debtor receives notification of the assignment.

(2) So far as the right to payment or a part thereof under an assigned contract has not been fully earned by performance, and notwithstanding notification of the assignment, any modification of or substitution for the contract made in good faith and in accordance with reasonable commercial standards is effective against an assignee unless the account debtor has otherwise agreed, but the assignee acquires corresponding rights under the modified or substituted contract. The assignment may provide that such modification or substitution is a breach by the assignor.

(3) The account debtor is authorized to pay the assignor until the account debtor receives notification that the amount due or to become due has been assigned and that payment is to be made to the assignee. A notification which does not reasonably identify the rights assigned is ineffective. If requested by the account debtor, the assignee must seasonably furnish reasonable proof that the assignment has been made; and unless he does so, the account debtor may pay the assignor.

(4) A term in any contract between an account debtor and an assignor is ineffective if it prohibits assignment of an account or prohibits creation of a security interest in a general intangible for money due or to become due or requires the account debtor's consent to such assignment or security interest.

Part 4

Filing

§ 9—401. Place of Filing; Erroneous Filing; Removal of Collateral

First Alternative Subsection (1)

(1) The proper place to file in order to perfect a security interest is as follows:

(a) when the collateral is timber to be cut or is minerals or the like (including oil and gas) or accounts subject to subsection (5) of Section 9—103, or when the financing statement is filed as a fixture filing (Section 9—313) and the collateral is goods which are or are to become fixtures, then in the office where a mortgage on the real estate would be filed or recorded;

(b) in all other cases, in the office of the [Secretary of State].

Second Alternative Subsection (1)

(1) The proper place to file in order to perfect a security interest is as follows:

(a) when the collateral is equipment used in farming operations, or farm products, or accounts or general intangibles arising from or relating to the sale of farm products by a farmer, or consumer goods, then in the office of the . . . . in the county of the debtor's residence or if the debtor is not a resident of this state then in the office of the . . . . in the county where the goods are kept, and in addition when the collateral is crops growing or to be grown in the office of the . . . . in the county where the land is located;

(b) when the collateral is timber to be cut or is minerals or the like (including oil and gas) or accounts subject to subsection (5) of Section 9—103, or when the financing statement is filed as a fixture filing (Section 9—313) and the collateral is goods which are or are to become fixtures, then in the office where a mortgage on the real estate would be filed or recorded;

(c) in all other cases, in the office of the [Secretary of State].

Third Alternative Subsection (1)

(1) The proper place to file in order to perfect a security interest is as follows:

(a) when the collateral is equipment used in farming operations, or farm products, or accounts or general intangibles arising from or relating to the sale of farm products by a farmer, or consumer goods, then in the office of the . . . . in the county of the debtor's residence or if the debtor is not a resident of this state then in the office of the . . . . in the county where the goods are kept, and in addition when the collateral is crops growing or to be grown in the office of the . . . . in the county where the land is located;

(b) when the collateral is timber to be cut or is minerals or the like (including oil and gas) or accounts subject to subsection (5) of Section 9—103, or when the financing statement is filed as a fixture filing (Section 9—313) and the collateral is goods which are or are to become fixtures, then in the office where a mortgage on the real estate would be filed or recorded;

(c) in all other cases, in the office of the [Secretary of State] and in addition, if the debtor has a place of business in only one county of this state, also in the office of . . . . of such county, or, if the debtor has no place of business in this state, but resides in the state, also in the office of . . . . of the county in which he resides.

Note: *One of the three alternatives should be selected as subsection (1).*

(2) A filing which is made in good faith in an improper place or not in all of the places required by this section is nevertheless effective with regard to any collateral as to which the filing complied with the requirements of this Article and is also effective with regard to collateral covered by the financing statement against any person who has knowledge of the contents of such financing statement.

(3) A filing which is made in the proper place in this state continues effective even though the debtor's residence or place of business or the location of the collateral or its use, whichever controlled the original filing, is thereafter changed.

Alternative Subsection (3)

[(3) A filing which is made in the proper county continues effective for four months after a change to another county of the debtor's residence or place of business or the location of the collateral, whichever controlled the original filing. It becomes ineffective thereafter unless a copy of the financing statement signed by the secured party is filed in the new county within said period. The security interest may also be perfected in the new county after the expiration of the four-month period; in such case, perfection dates from the time of perfection in the new county. A change in the use of the collateral does not impair the effectiveness of the original filing.]

(4) The rules stated in Section 9—103 determine whether filing is necessary in this state.

(5) Notwithstanding the preceding subsections, and subject to subsection (3) of Section 9–302, the proper place to file in order to perfect a security interest in collateral, including fixtures, of a transmitting utility is the office of the [Secretary of State]. This filing constitutes a fixture filing (Section 9—313) as to the collateral described therein which is or is to become fixtures.

(6) For the purposes of this section, the residence of an organization is its place of business if it has one or its chief executive office if it has more than one place of business.

Note: *Subsection (6) should be used only if the state chooses the Second or Third Alternative Subsection (1).*

§ 9—402. Formal Requisites of Financing Statement; Amendments; Mortgage as Financing Statement

(1) A financing statement is sufficient if it gives the names of the debtor and the secured party, is signed by the debtor, gives an address of the secured party from which information concerning the security interest may be obtained, gives a mailing address of the debtor and contains a statement indicating the types, or describing the items, of collateral. A financing statement may be filed before a security agreement is made or a security interest otherwise attaches. When the financing statement covers crops growing or to be grown, the statement must also contain a description of the real estate concerned. When the financing statement covers timber to be cut or covers minerals or the like (including oil and gas) or accounts subject to subsection (5) of Section 9—103, or when the financing statement is filed as a fixture filing (Section 9—313) and the collateral is goods which are or are to become fixtures, the statement must also comply with subsection (5). A copy of the security agreement is sufficient as a financing statement if it contains the above information and is signed by the debtor. A car-

bon, photographic or other reproduction of a security agreement or a financing statement is sufficient as a financing statement if the security agreement so provides or if the original has been filed in this state.

(2) A financing statement which otherwise complies with subsection (1) is sufficient when it is signed by the secured party instead of the debtor if it is filed to perfect a security interest in

(a) collateral already subject to a security interest in another jurisdiction when it is brought into this state, or when the debtor's location is changed to this state. Such a financing statement must state that the collateral was brought into this state or that the debtor's location was changed to this state under such circumstances; or

(b) proceeds under Section 9—306 if the security interest in the original collateral was perfected. Such a financing statement must describe the original collateral; or

(c) collateral as to which the filing has lapsed; or

(d) collateral acquired after a change of name, identity or corporate structure of the debtor (subsection (7)).

(3) A form substantially as follows is sufficient to comply with subsection (1):

Name of debtor (or assignor) ....
Address ....
Name of secured party (or assignee).......
Address ....
1. This financing statement covers the following types (or items) of property:
        (Describe)..........................
2. (If collateral is crops) The above described crops are growing or are to be grown on:
        (Describe Real Estate) ....
3. (If applicable) The above goods are to become fixtures on*
        (Describe Real Estate) ....
   and this financing statement is to be filed [for record] in the real estate records. (If the debtor does not have an interest of record) The name of a record owner is..........
4. (If products of collateral are claimed) Products of the collateral are also covered.

(use whichever is applicable)
        ....
        Signature of Debtor (or Assignor)
        ....
        Signature of Secured Party (or Assignee)

---

* Where appropriate substitute either "The above timber is standing on........" or "The above minerals or the like (including oil and gas) or accounts will be financed at the wellhead or minehead of the well or mine located on........"

(4) A financing statement may be amended by filing a writing signed by both the debtor and the secured party. An amendment does not extend the period of effectiveness of a financing statement. If any amendment adds collateral, it is effective as to the added collateral only from the filing date of the amendment. In this Article, unless the context otherwise requires, the term "financing statement" means the original financing statement and any amendments.

(5) A financing statement covering timber to be cut or covering minerals or the like (including oil and gas) or accounts subject to subsection (5) of Section 9—103, or a financing statement filed as a fixture filing (Section 9—313) where the debtor is not a transmitting utility, must show that it covers this type of collateral, must recite that it is to be filed [for record] in the real estate records, and the financing statement must contain a description of the real estate [sufficient if it were contained in a mortgage of the real estate to give constructive notice of the mortgage under the law of this state]. If the debtor does not have an interest of record in the real estate, the financing statement must show the name of a record owner.

(6) A mortgage is effective as a financing statement filed as a fixture filing from the date of its recording if

(a) the goods are described in the mortgage by item or type; and

(b) the goods are or are to become fixtures related to the real estate described in the mortgage; and

(c) the mortgage complies with the requirements for a financing statement in this section other than a recital that it is to be filed in the real estate records; and

(d) the mortgage is duly recorded.

No fee with reference to the financing statement is required other than the regular recording and satisfaction fees with respect to the mortgage.

(7) A financing statement sufficiently shows the name of the debtor if it gives the individual, partnership or corporate name of the debtor, whether or not it adds other trade names or names of partners. Where the debtor so changes his name or, in the case of an organization, its name, identity or corporate structure that a filed financing statement becomes seriously misleading, the filing is not effective to perfect a security interest in collateral acquired by the debtor more than four months after the change, unless a new appropriate financing statement is filed before the expiration of that time. A filed financing statement remains effective with respect to collateral transferred by the debtor even though the secured party knows of or consents to the transfer.

(8) A financing statement substantially complying with the requirements of this section is effective even though it contains minor errors which are not seriously misleading.

Note: *Language in brackets is optional.*

Note: *Where the state has any special recording system for real estate other than the usual grantor-grantee index (as, for instance, a tract system or a title registration or Torrens system) local adaptations of subsection (5) and Section 9—403(7) may be necessary. See Mass. Gen. Laws Chapter 106, Section 9—409.*

§ 9—403.   What Constitutes Filing; Duration of Filing; Effect of Lapsed Filing; Duties of Filing Officer

(1) Presentation for filing of a financing statement and tender of the filing fee or acceptance of the statement by the filing officer constitutes filing under this Article.

(2) Except as provided in subsection (6), a filed financing statement is effective for a period of five years from the date of filing. The effectiveness of a filed financing statement lapses on the expiration of the five-year period unless a continuation statement is filed prior to the lapse. If a security interest perfected by filing exists at the time insolvency proceedings are commenced by or against the debtor, the security interest remains perfected until termination of the insolvency proceedings and thereafter for a period of sixty days or until expiration of the five-year period, whichever occurs later. Upon lapse, the security interest becomes unperfected, unless it is perfected without filing. If the security interest becomes unperfected upon lapse, it is deemed to have been unperfected as against a person who became a purchaser or lien creditor before lapse.

(3) A continuation statement may be filed by the secured party within six months prior to the expiration of the five year period specified in subsection (2). Any such continuation statement must be signed by the secured party, identify the original statement by file number and state that the original statement is still effective. A continuation statement signed by a person other than the secured party of record must be accompanied by a separate written statement of assignment signed by the secured party of record and complying with subsection (2) of Section 9—405, including payment of the required fee. Upon timely filing of the continuation statement, the effectiveness of the original statement is continued for five years after the last date to which the filing was effective whereupon it lapses in the same manner as provided in subsection (2) unless another continuation statement is filed prior to such lapse. Succeeding continuation statements may be filed in the same manner to continue the effectiveness of the original statement. Unless a statute on disposition of public records provides otherwise, the filing officer may remove a lapsed statement from the files and destroy it immediately if he has retained a microfilm or other photographic record, or in other cases after one year after the lapse. The filing officer shall so arrange matters by physical annexation of financing statements to continuation statements or other related filings, or by other means, that if he physically destroys the financing statements of a period more than five years past, those which have been continued by a continuation statement or which are still effective under subsection (6) shall be retained.

(4) Except as provided in subsection (7), a filing officer shall mark each statement with a file number and with the date and hour of filing and shall hold the statement or a microfilm or other photographic copy thereof for public inspection. In addition, the filing officer shall index the statement according to the name of the debtor and shall note in the index the file number and the address of the debtor given in the statement.

(5) The uniform fee for filing and indexing and for stamping a copy furnished by the secured party to show the date and place of filing for an original financing statement or for a continuation statement shall be $........ if the statement is in the standard form prescribed by the [Secretary of State] and otherwise shall be $........, plus in each case, if the financing statement is subject to subsection (5) of Section 9—402, $........ The uniform fee for each name more than one required to be indexed shall be $........ The secured party may at his option show a trade name for any person and an extra uniform indexing fee of $........ shall be paid with respect thereto.

(6) If the debtor is a transmitting utility (subsection (5) of Section 9—401) and a filed financing statement so states, it is effective until a termination statement is filed. A real estate mortgage which is effective as a fixture filing under subsection (6) of Section 9—402 remains effective as a fixture filing until the mortgage is released or satisfied of record or its effectiveness otherwise terminates as to the real estate.

(7) When a financing statement covers timber to be cut or covers minerals or the like (including oil and gas) or accounts subject to subsection (5) of Section 9—103, or is filed as a fixture filing, [it shall be filed for record and] the filing officer shall index it under the names of the debtor and any owner of record shown on the financing statement in the same fashion as if they were the mortagagors in a mortgage of the real estate described, and, to the extent that the law of this state provides for indexing of mortgages under the name of the mortgagee, under the name of the secured party as if he were the mortgagee thereunder, or where indexing is by description in the same fashion as if the financing statement were a mortgage of the real estate described.

Note: *In states in which writings will not appear in the real estate records and indices unless actually recorded, the bracketed language in subsection (7) should be used.*

§ 9—404.   Termination Statement

If a financing statement covering consumer goods is filed on or after.............., then within one month or within ten days following written demand by the debtor after there is no outstanding secured obligation and no commitment to make advances, incur obligations or otherwise give value, the secured party must file with each filing officer with whom the financing statement was filed, a termination statement to the effect that he no longer claims a security interest under the financing statement, which shall be identified by file number. In other cases whenever there is no outstanding secured obligation and no commitment to make advances, incur obligations or otherwise give value, the secured party must on written demand by the debtor send the debtor, for each filing officer with whom the financing statement was filed, a termination statement to the effect that he no longer claims a security interest under the financing statement, which shall be identified by file number. A termination statement signed by a person other than the secured party of record must be accompanied by a separate written statement of assignment signed by the secured party of record complying with subsection (2) of Section 9—405, including payment of the required fee. If the affected secured party fails to file such a termination statement as required by this subsection, or to send such a termination statement within ten days after proper demand therefor, he shall be liable to the debtor for one hundred dollars, and in addition for any loss caused to the debtor by such failure.

(2) On presentation to the filing officer of such a termination statement, he must note it in the index. If he has received the termination statement in duplicate, he shall return one copy of the termination statement to the secured party stamped to show the time of receipt thereof. If the filing officer has a microfilm or other photographic record of the financing statement, and of any related continuation statement, statement of assignment and statement of release, he may remove the originals from the files at any time after receipt of the termination statement, or if he has no such record, he may remove them from the files at any time after one year after receipt of the termination statement.

(3) If the termination statement is in the standard form prescribed by the [Secretary of State], the uniform fee for filing and indexing the termination statement shall be $......, and otherwise shall be $......., plus in each case an additional fee of $....... for each name more than one against which the termination statement is required to be indexed.

Note: *The date to be inserted should be the effective date of the revised Article 9.*

§ 9—405. Assignment of Security Interest; Duties of Filing Officer; Fees

(1) A financing statement may disclose an assignment of a security interest in the collateral described in the financing statement by indication in the financing statement of the name and address of the assignee or by an assignment itself or a copy thereof on the face or back of the statement. On presentation to the filing officer of such a financing statement the filing officer shall mark the same as provided in Section 9—403(4). The uniform fee for filing, indexing and furnishing filing data for a financing statement so indicating an assignment shall be $....... if the statement is in the standard form prescribed by the [Secretary of State] and otherwise shall be $........., plus in each case an additional fee of $....... for each name more than one against which the financing statement is required to be indexed.

(2) A secured party may assign of record all or part of his rights under a financing statement by the filing in the place where the original financing statement was filed of a separate written statement of assignment signed by the secured party of record and setting forth the name of the secured party of record and the debtor, the file number and the date of filing of the financing statement and the name and address of the assignee and containing a description of the collateral assigned. A copy of the assignment is sufficient as a separate statement if it complies with the preceding sentence. On presentation to the filing officer of such a separate statement, the filing officer shall mark such separate statement with the date and hour of the filing. He shall note the assignment on the index of the financing statement, or in the case of a fixture filing, or a filing covering timber to be cut, or covering minerals or the like (including oil and gas) or accounts subject to subsection (5) of Section 9—103, he shall index the assignment under the name of the assignor as grantor and, to the extent that the law of this state provides for indexing the assignment of a mortgage under the name of the assignee, he shall index the assignment of the financing statement under the name of the assignee. The uniform fee for filing, indexing and furnishing filing data about such a separate statement of assignment shall be $........ if the statement is in the standard form prescribed by the [Secretary of State] and otherwise shall be $........, plus in each case an additional fee of $....... for each name more than one against which the statement of assignment is required to be indexed. Notwithstanding the provisions of this subsection, an assignment of record of a security interest in a fixture contained in a mortgage effective as a fixture filing (subsection (6) of Section 9—402) may be made only by an assignment of the mortgage in the manner provided by the law of this state other than this Act.

(3) After the disclosure or filing of an assignment under this section, the assignee is the secured party of record.

§ 9—406. Release of Collateral; Duties of Filing Officer; Fees

A secured party of record may by his signed statement release all or a part of any collateral described in a filed financing statement. The statement of release is sufficient if it contains a description of the collateral being released, the name and address of the debtor, the name and address of the secured party, and the file number of the financing statement. A statement of release signed by a person other than the secured party of record must be accompanied by a separate written statement of assignment signed by the secured party of record and complying with subsection (2) of Section 9—405, including payment of the required fee. Upon presentation of such a statement of release to the filing officer, he shall mark the statement with the hour and date of filing and shall note the same upon the margin of the index of the filing of the financing statement. The uniform fee for filing and noting such a statement of release shall be $........ if the statement is in the standard form prescribed by the [Secretary of State] and otherwise shall be $........, plus in each case an additional fee of $........ for each name more than one against which the statement of release is required to be indexed.

[§ 9—407. Information From Filing Officer]

[(1) If the person filing any financing statement, termination statement, statement of assignment, or statement of release, furnishes the filing officer a copy thereof, the filing officer shall upon request note upon the copy the file number and date and hour of the filing of the original and deliver or send the copy to such person.]

[(2) Upon request of any person, the filing officer shall issue his certificate showing whether there is on file on the date and hour stated therein, any presently effective financing statement naming a particular debtor and any statement of assignment thereof and if there is, giving the date and hour of filing of each such statement and the names and addresses of each secured party therein. The uniform fee for such a certificate shall be $........ if the request for the certificate is in the standard form prescribed by the [Secretary of State] and otherwise shall be $........ Upon request the filing officer shall furnish a copy of any filed financing statement or statement of assignment for a uniform fee of $........ per page.]

Note: *This section is proposed as an optional provision to require filing officers to furnish certificates. Local law and practices should be consulted with regard to the advisability of adoption.*

§ 9—408. Financing Statements Covering Consigned or Leased Goods

A consignor or lessor of goods may file a financing statement using the terms "consignor," "consignee," "lessor," "lessee" or the like instead of the terms specified in Section 9—402. The provisions of this Part shall apply as appropriate to such a financing statement but its filing shall not of itself be a factor in determining whether or not the consignment or lease is intended as security (Section 1—201(37)). However, if

it is determined for other reasons that the consignment or lease is so intended, a security interest of the consignor or lessor which attaches to the consigned or leased goods is perfected by such filing.

Part 5
Default

§ 9—501. Default; Procedure When Security Agreement Covers Both Real and Personal Property

(1) When a debtor is in default under a security agreement, a secured party has the rights and remedies provided in this Part and, except as limited by subsection (3), those provided in the security agreement. He may reduce his claim to judgment, foreclose or otherwise enforce the security interest by any available judicial procedure. If the collateral is documents, the secured party may proceed either as to the documents or as to the goods covered thereby. A secured party in possession has the rights, remedies and duties provided in Section 9—207. The rights and remedies referred to in this subsection are cumulative.

(2) After default, the debtor has the rights and remedies provided in this Part, those provided in the security agreement and those provided in Section 9—207.

(3) To the extent that they give rights to the debtor and impose duties on the secured party, the rules stated in the subsections referred to below may not be waived or varied except as provided with respect to compulsory disposition of collateral (subsection (3) of Section 9—504 and Section 9—505) and with respect to redemption of collateral (Section 9—506) but the parties may by agreement determine the standards by which the fulfillment of these rights and duties is to be measured if such standards are not manifestly unreasonable:

(a) subsection (2) of Section 9—502 and subsection (2) of Section 9—504 insofar as they require accounting for surplus proceeds of collateral;

(b) subsection (3) of Section 9—504 and subsection (1) of Section 9—505 which deal with disposition of collateral;

(c) subsection (2) of Section 9—505 which deals with acceptance of collateral as discharge of obligation;

(d) Section 9—506 which deals with redemption of collateral; and

(e) subsection (1) of Section 9—507 which deals with the secured party's liability for failure to comply with this Part.

(4) If the security agreement covers both real and personal property, the secured party may proceed under this Part as to the personal property or he may proceed as to both the real and the personal property in

accordance with his rights and remedies in respect of the real property, in which case the provisions of this Part do not apply.

(5) When a secured party has reduced his claim to judgment, the lien of any levy which may be made upon his collateral by virture of any execution based upon the judgment shall relate back to the date of the perfection of the security interest in such collateral. A judicial sale, pursuant to such execution, is a foreclosure of the security interest by judicial procedure within the meaning of this section, and the secured party may purchase at the sale and thereafter hold the collateral free of any other requirements of this Article.

§ 9 — 502. Collection Rights of Secured Party

(1) When so agreed, and in any event on default, the secured party is entitled to notify an account debtor or the obligor on an instrument to make payment to him whether or not the assignor was theretofore making collections on the collateral, and also to take control of any proceeds to which he is entitled under Section 9 — 306.

(2) A secured party who by agreement is entitled to charge back uncollected collateral or otherwise to full or limited recourse against the debtor and who undertakes to collect from the account debtors or obligors must proceed in a commercially reasonable manner and may deduct his reasonable expenses of realization from the collections. If the security agreement secures an indebtedness, the secured party must account to the debtor for any surplus, and unless otherwise agreed, the debtor is liable for any deficiency. But, if the underlying transaction was a sale of accounts or chattel paper, the debtor is entitled to any surplus or is liable for any deficiency only if the security agreement so provides.

§ 9 — 503. Secured Party's Right to Take Possession After Default

Unless otherwise agreed, a secured party has on default the right to take possession of the collateral. In taking possession, a secured party may proceed without judicial process if this can be done without breach of the peace or may proceed by action. If the security agreement so provides, the secured party may require the debtor to assemble the collateral and make it available to the secured party at a place to be designated by the secured party which is reasonably convenient to both parties. Without removal, a secured party may render equipment unusable and may dispose of collateral on the debtor's premises under Section 9 — 504.

§9 — 504. Secured Party's Right to Dispose of Collateral After Default; Effect of Disposition

(1) A secured party after default may sell, lease or otherwise dispose of any or all of the collateral in its then condition or following any commercially reasonable preparation or processing. Any sale of goods is subject to the Article on Sales (Article 2). The proceeds of disposition shall be applied in the order following to

(a) the reasonable expenses of retaking, holding, preparing for sale or lease, selling, leasing and the like and, to the extent provided for in the agreement and not prohibited by law, the reasonable attorneys' fees and legal expenses incurred by the secured party;

(b) the satisfaction of indebtedness secured by the security interest under which the disposition is made;

(c) the satisfaction of indebtedness secured by any subordinate security interest in the collateral if written notification of demand therefor is received before distribution of the proceeds is completed. If requested by the secured party, the holder of a subordinate security interest must seasonably furnish reasonable proof of his interest, and unless he does so, the secured party need not comply with his demand.

(2) If the security interest secures an indebtedness, the secured party must account to the debtor for any surplus, and, unless otherwise agreed, the debtor is liable for any deficiency. But if the underlying transaction was a sale of accounts or chattel paper, the debtor is entitled to any surplus or is liable for any deficiency only if the security agreement so provides.

(3) Disposition of the collateral may be by public or private proceedings and may be made by way of one or more contracts. Sale or other disposition may be as a unit or in parcels and at any time and place and on any terms but every aspect of the disposition including the method, manner, time, place and terms must be commercially reasonable. Unless collateral is perishable or threatens to decline speedily in value or is of a type customarily sold on a recognized market, reasonable notification of the time and place of any public sale or reasonable notification of the time after which any private sale or other intended disposition is to be made shall be sent by the secured party to the debtor, if he has not signed after default a statement renouncing or modifying his right to notification of sale. In the case of consumer goods, no other notification need be sent. In other cases, notification shall be sent to any other secured party from whom the secured party has received (before sending his notification to the debtor or before the debtor's renunciation of his rights) written notice of a claim of an interest in the collateral. The secured party may buy at any public sale; and if the collateral is of a type customarily sold in a recognized market or is of a type which is the subject of widely distributed standard price quotations, he may buy at private sale.

(4) When collateral is disposed of by a secured party after default, the disposition transfers to a pur-

chaser for value all of the debtor's rights therein, discharges the security interest under which it is made and any security interest or lien subordinate thereto. The purchaser takes free of all such rights and interests even though the secured party fails to comply with the requirements of this Part or of any judicial proceedings

    (a) in the case of a public sale, if the purchaser has no knowledge of any defects in the sale and if he does not buy in collusion with the secured party, other bidders or the person conducting the sale; or

    (b) in any other case, if the purchaser acts in good faith.

(5) A person who is liable to a secured party under a guaranty, indorsement, repurchase agreement or the like and who receives a transfer of collateral from the secured party or is subrogated to his rights thereafter the rights and duties of the secured party. Such a transfer of collateral is not a sale or disposition of the collateral under this Article.

§ 9—505. Compulsory Disposition of Collateral; Acceptance of the Collateral as Discharge of Obligation

(1) If the debtor has paid sixty percent of the cash price in the case of a purchase money security interest in consumer goods or sixty percent of the loan in the case of another security interest in consumer goods and has not signed after default a statement renouncing or modifying his rights under this Part, a secured party who has taken possession of collateral must dispose of it under Section 9—504; and if he fails to do so within ninety days after he takes possession, the debtor at his option may recover in conversion or under section 9—507(1) on secured party's liability.

(2) In any other case involving consumer goods or any other collateral, a secured party in possession may, after default, propose to retain the collateral in satisfaction of the obligation. Written notice of such proposal shall be sent to the debtor if he has not signed after default a statement renouncing or modifying his rights under this subsection. In the case of consumer goods, no other notice need be given. In other cases, notice shall be sent to any other secured party from whom the secured party has received (before sending his notice to the debtor or before the debtor's renunciation of his rights) written notice of a claim of an interest in the collateral. If the secured party receives objection in writing from a person entitled to receive notification within twenty-one days after the notice was sent, the secured party must dispose of the collateral under Section 9—504. In the absence of such written objection, the secured party may retain the collateral in satisfaction of the debtor's obligation.

§ 9—506. Debtor's Right to Redeem Collateral

At any time before the secured party has disposed of collateral or entered into a contract for its disposition under Section 9—504 or before the obligation has been discharged under Section 9—505(2), the debtor or any other secured party may, unless otherwise agreed in writing after default, redeem the collateral by tendering fulfillment of all obligations secured by the collateral as well as the expenses reasonably incurred by the secured party in retaking, holding and preparing the collateral for disposition, in arranging for the sale, and to the extent provided in the agreement and not prohibited by law, his reasonable attorneys' fees and legal expenses.

§ 9—507. Secured Party's Liability for Failure to Comply With This Part

(1) If it is established that the secured party is not proceeding in accordance with the provisions of this Part, disposition may be ordered or restrained on appropriate terms and conditions. If the disposition has occurred, the debtor or any person entitled to notification or whose security interest has been made known to the secured party prior to the disposition has a right to recover from the secured party any loss caused by a failure to comply with the provisions of this Part. If the collateral is consumer goods, the debtor has a right to recover in any event an amount not less than the credit service charge plus ten percent of the principal amount of the debt or the time price differential plus 10 percent of the cash price.

(2) The fact that a better price could have been obtained by a sale at a different time or in a different method from that selected by the secured party is not of itself sufficient to establish that the sale was not made in a commercially reasonable manner. If the secured party either sells the collateral in the usual manner in any recognized market therefor, or if he sells at the price current in such market at the time of his sale, or if he has otherwise sold in conformity with reasonable commercial practices among dealers in the type of property sold, he has sold in a commercially reasonable manner. The principles stated in the two preceding sentences with respect to sales also apply as may be appropriate to other types of disposition. A disposition which has been approved in any judicial proceeding or by any bona fide creditors' committee or representative of creditors shall conclusively be deemed to be commercially reasonable, but this sentence does not indicate that any such approval must be obtained in any case nor does it indicate that any disposition not so approved is not commercially reasonable.

ARTICLE 10

EFFECTIVE DATE AND REPEALER

See Article 11 for Transition Provisions for those juris-dictions adopting the 1972 amendments.

§ 10 — 101.   Effective Date

This Act shall become effective at midnight on December 31st following its enactment. It applies to transactions entered into and events occurring after that date.

§ 10 — 102.   Specific Repealer; Provision for Transition

(1) The following acts and all other acts and parts of acts inconsistent herewith are hereby repealed:

(Here should follow the acts to be specifically repealed including the following:

    Uniform Negotiable Instruments Act
    Uniform Warehouse Receipts Act
    Uniform Sales Act
    Uniform Bills of Lading Act
    Uniform Stock Transfer Act
    Uniform Conditional Sales Act
    Uniform Trust Receipts Act
    Also any acts regulating:
        Bank collections
        Bulk sales
        Chattel mortgages
        Conditional sales
        Factor's lien acts
        Farm storage of grain and similar acts
        Assignment of accounts receivable)

(2) Transactions validly entered into before the effective date specified in Section 10—101 and the rights, duties and interests flowing from them remain valid thereafter and may be terminated, completed, consummated or enforced as required or permitted by any statute or other law amended or repealed by this Act as though such repeal or amendment had not occurred.

Note: *Subsection (1) should be separately prepared for each state. The foregoing is a list of statutes to be checked.*

§ 10 — 103.   General Repealer

Except as provided in the following section, all acts and parts of acts inconsistent with this Act are hereby repealed.

§ 10 — 104.   Laws Not Repealed

[(1)] The Article on Documents of Title (Article 7) does not repeal or modify any laws prescribing the form or contents of documents of title or the services or facilities to be afforded by bailees, or otherwise regulating bailees' businesses in respects not specifically dealt with herein; but the fact that such laws are violated does not affect the status of a document of title which otherwise complies with the definition of a document of title (Section 1—201).

[(2) This act does not repeal . . . .
. . . .*, cited as the Uniform Act for the Simplification of Fiduciary Security Transfers, and if in any respect there is any inconsistency between that Act and the Article of this Act on investment securities (Article 8) the provisions of the former Act shall control.]

Note: *At* * *in subsection (2) insert the statutory reference to the Uniform Act for the Simplification of Fiduciary Security Transfers if such Act has previously been enacted. If it has not been enacted, omit subsection (2).*

ARTICLE 11

EFFECTIVE DATE AND TRANSITION PROVISIONS

This material has been numbered Article 11 to distinguish it from Article 10, the transition provision of the 1962 Code, which may still remain in effect in some states to cover transition problems from pre-Code law to the original Uniform Commercial Code. Adaptation may be necessary in particular states. The terms "[old Code]" and "[new Code]" and "[old U.C.C.]" and "[new U.C.C.]" are used herein and should be suitably changed in each state.

This draft was prepared by the Reporters and has not been passed upon by the Review Committee, the Permanent Editorial Board, the American Law Institute, or the National Conference of Commissioners or Uniform State Laws. It is submitted as a working draft which may be adapted as appropriate in each state.

§ 11 — 101.   Effective Date

This Act shall become effective at 12:01 A.M. on ____ , 19__ .

§ 11 — 102.   Preservation of Old Transition Provision

The provisions of [here insert reference to the original transition provision in the particular state] shall continue to apply to [the new U.C.C.] and for this purpose the [old U.C.C. and new U.C.C.] shall be considered one continuous statute.

§ 11 — 103.   Transition to [New Code] — General Rule

Transactions validly entered into after [effective date of old U.C.C.] and before [effective date of new U.C.C.], and which were subject to the provisions of [old U.C.C.] and which would be subject to this Act as amended if they had been entered into after the effective date of [new U.C.C.] and the rights, duties and interests flowing from such transactions remain valid after the latter date and may be terminated, completed, consummated or enforced as required or permitted by the [new U.C.C.]. Security interests arising out of such transactions which are perfected when [new U.C.C.] becomes effective shall remain perfected until they lapse as provided in [new U.C.C.], and may be continued as permitted by [new U.C.C.], except as stated in Section 11—105.

§ 11—104. Transition Provision on Change of Requirement of Filing

A security interest for the perfection of which filing or the taking of possession was required under [old U.C.C.] and which attached prior to the effective date of [new U.C.C.] but was not perfected shall be deemed perfected on the effective date of [new U.C.C.] if [new U.C.C.] permits perfection without filing or authorizes filing in the office or offices where a prior ineffective filing was made.

§ 11—105. Transition Provision on Change of Place of Filing

(1) A financing statement or continuation statement filed prior to [effective date of new U.C.C.] which shall not have lapsed prior to [the effective date of new U.C.C.] shall remain effective for the period provided in the [old Code], but not less than five years after the filing.

(2) With respect to any collateral acquired by the debtor subsequent to the effective date of [new U.C.C.], any effective financing statement or continuation statement described in this section shall apply only if the filing or filings are in the office or offices that would be appropriate to perfect the security interests in the new collateral under [new U.C.C.].

(3) The effectiveness of any financing statement or continuation statement filed prior to [effective date of new U.C.C.] may be continued by a continuation statement as permitted by [new U.C.C.], except that if [new U.C.C.] requires a filing in an office where there was no previous financing statement, a new financing statement conforming to Section 11—106 shall be filed in that office.

(4) If the record of a mortgage of real estate would have been effective as a fixture filing of goods described therein if [new U.C.C.] had been in effect on the date of recording the mortgage, the mortgage shall be deemed effective as a fixture filing as to such goods under subsection (6) of Section 9—402 of the [new U.C.C.] on the effective date of [new U.C.C.].

§ 11—106. Required Refilings

(1) If a security interest is perfected or has priority when this Act takes effect as to all persons or as to certain persons without any filing or recording, and if the filing of a financing statement would be required for the perfection or priority of the security interest

against those persons under [new U.C.C.], the perfection and priority rights of the security interest continue until 3 years after the effective date of [new U.C.C.]. The perfection will then lapse unless a financing statement is filed as provided in subsection (4) or unless the security interest is perfected otherwise than by filing.

(2) If a security interest is perfected when [new U.C.C.] takes effect under a law other than [U.C.C.] which requires no further filing, refiling or recording to continue its perfection, perfection continues until and will lapse 3 years after [new U.C.C.] takes effect, unless a financing statement is filed as provided in subsection (4) or unless the security interest is perfected otherwise than by filing, or unless under subsection (3) of Section 9—302 the other law continues to govern filing.

(3) If a security interest is perfected by a filing, refiling or recording under a law repealed by this Act which required further filing, refiling or recording to continue its perfection, perfection continues and will lapse on the date provided by the law so repealed for such further filing, refiling or recording unless a financing statement is filed as provided in subsection (4) or unless the security interest is perfected otherwise than by filing.

(4) A financing statement may be filed within six months before the perfection of a security interest would otherwise lapse. Any such financing statement may be signed by either the debtor or the secured party. It must identify the security agreement, statement or notice (however denominated in any statute or other law repealed or modified by this Act), state the office where and the date when the last filing, refiling or recording, if any, was made with respect thereto, and the filing number, if any, or book and page, if any, of recording and further state that the security agreement, statement or notice, however denominated, in another filing office under the [U.C.C.] or under any statute or other law repealed or modified by this Act is still effective. Section 9—401 and Section 9—103 determine the proper place to file such a financing statement. Except as specified in this subsection, the provisions of Section 9—403(3) for continuation statements apply to such a financing statement.

§ 11—107. Transition Provisions as to Priorities

Except as otherwise provided in [Article 11], [old U.C.C.] shall apply to any questions of priority if the positions of the parties were fixed prior to the effective date of [new U.C.C.]. In other cases questions of priority shall be determined by [new U.C.C.].

§ 11—108. Presumption that Rule of Law Continues Unchanged

Unless a change in law has clearly been made, the provisions of [new U.C.C.] shall be deemed declaratory of the meaning of the [old U.C.C.].

UNIFORM PARTNERSHIP ACT

Part 1

Preliminary Provisions

§ 1.   Name of Act

This act may be cited as Uniform Partnership Act.

§ 2.   Definition of Terms

In this act, "Court" includes every court and judge having jurisdiction in the case.

"Business" includes every trade, occupation, or profession.

"Person" includes individuals, partnerships, corporations, and other associations.

"Bankrupt" includes bankrupt under the Federal Bankruptcy Act or insolvent under any state insolvent act.

"Conveyance" includes every assignment, lease, mortgage, or encumbrance.

"Real property" includes land and any interest or estate in land.

§ 3.   Interpretation of Knowledge and Notice

(1) A person has "knowledge" of a fact within the meaning of this act not only when he has actual knowledge thereof, but also when he has knowledge of such other facts as in the circumstances shows bad faith.

(2) A person has "notice" of a fact within the meaning of this act when the person who claims the benefit of the notice

    (a) States the fact to such person, or

    (b) Delivers through the mail, or by other means of communication, a written statement of the fact to such person or to a proper person at his place of business or residence.

§ 4.   Rules of Construction

(1) The rule that statutes in derogation of the common law are to be strictly construed shall have no application to this act.

(2) The law of estoppel shall apply under this act.

(3) The law of agency shall apply under this act.

(4) This act shall be so interpreted and construed as to effect its general purpose to make uniform the law of those states which enact it.

(5) This act shall not be construed so as to impair the obligations of any contract existing when the act goes into effect, nor to affect any action or proceedings begun or right accrued before this act takes effect.

§ 5.   Rules for Cases Not Provided for in this Act

In any case not provided for in this act the rules of law and equity, including the law merchant, shall govern.

Part II

Nature of Partnership

§ 6.   Partnership Defined

(1) A partnership is an association of two or more persons to carry on as co-owners a business for profit.

(2) But any association formed under any other statute of this state, or any statute adopted by authority, other than the authority of this state, is not a partnership under this act, unless such association would have been a partnership in this state prior to the adoption of this act; but this act shall apply to limited partnerships except in so far as the statutes relating to such partnerships are inconsistent herewith.

§ 7.   Rules for Determining the Existence of a Partnership

In determining whether a partnership exists, these rules shall apply:

(1) Except as provided by Section 16 persons who are not partners as to each other are not partners as to third persons.

(2) Joint tenancy, tenancy in common, tenancy by the entireties, joint property, common property, or part ownership does not of itself establish a partnership, whether such co-owners do or do not share any profits made by the use of the property.

(3) The sharing of gross returns does not of itself establish a partnership, whether or not the persons sharing them have a joint or common right or interest in any property from which the returns are derived.

(4) The receipt by a person of a share of the profits of a business is prima facie evidence that he is a partner

in the business, but no such inference shall be drawn if such profits were received in payment:

> (a) As a debt by installments or otherwise,
> (b) As wages of an employee or rent to a landlord,
> (c) As an annuity to a widow or representative of a deceased partner,
> (d) As interest on a loan, though the amount of payment vary with the profits of the business,
> (e) As the consideration for the sale of a goodwill of a business or other property by installments or otherwise.

§ 8.   Partnership Property

(1) All property originally brought into the partnership stock or subsequently acquired by purchase or otherwise, on account of the partnership, is partnership property.

(2) Unless the contrary intention appears, property acquired with partnership funds is partnership property.

(3) Any estate in real property may be acquired in the partnership name. Title so acquired can be conveyed only in the partnership name.

(4) A conveyance to a partnership in the partnership name, though without words of inheritance, passes the entire estate of the grantor unless a contrary intent appears.

Part III

Relations of Partners to Persons Dealing with the Partnership

§ 9.   Partner Agent of Partnership as to Partnership Business

(1) Every partner is an agent of the partnership for the purpose of its business, and the act of every partner, including the execution in the partnership name of any instrument, for apparently carrying on in the usual way the business of the partnership of which he is a member binds the partnership, unless the partner so acting has in fact no authority to act for the partnership in the particular matter, and the person with whom he is dealing has knowledge of the fact that he has no such authority.

(2) An act of a partner which is not apparently for the carrying on of the business of the partnership in the usual way does not bind the partnership unless authorized by the other partners.

(3) Unless authorized by the other partners or unless they have abandoned the business, one or more but less than all the partners have no authority to:

> (a) Assign the partnership property in trust for creditors or on the assignee's promise to pay the debts of the partnership,

> (b) Dispose of the goodwill of the business,
> (c) Do any other act which would make it impossible to carry on the ordinary business of a partnership,
> (d) Confess a judgment,
> (e) Submit a partnership claim or liability to arbitration or reference.

(4) No act of a partner in contravention of a restriction on authority shall bind the partnership to persons having knowledge of the restriction.

§ 10.   Conveyance of Real Property of the Partnership

(1) Where title to real property is in the partnership name, any partner may convey title to such property by a conveyance executed in the partnership name; but the partnership may recover such property unless the partner's act binds the partnership under the provisions of paragraph (1) of section 9 or unless such property has been conveyed by the grantee or a person claiming through such grantee to a holder for value without knowledge that the partner, in making the conveyance, has exceeded his authority.

(2) Where title to real property is in the name of the partnership, a conveyance executed by a partner, in his own name, passes the equitable interest of the partnership, provided the act is one within the authority of the partner under the provisions of paragraph (1) of Section 9.

(3) Where title to real property is in the name of one or more but not all the partners, and the record does not disclose the right of the partnership, the partners in whose name the title stands may convey title to such property, but the partnership may recover such property if the partners' act does not bind the partnership under the provisions of paragraph (1) of section 9, unless the purchaser or his assignee, is a holder for value, without knowledge.

(4) Where the title to real property is in the name of one or more or all the partners, or in a third person in trust for the partnership, a conveyance executed by a partner in the partnership name, or in his own name, passes the equitable interest of the partnership, provided the act is one within the authority of the partner under the provisions of paragraph (1) of section 9.

(5) Where the title to real property is in the names of all the partners a conveyance executed by all the partners passes all their rights in such property.

§ 11.   Partnership Bound by Admission of Partner

An admission or representation made by any partner concerning partnership affairs within the scope of his authority as conferred by this act is evidence against the partnership.

§ 12. Partnership Charged with Knowledge of or Notice to Partner

Notice to any partner of any matter relating to partnership affairs, and the knowledge of the partner acting in the particular matter, acquired while a partner or then present to his mind, and the knowledge of any other partner who reasonably could and should have communicated it to the acting partner, operate as notice to or knowledge of the partnership, except in the case of a fraud on the partnership committed by or with the consent of that partner.

§ 13. Partnership Bound by Partner's Wrongful Act

Where, by any wrongful act or omission of any partner acting in the ordinary course of the business of the partnership or with the authority of his co-partners, loss or injury is caused to any person, not being a partner in the partnership, or any penalty is incurred, the partnership is liable therefor to the same extent as the partner so acting or omitting to act.

§ 14. Partnership Bound by Partner's Breach of Trust

The partnership is bound to make good the loss:

(a) Where one partner acting within the scope of his apparent authority receives money or property of a third person and misapplies it; and

(b) Where the partnership in the course of its business receives money or property of a third person and the money or property so received is misapplied by any partner while it is in the custody of the partnership.

§ 15. Nature of Partner's Liability

All partners are liable

(a) Jointly and severally for everything chargeable to the partnership under sections 13 and 14.

(b) Jointly for all other debts and obligations of the partnership; but any partner may enter into a separate obligation to perform a partnership contract.

§ 16. Partner by Estoppel

(1) When a person, by words spoken or written or by conduct, represents himself, or consents to another representing him to any one, as a partner in an existing partnership or with one or more persons not actual partners, he is liable to any such person to whom such representation has been made, who has, on the faith of such representation, given credit to the actual or apparent partnership, and if he has made such representation or consented to its being made in a public manner he is liable to such person, whether the representation has or has not been made or communicated to such person so giving credit by or with the knowl-edge of the apparent partner making the representation or consenting to its being made.

(a) When a partnership liability results, he is liable as though he were an actual member of the partnership.

(b) When no partnership liability results, he is liable jointly with the other persons, if any, so consenting to the contract or representation as to incur liability, otherwise separately.

(2) When a person has been thus represented to be a partner in an existing partnership, or with one or more persons not actual partners, he is an agent of the persons consenting to such representation to bind them to the same extent and in the same manner as though he were a partner in fact, with respect to persons who rely upon the representation. Where all the members of the existing partnership consent to the representation, a partnership act or obligation results; but in all other cases it is the joint act or obligation of the person acting and the persons consenting to the representation.

§ 17. Liability of Incoming Partner

A person admitted as a partner into an existing partnership is liable for all the obligations of the partnership arising before his admission as though he had been a partner when such obligations were incurred, except that this liability shall be satisfied only out of partnership property.

Part IV
Relations of Partners to One Another

§ 18. Rules Determining Rights and Duties of Partners

The rights and duties of the partners in relation to the partnership shall be determined, subject to any agreement between them, by the following rules:

(a) Each partner shall be repaid his contributions, whether by way of capital or advances to the partnership property and share equally in the profits and surplus remaining after all liabilities, including those to partners, are satisfied; and must contribute toward the losses, whether of capital or otherwise, sustained by the partnership according to his share in the profits.

(b) The partnership must indemnify every partner in respect of payments made and personal liabilities reasonably incurred by him in the ordinary and proper conduct of its business, or for the preservation of its business or property.

(c) A partner, who in aid of the partnership makes any payment or advance beyond the amount of capital which he agreed to contribute, shall be paid interest from the date of the payment or advance.

(d) A partner shall receive interest on the capital contributed by him only from the date when repayment should be made.

(e) All partners have equal rights in the management and conduct of the partnership business.

(f) No partner is entitled to remuneration for acting in the partnership business, except that a surviving partner is entitled to reasonable compensation for his services in winding up the partnership affairs.

(g) No person can become a member of a partnership without the consent of all the partners.

(h) Any difference arising as to ordinary matters connected with the partnership business may be decided by a majority of the partners; but no act in contravention of any agreement between the partners may be done rightfully without the consent of all the partners.

§ 19. Partnership Books

The partnership books shall be kept, subject to any agreement between the partners, at the principal place of business of the partnership, and every partner shall at all times have access to and may inspect and copy any of them.

§ 20. Duty of Partners to Render Information

Partners shall render on demand true and full information of all things affecting the partnership to any partner or the legal representative of any deceased partner or partner under legal disability.

§ 21. Partner Accountable as a Fiduciary

(1) Every partner must account to the partnership for any benefit, and hold as trustee for it any profits derived by him without the consent of the other partners from any transaction connected with the formation, conduct, or liquidation of the partnership or from any use by him of its property.

(2) This section applies also to the representatives of a deceased partner engaged in the liquidation of the affairs of the partnership as the personal representatives of the last surviving partner.

§ 22. Right to an Account

Any partner shall have the right to a formal account as to partnership affairs:

(a) If he is wrongfully excluded from the partnership business or possession of its property by his co-partners,

(b) If the right exists under the terms of any agreement,

(c) As provided by Section 21,

(d) Whenever other circumstances render it just and reasonable.

§ 23. Continuation of Partnership Beyond Fixed Term

(1) When a partnership for a fixed term or particular undertaking is continued after the termination of such term or particular undertaking without any express agreement, the rights and duties of the partners remain the same as they were at such termination, so far as is consistent with a partnership at will.

(2) A continuation of the business by the partners or such of them as habitually acted therein during the term, without any settlement or liquidation of the partnership affairs, is prima facie evidence of a continuation of the partnership.

Part V

Property Rights of a Partner

§ 24. Extent of Property Rights of a Partner

The property rights of a partner are (1) his rights in specific partnership property, (2) his interest in the partnership, and (3) his right to participate in the management.

§ 25. Nature of a Partner's Right in Specific Partnership Property

(1) A partner is co-owner with his partners of specific partnership property holding as a tenant in partnership.

(2) The incidents of this tenancy are such that:

(a) A partner, subject to the provisions of this act and to any agreement between the partners, has an equal right with his partners to possess specific partnership property for partnership purposes; but he has no right to possess such property for any other purpose without the consent of his partners.

(b) A partner's right in specific partnership property is not assignable except in connection with the assignment of rights of all the partners in the same property.

(c) A partner's right in specific partnership property is not subject to attachment or execution, except on a claim against the partnership. When partnership property is attached for a partnership debt the partners, or any of them, or the representatives of a deceased partner, cannot claim any right under the homestead or exemption laws.

(d) On the death of a partner his right in specific partnership property vests in the surviving partner or partners, except where the deceased was the last surviving partner or partners, or the legal representative of the last surviving partner, has no right to possess the partnership property for any but a partnership purpose.

(e) A partner's right in specific partnership property is not subject to dower, courtesy, or allowances to widows, heirs, or next of kin.

§ 26. Nature of Partner's Interest in the Partnership

A partner's interest in the partnership is his share of the profits and surplus, and the same is personal property.

§ 27. Assignment of Partner's Interest

(1) A conveyance by a partner of his interest in the partnership does not of itself dissolve the partnership, nor, as against the other partners in the absence of agreement, entitle the assignee, during the continuance of the partnership to interfere in the management or administration of the partnership business or affairs, or to require an information or account of partnership transactions, or to inspect the partnership books; but it merely entitles the assignee to receive in accordance with his contract the profits to which the assigning partner would otherwise be entitled.

(2) In case of a dissolution of the partnership, the assignee is entitled to receive his assignor's interest and may require an account from the date only of the last account agreed to by all the partners.

§ 28. Partner's Interest Subject to Charging Order

(1) On due application to a competent court by any judgment creditor of a partner, the court which entered the judgment, order, or decree, or any other court, may charge the interest of the debtor partner with payment of the unsatisfied amount of such judgment debt with interest thereon; and may then or later appoint a receiver of his share of the profits, and of any other money due or to fall due to him in respect of the partnership, and make all other orders, directions, accounts and inquiries which the debtor partner might have made, or which the circumstances of the case may require.

(2) The interest charged may be redeemed at any time before foreclosure, or in case of a sale being directed by the court may be purchased without thereby causing a dissolution:

(a) With separate property, by any one or more of the partners, or

(b) With partnership property, by any one or more of the partners with the consent of all the partners whose interests are not so charged or sold.

(3) Nothing in this act shall be held to deprive a partner of his right, if any, under the exemption laws, as regards his interest in the partnership.

Part VI
Dissolution and Winding Up

§ 29. Dissolution Defined

The dissolution of a partnership is the change in the relation of the partners caused by any partner ceasing to be associated in the carrying on as distinguished from the winding up of the business.

§ 30. Partnership Not Terminated by Dissolution

On dissolution the partnership is not terminated, but continues until the winding up of partnership affairs is completed.

§ 31. Causes of Dissolution

Dissolution is caused: (1) Without violation of the agreement between the partners,

(a) By the termination of the definite term or particular undertaking specified in the agreement,

(b) By the express will of any partner when no definite term or particular undertaking is specified,

(c) By the express will of all the partners who have not assigned their interests or suffered them to be charged for their separate debts, either before or after the termination of any specified term or particular undertaking,

(d) By the expulsion of any partner from the business bona fide in accordance with such a power conferred by the agreement between the partners;

(2) In contravention of the agreement between the partners, where the circumstances do not permit a dissolution under any other provision of this section, by the express will of any partner at any time;

(3) By any event which makes it unlawful for the business of the partnership to be carried on or for the members to carry it on in partnership;

(4) By the death of any partner;

(5) By the bankruptcy of any partner or the partnership;

(6) By decree of court under Section 32.

§ 32. Dissolution by Decree of Court

(1) On application by or for a partner the court shall decree a dissolution whenever:

(a) A partner has been declared a lunatic in any judicial proceeding or is shown to be of unsound mind,

(b) A partner becomes in any other way incapable of performing his part of the partnership contract,

(c) A partner has been guilty of such conduct as tends to affect prejudicially the carrying on of the business,

(d) A partner willfully or persistently commits a breach of the partnership agreement, or otherwise so conducts himself in matters relating to the partnership business that it is not reasonably practicable to carry on the business in partnership with him,

(e) The business of the partnership can only be carried on at a loss,

(f) Other circumstances render a dissolution equitable.

(2) On the application of the purchaser of a partner's interest under Sections 27 or 28:

(a) After the termination of the specified term or particular undertaking,

(b) At any time if the partnership was a partnership at will when the interest was assigned or when the charging order was issued.

§ 33. General Effect of Dissolution on Authority of Partner

Except so far as may be necessary to wind up partnership affairs or to complete transactions begun but not then finished, dissolution terminates all authority of any partner to act for the partnership,

(1) With respect to the partners,

(a) When the dissolution is not by the act, bankruptcy or death of a partner, or

(b) When the dissolution is by such act, bankruptcy or death of a partner, in cases where Section 34 so requires.

(2) With respect to persons not partners, as declared in Section 35.

§ 34. Right of Partner to Contribution from Copartners After Dissolution

Where the dissolution is caused by the act, death or bankruptcy of a partner, each partner is liable to his copartners for his share of any liability created by any partner acting for the partnership as if the partnership had not been dissolved unless

(a) The dissolution being by act of any partner, the partner acting for the partnership had knowledge of the dissolution, or

(b) The dissolution being by the death or bankruptcy of a partner, the partner acting for the partnership had knowledge or notice of the death or bankruptcy.

§ 35. Power of Partner to Bind Partnership to Third Persons After Dissolution

(1) After dissolution a partner can bind the partnership except as provided in Paragraph (3)

(a) By any act appropriate for winding up partnership affairs or completing transactions unfinished by dissolution;

(b) By any transaction which would bind the partnership if dissolution had not taken place, provided the other party to the transaction

(I) Had extended credit to the partnership prior to dissolution and had no knowledge or notice of the dissolution; or

(II) Though he had not so extended credit, had nevertheless known of the partnership prior to dissolution, and, having no knowledge or notice of dissolution, the fact of dissolution had not been advertised in a newspaper of general circulation in the place (or in each place if more than one) at which the partnership business was regularly carried on.

(2) The liability of a partner under paragraph (1b) shall be satisfied out of partnership assets alone when such partner had been prior to dissolution.

(a) Unknown as a partner to the person with whom the contract is made; and

(b) So far unknown and inactive in partnership affairs that the business reputation of the partnership could not be said to have been in any degree due to his connection with it.

(3) The partnership is in no case bound by any act of a partner after dissolution.

(a) Where the partnership is dissolved because it is unlawful to carry on the business, unless the act is appropriate for winding up partnership affairs; or

(b) Where the partner has become bankrupt; or

(c) Where the partner has no authority to wind up partnership affairs; except by a transaction with one who

(I) Had extended credit to the partnership prior to dissolution and had no knowledge or notice of his want of authority; or

(II) Had not extended credit to the partnership prior to dissolution, and, having no knowledge or notice of his want of authority, the fact of his want of authority has not been advertised in the manner provided for advertising the fact of dissolution in paragraph (1bII).

(4) Nothing in this section shall affect the liability under section 16 of any person who after dissolution represents himself or consents to another representing him as a partner in a partnership engaged in carrying on business.

§ 36. Effect of Dissolution on Partner's Existing Liability

(1) The dissolution of the partnership does not of itself discharge the existing liability of any partner.

(2) A partner is discharged from any existing liability upon dissolution of the partnership by an agree-

ment to that effect between himself, the partnership creditor and the person or partnership continuing the business; and such agreement may be inferred from the course of dealing between the creditor having knowledge of the dissolution and the person or partnership continuing the business.

(3) Where a person agrees to assume the existing obligations of a dissolved partnership, the partners whose obligations have been assumed shall be discharged from any liability to any creditor of the partnership who, knowing of the agreement, consents to a material alteration in the nature or time of payment of such obligations.

(4) The individual property of a deceased partner shall be liable for all obligations of the partnership incurred while he was a partner but subject to the prior payment of his separate debts.

§ 37. Right to Wind Up

Unless otherwise agreed the partners who have not wrongfully dissolved the partnership or the legal representative of the last surviving partner, not bankrupt, has the right to wind up the partnership affairs; provided, however, that any partner, his legal representative or his assignee, upon cause shown, may obtain winding up by the court.

§ 38. Rights of Partners to Application of Partnership Property

(1) When dissolution is caused in any way, except in contravention of the partnership agreement, each partner as against his co-partners and all persons claiming through them in respect of their interests in the partnership, unless otherwise agreed, may have the partnership property applied to discharge its liabilities, and the surplus applied to pay in cash the net amount owing to the respective partners. But if dissolution is caused by expulsion of a partner, bona fide under the partnership agreement and if the expelled partner is discharged from all partnership liabilities, either by payment or agreement under Section 36(2), he shall receive in cash only the net amount due him from the partnership.

(2) When dissolution is caused in contravention of the partnership agreement the rights of the partners shall be as follows:

(a) Each partner who has not caused dissolution wrongfully shall have,
  (I) All the rights specified in paragraph (1) of this section, and
  (II) The right, as against each partner who has caused the dissolution wrongfully, to damages for breach of the agreement.
(b) The partners who have not caused the dissolution wrongfully, if they all desire to continue the business in the same name, either by themselves or jointly with others, may do so, during the

agreed term for the partnership and for that purpose may possess the partnership property, provided they secure the payment by bond approved by the court, or pay to any partner who has caused the dissolution wrongfully, the value of his interest in the partnership at the dissolution, less any damages recoverable under clause (2aII) of the section, and in like manner indemnify him against all present or future partnership liabilities.

(c) A partner who has caused the dissolution wrongfully shall have:
  (I) If the business is not continued under the provisions of paragraph (2b) all the rights of a partner under paragraph (1), subject to clause (2aII), of this section,
  (II) If the business is continued under paragraph (2b) of this section the right as against his co-partners and all claiming through them in respect of their interests in the partnership, less any damages caused to his copartners by the dissolution, ascertained and paid to him in cash, or the payment secured by bond approved by the court, and to be released from all existing liabilities of the partnership; but in ascertaining the value of the partner's interest the value of the goodwill of the business shall not be considered.

§ 39. Rights Where Partnership is Dissolved for Fraud or Misrepresentation

Where a partnership contract is rescinded on the ground of the fraud or misrepresentation of one of the parties thereto, the party entitled to rescind is, without prejudice to any other right, entitled,

(a) To a lien on, or right of retention of, the surplus of the partnership property after satisfying the partnership liabilities to third persons for any sum of money paid by him for the purchase of an interest in the partnership and for any capital or advances contributed by him; and
(b) To stand, after all liabilities to third persons have been satisfied, in the place of the creditors of the partnership for any payments made by him in respect of the partnership liabilities; and
(c) To be indemnified by the person guilty of the fraud or making the representation against all debts and liabilities of the partnership.

§ 40. Rules for Distribution

In settling accounts between the partners after dissolution, the following rules shall be observed, sub-

ject to any agreement to the contrary:
- (a) The assets of the partnership are:
  - (I) The partnership property,
  - (II) The contributions of the partners necessary for the payment of all the liabilities specified in clause (b) of this paragraph.
- (b) The liabilities of the partnership shall rank in order of payment, as follows:
  - (I) Those owing to creditors other than partners,
  - (II) Those owing to partners other than for capital and profits,
  - (III) Those owing to partners in respect of capital,
  - (IV) Those owing to partners in respect of profits.
- (c) The assets shall be applied in the order of their declaration in clause (a) of this paragraph to the satisfaction of the liabilities.
- (d) The partners shall contribute, as provided by Section 18(a) the amount necessary to satisfy the liabilities; but if any, but not all, of the partners are insolvent, or, not being subject to process, refuse to contribute, the other parties shall contribute their share of the liabilities, and, in the relative proportions in which they share the profits, the additional amount necessary to pay the liabilities.
- (e) An assignee for the benefit of creditors or any person appointed by the court shall have the right to enforce the contributions specified in clause (d) of this paragraph.
- (f) Any partner or his legal representative shall have the right to enforce the contributions specified in clause (d) of this paragraph, to the extent of the amount which he has paid in excess of his share of the liability.
- (g) The individual property of a deceased partner shall be liable for the contributions specified in clause (d) of this paragraph.
- (h) When partnership property and the individual properties of the partners are in possession of a court for distribution, partnership creditors shall have priority on partnership property and separate creditors on individual property, saving the rights of lien or secured creditors as heretofore.
- (i) Where a partner has become bankrupt or his estate is insolvent the claims against his separate property shall rank in the following order:
  - (I) Those owing to separate creditors,
  - (II) Those owing to partnership creditors,
  - (III) Those owing to partners by way of contribution.

§ 41. Liability of Persons Continuing the Business in Certain Cases

(1) When any new partner is admitted into an existing partnership, or when any partner retires and assigns (or the representative of the deceased partner assigns) his rights in partnership property to two or more of the partners, or to one or more of the partners and one or more third persons, if the business is continued without liquidation of the partnership affairs, creditors of the first or dissolved partnership are also creditors of the partnership so continuing the business.

(2) When all but one partner retire and assign (or the representative of a deceased partner assigns) their rights in partnership property to the remaining partner, who continues the business without liquidation of partnership affairs, either alone or with others, creditors of the dissolved partnership are also creditors of the person or partnership so continuing the business.

(3) When any partner retires or dies and the business of the dissolved partnership is continued as set forth in paragraphs (1) and (2) of this section, with the consent of the retired partners or the representative of the deceased partner, but without any assignment of his right in partnership property, rights of creditors of the dissolved partnership and of the creditors of the person or partnership and of the creditors of the person or partnership continuing the business shall be as if such assignment had been made.

(4) When all the partners or their representatives assign their rights in partnership property to one or more third persons who promise to pay the debts and who continue the business of the dissolved partnership, creditors of the dissolved partnership are also creditors of the person or partnership continuing the business.

(5) When any partner wrongfully causes a dissolution and the remaining partners continue the business under the provisions of Section 38(2b), either alone or with others, and without liquidation of the partnership affairs, creditors of the dissolved partnership are also creditors of the person or partnership continuing the business.

(6) When a partner is expelled and the remaining partners continue the business either alone or with others, without liquidation of the partnership affairs, creditors of the dissolved partnership are also creditors of the person or partnership continuing the business.

(7) The liability of a third person becoming a partner in the partnership continuing the business, under this section, to the creditors of the dissolved partnership shall be satisfied out of partnership property only.

(8) When the business of a partnership after dissolution is continued under any conditions set forth in

this section the creditors of the dissolved partnership, as against the separate creditors of the retiring or deceased partner or the representative of the deceased partner, have a prior right to any claim of the retired partner or the representative of the deceased partner against the person or partnership continuing the business, on account of the retired partner or the representative of the deceased partner against the person or partnership continuing the business, on account of the retired or deceased partner's interest in the dissolved partnership or on account of any consideration promised for such interest or for his right in partnership property.

(9) Nothing in this section shall be held to modify any right of creditors to set aside any assignment on the ground of fraud.

(10) The use by the person or partnership continuing the business of the partnership name, or the name of a deceased partner as part thereof, shall not of itself make the individual property of the deceased partner liable for any debts contracted by such person or partnership.

§ 42. Rights of Retiring or Estate of Deceased Partner When the Business Is Continued

When any partner retires or dies, and the business is continued under any of the conditions set forth in Section 41(1, 2, 3, 5, 6), or Section 38(2b), without any settlement of accounts as between him or his estate and the person or partnership continuing the business, unless otherwise agreed, he or his legal representative as against such persons or partnership may have the value of his interest at the date of dissolution ascertained, and shall receive as an ordinary creditor an amount equal to the value of his interest in the dissolved partnership with interest, or, at his option or at the option of his legal representative, in lieu of interest, the profits attributable to the use of his right in the property of the dissolved partnership as against the separate creditors, or the representative of the retired or deceased partner, shall have priority on any claim arising under this section, as provided by Section 41(8) of this act.

§ 43. Accrual of Actions

The right to an account of his interest shall accrue to any partner, or his legal representative, as against the winding up partners or the surviving partners or the person or partnership continuing the business, at the date of dissolution, in the absence of any agreement to the contrary.

Part VII

Miscellaneous Provisions

§ 44. When Act Takes Effect

This act shall take effect on the ____ day of ____ one thousand nine hundred and ____.

§ 45. Legislation Repealed

All acts or parts of acts inconsistent with this act are hereby repealed.

UNIFORM LIMITED PARTNERSHIP ACT

---

§ 1. Limited Partnership Defined

A limited partnership is a partnership formed by two or more persons under the provisions of Section 2, having as members one or more general partners and one or more limited partners. The limited partners as such shall not be bound by the obligations of the partnership.

§ 2. Formation

(1) Two or more persons desiring to form a limited partnership shall

(a) Sign and swear to a certificate, which shall state

  (i) The name of the partnership,

  (ii) The character of the business,

  (iii) The location of the principal place of business,

  (iv) The name and place of residence of each member; general and limited partners being respectively designated,

  (v) The term for which the partnership is to exist,

  (vi) The amount of cash and a description of and the agreed value of the other property contributed by each limited partner,

  (vii) The additional contributions, if any, agreed to be made by each limited partner and the times at which or events on the happening of which they shall be made,

  (viii) The time, if agreed upon, when the contribution of each limited partner is to be returned,

  (ix) The share of the profits or the other compensation by way of income which each limited partner shall receive by reason of his contribution,

  (x) The right, if given, of a limited partner to substitute an assignee as con-

tributor in his place, and the terms and conditions of the substitution,

  (xi) The right, if given, of the partners to admit additional limited partners,

  (xii) The right, if given, of one or more of the limited partners to priority over other limited partners, as to contributions or as to compensation by way of income, and the nature of such priority,

  (xiii) The right, if given, of the remaining general partner or partners to continue the business on the death, retirement or insanity of a general partner, and

  (xiv) The right, if given, of a limited partner to demand and receive property other than cash in return for his contribution.

(b) File for record the certificate in the office of [here designate the proper office].

(2) A limited partnership is formed if there has been substantial compliance in good faith with the requirements of paragraph (1).

§ 3. Business Which May Be Carried On

A limited partnership may carry on any business which a partnership without limited partners may carry on, except [here designate the business to be prohibited].

§ 4. Character of Limited Partner's Contribution

The contributions of a limited partner may be cash or other property, but not services.

§ 5. A Name Not to Contain Surname of Limited Partner; Exceptions

(1) The surname of a limited partner shall not appear in the partnership name, unless

(a) It is also the surname of a general partner, or

(b) Prior to the time when the limited partner became such the business had been carried on under a name in which his surname appeared.

(2) A limited partner whose name appears in a partnership name contrary to the provisions of paragraph (1) is liable as a general partner to partnership creditors who extend credit to the partnership without actual knowledge that he is not a general partner.

§ 6.   Liability for False Statements in Certificate

If the certificate contains a false statement, one who suffers loss by reliance on such statement may hold liable any party to the certificate who knew the statement to be false.

(a) At the time he signed the certificate, or

(b) Subsequently, but within a sufficient time before the statement was relied upon to enable him to cancel or amend the certificate, or to file a petition for its cancellation or amendment as provided in Section 25(3).

§ 7.   Limited Partner Not Liable to Creditors

A limited partner shall not become liable as a general partner unless, in addition to the exercise of his rights and powers as a limited partner, he takes part in the control of the business.

§ 8.   Admission of Additional Limited Partners

After the formation of a limited partnership, additional limited partners may be admitted upon filing an amendment to the original certificate in accordance with the requirements of Section 25.

§ 9.   Rights, Powers, and Liabilities of a General Partner

(1) A general partner shall have all the rights and powers and be subject to all the restrictions and liabilities of a partner in a partnership without limited partners, except that without the written consent or ratification of the specific act by all the limited partners, a general partner or all of the general partners have no authority to

(a) Do any act in contravention of the certificate,

(b) Do any act which would make it impossible to carry on the ordinary business of the partnership,

(c) Confess a judgment against the partnership,

(d) Possess partnership property, or assign their rights in specific partnership property, for other than a partnership purpose,

(e) Admit a person as a general partner,

(f) Admit a person as a limited partner, unless the right so to do is given in the certificate,

(g) Continue the business with partnership property on the death, retirement or insanity of a general partner, unless the right so to do is given in the certificate.

§ 10.   Rights of a Limited Partner

(1) A limited partner shall have the same rights as a general partner to

(a) Have the partnership books kept at the principal place of business of the partnership, and at all times to inspect and copy any of them.

(b) Have on demand true and full information of all things affecting the partnership, and a formal account of partnership affairs whenever circumstances render it just and reasonable, and

(c) Have dissolution and winding up by decree of court.

(2) A limited partner shall have the right to receive a share of the profits or other compensation by way of income, and to the return of his contribution as provided in Sections 15 and 16.

§ 11.   Status of Person Erroneously Believing Himself a Limited Partner

A person who has contributed to the capital of a business conducted by a person or partnership erroneously believing that he has become a limited partner in a limited partnership, is not, by reason of his exercise of the rights of a limited partner, a general partner with the person or in the partnership carrying on the business, or bound by the obligations of such person or partnership; provided that on ascertaining the mistake he promptly renounces his interest in the profits of the business, or other compensation by way of income.

§ 12.   One Person Both General and Limited Partner

(1) A person may be a general partner and a limited partner in the same partnership at the same time.

(2) A person who is a general, and also at the same time a limited partner, shall have all the rights and powers and be subject to all the restrictions of a general partner; except that, in respect to his contribution, he shall have the rights against the other members which he would have had if he were not also a general partner.

§ 13.   Loans and Other Business Transactions with Limited Partner

(1) A limited partner also may loan money to and transact other business with the partnership, and, unless he is also a general partner, receive on account of resulting claims against the partnership, with general creditors, a pro rata share of the assets. No limited partner shall in respect to any such claim

(a) Receive or hold as collateral security any partnership property, or

(b) Receive from a general partner or the partnership any payment, conveyance, or release from liability, if at the time the assets of the partnership are not sufficient to discharge partnership liabilities to persons not claiming as general or limited partners.

(2) The receiving of collateral security, or a payment, conveyance, or release in violation of the provisions of paragraph (1) is a fraud on the creditors of the partnership.

§ 14. Relation of Limited Partners Inter Se

Where there are several limited partners the members may agree that one or more of the limited partners shall have a priority over other limited partners as to the return of their contributions, as to their compensation by way of income, or as to any other matter. If such an agreement is made it shall be stated in the certificate, and in the absence of such a statement all the limited partners shall stand upon equal footing.

§ 15. Compensation of Limited Partner

A limited partner may receive from the partnership the share of the profits or the compensation by way of income stipulated for in the certificate; provided, that after such payment is made, whether from the property of the partnership or that of a general partner, the partnership assets are in excess of all liabilities of the partnership except liabilities to limited partners on account of their contributions and to general partners.

§ 16. Withdrawal or Reduction of Limited Partner's Contribution

(1) A limited partner shall not receive from a general partner or out of partnership property any part of his contribution until

(a) All liabilities of the partnership, except liabilities to general partners and to limited partners on account of their contributions, have been paid or there remains property of the partnership sufficient to pay them,

(b) The consent of all members is had, unless the return of the contribution may be rightfully demanded under the provisions of paragraph (2), and

(c) The certificate is cancelled or so amended as to set forth the withdrawal or reduction.

(2) Subject to the provisions of paragraph (1) a limited partner may rightfully demand the return of his contribution

(a) On the dissolution of a partnership, or

(b) When the date specified in the certificate for its return has arrived, or

(c) After he has given six months' notice in writing to all other members, if no time is specified in the certificate either for the return of the contribution or for the dissolution of the partnership.

(3) In the absence of any statement in the certificate to the contrary or the consent of all members, a limited partner, irrespective of the nature of his contribution, has only the right to demand and receive cash in return for his contribution.

(4) A limited partner may have the partnership dissolved and its affairs wound up when

(a) He rightfully but unsuccessfully demands the return of his contribution, or

(b) The other liabilities of the partnership have not been paid, or the partnership property is insufficient for their payment as required by paragraph (1a) and the limited partner would otherwise be entitled to the return of his contribution.

§ 17. Liability of Limited Partner to Partnership

(1) A limited partner is liable to the partnership

(a) For the difference between his contribution as actually made and that stated in the certificate as having been made, and

(b) For any unpaid contribution which he agreed in the certificate to make in the future at the time and on the conditions stated in the certificate.

(2) A limited partner holds as trustee for the partnership

(a) Specific property stated in the certificate as contributed by him, but which was not contributed or which has been wrongfully returned, and

(b) Money or other property wrongfully paid or conveyed to him on account of his contribution.

(3) The liabilities of a limited partner as set forth in this section can be waived or compromised only by the consent of all members; but a waiver or compromise shall not affect the right of a creditor of a partnership who extended credit or whose claim arose after the filing and before a cancellation or amendment of the certificate, to enforce such liabilities.

(4) When a contributor has rightfully received the return in whole or in part of the capital of his contribution, he is nevertheless liable to the partnership for any sum, not in excess of such return with interest, necessary to discharge its liabilities to all creditors who extended credit or whose claims arose before such return.

§ 18. Nature of Limited Partner's Interest in Partnership

A limited partner's interest in the partnership is personal property.

§ 19. Assignment of Limited Partner's Interest

(1) A limited partner's interest is assignable.

(2) A substituted limited partner is a person ad-

mitted to all the rights of a limited partner who has died or has assigned his interest in a partnership.

(3) An assignee, who does not become a substituted limited partner, has no right to require any information or account of the partnership transactions or to inspect the partnership books; he is only entitled to receive the share of the profits or other compensation by way of income, or the return of his contribution, to which his assignor would otherwise be entitled.

(4) An assignee shall have the right to become a substituted limited partner if all the members (except the assignor) consent thereto or if the assignor, being thereunto empowered by the certificate, gives the assignee that right.

(5) An assignee becomes a substituted limited partner when the certificate is appropriately amended in accordance with Section 25.

(6) The substituted limited partner has all the rights and powers, and is subject to all the restrictions and liabilities of his assignor, except those liabilities of which he was ignorant at the time he became a limited partner and which could not be ascertained from the certificate.

(7) The substitution of the assignee as a limited partner does not release the assignor from liability to the partnership under Sections 6 and 17.

§ 20. Effect of Retirement, Death or Insanity of a General Partner

The retirement, death or insanity of a general partner dissolves the partnership, unless the business is continued by the remaining general partners

(a) Under a right so to do stated in the certificate, or

(b) With the consent of all members.

§ 21. Death of Limited Partner

(1) On the death of a limited partner his executor or administrator shall have all the rights of a limited partner for the purpose of settling his estate, and such power as the deceased had to constitute his assignee a substituted limited partner.

(2) The estate of a deceased limited partner shall be liable for all his liabilities as a limited partner.

§ 22. Rights of Creditors of Limited Partners

(1) On due application to a court of competent jurisdiction by any judgment creditor of a limited partner, the court may charge the interest of the indebted limited partner with payment of the unsatisfied amount of the judgment debt; and may appoint a receiver, and make all other orders, directions, and inquiries which the circumstances of the case may require.

(2) The interest may be redeemed with the separate property of any general partner, but may not be redeemed with partnership property.

(3) The remedies conferred by paragraph (1) shall not be deemed exclusive of others which may exist.

(4) Nothing in this act shall be held to deprive a limited partner of his statutory exemption.

§ 23. Distribution of Assets

(1) In settling accounts after dissolution the liabilities of the partnership shall be entitled to payment in the following order:

(a) Those to creditors, in the order of priority as provided by law, except those to limited partners on account of their contributions, and to general partners,

(b) Those to limited partners in respect to their share of the profits and other compensation by way of income on their contributions,

(c) Those to limited partners in respect to the capital of their contributions,

(d) Those to general partners other than for capital and profits,

(e) Those to general partners in respect to profits,

(f) Those to general partners in respect to capital.

(2) Subject to any statement in the certificate or to subsequent agreement, limited partners share in the partnership assets in respect to their claims for capital, and in respect to their claims for profits or for compensation by way of income on their contributions respectively, in proportion to the respective amounts of such claims.

§ 24. When Certificate Shall be Cancelled or Amended

(1) The certificate shall be cancelled when the partnership is dissolved or all limited partners cease to be such.

(2) A certificate shall be amended when

(a) There is a change in the name of the partnership or in the amount or character of the contribution of any limited partner,

(b) A person is substituted as a limited partner,

(c) An additional limited partner is admitted,

(d) A person is admitted as a general partner,

(e) A general partner retires, dies or becomes insane, and the business is continued under Section 20,

(f) There is a change in the character of the business of the partnership,

(g) There is a false or erroneous statement in the certificate,

(h) There is a change in the time as stated in the certificate for the dissolution of the partnership or for the return of a contribution,

(i) A time is fixed for the dissolution of the partnership, or the return of a contribution, no time having been specified in the certificate, or

(j) The members desire to make a change in any other statement in the certificate in order that it shall accurately represent the agreement between them.

§ 25. Requirements for Amendment and for Cancellation of Certificate

(1) The writing to amend a certificate shall

    (a) Conform to the requirements of Section 2 (1a) as far as necessary to set forth clearly the change in the certificate which it is desired to make, and

    (b) Be signed and sworn to by all members, and an amendment substituting a limited partner or adding a limited or general partner shall be signed also by the member to be substituted or added, and when a limited partner is to be substituted, the amendment shall also be signed by the assigning limited partner.

(2) The writing to cancel a certificate shall be signed by all members.

(3) A person desiring the cancellation or amendment of a certificate, if any person designated in paragraphs (1) and (2) as a person who must execute the writing refuses to do so, may petition the [here designate the proper court] to direct a cancellation or amendment thereof.

(4) If the court finds that the petitioner has a right to have the writing executed by a person who refuses to do so, it shall order the [here designate the responsible official in the office designated in Section 2] in the office where the certificate is recorded to record the cancellation or amendment of the certificate; and where the certificate is to be amended, the court shall also cause to be filed for record in said office a certified copy of its decree setting forth the amendment.

(5) A certificate is amended or cancelled when there is filed for record in the office [here designate the office designated in Section 2] where the certificate is recorded

    (a) A writing in accordance with the provisions of paragraph (1), or (2) or

    (b) A certified copy of the order of court in accordance with the provisions of paragraph (4).

(6) After the certificate is duly amended in accordance with this section, the amended certificate shall thereafter be for all purposes the certificate provided for by this act.

§ 26. Parties to Actions

A contributor, unless he is a general partner, is not a proper party to proceedings by or against a part-nership, except where the object is to enforce a limited partner's right against or liability to the partnership.

§ 27. Name of Act

This act may be cited as The Uniform Limited Partnership Act.

§ 28. Rules of Construction

(1) The rule that statutes in derogation of the common law are to be strictly construed shall have no application to this act.

(2) This act shall be so interpreted and construed as to effect its general purpose to make uniform the law of those states which enact it.

(3) This act shall not be so construed as to impair the obligations of any contract existing when the act goes into effect, not to affect any action or proceedings begun or right accrued before this act takes effect.

§ 29. Rules for Cases Not Provided for in This Act

In any case not provided for in this act the rules of law and equity, including the law merchant, shall govern.

§ 30. Provisions for Existing Limited Partnerships

(1) A limited partnership formed under any statute of this state prior to the adoption of this act, may become a limited partnership under this act by complying with the provisions of Section 2; provided the certificate set forth

    (a) The amount of the original contribution of each limited partner, and the time when the contribution was made, and

    (b) That the property of the partnership exceeds the amount sufficient to discharge its liabilities to persons not claiming as general or limited partners by an amount greater than the sum of the contributions of its limited partners.

(2) A limited partnership formed under any statute of this state prior to the adoption of this act, until or unless it becomes a limited partnership under this act, shall continue to be governed by the provisions of [here insert proper reference to the existing limited partnership act or acts], except that such partnership shall not be renewed unless so provided in the original agreement.

§ 31. Act (Acts) Repealed

Except as affecting existing limited partnerships to the extent set forth in Section 30, the act (acts) of [here designate the existing limited partnership act or acts] is (are) hereby repealed.

REVISED MODEL
BUSINESS CORPORATION ACT
(EXCERPTS)

§1.20. FILING REQUIREMENTS

(a) A document must satisfy the requirements of this section, and of any other section that adds to or varies from these requirements, to be entitled to filing by the secretary of state.

(b) This Act must require or permit filing the document in the office of the secretary of state.

(c) The document must contain the information required by this Act. It may contain other information as well.

(d) The document must be typewritten or printed.

(e) The document must be in the English language. A corporate name need not be in English if written in English letters or Arabic or Roman numerals, and the certificate of existence required of foreign corporations need not be in English if accompanied by a reasonably authenticated English translation.

(f) The document must be executed:

    (1) by the chairman of the board of directors of a domestic or foreign corporation, by its president, or by another of its officers;

    (2) if directors have not been selected or the corporation has not been formed, by an incorporator; or

    (3) if the corporation is in the hands of a receiver, trustee, or other court-appointed fiduciary, by that fiduciary.

(g) The person executing the document shall sign it and state beneath or opposite his signature his name and the capacity in which he signs. The document may but need not contain: (1) the corporate seal, (2) an attestation by the secretary or an assistant secretary, (3) an acknowledgment, verification, or proof.

(h) If the secretary of state has prescribed a mandatory form for the document under section 1.21, the document must be in or on the prescribed form.

(i) The document must be delivered to the office of the secretary of state for filing and must be accompanied by one exact or conformed copy (except as provided in sections 5.03 and 15.09), the correct filing fee, and any franchise tax, license fee, or penalty required by this Act or other law.

§1.21. FORMS

(a) The secretary of state may prescribe and furnish on request forms for: (1) an application for a certificate of existence, (2) a foreign corporation's application for a certificate of authority to transact business in this state, (3) a foreign corporation's application for a certificate of withdrawal, and (4) the annual report. If the secretary of state so requires, use of these forms is mandatory.

(b) The secretary of state may prescribe and furnish on request forms for other documents required or permitted to be filed by this Act but their use is not mandatory.

§1.23. EFFECTIVE TIME AND DATE OF DOCUMENT

(a) Except as provided in subsection (b) and section 1.24(c), a document accepted for filing is effective:

    (1) at the time of filing on the date it is filed, as evidenced by the secretary of state's date and time endorsement on the original document; or

    (2) at the time specified in the document as its effective time on the date it is filed.

(b) A document may specify a delayed effective time and date, and if it does so the document becomes effective at the time and date specified. If a delayed effective date but no time is specified, the document is effective at the close of business on that date. A delayed effective date for a document may not be later than the 90th day after the date it is filed.

§1.25. FILING DUTY OF SECRETARY OF STATE

(a) If a document delivered to the office of the secretary of state for filing satisfies the requirements of section 1.20, the secretary of state shall file it.

(b) The secretary of state files a document by stamping or otherwise endorsing "Filed," together with his name and official title and the date and time of receipt, on both the original and the document copy and on the receipt for the filing fee. After filing a document, except as provided in sections 5.03 and 15.10, the secretary of state shall deliver the document copy, with the filing fee receipt (or acknowledgment of receipt if no fee is required) attached, to the domestic or foreign corporation or its representative.

(c) If the secretary of state refuses to file a document, he shall return it to the domestic or foreign corporation or its representative within five days after the document was delivered, together with a brief, written explanation of the reason for his refusal.

(d) The secretary of state's duty to file documents under this section is ministerial. His filing or refusing to file a document does not:

    (1) affect the validity or invalidity of the document in whole or part;

    (2) relate to the correctness or incorrectness of information contained in the document;

    (3) create a presumption that the document is valid or invalid or that information contained in the document is correct or incorrect.

§1.40. ACT DEFINITIONS

In this Act:

(1) "Articles of incorporation" include amended and restated articles of incorporation and articles of merger.

(2) "Authorized shares" means the shares of all classes a domestic or foreign corporation is authorized to issue.

(3) "Conspicuous" means so written that a reasonable person against whom the writing is to operate should have noticed it. For example, printing in italics or boldface or contrasting color, or typing in capitals or underlined, is conspicuous.

(4) "Corporation" or "domestic corporation" means a corporation for profit, which is not a foreign corporation, incorporated under or subject to the provisions of this Act.

(5) "Deliver" includes mail.

(6) "Distribution" means a direct or indirect transfer of money or other property (except its own shares) or incurrence of indebtedness by a corporation to or for the benefit of its shareholders in respect of any of its shares. A distribution may be in the form of a declaration or payment of a dividend; a purchase, redemption, or other acquisition of shares; a distribution of indebtedness; or otherwise.

(7) "Effective date of notice" is defined in section 1.41.

(8) "Employee" includes an officer but not a director. A director may accept duties that make him also an employee.

(9) "Entity" includes corporation and foreign corporation; not-for-profit corporation; profit and not-for-profit unincorporated association; business trust, estate, partnership, trust, and two or more persons having a joint or common economic interest; and state, United States, and foreign government.

(10) "Foreign corporation" means a corporation for profit incorporated under a law other than the law of this state.

(11) "Governmental subdivision" includes authority, county, district, and municipality.

(12) "Includes" denotes a partial definition.

(13) "Individual" includes the estate of an incompetent or deceased individual.

(14) "Means" denotes an exhaustive definition.

(15) "Notice" is defined in section 1.41.

(16) "Person" includes individual and entity.

(17) "Principal office" means the office (in or out of this state) so designated in the annual report where the principal executive offices of a domestic or foreign corporation are located.

(18) "Proceeding" includes civil suit and criminal, administrative, and investigatory action.

(19) "Record date" means the date established under chapter 6 or 7 on which a corporation determines the identity of its shareholders for purposes of this Act.

(20) "Secretary" means the corporate officer to whom the board of directors has delegated responsibility under section 8.40(c) for custody of the minutes of the meetings of the board of directors and of the shareholders and for authenticating records of the corporation.

(21) "Shares" means the units into which the proprietary interests in a corporation are divided.

(22) "Shareholder" means the person in whose name shares are registered in the records of a corporation or the beneficial owner of shares to the extent of the rights granted by a nominee certificate on file with a corporation.

(23) "State," when referring to a part of the United States, includes a state and commonwealth (and their agencies and governmental subdivisions) and a territory and insular possession (and their agencies and governmental subdivisions) of the United States.

(24) "Subscriber" means a person who subscribes for shares in a corporation, whether before or after incorporation.

(25) "United States" includes district, authority, bureau, commission, department, and any other

agency of the United States.

(26) "Voting group" means all shares of one or more classes or series that under the articles of incorporation or this Act are entitled to vote and be counted together collectively on a matter at a meeting of shareholders. All shares entitled by the articles of incorporation or this Act to vote generally on the matter are for that purpose a single voting group.

§1.41. NOTICE

(a) Notice under this Act must be in writing unless oral notice is reasonable under the circumstances.

(b) Notice may be communicated in person; by telephone, telegraph, teletype, or other form of wire or wireless communication; or by mail or private carrier. If these forms of personal notice are impracticable, notice may be communicated by a newspaper of general circulation in the area where published; or by radio, television, or other form of public broadcast communication.

(c) Written notice by a domestic or foreign corporation to its shareholder, if in a comprehensible form, is effective when mailed, if mailed postpaid and correctly addressed to the shareholder's address shown in the corporation's current record of shareholders.

(d) Written notice to a domestic or foreign corporation (authorized to transact business in this state) may be addressed to its registered agent at its registered office or to the corporation or its secretary at its principal office shown in its most recent annual report or, in the case of a foreign corporation that has not yet delivered an annual report, in its application for a certificate of authority.

(e) Except as provided in subsection (c), written notice, if in a comprehensible form, is effective at the earliest of the following:

(1) when received;

(2) five days after its deposit in the United States Mail, as evidenced by the postmark, if mailed postpaid and correctly addressed;

(3) on the date shown on the return receipt, if sent by registered or certified mail, return receipt requested, and the receipt is signed by or on behalf of the addressee.

(f) Oral notice is effective when communicated if communicated in a comprehensible manner.

(g) If this Act prescribes notice requirements for particular circumstances, those requirements govern. If articles of incorporation or bylaws prescribe notice requirements, not inconsistent with this section or other provisions of this Act, those requirements govern.

§1.42. NUMBER OF SHAREHOLDERS

(a) For purposes of this Act, the following identi-fied as a shareholder in a corporation's current record of shareholders constitutes one shareholder:

(1) three or fewer coowners;

(2) a corporation, partnership, trust, estate, or other entity;

(3) the trustees, guardians, custodians, or other fiduciaries of a single trust, estate, or account.

(b) For purposes of this Act, shareholdings registered in substantially similar names constitute one shareholder if it is reasonable to believe that the names represent the same person.

§2.01. INCORPORATORS

One or more persons may act as the incorporator or incorporators of a corporation by delivering articles of incorporation to the secretary of state for filing.

§2.02. ARTICLES OF INCORPORATION

(a) The articles of incorporation must set forth:

(1) a corporate name for the corporation that satisfies the requirements of section 4.01;

(2) the number of shares the corporation is authorized to issue;

(3) the street address of the corporation's initial registered office and the name of its initial registered agent at that office; and

(4) the name and address of each incorporator.

(b) The articles of incorporation may set forth:

(1) the names and addresses of the individuals who are to serve as the initial directors;

(2) provisions not inconsistent with law regarding:

(i) the purpose or purposes for which the corporation is organized;

(ii) managing the business and regulating the affairs of the corporation;

(iii) defining, limiting, and regulating the powers of the corporation, its board of directors, and shareholders;

(iv) a par value for authorized shares or classes of shares;

(v) the imposition of personal liability on shareholders for the debts of the corporation to a specified extent and upon specified conditions; and

(3) any provision that under this Act is required or permitted to be set forth in the bylaws.

(c) The articles of incorporation need not set forth any of the corporate powers enumerated in this Act.

§2.03. INCORPORATION

(a) Unless a delayed effective date is specified,

the corporate existence begins when the articles of incorporation are filed.

(b) The secretary of state's filing of the articles of incorporation is conclusive proof that the incorporators satisfied all conditions precedent to incorporation except in a proceeding by the state to cancel or revoke the incorporation or involuntarily dissolve the corporation.

§2.04. LIABILITY FOR PRE-INCORPORATION TRANSACTIONS

All persons purporting to act as or on behalf of a corporation, knowing there was no incorporation under this Act, are jointly and severally liable for all liabilities created while so acting.

§2.05. ORGANIZATION OF CORPORATION

(a) After incorporation:
   (1) if initial directors are named in the articles of incorporation, the initial directors shall hold an organizational meeting, at the call of a majority of the directors, to complete the organization of the corporation by appointing officers, adopting bylaws, and carrying on any other business brought before the meeting;
   (2) if initial directors are not named in the articles, the incorporator or incorporators shall hold an organizational meeting at the call of a majority of the incorporators:
      (i) to elect directors and complete the organization of the corporation; or
      (ii) to elect a board of directors who shall complete the organization of the corporation.

(b) Action required or permitted by this Act to be taken by incorporators at an organizational meeting may be taken without a meeting if the action taken is evidenced by one or more written consents describing the action taken and signed by each incorporator.

(c) An organizational meeting may be held in or out of this state.

§2.06. BYLAWS

(a) The incorporators or board of directors of a corporation shall adopt initial bylaws for the corporation.

(b) The bylaws of a corporation may contain any provision for managing the business and regulating the affairs of the corporation that is not inconsistent with law or the articles of incorporation.

§2.07. EMERGENCY BYLAWS

(a) Unless the articles of incorporation provide otherwise, the board of directors of a corporation may adopt bylaws to be effective only in an emergency defined in subsection (d). The emergency bylaws, which are subject to amendment or repeal by the share-holders, may make all provisions necessary for managing the corporation during the emergency, including:
   (1) procedures for calling a meeting of the board of directors;
   (2) quorum requirements for the meeting; and
   (3) designation of additional or substitute directors.

(b) All provisions of the regular bylaws consistent with the emergency bylaws remain effective during the emergency. The emergency bylaws are not effective after the emergency ends.

(c) Corporate action taken in good faith in accordance with the emergency bylaws:
   (1) binds the corporation; and
   (2) may not be used to impose liability on a corporate director, officer, employee, or agent.

(d) An emergency exists for purposes of this section if a quorum of the corporation's directors cannot readily be assembled because of some catastrophic event.

§3.01. PURPOSES

(a) Every corporation incorporated under this Act has the purpose of engaging in any lawful business unless a more limited purpose is set forth in the articles of incorporation.

(b) A corporation engaging in a business that is subject to regulation under another statute of this state may incorporate under this Act only if permitted by, and subject to all limitations of, the other statute.

§3.02. GENERAL POWERS

Unless its articles of incorporation provide otherwise, every corporation has perpetual duration and succession in its corporate name and has the same powers as an individual to do all things necessary or convenient to carry out its business and affairs, including without limitation power:
   (1) to sue and be sued, complain and defend in its corporate name;
   (2) to have a corporate seal, which may be altered at will, and to use it, or a facsimile of it, by impressing or affixing it or in any other manner reproducing it;
   (3) to make and amend bylaws, not inconsistent with its articles of incorporation or with the laws of this state, for managing the business and regulating the affairs of the corporation;
   (4) to purchase, receive, lease, or otherwise acquire, and own, hold, improve, use, and otherwise deal with, real or personal property, or any legal or equitable interest in property, wherever located;
   (5) to sell, convey, mortgage, pledge, lease,

exchange, and otherwise dispose of all or any part of its property;

(6) to purchase, receive, subscribe for, or otherwise acquire; own, hold, vote, use, sell, mortgage, lend, pledge, or otherwise dispose of; and deal in and with shares or other interests in, or obligations of, any other entity;

(7) to make contracts and guarantees, incur liabilities, borrow money, issue its notes, bonds, and other obligations (which may be convertible into or include the option to purchase other securities of the corporation), and secure any of its obligations by mortgage or pledge of any of its property, franchises, or income;

(8) to lend money, invest and reinvest its funds, and receive and hold real and personal property as security for repayment;

(9) to be a promoter, partner, member, associate, or manager of any partnership, joint venture, trust, or other entity;

(10) to conduct its business, locate offices, and exercise the powers granted by this Act within or without this state;

(11) to elect directors and appoint officers, employees, and agents of the corporation, define their duties, fix their compensation, and lend them money and credit;

(12) to pay pensions and establish pension plans, pension trusts, profit sharing plans, share bonus plans, share option plans, and benefit or incentive plans for any or all of its current or former directors, officers, employees, and agents;

(13) to make donations for the public welfare or for charitable, scientific, or educational purposes;

(14) to transact any lawful business that will aid governmental policy;

(15) to make payments or donations, or do any other act, not inconsistent with law, that furthers the business and affairs of the corporation.

§3.03.   EMERGENCY POWERS

(a) In anticipation of or during an emergency defined in subsection (d), the board of directors of a corporation may:

(1) modify lines of succession to accommodate the incapacity of any director, officer, employee, or agent; and

(2) relocate the principal office, designate alternative principal offices or regional offices, or authorize the officers to do so.

(b) During an emergency defined in subsection (d), unless emergency bylaws provide otherwise:

(1) notice of a meeting of the board of directors need be given only to those directors whom it is practicable to reach and may be given in any practicable manner, including by publication and radio; and

(2) one or more officers of the corporation present at a meeting of the board of directors may be deemed to be directors for the meeting, in order of rank and within the same rank in order of seniority, as necessary to achieve a quorum.

(c) Corporate action taken in good faith during an emergency under this section to further the ordinary business affairs of the corporation:

(1) binds the corporation; and

(2) may not be used to impose liability on a corporate director, officer, employee, or agent.

(d) An emergency exists for purposes of this section if a quorum of the corporation's directors cannot readily be assembled because of some catastrophic event.

§3.04.   ULTRA VIRES

(a) Except as provided in subsection (b), the vailidity of corporate action may not be challenged on the ground that the corporation lacks or lacked power to act.

(b) A corporation's power to act may be challenged:

(1) in a proceeding by a shareholder against the corporation to enjoin the act;

(2) in a proceeding by the corporation, directly, derivatively, or through a receiver, trustee, or other legal representative, against an incumbent or former director, officer, employee, or agent of the corporation; or

(3) in a proceeding by the Attorney General under section 14.30.

(c) In a shareholder's proceeding under subsection (b)(1) to enjoin an unauthorized corporate act, the court may enjoin or set aside the act, if equitable and if all affected persons are parties to the proceeding, and may award damages for loss (other than anticipated profits) suffered by the corporation or another party because of enjoining the unauthorized act.

§4.01.   CORPORATE NAME

(a) A corporate name:

(1) must contain the word "corporation," "incorporated," "company," or "limited," or the abbreviation "corp.," "inc.," "co.," or "ltd.," or words or abbreviations of like import in another language; and

(2) may not contain language stating or implying that the corporation is organized

for a purpose other than that permitted by section 3.01 and its articles of incorporation.

(b) Except as authorized by subsections (c) and (d), a corporate name must be distinguishable upon the records of the secretary of state from:

(1) the corporate name of a corporation incorporated or authorized to transact business in this state;

(2) a corporate name reserved or registered under section 4.02 or 4.03;

(3) the fictitious name adopted by a foreign corporation authorized to transact business in this state because its real name is unavailable; and

(4) the corporate name of a not-for-profit corporation incorporated or authorized to transact business in this state.

(c) A corporation may apply to the secretary of state for authorization to use a name that is not distinguishable upon his records from one or more of the names described in subsection (b). The secretary of state shall authorize use of the name applied for if:

(1) the other corporation consents to the use in writing and submits an undertaking in form satisfactory to the secretary of state to change its name to a name that is distinguishable upon the records of the secretary of state from the name of the applying corporation; or

(2) the applicant delivers to the secretary of state a certified copy of the final judgment of a court of competent jurisdiction establishing the applicant's right to use the name applied for in this state.

(d) A corporation may use the name (including the fictitious name) of another domestic or foreign corporation that is used in this state if the other corporation is incorporated or authorized to transact business in this state and the proposed user corporation:

(1) has merged with the other corporation;

(2) has been formed by reorganization of the other corporation; or

(3) has acquired all or substantially all of the assets, including the corporate name, of the other corporation.

(e) This Act does not control the use of fictitious names.

§5.01. REGISTERED OFFICE AND REGISTERED AGENT

Each corporation must continuously maintain in this state:

(1) a registered office that may be the same as any of its places of business; and

(2) a registered agent, who may be:

(i) an individual who resides in this state and whose business office is identical with the registered office;

(ii) a domestic corporation or not-for-profit domestic corporation whose business office is identical with the registered office; or

(iii) a foreign corporation or not-for-profit foreign corporation authorized to transact business in this state whose business office is identical with the registered office.

§5.04. SERVICE ON CORPORATION

(a) A corporation's registered agent is the corporation's agent for service of process, notice, or demand required or permitted by law to be served on the corporation.

(b) If a corporation has no registered agent, or the agent cannot with reasonable diligence be served, the corporation may be served by registered or certified mail, return receipt requested, addressed to the secretary of the corporation at its principal office. Service is perfected under this subsection at the earliest of:

(1) the date the corporation receives the mail;

(2) the date shown on the return receipt, if signed on behalf of the corporation; or

(3) five days after its deposit in the United States Mail, as evidenced by the postmark, if mailed postpaid and correctly addressed.

(c) This section does not prescribe the only means, or necessarily the required means, of serving a corporation.

§6.01. AUTHORIZED SHARES

(a) The articles of incorporation must prescribe the classes of shares and the number of shares of each class that the corporation is authorized to issue. If more than one class of shares is authorized, the articles of incorporation must prescribe a distinguishing designation for each class, and, prior to the issuance of shares of a class, the preferences, limitations, and relative rights of that class must be described in the articles of incorporation. All shares of a class must have preferences, limitations, and relative rights identical with those of other shares of the same class except to the extent otherwise permitted by section 6.02.

(b) The articles of incorporation must authorize (1) one or more classes of shares that together have unlimited voting rights, and (2) one or more classes of shares (which may be the same class or classes as those with voting rights) that together are entitled to receive the net assets of the corporation upon dissolution.

(c) The articles of incorporation may authorize one or more classes of shares that:

(1) have special, conditional, or limited voting rights, or no right to vote, except to the extent prohibited by this Act;

(2) are redeemable or convertible as specified in the articles of incorporation (i) at the option of the corporation, the shareholder, or another person or upon the occurrence of a designated event; (ii) for cash, indebtedness, securities, or other property; (iii) in a designated amount or in an amount determined in accordance with a designated formula or by reference to extrinsic data or events;

(3) entitle the holders to distributions calculated in any manner, including dividends that may be cumulative, noncumulative, or partially cumulative;

(4) have preference over any other class of shares with respect to distributions, including dividends and distributions upon the dissolution of the corporation.

(d) The description of the designations, preferences, limitations, and relative rights of share classes in subsection (c) is not exhaustive.

§6.02. TERMS OF CLASS OR SERIES DETERMINED BY BOARD OF DIRECTORS

(a) If the articles of incorporation so provide, the board of directors may determine, in whole or part, the preferences, limitations, and relative rights (within the limits set forth in section 6.01) or (1) any class of shares before the issuance of any shares of that class or (2) one or more series within a class before the issuance of any shares of that series.

(b) Each series of a class must be given a distinguishing designation.

(c) All shares of a series must have preferences, limitations, and relative rights identical with those of other shares of the same series and, except to the extent otherwise provided in the description of the series, with those of other series of the same class.

(d) Before issuing any shares of a class or series created under this section, the corporation must deliver to the secretary of state for filing articles of amendment, which are effective without shareholder action, that set forth:

(1) the name of the corporation;

(2) the text of the amendment determining the terms of the class or series of shares;

(3) the date it was adopted; and

(4) a statement that the amendment was duly adopted by the board of directors.

§6.03. ISSUED AND OUTSTANDING SHARES

(a) A corporation may issue the number of shares of each class or series authorized by the articles of incorporation. Shares that are issued are outstanding shares until they are reacquired, redeemed, converted, or cancelled.

(b) The reacquisition, redemption, or conversion of outstanding shares is subject to the limitations of subsection (c) of this section and to section 6.40.

(c) At all times that shares of the corporation are outstanding, one or more shares that together have unlimited voting rights and one or more shares that together are entitled to receive the net assets of the corporation upon dissolution must be outstanding.

§6.04. FRACTIONAL SHARES

(a) A corporation may:

(1) issue fractions of a share or pay in money the value of fractions of a share;

(2) arrange for disposition of fractional shares by the shareholders;

(3) issue scrip in registered or bearer form entitling the holder to receive a full share upon surrendering enough scrip to equal a full share.

(b) Each certificate representing scrip must be conspicuously labeled "scrip" and must contain the information required by section 6.25(b).

(c) The holder of a fractional share is entitled to exercise the rights of a shareholder, including the right to vote, to receive dividends, and to participate in the assets of the corporation upon liquidation. The holder of scrip is not entitled to any of these rights unless the scrip provides for them.

(d) The board of directors may authorize the issuance of scrip subject to any condition considered desirable, including:

(1) that the scrip will become void if not exchanged for full shares before a specified date; and

(2) that the shares for which the scrip is exchangeable may be sold and the proceeds paid to the scripholders.

§6.20. SUBSCRIPTION FOR SHARES BEFORE INCORPORATION

(a) A subscription for shares entered into before incorporation is irrevocable for six months unless the subscription agreement provides a longer or shorter period or all the subscribers agree to revocation.

(b) The board of directors may determine the payment terms of subscriptions for shares that were entered into before incorporation, unless the subscription agreement specifies them. A call for payment by the board of directors must be uniform so far as practicable as to all shares of the same class or series, unless the subscription agreement specifies otherwise.

(c) Shares issued pursuant to subscriptions entered into before incorporation are fully paid and nonassessable when the corporation receives the consideration specified in the subscription agreement.

(d) If a subscriber defaults in payment of money or property under a subscription agreement entered into before incorporation, the corporation may collect the amount owed as any other debt. Alternatively, unless the subscription agreement provides otherwise, the corporation may rescind the agreement and may sell the shares if the debt remains unpaid more than 20 days after the corporation sends written demand for payment to the subscriber.

(e) A subscription agreement entered into after incorporation is a contract between the subscriber and the corporation subject to section 6.21.

§6.21. ISSUANCE OF SHARES

(a) The powers granted in this section to the board of directors may be reserved to the shareholders by the articles of incorporation.

(b) The board of directors may authorize shares to be issued for consideration consisting of any tangible or intangible property or benefit to the corporation, including cash, promissory notes, services performed, contracts for services to be performed, or other securities of the corporation.

(c) Before the corporation issues shares, the board of directors must determine that the consideration received or to be received for shares to be issued is adequate. That determination by the board of directors is conclusive insofar as the adequacy of consideration for the issuance of shares relates to whether the shares are validly issued, fully paid, and nonassessable.

(d) When the corporation receives the consideration for which the board of directors authorized the issuance of shares, the shares issued therefor are fully paid and nonassessable.

(e) The corporation may place in escrow shares issued for a contract for future services or benefits or a promissory note, or make other arrangements to restrict the transfer of the shares, and may credit distributions in respect of the shares against their purchase price, until the services are performed, the note is paid, or the benefits received. If the services are not performed, the note is not paid, or the benefits are not received, the shares escrowed or restricted and the distributions credited may be cancelled in whole or part.

§6.22. LIABILITY OF SHAREHOLDERS

(a) A purchaser from a corporation of its own shares is not liable to the corporation or its creditors with respect to the shares except to pay the consideration for which the shares were authorized to be issued (section 6.21) or specified in the subscription agreement (section 6.20).

(b) Unless otherwise provided in the articles of incorporation, a shareholder of a corporation is not personally liable for the acts or debts of the corporation except that he may become personally liable by reason of his own acts or conduct.

§6.30. SHAREHOLDERS' PREEMPTIVE RIGHTS

(a) The shareholders of a corporation do not have a preemptive right to acquire the corporation's unissued shares except to the extent the articles of incorporation so provide.

(b) A statement included in the articles of incorporation that "the corporation elects to have preemptive rights" (or words of similar import) means that the following principles apply except to the extent the articles of incorporation expressly provide otherwise:

(1) The shareholders of the corporation have a preemptive right, granted on uniform terms and conditions prescribed by the board of directors to provide a fair and reasonable opportunity to exercise the right, to acquire proportional amounts of the corporation's unissued shares upon the decision of the board of directors to issue them.

(2) A shareholder may waive his preemptive right. A waiver evidenced by a writing is irrevocable even though it is not supported by consideration.

(3) There is no preemptive right with respect to:

(i) shares issued as compensation to directors, officers, agents, or employees of the corporation, its subsidiaries or affiliates;

(ii) shares issued to satisfy conversion or option rights created to provide compensation to directors, officers, agents, or employees of the corporation, its subsidiaries or affiliates;

(iii) shares authorized in articles of incorporation that are issued within six months from the effective date of incorporation;

(iv) shares sold otherwise than for money.

(4) Holders of shares of any class without general voting rights but with preferential rights to distributions or assets have no preemptive rights with respect to shares of any class.

(5) Holders of shares of any class with general voting rights but without preferential rights to distributions or assets have no preemptive rights with respect to shares of any class with preferential rights to distributions or assets unless the shares with

preferential rights are convertible into or carry a right to subscribe for or acquire shares without preferential rights.

(6) Shares subject to preemptive rights that are not acquired by shareholders may be issued to any person for a period of one year after being offered to shareholders at a consideration set by the board of directors that is not lower than the consideration set for the exercise of preemptive rights. An offer at a lower consideration or after the expiration of one year is subject to the shareholders' preemptive rights.

(c) For purposes of this section, "shares" includes a security convertible into or carrying a right to subscribe for or acquire shares.

§6.31. CORPORATION'S ACQUISITION OF ITS OWN SHARES

(a) A corporation may acquire its own shares and shares so acquired constitute authorized but unissued shares.

(b) If the articles of incorporation prohibit the reissue of acquired shares, the number of authorized shares is reduced by the number of shares acquired, effective upon amendment of the articles of incorporation.

(c) The board of directors may adopt articles of amendment under this section without shareholder action and deliver them to the secretary of state for filing. The articles must set forth:

(1) the name of the corporation;

(2) the reduction in the number of authorized shares, itemized by class and series; and

(3) the total number of authorized shares, itemized by class and series, remaining after reduction of the shares.

§6.40. DISTRIBUTIONS TO SHAREHOLDERS

(a) A board of directors may authorize and the corporation may make distributions to its shareholders subject to restriction by the articles of incorporation and the limitation in subsection (c).

(b) If the board of directors does not fix the record date for determining shareholders entitled to a distribution (other than one involving a repurchase or reacquisition of shares), it is the date the board of directors authorizes the distribution.

(c) No distribution may be made if, after giving it effect:

(1) the corporation would not be able to pay its debts as they become due in the usual course of business; or

(2) the corporation's total assets would be less than the sum of its total liabilities plus (unless the articles of incorporation permit otherwise) the amount that would be needed, if the corporation were to be dissolved at the time of the distribution, to satisfy the preferential rights upon dissolution of shareholders whose preferential rights are superior to those receiving the distribution.

(d) The board of directors may base a determination that a distribution is not prohibited under subsection (c) either on financial statements prepared on the basis of accounting practices and principles that are reasonable in the circumstances or on a fair valuation or other method that is reasonable in the circumstances.

(e) The effect of a distribution under subsection (c) is measured:

(1) in the case of distribution by purchase, redemption, or other acquisition of the corporation's shares, as of the earlier of (i) the date money or other property is transferred or debt incurred by the corporation or (ii) the date the shareholder ceases to be a shareholder with respect to the acquired shares;

(2) in the case of any other distribution of indebtedness, as of the date the indebtedness is distributed;

(3) in all other cases, as of (i) the date the distribution is authorized if the payment occurs within 120 days after the date of authorization or (ii) the date the payment is made if it occurs more than 120 days after the date of authorization.

(f) A corporation's indebtedness to a shareholder incurred by reason of a distribution made in accordance with this section is at parity with the corporation's indebtedness to its general, unsecured creditors except to the extent subordinated by agreement.

§7.01. ANNUAL MEETING

(a) A corporation shall hold a meeting of shareholders annually at a time stated in or fixed in accordance with the bylaws.

(b) Annual shareholders' meetings may be held in or out of this state at the place stated in or fixed in accordance with the bylaws. If no place is stated in or fixed in accordance with the bylaws, annual meetings shall be held at the corporation's principal office.

(c) The failure to hold an annual meeting at the time stated in or fixed in accordance with a corporation's bylaws does not affect the validity of any corporate action.

§7.02. SPECIAL MEETING

(a) A corporation shall hold a special meeting of shareholders:

    (1) on call of its board of directors or the person or persons authorized to do so by the articles of incorporation or bylaws; or

    (2) if the holders of at least 10 percent of all the votes entitled to be cast on any issue proposed to be considered at the proposed special meeting sign, date, and deliver to the corporation's secretary one or more written demands for the meeting describing the purpose or purposes for which it is to be held.

(b) If not otherwise fixed under section 7.03 or 7.07, the record date for determining shareholders entitled to demand a special meeting is the date the first shareholder signs the demand.

(c) Special shareholders' meetings may be held in or out of this state at the place stated in or fixed in accordance with the bylaws. If no place is stated or fixed in accordance with the bylaws, special meetings shall be held at the corporation's principal office.

(d) Only business within the purpose or purposes described in the meeting notice required by section 7.05(c) may be conducted at a special shareholders' meeting.

§7.04. ACTION WITHOUT MEETING

(a) Action required or permitted by this Act to be taken at a shareholders' meeting may be taken without a meeting if the action is taken by all the shareholders entitled to vote on the action. The action must be evidenced by one or more written consents describing the action taken, signed by all the shareholders entitled to vote on the action, and delivered to the corporation for inclusion in the minutes or filing with the corporate records.

(b) If not otherwise fixed under section 7.03 or 7.07, the record date for determining shareholders entitled to take action without a meeting is the date the first shareholder signs the consent under subsection (a).

(c) A consent signed under this section has the effect of a meeting vote and may be described as such in any document.

(d) If this Act requires that notice of proposed action be given to nonvoting shareholders and the action is to be taken by unanimous consent of the voting shareholders, the corporation must give its nonvoting shareholders written notice of the proposed action at least 10 days before the action is taken. The notice must contain or be accompanied by the same material that, under this Act, would have been required to be sent to nonvoting shareholders in a notice of meeting at which the proposed action would have been submitted to the shareholders for action.

§7.05. NOTICE OF MEETING

(a) A corporation shall notify shareholders of the date, time, and place of each annual and special shareholders' meeting no fewer than 10 nor more than 60 days before the meeting date. Unless this Act or the articles of incorporation require otherwise, the corporation is required to give notice only to shareholders entitled to vote at the meeting.

(b) Unless this Act or the articles of incorporation require otherwise, notice of an annual meeting need not include a description of the purpose or purposes for which the meeting is called.

(c) Notice of a special meeting must include a description of the purpose or purposes for which the meeting is called.

(d) If not otherwise fixed under section 7.03 or 7.07, the record date for determining shareholders entitled to notice of and to vote at an annual or special shareholders' meeting is the close of business on the day before the first notice is delivered to shareholders.

(e) Unless the bylaws require otherwise, if an annual or special shareholders' meeting is adjourned to a different date, time, or place, notice need not be given of the new date, time, or place if the new date, time, or place is announced at the meeting before adjournment. If a new record date for the adjourned meeting is or must be fixed under section 7.07, however, notice of the adjourned meeting must be given under this section to persons who are shareholders as of the new record date.

§7.06. WAIVER OF NOTICE

(a) A shareholder may waive any notice required by this Act, the articles of incorporation, or bylaws before or after the date and time stated in the notice. The waiver must be in writing, be signed by the shareholder entitled to the notice, and be delivered to the corporation for inclusion in the minutes or filing with the corporate records.

(b) A shareholder's attendance at a meeting:

    (1) waives objection to lack of notice or

defective notice of the meeting, unless the shareholder at the beginning of the meeting objects to holding the meeting or transacting business at the meeting;

(2) waives objection to consideration of a particular matter at the meeting that is not within the purpose or purposes described in the meeting notice, unless the shareholder objects to considering the matter when it is presented.

§7.07. RECORD DATE

(a) The bylaws may fix or provide the manner of fixing the record date for one or more voting groups in order to determine the shareholders entitled to notice of a shareholders' meeting, to demand a special meeting, to vote, or to take any other action. If the bylaws do not fix or provide for fixing a record date, the board of directors of the corporation may fix a future date as the record date.

(b) A record date fixed under this section may not be more than 70 days before the meeting or action requiring a determination of shareholders.

(c) A determination of shareholders entitled to notice of or to vote at a shareholders' meeting is effective for any adjournment of the meeting unless the board of directors fixes a new record date, which it must do if the meeting is adjourned to a date more than 120 days after the date fixed for the original meeting.

(d) If a court orders a meeting adjourned to a date more than 120 days after the date fixed for the original meeting, it may provide that the original record date continues in effect or it may fix a new record date.

§7.21. VOTING ENTITLEMENT OF SHARES

(a) Except as provided in subsections (b) and (c) or unless the articles of incorporation provide otherwise, each outstanding share, regardless of class, is entitled to one vote on each matter voted on at a shareholders' meeting. Only shares are entitled to vote.

(b) Absent special circumstances, the shares of a corporation are not entitled to vote if they are owned, directly or indirectly, by a second corporation, domestic or foreign, and the first corporation owns, directly or indirectly, a majority of the shares entitled to vote for directors of the second corporation.

(c) Subsection (b) does not limit the power of a corporation to vote any shares, including its own shares, held by it in a fiduciary capacity.

(d) Redeemable shares are not entitled to vote after notice of redemption is mailed to the holders and a sum sufficient to redeem the shares has been deposited with a bank, trust company, or other financial institution under an irrevocable obligation to pay the holders the redemption price on surrender of the shares.

§7.22. PROXIES

(a) A shareholder may vote his shares in person or by proxy.

(b) A shareholder may appoint a proxy to vote or otherwise act for him by signing an appointment form, either personally or by his attorney-in-fact.

(c) An appointment of a proxy is effective when received by the secretary or other officer or agent authorized to tabulate votes. An appointment is valid for 11 months unless a longer period is expressly provided in the appointment form.

(d) An appointment of a proxy is revocable by the shareholder unless the appointment form conspicuously states that it is irrevocable and the appointment is coupled with an interest. Appointments coupled with an interest include the appointment of:

(1) a pledgee;

(2) a person who purchased or agreed to purchase the shares;

(3) a creditor of the corporation who extended it credit under terms requiring the appointment;

(4) an employee of the corporation whose employment contract requires the appointment; or

(5) a party to a voting agreement created under section 7.31.

(e) The death or incapacity of the shareholder appointing a proxy does not affect the right of the corporation to accept the proxy's authority unless notice of the death or incapacity is received by the secretary or other officer or agent authorized to tabulate votes before the proxy exercises his authority under the appointment.

(f) An appointment made irrevocable under subsection (d) is revoked when the interest with which it is coupled is extinguished.

(g) A transferee for value of shares subject to an irrevocable appointment may revoke the appointment if he did not know of its existence when he acquired the shares and the existence of the irrevocable appointment was not noted conspicuously on the certificate representing the shares or on the information statement for shares without certificates.

(h) Subject to section 7.24 and to any express limitation on the proxy's authority appearing on the face of the appointment form, a corporation is entitled to accept the proxy's vote or other action as that of the shareholder making the appointment.

§8.01. REQUIREMENT FOR AND DUTIES OF BOARD OF DIRECTORS

(a) Except as provided in subsection (c), each corporation must have a board of directors.

(b) All corporate powers shall be exercised by or under the authority of, and the business and affairs of the corporation managed under the direction of, its board of directors, subject to any limitation set forth in the articles of incorporation.

(c) A corporation having 50 or fewer shareholders may dispense with or limit the authority of a board of directors by describing in its articles of incorporation who will perform some or all of the duties of a board of directors.

§8.03. NUMBER AND ELECTION OF DIRECTORS

(a) A board of directors must consist of one or more individuals, with the number specified in or fixed in accordance with the articles of incorporation or bylaws.

(b) If a board of directors has power to fix or change the number of directors, the board may increase or decrease by 30 percent or less the number of directors last approved by the shareholders, but only the shareholders may increase or decrease by more than 30 percent the number of directors last approved by the shareholders.

(c) The articles of incorporation or bylaws may establish a variable range for the size of the board of directors by fixing a minimum and maximum number of directors. If a variable range is established, the number of directors may be fixed or changed from time to time, within the minimum and maximum, by the shareholders or the board of directors. After shares are issued, only the shareholders may change the range for the size of the board or change from a fixed to a variable-range size board or vice versa.

(d) Directors are elected at the first annual shareholders' meeting and at each annual meeting thereafter unless their terms are staggered under section 8.06.

§8.04. ELECTION OF DIRECTORS BY CERTAIN CLASSES OF SHAREHOLDERS

If the articles of incorporation authorize dividing the shares into classes, the articles may also authorize the election of all or a specified number of directors by the holders of one or more authorized classes of shares. A class (or classes) of shares entitled to elect one or more directors is a separate voting group for purposes of the election of directors.

§8.05. TERMS OF DIRECTORS GENERALLY

(a) The terms of the initial directors of a corporation expire at the first shareholders' meeting at which directors are elected.

(b) The terms of all other directors expire at the next annual shareholders' meeting following their election unless their terms are staggered under section 8.06.

(c) A decrease in the number of directors does not shorten an incumbent director's term.

(d) The term of a director elected to fill a vacancy expires at the next shareholders' meeting at which directors are elected.

(e) Despite the expiration of a director's term, he continues to serve until his successor is elected and qualifies or until there is a decrease in the number of directors.

§8.06. STAGGERED TERMS FOR DIRECTORS

If there are nine or more directors, the articles of incorporation may provide for staggering their terms by dividing the total number of directors into two or three groups, with each group containing one half or one-third of the total, as near as may be. In that event, the terms of directors in the first group expire at the first annual shareholders' meeting after their election, the terms of the second group expire at the second annual shareholders' meeting after their election, and the terms of the third group, if any, expire at the third annual shareholders' meeting after their election. At each annual shareholders' meeting held thereafter, directors shall be chosen for a term of two years or three years, as the case may be, to succeed those whose terms expire.

§8.08. REMOVAL OF DIRECTORS BY SHAREHOLDERS

(a) The shareholders may remove one or more directors with or without cause unless the articles of incorporation provide that directors may be removed only for cause.

(b) If a director is elected by a voting group of shareholders, only the shareholders of that voting group may participate in the vote to remove him.

(c) If cumulative voting is authorized, a director may not be removed if the number of votes sufficient to elect him under cumulative voting is voted against his removal. If cumulative voting is not authorized, a director may be removed only if the number of votes cast to remove him exceeds the number of votes cast not to remove him.

(d) A director may be removed by the shareholders only at a meeting called for the purpose of removing him and the meeting notice must state that the purpose, or one of the purposes, of the meeting is removal of the director.

§8.20. MEETINGS

(a) The board of directors may hold regular or special meetings in or out of this state.

(b) Unless the articles of incorporation or bylaws provide otherwise, the board of directors may permit any or all directors to participate in a regular or special meeting by, or conduct the meeting through the use of, any means of communication by which all directors participating may simultaneously hear each other during the meeting. A director participating in a meeting by this means is deemed to be present in person at the meeting.

§8.30. GENERAL STANDARDS FOR DIRECTORS

(a) A director shall discharge his duties as a director, including his duties as a member on a committee:
   (1) in good faith;
   (2) with the care an ordinarily prudent person in a like position would exercise under similar circumstances; and
   (3) in a manner he reasonably believes to be in the best interests of the corporation.

(b) In discharging his duties a director is entitled to rely on information, opinions, reports, or statements, including financial statements and other financial data, if prepared or presented by:
   (1) one or more officers or employees of the corporation whom the director reasonably believes to be reliable and competent in the matters presented;
   (2) legal counsel, public accountants, or other persons as to matters the director reasonably believes are within the person's professional or expert competence; or
   (3) a committee of the board of directors of which he is not a member if the director reasonably believes the committee merits confidence.

(c) A director is not acting in good faith if he has knowledge concerning the matter in question that makes reliance otherwise permitted by subsection (b) unwarranted.

(d) A director is not liable for any action taken as a director, or any failure to take any action, if he performed the duties of his office in compliance with this section.

§8.31. DIRECTOR CONFLICT OF INTEREST

(a) A conflict of interest transaction is a transaction with the corporation in which a director of the corporation has a direct or indirect interest. A conflict of interest transaction is not voidable by the corporation solely because of the director's interest in the transaction if any one of the following is true:
   (1) the material facts of the transaction and the director's interest were disclosed or known to the board of directors or a committee of the board of directors and the board of directors or committee authorized, approved, or ratified the transaction;
   (2) the material facts of the transaction and the director's interest were disclosed or known to the shareholders entitled to vote and they authorized, approved, or ratified the transaction; or
   (3) the transaction was fair to the corporation.

(b) For the purposes of this section, a director of the corporation has an indirect interest in a transaction if (1) another entity in which he has a material financial interest or in which he is a general partner is a party to the transaction or (2) another entity of which he is a director, officer, or trustee is a party to the transaction and the transaction is or should be considered by the board of directors of the corporation.

(c) For purposes of subsection (a)(1), a conflict of interest transaction is authorized, approved, or ratified if it receives the affirmative vote of a majority of the directors on the board of directors (or on the committee) who have no direct or indirect interest in the transaction, but a transaction may not be authorized, approved, or ratified under this section by a single director. If a majority of the directors who have no direct or indirect interest in the transaction vote to authorize, approve, or ratify the transaction, a quorum is present for the purpose of taking action under this section. The presence of, or a vote cast by, a director with a direct or indirect interest in the transaction does not affect the validity of any action taken under subsection (a)(1) if the transaction is otherwise authorized, approved, or ratified as provided in that subsection.

(d) For purposes of subsection (a)(2), a conflict of

interest transaction is authorized, approved, or ratified if it receives the vote of a majority of the shares entitled to be counted under this subsection. Shares owned by or voted under the control of a director who has a direct or indirect interest in the transaction, and shares owned by or voted under the control of an entity described in subsection (b)(1), may not be counted in a vote of shareholders to determine whether to authorize, approve, or ratify a conflict of interest transaction under subsection (a)(2). The vote of those shares, however, is counted in determining whether the transaction is approved under other sections of this Act. A majority of the shares, whether or not present, that are entitled to be counted in a vote on the transaction under this subsection constituted a quorum for the purpose of taking action under this section.

§8.33. LIABILITY FOR UNLAWFUL DISTRIBUTIONS

(a) Unless he complies with the applicable standards of conduct described in section 8.30, a director who votes for or assents to a distribution made in violation of this Act or the articles of incorporation is personally liable to the corporation for the amount of the distribution that exceeds what could have been distributed without violating this Act or the articles of incorporation.

(b) A director held liable for an unlawful distribution under subsection (a) is entitled to contribution:
   (1) from every other director who voted for or assented to the distribution without complying with the applicable standards of conduct described in section 8.30; and
   (2) from each shareholder for the amount the shareholder accepted knowing the distribution was made in violation of this Act or the articles of incorporation.

§8.40. REQUIRED OFFICERS

(a) A corporation has the officers described in its bylaws or appointed by the board of directors in accordance with the bylaws.

(b) A duly appointed officer may appoint one or more officers or assistant officers if authorized by the bylaws or the board of directors.

(c) The bylaws or the board of directors shall delegate to one of the officers responsibility for preparing minutes of the directors' and shareholders' meetings and for authenticating records of the corporation.

(d) The same individual may simultaneously hold more than one office in a corporation.

§8.41. DUTIES OF OFFICERS

Each officer has the authority and shall perform the duties set forth in the bylaws or, to the extent consistent with the bylaws, the duties prescribed by the board of directors or by direction of an officer authorized by the board of directors to presecribe the duties of other officers.

§8.42. STANDARDS OF CONDUCT FOR OFFICERS

(a) An officer with discretionary authority shall discharge his duties under that authority:
   (1) in good faith;
   (2) with the care an ordinarily prudent person in a like position would exercise under similar circumstances; and
   (3) in a manner he reasonably believes to be in the best interests of the corporation.

(b) In discharging his duties an officer is entitled to rely on information, opinions, reports, or statements, including financial statements and other financial data, if prepared or presented by:
   (1) one or more officers or employees of the corporation whom the officer reasonably believes to be reliable and competent in the matters presented; or
   (2) legal counsel, public accountants, or other persons as to matters the officer reasonably believes are within the person's professional or expert competence.

(c) An officer is not acting in good faith if he has knowledge concerning the matter in question that makes reliance otherwise permitted by subsection (b) unwarranted.

(d) An officer is not liable for any action taken as an officer, or any failure to take any action, if he performed the duties of his office in compliance with this section.

§11.01. MERGER

(a) One or more corporations may merge into another corporation if the board of directors of each corporation adopts and its shareholders (if required by section 11.03) approve a plan of merger.

(b) The plan of merger must set forth:
   (1) the name of each corporation planning to merge and the name of the surviving corporation into which each other corporation plans to merge;
   (2) the terms and conditions of the merger; and
   (3) the manner and basis of converting the shares of each corporation into shares, obligations, or other securities of the surviving or any other corporation or into cash or other property in whole or part.

(c) The plan of merger may set forth:
  (1) amendments to the articles of incorporation of the surviving corporation; and
  (2) other provisions relating to the merger.

§13.02. RIGHT TO DISSENT

(a) A shareholder is entitled to dissent from and obtain payment of the fair value of his shares in the event of, any of the following corporate actions:
  (1) consummation of a plan of merger to which the corporation is a party (i) if shareholder approval is required for the merger by section 11.03 or the articles of incorporation and the shareholder is entitled to vote on the merger or (ii) if the corporation is a subsidiary that is merged with its parent under section 11.04;
  (2) consummation of a plan of share exchange to which the corporation is a party as the corporation whose shares will be acquired, if the shareholder is entitled to vote on the plan;
  (3) consummation of a sale or exchange of all, or substantially all, of the property of the corporation other than in the usual and regular course of business, if the shareholder is entitled to vote on the sale or exchange, including a sale in dissolution, but not including a sale pursuant to court order or a sale for cash pursuant to a plan by which all or substantially all of the net proceeds of the sale will be distributed to the shareholders within one year after the date of sale;
  (4) an amendment of the articles of incorporation that materially and adversely affects rights in respect of a dissenter's shares because it:
    (i)   alters or abolishes a preferential right of the shares;
    (ii) creates, alters, or abolishes a right in respect of redemption, including a provision respecting a sinking fund for the redemption or repurchase, of the shares;
    (iii) alters or abolishes a preemptive right of the holder of the shares to acquire shares or other securities;
    (iv) excludes or limits the right of the shares to vote on any matter, or to cumulate votes, other than a limitation by dilution through issuance of shares or other securities with similar voting rights; or
    (v)   reduces the number of shares owned by the shareholder to a fraction of a share if the fractional share so created is to be acquired for cash under section 6.04; or
  (5) any corporate action taken pursuant to a shareholder vote to the extent the articles of incorporation, bylaws, or a resolution of the board of directors provides that voting or nonvoting shareholders are entitled to dissent and obtain payment for their shares.

(b) A shareholder entitled to dissent and obtain payment for his shares under this chapter may not challenge the corporate action creating his entitlement unless the action is unlawful or fraudulent with respect to the shareholder or the corporation.

§16.01. CORPORATE RECORDS

(a) A corporation shall keep as permanent records minutes of all meetings of its shareholders and board of directors, a record of all actions taken by the shareholders or board of directors without a meeting, and a record of all actions taken by a committee of the board of directors in place of the board of directors on behalf of the corporation.

(b) A corporation shall maintain appropriate accounting records.

(c) A corporation or its agent shall maintain a record of its shareholders, in a form that permits preparation of a list of the names and addresses of all shareholders, in alphabetical order by class of shares showing the number and class of shares held by each.

(d) A corporation shall maintain its records in written form or in another form capable of conversion into written form within a reasonable time.

(e) A corporation shall keep a copy of the following records at its principal office:
  (1) its articles or restated articles of incorporation and all amendments to them currently in effect;
  (2) its bylaws or restated bylaws and all amendments to them currently in effect;
  (3) resolutions adopted by its board of directors creating one or more classes or series of shares, and fixing their relative rights, preferences, and limitations, if shares issued pursuant to those resultions are outstanding;
  (4) the minutes of all shareholders' meetings, and records of all action taken by shareholders without a meeting, for the past three years;
  (5) all written communications to share-

holders generally within the past three years, including the financial statements furnished for the past three years under section 16.20;

(6) a list of the names and business addresses of its current directors and officers; and

(7) its most recent annual report delivered to the secretary of state under section 16.22.

§16.02. INSPECTION OF RECORDS BY SHAREHOLDERS

(a) A shareholder of a corporation is entitled to inspect and copy, during regular business hours at the corporation's principal office, any of the records of the corporation described in section 16.01(e) if he gives the corporation written notice of his demand at least five business days before the date on which he wishes to inspect and copy.

(b) A shareholder of a corporation is entitled to inspect and copy, during regular business hours at a reasonable location specified by the corporation, any of the following records of the corporation if the shareholder meets the requirements of subsection (c) and gives the corporation written notice of his demand at least five business days before the date on which he wishes to inspect and copy:

(1) excerpts from minutes of any meeting of the board of directors, records of any action of a committee of the board of directors while acting in place of the board of directors on behalf of the corporation, minutes of any meeting of the shareholders, and records of action taken by the shareholders or board of directors without a meeting, to the extent not subject to inspection under section 16.02(a);

(2) accounting records of the corporation; and

(3) the record of shareholders.

(c) A shareholder may inspect and copy the records described in subsection (b) only if:

(1) his demand is made in good faith and for a proper purpose;

(2) he describes with reasonable particularity his purpose and the records he desires to inspect; and

(3) the records are directly connected with his purpose.

(d) The right of inspection granted by this section

may not be abolished or limited by a corporation's articles of incorporation or bylaws.

(e) This section does not affect:

(1) the right of a shareholder to inspect records under section 7.20 or, if the shareholder is in litigation with the corporation, to the same extent as any other litigant;

(2) the power of a court, independently of this Act, to compel the production of corporate records for examination.

§16.20. FINANCIAL STATEMENTS FOR SHAREHOLDERS

(a) A corporation shall furnish its shareholders annual financial statements, which may be consolidated or combined statements of the corporation and one or more of its subsidiaries, as appropriate, that include a balance sheet as of the end of the fiscal year, an income statement for that year, and a statement of changes in shareholders' equity for the year unless that information appears elsewhere in the financial statements. If financial statements are prepared for the corporation on the basis of generally accepted accounting principles, the annual financial statements must also be prepared on that basis.

(b) If the annual financial statements are reported upon by a public accountant, his report must accompany them. If not, the statements must be accompanied by a statement of the president or the person responsible for the corporation's accounting records:

(1) stating his reasonable belief whether the statements were prepared on the basis of generally accepted accounting principles and, if not, describing the basis of preparation; and

(2) describing any respects in which the statements were not prepared on a basis of accounting consistent with the statements prepared for the preceding year.

(c) A corporation shall mail the annual financial statements to each shareholder within 120 days after the close of each fiscal year. Thereafter, on written request from a shareholder who was not mailed the statements, the corporation shall mail him the latest financial statements.

GLOSSARY

A

abandon: give up or leave employment; relinquish possession of personal property with intent to disclaim title.

abate: put a stop to a nuisance; reduce or cancel a legacy because the estate of the decedent is insufficient to make payment in full.

ab initio: from the beginning.

abrogate: Recall or repeal; make void or inoperative.

absolute liability: liability for an act that causes harm even though the actor was not at fault.

absolute privilege: protection from liability for slander or libel given under certain circumstances to statements regardless of the fact that they are false or maliciously made.

abstract of title: history of the transfers of title to a given piece of land, briefly stating the parties to and the effect of all deeds, wills, and judicial proceedings relating to the land.

acceleration clause: provision in a contract or any legal instrument that upon a certain event the time for the performance of specified obligations shall be advanced; for example, a provision making the balance due upon debtor's default.

acceptance: unqualified assent to the act or proposal of another; as the acceptance of a draft (bill of exchange), of an offer to make a contract, of goods delivered by the seller, or of a gift or a deed.

accession: acquisition of title to personal property by virtue of the fact that it has been attached to property already owned or was the offspring of an owned animal.

accessory after the fact: one who after the commission of a felony knowingly assists the felon.

accessory before the fact: one who is absent at the commission of the crime but who aided and abetted its commission.

accident: an event that occurs even though a reasonable person would not have foreseen its occurrence, because of which the law holds no one responsible for the harm caused.

accommodation party: a person who signs a commercial paper to lend credit to another party to the paper.

accord and satisfaction: an agreement to substitute a different performance for that called for in the contract and the performance of that substitute agreement.

accretion: the acquisition of title to additional land when the owner's land is built up by gradual deposits made by the natural action of water.

acknowledgment: an admission or confirmation, generally of an instrument and usually made before a person authorized to administer oaths, as a notary public; the purpose being to declare that the instrument was executed by the person making the instrument, or that it was a voluntary act or that that person desires that it be recorded.

action: a proceeding to enforce any right.

action in personam: an action brought to impose liability upon a person, such as a money judgment.

action in rem: an action brought to declare the status of a thing, such as an action to declare the title to property to be forfeited because of its illegal use.

action of assumpsit: a common-law action brought to recover damages for breach of a contract.

action of ejectment: a common-law action brought to recover the possession of land.

action of mandamus: a common-law action brought to compel the performance of a ministerial or clerical act by an officer.

action of quo warranto: a common-law action brought to challenge the authority of an officer to act or to hold office.

action of replevin: a common-law action brought to recover the possession of personal property.

action of trespass: a common-law action brought to recover damages for a tort.

act of bankruptcy: any of the acts specified by the national bankruptcy law which, when committed by the debtor within the four months preceding the filing of the petition in bankruptcy, is proper ground for declaring the debtor a bankrupt.

Act of God: a natural phenomenon that is not reasonably foreseeable.

administrative agency: a governmental commission or board given authority to regulate particular matters.

administrator–administratrix: the person (man–woman) appointed to wind up and settle the estate of a person who has died without a will.

adverse possession: the hostile possession of real estate, which when actual, visible, notorious, exclusive, and continued for the required time, will vest the title to the land in the person in such adverse possession.

advisory opinion: an opinion that may be rendered in a few states where there is no actual controversy before the court and the matter is submitted by private persons, or in some instances by the governor of the state, to obtain the court's opinion.

affidavit: a statement of facts set forth in written form and supported by the oath or affirmation of the person making the statement setting forth that such facts are true on the basis of actual knowledge or on information and belief. The affidavit is executed before a notary public or other person authorized to administer oaths.

affinity: the relationship that exists by virtue of marriage.

affirmative covenant: an express undertaking or promise in a contract or deed to do an act.

agency: the relationship that exists between a person identified as a principal and another by virtue of which the latter may make contracts with third persons on behalf of the principal. (Parties–principal, agent, third person)

agency coupled with an interest in the authority: an agency in which the agent has given a consideration or has paid for the right to exercise the authority granted to him.

agency coupled with an interest in the subject matter: an agency in which for a consideration the agent is given an interest in the property to which the agency relates.

agency shop: a union contract provision requiring that non-union employees pay to the union the equivalent of union dues in order to retain their employment.

agent: one who is authorized by the principal or by operation of law to make contracts with third persons on behalf of the principal.

allonge: a paper securely fastened to a commercial paper in order to provide additional space for indorsements.

alluvion: the additions made to land by accretion.

alteration: any material change of the terms of a writing fraudulently made by a party thereto.

ambulatory: not effective and therefore may be changed, as in the case of a will that is not final until its maker has died.

amicable action: an action that all parties agree should be brought and which is begun by the filing of such an agreement, rather than by serving the adverse parties with process. Although the parties agree to litigate, the dispute is real, and the decision is not an advisory opinion.

amicus curiae: literally, a friend of the court; one who is appointed by the court to take part in litigation and to assist the court by furnishing an opinion in the matter.

annexation: attachment of personal property to realty in such a way as to make it become real property and part of the realty.

annuity: a contract by which the insured pays a lump sum to the insurer and later receives fixed annual payments.

anomalous indorser: a person who signs a commercial paper but is not otherwise a party to the instrument.

anticipatory breach: the repudiation by a promisor of the contract prior to the time that performance is required when such repudiation is accepted by the promisee as a breach of the contract.

anti-injunction acts: statutes prohibiting the use of injunctions in labor disputes except under exceptional circumstances; notably the federal Norris-La Guardia Act of 1932.

Anti-Petrillo Act: a federal statute that makes it a crime to compel a radio broadcasting station to hire musicians not needed, to pay for services not performed, or to refrain from broadcasting music of school children or from foreign countries.

antitrust acts: statutes prohibiting combinations and contracts in restraint of trade, notably the federal Sherman Antitrust Act of 1890, now generally inapplicable to labor union activity.

appeal: taking the case to a reviewing court to determine whether the judgment of the lower court or administrative agency was correct. (Parties–appellant, appellee)

appellate jurisdiction: the power of a court to hear and decide a given class of cases on appeal from another court or administrative agency.

arbitration: the settlement of disputed questions, whether of law or fact, by one or more arbitrators by whose decision the parties agree to be bound. Increasingly used as a procedure for labor dispute settlement.

assignment: transfer of a right. Generally used in connection with personal property rights, as rights under a contract, commercial paper, an insurance policy, a mortgage, or a lease. (Parties–assignor, assignee)

assumption of risk: the common-law rule that an employee could not sue the employer for injuries caused by the ordinary risks of employment on the theory that the employee had assumed such risks by undertaking the work. The rule has been abolished in those areas governed by workmen's compensation laws and most employers' liability statutes.

attachment: the seizure of property of, or a debt owed to, the debtor by the service of process upon a third person who is in possession of the property or who owes a debt to the debtor.

attractive nuisance doctrine: a rule imposing liability on a landowner for injuries sustained by small children playing on the land when the landowner permits a condition to exist or maintains equipment that a reasonable person should realize would attract small children who could not realize the danger. The rule does not apply if an unreasonable burden would be imposed on the landowner in taking steps to protect the children.

authenticate: make or establish as genuine, official, or final, as by signing, countersigning, sealing, or any other act indicating approval.

B

bad check laws: laws making it a criminal offense to issue a bad check with intent to defraud.

baggage: such articles of necessity or personal convenience as are usually carried for personal use by passengers of common carriers.

bail: variously used in connection with the release of a person or property from the custody of the law, referring (a) to the act of releasing or bailing, (b) to the persons who assume liability in the event that the released person does not appear or it is held that the property should not be released, and (c) to the bond or sum of money that is furnished the court or other official as indemnity for nonperformance of the obligation.

bailee's lien: a specific, possessory lien of the bailee on the goods for work done to them. Commonly extended by statute to any bailee's claim for compensation and eliminating the necessity of retention of possession.

bailment: the relation that exists when personal property is delivered into the possession of another under an agreement, express or implied, that the identical property will be returned or will be delivered in accordance with the agreement. (Parties–bailor, bailee)

bankruptcy: a procedure by which one unable to pay debts may be declared a bankrupt, after which all assets in excess of any exemption claim are surrendered to the court for administration and distribution to creditors, and the debtor is given a discharge that releases from the unpaid balance due on most debts.

bearer: the person in physical possession of commercial paper payable to bearer, a document of title directing delivery to bearer, or an investment security in bearer form.

beneficiary: the person to whom the proceeds of a life insurance policy are payable, a person for whose benefit property is held in trust, or a person given property by a will.

bequest: a gift of personal property by will.

bill of exchange (draft): an unconditional order in writing by one person upon another, signed by the person giving it, and ordering the person to whom it is directed to pay on demand or at a definite time a sum certain in money to order or to bearer.

bill of lading: a document issued by a carrier reciting the receipt of goods and the terms of the contract of transportation. Regulated by the federal Bills of Lading Act or the Uniform Commercial Code.

bill of sale: a writing signed by the seller reciting that the personal property therein described has been sold to the buyer.

binder: a memorandum delivered to the insured stating the essential terms of a policy to be executed in the future, when it is agreed that the contract of insurance is to be effective before the written policy is executed.

blank indorsement: an indorsement that does not name the person to whom the paper, document of title, or investment security is negotiated.

blue-sky laws: state statutes designed to protect the public from the sale of worthless stocks and bonds.

boardinghouse keeper: one regularly engaged in the business of offering living accommodations to permanent lodgers or boarders.

bona fide: in good faith; without any fraud or deceit.

bond: an obligation or promise in writing and sealed, generally of corporations, personal representatives, trustees; fidelity bonds.

boycott: a combination of two or more persons to cause harm to another by refraining from patronizing or dealing with such other person in any way or inducing others to so refrain; commonly an incident of labor disputes.

bulk sales acts: statutes to protect creditors of a bulk seller. Notice must be given creditors, and the bulk sale buyer is liable to the seller's creditors if the statute is not satisfied. Expanded to "bulk transfers" under the UCC.

business trust: a form of business organization in which the owners of the property to be devoted to the business transfer the title of the property to trustees with full power to operate the business.

C

cancellation: a crossing out of a part of an instrument or a destruction of all legal effect of the instrument, whether by act of party, upon breach by the other party, or pursuant to agreement or decree of court.

capital: net assets of a corporation.

capital stock: the declared money value of the outstanding stock of the corporation.

cash surrender value: the sum paid the insured on the surrender of a policy to the insurer.

cause of action: the right to damages or other judicial relief when a legally protected right of the plaintiff is violated by an unlawful act of the defendant.

caveat emptor: let the buyer beware. This maxim has been nearly abolished by warranty and strict tort liability concepts.

certificate of protest: a written statement by a notary public setting forth the fact that the holder had presented the commercial paper to the primary party and that the latter had failed to make payment.

cestui que trust: the beneficiary or person for whose benefit the property is held in trust.

charter: the grant of authority from a government to exist as a corporation. Generally replaced today by a certificate of incorporation approving the articles of incorporation.

chattel mortgage: a security device by which the owner of personal property transfers the title to a creditor as security for the debt owed by the owner to the creditor. Replaced under the Uniform Commercial Code by a secured transaction. (Parties—chattel mortgagor, chattel mortgagee)

chattels personal: tangible personal property.

chattels real: leases of land and buildings.

check: an order by a depositor on a bank to pay a sum of money to a payee; a bill of exchange drawn on a bank and payable on demand.

chose in action: intangible personal property in the nature of claims against another, such as a claim for accounts receivable or wages.

chose in possession: tangible personal property.

circumstantial evidence: relates to circumstances surrounding the facts in dispute from which the trier of fact may deduce what had happened.

civil action: in many states a simplified form of action combining all or many of the former common-law actions.

civil court: a court with jurisdiction to hear and determine controversies relating to private rights and duties.

closed shop: a place of employment in which only union members may be employed. Now generally prohibited.

codicil: a writing by one who has made a will which is executed with all the formality of a will and is treated as an addition to or modification of the will.

coinsurance: a clause requiring the insured to maintain insurance on property up to a stated amount and providing that to the extent that this is not done the insured is to be deemed a coinsurer with the insurer, so that the latter is liable only for its proportionate share of the amount of insurance required to be carried.

collateral note: a note accompanied by collateral security.

collective bargaining: the process by which the terms of employment are agreed upon through negotiations between the employer or employers within a given industry or industrial area and the union or the bargaining representative of the employees.

collective bargaining unit: the employment area within which employees are by statute authorized to select a bargaining representative, who is then to represent all the employees in bargaining collectively with the employer.

collusion: an agreement between two or more persons to defraud the government or the courts, as by obtaining a divorce by collusion when no grounds for a divorce exist, or to defraud third persons of their rights.

color of title: circumstances that make a person appear to be the owner when in fact not the owner, as the existence of a deed appearing to convey the property to a given person gives color of title although the deed is worthless because it is in fact a forgery.

commission merchant: a bailee to whom goods are consigned for sale.

common carrier: a carrier that holds out its facilities to serve the general public for compensation without discrimination.

common law: the body of unwritten principles originally based on the usages and customs of the community which were recognized and enforced by the courts.

common stock: stock that has no right or priority over any other stock of the corporation as to dividends or distribution of assets, upon dissolution.

common trust fund: a plan by which the assets of small trust estates are pooled into a common fund, each trust being given certificates representing its proportionate ownership of the fund, and the pooled fund is then invested in investments of large size.

community property: the cotenancy held by husband and wife in property acquired during their marriage under the law of some of the states, principally in the southwestern United States.

complaint: the initial pleading filed by the plaintiff in many actions which in many states may be served as original process to acquire jurisdiction over the defendant.

composition of creditors: an agreement among creditors that each shall accept a part payment as full payment in consideration of the other creditors doing the same.

concealment: the failure to volunteer information not requested.

conditional estate: an estate that will come into being upon the satisfaction of a condition precedent or that will be terminated upon the satisfaction of a condition subsequent.

conditional sale: a credit transaction by which the buyer purchases on credit and promises to pay the purchase price in installments, while the seller retains the title to the goods, together with the right of repossession upon default, until the condition of payment in full has been satisfied. The conditional sale is replaced under the Uniform Commercial Code by a secured transaction.

confidential relationship: a relationship in which, because of the legal status of the parties or their respective physical or mental conditions or knowledge, one party places full confidence and trust in the other.

conflict of laws: the body of law that determines the law of which state is to apply when two or more states are involved in the facts of a given case.

confusion of goods: the mixing of goods of different owners that under certain circumstances results in one of the owners becoming the owner of all the goods.

consanguinity: relationship by blood.

consideration: the promise or performance that the promisor demands as the price of the promise.

consignment: a bailment made for the purpose of sale by the bailee. (Parties–consignor, consignee)

consolidation of corporations: a combining of two or more corporations in which the corporate existence of each one ceases and a new corporation is created.

constructive: an adjective employed to indicate that the noun which is modified by it does not exist but the law disposes of the matter as though it did; as a constructive bailment or a constructive trust.

contingent beneficiary: the person to whom the proceeds of a life insurance policy are payable in the event that the primary beneficiary dies before the insured.

contract: a binding agreement based upon the genuine assent of the parties, made for a lawful object, between competent parties, in the form required by law, and generally supported by consideration.

contract carrier: a carrier who transports on the basis of individual contracts that it makes with each shipper.

contract to sell: a contract to make a transfer of title in the future as contrasted with a present transfer.

contribution: the right of a co-obligor who has paid more than a proportionate share to demand that the other obligor pay the amount of the excess payment made.

contributory negligence: negligence of the plaintiff that contributes to injury and at common law bars from recovery from the defendant although the defendant may have been more negligent than the plaintiff.

conveyance: a transfer of an interest in land, ordinarily by the execution and delivery of a deed.

cooling-off period: a procedure designed to avoid strikes by requiring a specified period of delay before the strike may begin during which negotiations for a settlement must continue.

cooperative: a group of two or more persons or enterprises that act through a common agent with respect to a common objective, as buying or selling.

copyright: a grant to an author or artist of an exclusive right to publish and sell the copyrighted work for the life of the author or artist and fifty years thereafter.

corporation: an artificial legal person or being created by government grant, which for many purposes is treated as a natural person.

cost plus: a method of determining the purchase price or contract price by providing for the payment of an amount equal to the costs of the seller or contractor to which is added a stated percentage as the profit.

costs: the expenses of suing or being sued, recoverable in some actions by the successful party, and in others, subject to allocation by the court. Ordinarily they do not include attorney's fees or compensation for loss of time.

counterclaim: a claim that the defendant in an action may make against the plaintiff.

convenants of title: convenants of the grantor in a deed that guarantee such matters as the right to make the conveyance, ownership of the property, freedom of the property from encumbrances, or that the grantee will not be disturbed in the quiet enjoyment of the land.

crime: a violation of the law that is punished as an offense against the state or government.

cross complaint: a claim that the defendant may make against the plaintiff.

cross-examination: the examination made of a witness by the attorney for the adverse party.

cumulative voting: a system of voting for directors in which each shareholder has as many votes as the number of voting shares owned multiplied by the number of directors to be elected, which votes can be distributed for the various candidates as desired.

cy pres doctrine: the rule under which a charitable trust will be carried out as nearly as possible in the way the settlor desired, when for any reason it cannot be carried out exactly in the way or for the purposes expressed.

D

damages: a sum of money recovered to redress or make amends for the legal wrong or injury done.

damnum absque injuria: loss or damage without the violation of a legal right, or the mere fact that a person sustains a loss does not mean that legal rights have been violated.

declaratory judgment: a procedure for obtaining the decision of a court on a question before any action has been taken or loss sustained. It differs from an advisory opinion in that there must be an actual, imminent controversy.

dedication: acquisition by the public or a government of title to land when it is given over by its owner to use by the public and such gift is accepted.

deed: an instrument by which the grantor (owner of land) conveys or transfers the title to a grantee.

de facto: existing in fact as distinguished from as of right, as in the case of an officer or a corporation purporting to act as such without being elected to the office or having been properly incorporated.

deficiency judgment: a personal judgment for the amount still remaining due the mortgagee after foreclosure, which is entered against any person liable on the mortgage debt. Statutes generally require the mortgagee to credit the fair value of the property against the balance due when the mortgagee has purchased the property. Also, a similar judgment entered by a creditor against a debtor in a secured transaction under Article 9 of the UCC.

del credere agent: an agent who sells goods for the principal and who guarantees to the principal that the buyer will pay for the goods.

delegation: the transfer to another of the right and power to do an act.

de minimis non curat lex: a maxim that the law is not concerned with trifles. Not always applied, as in the case of the encroachment of a building over the property line, in which case the law will protect the landowner regardless of the extent of the encroachment.

demonstrative evidence: evidence that consists of visible, physical objects, as a sample taken from the wheat in controversy or a photograph of the subject matter involved.

demonstrative legacy: a legacy to be paid or distributed from a specified fund or property.

demurrage: a charge made by the carrier for the unreasonable detention of cars by the consignor or consignee.

demurrer: a pleading that may be filed to attack the sufficiency of the adverse party's pleading as not stating a cause of action or a defense.

dependent relative revocation: the doctrine recognized in some states that if a testator revokes or cancels a will in order to replace it with a later will, the earlier will is to be deemed revived if for any reason the later will does not take effect or no later will is executed.

deposition: the testimony of a witness taken out of court before a person authorized to administer oaths.

devise: a gift of real estate made by will.

directed verdict: a direction by the trial judge to the jury to return a verdict in favor of a specified party to the action.

directors: the persons vested with control of the corporation, subject to the elective power of the shareholders.

discharge in bankruptcy: an order of the bankruptcy court discharging the bankrupt debtor from the unpaid balance of most claims.

discharge of contract: termination of a contract by performance, agreement, impossibility, acceptance of breach, or operation of law.

discovery: procedures for ascertaining facts prior to the time of trial in order to eliminate the element of surprise in litigation.

dishonor by nonacceptance: the refusal of the drawee to accept a draft (bill of exchange).

dishonor by nonpayment: the refusal to pay a commercial paper when properly presented for payment.

dismiss: a procedure to terminate an action by moving to dismiss on the ground that the plaintiff has not pleaded a cause of action entitling the plaintiff to relief.

disparagement of goods: the making of malicious, false statements as to the quality of the goods of another.

distress for rent: the common-law right of the lessor to enter the premises when the rent has not been paid and to seize all personal property found on the premises. Statutes have modified or abolished this right in many states.

distributive share: the proportionate part of the estate of the decedent that will be distributed to an heir or legatee, and also as devisee in those jurisdictions in which real estate is administered as part of the decedent's estate.

domestic bill of exchange: a draft drawn in one state and payable in the same or another state.

domestic corporation: a corporation that has been incorporated by the state as opposed to incorporation by another state.

domicile: the home of a person or the state of incorporation, to be distinguished from a place where a person lives but does not regard as home, or a state in which a corporation does business but in which it was not incorporated.

double indemnity: a provision for payment of double the amount specified by the insurance contract if death is caused by an accident and occurs under specified circumstances.

double jeopardy: the principle that a person who has once been placed in jeopardy by being brought to trial at which the proceedings progressed at least as far as having the jury sworn cannot thereafter be tried a second time for the same offense.

draft: see bill of exchange.

draft-varying acceptance: one in which the acceptor's agreement to pay is not exactly in conformity with the order of the instrument.

due care: the degree of care that a reasonable person would exercise to prevent the realization of harm, which under all the circumstances was reasonably foreseeable in the event that such care was not taken.

due process of law: the guarantee by the 5th and 14th amendments of the federal Constitution and of many state constitutions that no person shall be deprived of life, liberty, or property without due process of law. As presently interpreted, this prohibits any law, either state or federal, that sets up an unfair procedure or the substance of which is arbitrary or capricious.

duress: conduct that deprives the victim of free will and which generally gives the victim the right to set aside any transaction entered into under such circumstances.

E

easement: a permanent right that one has in the land of another, as the right to cross another's land or easement of way.

eleemosynary corporation: a corporation organized for a charitable or benevolent purpose.

embezzlement: a statutory offense consisting of the unlawful conversion of property entrusted to the wrongdoer.

eminent domain: the power of a government and certain kinds of corporations to take private property against the objection of the owner, provided the taking is for a public purpose and just compensation is made therefor.

encumbrance: a right held by a third person in or a lien or charge against property, as a mortgage or judgment lien on land.

equity: the body of principles that originally developed because of the inadequacy of the rules then applied by the common-law courts of England.

erosion: the loss of land through a gradual washing away by tides or currents, with the owner losing title to the lost land.

escheat: the transfer to the state of the title to a decedent's property when the owner of property dies intestate not survived by anyone capable of taking the property as heir.

escrow: a conditional delivery of property or of a deed to a custodian or escrow holder, who in turn makes final delivery to the grantee or transferee when a specified condition has been satisfied.

estate: the extent and nature of one's interest in land; the assets constituting a decedent's property at the time of death, or the assets of a bankrupt.

estate in fee simple: the largest estate possible in which the owner has the absolute and entire property in the land.

estoppel: the principle by which a person is barred from pursuing a certain course of action or of disputing the truth of certain matters.

evidence: that which is presented to the trier of fact as the basis on which the trier is to determine what happened.

exception: an objection, as an exception to the admission of evidence on the ground that it was hearsay; a clause excluding particular property from the operation of a deed.

ex contractu: a claim or matter that is founded upon or arises out of a contract.

ex delicto: a claim or matter that is founded upon or arises out of a tort.

execution: the carrying out of a judgment of a court, generally directing that property owned by the defendant be sold and the proceeds first used to pay the execution or judgment creditor.

exemplary damages: damages in excess of the amount needed to compensate for the plaintiff's injury, which are awarded in order to punish the defendant for malicious or wanton conduct; also punitive.

exoneration: an agreement or provision in an agreement that one party shall not be held liable for loss; the right of the surety to demand that those primarily liable pay the claim for which the surety is secondarily liable.

expert witness: one who has acquired special knowledge in a particular field through practical experience, or study, or both, whose opinion is admissible as an aid to the trier of fact.

ex post facto law: a law making criminal an act that was lawful when done or that increases the penalty when done. Such laws are generally prohibited by constitutional provisions.

extraordinary bailment: a bailment in which the bailee is subject to unusual duties and liabilities, as a hotelkeeper or common carrier.

F

factor: a bailee to whom goods are consigned for sale.

factors' acts: statutes protecting persons who buy in good faith for value from a factor although the goods had not been delivered to the factor with the consent or authorization of their owner.

fair employment practice acts: statutes designed to eliminate discrimination in employment in terms of race, religion, national origin, or sex.

fair labor standards acts: statutes, particulary the federal statute, designed to prevent excessive hours of employment and low pay, the employment of young children, and other unsound practices.

featherbedding: the exaction of money for services not performed, which is made an unfair labor practice generally and a criminal offense in connection with radio broadcasting.

Federal Securities Act: a statute designed to protect the public from fraudulent securities.

Federal Securities Exchange Act: a statute prohibiting improper practices at and regulating security exchanges.

Federal Trade Commission Act: a statute prohibiting unfair methods of competition in interstate commerce.

fellow-servant rule: a common-law defense of the employer that barred an employee from suing an employer for injuries caused by a fellow employee.

felony: a criminal offense that is punishable by confinement in prison or by death, or that is expressly stated by statute to be a felony.

financial responsibility laws: statutes that require a driver involved in an automobile accident to prove financial responsibility in order to retain a license, which responsibility may be shown by procuring public liability insurance in a specified minimum amount.

financing factor: one who lends money to manufacturers on the security of goods to be manufactured thereafter.

firm offer: an offer stated to be held open for a specified time, which must be so held in some states even in the absence of an option contract, or under the Code, with respect to merchants.

fixture: personal property that has become so attached to or adapted to real estate that it has lost its character as personal property and is part of the real estate.

Food, Drug, and Cosmetic Act: a federal statute prohibiting the interstate shipment of misbranded or adulterated foods, drugs, cosmetics, and therapeutic devices.

forbearance: refraining from doing an act.

foreclosure: procedure for enforcing a mortgage resulting in the public sale of the mortgaged property and less commonly in merely barring the right of the mortgagor to redeem the property from the mortgage.

foreign (international) bill of exchange: a bill of exchange made in one nation and payable in another.

foreign corporation: a corporation incorporated under the laws of another state.

forgery: the fraudulent making or altering of an instrument that apparently creates or alters a legal liability of another.

franchise: (a) a privilege or authorization, generally exclusive, to engage in a particular activity within a particular geographic area, as a government franchise to operate a taxi company within a specified city, or a private franchise as the grant by a manufacturer of a right to sell products within a particular territory or for a particular number of years; (b) the right to vote.

fraud: the making of a false statement of a past or existing fact with knowledge of its falsity or with reckless indifference as to its truth with the intent to cause another to rely thereon, and such person does rely thereon and is harmed thereby.

freight forwarder: one who contracts to have goods transported and, in turn, contracts with carriers for such transportation.

fructus industriales: crops that are annually planted and raised.

fructus naturales: fruits from trees, bushes, and grasses growing from perennial roots.

fungible goods: goods of a homogeneous nature of which any unit is the equivalent of any other unit or is treated as such by mercantile usage.

future advance mortgage: a mortgage given to secure additional loans to be made in the future as well as an original loan.

G

garnishment: the name given in some states to attachment proceedings.

general creditor: a creditor who has a claim against the debtor but does not have any lien on any of the debtor's property, whether as security for debt or by way of a judgment or execution upon a judgment.

general damages: damages that in the ordinary course of events follow naturally and probably from the injury caused by the defendant.

general legacy: a legacy to be paid out of the assets generally of the decedent without specifying any particular fund or source from which the payment is to be made.

general partnership: a partnership in which the partners conduct as co-owners a business for profit, and each partner has a right to take part in the management of the business and has unlimited liability.

gift causa mortis: a gift made by the donor in the belief that death was immediate and impending, which gift is revoked or is revocable under certain circumstances.

grace period: a period generally of 30 or 31 days after the due date of a premium of life insurance in which the premium may be paid.

grand jury: a jury not exceeding 23 in number that considers evidence of the commission of crime and prepares indictments to bring offenders to trial before a petty jury.

grant: convey real property; an instrument by which such property has been conveyed, particularly in the case of a government.

gratuitous bailment: a bailment in which the bailee does not receive any compensation or advantage.

grievance settlement: the adjustment of disputes relating to the administration or application of existing contracts as compared with disputes over new terms of employment.

guarantor: one who undertakes the obligation of guaranty.

guaranty: an undertaking to pay the debt of another if the creditor first sues the debtor and is unable to recover the debt from the debtor or principal. (In some instances the liability is primary, in which case it is the same as suretyship.)

H

hearsay evidence: statements made out of court which are offered in court as proof of the information contained in the statements, which, subject to many exceptions, are not admissible in evidence.

hedging: the making of simultaneous contracts to purchase and to sell a particular commodity at a future date with the intention that the loss on one transaction will be offset by the gain on the other.

heirs: those persons specified by statute to receive the estate of a decedent not disposed of by will.

holder: the person in possession of a commercial paper payable to that person as payee or indorsee, or the person in possession of a commercial paper payable to bearer.

holder in due course: a holder of a commercial paper who is favored and is given an immunity from certain defenses.

holder through a holder in due course: a person who is not a holder in due course but is a holder of the paper after it was held by some prior party who was a holder in due course, and who is given the same rights as a holder in due course.

holographic will: a will written by hand.

hotelkeeper: one regularly engaged in the business of offering living accommodations to all transient persons.

hung jury: a petty jury that has been unable to agree upon a verdict.

I

ignorantia legis non excusat: ignorance of the law is not an excuse.

implied contract: a contract expressed by conduct or implied or deduced from the facts. Also used to refer to a quasi-contract.

imputed: vicariously attributed to or charged to another, as the knowledge of an agent obtained while acting in the scope of authority is imputed to the principal.

incidental authority: authority of an agent that is reasonably necessary to execute express authority.

incontestable clause: a provision that after the lapse of a specified time the insurer cannot dispute the policy on the ground of misrepresentation or fraud of the insured or similar wrongful conduct.

in custodia legis: in the custody of the law.

indemnity: the right of a person secondarily liable to require that a person primarily liable pay for loss sustained when the secondary party discharges the obligation which the primary party should have discharged; the right of an agent to be paid the amount of any loss or damage sustained without fault because of obedience to the principal's instructions; an undertaking by one person for a consideration to pay another person a sum of money to indemnify that person when a specified loss is incurred.

independent contractor: a contractor who undertakes to perform a specified task according to the terms of a contract but over whom the other contracting party has no control except as provided for by the contract.

indictment: a formal accusation of crime made by a grand jury which accusation is then tried by a petty or trial jury.

inheritance: the interest which passes from the decedent to the decedent's heirs.

injunction: an order of a court of equity to refrain from doing (negative injunction) or to do (affirmative or mandatory injunction) a specified act. Its use in labor disputes has been greatly restricted by statute.

in pari delicto: equally guilty; used in reference to a transaction as to which relief will not be granted to either party because both are equally guilty of wrongdoing.

insolvency: an excess of debts and liabilities over assets or inability to pay debts as they mature.

insurable interest: an interest in the nonoccurrence of the risk insured against, generally because such occurrence would cause financial loss, although sometimes merely because of the close relationship between the insured and the beneficiary.

insurance: a plan of security against risks by charging the loss against a fund created by the payments made by policyholders.

intangible personal property: an interest in an enterprise, such as an interest in a partnership or stock of a corporation, and claims against other persons, whether based on contract or tort.

interlineation: a writing between the lines or adding to the provisions of a document, the effect thereof depending upon the nature of the document.

interlocutory: an intermediate step or proceeding that does not make a final disposition of the action and from which ordinarily no appeal may be taken.

international bill of exchange: a bill or draft made in one nation and payable in another.

interpleader: a form of action or proceeding by which a person against whom conflicting claims are made may bring the claimants into court to litigate their claims between themselves, as in the case of a bailee when two persons each claim to be the owner of the bailed property, or an insurer when two persons each claim to be the beneficiary.

inter se: among or between themselves, as the rights of partners inter se or as between themselves.

inter vivos: any transaction which takes place between living persons and creates rights prior to the death of any of them.

intestate: the condition of dying without a will as to any property.

intestate succession: the distribution made as directed by statute of property owned by a decedent not effectively disposed of by will.

ipso facto: by the very act or fact in itself without any further action by any one.

irrebuttable presumption: a presumption which cannot be rebutted by proving that the facts are to the contrary; not a true presumption but merely a rule of law described in terms of a presumption.

irreparable injury to property: an injury that would be of such a nature or inflicted upon such an interest that it would not be reasonably possible to compensate the injured party by the payment of money damages because the property in question could not be purchased in the open market with the money damages which the defendant could be required to pay.

J

joint and several contract: a contract in which two or more persons are jointly and severally obligated or are jointly and severally entitled to recover.

joint contract: a contract in which two or more persons are jointly liable or jointly entitled to performance under the contract.

joint stock company: an association in which the shares of the members are transferable and control is delegated to a group or board.

joint tenancy: the estate held by two or more jointly with the right of survivorship as between them, unless modified by statute.

joint venture: a relationship in which two or more persons combine their labor or property for a single undertaking and share profits and losses equally unless otherwise agreed.

judgment: the final sentence, order, or decision entered into at the conclusion of the action.

judgment note: a promissory note containing a clause authorizing the holder of the note to enter judgment against the maker of the note if it is not paid when due. Also called cognovit note.

judgment n.o.v.: a judgment which may be entered after verdict upon the motion of the losing party on the ground that the verdict is so wrong that a judgment should be entered the opposite of the verdict, or non obstante verdicto (notwithstanding the verdict).

judgment on the pleadings: a judgment which may be entered after all the pleadings are filed when it is clear from the pleadings that a particular party is entitled to win the action without proceeding any further.

judicial sale: a sale made under order of court by an officer appointed to make the sale or by an officer having such authority as incident to the office. The sale may have the effect of divesting liens on the property.

jurisdiction: the power of a court to hear and determine a given class of cases; the power to act over a particular defendant.

jurisdictional dispute: a dispute between rival labor unions which may take the form of each claiming that particular work should be assigned to it.

justifiable abandonment by employee: the right of an employee to abandon employment because of nonpayment of wages, wrongful assault, the demand for the performance of services not contemplated, or injurious working conditions.

justifiable discharge of employee: the right of an employer to discharge an employee for nonperformance of duties, fraud, disobedience, disloyalty, or incompetence.

L

laches: the rule that the enforcement of equitable rights will be denied when the party has delayed so long that rights of third persons have intervened or the death or disappearance of witnesses would prejudice any party through the loss of evidence.

land: earth, including all things imbedded in or attached thereto, whether naturally or by the act of man.

last clear chance: the rule that a defendant who had the last clear chance to have avoided injuring the plaintiff is liable even though the plaintiff had also been contributorily negligent. In some states also called the humanitarian doctrine.

law of the case: matters decided in the course of litigation which are binding on the parties in the subsequent phases of litigation.

leading questions: questions which suggest the desired answer to the witness, or assume the existence of a fact which is in dispute.

lease: an agreement between the owner of property and a tenant by which the former agrees to give possession of the property to the latter in consideration of the payment of rent. (Parties–landlord or lessor, tenant or lessee)

leasehold: the estate or interest of a tenant in rented land.

legacy: a gift of personal property made by will.

legal tender: such form of money as the law recognizes as lawful and declares that a tender thereof in the proper amount is a proper tender which the creditor cannot refuse.

letters of administration: the written authorization given to an administrator as evidence of appointment and authority.

letters testamentary: the written authorization given to an executor as evidence of appointment and authority.

levy: a seizure of property by an officer of the court in execution of a judgment of the court, although in many states it is sufficient if the officer is physically in the presence of the property and announces the fact that it is "seized," but then allows the property to remain where it was found.

lex loci: the law of the place where the material facts occurred as governing the rights and liabilities of the parties.

lex loci contractus: the law of the place where the contract was made as governing the rights and liabilities of the parties to a contract with respect to certain matters.

lex loci fori: the law of the state in which the action is brought as determining the rules of procedure applicable to the action.

lex loci sitae rei: the law of the place where land is located as determining the validity of acts done relating thereto.

libel: written or visual defamation without legal justification.

license: a personal privilege to do some act or series of acts upon the land of another, as the placing of a sign thereon, not amounting to an easement or a right of possession.

lien: a claim or right against property existing by virtue of the entry of a judgment against its owner or by the entry of a judgment and a levy thereunder on the property, or because of the relationship of the claimant to the particular property, such as an unpaid seller.

life estate: an estate for the duration of a life.

limited jurisdiction: a court with power to hear and determine cases within certain restricted categories.

limited liability: loss of contributed capital or investment as maximum liability.

limited partnership: a partnership in which at least one partner has a liability limited to the loss of the capital contribution made to the partnership, and such a partner neither takes part in the management of the partnership nor appears to the public to be a partner.

lineal consanguinity: the relationship that exists when one person is a direct descendant from the other.

liquidated damages: a provision stipulating the amount of damages to be paid in event of default or breach of contract.

liquidation: the process of converting property into money whether of particular items of property or all the assets of a business or an estate.

lis pendens: the doctrine that certain types of pending actions are notice to everyone so that if any right is acquired from a party to such action, the transferee takes that right subject to the outcome of the pending action.

lobbying contract (illegal): a contract by which one party agrees to attempt to influence the action of a legislature or Congress, or any members thereof, by improper means.

lottery: any plan by which a consideration is given for a chance to win a prize.

lucri causa: with the motive of obtaining gain or pecuniary advantage.

M

majority: of age, as contrasted with being a minor; more than half of any group, as a majority of stockholders.

malice in fact: an intention to injure or cause harm.

malice in law: a presumed intention to injure or cause harm when there is no privilege or right to do the act in question, which presumption cannot be contradicted or rebutted.

maliciously inducing breach of contract: the wrong of inducing the breach of any kind of contract with knowledge of its existence and without justification.

malum in se: an offense that is criminal because contrary to the fundamental sense of a civilized community, as murder.

malum prohibitum: an offense that is criminal not because inherently wrong but is prohibited for the convenience of society, as overtime parking.

marshalling assets: the distribution of a debtor's assets in such a way as to give the greatest benefit to all creditors.

martial law: government exercised by a military commander over property and persons not in the armed forces, as contrasted with military law which governs the military personnel.

mechanics' lien: protection afforded by statute to various types of laborers and persons supplying materials, by giving them a lien on the building and land that has been improved or added to by them.

mens rea: the mental state that must accompany an act to make the act a crime. Sometimes described as the "guilty mind," although appreciation of guilt is not required.

merger by judgment: the discharge of a contract through being merged into a judgment which is entered in a suit on the contract.

merger of corporations: a combining of corporations by which one absorbs the other and continues to exist, preserving its original charter and identity while the other corporation ceases to exist.

misdemeanor: a criminal offense which is neither treason nor a felony.

misrepresentation: a false statement of fact although made innocently without any intent to deceive.

mobilia sequuntur personam: the maxim that personal property follows the owner and in the eyes of the law is located at the owner's domicile.

moratorium: a temporary suspension by statute of the enforcement of debts or the foreclosure of mortgages.

mortgage: an interest in land given by the owner to a creditor as security for the payment of the creditor of a debt, the nature of the interest depending upon the law of the state where the land is located. (Parties— mortgagor, mortgagee)

multiple insurers: insurers who agree to divide a risk so that each is only liable for a specified portion.

N

National Labor Management Relations Act: the federal statute, also known as the Taft-Hartley Act, designed to protect the organizational rights of labor and to prevent unfair labor practices by management or labor.

natural and probable consequences: those ordinary consequences of an act which a reasonable person would foresee.

negative covenant: an undertaking in a deed to refrain from doing an act.

negligence: the failure to exercise due care under the circumstances in consequence of which harm is proximately caused to one to whom the defendant owed a duty to exercise due care.

negligence per se: an action which is regarded as so improper that it is declared by law to be negligent in itself without regard to whether due care was otherwise exercised.

negotiable instruments: drafts, promissory notes, checks, and certificates of deposit in such form that greater rights may be acquired thereunder than by taking an assignment of a contract right; called negotiable commercial paper by the Code.

negotiation: the transfer of a commercial paper by indorsement and delivery by the person to whom then payable in the case of order paper, and by physical transfer in the case of bearer paper.

nominal damages: a nominal sum awarded the plaintiff in order to establish that legal rights have been violated although the plaintiff in fact has not sustained any actual loss or damages.

Norris-LaGuardia Anti-Injunction Act: a federal statute prohibiting the use of the injunction in labor disputes, except in particular cases.

notice of dishonor: notice given to parties secondarily liable that the primary party to the instrument has refused to accept the instrument or to make payment when it was properly presented for that purpose.

novation: the discharge of a contract between two parties by their agreeing with a third person that such third person shall be substituted for one of the original parties to the contract, who shall thereupon be released.

nudum pactum: a mere promise for which there is no consideration given and which therefore is ordinarily not enforceable.

nuisance: any conduct that harms or prejudices another in the use of his land or which harms or prejudices the public.

nuisance per se: an activity which is in itself a nuisance regardless of the time and place involved.

nuncupative will: an oral will made and declared by the testator in the presence of witnesses to be a will; generally made during the testator's last illness.

O

obiter dictum: that which is said in the opinion of a court in passing or by the way, but which is not necessary to the determination of the case and is therefore not regarded as authoritative as though it were actually involved in the decision.

obliteration: any erasing, writing upon, or crossing out that makes all or part of a will impossible to read, and which has the effect of revoking such part when done by the maker of the will with the intent of effecting a revocation.

occupation: taking and holding possession of property; a method of acquiring title to personal property after it has been abandoned.

open-end mortgage: a mortgage given to secure additional loans to be made in the future as well as the original loan.

operation of law: the attaching of certain consequences to certain facts because of legal principles that operate automatically, as contrasted with consequences which arise because of the voluntary action of a party designed to create those consequences.

opinion evidence: evidence not of what the witness observed but the conclusion drawn from what the witness has observed, or, in the case of expert witnesses, what has been observed in tests or experiments or what has been heard in court.

option contract: a contract to hold an offer to make a contract open for a fixed period of time.

P

paper title: the title of a person evidenced only by deeds or matter appearing of record under the recording statutes.

parol evidence rule: the rule that prohibits the introduction in evidence of oral or written statements made prior to or contemporaneously with the execution of a complete written contract, deed, or instrument, in the absence of clear proof of fraud, accident, or mistake causing the omission of the statement in question.

passive trust: a trust that is created without imposing any duty to be performed by the trustee and is therefore treated as an absolute transfer of the title to the trust beneficiary.

past consideration: something that has been performed in the past and which therefore cannot be consideration for a promise made in the present.

patent: the grant to an inventor of an exclusive right to make and sell an invention for a nonrenewable period of 17 years; a deed to land given by a government to a private person.

pawn: a pledge of tangible personal property rather than of documents representing property rights.

pecuniary legacy: a general legacy of a specified amount of money without indicating the source from which payment is to be made.

per autre vie: limitation of an estate. An estate held by A during the lifetime of B is an estate of A per autre vie.

per curiam opinion: an opinion written "by the court" rather than by a named judge when all the judges of the court are so agreed on the matter that it is not deemed to merit any discussion and may be simply disposed of.

perpetual succession: a phrase describing the continuing life of the corporation unaffected by the death of any stockholder or the transfer by stockholders of their stock.

perpetuities, rule against: a rule of law that prohibits the creation of an interest in property which will not become definite or vested until a date further away than 21 years after the death of persons alive at the time the owner of the property attempts to create the interest.

per se: in, through, or by itself.

person: a term that includes both natural persons, or living people, and artificial persons, as corporations which are created by act of government.

personal defenses: limited defenses that cannot be asserted by the defendant against a holder in due course. This term is not expressly used in Uniform Commercial Code.

per stirpes: according to the root or by way of representation. Distribution among heirs related to the decedent in different degrees, the property being divided into lines of descent from the decedent and the share of each line then divided within the line by way of representation.

petty jury: the trial jury of twelve. Also petit jury.

picketing: the placing of persons outside of places of employment or distribution so that by words or banners they may inform the public of the existence of a labor dispute.

pleadings: the papers filed by the parties in an action in order to set forth the facts and frame the issues to be tried, although under some systems, the pleadings merely give notice or a general indication of the nature of the issues.

pledge: a bailment given as security for the payment of a debt or the performance of an obligation owed to the pledgee. (Parties—pledgor, pledgee)

police power: the power to govern; the power to adopt laws for the protection of the public health, welfare, safety, and morals.

policy: the paper evidencing the contract of insurance.

polling the jury: the process of inquiring of each juror individually in open court as to whether the verdict announced in court was agreed to.

possession: exclusive dominion and control of property.

possessory lien: a right to retain possession of property of another as security for some debt or obligation owed the lienor which right continues only as long as possession is retained.

possibility of reverter: the nature of the interest held by the grantor after conveying land outright but subject to a condition or provision that may cause the grantee's interest to become forfeited and the interest to revert to the grantor or heirs.

postdate: to insert or place a later date on an instrument than the actual date on which it was executed.

power of appointment: a power given to another, commonly a beneficiary of a trust, to designate or appoint who shall be beneficiary or receive the fund after his death.

power of attorney: a written authorization to an agent by the principal.

precatory words: words indicating merely a desire or a wish that another use property for a particular purpose but which in law will not be enforced in the absence of an express declaration that the property shall be used for the specified purpose.

pre-emptive offer of shares: the right, subject to many exceptions, that each shareholder has that whenever the capital stock of the corporation is increased to be allowed to subscribe to such a percentage of the new shares as the shareholder's old shares bore to the former total capital stock.

preferred creditor: a creditor who by some statute is given the right to be paid first or before other creditors.

preferred stock: stock that has a priority or preference as to payment of dividends or upon liquidation, or both.

preponderance of evidence: the degree or quantum of evidence in favor of the existence of a certain fact when from a review of all the evidence it appears more probable that the fact exists than that it does not. The actual number of witnesses involved is not material nor is the fact that the margin of probability is very slight.

prescription: the acquisition of a right to use the land of another, as an easement, through the making of hostile, visible, and notorious use of the land, continuing for the period specified by the local law.

presumption: a rule of proof which permits the existence of a fact to be assumed from the proof that another fact exists when there is a logical relationship between the two or when the means of disproving the assumed fact are more readily within the control or knowledge of the adverse party against whom the presumption operates.

presumption of death: the rebuttable presumption which arises that a person has died when that person has been continuously absent and unheard of for a period of 7 years.

presumption of innocence: the presumption of fact that a person accused of crime is innocent until shown guilty of the offense charged.

presumption of payment: a rebuttable presumption that one performing continuing services which would normally be paid periodically, as weekly or monthly, has in fact been paid when a number of years have passed without any objection or demand for payment having been made.

presumptive heir: a person who would be the heir if the ancestor should die at that moment.

pretrial conference: a conference held prior to the trial at which the court and the attorneys seek to simplify the issues in controversy and eliminate matters not in dispute.

price: the consideration for sale of goods.

prima facie: such evidence as by itself would establish the claim or defense of the party if the evidence were believed.

primary beneficiary: the person designated as the first one to receive the proceeds of a life insurance policy, as distinguished from a contingent beneficiary who will receive the proceeds only if the primary beneficiary dies before the insured.

primary liability: the liability of a person whose act or omission gave rise to the cause of action and who in all fairness should therefore be the one to pay the victim even though others may also be liable for misconduct.

principal: one who employs an agent; the person who, with respect to a surety, is primarily liable to the third person or creditor.

principal in the first degree: one who actually engages in the commission or perpetration of a crime.

principal in the second degree: one who is actually or constructively present at the commission of the crime and who aids and abets in its commission.

private carrier: a carrier owned by the shipper, such as a company's own fleet of trucks.

privileged communication: information which the witness may refuse to testify to because of the relationship with the person furnishing the information, as husband-wife, attorney-client.

privilege from arrest: the immunity from arrest of parties, witnesses, and attorneys while present within the jurisdiction for the purpose of taking part in other litigation.

privity: a succession or chain of relationship to the same thing or right, as privity of contract, privity of estate, privity of possession.

probate: the procedure for formally establishing or proving that a given writing is the last will and testament of the person purporting to have signed it.

product liability: liability imposed upon the manufacturer or seller of goods for harm caused by a defect in the goods, embracing liability for (1) negligence, (2) fraud, (3) breach of warranty, and (4) strict tort.

profit à pendre: the right to take a part of the soil or produce of another's land, such as timber or water.

promissory estoppel: the doctrine that a promise will be enforced although it is not supported by consideration when the promisor should have reasonably expected that the promise would induce action or forbearance of a definite and substantial character on the part of the promisee, and injustice can only be avoided by enforcement of the promise.

promissory note: an unconditional promise in writing made by one person to another, signed by the maker engaging to pay on demand, or at a definite time, a sum certain in money to order or to bearer. (Parties—maker, payee)

promissory representation: a representation made by the applicant to the insurer as to what is to occur in the future.

promissory warranty: a representation made by the applicant to the insurer as to what is to occur in the future which the applicant warrants will occur.

promoters: the persons who plan the formation of the corporation and sell or promote the idea to others.

proof: the probative effect of the evidence; the conclusion drawn from the evidence as to the existence of particular facts.

property: the rights and interests one has in anything subject to ownership.

pro rata: proportionately, or divided according to a rate or standard.

protest: the formal certificate by a notary public or other authorized person that proper presentment of a commercial paper was made to the primary party and that such party defaulted, the certificate commonly also including a recital that notice was given to secondary parties.

proximate cause: the act which is the natural and reasonably foreseeable cause of the harm or event which occurs and injures the plaintiff.

proximate damages: damages which in the ordinary

course of events are the natural and reasonably fore-seeable result of the defendant's violation of the plaintiff's rights.

proxy: a written authorization by a shareholder to another person to vote the stock owned by the shareholder; the person who is the holder of such a written authorization.

public charge: a person who because of a personal disability or lack of means of support is dependent upon public charity or relief for sustenance.

public domain: public or government owned lands.

public easement: a right of way for use by members of the public at large.

public policy: certain objectives relating to health, morals, and integrity of government that the law seeks to advance by declaring invalid any contract which conflicts with those objectives even though there is no statute expressly declaring such contract illegal.

punitive damages: damages in excess of those required to compensate the plaintiff for the wrong done, which are imposed in order to punish the defendant because of the particularly wanton or willful character of wrongdoing; also exemplary.

purchase-money mortgage: a mortgage given by the purchaser of land to the seller to secure the seller for the payment of the unpaid balance of the purchase price, which the seller purports to lend the purchaser.

purchaser in good faith: a person who purchases without any notice or knowledge of any defect of title, misconduct, or defense.

Q

qualified acceptance: An acceptance of a draft that varies the order of the draft in some way.

qualified indorsement: an indorsement that includes words such as "without recourse" evidencing the intent that the indorser shall not be held liable for the failure of the primary party to pay the instrument.

quantum meruit: an action brought for the value of the services rendered the defendant when there was no express contract as to the payment to be made.

quantum valebant: an action brought for the value of goods sold the defendant when there was no express contract as to the purchase price.

quasi: as if, as though it were, having the characteristics of; a modifier employed to indicate that the subject is to be treated as though it were in fact the noun which follows the word "quasi:" as in quasi contract, quasi corporation, quasi public corporation.

quid pro quo: literally "what for what." An early form of the concept of consideration by which an action for debt could not be brought unless the defendant had obtained something in return for the obligation sued upon.

quitclaim deed: a deed by which the grantor purports only to give up whatever right or title the grantor may have in the property without specifying or warranting transfer of any particular interest.

quorum: the minimum number of persons, shares represented, or directors who must be present at a meeting in order that business may be lawfully transacted.

R

ratification by minor: the approval of a contract given by a minor after attaining majority.

ratification of agency: the approval of the unauthorized act of an agent or of a person who is not an agent for any purpose after the act has been done, which has the same effect as though the act had been authorized before it was done.

ratio decidendi: the reason or basis for deciding the case in a particular way.

ratio legis: the reason for a princple or rule of law.

real defenses: certain defenses (universal) that are available against any holder of a commercial paper, although this term is not expressly used by the Uniform Commercial Code.

real evidence: tangible objects that are presented in the courtroom for the observation of the trier of fact as proof of the facts in dispute or in support of the theory of a party.

real property: land and all rights in land.

reasonable care: the degree of care that a reasonable person would take under all the circumstances then known.

rebate: a refund made by the seller or the carrier of part of the purchase price or freight bill. Generally illegal as an unfair method of competition.

rebuttable presumption: a presumption which may be overcome or rebutted by proof that the actual facts were different than those presumed.

receiver: an impartial person appointed by a court to take possession of and manage property for the protection of all concerned.

recognizance: an obligation entered into before a court to do some act, such as to appear at a later date for a hearing. Also called a contract of record.

redemption: the buying back of one's property, which has been sold because of a default, upon paying the amount which had been originally due together with interest and costs.

referee: an impartial person selected by the parties or appointed by a court to determine facts or decide matters in dispute.

referee in bankruptcy: a referee appointed by a bankruptcy court to hear and determine various matters relating to bankruptcy proceedings.

reformation: a remedy by which a written instrument is corrected when it fails to express the actual intent of both parties because of fraud, accident, or mistake.

registration of titles: a system generally known as the Torrens system of permanent registration of title to all land within the state.

reimbursement: the right of one paying money on behalf of another, which such other person should have paid, to recover the amount of the payment from such other person.

release of liens: an agreement or instrument by which the holder of a lien on property such as a mortgage lien, releases the property from the lien although the debt itself is not discharged.

remedy: the action or procedure that is followed in order to enforce a right or to obtain damages for injury to a right.

remote damages: damages which were in fact caused by the defendant's act but the possibility that such damages should occur seemed so improbable and unlikely to a reasonable person that the law does not impose liability for such damages.

renunciation of duty: the repudiation of one's contractual duty in advance of the time for performance, which repudiation may be accepted as an anticipatory breach by the other contracting party.

renunciation of right: the surrender of a right or privilege, as the right to act as administrator or the right to receive a legacy under the will of a decedent.

reorganization of corporation: procedure devised to restore insolvent corporations to financial stability through readjustment of debt and capital structure either under the supervision of a court of equity or of bankruptcy.

repossession: any taking again of possession although generally used in connection with the act of a secured seller in taking back the property upon the default of the credit buyer.

representations: any statements, whether oral or written, made to give the insurer the information which it needs in writing the insurance, and which if false and relating to a material fact will entitle the insurer to avoid the contract.

representative capacity: action taken by one on behalf of another, as the act of a personal representative on behalf of a decedent's estate, or action taken both on one's behalf and on behalf of others, as a shareholder bringing a representative action.

rescission upon agreement: the setting aside of a contract by the action of the parties as though the contract had never been made.

rescission upon breach: the action of one party to a contract to set the contract aside when the other party is guilty of a breach of the contract.

residuary estate: the balance of the decedent's estate available for distribution after all administrative expenses, exemptions, debts, taxes, and legacies have been paid.

res inter alios acta: the rule that transactions and declarations between strangers having no connection with the pending action are not admissible in evidence.

res ipsa loquitur: the permissible inference that the defendant was negligent in that the thing speaks for itself when the circumstances are such that ordinarily the plaintiff could not have been injured had the defendant not been at fault.

res judicata: the principle that once a final judgment is entered in an action between the parties, it is binding upon them and the matter cannot be litigated again by bringing a second action.

respondeat superior: the doctrine that the principal or employer is vicariously liable for the unauthorized torts committed by an agent or employee while acting within the scope of the agency or the course of the employment, respectively.

restraints on alienation: limitations on the ability of the owner to convey freely as he chooses. Such limitations are generally regarded as invalid.

restrictive covenants: convenants in a deed by which the grantee agrees to refrain from doing specified acts.

restrictive indorsement: an indorsement that prohibits the further transfer, constitutes the indorsee the agent of the indorser, vests the title in the indorsee in trust for or to the use of some other person, is conditional, or is for collection or deposit.

resulting trust: a trust that is created by implication of law to carry out the presumed intent of the parties.

retaliatory statute: a statute that provides that when a corporation of another state enters the state it shall be subject to the same taxes and restrictions as would be imposed upon a corporation from the retaliating state if it had entered the other state. Also reciprocity statutes.

reversible error: an error or defect in court proceedings of so serious a nature that on appeal the appellate court will set aside the proceedings of the lower court.

reversionary interest: the interest that a lessor has in property which is subject to an outstanding lease.

revivial of judgment: the taking of appropriate action to preserve a judgment, in most instances to continue the lien of the judgment that would otherwise expire after a specified number of years.

revival of will: the restoration by the writer of a will which had previously been revoked.

rider: a slip of paper executed by the insurer and intended to be attached to the insurance policy for the purpose of changing it in some respect.

riparian rights: the right of a person through whose

land runs a natural watercourse to use the water free from unreasonable pollution or diversion by upper riparian owners and blocking by lower riparian owners.

risk: the peril or contingency against which the insured is protected by the contract of insurance.

Robinson-Patman Act: a federal statute designed to eliminate price discrimination in interstate commerce.

run with the land: the concept that certain covenants in a deed to land are deemed to "run" or pass with the land so that whoever owns the land is bound by or entitled to the benefit of the covenants.

S

sale or return: a sale in which the title to the property passes to the buyer at the time of the transaction but the buyer is given the option of returning the property and restoring the title to the seller.

scienter: knowledge, referring to those wrongs or crimes which require a knowledge of wrong in order to constitute the offense.

scope of employment: the area within which the employee is authorized to act with the consequence that a tort committed while so acting imposes liability upon the employer.

seal: at common law an impression on wax or other tenacious material attached to the instrument. Under modern law, any mark not ordinarily part of the signature is a seal when so intended, including the letters "L.S." and the word "seal," or a pictorial representation of a seal, without regard to whether they had been printed or typed on the instrument before its signing.

sealed verdict: a verdict that is rendered when the jury returns to the courtroom during an adjournment of the court, the verdict then being written down and sealed and later affirmed before the court when the court is in session.

secondary evidence: copies of original writings or testimony as to the contents of such writings which are admissible when the original cannot be produced and the inability to do so is reasonably explained.

secured transaction: a credit sale of goods or a secured loan that provides special protection for the creditor.

settlor: one who settles property in trust or creates a trust estate.

severable contract: a contract the terms of which are such that one part may be separated or severed from the other, so that a default as to one part is not necessarily a default as to the entire contract.

several contracts: separate or independent contracts made by different persons undertaking to perform the same obligation.

severalty: sole ownership of property by one person.

severed realty: real property that has been cut off and made moveable, as by cutting down a tree, and which thereby loses its character as real property and becomes personal property.

shareholder's action: an action brought by one or more shareholders on behalf of themselves and on behalf of all shareholders generally and of the corporation to enforce a cause of action of the corporation against third persons.

sheriff's deed: the deed executed and delivered by the sheriff to the purchaser at a sale conducted by the sheriff.

Sherman Antitrust Act: a federal statute prohibiting combinations and contracts in restraint of interstate trade, now generally inapplicable to labor union activity.

shop right: the right of an employer to use in business without charge an invention discovered by an employee during working hours and with the employer's material and equipment.

sight draft: a draft or bill of exchange payable on sight or when presented for payment.

sitdown strike: a strike in which the employees remain in the plant and refuse to allow the employer to operate it.

slander: defamation of character by spoken words or gestures.

slander of title: the malicious making of false statements as to a seller's title.

slowdown: a slowing down of production by employees without actual stopping work.

social security acts: statutes providing for assistance for the aged, blind, unemployed, and similar classes of persons in need.

special agent: an agent authorized to transact a specific transaction or to do a specific act.

special damages: damages that do not necessarily result from the injury to the plaintiff but at the same time are not so remote that the defendant should not be held liable therefor provided that the claim for special damages is properly made in the action.

special indorsement: an indorsement that specifies the person to whom the instrument is indorsed.

special jurisdiction: a court with power to hear and determine cases within certain restricted categories.

specific (identified) goods: goods which are so identified to the contract that no other goods may be delivered in performance of the contract.

specific lien: the right of a creditor to hold particular property or assert a lien on particular property of the debtor because of the creditor's having done work on or having some other association with the property; as distinguished from having a lien generally against the assets of the debtor merely because the debtor is indebted to the lienholder.

specific performance: an action brought to compel the adverse party to perform a contract on the theory that merely suing for damages for its breach will not be an adequate remedy.

spendthrift trust: a trust, which to varying degrees, provides that creditors of the beneficiary shall not be able to reach the principal or income held by the trustee and that the beneficiary shall not be able to assign any interest in the trust.

spoliation: an alteration or change made to a written instrument by a person who has no relationship to or interest in the writing. It has no effect as long as the terms of the instrument can still be ascertained.

stare decisis: the principle that the decision of a court should serve as a guide or precedent and control the decision of a similar case in the future.

status quo ante: the original positions of the parties to a contract prior to the making of the contract or the doing of some other act.

Statute of Frauds: a statute, which in order to prevent fraud through the use of perjured testimony, requires that certain types of transactions be evidenced in writing in order to be binding or enforceable.

Statute of Limitations: a statute that restricts the period of time within which an action may be brought.

stop delivery: the right of an unpaid seller under certain conditions to prevent a carrier or a bailee from delivering goods to the buyer.

stop payment: an order by a depositor to the bank to refuse to make payment of a check when presented for payment.

strict tort liability: a product liability theory which imposes liability on the manufacturer, seller, or distributor of goods for harm caused by defective goods.

sublease: a transfer of the premises by the lessee to a third person, the sublessee or subtenant, for a period of less than the term of the original lease.

subpoena: a court order directing a person to appear as a witness. In some states also it is the original process that is to be served on the defendant in order to give the court jurisdiction over the defendant.

subrogation: the right of a party secondarily liable to stand in the place of the creditor after making payment to the creditor and to enforce the creditor's right against the party primarily liable in order to obtain indemnity from such primary party.

subsidiary corporation: a corporation that is controlled by another corporation through the ownership by the latter of a controlling amount of the voting stock of the former.

subsidiary term: a provision of a contract that is not fundamental or does not go to the root of the contract.

substantial performance: the equitable doctrine that a contractor substantially performing a contract in good faith is entitled to recover the contract price less damages for noncompletion or defective work.

substantive law: the law that defines rights and liabilities.

substitution: discharge of contracts by substituting another in its place.

subtenant: one who rents the leased premises from the original tenant for a period of time less than the balance of the lease to the original tenant.

sui generis: in a class by itself, or its own kind.

sui juris: legally competent, possessing capacity.

summary judgment: a judgment entered by the court when no substantial dispute of fact is present, the court acting on the basis of affidavits or depositions which show that the claim or defense of a party is a sham.

summons: a writ by which an action was commenced under the common law.

supersedeas: a stay of proceedings pending the taking of an appeal or an order entered for the purpose of effecting such a stay.

suretyship: an undertaking to pay the debt or be liable for the default of another.

surrender: the yielding up of the tenant's leasehold estate to the lessor in consequence of which the lease terminates.

survival acts: statutes which provide that causes of action shall not terminate on death but shall survive and may be enforced by or against a decedent's estate.

survivorship: the right by which a surviving joint tenant or tenant by the entireties acquires the interest of the predeceasing tenant automatically upon the death of such tenant.

symbolic delivery: the delivery of goods by delivery of the means of control, as a key or relevant document of title, as a negotiable bill of lading.

syndicate: an association of individuals formed to conduct a particular business transaction, generally of a financial nature.

T

tacking: adding together successive periods of adverse possession of persons in privity with each other in order to constitute a sufficient period of continuous adverse possession to vest title thereby.

Taft-Hartley Act: popular name for the National Labor Management Relations Act of 1947.

tenancy at sufferance: the holding over by a tenant after a lease has expired of the rented land without the permission of the landlord and prior to the time that the landlord has elected to treat such possessor as a trespasser or a tenant.

tenancy at will: the holding of land for an indefinite period that may be terminated at any time by the landlord or by the landlord and tenant acting together.

tenancy for years: a tenancy for a fixed period of time, even though the time is less than a year.

tenancy from year to year: a tenancy which continues indefinitely from year to year until terminated.

tenancy in common: the relation that exists when two or more persons own undivided interests in property.

tenancy in partnership: the ownership relation that exists between partners under the Uniform Partnership Act.

tender of payment: an unconditional offer to pay the exact amount of money due at the time and place specified by the contract.

tender of performance: an unconditional offer to perform at the time and in the manner specified by the contract.

tentative trust: a trust which arises when money is deposited in a bank account in the name of the depositor "in trust for" a named person.

terminable fee: an estate that terminates upon the happening of a contingency without any entry by the grantor or heirs, as a conveyance for "so long as" the land is used for a specified purpose.

testamentary: designed to take effect at death, as by disposing of property or appointing a personal representative.

testate: the condition of leaving a will upon death.

testate succession: the distribution of an estate in accordance with the will of the decedent.

testator–testatrix: a man–woman who makes a will.

testimonium clause: a concluding paragraph in a deed, contract, or other instrument, reciting that the instrument has been executed on a specified date by the parties.

testimony: the answers of witnesses under oath to questions given at the time of the trial in the presence of the trier of fact.

theory of the case: the rule that when a case is tried on the basis of one theory, the appellant in taking an appeal cannot argue a different theory to the appellate court.

third party beneficiary: a third person whom the parties to a contract intend to benefit by the making of the contract and to confer upon such person the right to sue for breach of contract.

tie-in sale: the requirement imposed by the seller that the buyer of particular goods or equipment also purchase certain other goods from the seller in order to obtain the original property desired.

time draft: a bill of exchange payable at a stated time after sight or at a definite time.

title insurance: a form of insurance by which the insurer insures the buyer of real property against the risk of loss should the title acquired from the seller be defective in any way.

toll the statute: stop the running of the period of the Statute of Limitations by the doing of some act by the debtor.

Torrens System: see registration of titles.

tort: a private injury or wrong arising from a breach of a duty created by law.

trade acceptance: a draft or bill of exchange drawn by the seller of goods on the purchaser at the time of sale and accepted by the purchaser.

trade fixtures: articles of personal property which have been attached to the freehold by a tenant and which are used for or are necessary to the carrying on of the tenant's trade.

trademark: a name, device, or symbol used by a manufacturer or seller to distinguish goods from those of other persons.

trade name: a name under which a business is carried on and, if fictitious, it must be registered.

trade secrets: secrets of any character peculiar and important to the business of the employer that have been communicated to the employee in the course of confidential employment.

treason: an attempt to overthrow or betray the government to which one owes allegiance.

treasury stock: stock of the corporation which the corporation has reacquired.

trier of fact: in most cases a jury, although it may be the judge alone in certain classes of cases, as in equity, or in any case when jury trial is waived, or an administrative agency or commission is involved.

trust: a transfer of property by one person to another with the understanding or declaration that such property be held for the benefit of another, or the holding of property by the owner in trust for another, upon a declaration of trust, without a transfer to another person. (Parties—settlor, trustee, beneficiary.)

trust corpus: the fund or property that is transferred to the trustee or held by the settlor as the body or subject matter of the trust.

trust deed: a form of deed which transfers the trust property to the trustee for the purposes therein stated, particularly used when the trustee is to hold the title to the mortgagor's land in trust for the benefit of the mortgage bondholders.

trustee de son tort: a person who is not a trustee but who has wrongly intermeddled with property of another and who is required to account for the property as though an actual trustee.

trustee in bankruptcy: an impartial person elected to administer the bankrupt's estate.

trust receipt: a credit security device under which the wholesale buyer executes a receipt stating that the buyer holds the purchased goods in trust for the person financing the purchase. The trust receipt is replaced by the secured transaction under the UCC.

U

uberrima fides: utmost good faith, a duty to exercise the utmost good faith which arises in certain relationships, as that between an insurer and the applicant for insurance.

ultra vires: an act or contract which the corporation does not have authority to do or make.

underwriter: an insurer.

undisclosed principal: a principal on whose behalf an agent acts without disclosing to the third person the fact of agency or the identity of the principal.

undue influence: the influence that is asserted upon another person by one who dominates that person.

unfair competition: the wrong of employing competitive methods that have been declared unfair by statute or an administrative agency.

unfair labor practice acts: statutes that prohibit certain labor practices and declare them to be unfair labor practices.

unincorporated association: a combination of two or more persons for the furtherance of a common nonprofit purpose.

union contract: a contract between a labor union and an employer or group of employers prescribing the general terms of employment of workers by the latter.

union shop: under present unfair labor practice statutes, a place of employment where nonunion workers may be employed for a trial period of not more than 30 days after which the nonunion workers must join the union or be discharged.

universal agent: an agent authorized by the principal to do all acts that can lawfully be delegated to a representative.

usury: the lending of money at greater than the maximum rate of interest allowed by law.

V

vacating of judgment: the setting aside of a judgment.

valid: legal.

verdict: the decision of the trial or petty jury.

void: of no legal effect and not binding on anyone.

voidable: a transaction that may be set aside by one party thereto because of fraud or similar reason but which is binding on the other party until the injured party elects to avoid.

voidable preference: a preference given by the bankrupt to a creditor, but which may be set aside by the trustee in bankruptcy.

voir dire examination: the preliminary examination of a juror or a witness to ascertain fitness to act as such.

volenti non fit injuria: the maxim that the defendant's act cannot constitute a tort if the plaintiff has consented thereto.

voluntary nonsuit: a means of the plaintiff's stopping a trial at any time by moving for a voluntary nonsuit.

voting trust: the transfer by two or more persons of their shares of stock of a corporation to a trustee who is to vote the shares and act for such shareholders.

W

waiver: the release or relinquishment of a known right or objection.

warehouse receipt: a receipt issued by the warehouser for stored goods. Regulated by the Uniform Commercial Code, which clothes the receipt with some degree of negotiability.

warranties of indorser of commercial paper: the implied covenants made by an indorser of a commercial paper distinct from any undertaking to pay upon the default of the primary party.

warranties of insured: statements or promises made by the applicant for insurance which if false will entitle the insurer to avoid the contract of insurance in many jurisdictions.

warranties of seller of goods: warranties consisting of express warranties that relate to matters forming part of the basis of the bargain; warranties as to title and right to sell; and the implied warranties which the law adds to a sale depending upon the nature of the transaction.

warranty deed: a deed by which the grantor conveys a specific estate or interest to the grantee and makes one or more of the covenants of title.

warranty of authority: an implied warranty of an agent of the authority exercised by the agent.

warranty of principal: an implied warranty of an agent that the agent is acting for an existing principal who has capacity to contract.

watered stock: stock issued by a corporation as fully paid when in fact it is not.

will: an instrument executed with the formality required by law, by which a person makes a disposition of property to take effect upon death or appoints a personal representative.

willful: intentional as distinguished from accidental or involuntary. In penal statutes, with evil intent or legal malice, or without reasonable ground for believing one's act to be lawful.

Wool Products Labeling Act: a federal statute prohibiting the misbranding of woolen fabrics.

workmen's compensation: a system providing for payments to workers because they have been injured from a risk arising out of the course of their employment while they were employed at their employment or have contracted an occupational disease in that manner, payment being made without consideration of the negligence or lack of negligence of any party.

Y

year and a day: the common-law requirement that death result within a year and a day in order to impose criminal liability for homicide.

Z

zoning restrictions: restrictions imposed by government on the use of property for the advancement of the general welfare.

INDEX

A

absence of consideration, effect of, 254

absolute liability, 164

absolute, guaranty, 625; ownership, 382

abstract of title, 893

acceleration, of due date, 532

acceptance, by mail or telegraph, 215; by telephone, 217; communication of, 215; draft-varying, 575; general, 574; manner of, 213; nature of, 211; of an offer, 211; of offer to buy or sell goods, 445; of unordered goods and tickets, 214; silence as, 214

acceptance of draft, form of, 575; kinds of, 574; manner of presenting for, 574; necessity of presentment for, 574

acceptor, of a commercial paper, 524; of draft, 522

accessions, as a means of acquiring property, 390

accessories to a crime, 141; after the fact, 141; before the fact, 141

accommodation, public, 211

accommodation party, 524

accord, 343

accord and satisfaction, 343

act of God, 408

accountants, malpractice liability and, 370

ademption, of property, 933

adequacy of consideration, 258; exceptions to rule, 259

adhension contracts, 244

administration, letters of, 937

administrative agency(ies), 8, 90; constitutional limitations of investigations by, 98; finality of determination, 103; importance of, 90; living constitution and, 42; nature of, 90; open meetings, 93; open records of, 92; penalties imposed by compared to criminal fines, 143; public announcement of guidelines, 64; public knowledge of regulations, 92; public participation in adoption of regulations by, 95; regulation of contracts, 276; regulation of pollution, 111; uniqueness, 91

administrative dissolution, of a corporation, 820

administrative hearing, 100

administrative investigation, constitutional limitations of investigations by, 98; inspection of premises, 98; protection of papers, 98

administrative penalties, 143

administrative procedure, pattern of, 100

administrative regulations, 6

administrator, agency see agency administrator

administratrix, of decedent's estate, defined, 936; see also administrator of decedent's estate

administrator (agency), defined, 92; as a specialized court, 99; executive power of the, 96; judicial power of, 99; legislative power of, 93; liability of, 104; powers, of, 92; punishment and enforcement powers of, 102; regulation as law, 93

administrator (of decedent's estate), defined, 936; liability of, 941; powers and duties of, 939; of promise by, to pay a claim against estate from personal fund, 287

administrator pendente lite, 936

administratrix, 936; see also administrator of decedent's estate

adverse possession, 896

advertising, 122; corrective, 123; deception in, 122; retractive, 123; seals of approval and, 123

affirmative covenant, 895

after-acquired property, 615

Age Discrimination in Employment Act, 743

Agencies, administrative, 8; for enforcement of legal rights, 7; law and enforcement, 3; private, 8

agency, defined, 683; authorization by appointment, 687; authorization by conduct, 688; by operation of law, 692; by ratification, 690; coupled with an interest, 687; creating the, 687; nature of relationship, 683; nondisclosure, 527; proving the relationship, 693; power of attorney, 688; proving the relationship, 693; purpose of, 686; termination, 693

agency arrangements, and foreign markets, 74

agency contract, execution of, 721; expiration of, 693; rescission of, 695

agency status, of collecting bank, 596

agent, defined, 683; acts adverse to principal, 705; and foreign market, 74; as payee of commercial paper, 540; assumption of liability, 721; as transferee, 724; authority of, 703; classification of, 687; contrast with contract, 733; crimes of, 723, 731; death of, as terminating agency, 695; delegation of authority by, 707; disclosure of principal, 720; distinguished from bailees, 686; distinguished, from employees, 684; distinguished from independent contractors, 685; distinguished from real estate brokers, 686; duties and liabilities of, 708; duties and liabilities of principal to, 712; duty to account to principal, 710; duty to act with reasonable care, 710; duty to inform principal, 710; enforcement of claim by third person, 733; enforcement of liability of, 712; execution of contract, 721, 724; failure to obtain commitment of principal, 723; general, 687; insurance, 648; indemnification of corporate, 871; intending to be bound, 724; knowledge of, 727; liability of principal for torts and crimes of, 728; liability of third person to, 724; liability to third person, 718; liability to third person for torts and crimes, 723; limitation of authority, 706; loyalty of, 708; obedience and performance of, 709; of coroporation, 871; payment to, 726; principal's conduct as to, 688; renunciation by, 695; scope of authority, 703; soliciting, 733; special, 687; statement of, 727; unauthorized action, 719; universal, 687; who may be an, 687; wrongful receipt of money, 721

agent's authority, 703; duty to ascertain extent of, 704; limitations of, 706

agent's contracts, liability of principal to third person and, 725

aggrieved party, action of, 474

agreement, affecting public welfare, 271; cancellation of contract by,

341; contrary to public policy, 271; discharge of contract by, 340; effect of illegality, 267; for sale of real property, 286; illegal lobbying, 272; injuring public service, 272; intent to make a binding, 188; involving conflicts of interests, 272; noncompetition, 389; nondisclosure, 389; not to compete, 276; obstructing legal processes, 272; rescission by, 341; that cannot be performed within one year, 286; to commit crimes and civil wrongs, 268; to make a contract at a future date, 203; usurious, 278; void, 193; *see also* contracts

agreement, evading statutory protection, 272

airbill, 426

Aktiengesellschaft (A.G.), 74

alien, *defined*, 229; contractual capacity, 229; enemy, 229

alternate payee, 540

alteration, *defined*, 560

amending the constitution, 41

anatomical gifts, 393

animals, lease prohibiting the keeping of, 911; ownership of wild, 394

annuity policies, 673

answer, lawsuit and, 12

anticipatory breach, 351

anticipatory repudiation, 473

antidiscrimination, 211

antidumping laws, 81

antilapse statues, 933

anti-modification clause, 365

Anti-Tampering Act, 129

Antitrust Civil Process Act, 97

antitrust law, 75; exceptions to, 59; exemption, 769; foreign, 77

appeal, 17

appeal de novo, 9

appeals, court of, 10

appellate jurisdiction, *defined*, 7

arbitration, 8, partners and, 797

architects, malpractice liability and, 372

arson, 156

articles of copartnership, 780

articles of incorporation, 810; *illustrated*, 812

articles of partnership, 780

artistic works copyrightable, 385

assault, 177

assessments, duty of mortgagor and, 899; landlords duty to pay, 914

assets, distribution of dissolved partnership, 788

assignee, defenses of buyer against, 479; liability of, 327; obligation of sellers, as to performance, 479; of a commercial paper, 551; rights of, 325

assignment, *defined*, 322; defenses and setoffs, 327; delegation of duties

and, 325; for creditors, partnerships and, 797; form of, 322; increasing burden of performance, 324; notice of, 328; of a contract, 322; of a lease, 920; of commercial paper, 544; of fire insurance policy, 664; of future rights to money, 323; of personal services, 325; of rights, consent to, 323; of rights in a credit transaction, 325; of rights prohibition, 323; of right to a performance, 324; of right to money, 323; of sales contract, 478

assignor, 322; continuing liability of, 326; warranties of, 329

association, tribunals, 9; unincorporated, 768

assumed name, use of, 240

assurance, adequate, of performance, 474; failure to give, 475

attach, 610

attachment of wages, 747

attempts, criminal, 143

attestation, 929

attorneys, as officers of the court, 9; in-fact, 688; malpractice liability and, 369

attractive nuisance doctrine, 887

auction sales, 217, 465

authorities, public, 811

authority, agent's *see agent's authority*; housing, 811; municipal parking, 811

automatic teller machines, 601

automobile, leasing, 125; sales, 125; transfer of title, 394, 462

Automobile Dealder's Franchise Act, 762

automobile insurance, 666; collision and upset insurance, 667; comprehensive insurance, 673; financial responsibility laws, 666; fire, lighting, and transportation, 673; liability insurance, 667; nature of contract, 666; no fault insurance, 671; theft insurance, 672; uninsured motorist, 671

avoidance of holder in due course protection, 561

B

bad check laws, 591

bailed property, bailor's implied warranty and, 413; care of, 408; condition of, 412; maintenance of, 410; return of, 410; suits for damages to, 411; unauthorized use, 410

bailee, 403; distinguished from an agent, 686; duties of, 407; interest in bailed property, 405; liability of, 409; liability to third persons, 414; lien of, 411; rights against the, 412

bailiffs, 10

bailment, *defined*, 403; classification of, 405; constructive, 405; contract, 405; distinguished from sale, 442;

elements of, 404; extraordinary, 405; family purpose doctrine, 414; gratuitous, 405; of contents of container, 406; ordinary, 405; renting of space as distinguished from, 406; special, 419

bailor, 403; duties of, 412; implied warranty of, 413; interest in bailed property, 404; liability of to third party, 414; rights of the, 411

balance sheet test, 638

bank, agency status of collecting, 596; as drawee of check, 591; duties of drawee, 592; indemnity right of, 600; liability of, for improper payment and collection, 597; liability to drawer of check, 595; liability to holder of check, 595

bank accounts, multiple ownership of, 397

bank indorsements, 539

bankruptcy, balance sheet test, 638; commencement of the case, 635; corporation, 820; debtor's duties and exemptions, 640; discharge in, 640; discharge of contract claims and, 350; extended time payment plans, 643; involuntary, 636; number and claims of petitioning creditors, 636; partnership dissolution by, 784; preferences made to insiders, 638; preferential transfers, 638; protection against discrimination and, 643; reorganizations and payment plans under Chapters 11 and 13, 641; termination of agency and, 695; trustee in, 637; voidable transfers, 637; voluntary, 635

Bankruptcy Reform Act of 1978, 635

bankrupt's estate administration of, 639; priority of claims, 639; proof of claim, 639; provable claim, 639

bargaining, collective, 62

battery, 177

basis for decision, 14

bearer, commercial paper payable to, 530; of a commercial paper, 524

bearer paper, 531; negotiation of, 541

beneficiary, *defined*, 928; changing on life insurance policy, 675; contingent, 675; incidental distinguished, 321; of life insurance policy, 674; of trust, 946; of will, 929; primary, 675; third party, contracts, 320

benefits, present consideration versus past, 257

bequest, 928; residuary, 933

bigness, 58

bilateral contract, 193

billing, correction of errors, 129

billing methods, credit, 129

bill of exchange, *defined*, 522

bill of lading, 426; contents of, 426; negotiable, 426; nonnegotiable, 427; straight, 427; warranties, 427

bill of sale, 453

binding agreement, intent to make, 188

blackmail, *defined*, 150

blank indorsement, 537; *illustrated*, 538

blocking laws, 79

blue sky laws, 846

boarders, hotelkeepers liability and, 433

bonds, issued by a corporation, 830

books, rights of partners to inspect, 800

book value, of stock, 840

breach, anticipatory, 351; discharge of contract by acceptance, 351; effect of seller's, 463; of express warranty, 489

breach of contract, 351; distinguished from tort, 162; rescission of, 362; remedies for, 357; waiver of, 363

breach of duty, liability of partner for, 804

breach of warranty, action for, 508

bribery, *defined*, 149

broker, insurance, 648; real estate, 686; registration requirement of, 848

building, as real property, 882

bulk purchaser, liability of, 450

bulk transfers, 449

burglary, 155

burning to defraud, 156

burden of proof, 411

business, cessation of, 797; government ownership of, 46; government regulation of, 55, 247; limitations on state regulation of, 66; secrets, 387

business organizations, forms of, 73, 759

business relations, wrongful interference with, 177

business reorganizations under Chapter 11, 642

buyers, action for damages for nondelivery, 508; contract cancelled by, 509; contract for shipment to, 460; defenses, against sellers assignee, 479; duty to accept goods, 476; duty to pay for accepted goods, 477; marking goods for, 460; notice of third party action against, 509; remedies of the, 505; resale of goods, 510; right to consumer goods independent of default, 613; specifications, 492

bylaws, of a corporation, *defined*, 830

bystander, negligent conduct and, 171

C

cancellation, by agreement, 341; of commercial paper, 556, 585; of contract by buyer, 509; of contract by seller, 504; provision of contract, 254

capital, 840; distribution, 856; rights of partner and distribution of, 801

capital stock, 840

Capper-Volstead Act of 1922, 769

carrier, *defined*, 425; common, 425; contract, 425; private, 425

case law, *defined*, 6

cash surrender value, of life insurance policy, 676

casual relationship, 163

center of gravity, and contract lawsuits, 315

certificate of deposit, 522

certificate of incorporation, 810

certificate of stock, 840; shareholder's right to, 852

certified checks, 591

cestui que trust, 946

Chandler Act of 1938, 635

charge to the jury, 15

charge accounts, revolving, 279

charging order, 783

charitable contributions by corporations, 833

charitable subscriptions, 259

charitable trust, 951

charities, immunity from tort liability and, 170

charter, 810

cheats, 152

check, *defined*, 522, 590; bad check laws, 591; bank liability for alteration of, 599; bank's duty to pay on demand, 593; bank's liability to drawer of, 595; bank's liability to holder, 595; bank's payment on forged or missing indorsement, 599; bank's payment on forged signature of drawer, 597; bank's payment over stop payment order, 597; certified, 591; dishonor of, 595; duties of drawee bank, 592; forgery, reporting time, 600; liability of drawer, 592; nature of, 590; payment, after depositor's death, 593; payment by, 336; presentment for payment, 594; privacy concerning, 592; stale, 593; stopping payment of, 594; time of presentment for payment, 594; unauthorized collection of, 600; unauthorized signature on, 600

child, liability for tort of, 164

choses in action, 382

C.I.F. (cost, insurance, freight) contract, 477

civil court, *defined*, 8

civil disorders, 156

civil law, 7

civil penalties, improper consumer practice and, 134

Civil Rights Act of 1964, 743

civil wrongs, illegal agreement, 268

claim(s), against firm, 795; court, 11; false, 151; of firm, 795; priority, 639; proof of, 639; release of, 256

Clayton Act, bigness and, 58

clerk of the court, 10

close corporation, 811

codicil, 930

c.o.d. shipment, carriers and, 429

coinsurance clause, fire insurance and, 663

collateral, 531; classification of, 611; consumer goods as, 611; debtor rights in, 611; disposition of by sale, 619; equipment goods as, 611; farm products as, 611; impairment of, 584; inventory goods as, 611; proceeds of, 615; secured seller's repossession and resale of, 618; security interest and, 610

collateral heirs, intestate distribution and, 935

collection, improper methods, 130; liability of bank for improper payment and, 597; of check, bank liability for unauthorized, 600; of credit, 129

collective bargaining, contracts, 741; machinery to enforce, 62

collision insurance, 666, 669; exclusions, 670; notice and cooperation, 670; uninsured motorist coverage, 671

combinations, prevention of monopolies and, 58

comity, 76

commercial impracticability, 346

commercial influence, improper, 150

commercial paper, *defined*, 522; additional documents and, 532; adverse claims to, 560; agent or officer as payee, 540; alternate payee, 540; alteration of, 585; assignment of, 544; discharge of, 580; effect of incapacity or misconduct on negotiation, 543; effect of provisions for additional powers of benefits, 531; execution of, by a corporation, 830; forged and unauthorized indorsements, 541; impairment of right of recourse, 583; impostor rule, 542; joint payee, 540; kinds of, 521; kinds of holders, 550; kinds of indorsements, 536; liability of parties, 525; lost, 543; missing or incorrect date, 530; multiple payees and indorsees, 540; negotiability, 526; negotiation of bearer paper, 541; negotiation of order paper, 540; nondisclosure of agency, 527; ordinary holders and assignees, 551; parties to, 522; payable on demand, 529; payable to order of bearer, 530; payment by, 477; payment in money, 529; prior payment, 556; promise or order to pay, 528; reacquisition of paper by intermediate party, 585; signature required, 527; sum certain, 529; theft, 558; time for determining order or bearer character of paper, 540; time of payment, 529; transfer of, 536; unconditional promise or order, 528; warranties of transferor, 545; writing required, 527; commercial paper, *see also certificates of deposit, checks, drafts, indorsements, and promissory notes*

commission, 430

common carrier, 425; duties of, 427; liabilities of, 428; rights of, 427

common law, malpractice and, 370

common-law deed, 891

common stock, 841

community planning, 113; eminent domain, 115; nuisances and, 116; public zoning and, 113; restrictive covenants in private contracts, 113

community property, 398

compensation, rights of partners and, 800; of employees, 746

compensatory damages, 358

compete, agreements to not, 276

competition, crimes related to, 147; government regulation of, 56; unfair, 175

compliance verification, 103

composition of creditors, 256

Comprehensive Environmental Response, Compensation and Liability Act of 1980 (CERCL), 111

comprehensive insurance, 673

compromise, and release of claims, 256

compulsory nonsuit, 16

compulsory resale, 618

computer, defamation by, 173; raiding, 149; unauthorized use of, 148

computer crimes, 148

computer programs, copyrights, 387; patents and, 387; protection for, 387; trade secrets and, 388

Computer Software Copyright Act of 1980, 387

concealment, active, 239

concurrent conditions, 306

condition, implied in a sales contract, 447; of contract, 306

conditional, delivery, 557; promise, 254; sale, 443

condition precedent, 306; gifts and 393; to performance, in sales contract, 473

conditions, concurrent, 306

condition subsequent, 306; gifts and, 393

condominiums, 890; advantages of ownership, 890; collection of expenses from unit owner, 890; control and expense, 890; distinguished from cooperation, 890; freedom from enterprise liability, 890; tax deduction, 891; transferability of unit, 891; tort liability and, 890

conduct, liability-imposing, 164; of trial, 15

confidence games, 152

confidential relationship, 238

conflict of laws, 313; federal courts, 315; state courts, 313

conflict of interest, 867; agreements involving, 272

conglomerate, *defined*, 822

congress, borrowing power of, 45; currency power of, 46

consequential loss, breach of contract and, 357

consideration, *defined*, 252; adequacy of, 258; agreed exchange, 253; as determined by nature of contract, 252; compromise and release of claims, 256; effect of absence of, 254; exceptions to adequacy rule, 259; exceptions to requirement of, 259; failure of, 261; forbearance as, 257; legality of, 261; present versus past benefits, 257; promise as, 254; promise to perform existing obligation, 254; promissory estoppel, 260

consignee, 425, 430; consignment, selling on, 430

consignment sale, effect of sale on title, 466; sale or return, 465

consignor, 425, 430

consolidation, *defined*, 821

conspiracies, criminal acts and, 143

constable, 10

constitution, 38; administrative agencies of new, 42; amending the, 41; characteristics of new, 41; financial powers of federal government provided by, 44; equal protection of the laws, 49; protection of the person, 50; states and the, 38; what it is, 38

constitutional law, 6

constitutional limitations, on administrative investigation, 98; on state regulations of business, 66

constitutional protection of worker, 64

constructive bailments, 405

constructive delivery, 404

constructive eviction, 910

constructive trust, 952

consumer, action by, 134; action by state attorney general on behalf of, 133; credit transaction, 561; investigative report, 130; preservation of defense, 128; remedies, 133

Consumer Credit Protection Act, (CCPA), 6, 340

consumer goods, equipment classified as, 618; secured credit sale of, 612; used a collateral, 611

Consumer Leasing Act of 1976, 125

consumer liability, EFT card and, 602

Consumer Product Safety Act, 129

consumer protection, 121; civil and criminal penalties, 134; credit, collection, and billing methods, 129; contract terms, 126; corrective advertising, 123; credit cards, 127; deceptive advertising, 122; expansion of, 132; form of contract, 127; home solicited sales, 125; investigative consumer report, 130; labeling, 124; limitation of credit, 127; offers

and, 211; payments on open charge accounts, 128; preservation of consumer defense, 128; privacy, 130; product liability, 165; product safety, 129; property report, 132; protection from false information, 131; protection of credit standing and reputation, 130; real estate development sales, 132; referral sales, 126; seals of approval, 123; selling methods, 124; service contracts, 132; surcharge for use of credit card prohibited, 127; unauthorized use of credit card, 127; unconscionability, 126; unsolicited credit card, 127

consumer protection rescission, 339

consumer remedies, 133

contempt of court, 8

contingent beneficiary, 675

continuation statements, 617

contract, *defined*, 186; *illustrated*, 189; acceptance of offer, *acceptance*; agreement to make, at a future date, 203; adequacy of performance, 338; alteration of, 349; ambiguous terms of, 308; ambiguity in, 296; assignment of, 322; as it affects consideration, 252; auction sales, 217; assignment of sales, 478; avoidance, 223; bilateral, 194; breach of, 351, 356; by a partner, 795; cancellation by agreement, 341; cancellation by buyer, 509; cancellation provision of, 254; capacity of aliens, 229; capacity of insane persons, 228; capacity of intoxicated persons, 228; capacity of married women, 229; capacity to, 221; bargaining, collective, 741; communication of offer, 206; communication of revocation, 207; completion of, 255; concurrent conditions, 306; condition precedent, 306; conditions, 306; condition subsequent, 306; conduct and custom, 311; conflict between oral and written, 294; conflict of laws, 313; contradictory terms of, 307; consumer protection rescission, 339; counteroffer, 209; credit sale, 278; damages, 245; death or disability of either party, 210; definiteness, 204; delegation of duties, 325; destruction of the, 349; details of performance, 309; detrimental reliance on oral, 292; discharge by acceptance of breach, 351; discharge by agreement, 340; discharge by impossibility, 343; discharge by operation of law, 349; discharge by performance, 335; discharge by unilateral action, 340; divisible, 205, 306; duration of, 309; duress, 242; effect of enclosed printed matter, 188; effect of incompetence on, 228; effect of noncompliance, 290; effect of seller's breach, 463; elements of a, 186; exceptions to definiteness, 206; executed, 193; executory, 193; existence of, 296; expiration of agency, 693; express, 192; firm offer, 208; for credit sale, 278; formal,

190; form of, 127; for necessaries, 225; for sale of goods, modification to, 256; for services, 443; fraud, 239; guarantee of performance, 339; general rule of non-liability, 238; good faith, 310; governmental approval, 310; how a, arises, 187; illegal discrimination, 273; indemnity, 625; implied, 192; implied terms, 205, 309; incomplete, 295; individual employment, 741; informal, 190, 192; in restraint of trade, 276; insurance, 649; intention of parties to, 202, 303; intent to make a binding agreement, 188; interference with, 176; interpretation of, 302; joint, several, and joint and several, 312; innocent misrepresentation, 237; invitation to negotiate, 202; involving fraudulent sales, 276; lapse of time, 207; law applicable to a sale, 444; liability of partners and partnership as to, 801; maximum rate of interest, 278; minors cannot avoid certain, 227; minor's power to avoid, 223; minor's ratification of voidable, 226; modification of, 297; modification or termination of third party beneficiary, 321; mutual mistake and, 236; mutual recission of, 341; *n* factor, 270; nature of, 252; nature of writing, 307; negotiable instruments, 191; nondisclosure to a, 237; note or memorandum considered as, 288; of adhesion, 244, 312; offer to, 201; of record, 191; on two sides, 125; oppressive, 268; option, 208; oral *see oral contracts*; ordinary, defenses, 556; output and requirements, 446; parol evidence, 293; parties to a, 186; private, and community planning, 113; privity of, 186; prospective, 177; protection for computer programs and, 389; provision of original, 340; provisions on remedies, 511; quasi, 194; recovery of value conferred under, 290; reformation of, 365; reformation of by court, 245; rejection of offer, 209; remedies for breach of, 357; repudiation of, 473; rescission, 244, 341, 362; revocation of offer, 207; rules of construction and interpretation, 302; service, 132; several, 312; simple, 192; social consequences of, 270; statement of intention, 240; statement of opinion or value, 240; statutory regulation, 274; strict construction against drafting party, 308; subject matter of, 186; subsequent illegality, 210; subsidiary term, 351; substitution of, 342; terminable at will, 177; termination of offer, 207; terms, 126; that must be in writing, 285; the private, in society, 270; third part beneficiary, 320; time of performance, 337; tort liability to third person for nonperformance, 365; to sell, 443; unconscionable, 268; under seal, 191; undue influence, 214; unexpected costs of performing, 195; unilateral, 194; unilateral mis-

take and, 234; unimportant vague details ignored, 205; use of assumed name, 240; valid, 193; voidable, 193; waiver of breach as modification, 365; whole, 306; who may accept, 212; when license required, 274; with third person, 196; *see also agreements*; *sales contract*

contract bailments, 405

contract carrier, 425

contract for delivery, at destination, 460

contract for shipment, 459; to buyer, 460

contract provisions, 19

contractual intention, 202

contractual limitations, 350

conversion, 178, 396

conversion of goods, action for, 510

convertible shares, 841

cooperative, 769; antitrust law exemption, 769; apartment, 890; incorporated, 769

co-ownership, 781

copartnership, articles of, 780

copyright, 385; duration, 385; infringement of, 175; limitations on exclusive character of, 385; of computer programs, 387; of unpublished work, 385; what can be protected by, 386

Copyright Act of 1976, 387

corporate, debts and taxes, 873; directors, *see directors*; name, 829; powers, nature and limitations of, 828; stock, 840; seal, 830

corporate entity, ignoring the, 814

corporate powers, 828; acquire stock of other corporations, 832; acquisition of own stock, 832; acquisition of property, 831; adopt bylaws, 830; borrowing money, 830; charitable contributions, 833; engage in business in other states, 833; execution of commercial paper, 830; holding companies, 832; issue bonds, 830; issue stock, 830; nature and limitations of, 828; participation in enterprise, 833; particular, 828; perpetual succession, 829; seal, 830; select name, 829; transferring property, 831; ultra vires act, 833

corporate stock, *see stock*

corporation, 760; administratively dissolved, 820; advantages of, 816; agents of, 871; and governments, 813; application for incorporation, 818; articles of incorporation, 810; as a citizen, 814; as a legal person, 810; as a person, 813; bankruptcy, 820; by estoppel, 819; certificate of incorporation, 818; classifications of, 810; close, 811; conglomerate, 822; consolidation, 821; creation of the, 816; de facto, 819; defective incorporation, 818; de jure, 818; directors of, 865; disadvantages of, 761; domestic, 811; ef-

fect of irregular procedure, 874; employees of, 870, 871; federal antitrust legislation, 823; federal power to create, 813; financial troubles and, 820; foreign, 811; government power to regulate, 813; insolvency, 820; integrated industry, 822; judicial dissolution of, 821; legality of consolidation, merger, and asset acquisition, 823; liability for acts of management, 874; liability of component enterprise, 824; liability of management to third persons, 871; liability of successor enterprise, 823; merger, 821; nature and classes, 809; nonprofit, 811; officers of, 868; ownership rights, 852; private, 811; professional, 811; promoters, 816; proper incorporation, 818; public, 811; public authorities, 811; quasi public, 811; reorganization of, 820; responsibility for criminal acts and, 141; special service, 811; ultra vires act of, 833; wasting assets, 855

corporation code, general, 813

corrective advertising, 123

corrupt influence, 150

cosigner, liability of, on minor's contract, 227

Cost Savings Act, 125

cotenancy, 396

Council of Mutual Economic Cooperation (COMECON), 73

counterclaim, 13

Counterfeit Access Device and Computer Fraud and Abust Act of 1984, 149

counterfeiting, 151, 209

court, 7; administrator as a specialized, 99; civil, 8; claims, 11; contempt of, 8; contracts and conflict of state and federal, 315; county, 11; criers, 10; criminal, 8; federal, 11; federal district, 11; intermediate state, 11; not of record, 7; officers of, 9; of record, 7; organizations, 9; personnel of, 9; procedure, 12; state, 11; state district, 11; State Supreme, 11; Supreme Court of the United States, 10; tax, 11; territorial, 11

Court of International Trade, 11

Court of Military Appeals, 11

Court of Appeals, of the United States, 10

covenant, affirmative, 895; against encumbrances, 894; for further assurances, 894; for quiet enjoyment, 894, 910; grantee's, 895; of right to convey, 894; of tenant for repairs, 905; of seisin, 894; restrictive, 896; runs with the land, 895

credit, collection and billing methods, 129; letters of, 628; limitation of, 127; protection of standing and reputation, 130

credit card, 127; correction of errors, 129; crimes, 153; surcharge for use

of prohibited, 127; unauthorized use, 127; unsolicited, 127
Credit Card Act of 1970, 174
credit discrimination, 129
creditor, 625; claims, 458; composition of, 256; protection, 29
credit sale, contracts, 278; price, 278; revolving charge accounts and, 279; secured by consumer goods, 612; secured by equipment, 618; secured by inventory, 614; time-price differential, 278
credit transaction, 325; consumer, 561
crime, *defined*, 139; against property, 155; agreement to commit void, 268; classification of, 140; computer, 148; credit card, 153; distinguished from tort, 161; electronic fund transfer, 149; illegal agreement, 268; liability of partners and partnership as to, 803; nature of, 140; of agents, 723; of agent, liability of principal for, 728; of force, 155; parties to a, 141; related to production, competing, and marketing, 147; securities, 147; white collar, 146
crime-related property, foreiture of, 146
crimes mala in se, 140
crimes mala prohibita, 140
crime victim, indemnification of, 144
criminal acts, responsibility for, 141
criminal court, *defined*, 8
criminal law, source of, 140
criminal fines, 143
criminal liability, basis of, 140; environmental protection statutes and, 112
criminal libel, 153
criminal penalties, improper consumer practices and, 134
cross complaint, 13
cross-examination, 15
cumulative preferred stock, 841
cumulative voting, 852
currency power, of congress, 46
customary authority, of agent, 703
customer, of inventory used as security, protection of, 617; withdrawal of, 733
cy pres doctrine, 951

D

damages, 245; action for, 145; as remedy for voided agreement, 244; breach of contract and, 351; buyer's action for, and nondelivery, 508; compensatory, 358; consequential, 357; direct, 357; effect of failure to mitigate, 359; exclusion of in sales contract, 512; exemplary, 358; limitations of, in sales contract, 511; liquidated, 359; limitation of, 511; liquidation of, 511; measure of, in

breach of warranty, 508; mitigation of, 358; nominal, 358; punitive, 358; seller's action for, 504
death, discharge of contracts and, 345; of depositor, 593; of distributee after decedent, 936; partnership dissolved by, 784; presentment for payment not required, 569, simultaneous and intestacy, 936
debt, corporate, 873; promise to answer for another's, 287
debtor, duties and exemptions in bankruptcy, 640; has rights in collateral, 611; insolvent, 638; rehabilitation, 29; right of redemption, 619
decedent, debts and liabilities of, 939; murder of, 936
decedent's estate, administration of, 936
deception, in advertising, 122
declaratory judgment, 18
deed, *defined*, 891; acceptance of, 893; cancellation, 893; commonlaw, 891; delivery of, 892; execution of, 891; of trust, 947; quitclaim, 891; recording of, 893; transfer of real property by, 891; warranty, 891
deed of trust, 947
de facto corporation, 819
de facto dissolution, 820
defamation, *defined*, 172; computer, 173; by libel, 173; slander, 172
default, promise to answer for another's, 287
defect, necessity of showing, 493; notice of, 503
defective tender, cure of, 476
defendent, 12; improper products and, 485; incapacity of, 556; the indigent, 146
defense, preservation of, 514; waiver of, 514
defenses, and United States antitrust laws, 76; available against an ordinary holder, 555; limited, 555; universal, 555
definiteness, 204; by incorporation, 204; exceptions to, 206
defraud, burning to, 156; use of mails to, 153
de jure corporation, 819
delegation of duties, 325; under the UCC, 326
delivery, contract for, 460; rejection of improper, by buyer, 505
delivery at destination, 459
delivery of goods, place, time, and manner of, 475
demand, 529
demand paper, 591
democracy, and the protection of the person, 51
demurrage, 427
demurrer, 12
depositary bank, 539
deposition, *defined*, 4

depositor, payment after death of, 593; warehouse receipt and, 421
deposits, 512; direct, 601
derivative action, shareholder's, 857
destination, delivery at, 459
detention, 177
detrimental reliance, 209; on oral contract, 292
developing countries, regional trading groups of, 73
development sales, real estate, 132
development statement, real estate, 132
devise, 928
devisee, 928
direct damages, 357
direct deposit, and withdrawals, 601
directed verdict, 16
direct examination, 15
direct loss, breach of contract and, 357
directors, 865; action against, 868; conflict of interests, 867; indemnification of, 871; liability for conflict of interests, 868; liability of, 867; meetings of, 867; powers of, 866; removal of, 868; qualifications of, 866
disability, discharge of a contract and, 345; life insurance policy definition, 674; total permanent, 674
disability insurance, 674
discharge of commercial paper, 580
discharge of contract, 328, 334; by acceptance of breach, 351; by agreement, 340; by enconomic disappointment, 346; by impossibility, 343; by performance, 335; by unilateral action, 340
disclaimer of warranties, 494; postsale, 496; validity of, 494
disclosed principal, 720, 725; partially, 724
disclosure of transaction terms, 124
discovery, pretrial procedures of a lawsuit and, 14
discrimination credit, 129; illegal contracts, 273; sex, 61
dishonor, by nonacceptance, 576; notice of, 570; of check, 595; of note, 570; proof of, 572; protest of, 576
disinheritance, 934
disparagement, of goods and slander of title, 174
dissolution, administrative, 820; judicial, 821; de facto, 820; effects of, on partner's liability, 804; notice of partnership, 786; quasi, 820
distress, collecting rent and, 915
distribution, government regulation of business, 56; stirpital, 936
distribution per capita, 936
distributio per stripes, 936
distributorships, foreign, 74
District courts, federal, 11; state, 11
dividends, discretion of directors, 855;

effect of transfer of shares, 856; form of, 856; funds available for declaration of, 855; shareholder's right to, 855; unauthorized, 858

divisible contracts, *defined*, 205

D.O.C. coverage, automobile liability insurance and, 668

doctors, malpractice liabilities and, 369

documents of title, negotiable, 467; warehouse receipts as, 422

domestic corporations, 811

dominant tenement, 882

domiciled, 313, 568

donee, of a gift, 390

donor, of a gift, 390

dormant partners, 778

double aspect of contractual capacity, 222

double indemnity, 674

down payments, 512

draft, *defined*, 522; *illustrated*, 523; dishonor by nonacceptance, 576; drawee's liability for, 573; indorser's liability for, 574; presentment for acceptance, 572; presentment for payment, 576; protest of dishonor of, 576; waiver of protest, 576

draft-varying acceptance, *defined*, 575

drawee, liability of, 573; of a commercial paper, 523; of check, 591; of draft, 522

drawer, bank's liability to, of a check, 595; bank's payment on forged signature of drawer, 597; liability of, 573; of a commercial paper, 523; of draft, 522

drink, sale of, 492

due date, 568; acceleration of, 534

due process of law, 48

dumping, of foreign goods, 81

duress, contracts made under, 242; economic, 243; executed or indorsed commercial paper in response to, 559; physical, 242; remedies for, 244; signed or executed commercial paper under, 557

E

easements, 882; creation of, 882; dominant tenement, 882; servient tenement, 882; termination of, 883; ways of necessity, 882

economic disappointment, discharged contracts and, 346

economic duress, 242

economic frustration, discharged contracts and, 346

effects doctrine, 76

electronic fund transfer, *defined*, 601; consumer liability and, 602; crimes, 149; types of, 601

Electronic Fund Transfer Act (EFTA), 149, 601

embezzlement, *defined*, 154

eminent domain, 115, 896

employee, benefit and aid, corporations and, 833; compensation for injuries, 751; corporate, 870; distinguished from agent, 685; duties of, 744; duty to protect trade secrets, 745; exclusive and equal representation of all, 62; indemnification of corporate, 871; liability for tort of, 164; lien, 746; of the United States, 730; pension plans, 746; rights of, 746; right to compensation, 746; rights to invention, 745

employees health and safety, 749

Employees Retirement Income Security Act, 746

employee transfer, termination of a lease and, 908

employer, common-law status of, 751; defenses of, 752; modification of common-law defenses, 752; responsibility for criminal acts and, 141; statutory charges, 752; unfair practices, 63; worker's compensation, 752

employment, authority of partner and, 795; fair practices acts, 61; federal laws and, 743; relationship, 739; regulation of, 60; scope of, 730

employment contract, collective bargaining, 741; duration and termination of, 741; federal laws, 743; individual, 741; justifiable discharge, 743; remedies for wrongful discharge, 744

encumbrances, implied warranty against, 490

endowment insurance, 673

enemy alien, 229

enforcement, agencies, 3

enforcement powers of administrators, 102

entrustee, sale by, 467

environmental, impact statement, 111; protection, statutory, 110

environmental law, 109; criminal liability, 112; litigation, 111; regulation by administrative agencies, 111

Environmental Protection Act (EPA), 111

equal protection clause, 49

equipment, movable, 886; secured credit sales of, 618; used as collateral, 611

equitable circumstances, partnership dissolved by, 786

equitable title, 948

errors, correction of billing, 129

escheat, 395, 935

escrow payment of rent, 913

estate, administration expenses, as claims against, 939; administration of decedent's, 936; debts and liabilities of the decedent as claims against, 939; family allowances, as claims against, 939; fee simple, 884; leasehold, 884; life,

884; priority of claims against, 939; proof of claims against, 938

estoppel, effects of sale of on title, 467

ethics, *defined*, 22; societal, 23

European Economic Community (EEC), 73

eviction, constructive, 910; partial, 910

evidence, real, 14

examination, cross-, 15; direct, 15; re-cross-, 15; redirect, 15

exchanges, registration requirements of, 848

exclusion of damages, 512

exculpatory provisions, 361

executed contracts, *defined*, 193

execution, of agency contract, 721; of judgment, 17; of the law, 96

executive, branch of government, 38; power of administrator, 96

executor, *defined*, 936; liability of, 941; powers and duties of, 939; promise by, to pay claim against estate from personal funds, 287

executory contracts, *defined*, 193

executrix, *defined*, 936; *see executor*

exemplary damages, 358

Eximbank, 84

existing goods, 442, 458; identified at time of contracting, 459

exoneration, 626

exploitation, protection from, 28

expropriation, 83

Export Administration Act of 1979, 80

export controls, 80

export-import bank, United States, 84

export programs, government-assisted, 83

export sale, *defined*, 74

export subsidies, and antidumping laws, 81

Export Trading Company Act (ETCA), 84

ex post facto laws, 38

express authority, of agent, 703

express contracts, *defined*, 192

express waiver, 514

express warranty, *defined*, 486; effect of breach of, 489; federal regulation of, 488; form of, 486; seller's opinion on statement of value, 487; time of making, 487

extended coverage, fire insurance, 664

extortion, *defined*, 150

extraordinary bailments, 405

F

factor, *defined*, 430

factorage, 430

factor transaction, effects of, 430

facts, determination of, 14; trier of, 14

Fair Credit Reporting Act of 1970, 130, 174

fair employment practices acts, 61; allowable distinctions, 62; practices acts, sex discrimination, 61

Fair Labor Standards Act, 60

fairness, contracts and, 268

false claim and pretenses, 151

false imprisonment, 177

false information protection from, 131

family purpose doctrine, 414

family relationships, immunity from tort liability and, 169

farm products, used as collateral, 611

favored holders, 551

Federal Antitrust Act, 58

Federal Bill of Lading Act, 426

Federal Communications Act of 1934, 95

federal courts, 10; contract lawsuits and conflict of state laws, 315

Federal Deposit Insurance Corporation, 747

Federal Employees' Compensation Act, 752

Federal Employer's Liability Act, 752

federal government, financial powers of, 44; spending power of, 45

Federal Migrant and Seasonal Agricultural Work Protection Act, 61

Federal Register Act, 96

federal, supremacy, 38, 66

federal system, 37

Federal Tort Claims Act, 730

Federal Trade Commission (FTC), 122

Federal Trade Commission Rule, 561

fee simple, absolute, 884; estate, 884

felonies, defined, 140

field warehousing, 424

filing of financing statements, 615; central, 616; defective, 616; dual, 616; duration and continuation, 617; local, 616; place of, 616

financial institution, responsibility and liability of, 601

financial powers, of the federal government, 44

financial responsibility laws, automobile insurance and, 666

financing, government regulation of business, 56

financing statement, 616; filing, see filing of financing statements

fine print, 239

fines, criminal, 143

fire insurance, 662; amount of loss, 663; assignment of policy, 664; cancellation of, 666; coinsurance clause, 663; determination of insurer's liability, 663; extended coverage, 667; friendly fire, 662; hostile fire, 662; immediate or proximate cause by fire, 663; mortgage clause, 665; nature of contract, 662; motor vehi-

cle and, 673; replacement of property by insurer, 663; total loss, 663

firm offer, 208, 445

fixed payment, 781

fixtures, 884; as real property, 882; tests of a, 885; trade, 886

floating lien, 615

F.O.B. (free on board), 478

food, sale of, 492

Food, Drug, and Cosmestic Act, 873

forebearance, as consideration, 257

force, crimes of, 155

foreclosure, stay of, 900

foreign antitrust laws, 77

foreign corporation, 811

Foreign Corrupt Practices Act, 873

foreign distributorships, 74

foreign markets, agency arrangements and, 74

foreign policy, export controls as instruments of, 80

foreign sales corporation, 84

foreign secrecy laws, impact of, on SEC enforcement, 79

foreign trade, relief mechanisms for economic injury caused by, 81

Foreign Trade Antitrust Improvements Act of 1982, 77

forfeiture of crime-related property, 146

forged indorsements, 541; bank liability for, 599

forged signature of drawer, bank liability for, 597

forgery, defined, 151, 597; as universal defense against holder, 559; of commercial paper, 559; reporting time, 600

formal contracts, 190

four corners rule, 295

four installment rule, 124

franchise, defined, 762; duration and termination, 762; regulation, 763

franchise, defined, 762; and third persons, 765

franchisor, defined, 762; actual control by, 764; and third persons, 764; product liability of, 765

fraud, defined, 239; as to the nature of essential terms of a paper, 558; as universal defense against holder, 558; employer's liability for agent's, 729; in the inducement, 556; parole evidence and, 296; prevention of corporate, 814; product liability and, 496; proof of, 291; protection from, 28; remedies for, 511; sales contract and, 447; statement of intention, 240; statute of, 285; use of assumed name, 240

fraudulent sales, 276

freedom, of personal action, 27; of use of property, 27

Freedom of Information Act, 92

friendly fire, 662

full warranties, 488

funeral expenses, 938

fund, electronic transfer crimes, 149

fungible goods, 410

future goods, 442, 458, 460; contract for delivery at destination, 460; contract for shipment to buyer, 460; marking for buyer, 460

future rights, 323

future transactions, 611

G

garnishee, defined, 747

garnishment of wages, 747

gambling, 154

general acceptance, defined, 574

general agent, 687

General Agreement for Tariffs and Trade (GATT), 72, 80; foreign sales corporations and, 84

general jurisdiction, defined, 7

general legacies, 933

general partners, 765, 777

general partnership, 777

gifts, 390, 443; anatomical, 393; causa mortis, 391; conditional, 392; delivery of, 390; effect of donor's death on, 391; intent to make, 390; inter vivos, 390; symbolic delivery of, 391

good faith, adjustment to existing contract, 255; commercial paper and, 552; contracts required to be made in, 268; implied in a contract, 310; obligation of, 472; partner and, 798

goods, action for conversion, 510; action for recovery of, 510; buyer's action for damages for nondelivery, 508; buyer's duty to accept, 476; carrier of, 425; contract for delivery at destination, 460; contract for sale of, 287; contract for shipment to buyer, 460; creditor's claims to, 458; damage to, 457; damage to identified goods after risk of loss passes, 463; damage to identified goods before risk of loss passes, 462; damages to unidentified goods, 463; disparagement of, 74; disposition after revocation, 507; exclusion of warranties by examination of, 496; existing and identified at time of contract, 442, 458; future, 442, 458, 460; identified, 458; nature of, 442; nonresellable, 451; notice of revocation of acceptance, 506; place, time, and manner of delivery, 475; procedure for revoking acceptance, 506; receiving stolen, 154; rejected of improper delivery, 505; represented by negotiable document of title, 460; resale by buyer, 510; reservation of title or possession, 463; returnable, transactions, 464; revocation of acceptance, 505; right to examine by buyer, 476; sale of, 441; seller's duty to delivery, 475;

time for revocation of acceptance, 507; unidentified, 458, 460; un-ordered, 214; what constitutes acceptance of, 476

government, branches of, 38

government agency, and business practices, 133; *see administrative agency(ies)*

government approval of contracts, 310

Government in the Sunshine Act of 1976, 93

government-assisted export programs, 83

government ownership of business, 46

government regulation, of principals liability for torts and crimes of agent, 728; of production, distribution, and financing of businesses, 56

governments, corporations and, 813; immuned from tort liability, 169

grantee, 891; covenants, 895

grantor, 891; warranties, 894

gratuitous bailments, 405

gross returns, 781

group life insurance, 674

guarantee of performance, 339

guarantor, 524, 625; liability of, of payment, 526; of collection, 526; of a commercial paper, 524

guaranty, 624; absolute, 625; creation of relationship, 625

guardian, appointment of for incompetent person, 228

guest, hotel, *defined*, 431; duration of relationship, 431; hotelkeeper's liability for property of, 432

H

habitability, warranty of, 913

harm, and criminal liability, 140

hazardous wastes, dumping and criminal liability, 112

hearing, administrative, 100

heirs, collateral, intestate distribution and, 935

holder, 524; defenses available against an ordinary, 555; favored, 551; kinds of, 550; ordinary, 551; through a holder in due course, 551, 555; universal defenses available against, 558

holder in due course, 524, 551; avoidance of protection, 561; effect of discharge on, 586; good faith, 552; ignorance of defenses and adverse claims, 553; ignorance of paper overdue or dishonored, 553; limited defenses not available against, 555; value, 552

holding company, 832

holographic will, 932

holiday, instrument due on legal or business, 568

home solicited sales, 125

hostile fire, 662

hotel keeper, *defined*, 431; bailee's liability and, 430; liability for guest's property, 432; lien, 433

housing laws, 913

human rights, 42

I

identified goods, 458; damage to, after risk of loss passes, 463; damage to, before risk of loss passes, 462

illegality, agreements, 267; as universal defense against holder, 559; partial of an agreement, 268; partnership dissolved by, 784; prevention of corporate, 814; subsequent, of contract, 210

illegal discrimination contracts, 273

illegal lobbying agreement, 272

illegal sales, 448

immunity from liability, 169

impairment, of collateral, 584; of right of recourse, 583

implied conditions, in sales contract, 447

implied contracts, *defined*, 192

implied terms of contracts, 205

implied waiver, 514

implied warranty, *defined*, 489; additional, of merchant seller, 491; against encumbrances, 490; against infringement, 491; in particular sales, 492; of all sellers, 489; of fitness for a particular purpose, 490; of fitness for normal use, 491; of merchantability, 491; of title, 489; proving products defect, 493; sale of food or drink, 492; sale of second hand of used goods, 492; sale on buyer's specifications, 492

impostor rule, 542

impracticability, partnership dissolved by, 785

improvements, mortgagor and, 898

import injuries, relief from, 83

imprisonment, false, 177

improper delivery, rejection of, by buyers, 505

incapacitating self, 351

incapacity, 558; as universal defense against holder, 559; effect on negotiation, 543; of defendant, 556; partnership dissolved by, 785

incidental authority, of agent, 703

incidental beneficiary, of contract, 321

income, from property in trust, 946

incompetent, 228

incontestable clause, in life insurance policy, 676

incorporation, 817; application for, 818; articles of, 810; certificate of, 810, 818; cooperative, 769; defective, 818; definite by, 204, proper,

818; stock subscription after, 842; stock subscription before, 842

incorporator, 810

incorrect date, on commercial paper, 530

indemnification of officers, directors, employees, and agents of a corporation, 871

indemnity, 626; rights of partner and, 801

indemnity contract, 625

independent contractors, distinguished from an agent, 685; owner's liability for acts of, 731; undisclosed, 732

indorsee of commercial paper, 524; multiple, 540

indorsement, bank liability for missing, 599; correction of name by, 539; forged, 541; kinds of, 536; missing, 541; unauthorized, 541

indorser of a commercial paper, 524; liability of, 574; warranties of unqualified, 545

industrial activity, absolute liability of, 165

influence, undue, 241

informal contracts, 192

infringement, of copyrights, 175; of patents, 174; of trade and service marks, 174; warranty against, 491

in pari delicto, 267

insane persons, criminal responsibility and, 142

insanity, and contractural capacity, 228; partnership dissolved by, 785; termination of agency and, 695; termination of offer and, 210

insider, 638; information, 850; preferences made to, in bankruptcy, 638

Insider Trading Sanctions Act of 1984, 850

insolvent debtor, 638

insolvency, corporation and, 820; presentment for payment not required, 569

inspection of premises, by administrative officer, 98; by landlord, 912

instrument, due date, 568; negotiable, 191; nondelivery of, 556; sealed and written, 259

insurable interest, 648

insurance, 647; agent, 648; application as part of the contract, 650; broker, 648; coverage of policy, 654; insurance delivery of policy, 651; kinds of, 662; machine-vended, 652; mortgagor's duty to pay, 899; parties to, 648; partner's authority and, 795; rider, 653; sales transactions, and 458; statute of limitations, 656; *see also automobile insurance, fire insurance, liability insurance, life insurance*

insurance contract, 649; cancellation of, 654; duties of parties to, 651; interpretation of, 653; limitation on time for suit, 656; modification of,

652; statutory provisions as part of the, 650; when effective, 651

insurance claim, notification of, 656; proof of loss, 656

insurance, premiums, 654; nonforfeiture and antilapse provisions, 654; prepayment of, 651; return of unearned, 654; prepayment of, 651

insured, time limitations in making a claim, 656

insurer, 648; bad faith, 655; defenses of, 655; extent of liability, 654; subrogation of, 656

integrated industry, 822

intent, 162; as basis of tort liability, 162; enforcement of, 27; statement of, 240; to make a binding agreement, 188

intention, contractual, 202; to delegate duties, 326; statement of contractual, 203

interest, agents' in the authority, 687; agent's in the subject matter, 687; reservation of a security, 465; security, 610; maximum contract rate, 278, rights of partners and payment of, 801

interference with contract, 176

intermediate courts, 11

International Monetary Fund (IMF), 73

International Trade Commission (ITC), and dumping of foreign goods, 82

international trade organizations, conferences, and treaties, 72

interstate commerce, improper use of, 147

inter vivos gift, 390

inter vivos trust, 947

intestacy, 935

intestate, distribution, 935; collateral heirs, 935; death of distributee after decedent, 936; lineals, 935; murder of decendent, 935; per capita and per stripes, 936; parents, 935; simultaneous death, 936; spouses, 935

intestate sucession, 935

intoxicated persons, capacity to make a contract, 228; criminal responsibility and, 142

invasion of privacy, 171

inventions, contractual protection of, 387

inventory, secured credit sale of, 614; used for collateral, 611

investigative consumer report, 130

Investment Advisors Act of 1940, 846

Investment Company Act of 1940, 846, 857

investors, state and federal regulations to protect, 846

invitation, to negotiate, 202

invitees, liability for condition of real property and, 887

irresistible impulse test, 142

issuer, duty of, 629; warehouse receipts and, 421

J

joint and several contracts, 313

joint contracts, 312

joint payees, 540

joint tenancy, 396

joint ventures, 75, 767; duration of, 768; liability, 768

judge, 9; rent-a-, 19

judicial branch of government, 38

judicial dissolution of a corporation, 821

judicial power of administrator, 99

judicial procedure, streamlining, 18

judgment, and costs, 16; appeal of, 17; declaratory, 18; n.o.v., 16; execution of, 17; non obstante veredicto, 16; on the pleadings, 13

jurisdiction, defined, 7; appellate, 7; general, 7; of United States antitrust laws, 76; original, 7; special, 7

"jurisdictional rule of reason", 76

jury, defined, 10; charge to the, 15; list, 10; opening address to, 15; taking case from, 16; trial summary, 18; verdict, 15

L

labeling, 124

labels, false, 152

labor practices, unfair, 63

labor representation, 62

lack of success, partnership dissolved by, 786

land, 882; rights in other's, 882; trespass to, 178

land contract, part performance of, 291

landlord, defined, 905; distress, 915; duty to mitigate damages, 916; liability for crimes of third person, 917; liability to tenant, 917; liability to third person, 918; lien of, 915; recovery of possession, 916; remedies of, 915; suit for rent, 915

Land Sales Act, 132

larceny, defined, 155; by trick, 155

law, defined, 4; administrator's regulation as, 93; and enforcement agencies, 3; antidumping, 81; appliable to sale contracts, 444; as an evolutionary process, 32; as a synthesis, 33; as the crystallization of ethics, 23; case, 6; change of and discharging a contract, 345; classifications of, 7; conflicting objectives, 31; conflict of, 313; constitutional, 6; environmental, 109; ethics and, 22; execution of the, 96; foreign antitrust, 77; nature of, 4; objectives of, 24; of the forum, 313; procedural law, 7; secrecy, 79; societal ethics as the blueprint for future, 23; source of criminal, 140; statement of, 240; statutory, 6; substantive, 7; uniform state, 6; what is the law, 5

lease, defined, 904; assignment of, 920; automobile, 125; covenant for quiet enjoyment, 910; creation of relationship, 905; essential elements of, 906; improvements, 914; notice of termination, 908; renewal of, 909; possession and, 911; rights and duties of parties to, 909; taxes and assessments and, 914; termination of, 907; use of premises and, 911

leasehold estate, 884

legacy, 928; abatement of, 933; ademption of property, 933; antilapse statutes, 933; general, 933; specific, 933

legal holiday, instrument due on, 568

legal processes, agreements obstructing, 272

legal rights, 4; agencies for enforcement of, 7

legal system, streamlining within the, 18

legal tender, 335

legatee, 928

legislative branch of government, 38

legislative power of the administrator, 93

lessee, defined, 905

lessor, defined, 905

letters of administration, 937

letter of credit, 628; illustrated, 630

letters testamentary, 937

liability, absolute, 164; basis of criminal, 140; basis of tort, 162; division of, 168; malpractice, 368; no-fault, 165; immunity from, 169; of parties of commercial paper, 525; theories of, 483; vicarious, 728; see also product liability

liability-imposing conduct, 164

liability insurance, automobile, 666, 667; cancellation of, 669; exclusions, 669; insurer's duty to defend any suit, 669; notice and cooperation, 669; other drive clause, 668; person operating, 668; temporary replacement coverage, 668

libel, criminal, 153; defamation by, 173

license, nature of real property and, 883

licensed callings or dealings, 274

licensee, liability for condition of real property and, 887

licensing, as a means to do business in other countries, 74

lien, floating, 615; landlord's, 915; of hotelkeeper, 433; of warehouser, 421; real property and, 884; repair and storage, 612; seller's, 504

life estate, 884

life, insurable interest in, 648

life insurance, 673; annuity policies, 673; beneficiary, 674; cash surrender value of policy, 675; disability, 674; double indemnity, 674; endowment, 673; exclusions, 674; extended, 676; group, 674;

incontestable clause, 676; kinds of, 673; limited payment, 673; loan on policy, 676; ordinary, 673; paid-up policy, 676; reinstatement of lapsed policy, 677; retirement income insurance, 673; rights of creditors, 677; settlement options, 677; straight line, 673; term, 673

limitations, constitutional, on administrative investigation, 98; statute of, 502

limited defenses, 555; not available against a holder in due course, 555

limited (special) jurisdiction, *defined*, 7

limited partnership, 765

limited payment insurance, 673

limited warranties, 489

lineal descendants, intestate distribution and, 935

liquidated damages, 359

liquidation of damages, 511

liquidation under Chapter 7, 635

literary works, copyrightable, 385

litigation, and pollution, 111

living trust, 947

loans, by a partner, 795; on life insurance policy, 676; rights of partners and repayment of, 800

lobbying, illegal agreement, 272

lodgers, hotelkeeper's liability and, 433

loss, breach of contract and a consequential, 357; breach of contract and a direct, 357

lost property, 393; finder's right, 394; finding in public place, 393

lotteries, 154, 273

M

machinery, movable, 886

mail, acceptance of an offer by, 215; use of, to defraud, 153

maker, of a commercial paper, 523

malpractice, 171; liability, 368, 859; what constitutes, 368

management, rights of partners, 800

mark, *defined*, 382; abandonment of exclusive rights to, 384; injunction against improper use of, 383; registrable, 383

market value, of shares of stock, 840

marketing, crimes related to, 147

marriage, promise made in consideration of, 287

married women, capacity to contract, 229

marshals, 10

mask works, 389

material alteration, 349

maturity date, computing, 568

maximum contract rate of interest, 278

medical doctors, malpractice liability and, 369

mental distress, causing, 170

mental state, and criminal liability, 140

merchantability, implied warranty of, or fitness for normal use, 491

merchant seller, additional implied warranties of, 491

merger, *defined*, 821; and antitrust regulations, 59; of contract rights, 350

Mini-trial, 19

minor, *defined*, 223; contractual capacity, 223; contracts that cannot be avoided by, 227; criminal responsibility and, 142; gifts to, 391; immunity from tort liability and, 169; liability of cosigner for contract of, 227; liability of parents for contract of, 227; misrepresentation of age, 223; power to avoid contracts, 223; ratification of voidable contract, 226; recovery of property by, upon avoidance, 224; restitution by, after avoidance, 223; time for avoidance of contract, 223

misconduct, effect on negotiation, 543; partnership dissolved by, 785

misdemeanors, *defined*, 140

missing date, on commercial paper, 531

mistrial, 16

mitigation of damages, 358

model, warranty of conformity to, 488

Model Business Corporation Act, 813; revised, 818

modification, of contract, 297; of sales contract, 447

money, assignment of right to, 323; payment in, 529

monopolies, prevention of, 58

mortgage, *defined*, 897; characteristics of, 897; defeasance clause, 898; form of, 898; impairment of security, 899; fire insurance clause, 664; property subject to, 898; recording or filing of, 898; repairs and improvements under, 898; transfer of interest, 899

mortgagee, 897; rights of, after default, 900; transfer of interest and, 900

mortgagor, 897; duty to pay taxes, assessments, and insurance, 899; repairs and improvements and, 898; rights of, after default, 900; transfer of interest and, 899

most-favored nation clause, 72

motion, for judgment on the pleadings, 13; for summary judgment, 13; to dismiss, 12

motive, 162

Motor Vehicle Information and Cost Savings Act, 125, 175

murder, of decedent, 936

musical works, copyrightable, 385

mutual rescission, 341

N

National Environmental Policy Act of 1969 (NEPA), 110

National Labor Relations Act, 743

National Labor Relations Board, 62

necessaries, contract for, 225

negligence, 166; comparative, 167; contributory, 167; liability for agent's, 729; product liability and, 496; proof of, 168

negotiability, 526

negotiable bill of lading, 426

negotiable documents of title, 467; goods represented by, 460

negotiable draft, 522

negotiable instruments, 191

negotiable promissory note, 522

negotiable warehouse receipts, 422

negotiate, invitation to, 202

negotiation, *defined*, 540; effect of incapacity or misconduct on, 543; of bearer paper, 541; of commercial paper, 540; of order paper, 540

Newspaper Preservation Act, 60

new trial, 16

n factor, contracts, 270

no-fault insurance, 671; arbitration, 672; constitutionality, 672; harm to the insured, 671; other party injury, 671; suit against party at fault, 671

no-fault liability, 165

nominal damages, 358

nominal partners, 778

noncompetition agreement, 389

nonconforming use, *defined*, 114

nondisclosure, active concealment, 239; fraudulent, 238; general rule of non-liability, 238; of confidential relationship, 238; of terms in fine print, 239; of unknown defect or condition, 238

nondisclosure agreement, 389

nonnegotiable bill of lading, 427

nonnegotiable warehouse receipt, 422; *illustrated*, 423

nonprofit corporations, 811

nonresellable goods, 451

nonsuit, compulsory, 16; voluntary, 16

nontrading partnership, 777

note, dishonor of, 570; liability of maker, 566; presentment of for payment, 566

novation, 343

nuisance, 116

nuncupative will, 933

O

obedience, partner and, 799

objective intent, of parties to contract, 303

objectives of the law, 24; conflicting, 31

obligation, promise to perform existing, 254

obligee, 186

obligor, 186

occupation, 394

Occupational Safety and Health Administration, 750

Occupational Safety and Health Act of 1970, 749

odometer fraud, 125

offense, seriousness of, 140

offer, acceptance, 210; bids at auction sales as a, 217; communication of, 206; definiteness of, 204; effect of counteroffer on, 209; effect of death or disability of either party on, 210; effect of lapse of time on, 209; effect of subsequent illegality on, 210; firm, 208; manner of acceptance, 213; rejection of by offeree, 209; requirements of a, 201; revocation of by offeror, 207; sales contract, 445; termination of, 207; to make a contract at a future date, 203; who may accept an, 212

offeree, 187; counteroffer by, 209; privilege of, 210; rejection of offer by, 209

offeror, 187; revocation of offer by, 207

officer, as payee of commercial paper, 540; corporate president, 869; indemnification of corporate, 871; liability of corporate, 870; of corporation, 868; of the court, 9; powers of corporate, 868

omnibus clause, automobile liability insurance and, 668

opening addresses to jury, 15

operating companies, 832

opinion, statement of, 240

oppression, protection from, 28

option contracts, defined, 208

option to purchase, 443

oral contracts, 285, 451; conflict between written and, 294; detrimental reliance on, 292; proof of, permitted, 451

order, commercial paper payable to, 530

order paper, 531; negotiation of, 540

order to pay, 528

ordinary contract defenses, 556

ordinary holders, 551; defenses against, 555

ordinary life insurance, 673

Organizations, court, 9

Organization of Petroleum Exporting Countries (OPEC), 73

original jurisdiction, defined, 7

output contracts, 446

owners, rights of partners as, 800

ownership, absolute, 382; limitations on, 382

P

papers, protection against investigation, 99; see also commercial paper

parents, intestate distribution and, 935; liability on contract made by minor child, 227

parol evidence, defined, 293

parol evidence rule, 293; applied to sale of goods, 447; conflict between oral and written contracts, 294; four corners rule, 295; liberalization of, 294; reason for, 293; when it does not apply, 295

partial eviction, 910

participating preferred stock, 841

parties, to a contract, 186; to a crime, 141

party, action of aggrieved, 474

partners, 775, 778; adverse interest of, 797; assignment of interest, 783; as to third persons, 781; authority of, 794; authority to bind firm by admission, 796; authority to borrow money, 795; authority to hire employees and agents, 795; authority to insure firm property, 795; authority to make contracts, 795; authority to purchase, 795; authority to receive notice, 796; authority to sell, 795; authority to settle claims, 795; classification, 777; dormant, 778; duties of, 798; duty of loyalty and good faith, 798; duty of obedience, 799; duty to account, 799; duty to inform, 799; duty to use reasonable care, 799; effect of dissolution on liability, 804; enforcement of liability, 804; extent of liability, 803; general, 765, 777; liability for breach of duty, 804; liability for contracts, 801; liability for crimes, 803; liability for torts, 802; liability of, 801; liability of new, 804; limitation on authority, 796; nature of liability, 803; nominal, 778; prohibited transactions, 797; rights as owners, 800; right to inspect book of firm, 800; right to compensation, 800; right to contribution and indemnity, 801; right to share of distribution of capital, 801; right to share profits, 800; right to manage firm, 800; right to payment of interest, 801; right to repayment of loan, 800; secret, 778; silent, 778; who may be, 778

partnerships, 760, 775; advantages of, 760; agreement, 778, 780; agreement, illustrated, 779; articles of, 780; assignment of partner's interest, 783; characteristics of a, 775; classification of, 777; continuation of after dissolution, 789; control of, 780; co-ownership, 781; corporation as, 819; creation of, 778; determining existence of, 780; disadvantages, 760; dissolution and termination of, 783; dissolution by act of parties, 784; dissolution by agreement, 784; dissolution by death, 784; dissolution by decree of court, 784; disso-lution by expulsion of any partner, 784; dissolution by operation of law, 784; dissolved by bankruptcy, 784; dissolved by equitable circumstances, 786; dissolved by illegality, 784; dissolution by impracticability, 785; dissolved by incapacity of partner, 785; dissolution by lack of success, 786; dissolution by misconduct of a partner, 785; dissolved by insanity of partner, 785; dissolved by war, 784; dissolved by withdrawal of a partner, 784; distribution of assets, 788; effect of dissolution, 783; firm name, 777; fixed payment, 780; general, 777; gross returns, 781; liability of, 801; limited, 765; nature and creation, 775; nontrading, 777; notice of dissolution, 786; property, 782; purposes of a, 777; sharing profits and losses, 780; special, 777; tenancy in, 783; termination of, 797; trading, 777; winding up affairs, 787

part payment checks, 256

par value, 840

patent, 386; as protection for computer programs, 387; contractual protection of inventions, 387; infringement of, 174; loss of protection by publication, 387; secret business information, 387; trade secrets, 387; what can be protected by a, 386

payee, agent or office as, 540; alternate, 540; joint, 540; multiple, 540; of commercial paper, 524; of draft, 522

payment, as performance of contract, 335; by check, 336; by secondary party, 581; discharge of commercial paper by, 581; fixed, 781; in money, 529; in oral contract, 452; liability of bank for improper, 597; part, 256; presentment of note for, 567; tender of, 581; valid tender of, 335

penalties, administrative, 143; civil and criminal for improper consumer practices, 134

penalty, liquidated damages as, 360

pension plans, 746; enforcement, 747; federal regulation of, 746; fiduciary standards and reporting, 746; funding, 747; termination insurance, 747; vesting, 747

performance, adequacy, 338; details of implied in contract, 309; discharge of contract by, 335; guarantee of, 339; nature of, 335; substantial, 338; time of, 337; to satisfaction of third party, 338

perjury, defined, 151

permissive waste, 912

person, protection of, 50

personal property, 381; abandoned, 395; acquiring title to and protection of, 382; excheat, 395; gift of, 928; joint tenancy, 396; lost, 393; multiple ownership of, 396; occupation of, 394; tenancy by entirety,

398; tenancy in common, 396; transfer by nonowner, 394; trespass to, 178

personal representative, appointment of, 937; oath and bond, 938; person entitled to act as, 937; powers and duties of, 939; termination of authority of, 942

physical duress, 242

plaintiff, 12; improper product and identification of, 485

pleadings, 12; on the judgment, 13

point-of-sale terminals, 601

police power, 66

policy, insurance, 648

political influence, improper, 150

pollution, prevention of, 110

possession, adverse, 897; reservation of, 463

Postal Reorganization Act of 1970, 214

post-sale disclaimer, 496

power, executive, of the administrator, 96

power of attorney, 688

power to regulate, 56

precedent, *defined*, 6

preferred stock, 841; cumulative, 841; participating, 841

premerger notification, 59

premises, inspection of, by landlord, 912; repairs and condition of, 912

premiums, insurance, *see insurance premiums*

presentment of paper for payment and acceptance, 565; drafts, 572; notes for payment, 566; time of making, 568; when excused of unnecessary, 569

preservation of defenses, 514

preservation notice, 514

president, of corporation, 869

pretenses, 151

pretrial conference, 13

pretrial procedure, 13

price, determination of in a sale, 446

price discrimination, permitted, 57; prohibited, 57

price fixing, 59

prices, government regulation of, 57

primary beneficiary, 675

principal, 625, 946; acquiescence by, 689; agents and, 683; agency terminated by bankruptcy of, 695; agency terminated by death of, 695; agency terminated by insanity, 695; agent's communication to, 728; as parties to a crime, 141; bound by agent's knowledge, 727; bound by agent's statement, 727; conduct as to agent, 688; conduct as to third person, 688; disclosed, 725; disclosure of by agent, 720; duties and liabilities of, and agent, 708; duty to compensate agent, 712; duty to indemnify agent

for losses resulting from agency, 713; duty to provide agent with employment according to terms of contract, 712; duty to reimburse agent, 713; in the first degree, 141; in the second degree, 141; liability of, for torts and crimes of agent, 728; liability of, to third person, 725; nondisclosure of, 527; partially disclosed, 725; revocation of agency by, 693; undisclosed, 725; undisclosed by agent, 721; vicarious liability of, 728; who may be a, 686

privacy, invasion of, 171; of credit information, 130; the right of, 5

private agencies, 8

private carrier, 425

private contracts, community planning and, 113

private corporation, 811

private sale of collateral, 619

privity of contract, 186

probate, of will, 931

procedural law, *defined*, 7

proceeds, of collateral, 615

production, crimes related to, 147; government regulation of business, 56

product liability, cumulative theories of, 497; nature of harm, 484; theories of, 483; strict tort, 496; who may sue and be sued, 484

product safety, 129

professional corporations, 811, 859

profits, rights of partners to share, 800

promise, as consideration, 254; binding character of, 254; conditional, 254; to pay, 528; to perform existing obligation, 254

promisee, 186; satisfaction of, 338

promisor, 186; benefited by promise to pay debt of another, 291

promissory estoppel, 260

promissory notes, *defined*, 522; *illustrated*, 523; liability of maker of, 566

promoters, 810; corporations and, 816

proof of claim, 639

proof of loss, 656

proof of negligence, 168

property, *defined*, 381; acquired by accession, 390; acquired by gifts, 390; acquired by a corporation, 831; after-acquired, 615; ademption of, 933; bailed *see bailed property*; community, 398; contribution of, in a partnership, 781; crimes against, 155; destruction of, and lease termination, 908; forfeiture of crime-related, 146; insurable interest in, 648; lost, 393; partnership, 782; personal *see personal property*; real *see real property*; subject to mortgage, 898; unclaimed, 395; used as collateral, 611; use of, and extent of security interest, 615

property report, 132

property rights, 457; remedies for violation, 396

proprietorship, individual, 760

prospectus, 847

proxy, voting by, 853

public accommodation, offers and, 211

public announcement of agency guidelines, 93

publication, loss of trade secret protection and, 387

publication, of a will, 930

public authorities, 811

public corporation, 811

public knowledge of regulation, 96

public participation in adoption of regulation, 95

public policy, 271; agreement contrary to, 271; unconscionability and, 273

public sale of collateral, 619

public service, agreements injuring, 272

public utilities, offers and, 211

Public Utility Holding Company Act of 1935, 846

public warehousers, 420

public welfare, agreements affecting, 271

public zoning, 113

punishment powers of administrators, 102

punitive damages, 358

purchase, by a partner, 795; option to, 443

purchase money resulting trust, 952

purchase price, seller's action for the, 505

Q

qualified indorsement, 538; *illustrated*, 539

qualified indorser, warranties of, 546

quasi contract, *defined*, 194

quasi dissolution, 820

quasi public corporation, 811

quitclaim deed, 891

quorum, 865

R

ratification, minor's, of voidable contract, 226; form of, 226; time for, 226; what constitutes, 226

ratification, agency by, 690; conditions for, 691; effect of, 692; form of, 692

real estate, administration of, 941; broker, 686; development sales, 132

real evidence, *defined*, 14

real property, 381, 881; adverse possession, 896; agreement to sell or a sale of any interest, 286; building and fixtures, 882; condominiums, 890; co-ownership of, 889; duration and extent of ownership, 884; easements, 882; fixtures, 884; eminent domain, 896; gift of, 928; land, 882; property, liability to third persons for conditions of, 886; licenses, 883; lien on, 884; mortgages, 897; nature of, 881; transfer of, by deed, 891

reasonable care, partner and, 799

reasonable person, 166

receipt, warehouse, 421

receiving stolen goods, 154

recovery of goods, action for, 510

recross-examination, 15

redeemable shares, 841

redemption, debtor's right of, 619; mortgagor's right of, 900

redirect examination, 15

referral sales, 126

reformation of contract, 245, 365

registration, exemptions, 847; requirements, 847; statement, 847

regional trading groups of developing countries, 73

regulation of competition, 56; of employment, 60; of prices, 57; of production, distribution, and financing, 56

regulations, administrative, 6; public knowledge of, 96; public participation in adoption, 95

regulatory powers of state, local, and federal governments, 56

re ipsa loquitur, 168

rejection, of offer by offeree, 209

release, 343; of claims, 256

remedies, contract provisions on, 511; for breach of contract, 357; for breach of sales contracts, 502; for duress, 244; for fraud, 244; for fraud of seller, 511; for mistake, 244; for undue influence, 244; limitation of, 513; of buyer, 505; of seller, 503

rent, abatement and escrow payment of, 913; duty of tenant to pay, 911; suit for, 915

rent escalation, 911

renunciation, discharge of parties to commercial paper, 585; of contract, 351

repair, lien for charges to, 612

repairs, mortgagor's duty, 898

repossession, secured seller's, 618

repudiation, anticipatory, 473; of sales contract, 473

resale, by buyer's, 510; by seller, 504; compulsory, 618

rescission, as remedy for voidable contract, 244; of agency contract, 695; of contract, by agreement, 341

reservation of right, 364

reservation of title or possession, 463

residuary bequest, 933

restitution, by minor, after avoidance of contract, 223

restrictive covenant, 113, 895; scope of grantee's, 896

restrictive indorsement, 538; *illustrated*, 539

resulting trust, 952

retirement income insurance, 673

retractive advertising, 123

return, sale or, 465

returnable goods transactions, 464

returns, gross, 781

reversionary interest, 412

revocation, communication of, 207; of offer by offeror, 207; what constitutes a, 207

revocation of acceptances, 505; disposition of goods, 507; notice of, 506; procedure for, 506; time for, 507

revolving charge accounts, 279

right, of escheat, 935; of redemption, 900; of reentry, 916; reservation of, 364; to know, 92

right and wrong test, 142

right of recourse, impairment of, 583

rights, debtor, in collateral, 611; legal, 4; of the person, 50

riots, 156

robbery, *defined*, 155

Robinson-Patman Act of 1936, 57

S

sale, and estoppel, 467; bill of, 453; by entrustee, 467; conditional, 443; consignment, 466; contract law applicable to, 444; distinguished, 442; effect of, on title, 466; nature and form of, 441; of any interest in real property, evidenced by a writing, 286; of collateral, 619; of food or drink, 492; of goods, 287; of negotiable document of title, 460; on approval, 464; on buyer's specifications, 492; of secondhand or used goods, 492; or return, 465; point-of, terminals, 601

sales, auction, 217, 465; automobile, 125; by a partner, 795; credit, secured by consumer goods, 612; credit, secured by inventory, 614; export, 74; fraudulent, 276; home solicited, 125; illegal, 448; real estate development, 132; referral, 126; subject matter of, 442; warranties in particular, 492

sales contract, adequate assurance of performance, 474; assignment of, 478; buyer's duty to accept goods, 474; buyer's duty to pay, 477; buyer's right to examine goods, 476; cancellation by seller, 504; C.I.F. (cost, insurance, freight), 477; claim

for breach under UCC, 502; credit, 278; direct, 485; duties of the parties, 475; effect of noncompliance with statute of frauds, 451; exclusion of, 512; (F.O.B.), 478; form of, 450; limitation of damages in, 511; nature of the writing required, 450; obligation of good faith, 472; payment by commercial paper, 477; place, time, and manner of delivery, 475; quantity delivered, 475; remedies for breach of, 502; repudiation of the, 473; seller's duty to deliver, 475; statute of limitations, 502; warranty for future performance, 503; when proof of oral contract is permitted, 451

sales personnel, reasons for limitation on authority of, 733; transactions with, 733

sale price, credit, 278

sample, warranty of conformity to, 488

satisfaction, accord and, 343

seal, on a sales contract, 447

sealed instrument, as exception to requirement of consideration, 259; prohibited transactions of a partner and, 797

seals of approval, 123

secondhand goods, sale of, 492

secrecy laws, 79

secret partners, 778

secured credit sales, compulsory resale, 618; debtor's right of redemption, 619; disposition of collateral by sale, 619; of consumer goods, 612; of equipment, 618; of inventory, 614; rights of parties after default, 618; secured seller's repossession and resale of collateral, 618

secured credit sales of consumer goods, 612; filing not required, 612; interstate security interest, 612; protection of subpurchaser, 613; repair and storage lien, 612; rights as a debtor, 613; rights of the buyer independent of default, 613; rights of the seller independent of default, 612

secured credit sales of equipment, 618; use of collateral, 618

secured credit sales of inventory, 614; after-acquired property, 615; filing of financial statement, 615; proceeds of collateral, 615; protection of customers of the buyer, 617; termination of buyer's obligation, 617; use of property and extent of security interest, 615

secured party, 610

secured transaction, 610

securities, lost, destroyed, and stolen, 845

Securities Act of 1933, 846

securities crimes, 147

Securities Exchange Act of 1934, 846, 848; impact of foreign secrecy laws on, enforcement, 79; in an international environment, 79

securities brokers, dealers, and exchanges, registration requirements of, 848

securities regulations in an international environment, 79

security agreement, 610

security interest, 610; creation of, 610; interstate, 612; perfected, 611; reservation of a, 465

self-service stores, 461

sell, contract to, 443

seller, action for damages, 504; action for the purchase price, 505; cancellation by, 504; effect of breach of contract by, 463; duty to deliver, 475; implied warranties of, 489; implied warranties of merchant, 491; lien, 504; opinion or statement of value, 487; remedies for fraud of, 511; remedies of the, 503; resale by, 504

seller's assignee, obligation of, as to performance, 479; defenses of buyer against, 479

selling methods, 124

selling on consignment, 430

semiconductor chip product, 389

semiconductor chip protection, 389

Semiconductor Chip Protection Act of 1984, 389

sentencing, 145

service contracts, 132

servicemark, *defined*, 174, 382; infringement of, 174

servient tenement, 882

several contracts, 313

severalty, 396

sex discrimination, 61

shareholders, action, 857; exceptions to limited liability, 858; liabilities of, 858; limited liability of, 858; meetings of, 865; ownership rights, 852; preemptive offer of shares, 853; of professional corporation, 859; protection of, 874; rights to, 852; right to inspect books, 853; right to receive dividends, 855; right to share in capital distribution, 856; right to vote, 852

shares of stock, *see stock*

sheriff, 10

Sherman Antitrust Act, 58; bigness, 58; conduct prohibited by, 58; punishment and civil remedy, 60

shipment contract for, 459

short-swing profit, 851

silent partners, 778

slander, *defined*, 172; defamation by, 172; of title, 174

social security, 65

Social Security Act of 1935, unemployment insurance provisions of, 748

societal ethics, 23

socit anonyme (S.A.), 74

Soft Drink Interbrand Competition Act, 60

software, theft, 148

sogo shosha, 84

sole proprietorship, 760

solicited, home sales, 125

soliciting agent, 733

Sovereign Compliance Doctrine, 77

Sovereign Immunity Doctrine, 77

special agent, 687

special bailments, 419

Special Drawing Rights (SDR), 73

special indorsement, 537; *illustrated*, 538

special jurisdiction, *defined*, 7

special partnership, 777

special service corporations, 811

specific legacies, 933

specific lien, 421

specific performance, 362

spending power, of federal government, 45

spendthrift trust, 948

spot zoning, 115

spouses, intestate distribution and, 935

stale checks, 593

state, protection of, by law, 24; uniform laws, 6

state courts, 11; conflict of law and contract lawsuit, 313

states, and the constitution, 38

State Supreme Court, 11

statute, violation of, 168

statute of frauds, 285, 841

statute of limitations, 502; contract claim and, 350

statutory deed, 891

statutory law, 6

statutory protection, agreements evading, 272

statutory terms, contracts and, 310

stay of foreclosure, 900

stirpital distribution, 936

stock, 840; acquisition of, 841; blue sky laws, 846; book value, 840; capital, 840; certificate of, 840; common, 841; convertible shares, 841; corporate purchase of own, 832; cumulative preferred, 841; duration of, 841; effect of transfer on, 856; effect of transfer on negotiability, 845; fractional shares, 841; kinds of, 840; lost, destroyed, and stolen, 845; market value, 840; par value, 840; preferred, 841; redeemable shares, 841; statues of frauds, 841; transfer of, 842; valuation of, 840

stock subscriptions, 842; before incorporation, 842; after incorporation, 842

stop payment order, bank liability for payments over, 597; form of, 594

stopping payment of a check, 594; liability to holder, 594

straight bill of lading, 427

straight life insurance, 673

straight voting, 852

subrogation, 626

subscriptions, charitable, 259; stock, 842; unpaid, 858

subsidiaries, wholly-owned, and business abroad, 74

subsidiary companies, 832

substantial performance, 338

subjective intent, 303

sublease, 920

subpoena, 15

subpoena duces tecum, 15

subpurchaser, protection of, 613

substantive law, *defined*, 7

substitution of contract, 342

sue, improper products and who may, 484; who may, 169

suit for rent, 915

sum certain, 530

summary jury trial, 18

Supreme Court of the United States, 10

surcharge, for use of credit card prohibited, 127

surety, defenses of, 627; rights of, 626

suretyship, 624; creation of, 624; defenses, 627; prohibited transaction of a partner, 797

swindles, 152

symbolic delivery, of gift, 391

T

tangible personal property, as collateral, 611

tariff, *defined*, 80

taxes, corporate, 873; landlords duty to pay, 914; mortgagor's duty to pay, 899

taxing power, of federal government, 44

telegraph, acceptance of an offer by, 215

telephone, acceptance of an offer by, 217; electronic fund transfers by, 601

temporary replacement coverage, automobile liability insurance and, 668

tenancy, at will, 906; by entirety, 398; by sufferance, 906; for years, 906; from year to year, 906; in common, 396; in partnership, 783; joint, 396

tenant, *defined*, 905; abatement and escrow payment of rent, 913; assignment of lease and sublease, 920; deposit of, 914; duty to pay rent, 911; housing laws that protect, 913; liability to third person, 919; protection from retaliation, 915; right to acquire possession, 910; right to retain possession, 910; right to use of premises, 911; transfer of, and termination of lease, 908

tender, *defined*, 335; cure of defective, 476; legal, 335; of payment, 581; offers, 851; valid, 335

tentative trusts, 950

terms, contract, 126; disclosure of transaction, 124; implied in a contract, 205

termination of agency, *see agency, termination*

termination of offer, 207

termination statement, 617

term insurance, 673

territorial courts, 11

testamentary capacity, 928

testamentary intent, 929

testamentary trust, 947

testate distribution, 928

testator, *defined*, 928

testatrix, *defined*, 928

testimony, *defined*, 14

theft, of commercial paper, 558; of software, 148

theft insurance, 672

third party beneficiary contract, *defined*, 320; limitation on, 321; modification or termination, 321

tickets, unordered, 214

time payment, 529

time of performance, 337

time price differential, 278

tippee, insider information and, 850

title, acquiring for personal property, 382; document of, 422; effect of sale on, 466; goods represented by negotiable document of, 460; negotiable documents of, 467; reservation of, 463; voidable, 467; warranty of, 489

title transfer, of automobiles, 462

tort, 161; of agent, 723; product liability and strict, 496

tort liability, 162; of partners and partnership as to, 801; liability of principal of agent's, 728; to third persons for breach of contract, 365

total loss, fire insurance and, 663

total permanent disability, 674

trade, barriers, 80; combinations to divert, 176; contracts in restraint of, 276; furtherance of, 29; international organizations, conferences, and treaties, 72; relief mechanisms for economic injury caused by, 81

Trade Agreement Act of 1979, 82

trade fixtures, 886

trademark, *defined*, 174, 382; infringement of, 174

Trademark Counterfeiting Act of 1984, 152

trade secrets, 387; given to employees, 745

trading groups, regional, of developing countries, 73

trading partnerships, 777

transaction terms, disclosure of, 124

transferee, as agent, 724; participating, 561

transfer of tenant, termination of lease and, 908

transferor, warranties of, 546

transfers, voidable, 637

treason, *defined*, 140

treasury stock, 832

treaties, international trade organizations, conferences, and, 72

trespass, to land, 178; to personal property, 178; to the person, 177

trespassers, 887

trial, conduct of, 15; mini-, 19; new, 16

tribunals, association, 9

trust, *defined*, 946; acceptance of, 948; agreement, 947; charitable, 951; creation of, 947; defense of, 949; implied, 952; living, 947; nature of beneficiary's interest, 948; purchase money resulting, 952; remedies for breach of, 950; spendthrift, 948; tentative, 950; termination of, 950; testamentary, 947

trust corpus, 946

trustee, *defined*, 946; duties of, 949; duty of loyalty, 949; duty of performance, 949; duty to account and inform, 950; duty to defend trust, 949; duty to perserve trust property, 949; duty to produce income, 949; duty to use due care, 949; in bankruptcy, 637, powers of, 949

trust estate, 946

trust fund, 946

Trust Indenture Act of 1939, 846

trust property, possession and preservation of, 949

trust res, 946

Truth in Lending Act, 124; garnishment of employee's pay and, 748

U

ultra vires act, 833

unauthorized, indorsements, 541

unauthorized signature, reporting time, 600

unconscionability, 126; and public policy, 273

unconscionable contract, 269

underwriter, 648

undisclosed principal, 721, 724

undue influence, 241; remedies for, 244

unemployment benefits, 748

unemployment compensation, 748

unfair competition, 175

unfair employer practices, 63

unfair labor practices, 63

unfair union practices, 64

unidentified goods, 458, 460

Uniform Aeronautics Act, 882

Uniform Anatomical Gift Act, 393

Uniform Commercial Code, 6, 259; broken sales contract and Article 2 of, 505; bulk transfers and Article 6 of, 449; definition of good faith, 472; secured transaction and Article 9 of, 610; statue of limitations, 502; subject matter of sale under Article 2 of, 442; code, warranties governed by, 484

Uniform Disposition of Unclaimed Property Act, 395

Uniform Gifts to Minors Act, 391

Uniform Limited Partnership Act, 765

Uniform Probate Code, 927

Uniform Securities Act, 846

Uniform Simultaneous Death Act, 936

unilateral contract, 194

unilateral mistake, 234

unincorporated association, 768

uninsured motorist coverage, 671

union organization, 65

union practices, unfair, 64

universal agent, 687

universal defenses, 555

United Nations Conference on Trade and Development (UNCTAD), 72

United States export-import bank (eximbank), 84

unordered goods and tickets, 214

unpublished works, copyrights and, 385

unsecured claims, priority of, 639

unsolicited credit card, 127

used goods, sale of, 492

usurious agreements, 278

usury, *defined*, 278

utilities, public, 211

V

valid contracts, 193

valid tender of payment, 335

value, 610

vandalism, insurance against, 664

variance, zoning, 114

ventures, joint, 75, 767

verdict, 16; attaching, 16; directed, 16; of jury, 16

vesting, 747

vicarious liability, 728

victim, indemnification of crime, 144

Victims of Crime Act of 1984, 144

violation of statute, 168

voidable contracts, 193; minor's ratification of, 226

voidable title, sale of, 467
void agreements, 193
voluntary act, 162
voluntary bankruptcy, 635
voluntary nonsuit, 16
vote, shareholder's right to, 852
voting, by proxy, 853; cumulative, 852; straight, 852; trust, 853

W

wagers, 273
wages, attachment and garnishment of, 747
waiver, express, 514; implied, 514; of breach, 363; of breach as modification of contract, 365; of defenses, 513; of presentment for payment, 569; of protest, 576; prohibition of, 514; scope of, 364; term of a contract discharged by, 343
war, partnership dissolved by, 784; termination of agency and, 696
warehouser, *defined*, 420; lien of, 421; limitation of liability, 424; rights and duties of, 420
warehouse receipt, 421; depositor, 421; implied warranties of, 424; is-

suer, 421; negotiable, 422; nonnegotiable, 422; nonnegotiable, *illustrated*, 423; rights of holders of, 422
warehousing, field, 424
warranty, action for breach of, 508; against encumbrances, 490; against infringement, 491; bailor's implied, 413; bill of lading and implied, 427; disclaimer of, 494; exclusion of, by examination of goods, 496; express, 486; full, 488; federal regulation of, 488; for future performance, 503; full, 488; implied, 489; grantor's, 894; in particular sales, 492; liability, 484; limited, 489; of assignor, 329; of conformity to description, sample, or model, 488; of fitness for a particular purpose, 490; of habitability, 913; of merchantability of fitness for normal use, 491; of title, 489; of unqualified indorser, 545; transferor of warehouse receipt and implied, 424; transferred commercial paper 545
warrant deed, 891
waste control, 111
waste si cleanup, 111
wasting set corporation, 855
way of lessity, 882

weather, clauses, 349; discharged contracts and, 348
welfare, agreements affecting public, 271
white collar crimes, 146
wholly owned subsidiaries, and business abroad, 74
wild animals, absolute liability of keeper, 165; ownership of, 394
will, *defined*, 928; attestation, 929; construction of, 935; contest, 932; disinheritance by, 934; distribution under the, 933; election to take against the will, 934; form of, 929; holographic, 933; modification of, 930; nuncupative, 933; parties to, 928; probate of, 931; publication of, 929; revocation of, 931
withdrawals, direct, 601
women, married contracts and, 229
worker's compensation, 752
World Bank, 73
wrongful interference with business relations, 177

Z

zoning, *defined*, 113; spot, 115